W9-CNA-262

A
VISUAL DICTIONARY OF
ARCHITECTURE

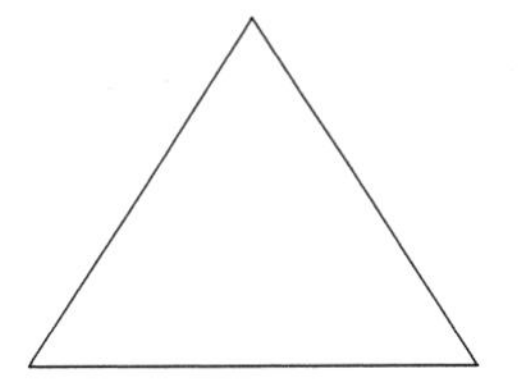

A VISUAL DICTIONARY OF ARCHITECTURE

FRANCIS D.K. CHING

VAN NOSTRAND REINHOLD

I(T)P™ A Division of International Thomson Publishing Inc.

New York • Albany • Bonn • Boston • Detroit • London • Madrid • Melbourne
Mexico City • Paris • San Francisco • Singapore • Tokyo • Toronto

Printed in the United States of America
For more information, contact:

Van Nostrand Reinhold
115 Fifth Avenue
New York, NY 10003

International Thomson Publishing GmbH
Königswinterer Strasse 418
53227 Bonn
Germany

International Thomson Publishing Europe
Berkshire House 168-173
High Holborn
London WCIV 7AA
England

International Thomson Publishing Asia
221 Henderson Road #05-10
Henderson Building
Singapore 0315

Thomas Nelson Australia
102 Dodds Street
South Melbourne, 3205
Victoria, Australia

International Thomson Publishing Japan
Hirakawacho Kyowa Building, 3F
2-2-1 Hirakawacho
Chiyoda-ku, 102 Tokyo
Japan

Nelson Canada
1120 Birchmount Road
Scarborough, Ontario
Canada M1K 5G4

International Thomson Editores
Campos Eliseos 385, Piso 7
Col. Polanco
11560 Mexico D.F. Mexico

1 2 3 4 5 6 7 8 9 10 QEB – KP 01 00 99 98 97 96 95

Library of Congress Cataloging-In-Publication Data

CONTENTS

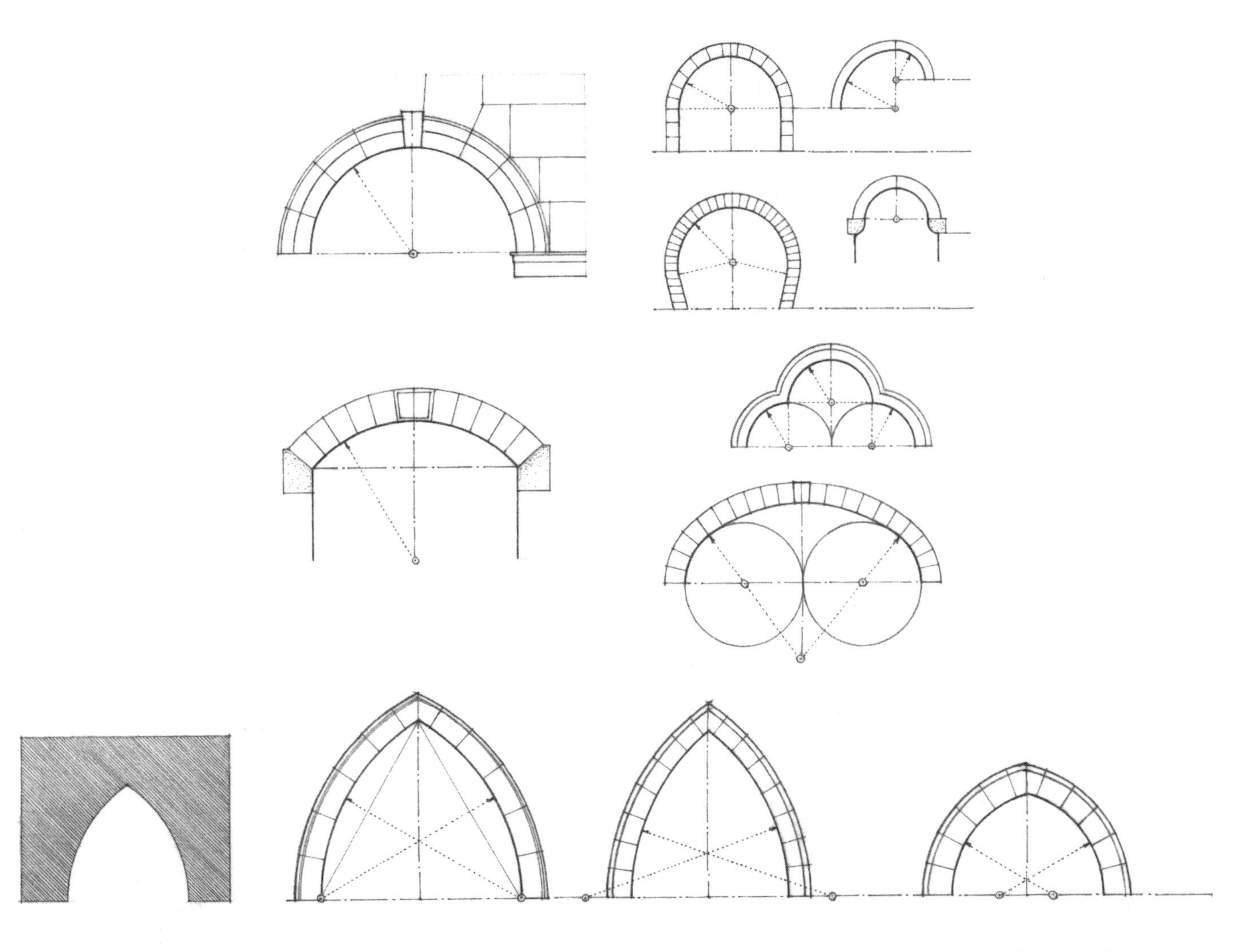

One picture is worth a thousand words

Just as a single image can be worth a thousand words, a single word can conjure up in the mind's eye a thousand images. Regardless of the power of a solitary word or image, however, each communicates meaning more effectively when brought together into a single presentation. The symbiotic relationship between graphic and verbal communication is the basis for this visual dictionary of architecture.

Instead of an alphabetical listing of entries as found in most dictionaries, the information is clustered around basic aspects of architecture as outlined in the table of contents. Within each section, words are placed in a visual context which further explains, clarifies, and completes their meaning.

The reader may use this dictionary in a number of ways. If one knows the exact term and wants to find out its meaning, then one can look it up in the index. Looking up one term will always present related terms arranged around one or more illustrations.

If one does not know the precise term, then one can look up the general subject either in the table of contents or the index. One can then refer to the appropriate section, browse the illustrations, and scan for the terms. While browsing, if one encounters an entry or a word used in a definition that is unfamiliar, one can look it up in the index.

Included are fundamental terms relating to architectural design, history, and technology. Since architecture is a visual art, most of the entries naturally lend themselves to graphic representation. Some are more abstract but are included to help clarify related terms or to complete the treatment of a subject. Others are inserted simply because they are of historical interest.

This is a book for the curious to browse as well as a desktop reference for the student of architecture. The compilation of words and definitions is not intended to be exhaustive. Rather, the selection is designed to be comprehensive enough to reflect the rich, complex, and multidimensional nature of architecture.

Architecture is an art for all to learn because all are concerned with it. –John Ruskin • **Architecture** depends on Order, Arrangement, Eurythmy, Symmetry, Propriety, and Economy. All of these must be built with due reference to durability, convenience, and beauty. Durability will be assured when foundations are carried down to the solid ground and materials wisely and liberally selected; convenience, when the arrangement of the apartments is faultless and presents no hindrance to use, and when each class of building is assigned to its suitable and appropriate exposure; and beauty, when the appearance of the work is pleasing and in good taste, and when its members are in due proportion according to correct principles of symmetry.–Vitruvius • **Architecture** is the masterly, correct and magnificent play of masses brought together in light. –Le Corbusier • Anyone entering on the study of **architecture** must understand that even though a plan may have abstract beauty on paper, the four facades may seem well-balanced and the total volume well-proportioned, the building itself may turn out to be poor **architecture**. Internal space, that space which cannot be completely represented in any form, which can be grasped and felt only through direct experience, is the protagonist of **architecture**. To grasp space, to know how to see it, is the key to the understanding of building. –Bruno Zevi • **Architecture**, painting, and sculpture are called the fine arts. They appeal to the eye as music does to the ear. But **architecture** is not judged by visual appeal alone. Buildings affect all of the human senses – sound, smell, touch, taste, and vision. –Forrest Wilson • It became apparent to us that **architecture** is generally assumed to be a highly specialized system with a set of prescribed technical goals rather than a sensual social art responsive to real human desires and feelings. This limitation is most frighteningly manifested in the reliance on two-dimensional diagrams that lay more stress on the quantifiable features of building organization than on the polychromatic and three-dimensional qualities of the whole architectural experience. –Kent Bloomer & Charles Moore • The only way you can build, the only way you can get the building into being, is through the measurable. You must follow the laws of nature and use quantities of brick, methods of construction, and engineering. But in the end, when the building becomes part of living, it evokes unmeasurable qualities, and the spirit of its existence takes over. –Louis Kahn • Built environments have various purposes: to shelter people and their activities and possessions from the elements, from human and animal enemies, and from supernatural powers; to establish place; to create a humanized, safe area in a profane and potentially dangerous world; to stress social identity and indicate status; and so on. Thus the origins of **architecture** are best understood if one takes a wider view and considers sociocultural factors, in the broadest sense, to be more important than climate, technology, materials, and economy. In any situation, it is the interplay of all these factors that best explains the form of buildings. No single explanation will suffice, because buildings – even apparently humble dwellings – are more than material objects or structures. They are institutions, basic cultural phenomena. People think environments before they build them. Thought orders space, time, activity, status, roles, and behavior. But giving physical expression to ideas is valuable. Encoding ideas makes them useful mnemonics; ideas help behavior by reminding people of how to act, how to behave, and what is expected of them. It is important to stress that all built environments – buildings, settlements, and landscapes – are one way of ordering the world by making ordering systems visible. The essential step, therefore, is the ordering or organizing of the environment.–Amos Rapaport • Ruskin said: 'Great nations write their autobiographies in three manuscripts, the book of their deeds, the book of their words and the book of their art. Not one of these books can be understood unless we read the two others, but of the three the only trustworthy one is the last.' On the whole I think this is true. If I had to say which was telling the truth about society, a speech by a minister of housing or the actual buildings put up in his time, I should believe the buildings. –Kenneth Clark • We require of any building, that it act well, and do the things it was intended to do in the best way; that it speak well, and say the things it was intended to say in the best words; that it look well, and please us by its presence, whatever it has to do or say. –John Ruskin • **Architecture** also exists without necessary assistance from an architect; and architects sometimes create buildings which are not **architecture**. –Norval White • **Architecture** is produced by ordinary people, for ordinary people; therefore it should be easily comprehensible to all. –Steen Eiler Rasmussen

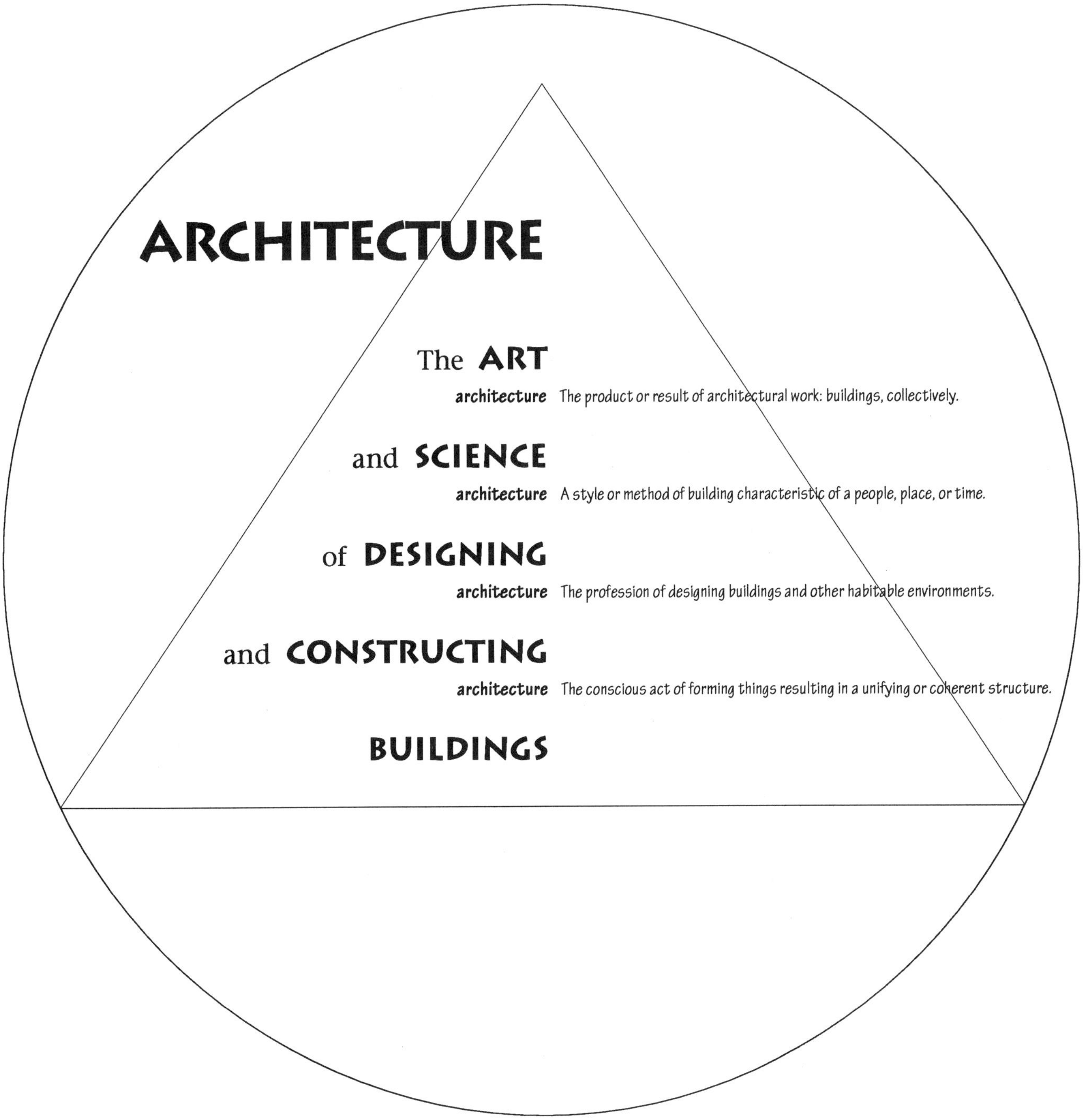

ARCHITECTURE

The **ART**

architecture The product or result of architectural work: buildings, collectively.

and **SCIENCE**

architecture A style or method of building characteristic of a people, place, or time.

of **DESIGNING**

architecture The profession of designing buildings and other habitable environments.

and **CONSTRUCTING**

architecture The conscious act of forming things resulting in a unifying or coherent structure.

BUILDINGS

art
The conscience use of skill, craft, and creative imagination in the production of what is beautiful, appealing, or of more than ordinary significance.

aesthetics
The branch of philosophy that deals with the nature of art, beauty, and taste, with a view to establishing the meaning and validity of critical judgments concerning works of art. Also, **esthetics**.

beauty
The aggregate of qualities in a person or thing that gives intense pleasure to the senses or deep satisfaction to the mind or spirit, whether arising from harmony of form or color, excellence of craft, truthfulness, originality, or other, often unspecifiable property.

taste
Critical judgment, discernment, or appreciation of what is fitting, harmonious, or beautiful prevailing in a culture or personal to an individual.

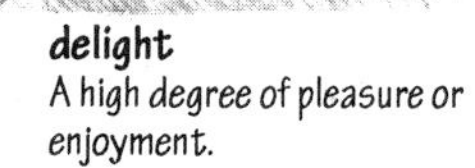

delight
A high degree of pleasure or enjoyment.

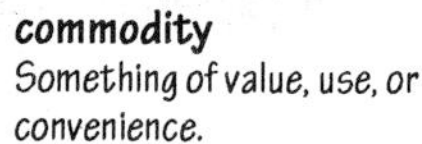

commodity
Something of value, use, or convenience.

environmental design
The ordering of the physical environment by means of architecture, engineering, construction, landscape architecture, urban design, and city planning.

urban design
The aspect of architecture and city planning that deals with the design of urban structures and spaces.

city planning
The activity or profession of determining the future physical arrangement and condition of a community, involving an appraisal of the current conditions, a forecast of future requirements, a plan for the fulfillment of these requirements, and proposals for legal, financial, and constructional programs to implement the plan. Also called **town planning**, **urban planning**.

interior design
The art, business, or profession of planning the design and supervising the execution of architectural interiors, including their color schemes, furnishings, fittings, finishes, and sometimes architectural features.

space planning
The aspect of architecture and interior design that deals with the planning, layout, design, and furnishing of spaces within a proposed or existing building.

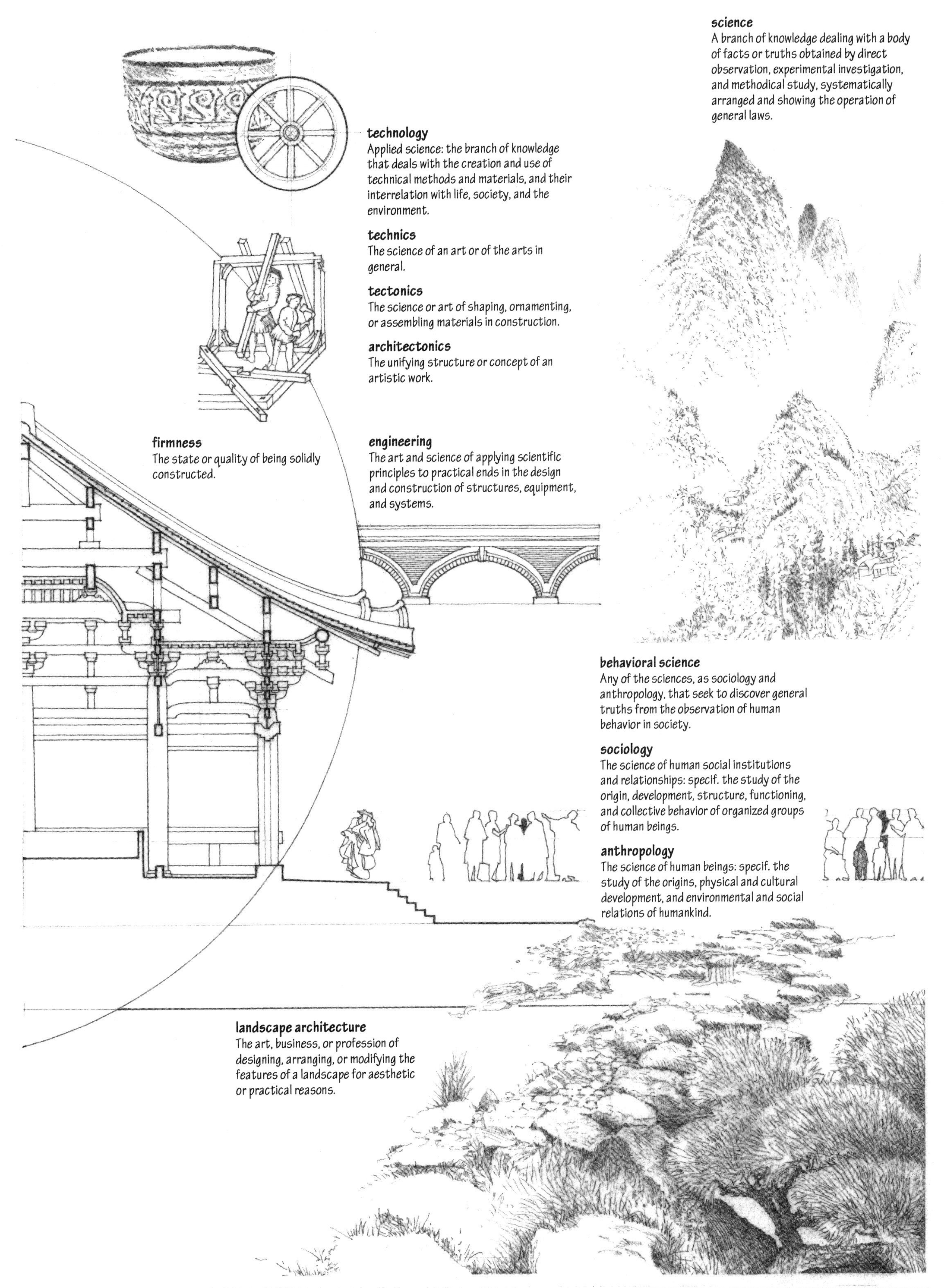

science
A branch of knowledge dealing with a body of facts or truths obtained by direct observation, experimental investigation, and methodical study, systematically arranged and showing the operation of general laws.

technology
Applied science: the branch of knowledge that deals with the creation and use of technical methods and materials, and their interrelation with life, society, and the environment.

technics
The science of an art or of the arts in general.

tectonics
The science or art of shaping, ornamenting, or assembling materials in construction.

architectonics
The unifying structure or concept of an artistic work.

firmness
The state or quality of being solidly constructed.

engineering
The art and science of applying scientific principles to practical ends in the design and construction of structures, equipment, and systems.

behavioral science
Any of the sciences, as sociology and anthropology, that seek to discover general truths from the observation of human behavior in society.

sociology
The science of human social institutions and relationships: specif. the study of the origin, development, structure, functioning, and collective behavior of organized groups of human beings.

anthropology
The science of human beings: specif. the study of the origins, physical and cultural development, and environmental and social relations of humankind.

landscape architecture
The art, business, or profession of designing, arranging, or modifying the features of a landscape for aesthetic or practical reasons.

ARCH

A curved structure for spanning an opening, designed to support a vertical load primarily by axial compression.

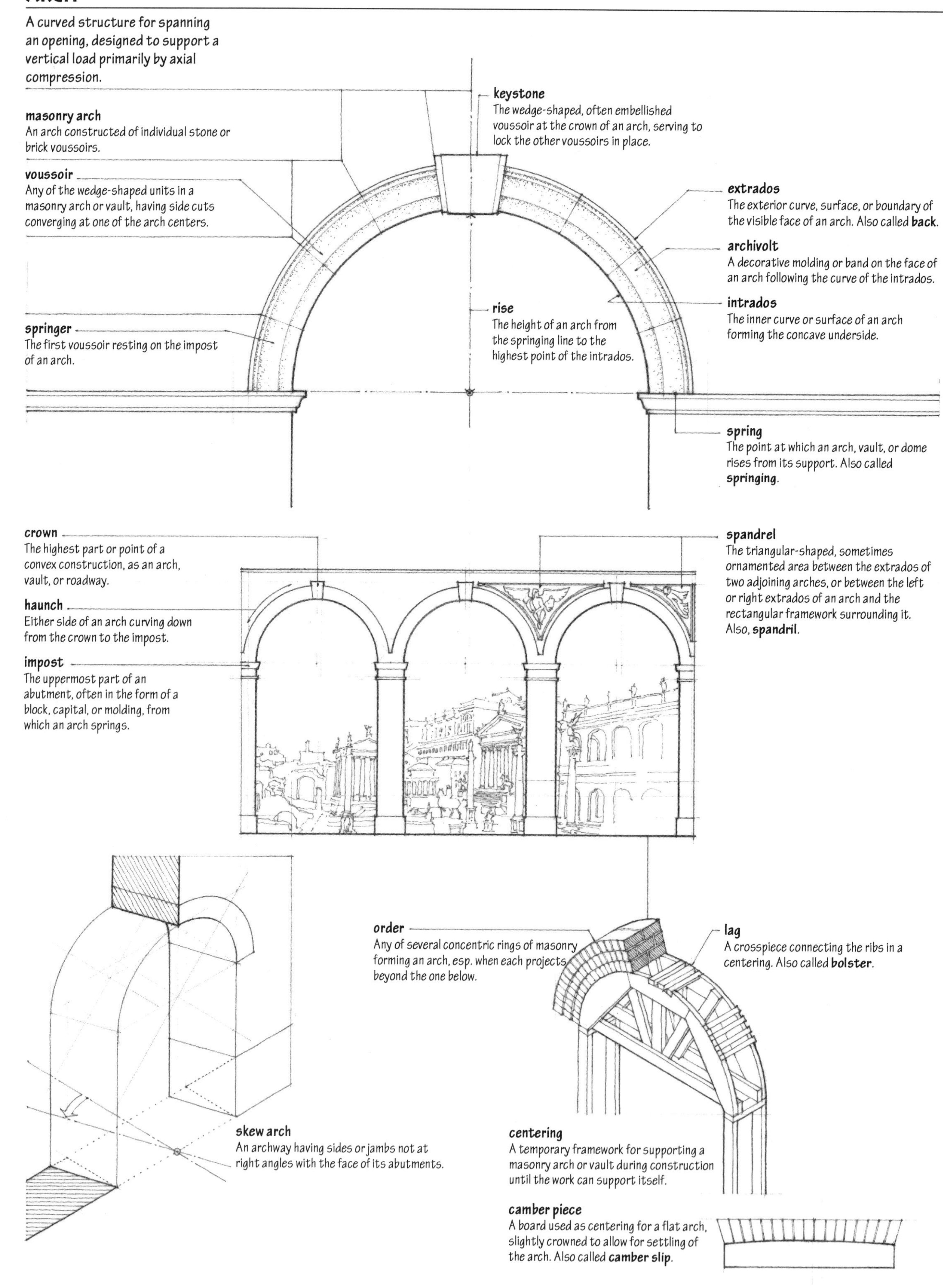

masonry arch
An arch constructed of individual stone or brick voussoirs.

voussoir
Any of the wedge-shaped units in a masonry arch or vault, having side cuts converging at one of the arch centers.

springer
The first voussoir resting on the impost of an arch.

keystone
The wedge-shaped, often embellished voussoir at the crown of an arch, serving to lock the other voussoirs in place.

rise
The height of an arch from the springing line to the highest point of the intrados.

extrados
The exterior curve, surface, or boundary of the visible face of an arch. Also called **back**.

archivolt
A decorative molding or band on the face of an arch following the curve of the intrados.

intrados
The inner curve or surface of an arch forming the concave underside.

spring
The point at which an arch, vault, or dome rises from its support. Also called **springing**.

crown
The highest part or point of a convex construction, as an arch, vault, or roadway.

haunch
Either side of an arch curving down from the crown to the impost.

impost
The uppermost part of an abutment, often in the form of a block, capital, or molding, from which an arch springs.

spandrel
The triangular-shaped, sometimes ornamented area between the extrados of two adjoining arches, or between the left or right extrados of an arch and the rectangular framework surrounding it. Also, **spandril**.

order
Any of several concentric rings of masonry forming an arch, esp. when each projects beyond the one below.

lag
A crosspiece connecting the ribs in a centering. Also called **bolster**.

skew arch
An archway having sides or jambs not at right angles with the face of its abutments.

centering
A temporary framework for supporting a masonry arch or vault during construction until the work can support itself.

camber piece
A board used as centering for a flat arch, slightly crowned to allow for settling of the arch. Also called **camber slip**.

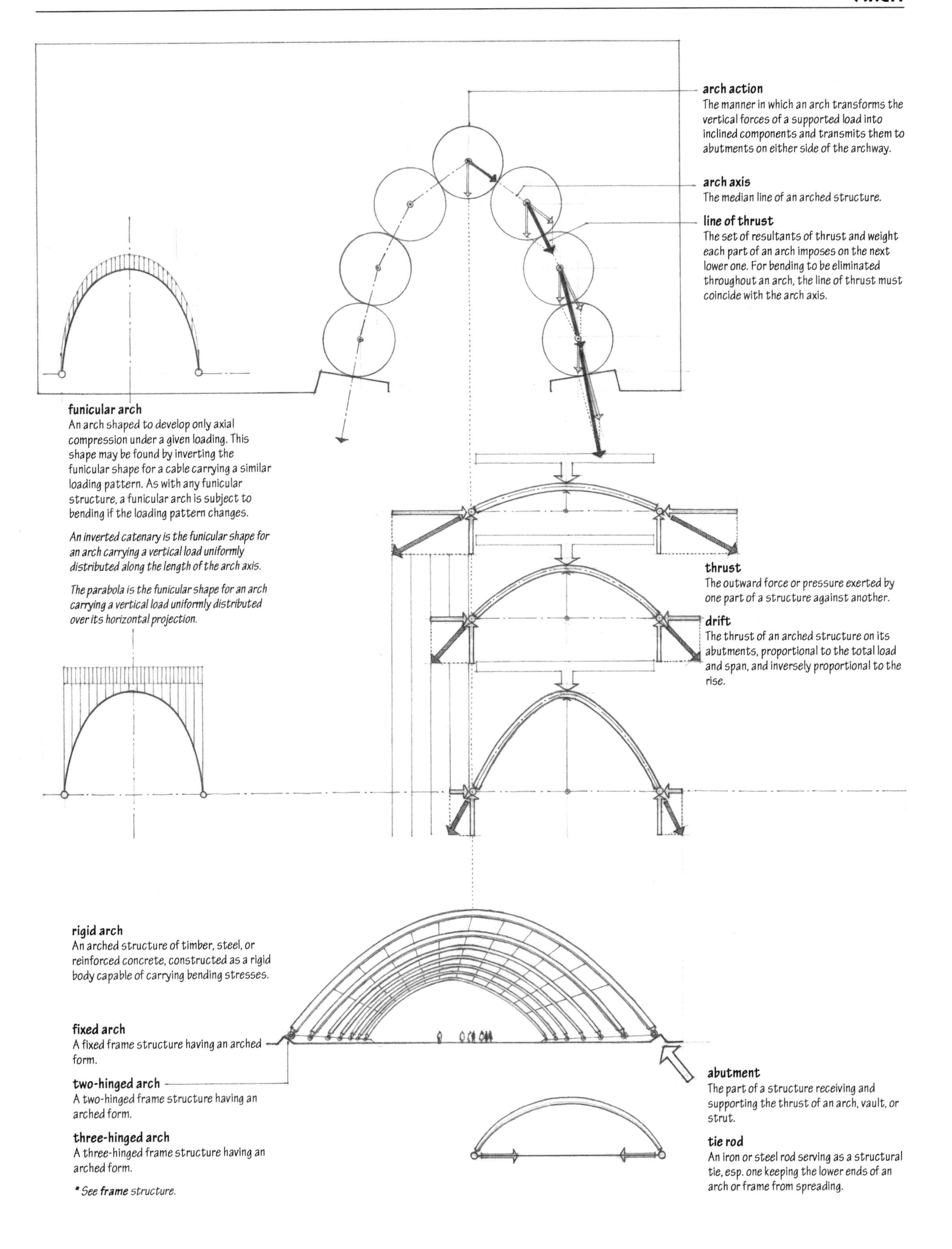

arch action
The manner in which an arch transforms the vertical forces of a supported load into inclined components and transmits them to abutments on either side of the archway.

arch axis
The median line of an arched structure.

line of thrust
The set of resultants of thrust and weight each part of an arch imposes on the next lower one. For bending to be eliminated throughout an arch, the line of thrust must coincide with the arch axis.

funicular arch
An arch shaped to develop only axial compression under a given loading. This shape may be found by inverting the funicular shape for a cable carrying a similar loading pattern. As with any funicular structure, a funicular arch is subject to bending if the loading pattern changes.

An inverted catenary is the funicular shape for an arch carrying a vertical load uniformly distributed along the length of the arch axis.

The parabola is the funicular shape for an arch carrying a vertical load uniformly distributed over its horizontal projection.

thrust
The outward force or pressure exerted by one part of a structure against another.

drift
The thrust of an arched structure on its abutments, proportional to the total load and span, and inversely proportional to the rise.

rigid arch
An arched structure of timber, steel, or reinforced concrete, constructed as a rigid body capable of carrying bending stresses.

fixed arch
A fixed frame structure having an arched form.

two-hinged arch
A two-hinged frame structure having an arched form.

three-hinged arch
A three-hinged frame structure having an arched form.

** See **frame** structure.*

abutment
The part of a structure receiving and supporting the thrust of an arch, vault, or strut.

tie rod
An iron or steel rod serving as a structural tie, esp. one keeping the lower ends of an arch or frame from spreading.

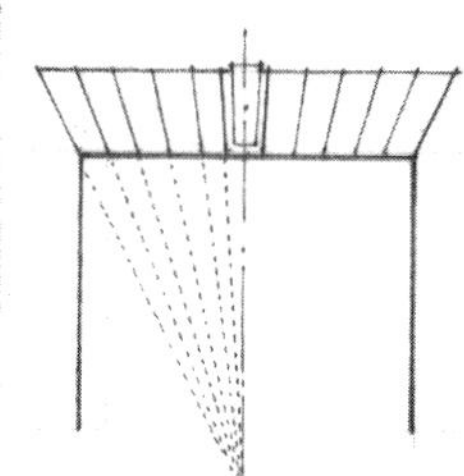

flat arch
An arch having a horizontal intrados with voussoirs radiating from a center below, often built with a slight camber to allow for settling. Also called **jack arch**.

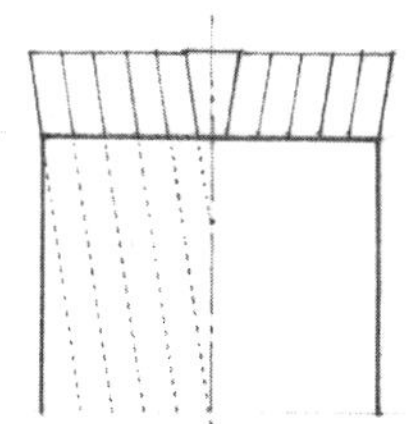

French arch
A flat arch having voussoirs inclined to the same angle on each side of the center.

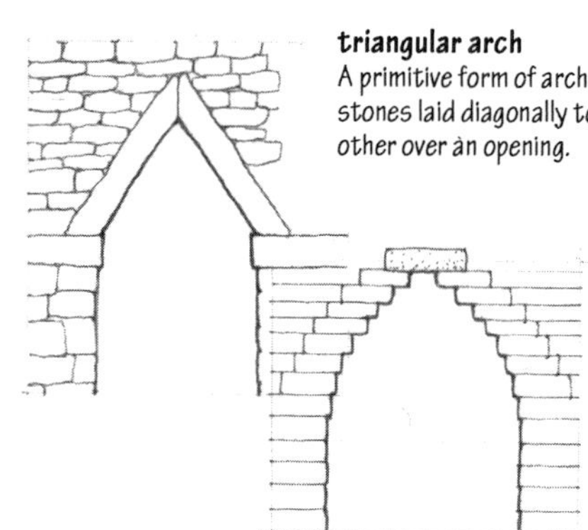

triangular arch
A primitive form of arch consisting of two stones laid diagonally to support each other over an opening.

corbel arch
A false arch constructed by corbeling courses from each side of an opening until they meet at a midpoint where a capstone is laid to complete the work. The stepped reveals may be smoothed, but no arch action is effected.

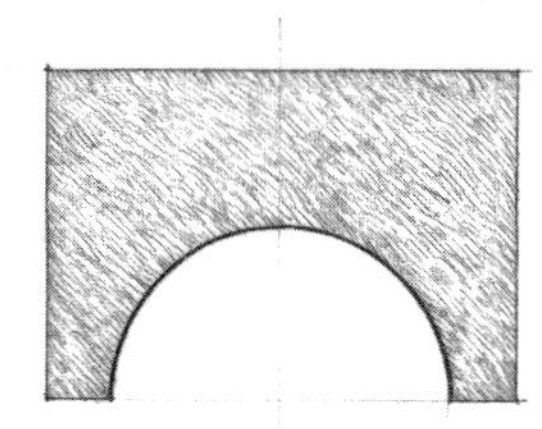

round arch
An arch having a continuously curved intrados, esp. a semicircular one.

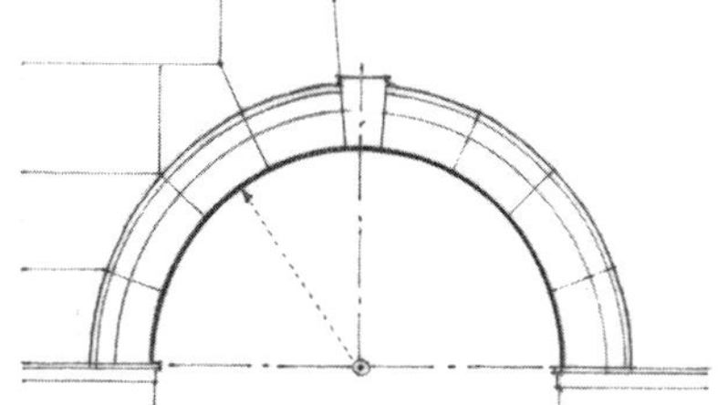

Roman arch
An arch having a semicircular intrados.

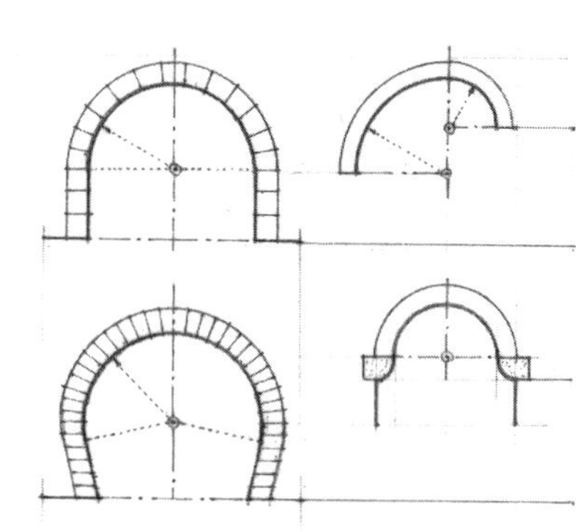

rampant arch
An arch having one impost higher than the other.

stilted arch
An arch resting on imposts treated as downward continuations of the archivolt.

bell arch
A round arch resting on two large corbels with curved faces.

horseshoe arch
An arch having an intrados that widens above the springing before narrowing to a rounded crown. Also called **Moorish arch**.

trefoil arch
An arch having a cusped intrados with three round or pointed foils.

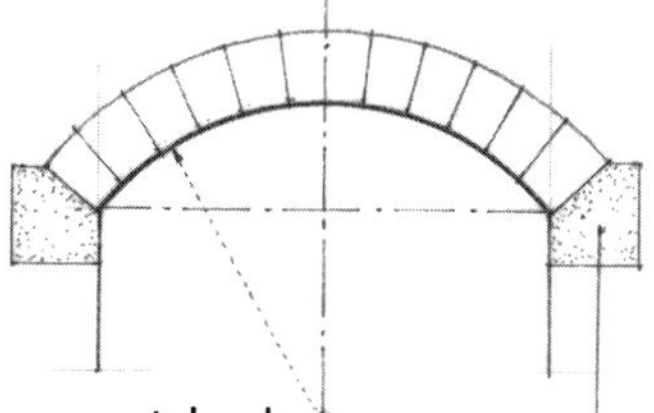

segmental arch
An arch struck from one or more centers below the springing line.

skewback
A stone or course of masonry having a sloping face against which the end of a segmental arch rests.

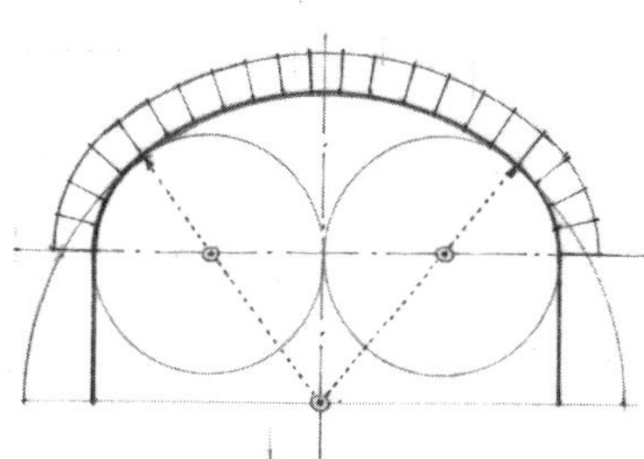

basket-handle arch
A three-centered arch having a crown with a radius much greater than that of the outer pair of curves. Also called **anse de panier**.

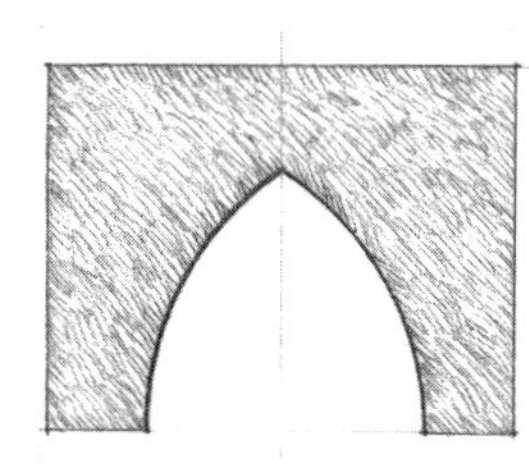

pointed arch
An arch having a pointed crown.

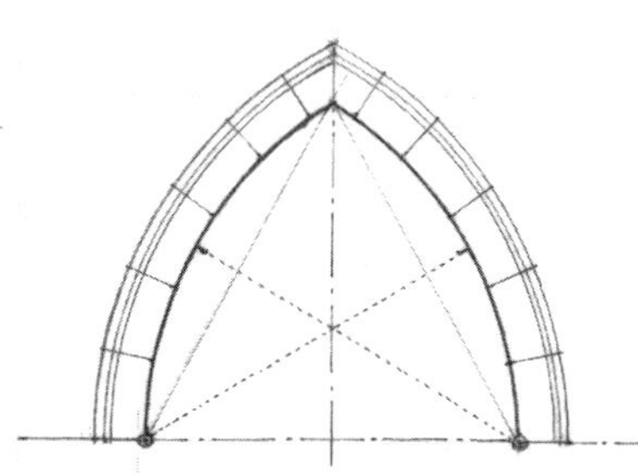

equilateral arch
A pointed arch having two centers and radii equal to the span.

Gothic arch
A pointed arch, esp. one having two centers and equal radii.

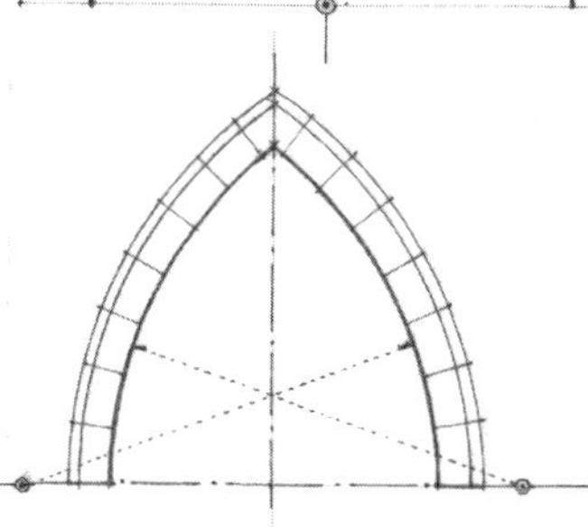

lancet arch
A pointed arch having two centers and radii greater than the span.

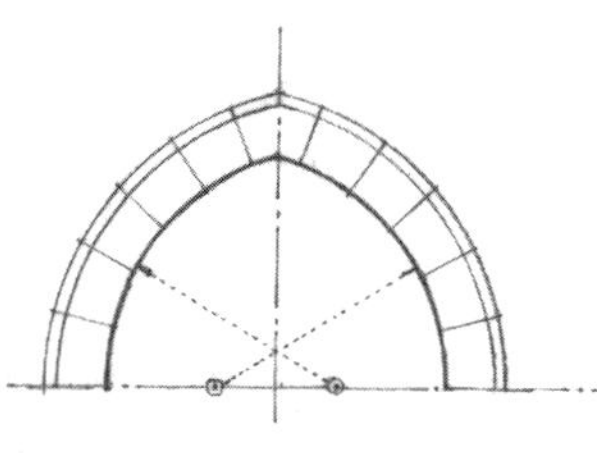

drop arch
A pointed arch having two centers and radii less than the span.

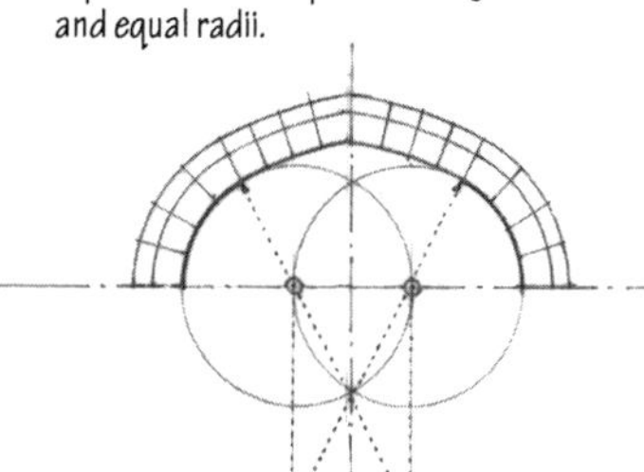

Tudor arch
A four-centered arch having an inner pair of curves with a radius much greater than that of the outer pair.

surbased arch
An arch having a rise of less than half the span.

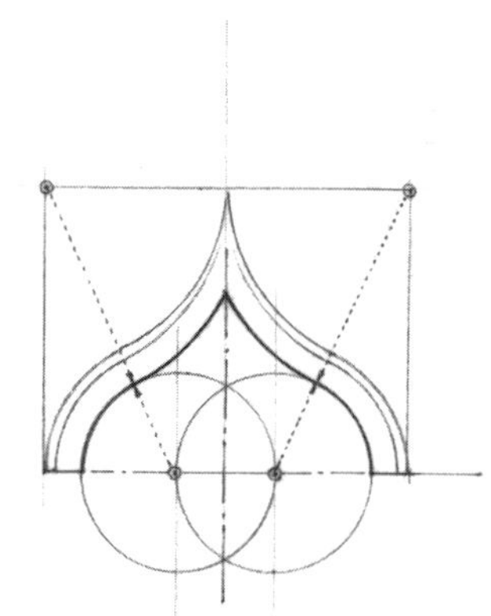

ogee arch
A pointed arch, each haunch of which is a double curve with the concave side uppermost.

BEAM

A rigid structural member designed to carry and transfer transverse loads across space to supporting elements.

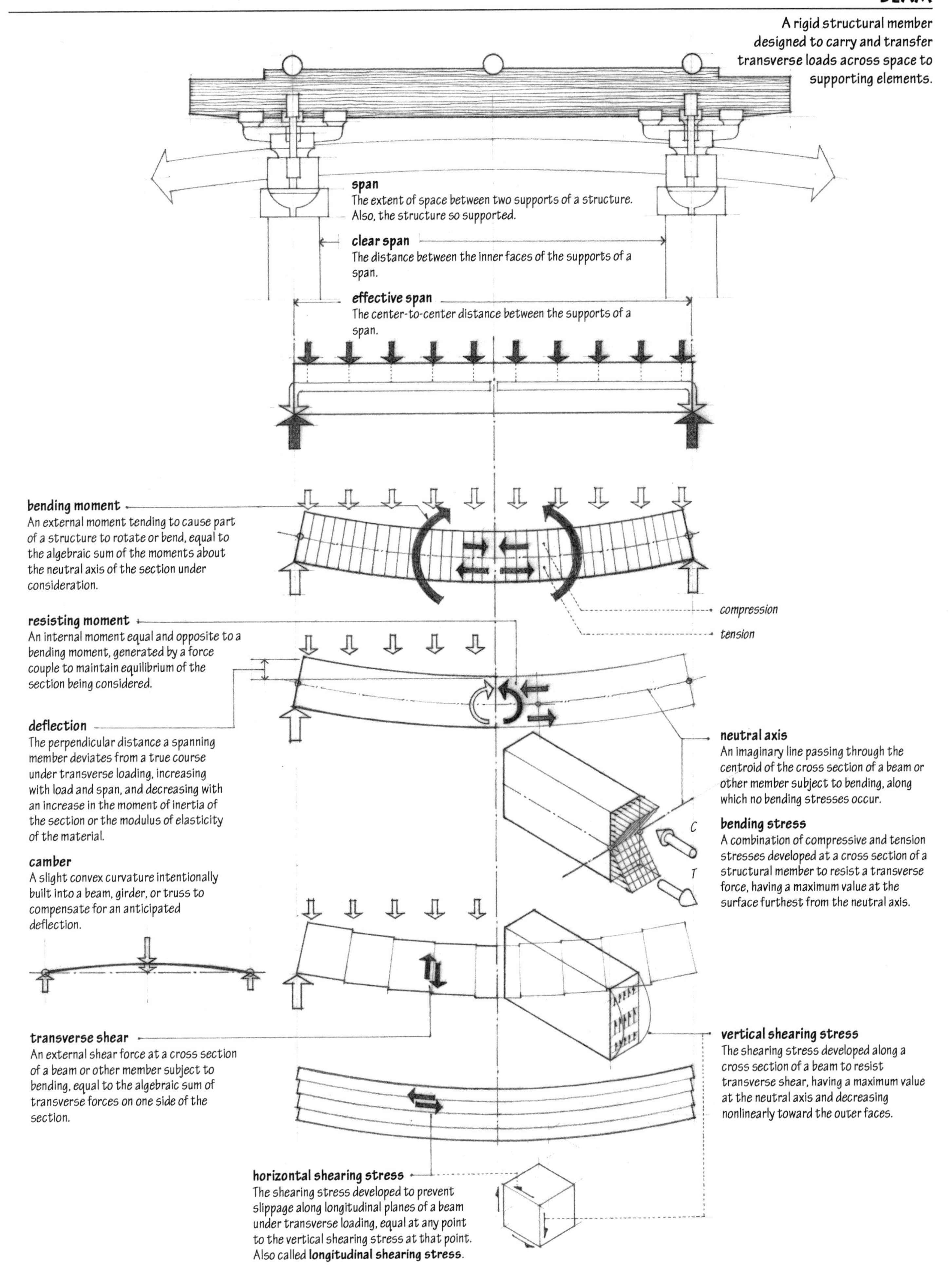

span
The extent of space between two supports of a structure. Also, the structure so supported.

clear span
The distance between the inner faces of the supports of a span.

effective span
The center-to-center distance between the supports of a span.

bending moment
An external moment tending to cause part of a structure to rotate or bend, equal to the algebraic sum of the moments about the neutral axis of the section under consideration.

resisting moment
An internal moment equal and opposite to a bending moment, generated by a force couple to maintain equilibrium of the section being considered.

deflection
The perpendicular distance a spanning member deviates from a true course under transverse loading, increasing with load and span, and decreasing with an increase in the moment of inertia of the section or the modulus of elasticity of the material.

camber
A slight convex curvature intentionally built into a beam, girder, or truss to compensate for an anticipated deflection.

neutral axis
An imaginary line passing through the centroid of the cross section of a beam or other member subject to bending, along which no bending stresses occur.

bending stress
A combination of compressive and tension stresses developed at a cross section of a structural member to resist a transverse force, having a maximum value at the surface furthest from the neutral axis.

transverse shear
An external shear force at a cross section of a beam or other member subject to bending, equal to the algebraic sum of transverse forces on one side of the section.

vertical shearing stress
The shearing stress developed along a cross section of a beam to resist transverse shear, having a maximum value at the neutral axis and decreasing nonlinearly toward the outer faces.

horizontal shearing stress
The shearing stress developed to prevent slippage along longitudinal planes of a beam under transverse loading, equal at any point to the vertical shearing stress at that point. Also called **longitudinal shearing stress**.

flexure formula
A formula defining the relationship between bending moment, bending stress, and the cross-sectional properties of a beam. Bending stress is directly proportional to bending moment and inversely proportional to the moment of inertia of a beam section.

$$f_b = Mc/I$$

where

f_b = *extreme fiber stress in bending*

M = *bending moment*

c = *distance from neutral axis to the outermost surface in bending*

If

$$I/c = S$$

then

$$f_b = M/S$$

moment of inertia
The sum of the products of each element of an area and the square of its distance from a coplanar axis of rotation. Moment of inertia is a geometric property that indicates how the cross-sectional area of a structural member is distributed and does not reflect the intrinsic physical properties of a material.

section modulus
A geometric property of a cross section, defined as the moment of inertia of the section divided by the distance from the neutral axis to the most remote surface.

While halving a beam span reduces the bending stresses by a factor of 2, doubling the depth reduces the bending stresses by a factor of 4.

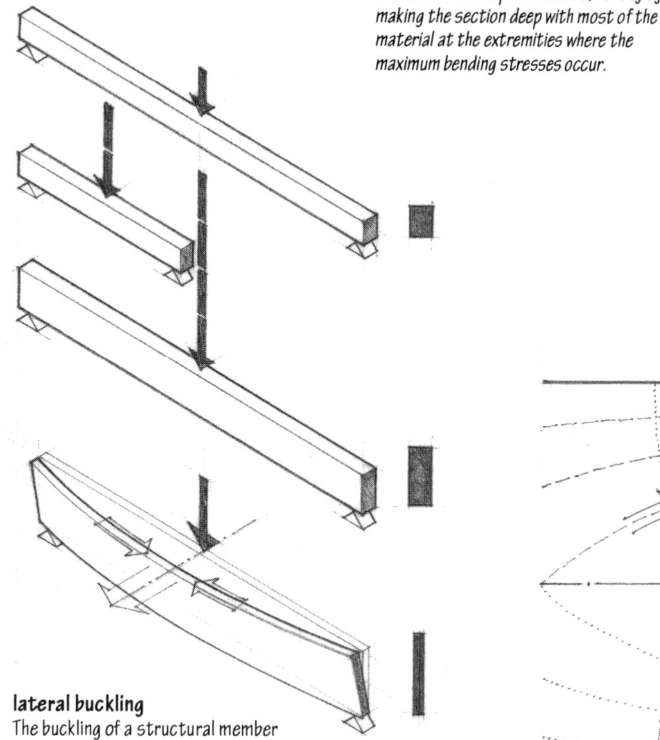

The efficiency of a beam is increased by configuring the cross section to provide the required moment of inertia or section modulus with the smallest possible area, usually by making the section deep with most of the material at the extremities where the maximum bending stresses occur.

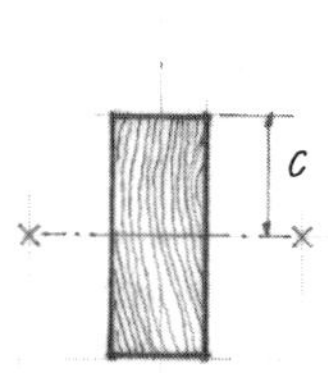

4 x 10 timber beam

$33.25\ in^2$ = *Area of section*

$250\ in^4$ = *I about x–x axis*

$52.6\ in^3$ = *S*

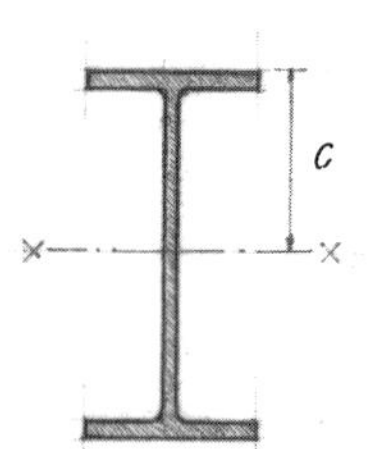

W 14 x 38 steel beam

$11.20\ in^2$ = *Area of section*

$386\ in^4$ = *I about x–x axis*

$54.7\ in^3$ = *S*

principal stresses
The tensile and compressive stresses resulting from the interaction of bending and shear stresses at a cross section of a beam.

At the extreme surfaces of a beam, only bending stresses exist and the principal stresses are equivalent to the tensile and compressive stresses resulting from bending.

At the neutral axis of the section, only shear stresses exist and these can be resolved into tensile and compressive stresses acting at 45° angles to the neutral axis.

For an intermediate element subject to both bending and shear stresses, the principal stresses have an inclination determined by the relative magnitudes of these stresses.

lateral buckling
The buckling of a structural member induced by compressive stresses acting on a slender portion insufficiently rigid in the lateral direction.

stress trajectories
Lines depicting the direction but not the magnitude of the principal stresses in a beam.

compression

tension

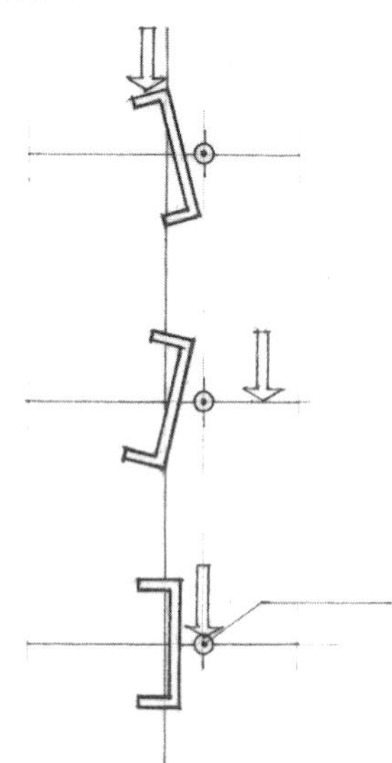

shear center
The point in the cross-sectional plane of a structural member through which a transverse load must pass in order to prevent torsion or twisting of the member about a longitudinal axis.

simple beam
A beam resting on simple supports at both ends, which are free to rotate and have no moment resistance. As with any statically determinate structure, the values of all reactions, shears, and moments for a simple beam are independent of its cross-sectional shape and material.

shear diagram
A graphic representation of the variation in magnitude of the external shears present in a structure for a given set of transverse loads and support conditions.

Concentrated loads produce external shears which are constant in magnitude between the loads.

Uniformly distributed loads produce linearly varying shears.

cantilever beam
A projecting beam supported at only one fixed end.

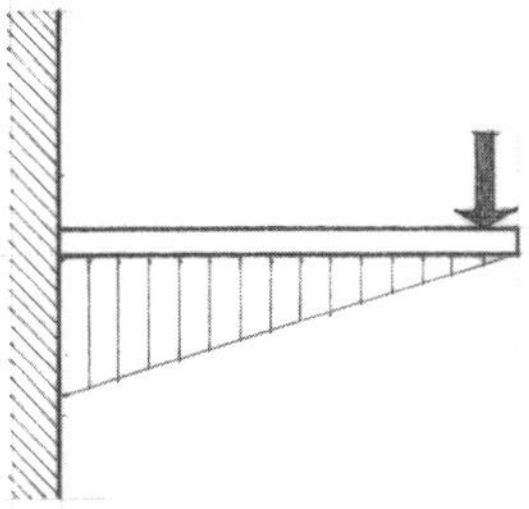

moment diagram
A graphic representation of the variation in magnitude of the bending moments present in a structure for a given set of transverse loads and support conditions. The overall deflected shape of a structure subject to bending can often be inferred from the shape of its moment diagram.

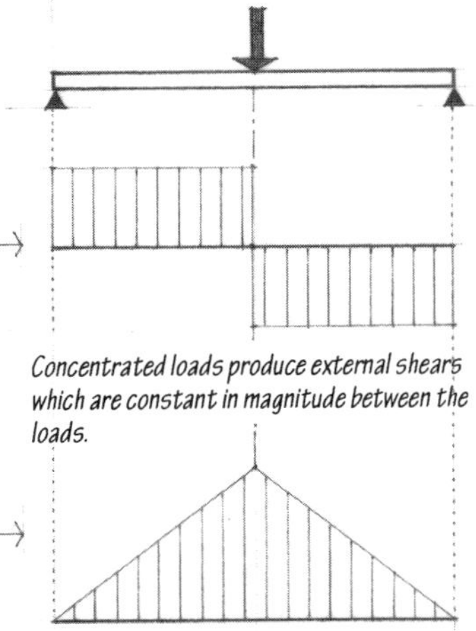

Concentrated loads produce bending moments which vary linearly between loads.

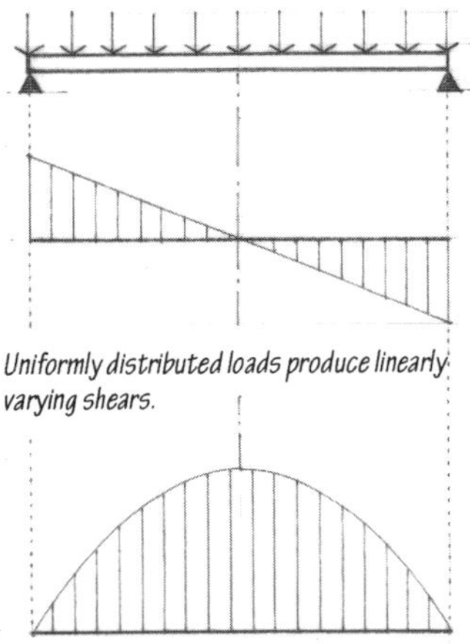

Uniformly distributed loads produce parabolically varying moments.

cantilever
A beam or other rigid structural member extending beyond a fulcrum and supported by a balancing member or a downward force behind the fulcrum.

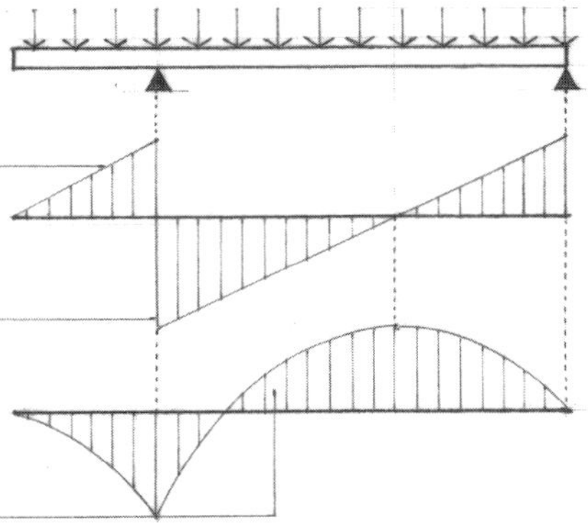

overhanging beam
A simple beam extending beyond one its supports. The overhang reduces the positive moment at midspan while developing a negative moment at the base of the cantilever over the support.

Assuming a uniformly distributed load, the projection for which the moment over the support is equal and opposite to the moment at midspan is approximately 3/8 of the span.

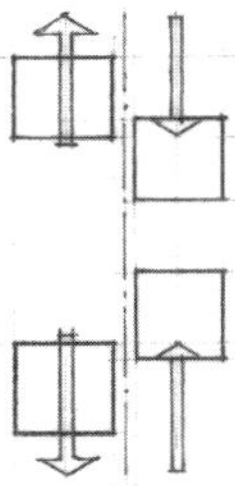

positive shear
A net resultant of shear forces that acts vertically upward on the left part of the structure being considered.

negative shear
A net resultant of shear forces that acts vertically downward on the left part of the structure being considered.

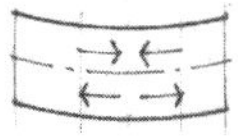

positive moment
A bending moment that produces a concave curvature at a section of a structure.

double overhanging beam
A simple beam extending beyond both of its supports.

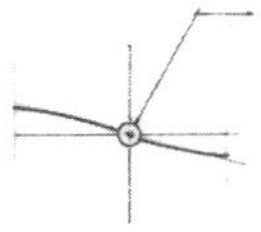

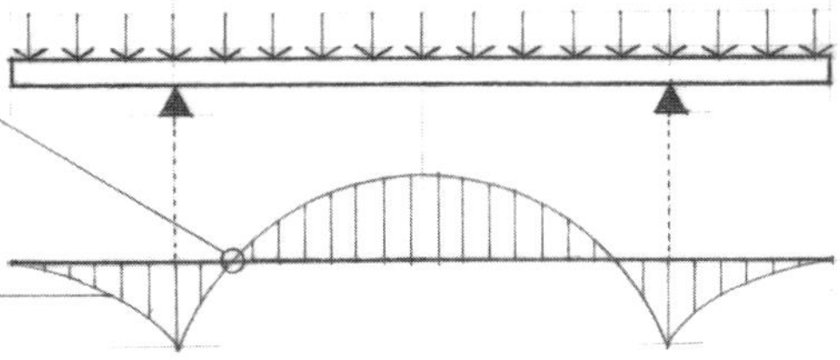

inflection point
A point at which a structure changes curvature from convex to concave or vice versa as it deflects under a transverse load: theoretically an internal hinge and therefore a point of zero moment.

Assuming a uniformly distributed load, the projections for which the moments over the supports are equal and opposite to the moment at midspan are approximately 1/3 of the span.

negative moment
A bending moment that produces a convex curvature at a section of a structure.

haunch
The part of a beam that is thickened or deepened to develop greater moment resistance. The efficiency of a beam can be increased by shaping its length in response to the moment and shear values which typically vary along its longitudinal axis.

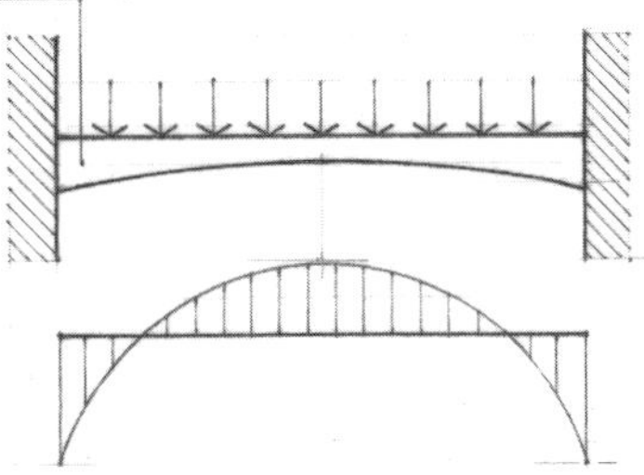

fixed-end beam
A beam having both ends restrained against translation and rotation. The fixed ends transfer bending stresses, increase the rigidity of the beam, and reduce its maximum deflection.

suspended-span
A simple beam supported by the cantilevers of two adjoining spans with pinned construction joints at points of zero moment. Also called **hung-span**.

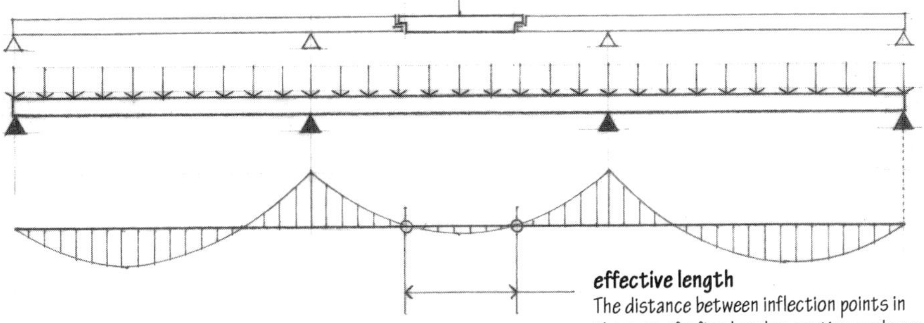

continuous beam
A beam extending over more than two supports in order to develop greater rigidity and smaller moments than a series of simple beams having similar spans and loading. Both fixed-end and continuous beams are indeterminate structures for which the values of all reactions, shears, and moments are dependent not only on span and loading but also on cross-sectional shape and material.

effective length
The distance between inflection points in the span of a fixed-end or continuous beam, equivalent in nature to the actual length of a simply supported beam.

A masonry unit of clay, formed into a rectangular prism while plastic and hardened by drying in the sun or firing in a kiln.

common brick
Brick made for general building purposes and not specially treated for color and texture. Also called **building brick**.

facing brick
Brick made of special clays for facing a wall, often treated to produce the desired color and surface texture. Also called **face brick**.

brick type
A designation indicating the permissible variation in size, color, chippage, and distortion allowed in a facing brick unit.

FBX
Facing brick suitable for use where a minimum variation in size, narrow color range, and high degree of mechanical perfection are required.

FBS
Facing brick suitable for use where a wider color range and greater variation in size are permitted than for type FBX.

FBA
Facing brick suitable for use where particular effects are desired resulting from nonuniformity in size, color, and texture of the individual units.

soft-mud process
The process of forming brick by molding relatively wet clay having a moisture content of 20% to 30%.

sandstruck brick
Brick formed in the soft-mud process with a mold lined with sand to prevent sticking, producing a matte-textured surface.

waterstruck brick
Brick formed in the soft-mud process with a mold lubricated with water to prevent sticking, producing a smooth, dense surface.

stiff-mud process
The process of forming brick and structural tile by extruding stiff but plastic clay having a moisture content of 12% to 15% through a die and cutting the extrusion to length with wires before firing.

dry-press process
The process of forming brick by molding relatively dry clay having a moisture content of 5% to 7% under high pressure, resulting in sharp-edged, smooth-surfaced bricks.

kiln
A furnace or oven for burning, baking, or drying something, esp. one for firing pottery, baking bricks, or drying timber.

flashing
Firing brick units alternately with too much or too little air to vary their face color.

cull
A brick or timber rejected as being of inferior quality.

brick grade
A designation indicating the durability of a brick unit when exposed to weathering. The U.S. is divided into three weathering regions – severe, moderate, and negligible – according to annual winter rainfall and the annual number of freezing-cycle days. Brick is graded for use in each region according to compressive strength, maximum water absorption, and maximum saturation coefficient.

MW
A brick grade suitable for exposure to moderate weathering, as when used above grade on surfaces unlikely to be permeated with water in subfreezing temperatures.

SW
A brick grade suitable for exposure to severe weathering, as when in contact with the ground or used on surfaces likely to be permeated with water in subfreezing temperatures.

NW
A brick grade suitable for exposure to negligible weathering, as when used as a backup or in interior masonry.

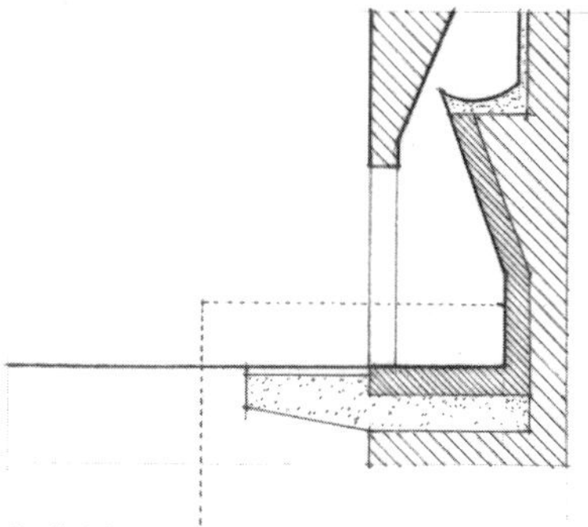

firebrick
A brick made of fire clay and used for lining furnaces and fireplaces.

fire clay
A refractory clay used in the making of firebricks, crucibles, and other objects exposed to high temperatures.

refractory
A material having the ability to retain its physical shape and chemical identity when subjected to high temperatures.

absorption
The weight of water absorbed by a clay masonry unit when immersed in either cold or boiling water for a stated length of time, expressed as a percentage of the weight of the dry unit.

saturation coefficient
The ratio of the weight of water absorbed by a clay masonry unit immersed in cold water to the weight absorbed when immersed in boiling water, indicating the probable resistance of the brick to the action of freezing and thawing.

suction
The weight of water absorbed by a clay masonry unit when partially immersed for one minute, expressed in grams or ounces per minute. Also called **initial rate of absorption**.

efflorescence
A white, powdery deposit that forms on an exposed masonry or concrete surface, caused by the leaching and crystallization of soluble salts from within the material.

clinker
A dense, hard-burned brick used esp. for paving.

nominal dimension
A brick dimension larger than the actual dimension to account for the thickness of a mortar joint.

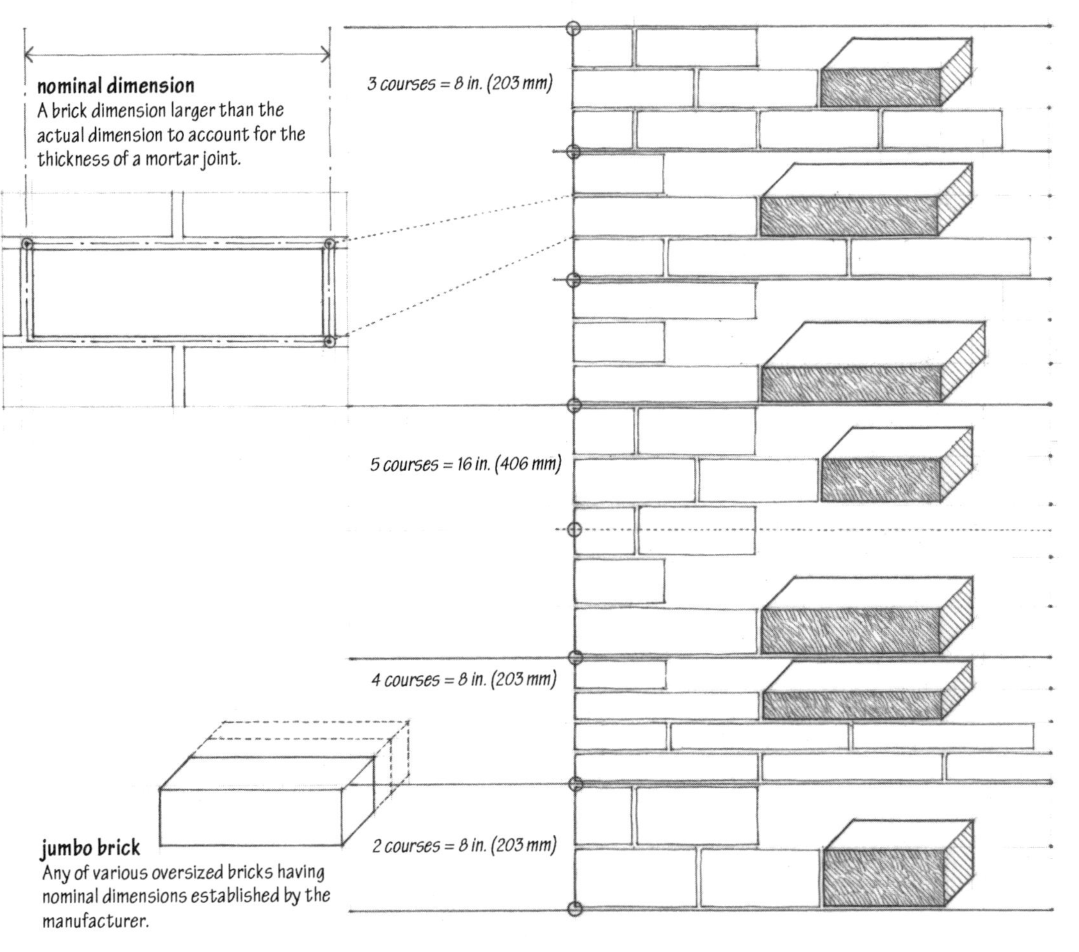

modular brick
A brick having nominal dimensions of 4 x 2⅔ x 8 in. (102 x 68 x 203 mm).

Norman brick
A brick having nominal dimensions of 4 x 2⅔ x 12 in. (102 x 68 x 305 mm).

SCR brick
Brick having nominal dimensions of 6 x 2⅔ x 12 in. (102 x 68 x 305 mm).

engineered brick
A brick having nominal dimensions of 4 x 3⅕ x 8 in. (102 x 81 x 203 mm).

Norwegian brick
A brick having nominal dimensions of 4 x 3⅕ x 12 in. (102 x 81 x 305 mm).

Roman brick
Brick having nominal dimensions of 4 x 2 x 12 in. (102 x 51 x 305 mm).

economy brick
A modular brick having nominal dimensions of 4 x 4 x 8 in. (102 x 102 x 203 mm).

jumbo brick
Any of various oversized bricks having nominal dimensions established by the manufacturer.

soap
A brick or tile having normal face dimensions but a nominal thickness of 2 in. (51 mm).

bat
A brick cut transversely so as to leave one end whole.

gauge
To chip or rub stones or bricks to a certain size or shape.

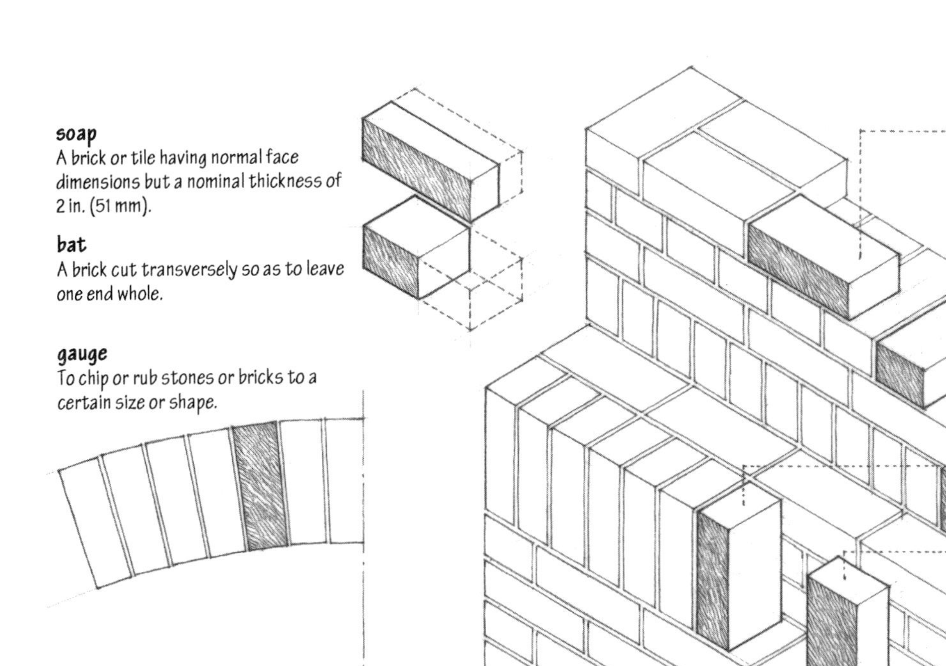

stretcher
A brick or other masonry unit laid horizontally in a wall with the longer edge exposed or parallel to the surface.

header
A brick or other masonry unit laid horizontally in a wall with the shorter end exposed or parallel to the surface.

rowlock
A brick laid horizontally on the longer edge with the shorter end exposed. Also, **rollock**.

soldier
A brick laid vertically with the longer face edge exposed.

sailor
A brick laid vertically with the broad face exposed.

shiner
A brick laid horizontally on the longer edge with the broad face exposed. Also called **bull stretcher**.

* See **masonry** for types of mortar joints.

brickwork
Brick construction, esp. the art of bonding bricks effectively.

bond
Any of various arrangements of masonry units having a regular, recognizable, usually overlapping pattern to increase the strength and enhance the appearance of the construction.

running bond
A brickwork or masonry bond composed of overlapping stretchers. Also called **stretcher bond**.

soldier course
A continuous course of soldiers in brickwork.

stack bond
A brickwork or masonry bond having successive courses of stretchers with all head joints aligned vertically. Also, **stacked bond**.

common bond
A brickwork bond having a course of headers between every five or six courses of stretchers. Also called **American bond**.

closer
A masonry unit specially formed or cut to finish a course or complete the bond at the corner of a wall. Also, **closure**.

stretching course
A continuous course of stretchers in brickwork.

heading course
A continuous course of headers in brickwork.

bond course
A continuous course of headers or bondstones overlapping more than one wythe of masonry.

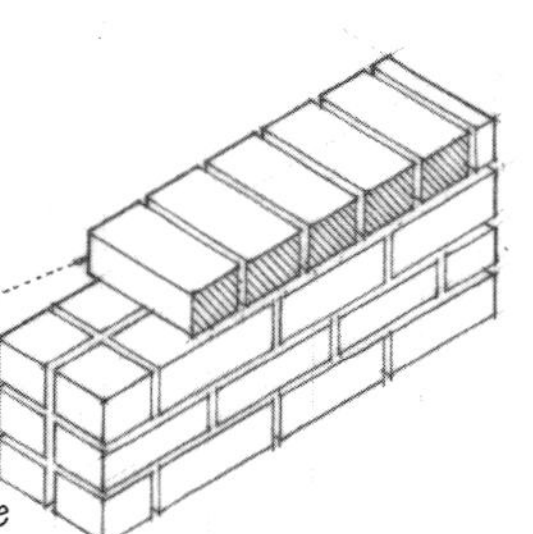

English bond
A brickwork bond having alternate courses of headers and stretchers in which the headers are centered on stretchers and the joints between stretchers line up vertically in all courses.

queen closer
A brick of half the normal width, used for completing a course or for spacing regular bricks. Also, **queen closure**.

English cross bond
A modified English bond in which the head joints in the stretching courses are offset by half the length of a stretcher. Also called **Dutch bond**.

Flemish bond
A brickwork bond having alternating headers and stretchers in each course, each header being centered above and below a stretcher.

king closer
A three-quarter brick for finishing a course or for spacing regular bricks. Also, **king closure**.

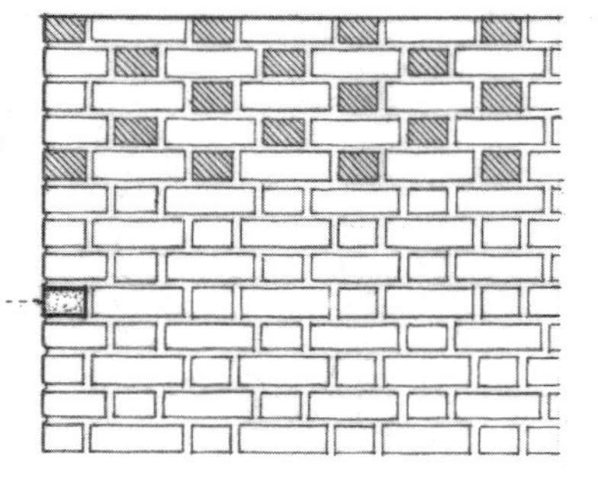

Flemish cross bond
A modified Flemish bond having courses of alternate headers and stretchers alternating with stretching courses.

flare header
A brick having a darker end exposed as a header in patterned brickwork.

Flemish diagonal bond
A form of Flemish cross bond in which the courses are offset to form a diamond pattern.

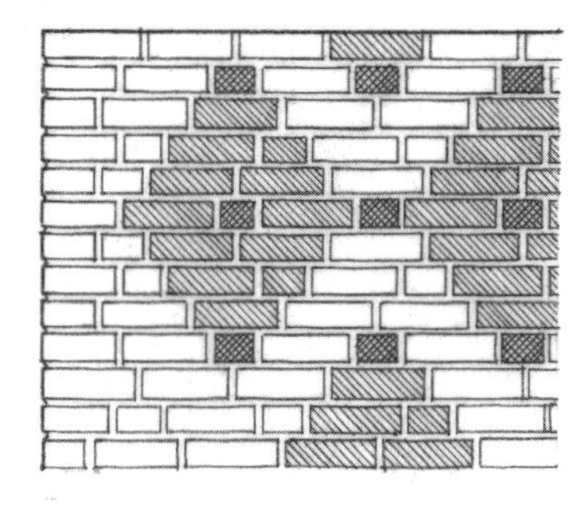

garden-wall bond
A brickwork bond for lightly loaded boundary walls, having a sequence of a header and three stretchers in each course, with each header being centered over a header in alternate courses.

BUILDING

A relatively permanent enclosed structure constructed over a plot of land for habitable use.

A building is a shelter from rain, sun, and wind. This implies a Roof, and Walls to support it. If the walls entirely enclose the space within, there are Doorways for access, and Windows for light. Roofs and walls, doors and windows are the essential features of buildings.

Roofs may be flat, sloping, or curved. A roof with one slope is called a Lean-to. When two sloping roofs rest upon parallel walls and lean against one another, they meet in a horizontal ridge at the top, and form a Gable at each end. If two walls make a projecting angle, their roofs intersect in an inclined line called a Hip. If the walls meet in a reentering angle, the inclined line of intersection is called a Valley. Circular walls carry conical or domical roofs.

If there is more than one story, the flat roof of the lower story becomes the Floor of the story above. If the roof extends beyond the wall that supports it, the projection is called the Eaves. If the wall also projects to support the extension of the roof, the projection is called a Cornice. The principal member of a cornice, which projects like a shelf and crowns the wall, is called a Corona.

Walls are generally made wider just at the bottom so as to get a better bearing on the ground. This projection is the Base. A similar projection at the top is called a Cap or, if it projects much, a Cornice, as has been said. A low wall is called a Parapet. A short piece of wall about as long as it is thick is called a Post, and if it supports something, a Pedestal; the part between its cap and base is then the Die. A tall post is called a Pier, if it is square, and a Column if it is round. Caps of piers and columns are called Capitals, and the part between the cap and the base, the shaft. The flat upper member of a capital is called the Abacus.

A beam that spans the space between two piers or columns or between a pier or column and a wall is called an Architrave, or Epistyle. Above it, between the architrave and the cornice, there is generally a little strip of wall called the Frieze. Architrave, frieze, and cornice constitute the Entablature. A series of columns is called a Colonnade. The spaces between piers or columns are sometimes spanned by Arches, a series of which is called an Arcade.

The space between two parallel walls is sometimes covered by a sort of continuous arch called a Vault, instead of by a floor or roof.

The Wall, the Pier, and the Column, with or without the pedestal, constitute the chief supporting members; the Frieze and Cornice, with the roof that rests upon them, constitute the chief part of the load they carry. The Architrave, the Arches, and the Spandrels form part of the load relative to what is below them, but are supporting members relative to what is above them.

Besides being valuable as a shelter, a building may be in itself a noble and delightful object, and architects are builders who, by giving a building good proportions and fine details, and by employing beautiful materials, make it valuable on its own account, independently of its uses.

—William Robert Ware
The American Vignola

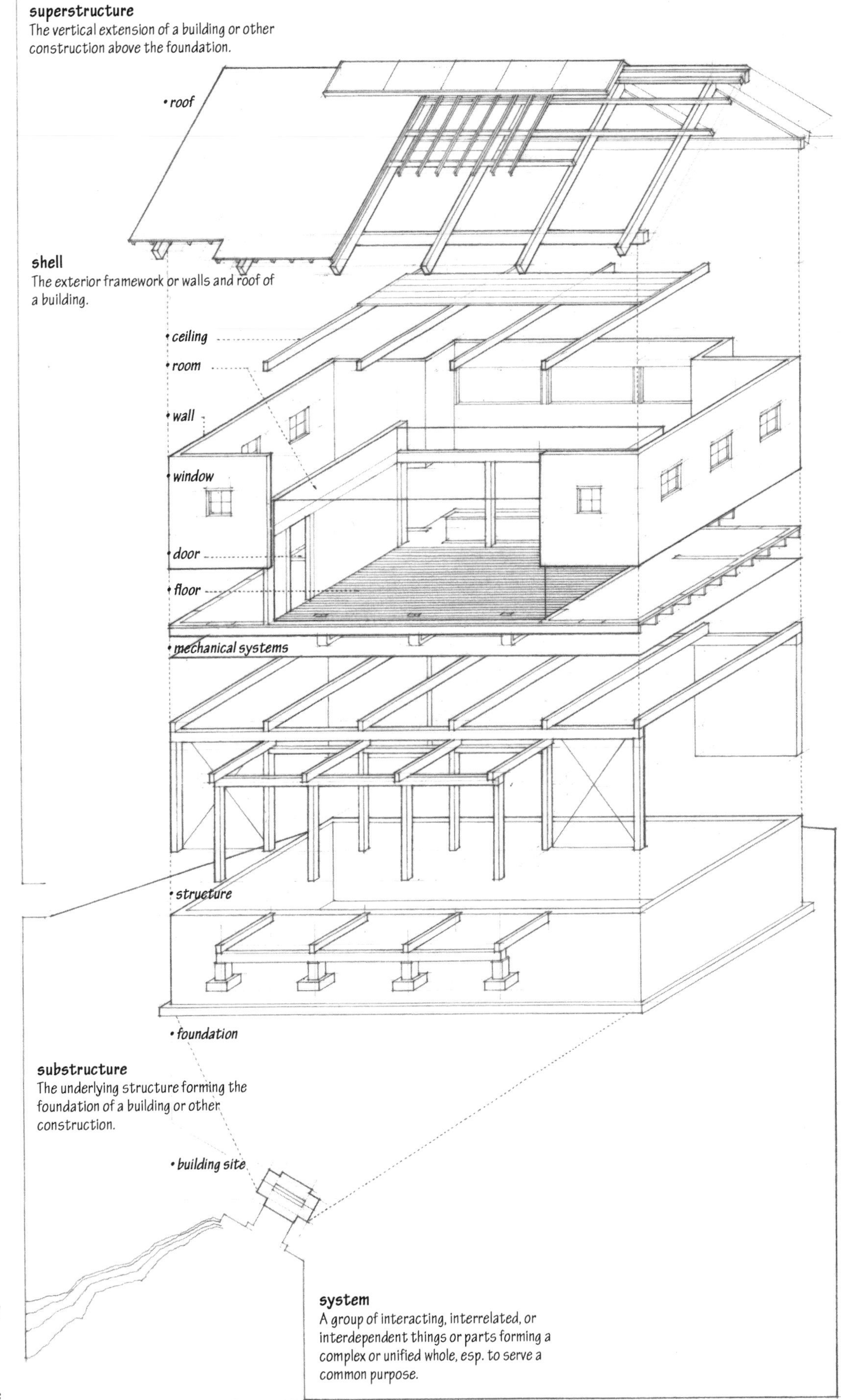

edifice
A building, esp. one of large size, massive structure, or imposing appearance.

skyscraper
A building of exceptional height and many stories, supported by a steel or concrete framework from which the walls are suspended.

high-rise
Describing a building having a comparatively large number of stories and equipped with elevators.

story
A complete horizontal division of a building, having a continuous or nearly continuous floor and comprising the space between two adjacent levels.

low-rise
Describing a building having one, two, or three stories and usually no elevator.

mid-rise
Describing a building having a moderately large number of stories, usually 5 to 10, and equipped with elevators.

loft
One of the upper floors of a warehouse or factory, typically unpartitioned and sometimes converted or adapted to other uses, as living quarters, artists' studios, or exhibition galleries.

loft building
A building having several floors with large areas of unobstructed space, originally rented out for light industrial purposes and now frequently converted to residential occupancy.

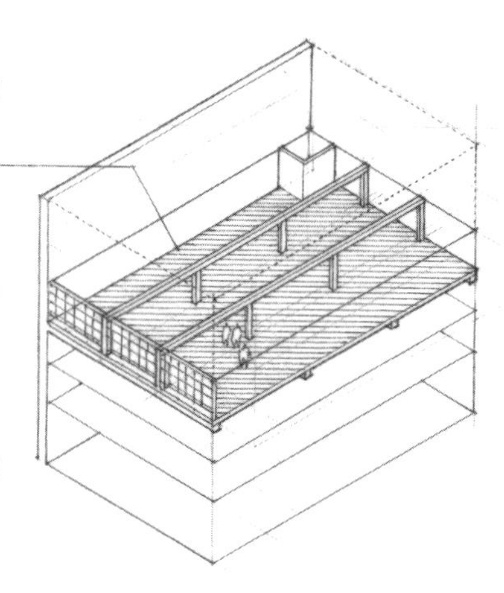

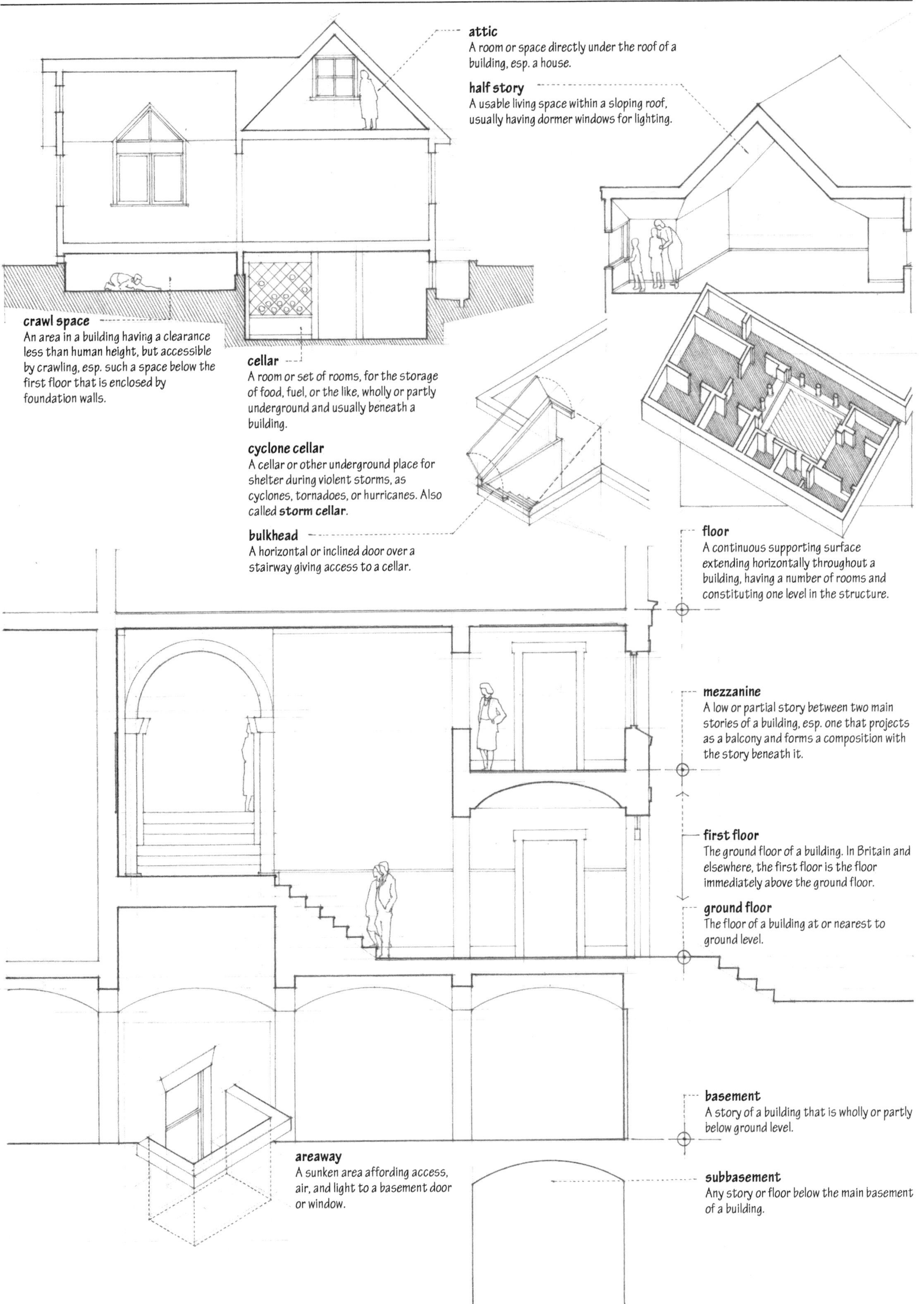

attic
A room or space directly under the roof of a building, esp. a house.

half story
A usable living space within a sloping roof, usually having dormer windows for lighting.

crawl space
An area in a building having a clearance less than human height, but accessible by crawling, esp. such a space below the first floor that is enclosed by foundation walls.

cellar
A room or set of rooms, for the storage of food, fuel, or the like, wholly or partly underground and usually beneath a building.

cyclone cellar
A cellar or other underground place for shelter during violent storms, as cyclones, tornadoes, or hurricanes. Also called **storm cellar**.

bulkhead
A horizontal or inclined door over a stairway giving access to a cellar.

floor
A continuous supporting surface extending horizontally throughout a building, having a number of rooms and constituting one level in the structure.

mezzanine
A low or partial story between two main stories of a building, esp. one that projects as a balcony and forms a composition with the story beneath it.

first floor
The ground floor of a building. In Britain and elsewhere, the first floor is the floor immediately above the ground floor.

ground floor
The floor of a building at or nearest to ground level.

basement
A story of a building that is wholly or partly below ground level.

areaway
A sunken area affording access, air, and light to a basement door or window.

subbasement
Any story or floor below the main basement of a building.

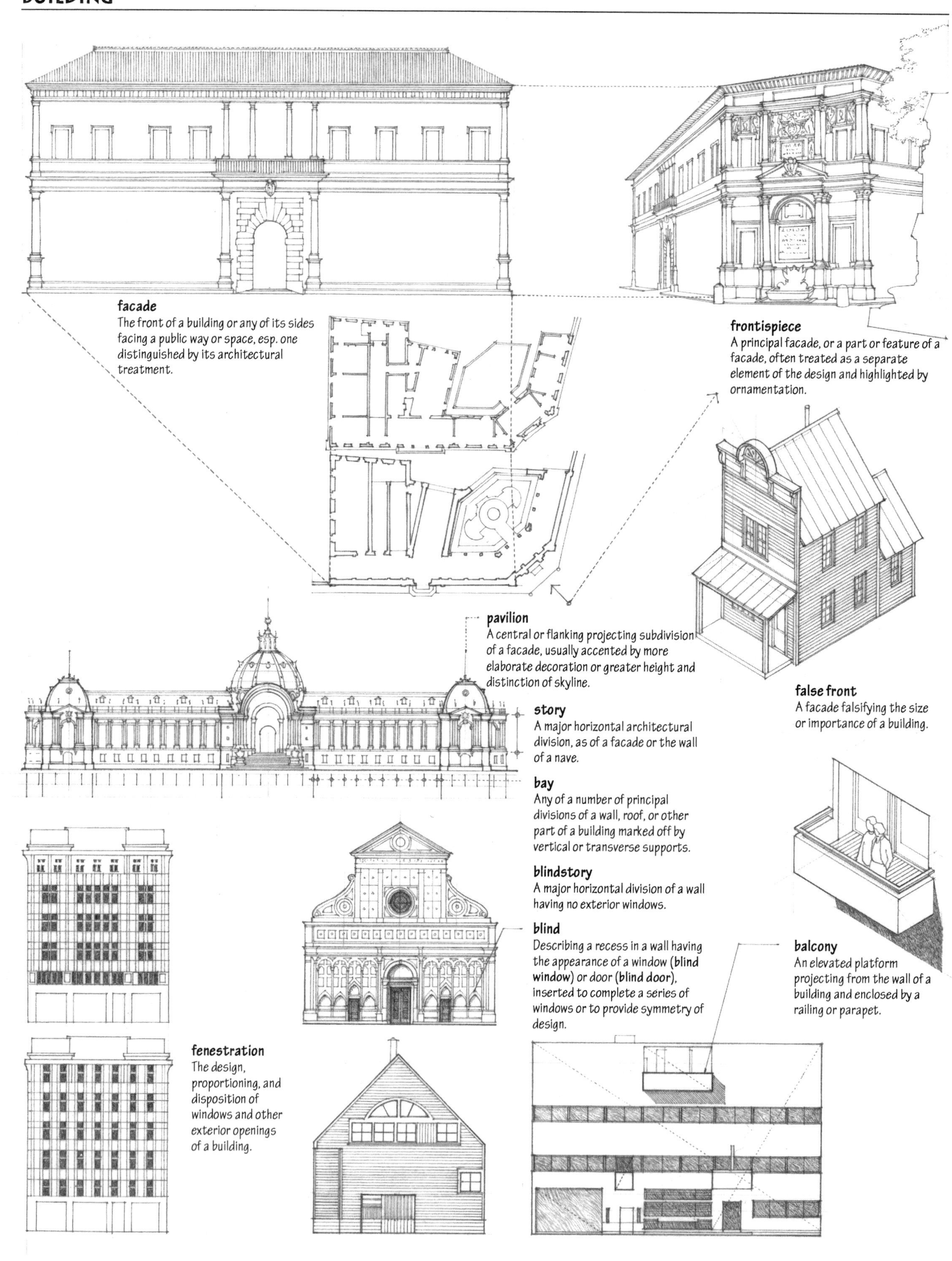

facade
The front of a building or any of its sides facing a public way or space, esp. one distinguished by its architectural treatment.

frontispiece
A principal facade, or a part or feature of a facade, often treated as a separate element of the design and highlighted by ornamentation.

pavilion
A central or flanking projecting subdivision of a facade, usually accented by more elaborate decoration or greater height and distinction of skyline.

false front
A facade falsifying the size or importance of a building.

story
A major horizontal architectural division, as of a facade or the wall of a nave.

bay
Any of a number of principal divisions of a wall, roof, or other part of a building marked off by vertical or transverse supports.

blindstory
A major horizontal division of a wall having no exterior windows.

blind
Describing a recess in a wall having the appearance of a window (**blind window**) or door (**blind door**), inserted to complete a series of windows or to provide symmetry of design.

balcony
An elevated platform projecting from the wall of a building and enclosed by a railing or parapet.

fenestration
The design, proportioning, and disposition of windows and other exterior openings of a building.

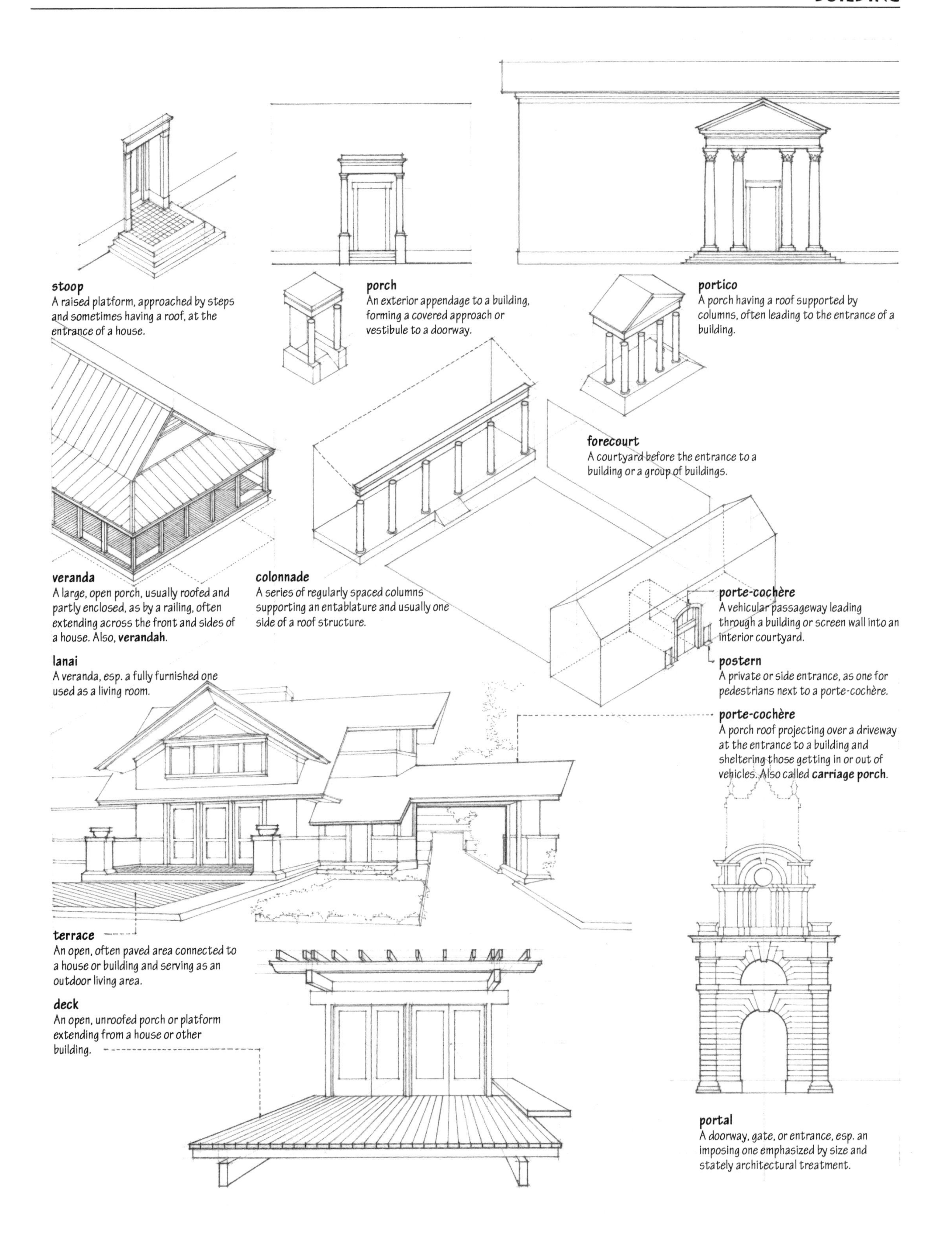

stoop
A raised platform, approached by steps and sometimes having a roof, at the entrance of a house.

porch
An exterior appendage to a building, forming a covered approach or vestibule to a doorway.

portico
A porch having a roof supported by columns, often leading to the entrance of a building.

forecourt
A courtyard before the entrance to a building or a group of buildings.

veranda
A large, open porch, usually roofed and partly enclosed, as by a railing, often extending across the front and sides of a house. Also, **verandah**.

lanai
A veranda, esp. a fully furnished one used as a living room.

colonnade
A series of regularly spaced columns supporting an entablature and usually one side of a roof structure.

porte-cochère
A vehicular passageway leading through a building or screen wall into an interior courtyard.

postern
A private or side entrance, as one for pedestrians next to a porte-cochère.

porte-cochère
A porch roof projecting over a driveway at the entrance to a building and sheltering those getting in or out of vehicles. Also called **carriage porch**.

terrace
An open, often paved area connected to a house or building and serving as an outdoor living area.

deck
An open, unroofed porch or platform extending from a house or other building.

portal
A doorway, gate, or entrance, esp. an imposing one emphasized by size and stately architectural treatment.

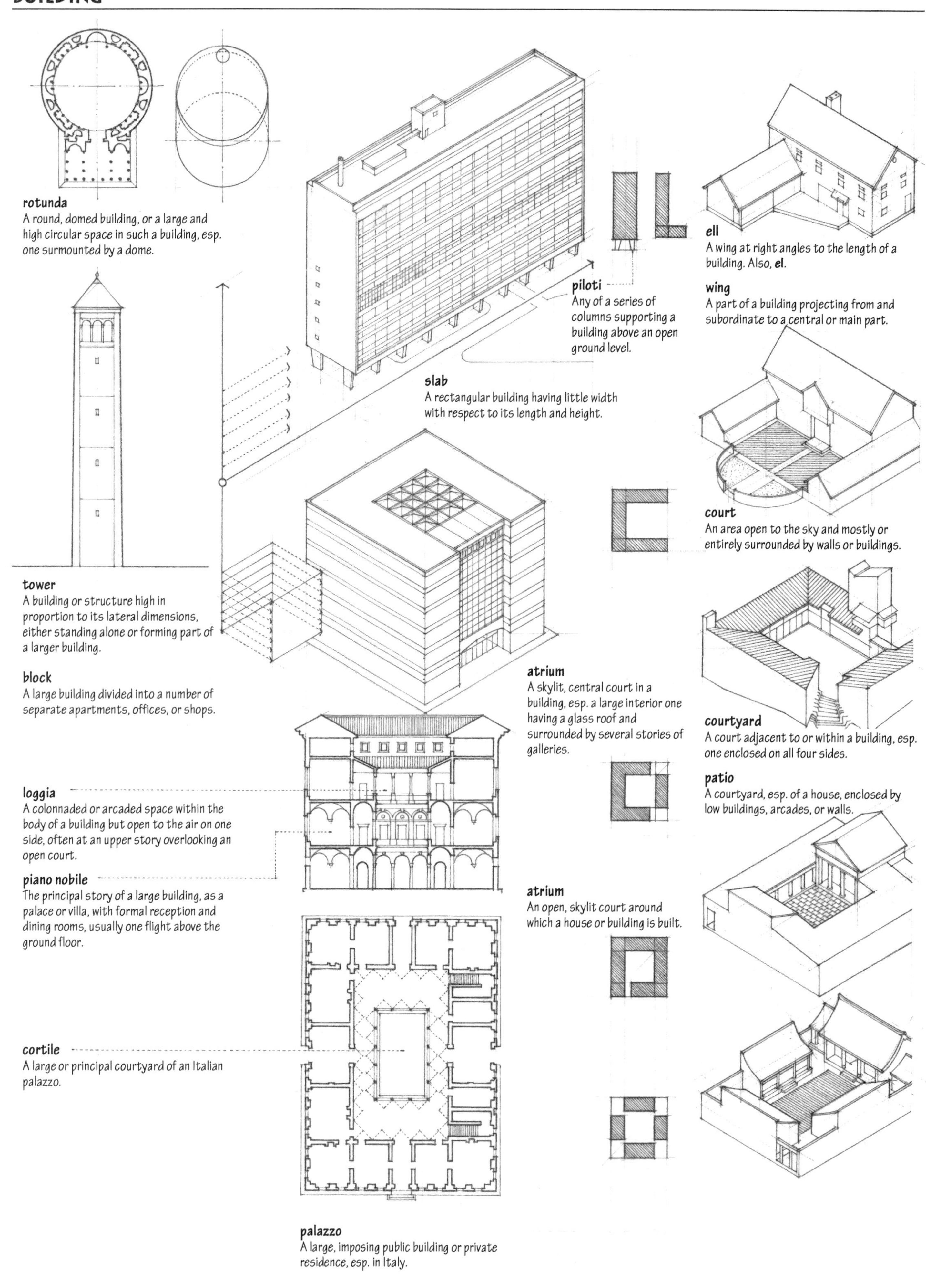

rotunda
A round, domed building, or a large and high circular space in such a building, esp. one surmounted by a dome.

tower
A building or structure high in proportion to its lateral dimensions, either standing alone or forming part of a larger building.

block
A large building divided into a number of separate apartments, offices, or shops.

loggia
A colonnaded or arcaded space within the body of a building but open to the air on one side, often at an upper story overlooking an open court.

piano nobile
The principal story of a large building, as a palace or villa, with formal reception and dining rooms, usually one flight above the ground floor.

cortile
A large or principal courtyard of an Italian palazzo.

slab
A rectangular building having little width with respect to its length and height.

piloti
Any of a series of columns supporting a building above an open ground level.

atrium
A skylit, central court in a building, esp. a large interior one having a glass roof and surrounded by several stories of galleries.

atrium
An open, skylit court around which a house or building is built.

palazzo
A large, imposing public building or private residence, esp. in Italy.

ell
A wing at right angles to the length of a building. Also, **el**.

wing
A part of a building projecting from and subordinate to a central or main part.

court
An area open to the sky and mostly or entirely surrounded by walls or buildings.

courtyard
A court adjacent to or within a building, esp. one enclosed on all four sides.

patio
A courtyard, esp. of a house, enclosed by low buildings, arcades, or walls.

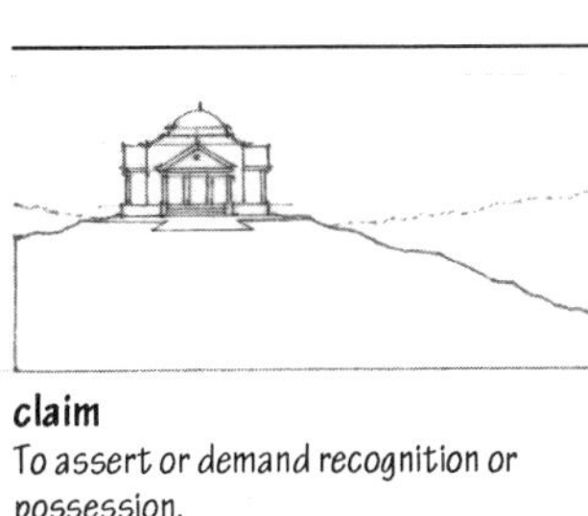

claim
To assert or demand recognition or possession.

merge
To combine, blend, or unite gradually by stages so as to blur identity or distinctions.

plaza
A public square or open space in a city or town.

piazza
An open square or public place in a city or town, esp. in Italy.

quadrangle
A square or quadrangular space or court surrounded by a building or buildings, as on a college campus. Also called **quad**.

galleria
A spacious promenade, court, or indoor mall, usually having a vaulted roof and lined with commercial establishments.

promenade
An area used for a stroll or walk, esp. in a public place, as for pleasure or display.

allée
French term for a broad walk planted with trees.

arbor
A shelter of shrubs and branches or of latticework intertwined with climbing vines and flowers.

trellis
A frame supporting open latticework, used as a screen or a support for growing vines or plants.

lattice
A structure of crossed strips arranged to form a regular pattern of open spaces.

front
To face in a specific direction or look out upon.

surround
To enclose or encompass on all sides.

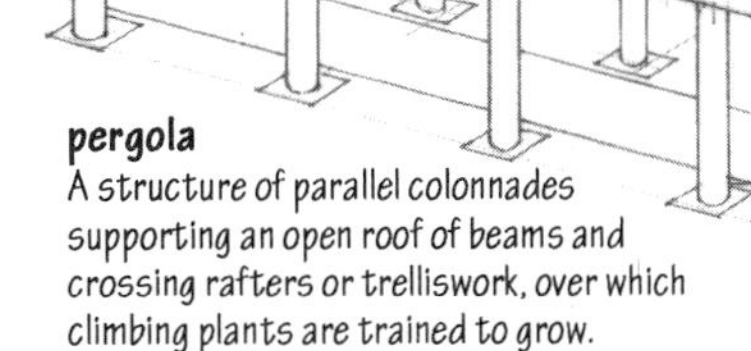

pergola
A structure of parallel colonnades supporting an open roof of beams and crossing rafters or trelliswork, over which climbing plants are trained to grow.

orientation
The position of a building on a site in relation to true north, to points on the compass, to a specific place or feature, or to local conditions of sunlight, wind, and drainage.

folly
A whimsical or extravagant structure built to serve as a conversation piece, lend interest to a view, or commemorate a person or event.

pavilion
A small, often ornamental building in a garden.

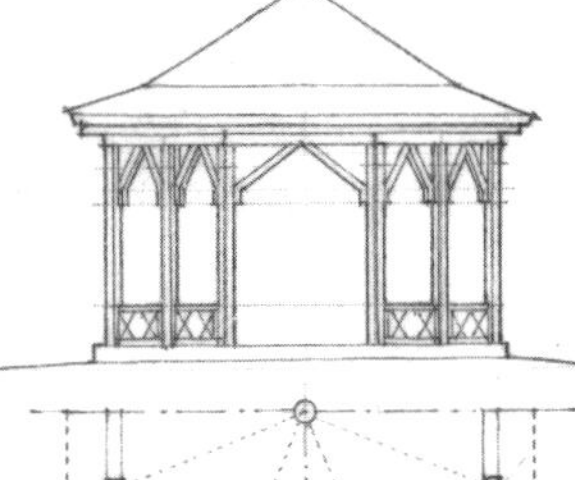

gazebo
A freestanding roofed structure, usually open on the sides, affording shade and rest in a garden or park.

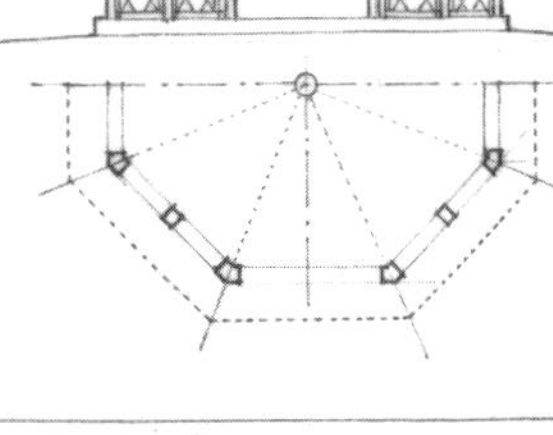

belvedere
A building, or architectural feature of a building, designed and situated to look out upon a pleasing scene.

topiary
Clipped or trimmed into ornamental and fantastic shapes, or the work or art of such clipping.

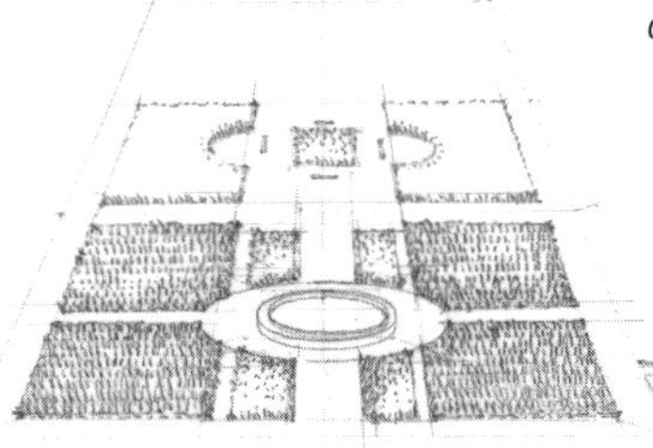

parterre
An ornamental arrangement of flower beds of different shapes and sizes.

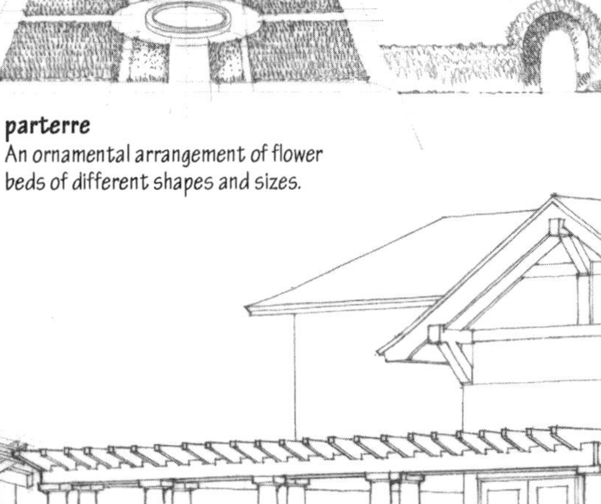

CABLE STRUCTURE

A structural system utilizing the cable as the principal means of support.

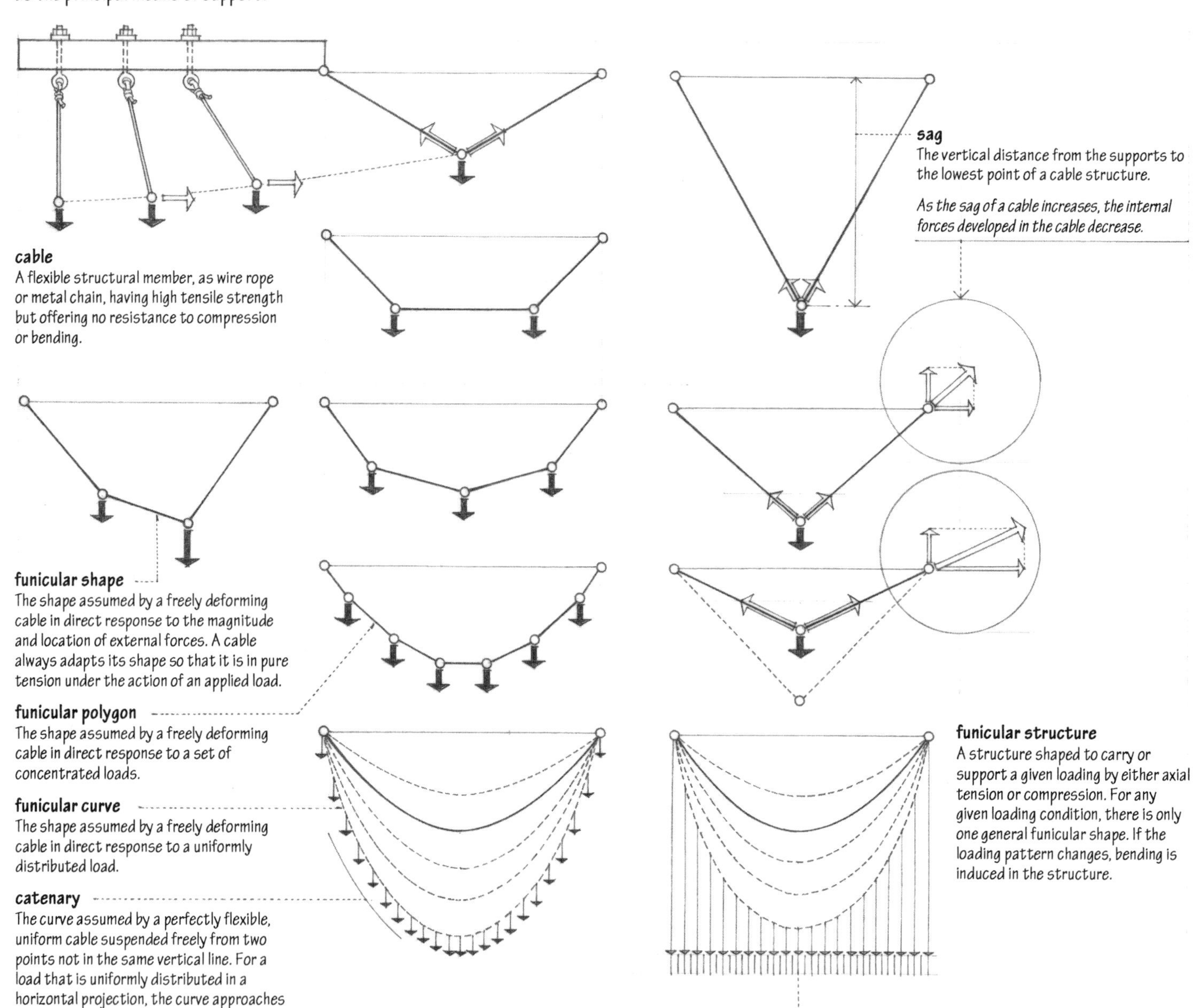

cable
A flexible structural member, as wire rope or metal chain, having high tensile strength but offering no resistance to compression or bending.

sag
The vertical distance from the supports to the lowest point of a cable structure.

As the sag of a cable increases, the internal forces developed in the cable decrease.

funicular shape
The shape assumed by a freely deforming cable in direct response to the magnitude and location of external forces. A cable always adapts its shape so that it is in pure tension under the action of an applied load.

funicular polygon
The shape assumed by a freely deforming cable in direct response to a set of concentrated loads.

funicular curve
The shape assumed by a freely deforming cable in direct response to a uniformly distributed load.

catenary
The curve assumed by a perfectly flexible, uniform cable suspended freely from two points not in the same vertical line. For a load that is uniformly distributed in a horizontal projection, the curve approaches that of a parabola.

funicular structure
A structure shaped to carry or support a given loading by either axial tension or compression. For any given loading condition, there is only one general funicular shape. If the loading pattern changes, bending is induced in the structure.

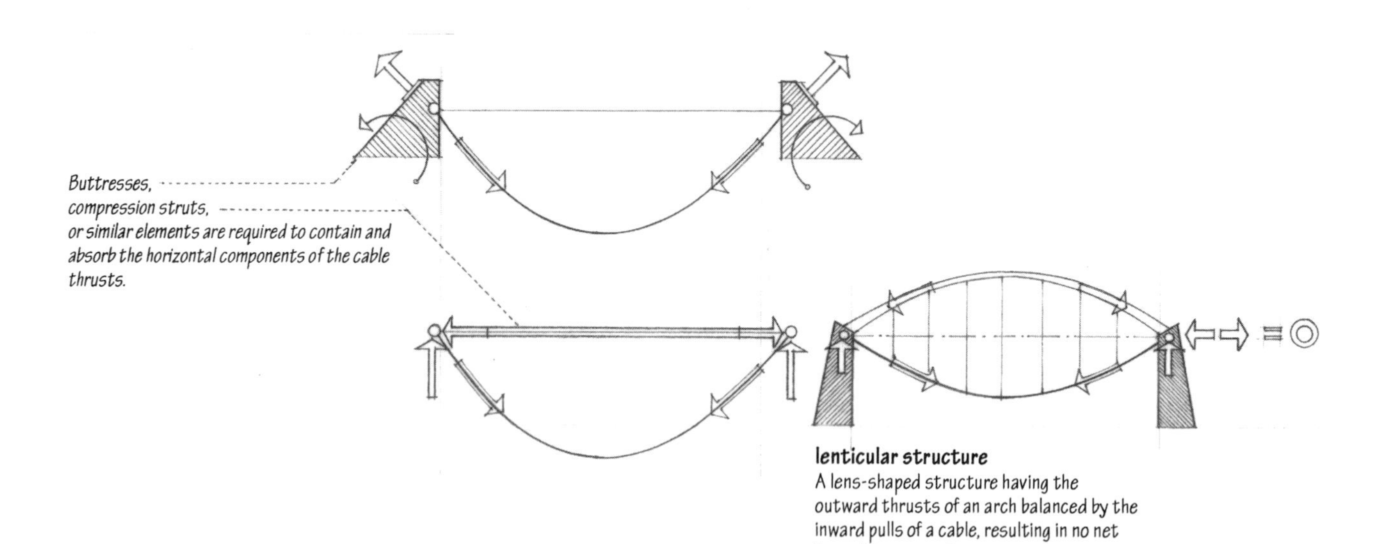

Buttresses,
compression struts,
or similar elements are required to contain and absorb the horizontal components of the cable thrusts.

lenticular structure
A lens-shaped structure having the outward thrusts of an arch balanced by the inward pulls of a cable, resulting in no net lateral forces at the supports.

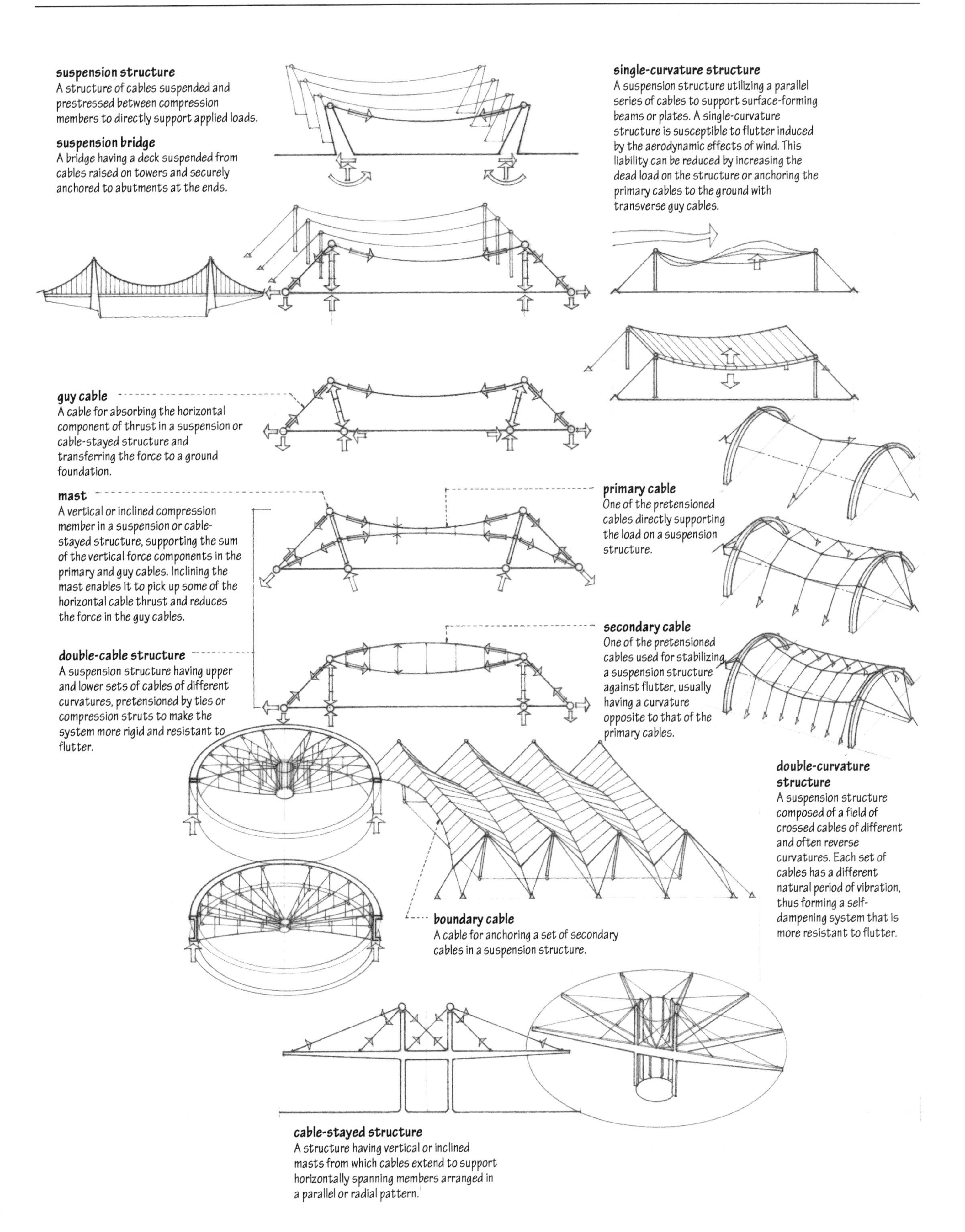

suspension structure
A structure of cables suspended and prestressed between compression members to directly support applied loads.

suspension bridge
A bridge having a deck suspended from cables raised on towers and securely anchored to abutments at the ends.

guy cable
A cable for absorbing the horizontal component of thrust in a suspension or cable-stayed structure and transferring the force to a ground foundation.

mast
A vertical or inclined compression member in a suspension or cable-stayed structure, supporting the sum of the vertical force components in the primary and guy cables. Inclining the mast enables it to pick up some of the horizontal cable thrust and reduces the force in the guy cables.

double-cable structure
A suspension structure having upper and lower sets of cables of different curvatures, pretensioned by ties or compression struts to make the system more rigid and resistant to flutter.

single-curvature structure
A suspension structure utilizing a parallel series of cables to support surface-forming beams or plates. A single-curvature structure is susceptible to flutter induced by the aerodynamic effects of wind. This liability can be reduced by increasing the dead load on the structure or anchoring the primary cables to the ground with transverse guy cables.

primary cable
One of the pretensioned cables directly supporting the load on a suspension structure.

secondary cable
One of the pretensioned cables used for stabilizing a suspension structure against flutter, usually having a curvature opposite to that of the primary cables.

double-curvature structure
A suspension structure composed of a field of crossed cables of different and often reverse curvatures. Each set of cables has a different natural period of vibration, thus forming a self-dampening system that is more resistant to flutter.

boundary cable
A cable for anchoring a set of secondary cables in a suspension structure.

cable-stayed structure
A structure having vertical or inclined masts from which cables extend to support horizontally spanning members arranged in a parallel or radial pattern.

CEILING

The overhead interior surface or lining of a room, often concealing the underside of the floor or roof above.

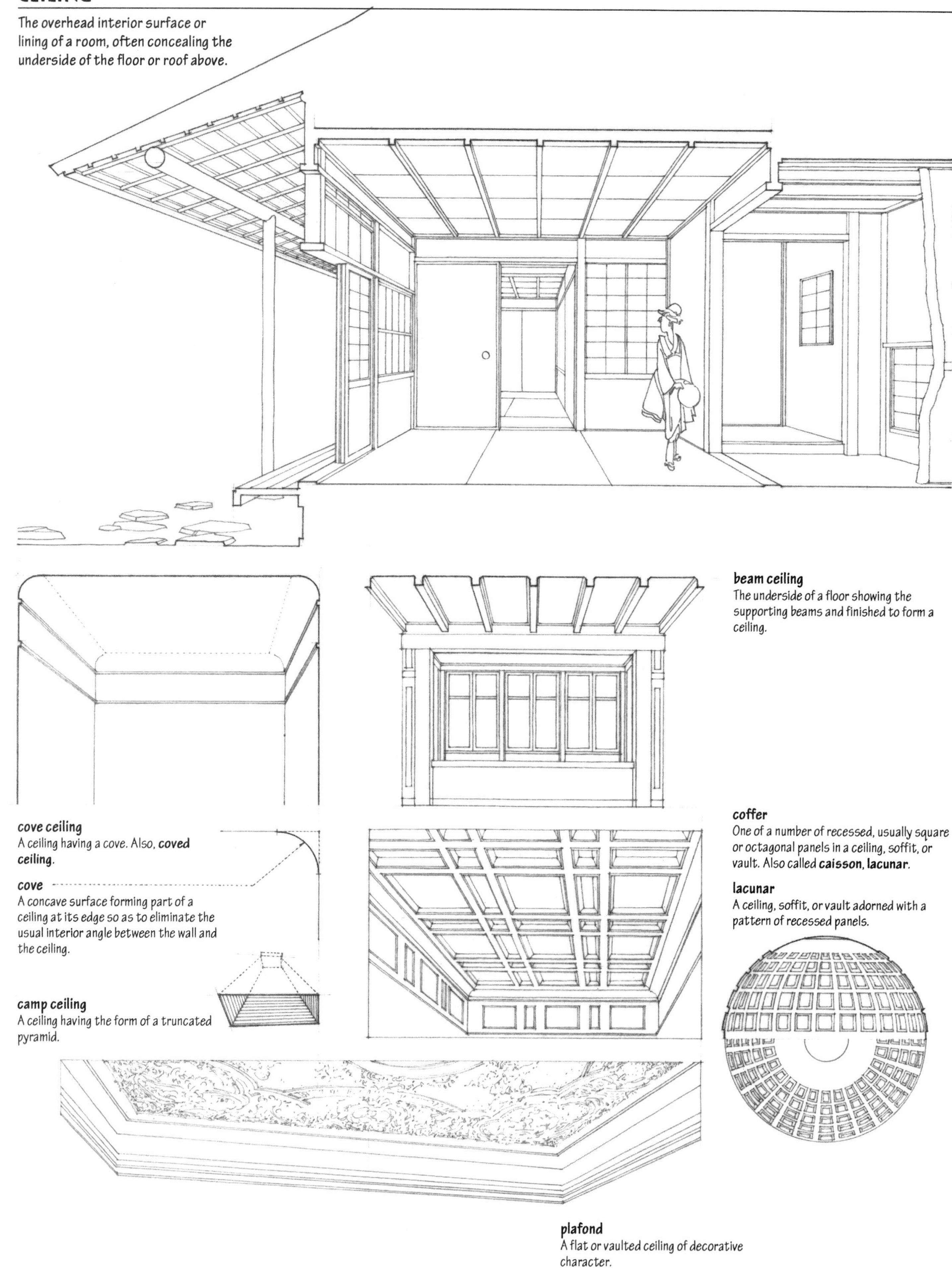

beam ceiling
The underside of a floor showing the supporting beams and finished to form a ceiling.

cove ceiling
A ceiling having a cove. Also, **coved ceiling**.

cove
A concave surface forming part of a ceiling at its edge so as to eliminate the usual interior angle between the wall and the ceiling.

camp ceiling
A ceiling having the form of a truncated pyramid.

coffer
One of a number of recessed, usually square or octagonal panels in a ceiling, soffit, or vault. Also called **caisson, lacunar**.

lacunar
A ceiling, soffit, or vault adorned with a pattern of recessed panels.

plafond
A flat or vaulted ceiling of decorative character.

drop ceiling
A secondary ceiling formed to provide space for piping or ductwork, or to alter the proportions of a room. Also, **dropped ceiling**.

suspended ceiling
A ceiling suspended from an overhead floor or roof structure to provide space for pipes, ductwork, lighting fixtures, or other service equipment.

plenum
The space between a suspended ceiling and the floor structure above, esp. one that serves as a receiving chamber for conditioned air to be distributed to inhabited spaces or for return air to be conveyed back to a central plant for processing.

acoustical ceiling
A ceiling of acoustical tile or other sound-absorbing material.

acoustical tile
Tile made in various sizes and textures from a soft, sound-absorbing material, as cork, mineral fiber, or glass fiber.

metal pan
An acoustical tile consisting of a steel or aluminum pan having a perforated face and containing a separate layer of sound-absorbing material.

exposed grid
A metal grid of inverted tees supporting the acoustical tiles of a suspended ceiling.

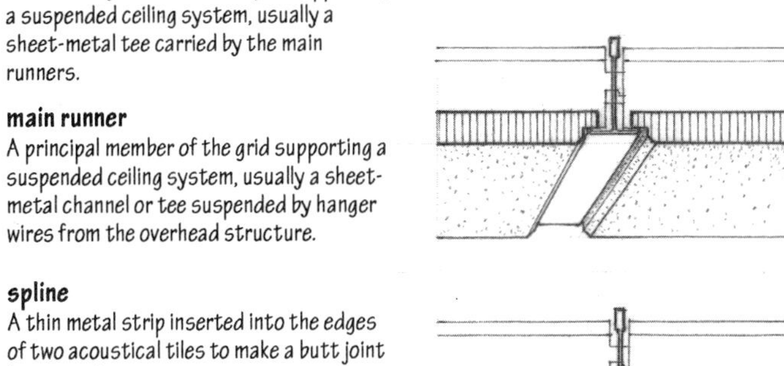

cross tee
A secondary member of the grid supporting a suspended ceiling system, usually a sheet-metal tee carried by the main runners.

main runner
A principal member of the grid supporting a suspended ceiling system, usually a sheet-metal channel or tee suspended by hanger wires from the overhead structure.

recessed grid
A metal grid for supporting a suspended ceiling of acoustical tiles having rabbeted joints.

spline
A thin metal strip inserted into the edges of two acoustical tiles to make a butt joint between them.

kerf
A groove cut into the edges of an acoustical tile to receive a spline or T-shaped member of a supporting grid.

concealed grid
A metal grid supporting the acoustical tiles of a suspended ceiling, hidden within kerfs cut into the edges of the tiles.

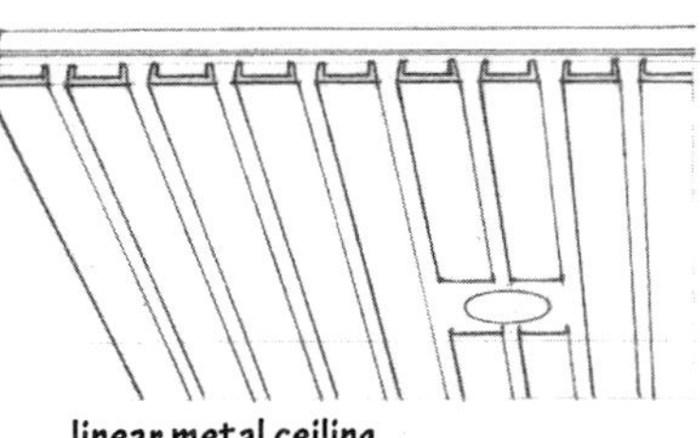

linear metal ceiling
A suspended ceiling system of narrow metal strips, usually incorporating modular lighting and air-handling components.

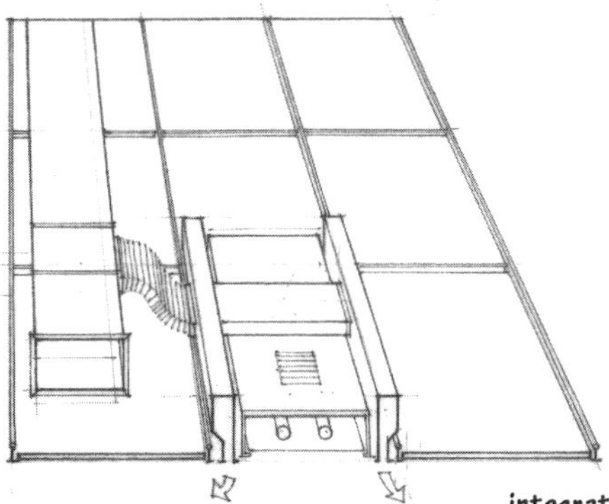

integrated ceiling
A suspended ceiling system incorporating acoustical, lighting, and air-handling components into a unified whole.

linear diffuser
A long, narrow diffuser designed to disperse air through slots between the panels of an integrated ceiling system. Also called **slot diffuser**.

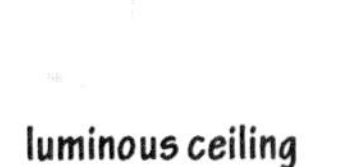

luminous ceiling
A suspended ceiling of translucent panels for diffusing the light from luminaires mounted above it.

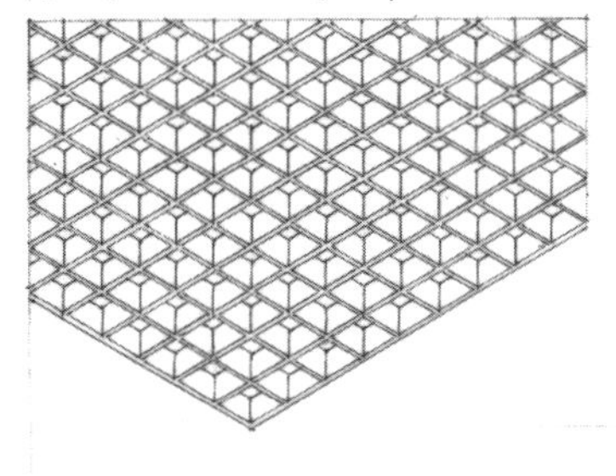

louvered ceiling
A suspended ceiling of multicellular louvers for shielding the light sources mounted above it.

Any of various hard, brittle, noncorrosive, and nonconductive materials formed by the ionic bonding of a metal and a nonmetal, as brick, concrete, and natural stone.

ceramic ware
Any of various products made by firing clay or similar materials in a kiln, as brick, tile, and pottery.

earthenware
Low-fired, opaque, nonvitreous ceramic ware.

stoneware
High-fired, opaque, vitrified ceramic ware.

porcelain
A hard, vitreous, translucent ceramic material consisting essentially of kaolin, feldspar, and quartz, fired at a very high temperature.

china
A translucent ceramic material, bisque-fired at a high temperature and glaze-fired at a lower temperature.

kaolin
A fine white clay used in the manufacture of porcelain and white portland cement. Also called **china clay**.

enamel
A vitreous, usually opaque, decorative or protective coating applied by fusion to the surface of metal, glass, or pottery.

porcelain enamel
An opaque, glassy coating bonded to metal by fusing at a high temperature. Also called **vitreous enamel**.

firing
The process of hardening or glazing ceramic ware by heating in a kiln to a specified temperature.

vitrify
To make a clay body vitreous by firing at a specified temperature.

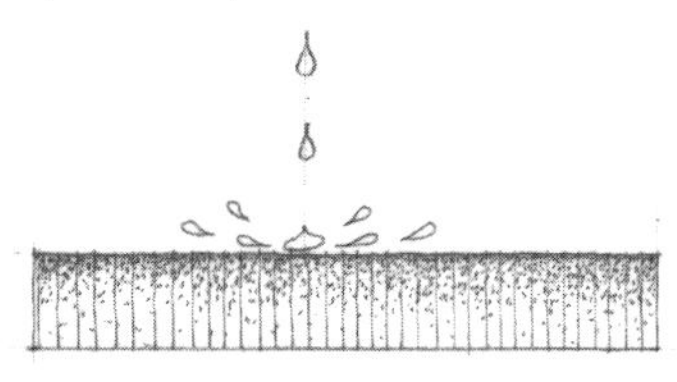

ceramic bond
A thermochemical bond between materials resulting from exposure to temperatures approaching the fusion point of the mixture.

body
The structural portion of a ceramic article or the clay material or mixture from which it is made.

hard-burned
Fired at a high temperature to near vitrification and having relatively low absorption and high compressive strength.

vitreous
Resembling glass, as in transparency, hardness, brittleness, luster, or having low or no porosity.

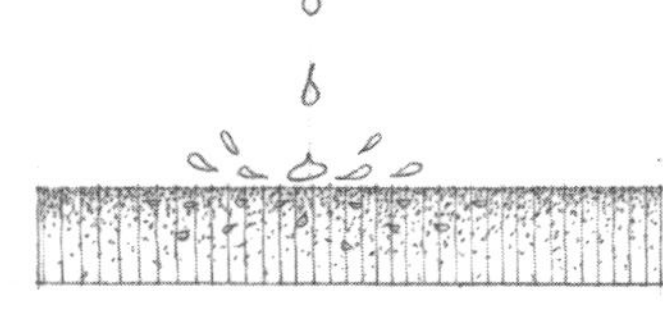

biscque-fired
Fired to harden a clay body.

bisque
Earthenware or porcelain that has been fired once but not glazed. Also called **biscuit**.

glaze-fired
Fired to fuse a glaze to a clay body.

glaze
A vitreous layer or coating fused to a clay body to color, decorate, waterproof, or strengthen its surface.

frit
A fused or partially fused material that is ground to introduce a soluble or unstable ingredients into glazes or enamels.

soft-burned
Fired at a low temperature and having relatively high absorption and low compressive strength.

semivitreous
Having a moderate water absorption of slightly under 6%.

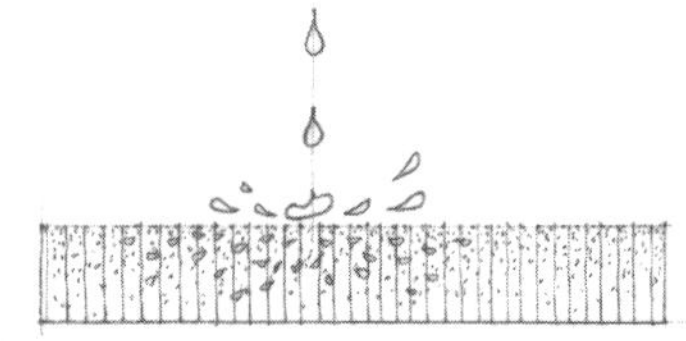

nonvitreous
Having a water absorption greater than 7%.

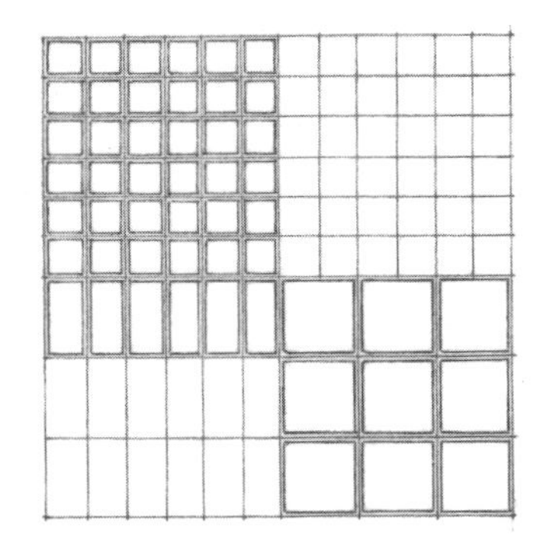

ceramic tile
Any of various fired clay tiles used for surfacing walls, floors, and countertops.

glazed wall tile
Ceramic tile having a nonvitreous body and a bright, matte, or crystalline glaze, used for surfacing interior walls and light-duty floors.

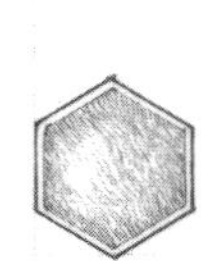

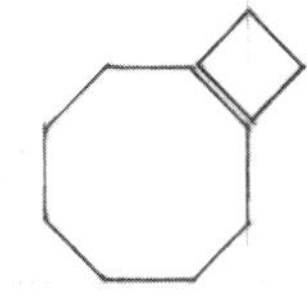

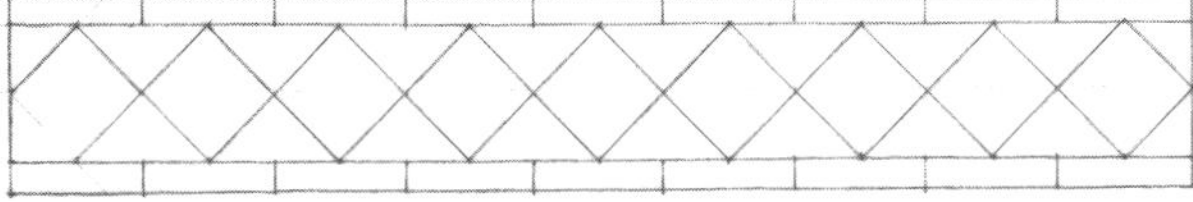

trimmer
Any of various specially shaped ceramic tiles for finishing an edge or angle.

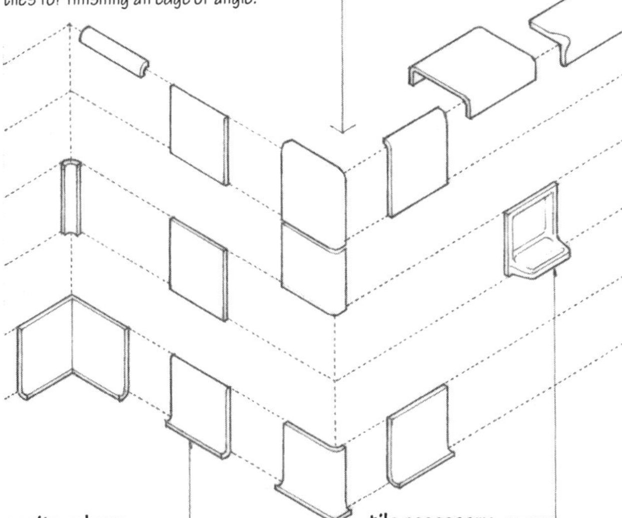

sanitary base
A coved tile set at the meeting of a floor and wall to prevent accumulation of dirt and to facilitate cleaning.

tile accessory
Any of the ceramic or nonceramic articles designed to be affixed to or inserted in tilework, as tower bars, soap holders, and the like.

ceramic mosaic tile
Small ceramic tile having a porcelain or natural clay body, glazed for surfacing walls or unglazed for use on both floors and walls, and usually face- or back-mounted on sheets to facilitate handling and speed installation.

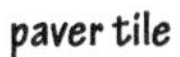

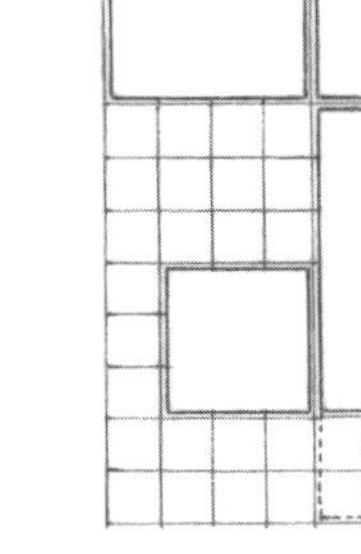

quarry tile
Unglazed ceramic floor tile having a natural clay body. Also called **promenade tile**.

paver tile
Unglazed ceramic floor tile similar in composition to ceramic mosaic tile but thicker and larger in surface area.

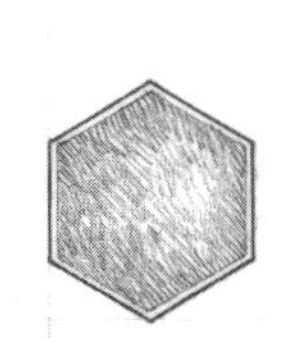

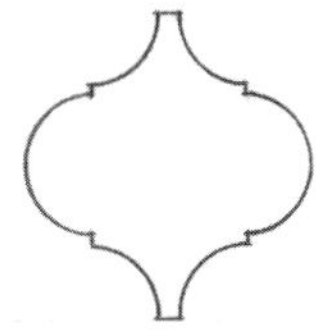

thick-set process
A tilesetting process in which ceramic tile is applied over a portland cement mortar bed 3/4 to 1 1/2 in. (19 to 38 mm) thick, which allows for accurate slopes and planes in the finished work.

portland cement mortar
A field mix of portland cement, sand, water, and sometimes hydrated lime, used for leveling or setting ceramic tile in the thick-set process.

bond coat
A thin coat of mortar for bonding ceramic tile to a backing.

thin-bed process
A tilesetting process in which ceramic tile is bonded to a continuous, stable backing with a thin coat of dry-set mortar, latex-portland cement mortar, epoxy mortar, or an organic adhesive, 1/32 to 1/8 in. (0.8 to 3.2 mm) thick.

tile grout
A cementitious or resinous mix for filling joints in ceramic tilework.

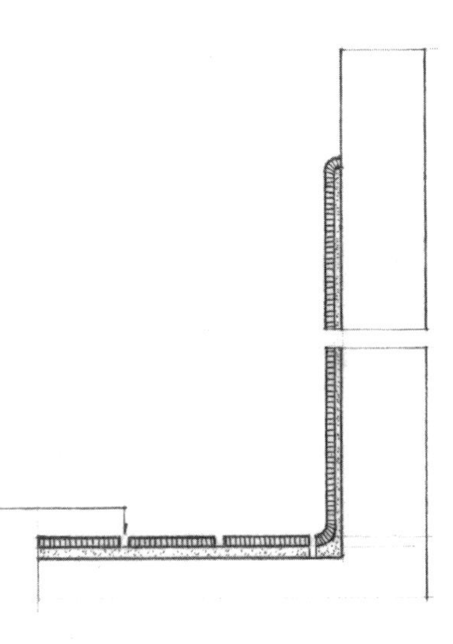

structural clay tile
A hollow tile of fired clay having parallel cells or cores, used in building walls and partitions.

LB
Load-bearing structural clay tile suitable for masonry walls not exposed to frost action, or in exposed masonry where protected by a facing of 3 in. (76.2 mm) or more of stone, brick, terra cotta, or other masonry.

LBX
Load-bearing structural clay tile suitable for masonry walls exposed to weathering or frost action.

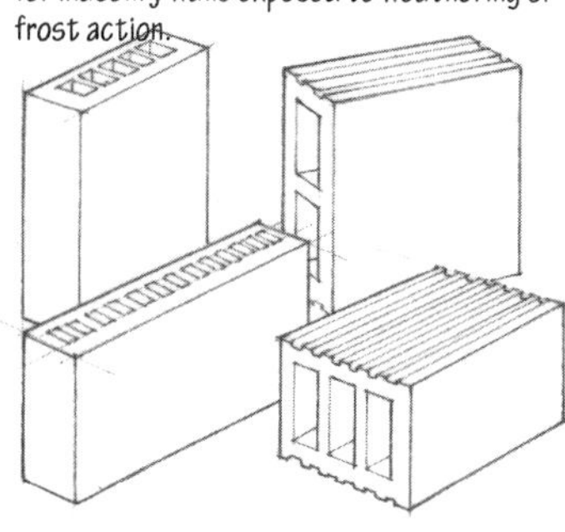

hollow tile
Any of various cellular building units of fired clay, concrete, or gypsum, used for building walls, floors, and roofs, or for fireproofing steelwork.

structural facing tile
Structural clay tile having a glazed surface, used for facing walls and partitions, esp. in areas subject to heavy wear, moisture problems, and strict sanitation requirements.

FTS
Structural facing tile suitable for exposed exterior and interior masonry walls and partitions where moderate absorption, slight variation in face dimensions, minor defects in surface finish, and medium color range are acceptable.

FTX
Smooth structural facing tile suitable for exposed exterior and interior masonry walls and partitions where low absorption and stain resistance are required, and where a high degree of mechanical perfection, minimum variation in face dimensions, and narrow color range are desired.

terra cotta
A hard, fired clay, reddish-brown in color when unglazed, used for architectural facings and ornaments, tile units, and pottery.

architectural terra cotta
Hard-burned, glazed or unglazed terra cotta, hand-molded or machine-extruded to order as a ceramic veneer for walls or for ornamentation.

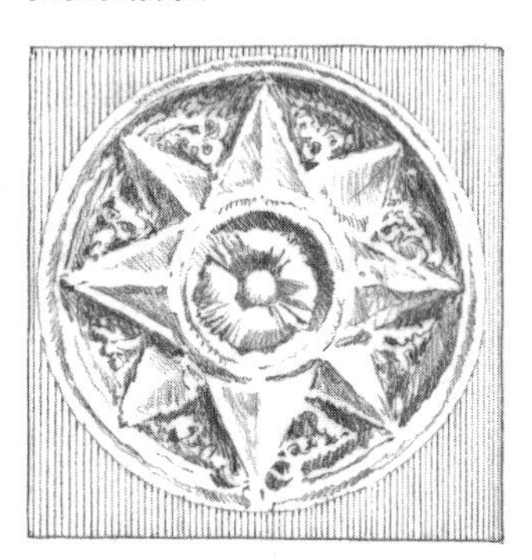

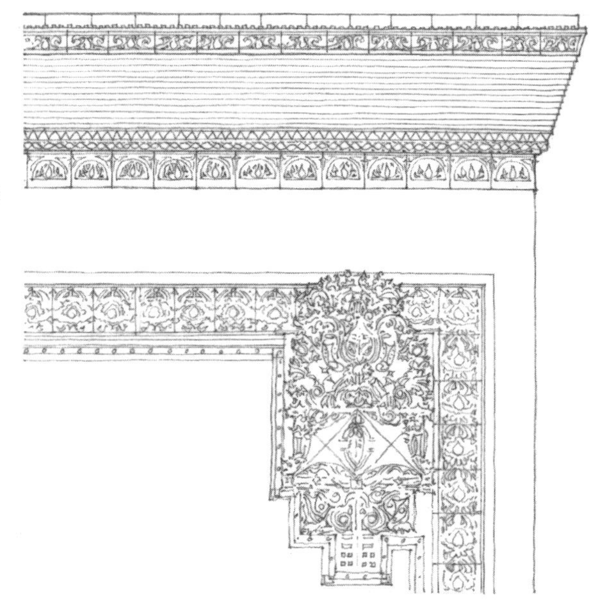

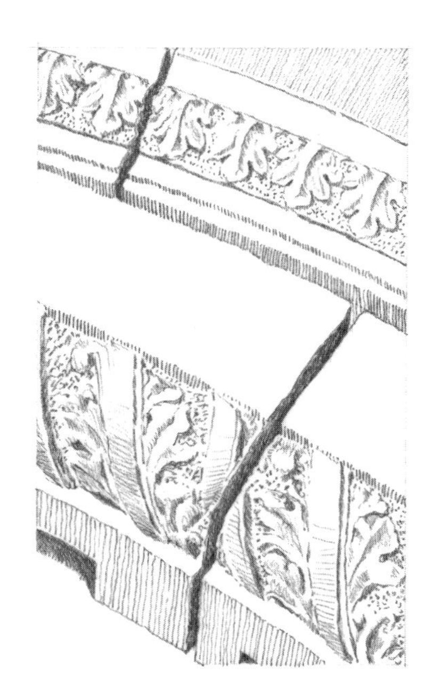

adobe
Sun-dried brick made of clay and straw, commonly used in countries with little rainfall.

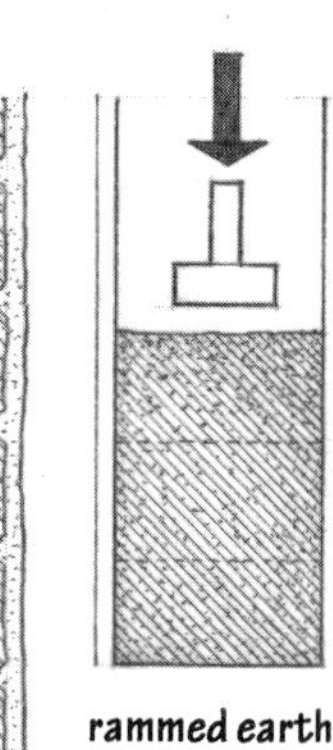

rammed earth
A stiff mixture of clay, sand or other aggregate, and water compressed and dried within forms as a wall construction. Also called **pisé**, **pisay**, **pisé de terre**.

A building for public Christian worship.

Christianity
The religion, founded on the teachings of Jesus Christ, including the Catholic, Protestant, and Eastern Orthodox churches.

basilica
An early Christian church, characterized by a long, rectangular plan, a high colonnaded nave lit by a clerestory and covered by a timbered gable roof, two or four lower side aisles, a semicircular apse at the end, a narthex, and often other features, as an atrium, a bema, and small semicircular apses terminating the aisles.

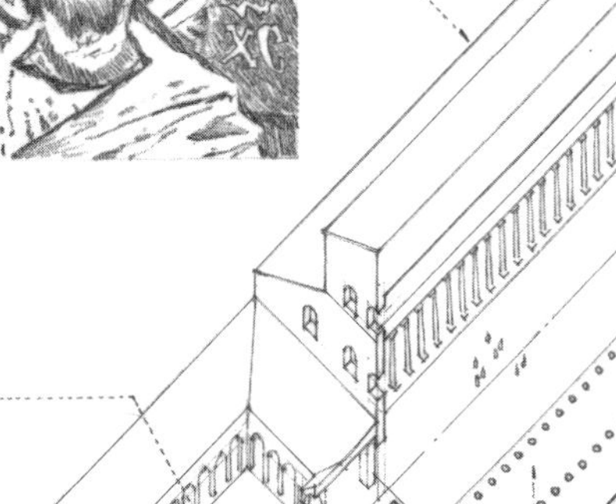

atrium
The forecourt of an early Christian church, flanked or surrounded by porticoes.

ambulatory
The covered walk of an atrium or cloister.

cantharus
A basin for a ritual cleansing with water in the atrium of an early Christian basilica.

apse
A semicircular or polygonal projection of a building, usually vaulted and used esp. at the sanctuary or east end of a church. Also, **apsis**.

tribune
The bishop's throne, occupying a recess or apse in an early Christian church.

bema
A transverse open space separating the nave and the apse of an early Christian church, developing into the transept of later cruciform churches.

sanctuary
A sacred or holy place, as that part of a church in which the principal altar is placed.

altar
The table in a Christian church upon which the Eucharist, the sacrament celebrating Christ's Last Supper, is celebrated. Also called **communion table**.

nave
The principal or central part of a church, extending from the narthex to the choir or chancel and usually flanked by aisles.

aisle
Any of the longitudinal divisions of a church, separated from the nave by a row of columns or piers.

baldachin
An ornamental canopy of stone or marble permanently placed over the altar in a church. Also, **baldachino**, **baldaquin**. Also called **ciborium**.

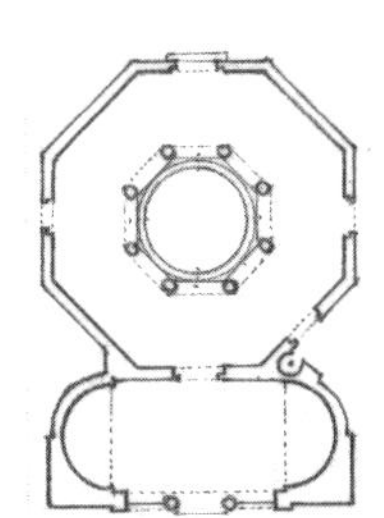

baptistery
A part of a church or a separate building in which baptism is administered. Also, **baptistry**.

baptism
A sacrament of initiation into Christianity, symbolic of spiritual regeneration, marked by a ceremonial immersion or application of water.

font
A basin, usually of stone, holding the water used in baptism.

narthex
The portico before the nave of an early Christian or Byzantine church, appropriated to penitents.

esonarthex
An inner narthex when two are present.

exonarthex
A covered walk or outer narthex situated before an inner narthex.

ambo
Either of two raised stands from which the Gospels or Epistles were read or chanted in an early Christian church. Also, **ambon**.

cancelli
A low screen in an early Christian basilica, separating the clergy and sometimes the choir from the congregation.

sarcophagus
A stone coffin, esp. one bearing sculpture or inscriptions and displayed as a monument.

icon
A representation of a sacred Christian personage, as Christ or a saint or angel, typically painted on a wood surface and itself venerated as being sacred, esp. in the tradition of the Eastern Church.

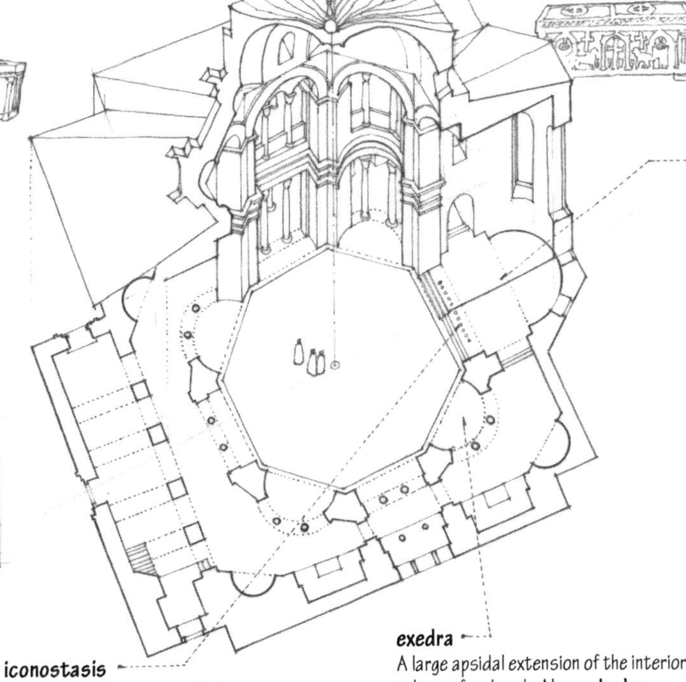

bema
The sanctuary space surrounding the altar of an Eastern church.

diaconicon
A sacristy in an early Christian or Eastern church, usually on the south side of the bema.

sacristy
A room in a church where the sacred vessels and vestments are kept. Also called **vestry**.

prothesis
A chapel in an Eastern Church where the Eucharistic elements are prepared, usually on the north side of the bema.

iconostasis
A screen or partition on which icons are placed, separating the bema from the nave of an Eastern church. Also, **iconostas**.

exedra
A large apsidal extension of the interior volume of a church. Also, **exhedra**.

transept
The major transverse part of a cruciform church, crossing the main axis at a right angle between the nave and choir.

crossing
The intersection of the nave and transept in a cruciform church.

spire
A tall, acutely tapering pyramidal structure surmounting a steeple or tower.

westwork
The monumental western front of a Romanesque church, treated as a tower or towers containing a low entrance hall below and a chapel open to the nave above.

campanile
A bell tower, usually one near but not attached to the body of a church.

steeple
A tall ornamental structure, usually ending in a spire and surmounting the tower of a church or other public building.

onion dome
A bulbous, domelike roof terminating in a sharp point, used esp. in Russian Orthodox church architecture to cover a cupola or tower.

wheel window
A rose window having distinctly radiating mullions or bars. Also called **Catherine wheel, marigold window**.

tympanum
The space between an arch and the horizontal head of a door or window below, often decorated with sculpture.

trumeau
A column supporting the tympanum of a doorway at its center.

tabernacle
A canopied recess for a religious image or icon.

gallery
A roofed promenade, esp. one extending inside or outside along the exterior wall of a building.

loft
A gallery or upper level in a church or hall.

stave church
An indigenous Scandinavian church of the 12th and 13th centuries, having a timber frame, plank walls, a tiered, steeply pitched roof, and few windows.

arcade
A series of arches supported on piers or columns.

arcuate
Curved or arched like a bow: a term used in describing the arched or vaulted structure of a Romanesque church or Gothic cathedral, as distinguished from the trabeated architecture of an Egyptian hypostyle hall or Greek Doric temple. Also, **arcuated**.

respond
A pier or pilaster projecting from a wall as a support for an arch or lintel, esp. at the termination of an arcade or colonnade.

dosseret
A thickened abacus or supplementary capital set above a column capital to receive the thrust of an arch. Also called **impost block**.

interlacing arcade
An arcade, esp. a blind one, composed of arches resting on alternate supports and overlapping in series where they cross. Also called **intersecting arcade**.

blind arcade
A series of arches superimposed on a wall for decoration. Also called **arcature**.

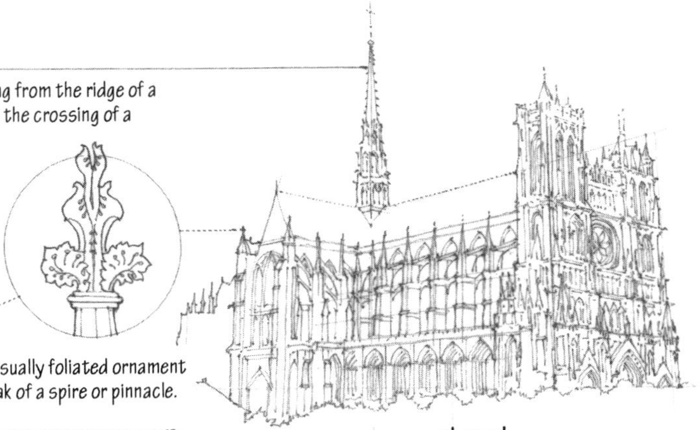

cathedral
The principal church of a diocese, containing the bishop's throne called the cathedra.

flèche
A slender spire rising from the ridge of a roof, esp. one above the crossing of a Gothic church.

finial
A relatively small, usually foliated ornament terminating the peak of a spire or pinnacle.

crocket
A projecting ornament, usually in the form of curved foliage, used esp. in Gothic architecture to decorate the outer angles of pinnacles, spires, and gables.

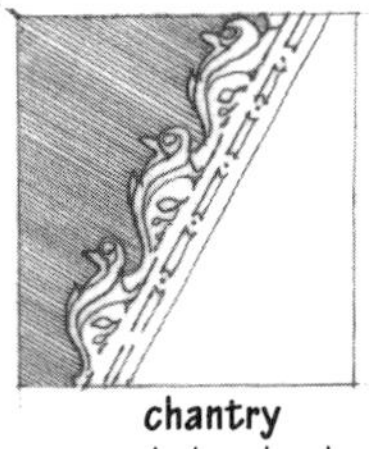

gargoyle
A grotesquely carved figure of a human or animal, esp. one with an open mouth that serves as a spout and projects from a gutter to throw rainwater clear of a building.

chapel
A separately dedicated part of a church for private prayer, meditation, or small religious services.

chancel
The space about the altar of a church for the clergy and choir, often elevated above the nave and separated from it by a railing or screen.

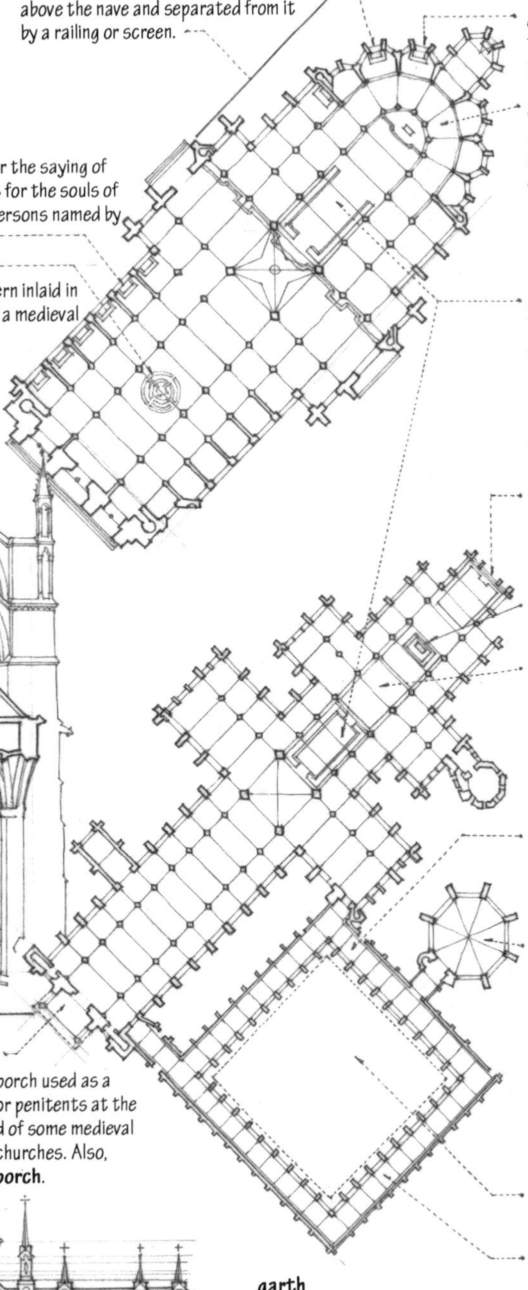

chevet
The rounded east end of a Gothic cathedral, including the apse and ambulatory.

ambulatory
An aisle encircling the end of the choir or chancel of a church. Also called **deambulatory**.

chantry
A chapel endowed for the saying of Masses and prayers for the souls of the founders or of persons named by them.

labyrinth
A mazelike pattern inlaid in the pavement of a medieval church.

choir
The part of a church occupied by the singers of a choir, usually part of the chancel.

retrochoir
A separate division behind the choir or high altar of a large church.

Lady chapel
A chapel dedicated to the Virgin Mary, usually located behind the high altar of a cathedral at the extremity of the apse.

rose window
A circular window, usually of stained glass and decorated with tracery symmetrical about the center.

stained glass
Glass colored or stained by having pigments baked onto its surface or by having various metallic oxides fused into it while in a molten state.

high altar
The main altar of a church.

presbytery
The part of a church reserved for the officiating clergy.

close
An enclosed place, esp. the land surrounding or beside a cathedral.

triforium
An arcaded story in a church, between the nave arches and clerestory and corresponding to the space between the vaulting and the roof of an aisle.

slype
A covered passage, esp. one between the transept and chapter house of a cathedral. Also, **slip**.

chapter house
The place where the chapter of a cathedral or monastery meets, usually a building attached to or a hall forming part of the cathedral or monastery.

crypt
An underground chamber or vault used as a burial place, esp. one beneath the main floor of a church.

galilee
A small porch used as a chapel for penitents at the west end of some medieval English churches. Also, **galilee porch**.

chapter
An assembly of the monks in a monastery, or the members of a religious house or order.

rood
A crucifix symbolizing the cross on which Christ was crucified, esp. a large one set above the entrance to the choir or chancel of a medieval church.

paradise
An atrium or cloister beside a church.

cloister
A covered walk having an arcade or colonnade on one side opening onto a courtyard.

rood screen
A screen, often elaborately adorned and properly surmounted by a rood, separating the chancel or choir from the nave of a medieval church.

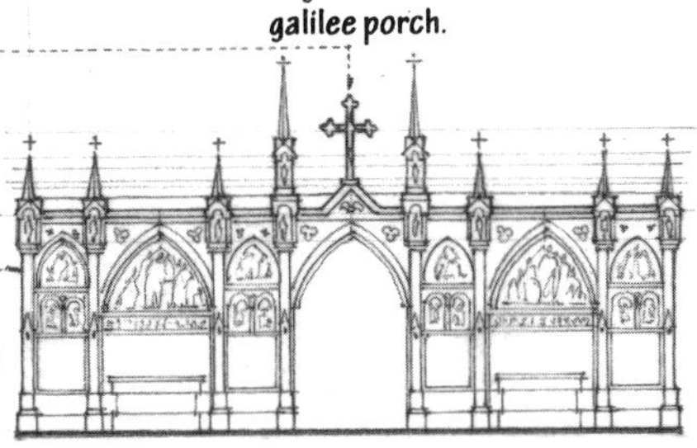

garth
A courtyard or quadrangle enclosed by a cloister. Also called **cloister garth**.

alure
A walk or passage, as along a cloister or behind the parapets of a castle. Also, **allure**.

COLOR

A phenomenon of light and visual perception that may be described in terms of an individual's perception of hue, saturation, and lightness for objects, and hue, saturation, and brightness for light sources.

spectrum
The distribution of energy emitted by a radiant source, arranged in order of wavelengths, esp. the band of colors produced when sunlight is refracted and dispersed by a prism, comprising red, orange, yellow, green, blue, indigo, and violet.

violet
indigo
blue
green
yellow
orange
red

pale
Designating a color having high lightness and low saturation.

brilliant
Designating a color having high lightness and strong saturation.

dark
Designating a color having low lightness and low saturation, and reflecting only a small fraction of incident light.

deep
Designating a color having low lightness and strong saturation.

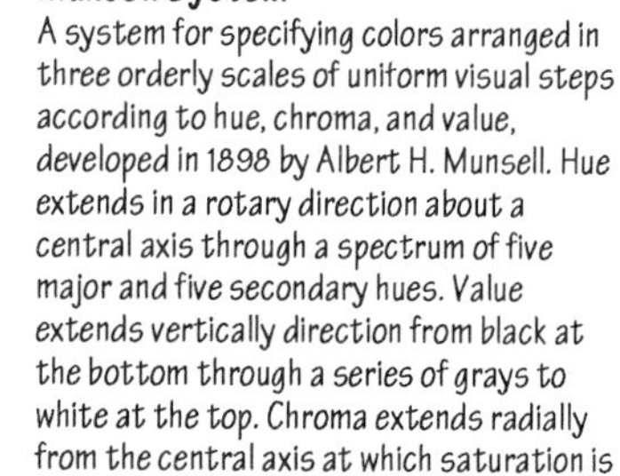

Munsell System
A system for specifying colors arranged in three orderly scales of uniform visual steps according to hue, chroma, and value, developed in 1898 by Albert H. Munsell. Hue extends in a rotary direction about a central axis through a spectrum of five major and five secondary hues. Value extends vertically direction from black at the bottom through a series of grays to white at the top. Chroma extends radially from the central axis at which saturation is zero, out to the strongest saturation attainable for each color's hue and value.

hue
One of the three dimensions of color: the property of light by which the color of an object is classified as being red, yellow, green, or blue, or an intermediate between any contiguous pair of these colors.

saturation
One of the three dimensions of color: the purity or vividness of a hue. Also called **intensity**.

chroma
The degree by which a color differs from a gray of the same lightness or brightness, corresponding to saturation of the perceived color.

reflected color
The perceived color of an object, determined by the wavelengths of the light reflected from its surface after selective absorption of other wavelengths of the incident light.

selective absorption
The absorption of certain wavelengths of the light incident on a colored surface, the remaining portion being reflected or transmitted.

lightness
The dimension of color by which an object appears to reflect more or less of the incident light, varying from black to white for surface colors and from black to colorless for transparent volume colors.

value
The degree by which a color appears to reflect more or less of the incident light, corresponding to lightness of the perceived color.

gray scale
A scale of achromatic colors having several, usually ten, equal gradations ranging from white to black.

brightness
The dimension of a color which is correlated with luminance and by which visual stimuli are ordered continuously from very dim to very bright. Pure white has the maximum brightness, and pure black the minimum brightness.

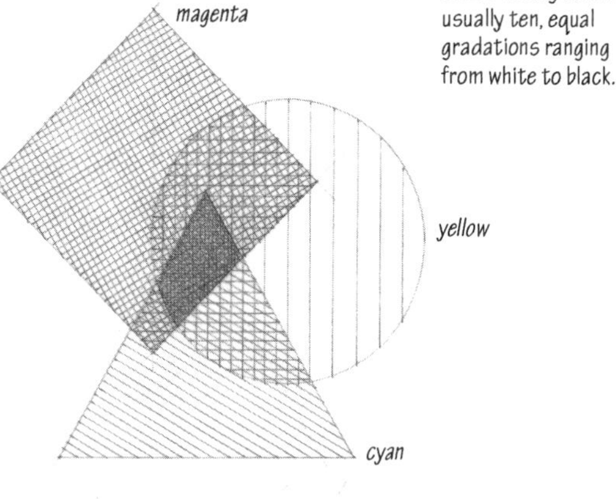

subtractive color
A color produced by mixing cyan, yellow, and magenta pigments, each of which absorbs certain wavelengths. A balanced mixture of these colorant or subtractive primaries theoretically yields black since it absorbs all wavelengths of visible light.

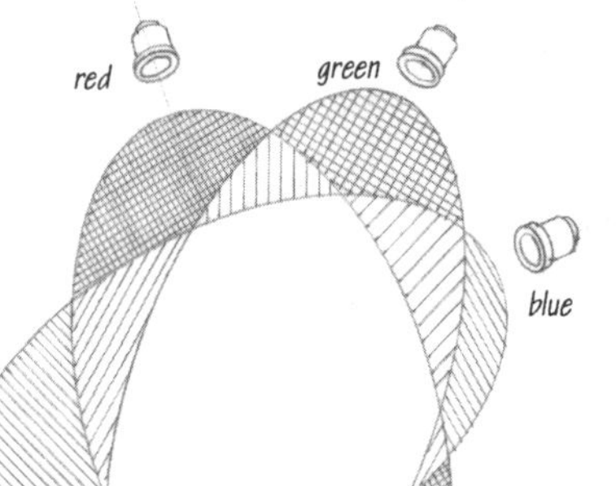

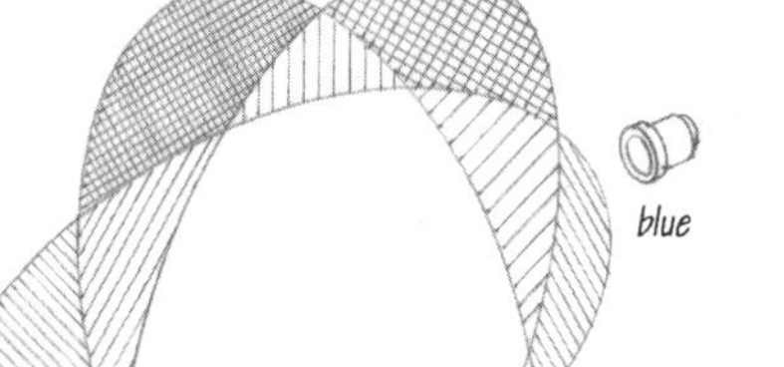

additive color
A color produced by combining lights of red, green, and blue wavelengths. These light or additive primaries contain all the wavelengths necessary to produce a colorless or white light.

optical mixing
The merging of juxtaposed dots or strokes of pure colors when seen from a distance to produce a hue often more luminous than that available from a premixed pigment.

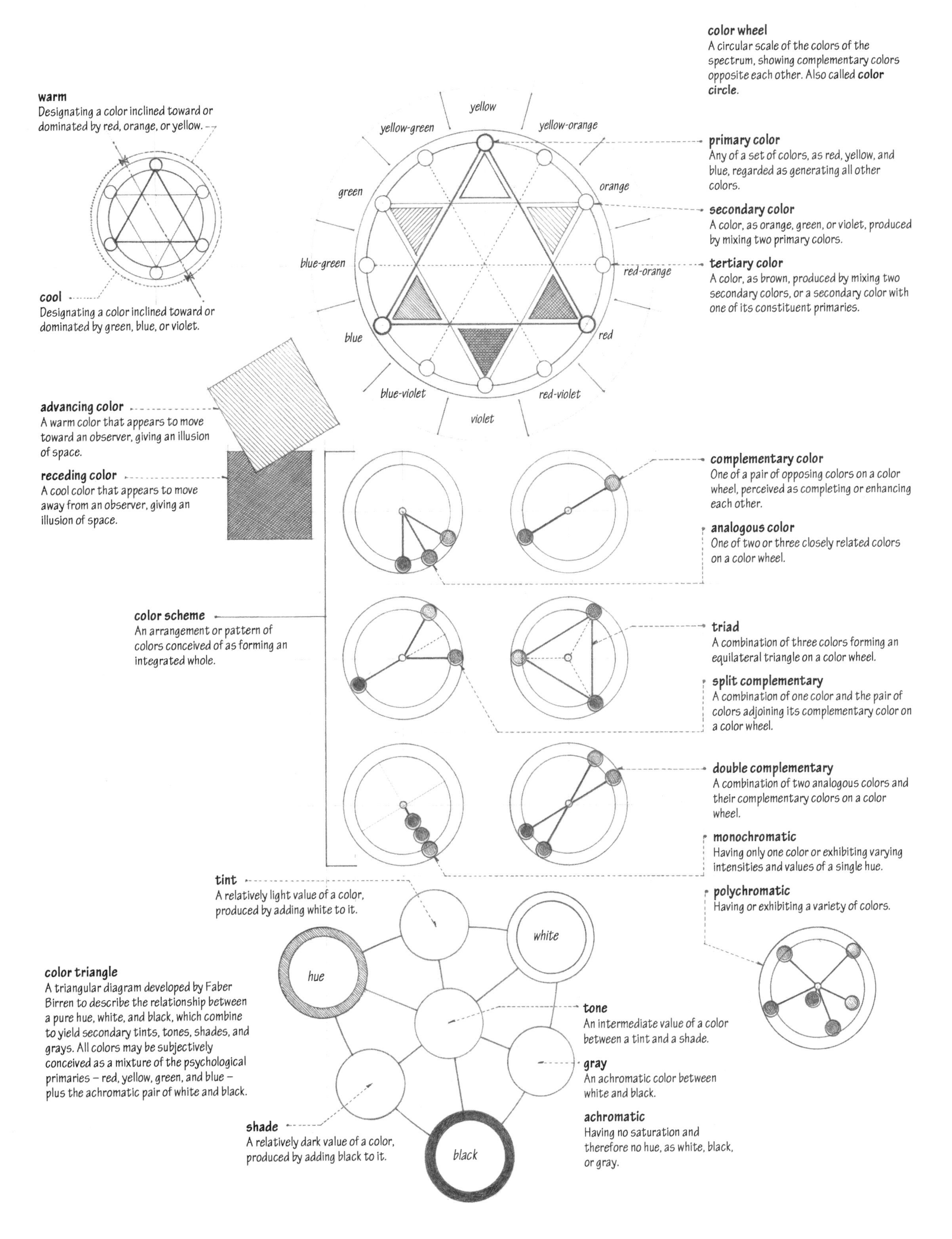

color wheel
A circular scale of the colors of the spectrum, showing complementary colors opposite each other. Also called **color circle**.

warm
Designating a color inclined toward or dominated by red, orange, or yellow.

cool
Designating a color inclined toward or dominated by green, blue, or violet.

primary color
Any of a set of colors, as red, yellow, and blue, regarded as generating all other colors.

secondary color
A color, as orange, green, or violet, produced by mixing two primary colors.

tertiary color
A color, as brown, produced by mixing two secondary colors, or a secondary color with one of its constituent primaries.

advancing color
A warm color that appears to move toward an observer, giving an illusion of space.

receding color
A cool color that appears to move away from an observer, giving an illusion of space.

complementary color
One of a pair of opposing colors on a color wheel, perceived as completing or enhancing each other.

analogous color
One of two or three closely related colors on a color wheel.

color scheme
An arrangement or pattern of colors conceived of as forming an integrated whole.

triad
A combination of three colors forming an equilateral triangle on a color wheel.

split complementary
A combination of one color and the pair of colors adjoining its complementary color on a color wheel.

double complementary
A combination of two analogous colors and their complementary colors on a color wheel.

monochromatic
Having only one color or exhibiting varying intensities and values of a single hue.

polychromatic
Having or exhibiting a variety of colors.

tint
A relatively light value of a color, produced by adding white to it.

color triangle
A triangular diagram developed by Faber Birren to describe the relationship between a pure hue, white, and black, which combine to yield secondary tints, tones, shades, and grays. All colors may be subjectively conceived as a mixture of the psychological primaries – red, yellow, green, and blue – plus the achromatic pair of white and black.

tone
An intermediate value of a color between a tint and a shade.

gray
An achromatic color between white and black.

shade
A relatively dark value of a color, produced by adding black to it.

achromatic
Having no saturation and therefore no hue, as white, black, or gray.

COLUMN

A rigid, relatively slender structural member designed primarily to support axial, compressive loads applied at the member ends.

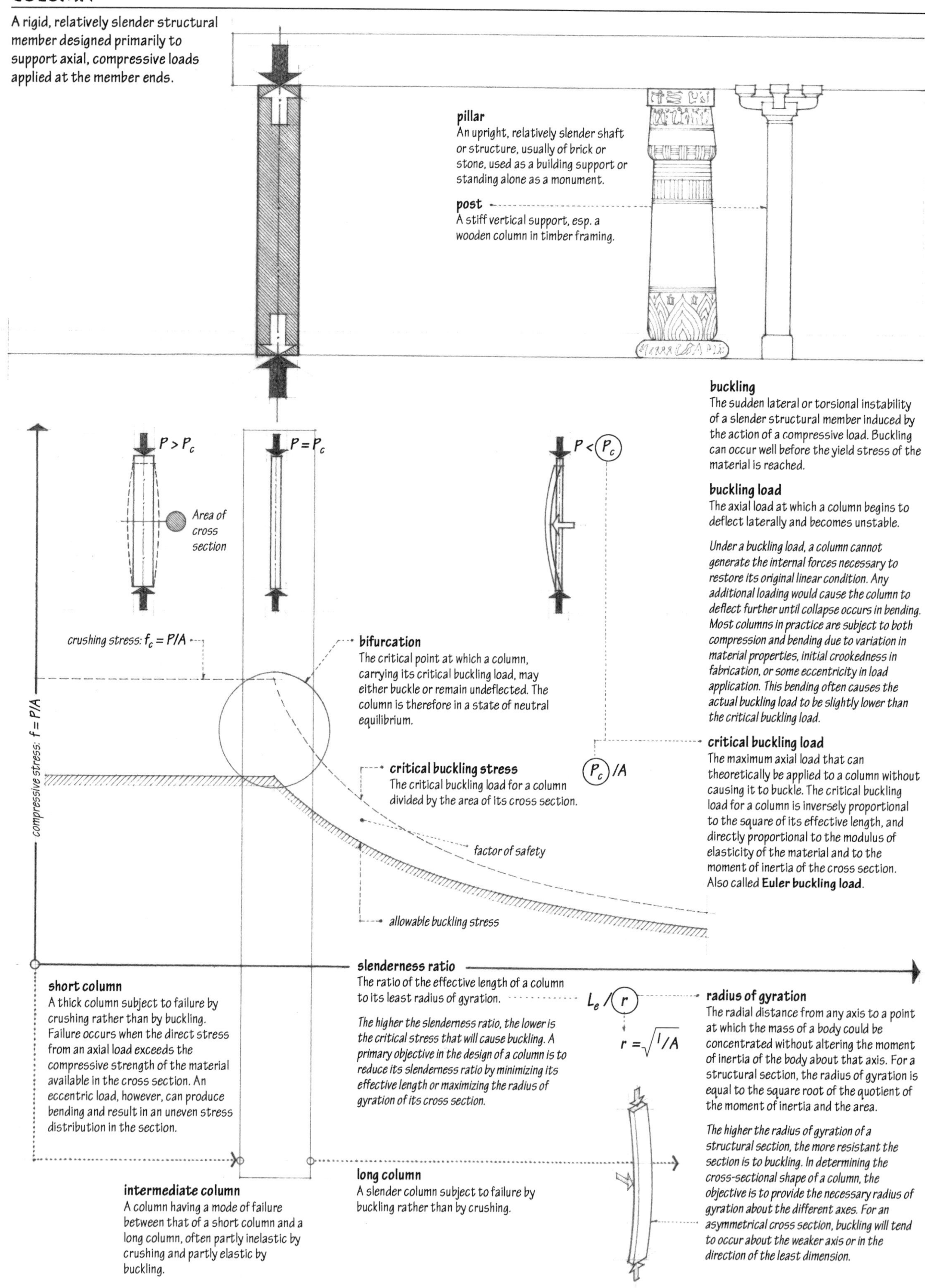

pillar
An upright, relatively slender shaft or structure, usually of brick or stone, used as a building support or standing alone as a monument.

post
A stiff vertical support, esp. a wooden column in timber framing.

buckling
The sudden lateral or torsional instability of a slender structural member induced by the action of a compressive load. Buckling can occur well before the yield stress of the material is reached.

buckling load
The axial load at which a column begins to deflect laterally and becomes unstable.

Under a buckling load, a column cannot generate the internal forces necessary to restore its original linear condition. Any additional loading would cause the column to deflect further until collapse occurs in bending. Most columns in practice are subject to both compression and bending due to variation in material properties, initial crookedness in fabrication, or some eccentricity in load application. This bending often causes the actual buckling load to be slightly lower than the critical buckling load.

bifurcation
The critical point at which a column, carrying its critical buckling load, may either buckle or remain undeflected. The column is therefore in a state of neutral equilibrium.

critical buckling stress
The critical buckling load for a column divided by the area of its cross section.

critical buckling load
The maximum axial load that can theoretically be applied to a column without causing it to buckle. The critical buckling load for a column is inversely proportional to the square of its effective length, and directly proportional to the modulus of elasticity of the material and to the moment of inertia of the cross section. Also called **Euler buckling load**.

slenderness ratio
The ratio of the effective length of a column to its least radius of gyration.

The higher the slenderness ratio, the lower is the critical stress that will cause buckling. A primary objective in the design of a column is to reduce its slenderness ratio by minimizing its effective length or maximizing the radius of gyration of its cross section.

radius of gyration
The radial distance from any axis to a point at which the mass of a body could be concentrated without altering the moment of inertia of the body about that axis. For a structural section, the radius of gyration is equal to the square root of the quotient of the moment of inertia and the area.

The higher the radius of gyration of a structural section, the more resistant the section is to buckling. In determining the cross-sectional shape of a column, the objective is to provide the necessary radius of gyration about the different axes. For an asymmetrical cross section, buckling will tend to occur about the weaker axis or in the direction of the least dimension.

short column
A thick column subject to failure by crushing rather than by buckling. Failure occurs when the direct stress from an axial load exceeds the compressive strength of the material available in the cross section. An eccentric load, however, can produce bending and result in an uneven stress distribution in the section.

intermediate column
A column having a mode of failure between that of a short column and a long column, often partly inelastic by crushing and partly elastic by buckling.

long column
A slender column subject to failure by buckling rather than by crushing.

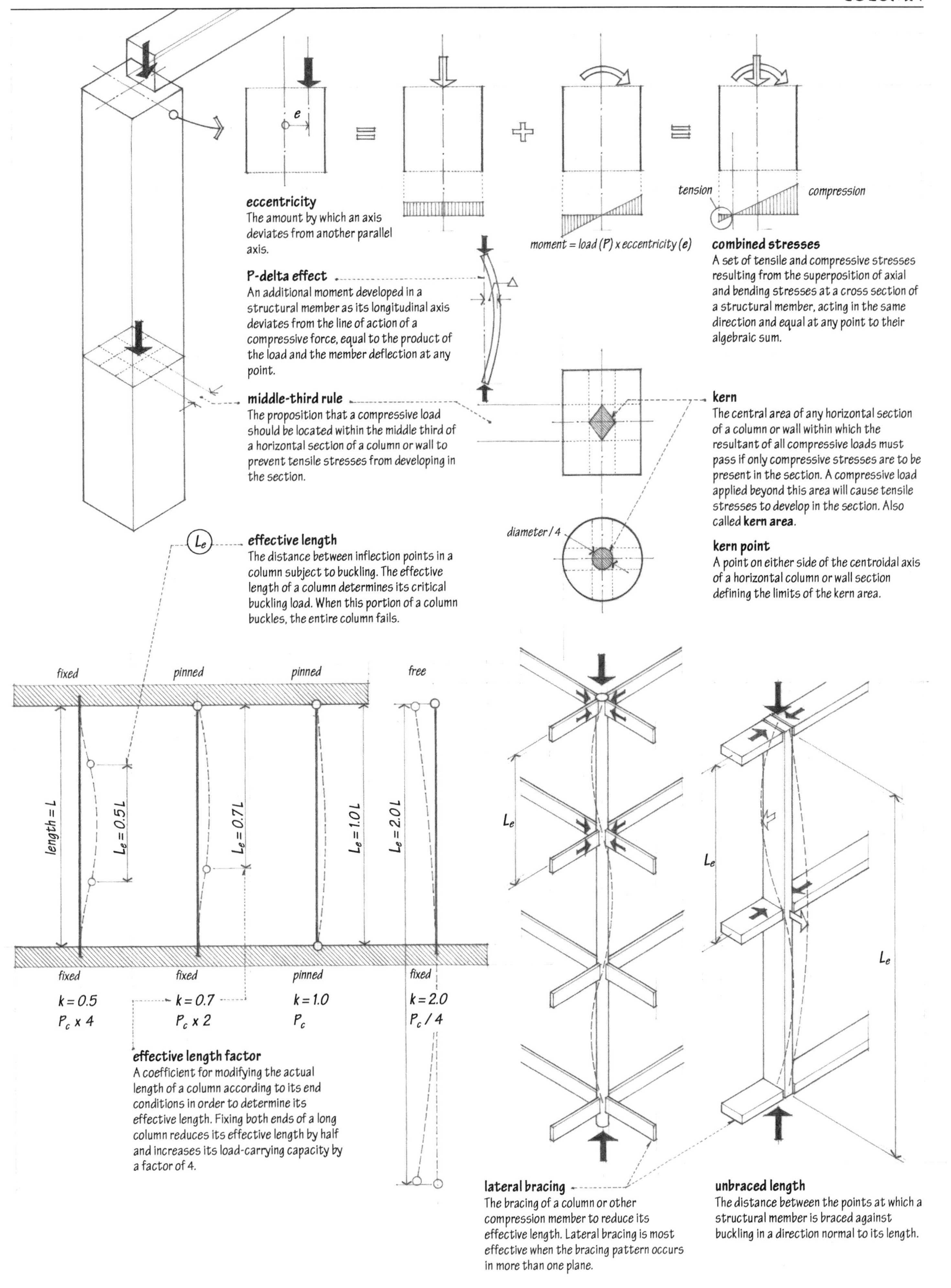

eccentricity
The amount by which an axis deviates from another parallel axis.

P-delta effect
An additional moment developed in a structural member as its longitudinal axis deviates from the line of action of a compressive force, equal to the product of the load and the member deflection at any point.

middle-third rule
The proposition that a compressive load should be located within the middle third of a horizontal section of a column or wall to prevent tensile stresses from developing in the section.

effective length
The distance between inflection points in a column subject to buckling. The effective length of a column determines its critical buckling load. When this portion of a column buckles, the entire column fails.

combined stresses
A set of tensile and compressive stresses resulting from the superposition of axial and bending stresses at a cross section of a structural member, acting in the same direction and equal at any point to their algebraic sum.

kern
The central area of any horizontal section of a column or wall within which the resultant of all compressive loads must pass if only compressive stresses are to be present in the section. A compressive load applied beyond this area will cause tensile stresses to develop in the section. Also called **kern area**.

kern point
A point on either side of the centroidal axis of a horizontal column or wall section defining the limits of the kern area.

effective length factor
A coefficient for modifying the actual length of a column according to its end conditions in order to determine its effective length. Fixing both ends of a long column reduces its effective length by half and increases its load-carrying capacity by a factor of 4.

lateral bracing
The bracing of a column or other compression member to reduce its effective length. Lateral bracing is most effective when the bracing pattern occurs in more than one plane.

unbraced length
The distance between the points at which a structural member is braced against buckling in a direction normal to its length.

CONCRETE

An artificial, stonelike building material made by mixing cement and various mineral aggregates with sufficient water to cause the cement to set and bind the entire mass.

natural cement
A naturally occurring clayey limestone which, when calcined and finely pulverized, produces a hydraulic cement.

pozzolan
A siliceous material, as fly ash, that reacts chemically with slaked lime in the presence of moisture to form a slow-hardening cement, named after a natural cement from Pozzuoli, an ancient Roman town near Vesuvius. Also, **pozzolona**, **pozzuolana**.

siliceous
Containing silica or a silicate.

fly ash
Fine particles of ash recovered from the waste gases of a solid-fuel furnace.

cement
A calcined mixture of clay and limestone, finely pulverized and used as an ingredient in concrete and mortar. The term is frequently used incorrectly for concrete.

tricalcium silicate
A compound constituting about half the volume of portland cement and responsible for the hardening or early gain in strength of the cement.

dicalcium silicate
A compound constituting about one-quarter of the volume of portland cement and responsible for the aging or long-term gain in strength of the cement.

tricalcium aluminate
A compound constituting about one-tenth of the volume of portland cement and responsible for the initial setting of the cement.

portland cement
A hydraulic cement made by burning a mixture of clay and limestone in a rotary kiln and pulverizing the resulting clinker into a very fine powder, named for its resemblance to a limestone quarried on the Isle of Portland, England.

hydraulic cement
Cement capable of setting and hardening by a reaction with water.

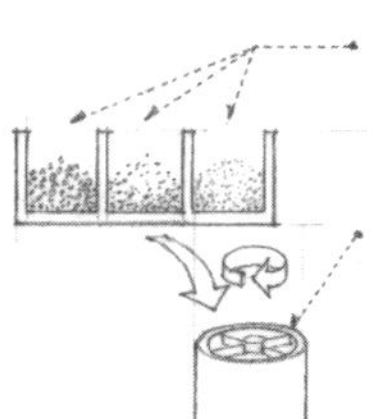

Raw materials consist of combinations of limestone, clay, shale, oyster shells, silica sand, and iron ore.

Raw materials are ground to powder and blended.

Burning in a rotary kiln changes raw mixture into cement clinker.

clinker
A fused mass of incombustible matter resulting from heating in a kiln or the burning of coal.

calcine
To heat a substance to a high temperature but without melting or fusing to drive off volatile matter or to cause oxidation or reduction.

Gypsum is added to clinker to retard setting.

Clinker is ground into portland cement.

Type I: normal
A portland cement used for general construction, having none of the distinguishing qualities of the other types.

Type II: moderate
A portland cement having a reduced content of tricalcium aluminate, making it more resistant to sulfates and causing it to generate less heat of hydration: used in general construction where resistance to moderate sulfate action is required or where heat buildup can be damaging, as in the construction of large piers and heavy retaining walls.

Type III: high early strength
A very finely ground portland cement having an increased content of tricalcium silicate, causing it to cure faster and gain strength earlier than normal portland cement: used when the early removal of formwork is desired, or in cold-weather construction to reduce the time required for protection from low temperatures.

Type IV: low heat
A portland cement having a reduced content of tricalcium silicate and an increased content of dicalcium silicate, causing it to generate less heat of hydration than normal portland cement: used in the construction of massive concrete structures, as gravity dams, where a large buildup in heat can be damaging.

Type V: sulfate resisting
A portland cement having a reduced content of tricalcium aluminate, lessening the need for gypsum, a sulfate normally added to cement to retard its setting time: used where resistance to severe sulfate action is required.

air-entraining portland cement
A Type I, Type II, or Type III portland cement to which a small quantity of an air-entraining agent has been interground during manufacture: designated by the suffix A, as Type IA, Type IIA, or Type IIIA.

white portland cement
A portland cement produced from raw materials low in iron oxide and manganese oxide, the substances that give concrete its gray color: used in precast concrete work and in the making of terrazzo, stucco, and tile grout.

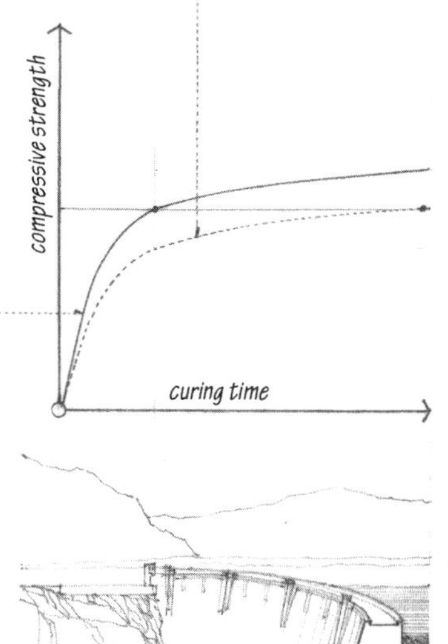

sulfate action
An expansive reaction occurring when the cement matrix of concrete or mortar comes in contact with sulfates dissolved in ground water or in soil.

entrained air
Microscopic, spherical air bubbles, typically 0.004 to 0.04 in. (0.1 to 1.0 mm) in diameter, intentionally dispersed in a concrete or mortar mix by an air-entraining agent.

mixing water
The water used in a concrete or mortar mix, exclusive of any absorbed by the aggregate and free of such harmful substances as organic material, clay, and salts. Water fit for drinking is generally acceptable.

cement paste
A mixture of cement and water for coating, setting, and binding the aggregate particles together in a concrete or mortar mix.

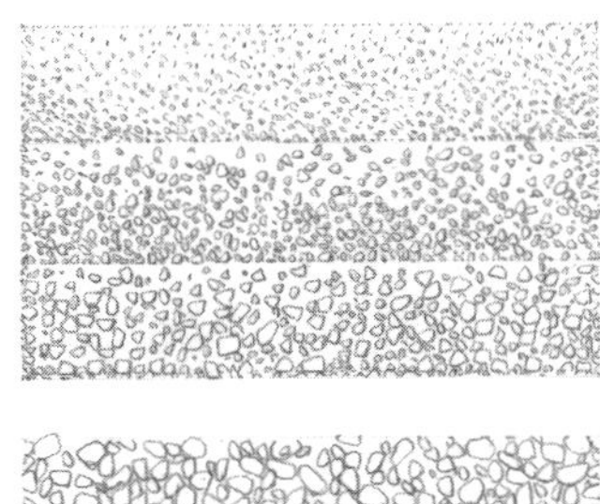

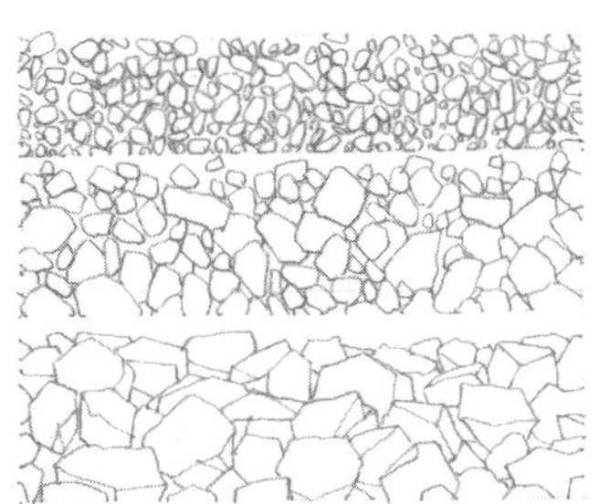

aggregate
Any of various hard, inert, mineral materials, as sand and gravel, added to a cement paste to make concrete or mortar. Since aggregate represents from 60% to 80% of the concrete volume, its properties are important to the strength, weight, and fire-resistance of the hardened concrete. Aggregate should be hard, dimensionally stable, and free of clay, silt, and organic matter which can prevent the cementing matrix from binding the particles together.

fine aggregate
Aggregate consisting of sand having a particle size smaller than 1/4 in. (6.4 mm): specif. the portion of aggregate that will pass through a 3/8 in. (9.5 mm) sieve, almost entirely through a No. 4 (4.8 mm) sieve, and be predominantly retained on a No. 200 (74μ) sieve.

coarse aggregate
Aggregate consisting of crushed stone, gravel, or blast-furnace slag having a particle size larger than 1/4 in. (6.4 mm): specif. the portion of aggregate that is retained on a No. 4 (4.8 mm) sieve. The maximum size of coarse aggregate in reinforced concrete is limited by the size of the section and the spacing of the reinforcing bars.

graded aggregate
Aggregate having a particle-size distribution characterized by uniform grading. Graded aggregate requires the least amount of cement paste to fill the voids and surround the particles.

particle-size distribution
The range of particle sizes in a granular material, expressed either as the cumulative percentage by weight of particles smaller or larger than a specified sieve opening, or as the percentage by weight of the particles that range between specified sieve openings.

uniform grading
A particle-size distribution in which aggregate particles vary uniformly from fine to coarse without a preponderance of any one size or group of sizes.

admixture
Any substance other than cement, water, or aggregate, added to a concrete or mortar mix to alter its properties or those of the hardened product. Also called **additive**.

- **air-entraining agent**
  An admixture that disperses entrained air in a concrete or mortar mix to increase workability, improve resistance of the cured product to the cracking induced by free-thaw cycles or the scaling caused by deicing chemicals, and in larger amounts, to produce lightweight insulating concrete.
- **accelerator**
  An admixture that hastens the setting and strength development of a concrete, mortar, or plaster mix.
- **retarder**
  An admixture that slows the setting of a concrete, mortar, or plaster mix in order to allow more time for placing and working the mix.
- **surface-active agent**
  An admixture for reducing the surface tension of the mixing water in a concrete mix, thereby facilitating the wetting and penetrating action of the water or aiding in the emulsifying and dispersion of other additives in the mix. Also called **surfactant**.
- **water-reducing agent**
  An admixture for reducing the amount of mixing water required for the desired workability of a concrete or mortar mix. Lowering the water-cement ratio in this manner generally results in increased strength. Also called **superplasticizer**.
- **coloring agent**
  A pigment or dye added to a concrete mix to alter or control its color.

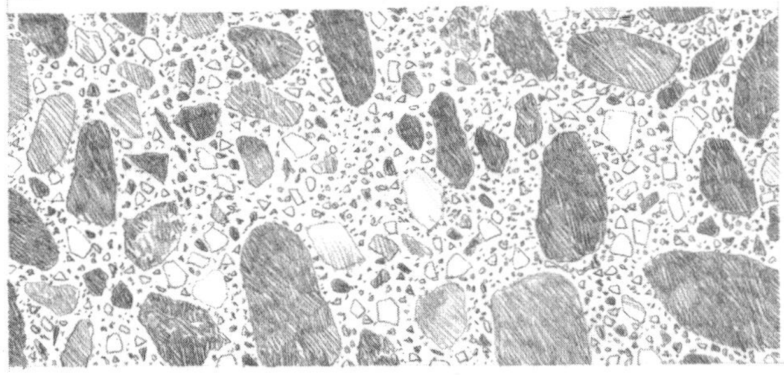

lightweight concrete
Concrete made with aggregate of low specific gravity and weighing less than normal concrete which has a unit weight of about 150 pcf (2,400 kg/ m^3).

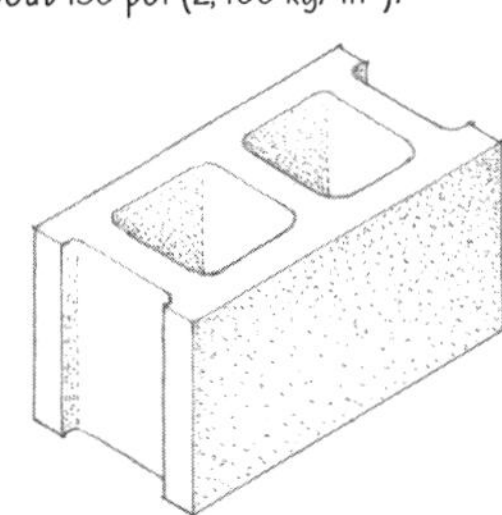

structural lightweight concrete
Concrete made with strong lightweight aggregate, as expanded shale or slate, having a unit weight from 85 to 115 pcf (1,362 to 1,840 kg/ m^3) and compressive strength comparable to that of normal concrete.

insulating concrete
Lightweight concrete having a unit weight of less than 60 pcf (960 kg/ m^3) and low thermal conductivity, made with lightweight aggregate, as perlite, or with a foaming agent or gas-forming chemical that infuses the mix with a homogeneous cellular structure.

expanded shale
A strong lightweight aggregate obtained by the exfoliation of clay or shale. Also called **expanded clay**.

expanded slate
A strong lightweight aggregate obtained by the exfoliation of slate.

exfoliation
The splitting or swelling of certain minerals into a scaly aggregate when heated.

perlite
A volcanic glass expanded by heat to form lightweight, spherical particles, used as nonstructural lightweight aggregate and as loose-fill thermal insulation. Also, **pearlite**.

vermiculite
Mica expanded by heat into very light, wormlike threads, used as nonstructural lightweight aggregate and as loose-fill thermal insulation.

mix design
The most economical selection and proportioning of cement, water, and aggregate to produce concrete or mortar having the required properties of workability, strength, durability, and watertightness.

Abram's law
A law postulating that, with given concrete materials, curing, and testing conditions, the compressive strength of concrete is inversely proportional to the ratio of water to cement: developed by D.A. Abrams in 1919 from experiments at Lewis Institute in Chicago.

water-cement ratio
The ratio of mixing water to cement in a unit volume of concrete or mortar mix, preferably expressed by weight as a decimal fraction but often stated in gallons of water per 94-lb. sack of cement. The water-cement ratio controls the strength, durability, and watertightness of hardened concrete.

cement — 7% – 15%
water — 16% – 21%
air — 1% – 3%
fine aggregate — 25% – 30%
coarse aggregate — 31% – 51%

cement content
The quantity of cement per unit volume of concrete or mortar mix, preferably expressed in pounds per cubic yard but often stated in sacks of cement per cubic yard of mix.

water content
The quantity of water per unit volume of concrete or mortar mix, preferably expressed in pounds per cubic yard but often stated in gallons per cubic yard of mix.

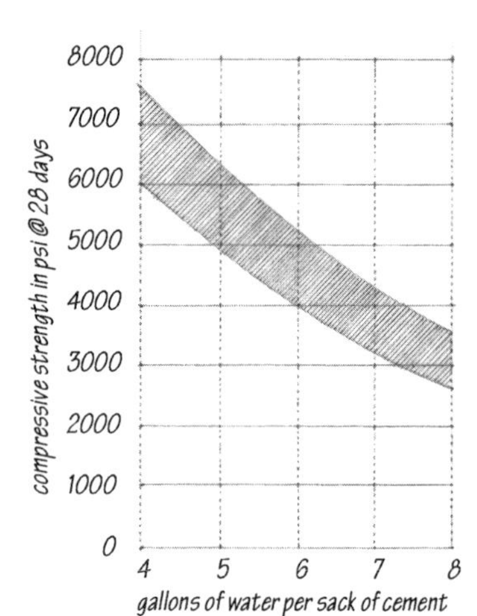

sack
A measure of portland cement: 94 lb. in the U.S., 87.5 lb. in Canada, 112 lb. in Britain, and 50 kg in countries using the metric system. Also called **bag**.

consistency
The relative ability of freshly mixed concrete or mortar to flow, usually measured by the slump test for concrete and by the flow test for grout or mortar. Consistency depends largely on the proportion of cement paste to aggregate in a mix.

workability
The relative ease with which freshly mixed concrete or mortar can be handled, placed in formwork, compacted, and finished. Workability depends partly on the water-cement ratio and partly on the grading of the aggregate in a mix.

slump test
A method for determining the consistency and workability of freshly mixed concrete by measuring the slump of a test specimen.

slump
A measure of the consistency and workability of freshly mixed concrete, expressed as the vertical settling, in inches, of a specimen after it has been placed in a slump cone, tamped in a prescribed manner, and the cone is lifted.

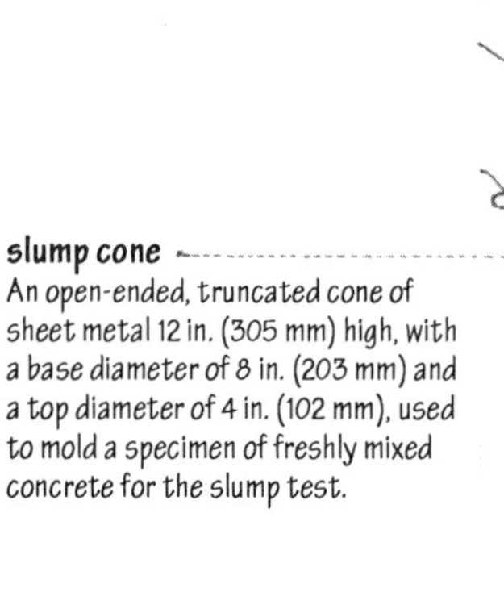

slump cone
An open-ended, truncated cone of sheet metal 12 in. (305 mm) high, with a base diameter of 8 in. (203 mm) and a top diameter of 4 in. (102 mm), used to mold a specimen of freshly mixed concrete for the slump test.

plastic mix
A concrete or mortar mix that flows sluggishly without segregating and is readily molded.

dry mix
A concrete or mortar mix containing little water or too much aggregate in relation to the other components and having little or no slump. Also called **stiff mix**.

wet mix
A concrete or mortar mix having a relatively high water content and runny consistency, yielding a product that is low in strength, durability, and watertightness.

compression test
A test for determining the compressive strength of a concrete batch, using a hydraulic press to measure the maximum load a test cylinder can support in axial compression before fracturing.

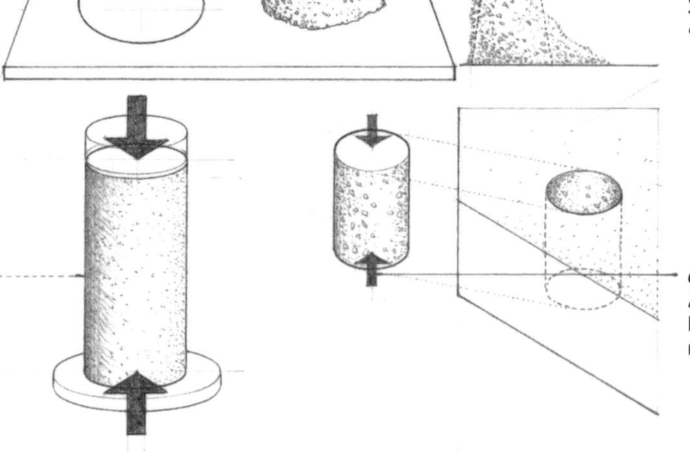

test cylinder
A cylinder of concrete 6 in. (152 mm) in diameter and 12 in. (305 mm) high, cast from a representative batch and cured in a laboratory or in the field under controlled conditions.

core test
A compression test of a cylinder cut from a hardened concrete structure, usually by means of a core drill.

form liner
Material for lining the inside face of a form, specially selected to impart a smooth or patterned finish to the concrete surface.

release agent
Any of various materials, as oil or silicone, for preventing the bonding of concrete to a surface. Also called **parting compound**.

bulkhead
A partition closing the end of a form or preventing the passage of newly place concrete at a construction joint.

keyway
A longitudinal groove or channel formed in a concrete footing or other member that has set, providing a shear-resisting key for newly placed concrete.

yoke
A clamping device for keeping column forms or the tops of wall forms from spreading under the fluid pressure of newly placed concrete.

spreader
A brace, usually of wood, for spacing and keeping wall or footing forms apart. Also called **spacer**.

wale
A horizontal timber or steel beam for reinforcing various vertical members, as in formwork or sheet piling, or for retaining earth at the edge of an embankment. Also called **breast timber**, **ranger**, **waler**.

strongback
A vertical support for aligning and reinforcing wales. Also called **stiffback**.

formwork
The temporary structure required to support newly placed concrete, including the forms and all necessary supporting members, bracing, and hardware.

form
Boarding or sheeting of wood, metal, plastic, or fiberglass for containing and giving a desired shape to newly placed concrete until it sets and gains sufficient strength to be self-supporting.

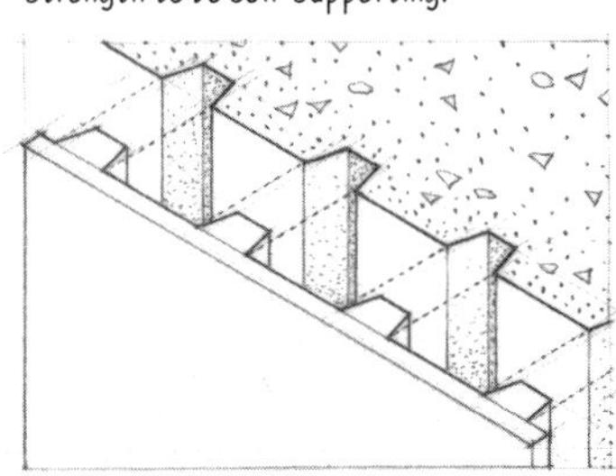

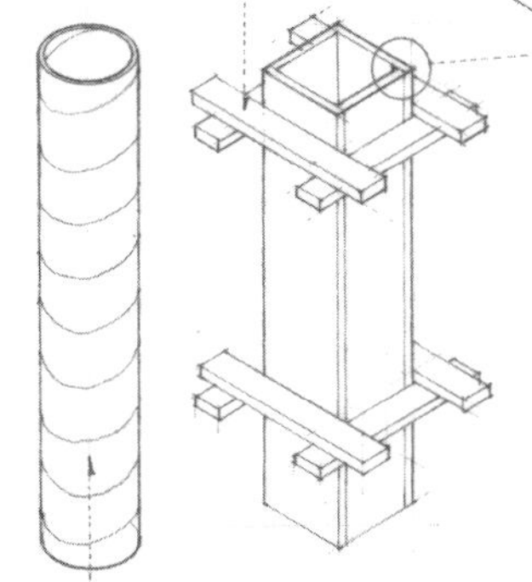

Sonotube
Trademark for a brand of cylindrical column form made of compressed, resin-impregnated paper.

chamfer strip
A strip of wood or other material attached to a form to produce a smooth, rounded or beveled edge on the outside corner of a concrete member.

rustication strip
A strip of wood or other material attached to the inside face of a form to produce a groove in the surface of a concrete member.

grade strip
A wood strip fixed to the inside face of a form to indicate the top of a concrete lift.

wedge
Any of a variety of slotted devices for tightening formwork and transferring the force in a form tie to the wales.

form tie
A metal tie for keeping wall forms from spreading under the fluid pressure of newly placed concrete.

snap tie
A form tie having notches or crimps which allow its ends to be snapped off below the concrete surface after stripping of the forms.

cone bolt
A form tie having cones at each end inside the forms which allow it to also serve as a spreader.

cone
A small, truncated cone of wood, steel, or plastic attached to a form tie to space and spread wall forms, leaving a neatly finished depression in the concrete surface to be filled or left exposed.

she bolt
A form tie consisting of waler rods which are inserted through the form and threaded onto the ends of an inner rod. After stripping, the waler rods are removed while the inner rod remains in the concrete.

chair
A device for supporting and holding steel reinforcement in proper position before and during the placing of concrete.

high chair
A tall chair for supporting top bars in a concrete beam or slab.

bolster
A wide chair for supporting and spacing bottom bars in a concrete beam or slab.

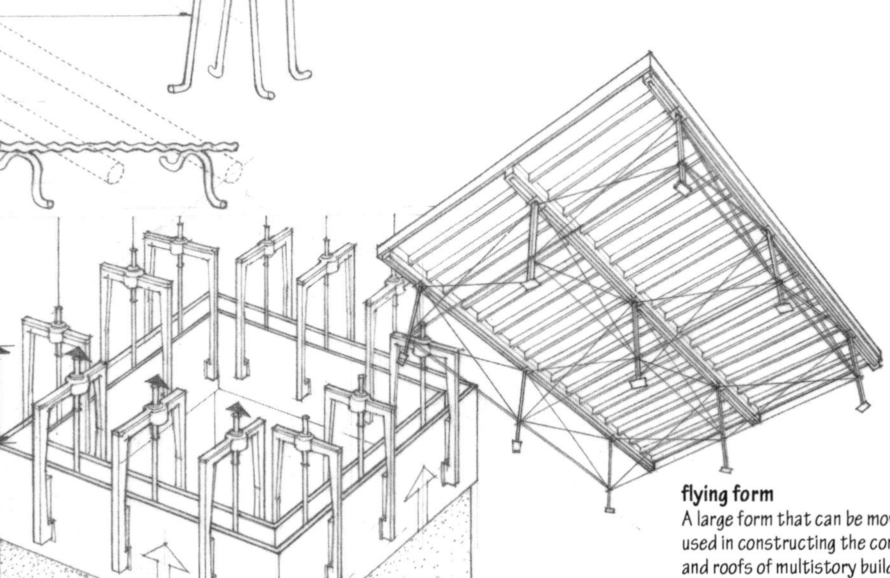

climbing form
A form that can be raised vertically for succeeding lifts of concrete during the construction of a multistory building.

lift
The height of a quantity of concrete placed in a form at one time.

slip form
A form that can be moved slowly and continuously as concrete is being placed during the construction of a concrete pavement or building.

flying form
A large form that can be moved by a crane, used in constructing the concrete floors and roofs of multistory buildings.

cast-in-place concrete
Concrete deposited, formed, cured, and finished in its final position as part of a structure. Also called **cast-in-situ concrete**.

time of haul
The period from first contact between mixing water and cement to completion of discharge of the freshly mixed concrete from a truck mixer.

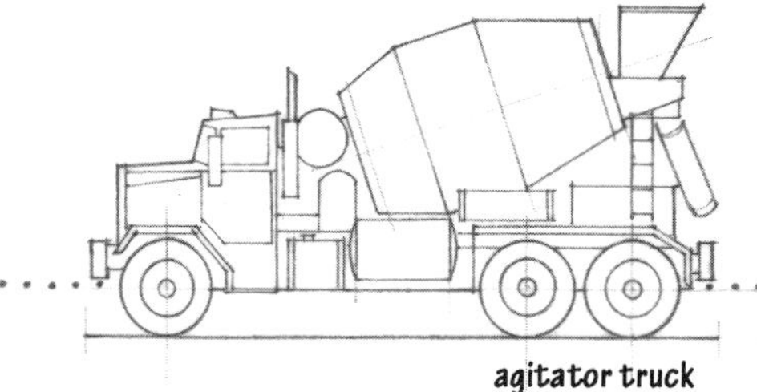

ready-mixed concrete
Concrete mixed at a batch plant for delivery by an agitator truck to a construction site.

shrink-mixed concrete
Concrete partially mixed at a batch plant and then mixed more completely in a truck mixer en route to a construction site.

transit-mixed concrete
Concrete dry batched at a batch plant and mixed in a truck mixer en route to a construction site.

agitator truck
A truck equipped with a rotating drum to prevent segregation or loss of plasticity of the ready-mixed concrete being delivered to a construction site.

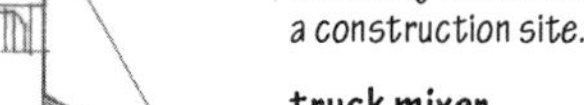

truck mixer
A truck equipped with a rotating drum and a separate water tank for mixing concrete en route to a construction site.

placement
The process of depositing and consolidating freshly mixed concrete in a form or in the final position where it is to harden.

concrete mixer
A machine having a revolving drum, often motor-driven, for mixing cement, aggregate, and water to produce concrete.

direct placement
The discharging of freshly mixed concrete directly into a form from a concrete mixer, buggy, or crane bucket.

buggy
A cart, often motor-driven, for transporting heavy materials, as freshly mixed concrete, for short distances at a construction site.

free fall
The descent of freshly mixed concrete into a form without the aid of a drop chute.

drop chute
A chute for containing and directing a falling stream of freshly mixed concrete so as not to cause segregation.

chute
An inclined trough or tube for conveying free-flowing materials to a lower level by gravity.

pneumatic placement
The delivery of concrete, slurry, or plaster by a pipeline or hose to the point of placement on a construction site, either in a plastic state for depositing in place or for spraying, or in a dry state with water added at the nozzle from which it is sprayed.

Gunite
A lightweight concrete construction consisting of a mixture of cement, sand or crushed slag, and water, pumped through a hose and sprayed at high velocity over reinforcement until the desired thickness is reached. Also called **shotcrete**.

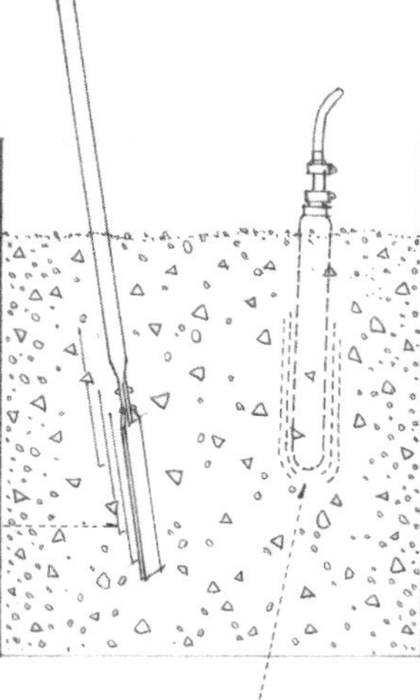

consolidation
The process of eliminating voids other than entrained air within newly placed concrete and ensuring close contact of the concrete with form surfaces and embedded reinforcement.

spading
Consolidation of newly placed concrete by the repeated insertions and withdrawals of a flat, spadelike tool.

rodding
Consolidation of newly placed concrete by the repeated insertions and withdrawals of a rod.

vibration
Consolidation of newly placed concrete by the moderately high-frequency oscillations of a vibrator.

vibrator
An electric or pneumatic oscillating tool for agitating and consolidating newly placed concrete.

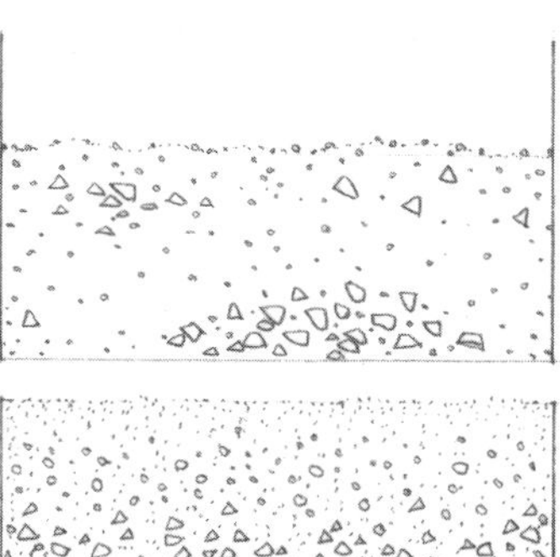

segregation
The separation of coarse aggregate from the mortar or of water from the other ingredients of freshly mixed concrete, resulting from excessive horizontal movement or free fall of the mix, or from overvibration after placement.

stratification
The separation of an excessively wet or overvibrated concrete mix into horizontal layers with increasingly lighter material migrating toward the top.

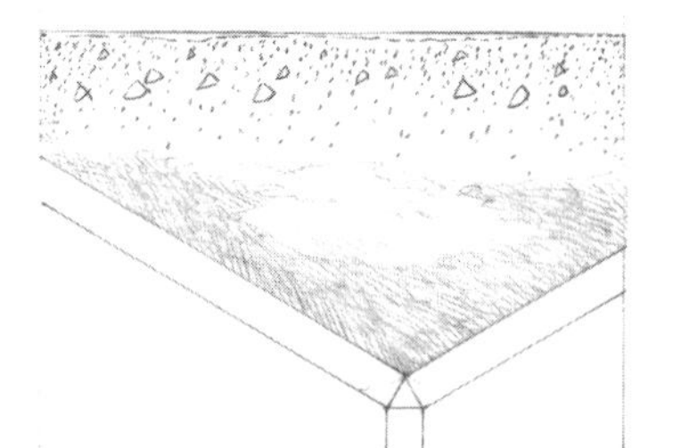

bleeding
The emergence of excess mixing water on the surface of newly placed concrete, caused by settlement of solids within the mass. Also called **water gain**.

laitance
A milky deposit containing cement and aggregate fines on the surface of new concrete, caused by the bleeding of excess mixing water, overworking of the mix, or improper finishing.

finishing
The process of leveling, smoothing, compacting, and treating a newly placed concrete surface to produce the desired texture and appearance.

darby
A long wooden or metal straightedge for smoothing a fresh concrete surface immediately after screeding.

screed
A wooden or metal straightedge drawn over a newly placed concrete slab to bring it to proper level.

screed
A firmly established grade strip or edge form serving as a guide for making a true level surface on a newly placed concrete slab.

float
A flat tool for spreading and smoothing a fresh concrete, stucco, or plaster surface.

bull float
A float having a large, flat blade attached to a long handle.

float finish
A fine-textured finish obtained by smoothing a fresh concrete, plaster, or stucco surface with a wood float.

trowel
Any of various flat-bladed hand tools for applying, spreading, working, or smoothing plastic material, as concrete, mortar, and plaster.

power trowel
A portable machine having steel trowels mounted on radial arms that rotate about a vertical shaft to smooth, compact, and finish a fresh concrete surface.

edger
A trowel having a long, curved lip for rounding the edges of a fresh concrete slab as it begins to set.

trowel finish
A dense, smooth finish obtained by working a fresh concrete or plaster surface with a steel trowel.

pavement saw
A wheel-mounted, rotary power saw equipped with a silicon-carbide or diamond blade for cutting a control joint in a hardened concrete slab.

set
The assumption of a rigid or hard state by concrete, mortar, plaster, or glue due to a physical or chemical change.

cure
To maintain newly placed concrete or mortar at the required temperature and humidity for the first seven days following placement, casting, or finishing to ensure satisfactory hydration of the cementitious materials and proper hardening.

heat of hydration
The heat generated by the process of hydration, as during the setting and curing of a concrete mix.

hydration
The process in which a substance combines chemically with water, as that occurring when cement is mixed with water.

dry-shake finish
A colored finish produced by sprinkling a dry mixture of cement, sand, and a pigment on a fresh concrete surface following screeding and after any free water has evaporated, and then working the mixture into the surface with a float.

broom finish
A striated finish obtained by stroking a broom or stiff brush over a freshly troweled concrete surface.

swirl finish
A textured finish given to a fresh plaster or concrete surface by troweling with a circular, overlapping motion.

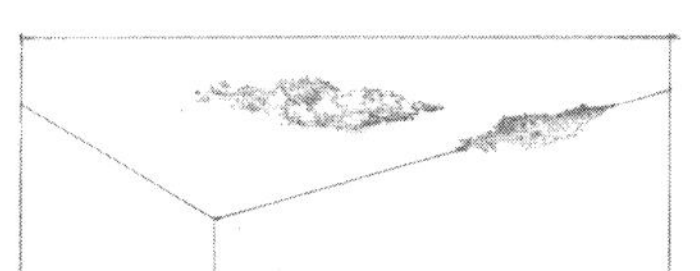

architectural concrete
Exposed concrete work requiring special care in the selection of materials, forming, placing, and finishing to acquire the desired appearance.

béton brut
Concrete left in its natural state after formwork is removed, esp. when the concrete surface reflects the texture, joints, and fasteners of a board form.

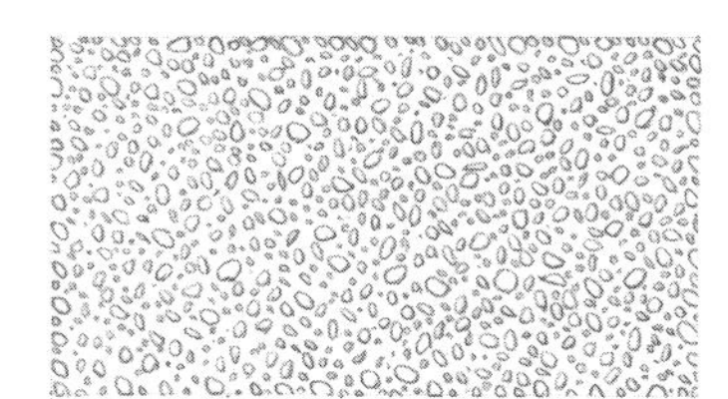

exposed aggregate finish
A decorative finish produced by sandblasting, etching with an acid, or scrubbing a concrete surface after the initial set in order to remove the outer layer of cement paste and expose the aggregate.

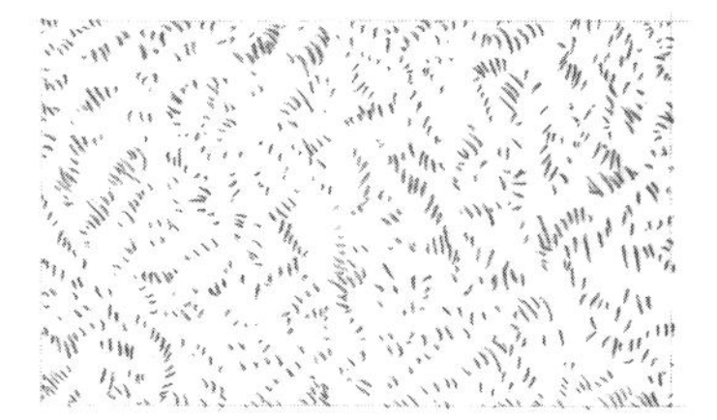

bushhammered finish
A coarse-textured finish obtained by fracturing a concrete or stone surface with a power-driven hammer having a rectangular head with a corrugated, serrated, or toothed face.

honeycomb
Voids on a formed concrete surface, caused by segregation during placement or by insufficient consolidation.

spalling
The chipping or scaling of a hardened concrete or masonry surface caused by freeze-thaw cycles or the application of deicing salts. Also called **scaling**.

crazing
Numerous hairline cracks occurring in the surface of a newly hardened concrete slab as a result of rapid drying shrinkage.

drying shrinkage
A reduction in volume of concrete, mortar, or plaster caused by a loss of moisture.

setting shrinkage
A reduction in volume of concrete prior to its final set, caused by hydration of the cement paste.

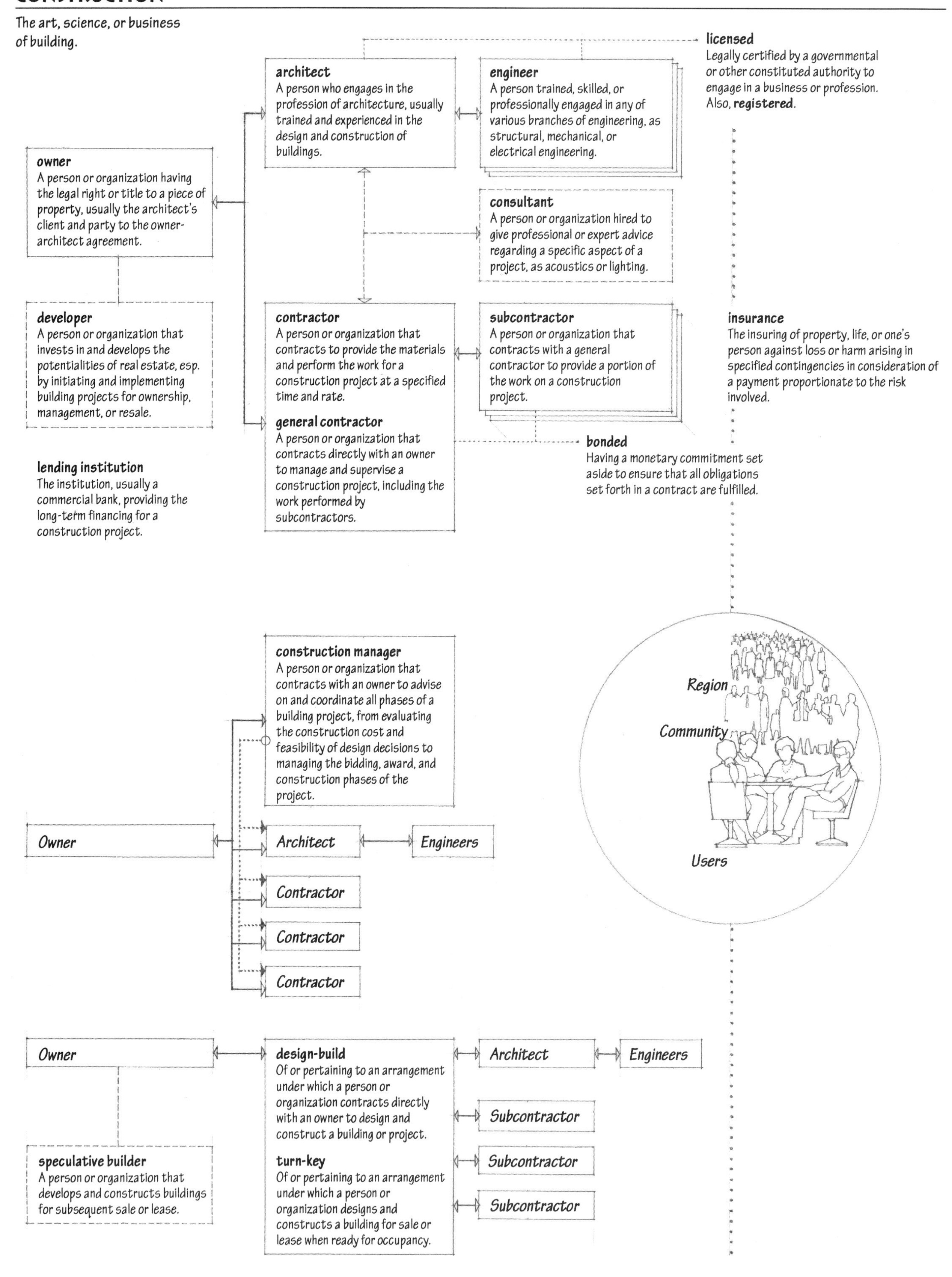
CONSTRUCTION
The art, science, or business of building.
architect
A person who engages in the profession of architecture, usually trained and experienced in the design and construction of buildings.
engineer
A person trained, skilled, or professionally engaged in any of various branches of engineering, as structural, mechanical, or electrical engineering.
licensed
Legally certified by a governmental or other constituted authority to engage in a business or profession. Also, registered.
owner
A person or organization having the legal right or title to a piece of property, usually the architect's client and party to the owner-architect agreement.
consultant
A person or organization hired to give professional or expert advice regarding a specific aspect of a project, as acoustics or lighting.
developer
A person or organization that invests in and develops the potentialities of real estate, esp. by initiating and implementing building projects for ownership, management, or resale.
contractor
A person or organization that contracts to provide the materials and perform the work for a construction project at a specified time and rate.
subcontractor
A person or organization that contracts with a general contractor to provide a portion of the work on a construction project.
insurance
The insuring of property, life, or one's person against loss or harm arising in specified contingencies in consideration of a payment proportionate to the risk involved.
general contractor
A person or organization that contracts directly with an owner to manage and supervise a construction project, including the work performed by subcontractors.
bonded
Having a monetary commitment set aside to ensure that all obligations set forth in a contract are fulfilled.
lending institution
The institution, usually a commercial bank, providing the long-term financing for a construction project.
construction manager
A person or organization that contracts with an owner to advise on and coordinate all phases of a building project, from evaluating the construction cost and feasibility of design decisions to managing the bidding, award, and construction phases of the project.
Region
Community
Owner
Architect
Engineers
Users
Contractor
Contractor
Contractor
Owner
design-build
Of or pertaining to an arrangement under which a person or organization contracts directly with an owner to design and construct a building or project.
Architect
Engineers
Subcontractor
speculative builder
A person or organization that develops and constructs buildings for subsequent sale or lease.
turn-key
Of or pertaining to an arrangement under which a person or organization designs and constructs a building for sale or lease when ready for occupancy.
Subcontractor
Subcontractor

CONSTRUCTION

The process of building, from site preparation through erection, assembly, and finishing operations.

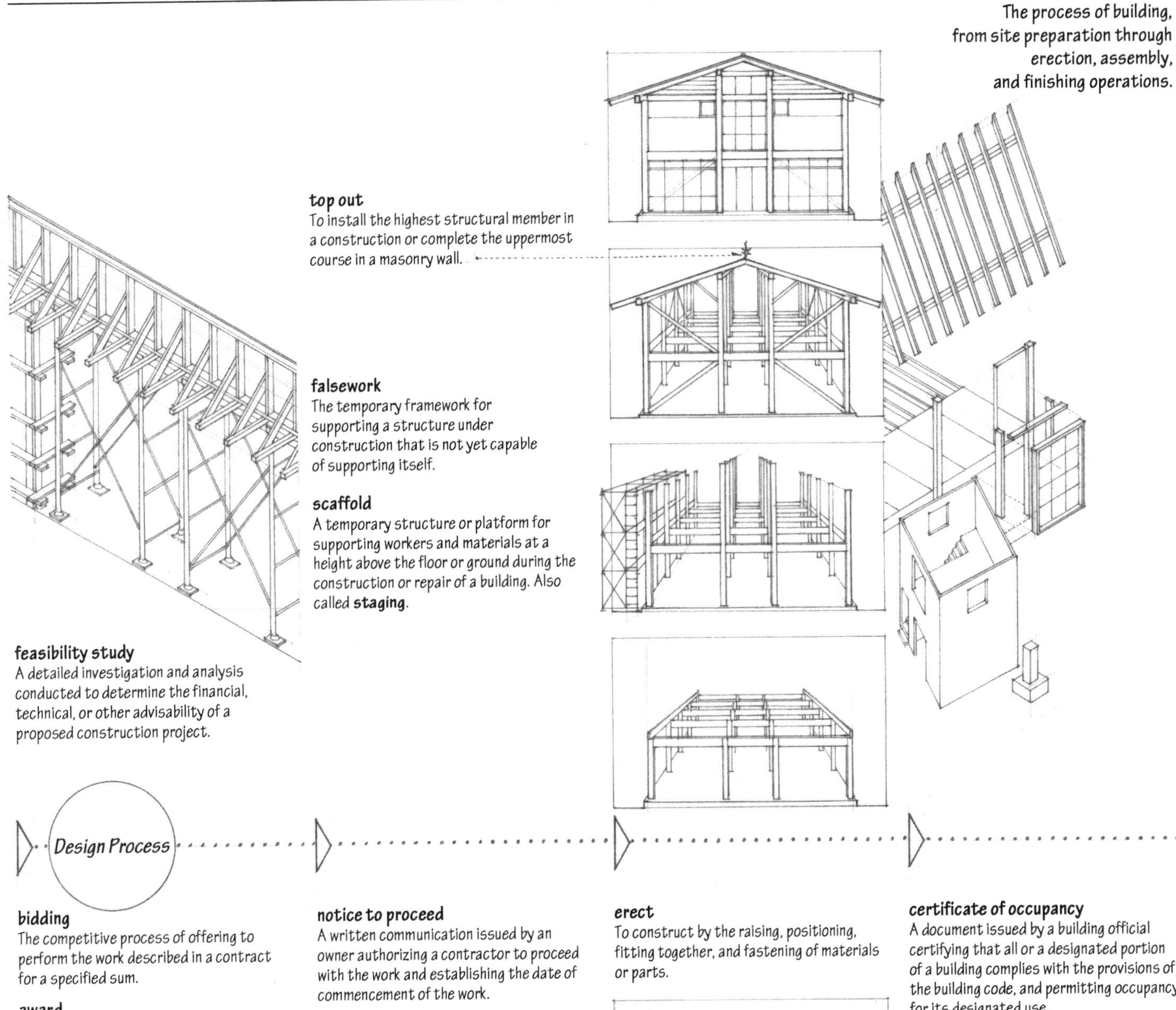

top out
To install the highest structural member in a construction or complete the uppermost course in a masonry wall.

falsework
The temporary framework for supporting a structure under construction that is not yet capable of supporting itself.

scaffold
A temporary structure or platform for supporting workers and materials at a height above the floor or ground during the construction or repair of a building. Also called **staging**.

feasibility study
A detailed investigation and analysis conducted to determine the financial, technical, or other advisability of a proposed construction project.

bidding
The competitive process of offering to perform the work described in a contract for a specified sum.

award
A formal acceptance of a bid or a negotiated proposal.

contract
A legally enforceable agreement, usually in written form, between two or more parties to do or not to do something specified.

notice to proceed
A written communication issued by an owner authorizing a contractor to proceed with the work and establishing the date of commencement of the work.

building permit
A written authorization to proceed with construction of a building project in accordance with approved drawings and specifications, issued by the local government agency having jurisdiction after plans have been filed and reviewed.

building official
A person designated by a governmental authority to administer and enforce the provisions of a building code.

erect
To construct by the raising, positioning, fitting together, and fastening of materials or parts.

certificate of occupancy
A document issued by a building official certifying that all or a designated portion of a building complies with the provisions of the building code, and permitting occupancy for its designated use.

postoccupancy evaluation
The process of diagnosing the technical, functional and behavioral aspects of a completed building in order to accumulate information for future programming and design activities.

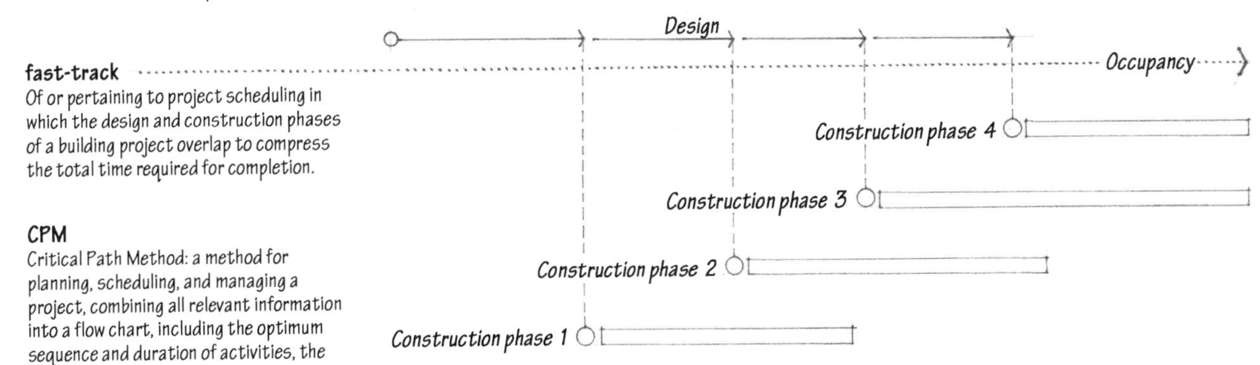

fast-track
Of or pertaining to project scheduling in which the design and construction phases of a building project overlap to compress the total time required for completion.

CPM
Critical Path Method: a method for planning, scheduling, and managing a project, combining all relevant information into a flow chart, including the optimum sequence and duration of activities, the relative significance of each event, and the coordination required for timely completion of the project.

CONSTRUCTION

The manner in which materials are ordered, assembled, and united into a whole, as frame construction.

systems building
A construction process using a high degree of prefabrication in the manufacture of standardized units or components to speed assembly and erection of a building. Also called **industrialized building**.

panel
A prefabricated section of a floor, wall, ceiling, or roof, handled as a single unit in the assembly and erection of a building.

sandwich panel
A structural panel consisting of a core of relatively light material enclosed between two sheets of a high-strength material, generally resulting in a high stiffness-to-weight ratio.

stressed-skin panel
A structural panel consisting of plywood facings glued to lumber stringers, used as floor, roof, or wall member subject to bending. The plywood facings and stringers act as a series of I-beams with the plywood resisting nearly all of the bending stresses. Cross bracing may be placed to support the edges of the skin and to help distribute concentrated loads.

prefabricate
To fabricate or manufacture beforehand, esp. in standardized units or components for quick assembly and erection.

fabricate
To construct by assembling diverse and usually standardized parts.

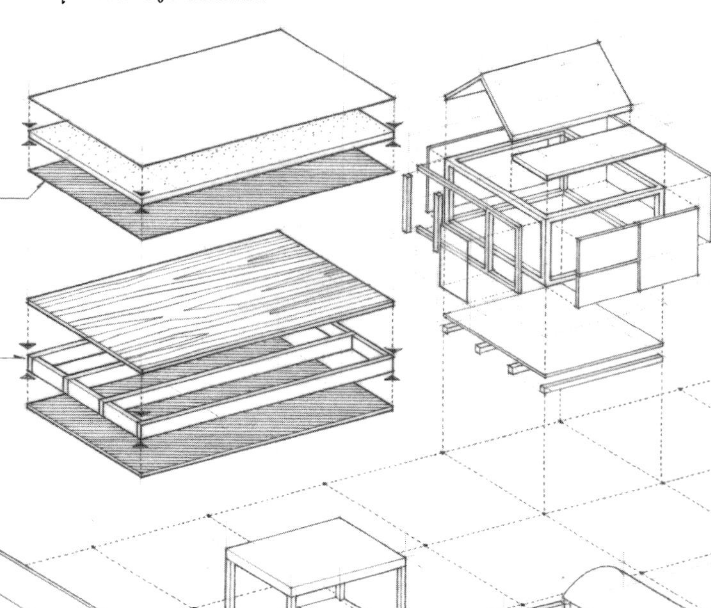

modular design
Planning and design utilizing prefabricated modules or modular coordination for ease of erection, flexible arrangement, or variety of use.

module
Any in a series of standardized, frequently interchangeable components used in assembling units of differing size, complexity, or function.

modular coordination
Correlating the dimensions of a structure and the unit sizes of its components, usually with the aid of a planning grid based on a 4-inch or 100-mm cubical module.

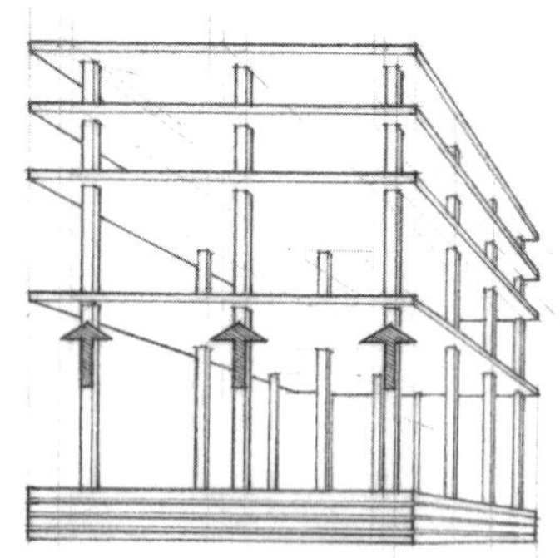

lift-slab construction
A technique of constructing multistory buildings in which all horizontal slabs are cast at ground level and, when cured, are raised into position by hydraulic jacks.

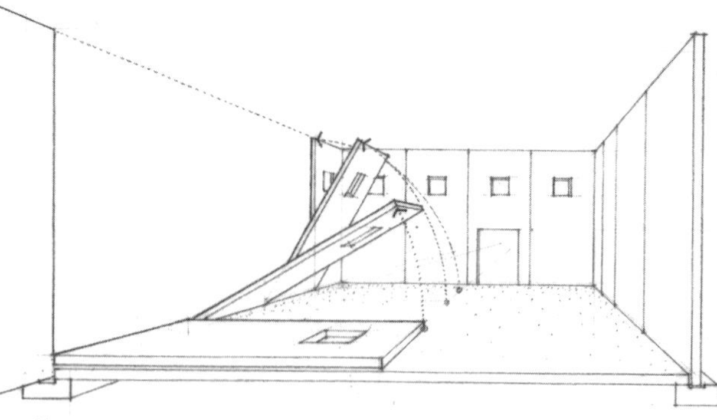

tilt-up construction
A method of casting reinforced concrete wall panels on site in a horizontal position, then tilting them up into their final position.

contract documents
The legal documents comprising a construction contract, including the owner-contractor agreement, conditions of the contract, and the construction drawings and specifications for the project, including all addenda, modifications, and any other items stipulated as being specifically included.

construction documents
The construction drawings and specifications setting forth in detail the requirements for the construction of a project.

specifications
The part of the contract documents consisting of a detailed description of the technical nature of the materials, standards, and quality of execution of the work to be placed under contract.

uniform system
A format developed by the Construction Specifications Institute for coordinating specifications, filing of technical data and product literature, and construction cost accounting, organized into 16 divisions based on an interrelationship of material, trade, or function. Also called **Masterformat**.

Division 1	*General Requirements*
Division 2	*Sitework*
Division 3	*Concrete*
Division 4	*Masonry*
Division 5	*Metals*
Division 6	*Wood & Plastics*
Division 7	*Thermal & Moisture Protection*
Division 8	*Doors & Windows*
Division 9	*Finishes*
Division 10	*Specialties*
Division 11	*Equipment*
Division 12	*Furnishings*
Division 13	*Special Construction*
Division 14	*Conveying Systems*
Division 15	*Mechanical*
Division 16	*Electrical*

performance specification
A specification that stipulates how a particular component or system must perform without giving the means to be employed to achieve the results.

descriptive specification
A specification that stipulates the exact quantities and qualities of materials to be furnished and how they are to be assembled in a construction.

reference specification
A specification that refers to a standard specification to indicate the properties desired in a material or component and the methods of testing required to substantiate the performance of products.

proprietary specification
A specification that stipulates the use of specific products, systems, or processes without provision for substitution.

building code
A code regulating the design, construction, alteration, and repair of buildings, adopted and enforced by a local government agency to protect the public safety, health, and welfare.

A building code generally establishes minimum standards for materials and methods of construction, specifications for structural and fire safety, and other requirements based on the type of construction and the occupancy of a building, often using standards established by the American Society for Testing and Materials (ASTM), the American National Standards Institute (ANSI), and various technical societies and trade associations.

model code
A building code developed by an organization of states, professional societies, and trade associations for adoption by local communities.

BOCA National Building Code
A building code developed and published by the Building Officials and Code Administrators International, Inc. (BOCA), and used primarily in the northeastern U.S.

Uniform Building Code
A building code developed and published by the International Conference of Building Officials (ICBO), and used primarily in the central and western U.S.

Standard Building Code
A building code developed and published by the Southern Building Code Conference (SBCC), and used primarily in the southeastern U.S.

energy code
A building code that sets minimum standards for energy conservation and the energy-efficient design of buildings.

Americans with Disabilities Act
An act of Congress that became law in 1992, establishing design standards and requirements for all buildings except single-family residences to ensure their accessibility by the physically disabled.

zoning ordinance
An ordinance regulating the division of land into zones, as to restrict the height, bulk, density, and use of buildings, and the provision of any ancillary facilities, as parking: a principal instrument in the implementation of a master plan. Also called **zoning code**.

restrictive covenant
A covenant with a clause that restricts the action of any party to it, as an agreement among property owners specifying the use to which a property can be put: racial and religious restrictions are legally unenforceable.

nonconforming
Of or pertaining to a material, type of construction, or occupancy or use not complying with the requirements set forth in a building code.

variance
An official permit to do something normally forbidden by regulations, esp. by building in a way or for a purpose normally forbidden by a building code or zoning ordinance.

noncombustible construction
Construction having a structure of steel, concrete or masonry, and walls, floors and a roof of noncombustible materials.

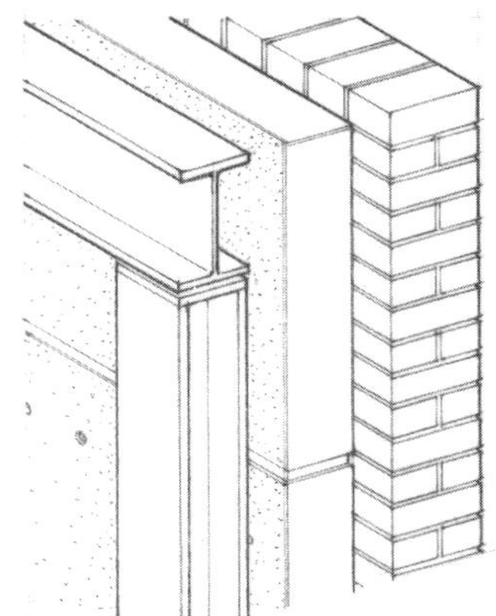

protected noncombustible construction
Noncombustible construction having a structure and major components with fire-resistance ratings at least equal to those specified by the appropriate authorities.

unprotected noncombustible construction
Noncombustible construction having no fire-resistance requirements except for fire walls and enclosures of fire exits and vertical shafts.

construction type
A classification of a building's construction according to the fire resistance of its major components: structural frame, exterior bearing and nonbearing walls, interior bearing walls, floors and ceilings, roofs, and enclosures of fire exits and vertical shafts. While each of the model codes differs in the detailed requirements for each construction type, they all limit the area and height of a building according to construction type and intended occupancy. Also called **construction class**.

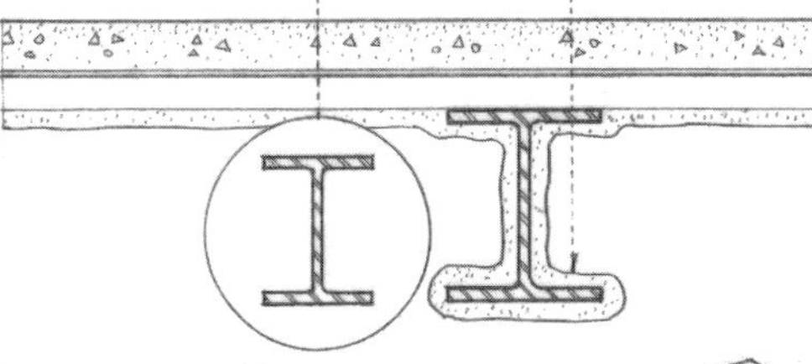

combustible construction
Any construction that does not fulfill the requirements for noncombustible construction.

ordinary construction
A construction type having noncombustible exterior walls and an interior structure wholly or partly of light wood framing.

protected ordinary construction
Ordinary construction having a structure and major components with fire-resistance ratings at least equal to those specified by the appropriate authorities.

unprotected ordinary construction
Ordinary construction having no fire-resistance requirements for the interior structure except for fire walls and enclosures of fire exits and vertical shafts.

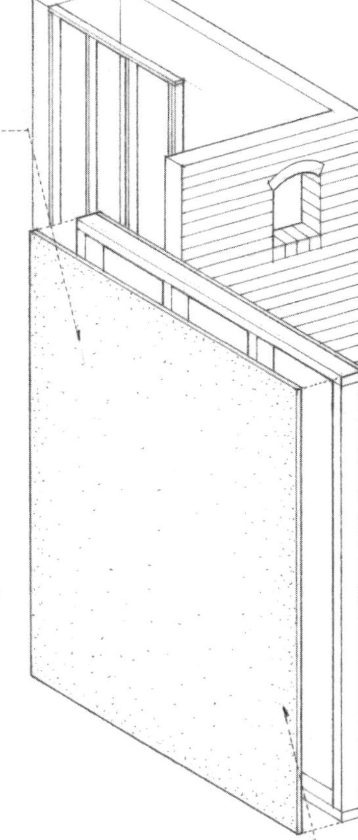

heavy-timber construction
A construction type having noncombustible exterior walls and an interior structure of timbers and decking of specified minimum sizes. Also called **mill construction**.

light wood frame construction
A construction type having a framework of wood members not meeting the requirements for heavy-timber construction.

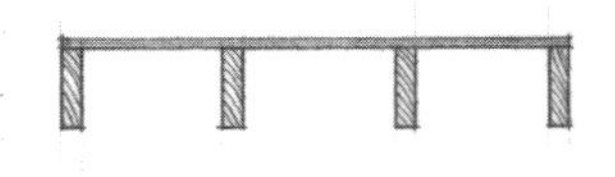

protected light wood frame construction
Light wood frame construction having a structure and major components with fire-resistance ratings at least equal to those specified by the appropriate authorities.

unprotected light wood frame construction
Light wood frame construction having no fire-resistance requirements except for fire walls and enclosures of fire exits and vertical shafts.

The creation and organization of formal elements in a work of art.

form
The shape and structure of something as distinguished from its substance or material.

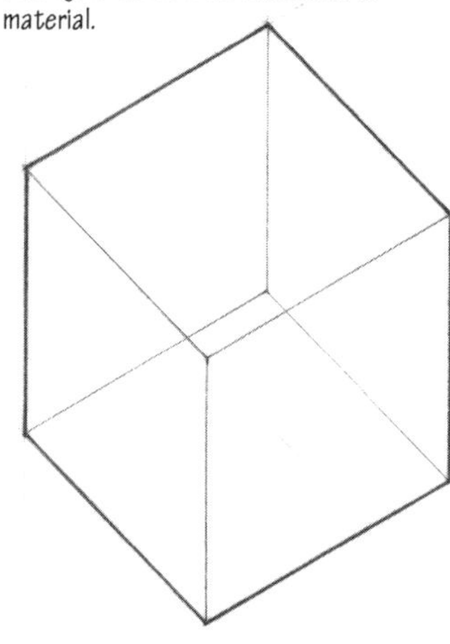

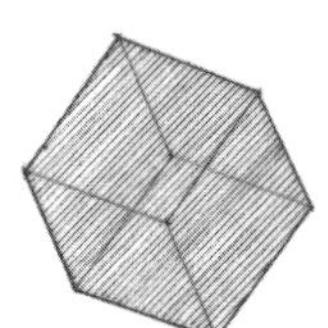

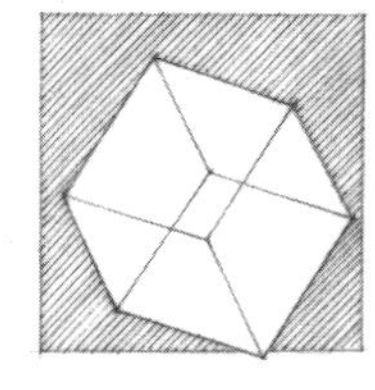

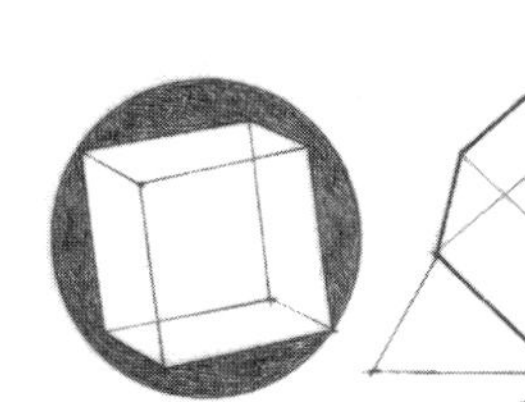

line
The edge or contour of a shape.

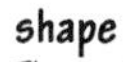

shape
The outline or surface configuration of a particular form or figure. While form usually refers to the principle that gives unity to a whole, and often includes a sense of mass or volume, shape suggests an outline with some emphasis on the enclosed area or mass.

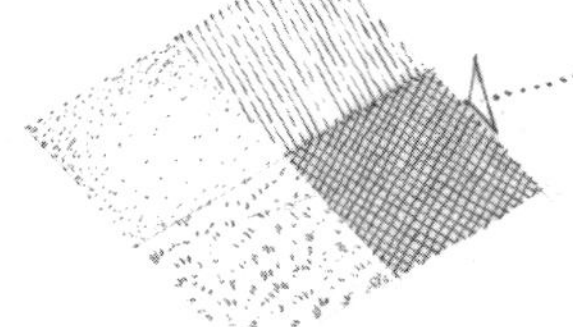

texture
The visual and esp. tactile quality of a surface, apart from its color or form.

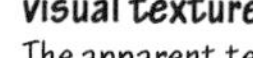

visual texture
The apparent texture of a surface resulting from the combination and interrelation of colors and tonal values.

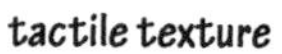

tactile texture
The physical, dimensional structure of a surface, apart from its color or form.

organic
Of or pertaining to shapes and forms having irregular contours which appear to resemble those of living plants or animals.

nonobjective
Of or pertaining to shapes and forms not representing natural or actual objects. Also, **nonrepresentational**.

geometric
Of or pertaining to shapes and forms which resemble or employ the simple rectilinear or curvilinear elements of geometry.

abstract
Of or pertaining to shapes and forms having an intellectual and affective content dependent solely on their intrinsic lines, colors, and relationship to one another.

symbol
Something that stands for or represents something else by association, resemblance, or convention, deriving its meaning chiefly from the structure in which it appears.

sign
A mark or figure having a conventional meaning and used in place of a word or phrase to express a complex notion.

massing
A unified compostion of two-dimensional shapes or three-dimensional volumes, esp. one that has or gives the impression of weight, density, and bulk.

articulation
A method or manner of jointing that makes the united parts clear, distinct, and precise in relation to each other.

additive
Characterized or produced by addition, accumulation, or uniting, often resulting in a new identity.

subtractive
Characterized or produced by removal of a part or portion without destroying a sense of the whole.

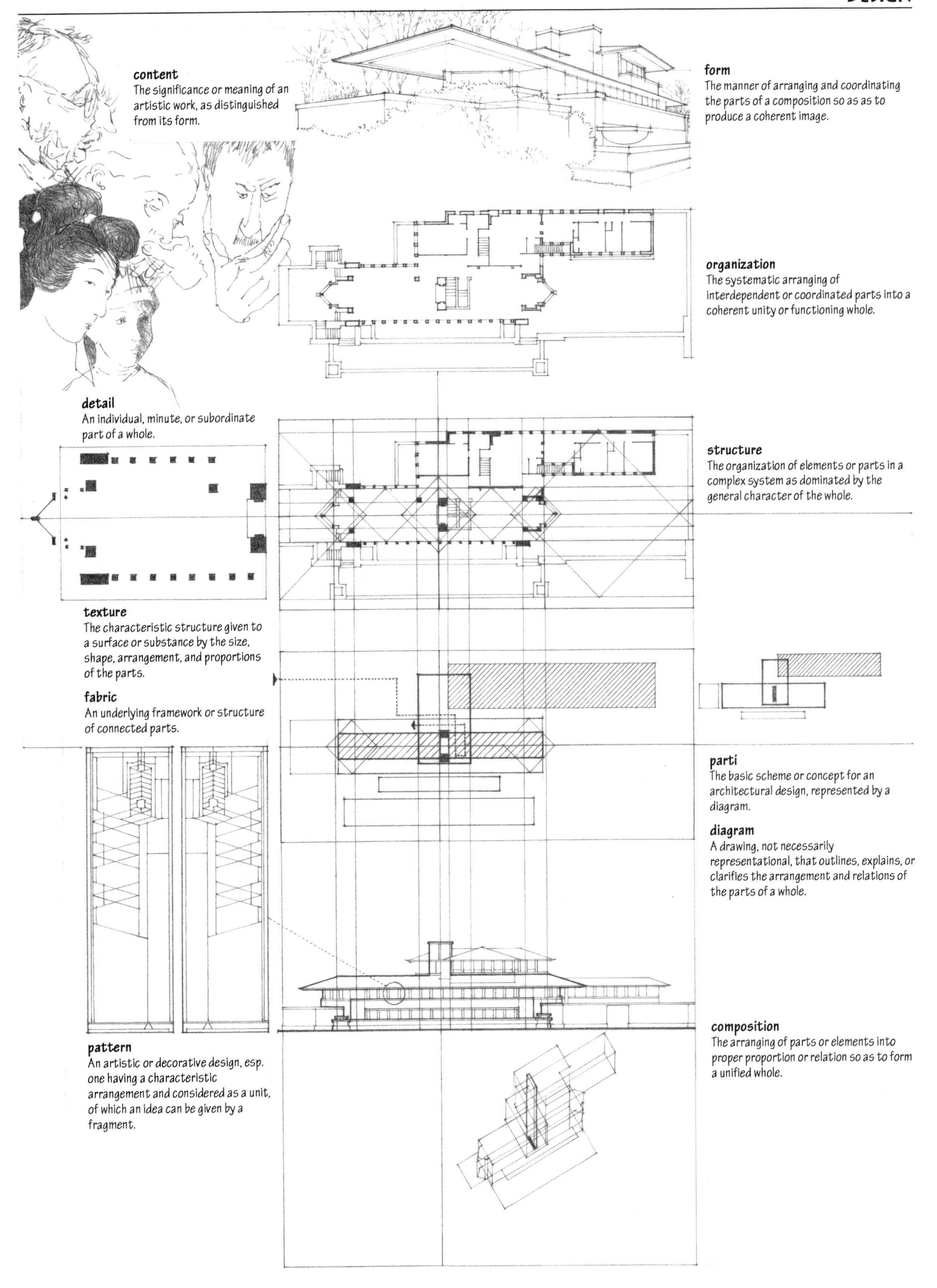

content
The significance or meaning of an artistic work, as distinguished from its form.

form
The manner of arranging and coordinating the parts of a composition so as to produce a coherent image.

organization
The systematic arranging of interdependent or coordinated parts into a coherent unity or functioning whole.

detail
An individual, minute, or subordinate part of a whole.

structure
The organization of elements or parts in a complex system as dominated by the general character of the whole.

texture
The characteristic structure given to a surface or substance by the size, shape, arrangement, and proportions of the parts.

fabric
An underlying framework or structure of connected parts.

parti
The basic scheme or concept for an architectural design, represented by a diagram.

diagram
A drawing, not necessarily representational, that outlines, explains, or clarifies the arrangement and relations of the parts of a whole.

composition
The arranging of parts or elements into proper proportion or relation so as to form a unified whole.

pattern
An artistic or decorative design, esp. one having a characteristic arrangement and considered as a unit, of which an idea can be given by a fragment.

design principle
A fundamental and comprehensive concept of visual perception for structuring an aesthetic composition.

order
A condition of logical, harmonious, or comprehensible arrangement in which each element of a group is properly disposed with reference to other elements and to its purpose.

harmony
The orderly, pleasing, or congruent arrangement of the elements or parts in an artistic whole.

repose
Harmony in the arrangement of parts or colors that is restful to the eye.

coherent
Logically or aesthetically ordered or integrated to afford comprehension or recognition.

unity
The state or quality of being combined into one, as the ordering of elements in an artistic work that constitutes a harmonious whole or promotes a singleness of effect.

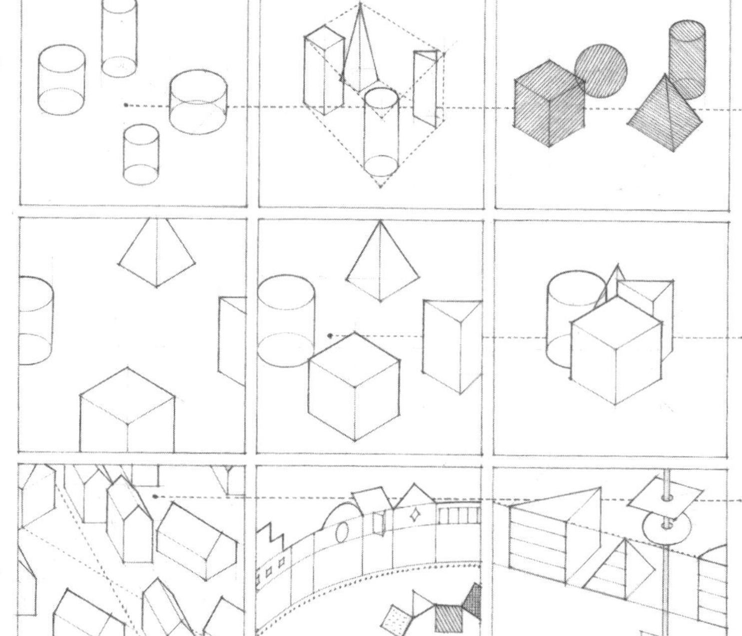

agreement
Correspondence in shape, size, or color among the elements in a work or art.

similarity
The state or quality of being alike in substance, essentials, or characteristics.

proximity
Nearness in place, order, or relation.

continuity
The state or quality of being continuous, as a line, edge, or direction.

alignment
Arrangement in or adjustment according to a straight line.

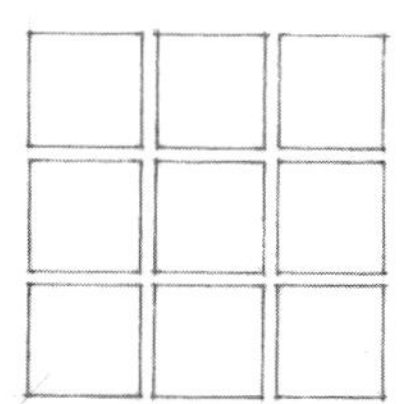

uniformity
The state or quality of being identical, homogeneous, or regular.

homogeneous
Uniform in structure throughout or composed of parts that are all of the same nature or kind.

regular
Uniformly or evenly formed or arranged.

monotony
The state or quality of lacking variety.

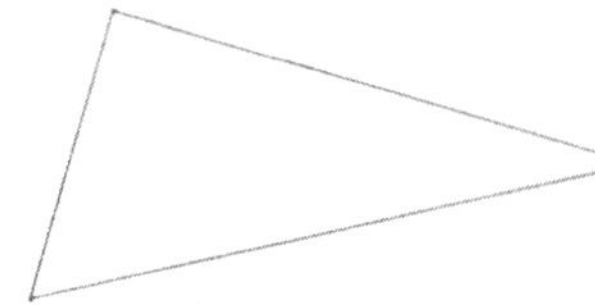

variety
The state or quality of having varied or diverse forms, types, or characteristics.

complexity
The state or quality of being a whole composed of complicated, intricate, or interconnected parts.

collage
An artistic composition of often diverse elements in unlikely or unexpected juxtaposition.

emphasis
Stress or prominence given to an element of a composition by means of contrast, anomaly, or counterpoint.

hierarchy
A system of elements ranked, classified, and organized one above another, according to importance or significance.

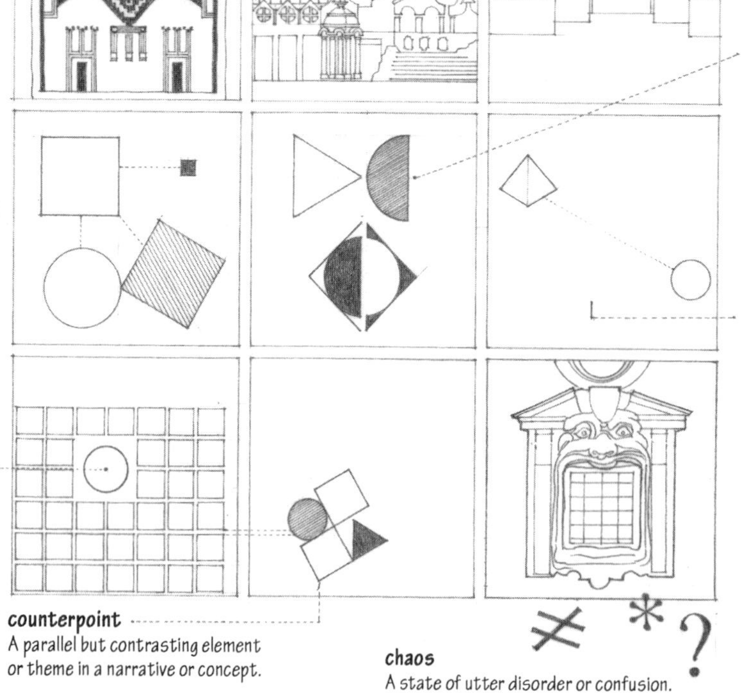

opposition
The state or position of being placed opposite another, or of lying in corresponding positions from an intervening space or object.

juxtaposition
The state or position of being placed close together or side by side, so as to permit comparison or contrast.

contrast
Opposition or juxtaposition of dissimilar elements in a work of art to intensify each element's properties and produce a more dynamic expressiveness.

tension
A tenuous balance maintained in an artistic work between opposing forces or elements, often causing anxiety or excitement.

anomaly
A deviation from the normal or expected form, order, or arrangement.

contradiction
The state or condition of being opposed, inconsistent, or logically incongruous.

point
The major idea, essential part, or salient feature of a narrative or concept.

salient
Prominent or conspicuous.

counterpoint
A parallel but contrasting element or theme in a narrative or concept.

chaos
A state of utter disorder or confusion.

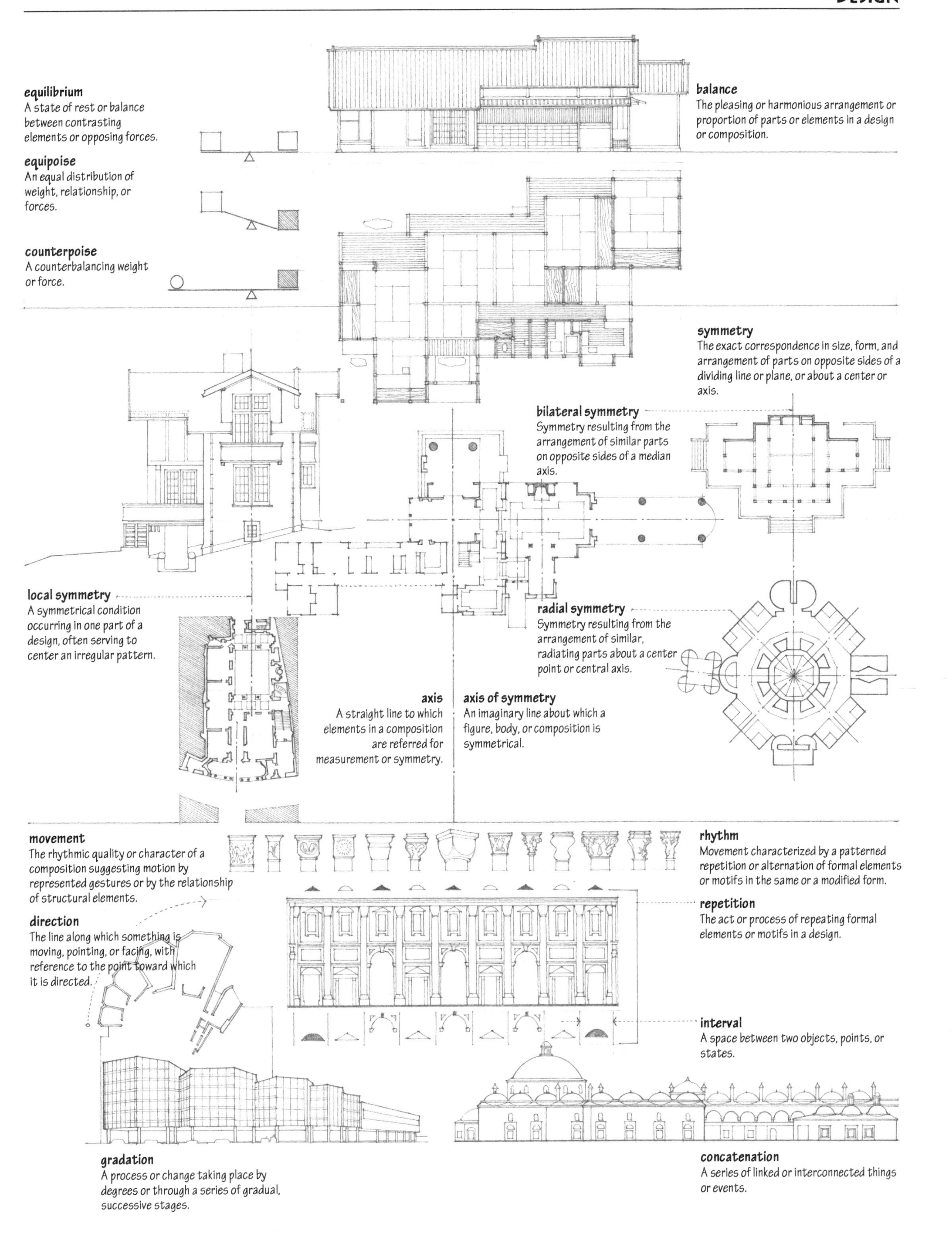
equilibrium
A state of rest or balance between contrasting elements or opposing forces.
equipoise
An equal distribution of weight, relationship, or forces.
counterpoise
A counterbalancing weight or force.
balance
The pleasing or harmonious arrangement or proportion of parts or elements in a design or composition.
symmetry
The exact correspondence in size, form, and arrangement of parts on opposite sides of a dividing line or plane, or about a center or axis.
bilateral symmetry
Symmetry resulting from the arrangement of similar parts on opposite sides of a median axis.
local symmetry
A symmetrical condition occurring in one part of a design, often serving to center an irregular pattern.
radial symmetry
Symmetry resulting from the arrangement of similar, radiating parts about a center point or central axis.
axis
A straight line to which elements in a composition are referred for measurement or symmetry.
axis of symmetry
An imaginary line about which a figure, body, or composition is symmetrical.
movement
The rhythmic quality or character of a composition suggesting motion by represented gestures or by the relationship of structural elements.
direction
The line along which something is moving, pointing, or facing, with reference to the point toward which it is directed.
rhythm
Movement characterized by a patterned repetition or alternation of formal elements or motifs in the same or a modified form.
repetition
The act or process of repeating formal elements or motifs in a design.
interval
A space between two objects, points, or states.
gradation
A process or change taking place by degrees or through a series of gradual, successive stages.
concatenation
A series of linked or interconnected things or events.

proportion
The comparative, proper, or harmonious relation of one part to another or to the whole with respect to magnitude, quantity, or degree.

$$A/B = B/(A+B)$$

proportion
The equality between two ratios in which the first of the four terms divided by the second equals the third divided by the fourth.

golden section
A proportion between the two dimensions of a plane figure or the two divisions of a line, in which the ratio of the smaller to the larger is the same as the ratio of the larger to the whole: a ratio of approximately 0.618 to 1.000. Also called **golden mean**.

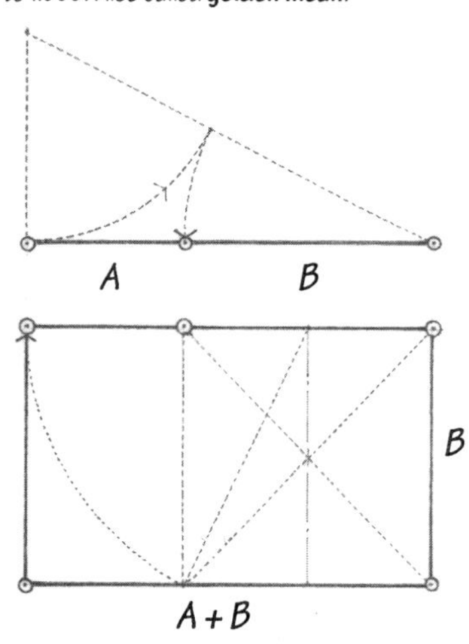

eurythmy
Harmony of proportion or movement.

ratio
Relation in magnitude, quantity, or degree between two or more similar things.

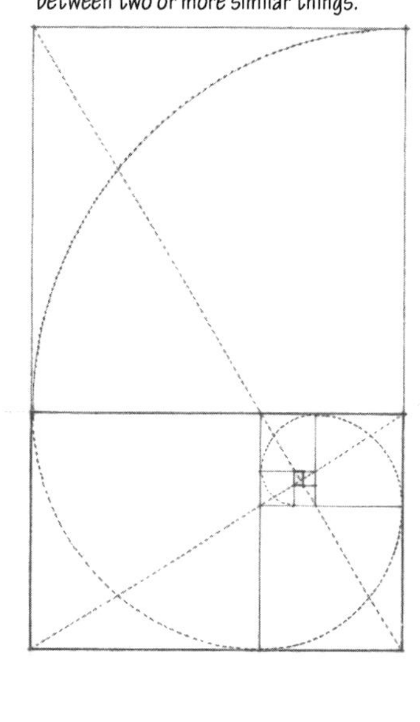

1, 1, 2, 3, 5, 8, 13, 21...

1/1, 1/2, 2/3, 3/5, 5/8, 8/13...

Fibonacci series
The unending sequence of numbers where the first two terms are 1 and 1, and each succeeding term is the sum of the two immediately preceding. Also called **Fibonacci sequence**.

harmonic series
A series in which the terms are in harmonic progression.

1, 1/3, 1/5, 1/7, 1/9

harmonic progression
A sequence of numbers the reciprocals of which form an arithmetic progression.

scale
A certain proportionate size, extent, or degree, usually judged in relation to some standard or point of reference.

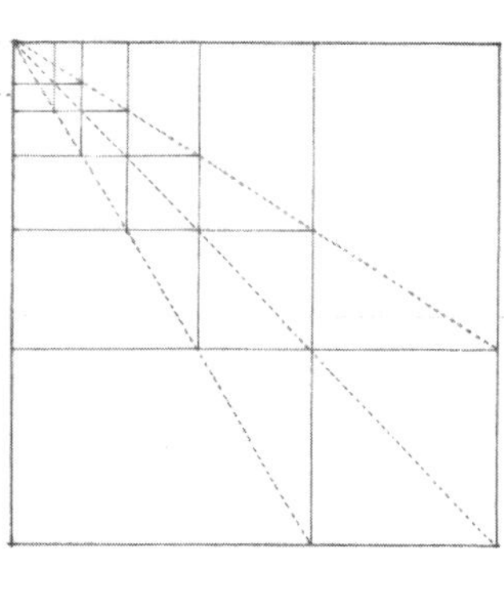

module
A unit of measurement used for standardizing the dimensions of building materials or regulating the proportions of an architectural composition.

human scale
The size or proportion of a building element or space, or an article of furniture, relative to the structural or functional dimensions of the human body.

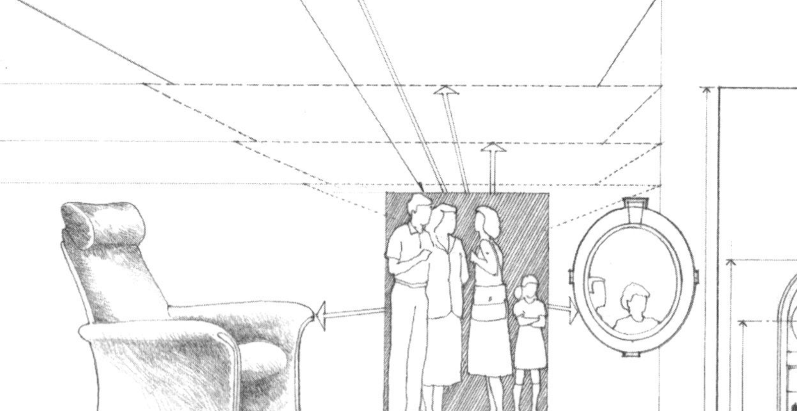

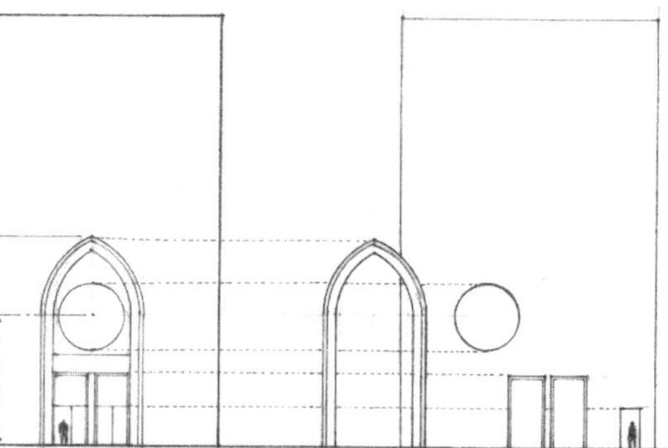

mechanical scale
The size or proportion of something relative to an accepted standard of measurement.

visual scale
The size or proportion a building element appears to have relative to other elements or components of known or assumed size.

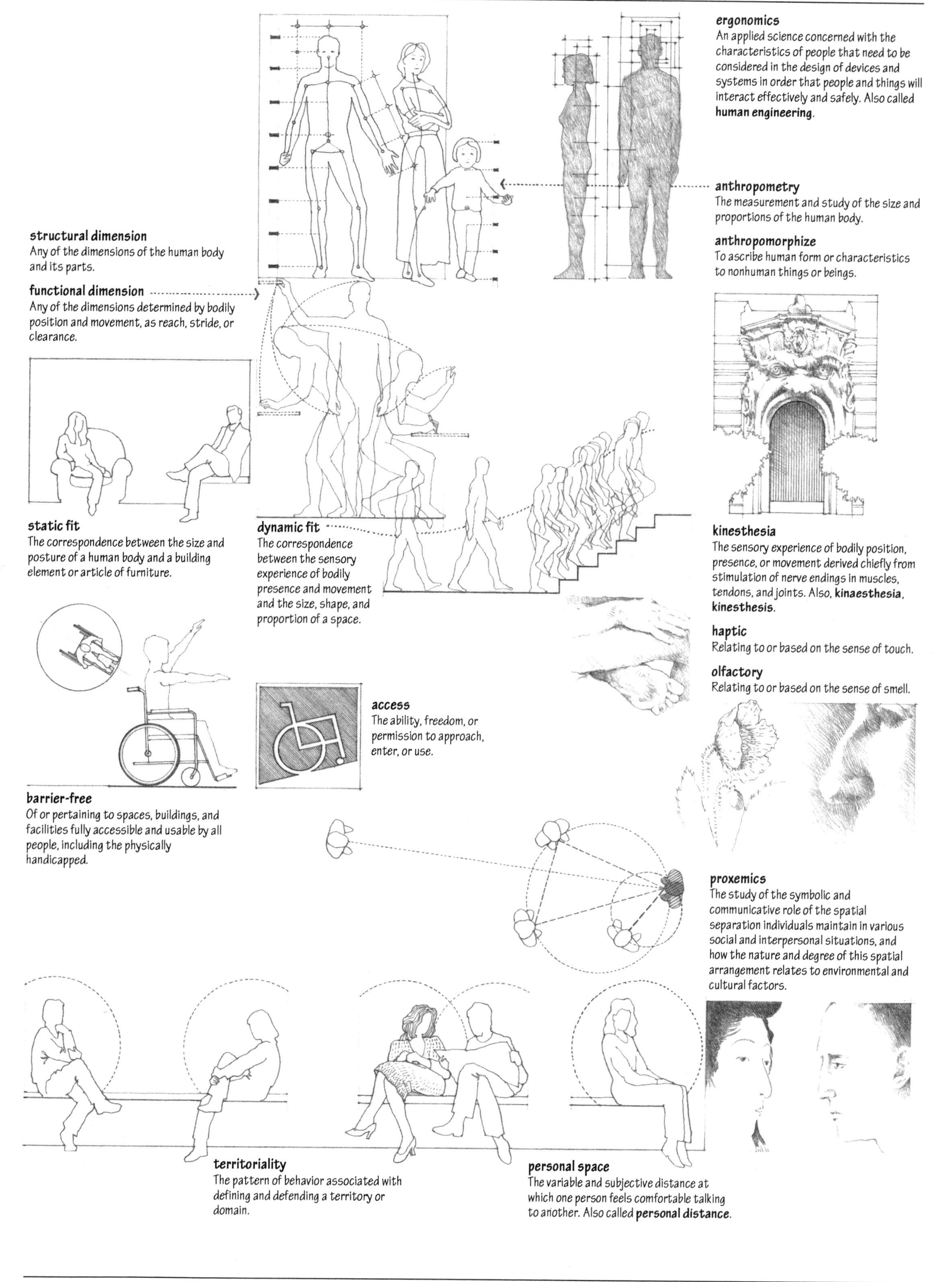

ergonomics
An applied science concerned with the characteristics of people that need to be considered in the design of devices and systems in order that people and things will interact effectively and safely. Also called **human engineering**.

anthropometry
The measurement and study of the size and proportions of the human body.

anthropomorphize
To ascribe human form or characteristics to nonhuman things or beings.

structural dimension
Any of the dimensions of the human body and its parts.

functional dimension
Any of the dimensions determined by bodily position and movement, as reach, stride, or clearance.

static fit
The correspondence between the size and posture of a human body and a building element or article of furniture.

dynamic fit
The correspondence between the sensory experience of bodily presence and movement and the size, shape, and proportion of a space.

kinesthesia
The sensory experience of bodily position, presence, or movement derived chiefly from stimulation of nerve endings in muscles, tendons, and joints. Also, **kinaesthesia**, **kinesthesis**.

haptic
Relating to or based on the sense of touch.

olfactory
Relating to or based on the sense of smell.

access
The ability, freedom, or permission to approach, enter, or use.

barrier-free
Of or pertaining to spaces, buildings, and facilities fully accessible and usable by all people, including the physically handicapped.

proxemics
The study of the symbolic and communicative role of the spatial separation individuals maintain in various social and interpersonal situations, and how the nature and degree of this spatial arrangement relates to environmental and cultural factors.

territoriality
The pattern of behavior associated with defining and defending a territory or domain.

personal space
The variable and subjective distance at which one person feels comfortable talking to another. Also called **personal distance**.

design
To conceive, contrive, or devise the form and structure of a building or other construction.

design process
A purposeful activity aimed at devising a plan for changing an existing situation into a future preferred state, esp. the cyclical, iterative process comprising the following phases.

process
A systematic series of actions or operations leading or directed to a particular end.

phase
A particular stage in a process of change or development.

program
A procedure for solving a problem, as a statement setting forth the context, conditions, requirements, and objectives for a design project.

initiation
Identifying a problem and its social, economic, and physical context.

preparation
Collecting and analyzing relevant information and establishing goals and criteria for an acceptable solution.

synthesis
Discovering constraints and opportunities, and hypothesizing possible alternative solutions.

conceive
To form an idea or conception in the mind.

contrive
To form in an artistic or ingenious manner.

devise
To form in the mind by new combinations or applications of existing ideas or principles.

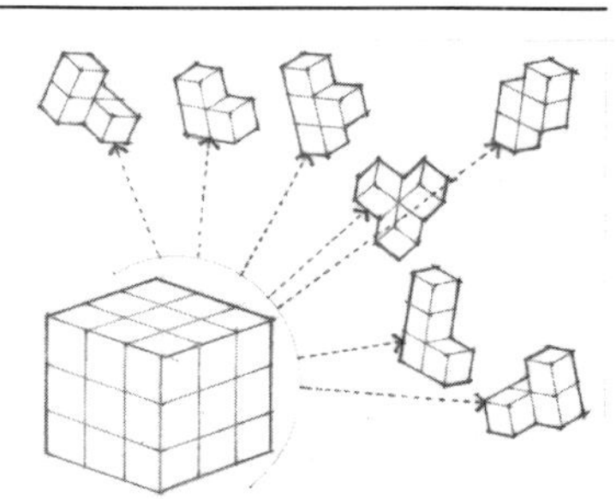

analysis
Separating of a whole into its constituent parts or elements, esp. as a method of studying the nature of the whole and determining its essential features and their relations.

synthesis
Combining of separate, often diverse parts or elements so as to form a single or coherent whole.

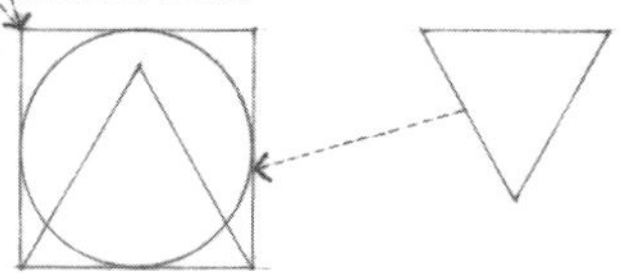

dynamics
The pattern of change, growth, or development of an object or phenomenon.

charrette
An intense effort to complete a design project within a specified time. Also, **charette**.

hypothesis
Formulating a tentative assumption in order to draw out and test its logical or empirical consequences.

alternative
One of the propositions or courses of action to be chosen from a set of two or more mutually exclusive possibilities.

develop
To work out, expand, or realize the capabilities or possibilities of so as to bring gradually to a fuller or more advanced or effective state.

modify
To change the form, character, or qualities of in order to give a new orientation to or to serve a new end.

refine
To improve or elaborate in order to make more fine or precise.

inflection
A bend, angle, or similar change in the shape of a configuration, by means of which a change of relationship to some context or condition is indicated.

reevaluation
Assessing how well an implemented solution in use satisfies the specified goals and criteria.

implement
To ensure the fulfillment of by means of a definite plan or procedure.

feedback
Evaluative information about an action or process prompting a return to a preceding phase for alteration or correction.

draft
A preliminary version of a plan or design.

transformation
The process of changing in form or structure through a series of discrete permutations and manipulations in response to a specific context or set of conditions without a loss of identity or concept.

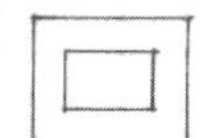
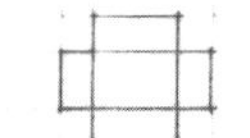
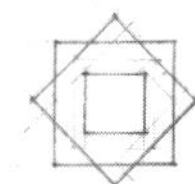

action
Selecting and implementing the most suitable solution.

evaluation
Simulating, testing, and modifying acceptable alternatives according to specified goals and criteria.

communicate
To express, convey, or interchange ideas, information, or the like by writing, speaking, or through a common system of signs or symbols, esp. in a way that is clearly and readily understood.

proposal
The offering of a plan for consideration, acceptance, or action.

select
To choose from a number of alternatives by fitness or preference.

judgment
The mental ability to perceive distinctions, comprehend relationships, or distinguish alternatives.

function
The natural or proper action for which something is designed, used, or exists.

purpose
The reason for which something exists or is done, made, or used.

amenity
Any feature that provides or increases comfort, convenience, or pleasure.

economy
Careful, thrifty, and efficient use and management of resources.

evaluate
To ascertain or assess the significance, worth, or quality of, usually by careful appraisal and study.

criterion
A standard, rule, or principle on which a judgment or decision may be based.

datum
An assumed, given, or otherwise determined fact or proposition from which conclusions may be drawn or decisions made.

simulate
To create a likeness or model of something anticipated for testing and evaluation.

model
A miniature representation, usually built to scale, to show the appearance or construction of something.

mock-up
A full-sized model of a building or structure, built accurately to scale for study, testing, or teaching.

test
To subject a system or process to such conditions or operations as will lead to a critical evaluation of abilities or performance and subsequent acceptance or rejection.

reason
The faculty or power of comprehending, inferring, or thinking in an orderly, rational way.

fancy
The play of the mind through which visions are summoned, esp. mental inventions that are whimsical, playful, and characteristically removed from reality.

creativity
The ability to transcend traditional ideas, patterns, or relationships and to initiate meaningful new ideas, forms, or interpretations.

originality
The creative ability to imagine or express in an independent and individual manner.

visualize
To form or recall a mental image of.

envision
To form a mental picture of a future possibility.

image
A mental representation of something previously perceived in the absence of the original stimulus.

reproductive imagination
The power of reproducing images stored in the memory under the suggestion of associated images.

creative imagination
The power of recombining former experiences in the creation of new images directed at a specific goal or aiding in the solution of a problem.

imagination
The faculty of forming mental images or concepts of what is not present to the senses or perceived in reality.

idea
A thought or notion resulting from mental awareness, understanding, or activity.

project
To regard an idea or concept as having some form of objective reality outside of the mind.

vision
The act or power of anticipating that which will or may come to be.

concept
A mental image or formulation of what something is or ought to be, esp. an idea generalized from particular characteristics or instances.

perspective
The faculty of seeing things in their true relations or of evaluating their relative significance.

inform
To animate or permeate with a particular form, substance, quality, or distinction.

design concept
A concept for the form, structure, and features of a building or other construction, represented graphically by diagrams, plans, or other drawings.

view
A particular manner or mode of looking at or regarding something.

address
To direct the efforts or attention of.

aspect
A way in which a thing may be viewed or regarded.

engage
To attract and hold fast by influence or power.

scheme
An underlying organizational pattern or structure for a design.

projet
The original scheme for a design presented in the form of a sketch outlining its specific character, to be developed in detail in later studies.

practice
Actual performance or application of principles, as distinguished from theory.

theory
Abstract thought or speculation resulting in a system of assumptions or principles used in analyzing, explaining, or predicting phenomena, and proposed or followed as the basis of action.

real
Having objective, verifiable, and independent existence, as opposed to being artificial or illusory.

metaphor
An object, activity, or idea used in place of another to suggest a likeness between them.

synectics
The study of creative processes, esp. as applied to the stating and solution of problems that involves free use of metaphor and analogy in informal interchange within a small group of diverse individuals.

abstract
Thought of without reference to concrete reality or a particular instance.

analogy
A similarity in some particulars between things otherwise dissimilar: specif., a logical inference based on the assumption that if two things are known to be alike in some respects, then they will probably be alike in other respects.

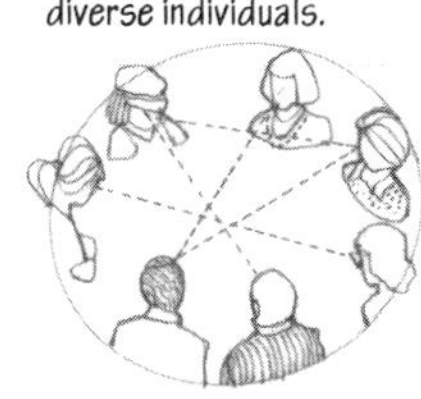

principle
A fundamental and comprehensive law, truth, or assumption governing action, procedure, or arrangement.

typology
A systematic classification or study of types according to structural features.

intuition
The power or faculty of knowing without evident rational thought and inference.

type
A number of things regarded as forming a group by reason of common attributes or characteristics.

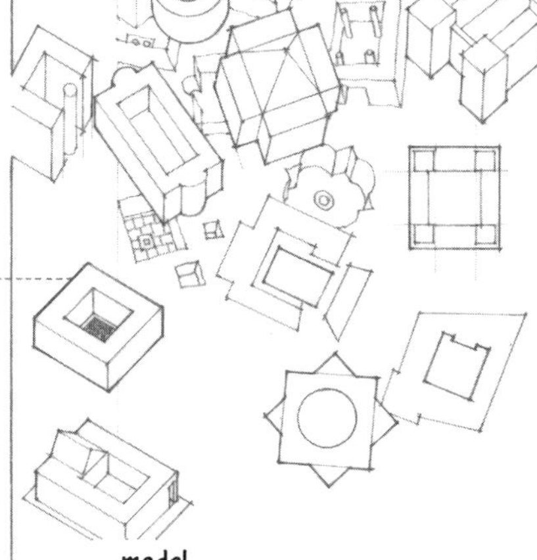

speculation
Meditation or reflection on a subject or idea, resulting in a conclusion inferred from incomplete or inconclusive evidence.

archetype
An original model or pattern on which all things of the same kind are copied or based.

ambiguity
The state or quality of being susceptible to uncertainty of meaning or multiple interpretation.

ectype
A reproduction of an original.

serendipity
An aptitude for making desirable and unexpected discoveries by accident.

prototype
An early and typical example that exhibits the essential features of a class or group and on which later stages are based or judged.

model
An example serving as a pattern for imitation or emulation in the creation of something.

connection
Contextual, causal, or logical relations or associations of something observed or imagined.

accident
A fortuitous circumstance, quality, or characteristic.

DOME

A vaulted structure having a circular plan and usually the form of a portion of a sphere, so constructed as to exert an equal thrust in all directions.

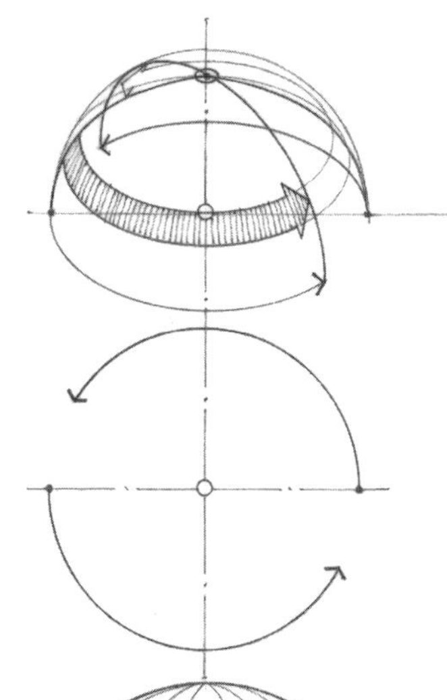

saucer dome
A dome having the form of a segment of a sphere, with its center well below the springing line. A saucer dome is particularly sensitive to buckling under an external load.

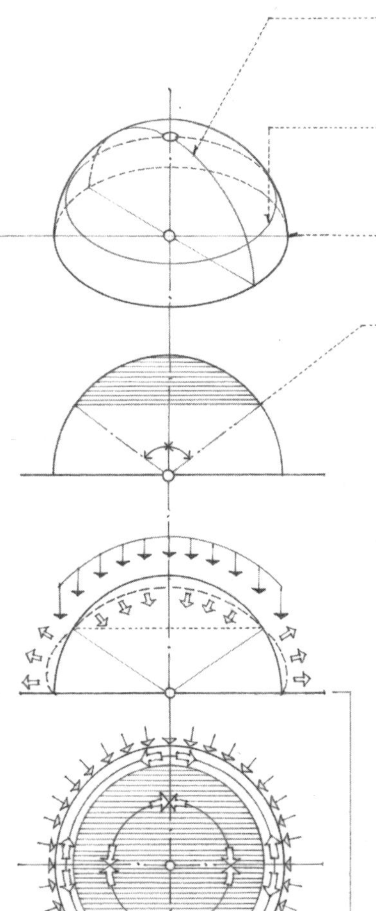

meridional line
A curved line describing a vertical section cut through the axis of a rotational surface.

hoop line
A circular line describing a horizontal section cut perpendicular to the axis of a rotational surface.

semicircular dome
A dome having the form of a hemisphere.

Transition from meridional to hoop forces occurs at an angle of from 45° to 60° from the vertical axis for most load conditions.

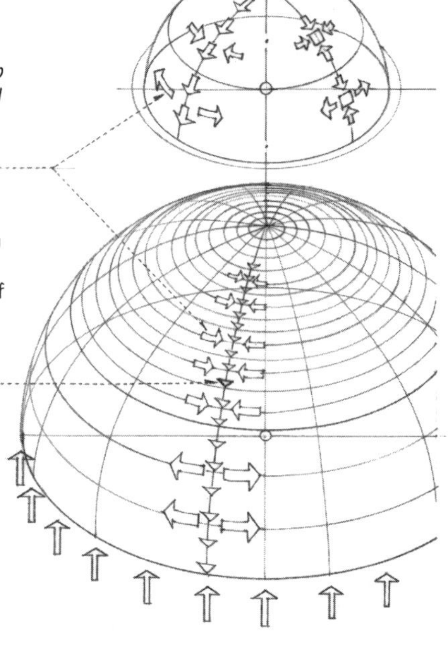

hoop force
A force acting along a hoop line of a dome structure, perpendicular to meridional forces. Hoop forces, which restrain the out-of-plane movement of the meridional strips in the shell of a dome, are compressive in the upper zone and tensile in the lower zone.

meridional force
A force acting along a meridional line of a dome structure, always compressive under full vertical loading.

tension ring
A ring encircling the base of a dome to contain the outward components of the meridional forces. In a concrete dome, this ring is thickened and reinforced to handle the bending stresses caused by the differing elastic deformations of the ring and shell.

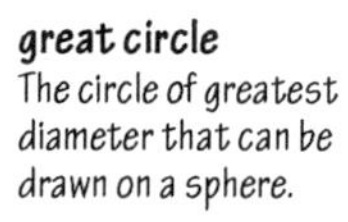

great circle
The circle of greatest diameter that can be drawn on a sphere.

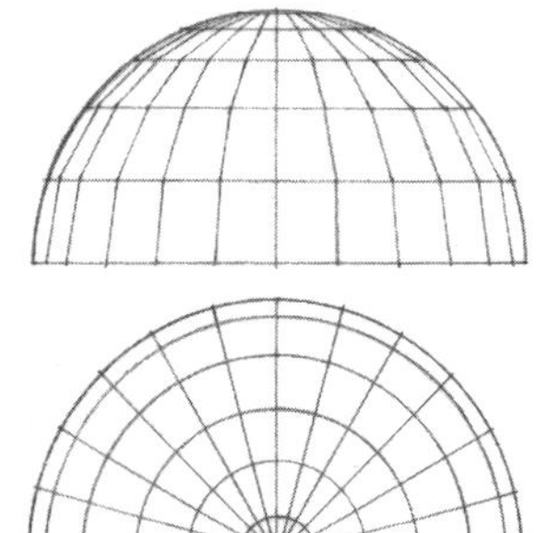

radial dome
A dome built with steel or timber trusses arranged in a radial manner and connected by polygonal rings at various heights.

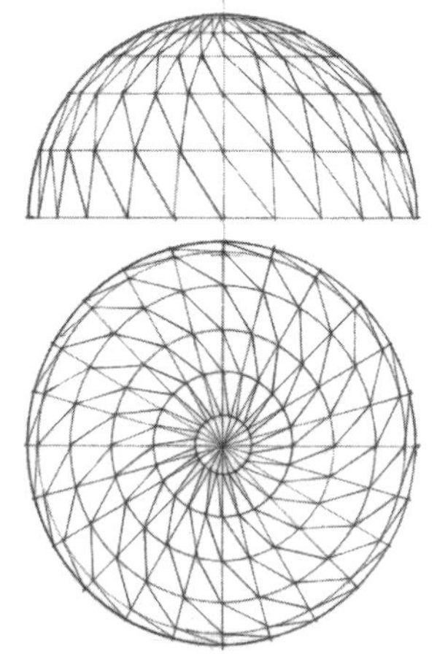

Schwedler dome
A steel dome having members which follow the lines of latitude and longitude, and a third set of diagonals completing the triangulation.

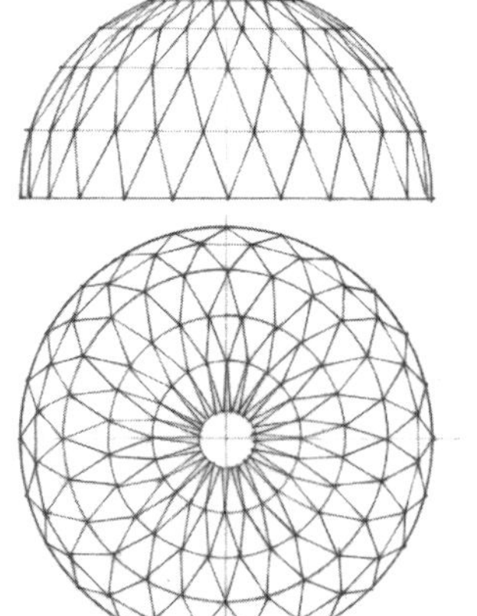

lattice dome
A steel dome structure having members which follow the circles of latitude, and two sets of diagonals replacing the lines of longitude and forming a series of isosceles triangles.

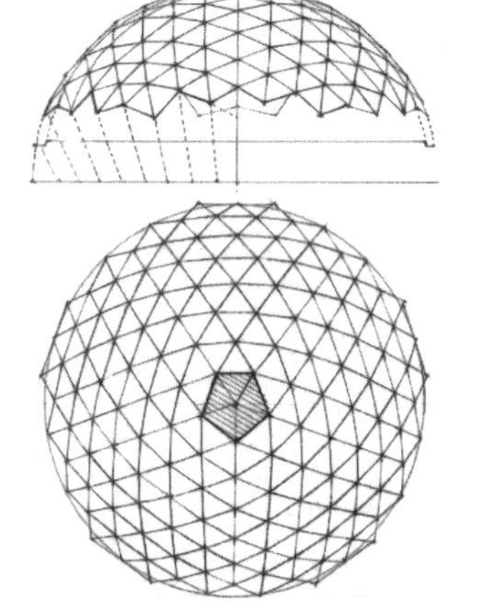

geodesic dome
A steel dome having members which follow three principal sets of great circles intersecting at 60°, subdividing the dome surface into a series of equilateral spherical triangles.

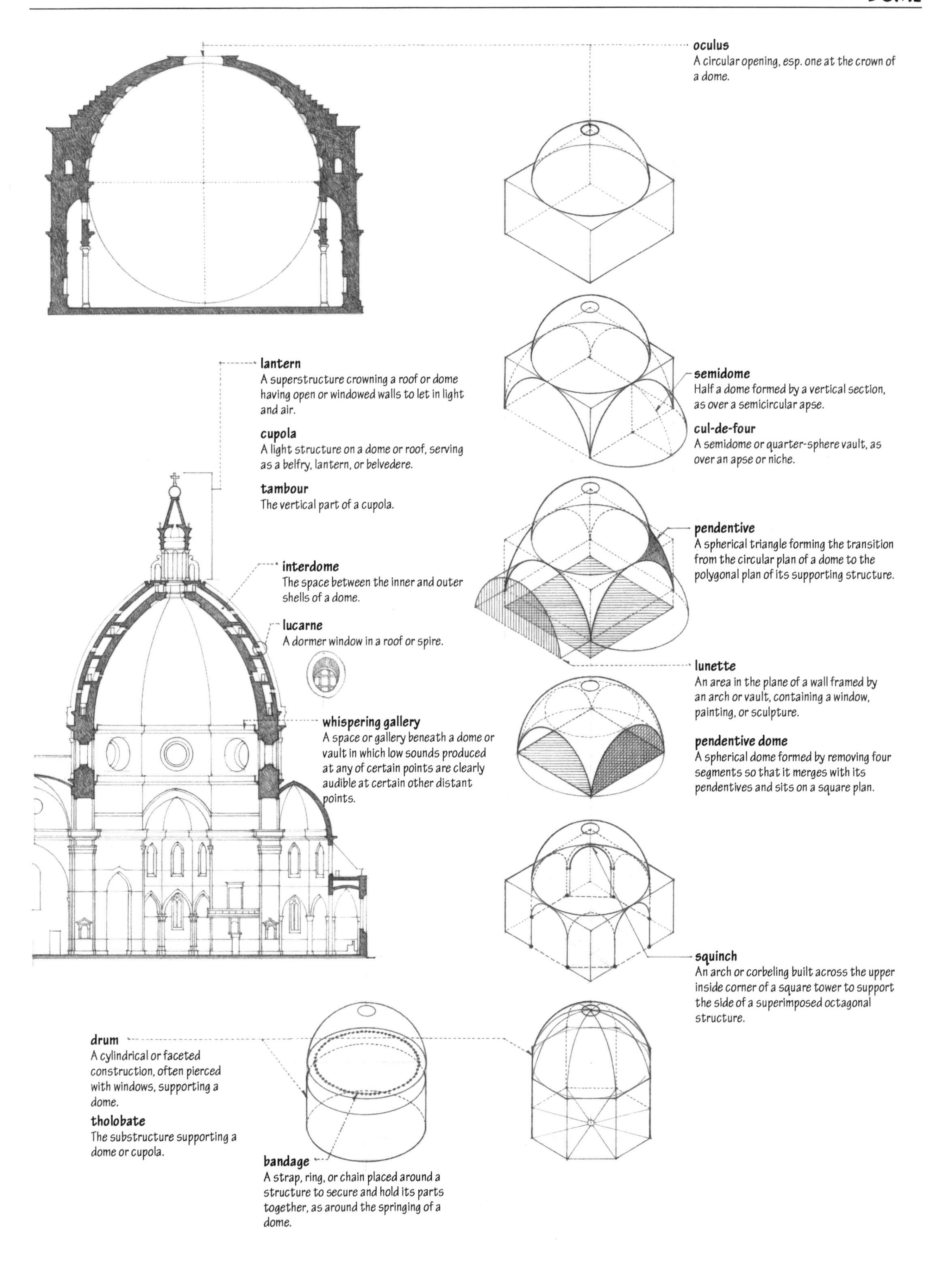

oculus
A circular opening, esp. one at the crown of a dome.

lantern
A superstructure crowning a roof or dome having open or windowed walls to let in light and air.

cupola
A light structure on a dome or roof, serving as a belfry, lantern, or belvedere.

tambour
The vertical part of a cupola.

interdome
The space between the inner and outer shells of a dome.

lucarne
A dormer window in a roof or spire.

whispering gallery
A space or gallery beneath a dome or vault in which low sounds produced at any of certain points are clearly audible at certain other distant points.

semidome
Half a dome formed by a vertical section, as over a semicircular apse.

cul-de-four
A semidome or quarter-sphere vault, as over an apse or niche.

pendentive
A spherical triangle forming the transition from the circular plan of a dome to the polygonal plan of its supporting structure.

lunette
An area in the plane of a wall framed by an arch or vault, containing a window, painting, or sculpture.

pendentive dome
A spherical dome formed by removing four segments so that it merges with its pendentives and sits on a square plan.

squinch
An arch or corbeling built across the upper inside corner of a square tower to support the side of a superimposed octagonal structure.

drum
A cylindrical or faceted construction, often pierced with windows, supporting a dome.

tholobate
The substructure supporting a dome or cupola.

bandage
A strap, ring, or chain placed around a structure to secure and hold its parts together, as around the springing of a dome.

A hinged, sliding, or folding barrier of wood, metal, or glass for opening and closing an entrance to a building, room, or cabinet.

swinging door
A door that turns on hinges or pivots about a vertical edge when pushed or pulled.

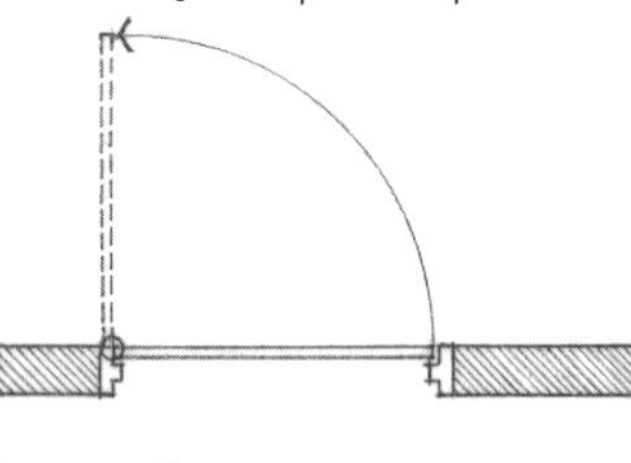

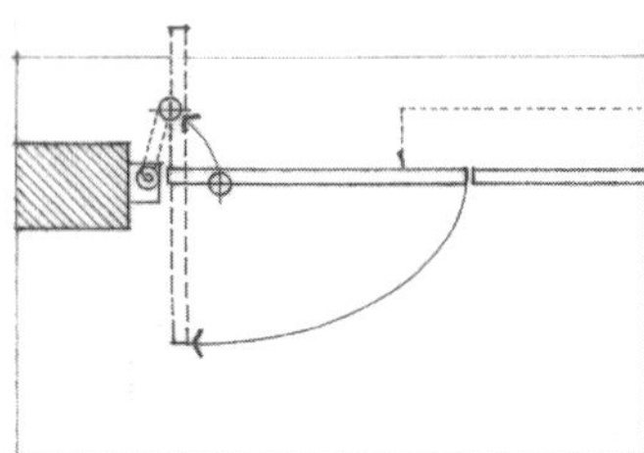

pivoted door
A door carried on and swinging about on a center or offset pivot, as distinguished from one hung on hinges.

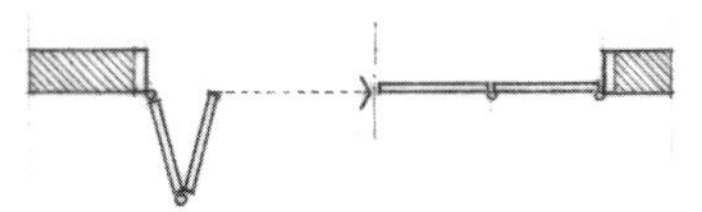

folding door
A door with hinged sections that can be folded flat against one another when opened.

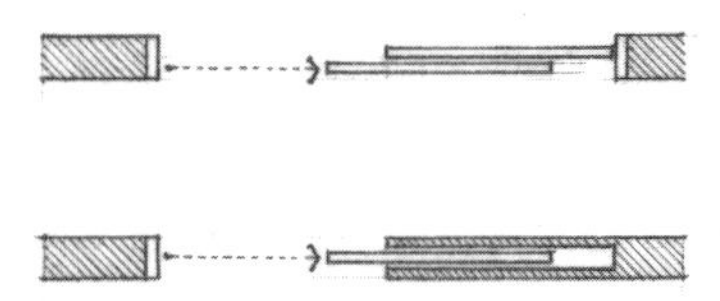

sliding door
A door that operates or moves by sliding on a track, usually parallel to a wall.

rolling door
A large door consisting of horizontal, interlocking metal slats guided by a track on either side, opening by coiling about an overhead drum at the head of the door opening.

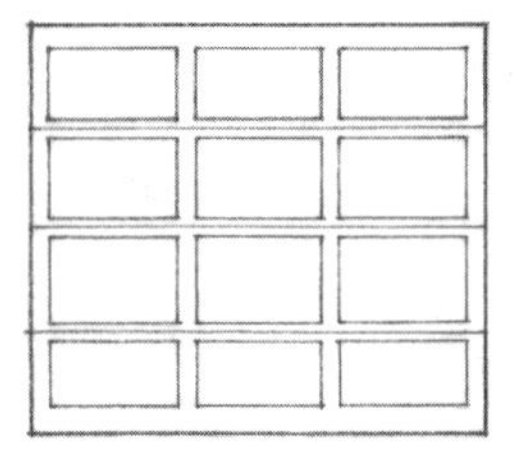

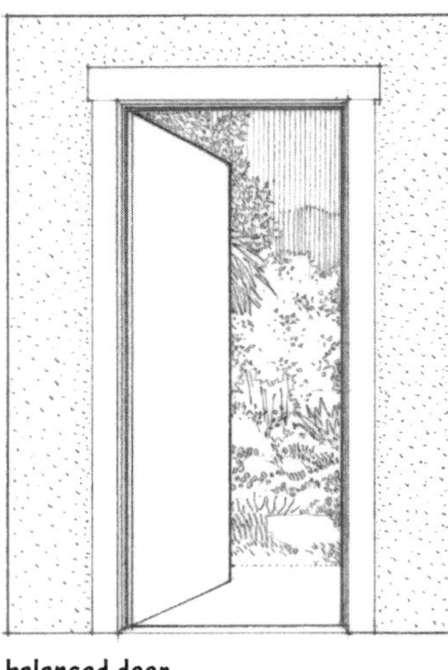

balanced door
A pivoted door that is partially counterbalanced for easier opening and closing.

automatic door
A door that opens automatically at the approach of a person or automobile.

door opener
A mechanism that automatically opens a door when actuated by a radio transmitter, electric eye, or other device.

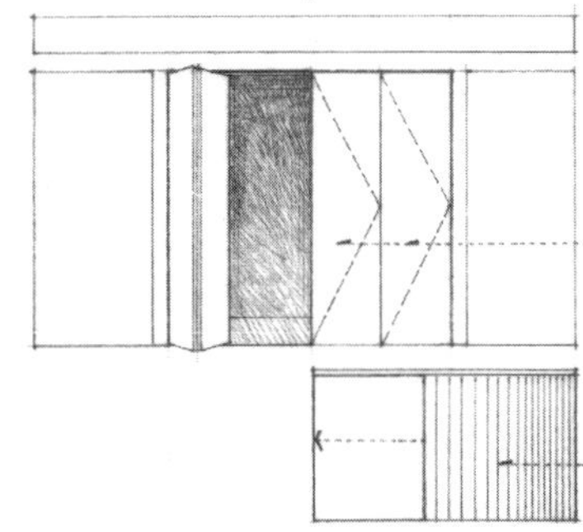

bifold door
A folding door that divides into two parts, the inner leaf of each part being hung from an overhead track and the outer leaf pivoted at the jamb.

accordion door
A multileafed door that is hung from an overhead track and opens by folding back in the manner of an accordion.

pocket door
A door that slides into and out of a recess in a doorway wall.

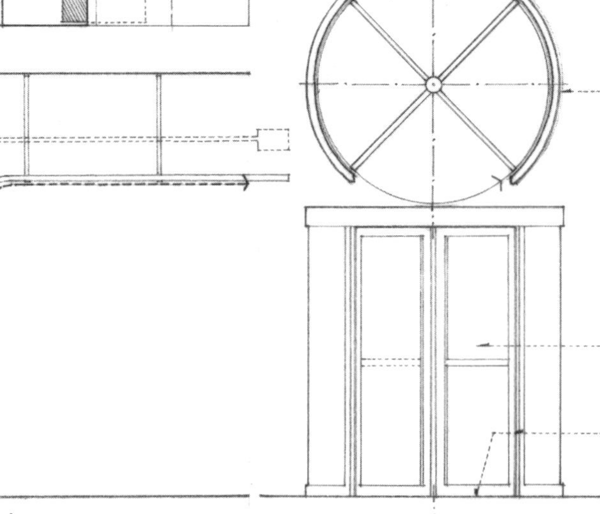

overhead door
A large door constructed of one or several leaves, opening by swinging or rolling up to a horizontal position above the door opening.

single-acting door
A door hung on hinges that permit it to swing in one direction only.

double-acting door
A door hung on hinges that permit it to swing in either direction from a closed position.

double doors
A pair of doors hung in the same doorframe.

leaf
A hinged or sliding section of a door or shutter.

active leaf
The leaf of a pair of double doors to which the latching or locking mechanism is attached. Also called **opening leaf**.

inactive leaf
The leaf of a pair of double doors to which the strike plate is fastened to receive the latch or bolt of the active leaf, usually fixed in a closed position by bolts at the top and bottom of the door. Also called **standing leaf**.

astragal
A molding attached to one or both meeting stiles of a pair of double doors to prevent drafts or the passage of light, noise, or smoke.

mullion
A slender vertical member dividing the opening for a pair of double doors, sometimes removable to permit the passage of large objects.

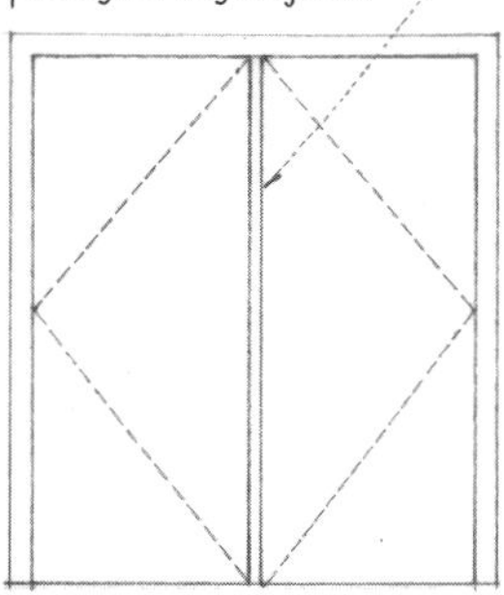

revolving door
An entrance door for excluding drafts from the interior of a building, consisting of four leaves set in the form of a cross and rotating about a central, vertical pivot within a cylindrically shaped vestibule. Some revolving doors automatically fold back in the direction of egress when pressure is applied, providing a legal passageway on both sides of the door pivot.

wing
One of the leaves of a double or revolving door.

sweep
The flexible weatherstripping along the edges of a revolving door.

air curtain
A stream of compressed air directed downward across a doorway so as to form a shield to exclude drafts.

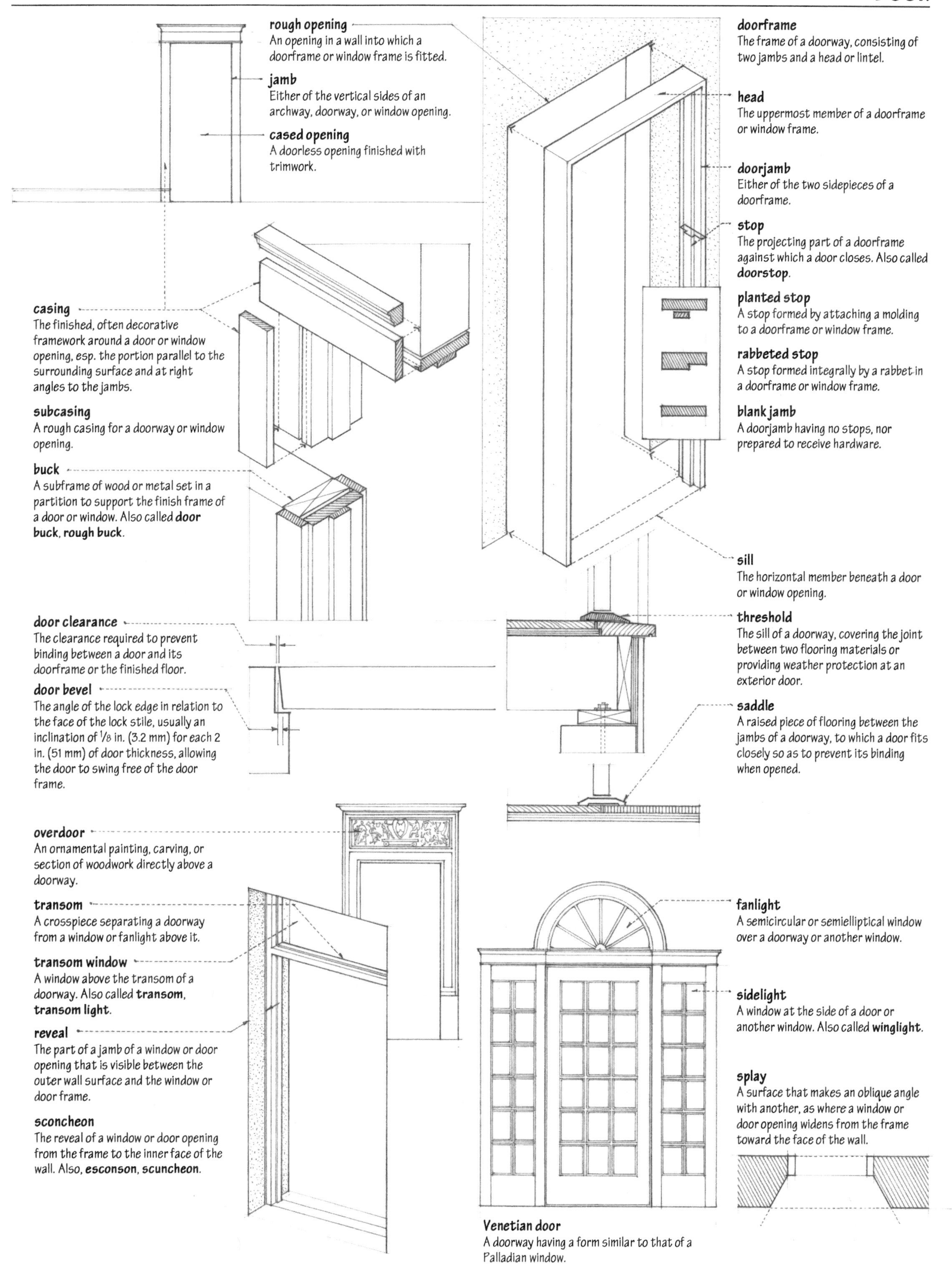

rough opening
An opening in a wall into which a doorframe or window frame is fitted.

jamb
Either of the vertical sides of an archway, doorway, or window opening.

cased opening
A doorless opening finished with trimwork.

casing
The finished, often decorative framework around a door or window opening, esp. the portion parallel to the surrounding surface and at right angles to the jambs.

subcasing
A rough casing for a doorway or window opening.

buck
A subframe of wood or metal set in a partition to support the finish frame of a door or window. Also called **door buck**, **rough buck**.

door clearance
The clearance required to prevent binding between a door and its doorframe or the finished floor.

door bevel
The angle of the lock edge in relation to the face of the lock stile, usually an inclination of 1/8 in. (3.2 mm) for each 2 in. (51 mm) of door thickness, allowing the door to swing free of the door frame.

overdoor
An ornamental painting, carving, or section of woodwork directly above a doorway.

transom
A crosspiece separating a doorway from a window or fanlight above it.

transom window
A window above the transom of a doorway. Also called **transom**, **transom light**.

reveal
The part of a jamb of a window or door opening that is visible between the outer wall surface and the window or door frame.

sconcheon
The reveal of a window or door opening from the frame to the inner face of the wall. Also, **esconson**, **scuncheon**.

doorframe
The frame of a doorway, consisting of two jambs and a head or lintel.

head
The uppermost member of a doorframe or window frame.

doorjamb
Either of the two sidepieces of a doorframe.

stop
The projecting part of a doorframe against which a door closes. Also called **doorstop**.

planted stop
A stop formed by attaching a molding to a doorframe or window frame.

rabbeted stop
A stop formed integrally by a rabbet in a doorframe or window frame.

blank jamb
A doorjamb having no stops, nor prepared to receive hardware.

sill
The horizontal member beneath a door or window opening.

threshold
The sill of a doorway, covering the joint between two flooring materials or providing weather protection at an exterior door.

saddle
A raised piece of flooring between the jambs of a doorway, to which a door fits closely so as to prevent its binding when opened.

fanlight
A semicircular or semielliptical window over a doorway or another window.

sidelight
A window at the side of a door or another window. Also called **winglight**.

splay
A surface that makes an oblique angle with another, as where a window or door opening widens from the frame toward the face of the wall.

Venetian door
A doorway having a form similar to that of a Palladian window.

paneled door
A door having a framework of stiles, rails, and sometimes muntins, filled with panels of a thinner material.

rail
Any of various horizontal members framing panels, as in a system of paneling, a paneled door, window sash, or chest of drawers.

top rail
The uppermost rail connecting the stiles of a paneled door or window sash.

lock rail
The rail of a door that meets the shutting stile at the level of the lockset.

bottom rail
The lowest rail connecting the stiles of a paneled door or window sash.

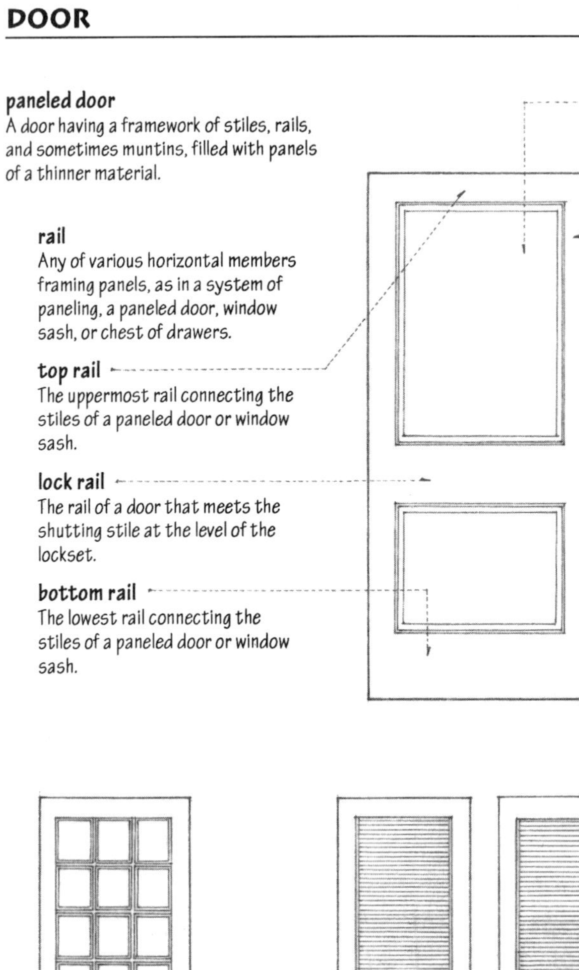

panel
A distinct section or division of a wall, ceiling, or door, recessed below or raised above the general level or enclosed by a frame.

stile
Any of various upright members framing panels, as in a system of paneling, a paneled door, window sash, or a chest of drawers.

hinge stile
The stile of a door by which it is hung. Also called **hanging stile**.

lock stile
The stile of a door that closes against the frame of the opening. Also called **shutting stile**.

muntin
A stile within the frame of a door.

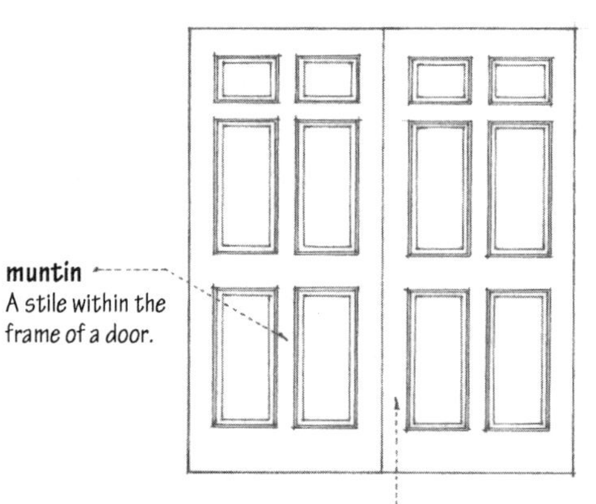

meeting stile
One of the abutting stiles in a pair of double doors.

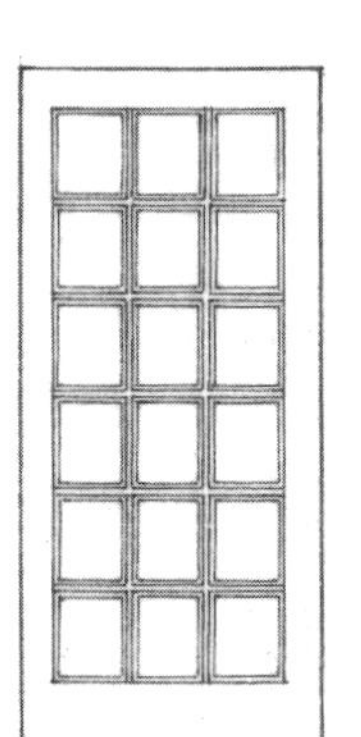

French door
A door having rectangular glass panes extending throughout its length, and often hung in pairs. Also called **casement door**.

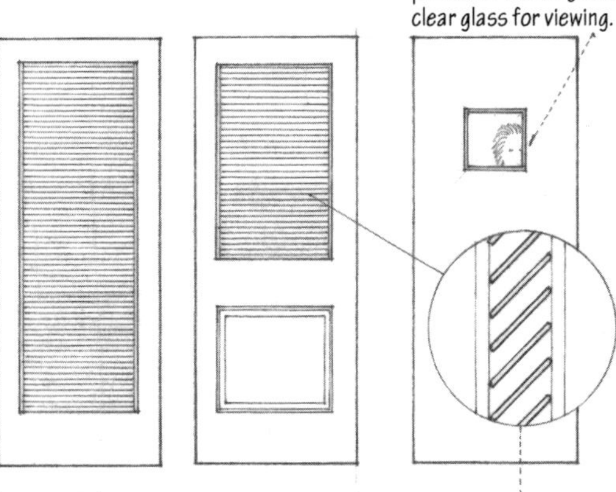

louvered door
A door having a louvered opening for the passage or circulation of air. Also called **blind door**.

vision light
A small light in the upper portion of a door glazed with clear glass for viewing.

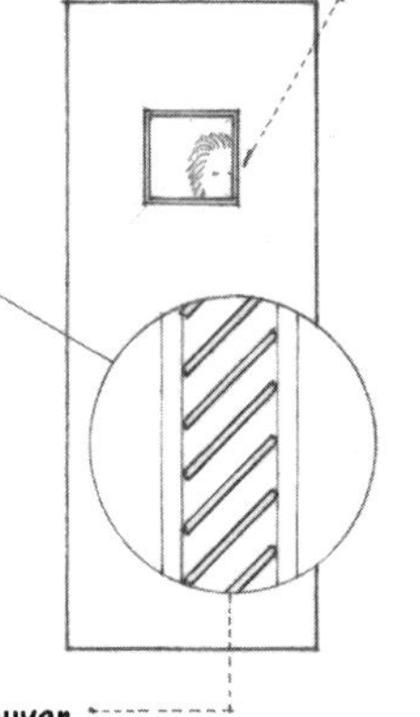

louver
An opening fitted with slanting, fixed or movable slats to admit air but exclude rain and snow or to provide privacy. Also, **louvre**.

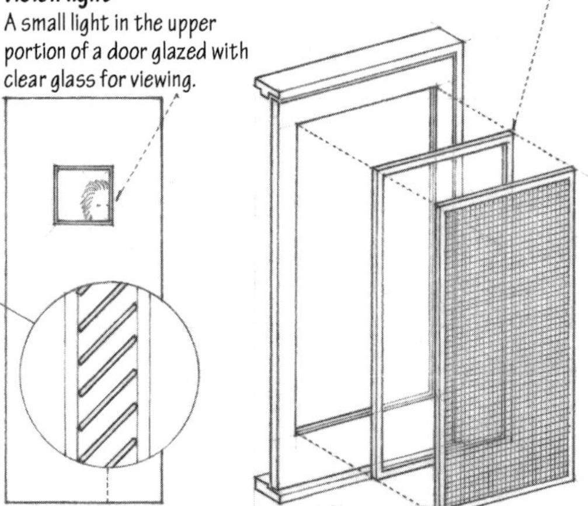

storm door
An outer or supplementary door, usually glazed, for protecting an entrance door from drafts, driving rain, or severe weather.

screen door
An exterior door having wood or aluminum stiles and rails that hold a wire or plastic mesh to admit air but exclude insects.

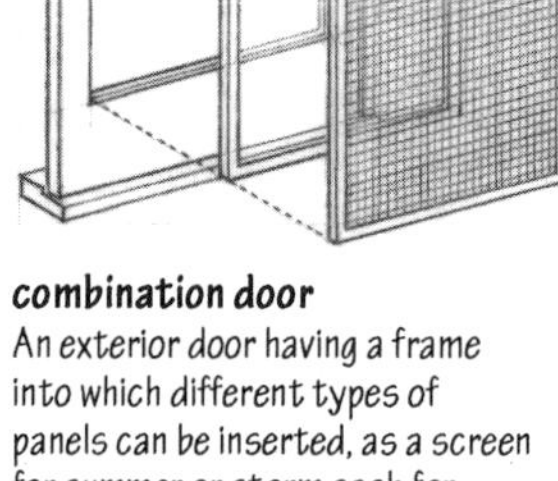

combination door
An exterior door having a frame into which different types of panels can be inserted, as a screen for summer or storm sash for winter.

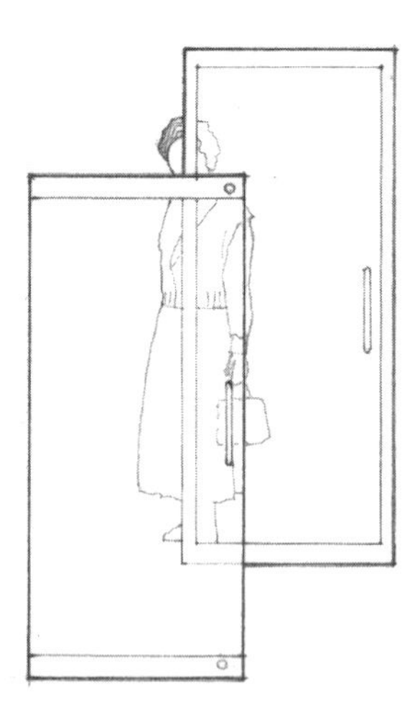

glass door
A door of heat-strengthened or tempered glass, with or without rails or stiles, used primarily as an entrance door.

Dutch door
A door divided horizontally so that the upper or lower part can be opened or closed separately.

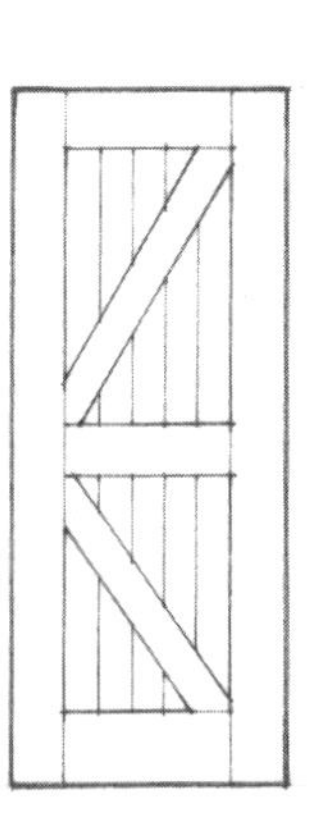

batten door
A door constructed of vertical boards held together by horizontal battens and diagonal bracing.

jib door
A door hinged to be flush with the wall on either side and treated so as to be indiscernible when closed. Also, **gib door**.

adjustable doorframe
A doorframe having a split head and jambs for installation in various wall thicknesses.

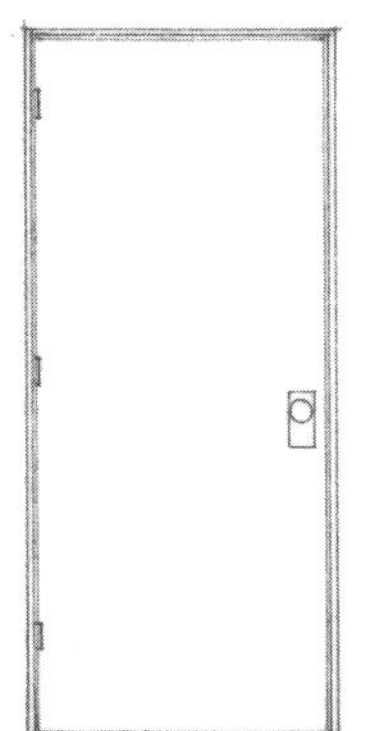

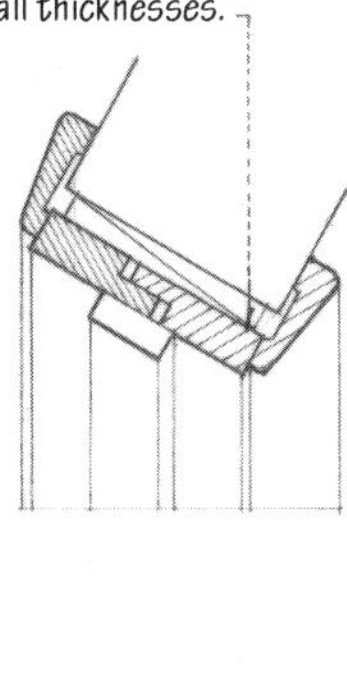

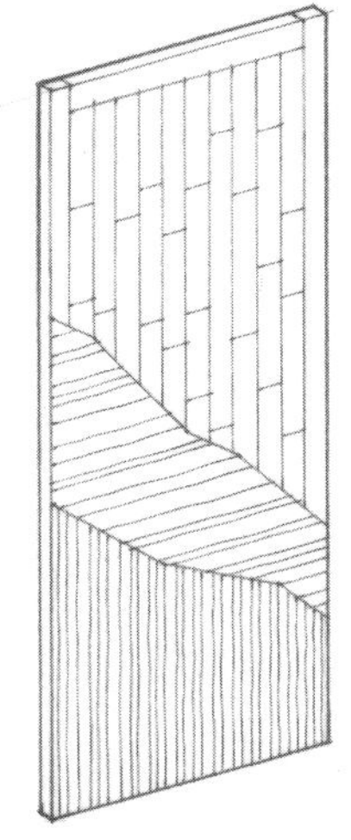

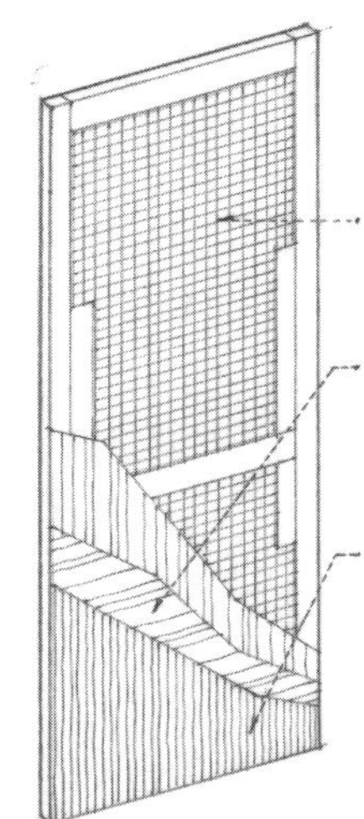

core
A wooden construction, as in a door, forming a backing for face veneers.

crossbanding
The plywood or hardboard veneer immediately beneath the face veneers of a flush door. Also, **crossband**.

doorskin
A surface veneer of plywood, hardboard, plastic laminate, or medium density overlay, bonded to the crossbanding or core of a flush door.

flush door
A door having smooth-surfaced faces.

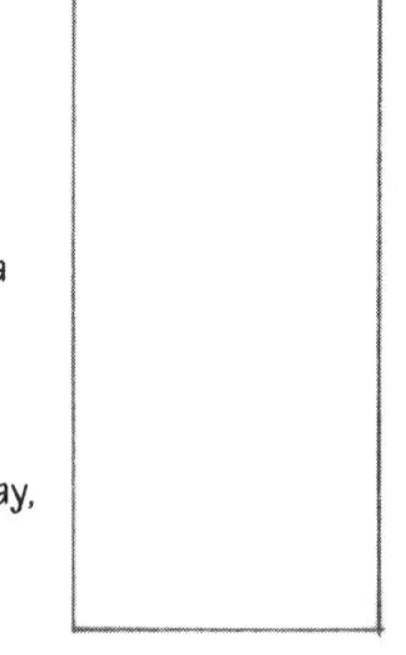

prehung door
A door hung in a doorframe before installation in a wall, sometimes prefinished and prefitted with all necessary hardware and casing trim.

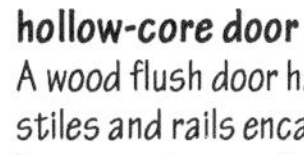

solid-core door
A wood flush door having a solid core of staved lumber, particle board, or a mineral composition.

hollow-core door
A wood flush door having a framework of stiles and rails encasing an expanded honeycomb core of corrugated fiberboard or a grid of interlocking horizontal and vertical wood strips.

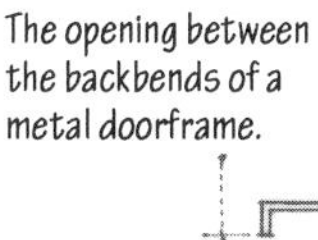

throat
The opening between the backbends of a metal doorframe.

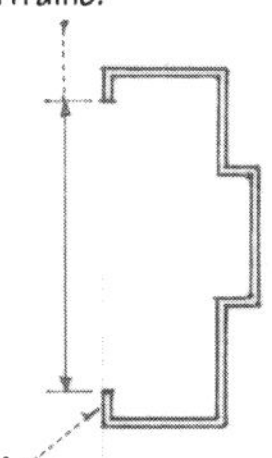

backbend
The face at the outer edge of a metal doorframe that returns to the wall surface.

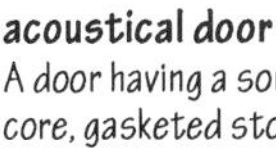

acoustical door
A door having a sound-deadening core, gasketed stops along the top and sides, and an automatic drop seal along the bottom. Also called **sound-insulating door**.

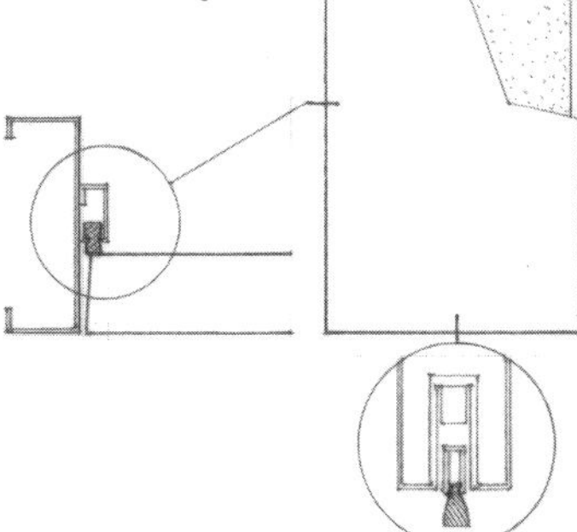

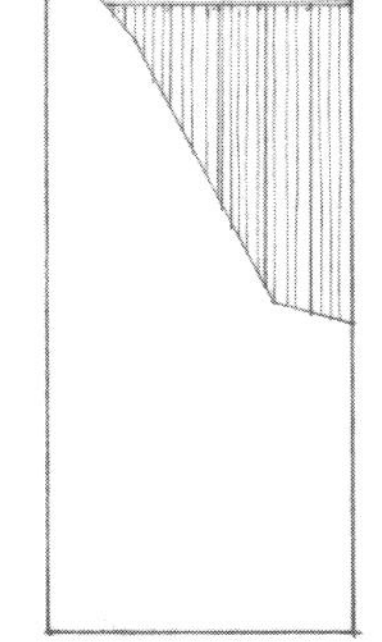

kalamein door
A door having a structural wood core clad with galvanized sheet metal.

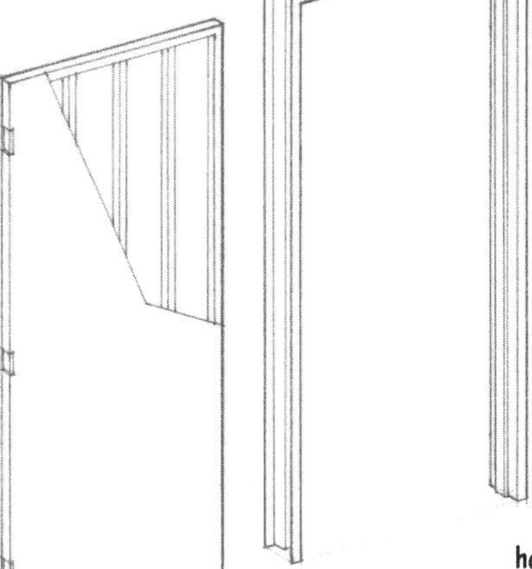

hollow metal door
A door having face sheets of light-gauge steel bonded to a steel channel frame, reinforced with channels, a kraft honeycomb structure, or a rigid plastic-foam core.

hollow metal frame
A doorframe having a head and jambs formed from a single piece of metal.

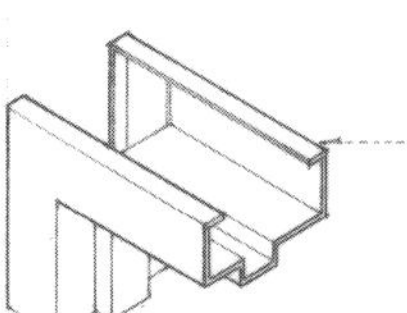

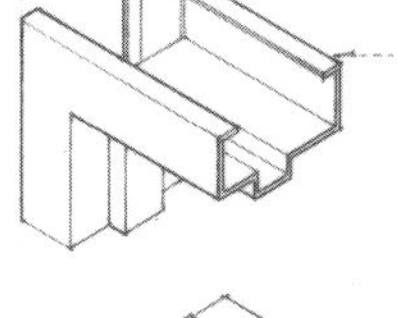

knockdown frame
A metal doorframe composed of three or more parts for assembly in the field.

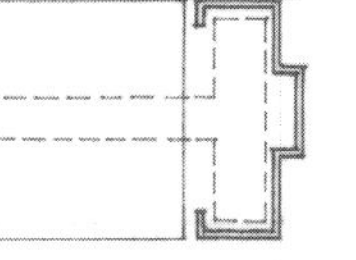

flush frame
A metal doorframe designed to be installed during the construction of a masonry or stud wall.

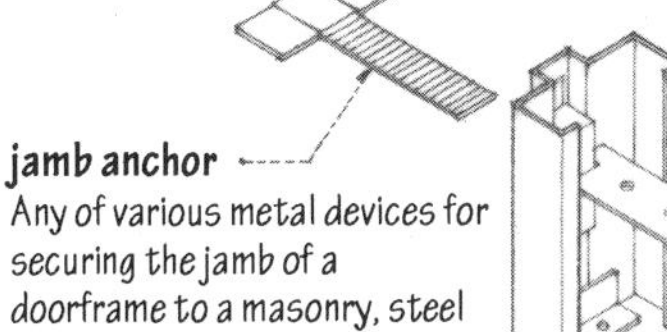

welded frame
A metal doorframe that is completely set up and welded at the factory.

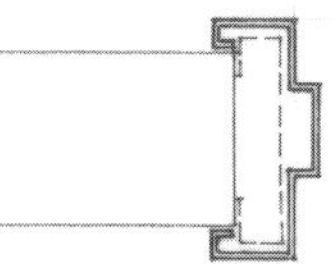

drywall frame
A knockdown frame having a double-return backbend for installation after a drywall partition is finished.

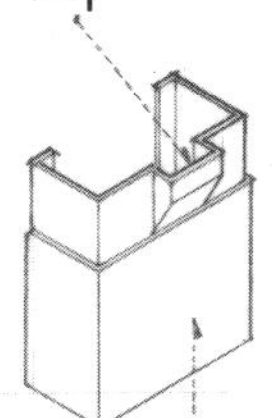

jamb anchor
Any of various metal devices for securing the jamb of a doorframe to a masonry, steel stud, or wood stud wall.

anchor
Any of various metal devices for binding one part of a structure to another.

base anchor
A metal clip or device for securing the base of a doorframe to the floor.

cutoff stop
A stop having a closed end that terminates above the floor line a 45° or 90° angle. Also called **hospital stop**, **sanitary stop**.

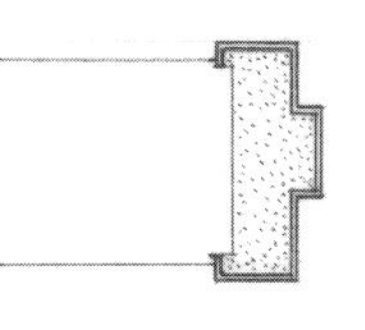

spat
A protective lining, usually of stainless steel, at the base of a doorframe.

grouted frame
A metal doorframe completely filled with plaster or mortar for structural rigidity and increased fire resistance.

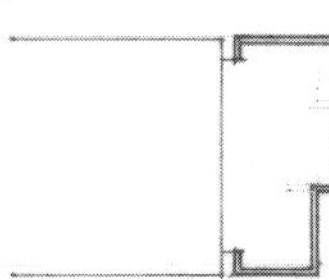

double egress frame
A metal doorframe prepared to receive a pair of single-acting doors that swing in opposite directions.

The art, process, or technique of representing an object, scene, or idea by means of lines on a surface.

technique
A method or procedure for accomplishing a desired aim or task, as that employed by an artist showing a high degree of skill or command of fundamentals.

contour drawing
The technique of drawing lines to represent the contours of a subject, without shading or modeling of form.

contour
The outline of a two-dimensional shape or bounding edges of a three-dimensional form.

freehand drawing
The art, process, or technique of drawing by hand without the aid of drafting instruments or mechanical devices, esp. for the representation of perceptions or the visualization of ideas.

image
A representation of the form or appearance of something, made visible in a sculpture, photograph, or drawing.

line
A thin, continuous mark made on a surface with a pencil, pen, or brush, as distinguished from shading or color.

outline
A line describing the outer boundary of a figure or object.

profile
An outline of a form or structure seen or represented from the side.

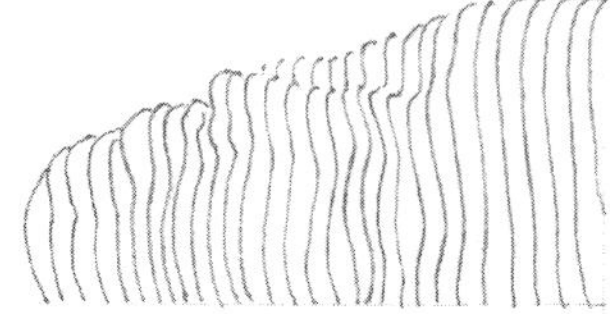

cross-contour drawing
The technique of drawing lines to represent a series of cuts across the surface of a form rather than its edges.

gesture drawing
The technique of drawing a single or multiple lines freely and quickly as a subject is scanned and perceptions of volume, mass, movement, and significant details are projected onto the drawing surface. In contrast to contour drawing, gesture drawing generally proceeds from the whole to the parts.

gesture
A movement of the hand, arm, head, face, or body that expresses an idea, opinion, or emotion.

movement
The effect or illusion of motion conveyed by the relationship of structural elements in a design or composition.

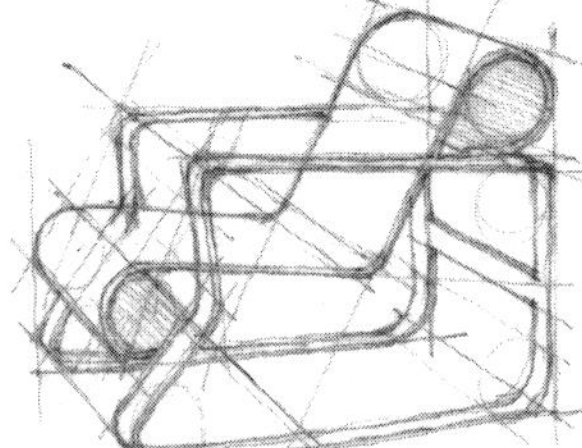

regulating line
A line drawn to measure or express alignment, scale, or proportion.

trace
A line lightly drawn to record alignment or measurement.

analytical drawing
The drawing of lines to represent the three-dimensional structure and geometry of a form, proceeding generally from the whole to the constituent parts.

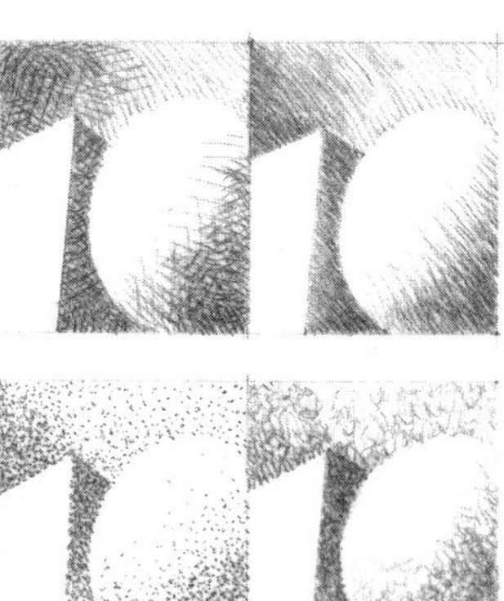

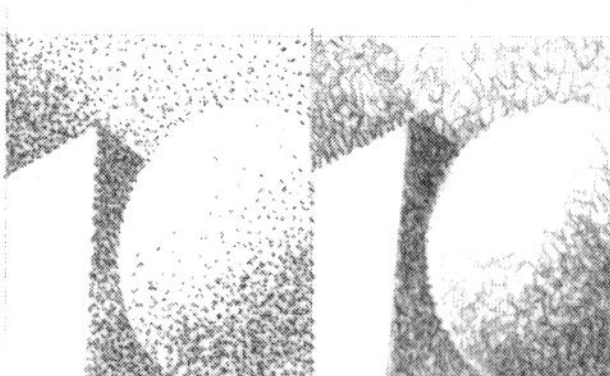

shading
The rendering of light and dark values in a drawing to create the illusion of three-dimensionality, represent light and shadow, or give the effect of color.

hatching
Shading composed of fine lines drawn in close proximity.

crosshatching
Shading composed of two or more series of intersecting parallel lines.

scribbling
Shading by means of a network of random, multidirectional lines.

stippling
Shading by means of dots, small spots, or short strokes.

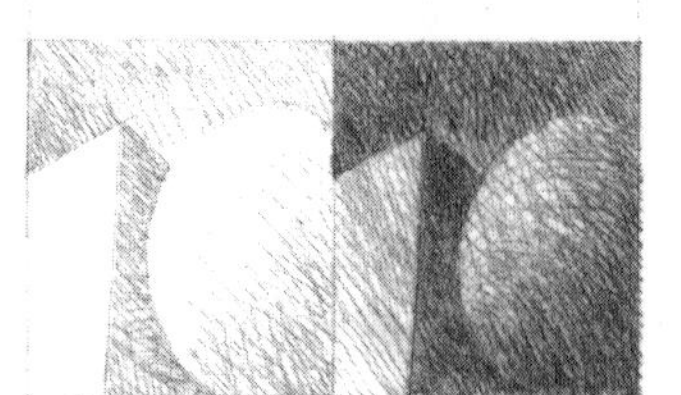

key
The dominant tonal value of a drawing or painting.

modeling
The technique of rendering the illusion of volume, depth, or solidity on a two-dimensional surface by shading.

grisaille
Monochromatic painting in shades of gray to produce a three-dimensional effect.

high-key
Having chiefly light tones with little contrast.

low-key
Having chiefly dark tones with little contrast.

sketch
A simply or hastily executed drawing or painting representing the essential features of an object or scene without the details, often made as a preliminary study.

study
A drawing executed as an educational exercise, produced as a preliminary to a final work, or made to record observations. Sometimes referred to as a **referential drawing**.

conception
A drawing of something that does not yet exist.

draft
A preliminary sketch of a design or plan, esp. one subject to revision.

esquisse
A sketch showing the general features of a design or plan.

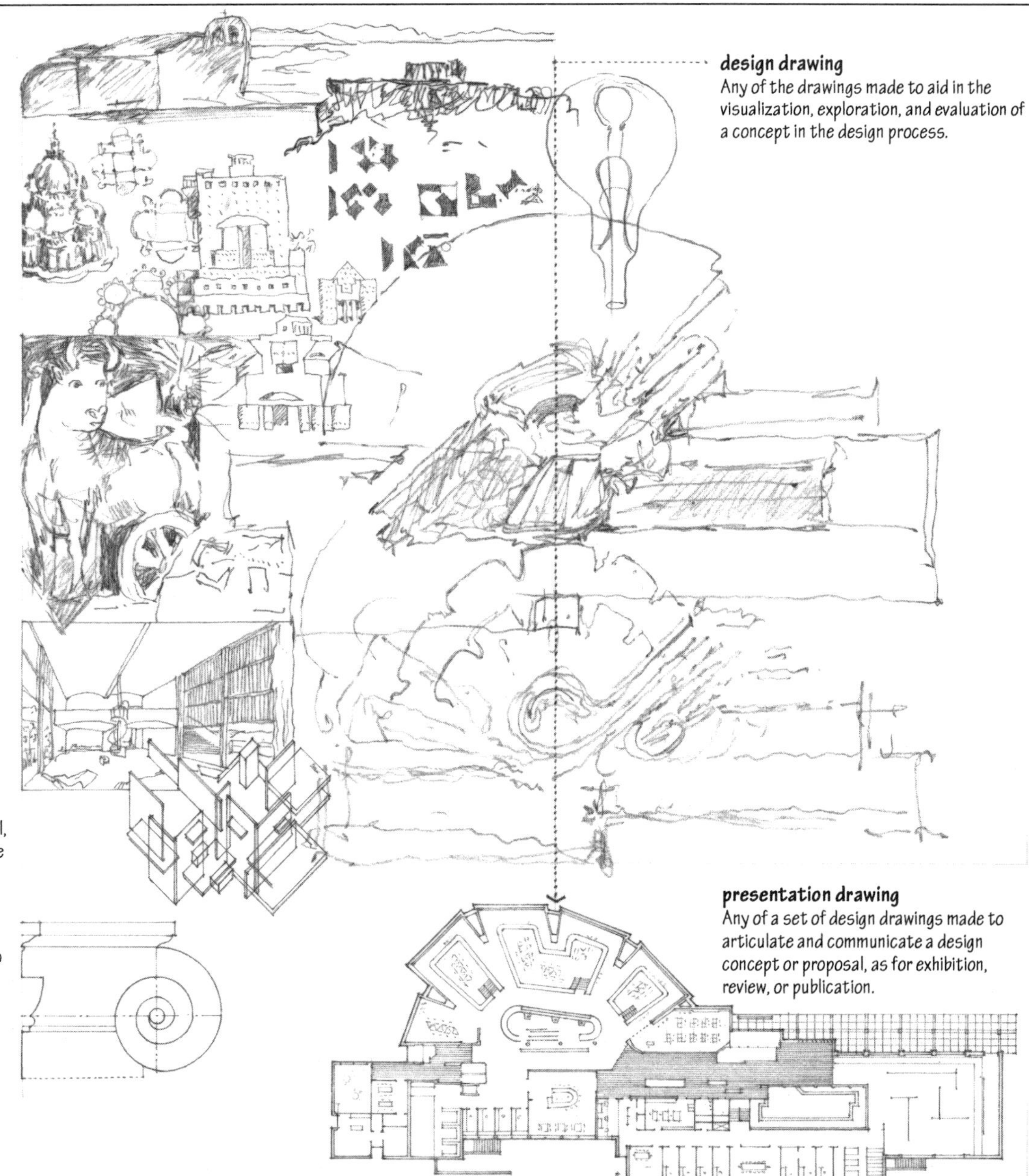

design drawing
Any of the drawings made to aid in the visualization, exploration, and evaluation of a concept in the design process.

épure
A full-scale, detailed drawing done on a wall, floor, or other large surface, from which are traced the patterns for various building elements.

cartoon
A full-scale drawing of a motif or design, to be transferred in preparation for a fresco, mosaic, or tapestry.

rendering
A drawing, esp. a perspective, of a building or interior space, artistically delineating materials, shades and shadows: usually done for the purposes of presentation and persuasion.

presentation drawing
Any of a set of design drawings made to articulate and communicate a design concept or proposal, as for exhibition, review, or publication.

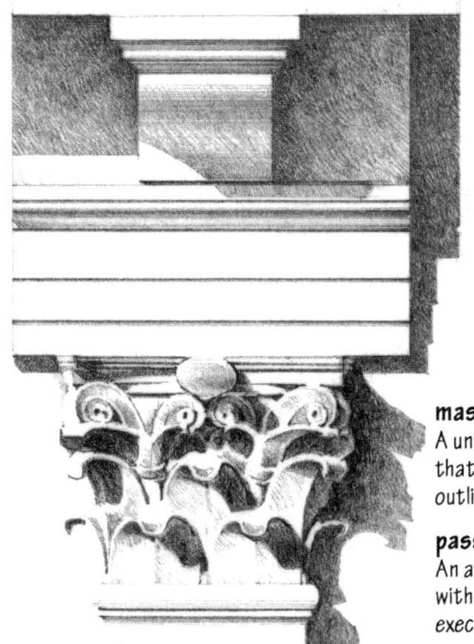

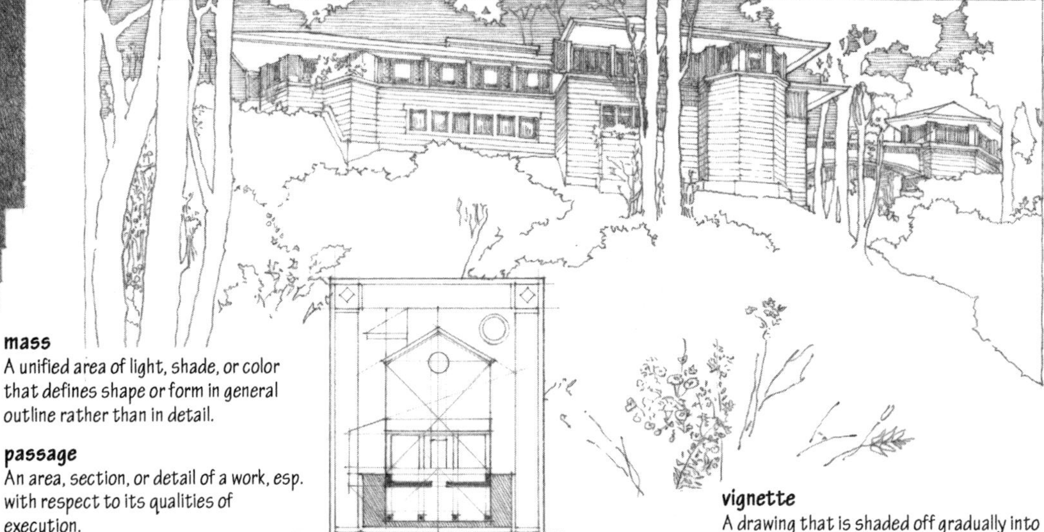

mass
A unified area of light, shade, or color that defines shape or form in general outline rather than in detail.

passage
An area, section, or detail of a work, esp. with respect to its qualities of execution.

vignette
A drawing that is shaded off gradually into the surrounding paper so as to leave no definite line at the border.

trompe l'oeil
A drawing or painting in which objects are rendered in extremely fine detail to emphasize the illusion of tactile and spatial qualities.

analytique
An elevation drawing of a facade, surrounded by a decorative arrangement of drawings of important details and sometimes a plan or section of the facade.

drafting
Drawing done with the aid of such instruments as T-squares, triangles, compasses, and scales, esp. for the systematic representation and dimensional specification of architectural and engineering structures. Also called **mechanical drawing**.

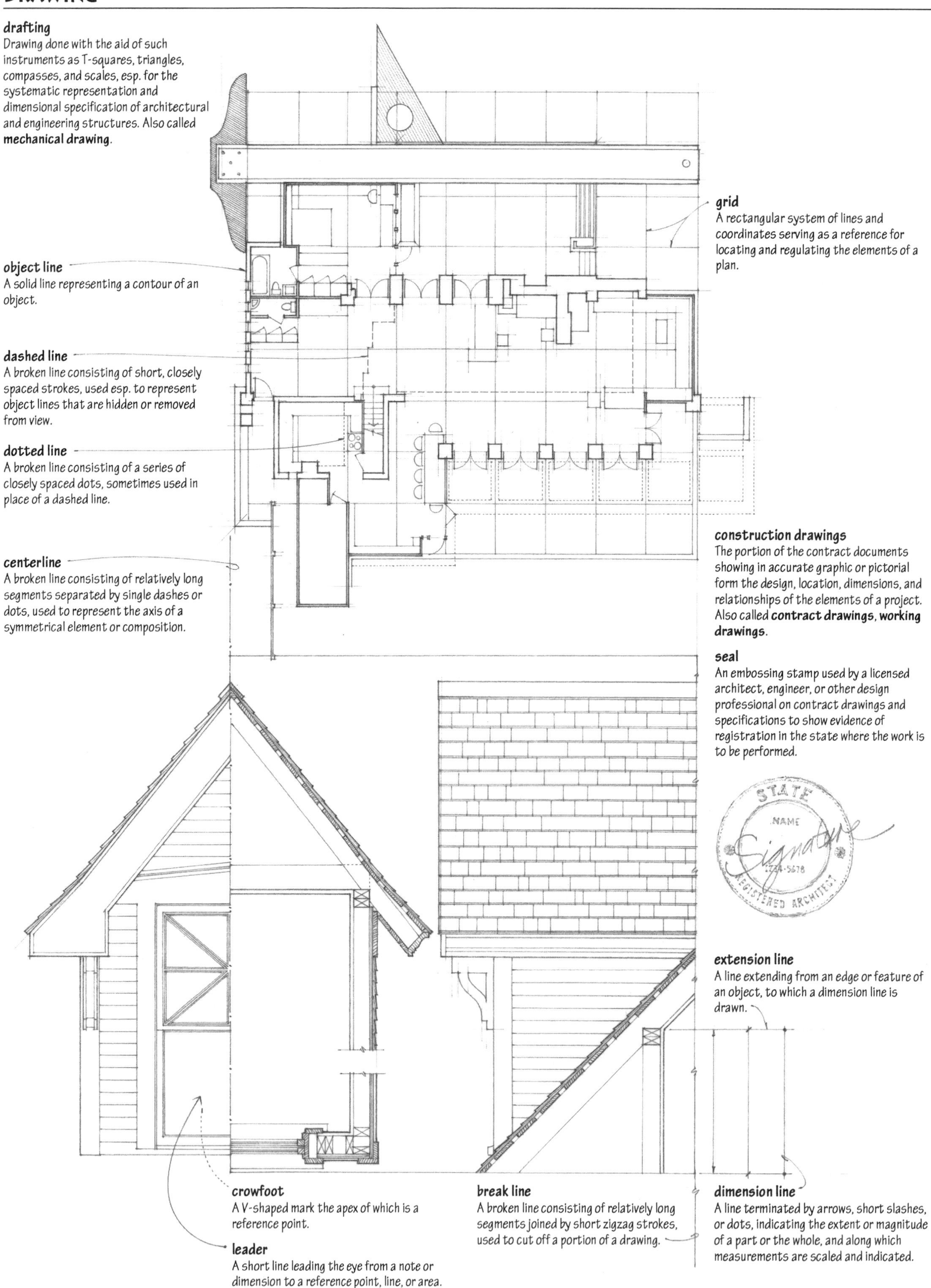

object line
A solid line representing a contour of an object.

dashed line
A broken line consisting of short, closely spaced strokes, used esp. to represent object lines that are hidden or removed from view.

dotted line
A broken line consisting of a series of closely spaced dots, sometimes used in place of a dashed line.

centerline
A broken line consisting of relatively long segments separated by single dashes or dots, used to represent the axis of a symmetrical element or composition.

grid
A rectangular system of lines and coordinates serving as a reference for locating and regulating the elements of a plan.

construction drawings
The portion of the contract documents showing in accurate graphic or pictorial form the design, location, dimensions, and relationships of the elements of a project. Also called **contract drawings, working drawings**.

seal
An embossing stamp used by a licensed architect, engineer, or other design professional on contract drawings and specifications to show evidence of registration in the state where the work is to be performed.

extension line
A line extending from an edge or feature of an object, to which a dimension line is drawn.

crowfoot
A V-shaped mark the apex of which is a reference point.

leader
A short line leading the eye from a note or dimension to a reference point, line, or area.

break line
A broken line consisting of relatively long segments joined by short zigzag strokes, used to cut off a portion of a drawing.

dimension line
A line terminated by arrows, short slashes, or dots, indicating the extent or magnitude of a part or the whole, and along which measurements are scaled and indicated.

descriptive geometry
The theory of making projections of three-dimensional objects on a plane surface in order to deduce their geometric properties and relationships.

projection
The process or technique of representing a three-dimensional object by projecting all its points by straight lines, either parallel or converging, to a picture plane.

orthographic projection
A method of projection in which a three-dimensional object is represented by projecting lines perpendicular to a picture plane. Also called **orthogonal projection**.

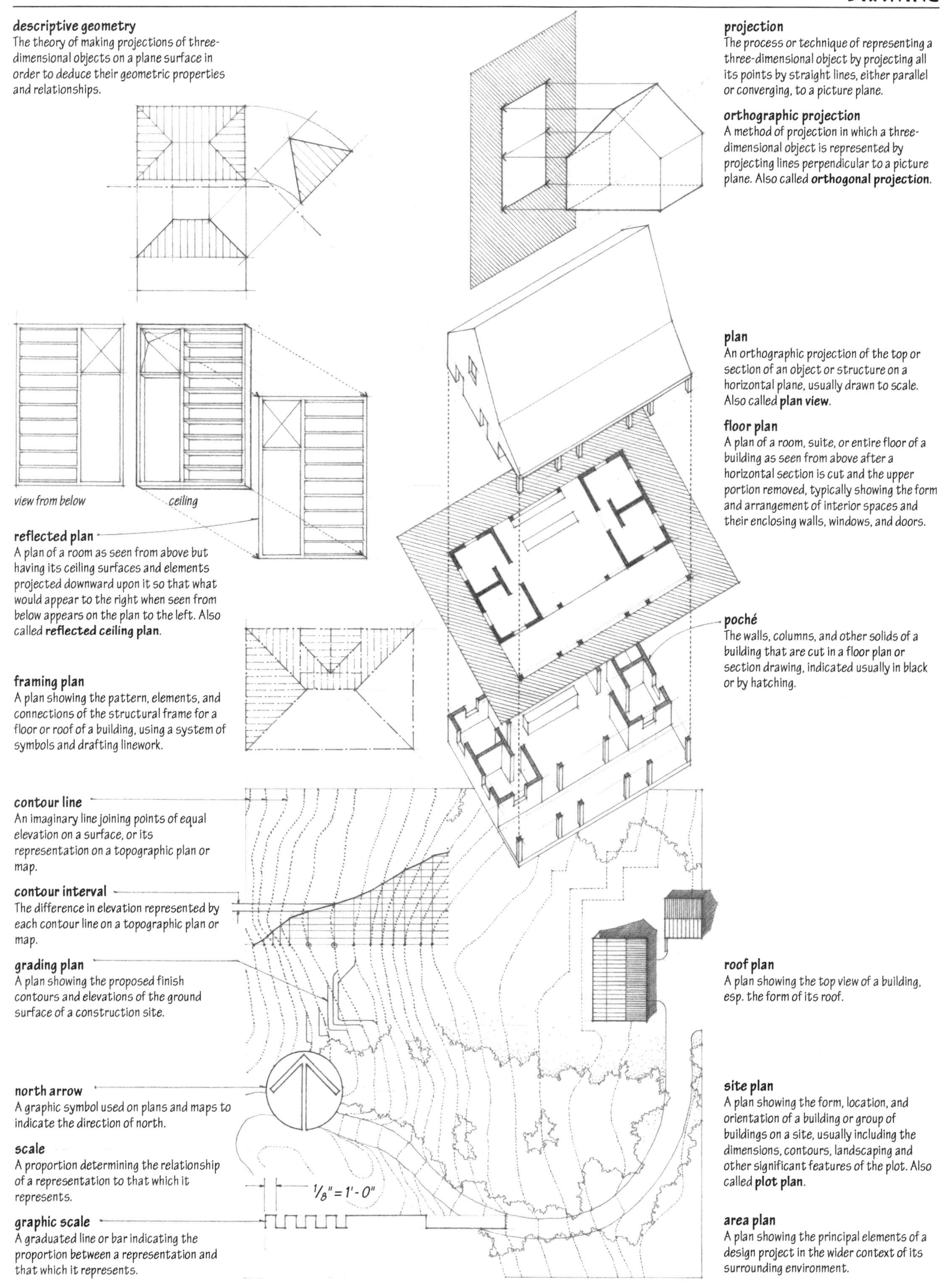

plan
An orthographic projection of the top or section of an object or structure on a horizontal plane, usually drawn to scale. Also called **plan view**.

floor plan
A plan of a room, suite, or entire floor of a building as seen from above after a horizontal section is cut and the upper portion removed, typically showing the form and arrangement of interior spaces and their enclosing walls, windows, and doors.

reflected plan
A plan of a room as seen from above but having its ceiling surfaces and elements projected downward upon it so that what would appear to the right when seen from below appears on the plan to the left. Also called **reflected ceiling plan**.

poché
The walls, columns, and other solids of a building that are cut in a floor plan or section drawing, indicated usually in black or by hatching.

framing plan
A plan showing the pattern, elements, and connections of the structural frame for a floor or roof of a building, using a system of symbols and drafting linework.

contour line
An imaginary line joining points of equal elevation on a surface, or its representation on a topographic plan or map.

contour interval
The difference in elevation represented by each contour line on a topographic plan or map.

grading plan
A plan showing the proposed finish contours and elevations of the ground surface of a construction site.

roof plan
A plan showing the top view of a building, esp. the form of its roof.

north arrow
A graphic symbol used on plans and maps to indicate the direction of north.

scale
A proportion determining the relationship of a representation to that which it represents.

graphic scale
A graduated line or bar indicating the proportion between a representation and that which it represents.

site plan
A plan showing the form, location, and orientation of a building or group of buildings on a site, usually including the dimensions, contours, landscaping and other significant features of the plot. Also called **plot plan**.

area plan
A plan showing the principal elements of a design project in the wider context of its surrounding environment.

section
An orthographic projection of an object or structure as it would appear if cut through by an intersecting plane to show its internal configuration, usually drawn to scale.

cross section
An orthographic projection of a section made by cutting transversely, esp. at right angles to the long axis of an object. Also called **transverse section**.

longitudinal section
An orthographic projection of a section made by cutting through the longest axis of an object.

section line
A centerline terminating in a perpendicular segment with an arrow, used to indicate where a section is cut in a plan or elevation view and the direction in which the section is to be viewed.

oblique section
An orthographic projection of a section made by cutting with a plane that is neither parallel nor perpendicular to the long axis of an object.

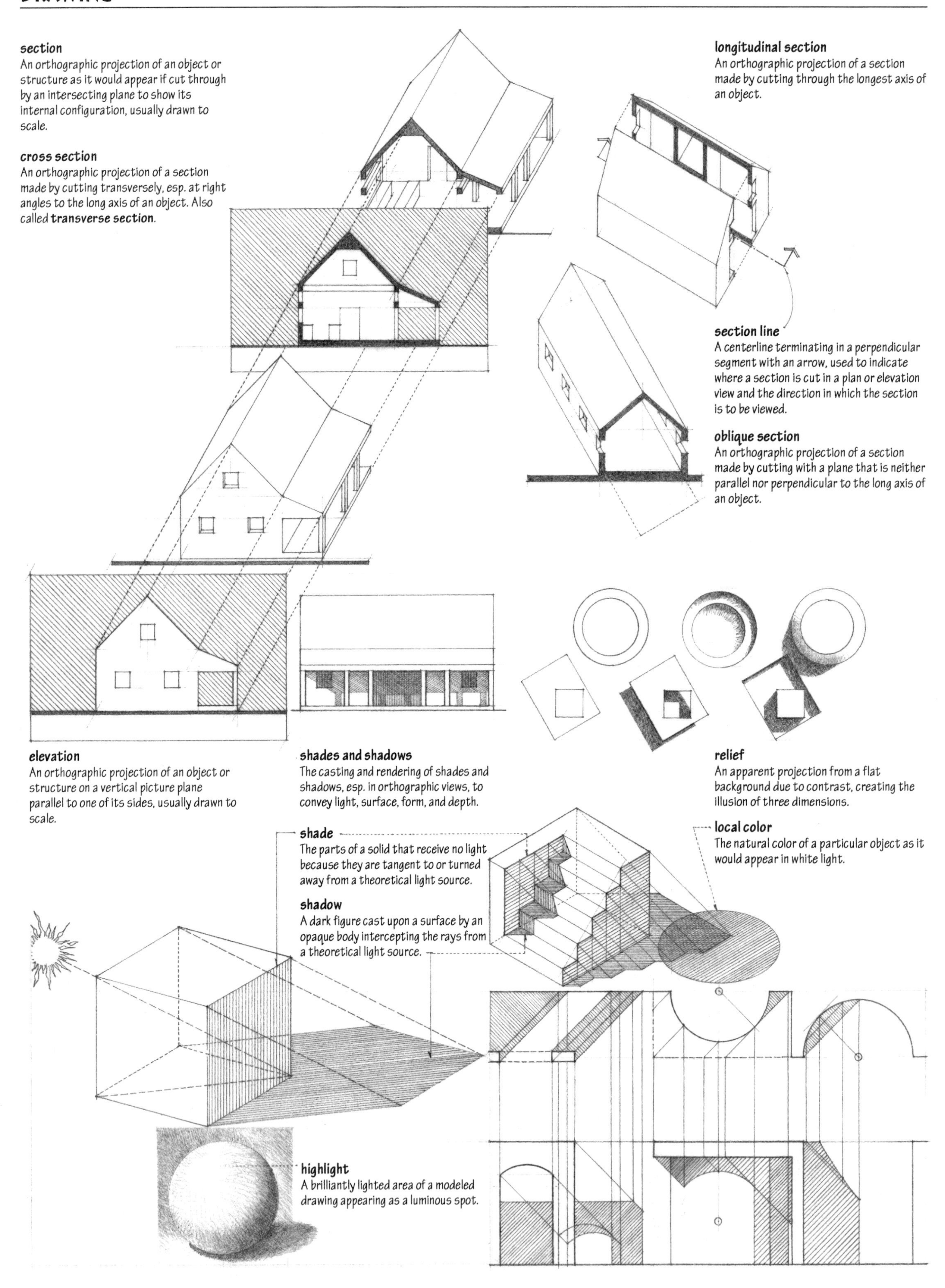

elevation
An orthographic projection of an object or structure on a vertical picture plane parallel to one of its sides, usually drawn to scale.

shades and shadows
The casting and rendering of shades and shadows, esp. in orthographic views, to convey light, surface, form, and depth.

relief
An apparent projection from a flat background due to contrast, creating the illusion of three dimensions.

shade
The parts of a solid that receive no light because they are tangent to or turned away from a theoretical light source.

local color
The natural color of a particular object as it would appear in white light.

shadow
A dark figure cast upon a surface by an opaque body intercepting the rays from a theoretical light source.

highlight
A brilliantly lighted area of a modeled drawing appearing as a luminous spot.

paraline drawing
Any of various single-view drawings characterized by parallel lines remaining parallel to each other rather than converging as in linear perspective.

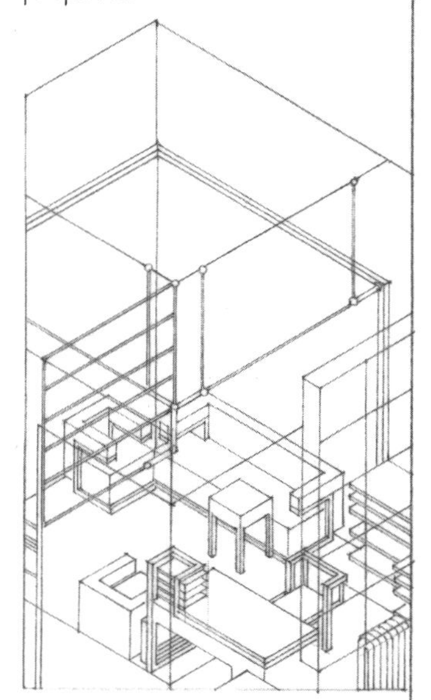

phantom
A part of a drawing that is made transparent to permit representation of details otherwise hidden from view.

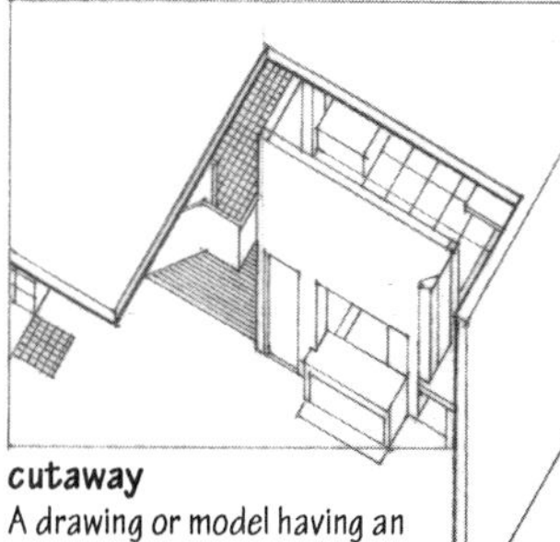

cutaway
A drawing or model having an outer section removed to display the interior.

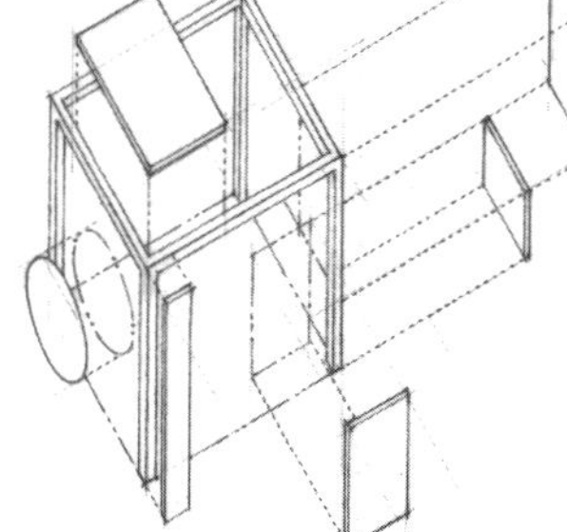

exploded view
A drawing that shows the individual parts of a structure or construction separately but indicates their proper relationships to each other and to the whole. Also called **expanded view**.

phantom line
A broken line consisting of relatively long segments separated by two short dashes or dots, used to represent a property line, an alternative position of a part of an object, or the relative position of an absent part.

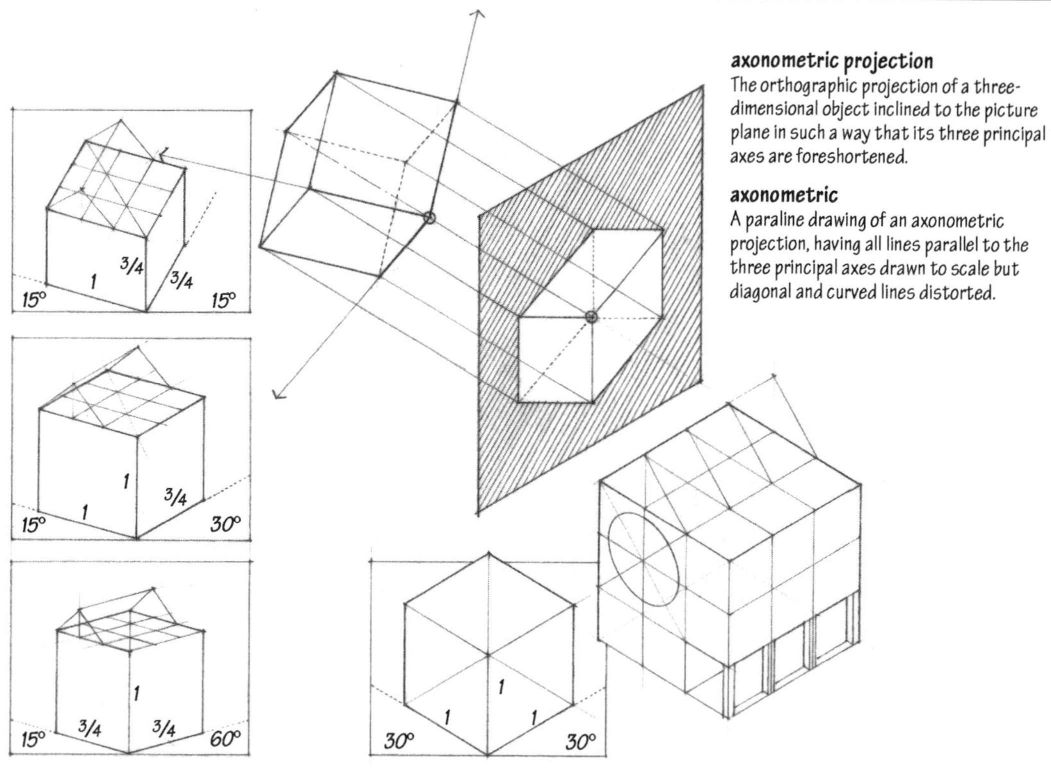

axonometric projection
The orthographic projection of a three-dimensional object inclined to the picture plane in such a way that its three principal axes are foreshortened.

axonometric
A paraline drawing of an axonometric projection, having all lines parallel to the three principal axes drawn to scale but diagonal and curved lines distorted.

dimetric projection
An axonometric projection of a three-dimensional object inclined to the picture plane in such a way that two of its principal axes are equally foreshortened and the third appears longer or shorter than the other two.

isometric
A paraline drawing of an isometric projection, having all lines parallel to the principal axes drawn to true length at the same scale.

isometric projection
An axonometric projection of a three-dimensional object having its principal faces equally inclined to the picture plane so that its three principal axes are equally foreshortened.

trimetric projection
An axonometric projection of a three-dimensional object inclined to the picture plane in such a way that all three principal axes are foreshortened at a different rate.

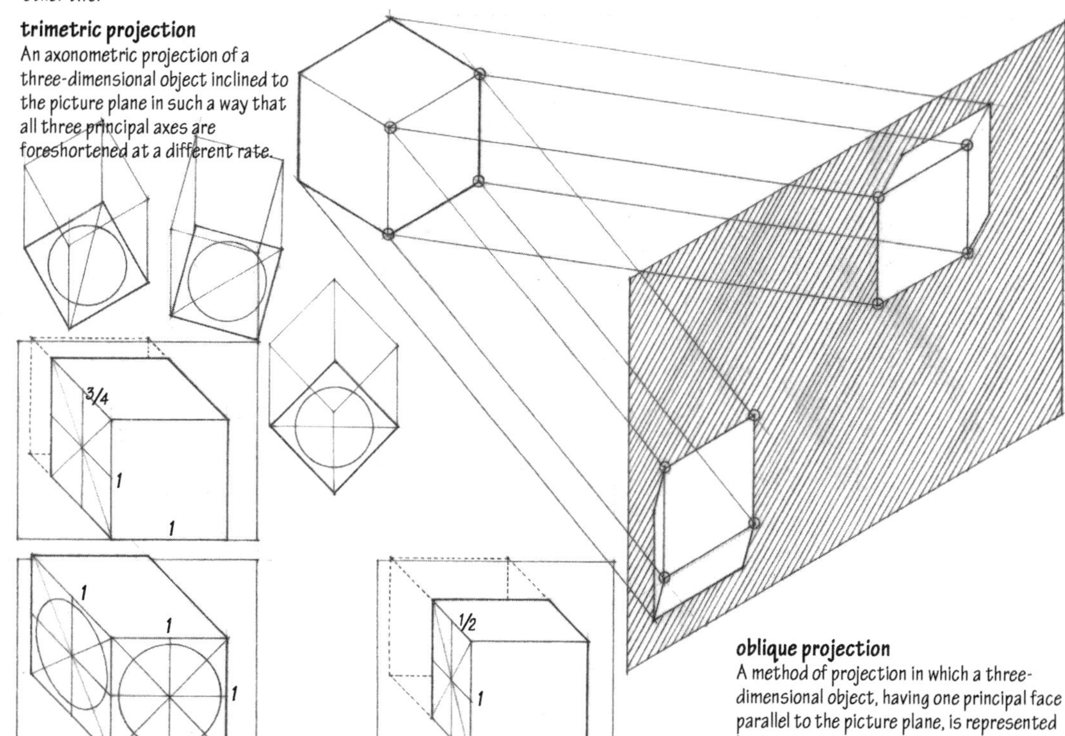

cavalier drawing
A paraline drawing of an oblique projection, having the receding lines perpendicular to the picture plane drawn to the same scale as the lines parallel to the picture plane.

cabinet drawing
A paraline drawing of an oblique projection, having all lines parallel to the picture plane drawn to exact scale, and the receding lines perpendicular to the picture plane reduced to half scale.

oblique projection
A method of projection in which a three-dimensional object, having one principal face parallel to the picture plane, is represented by projecting parallel lines at some angle other than 90° to the picture plane.

oblique
A paraline drawing of an oblique projection, having all lines and faces parallel to the picture plane drawn to exact scale, and all receding lines perpendicular to the picture plane shown at any convenient angle other than 90°, sometimes at a reduced scale to offset the appearance of distortion.

perspective
Any of various techniques for representing three-dimensional objects and spatial relationships on a two-dimensional surface as they might appear to the eye.

aerial perspective
A technique for rendering depth or distance by muting the hue, tone, and distinctness of objects perceived as receding from the picture plane. Also called **atmospheric perspective**.

pictorial space
The illusion of space or depth depicted on a two-dimensional surface by various graphic means, as aerial perspective, continuity of outline, or vertical location.

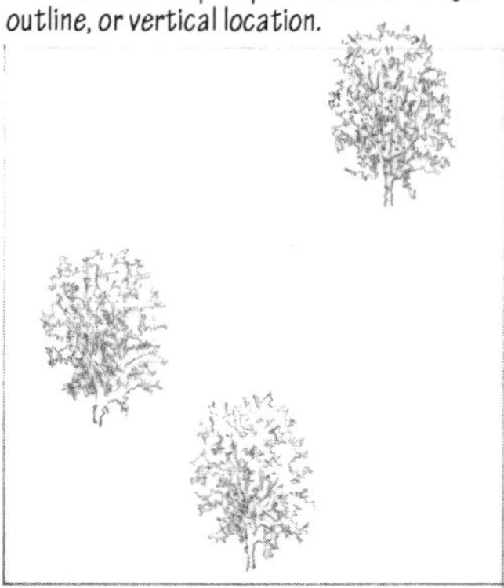

vertical location
A technique for representing depth or distance by placing distant objects higher in the picture plane than objects perceived as being closer.

size perspective
A technique for representing depth or distance by reducing the size of objects perceived as receding from the picture plane.

continuity of outline
A technique for representing depth or distance by emphasizing the continuity of the contour of a shape perceived as being in front and concealing a part of another behind it.

spatial edge
An edge of an object or surface separated from its background by an interval of space, delineated by a thicker line or by a sharp contrast in value or texture.

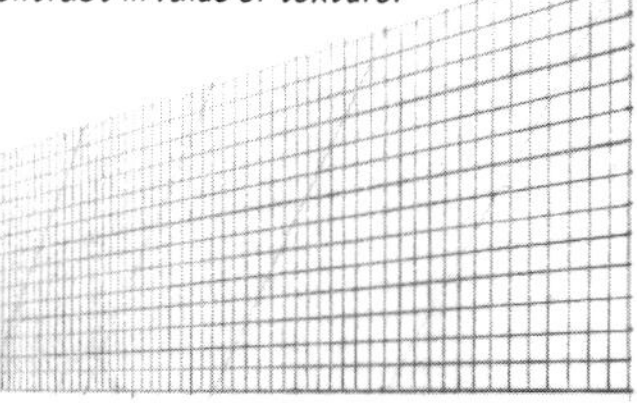

texture perspective
A technique for representing depth or distance by gradually increasing the density of the texture of a surface perceived as receding from the picture plane.

linear perspective
A mathematical system for representing three-dimensional objects and spatial relationships on a two-dimensional surface by means of perspective projection.

perspective projection
A method of projection in which a three-dimensional object is represented by projecting all its points to a picture plane by straight lines converging at an arbitrarily fixed point representing the eye of the viewer.

center of vision
A point representing the intersection of the central axis of vision and the picture plane in linear perspective.

station point
A fixed point in space representing a single eye of the viewer in linear perspective.

sightline
Any of the lines projecting from the eye of the viewer to various points on an object in linear perspective.

picture plane
An imaginary transparent plane, coexistent with the drawing surface, on which the image of a three-dimensional object is projected. In linear perspective, any line or plane coincident with the picture plane can be drawn to exact scale.

vanishing point
A point toward which receding parallel lines appear to converge in linear perspective, located at the point where a sightline parallel to the set of lines intersects the picture plane.

horizon line
A line representing the intersection of the picture plane and a horizontal plane through the eye of the viewer in linear perspective.

ground line
A horizontal line representing the intersection of the ground plane and the picture plane in linear perspective. Also called **base line**.

ground plane
A horizontal plane of reference from which vertical measurements can be taken in linear perspective, usually the plane supporting the object depicted or on which the viewer stands.

cone of vision
The field of vision radiating outward from the eye of the viewer in linear perspective, defined by sightlines forming a 15° to 30° angle with the central axis of vision. The cone of vision serves as a guide in determining what can be drawn in linear perspective without the appearance of distortion.

central axis of vision
The sightline indicating the direction in which the viewer is looking in linear perspective, perpendicular to the picture plane.

convergence
The apparent movement of parallel lines toward a common vanishing point as they recede, used in linear perspective to convey an illusion of space and depth.

Parallel lines perpendicular to the picture plane will appear to converge at the center of vision.

Parallel lines parallel to the picture plane retain their orientation and will not appear to converge.

perspective
A drawing of the perspective projection of an object or scene, characterized chiefly by convergence and foreshortening.

foreshortening
The apparent contraction or distortion of a represented line or shape that is not parallel to the picture plane, conveying an illusion of extension or projection in space.

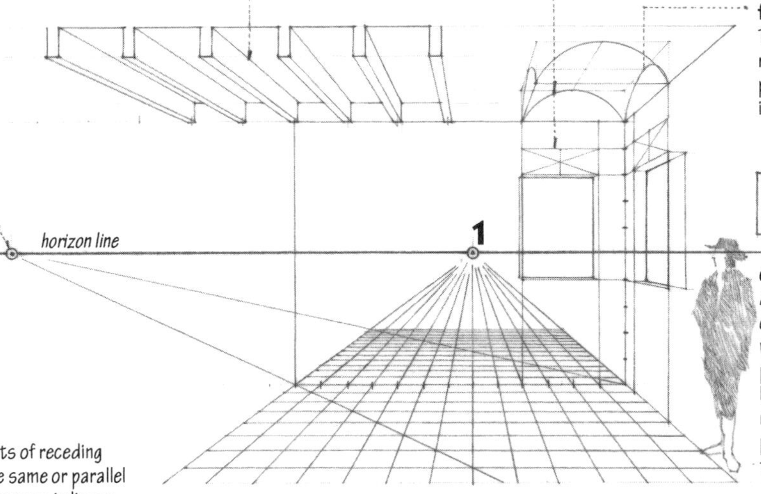

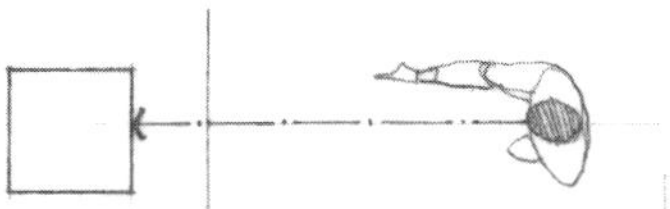

diagonal vanishing point
A vanishing point for a set of horizontal lines receding at a 45° angle to the picture plane in linear perspective. Also called **diagonal point, distance point.**

horizon line

1

one-point perspective
A linear perspective of a rectangular object or volume having a principal face parallel with the picture plane, so that vertical lines parallel to the picture plane remain vertical, horizontal lines parallel to the picture plane remain horizontal, and horizontal lines perpendicular to the picture plane appear to converge at the center of vision.

Parallel lines rising upward as they recede will appear to converge somewhere above the horizon line.

vanishing trace
A line along which all sets of receding parallel lines lying in the same or parallel planes will appear to converge in linear perspective.

Parallel lines which are horizontal but not perpendicular to the picture plane will appear to converge somewhere on the horizon line.

measuring point
A vanishing point for a set of parallel lines used in transferring scaled measurements in the picture plane to lines receding in linear perspective.

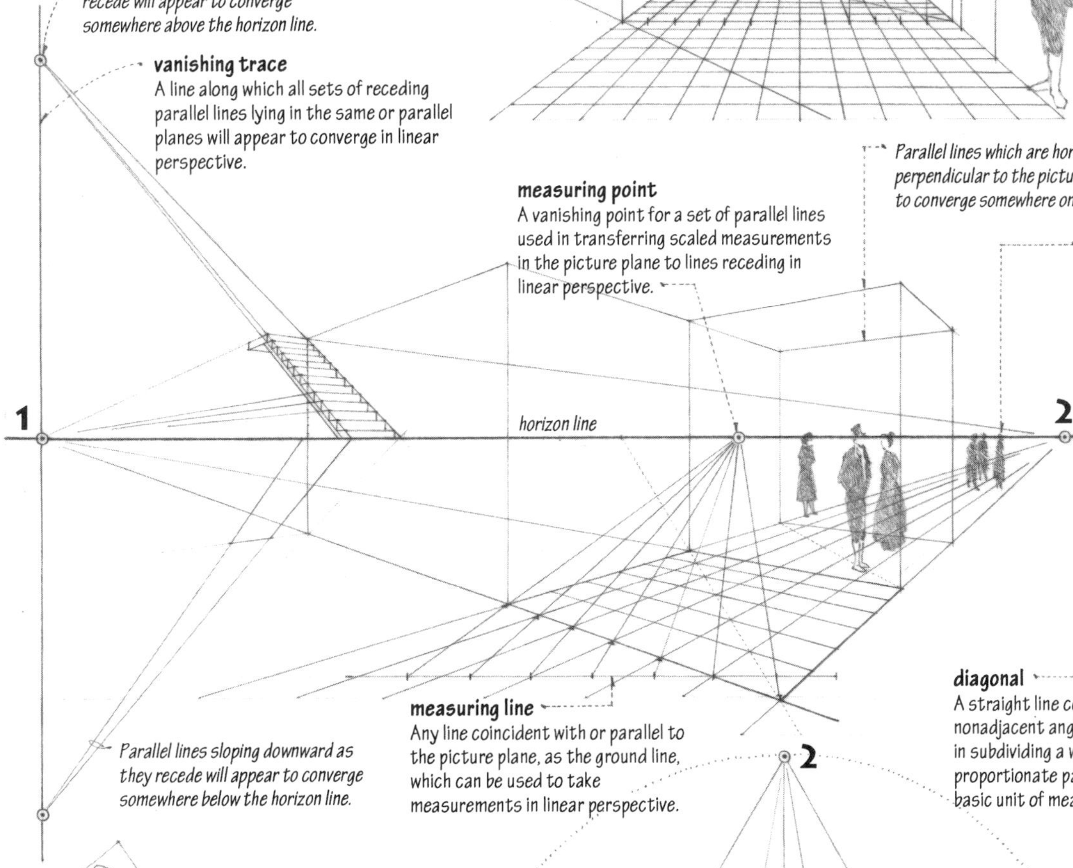

isocephalic
Having the heads of all figures at approximately the same level. Also, **isocephalous.**

1

horizon line

2

two-point perspective
A linear perspective of a rectangular object or volume having two principal faces oblique to the picture plane, so that vertical lines parallel to the picture plane remain vertical and two horizontal sets of parallel lines oblique to the picture plane appear to converge at two vanishing points, one to the left and the other to the right.

measuring line
Any line coincident with or parallel to the picture plane, as the ground line, which can be used to take measurements in linear perspective.

diagonal
A straight line connecting two nonadjacent angles of a rectangle, used in subdividing a whole into proportionate parts or multiplying a basic unit of measurement or space.

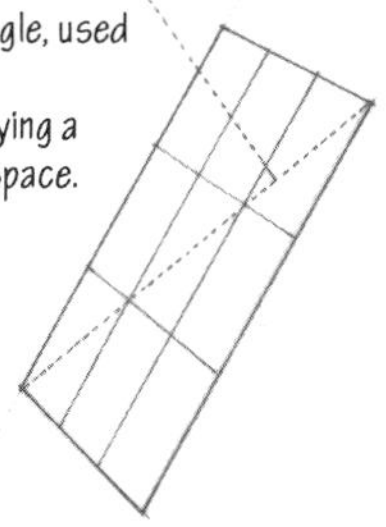

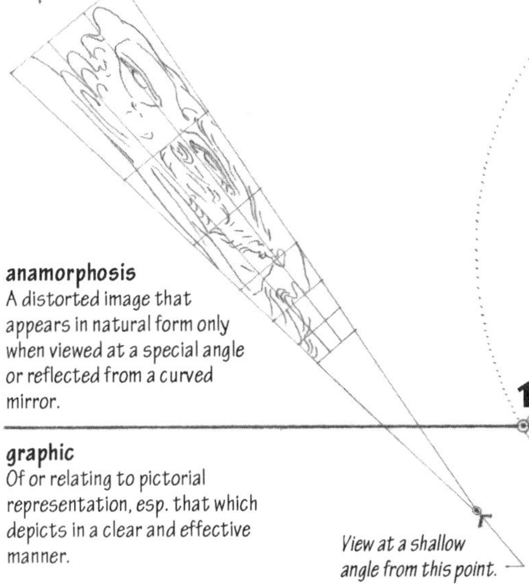

Parallel lines sloping downward as they recede will appear to converge somewhere below the horizon line.

2

anamorphosis
A distorted image that appears in natural form only when viewed at a special angle or reflected from a curved mirror.

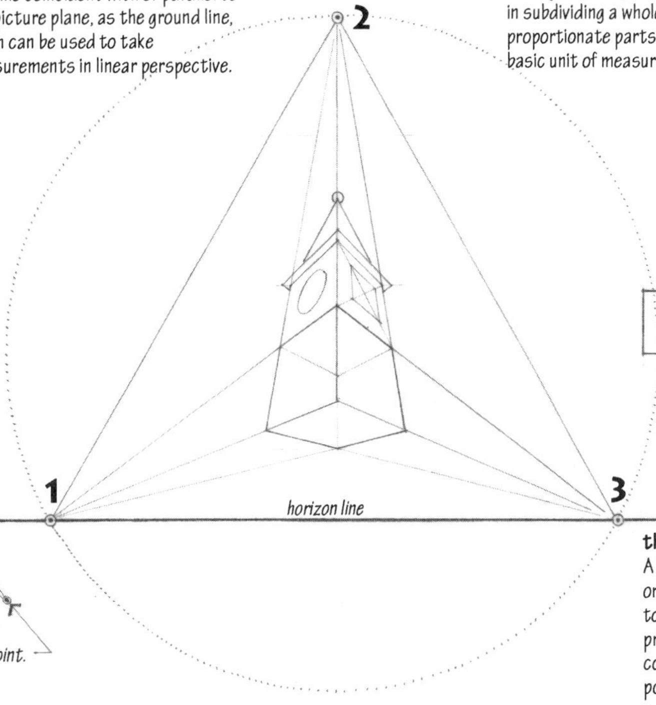

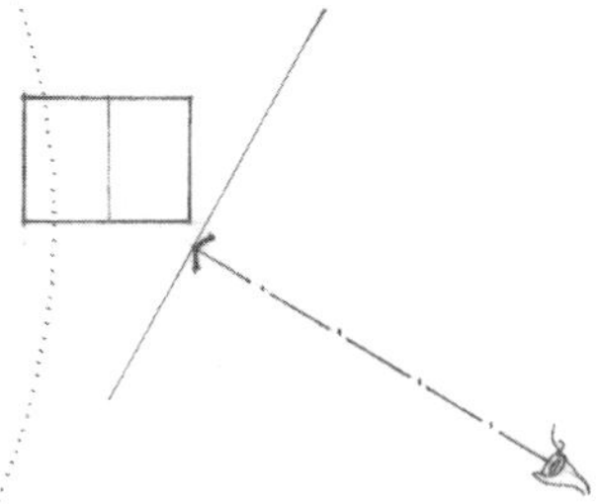

1

horizon line

3

graphic
Of or relating to pictorial representation, esp. that which depicts in a clear and effective manner.

View at a shallow angle from this point.

three-point perspective
A linear perspective of a rectangular object or volume having all principal faces oblique to the picture plane, so that the three principal sets of parallel lines appear to converge at three different vanishing points.

ELECTRICITY

The science dealing with the physical phenomena arising from the existence and interaction of electric charges.

electric charge
The intrinsic property of matter giving rise to all electric phenomena, occurring in two forms arbitrarily given positive and negative algebraic signs and measured in coulombs. Opposite charges attract while like charges repel each other.

coulomb
The SI unit of electric charge, equal to the quantity of electricity transferred across a conductor by a current of one ampere in one second. Abbr.: **C**

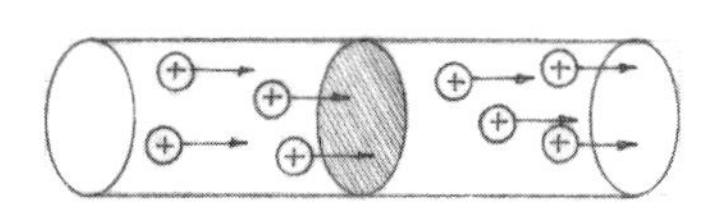

pressure : voltage

Hydraulic analogy to an electric circuit

valve : switch

flow : current

friction : resistance

$W = V \times A$

power
The product of potential difference and current in a direct-current circuit. In an alternating current circuit, power is equal to the product of the effective voltage, the effective current, and the cosine of the phase angle between current and voltage.

watt
The SI unit of power, equal to one joule per second or to the power represented by a current of one ampere flowing across a potential difference of one volt. Abbr.: **W**

wattage
An amount of power, esp. the power required to operate an electrical device or appliance, expressed in watts.

kilowatt
A unit of power, equal to 1,000 watts. Abbr.: **kW**

kilowatt-hour
A unit of energy, equal to the energy transferred or expended by one kilowatt in one hour: a common unit of electric power consumption. Abbr.: **kWh**

electromotive force
The energy per unit charge available for conversion from a chemical, mechanical, or other form of energy into electrical energy, or vice versa, in a conversion device as a battery, generator, or motor. Abbr.: **emf**

potential difference
The voltage difference between two points that represents the work involved in the transfer of a unit charge from one point to the other.

potential
The work required to move a unit charge from a reference point to a designated point.

voltage
Potential difference or electromotive force expressed in volts: analogous to pressure in water flow.

volt
The SI unit of potential difference and electromotive force, defined as the difference of electric potential between two points of a conductor carrying a constant current of one ampere, when the power dissipated between the points is equal to one watt. Abbr.: **V**

current
The rate of flow of electric charge in a circuit per unit time, measured in amperes.

Before the nature of electricity was fully understood, it was assumed that a direct current flowed from a positive point to a negative one. This convention is still used even though electrons flow in the opposite direction, from negative to positive.

ampere
The basic SI unit of electric current, equivalent to a flow of one coulomb per second or to the steady current produced by one volt applied across a resistance of one ohm. Abbr.: **A**

amperage
The strength of an electric current measured or expressed in amperes: analogous to the rate of water flow.

circuit
The complete path of an electric current, including the source of electric energy.

series
An arrangement of components in an electric circuit in which the same current flows through each component in turn without branching.

parallel
An arrangement of components in an electric circuit in which all positive terminals are connected to one conductor and all negative terminals are connected to a second conductor, the same voltage being applied to each component.

resistance
The opposition of a conductor to the flow of current, causing some of the electric energy to be transformed into heat and usually measured in ohms. Abbr.: **R**

ohm
The SI unit of electrical resistance, equal to the resistance of a conductor in which a potential difference of one volt produces a current of one ampere. Symbol: **Ω**

Ohm's law
The law that for any circuit the electric current is directly proportional to the voltage and inversely proportional to the resistance.

$I = V/R$

Joule's law
The principle that the rate of production of heat by a direct current is directly proportional to the resistance of the circuit and to the square of the current.

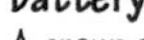

battery
A group of two or more cells connected together to produce electric current.

cell
A device for converting chemical into electric energy, usually consisting of a receptacle with electrodes in an electrolyte. Also called **electric cell, galvanic cell, voltaic cell.**

electrolyte
A nonmetallic conducting medium in which current is carried by the movement of ions.

electrode
A conductor through which a current enters or leaves a nonmetallic medium.

anode
The negative terminal of a primary cell or storage battery.

cathode
The positive terminal of a primary cell or storage battery.

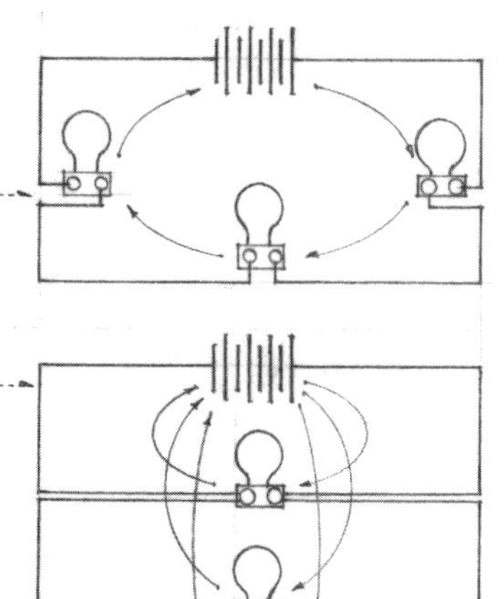

resistivity
The resistance per unit length of a substance with a unit cross-sectional area. Also called **specific resistance.**

conductivity
A measure of the ability of a substance to conduct electric current, equal to the reciprocal of the resistivity of the substance. Also called **specific conductance.**

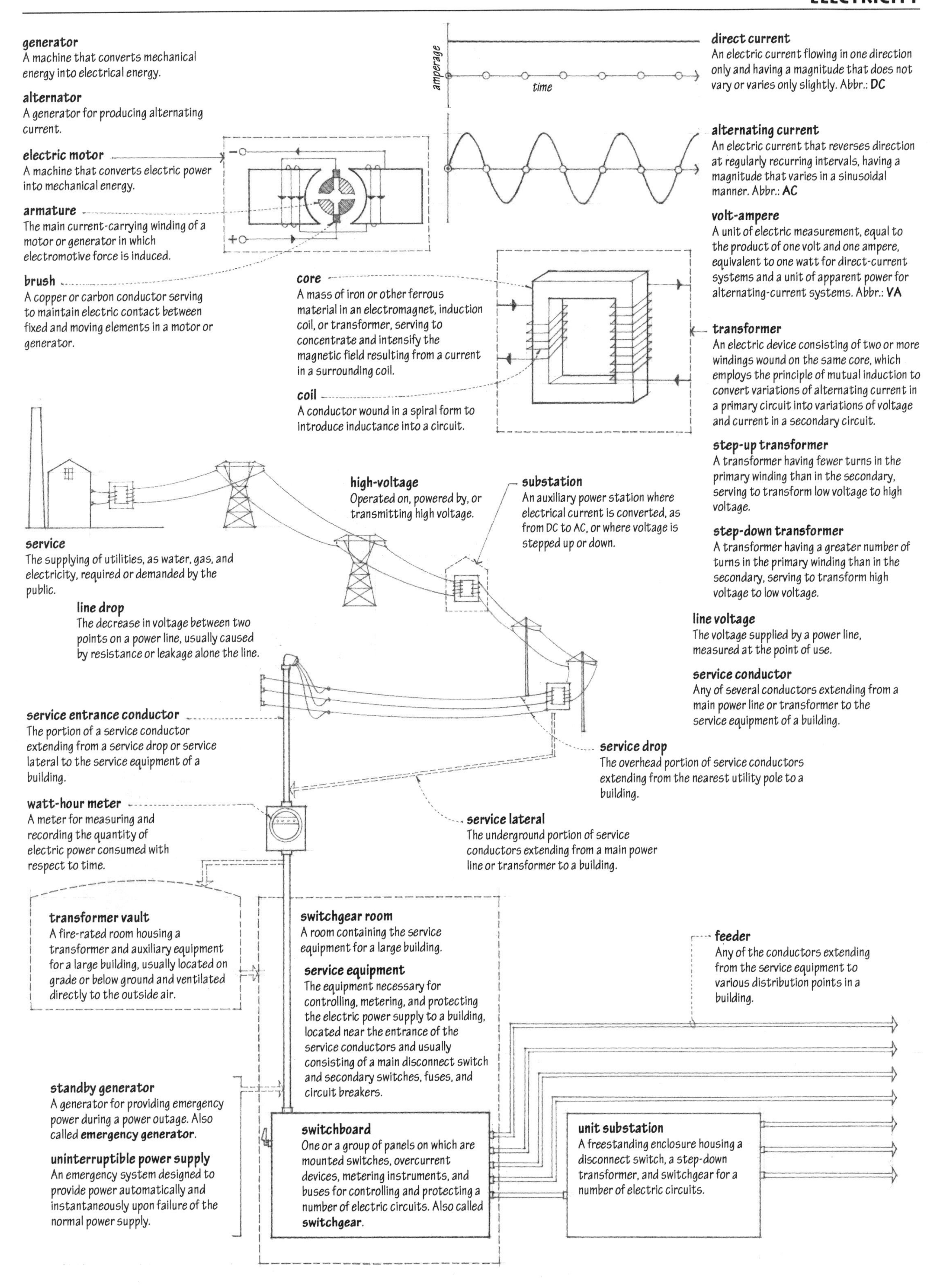

generator
A machine that converts mechanical energy into electrical energy.

alternator
A generator for producing alternating current.

electric motor
A machine that converts electric power into mechanical energy.

armature
The main current-carrying winding of a motor or generator in which electromotive force is induced.

brush
A copper or carbon conductor serving to maintain electric contact between fixed and moving elements in a motor or generator.

core
A mass of iron or other ferrous material in an electromagnet, induction coil, or transformer, serving to concentrate and intensify the magnetic field resulting from a current in a surrounding coil.

coil
A conductor wound in a spiral form to introduce inductance into a circuit.

direct current
An electric current flowing in one direction only and having a magnitude that does not vary or varies only slightly. Abbr.: **DC**

alternating current
An electric current that reverses direction at regularly recurring intervals, having a magnitude that varies in a sinusoidal manner. Abbr.: **AC**

volt-ampere
A unit of electric measurement, equal to the product of one volt and one ampere, equivalent to one watt for direct-current systems and a unit of apparent power for alternating-current systems. Abbr.: **VA**

transformer
An electric device consisting of two or more windings wound on the same core, which employs the principle of mutual induction to convert variations of alternating current in a primary circuit into variations of voltage and current in a secondary circuit.

step-up transformer
A transformer having fewer turns in the primary winding than in the secondary, serving to transform low voltage to high voltage.

step-down transformer
A transformer having a greater number of turns in the primary winding than in the secondary, serving to transform high voltage to low voltage.

high-voltage
Operated on, powered by, or transmitting high voltage.

substation
An auxiliary power station where electrical current is converted, as from DC to AC, or where voltage is stepped up or down.

service
The supplying of utilities, as water, gas, and electricity, required or demanded by the public.

line drop
The decrease in voltage between two points on a power line, usually caused by resistance or leakage alone the line.

line voltage
The voltage supplied by a power line, measured at the point of use.

service conductor
Any of several conductors extending from a main power line or transformer to the service equipment of a building.

service entrance conductor
The portion of a service conductor extending from a service drop or service lateral to the service equipment of a building.

service drop
The overhead portion of service conductors extending from the nearest utility pole to a building.

watt-hour meter
A meter for measuring and recording the quantity of electric power consumed with respect to time.

service lateral
The underground portion of service conductors extending from a main power line or transformer to a building.

transformer vault
A fire-rated room housing a transformer and auxiliary equipment for a large building, usually located on grade or below ground and ventilated directly to the outside air.

switchgear room
A room containing the service equipment for a large building.

service equipment
The equipment necessary for controlling, metering, and protecting the electric power supply to a building, located near the entrance of the service conductors and usually consisting of a main disconnect switch and secondary switches, fuses, and circuit breakers.

feeder
Any of the conductors extending from the service equipment to various distribution points in a building.

standby generator
A generator for providing emergency power during a power outage. Also called **emergency generator**.

uninterruptible power supply
An emergency system designed to provide power automatically and instantaneously upon failure of the normal power supply.

switchboard
One or a group of panels on which are mounted switches, overcurrent devices, metering instruments, and buses for controlling and protecting a number of electric circuits. Also called **switchgear**.

unit substation
A freestanding enclosure housing a disconnect switch, a step-down transformer, and switchgear for a number of electric circuits.

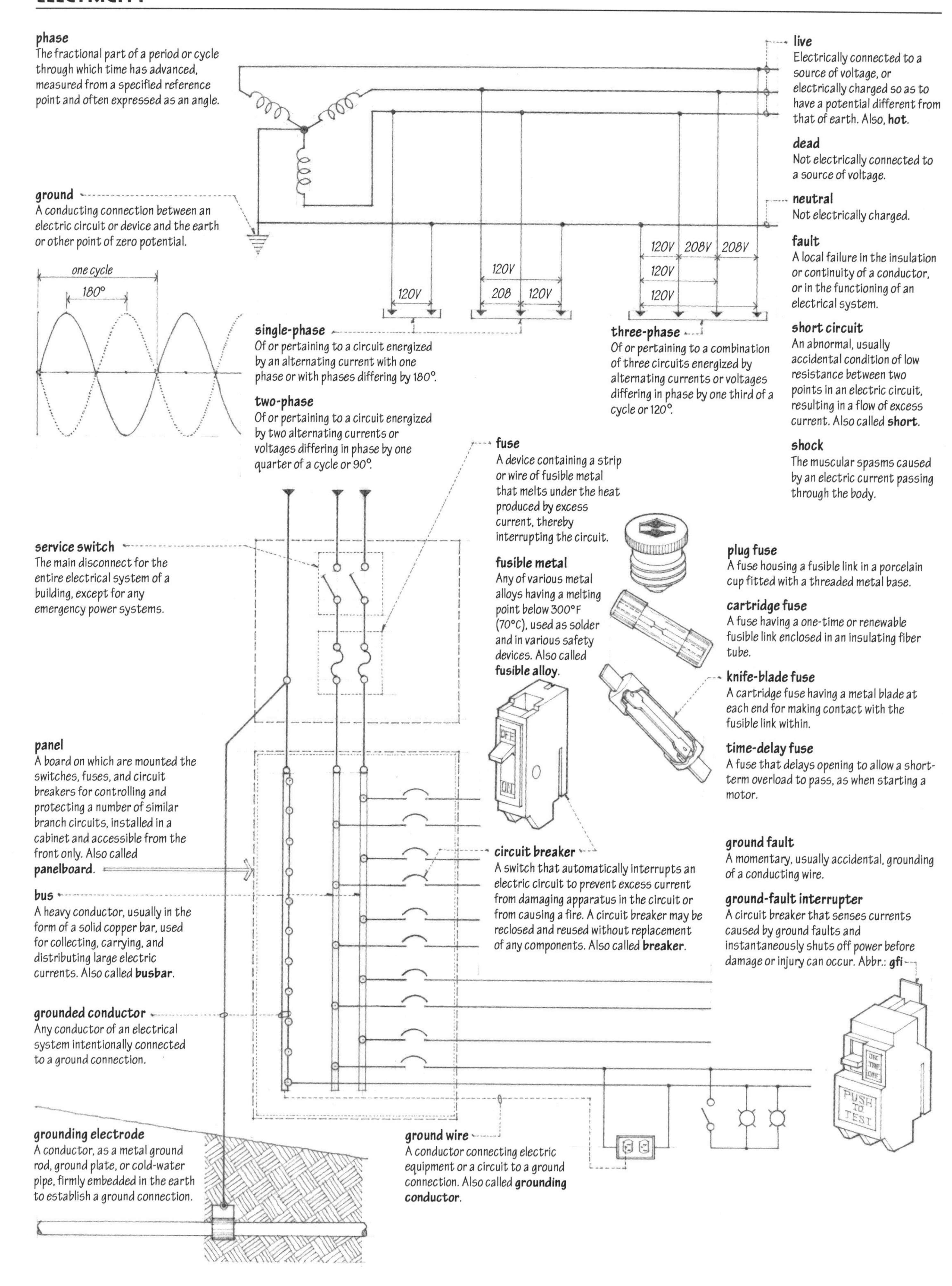

phase
The fractional part of a period or cycle through which time has advanced, measured from a specified reference point and often expressed as an angle.

ground
A conducting connection between an electric circuit or device and the earth or other point of zero potential.

single-phase
Of or pertaining to a circuit energized by an alternating current with one phase or with phases differing by 180°.

two-phase
Of or pertaining to a circuit energized by two alternating currents or voltages differing in phase by one quarter of a cycle or 90°.

three-phase
Of or pertaining to a combination of three circuits energized by alternating currents or voltages differing in phase by one third of a cycle or 120°.

live
Electrically connected to a source of voltage, or electrically charged so as to have a potential different from that of earth. Also, **hot**.

dead
Not electrically connected to a source of voltage.

neutral
Not electrically charged.

fault
A local failure in the insulation or continuity of a conductor, or in the functioning of an electrical system.

short circuit
An abnormal, usually accidental condition of low resistance between two points in an electric circuit, resulting in a flow of excess current. Also called **short**.

shock
The muscular spasms caused by an electric current passing through the body.

fuse
A device containing a strip or wire of fusible metal that melts under the heat produced by excess current, thereby interrupting the circuit.

fusible metal
Any of various metal alloys having a melting point below 300°F (70°C), used as solder and in various safety devices. Also called **fusible alloy**.

plug fuse
A fuse housing a fusible link in a porcelain cup fitted with a threaded metal base.

cartridge fuse
A fuse having a one-time or renewable fusible link enclosed in an insulating fiber tube.

knife-blade fuse
A cartridge fuse having a metal blade at each end for making contact with the fusible link within.

time-delay fuse
A fuse that delays opening to allow a short-term overload to pass, as when starting a motor.

service switch
The main disconnect for the entire electrical system of a building, except for any emergency power systems.

panel
A board on which are mounted the switches, fuses, and circuit breakers for controlling and protecting a number of similar branch circuits, installed in a cabinet and accessible from the front only. Also called **panelboard**.

bus
A heavy conductor, usually in the form of a solid copper bar, used for collecting, carrying, and distributing large electric currents. Also called **busbar**.

circuit breaker
A switch that automatically interrupts an electric circuit to prevent excess current from damaging apparatus in the circuit or from causing a fire. A circuit breaker may be reclosed and reused without replacement of any components. Also called **breaker**.

ground fault
A momentary, usually accidental, grounding of a conducting wire.

ground-fault interrupter
A circuit breaker that senses currents caused by ground faults and instantaneously shuts off power before damage or injury can occur. Abbr.: **gfi**

grounded conductor
Any conductor of an electrical system intentionally connected to a ground connection.

grounding electrode
A conductor, as a metal ground rod, ground plate, or cold-water pipe, firmly embedded in the earth to establish a ground connection.

ground wire
A conductor connecting electric equipment or a circuit to a ground connection. Also called **grounding conductor**.

lightning rod
Any of several conducting rods installed at the top of a structure and grounded to divert lightning away from the structure. Also called **air terminal**.

lightning arrester
A device for protecting electric equipment from damage by lightning or other high-voltage currents, using spark gaps to carry the current to the ground without passing through the device.

spark gap
A space between two terminals or electrodes, across which a discharge of electricity may pass at a prescribed voltage.

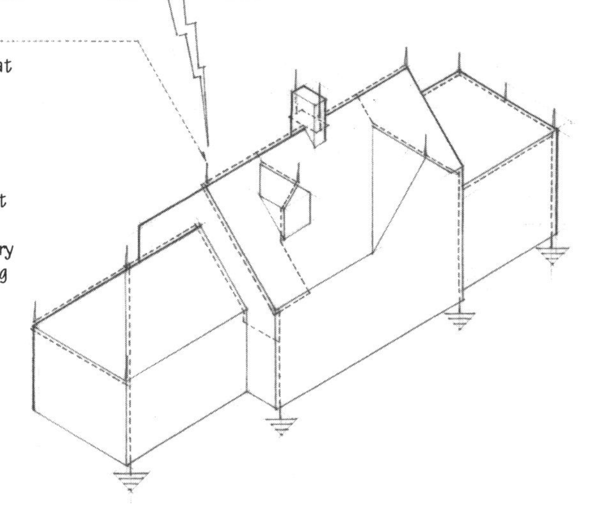

load
The power delivered by a generator or transformer, or the power consumed by an appliance or device.

connected load
The total load on an electrical system or circuit if all connected apparatus and equipment are energized simultaneously.

maximum demand
The greatest load delivered to an electrical system or circuit over a specified interval of time.

demand factor
The ratio of the maximum demand to the connected load of an electrical system, used in estimating the required capacity of the system to account for the probability that only a portion of the connected load may be applied at any time.

diversity factor
The ratio of the sum of the maximum demands on the various parts of an electrical system to the maximum demand on the whole.

load factor
The ratio of the average load on an electrical system over a specific period of time to the peak load occurring in that period.

branch circuit
The portion of an electrical system extending from the final overcurrent device protecting a circuit to the outlets served by the circuit.

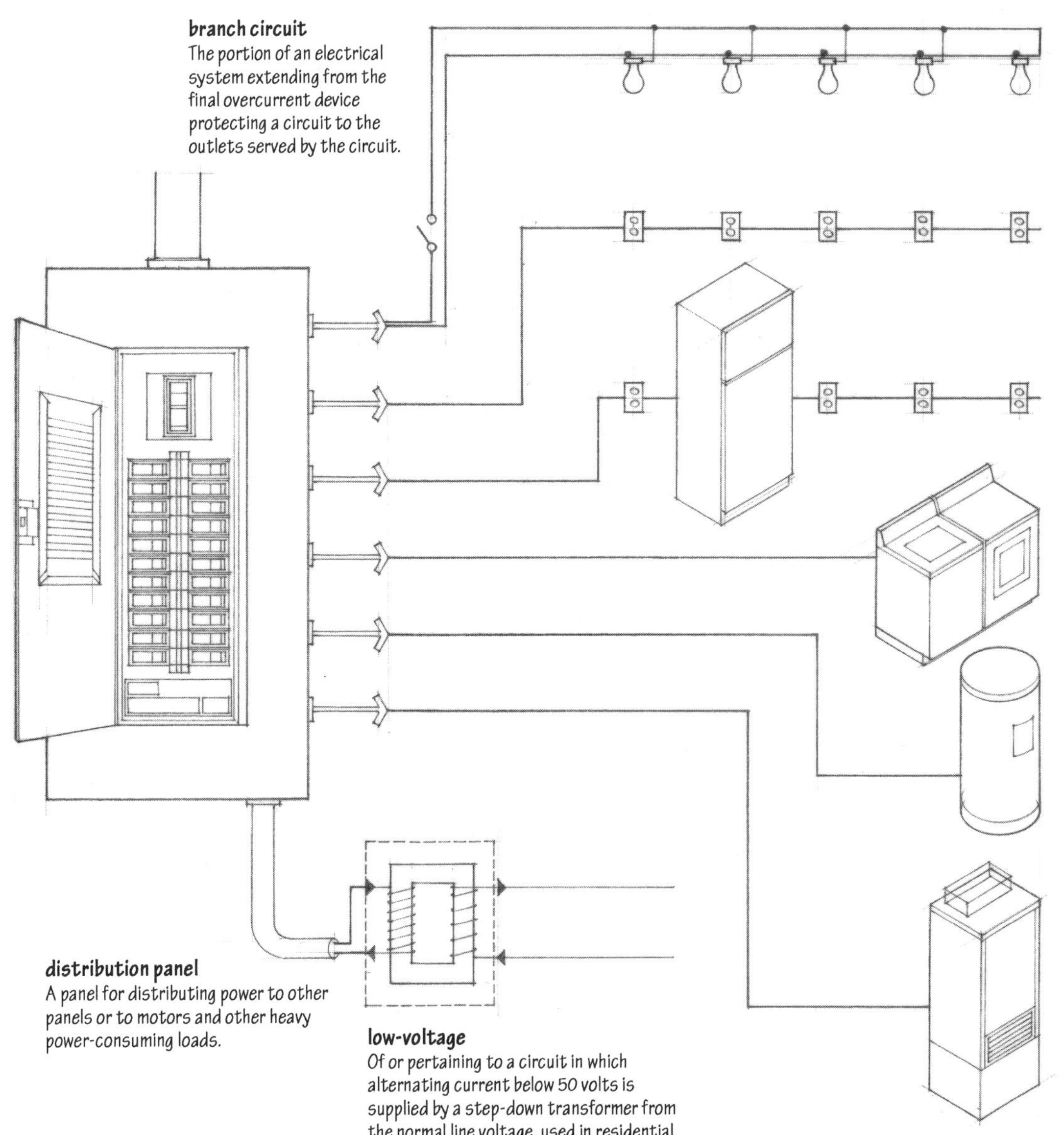

general purpose circuit
A branch circuit that supplies current to a number of outlets for lighting and appliances.

appliance circuit
A branch circuit that supplies current to one or more outlets specifically intended for appliances.

individual circuit
A branch circuit that supplies current only to a single piece of electrical equipment.

distribution panel
A panel for distributing power to other panels or to motors and other heavy power-consuming loads.

low-voltage
Of or pertaining to a circuit in which alternating current below 50 volts is supplied by a step-down transformer from the normal line voltage, used in residential systems to control doorbells, intercoms, heating and cooling systems, and remote lighting fixtures. Low-voltage circuits do not require a protective raceway.

cable
A single insulated conductor or a bound or sheathed combination of conductors insulated from one another.

armored cable
Electric cable consisting of two or more insulated conductors protected by a flexible, helically wound metal wrapping. Also called **BX cable**.

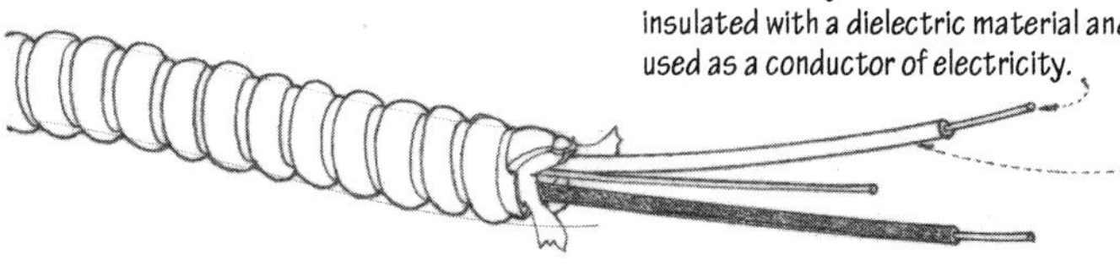

mineral-insulated cable
Electric cable consisting of a tubular copper sheath containing one or more conductors embedded in a highly compressed, insulating refractory mineral.

nonmetallic sheathed cable
Electric cable consisting of two or more insulated conductors enclosed in a nonmetallic, moisture-resistant, flame-retardant sheath. Also called **Romex cable**.

coaxial cable
A cable for transmitting high-frequency telephone, digital, or television signals, consisting of an insulated conducting tube enclosing an insulated conducting core.

shielded cable
An electric cable enclosed within a metallic sheath in order to reduce the effects of external electric or magnetic fields.

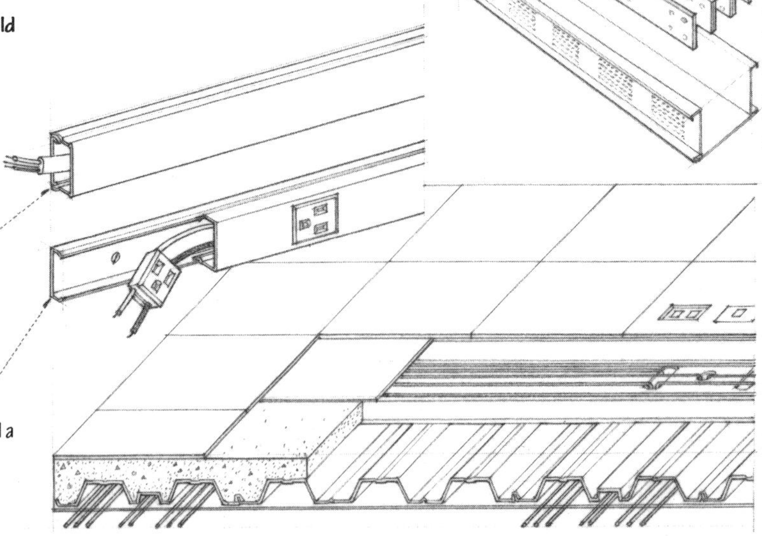

wire
A pliable metallic strand or a twisted or woven assembly of such strands, often insulated with a dielectric material and used as a conductor of electricity.

NM 12/2 WITH GROUND 600V

conductor
A substance, body, or device that conducts heat, sound, or electricity.

insulator
A material that is a poor conductor of electricity, used for separating or supporting conductors to prevent the undesired flow of current.

breakdown voltage
The minimum applied voltage at which a given insulator breaks down and permits current to pass.

dielectric strength
The maximum voltage that can be applied to a given material without causing it to break down, usually expressed in volts or kilovolts per unit of thickness.

dielectric
A nonconducting substance.

junction box
An enclosure for housing and protecting electric wires or cables that are joined together in connecting or branching electric circuits.

knockout
A panel in a casing or box that can readily be removed, as by punching, hammering, or cutting, to provide an opening into the interior.

grommet
A rubber or plastic washer inserted in a hole in a metal part to prevent grounding of a wire passing through the hole.

bushing
An insulating and protective lining for one or more conductors passing through a hole.

conduit
A tube, pipe, or duct for enclosing and protecting electric wires or cable.

rigid metal conduit
Heavy-walled, tubular steel conduit joined by screwing directly into a threaded hub with locknuts and bushings.

electrical metallic tubing
Thin-walled, tubular steel conduit joined by compression or setscrew couplings. Abbr.: EMT

flexible metal conduit
A flexible, helically wound metal conduit, used for connections to motors or other vibrating equipment. Also called **Greenfield conduit**.

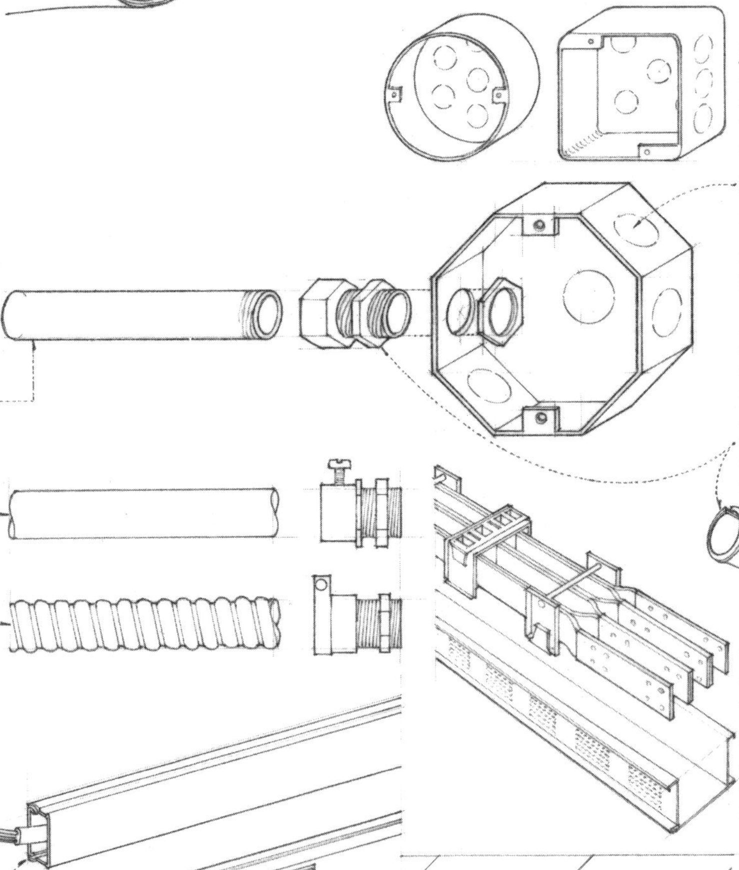

duct
An enclosed runway for housing conductors or cables.

bus duct
A rigid metal housing for a group of buses insulated from each other and the enclosure. Also called **busway**.

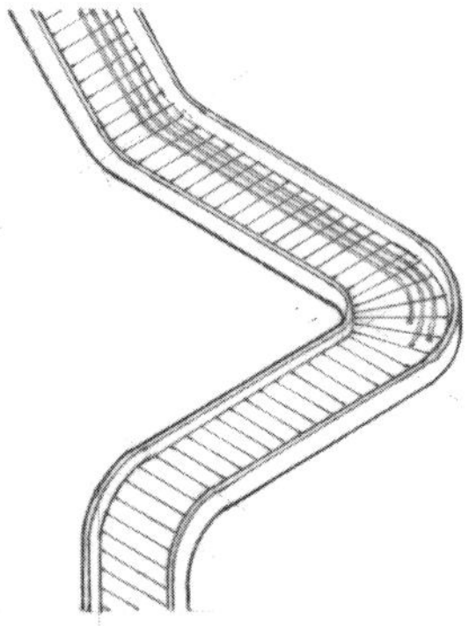

raceway
A channel expressly designed to hold and protect electric wires and cables.

surface raceway
A raceway designed for exposed installation in dry, nonhazardous, noncorrosive locations.

multi-outlet assembly
A surface-mounted raceway designed to house the electrical wires for a circuit and a series of receptacles.

underfloor raceway
A raceway suitable for installation under a floor, often used in office buildings to allow for the flexible placement of power, signal, and telephone outlets.

cable tray
An open metal framework for supporting insulated electrical conductors.

air switch
A switch in which the interruption of a circuit occurs in air.

knife switch
A form of air switch in which a hinged copper blade is placed between two contact clips.

float switch
A switch controlled by a conductor floating in a liquid.

mercury switch
An especially quiet switch that opens and closes an electric circuit by shifting a sealed glass tube of mercury so as to uncover or cover the contacts.

key switch
A switch operated only by inserting a key.

dimmer
A rheostat or similar device for regulating the intensity of an electric light without appreciably affecting spatial distribution. Also called **dimmer switch**.

rheostat
A resistor for regulating a current by means of variable resistances.

faceplate
A protective plate surrounding an electric outlet or light switch.

switch
A device for making, breaking, or directing an electric current.

toggle switch
A switch in which a lever or knob, moving through a small arc, causes the contacts to open or close an electric circuit.

three-way switch
A single-pole, double-throw switch used in conjunction with another to control lights from two locations.

four-way switch
A switch used in conjunction with two three-way switches to control lights from three locations.

knob-and-tube wiring
An obsolete wiring system consisting of single, insulated conductors secured to and supported on porcelain knobs and tubes.

loom
A flexible, nonmetallic, fire-resistant tubing for conductors in knob-and-tube wiring.

outlet
A point on a wiring system at which current is taken to supply an electric device or apparatus.

outlet box
A junction box designed to facilitate connecting an electric device or receptacle to a wiring system.

convenience outlet
An outlet usually mounted on a wall and housing one or more receptacles for portable lamps or appliances.

receptacle
A female fitting connected to a power supply and equipped to receive a plug. Also called **socket**.

lead
A flexible, insulated conductor for electrically connecting an apparatus to another or to a circuit.

pigtail
A short, flexible conductor used in connecting a stationery terminal with a terminal having a limited range of motion.

terminal
A conductive element or device for establishing an electric connection to an apparatus.

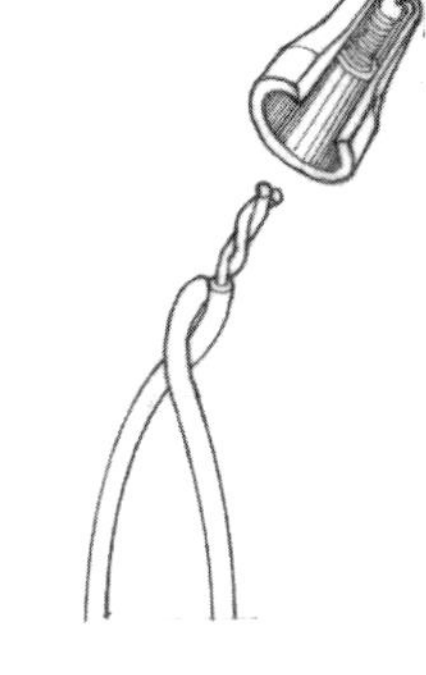

cord
A small, flexible, insulated cable fitted with a plug to connect a portable lamp or appliance to a receptacle.

wire nut
A plastic connector containing a threaded metal fitting for screwing onto the intertwined ends of two or more conductors.

connector
Any of various devices for joining two or more conductors without a permanent splice.

grounding outlet
An outlet having an additional contact for a ground connection.

plug
A male fitting for making an electrical connection to a circuit by insertion in a receptacle.

grounding plug
A plug having a blade for a ground connection.

polarized
Designed so that a plug and receptacle can fit together in only one way.

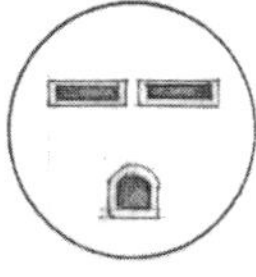

A moving platform or cage for carrying passengers or freight from one level of a building to another.

bulkhead
A boxlike structure on a roof providing access to a stairwell or an elevator shaft.

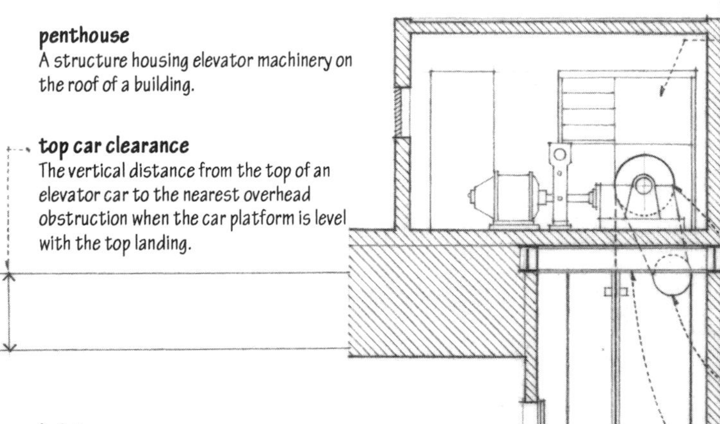

lift
British term for elevator.

passenger elevator
An elevator exclusively for the use of passengers.

freight elevator
An elevator for carrying heavy cargo, on which the operator and the persons necessary for unloading and loading the freight are permitted to ride.

dumbwaiter
A small elevator for conveying food, dishes, or other materials between the floors of a building.

bank
A row of elevators in a high-rise building, controlled by a common operating system and responding to a single call button.

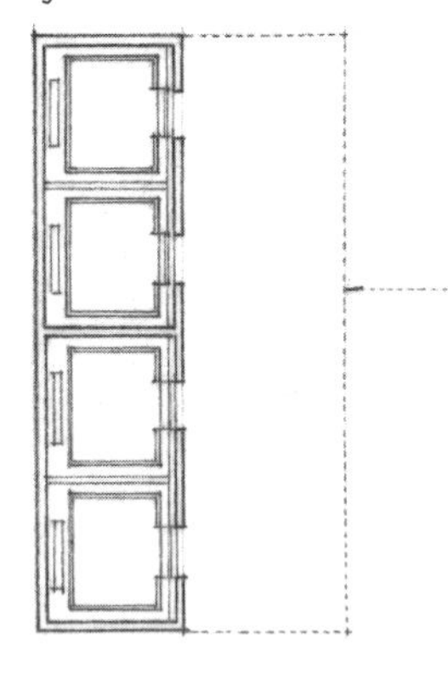

rise
The vertical distance traversed by an elevator car from the lowest to the highest landings of the hoistway. Also called **travel**.

electric elevator
An elevator system consisting of a car that is mounted on guide rails, supported by hoisting cables, and driven by electric hoisting machinery. Also called **traction elevator**.

penthouse
A structure housing elevator machinery on the roof of a building.

top car clearance
The vertical distance from the top of an elevator car to the nearest overhead obstruction when the car platform is level with the top landing.

hoistway
A vertical enclosed space for the travel of one or more elevators. Also called **elevator shaft**.

landing
The portion of a floor adjacent to an elevator hoistway, used for the receiving and discharge of passengers or freight.

elevator car safety
A mechanical device for slowing down and stopping an elevator car in the event of excessive speed or free fall, actuated by a governor and clamping the guide rails by a wedging action.

hoistway door
A door between a hoistway and an elevator landing, normally closed except when an elevator car is stopped at the landing.

elevator pit
The portion of a hoistway extending from the level of the lowest landing to the floor of the hoistway.

bottom car clearance
The vertical distance from the floor of an elevator pit to the lowest part of an elevator car platform when the car rests on fully compressed buffers.

control panel
A panel containing switches, buttons, and other equipment for regulating electrical devices.

hoisting machinery
The machinery for raising and lowering an elevator car, consisting of a motor-generator set, traction machine, speed governor, brake, drive shaft, driving sheave, and gears, if used.

driving sheave
A wheel or disk with a grooved rim, used as a pulley for hoisting.

idle sheave
A pulley for tightening and guiding the hoisting cables of an elevator system. Also called **deflector sheave**.

machine beam
One of the heavy steel beams supporting the hoisting machinery for an elevator.

hoisting cable
One of the wire cables or ropes used for raising and lowering an elevator car.

guide rail
One of the vertical steel tracks controlling the travel of an elevator car or counterweight.

traveling cable
One of the electric cables connecting an elevator car to a fixed electrical outlet in the hoistway.

counterweight
A weight balancing another weight, as the rectangular cast-iron blocks mounted in a steel frame to counterbalance the load placed on the hoisting machine by an elevator car.

limit switch
A switch that automatically cuts off current to an electric motor when an object moved by it, as an elevator car, has passed a given point.

buffer
A piston or spring device for absorbing the impact of a descending elevator car or counterweight at the extreme lower limit of travel.

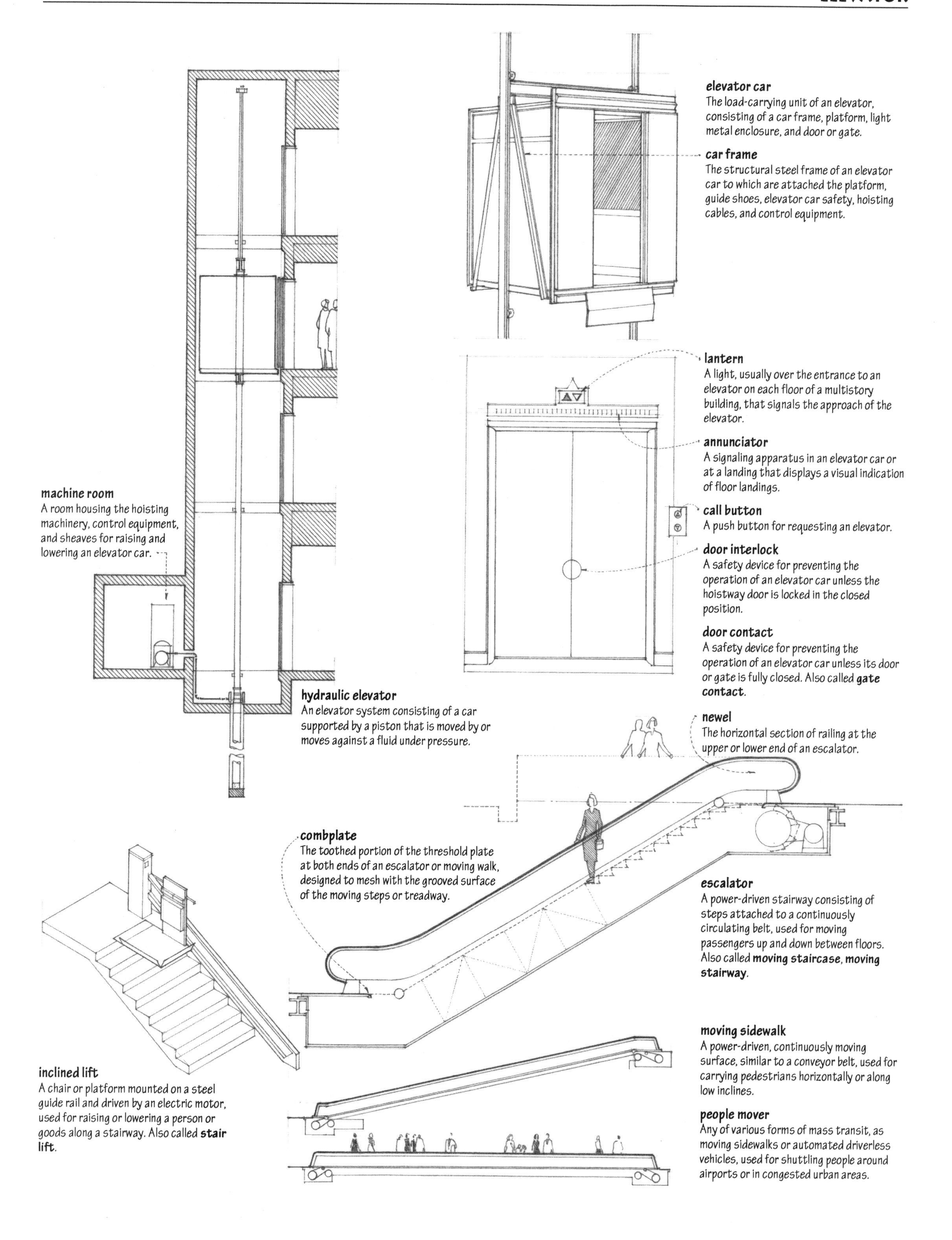

elevator car
The load-carrying unit of an elevator, consisting of a car frame, platform, light metal enclosure, and door or gate.

car frame
The structural steel frame of an elevator car to which are attached the platform, guide shoes, elevator car safety, hoisting cables, and control equipment.

lantern
A light, usually over the entrance to an elevator on each floor of a multistory building, that signals the approach of the elevator.

annunciator
A signaling apparatus in an elevator car or at a landing that displays a visual indication of floor landings.

call button
A push button for requesting an elevator.

door interlock
A safety device for preventing the operation of an elevator car unless the hoistway door is locked in the closed position.

door contact
A safety device for preventing the operation of an elevator car unless its door or gate is fully closed. Also called **gate contact**.

machine room
A room housing the hoisting machinery, control equipment, and sheaves for raising and lowering an elevator car.

hydraulic elevator
An elevator system consisting of a car supported by a piston that is moved by or moves against a fluid under pressure.

newel
The horizontal section of railing at the upper or lower end of an escalator.

combplate
The toothed portion of the threshold plate at both ends of an escalator or moving walk, designed to mesh with the grooved surface of the moving steps or treadway.

escalator
A power-driven stairway consisting of steps attached to a continuously circulating belt, used for moving passengers up and down between floors. Also called **moving staircase, moving stairway**.

inclined lift
A chair or platform mounted on a steel guide rail and driven by an electric motor, used for raising or lowering a person or goods along a stairway. Also called **stair lift**.

moving sidewalk
A power-driven, continuously moving surface, similar to a conveyor belt, used for carrying pedestrians horizontally or along low inclines.

people mover
Any of various forms of mass transit, as moving sidewalks or automated driverless vehicles, used for shuttling people around airports or in congested urban areas.

Holding together or uniting two or more parts or members, as by clamping with a mechanical fastener, by bonding with an adhesive, or by welding or soldering.

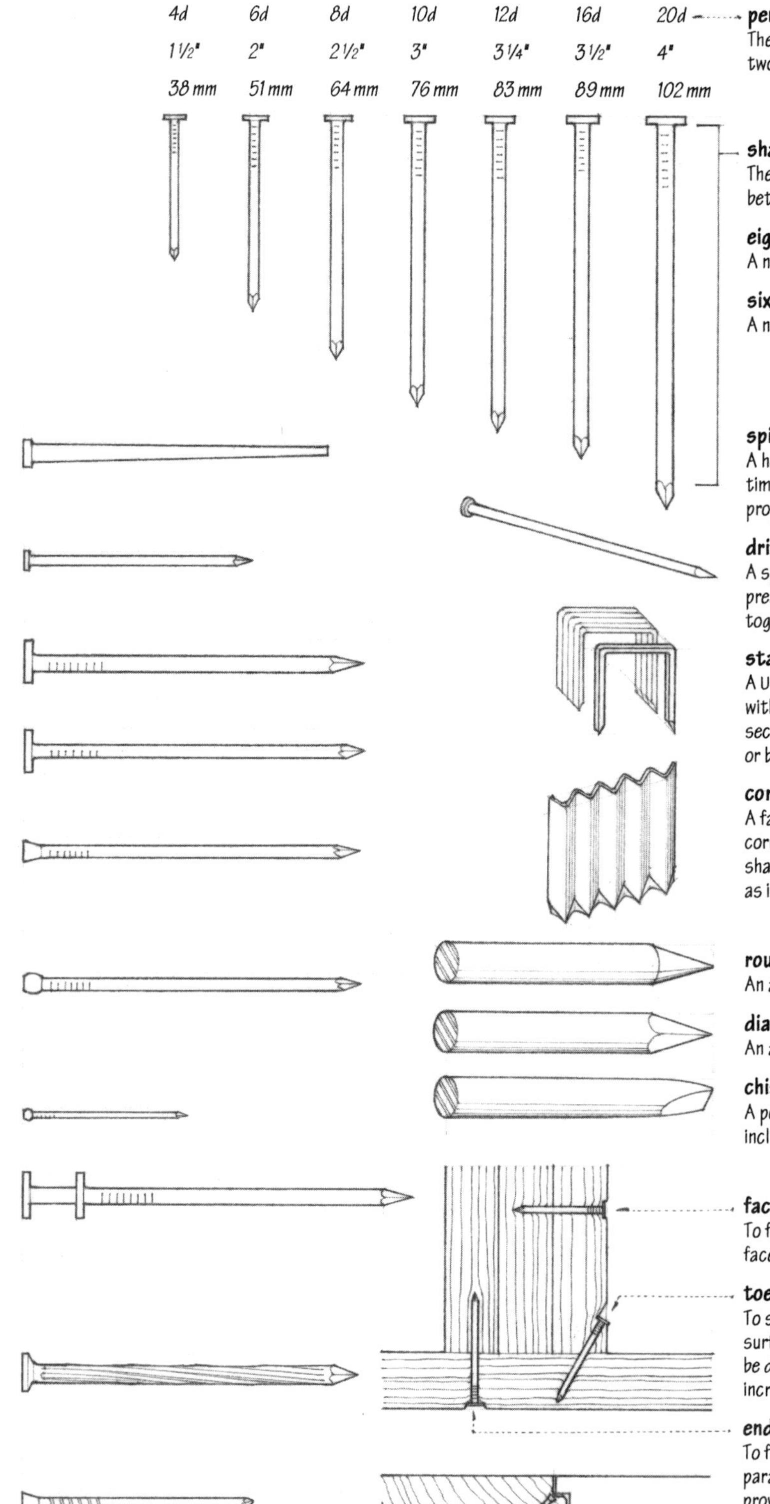

nail
A straight, slender piece of metal having one end pointed and the other enlarged and flattened for hammering into wood or other building materials as a fastener.

penny
The designated length of a nail, from twopenny to sixtypenny. Symbol: **d**

shank
The straight, narrow part of a nail or bolt, between the head and the point.

eightpenny nail
A nail 2½ inches (64 mm) long.

sixteenpenny nail
A nail 3½ inches (89 mm) long.

spike
A heavy nail for fastening together heavy timbers, 4 to 14 in. (102 to 356 mm) long and proportionally thicker than a common nail.

cut nail
A nail having a tapering rectangular shank with a blunt point, made by cutting from a rolled sheet of iron or steel.

wire nail
A nail made by cutting and shaping a piece of round or elliptical wire.

common nail
A nail having a slender shank, a flat head, and a diamond point.

box nail
A nail having a flat head and a shank more slender than a common nail of the same length.

casing nail
A nail having a small conical head and a shank more slender than a common nail of the same length, used in finish work in which the head may remain visible.

finishing nail
A nail having a slender shank and a small, barrel-shaped head that is driven slightly below the surface and covered with putty or the like.

brad
A small finishing nail.

double-headed nail
A nail used in building temporary structures, as scaffolding and formwork, having a flange on its shank to prevent it from being driven in all the way and to leave the head free for pulling. Also called **form nail**, **scaffold nail**.

concrete nail
A hardened-steel nail having a fluted or threaded shank and a diamond point for hammering into concrete or masonry. Also called **masonry nail**.

flooring nail
A nail for fastening floor boards, having a small conical head, a mechanically deformed shank, and a blunt diamond point.

ring-shank nail
A nail having a series of concentric grooves on its shank for increased holding power.

roofing nail
A nail having a barbed, threaded, or cement-coated shank and a broad, flat head for fastening shingles or the like.

drive screw
A metal fastener having a helically threaded shank that can be driven with a hammer and removed with a screw driver. Also called **screw nail**.

driftbolt
A spike having a round shank, driven into predrilled holes to fasten heavy timbers together. Also called **driftpin**.

staple
A U-shaped piece of metal or heavy wire with pointed ends, driven into a surface to secure sheet material or to hold a hasp, pin, or bolt.

corrugated fastener
A fastener consisting of a piece of corrugated sheet steel with one wavy edge sharpened, for uniting two pieces of wood, as in a miter joint. Also called **wiggle nail**.

round point
An acute, conical point on a nail or spike.

diamond point
An acute, pyramidal point on a nail or spike.

chisel point
A point on a nail or spike formed by two flat inclined sides meeting at a sharp angle.

face-nail
To fasten by nailing perpendicular to the face of the work.

toenail
To secure by nailing obliquely to the surfaces being joined. Alternate nails may be driven at opposite angles to provide increased holding power.

end-nail
To fasten by nailing into the end of a board, parallel to the grain of the wood. End-nailing provides poor resistance to withdrawal.

blind-nail
To secure by nailing in such a way that nailheads are not visible on the face of the work.

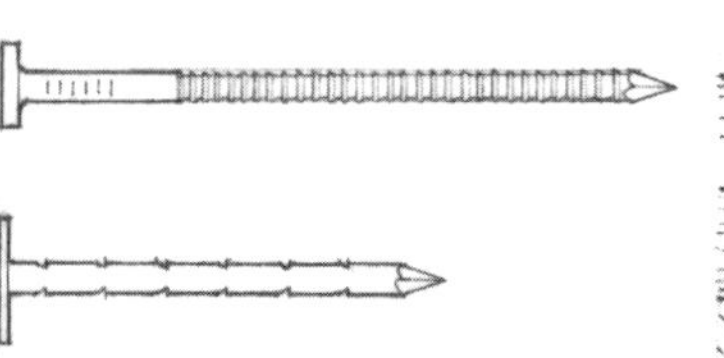

set
To sink a nailhead slightly below the surface with a nail set.

clinch
To secure a nail or screw in position by hammering down the protruding point.

nailing strip
A strip of wood or other partly yielding material attached to a hard surface, as of steel or concrete, so that objects may be fastened to the surface.

screw
A metal fastener having a tapered, helically threaded shank and a slotted head, designed to be driven into wood or the like by turning, as with a screwdriver.

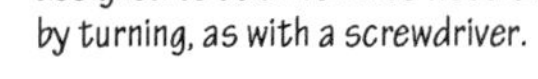

thread
The helical or spiral ridge of a screw, nut, or bolt.

pitch
The distance between two corresponding points on adjacent threads of a screw, nut, or bolt.

countersink
To enlarge the upper part of a drilled hole so that the head of screw or bolt will lie flush with or below the surface.

pilot hole
A guiding hole for a nail or screw, or for drilling a larger-size hole.

tap
To cut screw threads into an opening.

strip
To tear or damage the threads on a bolt or screw by applying too much force.

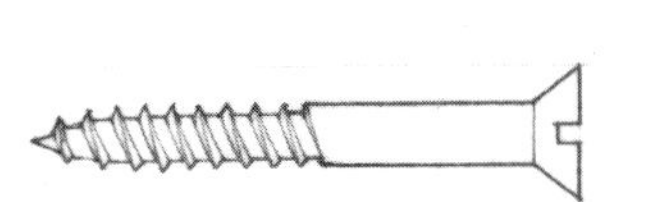

wood screw
A screw having a slotted head and a threaded point that permits it to form its own mating threads when driven into wood with a screwdriver.

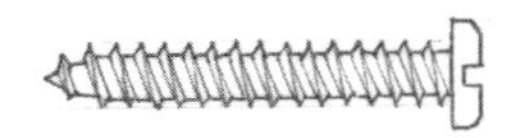

self-tapping screw
A coarse-threaded screw designed to tap its corresponding female thread as it is driven. Also called **tapping screw**.

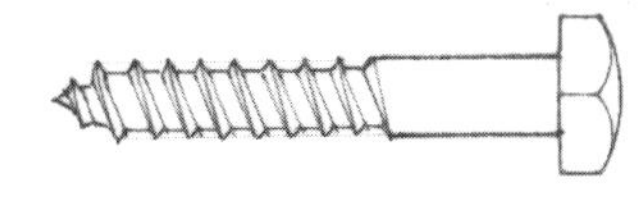

lag screw
A heavy, coarse-threaded screw having a square or hexagonal head driven by a wrench, used in areas inaccessible to the placement of a nut or where an exceptionally long bolt would be needed to penetrate a joint fully. Also called **coach screw, lag bolt**.

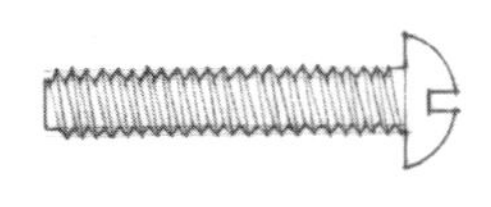

machine screw
A metal fastener used with a nut or driven into a tapped hole, having a straight, threaded shank and a slotted or Phillips head for turning with a screwdriver.

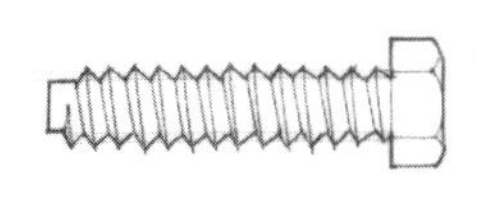

cap screw
A metal fastener for machine parts, having a straight, threaded shank held by threads tapped in the hole into which it is screwed.

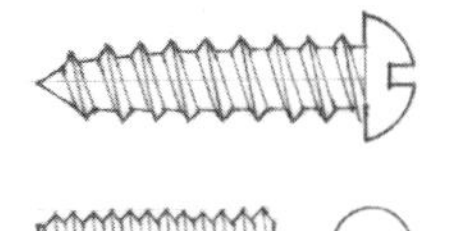

sheet-metal screw
A coarse-threaded screw for fastening sheet metal and other thin material.

setscrew
A screw, often without a head, threaded through a hole in one part tightly upon or into another part to prevent relative movement.

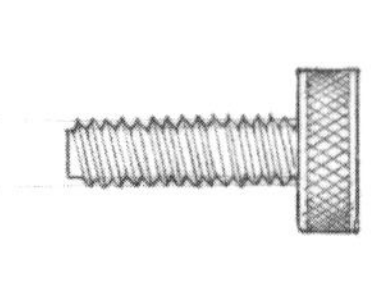

thumbscrew
A screw having a flattened, knurled head designed to be turned by the thumb and forefinger.

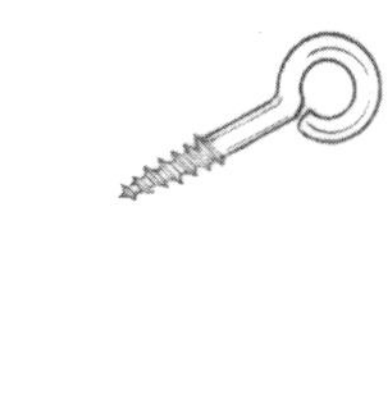

screw eye
A screw having a ring-shaped head.

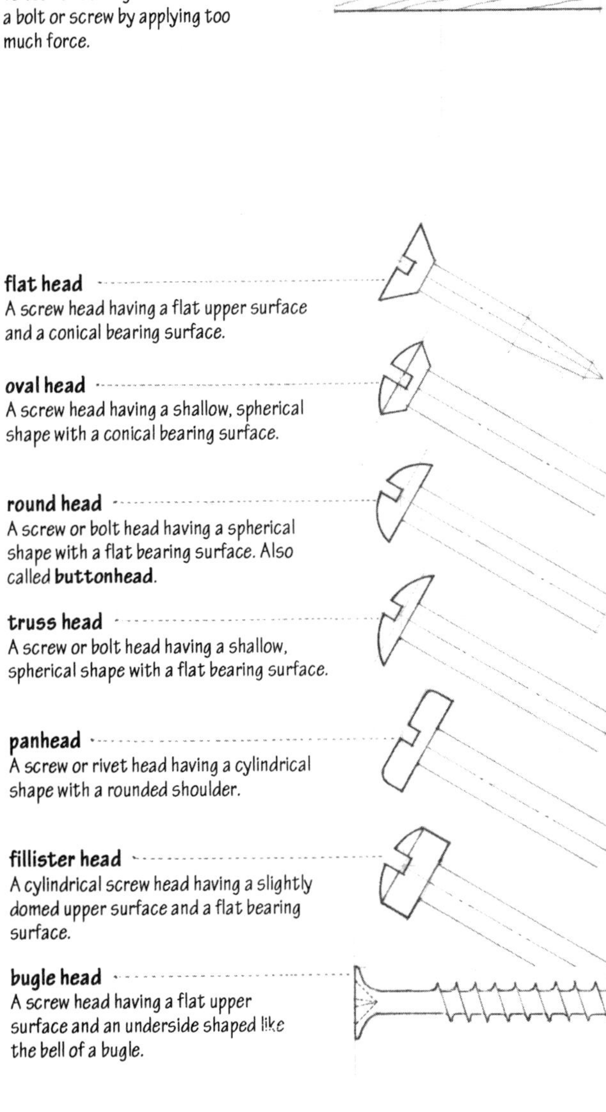

flat head
A screw head having a flat upper surface and a conical bearing surface.

oval head
A screw head having a shallow, spherical shape with a conical bearing surface.

round head
A screw or bolt head having a spherical shape with a flat bearing surface. Also called **buttonhead**.

truss head
A screw or bolt head having a shallow, spherical shape with a flat bearing surface.

panhead
A screw or rivet head having a cylindrical shape with a rounded shoulder.

fillister head
A cylindrical screw head having a slightly domed upper surface and a flat bearing surface.

bugle head
A screw head having a flat upper surface and an underside shaped like the bell of a bugle.

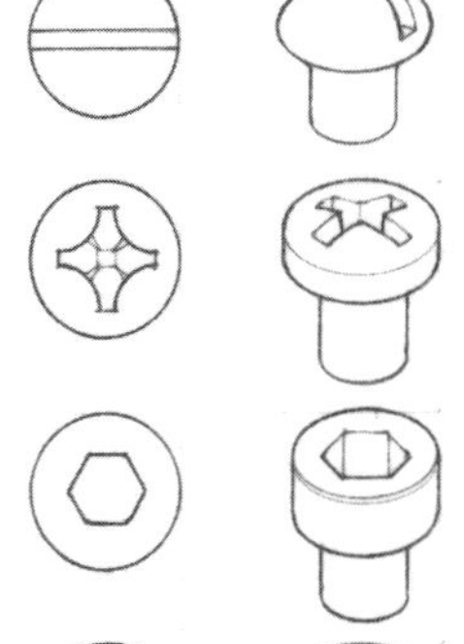

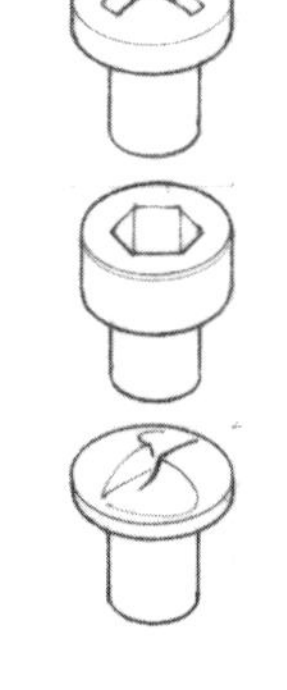

slotted head
A screw head having a single slot, driven by a flat-tipped screwdriver.

Phillips head
A screw head having two partial slots crossing at right angles, driven by a Phillips screwdriver.

Allen head
A screw head having an axial hexagonal recess, driven by an Allen wrench.

security head
A screw head designed to resist removal with a flat-tipped or Phillips screwdriver.

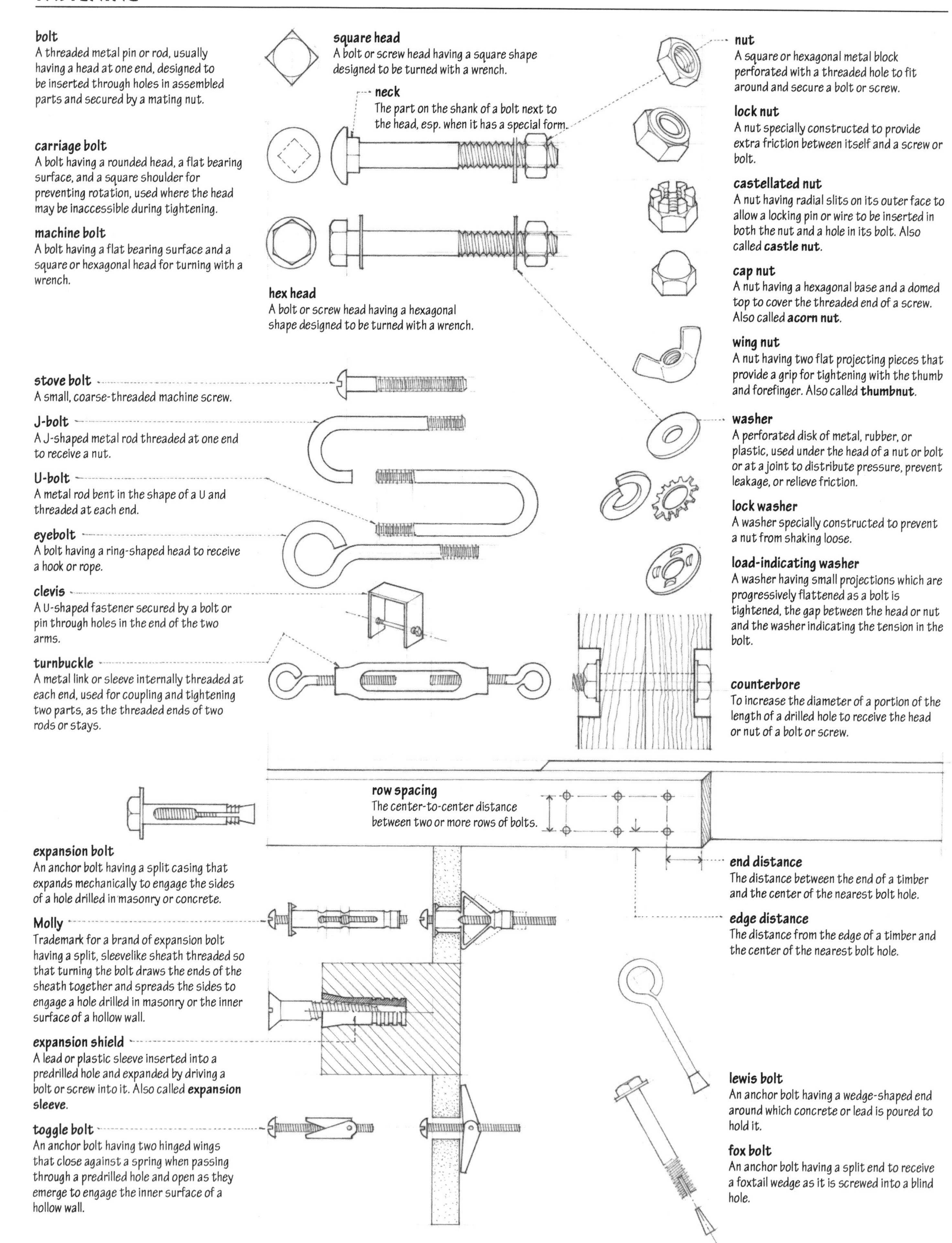

bolt
A threaded metal pin or rod, usually having a head at one end, designed to be inserted through holes in assembled parts and secured by a mating nut.

carriage bolt
A bolt having a rounded head, a flat bearing surface, and a square shoulder for preventing rotation, used where the head may be inaccessible during tightening.

machine bolt
A bolt having a flat bearing surface and a square or hexagonal head for turning with a wrench.

square head
A bolt or screw head having a square shape designed to be turned with a wrench.

neck
The part on the shank of a bolt next to the head, esp. when it has a special form.

hex head
A bolt or screw head having a hexagonal shape designed to be turned with a wrench.

nut
A square or hexagonal metal block perforated with a threaded hole to fit around and secure a bolt or screw.

lock nut
A nut specially constructed to provide extra friction between itself and a screw or bolt.

castellated nut
A nut having radial slits on its outer face to allow a locking pin or wire to be inserted in both the nut and a hole in its bolt. Also called **castle nut**.

cap nut
A nut having a hexagonal base and a domed top to cover the threaded end of a screw. Also called **acorn nut**.

wing nut
A nut having two flat projecting pieces that provide a grip for tightening with the thumb and forefinger. Also called **thumbnut**.

stove bolt
A small, coarse-threaded machine screw.

J-bolt
A J-shaped metal rod threaded at one end to receive a nut.

U-bolt
A metal rod bent in the shape of a U and threaded at each end.

eyebolt
A bolt having a ring-shaped head to receive a hook or rope.

clevis
A U-shaped fastener secured by a bolt or pin through holes in the end of the two arms.

turnbuckle
A metal link or sleeve internally threaded at each end, used for coupling and tightening two parts, as the threaded ends of two rods or stays.

washer
A perforated disk of metal, rubber, or plastic, used under the head of a nut or bolt or at a joint to distribute pressure, prevent leakage, or relieve friction.

lock washer
A washer specially constructed to prevent a nut from shaking loose.

load-indicating washer
A washer having small projections which are progressively flattened as a bolt is tightened, the gap between the head or nut and the washer indicating the tension in the bolt.

counterbore
To increase the diameter of a portion of the length of a drilled hole to receive the head or nut of a bolt or screw.

row spacing
The center-to-center distance between two or more rows of bolts.

end distance
The distance between the end of a timber and the center of the nearest bolt hole.

edge distance
The distance from the edge of a timber and the center of the nearest bolt hole.

expansion bolt
An anchor bolt having a split casing that expands mechanically to engage the sides of a hole drilled in masonry or concrete.

Molly
Trademark for a brand of expansion bolt having a split, sleevelike sheath threaded so that turning the bolt draws the ends of the sheath together and spreads the sides to engage a hole drilled in masonry or the inner surface of a hollow wall.

expansion shield
A lead or plastic sleeve inserted into a predrilled hole and expanded by driving a bolt or screw into it. Also called **expansion sleeve**.

toggle bolt
An anchor bolt having two hinged wings that close against a spring when passing through a predrilled hole and open as they emerge to engage the inner surface of a hollow wall.

lewis bolt
An anchor bolt having a wedge-shaped end around which concrete or lead is poured to hold it.

fox bolt
An anchor bolt having a split end to receive a foxtail wedge as it is screwed into a blind hole.

hanger
Any of various U-shaped metal brackets for supporting the end of a beam, joist, purlin, or truss at a girder or wall. The supported member transfers its reaction to the hanger through bearing, but load transfer to the supporting member is through shear in the special nails securing the hanger.

beam seat
A U-shaped metal bracket for anchoring a timber beam to a concrete support.

post cap
A U-shaped metal bracket for securing a timber beam to a supporting post. Also called **column cap**.

post base
A U-shaped metal bracket for supporting and anchoring a timber post to its base or foundation. Also called **column base**.

dowel
A cylindrical pin fitting snugly into holes in two adjacent pieces to prevent their slipping or to align them. Also called **dowel pin**.

toothed plate
A sheet-metal plate punched to produce a closely spaced grid of protruding teeth, used as a splice plate in the manufacture of light wood trusses.

spike grid
A flat or singly curved grid of spikes for joining heavy timbers, held in place by a single bolt. The resulting joint is resistant to loosening due to vibration, impact, and reversible lateral loads.

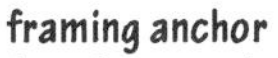

framing anchor
Any of various sheet-metal connectors for joining light wood framing members, using special nails which are loaded laterally rather than in withdrawal.

hurricane anchor
A framing anchor for tying a rafter or truss to a wall plate and securing it against lateral and uplifting wind and seismic forces. Also called **hurricane tie**.

joist anchor
A metal tie strap for securing the joists of a floor or roof diaphragm to a concrete or masonry wall in order to transmit lateral wind or seismic forces.

floor anchor
A metal tie strap for restraining a floor of a light wood frame structure against uplifting wind or seismic forces.

sill anchor
A framing anchor for securing a sill plate to a concrete slab or foundation wall.

holddown
A metal device for restraining a wood frame structure against uplifting wind or seismic forces, consisting of a stiffened steel angle bolted to a wall stud and secured by a threaded rod to a concrete foundation.

timber connector
A metal ring, plate, or grid for transferring shear between the faces of two timber members, used with a single bolt that serves to restrain and clamp the assembly together. Timber connectors are more efficient than bolts or lag screws used alone since they enlarge the area of wood over which a load is distributed.

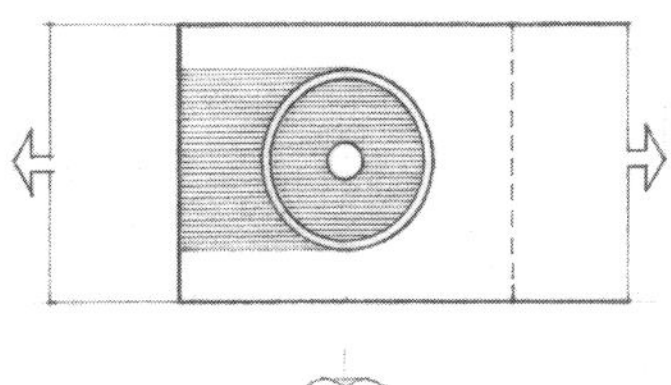

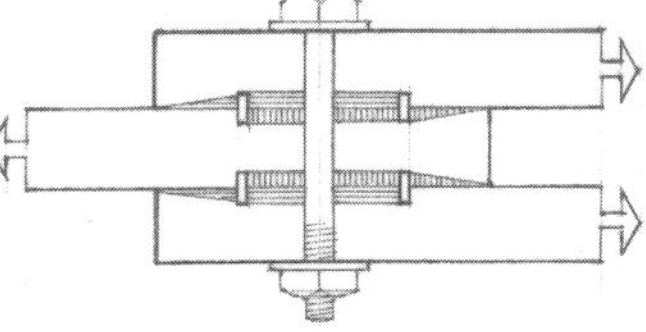

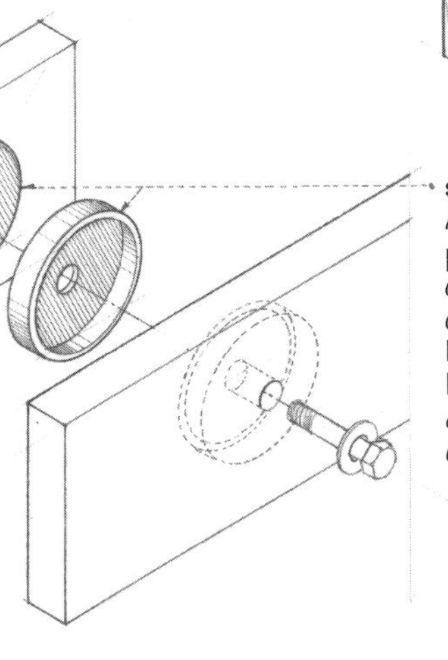

shear plate
A timber connector consisting of a round plate of malleable iron inserted into a corresponding groove, flush with the face of a timber, and held in place by a single bolt. Shear plates are used in back-to-back pairs to develop shear resistance in demountable wood-to-wood connections, or singly in a wood-to-metal connection.

split-ring
A timber connector consisting of a metal ring inserted into corresponding grooves cut into the faces of the joining members and held in place by a single bolt. The tongue-and-groove split in the ring permits it to deform slightly under loading and maintain bearing at all surfaces, while the beveled cross section eases insertion and ensures a tight-fitting joint after the ring is fully seated in the grooves.

solder
To unite two pieces of metal by applying any of various nonferrous solders, usually a tin-lead alloy, at a temperature below 800°F (427°C).

solder
Any of various fusible alloys applied in a molten state to the joint between two metal parts to unite them without heating the parts to the melting point. The molten solder flows into a joint by capillary attraction.

braze
To unite two pieces of metal by applying any of various nonferrous solders, usually a copper-zinc alloy, at a temperature above 800°F (427°C).

weld
To unite or fuse two pieces of metal by heating and allowing the metals to flow together, sometimes with pressure and the addition of an intermediate or filler metal.

gas welding
Any of a group of welding processes utilizing the heat produced by the combustion of a oxygen and a fuel gas, as acetylene.

arc welding
Any of a group of welding processes utilizing the heat of an arc between an electrode and the base metal.

arc
A sustained luminous discharge of electricity across a gap in a circuit or between two electrodes. Also called **electric arc**.

shielded metal arc welding
A method of arc welding using a consumable metal electrode that releases an inert gas to form a shield around the arc. This shield protects the weld area from oxygen and nitrogen in the air that would cause rapid oxidation of the liquid metal.

filler metal
The metal that is added during a welding, brazing, or soldering process, having a melting point either approximately the same as or below that of the metals being welded.

base metal
The principal metal to be welded, brazed, soldered, or cut, as distinguished from filler metal.

bead
A continuous deposit of fused metal. Also called **weld bead**.

fillet weld
A weld with a triangular cross section joining two surfaces that meet in an interior right angle.

lap weld
A weld made along the seams of two overlapping pieces of metal.

toe
The junction between the base metal and the face of a weld.

root
The point at which the back or bottom of a weld meets the base metal.

throat
The distance from the root of a weld to the face of the base metal.

welding rod
A wire or rod of filler metal used in gas-welding and brazing processes, and in those arc-welding processes in which the electrode does not furnish the filler metal.

flux
A substance, as rosin, applied to remove oxides from and prevent further oxidation of metal surfaces to be joined by welding, brazing, or soldering.

inert-gas shielded arc welding
A method of arc welding in which the weld area is shielded by the continuous flow of an inert gas from an external source, the filler metal being supplied by a consumable metal electrode or by a separate welding rod.

flux-cored arc welding
A method of arc welding using a tubular steel electrode containing a core of vaporizing flux that forms a gaseous shield around the weld area.

submerged arc welding
A method of arc welding in which the weld area is shielded by a blanket of fusible, granular metal that melts to form a layer of protective slag. The filler metal may be supplied by a consumable electrode or by a separate welding rod.

resistance welding
Any of a group of welding processes utilizing the heat generated by resistance to the passage of a electric current.

butt weld
A weld between two pieces of metal butted together.

partial-penetration weld
A butt weld having a depth less than the thickness of the smaller of the two members being joined.

full-penetration weld
A butt weld having a depth equal to the thickness of the smaller of the two members being joined.

puddle weld
A weld made by burning a hole in a piece of sheet metal and filling with a small pool of molten metal.

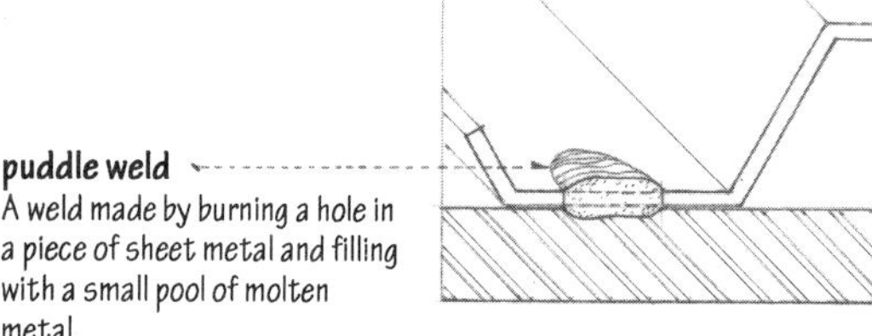

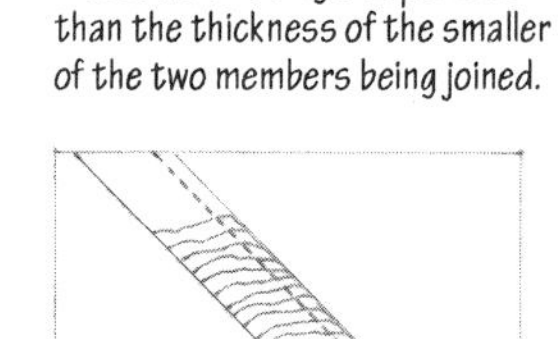

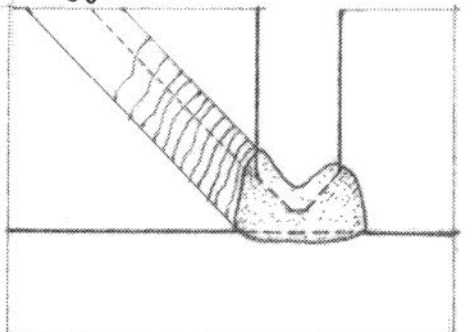

single-bevel weld
A groove weld in which the edge of one abutting member is beveled from one side.

double-bevel weld
A groove weld in which the edge of one abutting member is beveled from both sides.

single-vee weld
A groove weld in which the edge of each abutting member is beveled from the same side.

double-vee weld
A groove weld in which the edge of each abutting member is beveled from both sides.

groove weld
A weld made in a preformed indentation between two abutting pieces of metal.

rivet
A metal pin having a head at one end, used for uniting two or more plates by passing the shank through a hole in each piece and hammering down the plain end to form a second head.

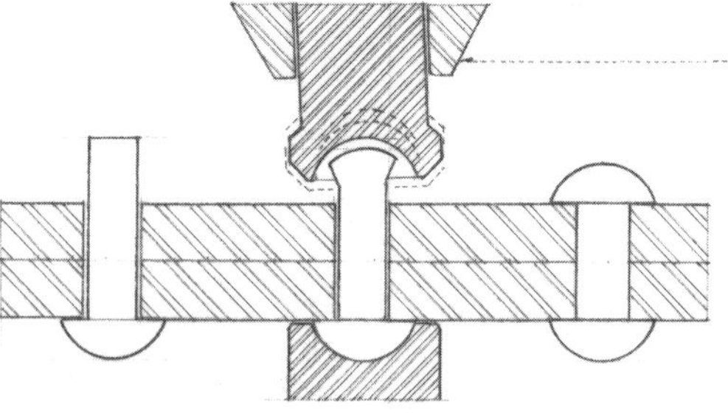

pneumatic riveter
A pneumatic hammer used with a rivet set to form the second head of a rivet.

rivet set
A tool for shaping the second head of a rivet.

drift
A round, tapering piece of metal for enlarging or aligning holes to receive rivets or bolts. Also called **driftpin**.

aligning punch
A drift for bringing holes in line to receive a rivet or bolt.

dolly
A tool for receiving and holding the head of a rivet while the other end is being headed.

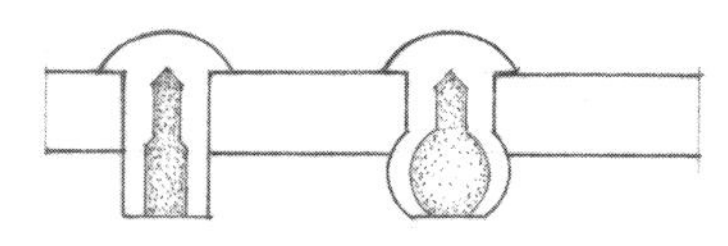

explosive rivet
A rivet for a joint accessible from one side only, having an explosive-filled shank that is detonated by striking the head with a hammer to expand the shank on the far side of the hole.

A framed opening made in a chimney to hold an open fire.

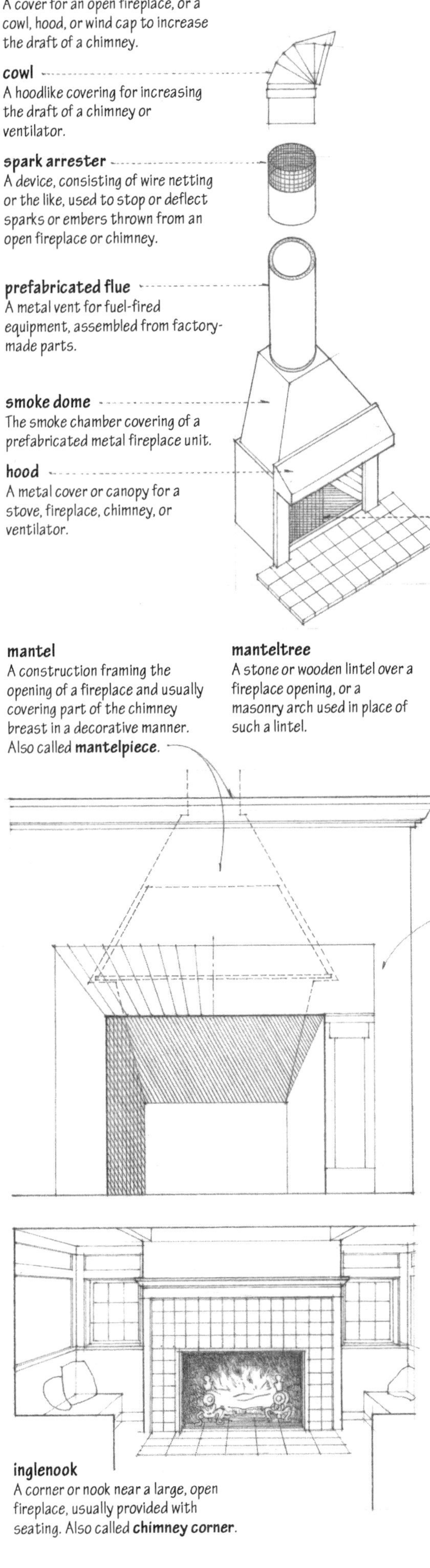

bonnet
A cover for an open fireplace, or a cowl, hood, or wind cap to increase the draft of a chimney.

cowl
A hoodlike covering for increasing the draft of a chimney or ventilator.

spark arrester
A device, consisting of wire netting or the like, used to stop or deflect sparks or embers thrown from an open fireplace or chimney.

prefabricated flue
A metal vent for fuel-fired equipment, assembled from factory-made parts.

smoke dome
The smoke chamber covering of a prefabricated metal fireplace unit.

hood
A metal cover or canopy for a stove, fireplace, chimney, or ventilator.

chimney
A vertical, incombustible structure containing a flue through which the smoke and gases of a fire or furnace are carried off to the outside and by means of which a draft is created, esp. the part of such a structure that rises above a roof.

smokestack
A pipe for the escape of the smoke or gases of combustion.

draft
A current of air in any enclosed space, as in a room, chimney, or stove, caused by the difference in temperature or pressure.

downdraft
A downward current of air in a chimney or flue, often carrying smoke with it.

fire screen
A screen placed in front of a fireplace to prevent sparks or embers from entering the room.

chimney cap
A raised cover for a chimney, usually in the form of a slab or cornice.

chimney pot
A cylindrical pipe of earthenware or metal, fitted on top of a chimney to increase draft and disperse smoke.

flue lining
A smooth-surfaced unit of heat-resistant fire clay or lightweight concrete, having a square, rectangular, or oval section, used for lining the flue of a chimney.

flue
An incombustible passage or duct for smoke in a chimney.

pargeting
A smooth lining of mortar or plaster for a chimney flue. Also, **parget**.

mantel
A construction framing the opening of a fireplace and usually covering part of the chimney breast in a decorative manner. Also called **mantelpiece**.

manteltree
A stone or wooden lintel over a fireplace opening, or a masonry arch used in place of such a lintel.

chimney breast
A part of a chimney or fireplace that projects out from a wall, usually inside a building.

chimney arch
An arch over a fireplace opening, supporting the breast.

chimney bar
A steel lintel for carrying the masonry above the fireplace opening. Also called **camber bar**, **turning bar**.

chimney cheek
The sides of a fireplace opening supporting the mantel.

hearth
The floor of a fireplace, usually of brick, tile, or stone, often extending a short distance into a room.

back hearth
The part of the hearth that is contained within the fireplace itself. Also called **inner hearth**.

front hearth
The part of the hearth that projects into the room. Also called **outer hearth**.

inglenook
A corner or nook near a large, open fireplace, usually provided with seating. Also called **chimney corner**.

draft
A device for regulating the current of air in a stove or fireplace.

damper
A movable plate for regulating the draft in a fireplace, stove, or furnace.

smoke chamber
An enlarged area between the throat of a fireplace and the flue of a chimney.

smoke shelf
A ledge at the bottom of a smoke chamber, so made as to deflect or break the downdrafts from the chimney.

throat
The narrow opening between a fireplace and its flue or smoke chamber, often closed with a damper.

firebox
The chamber containing the fire of a fireplace.

trimmer arch
An arch, usually of brick and in the form of half of a segmental arch, between a chimney and a header in a floor structure to support a hearth.

ashpit
A receptacle in the bottom of a fireplace or firebox for the collection and removal of ashes.

ashpit door
A cast-iron door providing access to an ashpit for removing ashes, or to a chimney for removing soot.

The measures taken to prevent fire or minimize the loss of life or property resulting from a fire, including limiting fire loads and hazards, confining the spread of fire with fire-resistant construction, the use of fire detection and extinguishing systems, the establishment of adequate firefighting services, and the training of building occupants in fire safety and evacuation procedures.

fire hazard
Any condition that increases the likelihood of a fire, obstructs access to firefighting equipment, or delays the egress of occupants in the event of fire.

fire load
The amount of combustible material in a building, measured in pounds per square foot of floor area.

combustible
Of or pertaining to a material capable of igniting and burning.

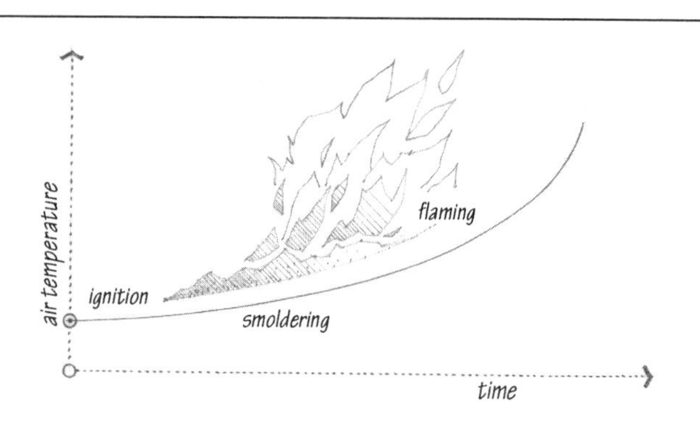

ignition point
The lowest temperature at which a substance will undergo spontaneous combustion and continue to burn without additional application of external heat.

flash point
The lowest temperature at which a combustible liquid will give off sufficient vapor to ignite momentarily when exposed to flame.

fire-rated
Noting or pertaining to a material, assembly, or construction having a fire-resistance rating required by its use. Also, **fire-resistive**.

fire-resistance rating
The time in hours a material or assembly can be expected to withstand exposure to fire without collapsing, developing any openings which permit the passage of flame or hot gases, or exceeding a specified temperature on the side away from the fire, determined by subjecting a full-size specimen to temperatures according to a standard time-temperature curve.

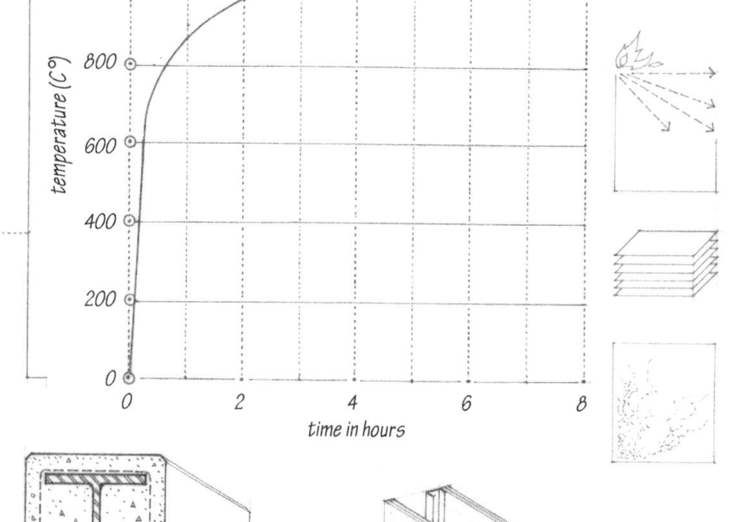

tunnel test
A test measuring the time it takes for a controlled flame to spread across the face of a test specimen, the amount of fuel the material contributes to the fire, and the density of the smoke developed by the fire. Also called **Steiner tunnel test**.

flame-spread rating
A rating of how quickly a fire can spread along the surface of an interior finish material. Red oak flooring has a flame-spread rating of 100 while a cement-asbestos board has a rating of 0.

fuel-contribution rating
A rating of the amount of combustible substances an interior finish material can contribute to a fire.

smoke-developed rating
A rating of the amount of smoke an interior finish material can produce when it burns. Materials having a smoke-developed rating above 450 are not permitted to be used inside buildings.

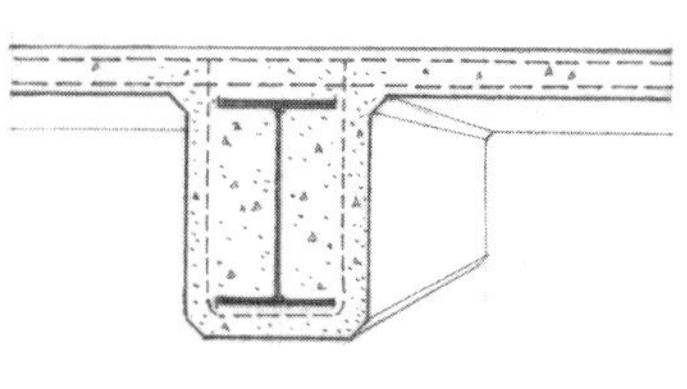

concrete

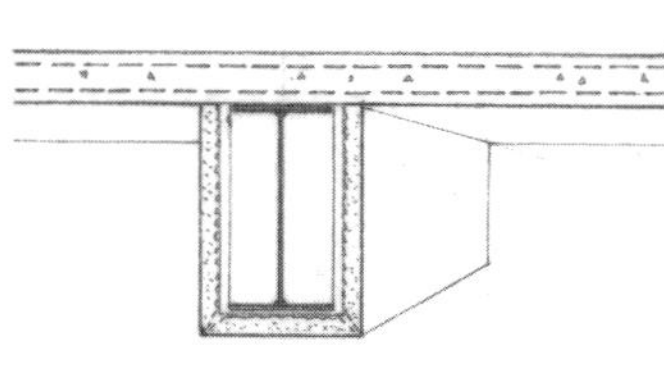

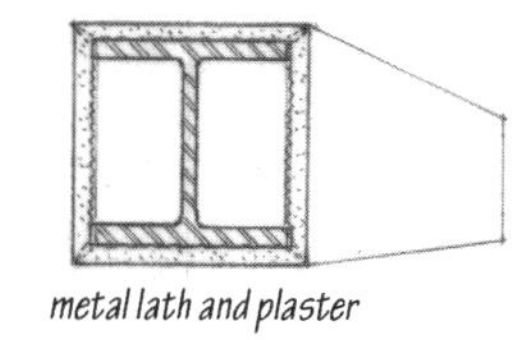

metal lath and plaster

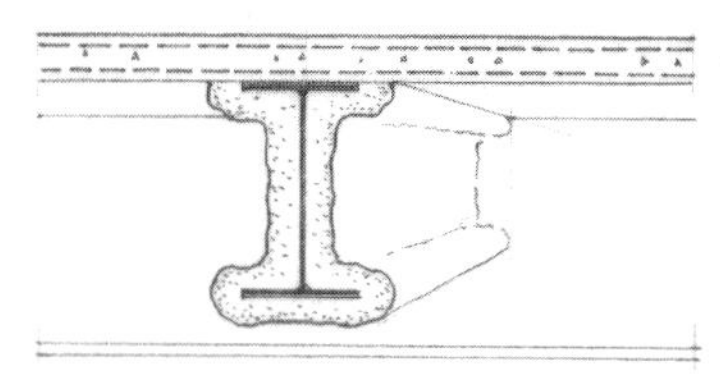

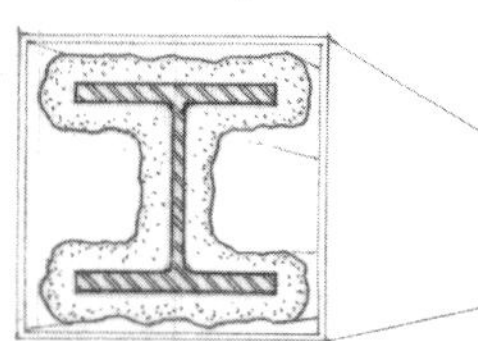

spray-on fireproofing
A mixture of mineral fibers and an inorganic binder, applied by air pressure with a spray gun to provide a thermal barrier to the heat of a fire.

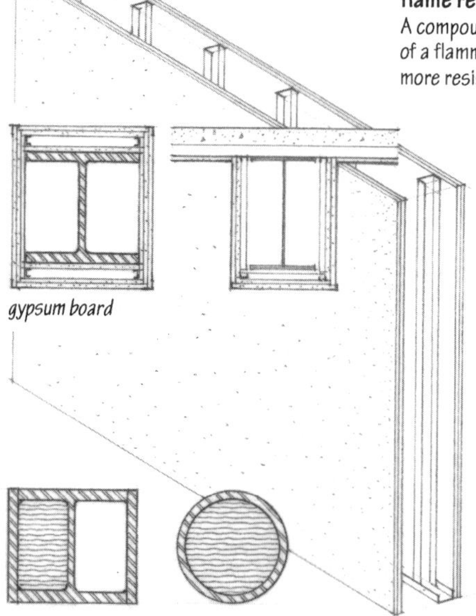

gypsum board

flame retardant
A compound used to raise the ignition point of a flammable material, thus making it more resistant to fire.

fireproofing
Any of various materials, as concrete, gypsum, or mineral fiber, used in making a structural member or system resistant to damage or destruction by fire.

intumescent paint
A coating that, when exposed to the heat of a fire, swells to form a thick insulating layer of inert gas bubbles that retards flame spread and combustion.

liquid-filled column
A hollow structural-steel column filled with water to increase its fire resistance. If exposed to flame, the water absorbs heat, rises by convection to remove the heat, and is replaced with cooler water from a storage tank or a city water main.

fire zone
A zone of a city within which certain construction types are prohibited because of fire hazards present in the zone.

firebreak
An open space established to prevent the spread of fire from a building, a group of buildings, or an area of a city to another.

fire separation
Any floor, wall, or roof-ceiling construction having the required fire-resistance rating to confine the spread of fire.

occupancy separation
A vertical or horizontal construction having the required fire-resistance rating to prevent the spread of fire from one occupancy to another in a mixed-occupancy building.

distance separation
The separation required between an exterior wall of a building and a property line, the center line of an adjacent street or public space, or the exterior wall of an adjacent building, all measured at right angles to the exterior wall.

fire area
An area of a building enclosed by fire-rated construction capable of confining the spread of fire.

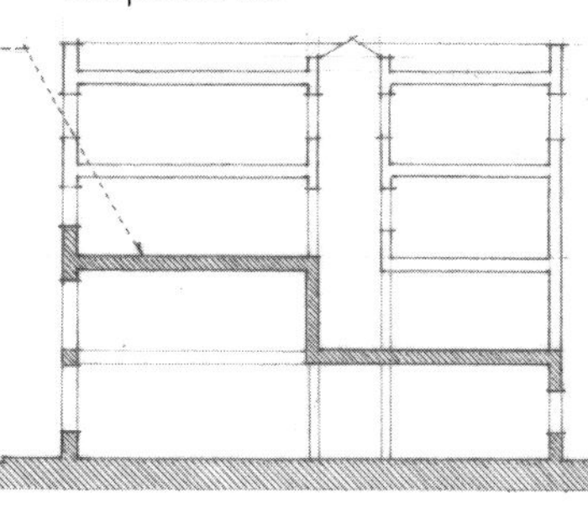

fire wall
A wall having the required fire-resistance rating to prevent the spread of fire from one part of a building to another, extending from the foundation to a parapet above the roof and having all openings restricted to a certain percentage of the wall length and protected by a self-closing or automatic-closing fire assembly. Each portion of a building separated by one or more fire walls may be considered a separate building when calculating the floor area and height allowed by a building code.

draft stop
A fire-rated partition dividing an enclosed attic space of combustible construction, or the concealed space between a suspended ceiling and a wood-frame floor above.

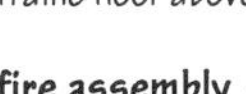

fire assembly
The assembly of a fire door, fire window, or fire damper, including all required hardware, anchorage, frames, and sills.

protected opening
An opening in a wall, floor, or roof-ceiling construction that is fitted with a fire assembly having the required fire-resistance rating for its location and use.

self-closing fire assembly
A fire assembly that is normally kept in a closed position and is equipped with an approved device to insure closing and latching after having been opened for use.

automatic-closing fire assembly
A fire assembly that may remain in an open position and will close automatically if subjected to an increase in temperature or actuated by a smoke detector.

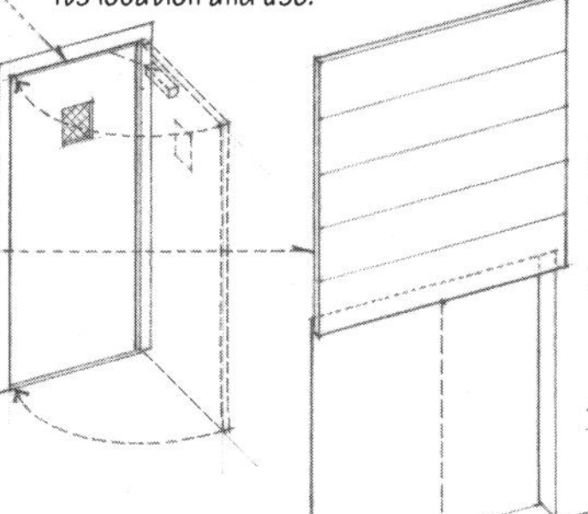

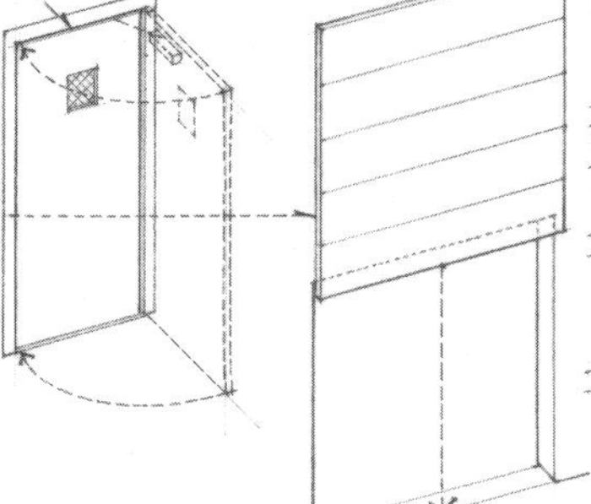

class A
Classification for a fire assembly having a 3-hour fire-resistance rating for protecting openings in 3-hour or 4-hour fire walls and occupancy separations.

class B
Classification for a fire assembly having a 1-hour or 1 ½-hour fire-resistance rating for protecting openings in 1-hour or 2-hour fire separations, exit stairways, and vertical shafts.

class C
Classification for a fire assembly having a ¾-hour fire-resistance rating for protecting openings in 1-hour walls, corridors, and hazardous areas.

class D
Classification for a fire assembly having a 1 ½-hour fire-resistance rating for protecting openings in exterior walls subject to severe fire exposure from outside the building.

class E
Classification for a fire assembly having a ¾-hour fire-resistance rating for protecting openings in exterior walls subject to light or moderate fire exposure from outside the building.

UL label
A label affixed to a building material, component, or device with the authorization of Underwriters' Laboratories, Inc., indicating that the product (a) has a rating based on performance tests of such products; (b) is from a production lot found by examination to be made from materials and by processes essentially identical to those of representative products which have been subjected to appropriate fire, electrical hazard, or other tests for safety; and (c) is subject to the reexamination service of UL.

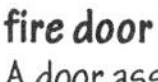

labeled
Of or pertaining to a building material or assembly having a fire-resistance rating certified by Underwriters' Laboratories, Inc. or other recognized testing laboratory.

fire door
A door assembly, including all required hardware, anchorage, frames and sills, having the required fire-resistance rating for its location and use.

fire window
A window assembly, including all required hardware, anchorage, frames and sills, having the required fire-resistance rating for its location and use.

smoke vent
A vent designed to open automatically in the event of fire in order to remove smoke and heat from a building.

fire damper
A damper that closes an air duct automatically in the event of fire to restrict the passage of fire and smoke, required where a duct penetrates a fire wall, fire-rated shaft, or other fire separation.

fusible link
A link made of a fusible metal. When exposed to the heat of a fire, the link melts and causes a fire door, fire damper, or the like to close.

fire-alarm system
An electrical system installed in a building to automatically sound an alarm when actuated by a fire-detection system.

fire-detection system
A system of thermostats or other approved sensors for detecting the presence of fire and automatically signaling an alarm.

smoke detector
An electronic fire alarm that is activated by the presence of smoke.

standpipe
A water pipe extending vertically through a building to supply fire hoses at every floor.

wet standpipe
A standpipe containing water under pressure and fitted with fire hoses for emergency use by building occupants.

dry standpipe
A standpipe containing no water and used by the fire department to connect fire hoses to a fire hydrant or pumper truck.

fire hose
A heavy-duty hose for use in fighting a fire.

hydrant
An upright pipe with one or more nozzles or spouts for drawing water from a main, esp. for fighting fires. Also called **fire hydrant**, **fireplug**.

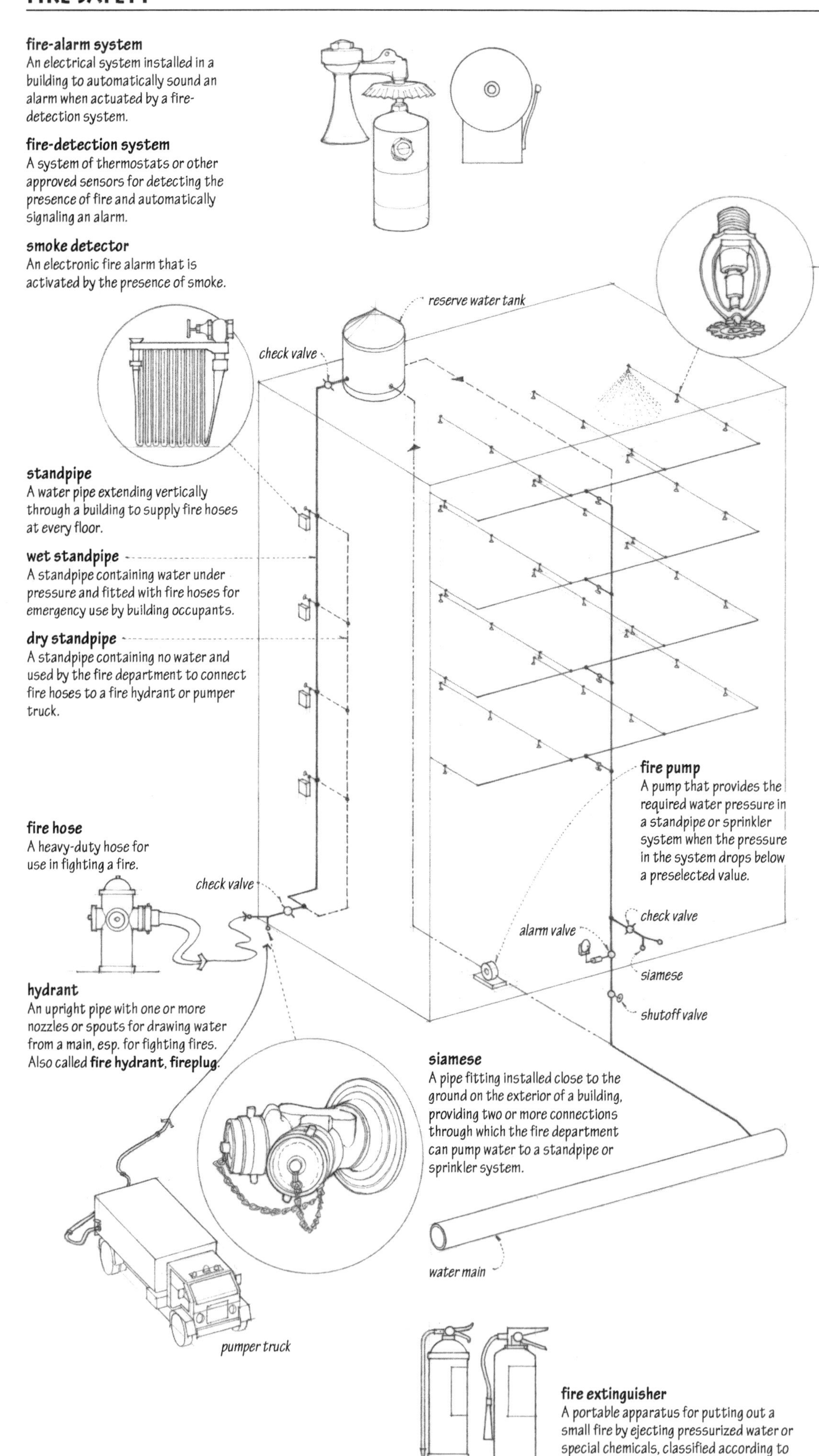

fire pump
A pump that provides the required water pressure in a standpipe or sprinkler system when the pressure in the system drops below a preselected value.

siamese
A pipe fitting installed close to the ground on the exterior of a building, providing two or more connections through which the fire department can pump water to a standpipe or sprinkler system.

fire extinguisher
A portable apparatus for putting out a small fire by ejecting pressurized water or special chemicals, classified according to the type of fire it is able to extinguish.

sprinkler system
Apparatus for automatically extinguishing fires in a building, consisting of a system of pipes in or below the ceilings, connected to a suitable water supply, and supplied with valves or sprinkler heads made to open automatically at a certain temperature.

sprinklered
Of or pertaining to a building or building area that has or is protected by a properly maintained sprinkler system.

sprinkler head
A nozzle in a sprinkler system for dispersing a stream or spray of water, usually controlled by a fusible link that melts at a predetermined temperature.

automatic fire-extinguishing system
A system of devices and equipment which automatically detects a fire and discharges an approved fire-extinguishing agent onto or in the area of a fire.

wet-pipe system
A sprinkler system containing water at sufficient pressure to provide an immediate, continuous discharge through sprinkler heads that open automatically in the event of fire.

dry-pipe system
A sprinkler system containing pressurized air that is released when a sprinkler head opens in the event of fire, allowing water to flow through the piping and out the opened nozzle. Dry-pipe systems are used where the piping is subject to freezing.

preaction system
A dry-pipe sprinkler system through which water flow is controlled by a valve operated by fire-detection devices more sensitive than those in the sprinkler heads. Preaction systems are used when an accidental discharge would damage valuable materials.

deluge system
A sprinkler system having sprinkler heads open at all times, through which water flow is controlled by a valve operated by a heat-, smoke-, or flame-sensing device.

class A fire
A fire involving ordinary combustible materials, as wood, paper and cloth, on which the quenching or cooling effect of water is of primary importance.

class B fire
A fire involving flammable liquids, as gasoline, oil and grease, which must be extinguished by excluding air and inhibiting the release of combustible vapors.

class C fire
A fire involving live electrical equipment, which requires a nonconducting extinguishing medium.

class D fire
A fire involving certain combustible metals, as magnesium or sodium, which requires a nonreactive, heat-absorbing extinguishing medium.

exit access
That portion of a means of egress that leads to an exit. Building codes specify the maximum distance of travel to an exit and the minimum distance between exits when two or more are required.

well
A shaft for air, light, stairs, or an elevator, extending vertically through the floors of a building.

exit light
An illuminated sign identifying a required exit.

emergency lighting
A lighting system designed to supply the illumination required for safe egress from a building in the event of a power failure.

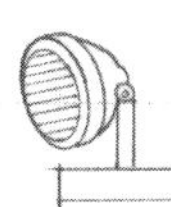
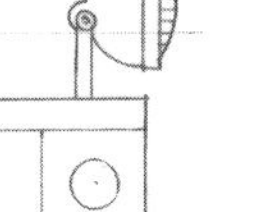

occupant load
The total number of persons that may occupy a building or portion thereof at any one time, determined by dividing the floor area assigned to a particular use by the square feet per occupant permitted in that use. Building codes use occupant load to establish the required number and width of exits for a building.

horizontal exit
A passage through or around a wall constructed as required for an occupancy separation, protected by an automatic-closing fire door, and leading to an area of refuge in the same building or on approximately the same level in an adjacent building.

area of refuge
An area affording safety from fire or smoke coming from the area from which escape is made.

exit corridor
A passageway serving as a required exit, enclosed by walls of fire-resistive construction. Building codes limit the length of dead-end corridors.

exit door
A door providing access to a means of egress, swinging in the direction of exit travel, and usually equipped with a panic bar.

exit passageway
A means of egress connecting a required exit or exit court with a public way, having no openings other than required exits and enclosed by fire-resistive construction as required for the walls, floors, and ceiling of the building served.

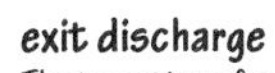

exit discharge
That portion of a means of egress that leads from an exit to an exit court or public way.

means of egress
A continuous path of travel from any point in a building to the outside at ground level.

exit
An enclosed and protected path of escape for the occupants of a building in the event of fire, leading from an exit access to an exit discharge.

smokeproof enclosure
The enclosing of an exit stairway by walls of fire-resistive construction, accessible by a vestibule or by an open exterior balcony, and ventilated by natural or mechanical means to limit the penetration of smoke and heat. Building codes usually require one or more of the exit stairways for a high-rise building be protected by a smokeproof enclosure.

exit stairway
A stairway leading to an exit passageway, an exit court, or public way, enclosed by fire-resistive construction with self-closing fire doors that swing in the direction of exit travel.

exterior exit balcony
A landing or porch projecting from the wall of a building and serving as a required means of egress.

fire escape
An exit stairway down an outside wall of a building, constructed to the same standards as an interior exit stairway.

exterior exit
An exit door opening directly to an exit court or public way.

exit court
A yard or court providing egress to a public way for one or more required exits.

public way
A street, alley, or similar parcel of land open to the sky and deeded, dedicated, or otherwise permanently appropriated for the free passage and use of the general public.

FLOOR

The level, base surface of a room or hall upon which one stands or walks.

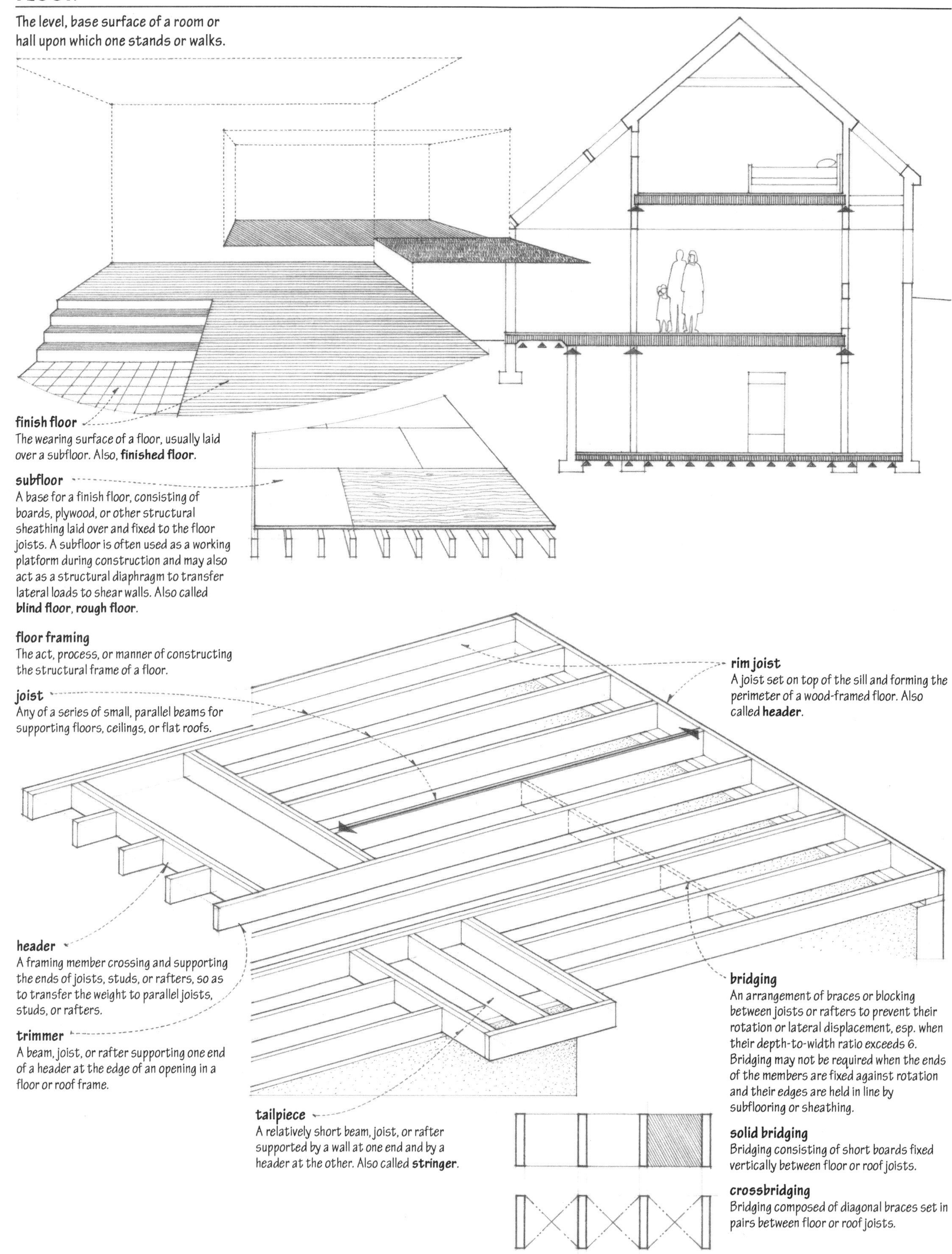

finish floor
The wearing surface of a floor, usually laid over a subfloor. Also, **finished floor**.

subfloor
A base for a finish floor, consisting of boards, plywood, or other structural sheathing laid over and fixed to the floor joists. A subfloor is often used as a working platform during construction and may also act as a structural diaphragm to transfer lateral loads to shear walls. Also called **blind floor**, **rough floor**.

floor framing
The act, process, or manner of constructing the structural frame of a floor.

joist
Any of a series of small, parallel beams for supporting floors, ceilings, or flat roofs.

rim joist
A joist set on top of the sill and forming the perimeter of a wood-framed floor. Also called **header**.

header
A framing member crossing and supporting the ends of joists, studs, or rafters, so as to transfer the weight to parallel joists, studs, or rafters.

trimmer
A beam, joist, or rafter supporting one end of a header at the edge of an opening in a floor or roof frame.

tailpiece
A relatively short beam, joist, or rafter supported by a wall at one end and by a header at the other. Also called **stringer**.

bridging
An arrangement of braces or blocking between joists or rafters to prevent their rotation or lateral displacement, esp. when their depth-to-width ratio exceeds 6. Bridging may not be required when the ends of the members are fixed against rotation and their edges are held in line by subflooring or sheathing.

solid bridging
Bridging consisting of short boards fixed vertically between floor or roof joists.

crossbridging
Bridging composed of diagonal braces set in pairs between floor or roof joists.

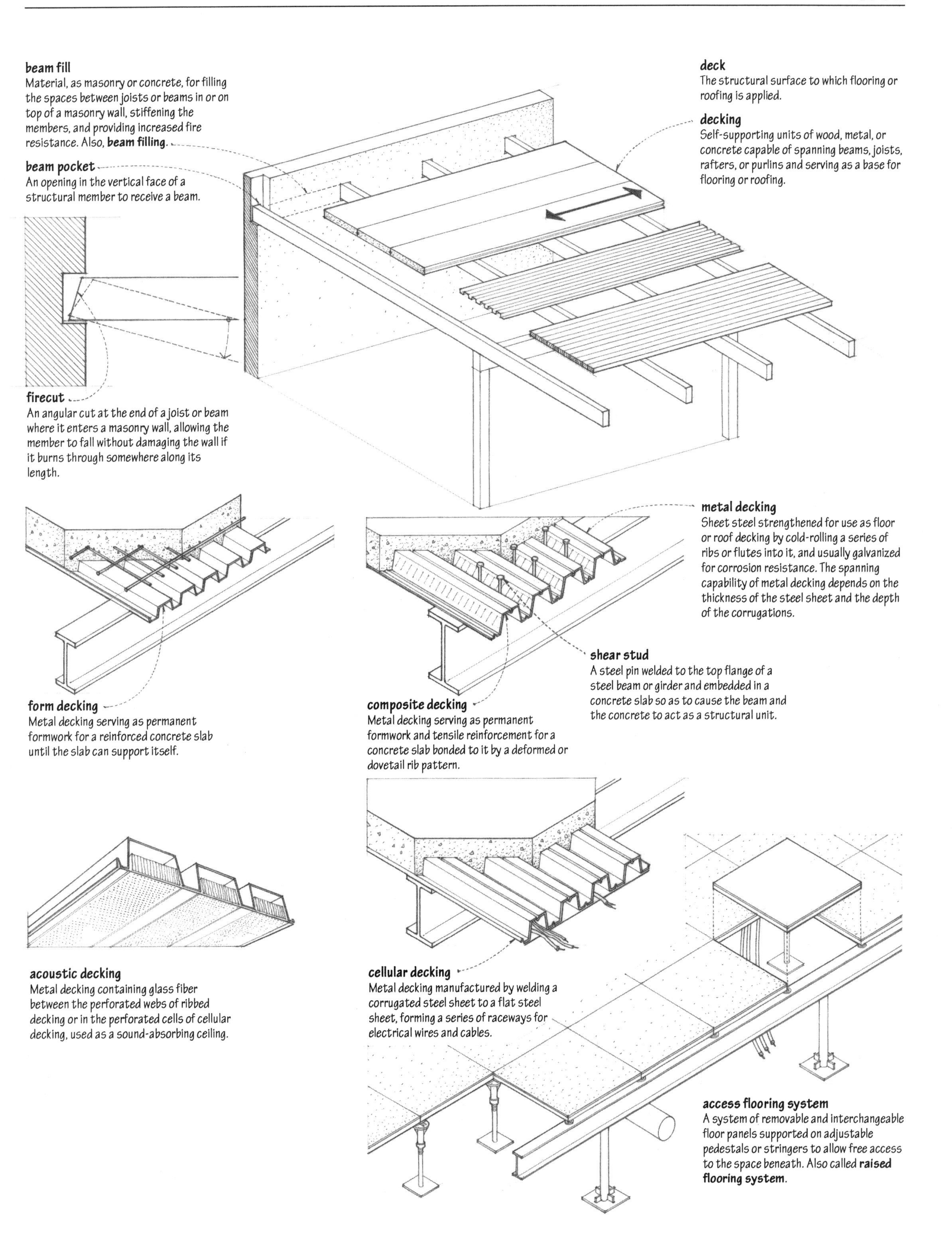

beam fill
Material, as masonry or concrete, for filling the spaces between joists or beams in or on top of a masonry wall, stiffening the members, and providing increased fire resistance. Also, **beam filling.**

beam pocket
An opening in the vertical face of a structural member to receive a beam.

firecut
An angular cut at the end of a joist or beam where it enters a masonry wall, allowing the member to fall without damaging the wall if it burns through somewhere along its length.

deck
The structural surface to which flooring or roofing is applied.

decking
Self-supporting units of wood, metal, or concrete capable of spanning beams, joists, rafters, or purlins and serving as a base for flooring or roofing.

metal decking
Sheet steel strengthened for use as floor or roof decking by cold-rolling a series of ribs or flutes into it, and usually galvanized for corrosion resistance. The spanning capability of metal decking depends on the thickness of the steel sheet and the depth of the corrugations.

form decking
Metal decking serving as permanent formwork for a reinforced concrete slab until the slab can support itself.

composite decking
Metal decking serving as permanent formwork and tensile reinforcement for a concrete slab bonded to it by a deformed or dovetail rib pattern.

shear stud
A steel pin welded to the top flange of a steel beam or girder and embedded in a concrete slab so as to cause the beam and the concrete to act as a structural unit.

acoustic decking
Metal decking containing glass fiber between the perforated webs of ribbed decking or in the perforated cells of cellular decking, used as a sound-absorbing ceiling.

cellular decking
Metal decking manufactured by welding a corrugated steel sheet to a flat steel sheet, forming a series of raceways for electrical wires and cables.

access flooring system
A system of removable and interchangeable floor panels supported on adjustable pedestals or stringers to allow free access to the space beneath. Also called **raised flooring system.**

finish flooring
Material used for the wearing surface of a floor, as hardwood, terrazzo, or floor tile.

wood flooring
Finish flooring in the form of wood strips, planks, or blocks.

strip flooring
Flooring composed of long, narrow wood strips, usually side- and end-matched.

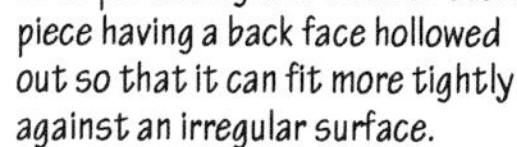

plank flooring
Flooring composed of boards wider than strip flooring, usually side- and end-matched.

hollow-backed
Of or pertaining to a wood or stone piece having a back face hollowed out so that it can fit more tightly against an irregular surface.

sleeper
Any of a number of wooden strips laid upon a concrete slab to provide a means of attaching a subfloor or flooring.

solid block flooring
Long-wearing flooring composed of solid wood blocks set in adhesive with their grain oriented vertically.

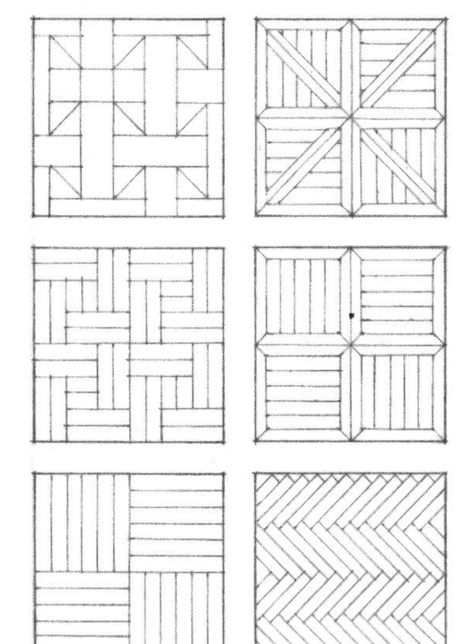

parquet
A floor composed of short strips or blocks of wood forming a pattern, sometimes with inlays of other woods or other materials.

parquetry
Mosaic work of wood used for floors and wainscoting.

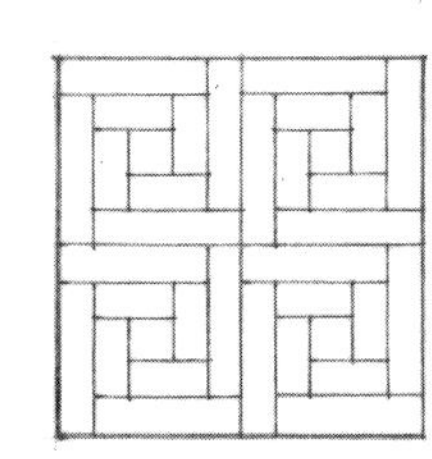

block flooring
Flooring composed of square units preassembled at the mill and usually installed with mastic over a wood subfloor or concrete slab.

unit block
A flooring block made by joining short lengths of strip flooring edgewise, usually tongued on two adjoining sides and grooved on the other two to ensure proper alignment in setting.

laminated block
A flooring block made by bonding three or more wood veneers with a moisture-resistant adhesive, usually tongued on two opposing sides and grooved on the other two to ensure proper alignment in setting.

slat block
A flooring block made by assembling narrow slats or fingers of hardwood into larger units.

terrazzo
A mosaic floor or paving composed of marble or other stone chips, set in a cementitious or resinous matrix and ground when dry.

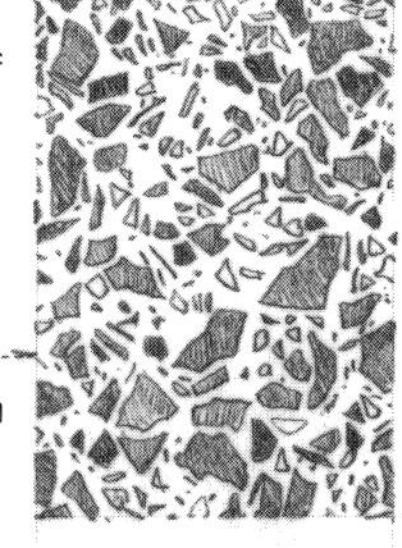

standard terrazzo
A ground and polished terrazzo finish consisting mainly of relatively small stone chips.

Venetian terrazzo
A ground and polished terrazzo finish consisting mainly of large stone chips, with smaller chips filling the spaces between.

rustic terrazzo
A uniformly textured terrazzo finish produced by washing the matrix prior to setting so as to expose the chips, which are not ground.

Palladiana
A mosaic terrazzo finish consisting of cut or fractured marble slabs set by hand in the desired pattern, with smaller chips filling the spaces between.

topping
The mixture of stone chips and cementitious or resinous matrix that produces a terrazzo surface.

bonding agent
A chemical substance applied to a substrate to create a bond between it and a succeeding layer, as between a terrazzo topping and a subfloor.

underbed
The mortar base on which a terrazzo topping is applied.

resinous matrix
A latex, polyester, or epoxy binder combined with stone chips to from a terrazzo topping especially resistant to chemicals and abrasion.

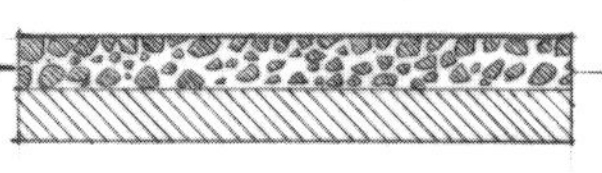

thin-set terrazzo
A thin resinous terrazzo topping directly over a sound wood, metal, or concrete subfloor.

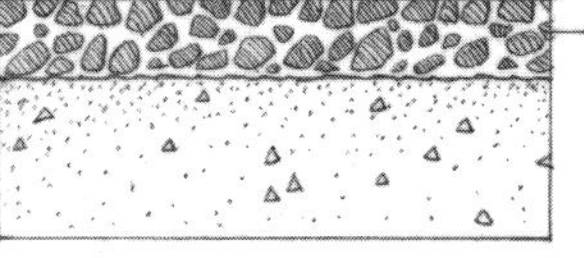

monolithic terrazzo
A terrazzo topping installed directly over a rough-finished concrete slab. A chemical bonding agent is used if the concrete surface is too smooth for a mechanical bond.

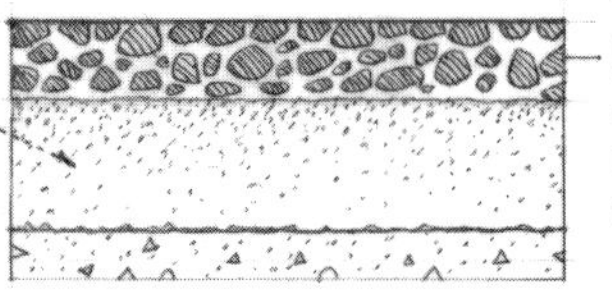

bonded terrazzo
A terrazzo topping installed over a mortar underbed that is bonded to a rough-finished concrete slab.

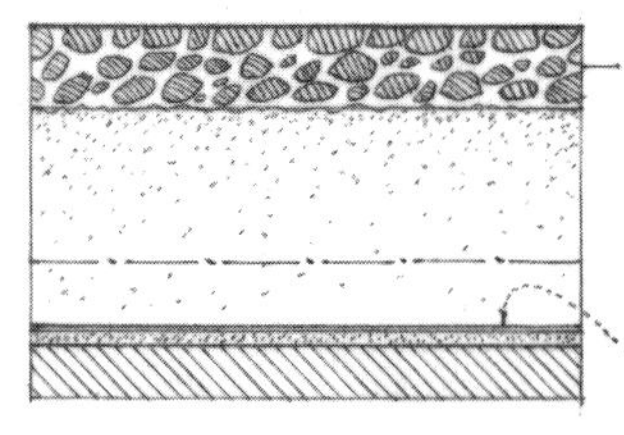

sand-cushion terrazzo
A terrazzo system for controlling cracking when structural movement is expected, consisting of a terrazzo topping installed over a reinforced mortar underbed that is separated from the subfloor by an isolation membrane and a thin layer of sand.

linoleum
A resilient floor covering formed by coating burlap or canvas with heated linseed oil, powdered cork, and rosin, and adding pigments to achieve the desired colors and patterns. Linoleum should be used only on a subfloor suspended above grade.

vinyl sheet
A resilient floor covering composed principally of polyvinyl chloride in combination with mineral fillers, pigments, and a fiber, felt, or foam backing.

vinyl tile
A resilient floor tile composed principally of polyvinyl chloride in combination with mineral fillers and pigments.

cork tile
A resilient floor tile composed of granulated cork and synthetic resin binders, finished with a protective coat of wax or a film of clear polyvinyl chloride. Cork tile should be used only on a subfloor suspended above grade.

rubber tile
A resilient floor tile composed of natural or synthetic rubber with mineral fillers.

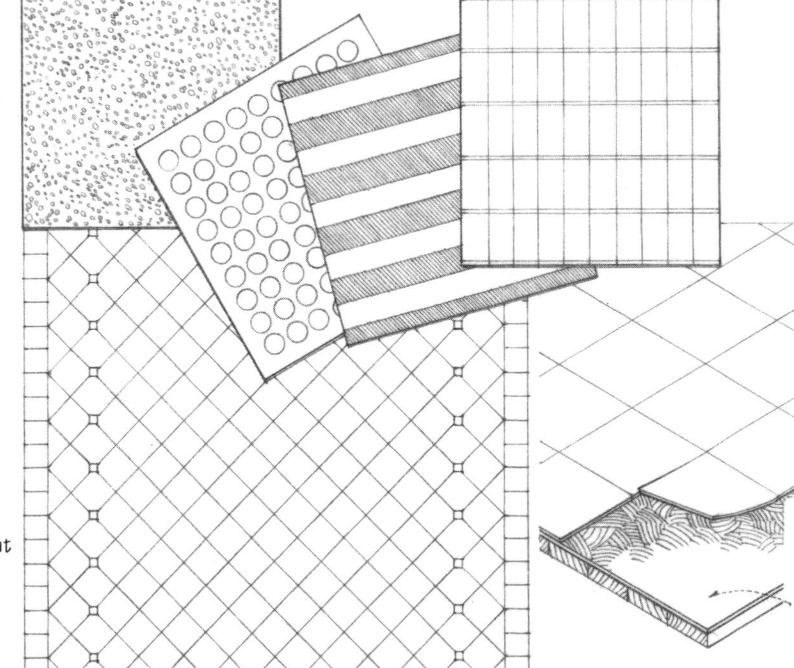

resilient flooring
Any of various floor coverings capable of springing back to the original form after being bent or compressed, available in either tile or sheet form and set in mastic over a suitable underlayment.

floor covering
Material, esp. a nonfabric material, as vinyl or ceramic tile, used to cover a floor.

mastic
Any of various pasty substances used as a sealant, adhesive, or protective coating.

underlayment
A material, as plywood or hardboard, laid over a subfloor to provide a smooth, even base for resilient flooring, carpet, or other nonstructural flooring.

carpet
A heavy woven, knitted, needle-tufted, or felted fabric for covering a floor.

pile weight
The average weight of pile yarn in a carpet, stated in ounces per square yard.

pile density
The weight of pile yarn per unit volume of carpet, stated in ounces per cubic yard.

pitch
The crosswise number of tuft-forming pile yarns in a 27-inch (686 mm) width of woven carpet.

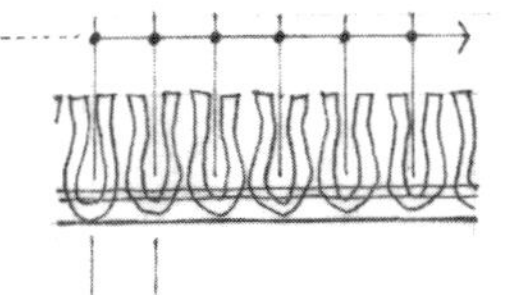

gauge
The spacing of tufts across the width of a tufted or knitted carpet, expressed in fractions of an inch.

woven carpet
Carpet made by simultaneously interweaving the backing and pile yarns on a loom.

tufted carpet
Carpet made by mechanically stitching pile yarn through a primary fabric backing and bonded with latex to a secondary backing.

knitted carpet
Carpet made by looping the backing, stitching, and pile yarns with three sets of needles.

fusion-bonded carpet
Carpet made by heat-fusing face yarns to a vinyl backing supported by other materials.

flocked carpet
Carpet made by propelling short strands of pile fiber electrostatically against an adhesive-coated backing.

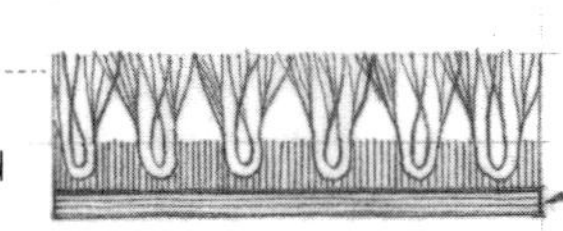

needlepunched carpet
Carpet made by punching carpet fibers back and forth through a woven polypropylene sheet with barbed needles to form a felted fiber mat.

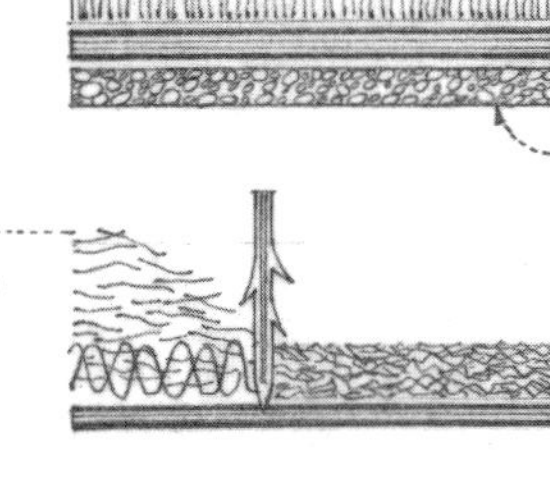

carpet tile
A flooring tile made of carpeting material.

pile
The upright tufts of yarn forming the surface of a carpet or fabric.

loop pile
A carpet texture created by weaving, tufting, or knitting the pile yarn into loops.

cut pile
A carpet texture created by cutting each loop of pile yarn, producing a range of textures from informal shags to short, dense velvets.

backing
The foundation material securing the pile yarns of a carpet and providing it with stiffness, strength, and dimensional stability.

carpet pad
A pad of cellular rubber or felted animal hair, over which carpet is installed to increase resilience, improve durability, and reduce impact sound transmission. Also called **carpet cushion**.

FORCE

An influence on a body producing or tending to produce a change in shape or movement.

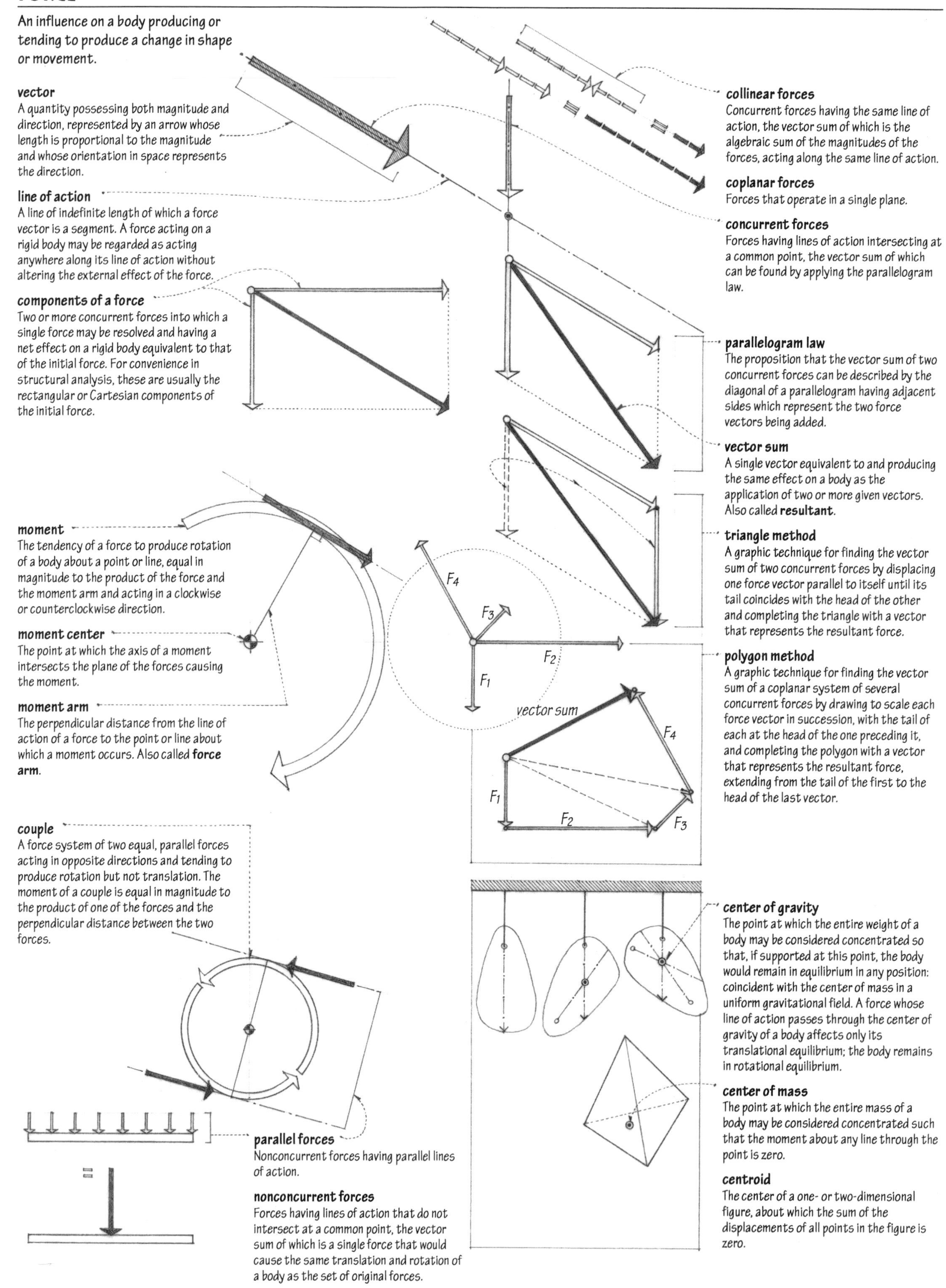

vector
A quantity possessing both magnitude and direction, represented by an arrow whose length is proportional to the magnitude and whose orientation in space represents the direction.

line of action
A line of indefinite length of which a force vector is a segment. A force acting on a rigid body may be regarded as acting anywhere along its line of action without altering the external effect of the force.

components of a force
Two or more concurrent forces into which a single force may be resolved and having a net effect on a rigid body equivalent to that of the initial force. For convenience in structural analysis, these are usually the rectangular or Cartesian components of the initial force.

moment
The tendency of a force to produce rotation of a body about a point or line, equal in magnitude to the product of the force and the moment arm and acting in a clockwise or counterclockwise direction.

moment center
The point at which the axis of a moment intersects the plane of the forces causing the moment.

moment arm
The perpendicular distance from the line of action of a force to the point or line about which a moment occurs. Also called **force arm**.

couple
A force system of two equal, parallel forces acting in opposite directions and tending to produce rotation but not translation. The moment of a couple is equal in magnitude to the product of one of the forces and the perpendicular distance between the two forces.

parallel forces
Nonconcurrent forces having parallel lines of action.

nonconcurrent forces
Forces having lines of action that do not intersect at a common point, the vector sum of which is a single force that would cause the same translation and rotation of a body as the set of original forces.

collinear forces
Concurrent forces having the same line of action, the vector sum of which is the algebraic sum of the magnitudes of the forces, acting along the same line of action.

coplanar forces
Forces that operate in a single plane.

concurrent forces
Forces having lines of action intersecting at a common point, the vector sum of which can be found by applying the parallelogram law.

parallelogram law
The proposition that the vector sum of two concurrent forces can be described by the diagonal of a parallelogram having adjacent sides which represent the two force vectors being added.

vector sum
A single vector equivalent to and producing the same effect on a body as the application of two or more given vectors. Also called **resultant**.

triangle method
A graphic technique for finding the vector sum of two concurrent forces by displacing one force vector parallel to itself until its tail coincides with the head of the other and completing the triangle with a vector that represents the resultant force.

polygon method
A graphic technique for finding the vector sum of a coplanar system of several concurrent forces by drawing to scale each force vector in succession, with the tail of each at the head of the one preceding it, and completing the polygon with a vector that represents the resultant force, extending from the tail of the first to the head of the last vector.

center of gravity
The point at which the entire weight of a body may be considered concentrated so that, if supported at this point, the body would remain in equilibrium in any position: coincident with the center of mass in a uniform gravitational field. A force whose line of action passes through the center of gravity of a body affects only its translational equilibrium; the body remains in rotational equilibrium.

center of mass
The point at which the entire mass of a body may be considered concentrated such that the moment about any line through the point is zero.

centroid
The center of a one- or two-dimensional figure, about which the sum of the displacements of all points in the figure is zero.

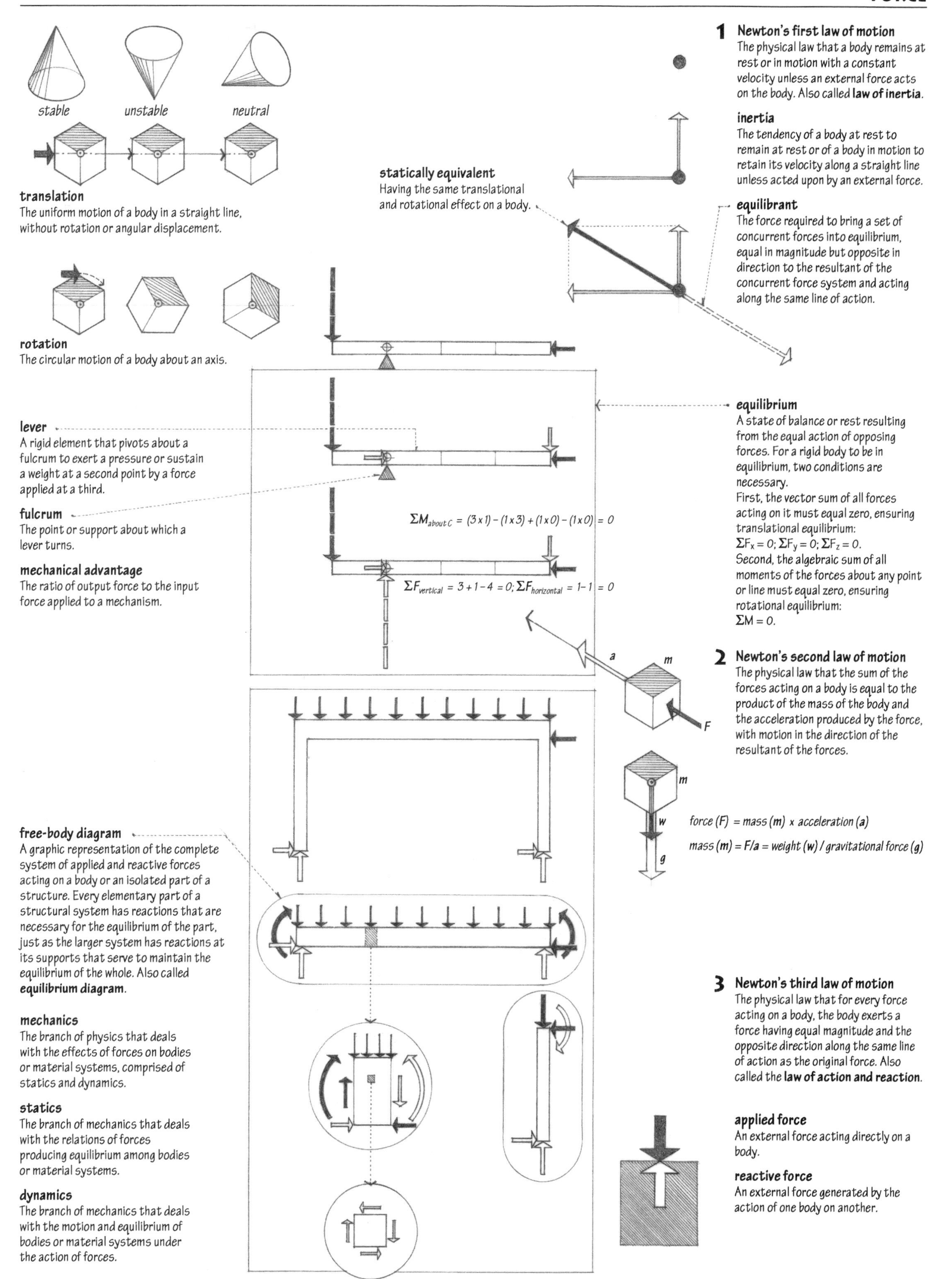

translation
The uniform motion of a body in a straight line, without rotation or angular displacement.

rotation
The circular motion of a body about an axis.

lever
A rigid element that pivots about a fulcrum to exert a pressure or sustain a weight at a second point by a force applied at a third.

fulcrum
The point or support about which a lever turns.

mechanical advantage
The ratio of output force to the input force applied to a mechanism.

free-body diagram
A graphic representation of the complete system of applied and reactive forces acting on a body or an isolated part of a structure. Every elementary part of a structural system has reactions that are necessary for the equilibrium of the part, just as the larger system has reactions at its supports that serve to maintain the equilibrium of the whole. Also called **equilibrium diagram**.

mechanics
The branch of physics that deals with the effects of forces on bodies or material systems, comprised of statics and dynamics.

statics
The branch of mechanics that deals with the relations of forces producing equilibrium among bodies or material systems.

dynamics
The branch of mechanics that deals with the motion and equilibrium of bodies or material systems under the action of forces.

statically equivalent
Having the same translational and rotational effect on a body.

1 Newton's first law of motion
The physical law that a body remains at rest or in motion with a constant velocity unless an external force acts on the body. Also called **law of inertia**.

inertia
The tendency of a body at rest to remain at rest or of a body in motion to retain its velocity along a straight line unless acted upon by an external force.

equilibrant
The force required to bring a set of concurrent forces into equilibrium, equal in magnitude but opposite in direction to the resultant of the concurrent force system and acting along the same line of action.

equilibrium
A state of balance or rest resulting from the equal action of opposing forces. For a rigid body to be in equilibrium, two conditions are necessary.
First, the vector sum of all forces acting on it must equal zero, ensuring translational equilibrium:
$\Sigma F_x = 0; \Sigma F_y = 0; \Sigma F_z = 0$.
Second, the algebraic sum of all moments of the forces about any point or line must equal zero, ensuring rotational equilibrium:
$\Sigma M = 0$.

2 Newton's second law of motion
The physical law that the sum of the forces acting on a body is equal to the product of the mass of the body and the acceleration produced by the force, with motion in the direction of the resultant of the forces.

3 Newton's third law of motion
The physical law that for every force acting on a body, the body exerts a force having equal magnitude and the opposite direction along the same line of action as the original force. Also called the **law of action and reaction**.

applied force
An external force acting directly on a body.

reactive force
An external force generated by the action of one body on another.

FORTIFICATION

A defensive military work constructed for the purpose of strengthening a position.

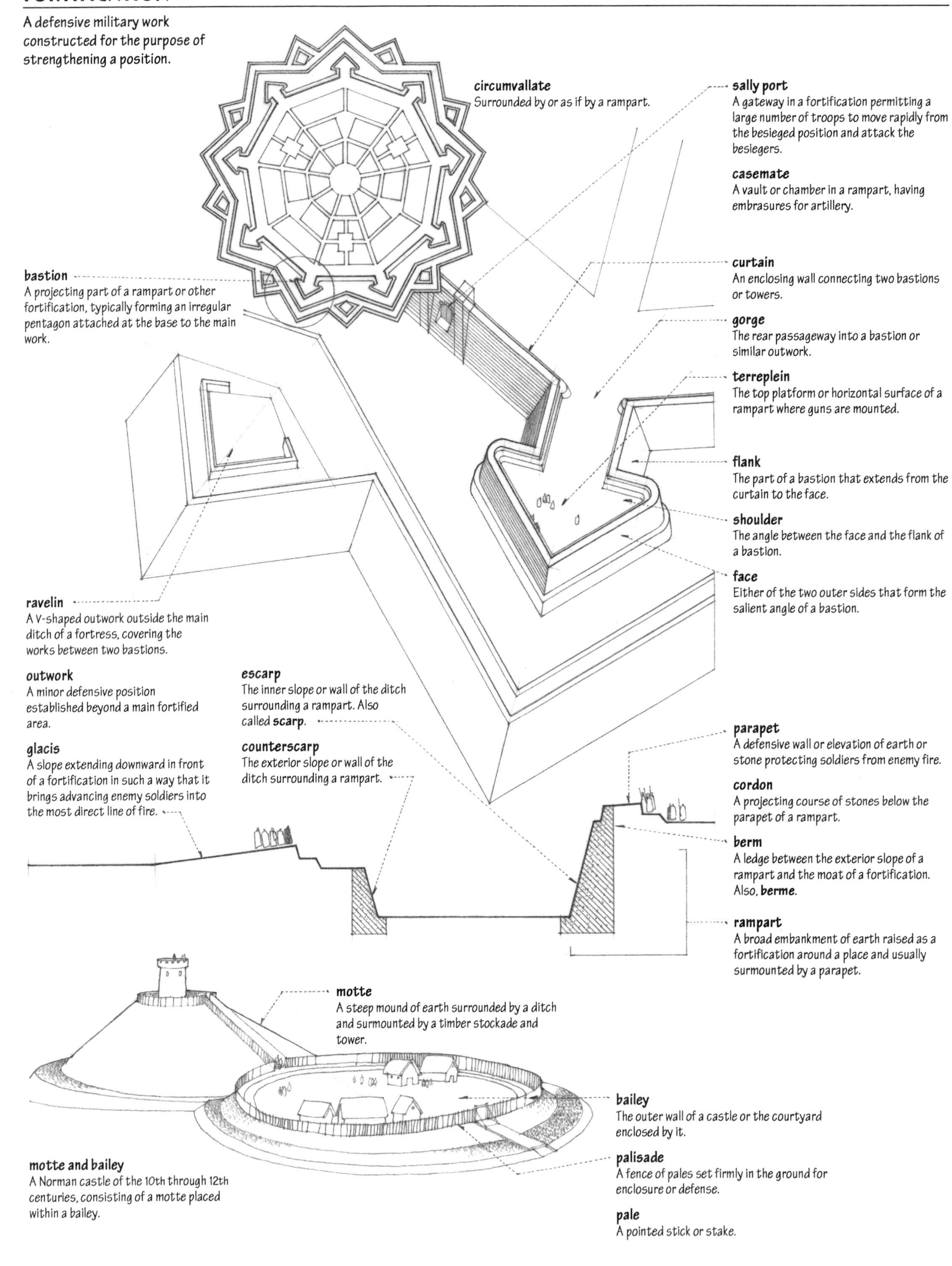

circumvallate
Surrounded by or as if by a rampart.

sally port
A gateway in a fortification permitting a large number of troops to move rapidly from the besieged position and attack the besiegers.

casemate
A vault or chamber in a rampart, having embrasures for artillery.

bastion
A projecting part of a rampart or other fortification, typically forming an irregular pentagon attached at the base to the main work.

curtain
An enclosing wall connecting two bastions or towers.

gorge
The rear passageway into a bastion or similar outwork.

terreplein
The top platform or horizontal surface of a rampart where guns are mounted.

flank
The part of a bastion that extends from the curtain to the face.

shoulder
The angle between the face and the flank of a bastion.

face
Either of the two outer sides that form the salient angle of a bastion.

ravelin
A V-shaped outwork outside the main ditch of a fortress, covering the works between two bastions.

outwork
A minor defensive position established beyond a main fortified area.

glacis
A slope extending downward in front of a fortification in such a way that it brings advancing enemy soldiers into the most direct line of fire.

escarp
The inner slope or wall of the ditch surrounding a rampart. Also called **scarp**.

counterscarp
The exterior slope or wall of the ditch surrounding a rampart.

parapet
A defensive wall or elevation of earth or stone protecting soldiers from enemy fire.

cordon
A projecting course of stones below the parapet of a rampart.

berm
A ledge between the exterior slope of a rampart and the moat of a fortification. Also, **berme**.

rampart
A broad embankment of earth raised as a fortification around a place and usually surmounted by a parapet.

motte
A steep mound of earth surrounded by a ditch and surmounted by a timber stockade and tower.

bailey
The outer wall of a castle or the courtyard enclosed by it.

motte and bailey
A Norman castle of the 10th through 12th centuries, consisting of a motte placed within a bailey.

palisade
A fence of pales set firmly in the ground for enclosure or defense.

pale
A pointed stick or stake.

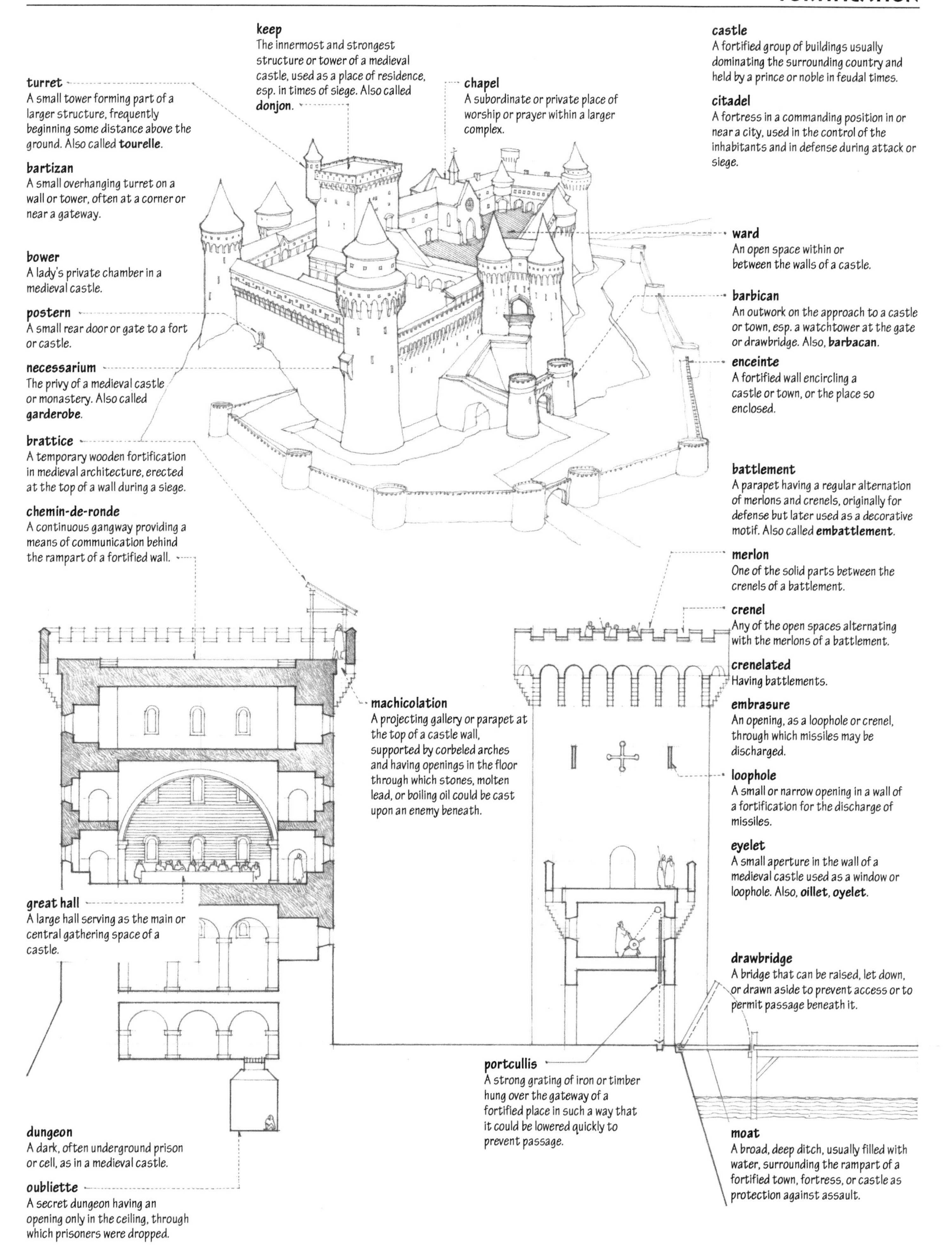
keep
The innermost and strongest structure or tower of a medieval castle, used as a place of residence, esp. in times of siege. Also called donjon.
chapel
A subordinate or private place of worship or prayer within a larger complex.
castle
A fortified group of buildings usually dominating the surrounding country and held by a prince or noble in feudal times.
citadel
A fortress in a commanding position in or near a city, used in the control of the inhabitants and in defense during attack or siege.
turret
A small tower forming part of a larger structure, frequently beginning some distance above the ground. Also called tourelle.
bartizan
A small overhanging turret on a wall or tower, often at a corner or near a gateway.
bower
A lady's private chamber in a medieval castle.
postern
A small rear door or gate to a fort or castle.
necessarium
The privy of a medieval castle or monastery. Also called garderobe.
brattice
A temporary wooden fortification in medieval architecture, erected at the top of a wall during a siege.
chemin-de-ronde
A continuous gangway providing a means of communication behind the rampart of a fortified wall.
ward
An open space within or between the walls of a castle.
barbican
An outwork on the approach to a castle or town, esp. a watchtower at the gate or drawbridge. Also, barbacan.
enceinte
A fortified wall encircling a castle or town, or the place so enclosed.
battlement
A parapet having a regular alternation of merlons and crenels, originally for defense but later used as a decorative motif. Also called embattlement.
merlon
One of the solid parts between the crenels of a battlement.
crenel
Any of the open spaces alternating with the merlons of a battlement.
crenelated
Having battlements.
embrasure
An opening, as a loophole or crenel, through which missiles may be discharged.
loophole
A small or narrow opening in a wall of a fortification for the discharge of missiles.
eyelet
A small aperture in the wall of a medieval castle used as a window or loophole. Also, oillet, oyelet.
machicolation
A projecting gallery or parapet at the top of a castle wall, supported by corbeled arches and having openings in the floor through which stones, molten lead, or boiling oil could be cast upon an enemy beneath.
great hall
A large hall serving as the main or central gathering space of a castle.
drawbridge
A bridge that can be raised, let down, or drawn aside to prevent access or to permit passage beneath it.
portcullis
A strong grating of iron or timber hung over the gateway of a fortified place in such a way that it could be lowered quickly to prevent passage.
moat
A broad, deep ditch, usually filled with water, surrounding the rampart of a fortified town, fortress, or castle as protection against assault.
dungeon
A dark, often underground prison or cell, as in a medieval castle.
oubliette
A secret dungeon having an opening only in the ceiling, through which prisoners were dropped.

The lowest division of a building or other construction, partly or wholly below the surface of the ground, designed to support and anchor the superstructure and transmit its loads directly to the earth.

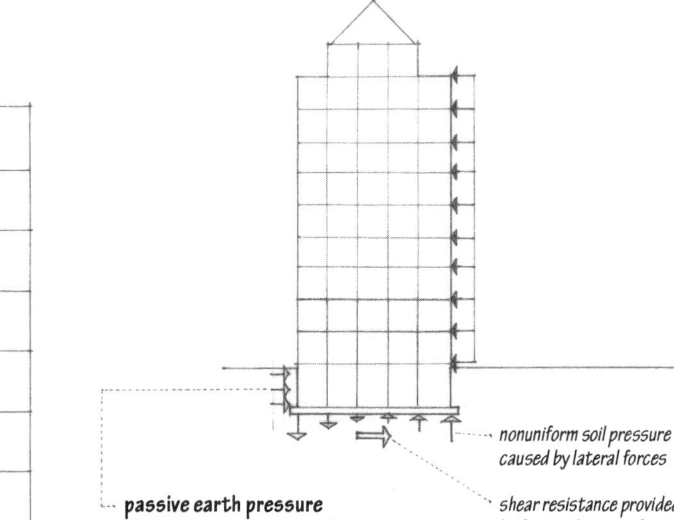

shallow foundation
A foundation system placed directly below the lowest part of a substructure and transferring building loads directly to the supporting soil by vertical pressure.

passive earth pressure
The horizontal component of resistance developed by a soil mass against the horizontal movement of a vertical structure through the soil.

footing
The part of a foundation bearing directly upon the supporting soil, set below the frostline and enlarged to distribute its load over a greater area.

active earth pressure
The horizontal component of pressure that a soil mass exerts on a vertical retaining structure.

settlement
The gradual subsiding of a structure as the soil beneath its foundation consolidates under loading.

consolidation
The gradual reduction in the volume of a soil mass resulting from the application of a sustained load and an increase in compressive stress.

primary consolidation
A reduction in volume of a soil mass under the action of a sustained load, due chiefly to a squeezing out of water from the voids within the mass and a transfer of the load from the soil water to the soil solids. Also called **primary compression**.

secondary consolidation
A reduction in volume of a soil mass under the action of a sustained load, due chiefly to adjustment of the internal structure of the soil mass after most of the load has been transferred from the soil water to the soil solids.

soil pressure
The actual pressure developed between a footing and the supporting soil mass, equal to the quotient of the magnitude of the forces transmitted and the area of contact. Also called **contact pressure**.

allowable bearing pressure
The maximum unit pressure a foundation is permitted to impose vertically or laterally on a supporting soil mass. Allowable bearing pressures for various soil classifications are conservative values permitted by building codes in the absence of geotechnical investigation and testing of the soil. Also called **allowable bearing capacity, allowable soil pressure**.

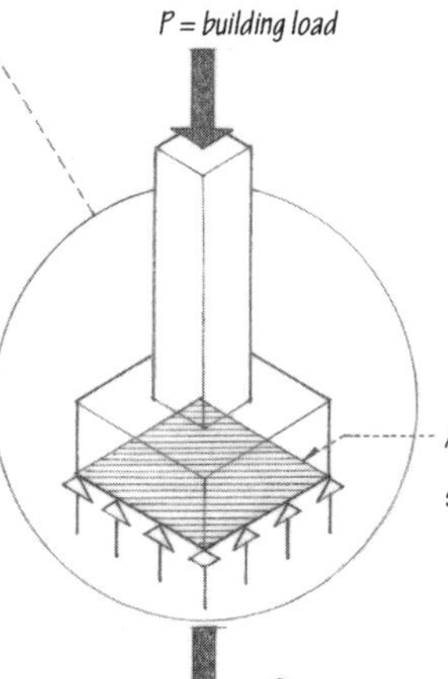

differential settlement
The relative movement of different parts of a structure caused by uneven settlement or failure of its foundation.

Overlapping soil stresses may be caused by closely spaced footings or by adjacent footings located at different levels.

frostline
The maximum depth at which soil is frozen or frost penetrates the ground.

frost heave
An uplift in soil caused by the freezing of internal moisture.

frost boil
A softening of soil resulting from the thawing of frozen groundwater.

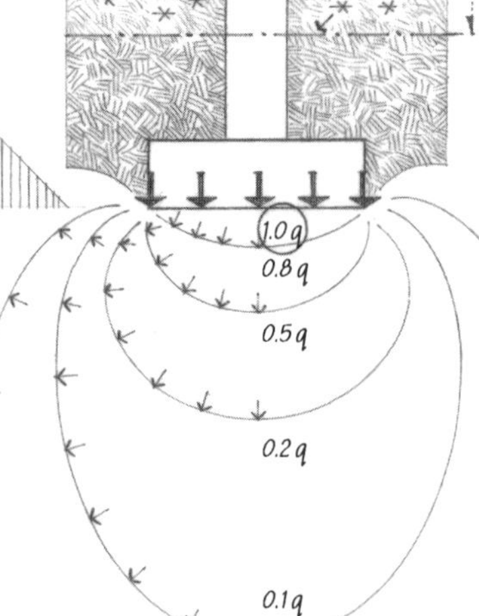

arching
The transfer of stress from a yielding part of a soil mass to adjoining, less yielding or restrained parts of the mass.

foundation wall
A wall occurring below the floor nearest grade, designed to support and anchor the superstructure.

ground slab
A concrete slab placed over a dense or compacted base and supported directly by the ground, usually reinforced with welded wire fabric or a grid of reinforcing bars to control any cracking caused by drying shrinkage or thermal stresses. Separate or integral footings are required for heavy or concentrated loads. Over problem soils, the slab must be designed as a mat or raft foundation. Also called **slab on grade**.

base course
A layer of coarse granular materials placed and compacted on undisturbed soil or prepared fill to prevent the capillary rise of moisture to a concrete ground slab.

substratum
Something that underlies or serves as a base or foundation. Also called **substrate**.

spread footing
A concrete footing extended laterally to distribute the foundation load over a wide enough area that the allowable bearing capacity of the supporting soil is not exceeded.

critical section assumed for shear
actual punching shear
compression
tension
d/2
d

strip footing
The continuous spread footing of a foundation wall.

isolated footing
A single spread footing supporting a freestanding column or pier.

continuous footing
A reinforced concrete footing extended to support a row of columns.

grade beam
A reinforced concrete beam supporting a superstructure at or near ground level and transferring the load to isolated footings, piers, or piles. Also called **ground beam**.

stepped footing
A continuous or strip footing that changes levels in stages to accommodate a sloping site or bearing stratum.

cantilever footing
A reinforced concrete footing connected by a tie beam to another footing in order to balance an asymmetrically imposed load, as at the perimeter of a building site. Also called **strap footing**.

combined footing
A reinforced concrete footing for a perimeter column or foundation wall extended to support an interior column load.

To avoid rotation or differential settlement, continuous and cantilever footings are proportioned to generate uniform soil pressure.

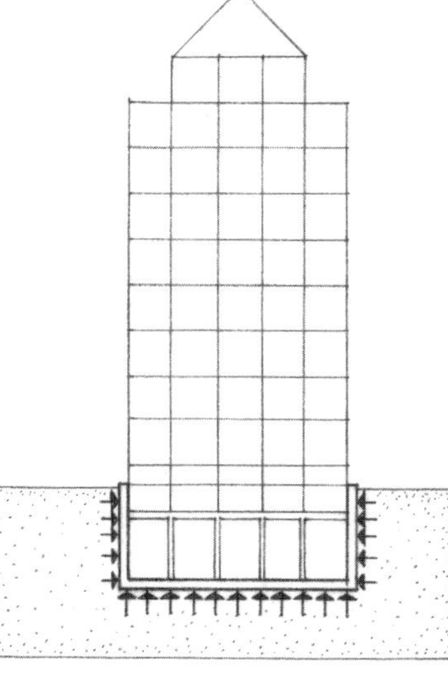

floating foundation
A foundation used in yielding soil, having for its footing a raft placed deep enough that the weight of the excavated soil is equal to or greater than the weight of the construction supported.

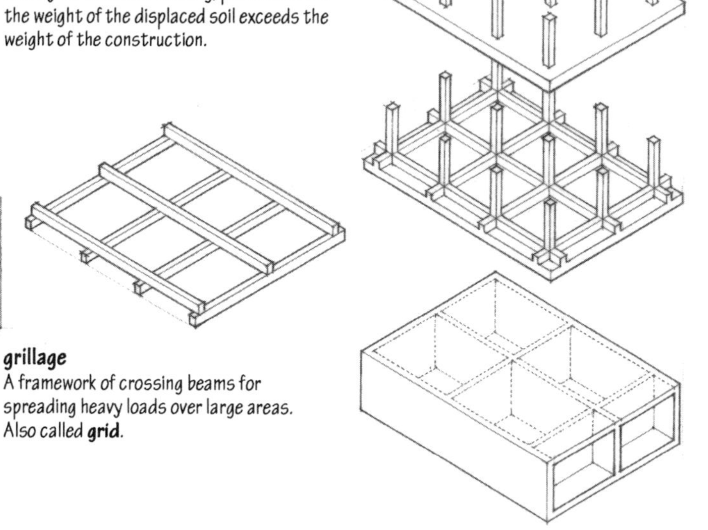

raft
A mat providing a footing on yielding soil, usually for an entire building, placed so that the weight of the displaced soil exceeds the weight of the construction.

grillage
A framework of crossing beams for spreading heavy loads over large areas. Also called **grid**.

mat
A thick, slablike footing of reinforced concrete supporting a number of columns or an entire building.

ribbed mat
A mat foundation reinforced by a grid of ribs above or below the slab.

cellular mat
A composite structure of reinforced concrete slabs and basement walls serving as a mat foundation.

deep foundation
A foundation system that extends down through unsuitable soil to transfer building loads to a more appropriate bearing stratum well below the superstructure.

pile foundation
A system of piles, pile caps, and tie beams for transferring building loads down to a suitable bearing stratum, used esp. when the soil mass directly below the construction is not suitable for the direct bearing of footings.

bearing stratum
A stratum of soil or rock on which a footing bears, or to which a building load is transferred by a pile or caisson.

batter pile
A pile driven at a specified angle to the vertical in order to provide resistance against lateral forces.

drive band
A steel band encircling the head of a timber pile to prevent it from splitting when driven. Also called **pile ring**.

anvil
The component of a pile hammer, located just below the ram, that transfers the driving force to the pile head.

cushion
A cap for protecting a pile head as well as the pile hammer during a driving operation. Also called **cushion block**, **cushion head**.

pile driver
A machine for driving piles, usually composed of a tall framework supporting machinery for lifting a pile in position before driving, a driving hammer, and vertical rails or leads for guiding the hammer.

pile
A long slender column of wood, steel, or reinforced concrete, driven or hammered vertically into the earth to form part of a foundation system.

end-bearing pile
A pile depending principally on the bearing resistance of soil or rock beneath its foot for support. The surrounding soil mass provides a degree of lateral stability for the long compression member. Also called **point-bearing pile**.

allowable pile load
The maximum axial and lateral loads permitted on a pile, as determined by a dynamic pile formula, a static load test, or a geotechnical investigation of the foundation soil.

pile eccentricity
The deviation of a pile from its plan location or from the vertical, resulting in a reduction of its allowable load.

pile tolerance
The permitted deviation of a pile from the vertical, for which a reduction in allowable load is not required.

timber pile
A log driven usually as a friction pile, often fitted with a steel shoe and a drive band to prevent it from splitting or shattering.

shoe
The hard, pointed or rounded foot of a pile or caisson for piercing underlying soil. Also called **drive shoe**.

precast concrete pile
A precast, often prestressed concrete column, having a round, square, or polygonal section and sometimes an open core, driven into the earth by a pile driver until it meets the required resistance.

pipe pile
A heavy steel pipe driven with the lower end either open or closed by a heavy steel plate or point and filled with concrete. An open-ended pipe pile requires inspection and excavation before being filled with concrete.

H-pile
A steel H-section driven as a pile, sometimes encased in concrete to a point below the water table to prevent corrosion. H-sections can be welded together in the driving process to form any length of pile.

composite pile
A pile constructed of two materials, as a timber pile having a concrete upper section to prevent the portion of the pile above the water table from deteriorating.

friction pile
A pile depending principally on the frictional resistance of surrounding earth for support.

skin friction
The friction developed between the sides of a pile and the soil into which the pile is driven, limited by the adhesion of soil to the pile sides and the shear strength of the surrounding soil mass.

negative friction
An additional load on a pile resulting from settling of fill, which tends to drag the pile downward into the soil.

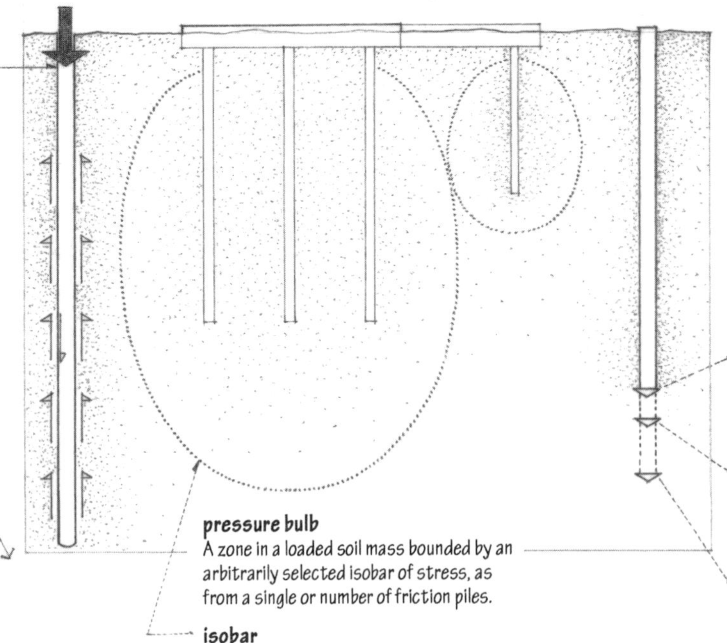

pressure bulb
A zone in a loaded soil mass bounded by an arbitrarily selected isobar of stress, as from a single or number of friction piles.

isobar
A line connecting points of equal pressure.

dynamic pile formula
Any of several formulas by which the allowable axial load on a pile can be calculated from the energy required for a pile hammer to advance the pile foot a specified distance into the subsoil.

static load test
A test for determining the allowable axial load on a single pile, usually a fraction of the load required to reach a yield point, a point of resistance, or a point of refusal.

point of resistance
The point at which a pile load causes a specified net settlement after being applied continuously for a specified period of time.

point of refusal
The point at which no additional settlement takes place after a pile has been loaded continuously for a specified period of time.

yield point
The point at which an increase in pile load produces a disproportionate increase in settlement.

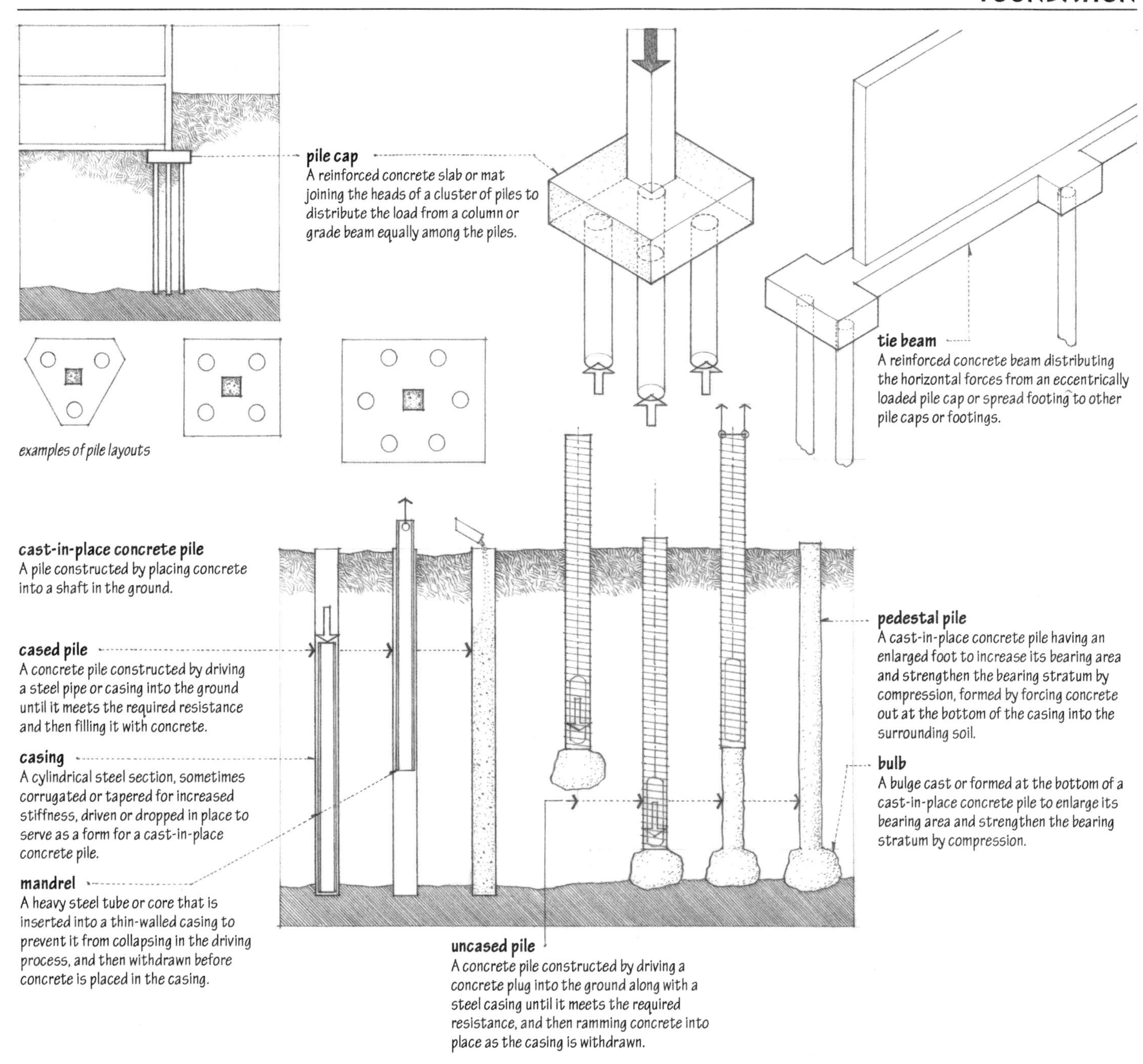

pile cap
A reinforced concrete slab or mat joining the heads of a cluster of piles to distribute the load from a column or grade beam equally among the piles.

tie beam
A reinforced concrete beam distributing the horizontal forces from an eccentrically loaded pile cap or spread footing to other pile caps or footings.

examples of pile layouts

cast-in-place concrete pile
A pile constructed by placing concrete into a shaft in the ground.

cased pile
A concrete pile constructed by driving a steel pipe or casing into the ground until it meets the required resistance and then filling it with concrete.

casing
A cylindrical steel section, sometimes corrugated or tapered for increased stiffness, driven or dropped in place to serve as a form for a cast-in-place concrete pile.

mandrel
A heavy steel tube or core that is inserted into a thin-walled casing to prevent it from collapsing in the driving process, and then withdrawn before concrete is placed in the casing.

uncased pile
A concrete pile constructed by driving a concrete plug into the ground along with a steel casing until it meets the required resistance, and then ramming concrete into place as the casing is withdrawn.

pedestal pile
A cast-in-place concrete pile having an enlarged foot to increase its bearing area and strengthen the bearing stratum by compression, formed by forcing concrete out at the bottom of the casing into the surrounding soil.

bulb
A bulge cast or formed at the bottom of a cast-in-place concrete pile to enlarge its bearing area and strengthen the bearing stratum by compression.

pier
A cast-in-place concrete foundation formed by boring with a large auger or excavating by hand a shaft in the earth to a suitable bearing stratum and filling the shaft with concrete.

caisson
A pier, esp. when the boring is 2 ft. (610 mm) or larger in diameter to permit inspection of the bottom.

bell
The base of a caisson enlarged to increase its bearing area.

bell bucket
An attachment to an earth auger having expanding blades for excavating a bell at the bottom of a caisson shaft.

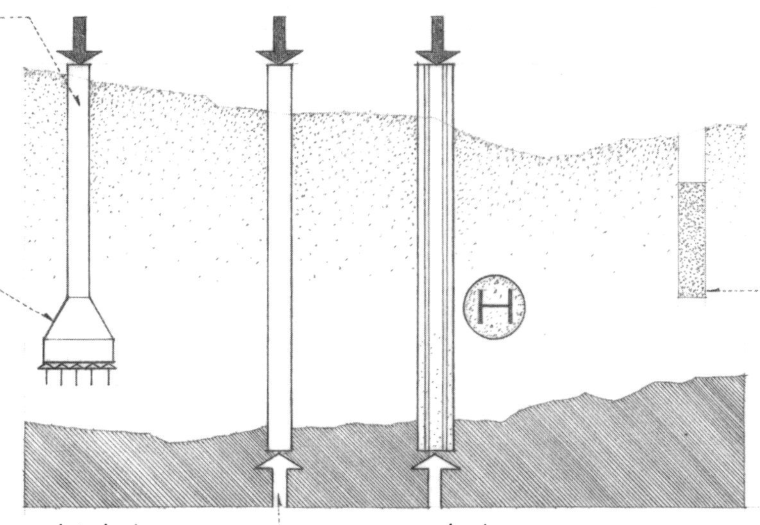

sand pile
A base for a footing in soft soil, made by compacting sand in a cavity left by a timber pile.

socketed caisson
A caisson that is drilled into a stratum of solid rock rather than belled.

rock caisson
A socketed caisson having a steel H-section core within a concrete-filled pipe casing.

FRAME

A skeletal structure of relatively slender members designed to give shape and support to a building or other construction.

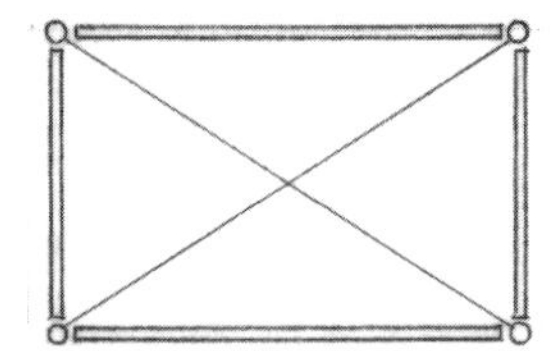

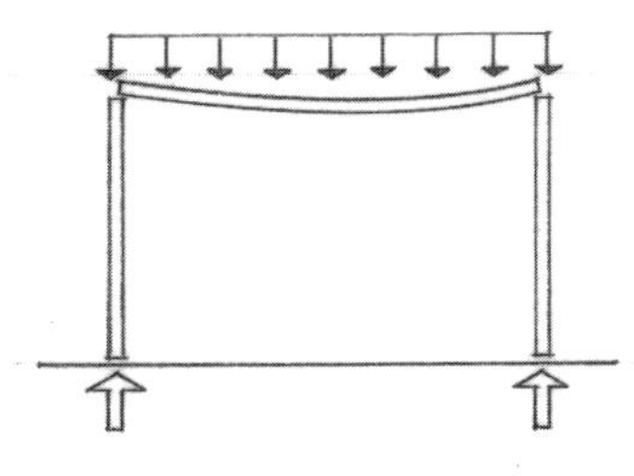

braced frame
A structural frame whose resistance to lateral forces is provided by diagonal or other type of bracing.

plastic hinge
A virtual hinge that develops when all fibers are fully yielded at a cross section of a structural member.

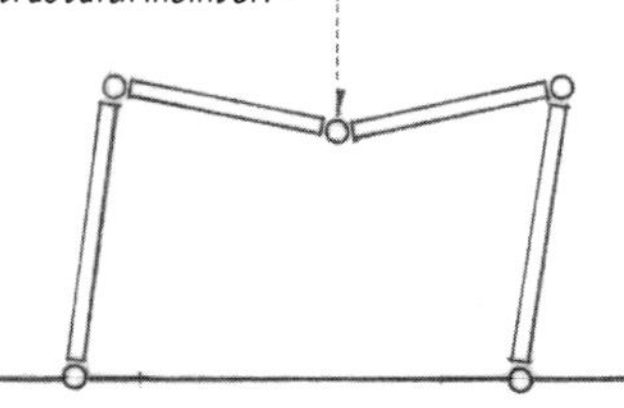

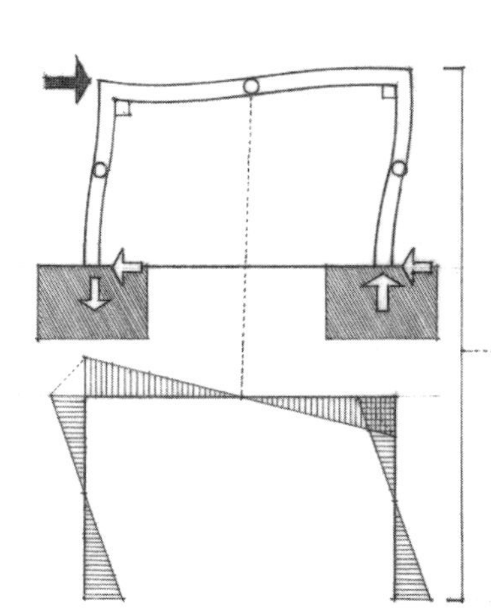

rigid frame
A structural frame of linear members rigidly connected at their joints. Applied loads produce axial, bending, and shear forces in all members of the frame since the rigid joints restrain the ends of the members from rotating freely. In addition, vertical loads cause a rigid frame to develop horizontal thrusts at its base. A rigid frame is statically indeterminate and rigid only in its plane. Also called **moment-resisting frame**.

fixed frame
A rigid frame connected to its supports with fixed joints. A fixed frame is more resistant to deflection than a hinged frame but also more sensitive to support settlements and thermal expansion and contraction.

sidesway
The lateral displacement produced in a rigid frame by lateral loads or asymmetrical vertical loading.

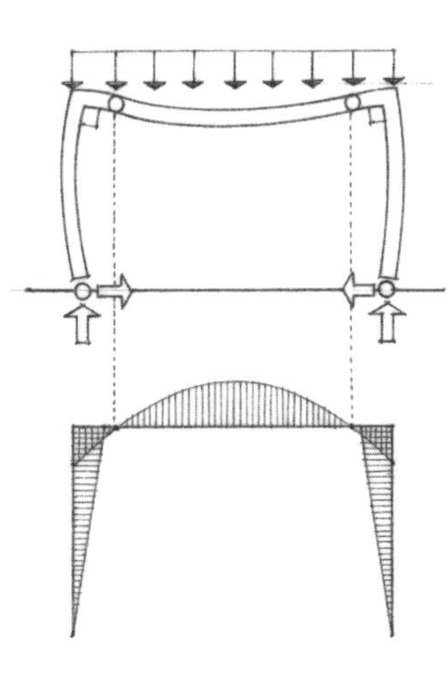

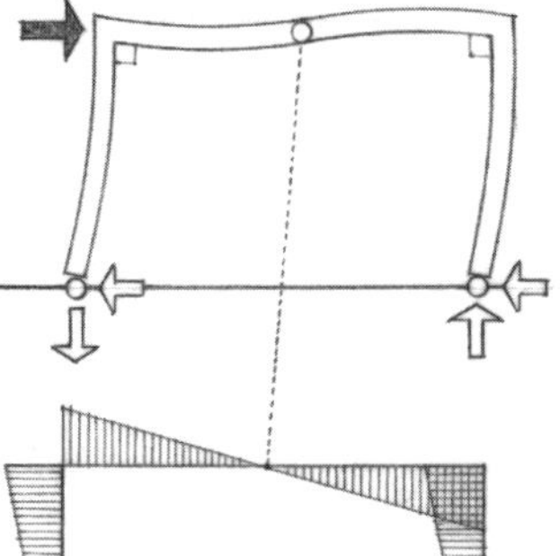

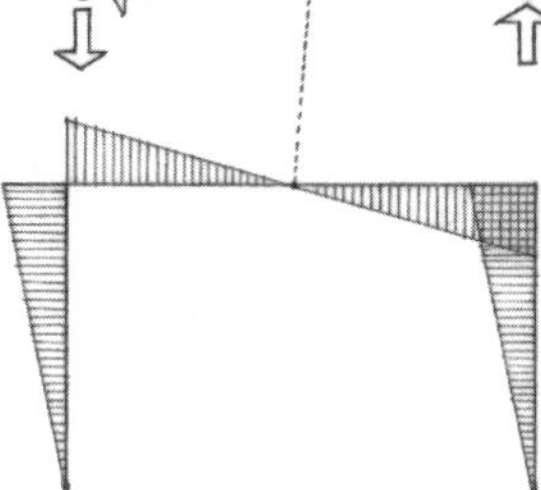

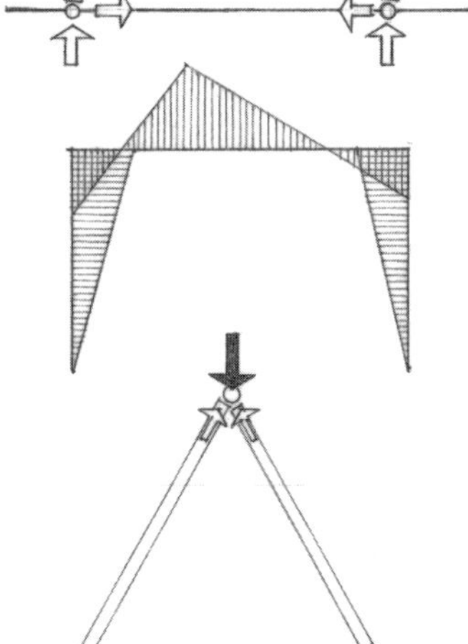

hinged frame
A rigid frame connected to its supports with pin joints. The pin joints prevent high bending stresses from developing by allowing the frame to rotate as a unit when strained by support settlements, and to flex slightly when stressed by changes in temperature.

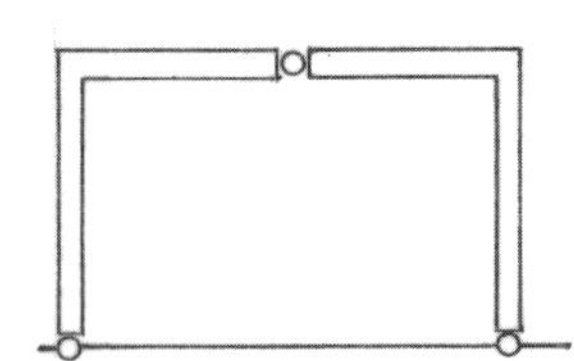

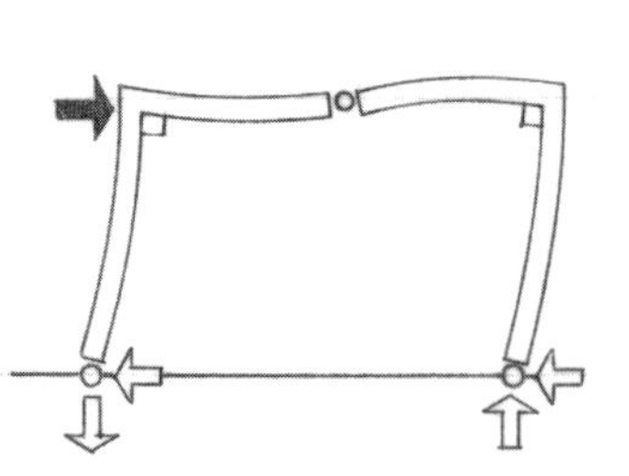

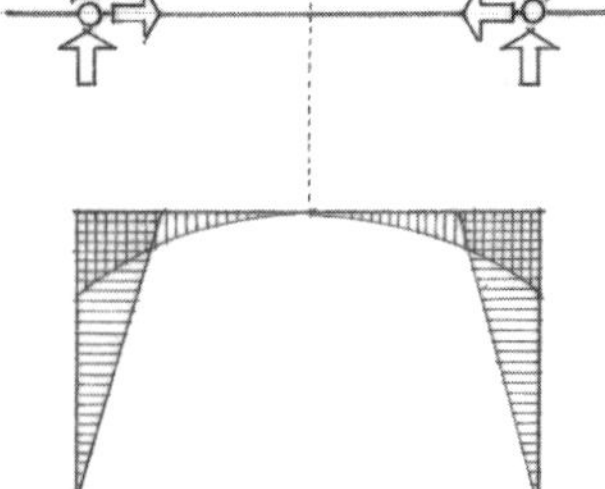

three-hinged frame
A structural assembly of two rigid sections connected to each other and to its supports with pin joints. While more sensitive to deflection than either the fixed or hinged frame, the three-hinged frame is least affected by support settlements and thermal stresses. The three pin joints also permit the frame to be analyzed as a statically determinate structure.

A-frame
A building constructed with a steep triangular frame resting directly on a foundation.

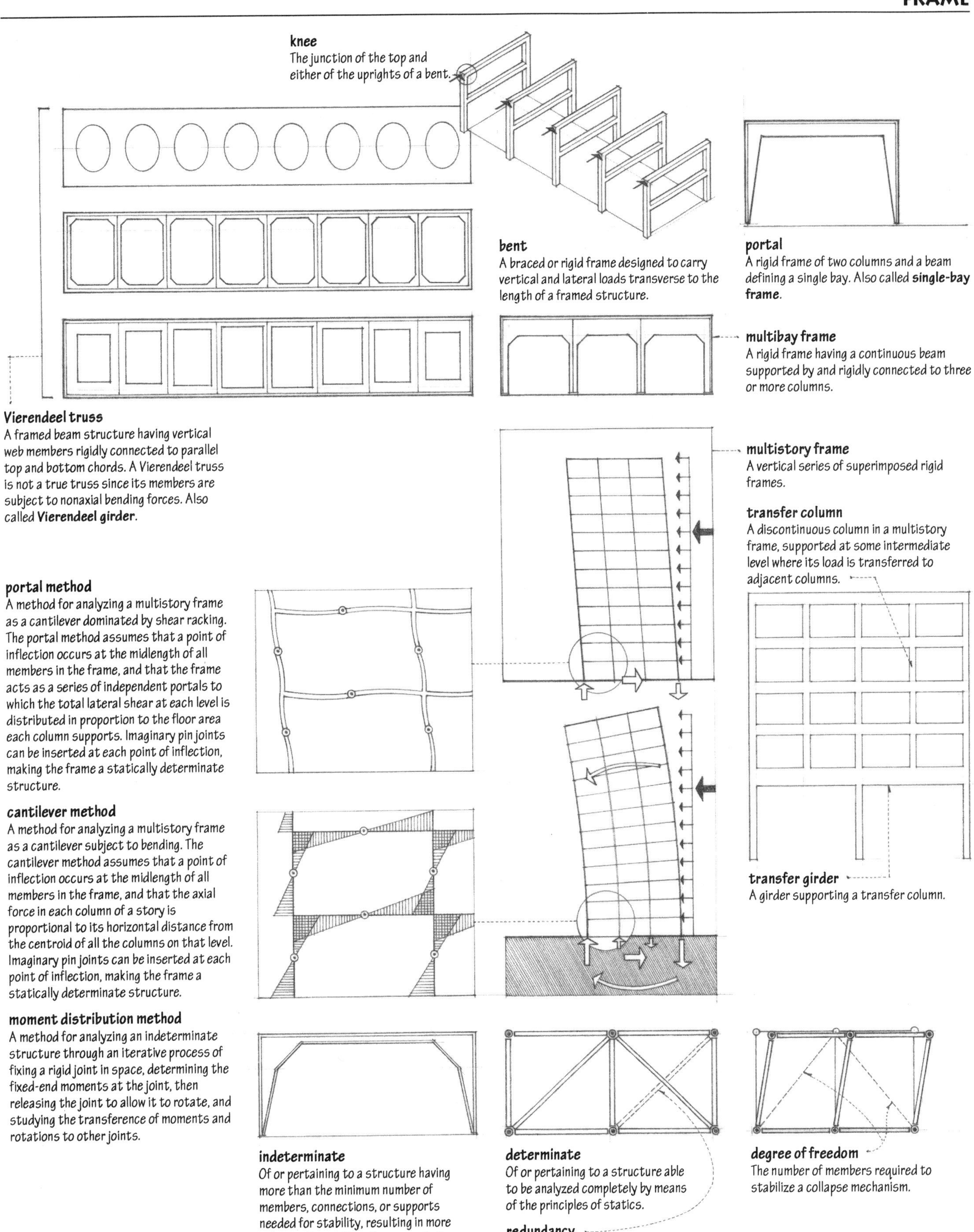

knee
The junction of the top and either of the uprights of a bent.

Vierendeel truss
A framed beam structure having vertical web members rigidly connected to parallel top and bottom chords. A Vierendeel truss is not a true truss since its members are subject to nonaxial bending forces. Also called **Vierendeel girder**.

bent
A braced or rigid frame designed to carry vertical and lateral loads transverse to the length of a framed structure.

portal
A rigid frame of two columns and a beam defining a single bay. Also called **single-bay frame**.

multibay frame
A rigid frame having a continuous beam supported by and rigidly connected to three or more columns.

multistory frame
A vertical series of superimposed rigid frames.

transfer column
A discontinuous column in a multistory frame, supported at some intermediate level where its load is transferred to adjacent columns.

transfer girder
A girder supporting a transfer column.

portal method
A method for analyzing a multistory frame as a cantilever dominated by shear racking. The portal method assumes that a point of inflection occurs at the midlength of all members in the frame, and that the frame acts as a series of independent portals to which the total lateral shear at each level is distributed in proportion to the floor area each column supports. Imaginary pin joints can be inserted at each point of inflection, making the frame a statically determinate structure.

cantilever method
A method for analyzing a multistory frame as a cantilever subject to bending. The cantilever method assumes that a point of inflection occurs at the midlength of all members in the frame, and that the axial force in each column of a story is proportional to its horizontal distance from the centroid of all the columns on that level. Imaginary pin joints can be inserted at each point of inflection, making the frame a statically determinate structure.

moment distribution method
A method for analyzing an indeterminate structure through an iterative process of fixing a rigid joint in space, determining the fixed-end moments at the joint, then releasing the joint to allow it to rotate, and studying the transference of moments and rotations to other joints.

indeterminate
Of or pertaining to a structure having more than the minimum number of members, connections, or supports needed for stability, resulting in more unknown forces than there are static equations for solution.

degree of indeterminacy
The difference between the number of unknown forces in an indeterminate structure and the number of static equations available for solution.

determinate
Of or pertaining to a structure able to be analyzed completely by means of the principles of statics.

redundancy
A structural member, connection, or support not required for a statically determinate structure.

degree of redundancy
The number of members beyond that required for the stability of a statically determinate structure.

degree of freedom
The number of members required to stabilize a collapse mechanism.

framing
The act, process, or manner of fitting and joining together relatively slender members to give shape and support to a structure.

framework
A skeletal structure of parts fitted and joined together in order to support, define, or enclose.

light frame construction
A system of construction utilizing closely spaced and sheathed members of dimension lumber or light-gauge metal to form the structural elements of a building.

*See balloon frame
floor framing
platform frame
roof framing

skeleton construction
A system of construction utilizing a framework of columns and beams to transmit building loads down to the foundation.

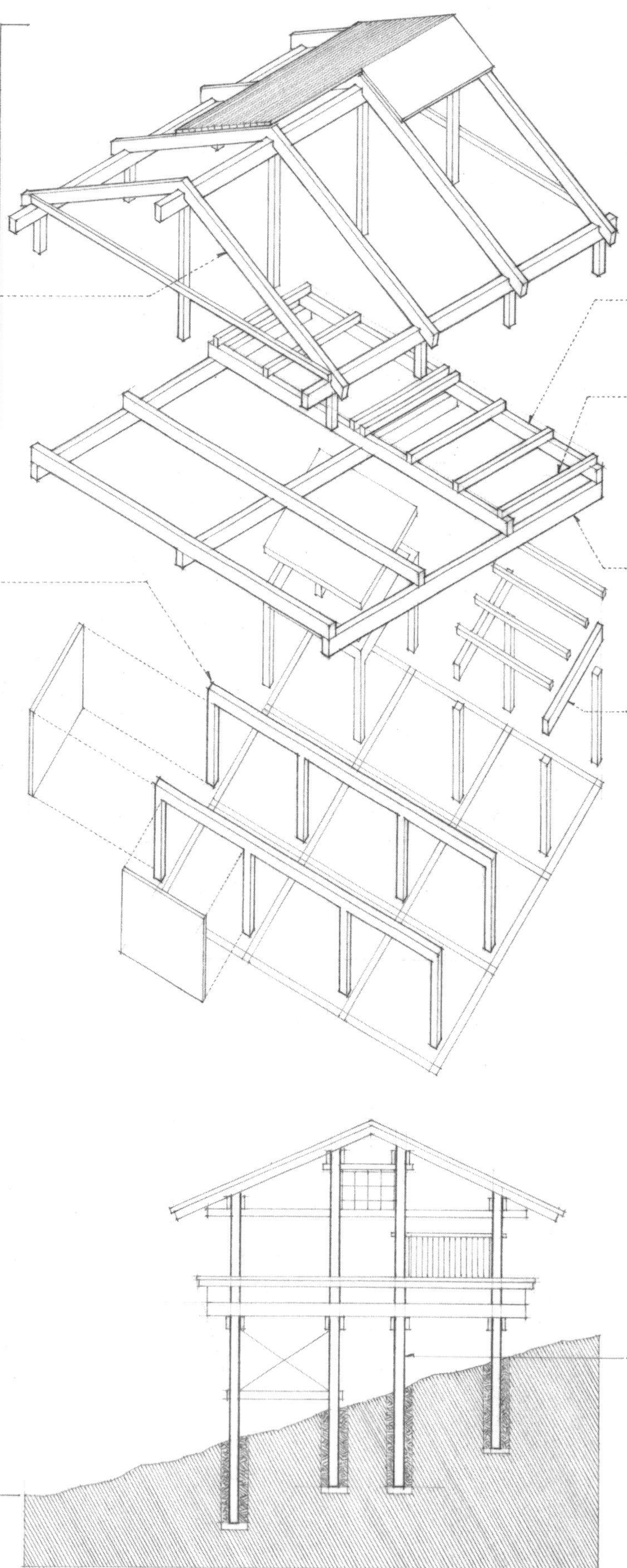

plank-and-beam construction
Floor or roof construction utilizing a framework of timber beams to support wood planks or decking.

principal beam
Any large beam in a structural frame that supports secondary beams or joists. Also called **primary beam**.

secondary beam
Any beam that transmits its load to a principal beam.

tertiary beam
Any beam that transmits its load to a secondary beam.

girder
A large principal beam designed to support concentrated loads at isolated points along its length.

post-and-beam construction
Wall construction utilizing a framework of vertical posts and horizontal beams to carry floor and roof loads. Also called **post-and-lintel construction**.

trabeate
Of or pertaining to a system of construction employing beams or lintels. Also, **trabeated**.

arcuate
Of or pertaining to a system of construction employing arches or arched forms. Also, **arcuated**.

pole construction
A system of construction employing a vertical structure of pressure-treated wood poles which are firmly embedded in the ground as a pier foundation.

pole house
A house of pole construction.

pole
A long, cylindrical, often slender piece of wood or metal.

stilt
One of several piles or posts for supporting a structure above the surface of land or water.

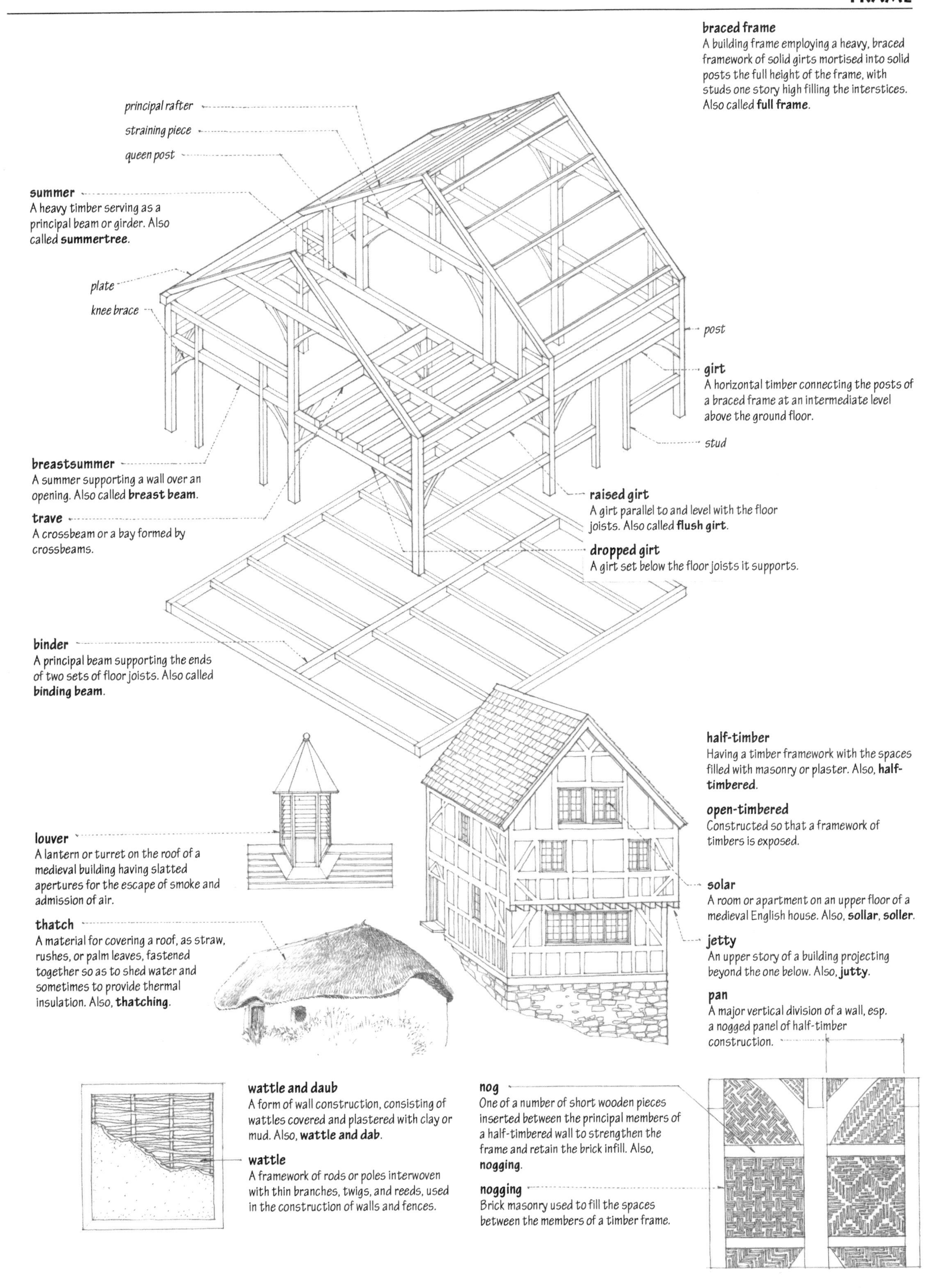

braced frame
A building frame employing a heavy, braced framework of solid girts mortised into solid posts the full height of the frame, with studs one story high filling the interstices. Also called **full frame**.

summer
A heavy timber serving as a principal beam or girder. Also called **summertree**.

girt
A horizontal timber connecting the posts of a braced frame at an intermediate level above the ground floor.

breastsummer
A summer supporting a wall over an opening. Also called **breast beam**.

trave
A crossbeam or a bay formed by crossbeams.

raised girt
A girt parallel to and level with the floor joists. Also called **flush girt**.

dropped girt
A girt set below the floor joists it supports.

binder
A principal beam supporting the ends of two sets of floor joists. Also called **binding beam**.

half-timber
Having a timber framework with the spaces filled with masonry or plaster. Also, **half-timbered**.

open-timbered
Constructed so that a framework of timbers is exposed.

louver
A lantern or turret on the roof of a medieval building having slatted apertures for the escape of smoke and admission of air.

solar
A room or apartment on an upper floor of a medieval English house. Also, **sollar**, **soller**.

thatch
A material for covering a roof, as straw, rushes, or palm leaves, fastened together so as to shed water and sometimes to provide thermal insulation. Also, **thatching**.

jetty
An upper story of a building projecting beyond the one below. Also, **jutty**.

pan
A major vertical division of a wall, esp. a nogged panel of half-timber construction.

wattle and daub
A form of wall construction, consisting of wattles covered and plastered with clay or mud. Also, **wattle and dab**.

wattle
A framework of rods or poles interwoven with thin branches, twigs, and reeds, used in the construction of walls and fences.

nog
One of a number of short wooden pieces inserted between the principal members of a half-timbered wall to strengthen the frame and retain the brick infill. Also, **nogging**.

nogging
Brick masonry used to fill the spaces between the members of a timber frame.

GEOMETRY

A branch of mathematics that deals with the properties, measurement, and relationships of points, lines, angles, and solids, deduced from their defining conditions by means of certain assumed properties of space.

point
A dimensionless geometric element that has no property but location, as the intersection of two lines.

y-axis
The axis along which ordinates or y-values are measured in a Cartesian coordinate system. Also called **axis of ordinates**.

z-coordinate
A coordinate determined by measuring parallel to the z-axis.

z-axis
The axis along which z-values are measured in a three-dimensional Cartesian coordinate system.

rectangular coordinate system
A Cartesian coordinate system in which the axes or coordinate planes are perpendicular.

x-axis
The axis along which abscissas or x-values are measured in a Cartesian coordinate system. Also called **axis of abscissas**.

abscissa
A coordinate determined by measuring parallel to the x-axis. Also called **x-coordinate**.

coordinate
Any of a set of numbers that serve to specify the location of a point on a line, surface, or in space by reference to a fixed figure or system of lines.

Cartesian coordinate
Any of the coordinates for locating a point on a plane by its distance from each of two intersecting lines, or in space by its distance from each of three planes intersecting at a point.

ordinate
A coordinate determined by measuring parallel to the y-axis. Also called **y-coordinate**.

Euclidean geometry
Geometry based upon the postulates of Euclid, esp. the postulate that only one line may be drawn through a given point parallel to a given line.

radius vector
A straight line segment that joins a variable point to the fixed origin of a polar coordinate system.

polar angle
The angle formed by the polar axis and a radius vector in a polar coordinate system.

polar axis
The reference axis from which the polar angle is measured in a polar coordinate system.

polar coordinate system
A system for locating a point on a plane by its radius vector and polar angle.

line
A geometric element generated by a moving point and having extension without breadth or thickness.

vertical
Perpendicular to the plane of the horizon.

oblique
Neither parallel nor perpendicular to a given line or surface.

horizontal
Parallel to or operating in a plane parallel to the horizon.

parallel
Extending in the same direction, equidistant at all points, and never converging or diverging.

skew lines
Any lines in space that are neither parallel nor intersecting.

angle
The space between two lines diverging from a common point, or within two planes diverging from a common line: the figure so formed.

vertex
The point at which the sides of an angle intersect.

angle
The amount of rotation needed to bring one line or plane into coincidence with another, measured in radians or in degrees, minutes, and seconds.

radian
A unit of angular measure equal to the central angle subtending an arc equal in length to the radius: $360/2\pi$ or approx. 57.3°.

degree
A unit of angular measure, equal to $1/360$th of a complete angle or turn, or of the circumference of a circle.

minute
The 60th part of a degree of angular measure.

second
The 60th part of a minute of angular measure.

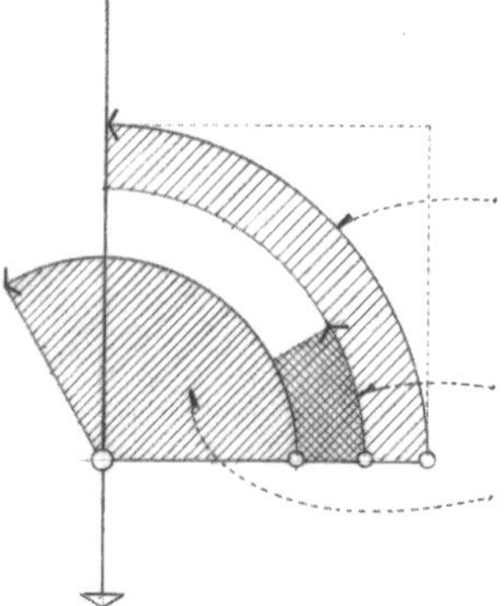

right angle
An angle of 90° formed by the perpendicular intersection of two straight lines.

acute angle
An angle less than 90°.

obtuse angle
An angle greater than 90° but less than 180°.

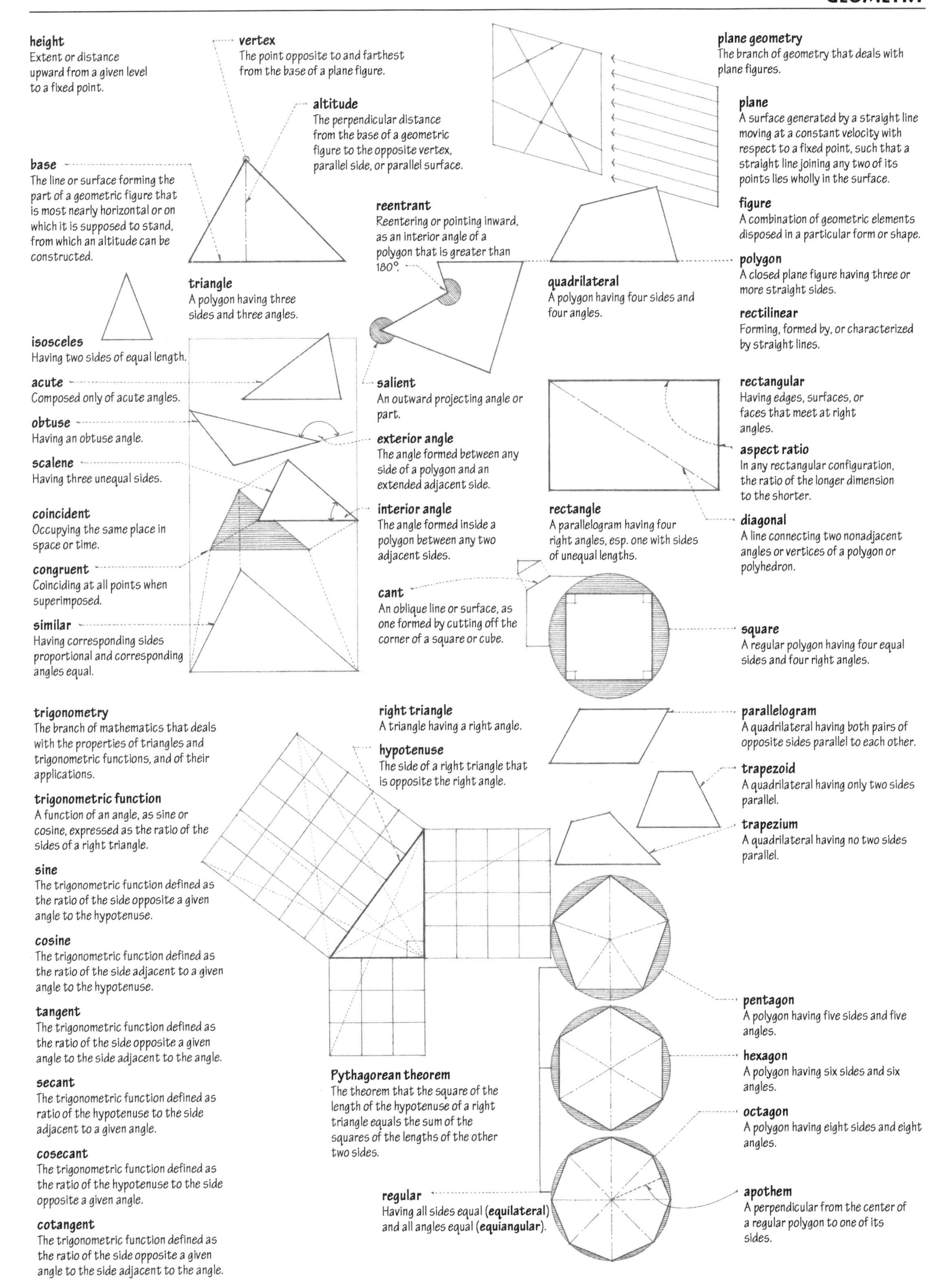

height
Extent or distance upward from a given level to a fixed point.

vertex
The point opposite to and farthest from the base of a plane figure.

altitude
The perpendicular distance from the base of a geometric figure to the opposite vertex, parallel side, or parallel surface.

base
The line or surface forming the part of a geometric figure that is most nearly horizontal or on which it is supposed to stand, from which an altitude can be constructed.

triangle
A polygon having three sides and three angles.

isosceles
Having two sides of equal length.

acute
Composed only of acute angles.

obtuse
Having an obtuse angle.

scalene
Having three unequal sides.

coincident
Occupying the same place in space or time.

congruent
Coinciding at all points when superimposed.

similar
Having corresponding sides proportional and corresponding angles equal.

reentrant
Reentering or pointing inward, as an interior angle of a polygon that is greater than 180°.

salient
An outward projecting angle or part.

exterior angle
The angle formed between any side of a polygon and an extended adjacent side.

interior angle
The angle formed inside a polygon between any two adjacent sides.

cant
An oblique line or surface, as one formed by cutting off the corner of a square or cube.

quadrilateral
A polygon having four sides and four angles.

rectangle
A parallelogram having four right angles, esp. one with sides of unequal lengths.

plane geometry
The branch of geometry that deals with plane figures.

plane
A surface generated by a straight line moving at a constant velocity with respect to a fixed point, such that a straight line joining any two of its points lies wholly in the surface.

figure
A combination of geometric elements disposed in a particular form or shape.

polygon
A closed plane figure having three or more straight sides.

rectilinear
Forming, formed by, or characterized by straight lines.

rectangular
Having edges, surfaces, or faces that meet at right angles.

aspect ratio
In any rectangular configuration, the ratio of the longer dimension to the shorter.

diagonal
A line connecting two nonadjacent angles or vertices of a polygon or polyhedron.

square
A regular polygon having four equal sides and four right angles.

trigonometry
The branch of mathematics that deals with the properties of triangles and trigonometric functions, and of their applications.

trigonometric function
A function of an angle, as sine or cosine, expressed as the ratio of the sides of a right triangle.

sine
The trigonometric function defined as the ratio of the side opposite a given angle to the hypotenuse.

cosine
The trigonometric function defined as the ratio of the side adjacent to a given angle to the hypotenuse.

tangent
The trigonometric function defined as the ratio of the side opposite a given angle to the side adjacent to the angle.

secant
The trigonometric function defined as ratio of the hypotenuse to the side adjacent to a given angle.

cosecant
The trigonometric function defined as the ratio of the hypotenuse to the side opposite a given angle.

cotangent
The trigonometric function defined as the ratio of the side opposite a given angle to the side adjacent to the angle.

right triangle
A triangle having a right angle.

hypotenuse
The side of a right triangle that is opposite the right angle.

Pythagorean theorem
The theorem that the square of the length of the hypotenuse of a right triangle equals the sum of the squares of the lengths of the other two sides.

regular
Having all sides equal (**equilateral**) and all angles equal (**equiangular**).

parallelogram
A quadrilateral having both pairs of opposite sides parallel to each other.

trapezoid
A quadrilateral having only two sides parallel.

trapezium
A quadrilateral having no two sides parallel.

pentagon
A polygon having five sides and five angles.

hexagon
A polygon having six sides and six angles.

octagon
A polygon having eight sides and eight angles.

apothem
A perpendicular from the center of a regular polygon to one of its sides.

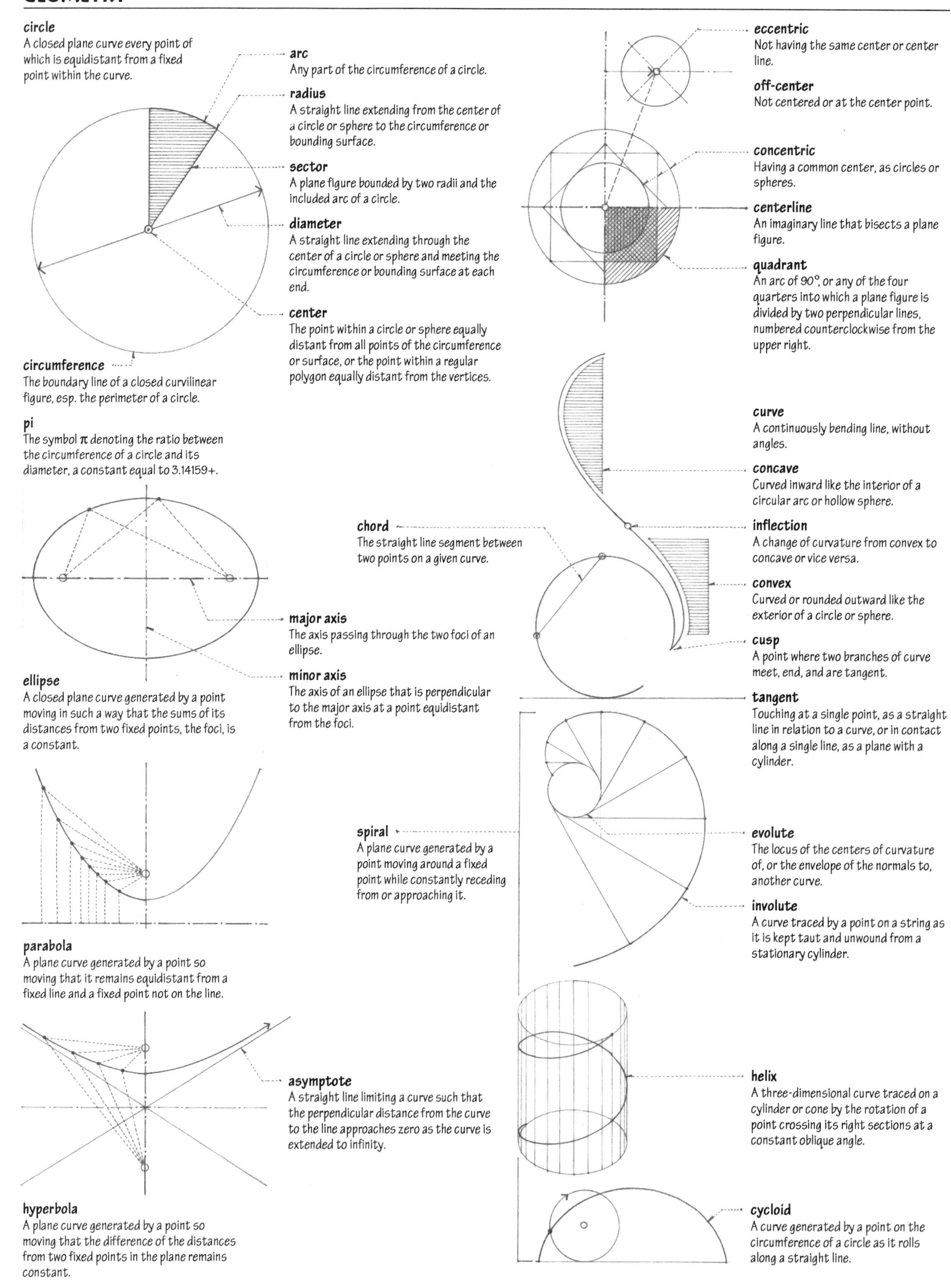

circle
A closed plane curve every point of which is equidistant from a fixed point within the curve.

circumference
The boundary line of a closed curvilinear figure, esp. the perimeter of a circle.

pi
The symbol π denoting the ratio between the circumference of a circle and its diameter, a constant equal to 3.14159+.

arc
Any part of the circumference of a circle.

radius
A straight line extending from the center of a circle or sphere to the circumference or bounding surface.

sector
A plane figure bounded by two radii and the included arc of a circle.

diameter
A straight line extending through the center of a circle or sphere and meeting the circumference or bounding surface at each end.

center
The point within a circle or sphere equally distant from all points of the circumference or surface, or the point within a regular polygon equally distant from the vertices.

ellipse
A closed plane curve generated by a point moving in such a way that the sums of its distances from two fixed points, the foci, is a constant.

major axis
The axis passing through the two foci of an ellipse.

minor axis
The axis of an ellipse that is perpendicular to the major axis at a point equidistant from the foci.

parabola
A plane curve generated by a point so moving that it remains equidistant from a fixed line and a fixed point not on the line.

hyperbola
A plane curve generated by a point so moving that the difference of the distances from two fixed points in the plane remains constant.

asymptote
A straight line limiting a curve such that the perpendicular distance from the curve to the line approaches zero as the curve is extended to infinity.

chord
The straight line segment between two points on a given curve.

spiral
A plane curve generated by a point moving around a fixed point while constantly receding from or approaching it.

eccentric
Not having the same center or center line.

off-center
Not centered or at the center point.

concentric
Having a common center, as circles or spheres.

centerline
An imaginary line that bisects a plane figure.

quadrant
An arc of 90°, or any of the four quarters into which a plane figure is divided by two perpendicular lines, numbered counterclockwise from the upper right.

curve
A continuously bending line, without angles.

concave
Curved inward like the interior of a circular arc or hollow sphere.

inflection
A change of curvature from convex to concave or vice versa.

convex
Curved or rounded outward like the exterior of a circle or sphere.

cusp
A point where two branches of curve meet, end, and are tangent.

tangent
Touching at a single point, as a straight line in relation to a curve, or in contact along a single line, as a plane with a cylinder.

evolute
The locus of the centers of curvature of, or the envelope of the normals to, another curve.

involute
A curve traced by a point on a string as it is kept taut and unwound from a stationary cylinder.

helix
A three-dimensional curve traced on a cylinder or cone by the rotation of a point crossing its right sections at a constant oblique angle.

cycloid
A curve generated by a point on the circumference of a circle as it rolls along a straight line.

spheroid
A solid geometrical figure similar in shape to a sphere, as an ellipsoid.

solid geometry
The branch of geometry that deals with solid figures and three-dimensional space.

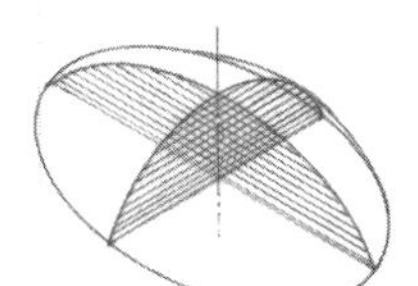

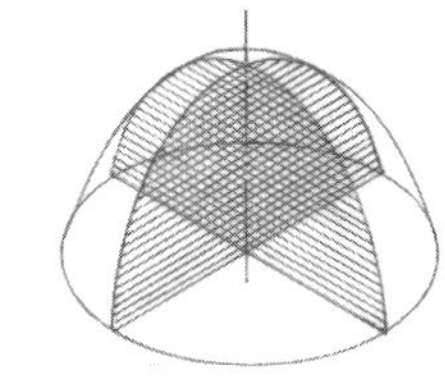

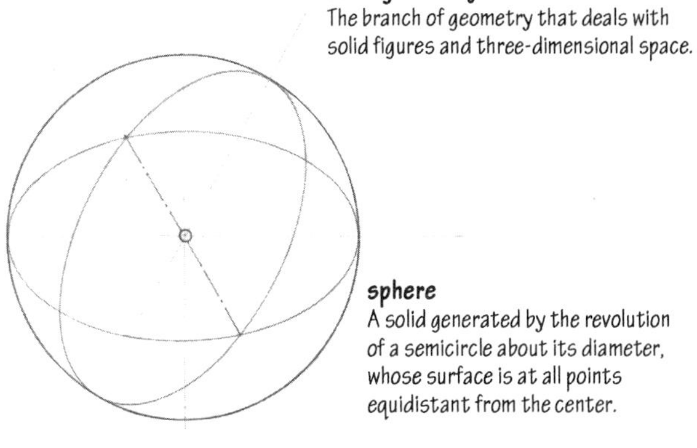

ellipsoid
A solid figure all plane sections of which are ellipses.

prolate spheroid
A spheroid generated by rotating an ellipse about its major axis.

prolate
Elongated along the polar diameter.

oblate spheroid
A spheroid generated by rotating an ellipse about its minor axis.

oblate
Flattened at the poles.

sphere
A solid generated by the revolution of a semicircle about its diameter, whose surface is at all points equidistant from the center.

cylinder
A solid bounded by two parallel planes and a surface generated by a straight line moving parallel to a fixed straight line and intersecting a closed plane curve in one of the planes.

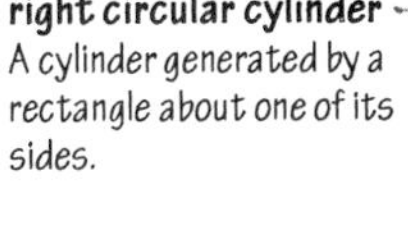

right circular cylinder
A cylinder generated by a rectangle about one of its sides.

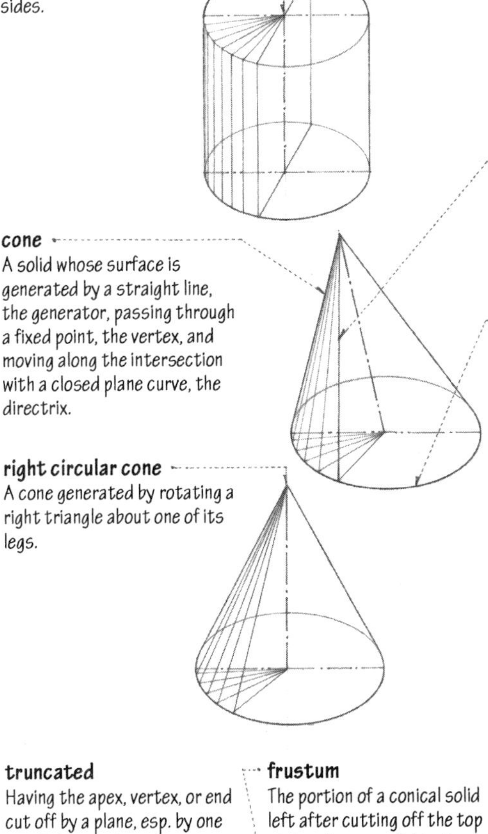

cone
A solid whose surface is generated by a straight line, the generator, passing through a fixed point, the vertex, and moving along the intersection with a closed plane curve, the directrix.

right circular cone
A cone generated by rotating a right triangle about one of its legs.

solid
A geometric figure having the three dimensions of length, breadth, and thickness. Also called **body**.

volume
The extent of a three-dimensional object or the amount of space that it occupies, measured in cubic units.

surface
Any figure having only two dimensions, as a plane or curved two-dimensional locus of points defining the boundary of a solid.

generator
An element that generates a geometric figure, esp. a straight line that generates a surface by moving in a specified fashion. Also called **generatrix**.

directrix
A fixed line used in the description of a curve or surface.

center
The point within a regular polygon equally distant from the vertices.

edge
A line at which a surface terminates or at which two surfaces of a solid meet.

vertex
A point in a geometric solid common to three or more sides.

polyhedron
A solid geometric figure bounded by plane faces.

regular
Having all faces congruent regular polygons and all solid angles congruent.

pyramid
A polyhedron having a polygonal base and triangular faces meeting at a common point or vertex.

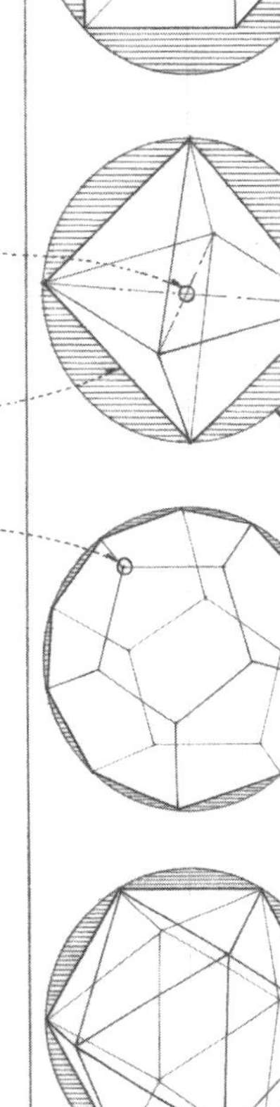

tetrahedron
A regular polyhedron bounded by four plane faces.

cube
A solid bounded by six equal square sides, the angle between any two adjacent faces being a right angle.

hexahedron
A regular polyhedron having six faces.

prism
A polyhedron having ends that are parallel, congruent polygons and sides that are parallelograms.

Platonic solid
One of the five regular polyhedrons: tetrahedron, hexahedron, octahedron, dodecahedron, or icosahedron.

octahedron
A regular polyhedron having eight faces.

dodecahedron
A regular polyhedron having 12 faces.

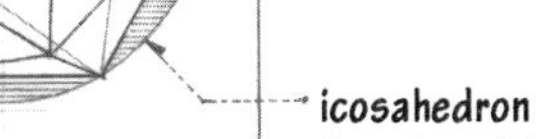

icosahedron
A regular polyhedron having 20 faces.

truncated
Having the apex, vertex, or end cut off by a plane, esp. by one parallel to the base.

frustum
The portion of a conical solid left after cutting off the top with a plane parallel to the base.

conic section
A plane curve formed by the intersection of a right circular cone with a plane.

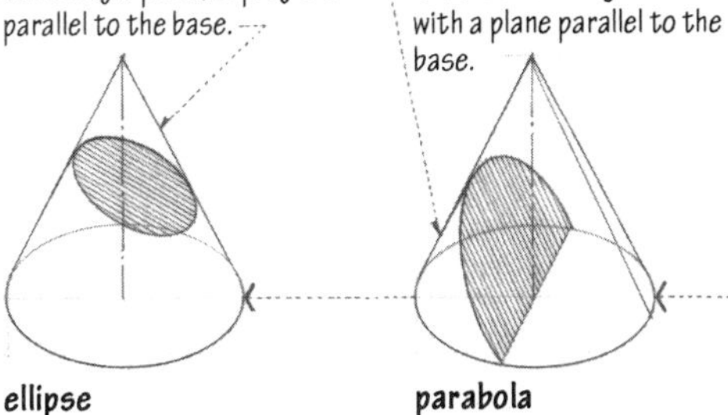

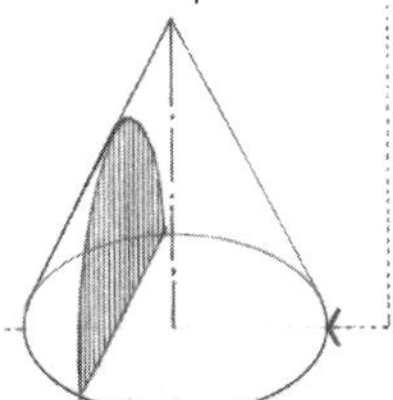

ellipse
A conic section formed by the intersection of a right circular cone with a plane that cuts through both the axis and the surface of the cone.

parabola
A conic section formed by the intersection of a right circular cone with a plane parallel to a generator of the cone.

hyperbola
A conic section formed by the intersection of a right circular cone with a plane that makes a greater angle with the base than does the generator of the cone.

A hard, brittle, usually transparent or translucent substance, produced by fusing silica together with a flux and a stabilizer into a mass that cools to a rigid condition without crystallization.

crown glass
An old form of window glass formed by blowing and whirling a hollow sphere of glass into a flat, circular disk with a center lump left by the worker's rod.

sheet glass
A flat, soda-lime-silica glass fabricated by drawing the molten glass from a furnace (**drawn glass**), or by forming a cylinder, dividing it lengthwise, and flattening it (**cylinder glass**). The fire-polished surfaces are not perfectly parallel, resulting in some distortion of vision.

plate glass
A flat, soda-lime-silica glass formed by rolling molten glass into a plate (**rolled glass**) that is subsequently ground and polished after cooling.

float glass
A flat, soda-lime-silica glass that is extremely smooth and nearly distortion-free, manufactured by pouring molten glass onto a surface of molten tin and allowing it to cool slowly. Float glass is the successor to plate glass and accounts for the majority of flat-glass production.

insulating glass
A glass unit consisting of two or more sheets of glass separated by hermetically-sealed airspaces.

hermetic
Made airtight by fusing or sealing.

tinted glass
Glass having a chemical admixture to absorb a portion of the radiant heat and visible light that strike it. Iron oxide gives the glass a pale blue-green tint; cobalt oxide and nickel imparts a grayish tint; selenium infuses a bronze tint. Also called **heat-absorbing glass**.

reflective glass
Glass having a thin, translucent metallic coating bonded to the exterior or interior surface to reflect a portion of the light and radiant heat that strike it.

low-emissivity glass
Glass that transmits visible light while selectively reflecting the longer wavelengths of radiant heat, produced by depositing a low-emissivity coating either on the glass itself or over a transparent plastic film suspended in the sealed air space of insulating glass. Also called **low-e glass**.

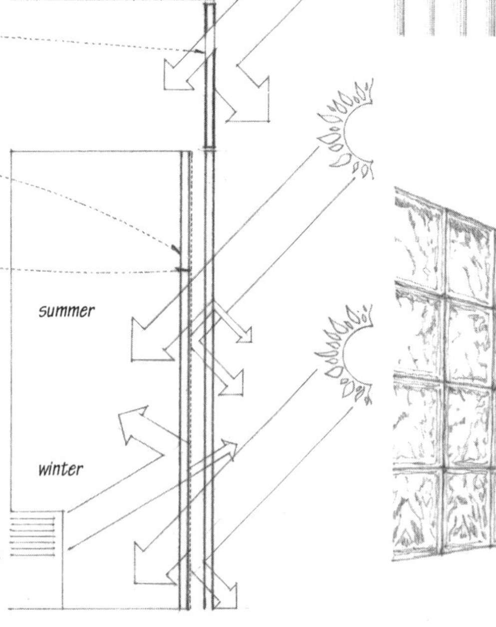

emissivity
The relative ability of a surface to emit radiant heat, measured against a black body at the same temperature.

shading coefficient
The ratio of solar heat transmission through a particular glass to the solar heat transmission through double-strength clear glass.

single-strength glass
Sheet glass having a thickness of 3/32 in. (2.4 mm).

double-strength glass
Sheet glass having a thickness of 1/8 in. (3.2 mm).

annealed glass
Glass that is cooled slowly to relieve internal stresses.

heat-strengthened glass
Annealed glass that is partially tempered by a process of reheating and sudden cooling. Heat-strengthened glass has about twice the strength of annealed glass of the same thickness.

tempered glass
Annealed glass that is reheated to just below the softening point and then rapidly cooled to induce compressive stresses in the surfaces and edges of the glass and tensile stresses in the interior. Tempered glass has three to five times the resistance of annealed glass to impact and thermal stresses but cannot be altered after fabrication. When fractured, it breaks into relatively harmless particles.

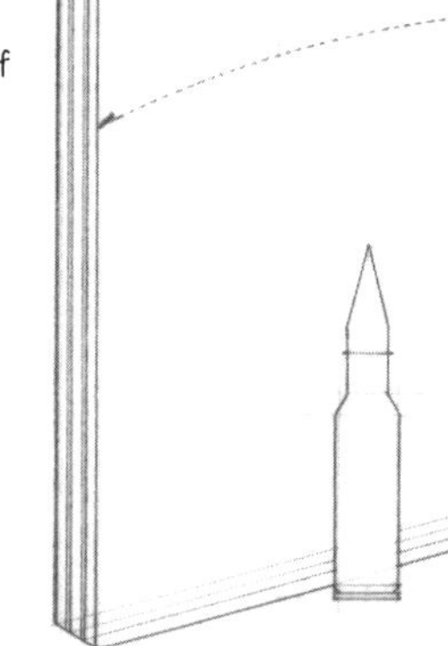

laminated glass
Two or more plies of flat glass bonded under heat and pressure to interlayers of polyvinyl butyral resin that retains the fragments if the glass is broken. Also called **safety glass**.

security glass
Laminated glass having exceptional tensile and impact strength, consisting of multiple plies of glass bonded under heat and pressure to interlayers of polyvinyl butyral resin.

acoustical glass
Laminated or insulating glass used for sound control.

wire glass
Flat or patterned glass having a square or diamond wire mesh embedded within it to prevent shattering in the event of breakage or excessive heat. Wire glass is considered a safety glazing material.

patterned glass
Glass having an irregular surface pattern formed in the rolling process to obscure vision or to diffuse light. Also called **figured glass**.

obscure glass
Glass having one or both sides acid-etched or sandblasted to obscure vision.

spandrel glass
An opaque glass for concealing the structural elements in curtain wall construction, produced by fusing a ceramic frit to the interior surface of tempered or heat-strengthened glass.

glass block
A translucent, hollow block of glass with clear, textured, or patterned faces, made by fusing two halves together with a partial vacuum inside and used for glazing openings.

glass brick
A solid, impact-resistant glass block unit, sometimes having an insert or coated to reduce solar heat transmission.

face glazing
The setting of a glass pane in a rabbeted frame, holding it in place with glazier's points, and sealing it with a beveled bead of putty or glazing compound.

face putty
The putty or glazing compound formed on the exterior side of a glass pane.

bedding
A thin layer of putty or glazing compound laid in the rabbet of a window sash to give a pane of glass an even backing.

glazier's point
A small, pointed piece of sheet metal for holding a glass pane in a wood sash until the face putty has hardened. Also called **glazing brad, sprig**.

putty
A compound of whiting and linseed oil, of doughlike consistency when fresh, used in securing windowpanes or patching woodwork defects.

glazing compound
An adhesive compound used as putty, formulated so as not to become brittle with age.

double glazing
The installation of two parallel panes of glass with a sealed air space between to reduce the transmission of heat and sound.

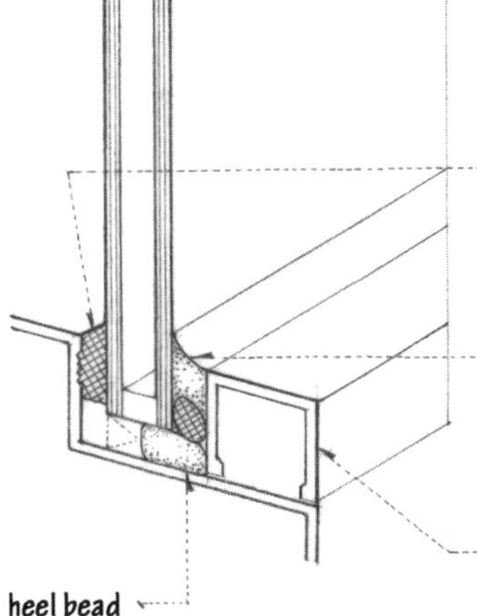

heel bead
An adhesive liquid of synthetic rubber injected between a glass pane or unit and a glazing bead, curing to form an airtight seal.

glazing
The panes or sheets of glass or other transparent material made to be set in frames, as in windows, doors, or mirrors.

wet glazing
The setting of glass in a window frame with glazing tape or a liquid sealant.

glazing tape
A preformed ribbon of synthetic rubber having adhesive properties and used in glazing to form a watertight seal between glass and frame.

cap sealant
An adhesive liquid of synthetic rubber injected into the joint between a glass pane or unit and a window frame, curing to form a watertight seal. Also called **cap bead**.

glazing bead
A wood molding or metal section secured against the edge of a glass pane or unit to hold it in place. Also called **glazing stop**.

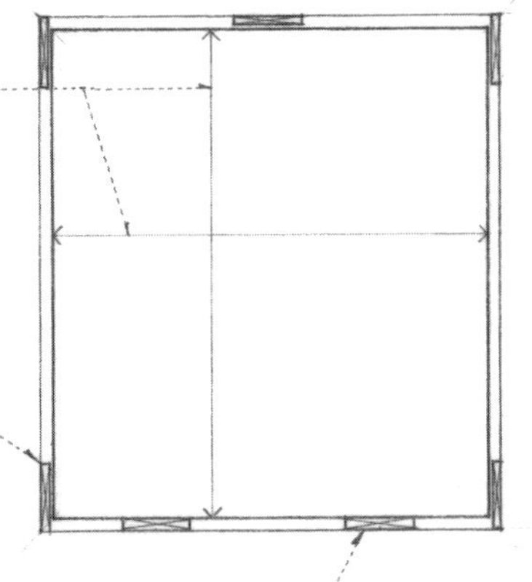

glass size
The size of a glass pane or unit required for glazing an opening, allowing for adequate edge clearances. Also called **glazing size**.

united inches
The sum of one length and one width of a rectangular glass pane or unit, measured in inches.

edge block
One of the small blocks of synthetic rubber placed between the side edges of a glass pane or unit and a frame to center it, maintain a uniform width of sealant, and limit lateral movement caused by building vibrations or thermal expansion or contraction. Also called **centering shim, spacer**.

setting block
One of the small blocks of lead or synthetic rubber placed under the lower edge of a glass pane or unit to support it within a frame.

dry glazing
The setting of glass in a window frame with a compression gasket instead of glazing tape or a liquid sealant.

compression gasket
A preformed strip of synthetic rubber or plastic compressed between a glass pane or unit and a window frame to form a watertight seal and cushion for the glass.

lockstrip gasket
A preformed gasket of synthetic rubber for securing a glass pane or unit in a window frame or opening, held in compression by forcing a keyed locking strip into a groove in the gasket.

face clearance
The distance between the face of a glass pane or unit and the nearest face of its frame or stop, measured normal to the plane of the glass.

bite
The amount of overlap between the edge of a glass pane or unit and a window frame, stop, or lock-strip gasket.

edge clearance
The distance between the edge of a glass pane or unit and a window frame, measured in the plane of the glass.

flush glazing
A glazing system in which the framing members are set entirely behind the glass panes or units to form a flush exterior surface, the glass adhering to the framing with a structural silicone sealant.

structural sealant
A high-strength silicone sealant capable of adhering glass to a supporting frame.

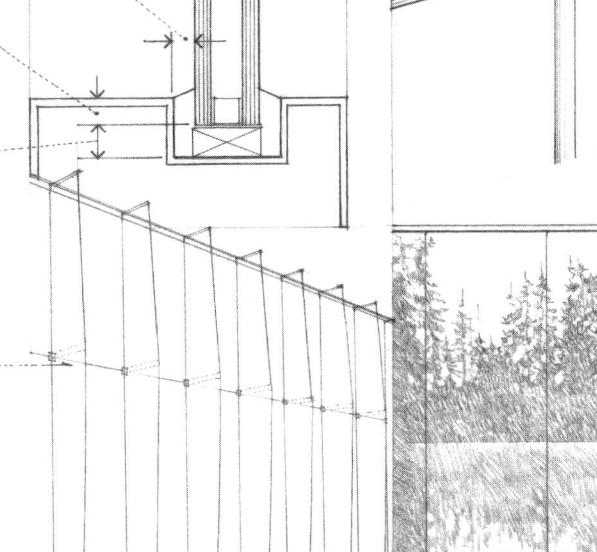

glass mullion system
A glazing system in which sheets of tempered glass are suspended from special clamps, stabilized by perpendicular stiffeners of tempered glass, and joined by a structural silicone sealant and sometimes by metal patch plates.

butt-joint glazing
A glazing system in which the glass panes or units are supported at the head and sill in a conventional manner, with their vertical edges being joined with a structural silicone sealant without mullions.

HARDWARE

The metal tools, fastenings, and fittings used in construction.

rough hardware
Bolts, screws, nails, and other metal fittings that are concealed in a finished construction.

finish hardware
Exposed hardware serving a decorative as well as a utilitarian purpose, as the locks, hinges, and other accessories for doors, windows, and cabinetwork. Also called **architectural hardware**.

door hardware
The finish hardware required for hanging and operating a door.

push plate
A protective plate of metal or plastic mounted vertically on the lock stile of a door.

door pull
A handle for opening a door.

pull bar
A bar fixed across a glazed door, used for opening or closing the door and providing protection for the glass.

kick plate
A protective metal plate fastened to the bottom of a door to resist blows and scratches.

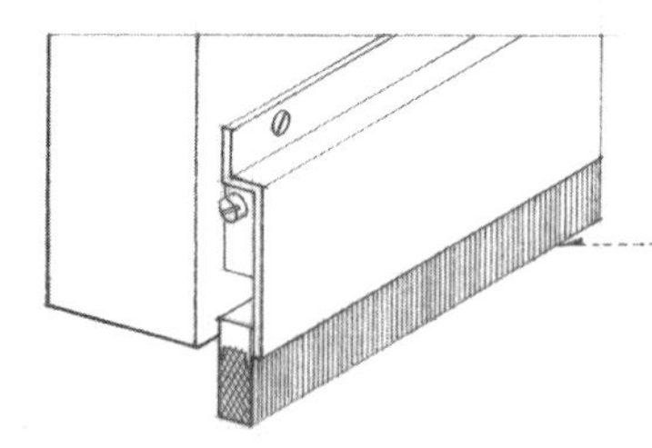

door closer
A hydraulic or pneumatic device for controlling the closing of a door and preventing it from slamming. Also called **door check**.

floor closer
A door closer installed in a recess in the floor.

automatic door bottom
A horizontal bar at the bottom of a door that drops automatically when the door is closed in order to seal the threshold and reduce noise transmission.

overhead concealed closer
A door closer concealed in the head of a doorframe.

backcheck
A device in a hydraulic door closer for slowing the speed with which a door may be opened.

knocker
A hinged ring, bar, or knob on a door for use in knocking.

doorplate
A small identifying plate on the outside door of a house or room, bearing the occupant's name, the house or apartment number, or the like.

judas
A peephole, as in an entrance door or the door of a prison cell. Also called **judas hole**.

door chain
A short chain with a removable slide fitting that can be attached between the inside of a door and the doorjamb to prevent the door from being opened more than a few inches without the chain being removed.

mail slot
A small opening in an exterior door or wall, often with a hinged closer, through which mail is delivered. Also called **letter slot**.

doorstop
A device for holding a door open, as a wedge or small weight.

bumper
A projecting rim, guard, pad, or disk for absorbing shock or preventing damage from bumping.

hand
The position of the hinges of a door, in terms of right and left, when seen from the exterior of the building or room to which the doorway leads.

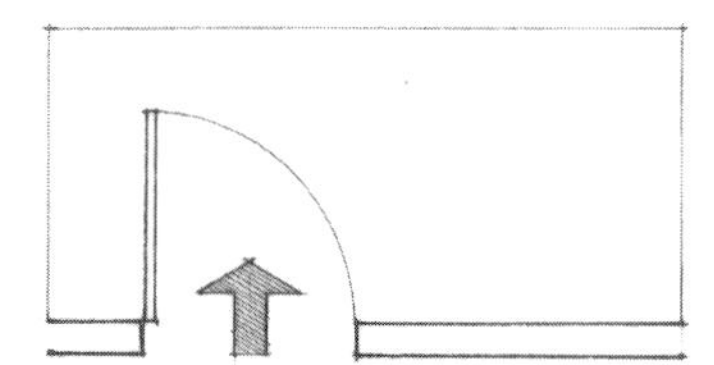

left-hand
Having the hinges on the left of an inward opening door when seen from the exterior of the building or room to which the doorway leads.

right-hand
Having the hinges on the right of an inward opening door when seen from the exterior of the building or room to which the doorway leads.

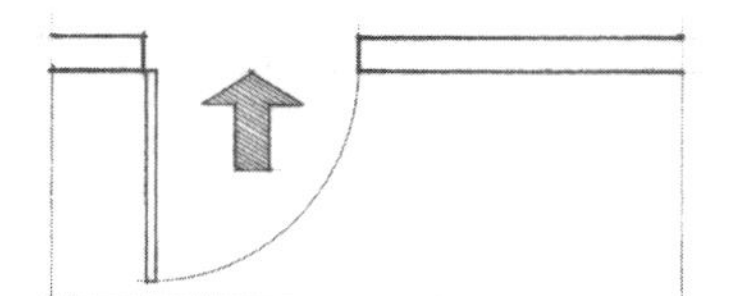

left-hand reverse
Having the hinges on the left of an outward opening door when seen from the exterior of the building or room to which the doorway leads.

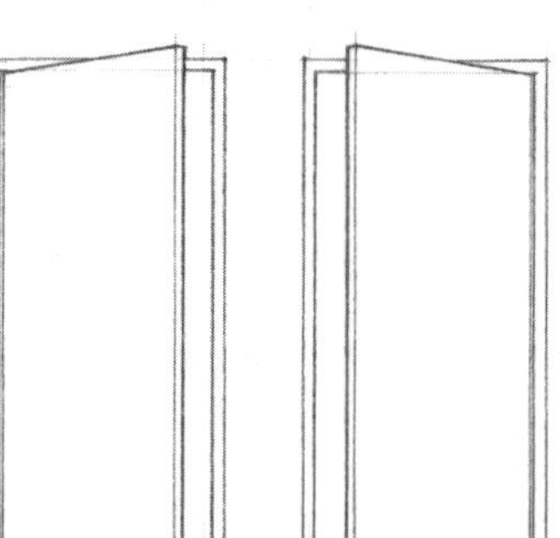

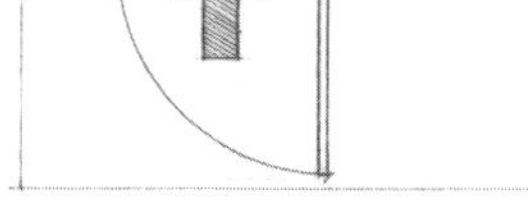

right-hand reverse
Having the hinges on the right of an outward opening door when seen from the exterior of the building or room to which the doorway leads.

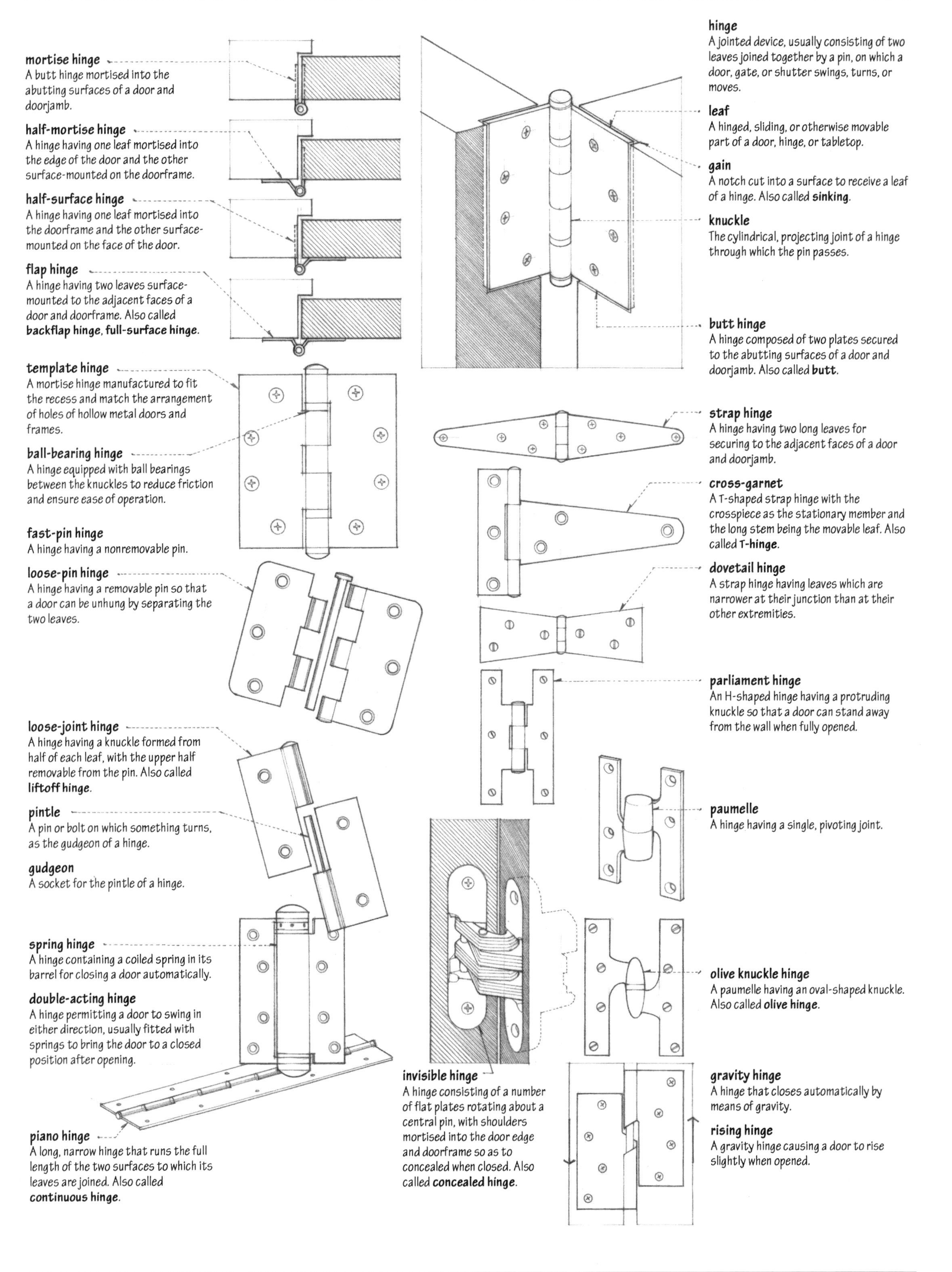

mortise hinge
A butt hinge mortised into the abutting surfaces of a door and doorjamb.

half-mortise hinge
A hinge having one leaf mortised into the edge of the door and the other surface-mounted on the doorframe.

half-surface hinge
A hinge having one leaf mortised into the doorframe and the other surface-mounted on the face of the door.

flap hinge
A hinge having two leaves surface-mounted to the adjacent faces of a door and doorframe. Also called **backflap hinge**, **full-surface hinge**.

template hinge
A mortise hinge manufactured to fit the recess and match the arrangement of holes of hollow metal doors and frames.

ball-bearing hinge
A hinge equipped with ball bearings between the knuckles to reduce friction and ensure ease of operation.

fast-pin hinge
A hinge having a nonremovable pin.

loose-pin hinge
A hinge having a removable pin so that a door can be unhung by separating the two leaves.

loose-joint hinge
A hinge having a knuckle formed from half of each leaf, with the upper half removable from the pin. Also called **liftoff hinge**.

pintle
A pin or bolt on which something turns, as the gudgeon of a hinge.

gudgeon
A socket for the pintle of a hinge.

spring hinge
A hinge containing a coiled spring in its barrel for closing a door automatically.

double-acting hinge
A hinge permitting a door to swing in either direction, usually fitted with springs to bring the door to a closed position after opening.

piano hinge
A long, narrow hinge that runs the full length of the two surfaces to which its leaves are joined. Also called **continuous hinge**.

invisible hinge
A hinge consisting of a number of flat plates rotating about a central pin, with shoulders mortised into the door edge and doorframe so as to concealed when closed. Also called **concealed hinge**.

hinge
A jointed device, usually consisting of two leaves joined together by a pin, on which a door, gate, or shutter swings, turns, or moves.

leaf
A hinged, sliding, or otherwise movable part of a door, hinge, or tabletop.

gain
A notch cut into a surface to receive a leaf of a hinge. Also called **sinking**.

knuckle
The cylindrical, projecting joint of a hinge through which the pin passes.

butt hinge
A hinge composed of two plates secured to the abutting surfaces of a door and doorjamb. Also called **butt**.

strap hinge
A hinge having two long leaves for securing to the adjacent faces of a door and doorjamb.

cross-garnet
A T-shaped strap hinge with the crosspiece as the stationary member and the long stem being the movable leaf. Also called **T-hinge**.

dovetail hinge
A strap hinge having leaves which are narrower at their junction than at their other extremities.

parliament hinge
An H-shaped hinge having a protruding knuckle so that a door can stand away from the wall when fully opened.

paumelle
A hinge having a single, pivoting joint.

olive knuckle hinge
A paumelle having an oval-shaped knuckle. Also called **olive hinge**.

gravity hinge
A hinge that closes automatically by means of gravity.

rising hinge
A gravity hinge causing a door to rise slightly when opened.

lock
A device for securing a door, drawer, or lid in position when closed, consisting of a bolt or combination of bolts propelled and withdrawn by a key- or combination-operated mechanism.

rim lock
A lock fastened to the face of a door, as opposed to one built into its edge.

cylinder lock
A lock housed within two holes bored at right angles to each other, one through the face of a door and the other in the door edge.

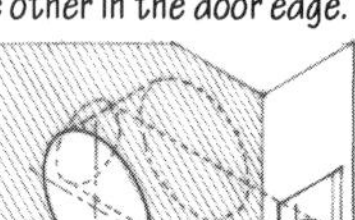

unit lock
A lock housed within a rectangular notch cut into the edge of a door.

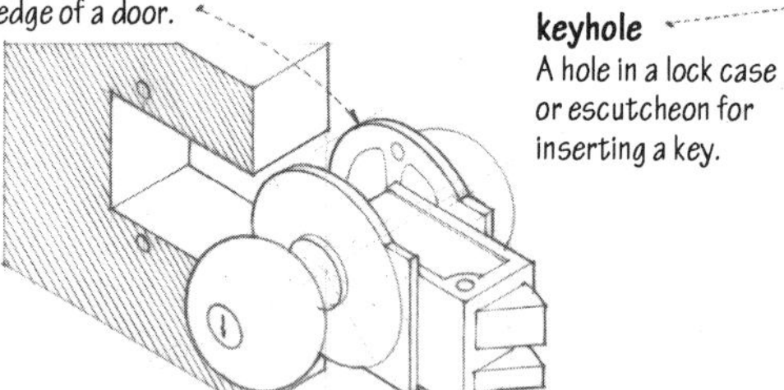

mortise lock
A lock housed within a mortise cut into a door edge so that the lock mechanism is covered on both sides.

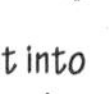

spindle
The bar or shaft that carries the knobs and actuates the latch or bolt of a lock.

panic bar
A horizontal bar that spans the interior of an emergency exit door at waist height and that opens the latch when pressure is applied. Also called **panic bolt, panic hardware**.

lockset
An assembly of parts making up a complete locking system, including knobs, plates and a locking mechanism.

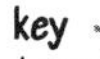

doorknob
The knob-shaped handle by which a door is opened or closed.

keyhole
A hole in a lock case or escutcheon for inserting a key.

rose
An ornamental plate surrounding the shaft of a doorknob at the face of a door.

escutcheon
A protective or ornamental plate, as around a keyhole, doorknob, drawer pull, or light switch. Also, **scutcheon.**

backset
The horizontal distance from the face of a lock through which the bolt passes to the centerline of the knob stem, keyhole, or lock cylinder.

lever handle
A horizontal handle for operating the bolt of a lock.

strike
A metal plate on a doorjamb having a hole for receiving the end of a lock bolt when the door is closed. Also called **strike plate.**

lip
The projecting edge or rim of a strike.

box strike
A metal box recessed into a doorjamb to receive the end of a lock bolt when the door is closed.

latch
A device for holding a door closed, consisting essentially of a bar that falls or slides into a groove or hole.

key
A small metal instrument specially cut to fit into a lock and move its bolt.

bit
One of the projecting blades cut to engage with and actuate either or both the bolt and the tumblers of a lock.

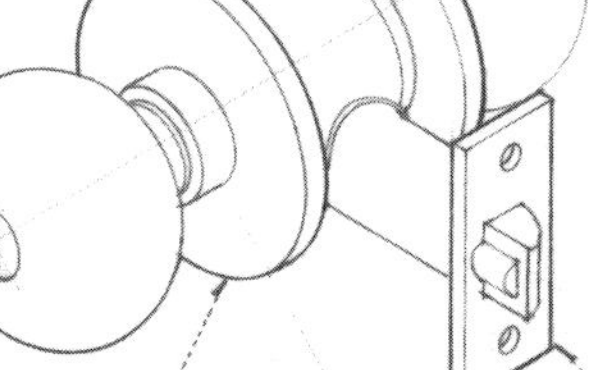

faceplate
The edge plate or surface through which the bolt of a lock passes. Also called **selvage.**

bolt
A metal bar or rod in the mechanism of a lock that is propelled or withdrawn, as by turning a knob or key.

deadbolt
A lock bolt having a square head that is moved into position by the turning of a knob or key rather than by spring action. Also called **deadlock.**

bevel
The oblique end of a latchbolt that hits a strike plate.

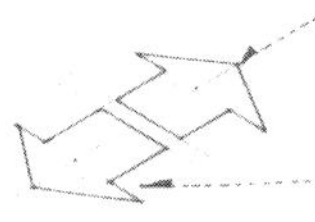

latchbolt
A lock bolt having a beveled head that is moved into position by a spring except when retracted by a doorknob, or when pushed against the lip of the strike plate as the door is closed.

flush bolt
A bolt set flush with the face or edge of a door.

extension bolt
A flush bolt fitted into a mortise in a door, sliding into a socket in the head or the sill.

coordinator
A device for ensuring that the inactive leaf of a pair of doors is permitted to close before the active leaf.

cylinder
A cylindrical device for retaining the bolt of a lock until the tumblers have been pushed out of its way.

tumbler
An obstructing part in a lock that prevents a bolt from being propelled or withdrawn until it is moved by the action of a key.

lever tumbler
A flat metal tumbler having a pivoting motion actuated by the turning of a key.

cam
A disk or cylinder having an irregular form that rotates or slides to impart motion to a roller moving against its edge or to a pin free to move in a groove on its face.

keyway
A slot in a lock for receiving and guiding a key.

ward
A projecting ridge of metal in a lock or keyhole that prevents the insertion of any key that does not have a corresponding notch.

reversible lock
A lock having a latchbolt that can be reversed for installation in either a right-hand or left-hand door.

bevel
The side of a lock facing in the same direction as the bevel at the end of the latchbolt.

regular bevel
The bevel of a bolt or lock on a door opening into the building or room to which the doorway leads.

reverse bevel
The bevel of a bolt or lock on a door opening outward from the building or room to which the doorway leads.

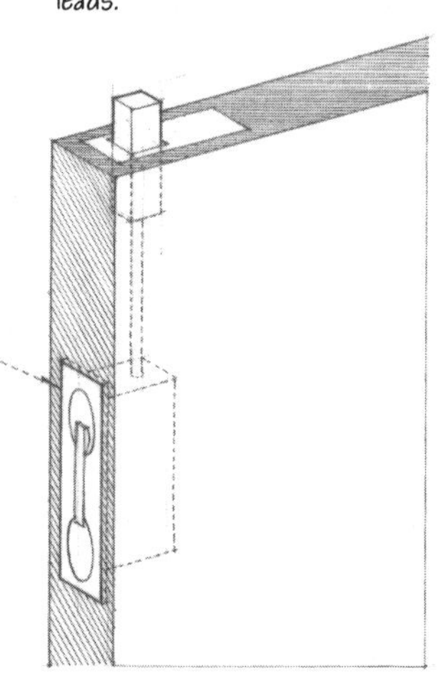

A form of energy associated with the random motion of atoms or molecules, capable of being transmitted by convection, conduction, or radiation and causing substances to rise in temperature, fuse, expand, or evaporate.

temperature
A measure of the warmth or coldness of a substance, object, or environment with reference to some standard value.

thermometer
An instrument for measuring temperature, consisting typically of a glass tube with a numbered scale and a bulb containing a liquid, as mercury, that rises and falls with changes in temperature.

British thermal unit
The quantity of heat required to raise the temperature of one pound (0.4 kg) of water 1°F. Abbr.: **Btu**

therm
A unit of heat equal to 100,000 British thermal units.

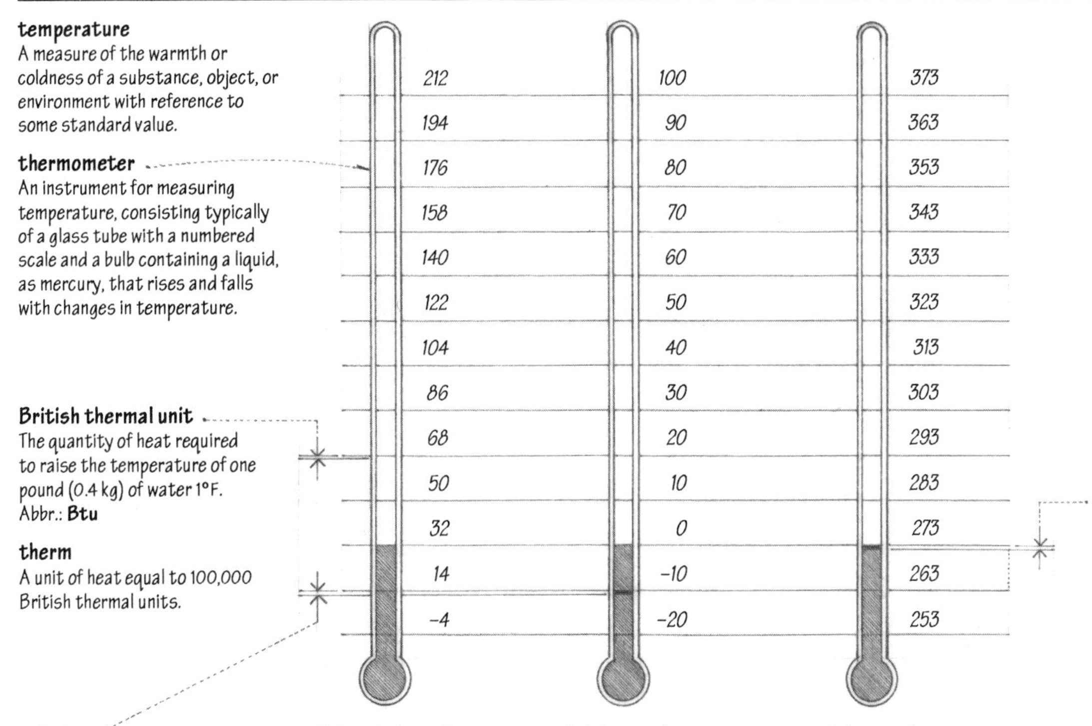

kelvin
The base SI unit of temperature equal to 1/273.16 of the triple point of water. Symbol: **K**

triple point
The particular temperature and pressure at which the liquid, gaseous, and solid phases of a substance can exist in equilibrium.

calorie
A unit of heat equal to the quantity of heat required to raise the temperature of one gram of water 1°C at a pressure of one atmosphere, equivalent to 4.186 joules. Abbr.: **cal.** Also called **gram calorie, small calorie.**

kilocalorie
A unit of heat equal to the quantity of heat required to raise the temperature of one kilogram of water 1°C at a pressure of one atmosphere, equivalent to 1000 small calories. Abbr.: **Cal.** Also called **kilogram calorie, large calorie.**

Fahrenheit scale
A temperature scale in which 32°F represents the freezing point and 212°F the boiling point of water under standard atmospheric pressure.

When you know degrees Fahrenheit, first subtract 32 and then multiply by 5/9 to find degrees Celsius.

Celsius scale
A temperature scale divided into 100 degrees, in which 0°C represents the freezing point and 100°C the boiling point of water under standard atmospheric pressure. Also called **Centigrade scale.**

When you know degrees Celsius, first multiply by 9/5 and then add 32 to find degrees Fahrenheit.

Kelvin scale
An absolute scale of temperature having a zero point of -273.16°C.

absolute scale
A temperature scale based on absolute zero with scale units equal in magnitude to centigrade degrees.

absolute zero
The hypothetical lowest limit of physical temperature characterized by complete absence of heat, equal to -273.16°C or -459.67°F.

absolute temperature
Temperature as measured on a absolute scale.

heat capacity
The quantity of heat required to raise the temperature of a substance by one degree.

specific heat
Heat capacity per unit mass of a substance: the number of Btu required to raise the temperature of one pound of a substance 1°F, or the number of calories per gram per degree centigrade.

gaseous phase (steam)
liquid phase (water)
solid phase (ice)
temperature (°C)
125
100
75
50
25
0
-25
time

latent heat
The quantity of heat absorbed or released by a substance during a change in phase at constant temperature and pressure.

sensible heat
The quantity of heat absorbed or released by a substance during a change in temperature without a change in phase.

conduction
The transfer of heat from the warmer to the cooler particles of a medium or of two bodies in direct contact, occurring without perceptible displacement of the particles themselves.

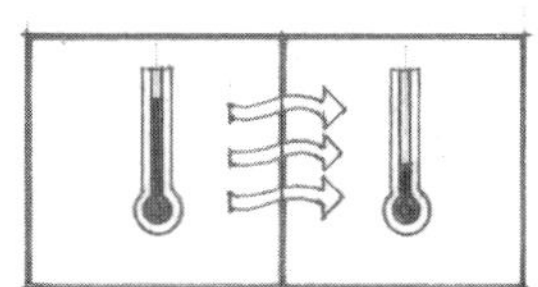

convection
The transfer of heat by the circulatory motion of the heated parts of a liquid or gas owing to a variation in density and the action of gravity.

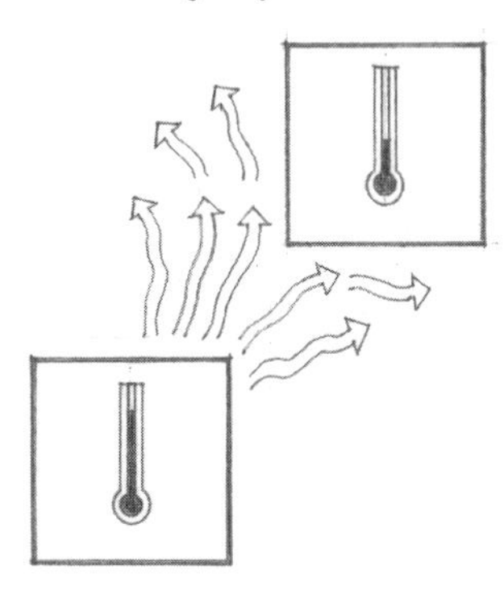

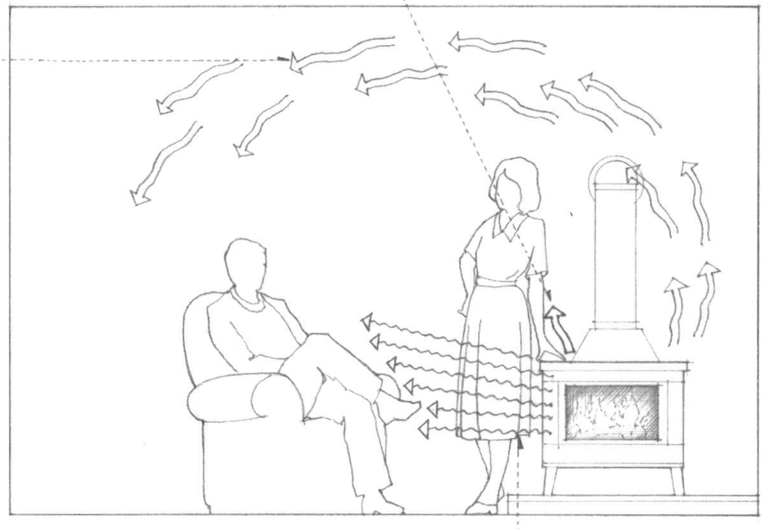

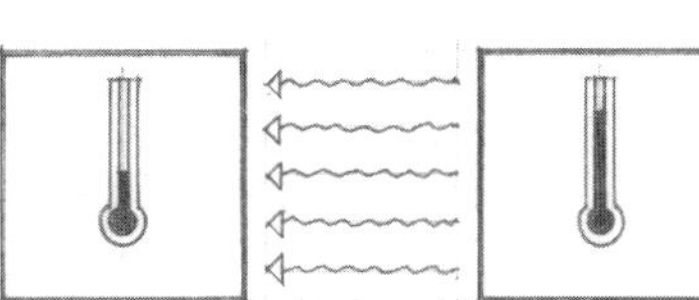

radiation
The process in which energy in the form of waves or particles is emitted by one body, passed through an intervening medium or space, and absorbed by another body.

thermal conductivity
The time rate of heat flow through a unit area of a given material of unit thickness when the temperature difference across the thickness is one unit of temperature.

thermal conductance
The time rate of heat flow through a unit area of a given material when the temperature difference across a specified thickness of the material is one unit of temperature.

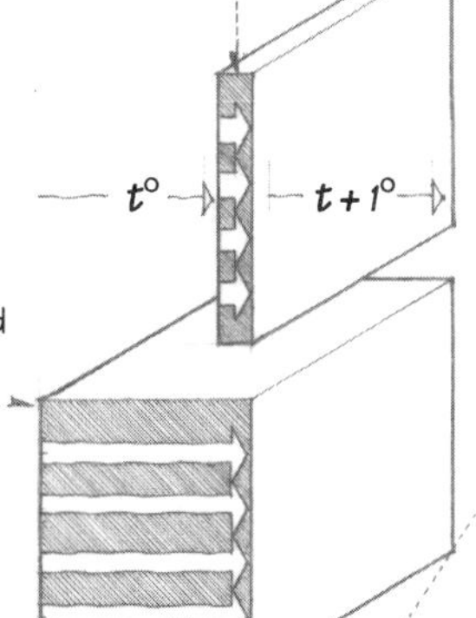

thermal resistance
The reciprocal of thermal conductance, expressed as the temperature difference required to cause heat to flow through a unit area of a material of given thickness at the rate of one heat unit per unit time.

R-value
A measure of thermal resistance of a given material, used esp. to specify the performance of thermal insulation. The total R-value for a building component or assembly is the sum of the R-values for each layer in the component or assembly.

thermal transmittance
The time rate of heat flow through a unit area of a building component or assembly when the difference between the air temperatures on the two sides of the component or assembly is one unit of temperature. Also called **coefficient of heat transfer**.

U-value
A measure of the thermal transmittance of a building component or assembly, equal to the reciprocal of the total R-value of the component or assembly.

$C = 1/R$

$1/R(total) = U$

thermal break
An element of low thermal conductivity placed in an assembly to reduce the flow of heat between highly conductive materials. Also called **thermal barrier**.

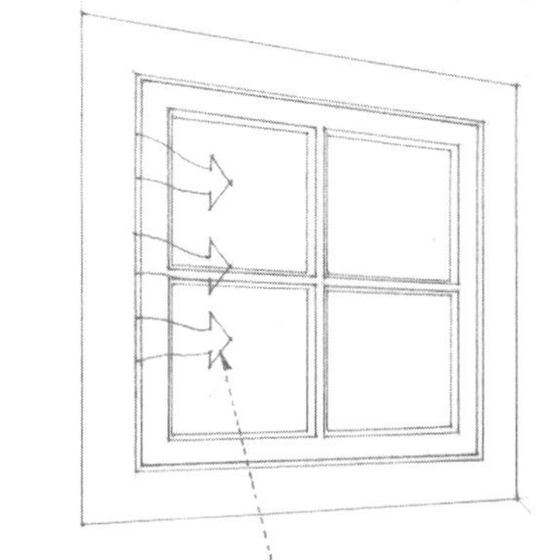

infiltration
The flow of outside air into an interior space through cracks around windows and doors or other openings in the envelope of a building.

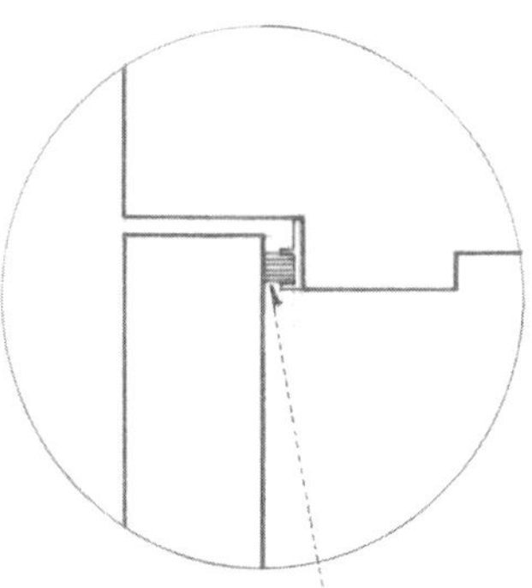

weather strip
A strip of metal, felt, vinyl, or foam rubber, placed between a door or window sash and its frame to provide a seal against windblown rain and air infiltration. Also, **weather stripping**.

mineral wool
Any of various lightweight, inorganic, fibrous materials used esp. for thermal and sound insulation, as glass wool and rock wool.

glass wool
Spun glass fibers resembling wool and used for thermal insulation and air filters.

fiberglass
A material consisting of extremely fine filaments of glass, woven into fabric, massed for use as a thermal and acoustical insulator, or embedded to reinforce various materials.

Fiberglas
Trademark for a brand of fiberglass.

rock wool
Mineral wool made by blowing steam or air through molten slag or rock.

airway
The passageway required for the circulation of air between batt insulation and roof sheathing.

batt insulation
Flexible, fibrous thermal insulation of glass or mineral wool, made in various thicknesses and lengths and in 16-in. (406 mm) or 24-in. (610 mm) widths to fit between studs, joists, and rafters in light wood frame construction, sometimes faced with a vapor retarder of kraft paper, metal foil, or plastic sheet. Batt insulation is also as a component in sound-insulating construction. Also called **blanket insulation**.

kraft paper
A strong, usually brown paper, processed from wood pulp and sized with resin.

thermal insulation
A material providing high resistance to heat flow, as mineral wool, vermiculite, or foamed plastic, fabricated in the form of batts, blankets, boards, or loose fill.

weatherize
To make a house or building secure against cold or stormy weather, as by adding thermal insulation or storm windows, or by sealing joints.

foamed plastic
Plastic, as polyurethane or polystyrene, made light and cellular by the introduction of pockets of gas or air and used as thermal insulation. Also called **expanded plastic**, **plastic foam**.

polyurethane foam
A rigid expanded polyurethane having a closed-cell structure and used as thermal insulation.

molded polystyrene
A rigid polystyrene foam having an open-cell structure and used as thermal insulation.

extruded polystyrene
A rigid polystyrene foam having a closed-cell structure and used as thermal insulation.

Styrofoam
Trademark for a brand of foamed plastic made from polystyrene.

foam glass
Cellular glass made by foaming softened glass and molding it into boards or blocks for use as thermal insulation.

rigid board insulation
A preformed, nonstructural insulating board of foamed plastic or cellular glass. Cellular glass insulation is fire-resistant, impervious to moisture, and dimensionally stable, but has a lower thermal-resistance value than foamed plastic insulations, which are flammable and must be protected by a thermal barrier when used on the interior surfaces of a building. Rigid insulation having closed-cell structures, as extruded polystyrene and cellular glass, are moisture-resistant and may be used in contact with the earth.

fiberboard
An insulating board made of wood or cane fibers compressed and cemented into rigid sheets, used as an inexpensive wall finish or as ceiling tiles.

fiberboard sheathing
Insulating fiberboard treated or impregnated with asphalt for water resistance and used primarily for sheathing light wood frame walls.

foamed-in-place insulation
Thermal insulation in the form of a foamed plastic, as polyurethane, that is sprayed or injected into a cavity where it adheres to the surrounding surfaces.

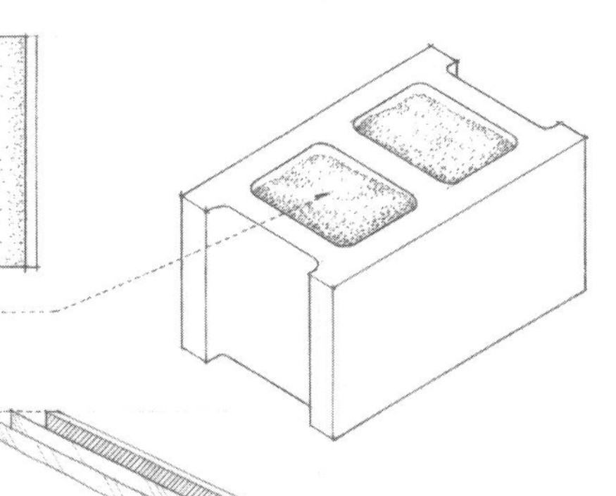

loose-fill insulation
Thermal insulation in the form of mineral wool fibers, granular vermiculite or perlite, or treated cellulosic fibers, poured by hand or blown through a nozzle into a cavity or over a supporting membrane.

wood wool
Fine wood shavings, usually of pine or chemically treated wood fibers, used as an insulating material, as a binder in plaster, and for packing. Also called **excelsior**.

reflective insulation
Thermal insulation in the form of a material of high reflectivity and low emissivity, as paper-backed aluminum foil or foil-backed gypsum board, used in conjunction with a dead-air space to reduce the transfer of heat by radiation.

emissivity
The ability of a surface to emit heat by radiation, equal to the ratio of the radiant energy emitted to that emitted by a black body at the same temperature.

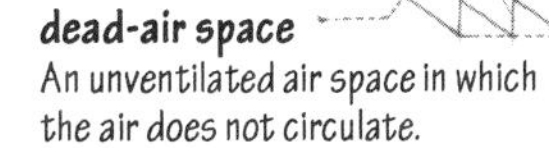

dead-air space
An unventilated air space in which the air does not circulate.

thermal comfort
Human comfort as determined by the ability of the body to dissipate the heat and moisture it produces by metabolic action.

effective temperature
A temperature representing the combined effect of ambient temperature, relative humidity, and air movement on the sensation of warmth or cold felt by the human body, equivalent to the dry-bulb temperature of still air at 50% relative humidity which induces an identical sensation.

wet-bulb temperature
The temperature recorded by the wet-bulb thermometer in a psychrometer.

dew point
The temperature at which air becomes saturated with water vapor. Also called **dew-point temperature**.

comfort zone
The range of dry-bulb temprature, relative humidity, mean radiant temperature, and air movement judged to be comfortable by a majority of Americans and Canadians tested. This comfort zone varies with climate, the season of the year, the type of clothing worn, and the activity level of the individual. Also called **comfort envelope**.

humidity ratio
The ratio of the mass of water vapor to the mass of dry air in a mixture of air and water vapor. Also called **mixing ratio**.

enthalpy
A measure of the total heat contained in a substance, equal to the internal energy of the substance plus the product of its volume and pressure. The enthalpy of air is equal to the sensible heat of the air and the water vapor present in the air plus the latent heat of the water vapor, expressed in Btu per pound (kilojoules per kilogram) of dry air. Also called **heat content**.

psychrometric chart
A chart relating the wet-bulb and dry-bulb readings from a psychrometer to relative humidity, absolute humidity, and dew point.

dry-bulb temperature
The temperature recorded by the dry-bulb thermometer in a psychrometer.

psychrometer
An instrument for measuring atmospheric humidity, consisting of two thermometers, the bulb of one being dry and the bulb of the other being kept moist and ventilated so that the cooling that results from evaporation makes it register a lower temperature than the dry one, with the difference between the readings being a measure of atmospheric humidity.

relative humidity
The ratio of the amount of water vapor actually present in the air to the maximum amount that the air could hold at the same temperature, expressed as a percentage. Abbr.: **rh**

absolute humidity
The mass of water vapor present in a unit volume of air.

specific humidity
The ratio of the mass of water vapor in air to the total mass of the mixture of air and water vapor.

hygrometer
Any of various instruments for measuring the humidity of the atmosphere.

adiabatic heating
A rise in temperature occurring without the addition or removal of heat, as when excess water vapor in the air condenses and the latent heat of vaporization of the water vapor is converted to sensible heat in the air.

mean radiant temperature
The sum of the temperatures of the surrounding walls, floor, and ceiling of a room, weighted according to the solid angle subtended by each at the point of measurement. Mean radiant temperature is important to thermal comfort since the human body receives radiant heat from or loses heat by radiation to the surrounding surfaces if their mean radiant temperature is significantly higher or lower than the air temperature.

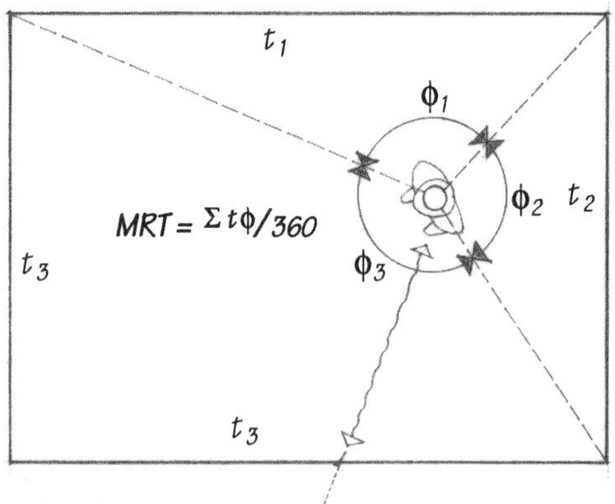

radiant heat
Heat energy transmitted by the radiation of electromagnetic waves in contrast to heat transmitted by conduction or convection.

evaporative cooling
A drop in temperature occurring without the addition or removal of heat, as when water evaporates and the sensible heat of the liquid is converted to latent heat in the vapor. Also called **adiabatic cooling**.

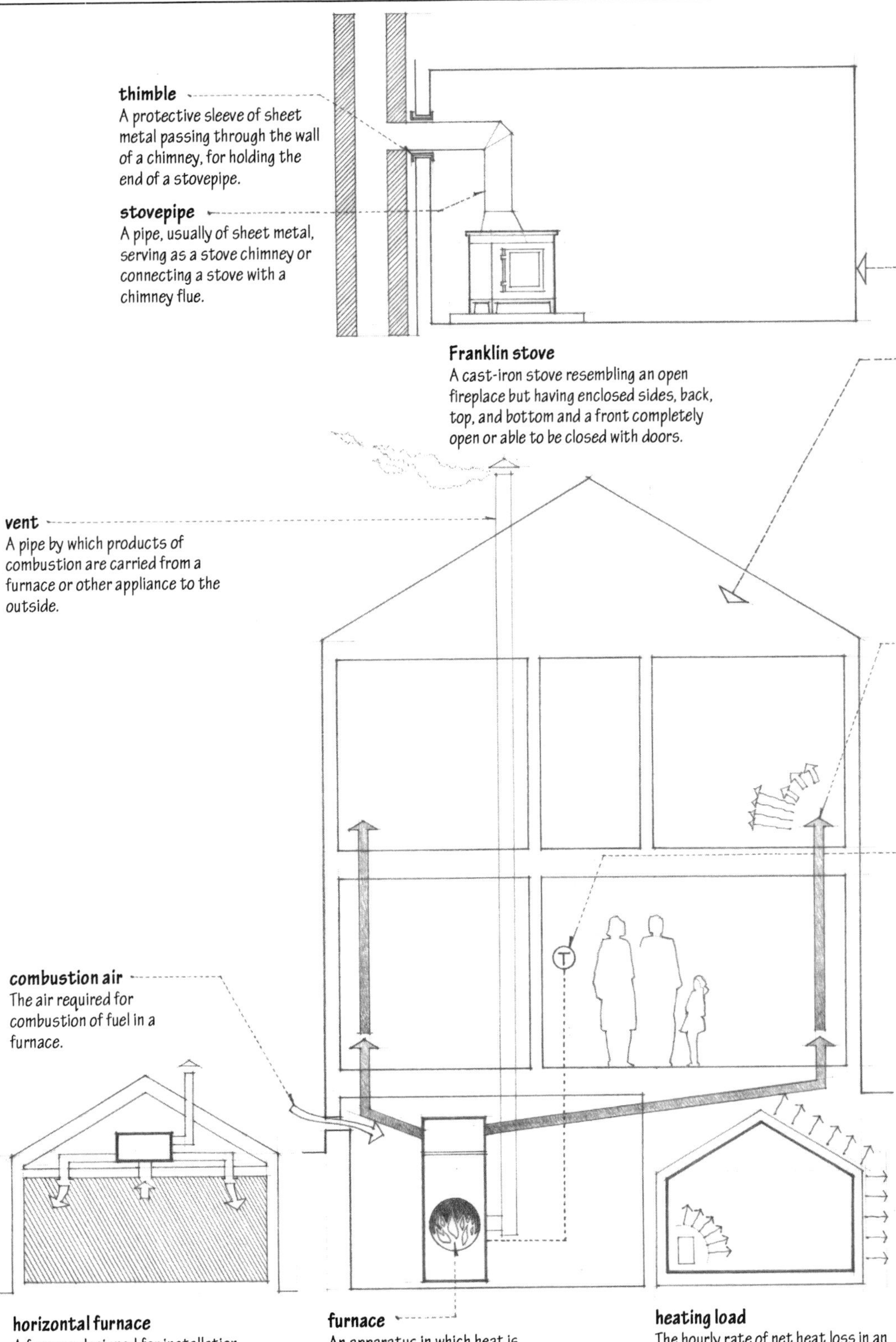

thimble
A protective sleeve of sheet metal passing through the wall of a chimney, for holding the end of a stovepipe.

stovepipe
A pipe, usually of sheet metal, serving as a stove chimney or connecting a stove with a chimney flue.

Franklin stove
A cast-iron stove resembling an open fireplace but having enclosed sides, back, top, and bottom and a front completely open or able to be closed with doors.

mechanical system
Any of the systems that provide essential services to a building, as water supply, sewage disposal, electric power, heating, ventilation, air-conditioning, vertical transportation, or fire fighting.

space heating
The heating of a limited area, as a room, esp. by means of a heat source located within the space.

central heating
A mechanical system that supplies heat to an entire building from a single source through a network of ducts or pipes.

vent
A pipe by which products of combustion are carried from a furnace or other appliance to the outside.

heating medium
A fluid substance, as warm air, hot water, or steam, capable of conveying heat from a source to the space being heated.

thermostat
A device that automatically responds to changes in temperature and activates switches controlling such equipment as furnaces, refrigerators, and air conditioners.

thermocouple
A device for measuring temperature in which a pair of dissimilar metals, as copper and iron, are joined so that a potential difference generated between the points of contact is a measure of the temperature difference between the points.

bimetallic element
A material made by bonding two metallic strips having different coefficients of expansion, used in temperature-indicating and temperature-controlling devices.

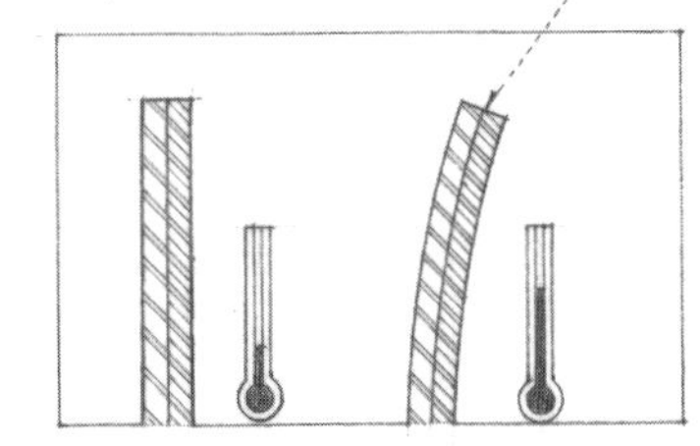

combustion air
The air required for combustion of fuel in a furnace.

horizontal furnace
A furnace designed for installation in a low attic or crawl space.

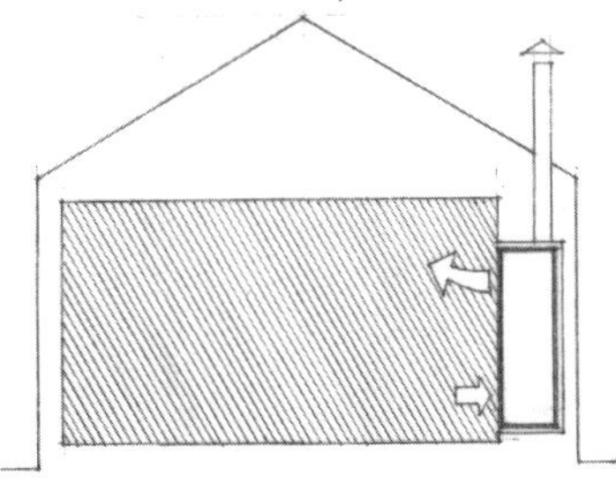

wall furnace
A furnace recessed in or mounted on a wall and supplying heated air directly to a space without the use of ducts.

furnace
An apparatus in which heat is produced, as for heating a house or producing steam.

electric furnace
A furnace in which the heat required is produced through electricity.

gas furnace
A furnace using gas as a fuel.

oil burner
A furnace or boiler that burns fuel oil.

conversion burner
A burner designed for installation in a furnace that originally used another fuel.

heating load
The hourly rate of net heat loss in an enclosed space, expressed in Btu per hour and used as the basis for selecting a heating unit or system.

heating degree day
A degree-day below the standard temperature of 65°F (19°C), used in estimating fuel or power consumption by a heating system.

degree day
A unit that represents one degree of departure in the mean daily outdoor temperature from a given standard temperature.

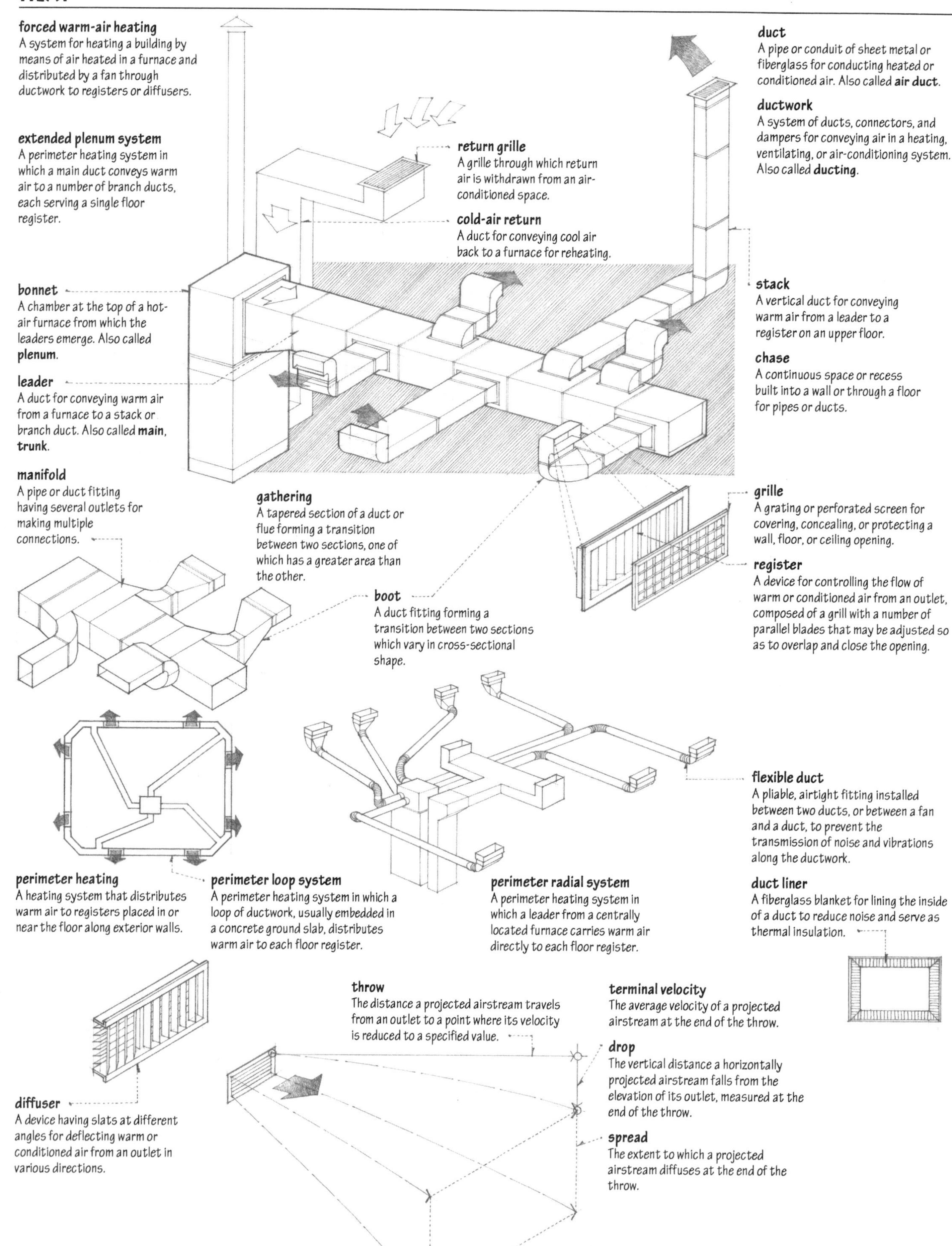

forced warm-air heating
A system for heating a building by means of air heated in a furnace and distributed by a fan through ductwork to registers or diffusers.

extended plenum system
A perimeter heating system in which a main duct conveys warm air to a number of branch ducts, each serving a single floor register.

bonnet
A chamber at the top of a hot-air furnace from which the leaders emerge. Also called **plenum**.

leader
A duct for conveying warm air from a furnace to a stack or branch duct. Also called **main**, **trunk**.

return grille
A grille through which return air is withdrawn from an air-conditioned space.

cold-air return
A duct for conveying cool air back to a furnace for reheating.

duct
A pipe or conduit of sheet metal or fiberglass for conducting heated or conditioned air. Also called **air duct**.

ductwork
A system of ducts, connectors, and dampers for conveying air in a heating, ventilating, or air-conditioning system. Also called **ducting**.

stack
A vertical duct for conveying warm air from a leader to a register on an upper floor.

chase
A continuous space or recess built into a wall or through a floor for pipes or ducts.

manifold
A pipe or duct fitting having several outlets for making multiple connections.

gathering
A tapered section of a duct or flue forming a transition between two sections, one of which has a greater area than the other.

boot
A duct fitting forming a transition between two sections which vary in cross-sectional shape.

grille
A grating or perforated screen for covering, concealing, or protecting a wall, floor, or ceiling opening.

register
A device for controlling the flow of warm or conditioned air from an outlet, composed of a grill with a number of parallel blades that may be adjusted so as to overlap and close the opening.

perimeter heating
A heating system that distributes warm air to registers placed in or near the floor along exterior walls.

perimeter loop system
A perimeter heating system in which a loop of ductwork, usually embedded in a concrete ground slab, distributes warm air to each floor register.

perimeter radial system
A perimeter heating system in which a leader from a centrally located furnace carries warm air directly to each floor register.

flexible duct
A pliable, airtight fitting installed between two ducts, or between a fan and a duct, to prevent the transmission of noise and vibrations along the ductwork.

duct liner
A fiberglass blanket for lining the inside of a duct to reduce noise and serve as thermal insulation.

diffuser
A device having slats at different angles for deflecting warm or conditioned air from an outlet in various directions.

throw
The distance a projected airstream travels from an outlet to a point where its velocity is reduced to a specified value.

terminal velocity
The average velocity of a projected airstream at the end of the throw.

drop
The vertical distance a horizontally projected airstream falls from the elevation of its outlet, measured at the end of the throw.

spread
The extent to which a projected airstream diffuses at the end of the throw.

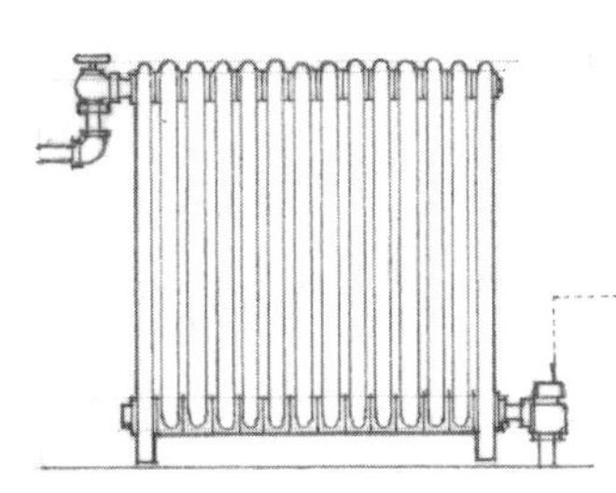

radiator
A heating device consisting of a series or coil of pipes through which hot water or steam passes.

venturi tee
A special fitting used in a one-pipe system to induce the flow of water from a return branch into the supply main.

bucket trap
A valve for eliminating air and condensed moisture from a radiator without allowing steam to escape. Also called **steam trap**.

bleeder
A valve for draining a pipe, radiator, or tank. Also called **bleeder valve**.

hot-water heating
A system for heating a building by means of water heated in a boiler and circulated by a pump through pipes to radiators or convectors. Also called **hydronic heating**.

steam heating
A system for heating a building by means of steam generated in a boiler and circulated through pipes to radiators.

one-pipe system
A hot-water heating system in which a single pipe supplies hot water from a boiler to each radiator or convector in sequence.

two-pipe system
A hot-water heating system in which one pipe supplies hot water from a boiler to the radiators or convectors and a second pipe returns the water to the boiler.

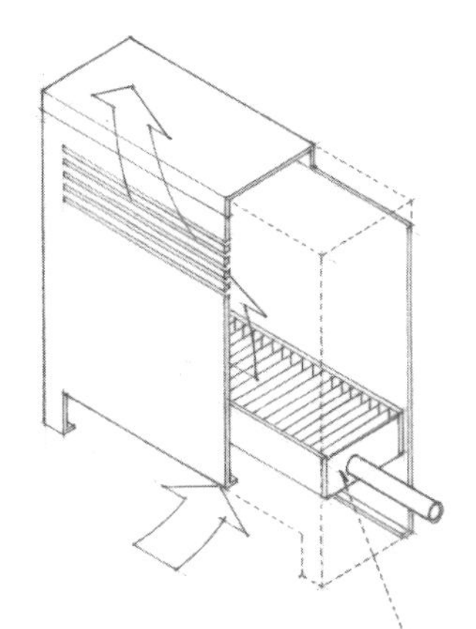

reverse return
A two-pipe hot-water system in which the lengths of the supply and return pipes for each radiator or convector are nearly equal.

direct return
A two-pipe hot-water system in which the return pipe from each radiator or convector takes the shortest route back to the boiler.

dry return
A return pipe in a steam-heating system that carries both air and water of condensation.

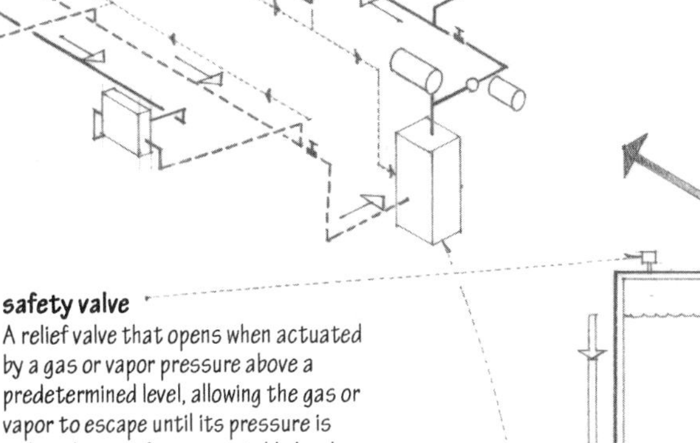

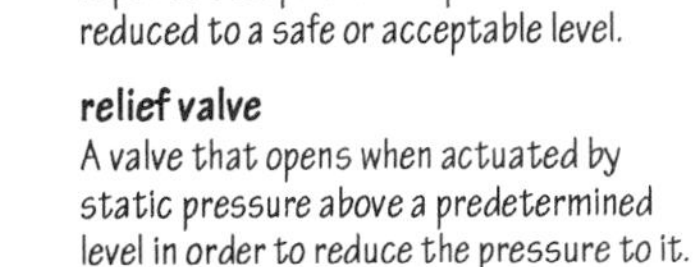

convector
A heating unit in which air heated by contact with a radiator or fin tube circulates by convection.

fin tube
A type of radiator having horizontal tubes with closely spaced vertical fins to maximize heat transfer to the surrounding air.

baseboard heater
A long, narrow hydronic or electric convector designed for installation along the base of a wall.

safety valve
A relief valve that opens when actuated by a gas or vapor pressure above a predetermined level, allowing the gas or vapor to escape until its pressure is reduced to a safe or acceptable level.

relief valve
A valve that opens when actuated by static pressure above a predetermined level in order to reduce the pressure to it.

petcock
A small faucet or valve for draining or releasing compression in pipes, radiators, and boilers.

boiler
A closed vessel or arrangement of vessels and tubes in which water is heated or steam is generated to supply heat or power.

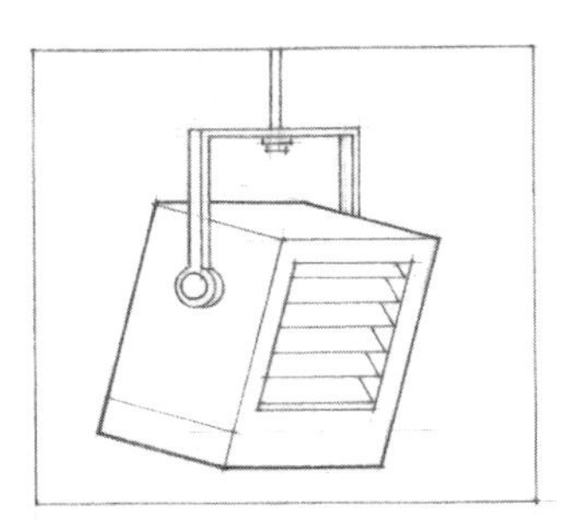

unit heater
A self-contained electric or gas-fired space heater, consisting of a heating element, fan, and a directional outlet.

space heater
A device for heating the space in which it is located, esp. a unit that has no external heating ducts or connection to a chimney.

quartz heater
An electric space heater having heating elements sealed in quartz-glass tubes that produce infrared radiation in front of a reflective backing.

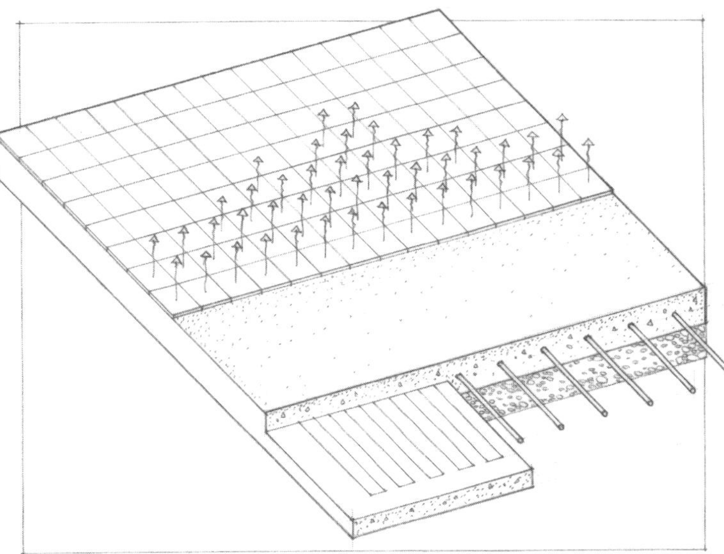

radiant heating
A system for heating by radiation from a surface, esp. one that is heated by means of electric resistance or hot water.

electric heat
Heat generated by the resistance of a conductor to the flow of electric current.

panel heating
The radiant heating of a room or building by means of wall, floor, baseboard, or ceiling panels containing electrical conductors, hot-water pipes, or hot-air ducts.

air conditioning
A system or process for simultaneously controlling the temperature, humidity, purity, distribution, and motion of the air in an interior space, esp. one capable of cooling.

air conditioner
Any device or apparatus for controlling, esp. lowering, the temperature and humidity of a space.

packaged air conditioner
A factory-assembled air conditioner having a fan, filters, compressor, condenser, and evaporator coils for cooling. For heating, the unit may operate as a heat pump or contain auxiliary heating elements.

load
The demand placed on a heating, ventilating, or air-conditioning system in order to maintain the desired conditions of thermal comfort in a building.

cooling load
The hourly rate of heat gain in an enclosed space, expressed in Btu per hour and used as the basis for selecting an air-conditioning unit or system.

cooling degree-day
A degree-day above the standard temperature of 75°F (24°C), used in estimating energy requirements for air-conditioning and refrigeration.

cooling medium
A fluid substance, as chilled water or cool air, for removing heat, as from the interior spaces of a building.

ton of refrigeration
The cooling effect obtained when 1 ton of ice at 32°F (0°C) melts to water at the same temperature in 24 hours, equivalent to 12,000 Btu/hr. (3.5 kW).

energy efficiency rating
An index of the efficiency of a refrigerating unit, expressing the Btu removed per watt of electrical energy input.

compressive refrigeration
A refrigeration process in which cooling is effected by the vaporization and expansion of a liquid refrigerant.

expansion valve
A valve that reduces the pressure and evaporation temperature of a refrigerant as it flows to the evaporator.

refrigerant
A liquid capable of vaporizing at a low temperature, as ammonia, used in mechanical refrigeration.

evaporator
The component of a refrigeration system in which the refrigerant absorbs heat from a cooling medium and changes from a liquid to a gas.

compressor
A pump or other machine for reducing the volume and increasing the pressure of a gas.

condenser
A device for reducing a vapor or gas to liquid or solid form.

coolant
A fluid agent for reducing the temperature of a system below a specified value by conducting away the heat produced in the operation of the system.

heat sink
A medium or environment for the absorption or dissipation of unwanted heat.

heat pump
A device that uses a compressible refrigerant to transfer heat from one reservoir to another, with the process being reversible so that it can be used for both heating and cooling a building.

absorption refrigeration
A refrigeration process that uses a generator and an absorber instead of a compressor to transfer heat.

heat exchanger
A device for transferring the heat of a fluid flowing on one side of a barrier to a fluid flowing on the other.

absorber
The component of an absorption-refrigeration system that uses a saline solution to draw water vapor from the evaporator, cooling the remaining water in the process.

generator
The component of an absorption-refrigeration system that uses a heat source to remove excess water vapor from a saline solution.

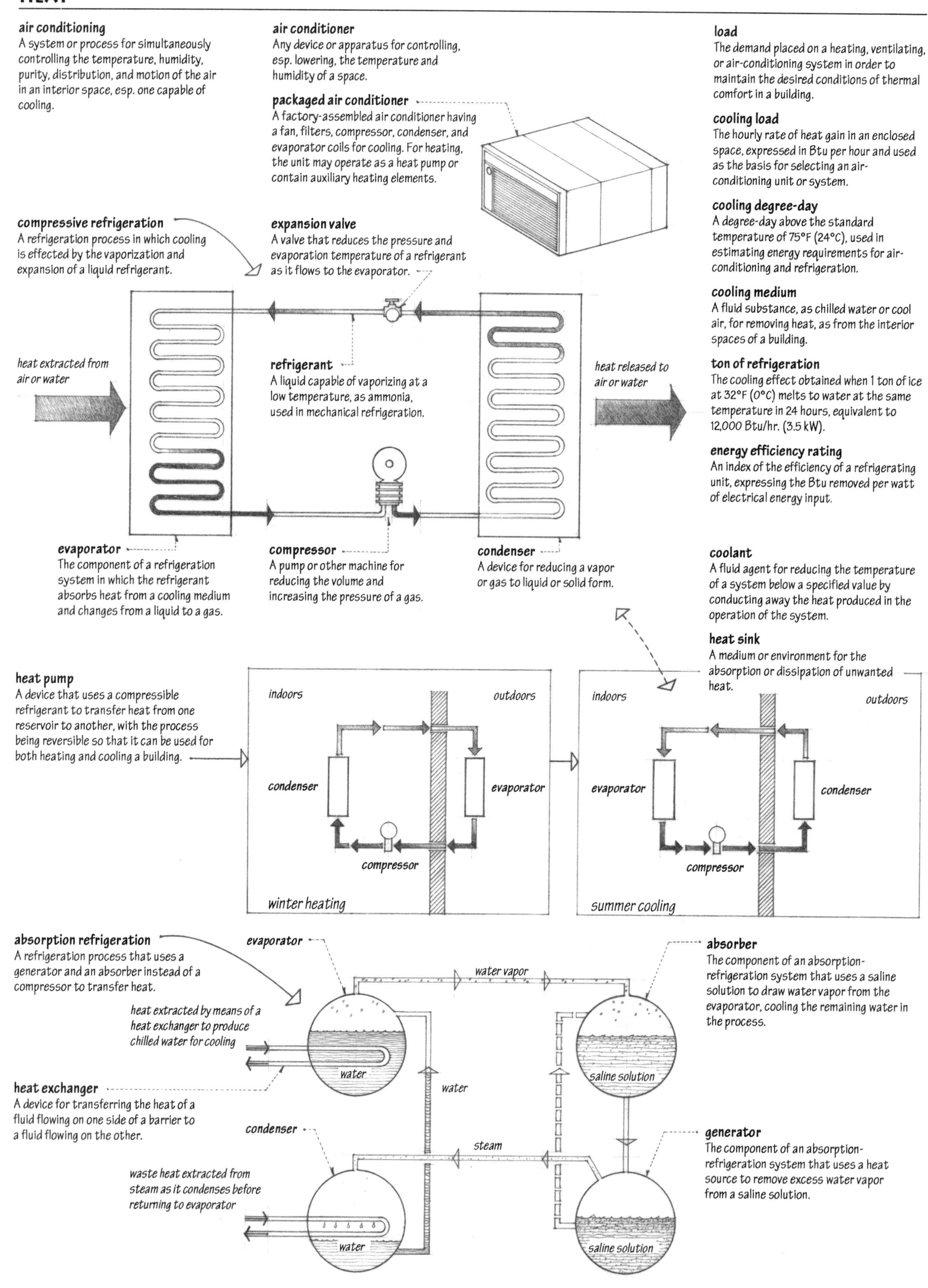

central air conditioning
An air-conditioning system that treats air at a central location and distributes the conditioned air to an entire building by means of fans and ductwork.

HVAC
Abbreviation for heating, ventilating, and air conditioning.

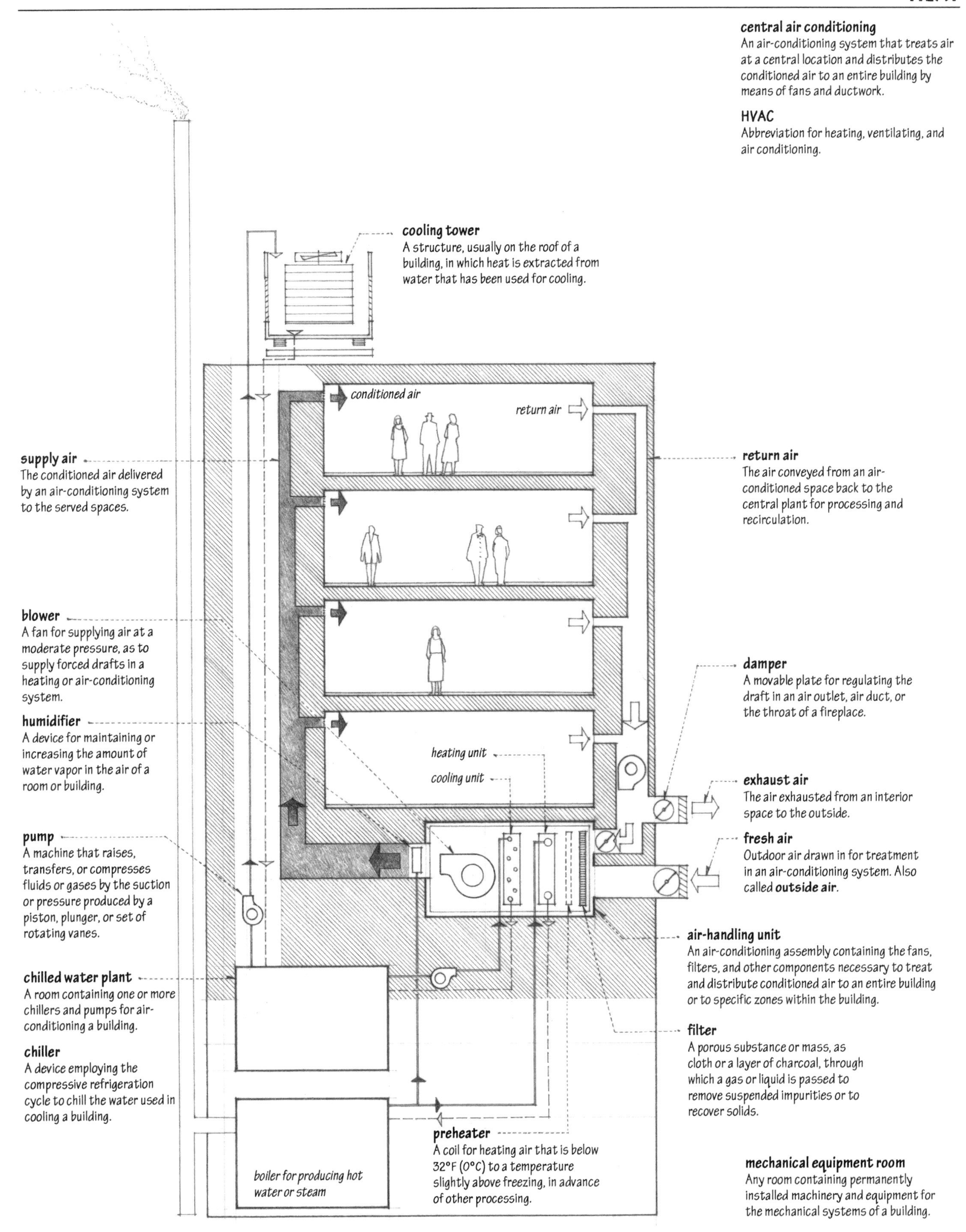

cooling tower
A structure, usually on the roof of a building, in which heat is extracted from water that has been used for cooling.

supply air
The conditioned air delivered by an air-conditioning system to the served spaces.

return air
The air conveyed from an air-conditioned space back to the central plant for processing and recirculation.

blower
A fan for supplying air at a moderate pressure, as to supply forced drafts in a heating or air-conditioning system.

humidifier
A device for maintaining or increasing the amount of water vapor in the air of a room or building.

damper
A movable plate for regulating the draft in an air outlet, air duct, or the throat of a fireplace.

exhaust air
The air exhausted from an interior space to the outside.

fresh air
Outdoor air drawn in for treatment in an air-conditioning system. Also called **outside air**.

pump
A machine that raises, transfers, or compresses fluids or gases by the suction or pressure produced by a piston, plunger, or set of rotating vanes.

air-handling unit
An air-conditioning assembly containing the fans, filters, and other components necessary to treat and distribute conditioned air to an entire building or to specific zones within the building.

chilled water plant
A room containing one or more chillers and pumps for air-conditioning a building.

chiller
A device employing the compressive refrigeration cycle to chill the water used in cooling a building.

filter
A porous substance or mass, as cloth or a layer of charcoal, through which a gas or liquid is passed to remove suspended impurities or to recover solids.

preheater
A coil for heating air that is below 32°F (0°C) to a temperature slightly above freezing, in advance of other processing.

mechanical equipment room
Any room containing permanently installed machinery and equipment for the mechanical systems of a building.

all-water system
An air-conditioning system in which either hot or chilled water is piped to fan-coil units in the served spaces, where air is circulated locally.

two-pipe system
An all-water system in which one pipe supplies the hot or chilled water to fan-coil units, and the other pipe returns it to the boiler or chilled water plant.

four-pipe system
An all-water system in which separate hot-water and chilled-water piping circuits provide for simultaneous heating and cooling as needed in various zones of a building.

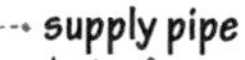

supply pipe
A pipe for conveying hot or chilled water from the boiler or chilled-water plant to a fan-coil unit.

return pipe
A pipe for conveying water from a fan-coil unit to the boiler or chilled-water plant.

terminal unit
Any of various devices for delivering a heating or cooling medium to a space.

fan-coil unit
A terminal unit containing an air filter, heating or cooling coils, and a centrifugal fan for drawing in a mixture of room air and outside air.

coil
A connected series of pipes or tubing in rows or layers, often having fins attached to dissipate heat.

all-air system
An air-conditioning system in which central fans distribute conditioned air to the served spaces by means of ductwork.

single-duct system
An all-air system in which a single duct conveys conditioned air to the served spaces.

constant-air-volume system
An all-air system in which a master thermostat automatically regulates the quantity of conditioned air supplied to each zone.

variable-air-volume system
An all-air system in which a thermostatically controlled variable-volume box regulates the quantity of conditioned air supplied to each zone.

multizone system
A central air-handling unit capable of serving up to eight zones simultaneously.

zone
A space or group of spaces in a building whose temperature and air quality is regulated by a single control.

mixing box
A chamber for proportioning and blending cold and warm air under thermostatic control to reach the desired temperature.

dual-duct system
An all-air system in which separate cold-air and warm-air supply ducts meet at a mixing box where the air is blended before distribution to each zone.

reheat coil
An electric or hot-water coil for raising the temperature of the air in the supply duct of an air-conditioning system.

terminal reheat system
An all-air system in which a reheat coil regulates the temperature of the air being furnished to each individually controlled zone.

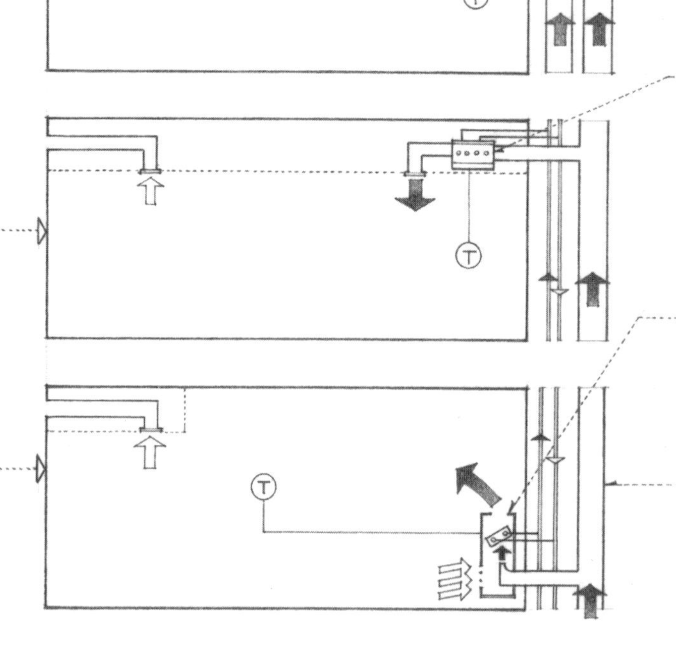

air-water system
An air-conditioning system in which high-velocity ducts supply conditioned air from a central plant to each zone where it mixes with room air and is further heated or cooled in an induction or fan-coil unit.

induction unit
A terminal unit in which primary air draws in room air through a filter and the mixture passes over coils that are either heated or chilled by secondary water from a boiler or chilled water plant.

high-velocity duct
A small duct capable of conveying primary air at a velocity of 2,400 ft. (730 m) per minute or higher.

primary air
The conditioned air supplied at a high pressure and high velocity by a central air handling unit.

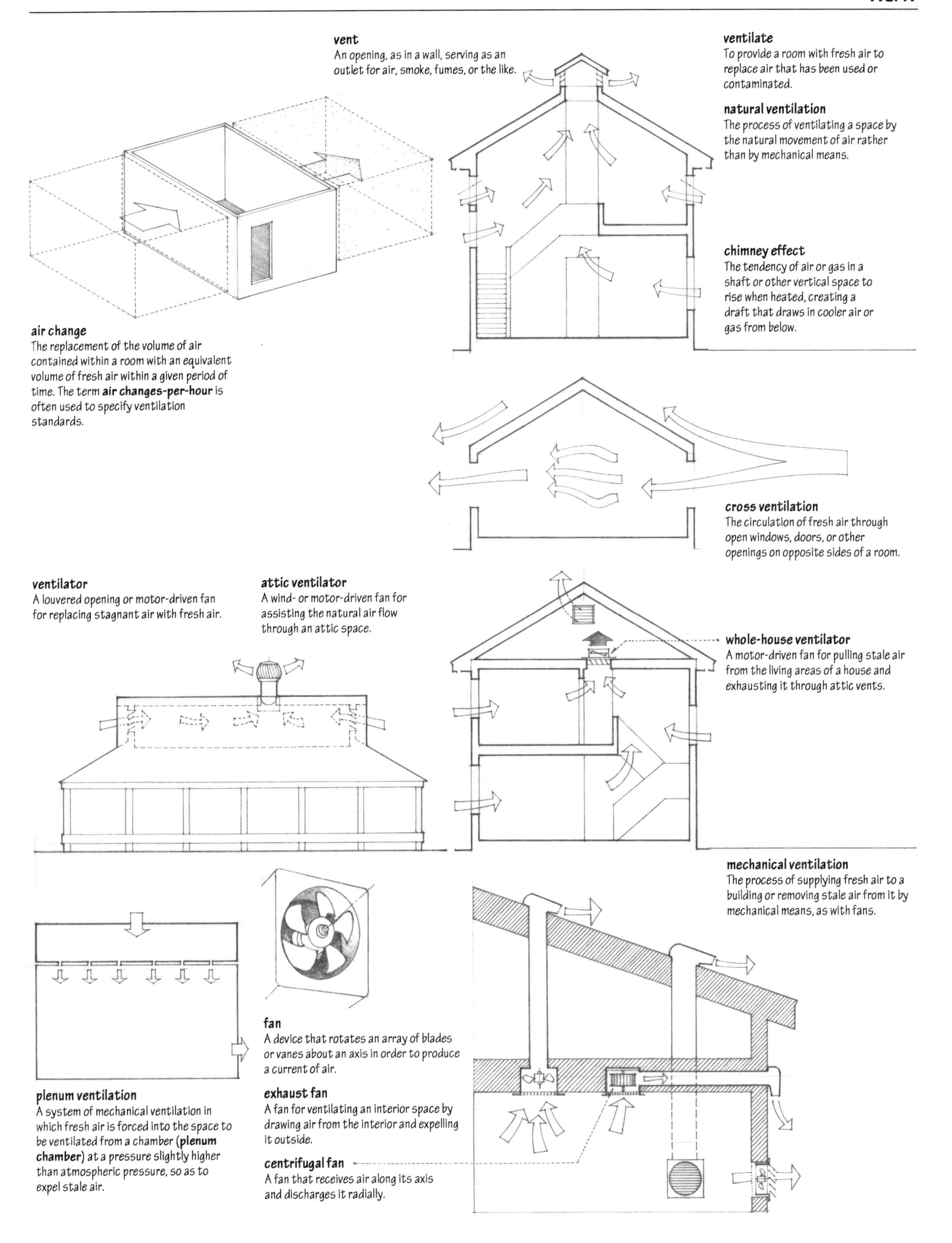

vent
An opening, as in a wall, serving as an outlet for air, smoke, fumes, or the like.

ventilate
To provide a room with fresh air to replace air that has been used or contaminated.

natural ventilation
The process of ventilating a space by the natural movement of air rather than by mechanical means.

chimney effect
The tendency of air or gas in a shaft or other vertical space to rise when heated, creating a draft that draws in cooler air or gas from below.

air change
The replacement of the volume of air contained within a room with an equivalent volume of fresh air within a given period of time. The term **air changes-per-hour** is often used to specify ventilation standards.

cross ventilation
The circulation of fresh air through open windows, doors, or other openings on opposite sides of a room.

ventilator
A louvered opening or motor-driven fan for replacing stagnant air with fresh air.

attic ventilator
A wind- or motor-driven fan for assisting the natural air flow through an attic space.

whole-house ventilator
A motor-driven fan for pulling stale air from the living areas of a house and exhausting it through attic vents.

mechanical ventilation
The process of supplying fresh air to a building or removing stale air from it by mechanical means, as with fans.

fan
A device that rotates an array of blades or vanes about an axis in order to produce a current of air.

plenum ventilation
A system of mechanical ventilation in which fresh air is forced into the space to be ventilated from a chamber (**plenum chamber**) at a pressure slightly higher than atmospheric pressure, so as to expel stale air.

exhaust fan
A fan for ventilating an interior space by drawing air from the interior and expelling it outside.

centrifugal fan
A fan that receives air along its axis and discharges it radially.

A systematic, often chronological narrative of significant events as relating to a particular people, country, or period, often including an explanation of their causes.

civilization
An advanced state of human society marked by a relatively high level of cultural, technical, and political development.

society
An enduring and cooperating large-scale community of people having common traditions, institutions, and identity, whose members have developed collective interests and beliefs through interaction with one another.

culture
The integrated pattern of human knowledge, beliefs, and behaviors built up by a group of human beings and transmitted from one generation to the next.

style
A particular or distinctive form of artistic expression characteristic of a person, people, or period.

expression
The manner in which meaning, spirit, or character is symbolized or communicated in the execution of an artistic work.

Mesopotamia
An ancient region in western Asia between the Tigris and Euphrates rivers, comprising the lands of Sumer and Akkad and occupied successively by the Sumerians, Babylonians, Assyrians, and Persians: now part of Iraq.

Fertile Crescent
An agricultural region arching from the eastern shores of the Mediterranean Sea in the west to Iraq in the east: the location of humankind's earliest cultures.

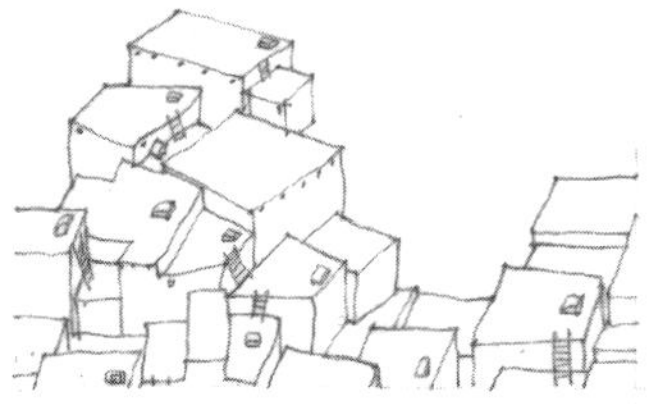

Catal Hüyük
A Neolithic settlement in Anatolia, dated 6500–5000 B.C. One of the world's earliest cities, it had mud-brick fortifications and houses, frescoed shrines, a fully developed agriculture, and extensive trading in obsidian, the chief material for tool-making.

Anatolia
A vast plateau between the Black, Mediterranean, and Aegean Seas, synonymous with the peninsula of Asia Minor: today comprises most of Turkey.

Sumerian architecture
The architecture developed by the Sumerians who dominated southern Mesopotamia from the 4th to the end of the 3rd millennium B.C., characterized by monumental temples of sun-dried brick faced with burnt or glazed brick, often built upon the ruins of their predecessors.

Sumer
An ancient region in southern Mesopotamia, where a number of independent cities and city-states were established as early as 5000 B.C. A number of its cities, as Eridu, Uruk, and Ur, are major archeological sites.

tell
An artificial mound accumulated from the remains of one or more ancient settlements: often used in the Middle East as part of a place name.

Egyptian Architecture
The architecture of the ancient civilization that flourished along the Nile River in northwest Africa from before 3000 B.C. to its annexation by Rome in 30 B.C., characterized esp. by the axial planning of massive masonry tombs and temples, the use of trabeated construction with precise stonework, and the decoration of battered walls with pictographic carvings in relief. A preoccupation with eternity and the afterlife dominated the building of these funerary monuments and temples, which reproduced the features of domestic architecture but on a massive scale using stone for permanence.

Minoan architecture
The architecture of the Bronze Age civilization that flourished on Crete from about 3000 to 1100 B.C., named after the legendary King Minos of Knossos and characterized by the elaborate palaces at Knossus and Phaetus.

3000 BC

prehistoric
Of, pertaining to, or existing in the time prior to the recording of human events, knowledge of which is gained mainly through archaeological discoveries, study, and research.

Stone Age
The earliest known period of human culture, preceding the Bronze Age and the Iron Age and characterized by the use of stone implements and weapons.

Neolithic
Of or relating to the last phase of the Stone Age, characterized by the cultivation of grain crops, domestication of animals, settlement of villages, manufacture of pottery and textiles, and use of polished stone implements: thought to have begun c9000–8000 B.C.

Lascaux Cave
A cave in Lascaux, France, containing wall paintings and engravings thought to date from c13,000–8500 B.C.

Bronze Age
A period of human history that began c4000–3000 B.C., following the Stone Age and preceding the Iron Age, characterized by the use of bronze implements.

Yang-shao
A Neolithic culture in China centered around the fertile plains of the Yellow River, characterized by pit dwellings and fine pottery painted in geometric designs.

Xia
A legendary dynasty in China, 2205–1766 B.C. Also, **Hsia**.

Shang
A Chinese dynasty, c1600 B.C.–1030 B.C., marked by the introduction of writing, the development of an urban civilization, and a mastery of bronze casting. Also, **Yin**.

Harappa
A Bronze Age culture that flourished in the Indus valley c2300–1500 B.C.

Chinese architecture
The indigenous architecture of a vast country in eastern Asia whose civilization has continually evolved and survived longer than any other nation in the world. Despite the marked diversity in the architecture of various regions caused by differences in geographic and climatic conditions, a unique system of wood frame construction gradually took shape over several millennia of innovation and synthesis and exerted a profound influence over the architecture of Korea, Japan, and Southeast Asia.

Preclassic
Of or pertaining to Mesoamerican culture from 2200 B.C. to A.D. 100.

Hittite architecture
The architecture of the Hittite Empire which dominated Asia Minor and northern Syria from about 2000 to 1200 B.C., characterized by fortifications of cyclopean stone masonry and gateways with portal sculptures.

Code of Hammurabi
A Babylonian legal code instituted by Hammurabi in the mid-18th century B.C., based on principles absorbed from Sumerian culture.

Mycenaean architecture
The architecture of the Aegean civilization that spread its influence from Mycenae in southern Greece to many parts of the Mediterranean region from about 1600 to 1100 B.C., characterized by shaft graves, monumental beehive tombs, and palaces fortified with cyclopean walls.

Assyrian architecture
The Mesopotamian architecture developed under the Assyrian king-emperors of the 9th to 7th centuries B.C. Within city walls strengthened by towers with crenelated battlements, palaces took precedence over religious buildings. Vaulting played a greater role than in southern Mesopotamia and polychrome glazed brickwork showed the influence of Egyptian decoration.

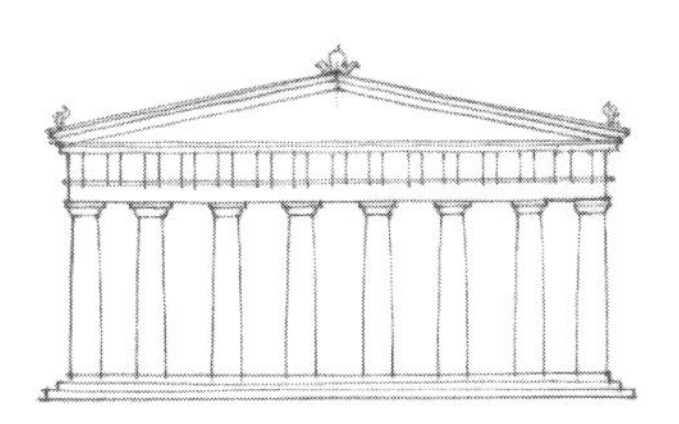

Greek architecture
The architecture of the civilization that flourished on the Greek peninsula, in Asia Minor, on the north coast of Africa, and in the western Mediterranean until the establishment of Roman dominion in A.D. 146, characterized by a system of construction based on rules of form and proportion. Temples of post-and-lintel construction were continually refined in a quest for perfection and their design influenced a wide range of secular, civic buildings.

Neo-Babylonian architecture
The Mesopotamian architecture that developed after the decline of the Assyrian Empire, deriving much from Assyrian architecture and enhanced by figured designs of heraldic animals in glazed brickwork.

Hanging Gardens of Babylon
A series of irrigated ornamental gardens planted on the terraces of the Citadel, the palace complex in ancient Babylon: regarded as one of the Seven Wonders of the World.

Hellenic
Of or pertaining to ancient Greek history, culture, and art, esp. before the time of Alexander the Great.

Hellenistic
Of or pertaining to Greek history, culture, and art from the time of Alexander the Great's death in 323 B.C. through the 1st century B.C., during which Greek dynasties were established in Egypt, Syria, and Persia, and Greek culture was modified by foreign elements.

Persian architecture
The architecture developed under the Achaemenid dynasty of kings who ruled ancient Persia from 550 B.C. until its conquest by Alexander the Great in 331 B.C., characterized by a synthesis of architectural elements of surrounding countries, as Assyria, Egypt, and Ionian Greece.

Persian
A telamon portrayed in Persian dress.

Parthian architecture
The architecture developed under Parthian rule in Iran and western Mesopotamia, from the 3rd century B.C. to the 3rd century A.D., combining classical with indigenous features.

Etruscan architecture
The architecture of the Etruscan people in west-central Italy from the 8th to 3rd centuries B.C., before the rise of Rome. Its construction methods, esp. that of the true stone arch, influenced later Roman architecture.

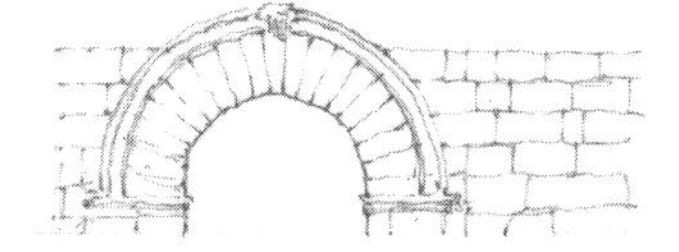

4 BC

Zhou
A Chinese dynasty, c1030 B.C.–256 B.C., marked by the division of China into separate feudal states and the emergence of Confucianism and Taoism, which gave thrust to all subsequent Chinese culture. Also, **Chou**.

Confucianism
A philosophy that dominated China until the early 20th century: an ethical system based on the teachings of the Chinese philosopher, Confucius, c551–478 B.C, emphasizing love for humanity, harmony in thought and conduct, devotion to family, and reverence for parents, including the spirits of one's ancestors.

Olmec architecture
The architecture of the Mesoamerican civilization which flourished c1200–500 B.C. in the tropical lowlands of the Mexican Gulf Coast, characterized by temple-pyramids and large ceremonial centers.

Indian architecture
The architecture of the Indian subcontinent, from the Indus valley culture of the Harappa to the Mauryan era, and later to periods of foreign domination and indigenous rule, characterized esp. by Hindu and Buddhist monuments, sometimes sharing the same site, and rhythmic, stratified multiplication of motifs and profuse carved ornamentation, often combining the religious and the sensuous.

Taoism
Chinese philosophy and religion considered next to Confucianism in importance. Based on the teachings of the Chinese philosopher, Lao-tzu, c604–531 B.C., it emphasizes a life of simplicity and noninterference with the course of natural events in order to attain a happy existence in harmony with the Tao. As a religion, it dates from A.D. 143, becoming popular during the decline of the Han dynasty and the introduction of Buddhism to China.

Tao
The Way: the creative principle that orders the universe.

Great Wall of China
A fortified wall commenced under the Zhou dynasty to protect China against nomads from the north and serve as a means of communication. Various sections were built and connected until, during the Ming dynasty, 1368–1644, it extended for 1,500 miles (2,415 km), from southern Kansu province to the coast east of Peking. Rebuilt and refaced repeatedly, it is the only human-made construction visible from outer space.

Chavin
A Peruvian culture lasting from c1000 B.C. to c200 B.C., based on the worship of the jaguar god and characterized by excellent stone sculpture, elaborate gold work, and remarkable ceramics: named after the town of that name in central Peru, where a complex of massive stone buildings with subterranean galleries surround formal courtyards.

Maurya
A member of an ancient Indian people who united northern India and established an empire c320 B.C.: architecture from this period shows the cultural influence of Achaemenid Persia and the first use of dressed stone.

Qin
A dynasty in China, 221–206 B.C., marked by the emergence of a centralized government and the construction of much of the Great Wall of China. Also, **Ch'in**.

Mochica
A pre-Incan culture that flourished on the northern coast of Peru from c200 B.C. to A.D. 700, noted for its fine pottery and the colossal Temple of the Sun, a terraced pyramid made entirely of adobe bricks. Also called **Moche**.

Classical architecture
The architecture of ancient Greece and Rome, on which the Italian Renaissance and subsequent styles, as the Baroque and the Classic Revival, based their development.

Roman architecture
The architecture of the ancient Roman people, characterized by massive brick and concrete construction employing such features as the semicircular arch, the barrel and groin vaults, and the dome, a simplicity and grandeur of massing often combined with elaborate detailing, the elaboration of the Greek orders as purely decorative motifs for the adornment of facades and interiors, and the use of marble linings, mosaics, and molded stucco in interiors.

Rome
A city in the central part of Italy which, according to tradition, was founded by Romulus and Remus in 758 B.C.: ancient capital of the Roman Empire and site of Vatican City, the seat of authority of the Roman Catholic Church.

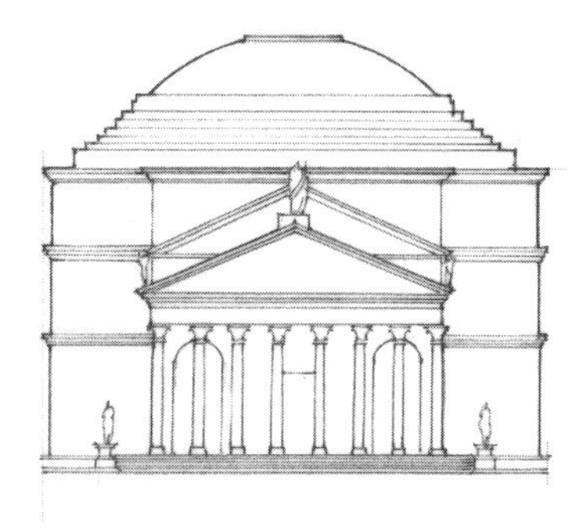

Sassanian architecture
The architecture prevalent in Persia under the Sassanian dynasty that ruled A.D. 226–651, forming a link between the older Mesopotamian traditions and the Byzantine, and characterized by palaces with elliptical vaults and domes set on squinches and stuccoed masonry walls articulated by pilasters and cornices.

Early Christian architecture
The final phase of Roman architecture, following the adoption of Christianity as the state religion by Constantine in A.D. 313 and lasting until the coronation of Charlemagne in A.D. 800 as emperor of the Holy Roman Empire, characterized by churches planned for congregational worship, esp. the basilica: coincident with and related to the rise of Byzantine architecture.

Byzantine architecture
The architecture of the eastern sphere of the later Roman Empire, developing from late Roman and early Christian antecedents in the 5th century and influencing church building in Greece, Italy, and elsewhere for more than a thousand years: characterized by masonry construction, round arches, shallow domes carried on pendentives, and the extensive use of rich frescoes, colored glass mosaics, and marble revetments to cover whole interiors.

Medieval architecture
The architecture of the European Middle Ages, comprising the architecture of the Byzantine, pre-Romanesque, Romanesque, and Gothic periods.

Middle Ages
The time in European history between classical antiquity and the Renaissance, often dated from A.D. 476 when Romulus Augustulus, the last Roman emperor of the Western Roman Empire, was deposed, to about 1500.

Dark Ages
The early part of the Middle Ages, from about A.D. 476 to c1100.

AD 100

Gupta
The dynasty of the Mauryan empire in northern India, A.D. 320–540, whose court was the center of classical Indian art and literature: the earliest substantial architectural remains are from this period.

Pallava
A Hindu state established in southern India about A.D. 350: contributed to the expansion of Indian culture into Southeast Asia.

Dravidian
A style of Indian architecture in the Pallava period, named after the language spoken in southern India.

Pre-Columbian
Of or pertaining to the Americas before the voyages of Columbus.

Mesoamerica
The area extending from central Mexico and the Yucatán Peninsula to Honduras and Nicaragua in which pre-Columbian civilizations flourished. These cultures excelled in astronomy and the measurement of time, and shared temple-pyramids and a pantheon of deities including sun, wind, and rain gods.

Classic
Of or pertaining to Mesoamerican culture from A.D. 100 to 900.

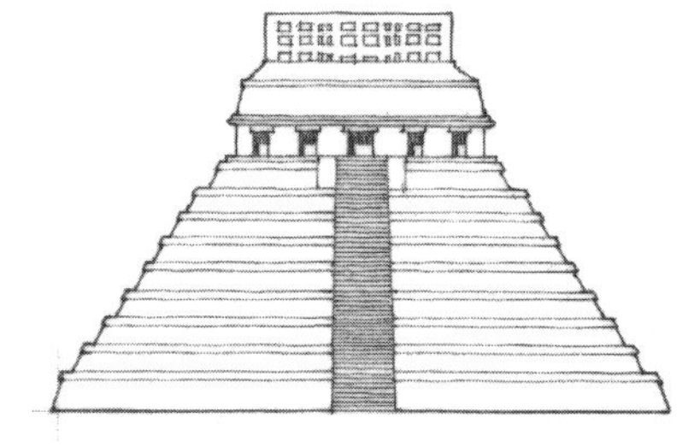

Mayan architecture
The architecture of the Mesoamerican civilization of the Yucatán Peninsula, Guatemala, and part of Honduras, from the 1st century A.D. to its peak in the 9th century, characterized by magnificent ceremonial centers with temple-pyramids, ritual ball courts, spacious plazas, and palaces with sculptured facades.

Zapotec architecture
The eclectic architecture of the Amerindian civilization which flourished c500 B.C.–A.D. 1000 in the highland valley of Oaxaca in southern Mexico, assimilating influences from the Olmecs and from Teotihuacán during the Classic period.

Tiahuanaco
A pre-Incan culture existing from about 300 B.C. to A.D. 900, chiefly in Peru and Bolivia, characterized by monolithic stone carving, polychrome pottery, and bronze artifacts.

Romanesque architecture
A style of architecture emerging in Italy and western Europe in the 9th century and lasting until the advent of Gothic architecture in the 12th century, comprising a variety of related regional styles and characterized by heavy, articulated masonry construction with narrow openings, the use of the round arch and barrel vault, the development of the vaulting rib and shaft, and the introduction of central and western towers for churches.

Carolingian architecture
The early Romanesque architecture of the Frankish dynasty that reigned in France A.D. 751–987 and in Germany until A.D. 911, characterized by a revival of the forms of classical antiquity modified by ecclesiastical requirements.

Lombard architecture
The early Romanesque architecture of northern Italy during the 7th and 8th centuries, characterized by the use of Early Christian and Roman forms and the development of the ribbed vault and vaulting shaft.

Ottonian architecture
The early Romanesque architecture of the German dynasty that ruled as emperors of the Holy Roman Empire from A.D. 962–1002, characterized by the development of forms derived from Carolingian and Byzantine concepts.

Islamic architecture
The architecture of the Muslim peoples from the 7th century on, developing in the wake of Muhammadan conquests of diverse territories from Spain in the west to India in the east and absorbing elements of art and architecture from each region: characterized by the development of the mosque as a distinct building type, masonry domes and tunnel vaults, round and horseshoe arches, and rich surface decorations incorporating calligraphy and floral motifs in a geometric framework because of the ban on human and animal representations. Also referred to as **Muslim architecture**.

Anglo-Saxon architecture
The early Romanesque architecture of England before the Norman Conquest in 1066, characterized by the translation of timber prototypes into stone.

Norman architecture
The Romanesque architecture introduced from Normandy into England before the Norman Conquest and flourishing until the rise of Gothic architecture c1200, characterized by the building of great Benedictine abbeys, the two-tower facade supplementing a central tower over the crossing, and the use of geometric ornamentation.

Norman Conquest
The conquest of England by the Normans under William the Conqueror, in 1066.

1000

Islam
The religious faith of Muslims, based on the teachings of the prophet Muhammad, the central themes of which are belief in the one God, Allah, the existence of Paradise and Hell, and the universal Judgment Day to come. Also, the civilization built on Islamic faith. Also called **Muhammadanism**.

Muhammad
Arab prophet and founder of Islam, A.D. 570–632. Also, Mohammed.

Moorish architecture
The Islamic architecture of North Africa and esp. of the regions of Spain under Moorish domination, characterized by the building of large mosques and elaborate fortress-palaces.

Moor
A member of the Muslim people of northwest Africa who invaded Spain in the 8th century and occupied it until 1492.

Mozarabic style
A style of Spanish architecture produced from the 9th to 15th centuries by Christians under Moorish influence, characterized by the horseshoe arch and other Moorish features.

Nara
A period in Japanese history, A.D. 710–794, characterized by the adoption of Chinese culture and form of government: named after the first permanent capital and chief Buddhist center in ancient Japan.

Japanese architecture
The architecture of the civilization that emerged on the Japanese archipelago off the east coast of Asia, characterized by a synthesis of seminal ideas from China and native conditions producing a distinctive style characterized by lightness, delicacy, and refinement.

Heian
Of or pertaining to the period in Japan, A.D. 785–1185, characterized by the modification and naturalization of ideas and institutions that were earlier introduced from China. During this time indigenous feudalism superseded Chinese-based social order and Japanese architecture developed in isolation from China.

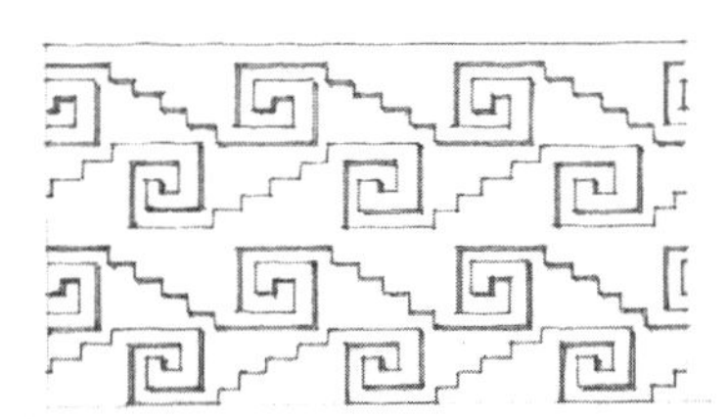

Mixtec architecture
The architecture of the Amerindian culture centered in the Oaxaca Valley of Mexico from about A.D. 800 to the Spanish conquest, characterized by great stone masses, the use of interior stone columns, and the highly detailed fretwork of interior and exterior friezes.

Toltec architecture
The architecture of the Amerindian people who settled in central Mexico around A.D. 900 and who are traditionally credited with laying the foundation of Aztec culture: characterized by colossal basalt telemones of Toltec warriors, colonnades several ranks deep, and stone panels carved with human-headed jaguars and symbols of Quetzatlcóatl, set in plain wall surfaces.

Quetzatlcóatl
Priest-ruler of the Toltec people, who was deified as the feathered-serpent god called by that name.

Gothic architecture
The style of architecture originating in France in the 12th century and existing in the western half of Europe through the middle of the 16th century, characterized by the building of great cathedrals, a progressive lightening and heightening of structure, and the use of the pointed arch, ribbed vault, and a system of richly decorated fenestration.

Early French style
The first of the three phases of French Gothic architecture, characterized by the pointed arch and geometric tracery.

Rayonnant style
The middle phase of French Gothic architecture from the end of the 13th through the late 14th centuries, characterized by circular windows with radiating lines of tracery.

Flamboyant style
The final phase of French Gothic architecture from the late 14th through the middle of the 16th centuries, characterized by flamelike tracery, intricacy of detailing, and frequent complication of interior space.

Early English style
The first of the three phases of English Gothic architecture from the late 12th through the 13th centuries, characterized by the lancet window and plate tracery.

Decorated style
The second of the three phases of English Gothic architecture from the late 13th through the late 14th centuries, characterized by rich tracery, elaborate ornamental vaulting, and refinement of stonecutting techniques.

Perpendicular style
The final phase of English Gothic architecture prevailing from the late 14th through the early 16th centuries, characterized by perpendicular tracery, fine intricate stonework, and elaborate fan vaults. Also called **Rectilinear style**.

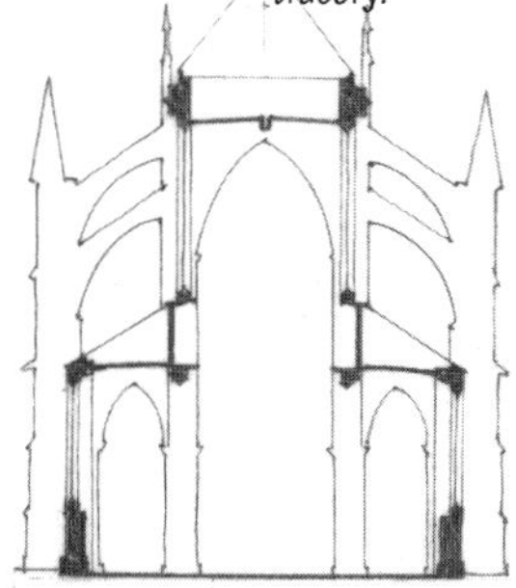

Geometric style
The early development of the Decorated style in the late 13th and early 14th centuries, characterized by the use of geometric tracery.

Curvilinear style
The later development of the Decorated style in the second half of the 14th century, characterized by use of curvilinear tracery.

minster
Originally, a monastery church; later, any large or important church, as a cathedral or the principal church of a town.

Renaissance
The activity, spirit, or time of the humanistic revival of classical art, literature, and learning originating in Italy in the 14th century and extending to the 17th century, marking the transition from the medieval to the modern world.

Renaissance architecture
The various adaptations of Italian Renaissance architecture that occurred throughout Europe until the advent of Mannerism and the Baroque in the 16th and 17th centuries, characterized by the use of Italian Renaissance forms and motifs in more or less traditional buildings.

Italian Renaissance architecture
The group of architectural styles that originated in Italy in the 15th and 16th centuries, characterized by an emphasis on symmetry, exact mathematical relationships between parts, and an overall effect of simplicity and repose.

Early Renaissance
A style of Italian Renaissance art and architecture developed during the 15th century, characterized by the development of linear perspective, chiaroscuro, and in building, by the free and inventive use of classical details.

duomo
Italian designation for a true cathedral.

1100

Mudéjar architecture
A style of Spanish architecture produced from the 13th to 16th centuries by Mudéjars and Christians working within the Muslim tradition, characterized by a fusion of Romanesque and Gothic with Islamic elements.

Mudéjar
A Muslim permitted to remain in Spain after the Christian reconquest, esp. during the 8th to 13th centuries.

Seljuk architecture
The Islamic architecture of several Turkish dynasties that ruled over central and western Asia from the 11th to 13th centuries, much influenced by Persian architecture.

Ottoman architecture
The Islamic architecture of the Ottoman Empire from the 14th century on, much influenced by Byzantine architecture.

Quattrocento architecture
The Italian Renaissance architecture of the 15th century.

Chimu
An Amerindian people inhabiting the northern coast of Peru and having a highly developed urban culture that lasted from about A.D.1000 to its destruction by the Incas c1470.

Postclassic
Of or pertaining to Mesoamerican culture from A.D. 900 to the Spanish conquest in 1519.

Inca architecture
The architecture of the Quechuan people who migrated into the Cuzco area about A.D. 1100 and ruled Peru until the Spanish conquest in the 16th century, characterized esp. by strong simple forms of smooth ashlar or polygonal masonry which was cut, finished, and fitted with great precision without the use of iron chisels.

Aztec architecture
The architecture of the Amerindian people who settled near the shore of Lake Texcoco in central Mexico c1352 and who rose to dominance c1450: characterized chiefly by the pyramid supporting twin temples on a common platform, approached by parallel stairways. The destruction of Aztec architecture by the Spanish conquistadors have left few remains.

High Renaissance
A style of Italian Renaissance art and architecture developed in the late 15th and early 16th centuries, characterized by an emphasis on draftsmanship, the illusion of sculptural volume in painting, and in building, by the imitative use of whole orders and compositional arrangements in the classical style, with great attention to the formulation of compositional rules after the precepts of Vitruvius and the precedents of existing ruins.

Tudor architecture
A transitional style of English architecture that developed during the reign of the royal house of Tudor in the second half of the 16th century, characterized by the Tudor arch and the application of Renaissance details to buildings otherwise late Perpendicular in style.

zwinger
A protective fortress in or adjoining a German city: by extension, a term for several German palaces or parts of palaces, as in Dresden.

Baroque architecture
A style of architecture originating in Italy in the early 17th century and variously prevalent in Europe and the New World for a century and a half, characterized by free and sculptural use of the classical orders and ornament, dynamic opposition and interpenetration of spaces, and the dramatic combined effects of architecture, sculpture, painting, and the decorative arts.

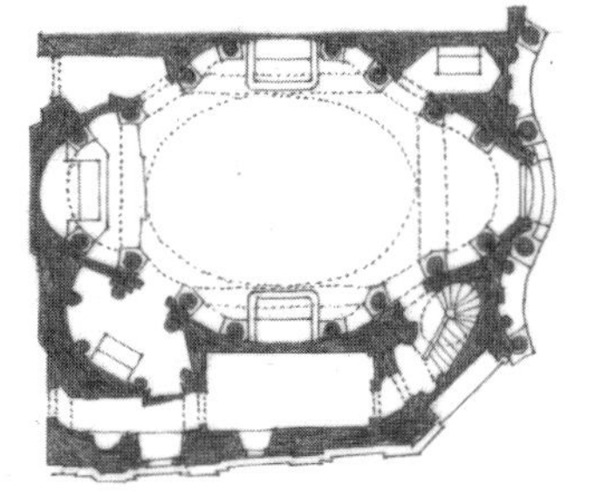

Rococo
A style of decorative art that evolved from the Baroque, originating in France about 1720 and distinguished by fanciful, curved spatial forms and elaborate, profuse designs of shellwork and foliage intended for a delicate overall effect.

classicism
The principles or styles characteristic of the culture, art, and literature of ancient Greece and Rome.

Classic Revival
Art and architecture in the style of the ancient Greeks and Romans, as that of the Italian Renaissance and the neoclassical movements in England and the United States in the late 18th and early 19th centuries. Also, **Classical Revival**.

Neoclassicism
The classicism prevailing in the architecture of Europe, America, and various European colonies during the late 18th and early 19th centuries, characterized by the introduction and widespread use of Greek and Roman orders and decorative motifs, the subordination of detail to simple, strongly geometric compositions, and the frequent shallowness of relief in ornamental treatment of facades.

Cinquecento architecture
The Italian Renaissance architecture of the 16th century.

Mogul architecture
The Indo-Islamic architecture of the Mogul dynasty, 1526–1857, typified by monumental palaces and mosques with highly detailed decorative work.

Mannerism
A transitional style in European architecture in the late 16th century, particularly in Italy, characterized by the unconventional use of classical elements. In the fine arts, Mannerism was chiefly characterized by a distortion of perspective, elongated forms, and intense, often strident color.

chinoiserie
A style of ornament prevalent chiefly in 18th-century Europe, characterized by intricate patterns and extensive use of motifs identified as Chinese.

Georgian architecture
The prevailing style of architecture, furniture, and crafts current in England and the North American colonies, esp. from 1714 to 1811, derived from classical, Renaissance, and Baroque forms: named after the four kings named George who reigned successively during this period.

Directoire style
A style of French furnishings and decoration preceding the Empire style, characterized by an increasing use of Greco-Roman forms along with an introduction, toward the end, of Egyptian motifs: named after the Directory, the body of five directors forming the executive power of France from 1795–99.

Colonial architecture
The style of architecture, decoration, and furnishings of the British colonies in America in the 17th and 18th centuries, mainly adapted to local materials and demands from prevailing English styles.

Federal style
The Classic Revival style of the decorative arts and architecture current in the U.S. from c1780 to c1830.

Regency style
The neoclassic style of architecture, furnishings, and decoration during the period in British history, 1811–20, during which George, Prince of Wales (later George IV) was regent: similar to the Directoire and Empire styles and characterized by close imitation of ancient Greek forms as well as by less frequent and looser adaptations of ancient Roman, Gothic, Chinese, and ancient Egyptian forms.

Empire style
The neoclassic style of architecture, furnishings, and decoration prevailing in France and imitated in various other countries during the first French Empire, c1800–30, characterized by the use of delicate but elaborate ornamentation imitated from Greek and Roman examples and by the occasional use of military and Egyptian motifs.

Gothic Revival
A movement aimed at reviving the spirit and forms of Gothic architecture, originating in the late 18th century but flourishing mainly in the 19th century in France, Germany, England and to a lesser extent in the U.S. Gothic remained the accepted style for churches well into the 20th century.

Victorian architecture
The revival and eclectic architecture, decor, and furnishings popular in English-speaking countries during the reign of Queen Victoria of England, 1837–1901, characterized by rapid changes of style as a consequence of aesthetic controversy and technological innovations, by the frequent presence of ostentatious ornament, and by an overall trend from classicism at the start to romanticism and eclecticism at the middle of the period and thence to classicism again.

Beaux-Arts architecture
A style of architecture favored by the Ecole des Beaux-Arts in late 19th-century France and adopted in the U.S. and elsewhere c1900, characterized by symmetrical plans and the eclectic use of architectural features combined so as to give a massive, elaborate, and often ostentatious effect. The term is often used in a pejorative sense to designate excessive formalism disregarding considerations of structural truth, advanced aesthetic theory, rational planning, or economy.

Steamboat Gothic
A florid architectural style used for homes built in the middle of the 19th century in the Ohio and Mississippi river valleys, suggesting the gingerbread-decorated construction of riverboats of the Victorian period.

gingerbread
Heavily, gaudily, and superfluously ornamented, esp. in architecture.

collegiate Gothic
A secular version of Gothic architecture, as in the older colleges of Cambridge and Oxford.

Carpenter Gothic
A style of Victorian Gothic architecture in the 19th century adapted by artisan-builders to the resources of contemporary woodworking tools and machinery.

eclecticism
A tendency in architecture and the decorative arts to freely mix various historical styles with the aim of combining the virtues of diverse sources, or of increasing allusive content, particularly during the second half of the 19th century in Europe and the U.S.

eclectic
Of or pertaining to works of architecture and the decorative arts that derive from a wide range of historic styles, the style in each instance being chosen for its deemed appropriateness to local tradition, geography, or culture.

1800

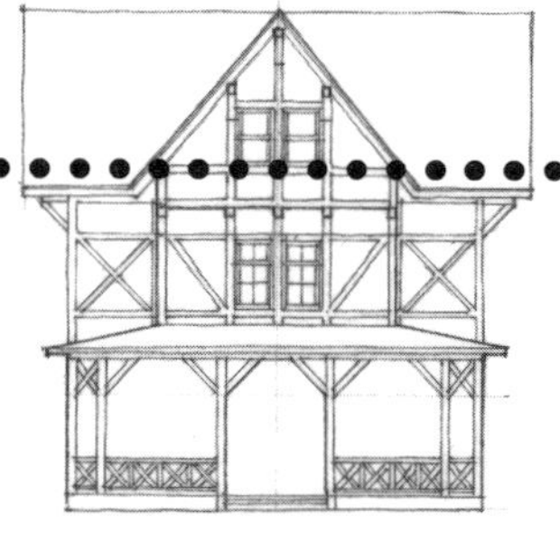

Rationalism
A design movement of the mid-19th century that emphasized the decorative use of materials and textures and the development of ornament as an integral part of a structure rather than as applied adornment.

Stick style
An eclectic style of American architecture in the second half of the 19th century, characterized esp. by the use of vertical board siding with battens or grids of boards over horizontal siding to express the frame construction beneath.

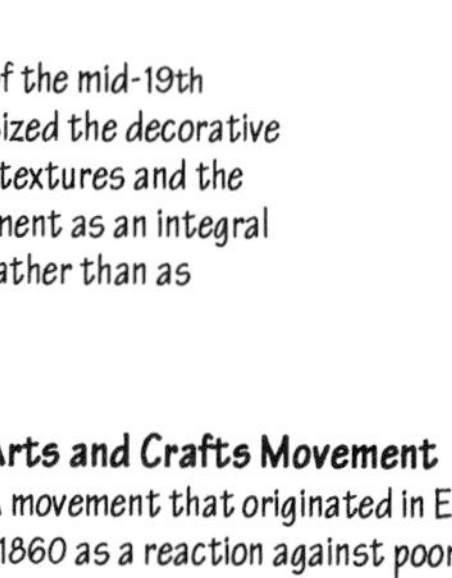

Arts and Crafts Movement
A movement that originated in England c1860 as a reaction against poor-quality mass-produced goods, conceiving of craft and decoration as a single entity in the handcrafting of both utilitarian and decorative objects.

Shingle style
An American style of domestic architecture during the second half of the 19th century, characterized by the extensive use of wood shingles as exterior cladding over a timber frame and frequently asymmetrical and fluid plan arrangements.

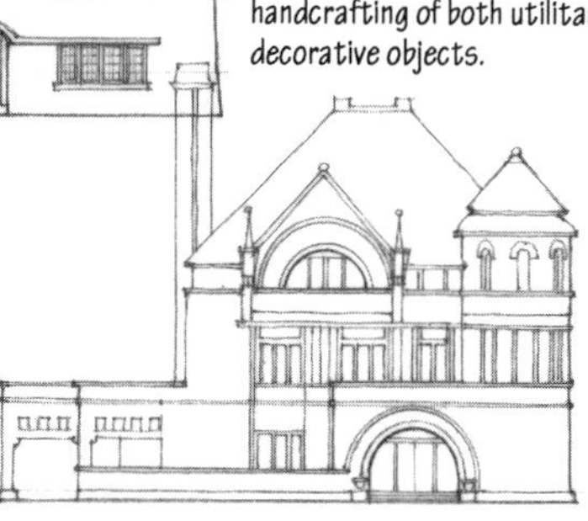

Mission Style
A style of architecture associated with that of early Spanish colonial missions in Mexico and the southwestern U.S., mainly in the 18th century.

Richardsonian Romanesque
The revival of the Romanesque style in the U.S. by Henry Hobson Richardson, 1838–86, and his followers, characterized by heavy arches, rusticated masonry walls, and dramatic asymmetrical effects.

Rundbogenstil
A style of architecture in the mid-19th century, esp. in Germany, characterized by the use of the round-arch motif and combining in various degrees elements from the Early Christian, Byzantine, Romanesque, and Early Renaissance styles: from the German term for round-arched style.

Art Nouveau
A style of fine and applied art current in the late 19th and early 20th centuries, characterized by fluid, undulating motifs, often derived from natural forms.

Stile Liberty
The Italian version of Art Nouveau, named after the firm of Liberty and Co. in London.

Sezession
The Austrian version of Art Nouveau, so named because its adherents seceded from the official Academy of Art in Vienna.

Modernismo
The Spanish, particularly Catalan, version of Art Nouveau.

Jugendstil
Art Nouveau as practiced in German-speaking countries: from the German term for youth style.

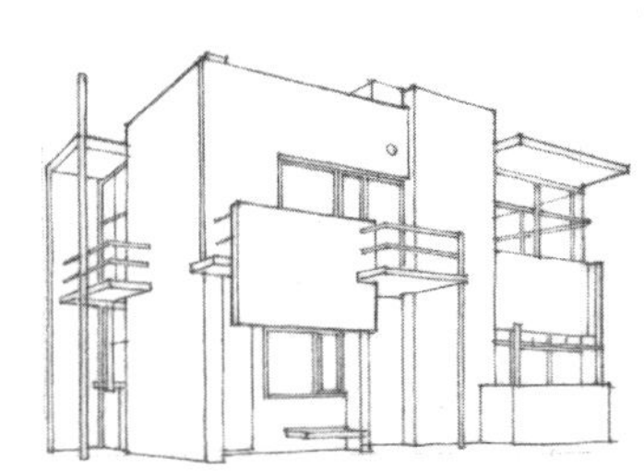

de Stijl
A school of art that was founded in the Netherlands in 1917, embracing painting, sculpture, architecture, furniture, and the decorative arts, marked esp. by the use of black and white with the primary colors, rectangular forms, and asymmetry. From 'the style', the name of a magazine published by participants in the movement.

cubism
A style of painting and sculpture developed in the early 20th century, characterized by an emphasis on formal structure, the reduction of natural forms to their geometrical equivalents, and the organization of the planes of a represented object independently of representational requirements.

Bauhaus
A school of design established in Weimar, Germany, in 1919 by Walter Gropius, moved to Dessau in 1926, and closed in 1933 as a result of Nazi hostility. The concepts and ideas developed at the Bauhaus were characterized chiefly by the synthesis of technology, craft, and design aesthetics, with an emphasis on functional design in architecture and the applied arts.

abstract expressionism
A movement in experimental, nonrepresentational painting originating in the U.S. in the 1940's, embracing many individual styles marked in common by freedom of technique, a preference for dramatically large canvases, and a desire to give spontaneous expression to the unconscious.

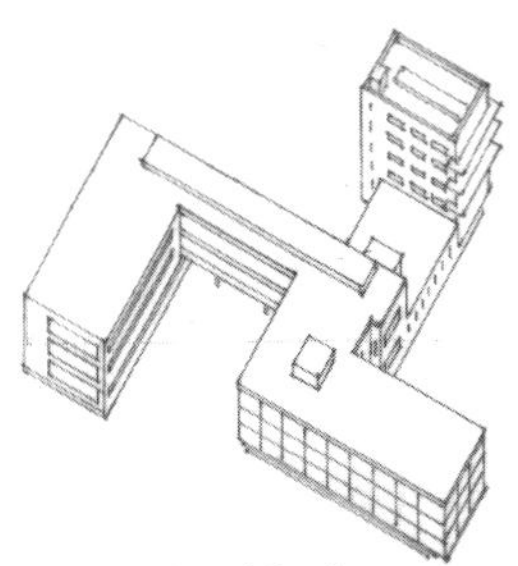

International Style
A functional architecture devoid of regional characteristics, developed in the 1920's and 1930's in Western Europe and the U.S. and applied throughout the world: characterized by simple geometric forms, large untextured, often white surfaces, large areas of glass, and general use of steel or reinforced concrete construction.

brutalism
A movement in architecture in the 1950's, emphasizing the aesthetic use of basic building processes, esp. of cast-in-place concrete, with no apparent concern for visual amenity.

modernism
A deliberate philosophical and practical estrangement from the past in the arts and literature occurring in the course of the 20th century and taking form in any of various innovative movements and styles.

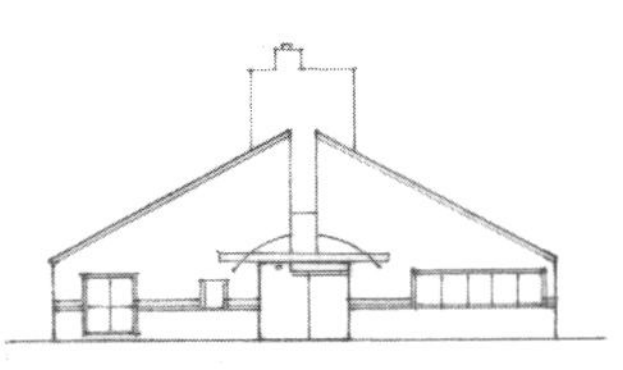

post-modernism
A movement in architecture and the decorative arts that developed in the 1970's in reaction to the principles and practices of modernism, esp. the influence of the International Style, encouraging the use of elements from historical vernacular styles and often playful illusion, decoration, and complexity.

decorated shed
A design concept characterized by buildings of utilitarian design but having fronts intended to elevate their importance or to announce their functions.

1900

Chicago School
A group of U.S. architects active c1880–1910 and known for major innovations in high-rise construction and for the development of modern commercial building design.

Constructivism
A movement which originated in Moscow after 1917, primarily in sculpture but with broad application to architecture. The expression of construction was to be the basis for all building design, with emphasis on functional machine parts.

Functionalism
A design movement that evolved from several previous movements in Europe in the early 20th century, advocating the design of buildings, furnishings, or the like as direct fulfillment of functional requirements, with the construction, materials, and purpose clearly expressed, and with aesthetic effect derived chiefly from proportions and finish to the exclusion or subordination of purely decorative effects.

Organic architecture
A philosophy of architectural design that emerged in the early 20th century, asserting that a building should have a structure and plan that fulfill its functional requirements, harmonize with its natural environment, and form an intellectually lucid, integrated whole. The shapes or forms in such a work are often of irregular contour and seem to resemble or suggest forms found in nature.

Art Deco
A style of decorative art developed originally in the 1920's with a revival in the 1960's, marked chiefly by geometric motifs, streamlined and curvilinear forms, sharply defined outlines, often bold colors, and the use of synthetic materials, as plastics: shortened from Exposition Internationale Des Arts Décoratifs et Industriels Modernes, an exposition of modern and decorative arts held in Paris, France, in 1925. Also called **Style Moderne**.

vernacular architecture
A style of architecture exemplifying the commonest building techniques based on the forms and materials of a particular historical period, region, or group of people.

avant-garde
The advance group in any field, esp. in the visual, literary, or musical arts, whose works are characterized chiefly by unorthodox and experimental methods.

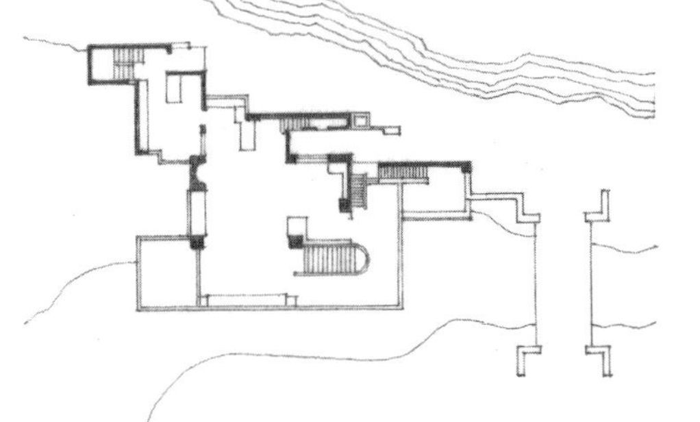

high-tech
A style of design incorporating industrial, commercial, and institutional fixtures, equipment, materials, or other elements having the utilitarian appearance characteristic of industrial design.

deconstruction
A philosophical and critical movement that started in the 1960's, esp. in the study of literature, questioning traditional assumptions about the ability of language to represent reality and emphasizing that a text has no stable reference because words essentially refer only to other words. A reader must therefore approach a text by eliminating any abstract reasoning or ethnocentric assumptions through an active role of defining meaning, sometimes by a reliance on etymology and new word construction.

HOUSE

A building in which people live.

shelter
Something beneath, behind, or within which a person is protected from storms or other adverse conditions.

hut
A small, simple dwelling or shelter, esp. one made of natural materials.

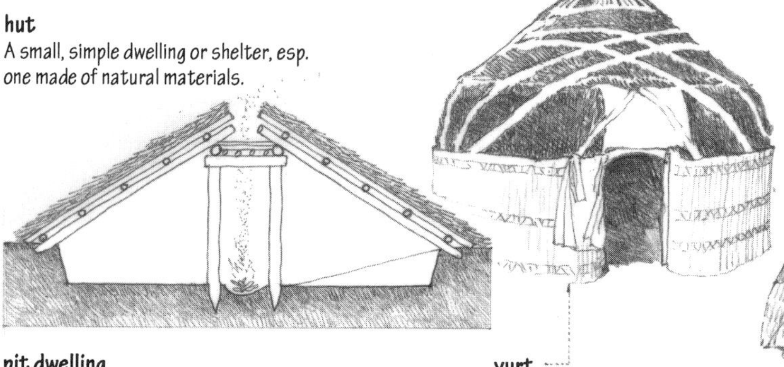

pit dwelling
A primitive form of shelter consisting of a pit excavated in the earth and roofed over. Also called **pit house**.

lake dwelling
A dwelling, esp. of prehistoric times, built on piles or other supports over the water of a lake.

yurt
A circular, tentlike dwelling of the Mongol nomads of central Asia, consisting of a cylindrical wall of poles in a lattice arrangement with a conical roof of poles, both covered by felt or animal skins.

tepee
A tent of the American Indians, made usually from animal skins laid on a conical frame of long poles and having an opening at the top for ventilation and a flap door. Also, **teepee**.

wigwam
An American Indian dwelling, usually of round or oval shape, formed of poles overlaid with bark, rush mats, or animal skins.

hogan
A Navaho Indian dwelling constructed usually of earth and logs and covered with mud and sod.

sod house
A house built of strips of sod, laid like brickwork, and used esp. by settlers on the Great Plains when timber was scarce.

longhouse
A communal dwelling characteristic of many early cultures, esp. that of the Iroquois and various other North American Indian peoples, consisting of a wooden, bark-covered framework often as much as 100 ft. (30.5 m) in length.

totem pole
A pole or post carved and painted with totemic figures, erected by Indians of the northwest coast of North America, esp. in front of their houses.

totem
An animal, plant, or natural object serving as an emblem of a family or clan by virtue of an ancestral relationship.

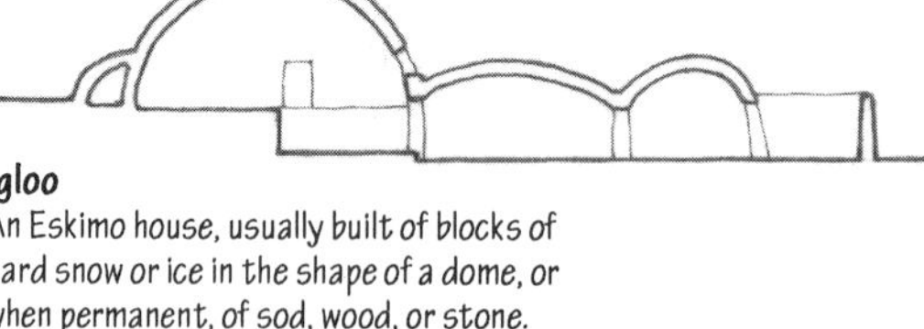

igloo
An Eskimo house, usually built of blocks of hard snow or ice in the shape of a dome, or when permanent, of sod, wood, or stone. Also, **iglu**.

plank house
A large, usually rectangular house constructed of timber planks, built and used by Indians and, less frequently, by Eskimos.

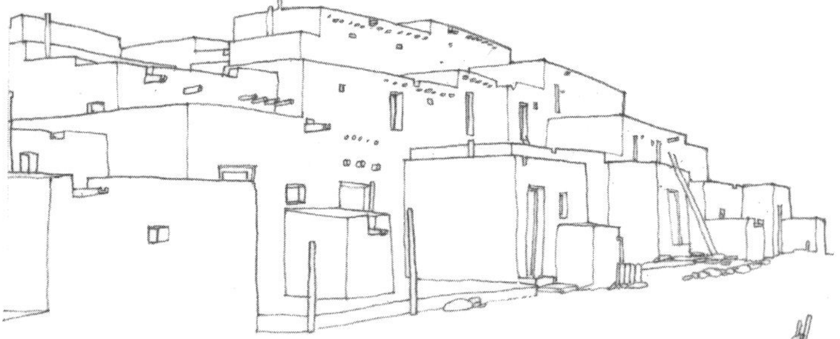

pueblo
A communal dwelling and defensive structure of the Pueblo Indians of the southwestern U.S., built of adobe or stone, typically many-storied, and terraced, with entry through the flat roofs of the chambers by ladder. Pueblo structures were built on the desert floor, in valleys, or in the more easily defended cliff walls of mesas.

mesa
A natural flat-topped elevation with one or more clifflike sides, common in arid and semiarid parts of the southwestern U. S. and Mexico.

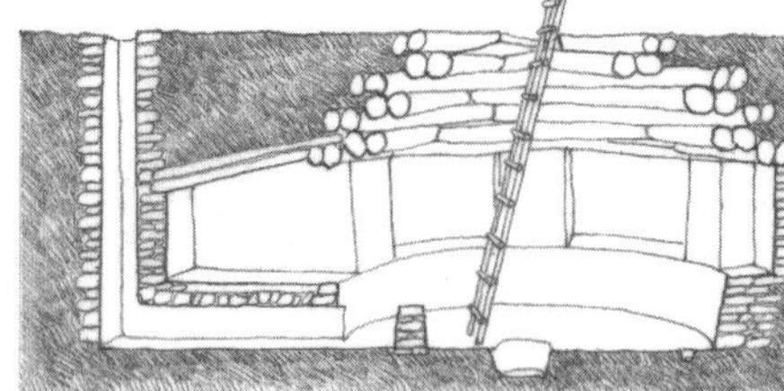

kiva
A large underground or partly underground chamber in a Pueblo Indian village, used by the men for religious ceremonies or councils.

trullo
A circular stone shelter of the Apulia region of southern Italy, roofed with conical constructions of corbeled dry masonry, usually whitewashed and painted with figures or symbols. Many trulli are over 1,000 years old and still in use today, usually located among vineyards to serve as storage structures or as temporary living quarters during the harvest.

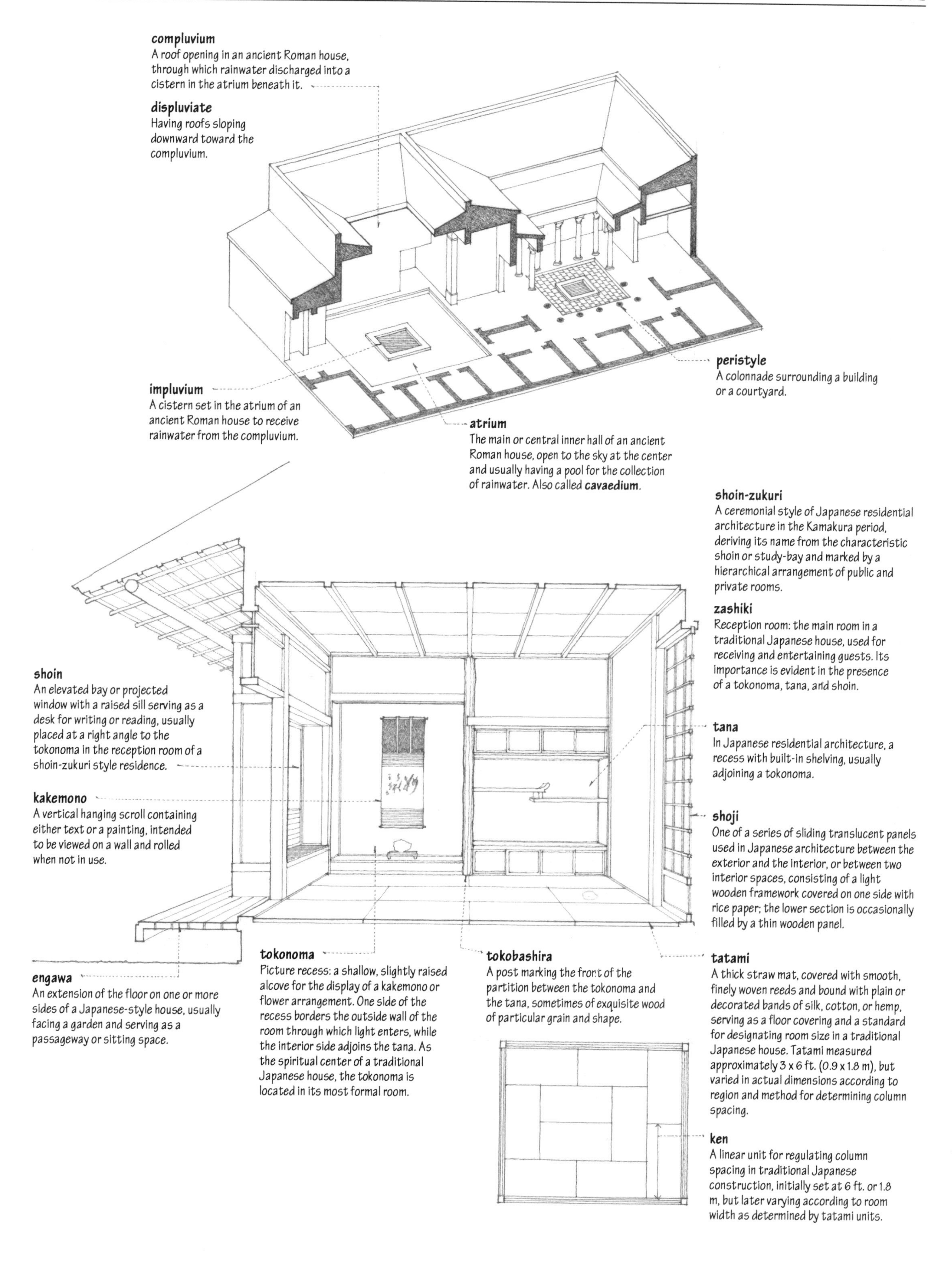

compluvium
A roof opening in an ancient Roman house, through which rainwater discharged into a cistern in the atrium beneath it.

displuviate
Having roofs sloping downward toward the compluvium.

impluvium
A cistern set in the atrium of an ancient Roman house to receive rainwater from the compluvium.

atrium
The main or central inner hall of an ancient Roman house, open to the sky at the center and usually having a pool for the collection of rainwater. Also called **cavaedium**.

peristyle
A colonnade surrounding a building or a courtyard.

shoin-zukuri
A ceremonial style of Japanese residential architecture in the Kamakura period, deriving its name from the characteristic shoin or study-bay and marked by a hierarchical arrangement of public and private rooms.

zashiki
Reception room: the main room in a traditional Japanese house, used for receiving and entertaining guests. Its importance is evident in the presence of a tokonoma, tana, and shoin.

shoin
An elevated bay or projected window with a raised sill serving as a desk for writing or reading, usually placed at a right angle to the tokonoma in the reception room of a shoin-zukuri style residence.

kakemono
A vertical hanging scroll containing either text or a painting, intended to be viewed on a wall and rolled when not in use.

tana
In Japanese residential architecture, a recess with built-in shelving, usually adjoining a tokonoma.

shoji
One of a series of sliding translucent panels used in Japanese architecture between the exterior and the interior, or between two interior spaces, consisting of a light wooden framework covered on one side with rice paper; the lower section is occasionally filled by a thin wooden panel.

engawa
An extension of the floor on one or more sides of a Japanese-style house, usually facing a garden and serving as a passageway or sitting space.

tokonoma
Picture recess: a shallow, slightly raised alcove for the display of a kakemono or flower arrangement. One side of the recess borders the outside wall of the room through which light enters, while the interior side adjoins the tana. As the spiritual center of a traditional Japanese house, the tokonoma is located in its most formal room.

tokobashira
A post marking the front of the partition between the tokonoma and the tana, sometimes of exquisite wood of particular grain and shape.

tatami
A thick straw mat, covered with smooth, finely woven reeds and bound with plain or decorated bands of silk, cotton, or hemp, serving as a floor covering and a standard for designating room size in a traditional Japanese house. Tatami measured approximately 3 x 6 ft. (0.9 x 1.8 m), but varied in actual dimensions according to region and method for determining column spacing.

ken
A linear unit for regulating column spacing in traditional Japanese construction, initially set at 6 ft. or 1.8 m, but later varying according to room width as determined by tatami units.

detached dwelling
A house having no wall in common with another house.

Dutch Colonial
Of or pertaining to the domestic architecture of Dutch settlers in New York and New Jersey in the 17th century, often characterized by gambrel roofs having curved eaves over porches on the long sides.

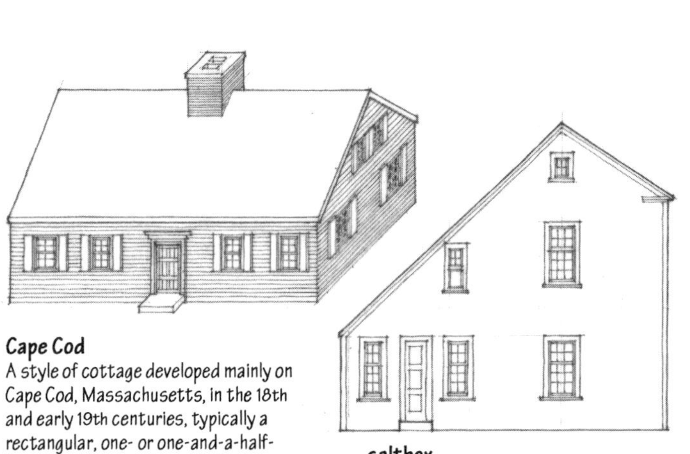

Cape Cod
A style of cottage developed mainly on Cape Cod, Massachusetts, in the 18th and early 19th centuries, typically a rectangular, one- or one-and-a-half-story, wood-frame house with white clapboarded or shingle walls, a gable roof with low eaves and usually no dormer, a large central chimney, and a front door located on one of the long sides.

saltbox
A type of wood-framed house found esp. in New England, generally two full stories high in front and one story high in back, the roof having about the same pitch in both directions so that the ridge is well toward the front of the house.

bungalow
A derivative of the Indian bungalow, popular esp. in the first quarter of the 20th century, usually having one or one-and-a-half stories, a widely bracketed gable roof, a large porch, and often built of rustic materials.

bungalow court
A group of three or more detached, one-story, single-family dwellings, arranged with common utilities and accessories under a common ownership.

Prairie School
A group of early 20th-century architects, notably Frank Lloyd Wright, who designed houses and other buildings with emphasized horizontal lines responding to the flatness of the Midwestern prairie.

split-level
A house having a room or rooms somewhat above or below adjacent rooms, with the floor levels usually differing by approximately half a story.

bi-level
A two-story house having the lower level sunken below grade and an entry at grade halfway between the two floor levels.

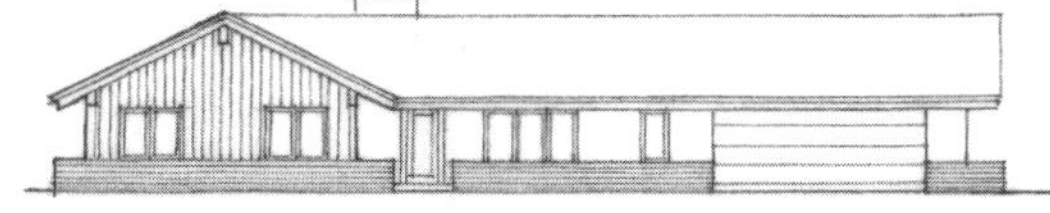

rambler
A one-story house with a low-pitched roof, esp. one built in the suburbs.

tract house
A house forming part of a real-estate development, usually having a plan and appearance common to some or all of the houses in the development.

semidetached dwelling
A house joined by a party wall to another house or row of houses.

duplex house
A house having separate apartments for two families, esp. a two-story house having a complete apartment on each floor and two separate entrances. Also called **duplex**.

triplex
A building having three apartments, an apartment having three floors, or a multiplex of three theaters.

dogtrot
A breezeway linking two parts of a house.

breezeway
A porch or roofed passageway open on the sides, for connecting two buildings or parts of a building.

multifamily
Designed or suitable for use by several or many families.

housing unit
A house, apartment, suite of rooms, or a single room, occupied or intended for occupancy as separate living quarters.

condominium
An apartment house, office building, or other multiple-unit complex, the units of which are individually owned, each owner receiving a recordable deed to the individual unit purchased, including the right to sell or mortgage that unit, and sharing in the joint ownership of any common elements, as hallways, elevators, mechanical and plumbing systems, or the like.

cooperative
A building owned and managed by a nonprofit corporation in which shares are sold, entitling the shareholders to occupy units in the building. Also called **co-op**, **cooperative apartment**.

townhouse
One of a row of houses in a city joined by common sidewalls.

brownstone
A building, esp. a row house, fronted with a reddish-brown sandstone.

mew
A street having small apartments converted from stables. Also, **mews**.

row house
One of a row of houses having at least one sidewall in common with a neighboring dwelling, and usually uniform or nearly uniform plans, fenestration, and architectural treatment.

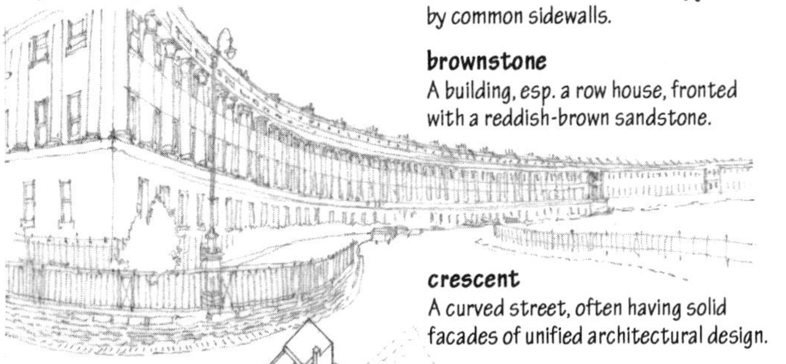

crescent
A curved street, often having solid facades of unified architectural design.

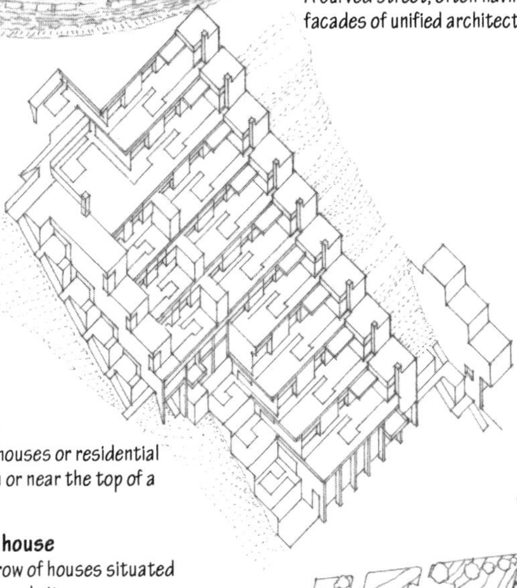

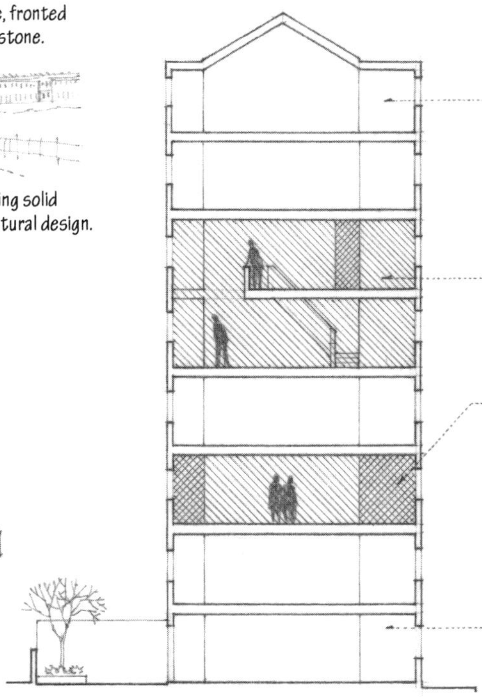

penthouse
An apartment or residence on the top floor or roof of a building, often set back from the outer walls and opening onto a terrace.

duplex apartment
An apartment with rooms on two connected floors. Also called **duplex**.

flat
An apartment or suite of rooms on one floor forming a residence.

walk-up
An apartment above the ground floor in a building that has no elevator.

terrace
A row of houses or residential street on or near the top of a slope.

terrace house
One of a row of houses situated on a terraced site.

garden apartment
An apartment on the ground floor of an apartment building having access to a backyard or garden.

apartment house
A building containing a number of apartment units. Also called **apartment building**.

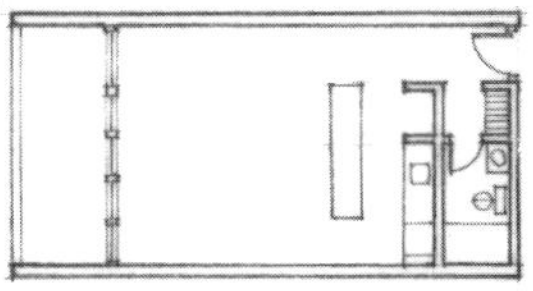

studio apartment
An apartment consisting of a single, multifunctional room, a kitchen or kitchenette, and a bathroom. Also called **efficiency apartment**.

cluster housing
A group of buildings and esp. houses built close together to form relatively compact units on a sizable tract in order to preserve open spaces larger than the individual yard for common recreation.

commons
A tract of land owned or used jointly by the residents of a community, usually a central square or park in a city or town.

The art or craft of forming joints, esp. in woodwork.

woodwork
The work produced by the carpenter's and joiner's art, generally applied to objects or parts of a wooden structure, as stairways, furniture, or moldings.

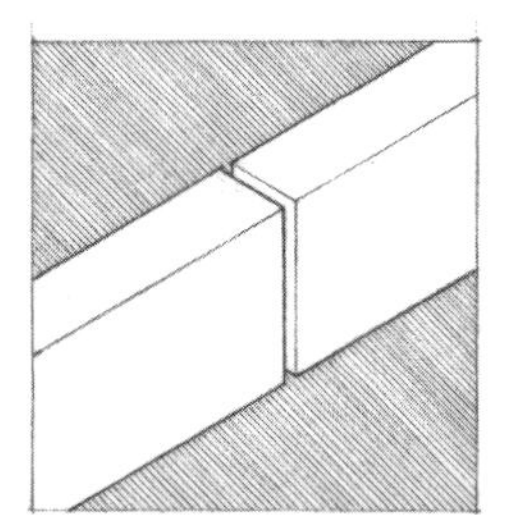

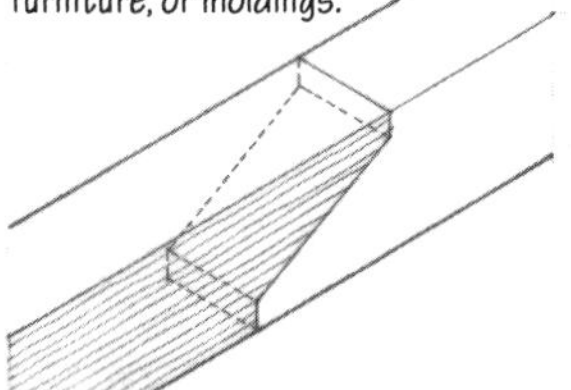

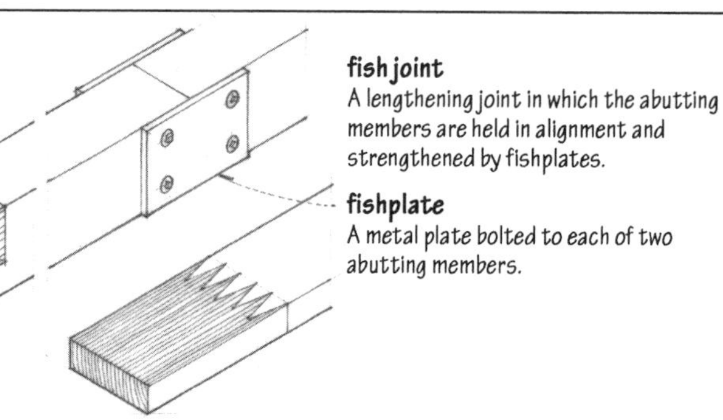

fish joint
A lengthening joint in which the abutting members are held in alignment and strengthened by fishplates.

fishplate
A metal plate bolted to each of two abutting members.

end joint
Any joint formed by uniting two members end to end so as to increase their length. Also called **lengthening joint**.

scarf joint
A lengthening joint made by overlapping the tapered, notched, or halved ends of two members and holding them in place with bolts, straps, keys, or fishplates, to resist tension or compression.

square splice
A halved scarf joint used esp. to resist tension, having a thicker and a thinner section for each member, the thicker one being on the end.

finger joint
A lengthening joint formed by interlacing finger-like projections on the ends of the joined members.

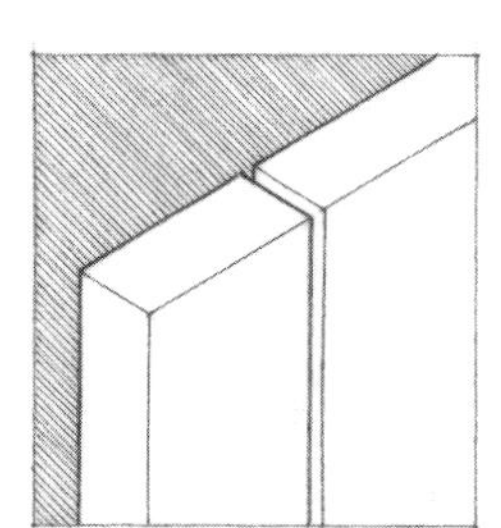

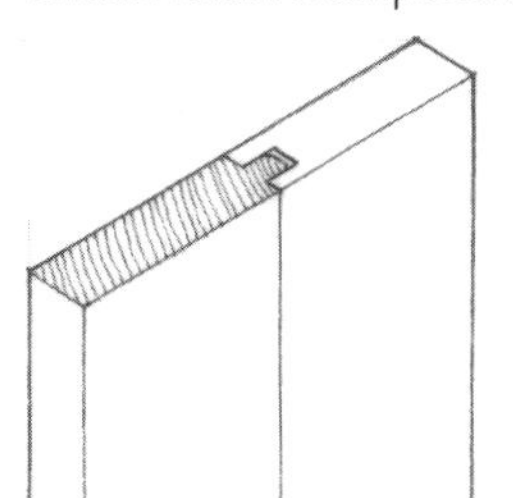

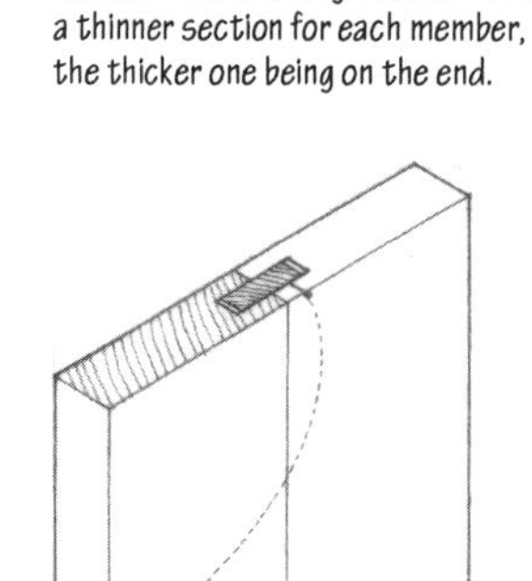

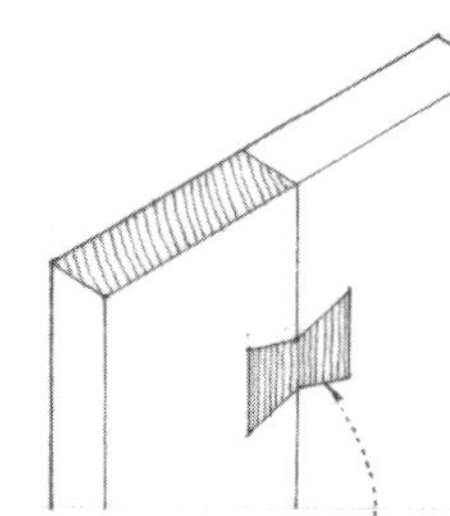

butt joint
Any of various joints formed by abutting the surfaces of two members squarely together without overlapping.

flush joint
Any joint finished even or level with the surrounding surfaces.

edge joint
Any joint formed by uniting two members edge to edge so as to increase their width.

tongue and groove
A joint made by fitting a raised area or tongue on the edge of one member into a corresponding groove in the edge of another member to produce a flush surface. Abbr.: **T & G**

spline
A thin strip of material inserted into the grooved edges of two members to make a butt joint between them. Also called **feather**.

butterfly wedge
A fastener in the form of a double dovetail for joining two members at their edges. Also called **butterfly**.

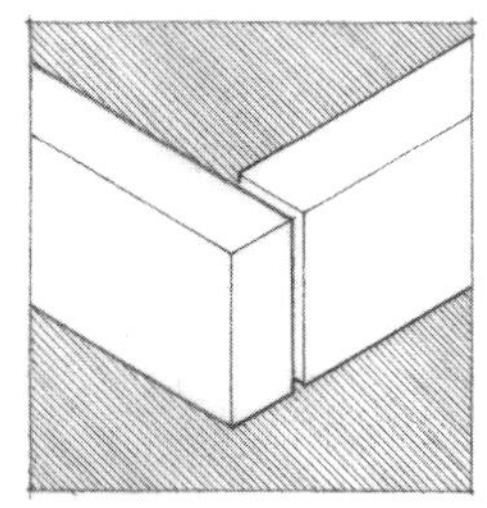

dado
A rectangular groove cut in a member to receive the end of another.

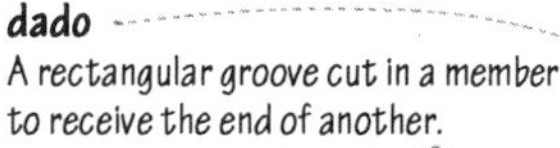

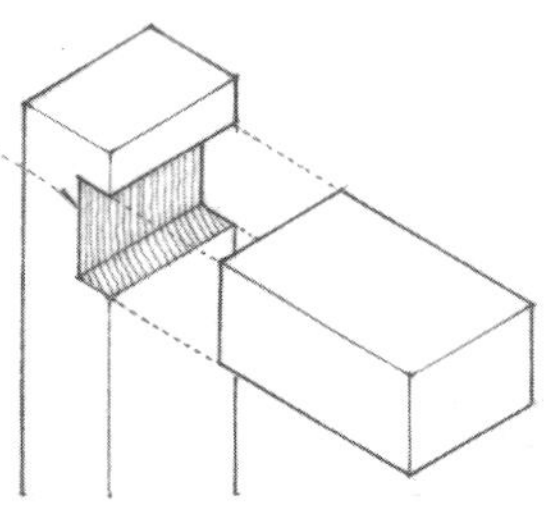

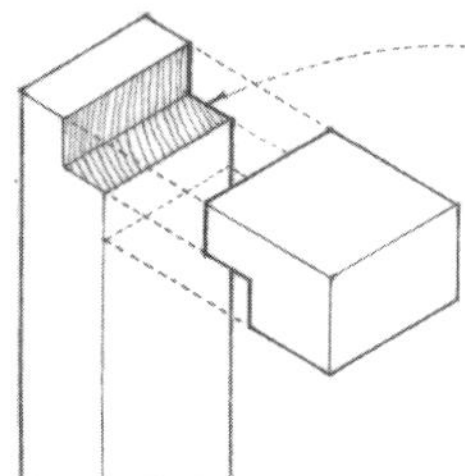

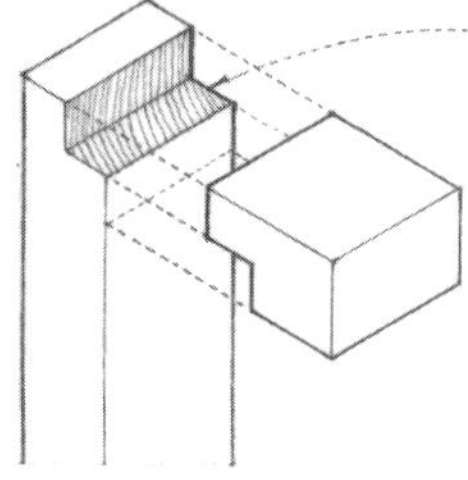

rabbet
A channel, groove, or notch cut along or near one edge of a member so that something else can be fitted into it. Also, **rebate**.

rout
To groove or hollow out with a gouge or machine.

angle joint
Any joint formed by uniting two members at a corner so as to change direction.

stopped dado
A dado that is not cut across the full width of a member.

dado joint
A joint made by inserting the end or edge of one member into a corresponding dado in the other. Also called **housed joint**.

rabbet joint
A joint between rabbeted parts.

miter
An oblique surface formed so as to butt against another oblique surface to be joined with it.

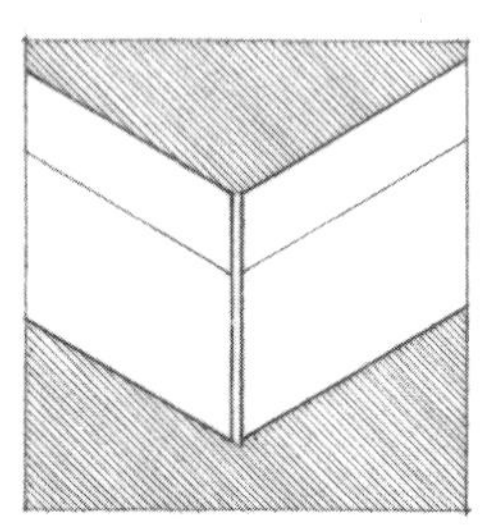

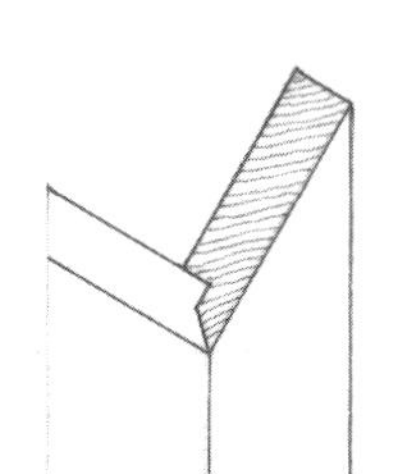

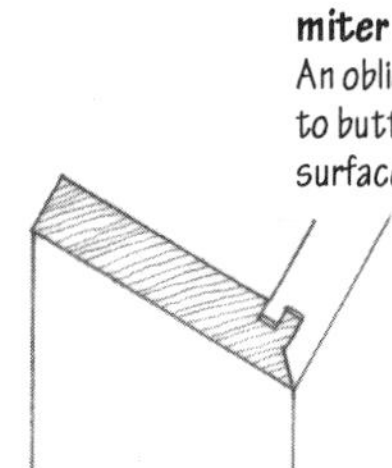

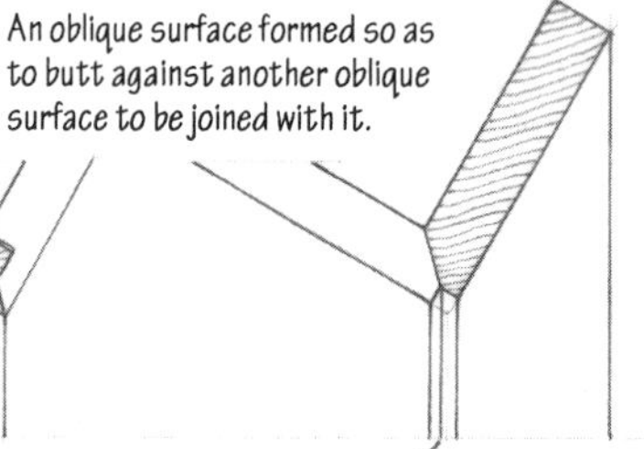

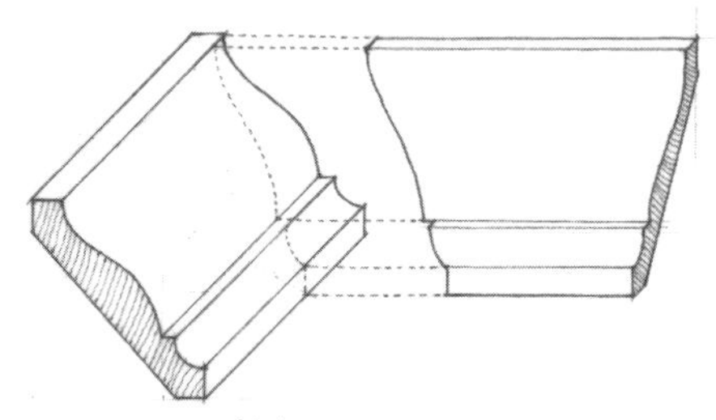

miter joint
A joint between two members meeting at an angle, made by cutting each of the butting surfaces to an angle equal to half the angle of junction.

shoulder miter
A miter joint having a raised surface to limit motion between the joined parts.

tongued miter
A miter joint that incorporates a tongue and groove.

quirk
An acute angle or groove separating one element from another.

coped joint
A joint between two moldings made by undercutting the end of one of them to the profile of the other. Also called **scribed joint**.

easement
A curved joint forming a smooth transition between surfaces that would otherwise intersect at an angle.

eased edge
A slightly rounded edge.

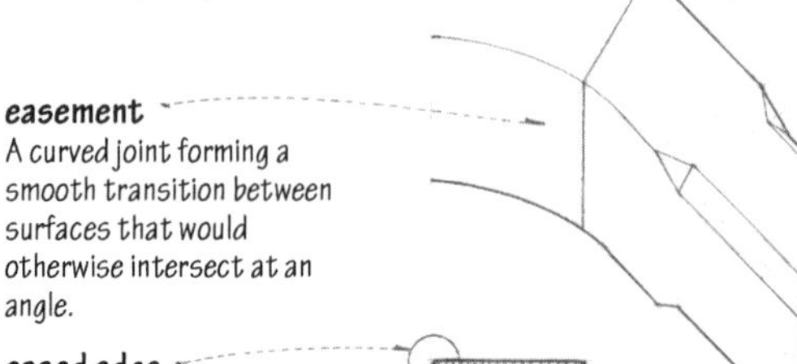

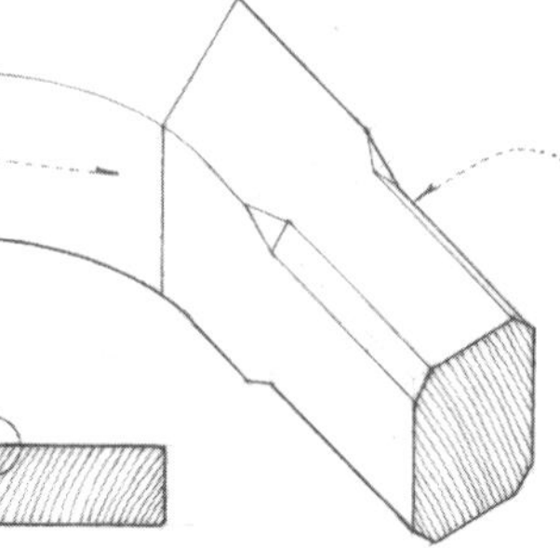

stop chamfer
A chamfer that narrows gradually to merge with a sharp arris. Also, **stopped chamfer**.

chamfer
A beveled surface, usually formed or cut at a 45° angle to the adjacent principal faces.

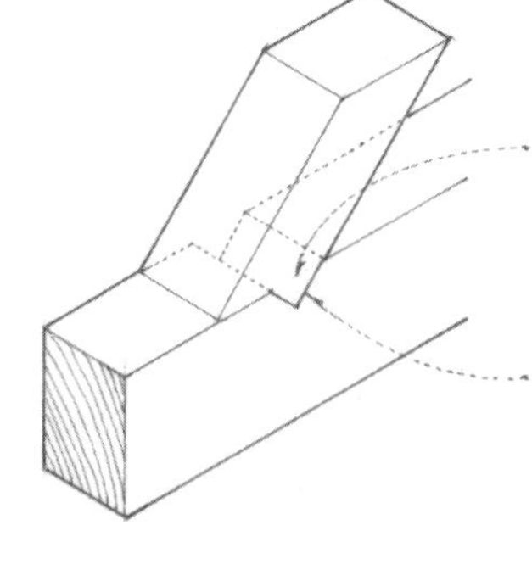

joggle
A projection on one of two joining members fitting into a corresponding recess in the other to prevent slipping.

dap
A notch cut in a timber to receive a timber connector or part of another timber.

halved joint
A lap joint formed by cutting away half of each member at the place of joining so that a flush surface results. Also called **half-lap joint**.

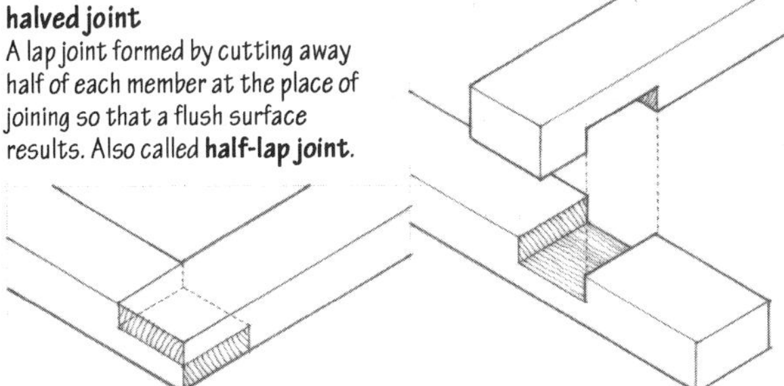

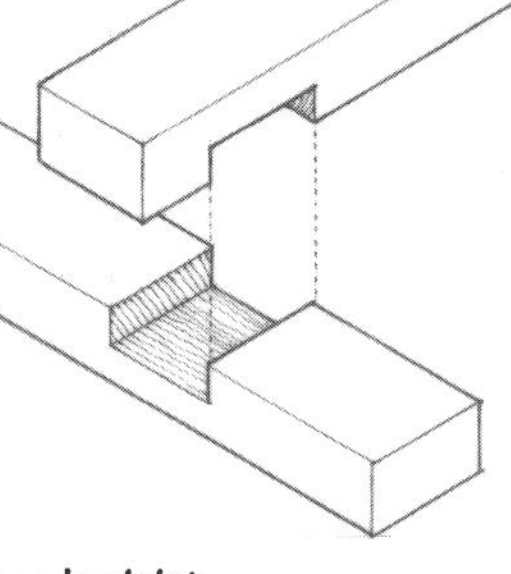

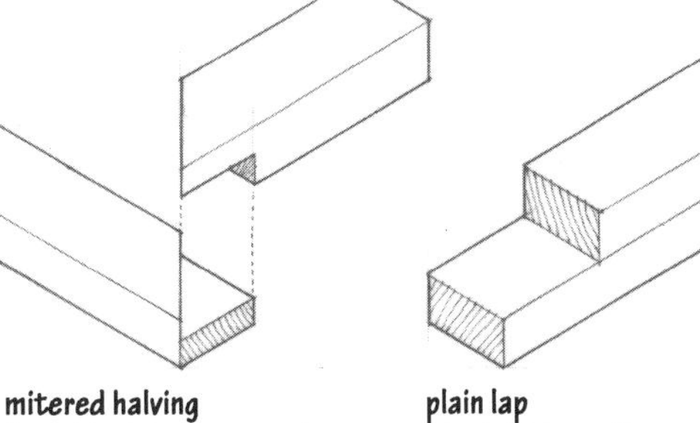

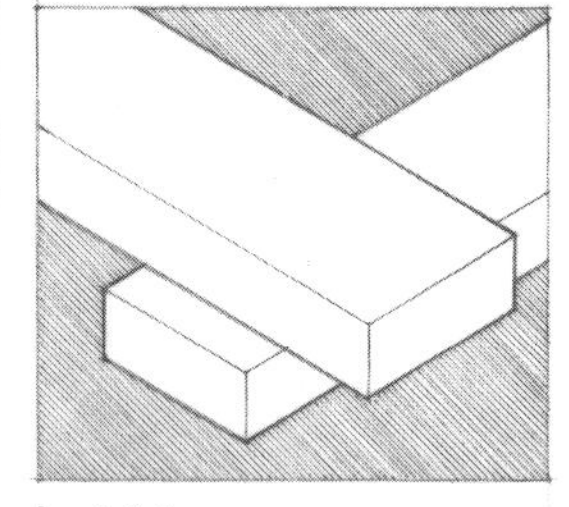

end-lap joint
An angle joint formed by halving each member for a length equal to the width of the other.

cross-lap joint
A halved joint formed by two crossing members.

mitered halving
An end-lap joint incorporating a miter on one face.

plain lap
A lap joint formed by overlapping two members without any change in form.

lap joint
Any of various joints formed by overlapping the ends or edges of two members.

dovetail
A fan-shaped tenon broader at its end than at its base.

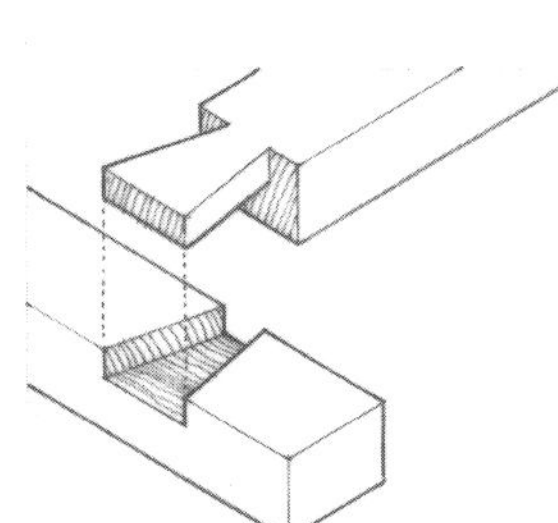

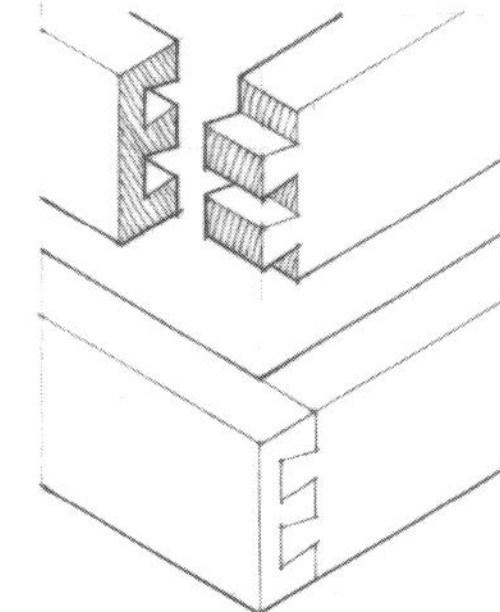

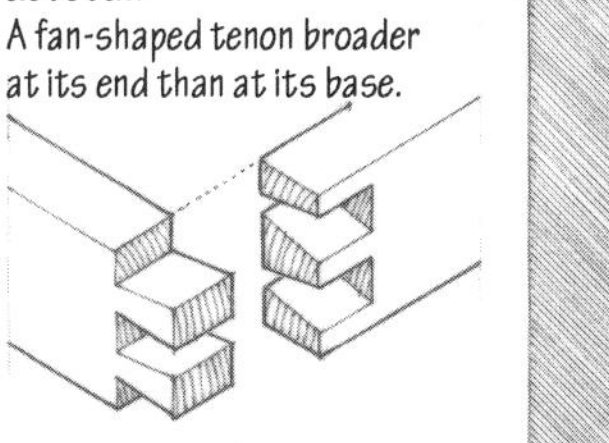

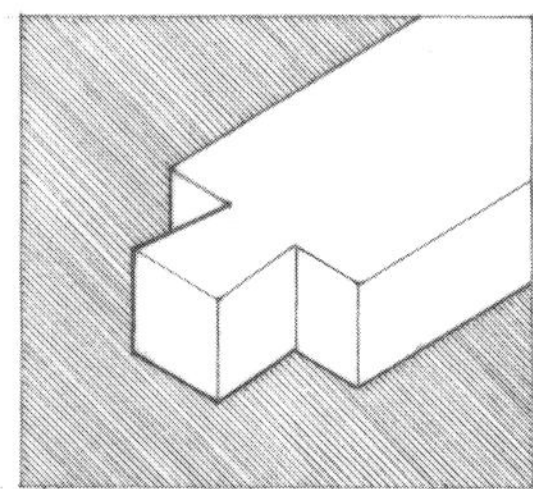

dovetail halving
A halved joint made by fitting a dovetail at the end of one member into a corresponding mortise in the second member.

secret dovetail
A corner dovetail joint showing only the line of a miter. Also called **miter dovetail**.

lap dovetail
A corner dovetail joint visible on one face only. Also called **half-blind dovetail**.

common dovetail
A corner dovetail joint visible on both faces.

dovetail joint
A joint formed by one or more dovetails fitting tightly within corresponding mortises.

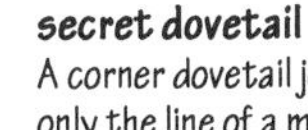

blind mortise
A mortise that does not pass completely through a member. Also called **stopped mortise**.

chase mortise
A blind mortise having one inclined narrow side so that a tenon can be slid into it sideways.

open mortise
A mortise open on three sides. Also called **slip mortise**, **slot mortise**.

mortise
A notch or hole, usually rectangular, cut into a piece to receive a tenon of the same dimensions.

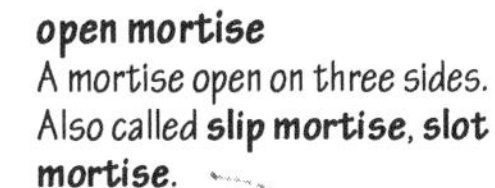

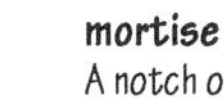

stub tenon
A short tenon for fitting into a blind mortise.

shoulder
The end surface from which a tenon projects.

mortise joint
Any of various joints between two members made by housing a tenon in a mortise. Also called **mortise-and-tenon joint**.

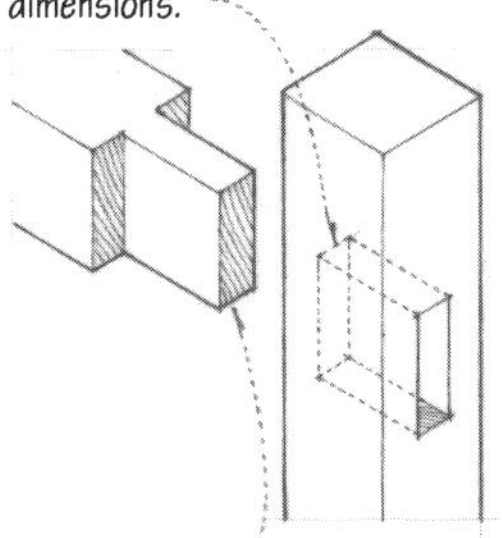

undercut tenon
A tenon having its shoulder cut at an angle to ensure that it bears on the mortised piece.

bevel
A line or surface that meets another at any angle other than a right angle.

through tenon
A tenon that extends completely through or beyond the piece into which its corresponding mortise is cut.

tenon
A projection formed on the end of a member for insertion into a mortise of the same dimensions.

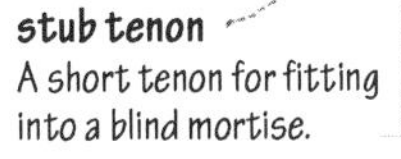

haunched tenon
A tenon that is narrower at its tip than at its root.

tusk
A beveled shoulder for strengthening a tenon.

root
The widened portion of a tenon in the plane of the shoulders.

key
A piece of wood or metal used as a wedge to tighten a joint or to prevent motion between parts.

gain
A notch, dado, or mortise cut into a member to receive another part.

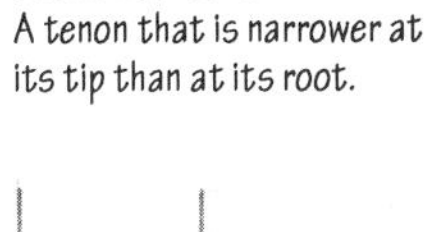

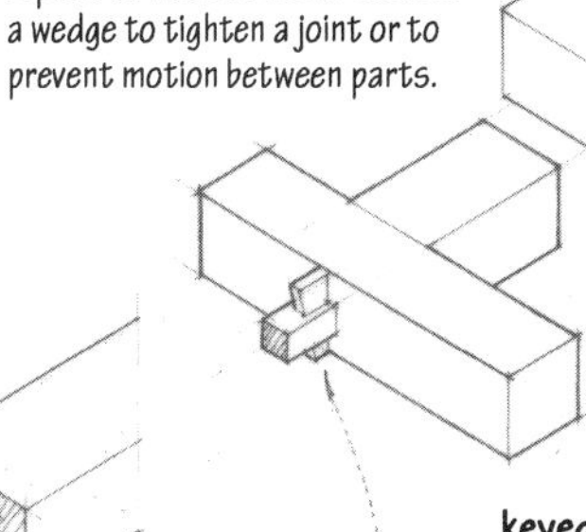

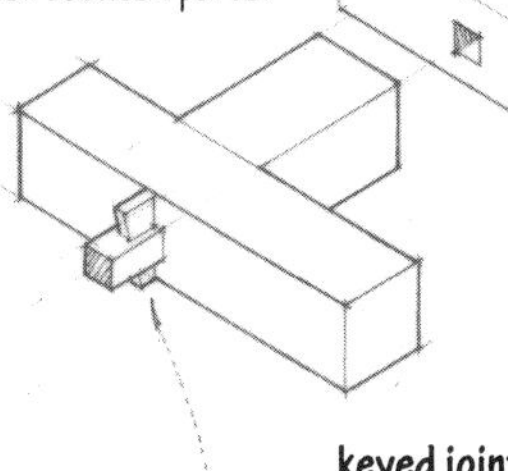

keyed joint
A joint fastened or secured by a key.

drawbore
A hole in a tenon bored eccentric with the corresponding holes in the mortise so that the two pieces being joined will be forced tightly together when the **drawbore pin** is hammered into place.

bridle joint
A joint formed by fitting the end of one member, notched to form two parallel tenons, into two gains cut into the edge of a second member.

foxtail wedge
A small wedge in the split end of a stub tenon for spreading and securing it when driven into a blind mortise. Also called **fox wedge**.

articulate
To unite by means of a joint or joints, esp. so as to make distinct or reveal how the parts fit into a systematic whole.

LIGHT

Electromagnetic radiation that the unaided human eye can perceive, having a wavelength in the range from about 370 to 800 nm and propagating at a speed of 186,281 mi./sec (299,972 km/sec).

nanometer
A unit of length equal to one billionth of a meter, used esp. to express the wavelengths of light in or near the visible spectrum. Abbr.: **nm**

angstrom
A unit of length equal to one ten-billionth of a meter, used esp. to express the wavelengths of radiation. Symbol: **Å**

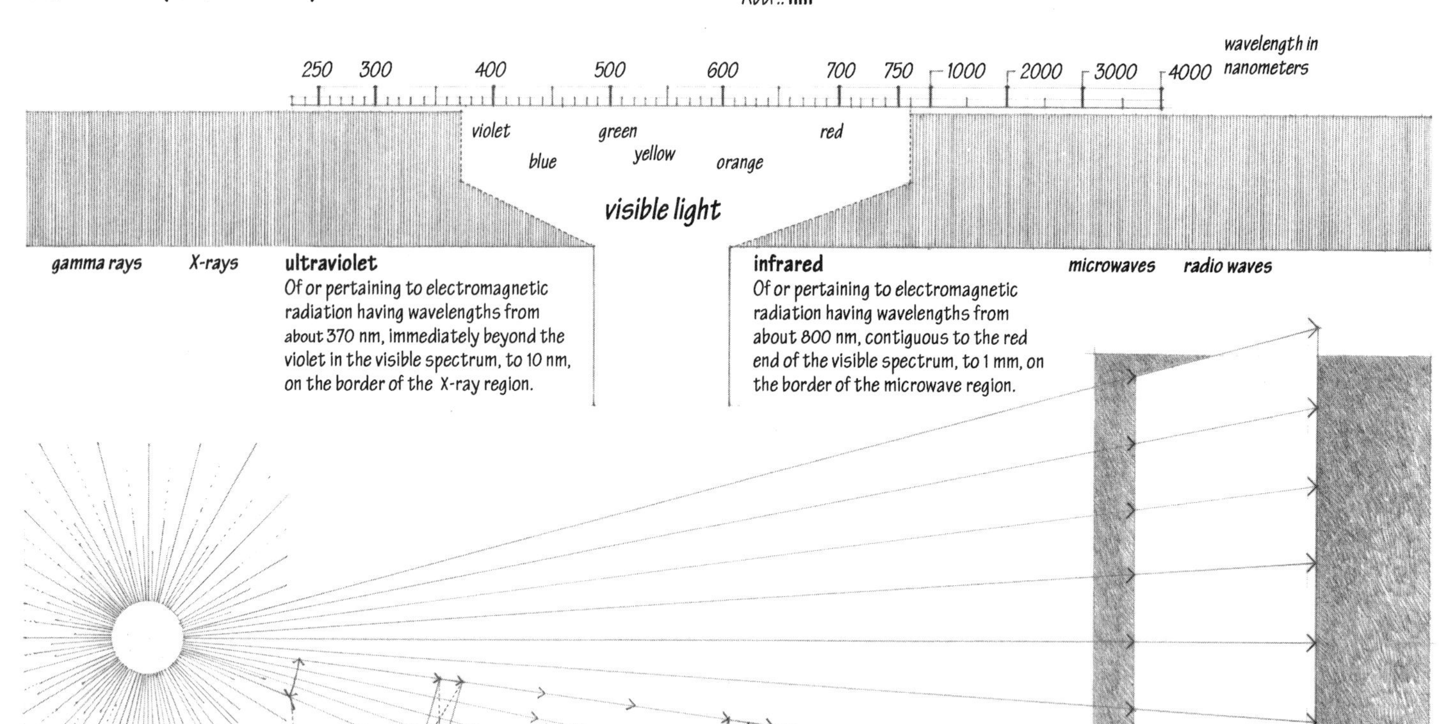

ultraviolet
Of or pertaining to electromagnetic radiation having wavelengths from about 370 nm, immediately beyond the violet in the visible spectrum, to 10 nm, on the border of the X-ray region.

infrared
Of or pertaining to electromagnetic radiation having wavelengths from about 800 nm, contiguous to the red end of the visible spectrum, to 1 mm, on the border of the microwave region.

luminous intensity
The luminous flux emitted per unit solid angle by a light source, expressed in candelas.

candlepower
Luminous intensity expressed in candelas.

candle
A unit of luminous intensity used prior to 1948, equal to the luminous intensity of a wax candle of standard specifications.

candela
The basic SI unit of luminous intensity, equal to the luminous intensity of a source that emits monochromatic radiation of frequency 540 x 10^{12} hertz and that has a radiant intensity of 1/683 watt per steradian. Also called **standard candle**. Abbr.: **Cd**

solid angle
An angle formed by three or more planes intersecting at a common point.

steradian
A solid angle at the center of a sphere subtending an area on the surface equal to the square of the radius of the sphere. Abbr.: **sr**

luminous flux
The rate of flow of visible light per unit time, expressed in lumens.

lumen
The SI unit of luminous flux, equal to the light emitted in a solid angle of one steradian by a uniform point source having an intensity of one candela. Abbr.: **lm**

cosine law
The law that the illumination produced on a surface by a point source is proportional to the cosine of the angle of incidence. Also called **Lambert's law**.

inverse square law
One of several laws relating two quantities such that one quantity varies inversely as the square of the other, as the law that the illumination produced on a surface by a point source varies inversely as the square of the distance of the surface from the source.

illumination
The intensity of light falling at any given place on a lighted surface, equal to the luminous flux incident per unit area and expressed in lumens per unit of area. Also called **illuminance**.

lux
The SI unit of illumination, equal to one lumen per square meter. Abbr.: **lx**

foot-candle
A unit of illumination on a surface that is everywhere one foot from a uniform point source of one candela and equal to one lumen incident per square foot. Abbr.: **FC**

luminance
The quantitative measure of brightness of a light source or an illuminated surface, equal to the luminous intensity per unit projected area of the source or surface viewed from a given direction.

lambert
A unit of luminance or brightness equal to 0.32 candela per square centimeter. Abbr.: **L**

foot-lambert
A unit of luminance or brightness equal to 0.32 candela per square foot. Abbr.: **fL**

brightness
The sensation by which an observer is able to distinguish between differences in luminance.

incidence
The striking of a ray of light or sound wave on a surface.

reflection
The return of light, sound, or radiant heat after striking a surface.

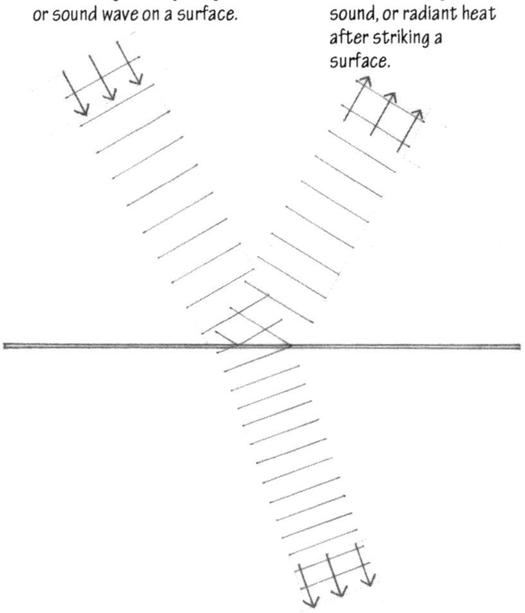

angle of incidence
The angle that a straight line, as a ray of light falling on a surface, makes with a normal to the surface at the point of incidence.

angle of reflection
The angle that a reflected ray makes with a normal to a reflecting surface at the point of incidence.

law of reflection
The principle that when light or sound is reflected from a smooth surface, the angle of incidence is equal to the angle of reflection, and the incident ray, the reflected ray, and the normal to the surface all lie in the same plane.

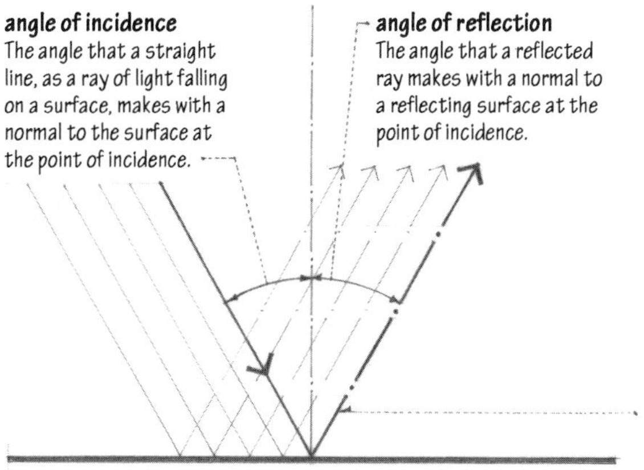

specular
Directed from a smooth, polished surface.

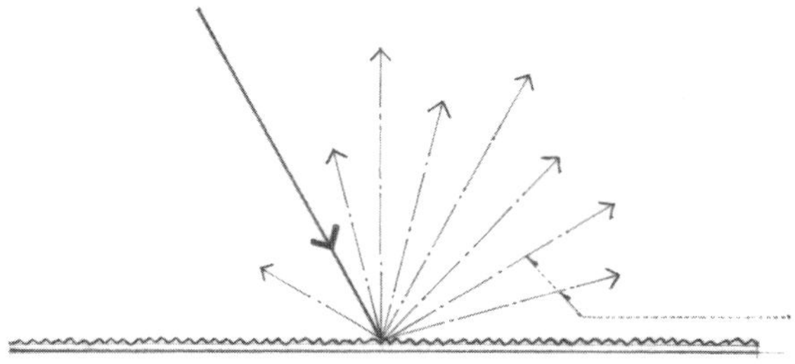

diffusion
A scattered reflection of light from an irregular surface or an erratic dispersion through a translucent material.

diffuse
Dispersed from an irregular surface.

refraction
The change of direction of a ray of light as it passes obliquely from one medium into another in which its velocity is different.

reflectance
The ratio of the radiation reflected by a surface to the total incident on the surface.

absorptance
The ratio of the radiation absorbed by a surface to the total incident on the surface.

transmittance
The ratio of the radiation transmitted through and emerging from a body to the total incident on it, equivalent to one minus the absorptance.

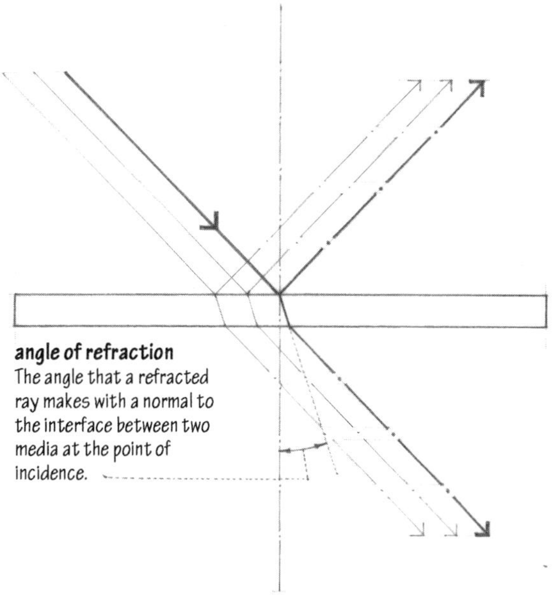

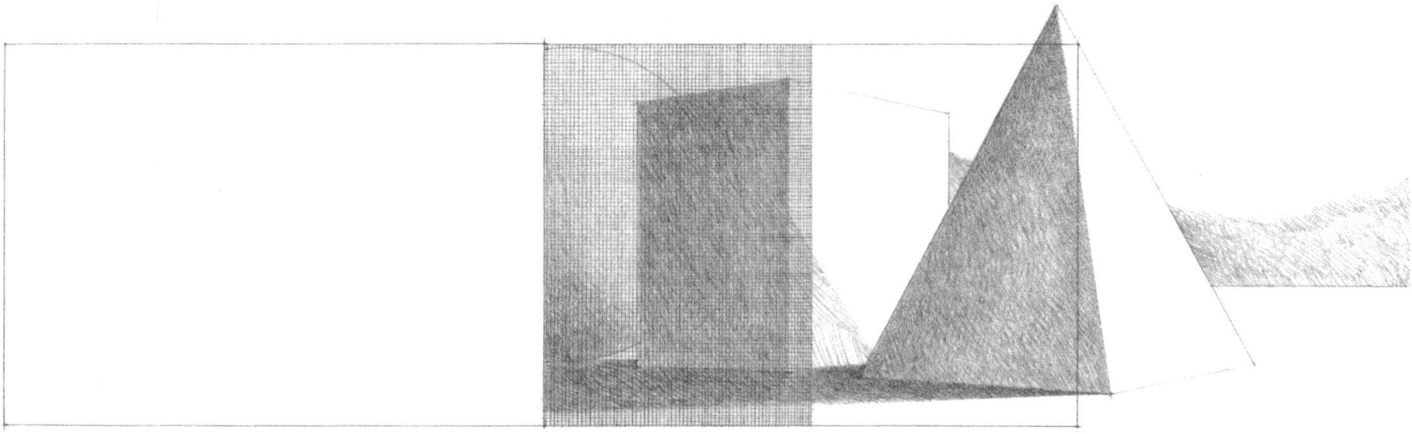

angle of refraction
The angle that a refracted ray makes with a normal to the interface between two media at the point of incidence.

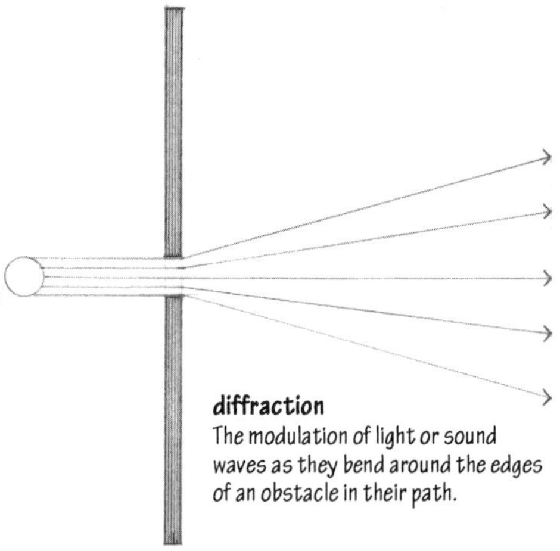

diffraction
The modulation of light or sound waves as they bend around the edges of an obstacle in their path.

opaque
Impenetrable to light.

translucent
Transmitting and diffusing light so that bodies on the opposite side are not clearly visible.

transparent
Capable of transmitting light so that bodies situated beyond or behind can be distinctly seen.

lamp
Any of various devices for producing light or heat, as by electricity or gas.

incandescent lamp
A lamp in which a filament gives off light when heated to incandescence by an electric current. Also called **light bulb**.

filament
The threadlike conductor of an electric lamp that is heated to incandescence by the passage of an electric current.

incandescence
The emission of visible light by a body when heated to a high temperature.

extended-service lamp
A lamp designed for reduced energy consumption and a life longer than the conventionally set value for its general class. Also called **long-life lamp**.

efficacy
A measure of the effectiveness with which a lamp converts electric power into luminous flux, equal to the ratio of flux emitted to power input and expressed in lumens per watt.

rated life
The average life in hours of a given type of lamp, based on laboratory tests of a representative group under controlled conditions.

three-way lamp
An incandescent lamp having two filaments so that it can be switched to three successive degrees of illumination.

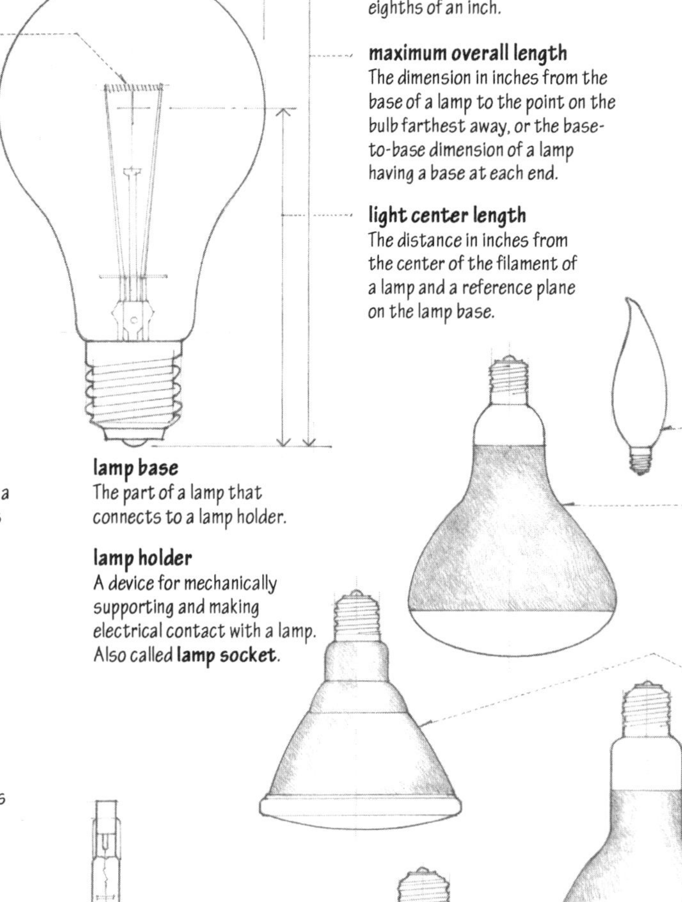

bulb
The glass housing of an incandescent lamp, filled with an inert gas mixture, usually of argon and nitrogen, to retard evaporation of the filament. Its shape is designated by a letter, followed by a number that indicates the lamp diameter.

lamp diameter
The maximum diameter of a lamp bulb, measured in eighths of an inch.

maximum overall length
The dimension in inches from the base of a lamp to the point on the bulb farthest away, or the base-to-base dimension of a lamp having a base at each end.

light center length
The distance in inches from the center of the filament of a lamp and a reference plane on the lamp base.

lamp base
The part of a lamp that connects to a lamp holder.

lamp holder
A device for mechanically supporting and making electrical contact with a lamp. Also called **lamp socket**.

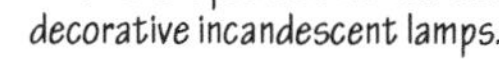

A bulb
The standard rounded shape for the bulbs of general-service incandescent lamps.

B bulb
A flame-shaped bulb for low-wattage, decorative incandescent lamps.

C bulb
A cone-shaped bulb for low-wattage, decorative incandescent lamps.

CA bulb
A candle-shaped bulb for low-wattage, decorative incandescent lamps.

R bulb
A reflector bulb of blown glass for incandescent and high-intensity-discharge lamps, having an internal reflective coating and either a clear or frosted glass front to provide the desired beam spread.

PAR bulb
A parabolic aluminized reflector bulb of cast glass for incandescent and high-intensity-discharge lamps, having a precisely formed internal reflector and a lensed front to provide the desired beam spread.

ER bulb
An ellipsoidal reflector bulb for incandescent lamps, having a precisely formed internal reflector that collects light and redirects it into a dispersed pattern at some distance in front of the light source.

A/SB bulb
An A bulb having a hemispherical, reflective silver bowl opposite the lamp base to decrease glare.

G bulb
A globe-shaped bulb for incandescent lamps, having a low brightness for exposed use.

PS bulb
A pear-shaped bulb for large incandescent lamps.

S bulb
A straight-sided bulb for low-wattage, decorative incandescent lamps.

tungsten lamp
An incandescent lamp having a tungsten filament.

tungsten-halogen lamp
A tungsten lamp having a quartz bulb containing a small amount of a halogen that vaporizes on heating and redeposits any evaporated tungsten particles back onto the filament. Also called **halogen lamp, quartz lamp**.

IR lamp
A tungsten-halogen lamp having an infrared dichroic coating for reflecting infrared energy back to the filament, raising lamp efficiency, and reducing radiant heat in the emitted light beam.

infrared lamp
An incandescent lamp having a higher percentage of its radiant power in the infrared region than a standard incandescent lamp, often having a red glass bulb to reduce the radiated visible light.

TB bulb
A quartz bulb for tungsten-halogen lamps, similar in shape to the A bulb but having an angular profile.

MR bulb
A multifaceted reflector bulb for tungsten-halogen lamps, having highly polished reflectors arranged in discrete segments to provide the desired beam spread.

ballast
A device for maintaining the current through a fluorescent or HID lamp at the desired constant value, and sometimes also providing the required starting voltage and current.

starter
A device used with a ballast to provide the starting voltage for a preheat fluorescent lamp.

T bulb
A tubular bulb for incandescent, fluorescent, and high-intensity-discharge lamps.

circline lamp
A doughnut-shaped fluorescent lamp for circular luminaires.

U-bent lamp
A U-shaped fluorescent lamp for square or rectangular luminaires.

compact fluorescent lamp
Any of various small, improved efficiency fluorescent lamps having a single, double, or U-shaped tube, and often an adapter for fitting an incandescent lampholder.

phosphor
Any of a number of substances that emit light when excited by radiation.

triphosphor
A phosphor having peaks in three specific color regions, red, blue, and green, used to improve the color rendering of a fluorescent lamp.

discharge lamp
A lamp in which light is produced by the discharge of electricity between electrodes in a gas-filled glass enclosure.

fluorescent lamp
A tubular discharge lamp in which light is produced by the fluorescence of phosphors coating the inside of the tube.

fluorescence
The emission of radiation, esp. of visible light, by a substance during exposure to external radiation.

preheat lamp
A fluorescent lamp that requires a separate starter to preheat the cathodes before opening the circuit to the starting voltage.

rapid-start lamp
A fluorescent lamp designed to operate with a ballast having a low-voltage winding for continuous heating of the cathodes, which allows the lamp to be started more rapidly than a preheat lamp.

instant-start lamp
A fluorescent lamp designed to operate with a ballast having a high-voltage transformer to initiate the arc directly without any preheating of the cathodes.

high-output lamp
A rapid-start fluorescent lamp designed to operate on a current of 800 milliamperes, resulting in a corresponding increase in luminous flux per unit length of lamp.

very-high-output lamp
A rapid-start fluorescent lamp designed to operate on a current of 1500 milliamperes, providing a corresponding increase in luminous flux per unit length of lamp.

color temperature
The temperature at which a blackbody emits light of a specified spectral distribution, used to specify the color of a light source.

spectral distribution curve
A curve plotting the radiant energy in each wavelength of a particular light source.

color rendering index
A measure of the ability of an electric lamp to render color accurately when compared with a reference light source of similar color temperature. A tungsten lamp operating at a color temperature of 3200°K, noon sunlight having a color temperature of 4800°K, and average daylight having a color temperature of 7000°K all have an index of 100 and are considered to render color perfectly.

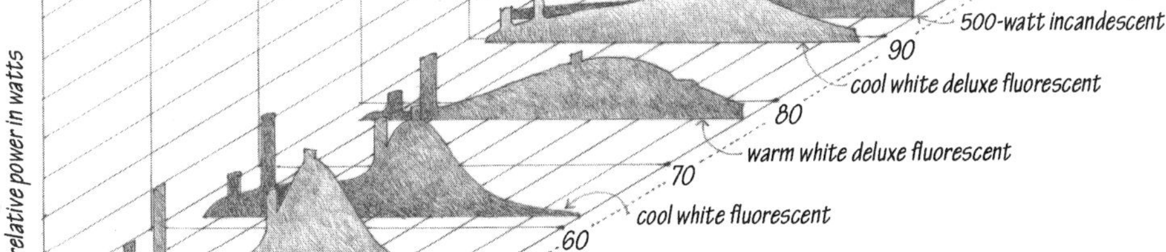

high-intensity discharge lamp
A discharge lamp in which a significant amount of light is produced by the discharge of electricity through a metallic vapor in a sealed glass enclosure. Also, **HID lamp**.

mercury lamp
A high-intensity discharge lamp producing light by means of an electric discharge in mercury vapor. Also called **mercury-vapor lamp**.

sodium lamp
A high-intensity discharge lamp producing light by means of an electric discharge in sodium vapor. Also called **sodium-vapor lamp**.

low-pressure sodium lamp
A sodium lamp producing a yellow, glareless light and used esp. to illuminate roadways. Also, **LPS lamp**.

high-pressure sodium lamp
A sodium lamp producing a broader-spectrum, golden-white light than a low-pressure sodium lamp. Also, **HPS lamp**.

metal halide lamp
A high-intensity discharge lamp similar in construction to a mercury lamp, but having an arc tube to which various metal halides are added to produce more light and improve color rendering.

neon lamp
A cold-cathode lamp emitting a glow when a high voltage is applied across two electrodes in a neon-filled glass tube.

cold-cathode lamp
A discharge lamp having cathodes that emit electrons without having to be heated.

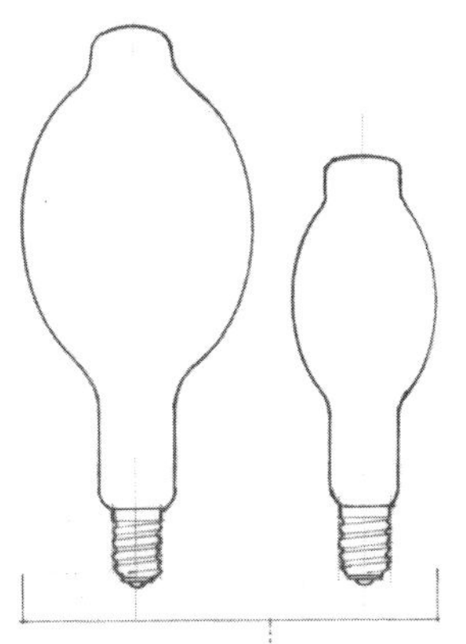

BT bulb
A bulged tubular bulb for high-intensity-discharge lamps.

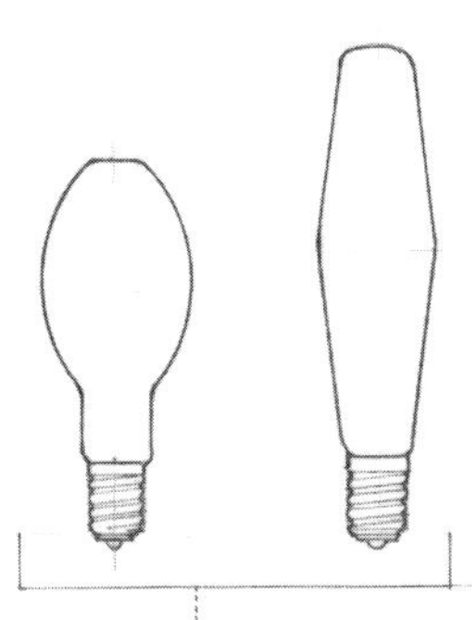

E bulb
An ellipsoidal bulb for high-intensity-discharge lamps.

luminaire
A lighting unit consisting of one or more electric lamps with all of the necessary parts and wiring for positioning and protecting the lamps, connecting the lamps to a power supply, and distributing the light. Also called **lighting fixture**.

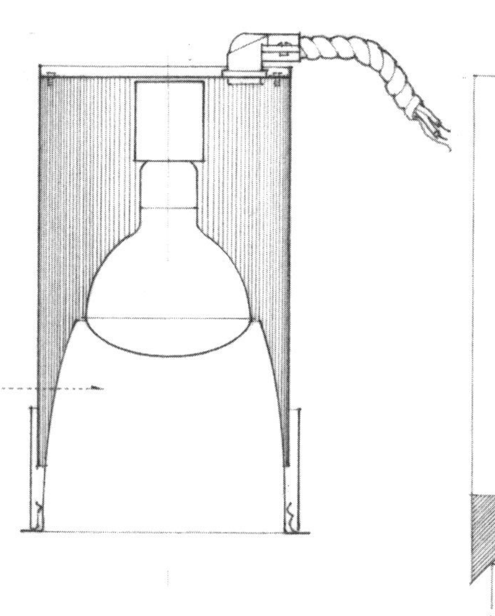

reflector
A surface for reflecting light, heat, or sound, esp. the device on a luminaire having such a surface for controlling the distribution of light emitted by a lamp.

parabolic reflector
A reflector having a parabolic surface to collimate, spread, or focus the rays from a light source, depending on the location of the source.

lens
A piece of transparent material, as glass or plastic, having two opposite surfaces either or both of which are curved, used in luminaires to focus, disperse, or collimate the emitted light.

collimate
To make rays of light parallel.

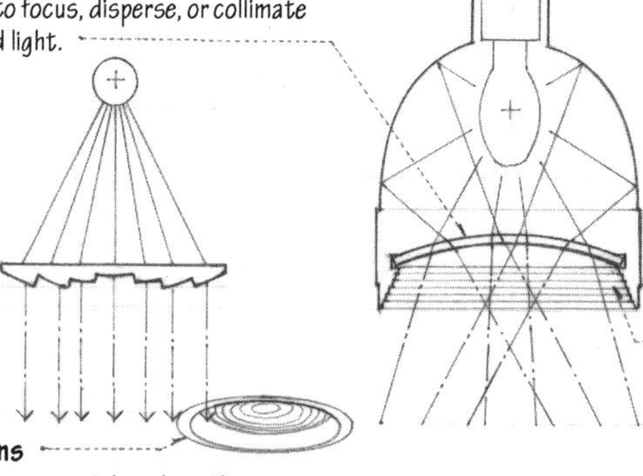

elliptical reflector
A reflector having an elliptical surface to focus the rays from a light source.

ridged baffle
A series of circular ridges for reducing the brightness of a light source at an aperture.

Fresnel lens
A lens having concentric, prismatic grooves to concentrate light from a small source.

prismatic lens
A lens having a multifaceted surface with parallel prisms to redirect the rays from a light source.

diffuser
Any of a variety of translucent materials for filtering glare from a light source and distributing the light over an extended area.

louver
A finned or vaned device for controlling the radiation from a light source.

candlepower distribution curve
A polar plot of the luminous intensity emitted by a lamp, luminaire, or window in a given direction from the center of the light source, measured in a single plane for a symmetrical light source, and in a perpendicular, parallel, and sometimes a 45° plane for an asymmetrical source.

eggcrate
A louvered construction divided into cell-like areas and used for redirecting the light emitted by an overhead source.

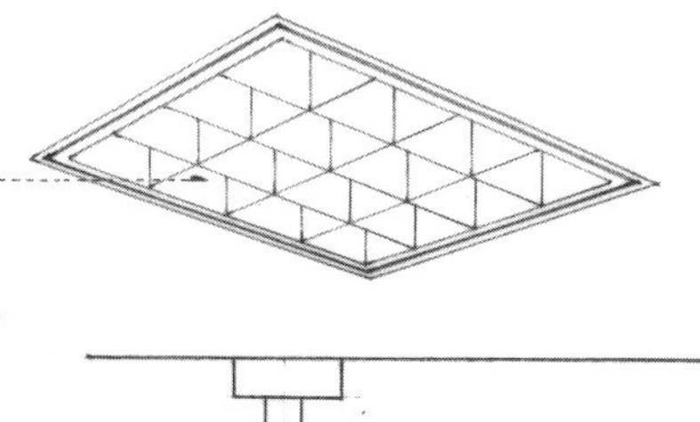

baffle
A louvered device for shielding a light source from view at certain angles.

shielding angle
The angle below which a light source can be seen.

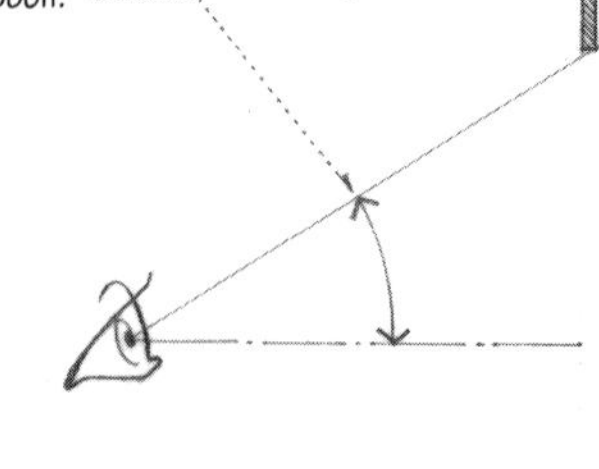

isochart
A graphic plot of the pattern of illumination produced on a surface by a lamp or luminaire.

isolux line
A line through all points on a surface where the level of illumination is the same. Called **isofootcandle line** if illumination is expressed in footcandles.

luminaire efficiency
The ratio of luminous flux emitted by a luminaire to the total flux emitted by the lamps in the luminaire.

wall washer
A downlight mounted close to the plane of a wall and equipped with a reflector, baffle, or lens to illuminate the vertical surface.

floodlight
A lamp designed to project or diffuse a comparatively uniform level of illumination over a large area. Also called **flood, flood lamp**.

downlight
A luminaire consisting of a lamp set in a metal cylinder, recessed into or mounted on a ceiling to direct a beam of light downward.

spotlight
A lamp designed to project a strong, focused beam of light on an object or area. Also called **spot**.

spill
Superfluous or useless light rays, as from a spotlight or other focused light source. Also called **spill light**.

point source
A light source having a maximum dimension less than one fifth the distance from the source to the surface illuminated.

track lighting
Lighting provided by adjustable spotlights mounted along a narrow, ceiling- or wall-mounted metal track through which current is conducted.

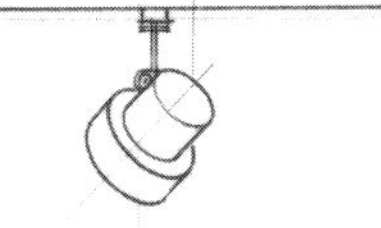

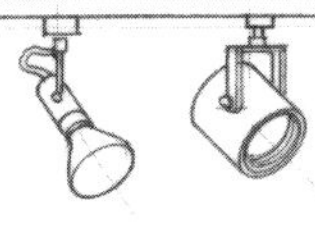

light strip
A rigid or flexible tape with exposed low-voltage light sources of 1 to 10 watts.

cove lighting
Indirect lighting directed upward from an interior cornice at the edge of a ceiling.

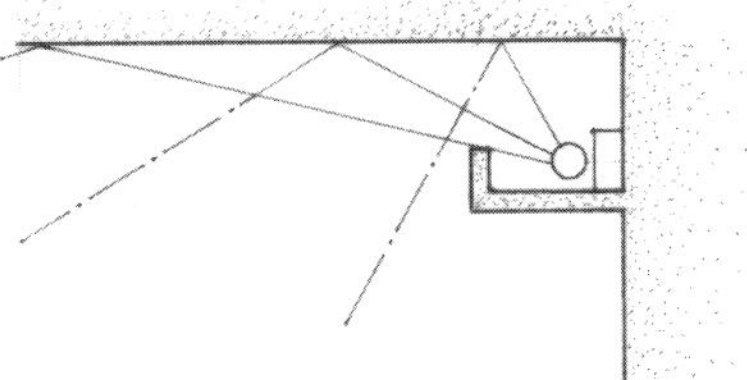

troffer
A luminaire having a trough-shaped reflector holding one or more fluorescent lamps.

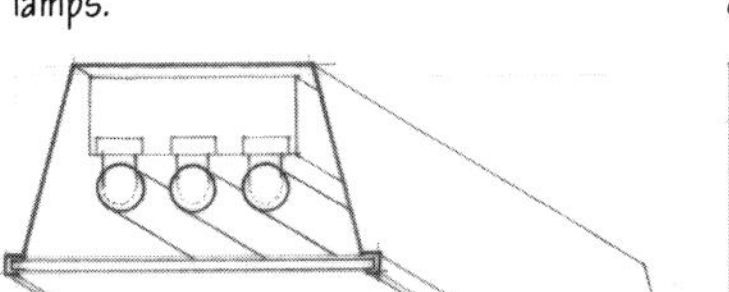

linear source
A light source having one dimension significantly greater than its other dimensions, as a fluorescent lamp.

valance lighting
Indirect lighting directed upward or downward from a light source concealed by a horizontal board or band.

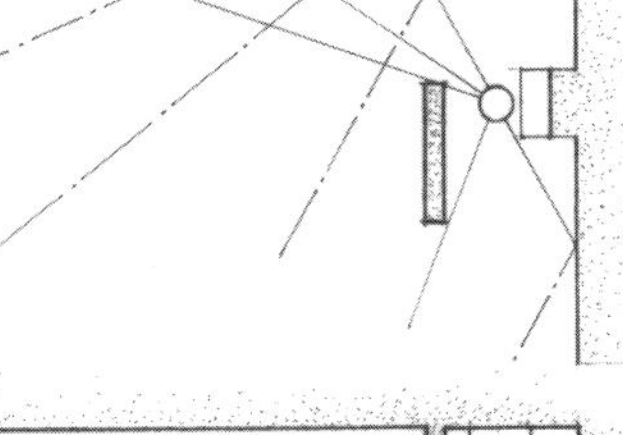

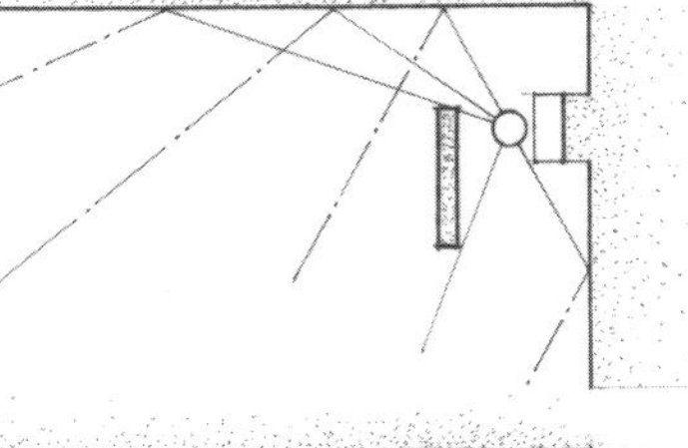

area source
A light source having significant dimensions in two directions, as a large window or a luminous ceiling.

cornice lighting
Indirect lighting directed downward from an interior cornice at the edge of a ceiling.

droplight
A lighting fixture suspended from a ceiling or wall by a flexible cord, by which it can be raised or lowered.

pendant
A lighting fixture suspended from a ceiling.

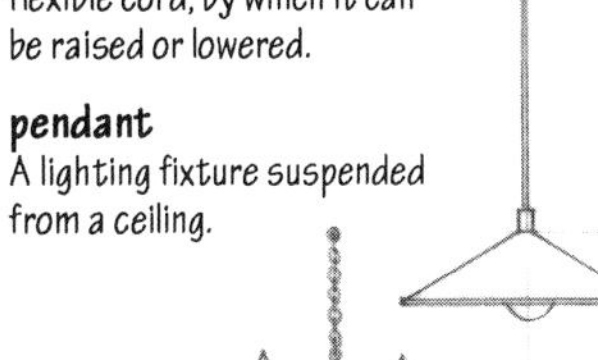

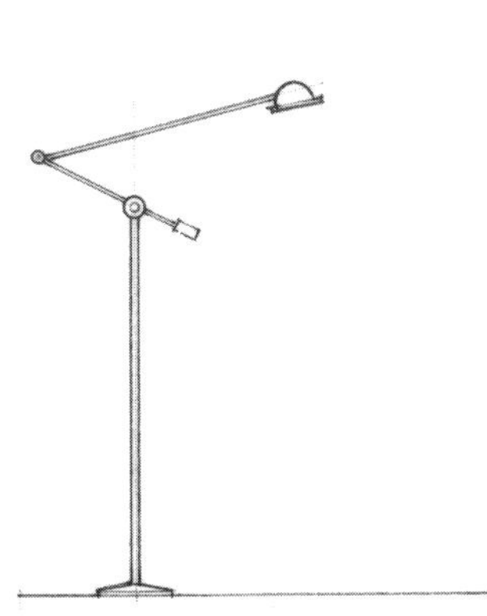

bridge lamp
A floor lamp having the light source on a hinged, horizontally adjustable arm.

gooseneck lamp
A desk lamp having a flexible shaft resembling the neck of a goose.

torchiere
A floor lamp having its light source within a reflecting bowl that directs the light upward. Also, **torchère, torchier´**.

chandelier
A decorative lighting fixture suspended from a ceiling, usually having branched supports for a number of lamps.

sconce
A decorative wall bracket for candles or other lights.

lighting
The science, theory, or method of providing illumination through the use of electric lamps.

general lighting
Lighting designed to provide a uniform level of illumination throughout an area.

local lighting
Lighting designed to provide a relatively high level of illumination over a small area, with a surrounding area of lower intensity from spill light.

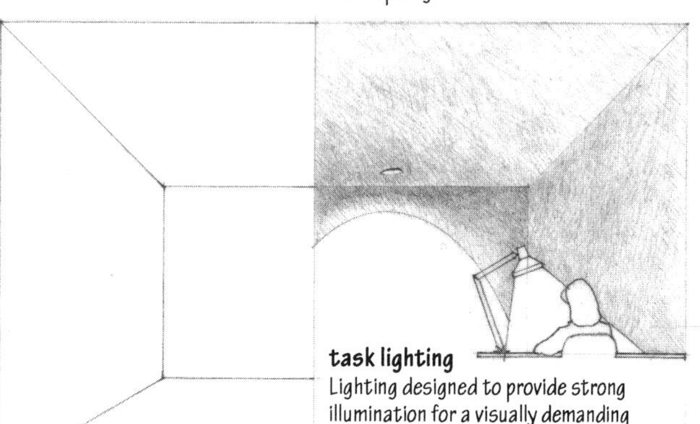

task lighting
Lighting designed to provide strong illumination for a visually demanding activity, as reading or drafting.

accent lighting
Lighting that calls attention to a particular object or feature in the visual field, or that forms a decorative pattern on a surface.

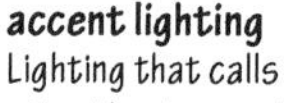

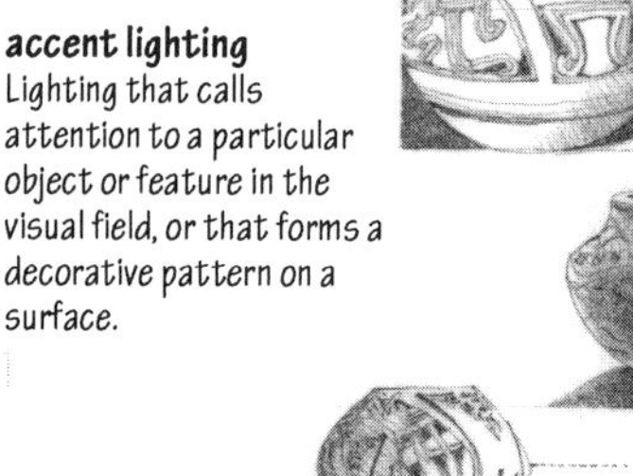

highlight
To emphasize by illuminating with a strong light.

backlight
To illuminate something from behind in order to enhance depth or to separate the subject from its background.

sidelight
Light coming or produced from the side.

soft light
Diffuse light that produces little contrast and poorly defined shadows on the subject.

hard light
Direct light that produces high contrast and distinct shadows on the subject.

direct lighting
Lighting in which luminaires distribute 90% to 100% of the emitted light downward on the surface or area to be illuminated.

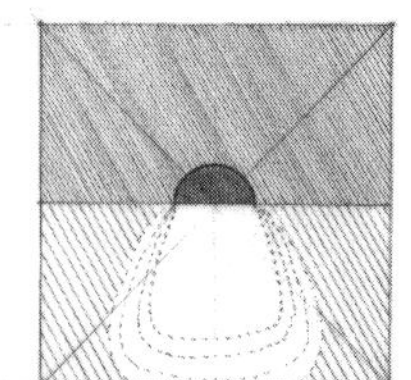

semidirect lighting
Lighting in which luminaires distribute 60% to 90% of the emitted light downward.

general diffuse lighting
Lighting from luminaires that emit an approximately equal distribution of light upward and downward.

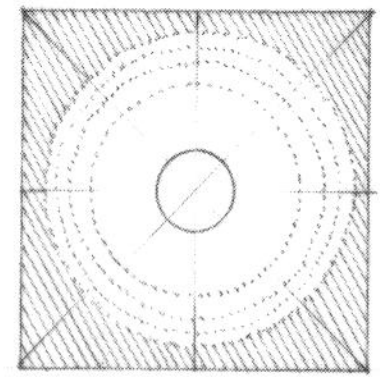

direct-indirect lighting
General diffuse lighting in which little light is emitted in the horizontal plane of the luminaires.

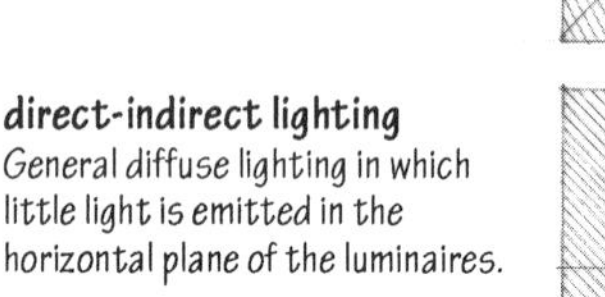

semi-indirect lighting
Lighting in which luminaires distribute 60% to 90% of the emitted light upward.

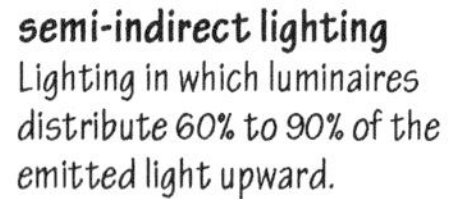

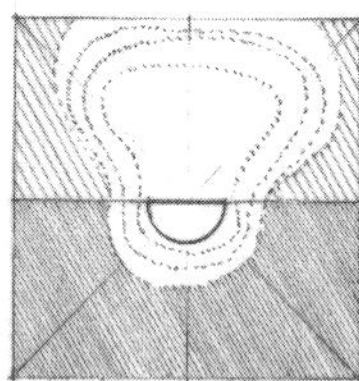

indirect lighting
Lighting in which luminaires distribute 90% to 100% of the emitted light upward, esp. to avoid glare or prevent shadows.

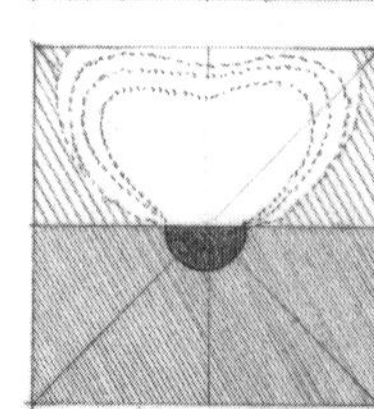

glare
The sensation produced by any brightness within the visual field that is sufficiently greater than the luminance to which the eyes are adapted to cause annoyance, discomfort, or loss of visibility.

adaptation
The regulating by the pupil of the quantity of light entering the eye, resulting in a change in the sensitivity of the eye's photoreceptors to light.

visual comfort probability
A rating of the likelihood that a lighting system will not cause direct glare, expressed as the percentage of people who may be expected to experience visual comfort when seated in the least favorable visual position.

brightness ratio
The ratio between the luminance of an object and that of its background. Also called **contrast ratio**.

blinding glare
Glare so intense that, for an appreciable length of time after it has been removed, visibility is lost.

disability glare
Glare that reduces visibility or impairs visual performance, often accompanied by discomfort.

discomfort glare
Glare that produces discomfort but does not necessarily interfere with visibility or visual performance.

CONTRAST

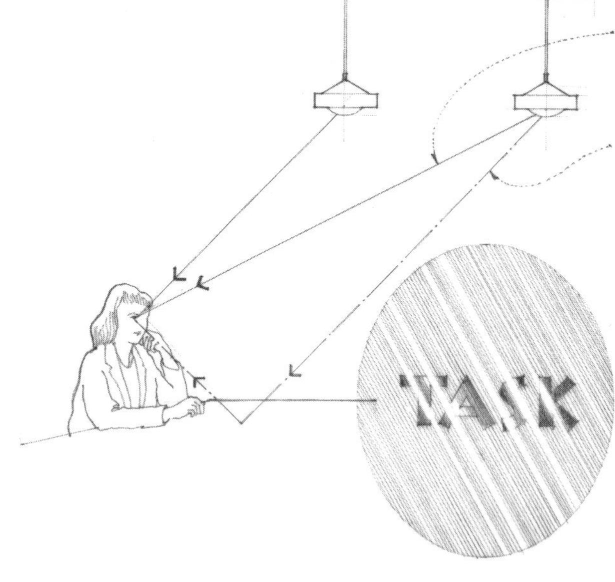

direct glare
Glare resulting from a high brightness ratio or an insufficiently shielded light source in the visual field.

reflected glare
Glare resulting from the specular reflection of a light source within the visual field. Also called **indirect glare**.

veiling reflectance
Reflected glare on a task surface that reduces the contrast necessary for seeing details.

beam spread
The angle of a light beam that intersects the candlepower distribution curve at points where the luminous intensity equals a stated percent of a maximum reference intensity.

spacing criteria
A formula for determining how far apart luminaires may be installed for uniform lighting of a surface or area, based on mounting height.

spacing criteria (sc) = spacing (s) / mounting height (mh)

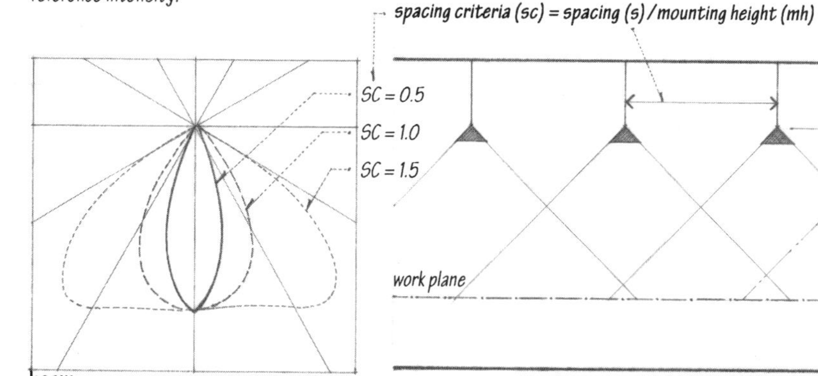

point method
A procedure for calculating the illumination produced on a surface by a point source from any angle, based on the inverse square and cosine laws.

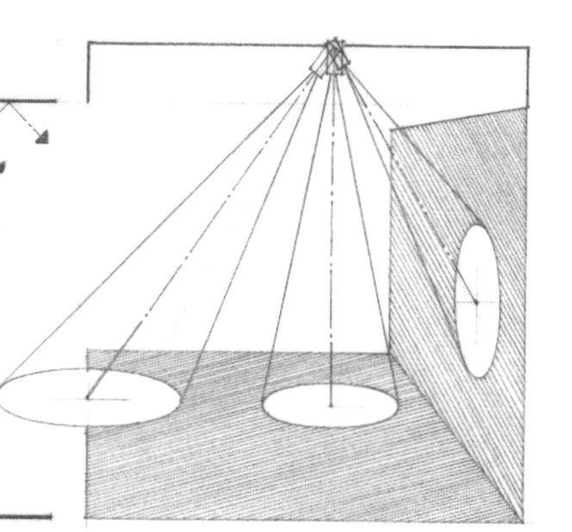

beam
A group of nearly parallel rays of light.

throw
The effective length of a beam of light.

ceiling cavity
The cavity formed by the ceiling, a plane of suspended luminaires, and the wall surfaces between these two planes.

room cavity
The cavity formed by a plane of luminaires, the work plane, and the wall surfaces between these two planes.

floor cavity
The cavity formed by the work plane, the floor, and the wall surfaces between these two planes.

lumen method
A procedure for determining the number and types of lamps, luminaires, or windows required to provide a uniform level of illumination on a work plane, taking into account both direct and reflected luminous flux. Also called **zonal cavity method**.

work plane
The horizontal plane at which work is done and on which illumination is specified and measured, usually assumed to be 30 in. (762 mm) above the floor.

room cavity ratio
A single number derived from the dimensions of a room cavity for use in determining the coefficient of utilization.

coefficient of utilization
The ratio of the luminous flux reaching a specified work plane to the total lumen output of a luminaire, taking into account the proportions of a room and the reflectances of its surfaces.

light loss factor
Any of several factors used in calculating the effective illumination provided by a lighting system after a given period of time and under given conditions. Formerly called **maintenance factor**.

recoverable light loss factor
A light loss factor that may be recovered by relamping or maintenance, as lamp lumen depreciation, luminaire dirt depreciation, and room surface dirt depreciation.

lamp lumen depreciation
A light loss factor representing the decrease in luminous output of a lamp during its operating life, expressed as a percentage of initial lamp lumens.

luminaire dirt depreciation
A light loss factor representing the decrease in luminous output of a luminaire resulting from the accumulation of dirt on its surfaces, expressed as a percentage of the illumination from the luminaire when new or clean.

room surface dirt depreciation
A light loss factor representing the decrease in reflected light resulting from the accumulation of dirt on a room's surfaces, expressed as a percentage of the light reflected from the surfaces when clean.

$$\text{average maintained illuminance} = \frac{\text{initial lamp lumens} \times CU \times RLLF \times NRLLF}{\text{work area}}$$

$$\text{initial lamp lumens} = \text{lumens per lamp} \times \text{lamps per luminaire}$$

nonrecoverable light loss factor
Any of several permanent light loss factors that take into account the effects of temperature, voltage drops or surges, ballast variations, and partition heights.

daylighting
The science, theory, or method of providing illumination through the use of light of day.

daylight
To provide an interior space with daylight from both direct and indirect sources.

skylight
The light from the sky, reflected and diffused by air molecules.

sunlight
The direct light of the sun.

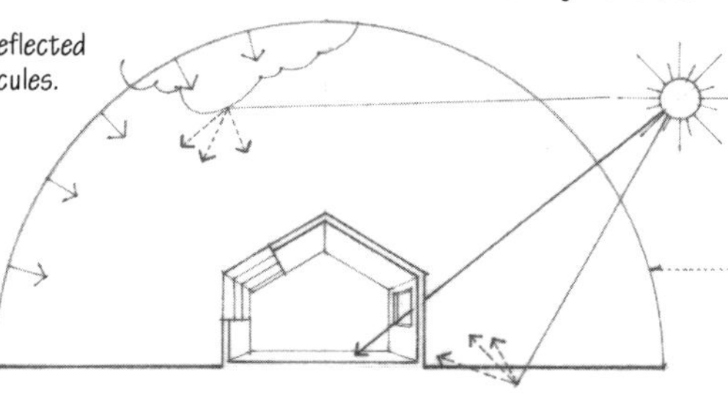

clear sky
A sky having less than 30% cloud cover with the solar disk unobstructed. Also, the CIE standard for a reference cloudless sky condition, having the greatest luminance near the sun and least luminance 90° from the sun.

ground light
Sunlight or skylight reflected by surfaces below the plane of the horizon.

zenith
The point on the celestial sphere vertically above a given position or observer.

cloudy sky
A sky having between 30% and 70% cloud cover, with the solar disk obstructed.

counterlight
Light originating from sources facing each other, as from windows in opposite walls.

crosslight
Light originating from sources not facing each other, as from windows in adjacent walls.

overcast sky
A sky having 100% cloud cover. Also, the CIE standard for a reference sky having a luminance distribution three times brighter near the zenith than at the horizon.

CIE
Commission Internationale de l'Eclairage, an international commission developing definitions, standards, and procedures for the art, science, and technology of lighting.

IES
Illuminating Engineering Society, a professional society in North America devoted to the development and dissemination of standards and procedures relating to the art, science, and technology of lighting.

daylight factor method
A method for calculating the performance of a daylighting system, based on the daylight factor.

sky component
A component of the daylight factor, equal to the ratio of daylight illumination at a point on a given plane received directly from a sky of assumed or known luminance distribution to the simultaneously measured illuminance on a horizontal plane from an unobstructed hemisphere of this sky.

artificial sky
A hemispherical dome or similar enclosure illuminated by concealed light sources that simulate the luminance distribution of a clear or overcast sky, used for studying and testing daylighting techniques on architectural models placed near its center.

daylight factor
A measure of daylight illuminance, expressed as the ratio of daylight illumination at a point on a given plane to the simultaneously measured illuminance on a horizontal plane from an unobstructed sky of assumed or known luminance distribution.

heliodon
A device for orienting an architectural model to a light source representing the sun, calibrated with respect to latitude, time of day, and season of the year and used for studying daylighting techniques and shadows cast by the sun.

external reflected component
A component of the daylight factor, equal to the ratio of the daylight illumination at a point on a given plane received directly from exterior reflecting surfaces to the simultaneously measured illuminance on a horizontal plane from an unobstructed sky of assumed or known luminance distribution.

internal reflected component
A component of the daylight factor, equal to the ratio of the daylight illumination at a point on a given plane received directly or indirectly from interior reflecting surfaces to the simultaneously measured illuminance on a horizontal plane from an unobstructed sky of assumed or known luminance distribution.

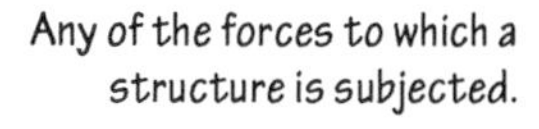

Any of the forces to which a structure is subjected.

concentrated load
A load acting on a very small area or particular point of a supporting structural element.

distributed load
A load extending over the length or area of the supporting structural element.

uniformly distributed load
A distributed load of uniform magnitude.

static load
A load applied slowly to a structure until it reaches its peak value without fluctuating rapidly in magnitude or position. Under a static load, a structure responds slowly and its deformation reaches a peak when the static force is maximum.

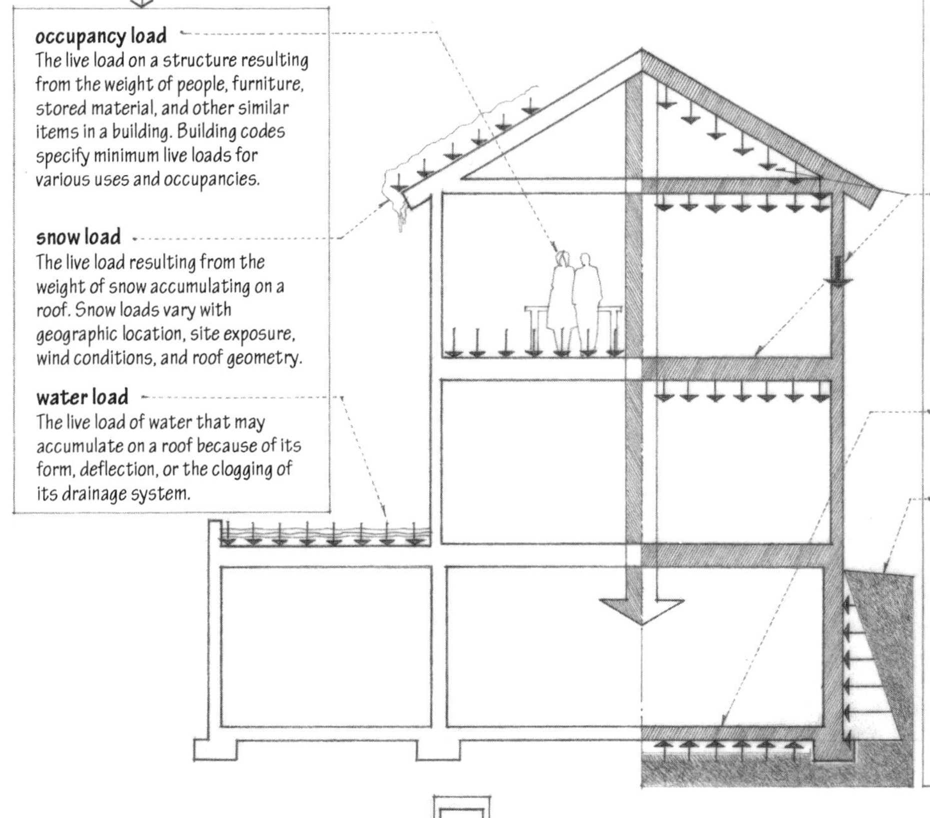

live load
Any moving or movable load on a structure resulting from occupancy, collected snow and water, or moving equipment. A live load typically acts vertically downward, but may act horizontally as well to reflect the dynamic nature of a moving load.

occupancy load
The live load on a structure resulting from the weight of people, furniture, stored material, and other similar items in a building. Building codes specify minimum live loads for various uses and occupancies.

snow load
The live load resulting from the weight of snow accumulating on a roof. Snow loads vary with geographic location, site exposure, wind conditions, and roof geometry.

water load
The live load of water that may accumulate on a roof because of its form, deflection, or the clogging of its drainage system.

dead load
The static load acting vertically downward on a structure, comprising the self-weight of the structure and the weight of building elements, fixtures, and equipment permanently attached to it.

water pressure
The uplifting force a water table exerts on a foundation system.

earth pressure
The horizontal force a soil mass exerts on a vertical retaining structure.

settlement load
A load imposed on a structure by subsidence of a portion of the supporting soil and the resulting differential settlement of its foundation.

equivalent load
A load substituted by a building code for an actual load, derived on the basis of statistical evidence for given types of buildings. For safety, the equivalent load is usually a multiple of the load that would produce failure or unacceptable deflection.

load combination
The dead load and two or more live loads assumed to occur simultaneously on a structure when their combined effect can be reasonably expected to be less than the sum of their separate actions.

1.00 (dead + live + snow loads)

0.75 (dead + live + snow + wind or seismic loads)

load reduction
A reduction in design loading allowed by building codes for certain load combinations, based on the assumption that not all live loads will act simultaneously on a structure at their full value. After all possible load combinations are considered, a structure is designed to carry the most severe but realistic distribution, concentration, and combination of loads.

wind load

earthquake load

dynamic load
A load applied suddenly to a structure, often with rapid changes in magnitude and location. Under a dynamic load, a structure develops inertial forces in relation to its mass and its maximum deformation does not necessarily correspond to the maximum magnitude of the applied force.

moving load
A kinetic load of short duration due to moving vehicles, equipment, and machinery. Building codes treat this load as a static load, compensating for its dynamic nature by amplifying the static load. Also called **impact load**.

impact factor
A factor by which the effect of a static load is multiplied to approximate the effect of applying the same load dynamically.

erection stress
The stress induced on a building unit or component by loads applied during the erection process.

erection bracing
The temporary bracing required to secure the units or components of a building until permanently fastened in place.

construction load
A temporary load on a structure occurring during its erection, as from wind or the weight of construction equipment and stored materials.

lateral load
A load acting horizontally on a structure, as a wind or earthquake load.

earthquake load
The forces exerted on a structure by an earthquake.

earthquake
A series of longitudinal and transverse vibrations induced in the earth's crust by the abrupt movement of plates along fault lines. The shocks of an earthquake propagate along the earth's surface in the form of waves and attenuate logarithmically with distance from its source.

epicenter
A point directly above the hypocenter, from which the shock waves of an earthquake apparently emanate.

hypocenter
The point of origin of an earthquake. Also called **focus**.

fault
A break in the earth's crust accompanied by a dislocation in the plane of the fracture.

plate
Any of the huge movable segments into which the earth's crust is divided.

seismic
Of, pertaining to, or caused by an earthquake or vibration of the earth.

seismic force
Any of the forces caused by the vibratory ground motions of an earthquake. While these motions are three-dimensional in nature, their horizontal components are considered to be the most important in structural design; the vertical load-carrying elements of a structure usually have considerable reserve for resisting additional vertical loads. During an earthquake, the mass of a structure develops an inertial force as it tries to resist ground acceleration. From Newton's second law, this force is equal to the product of mass and acceleration. For design purposes, a statically equivalent lateral force, base shear, is computed by formula.

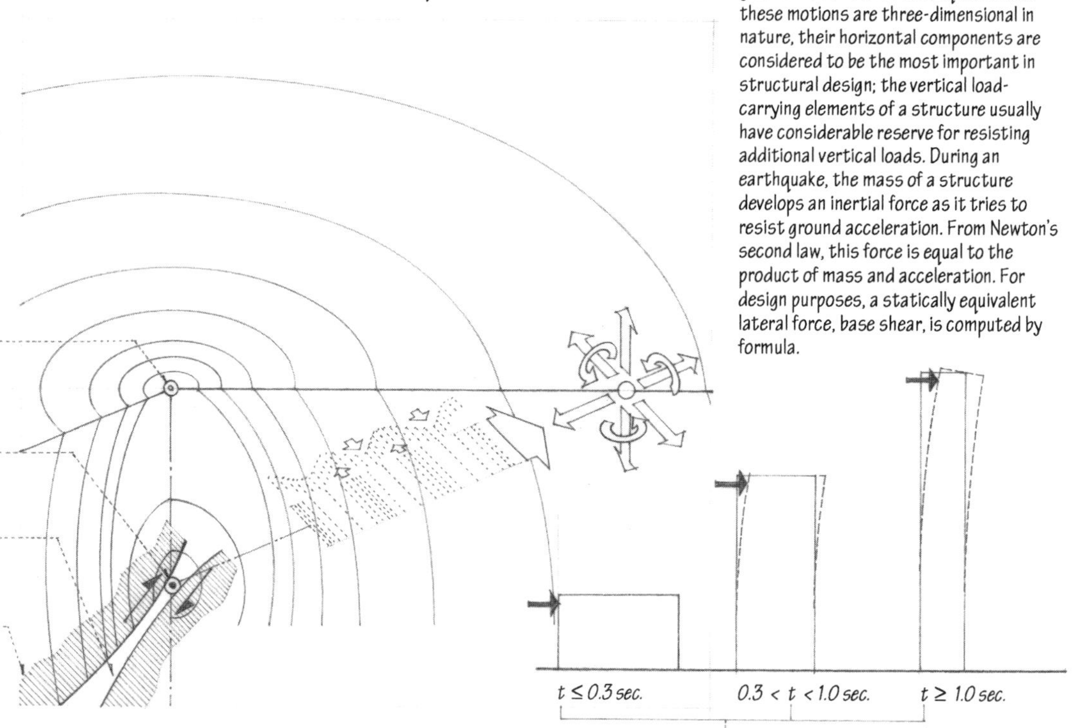

$t \leq 0.3$ sec. $0.3 < t < 1.0$ sec. $t \geq 1.0$ sec.

vibration
The oscillating, reciprocating, or other periodic motion of an elastic body or medium when forced from a position or state of equilibrium.

periodic motion
Any motion that recurs in the same form at equal intervals of time.

harmonic motion
Periodic motion consisting of one or more vibratory motions that are symmetric about a region of equilibrium, as the motion of a vibrating string of a musical instrument.

period
The time required for one complete cycle of a wave or oscillation.

natural period of vibration
The time required for a body subject to a vibratory force to go through one oscillation in the direction under consideration. A structure's natural period of vibration varies according to its height above the base and its dimension parallel to the direction of the applied forces. A relatively stiff structure tends to oscillate rapidly and has a short period of vibration while a more flexible structure tends to oscillate slowly and has a longer period. Also called **fundamental period of vibration**.

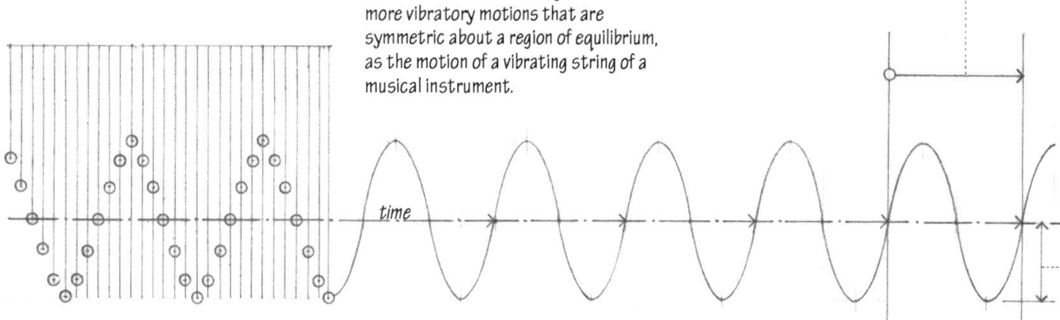

time

amplitude
The maximum displacement from the mean position during one period of an oscillation.

drift
The lateral deflection or movement of a structure due to wind, earthquake, or asymmetrical vertical loading.

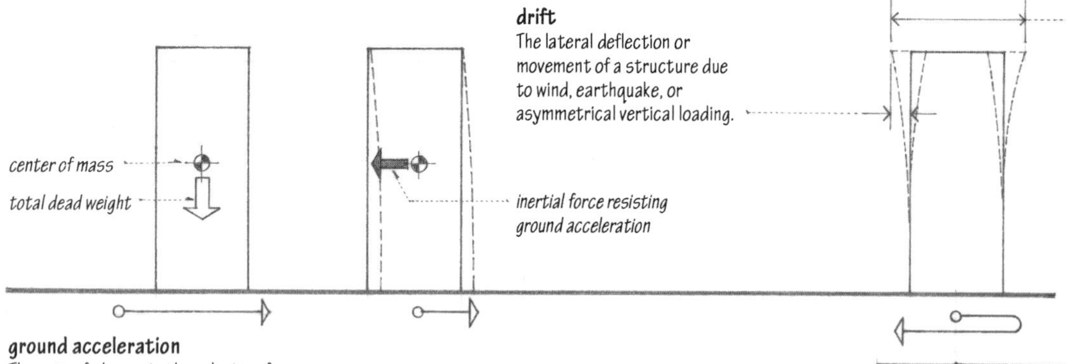

oscillation
A single swing of an oscillating body from one extreme limit to another.

oscillate
To swing back and forth like a pendulum between alternating extremes.

center of mass

total dead weight

inertial force resisting ground acceleration

resonance
An abnormally large vibration in a system caused by a relatively small vibratory force of the same or nearly the same period as the natural period of vibration of the system.

ground acceleration
The rate of change in the velocity of ground movement with respect to time. High accelerations are the most damaging to a structure, which must try to follow the rapid changes in ground movement during an earthquake.

damping
The absorption or dissipation of energy to progressively diminish successive oscillations or waves of a vibrating structure.

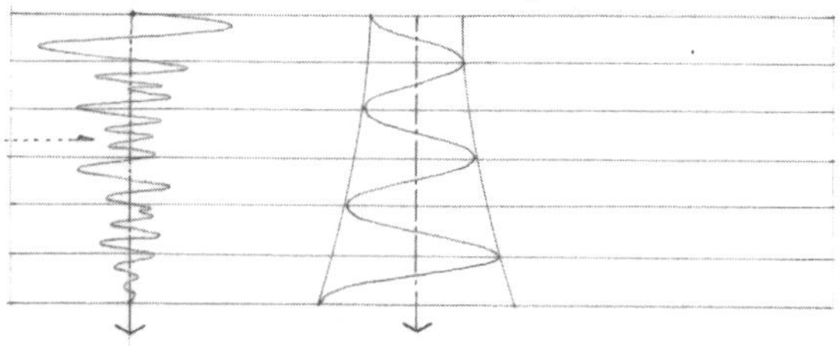

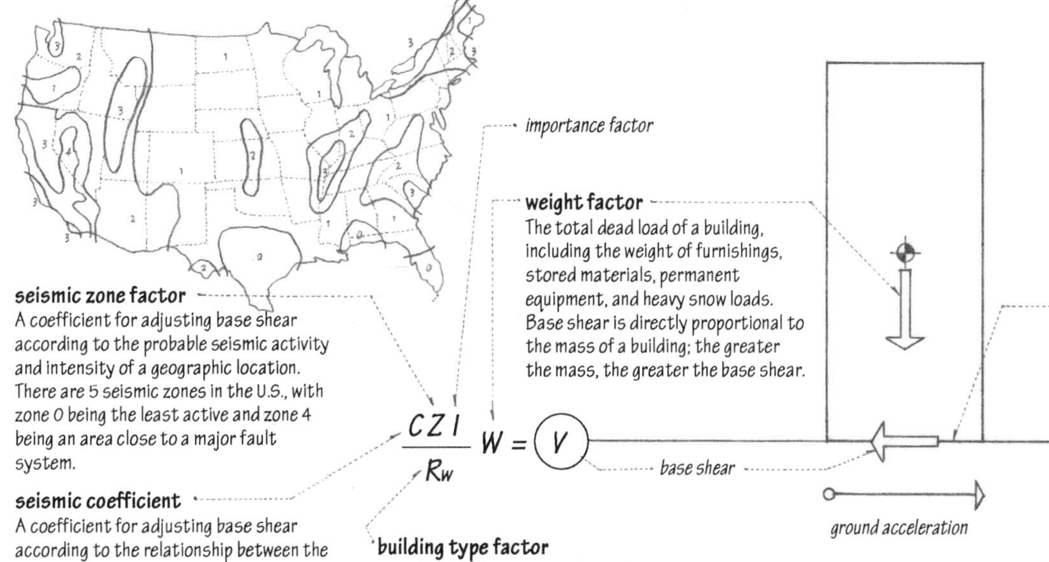

seismic zone factor
A coefficient for adjusting base shear according to the probable seismic activity and intensity of a geographic location. There are 5 seismic zones in the U.S., with zone 0 being the least active and zone 4 being an area close to a major fault system.

seismic coefficient
A coefficient for adjusting base shear according to the relationship between the natural period of vibration of a structure and that of the underlying soil on which the structure rests. When these periods are similar, base shear is increased to reflect the likelihood of destructive resonances occurring in the structure. Also called **base shear coefficient**.

site coefficient
A coefficient reflecting the nature and profile of the foundation soil, usually based on a geotechnical investigation. Ground movements are potentially much greater in alluvial soils than in rocky areas or diluvial soils.

liquefaction
The sudden loss of shearing resistance in a cohesionless soil, causing the soil mass to behave as a liquid.

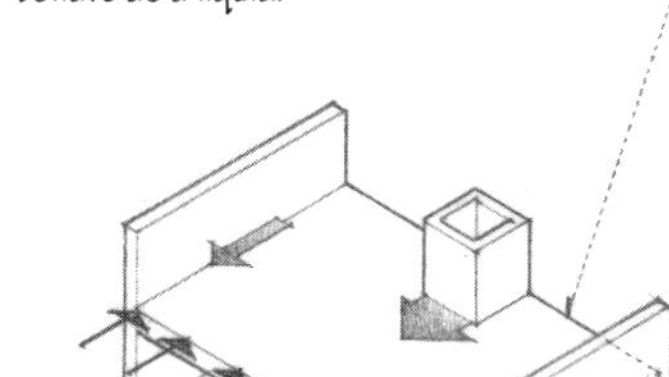

weight factor
The total dead load of a building, including the weight of furnishings, stored materials, permanent equipment, and heavy snow loads. Base shear is directly proportional to the mass of a building; the greater the mass, the greater the base shear.

building type factor
A coefficient for adjusting base shear according to construction type and material, and the energy-absorbing capacity of the structural and lateral force-resisting systems used. Base shear is inversely proportional to the energy-absorbing capacity of a structure; the greater the structure's stiffness or ductility, the lower the base shear.

horizontal force factor
A coefficient used in calculating the lateral seismic force on structural elements, nonstructural components, or their connections, according to their weight and function.

story shear
The total shear in any horizontal plane of a structure subject to lateral loads, distributed according to the various lateral force-resisting elements in proportion to their rigidities. Story shear is cumulative and increases from its minimum value at the top to its maximum at the base.

building separation
The distance required to avoid contact between separated structures under deflection from seismic action or wind forces.

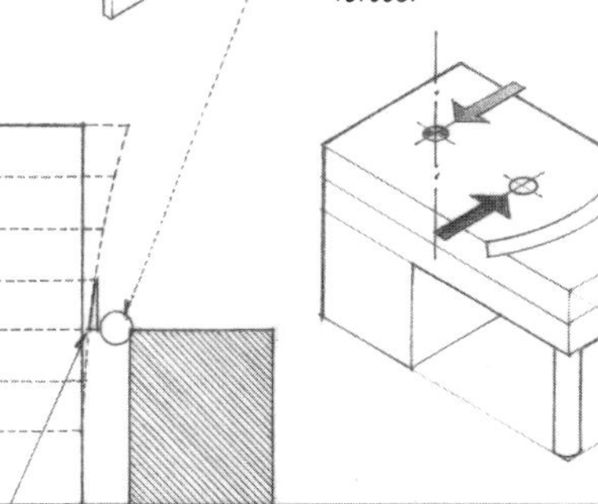

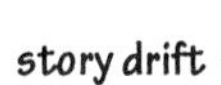

story drift
The horizontal movement of one level of a structure relative to the level above or below.

drift index
The maximum ratio of story drift to story height allowed by a building code in order to minimize damage to building components or adjacent structures. Also called **drift limitation**.

horizontal torsion
The torsion resulting from a lateral load acting on a structure having noncoincident centers of mass and resistance. To avoid destructive torsional effects, structures subject to lateral loads should be arranged and braced symmetrically with centers of mass and resistance as coincident as possible. In asymmetrical layouts, bracing elements should be distributed with stiffnesses that correspond to the distribution of the mass.

restoring moment
A resisting moment provided by the dead load of a structure acting about the same point of rotation as the overturning movement. Building codes usually require that the restoring moment be at least 50% greater than the overturning moment. Also called **righting moment**, **stabilizing moment**.

base
The level at which earthquake motions are assumed to be imparted to a structure.

base shear
The shearing force developed at the base of a structure by the tendency of its upper mass to remain at rest while the base is translated by ground motions during an earthquake. Base shear is the minimum design value for the total lateral seismic force on a structure, and is assumed to act nonconcurrently in the direction of each of the main axes of the structure. It is computed by multiplying the total dead load of the structure by a number of coefficients to reflect the character and intensity of the ground motions, the mass and stiffness of the structure and the way these are distributed, the type of soil underlying the foundation, and the presence of damping mechanisms in the structure.

distribution of base shear
The manner in which base shear is distributed over the height of a structure according to the displacements that would occur during an earthquake. For a building of regular rectangular shape with equal floor weights and heights and no irregularities in stiffness or mass, base shear is distributed to each horizontal diaphragm above the base in proportion to the floor weight at each level and its distance from the base. This results in a triangular load configuration varying from zero at the base to a maximum value at the top. For structures having a natural period of vibration greater than 0.7 seconds, a portion of the total base shear is assumed to be concentrated at the top of the structure to account for the whiplash effect of seismic forces. For structures with irregular shapes or framing systems, the distribution of lateral forces should be determined according to the relative stiffnesses of adjacent floor levels and the dynamic characteristics of the structure.

overturning moment
An external moment generated at the base of a structure by a lateral load applied at a distance above grade. For equilibrium, the overturning moment must be counterbalanced by an external restoring moment and an internal resisting moment provided by forces developed in column members and shear walls.

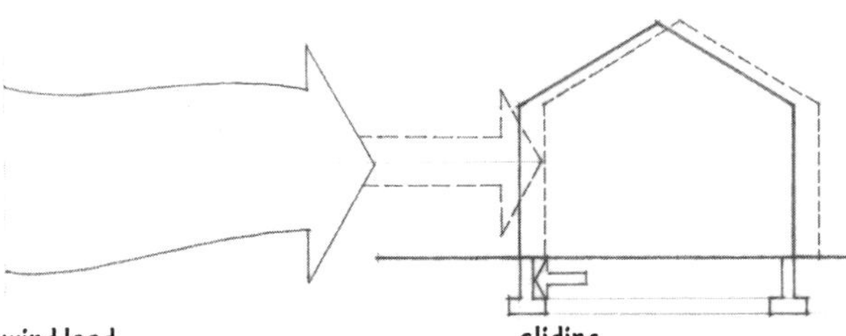

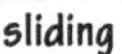

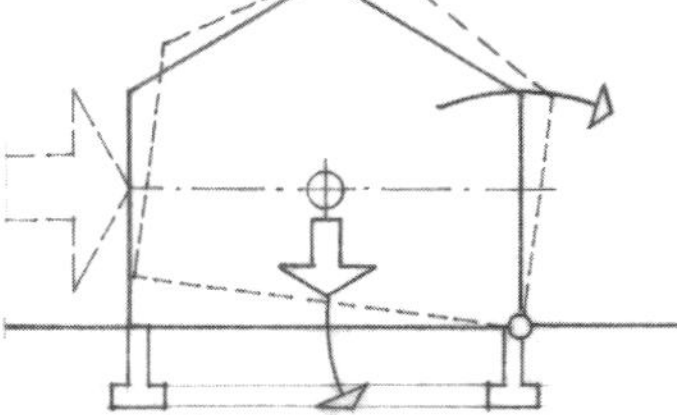

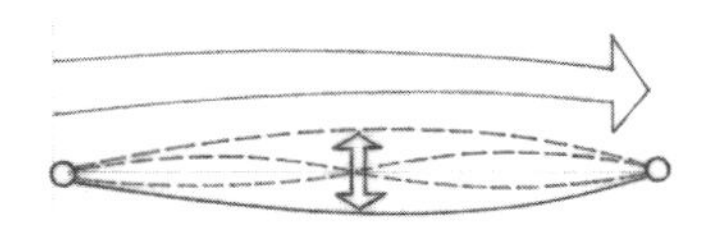

wind load
Any of the forces exerted by the kinetic energy of a moving mass of air, resulting in pressure on certain parts of a structure and suction on others.

sliding
The horizontal movement of a structure in response to a lateral load.

uplift
The raising of a structure or portion of structure in response to an overturning moment or wind suction.

flutter
The rapid oscillations of a flexible cable or membrane structure caused by the aerodynamic effects of wind. Also called **aerodynamic oscillation**.

Bernoulli equation
An expression of the conservation of energy in streamline flow, stating that the sum of the ratio of pressure to mass density, the square of the velocity divided by 2, and the product of the gravitational constant and vertical height, remains constant. Also called **Bernoulli's theorem**.

dynamic wind pressure
The pressure exerted by a moving mass of air, derived from Bernoulli's equation and equal to the product of the mass density of the air and the square of the velocity at a given height divided by 2.

design wind pressure
A minimum design value for the equivalent static pressure on the exterior surfaces of a structure resulting from a critical wind velocity, equal to the wind stagnation pressure modified by a number of coefficients to account for the effects of exposure condition, building height, wind gusts, and the geometry and orientation of the structure to the impinging air flow.

$$P = C_e C_q q_s I$$

height factor
A coefficient increasing design wind pressure to account for the increase in wind velocity with height above the ground.

gust factor
A coefficient increasing design wind pressure to account for the dynamic effects of wind gusts.

exposure condition
One of four conditions modifying design wind pressure according to obstructions in the area surrounding a building site.

exposure A: urban areas with high-rise buildings, or rough, hilly terrain;

exposure B: suburban sites, wooded areas, or rolling terrain;

exposure C: flat, open terrain with minimal obstructions;

exposure D: flat, unobstructed terrain facing large bodies of water.

The more open a site, the greater the wind speed and the resulting design wind pressure.

building height

0 0.5 1.0 1.5 2.0 2.5 3.0

importance factor
A coefficient for increasing the design values for wind or seismic forces on a building because of its large occupancy, its potentially hazardous contents, or its essential nature in the wake of a hurricane or earthquake.

wind stagnation pressure
The static equivalent to dynamic wind pressure used as a reference in calculating design wind pressure, specified in pounds per square foot and equal to 0.00256 times the square of the basic wind speed for the geographic location. Wind velocity approaches zero as the moving air mass parts to flow around an obstruction. Since the sum of static and dynamic pressures remains constant in streamline flow, all of the energy in the flow at this point of stagnation is in the form of static pressure.

pressure coefficient
A coefficient modifying design wind pressure to reflect how the geometry and orientation of the various parts of a structure alter the effects of an impinging air flow. Inward or positive coefficients result in wind pressure while outward or negative coefficients result in wind suction.

basic wind speed
The wind velocity used in calculating wind stagnation pressure, usually the extreme fastest-mile wind speed recorded for a geographic location at a standard height of 33 ft. (10 m) and based on a 50-year mean occurrence interval. Also called **design wind velocity**.

fastest-mile wind speed
The average speed of a one-mile-long column of air that passes over a given point, measured in miles per hour.

leeward
Pertaining to, being in, or facing the direction toward which the wind is blowing.

wind suction
The negative pressure exerted by wind on the sides and leeward vertical surfaces of a building and normal to windward roof surfaces having a slope less than 30°.

30°

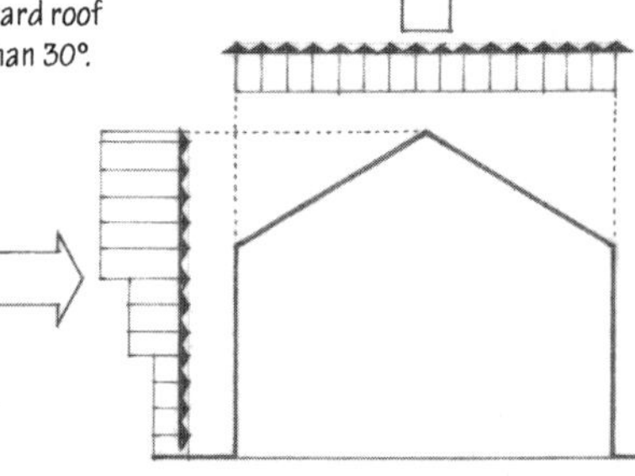

windward
Pertaining to, being in, or facing the direction from which the wind blows.

wind pressure
The pressure exerted by wind horizontally on the windward vertical surfaces of a building and normal to windward roof surfaces having a slope greater than 30°.

normal force method
A design method for applying design wind pressure to the primary frame and bracing systems of a building, in which wind pressures are assumed to act simultaneously normal to all exterior surfaces. This method may be used for any structure, but is required for gabled rigid frames.

Tall, slender buildings, structures with unusual or complex shapes, and lightweight, flexible structures subject to flutter require wind tunnel testing or computer modeling to investigate how they respond to the distribution of wind pressure.

projected area method
A design method for applying design wind pressure to the primary frame and bracing systems of a building, in which the total wind effect is considered to be a combination of a single inward or positive horizontal pressure acting on the full vertical projected area of the building and an outward or negative pressure acting on the full horizontal projected area of the building. This method may be used for any structure less than 200 ft. (61 m) high, except for gabled rigid frames.

Building with units of various natural or manufactured products, as stone, brick, or concrete block, usually with the use of mortar as a bonding agent.

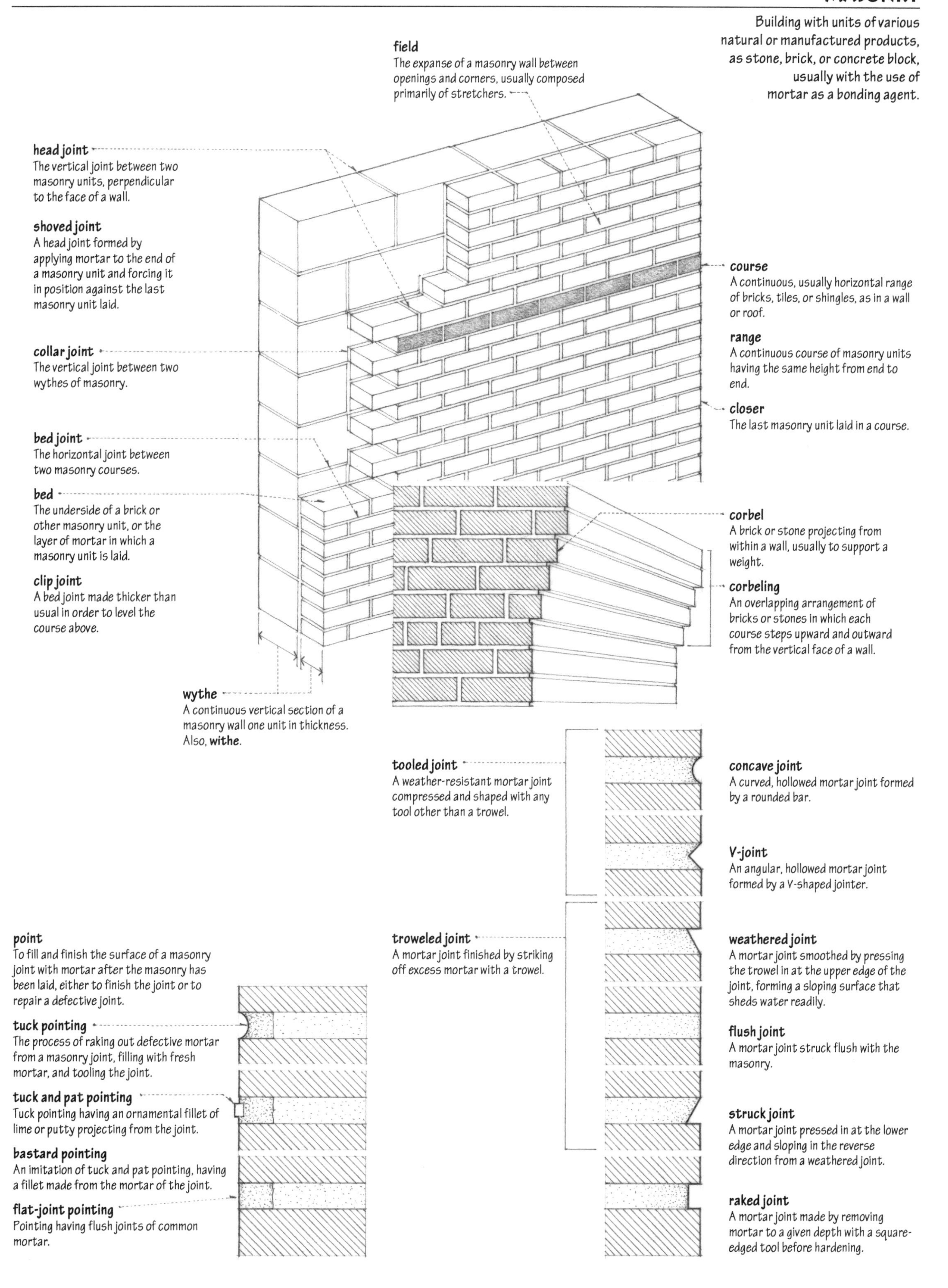

field
The expanse of a masonry wall between openings and corners, usually composed primarily of stretchers.

head joint
The vertical joint between two masonry units, perpendicular to the face of a wall.

shoved joint
A head joint formed by applying mortar to the end of a masonry unit and forcing it in position against the last masonry unit laid.

collar joint
The vertical joint between two wythes of masonry.

bed joint
The horizontal joint between two masonry courses.

bed
The underside of a brick or other masonry unit, or the layer of mortar in which a masonry unit is laid.

clip joint
A bed joint made thicker than usual in order to level the course above.

wythe
A continuous vertical section of a masonry wall one unit in thickness. Also, **withe**.

course
A continuous, usually horizontal range of bricks, tiles, or shingles, as in a wall or roof.

range
A continuous course of masonry units having the same height from end to end.

closer
The last masonry unit laid in a course.

corbel
A brick or stone projecting from within a wall, usually to support a weight.

corbeling
An overlapping arrangement of bricks or stones in which each course steps upward and outward from the vertical face of a wall.

tooled joint
A weather-resistant mortar joint compressed and shaped with any tool other than a trowel.

concave joint
A curved, hollowed mortar joint formed by a rounded bar.

V-joint
An angular, hollowed mortar joint formed by a V-shaped jointer.

troweled joint
A mortar joint finished by striking off excess mortar with a trowel.

weathered joint
A mortar joint smoothed by pressing the trowel in at the upper edge of the joint, forming a sloping surface that sheds water readily.

flush joint
A mortar joint struck flush with the masonry.

struck joint
A mortar joint pressed in at the lower edge and sloping in the reverse direction from a weathered joint.

raked joint
A mortar joint made by removing mortar to a given depth with a square-edged tool before hardening.

point
To fill and finish the surface of a masonry joint with mortar after the masonry has been laid, either to finish the joint or to repair a defective joint.

tuck pointing
The process of raking out defective mortar from a masonry joint, filling with fresh mortar, and tooling the joint.

tuck and pat pointing
Tuck pointing having an ornamental fillet of lime or putty projecting from the joint.

bastard pointing
An imitation of tuck and pat pointing, having a fillet made from the mortar of the joint.

flat-joint pointing
Pointing having flush joints of common mortar.

solid masonry
A wall constructed of brick or other solid masonry units laid contiguously with all joints solidly filled with mortar and adjacent wythes bonded by masonry headers or metal ties.

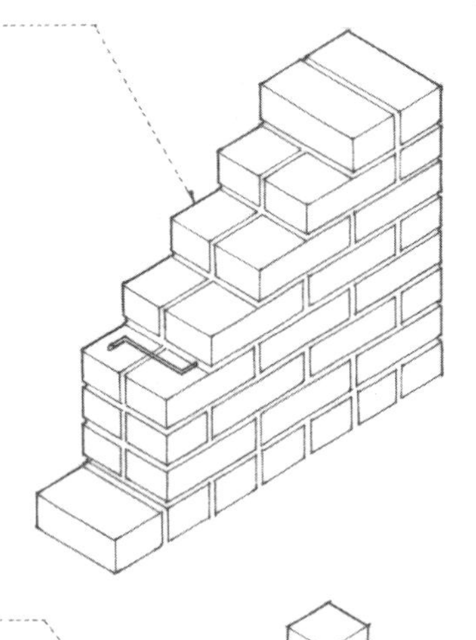

economy wall
A brick wall 4 in. (102 mm) thick, plastered and strengthened at intervals with 8-in. (203-mm) pilasters to support roof trusses.

cavity wall
A masonry wall having a facing and backing completely separated except for metal ties and enclosing an inner space serving to prevent penetration by water.

facing
An ornamental or protective layer, as the outer wythe of a masonry wall.

backing
Something that forms the back or provides support, strength, or protection from the back, as the inner wythe or wythes of a masonry wall.

weep hole
A small opening in a cavity wall, retaining wall, or other construction for draining off accumulated moisture, as from condensation or leakage.

composite wall
A masonry wall having at least one wythe dissimilar to the other wythe or wythes with respect to type or grade of masonry unit or mortar.

adjustable tie
A metal tie consisting of two interlocking parts which enable it to adapt to bed joints at different elevations.

tie
Any of various corrosive-resistant metal devices for holding two parts of a construction together, as the wythes of a masonry wall.

back plaster
To parge a part of a wall that is not seen, as behind the outer wythe of a cavity wall in order to exclude air and moisture from the interior of the wall.

faced wall
A wall having a masonry facing bonded to a backing so as to exert a common action under load.

adhered veneer
A veneer supported by and secured to a backing by means of a bonding material.

veneer
A nonstructural facing of brick, stone, concrete, or tile attached to a backing for the purpose of ornamentation, protection, or insulation.

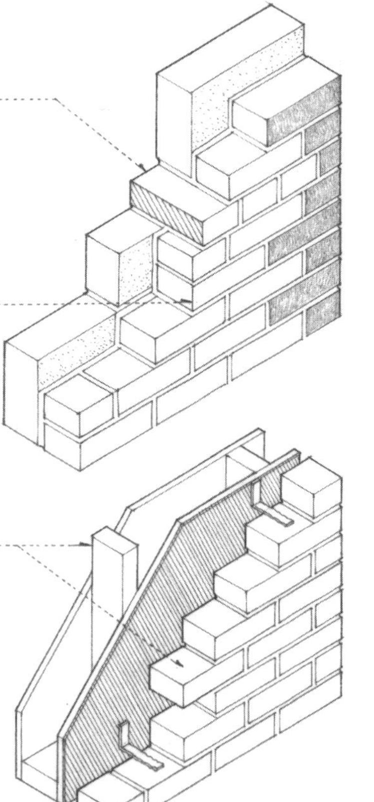

veneered wall
A wall having a nonstructural facing attached but not bonded to a supporting structure.

anchored veneer
A veneer supported by and secured to a backing by means of mechanical fasteners.

panel wall
A non-load-bearing exterior masonry wall wholly supported at each story.

lewis
A device for lifting a dressed stone or precast concrete panel, consisting of a number of pieces fitting together to fill a dovetailed recess cut into the stone or panel.

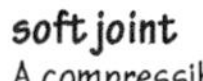

soft joint
A compressible joint directly below a supporting shelf or relieving angle, allowing for the expansion and contraction of a panel wall and preventing the weight of higher courses from being transmitted to the masonry below.

mortar
A plastic mixture of lime or cement, or a combination of both, with sand and water, used as a bonding agent in masonry construction.

cement mortar
A mortar made by mixing portland cement, sand, and water.

cement-lime mortar
A cement mortar to which lime is added to increase its plasticity and water-retentivity.

masonry cement
A proprietary mix of portland cement and other ingredients, as hydrated lime, plasticizers, air-entraining agents, and gypsum, requiring only the addition of sand and water to make cement mortar.

epoxy mortar
A mortar consisting of epoxy resin, a catalyst, and fine aggregate.

nonstaining mortar
A mortar having a low free-alkali content to minimize efflorescence or the staining of adjacent masonry by the migration of soluble materials.

lime mortar
A mixture of lime, sand, and water that is rarely used because of its slow rate of hardening and low compressive strength.

lime
A white or grayish white, caustic, odorless solid obtained by heating forms of calcium carbonate, as shells or limestone, at a high temperature. Also called **calcium oxide**, **calx**, **caustic lime**, **quicklime**.

hydrated lime
A soft, crystalline powder obtained by the action of water on lime and used in making mortar, plaster, and cement. Also called **calcium hydroxide**, **slaked lime**.

green
Of or pertaining to concrete or mortar that is freshly set but not completely hardened.

fat mix
A concrete or mortar mix that is easy to work or spread because of a relatively high cement or lime content. Also called **rich mix**.

lean mix
A concrete or mortar mix that is difficult to work or spread because of a shortness of cement or lime.

plasticizer
An admixture for making a concrete or mortar mix workable with little water.

Type M mortar
A high-strength mortar recommended for use in reinforced masonry below grade or in contact with the earth, as foundation and retaining walls subject to frost action or to high lateral or compressive loads.

Type S mortar
A medium-high-strength mortar recommended for use in masonry where bond and lateral strength are more important than compressive strength.

Type N mortar
A medium-strength mortar recommended for general use in exposed masonry above grade where high compressive and lateral strength are not required.

Type O mortar
A low-strength mortar suitable for use in interior non-load-bearing walls and partitions.

Type K mortar
A very-low-strength mortar suitable only for use in interior non-load-bearing walls where permitted by the building code.

grout
A fluid cement mortar that will flow easily without segregation of the ingredients, used to fill narrow cavities in masonry and consolidate the adjoining materials into a solid mass.

bond
The adhesion between mortar or grout and the masonry units or steel reinforcement being cemented.

grouted masonry
A wall constructed of brick or concrete brick units with all interior joints being filled with grout as the work progresses.

high-lift grouting
A technique for grouting a masonry wall constructed a story at a time in lifts not exceeding 6 feet (1.8 m).

low-lift grouting
A technique for grouting a masonry wall in lifts not exceeding six times the width of the grout space or a maximum of 8 inches (203 mm) as the wall is built.

grout pour
The total height of masonry to be filled with grout before the erection of additional masonry, consisting of one or more grout lifts.

grout lift
An increment of grout height within a total grout pour.

cleanout
Any of a series of temporary openings at the bottom of a masonry wall large enough to permit the removal of debris or obstructions from a cavity or cell prior to grouting.

reinforced grouted masonry
A masonry wall constructed with horizontal and vertical steel reinforcement fully embedded in grout for increased resistance to buckling and lateral wind and seismic loads.

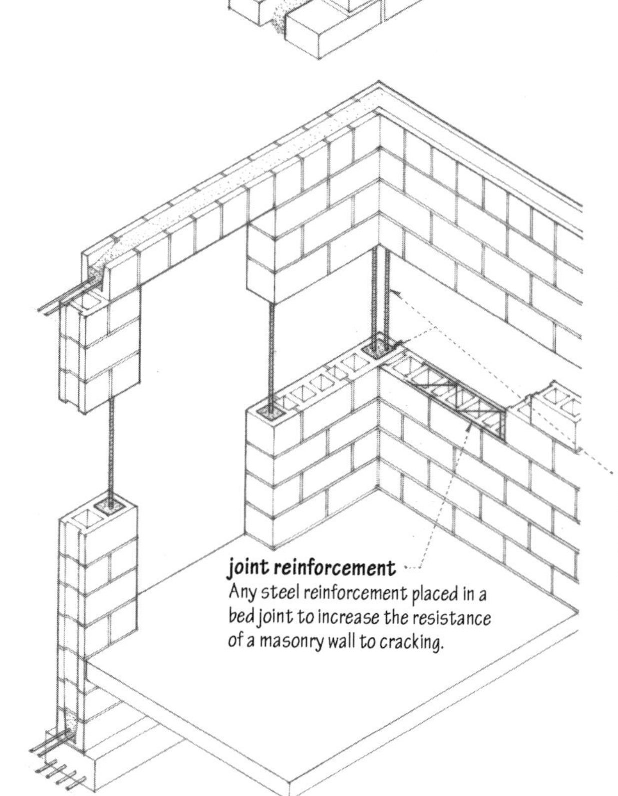

hollow unit masonry
A wall constructed of hollow masonry units laid and set with mortar, with adjacent wythes bonded by masonry headers or metal ties.

reinforced hollow-unit masonry
Hollow unit masonry having certain cells continuously filled with concrete or grout, in which reinforcing steel is embedded for increased resistance to buckling and lateral wind and seismic loads.

joint reinforcement
Any steel reinforcement placed in a bed joint to increase the resistance of a masonry wall to cracking.

rubble
Rough fragments of broken stone or the masonry built of such stones.

gallet
To embed small stone chips in the mortar joints of rough masonry to wedge larger stones in position or add detail to the appearance. Also, **garret**.

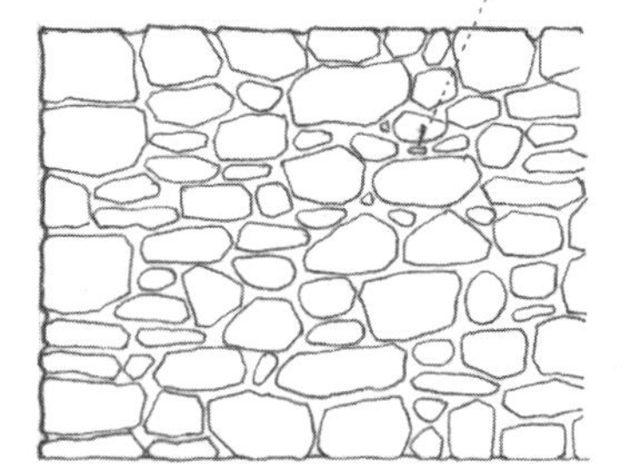

random rubble
A rubble wall having discontinuous but approximately level beds or courses.

coursed rubble
A rubble wall having approximately level beds and brought at intervals to continuous level courses.

squared rubble
A rubble wall built of squared stones of varying sizes and coursed at every third or fourth stone.

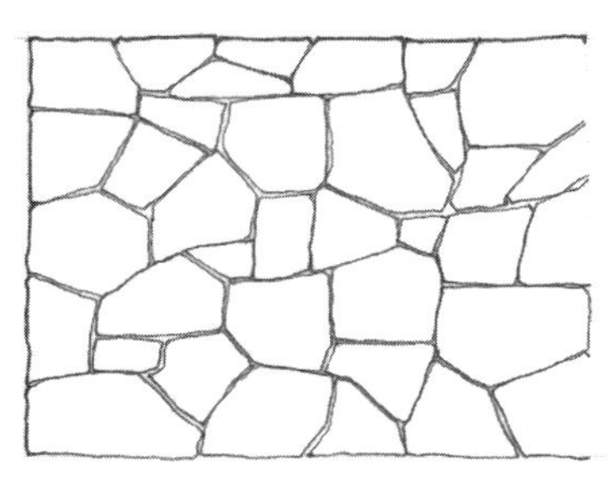

cyclopean
Formed with large, irregular blocks of stones fitted closely together without the use of mortar.

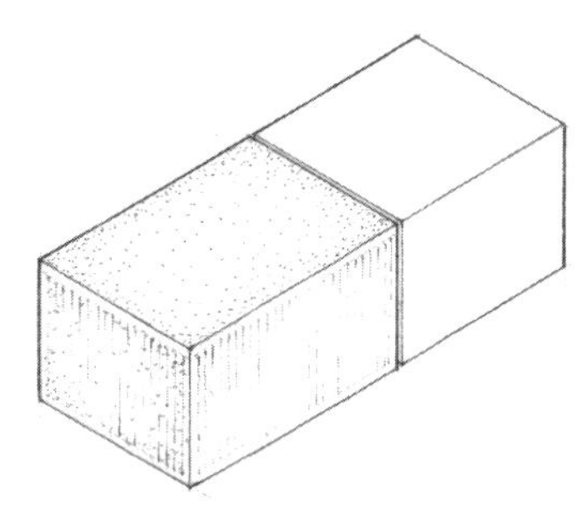

ashlar
A squared building stone finely dressed on all faces adjacent to those of other stones so as to permit very thin mortar joints.

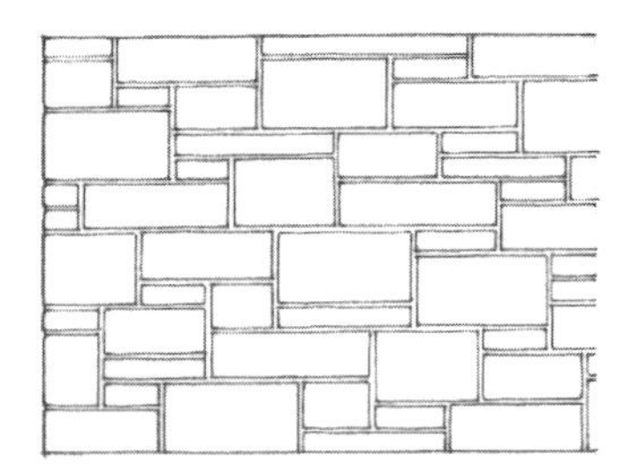

random ashlar
Ashlar masonry built in discontinuous courses.

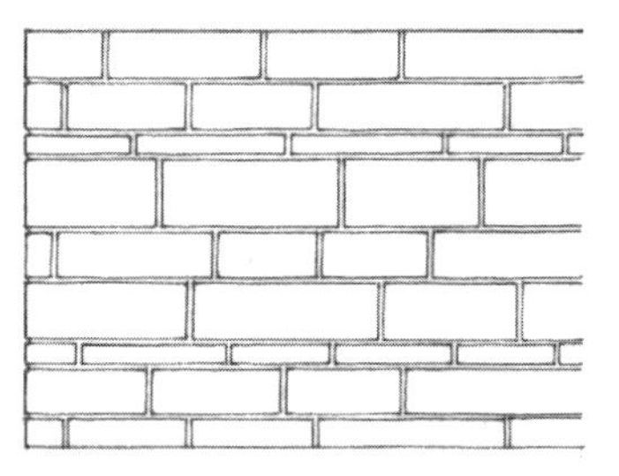

coursed ashlar
Ashlar masonry built of stones having the same height within each course, but each course varying in height.

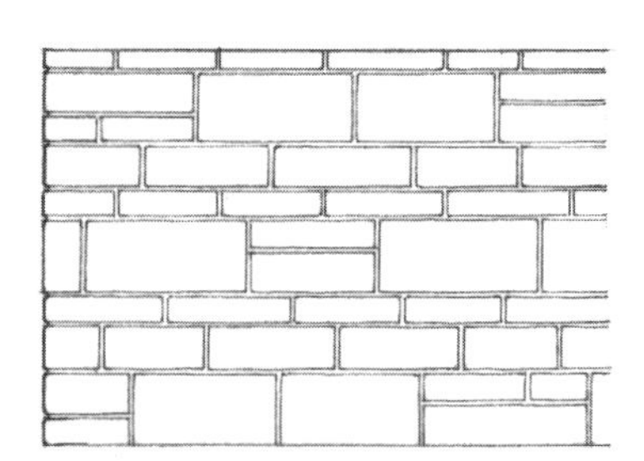

broken rangework
Ashlar masonry laid in horizontal courses of varying heights, any one of which may be broken at intervals into two or more courses.

quoin
An exterior angle of a masonry wall, or one of the stones or bricks forming such an angle, usually differentiated from adjoining surfaces by material, texture, color, size, or projection.

perpend
A large stone passing through the entire thickness of a wall and exposed on both faces. Also called **through stone**.

bondstone
A stone for bonding facing masonry to a masonry backing. Also called **binder**.

long-and-short work
An arrangement of rectangular quoins or jambstones set alternately horizontally and vertically.

in-and-out bond
A masonry bond having headers and stretchers alternating vertically.

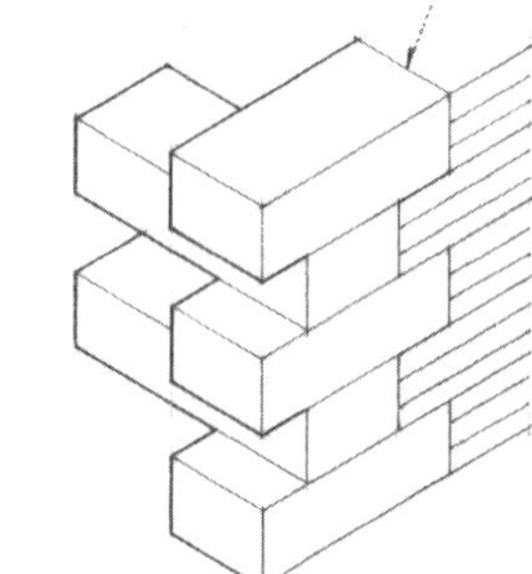

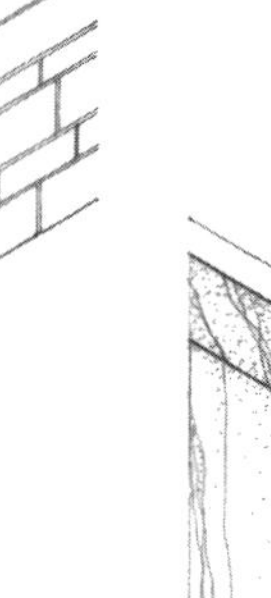

rustication
Ashlar masonry having the visible faces of the dressed stones raised or otherwise contrasted with the horizontal and usually the vertical joints, which may be rabbeted, chamfered, or beveled.

rustic joint
A mortar joint between stones recessed from the adjacent faces between sunken drafts or bevels.

rustic
Having rough, irregular surfaces and sunken or beveled joints.

interlocking joint
A joint in ashlar masonry made by fitting a projection on one stone into a routed groove on the next stone.

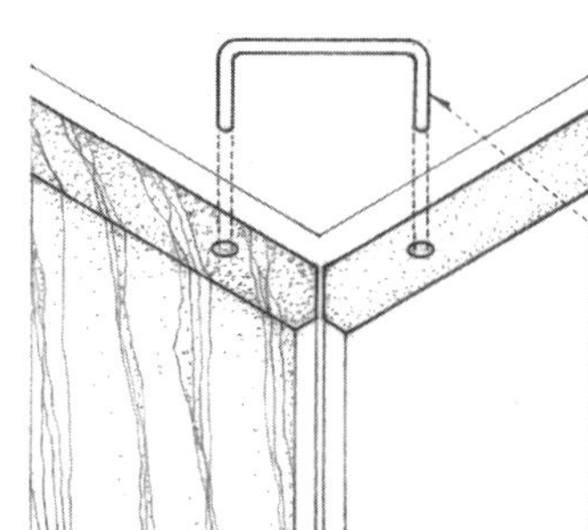

cramp iron
An iron bar or rod with bent ends for holding together stone masonry units.

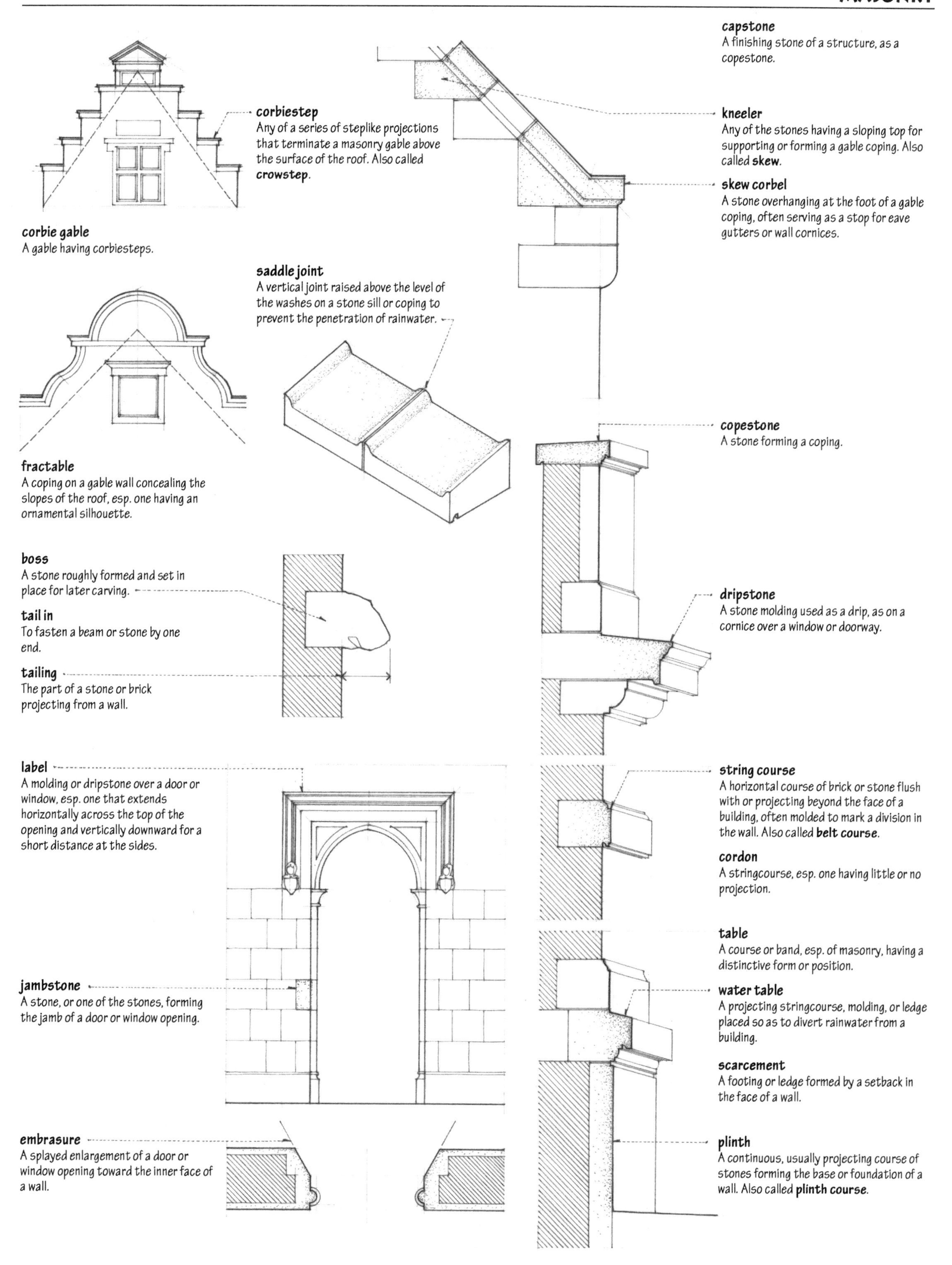

corbie gable
A gable having corbiesteps.

corbiestep
Any of a series of steplike projections that terminate a masonry gable above the surface of the roof. Also called **crowstep**.

capstone
A finishing stone of a structure, as a copestone.

kneeler
Any of the stones having a sloping top for supporting or forming a gable coping. Also called **skew**.

skew corbel
A stone overhanging at the foot of a gable coping, often serving as a stop for eave gutters or wall cornices.

saddle joint
A vertical joint raised above the level of the washes on a stone sill or coping to prevent the penetration of rainwater.

fractable
A coping on a gable wall concealing the slopes of the roof, esp. one having an ornamental silhouette.

copestone
A stone forming a coping.

boss
A stone roughly formed and set in place for later carving.

tail in
To fasten a beam or stone by one end.

tailing
The part of a stone or brick projecting from a wall.

dripstone
A stone molding used as a drip, as on a cornice over a window or doorway.

label
A molding or dripstone over a door or window, esp. one that extends horizontally across the top of the opening and vertically downward for a short distance at the sides.

string course
A horizontal course of brick or stone flush with or projecting beyond the face of a building, often molded to mark a division in the wall. Also called **belt course**.

cordon
A stringcourse, esp. one having little or no projection.

table
A course or band, esp. of masonry, having a distinctive form or position.

jambstone
A stone, or one of the stones, forming the jamb of a door or window opening.

water table
A projecting stringcourse, molding, or ledge placed so as to divert rainwater from a building.

scarcement
A footing or ledge formed by a setback in the face of a wall.

embrasure
A splayed enlargement of a door or window opening toward the inner face of a wall.

plinth
A continuous, usually projecting course of stones forming the base or foundation of a wall. Also called **plinth course**.

concrete masonry unit
A precast masonry unit of portland cement, fine aggregate, and water, molded into various shapes.

stretcher block
A concrete masonry unit having nominal dimensions of 8 x 8 x 16 in. (203 x 203 x 406 mm).

partition block
A concrete masonry unit used in constructing non-load-bearing walls, usually having a nominal thickness of 4 or 6 in. (102 or 152 mm).

bullnose block
A concrete masonry unit having one or more rounded exterior corners.

corner block
A concrete masonry unit having a solid end face and used in constructing the end or corner of a wall.

return-corner block
A concrete masonry unit used at the corners of walls to maintain horizontal coursing with the appearance of full- and half-length units.

double-corner block
A concrete masonry unit having solid faces at both ends and used in constructing a masonry pier.

pilaster block
Any of various concrete masonry units used in constructing a plain or reinforced masonry pilaster.

coping block
A solid concrete masonry unit used in constructing the top or finishing course of a masonry wall.

sash block
A concrete masonry unit having an end slot or rabbet to receive the jamb of a door or window frame. Also called **jamb block**.

sill block
A solid concrete masonry unit having a wash to shed rainwater from a sill.

wash
An upper surface inclined to shed rain water from a building. Also called **weathering**.

cap block
A concrete masonry unit having a solid top for use as a bearing surface in the finishing course of a foundation wall. Also called **solid-top block**.

control-joint block
Any of various concrete masonry units used in constructing a vertical control joint.

bond-beam block
A concrete masonry unit used in constructing a bond beam, having a depressed section in which reinforcing steel can be placed for embedment in grout.

bond beam
A masonry course grouted and reinforced to serve as a beam, a horizontal tie, or a bearing course for structural members.

concrete block
A hollow or solid concrete masonry unit, often incorrectly referred to as cement block.

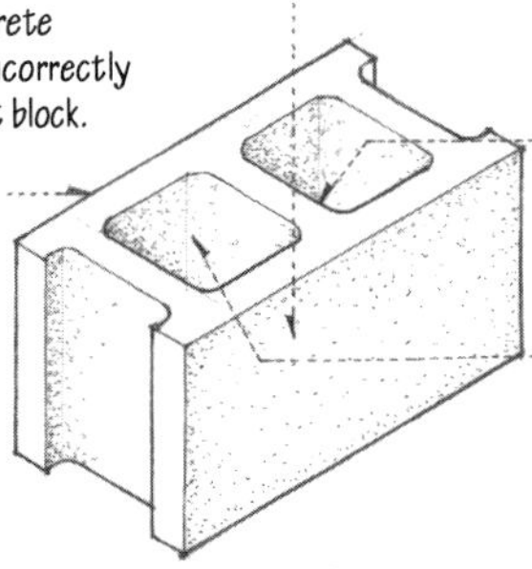

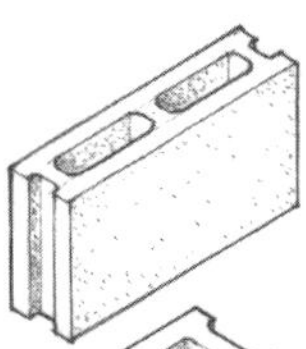

face shell
One of the two sidewalls of a hollow concrete masonry unit.

web
One of the cross walls connecting the face shells of a hollow masonry unit.

core
The molded open space in a concrete masonry unit. Also called **cell**.

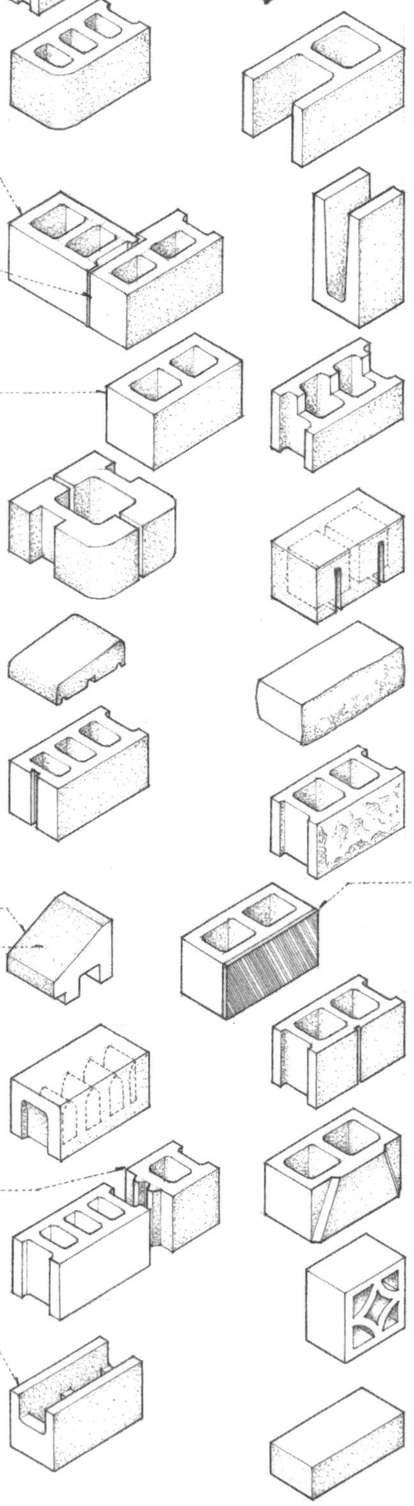

open-end block
A concrete masonry unit having one end open in which vertical steel reinforcement can be placed for embedment in grout.

lintel block
A concrete masonry unit used in constructing a lintel or bond beam, having a U-shaped section in which reinforcing steel can be placed for embedment in grout.

header block
A concrete masonry unit having a portion of one face shell removed to receive headers in a bonded masonry wall.

sound-absorbing masonry unit
A concrete masonry unit having a solid top and a slotted face shell, and sometimes a fibrous filler, for increased sound absorption.

slump block
A concrete masonry unit having an irregular face and surface texture caused by the settlement of a wet mix during curing.

split-face block
A concrete masonry unit, split lengthwise by a machine after curing to produce a rough, fractured face texture.

faced block
A concrete masonry unit having a special ceramic, glazed, or polished face.

scored block
Any of various concrete masonry units having one or more vertical grooves which simulate raked joints.

shadow block
Any of various concrete masonry units having a face shell with a pattern of beveled recesses.

screen block
A concrete masonry unit used esp. in tropical architecture, having a decorative pattern of transverse openings for admitting air and excluding sunlight.

concrete brick
A solid rectangular concrete masonry unit, usually not larger than 4 x 4 x 12 in. (102 x 102 x 305 mm).

sand-lime brick
A hard, light-colored brick made by molding a mixture of damp sand and slaked lime under high pressure and curing in a steam oven.

solid masonry unit
A masonry unit having a net cross-sectional area in any plane parallel to the bearing surface that is 75% or more of the gross cross-sectional area measured in the same plane.

hollow masonry unit
A masonry unit having a net cross-sectional area in any plane parallel to the bearing surface less than 75% of the gross cross-sectional area measured in the same plane.

gross cross-sectional area
The total cross-sectional area of a hollow masonry unit perpendicular to the direction of loading, including cellular and reentrant spaces, except when these spaces are to be occupied by portions of adjacent masonry.

net cross-sectional area
The gross cross-sectional area of a hollow masonry unit minus the area of ungrouted cores of cellular spaces.

equivalent thickness
The thickness that would be obtained if the amount of concrete contained in a hollow masonry unit were recast without any cellular spaces, used esp. to determine the fire resistance of a wall constructed with such units.

absorption
The weight of water absorbed by a concrete masonry unit when immersed in water, expressed in pounds of water per cubic foot of concrete.

Grade N
A grade of load-bearing concrete masonry unit suitable for general use, as in exterior walls above and below grade.

Grade S
A grade of load-bearing concrete masonry unit limited to use above grade, in exterior walls with weather-protective coatings, or in walls not exposed to the weather.

Type I
A concrete masonry unit manufactured to a specified limit of moisture content in order to minimize the drying shrinkage that can cause cracking.

Type II
A concrete masonry unit not manufactured to a specified limit moisture content.

normal-weight block
A concrete masonry unit made with sand, gravel, or other dense aggregate and weighing more than 125 pcf (2000 kg/m^3).

lightweight block
A concrete masonry unit made with lightweight aggregate, as cinder or expanded slag, and weighing less than 125 pcf (2000 kg/m^3).

surface bonding
The bonding of a concrete masonry wall by stacking the units without mortar and troweling on a stucco-like compound of white portland cement and glass fiber.

Matter having unique qualities by which it may be categorized.

bond
The attractive force by which atoms, ions, or groups of atoms are bound together in a molecule or crystalline structure. Also called **chemical bond**.

ionic bond
A chemical bond characteristic of salts and ceramic materials, formed by the complete transfer of one or more electrons from one kind of ion to another. Also called **electrovalent bond**.

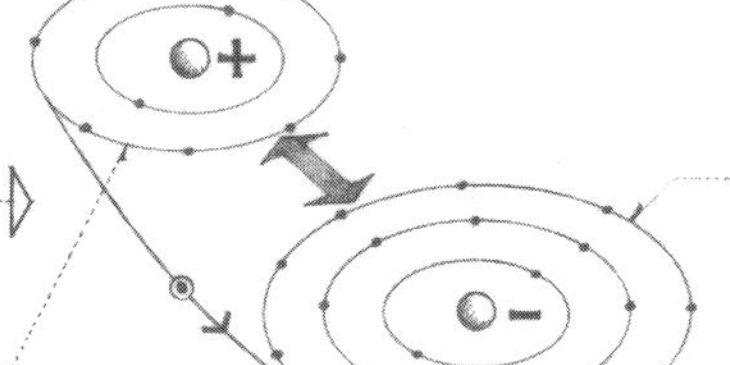

positive ion
A positively charged ion created by electron loss. Also called **cation**.

ion
An electrically charged atom or group of atoms formed by the loss or gain of one or more electrons.

negative ion
A negatively charged ion created by electron gain. Also called **anion**.

valence
A measure of the capacity of an atom or group to combine with other atoms or groups, equal to the number of chemical bonds the atom or group can form.

covalent bond
A chemical bond formed by the sharing of pairs of electrons between two atoms.

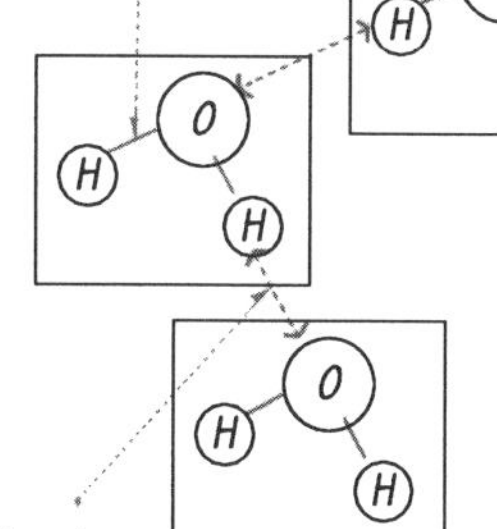

hydrogen bond
An electrostatic bond between an electronegative atom and a hydrogen atom already linked to another electronegative atom by a covalent bond.

molecule
The smallest particle of a substance that displays all of the characteristic physical and chemical properties of the substance, consisting of one or more like atoms in an element, or two or more different atoms in a compound.

molecular weight
The average weight of a molecule of an element or compound calculated as the sum of the atomic weights of the molecule's constituent atoms. Also called **formula weight**.

mole
The molecular weight of a substance expressed in grams; gram molecule. Also, **mol**.

valence electron
An electron located in the outer shell of an atom that can be transferred or shared in forming a chemical bond with another atom.

inert gas configuration
The stable configuration of an element in which the outer shells of its atoms or ions are filled with the maximum number of electron pairs. Nature moves atoms and ions toward this configuration by capturing, surrendering, or sharing electrons with neighboring atoms or ions in an effort to achieve a relatively inert state of low energy.

noble gas
Any of the chemically inert gaseous elements: helium, neon, argon, krypton, xenon, and radon. Also called **inert gas**.

matter
That which occupies space, can be perceived by the senses, and constitutes the substance of a physical body.

shell
Any of up to seven spherical surfaces containing the orbits of electrons of approximately equal energy about the nucleus of an atom.

electron
A fundamental particle of matter having a negative charge.

neutron
A fundamental particle having no charge.

proton
A positively charged particle that is a fundamental constituent of all atomic nuclei.

periodic table
A tabular arrangement of the chemical elements in related groups, formerly in the order of their atomic weights and now according to their atomic numbers.

atom
The smallest unit of an element that can exist either alone or in combination, consisting of a nucleus of neutrons and protons surrounded by one or more electrons bound to the nucleus by electrical attraction.

atomic number
The number of protons in the nucleus of an atom of a given element, which equals the number of electrons normally surrounding the nucleus. Also called **proton number**.

element
One of a class of substances that cannot be separated into simpler substances by chemical means, composed of atoms having an identical number of protons in each nucleus.

6
CARBON
C
12

atomic weight
The average weight of an atom of an element based on 1/12 the weight of the carbon-12 atom.

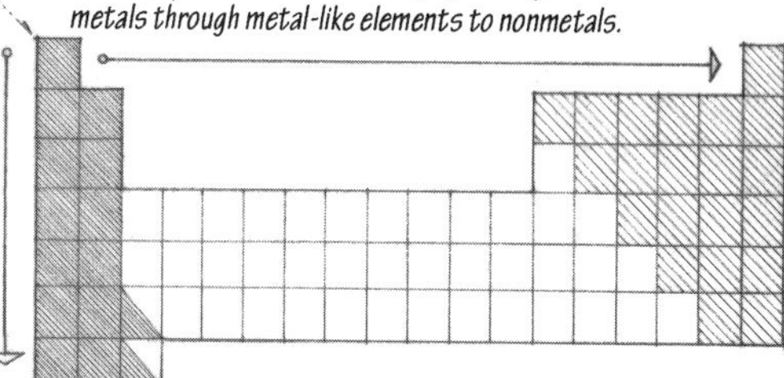

Across a period, elements change gradually from metals through metal-like elements to nonmetals.

Down a group, elements share certain characteristics and behave in a similar manner because of the way electrons are arranged in their outer shells.

fluid
A substance, as a gas or liquid, that is capable of flowing, yields easily to pressure, and conforms to the shape of its container.

gas
Matter having neither independent shape nor volume, possessing perfect molecular mobility and the tendency to expand indefinitely.

solid
Matter having relative firmness, coherence of particles, or persistence of form.

metallic bond
A chemical bond characteristic of metals, produced by the sharing of valence electrons which move freely through the lattice of a usually stable crystalline structure.

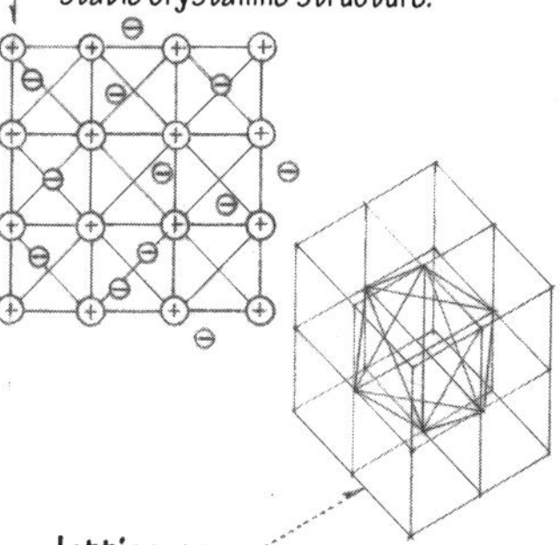

condense
To reduce to a denser form, as a gas or vapor to a liquid or solid state.

heat of condensation
The heat liberated by a unit mass of gas at its boiling point as it condenses to a liquid.

heat of vaporization
The quantity of heat required to convert a unit mass of liquid at its boiling point into vapor at the same temperature: equal to the heat of condensation.

evaporate
To change or convert from a liquid or solid into a vapor.

solidify
To change or convert from a liquid or gas into a solid.

liquid
Matter distinguished from the solid or gaseous states by a characteristic readiness to flow, little or no tendency to disperse, and relatively high incompressibility.

heat of solidification
The heat liberated by a unit mass of liquid at its freezing point as it solidifies.

heat of fusion
The quantity of heat required to convert a unit mass of a solid at its melting point into a liquid at the same temperature: equal to the heat of solidification.

lattice
A regular pattern of isolated points in space showing the location of atoms, ions, or molecules in a crystalline solid.

crystal
A solid having a regularly repeating internal structure of atoms, ions, or molecules and enclosed by symmetrically arranged plane surfaces.

amorphous
Not crystalline in structure.

property
An essential or distinctive attribute or quality belonging specifically in the constitution of, or found in, the behavior of a thing.

mechanical property
Any of the physical properties of a material that exhibit a response to applied forces.

strength
The capability of a material to resist the forces imposed on it, esp. the ability to sustain a high stress without yielding or rupturing.

strength of materials
The study of the relationship between applied external forces and the internal effects produced by these forces in a body.

isotropic
Exhibiting the same physical properties along all axes.

anisotropic
Having different physical properties along different axes, as wood and other fibrous materials.

tension
The act of stretching or state of being pulled apart, resulting in the elongation of an elastic body.

tensile force
An applied force producing or tending to produce tension in an elastic body.

axial force
A tensile or compressive force acting along the longitudinal axis of a structural member and at the centroid of the cross section, producing axial stress without bending, torsion, or shear. Also called **axial load**.

axial stress
The tensile or compressive stress that develops to resist an axial force, assumed to be normal to and uniformly distributed over the area of the cross section. Also called **direct stress**, **normal stress**.

compression
The act of shortening or state of being pushed together, resulting in a reduction in size or volume of an elastic body.

compressive force
An applied force producing or tending to produce compression in an elastic body.

eccentric force
A force applied parallel to the longitudinal axis of a structural member but not to the centroid of the cross section, producing bending and an uneven distribution of stresses in the section. Also called **eccentric load**.

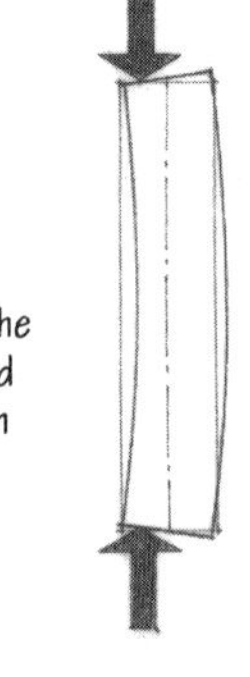

stress
The internal resistance or reaction of an elastic body to external forces applied to it, equal to the ratio of force to area and expressed in units of force per unit of cross-sectional area. Also called **unit stress**.

tensile stress
The axial stress that develops at the cross section of an elastic body to resist the collinear tensile forces tending to elongate it.

tensile strain
The elongation of a unit length of material produced by a tensile stress.

strain
The deformation of a body under the action of an applied force. Strain is a dimensionless quantity, equal to the ratio of the change in size or shape to the original size or shape of a stressed element.

Young's modulus
A coefficient of elasticity of a material, expressing the ratio of longitudinal stress to the corresponding longitudinal strain caused by the stress.

Poisson's ratio
The ratio of lateral strain to the corresponding longitudinal strain in an elastic body under longitudinal stress.

compressive stress
The axial stress that develops at the cross section of an elastic body to resist the collinear compressive forces tending to shorten it.

compressive strain
The shortening of a unit length of material produced by a compressive stress.

tensile test
A test for determining the behavior of a material under axial tension, in which a specimen is gripped at both ends and pulled apart until rupture occurs: the most common test for structural materials.

tensile strength
The resistance of a material to longitudinal stress, measured by the minimum amount of longitudinal stress required to rupture the material.

elongation
A measure of the ductility of a material, expressed as the percentage increase in length of a test specimen after failure in a tensile test.

reduction of area
A measure of the ductility of a material, expressed as the percentage decrease in cross-sectional area of a test specimen after rupturing in a tensile test.

compression test
A test for determining the behavior of a material under axial compression, in which a specimen is crushed until fracture or disintegration occurs. The compression test is used for brittle materials since their low tensile strength is difficult to measure accurately.

strain gauge
An instrument for measuring minute deformations in a test specimen caused by tension, compression, bending, or twisting. Also called **extensometer**.

bulk modulus
A coefficient of elasticity of a material, expressing the ratio between a pressure and the corresponding fractional change in volume produced.

compressibility
The reciprocal of bulk modulus, equal to the ratio of the fractional change in volume to the pressure applied to a substance.

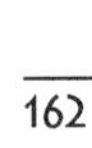

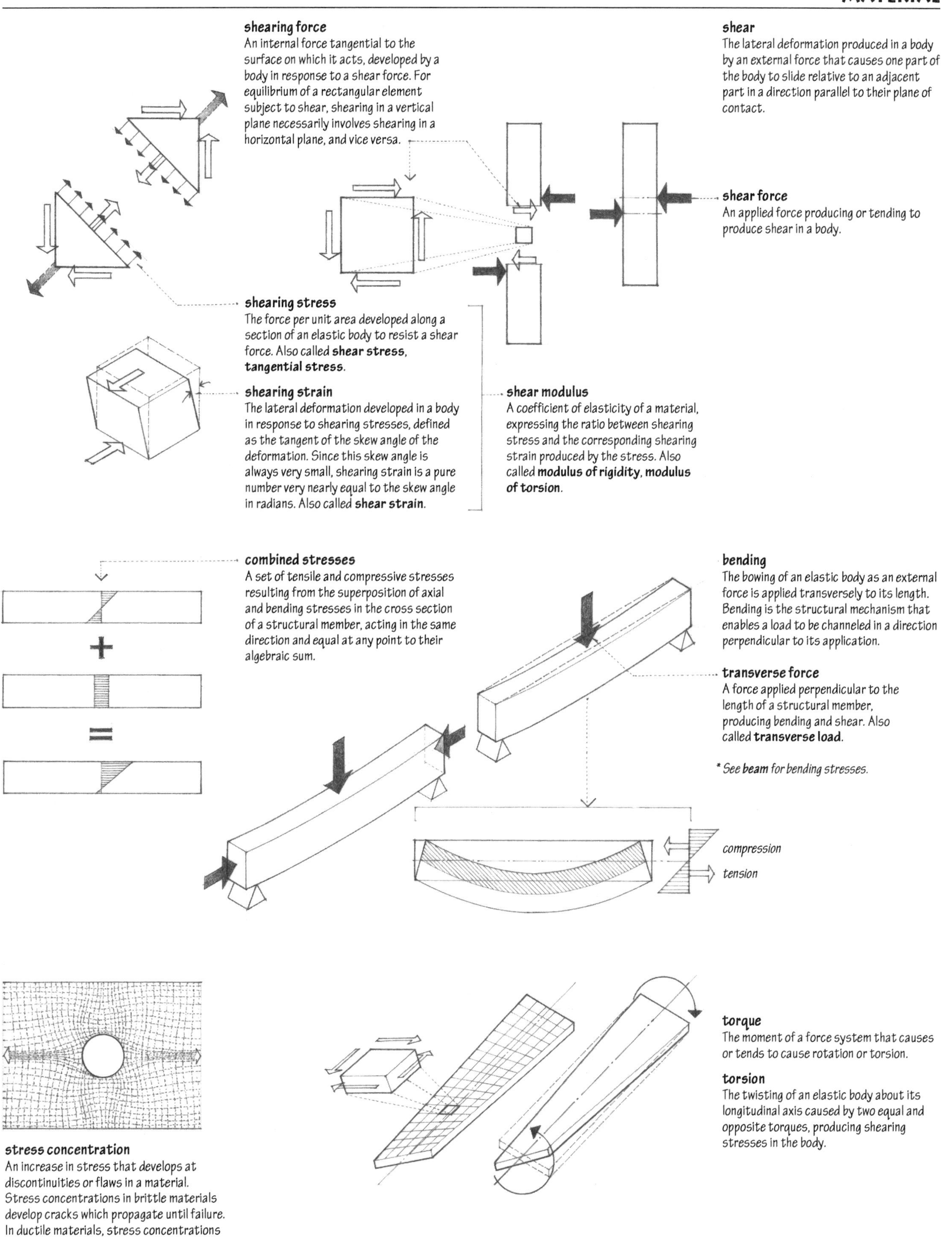

shearing force
An internal force tangential to the surface on which it acts, developed by a body in response to a shear force. For equilibrium of a rectangular element subject to shear, shearing in a vertical plane necessarily involves shearing in a horizontal plane, and vice versa.

shear
The lateral deformation produced in a body by an external force that causes one part of the body to slide relative to an adjacent part in a direction parallel to their plane of contact.

shear force
An applied force producing or tending to produce shear in a body.

shearing stress
The force per unit area developed along a section of an elastic body to resist a shear force. Also called **shear stress**, **tangential stress**.

shearing strain
The lateral deformation developed in a body in response to shearing stresses, defined as the tangent of the skew angle of the deformation. Since this skew angle is always very small, shearing strain is a pure number very nearly equal to the skew angle in radians. Also called **shear strain**.

shear modulus
A coefficient of elasticity of a material, expressing the ratio between shearing stress and the corresponding shearing strain produced by the stress. Also called **modulus of rigidity**, **modulus of torsion**.

combined stresses
A set of tensile and compressive stresses resulting from the superposition of axial and bending stresses in the cross section of a structural member, acting in the same direction and equal at any point to their algebraic sum.

bending
The bowing of an elastic body as an external force is applied transversely to its length. Bending is the structural mechanism that enables a load to be channeled in a direction perpendicular to its application.

transverse force
A force applied perpendicular to the length of a structural member, producing bending and shear. Also called **transverse load**.

* *See* ***beam*** *for bending stresses.*

stress concentration
An increase in stress that develops at discontinuities or flaws in a material. Stress concentrations in brittle materials develop cracks which propagate until failure. In ductile materials, stress concentrations develop local deformations which serve to redistribute and relieve the stresses.

torque
The moment of a force system that causes or tends to cause rotation or torsion.

torsion
The twisting of an elastic body about its longitudinal axis caused by two equal and opposite torques, producing shearing stresses in the body.

stress-strain diagram
A graphic representation of the relationship between unit stress values and the corresponding unit strains for a specific material.

elastic range
The range of unit stresses for which a material exhibits elastic deformation.

deformation
A change in the shape or dimensions of a body or structure resulting from stress.

elastic deformation
A temporary change in the dimensions or shape of a body produced by a stress less than the elastic limit of the material.

plastic range
The range of unit stresses for which a material exhibits plastic deformation.

strain-hardening range
The range of unit stresses for which a material exhibits increased stength with some loss of ductility.

plastic deformation
A permanent change in the dimensions or shape of a body produced by a stress greater than the elastic limit of the material, remaining rigid under stresses of less than a certain intensity. The molecular bonds in a material that exhibits plastic behavior reform after being stressed beyond the elastic limit. The material thus retains a measure of reserve strength. Also called **plastic flow**.

ultimate strength
The maximum tensile, compressive, or shearing stress a material can be expected to bear without rupturing or fracturing. Also called **ultimate stress**.

brittleness
The property of a material that causes it to rupture suddenly under stress with little evident deformation. Since brittle materials lack the plastic behavior of ductile materials, they can give no advance warning of impending failure.

yield point
The stress beyond which a marked increase in strain occurs in a material without a concurrent increase in stress. Many materials do not have clearly defined yield points. For these materials, a theoretical yield strength is calculated from the stress-strain curve.

fracture
The breaking of a material resulting from the rupturing of its atomic bonds when stressed beyond its ultimate strength.

proportional limit
The stress beyond which the ratio of stress to strain for a material no longer remains constant.

STRESS (psi)

stiffness
A measure of a material's resistance to deformation when stressed within its elastic range.

elastic limit
The maximum stress that can be applied to a material without causing permanent deformation.

ductility
The property of a material that enables it to undergo plastic deformation after being stressed beyond the elastic limit and before rupturing. Ductility is a desirable property of a structural material since plastic behavior is an indicator of reserve strength and can serve as a visual warning of impending failure.

STRAIN (in./in.)

allowable stress
The maximum unit stress permitted for a material in the design of a structural member, usually a fraction of the material's elastic limit, yield strength, or ultimate strength. The allowable stresses for various materials are specified by building codes, engineering societies, and trade associations, based on specifications and methods of testing established by the American Society for Testing and Materials. Also called **allowable unit stress, working stress.**

elasticity
The property of a material that enables it to deform in response to an applied force and to recover its original size and shape upon removal of the force.

modulus of elasticity
A coefficient of elasticity of a material, expressing the ratio between a unit stress and the corresponding unit strain caused by the stress, as derived from Hooke's law and represented by the slope of the straight-line portion of the stress-strain diagram. Also called **coefficient of elasticity, elastic modulus.**

Hooke's law
The law stating that the stress on a body is directly proportional to the strain produced, provided the stress does not exceed the elastic limit of the material.

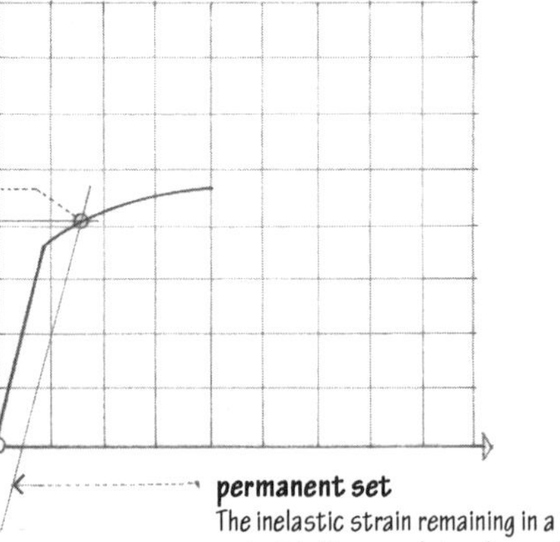

yield strength
The stress necessary to produce a specified limiting permanent set in a material, usually 0.2% of its original length when tested in tension. Yield strength is used to determine the limit of usefulness of a material having a poorly defined yield point. Also called **proof stress.**

permanent set
The inelastic strain remaining in a material after complete release of the stress producing the deformation.

strong but brittle

ductile and tough

toughness
The property of a material that enables it to absorb energy before rupturing, represented by the area under the stress-strain curve derived from a tensile test of the material. Ductile materials are tougher than brittle materials.

moisture expansion
An increase in the bulk of a material caused by the absorption of water or water vapor. Also called **bulking**.

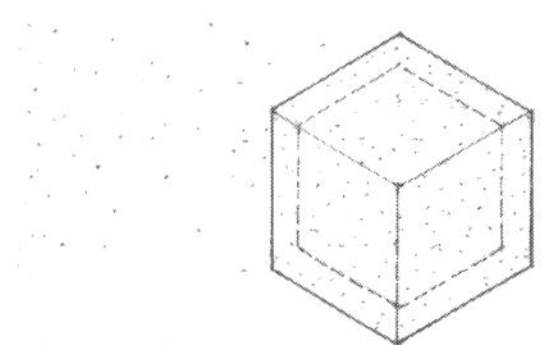

absorption
The taking in or reception of a gas or liquid by molecular or chemical action.

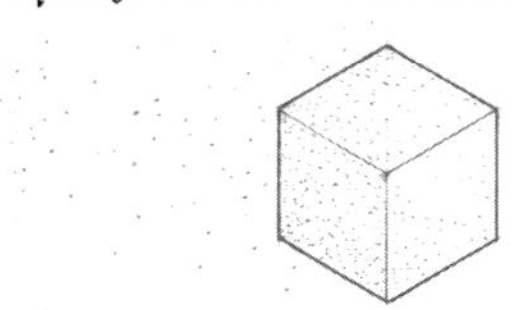

adsorption
The adhesion of a thin, condensed layer of gas, liquid, or dissolved substance to the surface of a solid, usually without any physical or chemical change in the material.

coefficient of expansion
The fractional change in length, area, or volume of a material per unit change in temperature at a given constant pressure. Also called **expansivity**.

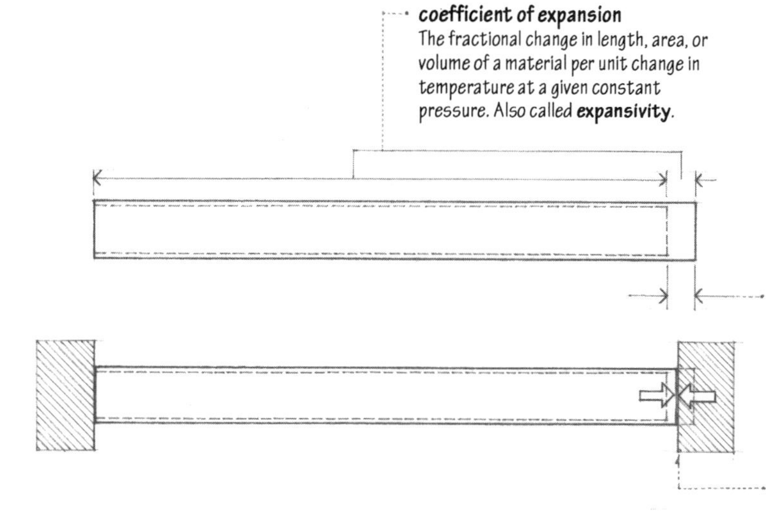

dimensional stability
The property of a material that enables it to maintain its original shape and dimensions when subjected to changes in temperature or humidity.

kinetic theory of heat
The theory that the temperature of a substance increases with an increase of the average kinetic energy of its particles when heat is absorbed.

thermal expansion
An increase in length, area, or volume of a material caused by a rise in temperature.

thermal contraction
A decrease in length, area, or volume of a material caused by a drop in temperature.

thermal stress
The tensile or compressive stress developed in a material constrained against thermal expansion or contraction.

thermal shock
The sudden stress a rapid change in temperature can produce in a material.

weatherability
The property of a material that enables it to to retain its appearance and integrity when exposed to the effects of sun, wind, moisture, and changes in temperature.

weatherometer
A device for determining the weather resistance of a material by subjecting a test specimen to accelerated weathering.

accelerated weathering
A process for exposing a material to ultraviolet rays, water sprays, and heating elements in order to simulate the long-term effects of sun, rain, and temperature changes. Also called **accelerated aging**.

abrasion resistance
The property of a material that enables it to resist being worn away by friction when rubbed with another object. Abrasion resistance is a measure of toughness rather than hardness and is a necessary quality of flooring materials and surface finishes.

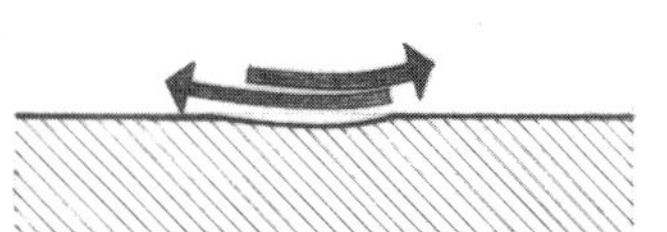

abrasion-resistance index
A measure of the abrasion resistance of a material, commonly expressed as the depth of penetration or material loss after testing with a weighted abrasive wheel for a specified number of cycles.

hardness
The property of a material that enables it to resist deformation by compression, indentation, or penetration.

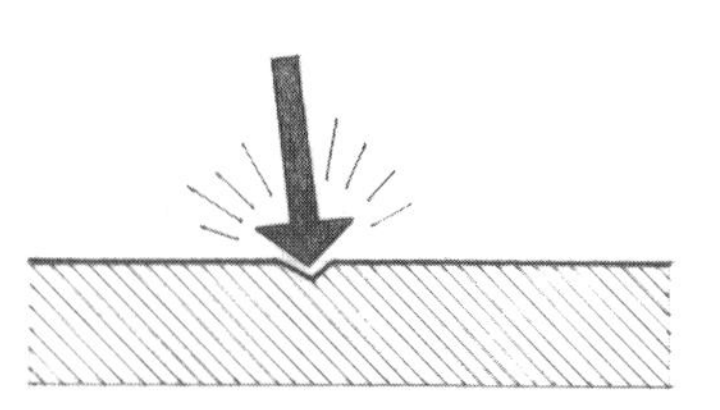

Mohs' scale
A scale for measuring the hardness of a mineral. Its degrees, in increasing hardness, are: 1, talc; 2, gypsum; 3, calcite; 4, fluorite; 5, apatite; 6, feldspar; 7, quartz; 8,topaz; 9, sapphire; 10, diamond.

Brinell number
A measure of the hardness of a material, determined by pressing a standard steel ball into a test piece using a standard force and dividing the load by the area of indentation. The higher the number, the harder the material.

Rockwell number
A measure of the hardness of a material, determined by indenting a test piece with a conoidal diamond indenter, or with a standard steel ball, under two successive loads and measuring the net increase in depth of the impressions: the higher the number, the harder the material.

Vickers number
A measure of the hardness of a material, determined by indenting a test piece with the point of a diamond using a known force and dividing the load by the surface area of indentation: the higher the number, the harder the material.

strain-rate effect
The brittle behavior an increased rate of load application can cause in a normally ductile material.

temperature effect
The brittle behavior low temperatures can cause in a normally ductile material.

stress relaxation
The time-dependent decrease in stress in a constrained material under a constant load.

creep
The gradual and permanent deformation of a body produced by a continued application of stress or prolonged exposure to heat. Creep deflection in a concrete structure continues over time and can be significantly greater than the initial elastic deflection.

fatigue
The weakening or failure of a material at a stress below the elastic limit when subjected to a repeated series of stresses.

fatigue limit
The maximum stress to which a material can be subjected for an indefinite number of cycles without failing.

fatigue ratio
The ratio between the fatigue limit and the tensile strength of a material. Also called **endurance ratio**.

MEASURE

A unit or standard of measurement used to ascertain the dimensions, quantity, or capacity of something.

metric system
A decimal system of weights and measures, adopted first in France but now widespread and universally used in science.

International System of Units
An internationally accepted system of coherent physical units, using the meter, kilogram, second, ampere, kelvin, and candela as the basic units of the fundamental quantities of length, mass, time, electric current, temperature, and luminous intensity.

length
The extent of anything measured along its greatest dimension.

conversion table
A tabular arrangement of the equivalent values of the weight or measure units of different systems.

SI unit
One of the basic units of the International System of Units.

meter
The basic unit of length in the metric system, equivalent to 39.37 inches, originally defined as one ten-millionth of the distance from the equator to the pole measured on the meridian, later as the distance between two lines on a platinum-iridium bar preserved at the International Bureau of Weights and Measures near Paris, and now as 1/299,972,458 of the distance light travels in a vacuum in one second. Abbr.: **m**

kilometer
A unit of length and distance equal to 1000 meters and equivalent to 3280.8 feet or 0.621 mile. Abbr.: **km**

scale
A system of ordered marks laid down at known intervals and used as a standard reference in measuring.

centimeter
A metric unit of length equal to 1/100 of a meter or 0.3937 inch. The use of the centimeter is not recommended for use in construction. Abbr.: **cm**

millimeter
A metric unit of length equal to 1/1000 of a meter or 0.03937 of an inch. Abbr.: **mm**

micron
The millionth part of a meter. Also called **micrometer**. Symbol: **mu, µ**

foot
A unit of length originally derived from the length of the human foot, divided into 12 inches and equal to 304.8 millimeters. Abbr.: **ft.**

inch
A unit of length, 1/12th of a foot, equivalent to 25.4 millimeters. Abbr.: **in.**

mil
A unit of length equal to 0.001 of an inch or 0.0254 mm, used in measuring the diameter of wires and the thickness of very thin sheet materials.

yard
A unit of length equal to 3 feet or 36 inches, and equivalent to 0.9144 meter. Abbr.: **yd.**

rod
A unit of length equal to 5½ yards or 16½ feet, and equivalent to 5.029 meters.

mile
A unit of distance on land equal to 5280 feet or 1760 yards, and equivalent to 1.609 km. Also called **statute mile**. Abbr.: **mi**

nautical mile
A unit of distance used in sea or air navigation, equal to 1.852 kilometers or about 6,076 feet. Also called **air mile**.

square measure
A unit or system of units for measuring area, derived from units of linear measure.

area
A quantitative measure of a plane or curved surface.

are
A metric unit of area equal to 1/100 of a hectare, 100 square meters, or 119.6 square yards. Abbr.: **a**

hectare
A metric unit of area equal to 10,000 square meters or 2.47 acres. Abbr.: **ha**

acre
A unit of land area equal to 1/640 of a square mile, 4840 square yards, 43,560 square feet, or 4047 square meters.

circular mil
A unit used principally for measuring the cross-sectional area of wire, equal to the area of a circle having a diameter of one mil.

cubic measure
A unit or system of units for measuring volume or capacity, derived from units of linear measure.

volume
The size or extent of a three-dimensional object or region of space, measured in cubic units.

liter
A metric unit of capacity equal to 1/1000 of a cubic meter or 61.02 cubic inches. Abbr.: **L**

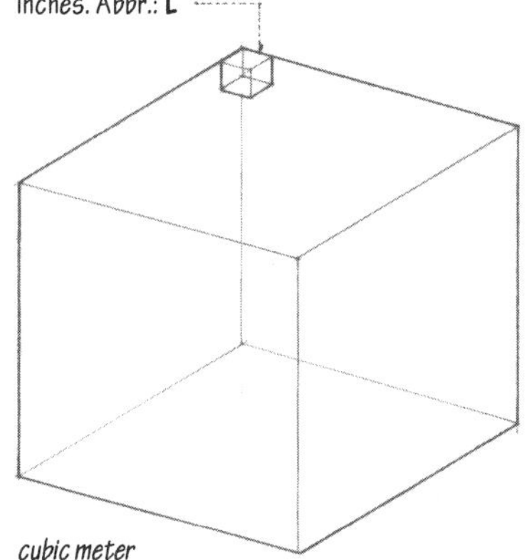
cubic meter

milliliter
A metric unit of capacity equal to 1/1000 of a liter or 0.0162 cubic inch. Abbr.: **ml**

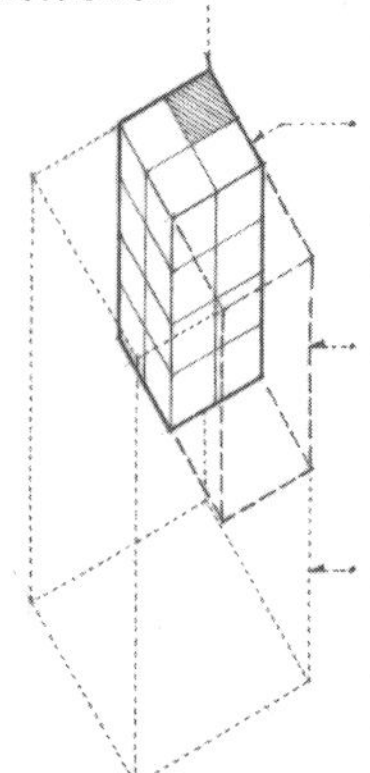

fluid ounce
A unit of liquid capacity equal to 1.805 cubic inches or 29.573 milliliters. Abbr.: **fl. oz.**

pint
A unit of liquid capacity equal to 16 fluid ounces, 28.875 cubic inches, or 0.473 liter. Abbr.: **pt.**

quart
A unit of liquid capacity equal to two pints, 57.75 cubic inches, or 0.946 liter. Abbr.: **qt.**

gallon
A unit of liquid capacity equal to 4 quarts, 231 cubic inches, or 3.875 liters. Abbr.: **gal.**

density
The mass of a substance per unit volume.

specific volume
The reciprocal of density, equal to volume per unit mass.

specific gravity
The ratio of the density of a substance to the density of another substance taken as a standard, usually distilled water for liquids and solids, and air or hydrogen for gases.

metric ton
A unit of mass equal to 1,000 kilograms and equivalent to 2,204.62 avoirdupois pounds. Also called **tonne**. Abbr.: **m.t.**

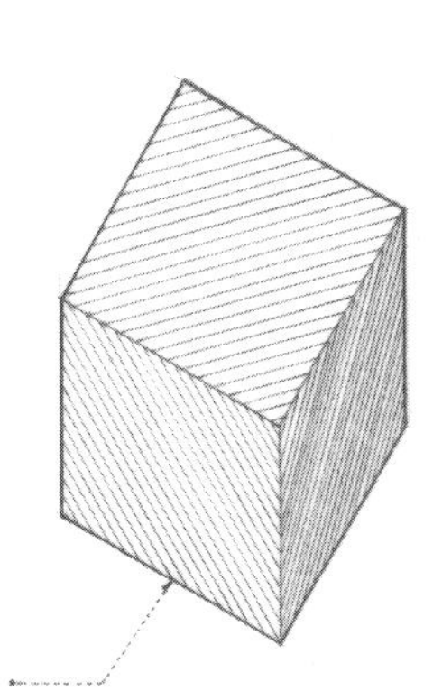

gram
A metric unit of mass equal to 1/1000 of a kilogram or 0.035 ounce. Abbr.: **g**

mass
A measure of a body's inertia, as determined by the quantity of material it contains and its weight in a field of constant gravitational acceleration. Abbr.: **M**

kilogram
The base SI unit of mass, equal to the mass of a platinum-iridium cylinder kept at the International Bureau of Weights and Measures near Paris; equivalent to 2.205 avoirdupois pounds. Abbr.: **kg**

pound
A unit of force equal to the weight of a one-pound mass under the acceleration of gravity. Abbr.: **lb**

newton
The SI unit of force equal to the force required to accelerate a mass of one kilogram at the rate of one meter per second per second. Abbr.: **N**

kilogram
A unit of force and weight equal to the weight of a kilogram mass under the acceleration of gravity. Abbr.: **kg**

pound
A unit of weight equal to 16 ounces and equivalent to 0.453 kg. Abbr.: **lb**.

kip
A unit of weight equal to 1000 pounds or 453.6 kg.

ton
A unit of weight equal to 2,000 pounds or 0.907 metric ton. Also called **short ton**.

weight
The gravitational force exerted by the earth on a body, equal to the mass of the body times the local acceleration of gravity.

gravity
The central force of attraction exerted by the mass of the earth on a body near its surface.

acceleration of gravity
The acceleration of a freely falling body in the earth's gravitational field, having an approximate value at sea level of 32 ft. (9.8 m) per second per second.

atmosphere
A unit of pressure equal to the normal pressure of the air at sea level, equal to 1.01325 x 105 N/m^2 or about 14.7 pounds per square inch. Abbr.: **atm**.

standard atmosphere
A standard unit of atmospheric pressure, having a value of 29.92 in. (760 mm) of mercury.

atmospheric pressure
The pressure exerted by the earth's atmosphere at any given point, usually expressed in terms of the height of a column of mercury. Also called **barometric pressure.**

barometer
An instrument for measuring atmospheric pressure, used in weather forecasting and determining elevation.

Boyle's law
The principle that, at relatively low pressures and a fixed temperature, the pressure of a confined ideal gas varies inversely with its volume.

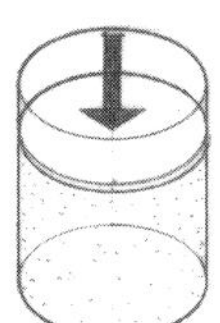

pressure
The force exerted over a surface, measured as force per unit area.

pascal
The SI unit of pressure equal to one newton per square meter. Abbr.: **Pa**

foot-pound
A unit of energy equal to the work done when the point of application of a force of one pound moves through a distance of one foot in the direction of the force. Abbr.: **ft-lb**

inch-pound
One-twelfth of a foot-pound. Abbr.: **in-lb**

energy
The work a physical system is capable of doing in changing from its actual state to a specified reference state.

joule
The SI unit of work or energy equal to the work done when the point of application of a force of one newton moves through a distance of one meter in the direction of the force: approximately 0.7375 ft-lb. Also called **newton-meter**. Abbr.: **J**

watt-hour
A unit of energy equal to energy of one watt operating for one hour and equivalent to 3,600 joules. Abbr.: **Wh**

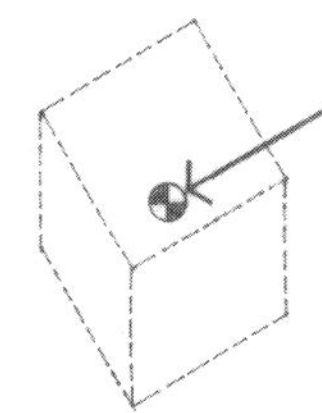

horsepower
A unit of power equal to 550 foot-pounds per second or 745.7 watts. Abbr.: **hp**

mechanical equivalent of heat
The number of units of work or energy equal to one unit of heat, as 778.2 ft-lb, which equals one Btu, or 4.1858 joules, which equals one calorie.

power
The amount of work done or energy transferred per unit of time, usually expressed in watts or horsepower.

work
The transfer of energy produced by the motion of the point of application of a force, equal to the product of the component of the force that acts in the direction of the motion of the point of action and the distance through which the point of application moves.

MEMBRANE

A thin, flexible surface that carries loads primarily through the development of tensile stresses.

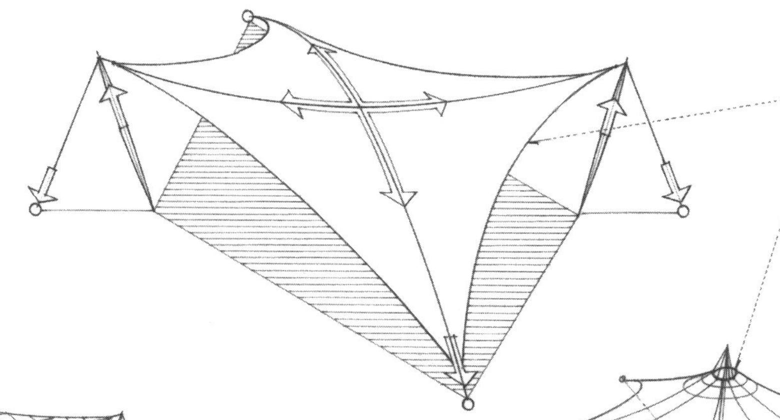

tent structure
A membrane structure prestressed by externally applied forces so that it is held completely taut under all anticipated load conditions. To avoid extremely high tensile forces, a membrane structure should have relatively sharp curvatures in opposite directions.

reinforcing edge cable
A cable stiffening the free edges of a prestressed membrane structure.

cable loop
A reinforcing edge cable tied to the mast support of a membrane structure.

distribution cap
The broadened end of a mast over which a prestressed membrane structure is stretched.

net structure
A membrane structure having a surface of closely spaced cables instead of a fabric material.

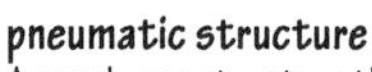

pneumatic structure
A membrane structure that is placed in tension and stabilized by the pressure of compressed air.

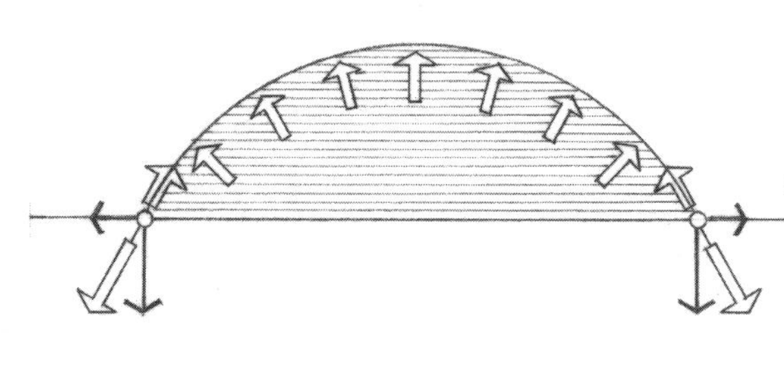

air-supported structure
A pneumatic structure consisting of a single membrane supported by an internal air pressure slightly higher than normal atmospheric pressure, and securely anchored and sealed along the perimeter to prevent leaking. Air locks are required at entrances to maintain the internal air pressure.

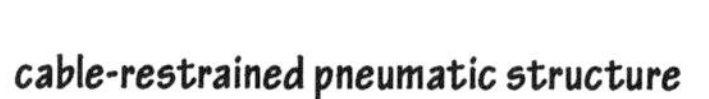

cable-restrained pneumatic structure
An air-supported structure that uses a net of cables placed in tension by the inflating force to restrain the membrane from developing its natural inflated profile.

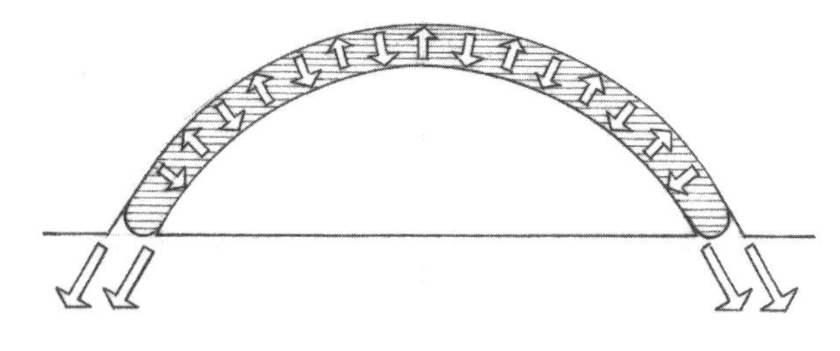

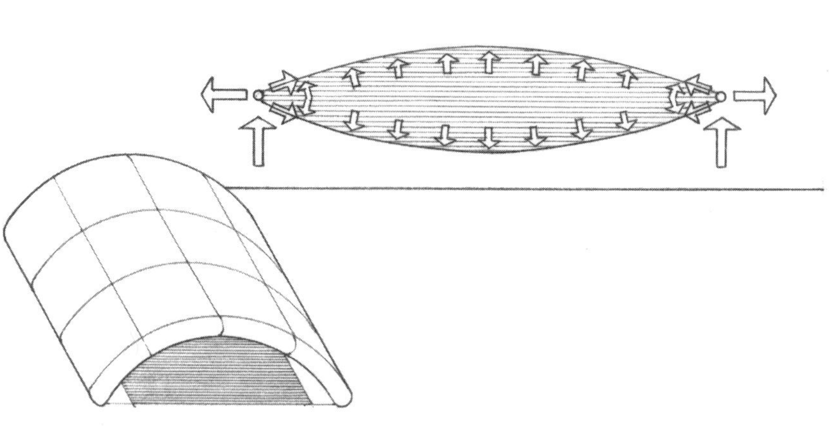

air-inflated structure
A pneumatic structure supported by pressurized air within inflated building elements, which are shaped to carry loads in a traditional manner, while the enclosed volume of building air remains at normal atmospheric pressure. The tendency for a double-membrane structure to bulge in the middle is restrained by a compression ring or by internal ties or diaphragms.

Any of a class of elementary substances, as gold, silver, or copper, all of which are crystalline when solid and many of which are characterized by opacity, ductility, conductivity, and a unique luster when freshly fractured.

ingot
A mass of metal cast into a convenient shape for storage or transportation before further processing.

blank
A piece of metal ready to be drawn, pressed, or machined into a finished object.

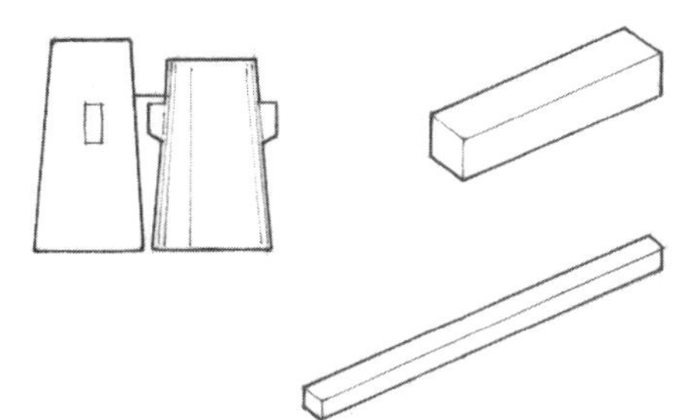

bloom
A bar of steel reduced from an ingot to dimensions suitable for further rolling.

blooming mill
A mill for rolling ingots into blooms.

billet
A narrow, generally square, bar of steel, forged or hot-rolled from an ingot or bloom.

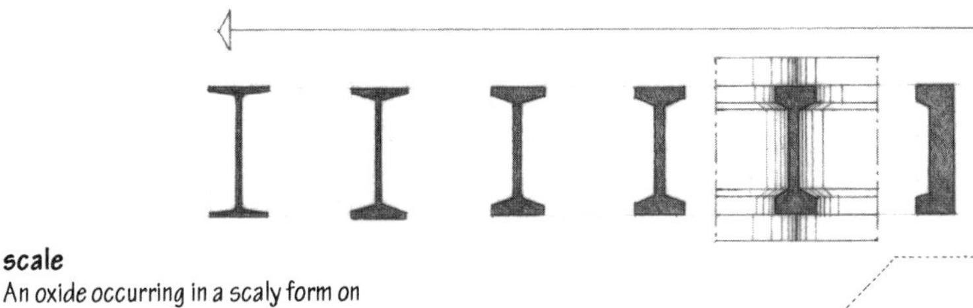

hot-roll
To roll metal at a heat high enough to permit recrystallization.

hot-rolled finish
The dark, oxidized, relatively rough finish obtained by rolling metal while hot.

die casting
The process or product of forcing molten metal into a metallic mold under hydraulic pressure to give it a particular shape or form.

casting
The process or product of forming a material into a particular shape by pouring it into a mold in a fluid state and letting it harden.

mold
A hollow form or matrix for giving a particular shape to something in a molten or plastic state.

forge
To form metal by heating and hammering.

hot-working
The working of a metal at a temperature high enough to permit recrystallization.

recrystallize
To acquire a new granular structure with new crystals because of plastic deformation, as when worked after being heated.

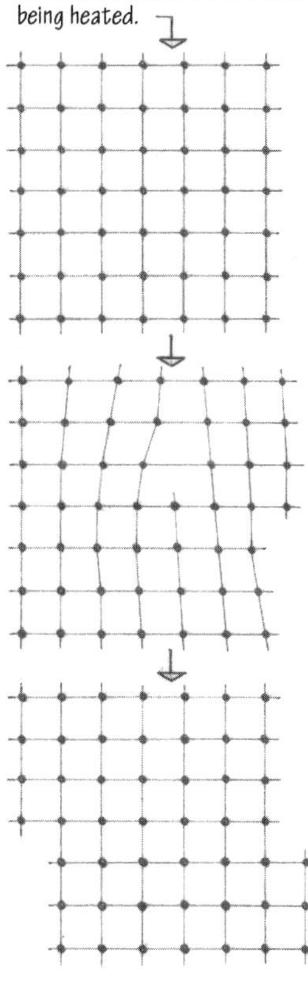

scale
An oxide occurring in a scaly form on the surface of metal when brought to a high temperature.

mill scale
A loose coating of iron oxide that forms on iron or steel during hot-rolling. Mill scale increases the bond between steel and concrete in reinforced concrete or in structural steelwork encased in concrete for fire protection.

heat treatment
The controlled heating and cooling of a metal to develop certain desirable physical or mechanical properties.

anneal
To remove internal stress from metal or glass by heating to a temperature below that of recrystallization and then gradually cooling in a liquid or air, esp. to make the material more ductile.

quench
To rapidly cool a heated metal by immersion in water, esp. to increase its hardness.

temper
To strengthen or toughen a metal by reheating at a lower temperature and slowly cooling the material.

stress relieving
The tempering of a metal at a temperature high enough to relieve residual stresses, followed by slow, uniform cooling.

residual stress
Microscopic stress in a metal resulting from nonuniform thermal changes, plastic deformation, or other causes aside from external forces or applications of heat.

case-harden
To make the outside surface of an iron-based alloy hard by carburization and heat treatment, leaving the interior tough and ductile.

cold-roll
To roll metal at a temperature below that at which recrystallization occurs, so as to increase its tensile strength or improve its surface finish.

mill finish
The striated finish that cold rolling or extrusion imparts to a metal surface.

extrusion
The process or product of forming a metal or plastic with a desired cross section by forcing it through a die with a pressure ram.

cold-draw
To draw metal through a set of dies to reduce its cross-sectional area without preheating, as in the fabrication of wire or tubing.

drawn finish
A smooth, bright finish produced by drawing metal through a die.

die
A steel block or plate having small conical holes through which metal or plastic is extruded or drawn for shaping.

cold-working
The working of metal below the temperature at which recrystallization occurs, as in drawing, pressing, or stamping.

ferrous metal
A metal containing iron as a principal element.

iron
A malleable, ductile, magnetic, silver-white metallic element from which pig iron and steel are made. Symbol: **Fe**

smelt
To melt or fuse ore in order to separate the metal constituents.

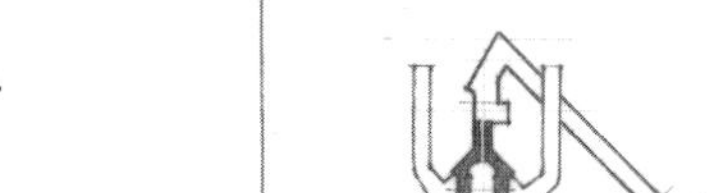

coke
The solid residue of coal left after destructive distillation, used as a fuel.

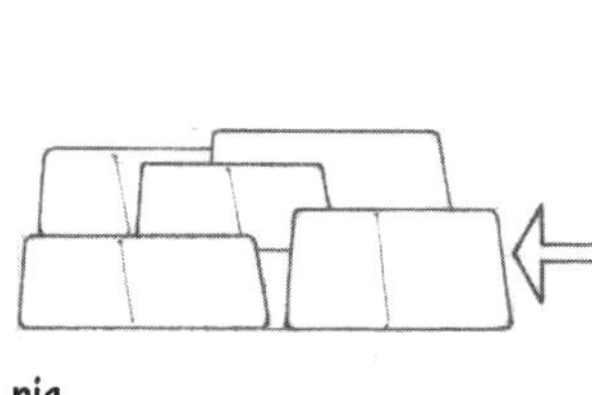

pig iron
Crude iron that is drawn from a blast furnace and cast into pigs in preparation for conversion into cast iron, wrought iron, or steel.

pig
An oblong mass of metal that has been poured while still molten into a mold of sand, esp. such a mass of iron from a blast furnace.

blast furnace
A large vertical furnace for smelting iron from ore, in which combustion is intensified by a continuous blast of air through the fuel.

blast-furnace slag
Slag left as a residue by the smelting of iron ore in a blast furnace.

slag
The vitrified matter left as a residue from the smelting of a metallic ore. Also called **cinder**.

cast iron
A hard, brittle, nonmalleable iron-based alloy containing 2.0% to 4.5% carbon and 0.5% to 3% silicon, cast in a sand mold and machined to make many building products.

malleable cast iron
Cast iron that has been annealed by transforming the carbon content into graphite or removing it completely.

malleable
Capable of being shaped or formed by hammering or by pressure from rollers.

wrought iron
A tough, malleable, relatively soft iron that is readily forged and welded, having a fibrous structure containing approximately 0.2% carbon and a small amount of uniformly distributed slag.

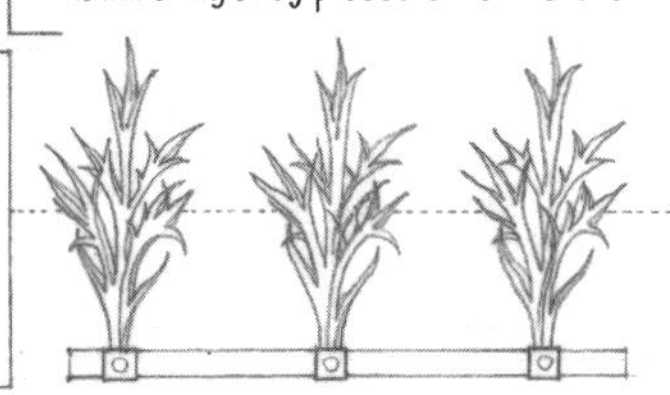

steel
Any of various iron-based alloys having a carbon content less than that of cast iron and more than that of wrought iron, and having qualities of strength, hardness, and elasticity varying according to composition and heat treatment.

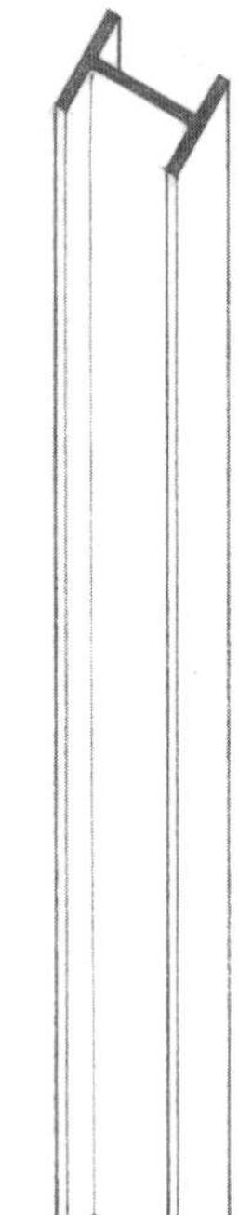

carbon steel
Ordinary, unalloyed steel in which the residual elements, as carbon, manganese, phosphorus, sulfur, and silicon, are controlled. Any increase in carbon content increases the strength and hardness of the steel but reduces its ductility and weldability.

carbon
A nonmetallic element occurring in a pure state as diamond and graphite, or as a constituent of coal and petroleum. Symbol: **C**

mild steel
A low-carbon steel containing from 0.15% to 0.25% carbon. Also called **soft steel**.

medium steel
A carbon steel containing from 0.25% to 0.45% carbon.

hard steel
A high-carbon steel containing from 0.45% to 0.85% carbon.

spring steel
A high-carbon steel containing 0.85% to 1.80% carbon.

alloy steel
Carbon steel to which various elements, as chromium, cobalt, copper, manganese, molybdenum, nickel, tungsten, or vanadium, have been added in a sufficient amount to obtain particular physical or chemical properties.

alloy
A substance composed of two or more metals, or of a metal and a nonmetal, intimately mixed, as by fusing or electrodeposition.

base metal
The principal metal of an alloy or a piece underlying a coating of another metal.

stainless steel
An alloy steel containing a minimum of 12% chromium, sometimes with nickel, manganese, or molybdenum as additional alloying elements, so as to be highly resistant to corrosion.

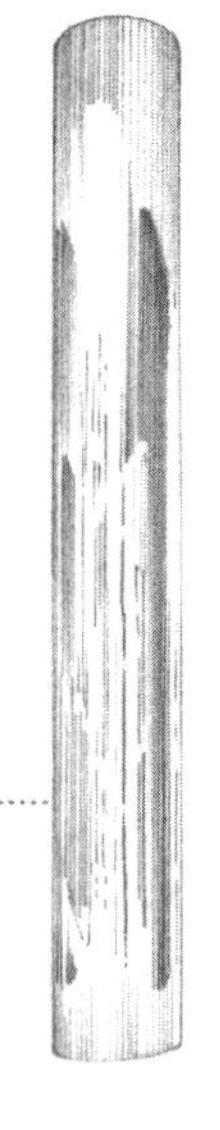

high-strength low-alloy steel
Any of a group of low-carbon steels containing less than 2% alloys in a chemical composition specifically developed for increased strength, ductility, and resistance to corrosion.

weathering steel
A high-strength, low-alloy steel that forms an oxide coating when exposed to rain or moisture in the atmosphere, which adheres firmly to the base metal and protects it from further corrosion. Structures using weathering steel should be detailed to prevent the small amounts of oxide carried off by rainwater from staining adjoining materials.

rust
The reddish brittle coating formed on the surface of iron esp. when exposed to moisture and air, consisting essentially of hydrated ferric oxide formed by oxidation.

oxidation
The process or result of combining with oxygen to form an oxide.

oxide
A binary compound of oxygen with another element.

noble metal
A metal, as gold, silver, and mercury, that resists oxidation when heated in air, and solution by inorganic acids.

cathode (−) (most noble)

- GOLD & PLATINUM
- TITANIUM
- SILVER
- STAINLESS STEEL
- BRONZE
- COPPER
- BRASS
- NICKEL
- TIN
- LEAD
- IRON & STEEL
- CADMIUM
- ALUMINUM
- ZINC
- MAGNESIUM

(least noble) anode (+)

corrosion
The gradual deterioration of metal by chemical action, as when exposed to weather, moisture, or other corroding agents.

galvanic corrosion
An accelerated corrosive action that takes place when dissimilar metals are in contact in the presence of an electrolyte.

galvanic series
A list of metals arranged in order from least noble to most noble. The farther apart two metals are on the list, the more susceptible the least noble one is to corrosive deterioration.

sacrificial anode
An anode that is attached to a metal object subject to electrolysis and is decomposed instead of the object.

cathodic protection
The protection of ferrous metals against electrolysis by the attachment of sacrificial anodes. Also called **electrolytic protection**.

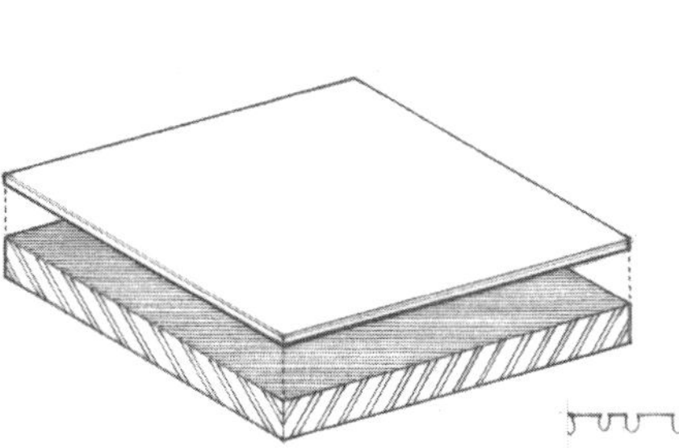

cladding
The process or product of bonding one metal to another, usually to protect the inner metal form corrosion.

pickle
An acid or other chemical solution in which a metal object is dipped to remove oxide scale or other adhering substances.

bonderize
To coat steel with an anticorrosive phosphate solution in preparation for the application of paint, enamel, or lacquer.

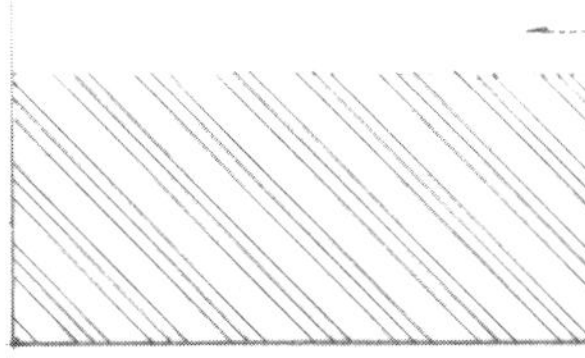

anodize
To coat a metal, esp. aluminum or magnesium, with a hard, noncorrosive film by electrolytic or chemical action.

chrome
To coat or plate a metal surface with a compound of chromium. Also called **chromeplate**.

chromium
A lustrous, hard, brittle metallic element used in alloy steels for hardness and corrosion resistance, and for electroplating other metals.

galvanize
To coat metal, esp. iron or steel, with zinc, esp. to immerse in molten zinc to produce a coating of zinc–iron alloy.

hot-dip galvanizing
The protective coating of ferrous metal by dipping in a bath of molten zinc.

galvanized iron
Iron coated with zinc to prevent rust.

zinc
A ductile, crystalline, bluish-white metallic element, used for galvanizing iron and steel and in making other alloys. Symbol: **Zn**

tinplate
Thin iron or steel sheet plated with tin for protection against oxidation.

tin
A lustrous, low-melting, bluish-white metallic element that is malleable and ductile at ordinary temperatures and used in plating and in making alloys and soft solders. Symbol: **Sn**

electroplate
To plate with an adherent metallic coating by electrolysis, usually to increase the hardness, improve the durability, or enhance the appearance of the base metal.

electrolysis
The producing of chemical changes by the passage of an electric current through an electrolyte, with subsequent migration of positively and negatively charged ions to the negative and positive electrodes.

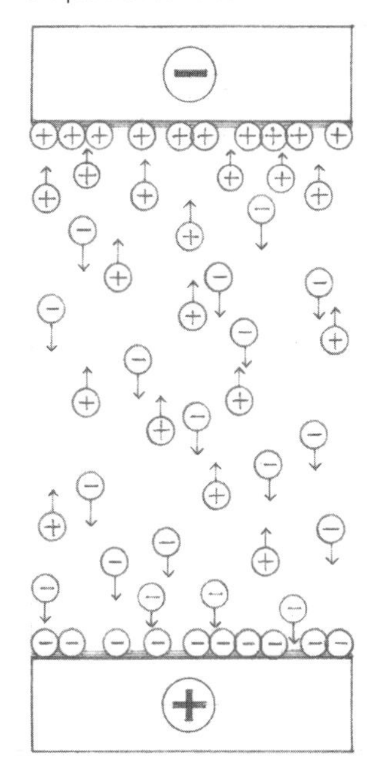

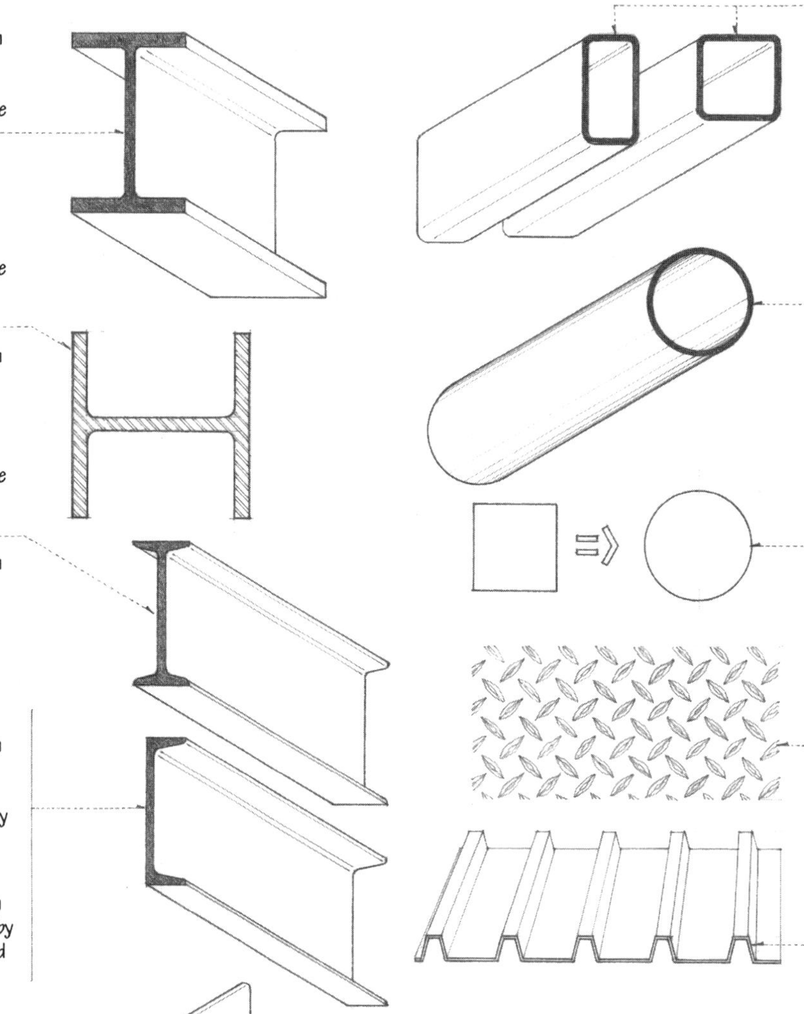

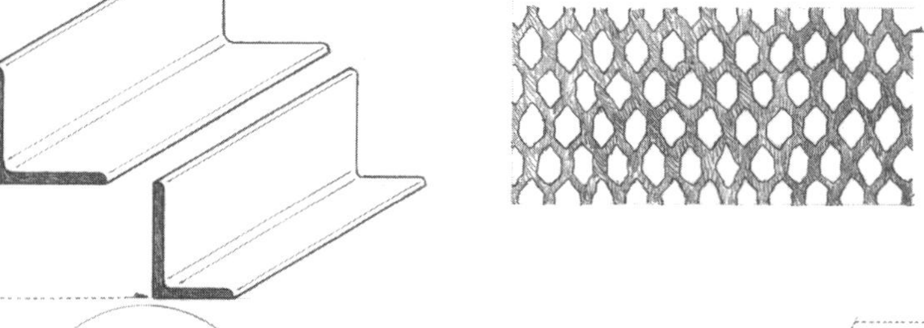

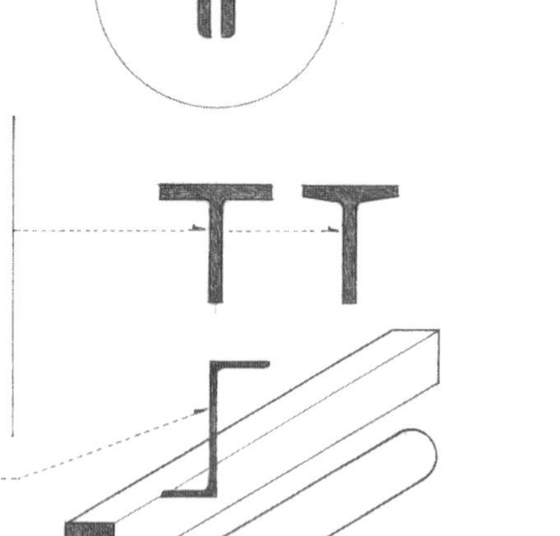

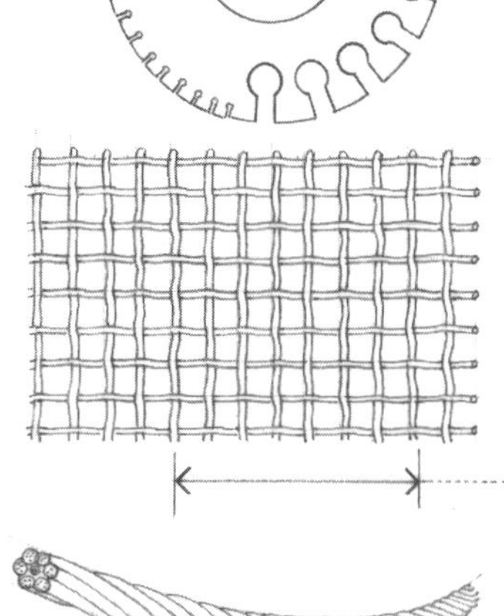

W-shape
A hot-rolled structural steel section having an H-shape with wide parallel flanges, designated by the prefix W followed by the size and weight of the member. Also called **wide flange**.

M-shape
A hot-rolled structural steel shape similar to but not classified as a W-shape, designated by the prefix M followed by the size and weight of the member.

HP-shape
A hot-rolled structural steel section similar to a W-shape but having flanges and web of equal thickness and typically used as a load-bearing pile, designated by the prefix HP followed by the size and weight of the member.

S-shape
A hot-rolled structural steel section having an I-shape with sloped inner flange surfaces, designated by the prefix S followed by the size and weight of the member. Also called **American standard beam**.

American standard channel
A hot-rolled structural steel section having a rectangular C-shape with sloped inner flange surfaces, designated by the prefix C followed by the size and weight of the member.

miscellaneous channel
A hot-rolled structural steel section similar to a C-shape but designated by the prefix MC followed by the size and weight of the member.

angle
A hot-rolled structural steel section having an L-shape, designated by the prefix L followed by the length of each leg and their thickness. Also called **angle iron**.

equal leg angle
An angle iron having legs of equal length.

unequal leg angle
An angle iron having legs of unequal length.

double angle
A structural member consisting of a pair of angles joined back to back. The parallel legs may be in contact or slightly separated.

structural tee
A structural steel section cut from a W-, S-, or M-shape and having a T-shape. It is designated by the prefix WT, ST, or MT, depending on the section from which it is cut, followed by the size and weight of the member.

tee
A rolled metal bar having a T-shaped cross section. Also called **T-bar**.

zee
A rolled metal bar having a Z-shaped cross section with internal right angles. Also called **Z-bar**.

bar
A long, solid piece of metal, esp. one having a square, rectangular, or other simple cross-sectional shape.

structural tubing
A hollow structural steel shape of square, rectangular, or circular cross section. It is designated by the prefix TS followed by the side dimensions or diameter and the wall thickness.

standard pipe
A structural steel pipe of standard weight and wall thickness, designated as Pipe (nominal inside diameter) Std.

extra-strong pipe
A structural steel pipe having increased wall thickness for greater strength, designated as Pipe (nominal inside diameter) X-Strong.

double-extra-strong pipe
A structural steel pipe having a wall thickness greater than that of extra-strong pipe, designated as Pipe (nominal inside diameter) XX-Strong.

equivalent round
The diameter of a circle having a circumference equal to the perimeter of a noncircular tube.

plate
A thin, flat sheet or piece of metal, esp. one of uniform thickness.

checkered plate
A steel or cast-iron plate having a wafflelike pattern.

sheet metal
Metal in thin sheets or plates, used in the manufacture of ductwork, flashing, and roofing.

corrugated metal
Sheet metal drawn or rolled into parallel ridges and furrows for additional mechanical strength.

expanded metal
Sheet metal slotted and stretched into a stiff, open mesh or lattice, used esp. as lath.

blackplate
Cold-rolled sheet steel before pickling or cleaning, used for coating with zinc, tin, or terne metal.

gauge
Any of various standards for designating the thickness or diameter of a thin object, as the thickness of sheet metal or the diameter of a wire or screw. Also, **gage**.

wire gauge
A gauge calibrated for determining the diameter of wire or thickness of sheet metal, consisting of a steel plate with a series of standard-sized notches around the edge.

wire cloth
A fabric of woven metallic wire, used in screens, sieves, or the like.

hardware cloth
A galvanized steel wire cloth with a mesh between 0.25 and 0.50 in. (6.4 to 12.7 mm).

mesh
The number of openings per inch in wire cloth.

wire rope
A heavy rope made of or containing wire strands twisted around a central core.

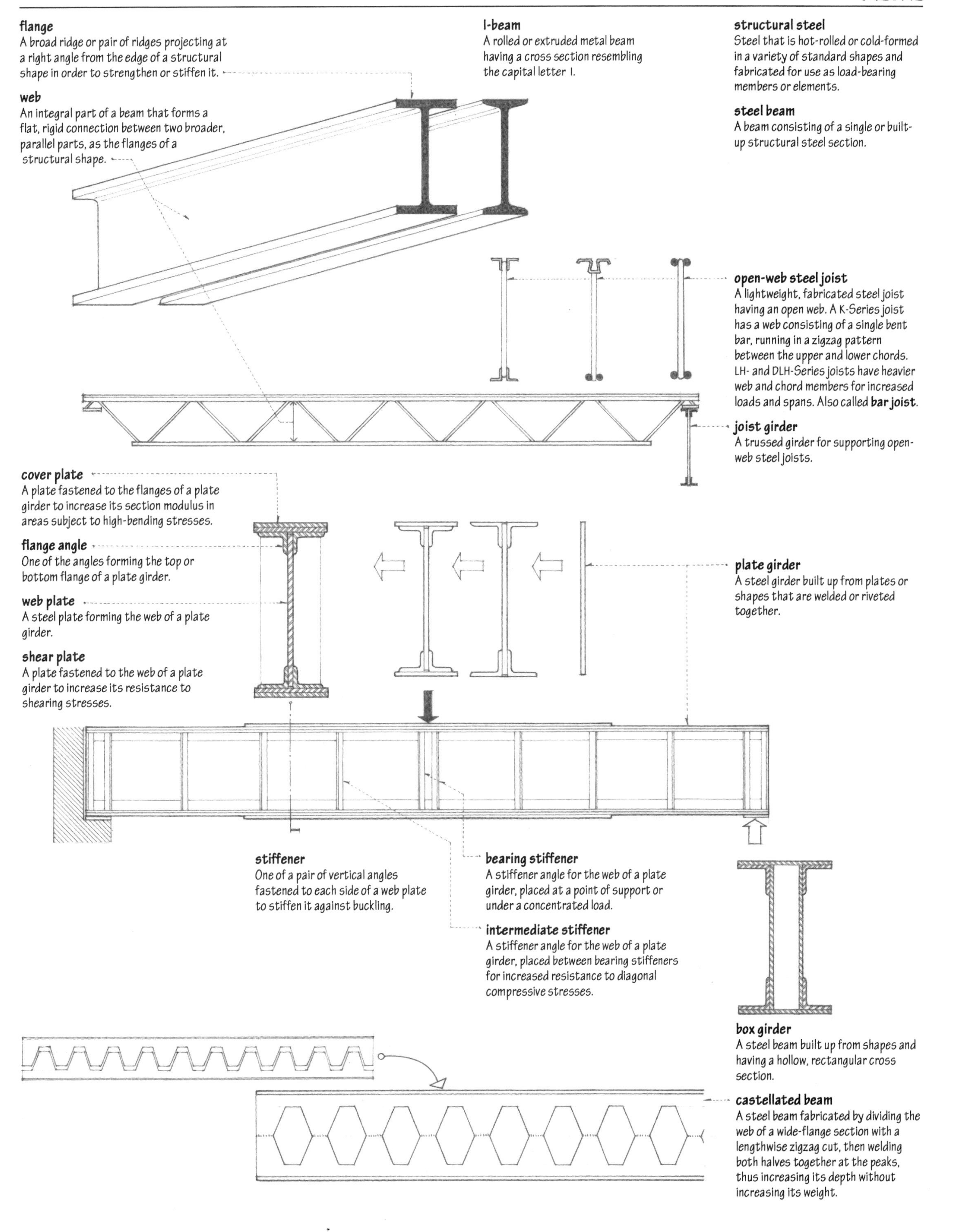

flange
A broad ridge or pair of ridges projecting at a right angle from the edge of a structural shape in order to strengthen or stiffen it.

web
An integral part of a beam that forms a flat, rigid connection between two broader, parallel parts, as the flanges of a structural shape.

I-beam
A rolled or extruded metal beam having a cross section resembling the capital letter I.

structural steel
Steel that is hot-rolled or cold-formed in a variety of standard shapes and fabricated for use as load-bearing members or elements.

steel beam
A beam consisting of a single or built-up structural steel section.

open-web steel joist
A lightweight, fabricated steel joist having an open web. A K-Series joist has a web consisting of a single bent bar, running in a zigzag pattern between the upper and lower chords. LH- and DLH-Series joists have heavier web and chord members for increased loads and spans. Also called **bar joist**.

joist girder
A trussed girder for supporting open-web steel joists.

cover plate
A plate fastened to the flanges of a plate girder to increase its section modulus in areas subject to high-bending stresses.

flange angle
One of the angles forming the top or bottom flange of a plate girder.

web plate
A steel plate forming the web of a plate girder.

shear plate
A plate fastened to the web of a plate girder to increase its resistance to shearing stresses.

plate girder
A steel girder built up from plates or shapes that are welded or riveted together.

stiffener
One of a pair of vertical angles fastened to each side of a web plate to stiffen it against buckling.

bearing stiffener
A stiffener angle for the web of a plate girder, placed at a point of support or under a concentrated load.

intermediate stiffener
A stiffener angle for the web of a plate girder, placed between bearing stiffeners for increased resistance to diagonal compressive stresses.

box girder
A steel beam built up from shapes and having a hollow, rectangular cross section.

castellated beam
A steel beam fabricated by dividing the web of a wide-flange section with a lengthwise zigzag cut, then welding both halves together at the peaks, thus increasing its depth without increasing its weight.

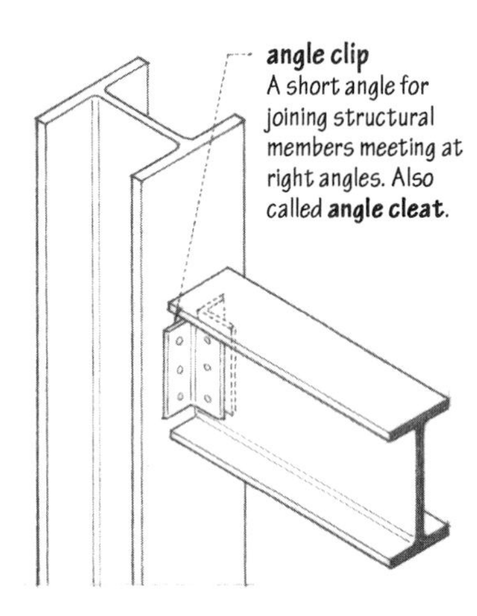

angle clip
A short angle for joining structural members meeting at right angles. Also called **angle cleat**.

framed connection
A shear-resisting steel connection made by welding or bolting the web of a beam to the supporting column or girder with two angles.

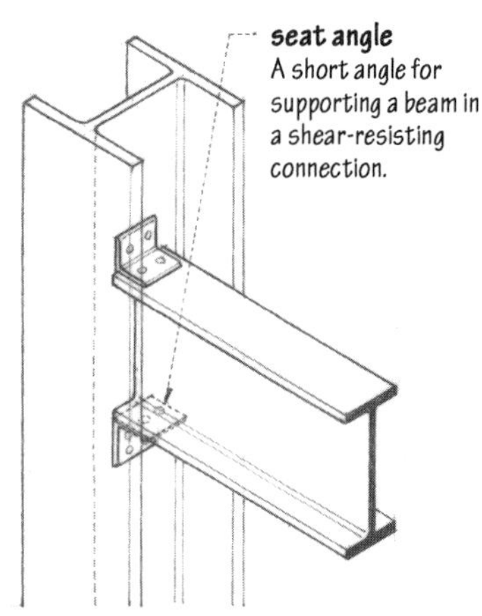

seat angle
A short angle for supporting a beam in a shear-resisting connection.

seated connection
A shear-resisting steel connection made by welding or bolting the flanges of a beam to the supporting column with a seat angle below and a stabilizing angle above.

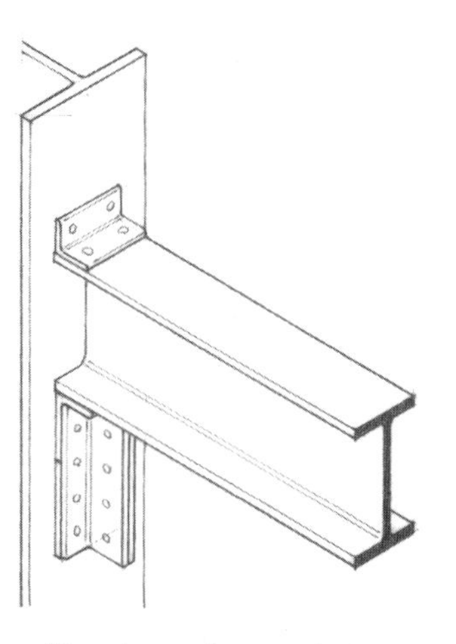

stiffened seated connection
A seated connection stiffened to resist large beam reactions, usually by means of a vertical plate or pair of angles directly below the horizontal component of the seat angle.

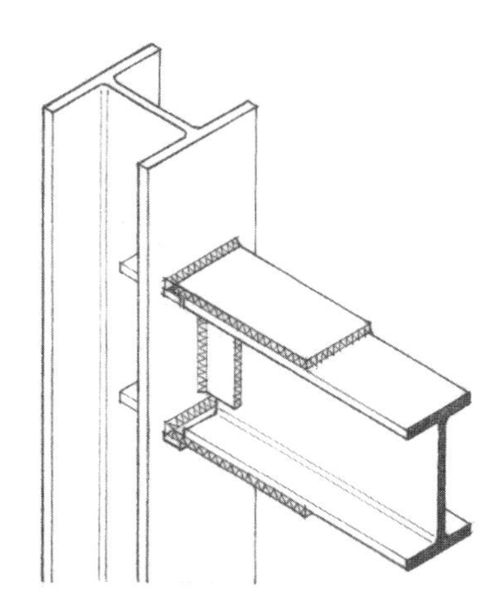

moment connection
A steel connection made so as to develop a specified resisting moment, usually by means of plates welded or bolted to the beam flanges and the supporting column.

steel column
A column consisting of a single- or built-up structural steel section. The allowable compressive load on a steel column depends not only on the area of the cross section but also on its shape. The slenderness ratio for a primary column should generally not exceed 120. For bracing and other secondary members, the slenderness ratio should not exceed 200.

built-up column
A steel column fabricated from a number of structural steel shapes, as W-shapes, channels, angles, and plates. The arrangement of elements and cross-sectional shape of a built-up steel column is not only a response to constructional and aesthetic conditions, but must also provide the largest possible radius of gyration in response to buckling conditions.

box column
A built-up steel column consisting of a single or multiple shafts rigidly connected by lacing or cover plates.

lacing
Any member or members uniting the angles or flanges of a composite steel column, girder, or strut.

pipe column
A section of structural steel pipe used as a vertical support.

Lally column
Trademark for a brand of steel pipe column, usually filled with concrete.

cap plate
A steel plate fixed atop a column to provide a bearing surface for a crossing beam or girder.

filler plate
A steel plate or shim used in splicing steel columns with different flange thicknesses.

splice plate
A steel plate aligning and uniting the flanges of two steel sections at a column splice. Horizontal surfaces in contact must be milled to provide full bearing areas. To avoid conflicting with beam and girder connections, a column splice is usually made two to three feet (0.6 to 0.9 m) above a floor level.

butt plate
A horizontal steel plate providing a full bearing area for a smaller column section being joined to a larger section.

base plate
A steel plate for transmitting and distributing a column load to the supporting foundation material.

dry-pack
To ram a stiff, high-strength, low-shrinkage concrete or grout mix into a confined space, as under a bearing plate, to transmit a compressive load.

high-strength bolt
A bolt made of high-strength low-alloy steel for making structural steel connections.

high-tension bolt
A high-strength bolt tightened with a calibrated torsion wrench and providing the clamping force necessary for the surfaces of the connected members to transfer the load between them by friction.

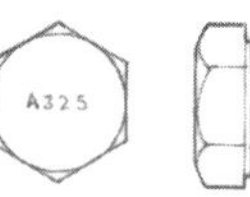

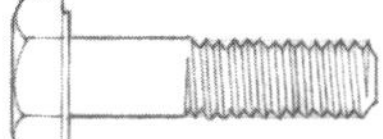

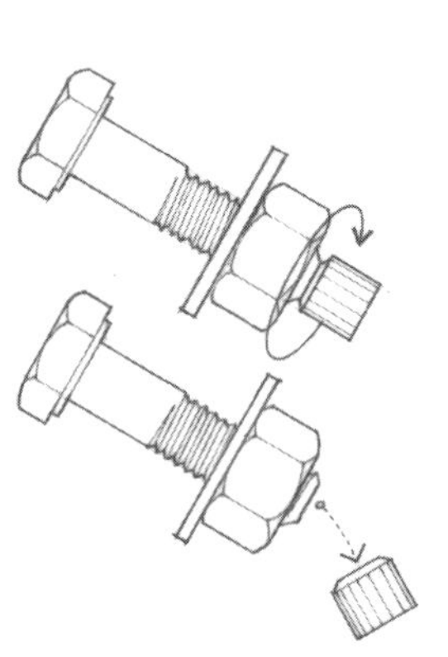

tension-control bolt
A high-tension bolt having a splined end that twists off when the required torque has been reached.

nonferrous metal
Any metal containing little or no iron.

bauxite
The principal ore of aluminum, consisting of 45% to 60% aluminum oxide, ferric oxide, and various other impurities.

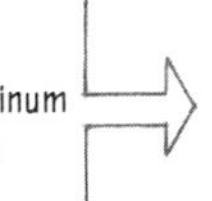

alumina
A natural or synthetic oxide of aluminum, used in aluminum production, ceramics, and electrical insulation. Also called **aluminum oxide**.

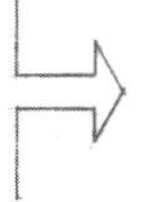

aluminum
A ductile, malleable, silver-white metallic element that is used in forming many hard, light alloys, often anodized for better corrosion resistance, color, and surface hardness. Symbol: **Al**

Bayer process
The process generally employed to refine alumina from bauxite.

reduction
The process of bringing to the metallic state by removing nonmetallic constituents, as the electrolytic process used in refining aluminum from alumina.

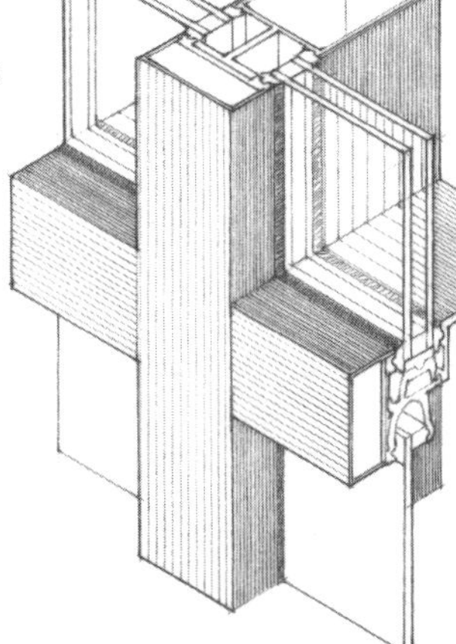

heat-treatable alloy
An aluminum alloy capable of gaining strength by heat treatment.

non-heat-treatable alloy
An aluminum alloy capable of gaining strength by cold-working. Also called **common alloy**.

alclad
An aluminum product clad with an aluminum alloy that is anodic to the core alloy, thus protecting it physically and electrolytically against corrosion.

duralumin
A light, strong alloy of aluminum, copper, manganese, and magnesium.

patina
A greenish film or encrustation produced by oxidation on the surface of old bronze and copper and often admired for its ornamental value.

antimony
A brittle, crystalline, silvery white metallic element used chiefly in alloys. Symbol: **Sb**

cadmium
A white, ductile metallic element resembling tin, used in plating and making certain alloys.

carbide
A very hard material made of carbon and one or more heavy metals, as tungsten carbide, used for cutting edges and dies.

magnesium
A light, ductile, silver-white metallic element used in lightweight alloys. Symbol: **Mg**

manganese
A hard, brittle metallic element, used chiefly as an alloying agent to increase the hardness and toughness of steel. Symbol: **Mn**

nickel
A hard, silvery-white, malleable and ductile metallic element, used in steel and cast-iron alloys and in electroplating metals which require corrosion resistance. Symbol: **Ni**

silicon
A nonmetallic element having amorphous or crystalline forms, used esp. in electronic devices and to strengthen low-alloy steels. Symbol: **Si**

tungsten
A heavy, brittle, gray-white metallic element having a high melting point and used in electrical elements and for hardening alloys. Symbol: **W**

vanadium
A malleable, ductile, grayish metallic element used in forming alloys. Symbol: **V**

bronze
Traditionally, any of various alloys consisting essentially of copper and tin, and sometimes traces of other metals. Now, any of various alloys having a large copper content with little or no tin.

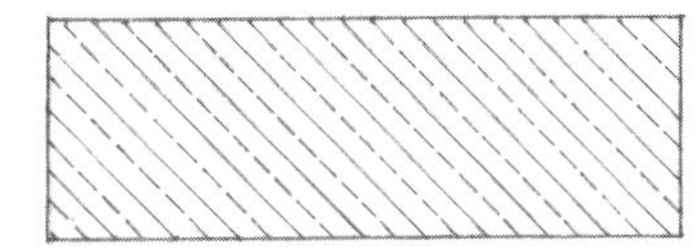

silicon bronze
An alloy of 97% copper with 3% silicon.

gold bronze
An alloy of about 90% copper, 5% zinc, 3% lead, and 2% tin.

phosphor bronze
A hard, corrosion-resistant alloy of about 80% copper, 10% tin, 9% antimony, and 1% phosphorus.

aluminum bronze
Any of various alloys containing a high percentage of copper with from 5% to 11% aluminum and varying amounts of iron, nickel, and manganese. Also called **albronze**.

brass
Any of various alloys consisting essentially of copper and zinc, used for windows, railing, trim, and finish hardware. Alloys that are brass by definition may have names that include the word bronze, as architectural bronze.

commercial bronze
An alloy of about 90% copper and 10% zinc.

red brass
An alloy of from 77% to 86% copper with the balance zinc.

aluminum brass
An alloy of about 75% copper, 2% aluminum, small amounts of other elements, with the balance zinc.

common brass
An alloy of about 65% copper and 35% zinc.

naval brass
An alloy of about 60% copper and 40% zinc.

architectural bronze
An alloy of about 57% copper, 40% zinc, 2.75% lead, and 0.25% tin.

Muntz metal
An alloy of from 55% to 61% copper with from 39% to 45% zinc. Also called **alpha-beta brass**.

manganese bronze
An alloy of about 55% copper, 40% zinc, and up to 3.5% manganese.

copper
A ductile, malleable, reddish-brown metallic element that is an excellent conductor of heat and electricity and is widely used for electrical wiring, water piping, and in the manufacture of alloys, as bronze and brass. Symbol: **Cu**

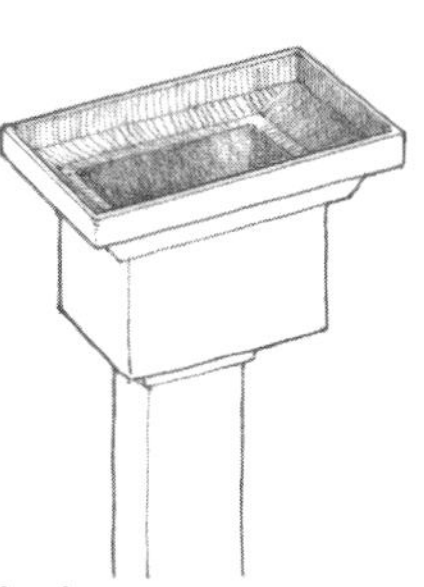

lead
A heavy, soft, malleable, bluish-gray metallic element used in solder and radiation shielding. Symbol: **Pb**

terne metal
An alloy of about 80% lead and 20% tin, used for plating.

terneplate
Steel plate coated with terne metal for use as a roofing material.

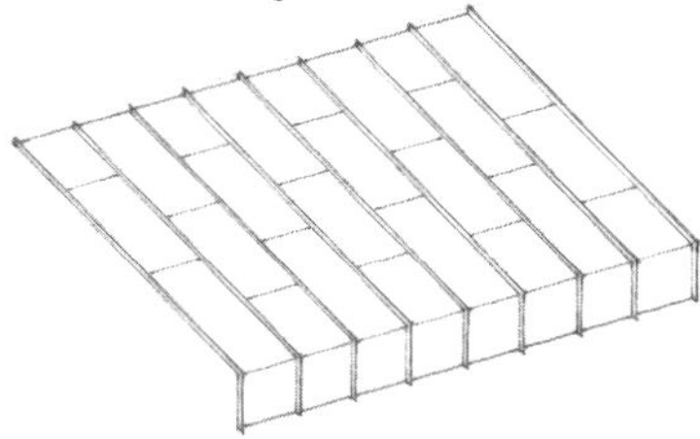

MOISTURE PROTECTION

Restricting by various means the passage or migration of water or water vapor through a building assembly or construction.

dew-point gradient

outdoor air temperature

vapor retarder
A material of low permeance, as plastic film or foil, installed in a construction to retard the transmission of moisture from the interior environment to a point where it can condense into water. Also called **vapor barrier**.

permeance
The time rate at which water vapor, under a unit pressure difference, is transmitted through a unit area of material of a given thickness.

perm
A unit of permeance, equal to 1 grain of water vapor transmitted per 1 sq. ft. per hour per inch of mercury pressure difference.

saturated air
Air containing the maximum amount of water vapor possible at a given temperature.

vapor migration
The movement of a vapor through a porous medium resulting from a difference in vapor pressure and temperature.

indoor air temperature

vapor pressure
The pressure exerted by the molecules of a vapor in a mixture of gases, as by water vapor in air.

condensation
A liquid reduced from a vapor or vapor mixture, as the water that forms when relatively humid air migrates into a region at or below the dew point of the air. Also called **condensate**.

surface condensation
The condensation that occurs when relatively humid air comes into contact with a surface at or below the dew point of the air.

sweating
The gathering of moisture from the surrounding air on a surface by condensation.

water vapor
A dispersion in air of water molecules, esp. as produced by evaporation at ambient temperatures rather than by boiling.

vapor
A gas at a temperature below its critical temperature.

mildew
A discoloration caused by fungi, as that which appears on a surface when exposed to moisture.

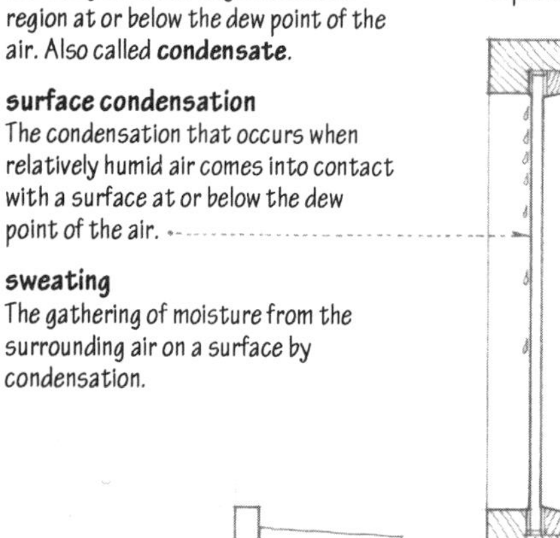

dampproofing
The treatment of a masonry or concrete surface to retard the absorption of water or penetration of water vapor, either by applying a waterproof coating or by using a suitable admixture.

parging
A thin coat of cement mortar for smoothing the surface of rough masonry or for sealing a masonry wall against moisture. Also called **parget**.

waterproofing
A membrane or coating applied to render a surface impervious to water.

asphalt mastic
A mixture of asphalt, graded mineral aggregate, and fine mineral matter that can be poured when heated and hardens when exposed to air, used as an adhesive, as a joint sealant, and in waterproofing.

mastic
Any of various pasty preparations containing bituminous materials and used as an adhesive or sealant.

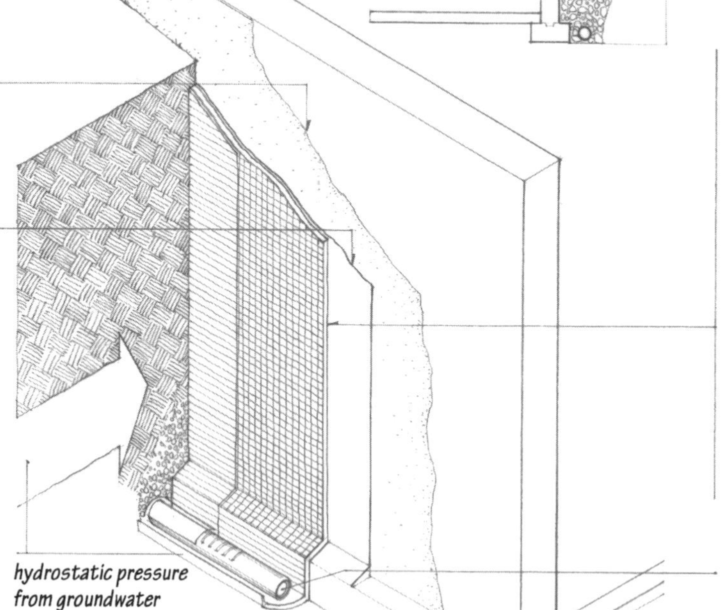

gravel drain
A layer or fill of crushed rock or gravel placed to ensure adequate drainage of groundwater while preventing the entry and flow of sediment and silt.

drainage mat
A two-part material for draining groundwater, as from behind a foundation or retaining wall, consisting of synthetic matting or an eggcrate core, faced on one or both sides with a filter fabric.

filter fabric
A geotextile fabric that allows water to pass freely into an underground drainage medium but prevents fine soil particles from entering and clogging the system.

geotextile
Any of a class of synthetic fabrics used to separate soil materials, filter fine soil particles from a drainage medium, or control soil erosion.

foundation drain
Open-jointed tile or perforated pipe laid around the foundation of a building for the collection and conveyance of groundwater to a point of disposal.

cap receiver
A metal strip interlocking with and securing a cap flashing.

cap flashing
Flashing turned down to protect base flashing and prevent water from entering the joint. Also called **counterflashing**.

base flashing
Flashing covering and protecting the joint between a roof and the vertical surface of a wall, parapet, or chimney.

parapet skirting
Roofing felt turned up against a parapet wall.

cant strip
An inclined or beveled strip changing the pitch of a roof slope or rounding out the angle between a flat roof and a parapet.

tag
A strip of sheet metal folded over and used as a wedge to secure flashing in a masonry joint.

lead wedge
A tapered piece of lead for securing flashing in a reglet.

reglet
A groove cut or formed in a vertical surface to receive flashing.

step flashing
Flashing covering and protecting the intersection of a wall and the sloping part of a roof, consisting of L-shaped pieces that step down to follow the slope of the roof. Also, **stepped flashing**.

passing
The distance by which one sheet of flashing overlaps another.

filleting
Material, as mortar, used as a substitute for flashing where a sloping roof meets a wall.

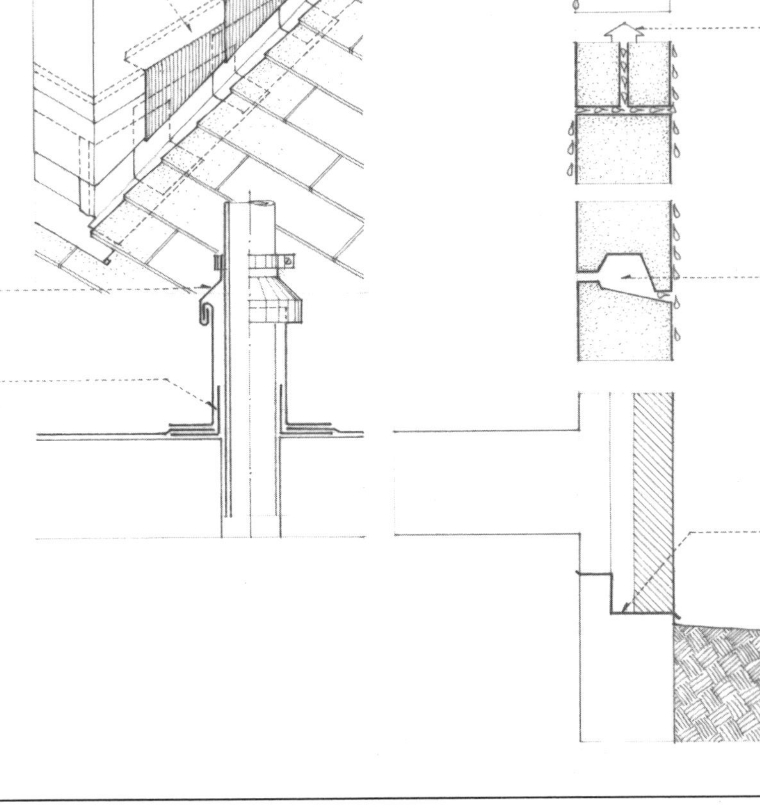

collar
A metal flashing for a vent pipe projecting above a roof deck.

roof flange
A flange that fits around and provides a raintight seal for a vent pipe penetrating a roof deck.

flashing
Pieces of sheet metal or other thin, impervious material installed to prevent the passage of water into a structure from an angle or joint.

through-wall flashing
Flashing that extends from one side of a wall to the other.

feint
A slight bend in the edge of a flashing forming a capillary break.

pressure-equalized design
Wall construction employing a rainscreen to eliminate any difference in air pressure between the exterior and the interior that would cause rainwater to move through joints in the wall.

rainscreen principle
A concept for preventing the penetration of wind-driven rain through a wall, utilizing a rainscreen backed by a confined air space to shield an inner barrier where the primary air and vapor seals are located.

rainscreen
An exposed outer layer of a wall, having openings designed to deter the penetration of rainwater and to equalize the air pressures on opposite sides of the facing.

surface tension
The elasticlike force existing in the free surface of a liquid, tending to minimize the area of the surface, caused by unbalanced intermolecular forces at or near the surface.

capillary action
A manifestation of surface tension by which the greater adhesion of a liquid to a solid surface than internal cohesion of the liquid itself causes the liquid to be elevated against a vertical surface. Also called **capillarity, capillary attraction**.

wick
To draw off liquid by capillary action.

capillary break
A space between two solid surfaces made wide enough to prevent the capillary action of moisture through the space.

damp course
A horizontal layer of impervious material laid in a masonry wall to prevent the capillary rise of moisture from the ground or a lower course. Also called **damp check**.

joint sealant
Any of various viscous substances injected into a building joint, curing to form a flexible material that adheres to the surrounding surfaces and seals the joint against the passage of air and water.

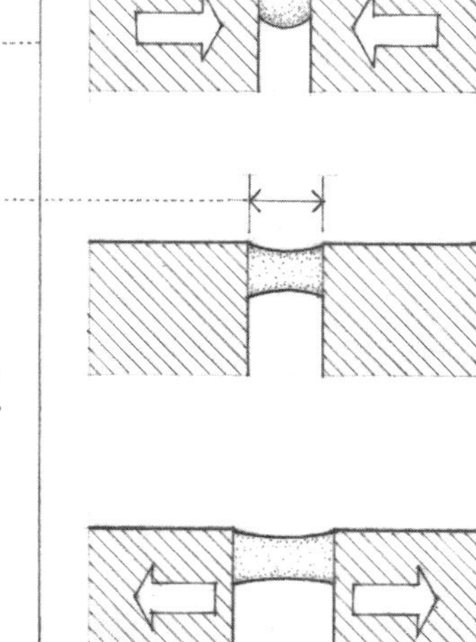

joint movement
The change in width of a building joint resulting from a change in temperature.

extensibility
The capacity of a sealant to be extended in tension.

high-range sealant
A joint sealant of polysulfide, polyurethane, or silicone capable of elongations up to 25%, used for sealing joints in curtain-wall systems.

medium-range sealant
A joint sealant of butyl rubber or acrylic capable of elongations up to 10%, used for sealing nonworking or mechanically fastened joints.

caulk
A low-range joint sealant used for filling or closing a seam, crevice or crack in order to make it watertight and airtight. Also, **caulking**.

bead
A narrow deposit of sealant applied to a building joint.

bond face
The surface of a building component or joint that serves as a substrate for a sealant and to which the sealant is bonded.

substrate
Any material that underlies and serves as a base or foundation.

primer
A liquid for improving the adhesion of a sealant to a substrate.

joint filler
A compressible strip, rod, or tube of resilient material, as neoprene or butyl, used for filling a joint and controlling the depth of a sealant. Also called **backup rod**.

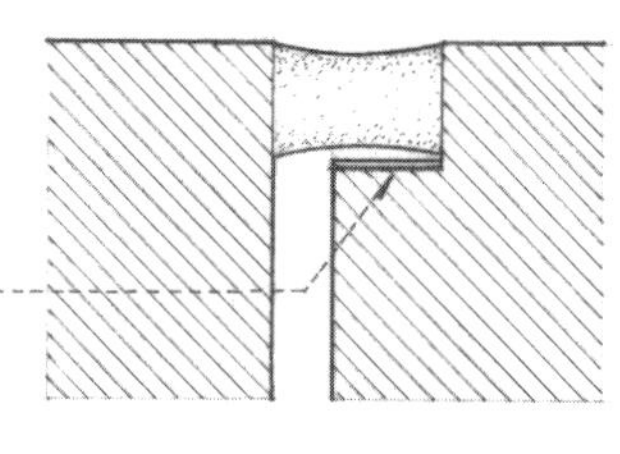

bond breaker
Any of various materials, as polyethylene tape, used for preventing the adhesion of a sealant to the bottom of a joint.

construction joint
A joint between two successive placements of concrete, often keyed or doweled to provide lateral stability across the joint.

dowel
A short reinforcing bar extending equally into two abutting sections of concrete to prevent differential movement.

expansion sleeve
A pipe sleeve that allows the housed element to move freely in a longitudinal direction.

waterstop
A flexible strip of rubber or plastic inserted across a concrete or masonry joint to prevent the passage of water.

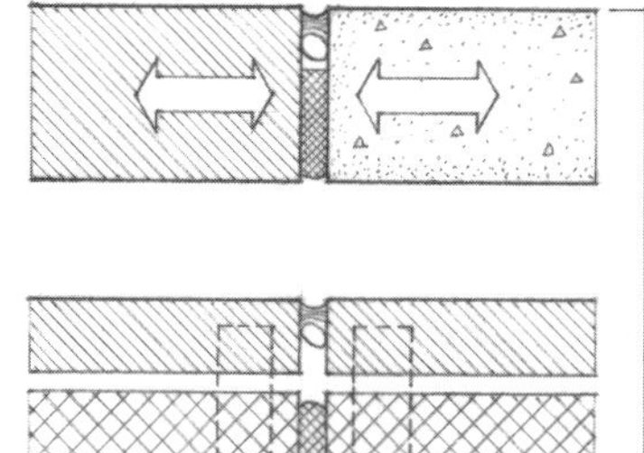

expansion joint
A joint between two parts of a building or structure permitting thermal or moisture expansion to occur without damage to either part. Expansion joints also serve as isolation joints and control joints.

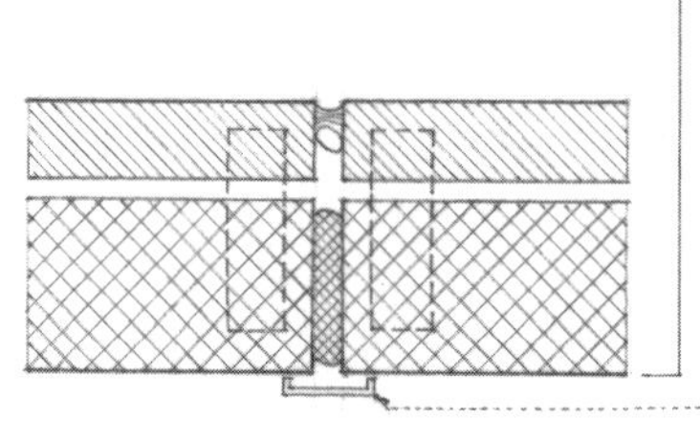

expansion joint cover
A prefabricated cover for protecting an expansion joint while allowing relative movement between the two parts being connected.

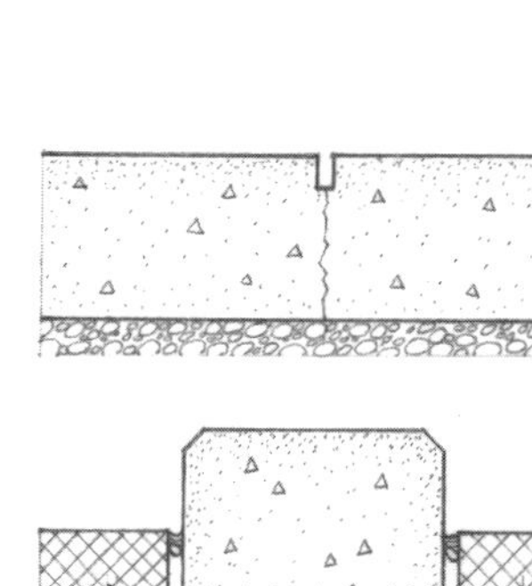

control joint
A continuous groove or separation formed, sawed, or tooled in a concrete or masonry structure to form a plane of weakness and thus regulate the location and amount of cracking resulting from drying shrinkage or thermal stresses.

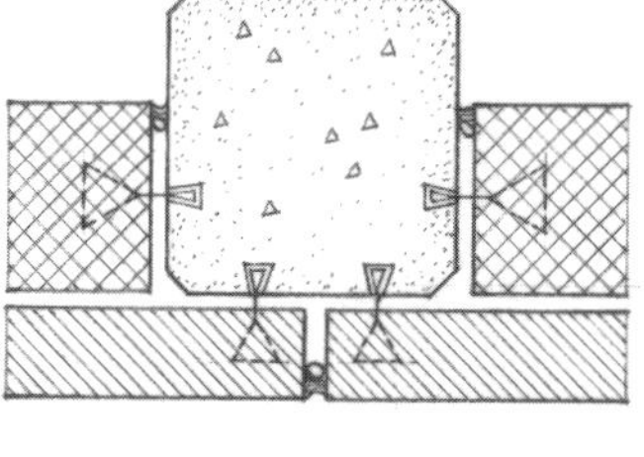

contraction joint
A joint between two parts of a structure, designed to compensate for the contraction of either part.

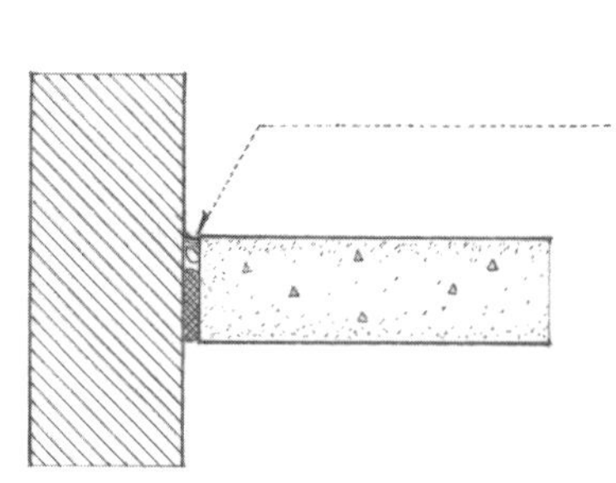

isolation joint
A joint separating two sections of a structure so that differential movement or settlement can occur between the parts.

Any of five styles of classical architecture characterized by the type and arrangement of columns and entablatures employed, as the Doric, Ionic, Corinthian, Tuscan, and Composite orders.

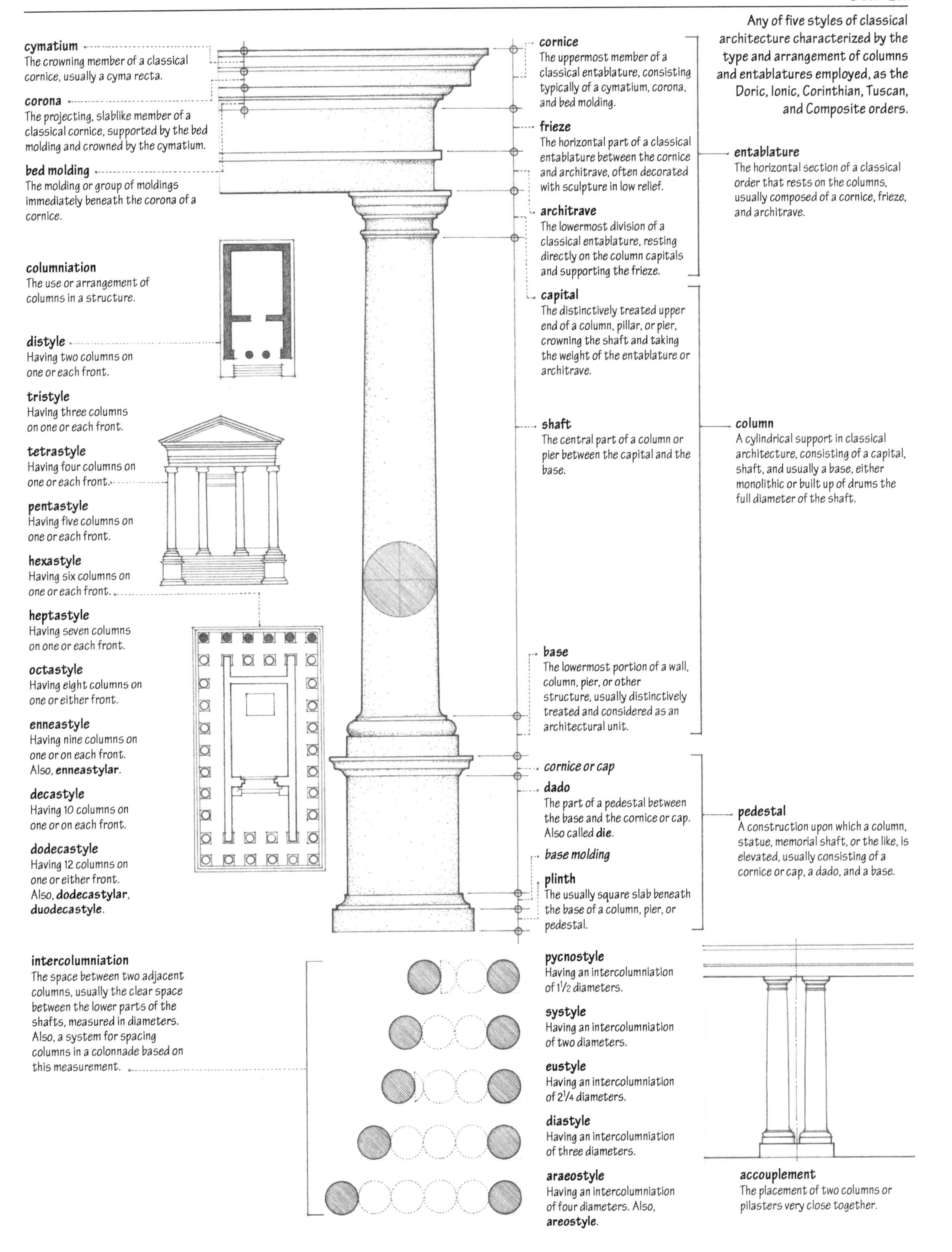

cymatium
The crowning member of a classical cornice, usually a cyma recta.

corona
The projecting, slablike member of a classical cornice, supported by the bed molding and crowned by the cymatium.

bed molding
The molding or group of moldings immediately beneath the corona of a cornice.

columniation
The use or arrangement of columns in a structure.

distyle
Having two columns on one or each front.

tristyle
Having three columns on one or each front.

tetrastyle
Having four columns on one or each front.

pentastyle
Having five columns on one or each front.

hexastyle
Having six columns on one or each front.

heptastyle
Having seven columns on one or each front.

octastyle
Having eight columns on one or either front.

enneastyle
Having nine columns on one or on each front. Also, **enneastylar**.

decastyle
Having 10 columns on one or on each front.

dodecastyle
Having 12 columns on one or either front. Also, **dodecastylar**, **duodecastyle**.

cornice
The uppermost member of a classical entablature, consisting typically of a cymatium, corona, and bed molding.

frieze
The horizontal part of a classical entablature between the cornice and architrave, often decorated with sculpture in low relief.

architrave
The lowermost division of a classical entablature, resting directly on the column capitals and supporting the frieze.

entablature
The horizontal section of a classical order that rests on the columns, usually composed of a cornice, frieze, and architrave.

capital
The distinctively treated upper end of a column, pillar, or pier, crowning the shaft and taking the weight of the entablature or architrave.

shaft
The central part of a column or pier between the capital and the base.

base
The lowermost portion of a wall, column, pier, or other structure, usually distinctively treated and considered as an architectural unit.

column
A cylindrical support in classical architecture, consisting of a capital, shaft, and usually a base, either monolithic or built up of drums the full diameter of the shaft.

cornice or cap

dado
The part of a pedestal between the base and the cornice or cap. Also called **die**.

base molding

plinth
The usually square slab beneath the base of a column, pier, or pedestal.

pedestal
A construction upon which a column, statue, memorial shaft, or the like, is elevated, usually consisting of a cornice or cap, a dado, and a base.

intercolumniation
The space between two adjacent columns, usually the clear space between the lower parts of the shafts, measured in diameters. Also, a system for spacing columns in a colonnade based on this measurement.

pycnostyle
Having an intercolumniation of 1½ diameters.

systyle
Having an intercolumniation of two diameters.

eustyle
Having an intercolumniation of 2¼ diameters.

diastyle
Having an intercolumniation of three diameters.

araeostyle
Having an intercolumniation of four diameters. Also, **areostyle**.

accouplement
The placement of two columns or pilasters very close together.

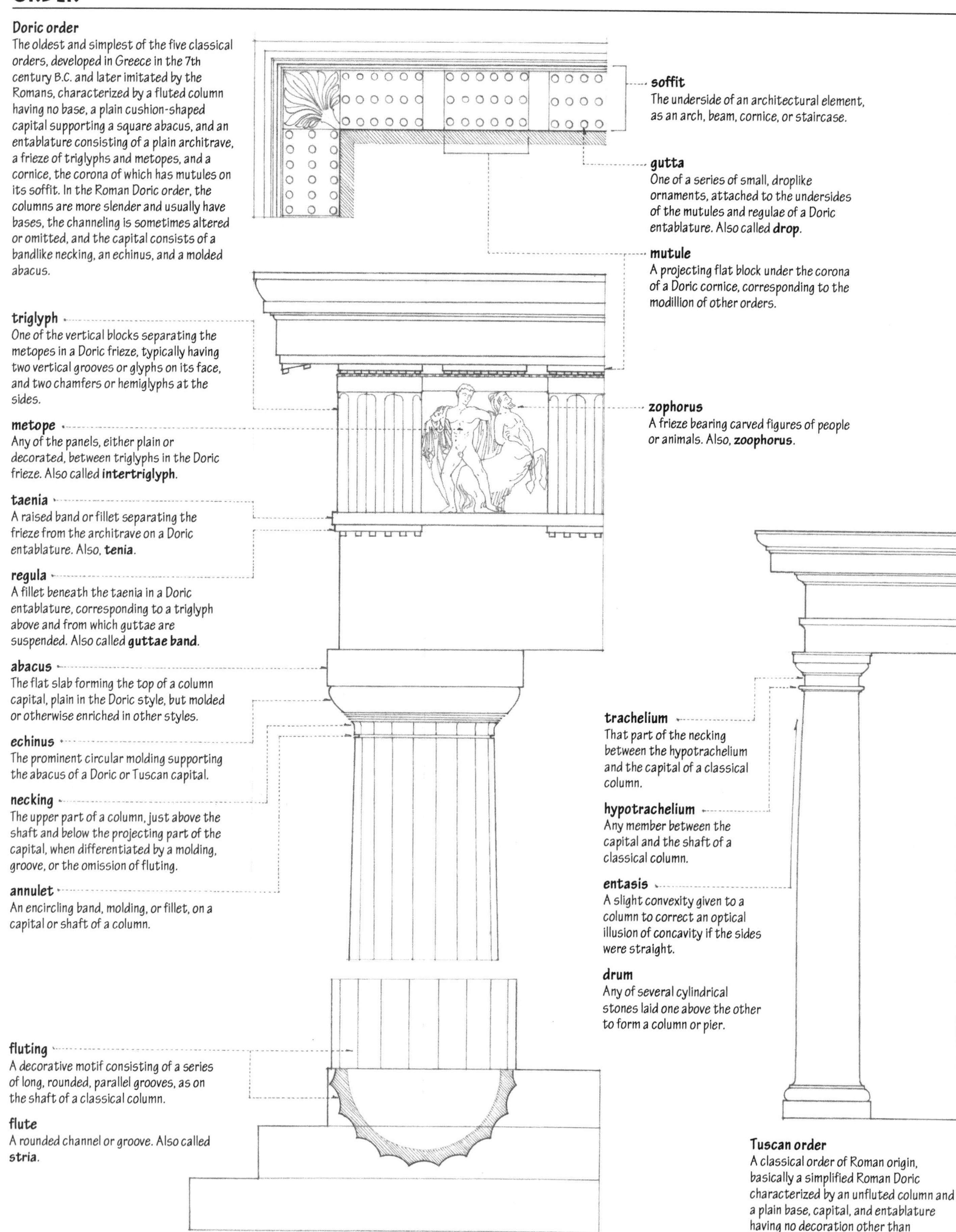

Doric order
The oldest and simplest of the five classical orders, developed in Greece in the 7th century B.C. and later imitated by the Romans, characterized by a fluted column having no base, a plain cushion-shaped capital supporting a square abacus, and an entablature consisting of a plain architrave, a frieze of triglyphs and metopes, and a cornice, the corona of which has mutules on its soffit. In the Roman Doric order, the columns are more slender and usually have bases, the channeling is sometimes altered or omitted, and the capital consists of a bandlike necking, an echinus, and a molded abacus.

triglyph
One of the vertical blocks separating the metopes in a Doric frieze, typically having two vertical grooves or glyphs on its face, and two chamfers or hemiglyphs at the sides.

metope
Any of the panels, either plain or decorated, between triglyphs in the Doric frieze. Also called **intertriglyph**.

taenia
A raised band or fillet separating the frieze from the architrave on a Doric entablature. Also, **tenia**.

regula
A fillet beneath the taenia in a Doric entablature, corresponding to a triglyph above and from which guttae are suspended. Also called **guttae band**.

abacus
The flat slab forming the top of a column capital, plain in the Doric style, but molded or otherwise enriched in other styles.

echinus
The prominent circular molding supporting the abacus of a Doric or Tuscan capital.

necking
The upper part of a column, just above the shaft and below the projecting part of the capital, when differentiated by a molding, groove, or the omission of fluting.

annulet
An encircling band, molding, or fillet, on a capital or shaft of a column.

fluting
A decorative motif consisting of a series of long, rounded, parallel grooves, as on the shaft of a classical column.

flute
A rounded channel or groove. Also called **stria**.

soffit
The underside of an architectural element, as an arch, beam, cornice, or staircase.

gutta
One of a series of small, droplike ornaments, attached to the undersides of the mutules and regulae of a Doric entablature. Also called **drop**.

mutule
A projecting flat block under the corona of a Doric cornice, corresponding to the modillion of other orders.

zophorus
A frieze bearing carved figures of people or animals. Also, **zoophorus**.

trachelium
That part of the necking between the hypotrachelium and the capital of a classical column.

hypotrachelium
Any member between the capital and the shaft of a classical column.

entasis
A slight convexity given to a column to correct an optical illusion of concavity if the sides were straight.

drum
Any of several cylindrical stones laid one above the other to form a column or pier.

Tuscan order
A classical order of Roman origin, basically a simplified Roman Doric characterized by an unfluted column and a plain base, capital, and entablature having no decoration other than moldings.

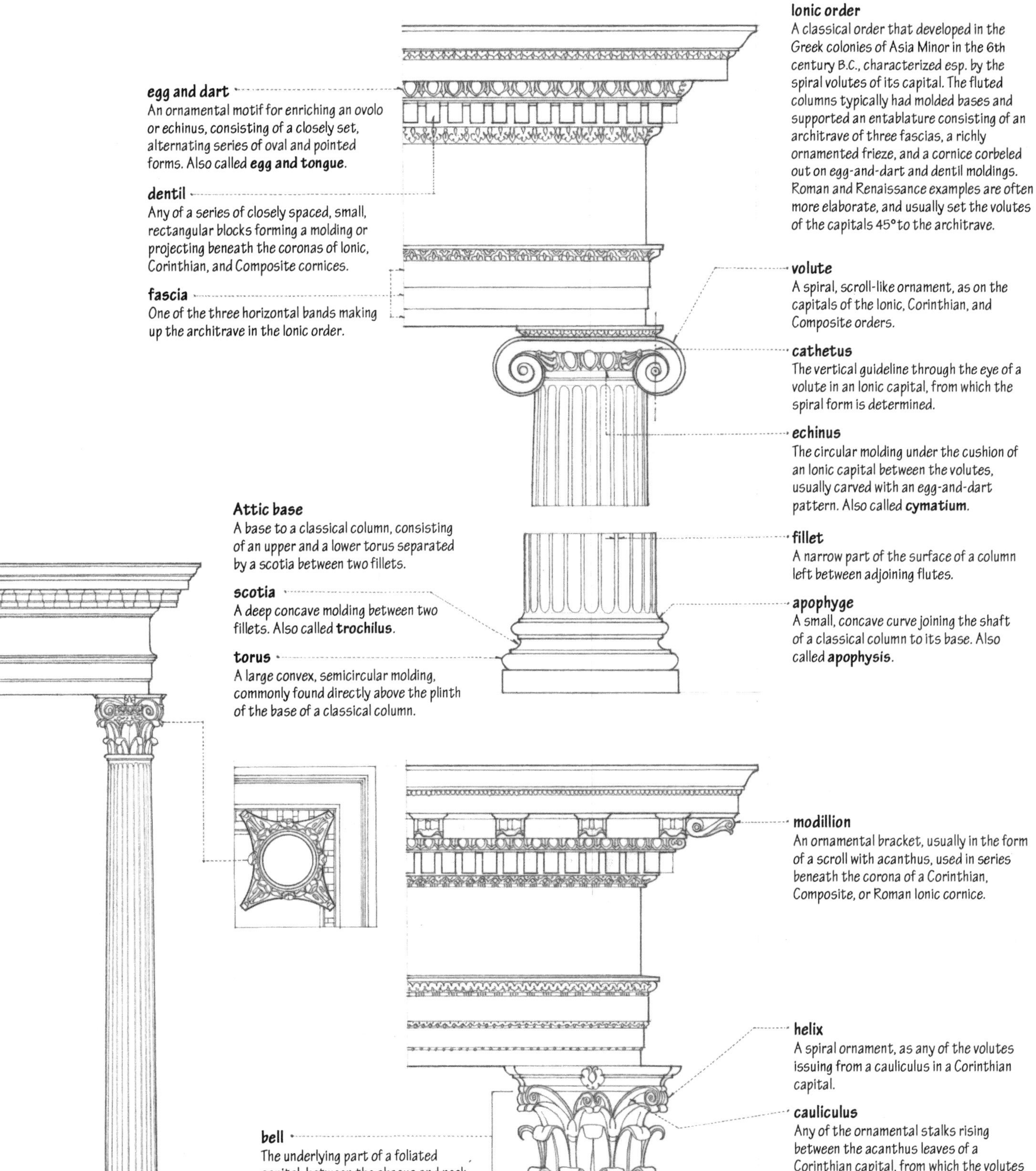

Ionic order
A classical order that developed in the Greek colonies of Asia Minor in the 6th century B.C., characterized esp. by the spiral volutes of its capital. The fluted columns typically had molded bases and supported an entablature consisting of an architrave of three fascias, a richly ornamented frieze, and a cornice corbeled out on egg-and-dart and dentil moldings. Roman and Renaissance examples are often more elaborate, and usually set the volutes of the capitals 45° to the architrave.

egg and dart
An ornamental motif for enriching an ovolo or echinus, consisting of a closely set, alternating series of oval and pointed forms. Also called **egg and tongue**.

dentil
Any of a series of closely spaced, small, rectangular blocks forming a molding or projecting beneath the coronas of Ionic, Corinthian, and Composite cornices.

fascia
One of the three horizontal bands making up the architrave in the Ionic order.

volute
A spiral, scroll-like ornament, as on the capitals of the Ionic, Corinthian, and Composite orders.

cathetus
The vertical guideline through the eye of a volute in an Ionic capital, from which the spiral form is determined.

echinus
The circular molding under the cushion of an Ionic capital between the volutes, usually carved with an egg-and-dart pattern. Also called **cymatium**.

Attic base
A base to a classical column, consisting of an upper and a lower torus separated by a scotia between two fillets.

scotia
A deep concave molding between two fillets. Also called **trochilus**.

torus
A large convex, semicircular molding, commonly found directly above the plinth of the base of a classical column.

fillet
A narrow part of the surface of a column left between adjoining flutes.

apophyge
A small, concave curve joining the shaft of a classical column to its base. Also called **apophysis**.

modillion
An ornamental bracket, usually in the form of a scroll with acanthus, used in series beneath the corona of a Corinthian, Composite, or Roman Ionic cornice.

helix
A spiral ornament, as any of the volutes issuing from a cauliculus in a Corinthian capital.

cauliculus
Any of the ornamental stalks rising between the acanthus leaves of a Corinthian capital, from which the volutes spring. Also called **caulcole**.

bell
The underlying part of a foliated capital, between the abacus and neck molding.

acanthus
An ornament, as on the Corinthian capital, patterned after the large, toothed leaves of a Mediterranean plant of the same name.

Composite order
One of the five classical orders, popular esp. since the beginning of the Renaissance but invented by the ancient Romans, in which the Corinthian order is modified by superimposing four diagonally set Ionic volutes on a bell of Corinthian acanthus leaves.

Corinthian order
The most ornate of the five classical orders, developed by the Greeks in the 4th century B.C. but used more extensively in Roman architecture, similar in most respects to the Ionic but usually of slenderer proportions and characterized esp. by a deep bell-shaped capital decorated with acanthus leaves and an abacus with concave sides.

ORNAMENT

An accessory, article, or detail that lends grace or beauty to something to which it is added or of which it is an integral part.

pictograph
A pictorial sign or symbol.

graffito
An ancient drawing or writing scratched on stone, plaster, or other hard surface.

graffiti
Inscriptions or drawings spray-painted or sketched on a public surface, as a sidewalk or wall of a building.

sgraffito
Decoration produced by cutting or scratching through a surface layer of paint or plaster to reveal a ground of contrasting color.

mural
A large picture painted on or applied directly to a wall or ceiling surface.

fresco
The art or technique of painting on a freshly spread, moist plaster surface with pigments ground up in water or a limewater mixture. Also, a picture or design so painted.

opus sectile
Any mosaic of regularly cut material.

opus Alexandrinum
A form of opus sectile having a geometric pattern formed with few colors, as black and white, or dark green and red.

mosaic
A picture or decorative pattern made by inlaying small, usually colored pieces of tile, enamel, or glass in mortar.

tessera
One of the small pieces of colored marble, glass, or tile used in mosaic work.

smalto
Colored glass or enamel, esp. in the form of minute squares, used in mosaic work.

opus vermiculatum
A mosaic of tessera arranged in waving lines resembling the form or tracks of a worm.

Florentine mosaic
A mosaic made by inlaying fine, delicately colored stones into a white or black marble surface.

relief
The projection of a figure or form from the flat background on which it is formed.

cavo-relievo
Sculptural relief in which the highest points of the modeled forms are below or level with the original surface. Also called **sunk relief**.

alto-relievo
Sculptural relief in which the modeled forms project from the background by at least half their depth. Also called **high relief**.

mezzo-relievo
Sculptural relief intermediate between high relief and bas-relief. Also called **demirelief**, **half relief**.

bas-relief
Sculptural relief that projects very slightly from the background. Also called **basso-relievo**, **low relief**.

anaglyph
An ornament carved or embossed in low relief.

appliqué
A decoration or ornament made by cutting out a design and fastening it to a larger piece of material.

inlay
To decorate by setting pieces of wood, ivory, or the like into a surface, usually at the same level.

emboss
To raise, mold, or carve a surface design in relief.

engrave
To carve, cut, or etch designs on a hard surface, as of metal, stone, or the end grain of wood.

intaglio
A figure or design incised into the surface of a stone or metal plate so that an impression yields a figure in relief.

openwork
Ornamental or structural work having a latticelike nature or showing openings through its substance.

filigree
Ornamental openwork of delicate or intricate design. Also, **filagree**.

pastiche
An artistic composition consisting of forms or motifs borrowed from different sources.

postiche
Artificial, counterfeit, or false, as an architectural ornament that is added superfluously or inappropriately.

grotesque
A decorative style characterized by the fantastic shaping and combining of incongruous human and animal forms with foliage or similar figures, often distorting the natural into caricature or absurdity.

antic
A grotesque sculpture of animal, human, or foliated forms, as a gargoyle.

mask
An often grotesque representation of a head or face, used as an architectural ornament. Also called **mascaron**.

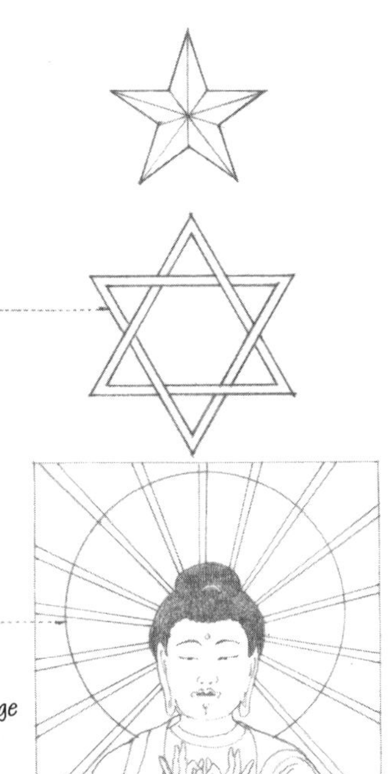

star
A conventional figure usually having five or more points radiating from a center, often used as an ornament and symbol.

Star of David
A hexagram used as a symbol of Judaism. Also called **Magen David**, **Mogen David**.

hexagram
A six-pointed starlike figure, formed by extending each of the sides of a regular hexagon into equilateral triangles.

griffin
A mythological animal typically having the head and wings of an eagle and the body and tail of a lion. Also, **griffon**, **gryphon**.

griffe
An ornament projecting from the round base of a column toward a corner of a square or polygonal plinth. Also called **spur**.

glory
A ring, circle, or surrounding radiance of light, as a halo, nimbus, or aureole.

halo
A disk or ring of radiant light around or above the head, traditionally symbolizing the sanctity of a divine or sacred personage in religious paintings and sculptures. Also called **nimbus**.

aureole
A circle of light or radiance surrounding the head or body in the representation of a sacred personage.

ballflower
A medieval English ornament suggesting a flower of three or four petals enclosing and partially concealing a ball.

vesica piscis
An elliptical, pointed figure used esp. in early Christian art as an emblem of Christ. Also called **mandorla**.

Chi-Rho
A Christian monogram and symbol formed by superimposing the first two letters of the Greek word for Christ. Also called **chrismon**.

cross
An object or figure consisting essentially of an upright and a transverse piece at right angles to each another: often used as a symbol of Christianity.

Latin cross
A cross having an upright or vertical shaft crossed near the top by a shorter horizontal bar.

Celtic cross
A cross shaped like a Latin cross and having a ring about the intersection of the shaft and crossbar.

Greek cross
A cross consisting of an upright crossed in the middle by a horizontal of the same length.

Jerusalem cross
A cross whose four arms each terminate in a crossbar, often with a small Greek cross centered in each quadrant.

Maltese cross
A cross formèe having the outer face of each arm indented in a V.

cross formèe
A cross having arms of equal length, each expanding outward from the center.

table
A raised or sunken rectangular panel on a wall, distinctively treated or ornamented with inscriptions, painting, or sculpture.

tablet
A flat slab or plaque having a surface suitable for or bearing an inscription, carving, or the like.

medallion
A usually oval or circular tablet, often bearing a figure or ornament in relief.

cartouche
An oval or oblong, slightly convex surface, usually surrounded with ornamental scrollwork, for receiving a painted or low-relief decoration. Also, **cartouch**.

motif
A distinctive and recurring shape, form, or color in a design.

checker
To mark or decorate with a squared pattern.

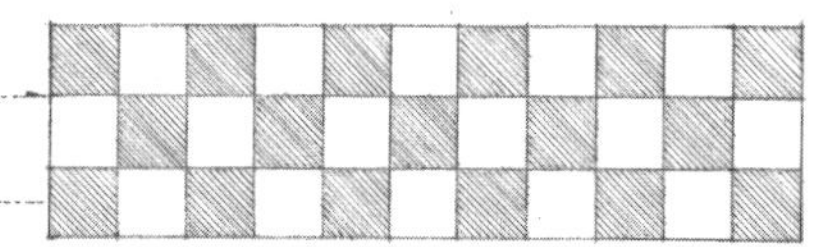

reticulate
Resembling or covered with a network of regularly intersecting lines.

diaper
A pattern of small, repeated figures connecting or growing out of one another, originally used in the Middle Ages in weaving silk and gold.

imbrication
A pattern or design resembling the regular overlapping of tiles or shingles.

herringbone
A pattern consisting of rows of short, parallel lines which in any two adjacent rows slant in opposite directions, used in masonry, parquetry, and weaving.

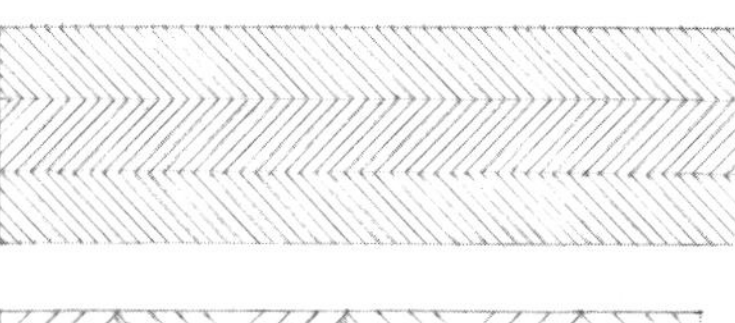

chevron
A V-shaped pattern used in heraldry and as ornamentation.

dancette
An ornamental zigzag, as in a molding.

fret
A decorative design contained within a band or border, consisting of repeated, often geometric figures. Also called **key pattern**.

meander
A running ornament consisting of an intricate variety of fret or fretwork.

guilloche
An ornamental border formed of two or more interlaced bands around a series of circular voids.

dentil band
A molding occupying the position of a row of dentils, and often carved to resemble one.

Venetian dentil
Any of a series of small rectangular blocks alternating with sloping surfaces on an archivolt or molding.

scroll
An ornament having a spiral or convoluted form resembling a partly or loosely rolled parchment.

Vitruvian scroll
A series of scrolls forming a stylized wave pattern. Also called **Vitruvian wave, wave scroll**.

banderole
A sculptured band resembling a long ribbon or scroll, adapted to receive an inscription. Also, **banderol, bandrole**.

strapwork
Ornamentation composed of folded, crossed, and interlaced bands, sometimes cut with foliations.

foliated
Ornamented with foils or representations of foliage. Also, **foliate**.

wreath
A decorative band or garland of flowers, foliage, or other ornamental material.

festoon
A decorative representation of a string or garland of flowers, foliage, ribbon, or the like, suspended in a curve between two points.

fleur-de-lis
A stylized three-petaled iris flower tied by an encircling band, used as the heraldic bearing of the royal family of France. Also, **fleur-de-lys**.

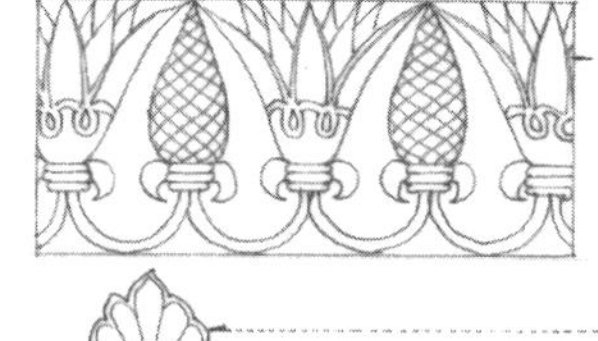

lotus
A representation of various aquatic plants in the water lily family, used as a decorative motif in ancient Egyptian and Hindu art and architecture.

anthemion
An ornament of honeysuckle or palm leaves in a radiating cluster. Also called **honeysuckle ornament**.

palmette
A stylized palm leaf shape used as a decorative element in classical art and architecture.

rosette
An ornament having a generally circular combination of parts resembling a flower or plant. Also, **rose**.

dogtooth
Any of a series of closely spaced, pyramidal ornaments, formed by sculptured leaves radiating from a raised center, used esp. in early English Gothic architecture.

arabesque
A complex and ornate design that employs flowers, foliage, and sometimes animal and geometric figures to produce an intricate pattern of interlaced lines.

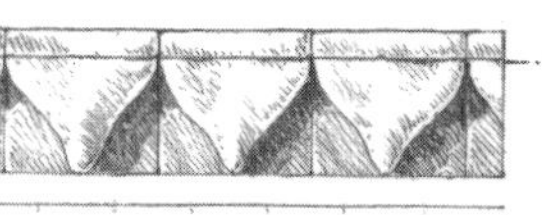

calf's-tongue
A molding having pendant, tonguelike elements carved in relief against a flat or curved surface.

scallop
Any of a series of curved projections forming an ornamental border.

purfle
To decorate a shrine or tabernacle with miniature architectural forms so as to produce a lacy effect.

arris
A sharp edge or ridge formed by two surfaces meeting at an exterior angle. Also called **piend**.

bullnose
A rounded or obtuse exterior angle. Also, **bull's-nose**.

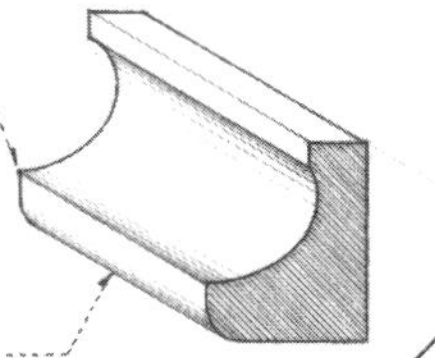

splay
A surface that makes an oblique angle with another.

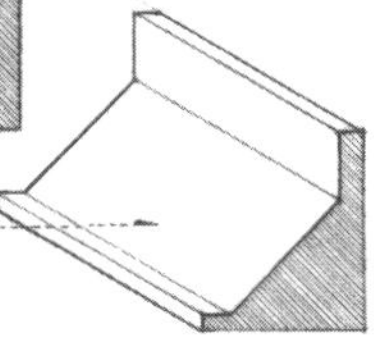

fillet
A narrow flat molding or area, raised or sunk to separate larger moldings or areas. Also called **list**.

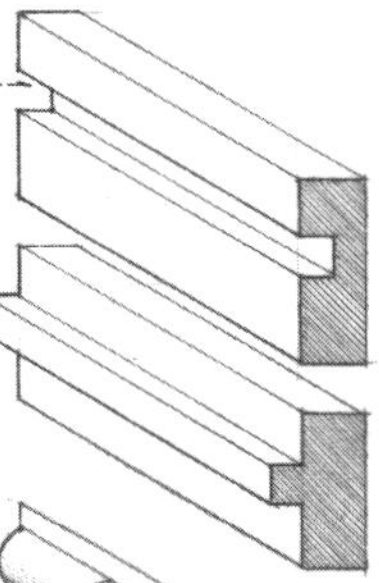

billet
Any of a series of closely spaced cylindrical forms ornamenting a hollow molding or cornice.

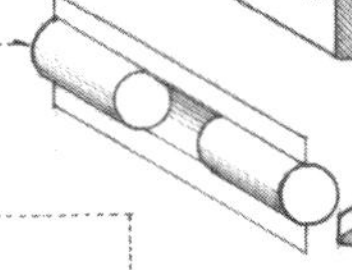

cove
A concave surface or molding, esp. at the transition from wall to ceiling.

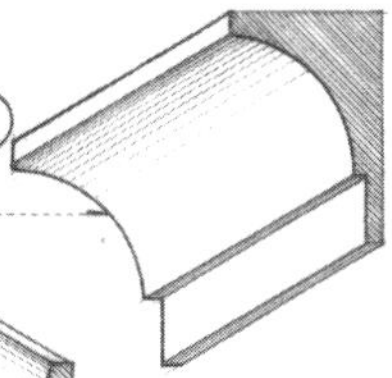

cavetto
A concave molding having an outline that approximates a quarter circle.

congé
A concave molding having the form of a quadrant curving away from a given surface and terminating perpendicular to a fillet parallel to that surface. Also, **congee**.

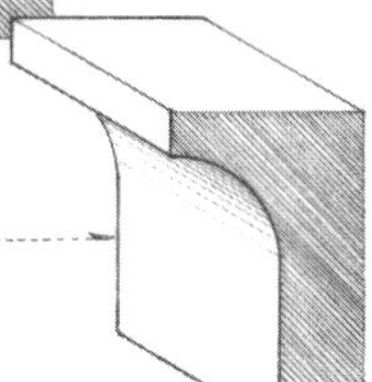

ogee
A molding having a profile of a double curve in the shape of an elongated S. Also called **gula**.

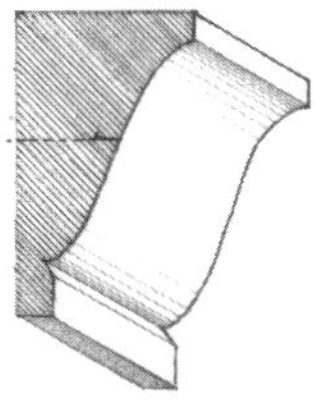

cyma
A projecting molding having the profile of a double curve formed by the union of a convex line and a concave line.

cyma recta
A cyma having the concave part projecting beyond the convex part. Also called **Doric cyma**.

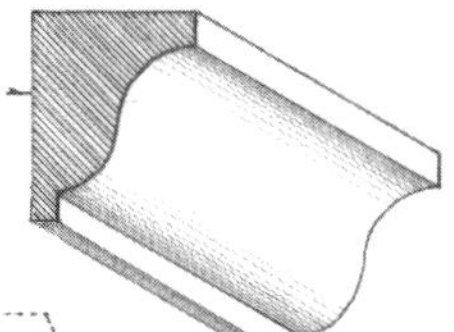

cyma reversa
A cyma having the convex part projecting beyond the concave part. Also called **Lesbian cyma**.

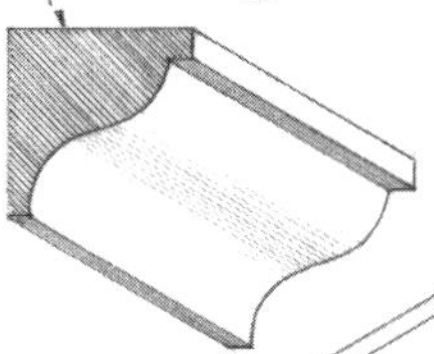

beak
A small pendant molding forming a drip and casting a deep shadow, as on the soffit of a cornice. Also called **bird's beak**.

brace molding
A projecting molding having a profile formed by two ogees symmetrically disposed about an arris or fillet. Also called **keel**.

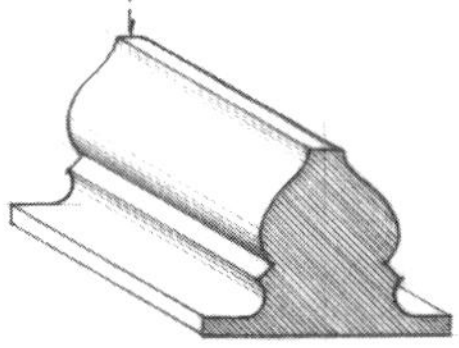

profile
An outline of an object formed on a vertical plane passed through the object at right angles to one of its principal horizontal dimensions.

molding
Any of various long, narrow, ornamental surfaces with uniform cross sections and a profile shaped to produce modulations of light, shade, and shadow. Almost all moldings derive at least in part from wood prototypes, as those in classical architecture, or stone prototypes, as those in Gothic architecture. By extension, the term now refers to a slender strip of wood or other material having such a surface and used for ornamentation and finishing. Also, **mold**, **moulding**.

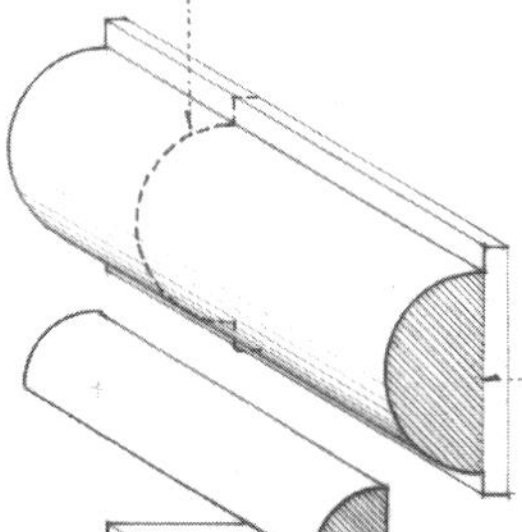

half round
A molding having a semicircular cross section.

quarter round
A convex molding whose section is a quarter circle.

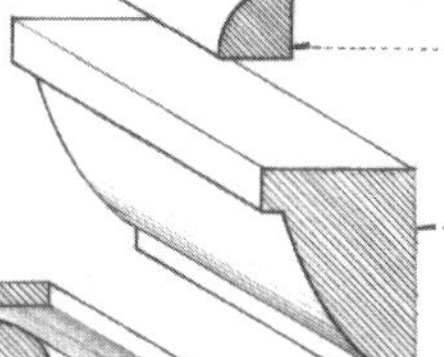

ovolo
A convex molding having a profile approximating a quarter section of a circle or ellipse.

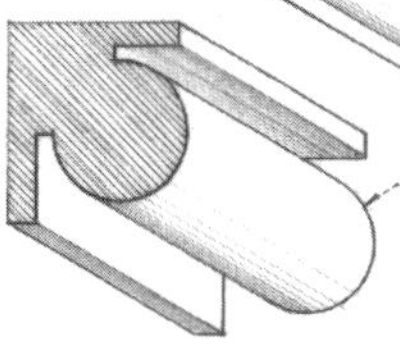

boltel
A convex, rounded molding. Also, **boutel**, **bowtel**.

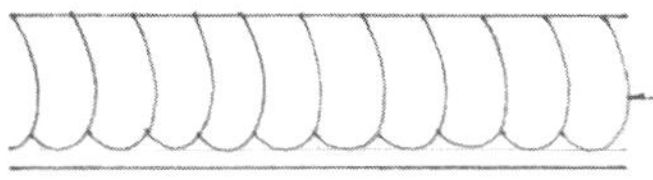

gadroon
A convex molding elaborately carved with reeding or indented with notches. Also, **godroon**.

Aaron's rod
A convex molding having pointed leaves or scrollwork emerging at regular intervals.

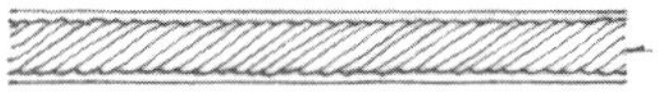

cable molding
A convex molding having the form of a rope.

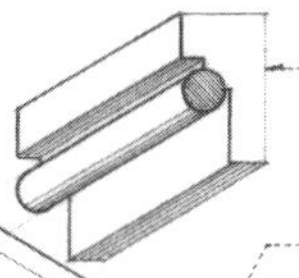

bead
A small convex molding usually having a continuous cylindrical surface.

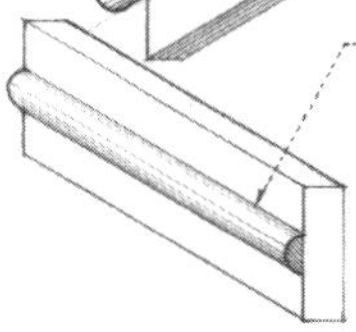

astragal
A small convex molding usually semicircular in section.

baguette
A small convex molding of semicircular section, smaller than an astragal. Also, **baguet**.

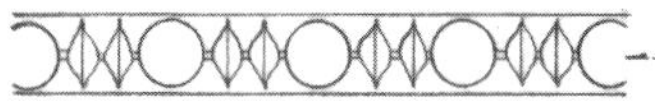

bead and reel
A convex molding having the form of disks alternating with spherical or elongated beads.

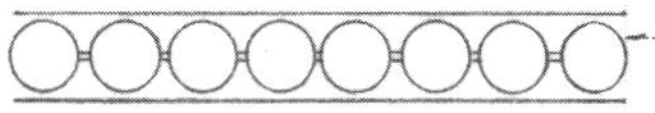

pearl molding
A molding having the form of a row of pearls or beads. Also called **bead molding**, **Paternoster**.

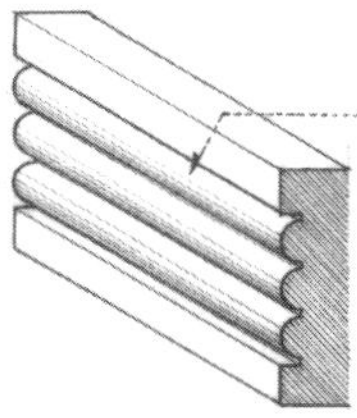

reeding
A parallel set of small convex moldings for ornamenting a plane or curved surface.

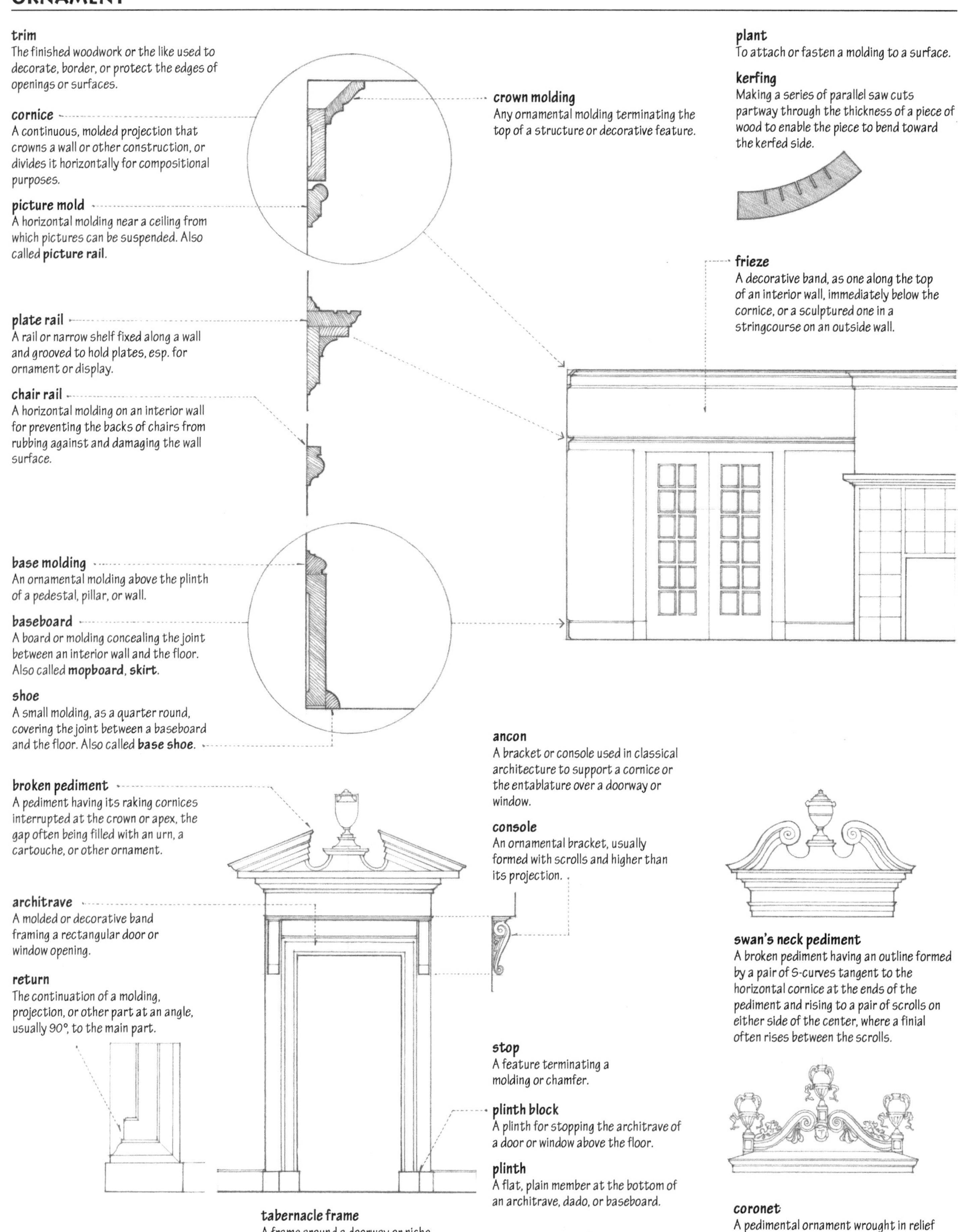

trim
The finished woodwork or the like used to decorate, border, or protect the edges of openings or surfaces.

cornice
A continuous, molded projection that crowns a wall or other construction, or divides it horizontally for compositional purposes.

picture mold
A horizontal molding near a ceiling from which pictures can be suspended. Also called **picture rail**.

plate rail
A rail or narrow shelf fixed along a wall and grooved to hold plates, esp. for ornament or display.

chair rail
A horizontal molding on an interior wall for preventing the backs of chairs from rubbing against and damaging the wall surface.

base molding
An ornamental molding above the plinth of a pedestal, pillar, or wall.

baseboard
A board or molding concealing the joint between an interior wall and the floor. Also called **mopboard**, **skirt**.

shoe
A small molding, as a quarter round, covering the joint between a baseboard and the floor. Also called **base shoe**.

crown molding
Any ornamental molding terminating the top of a structure or decorative feature.

plant
To attach or fasten a molding to a surface.

kerfing
Making a series of parallel saw cuts partway through the thickness of a piece of wood to enable the piece to bend toward the kerfed side.

frieze
A decorative band, as one along the top of an interior wall, immediately below the cornice, or a sculptured one in a stringcourse on an outside wall.

broken pediment
A pediment having its raking cornices interrupted at the crown or apex, the gap often being filled with an urn, a cartouche, or other ornament.

architrave
A molded or decorative band framing a rectangular door or window opening.

return
The continuation of a molding, projection, or other part at an angle, usually 90°, to the main part.

tabernacle frame
A frame around a doorway or niche, having two columns or pilasters on a base supporting a pediment.

ancon
A bracket or console used in classical architecture to support a cornice or the entablature over a doorway or window.

console
An ornamental bracket, usually formed with scrolls and higher than its projection.

stop
A feature terminating a molding or chamfer.

plinth block
A plinth for stopping the architrave of a door or window above the floor.

plinth
A flat, plain member at the bottom of an architrave, dado, or baseboard.

swan's neck pediment
A broken pediment having an outline formed by a pair of S-curves tangent to the horizontal cornice at the ends of the pediment and rising to a pair of scrolls on either side of the center, where a finial often rises between the scrolls.

coronet
A pedimental ornament wrought in relief over a window or door.

A mixture of a solid pigment suspended in a liquid vehicle, applied as a thin, usually opaque coating to a surface for protection and decoration.

gloss
The degree of surface luster of a dried paint film, ranging in decreasing order of gloss from high gloss, semigloss, eggshell, to flat.

high gloss
Having a brilliant sheen or luster.

enamel
Any paint or varnish drying to a very smooth, hard, usually glossy finish.

semigloss
Having a moderate, satiny luster, producing a finish midway between high gloss and eggshell. Also called **satin finish**.

eggshell
Having little or no gloss, producing a finish midway between semigloss and flat.

flat
Without gloss or sheen.

colorfast
Having color that will not fade or run with washing, age, or exposure to light, esp. sunlight.

actinic ray
A ray of light, as ultraviolet, that produces photochemical effects, as the yellowing, chalking, and disintegration of paint coatings.

photochemical
Of or pertaining to the chemical action of radiant energy, esp. light.

coverage
A measure of the area over which a gallon of paint may be spread at a given thickness, usually expressed in square feet per gallon.

hiding power
The ability of a paint film to conceal any marks, pattern, or color on the surface to which it is applied. Also called **covering power**.

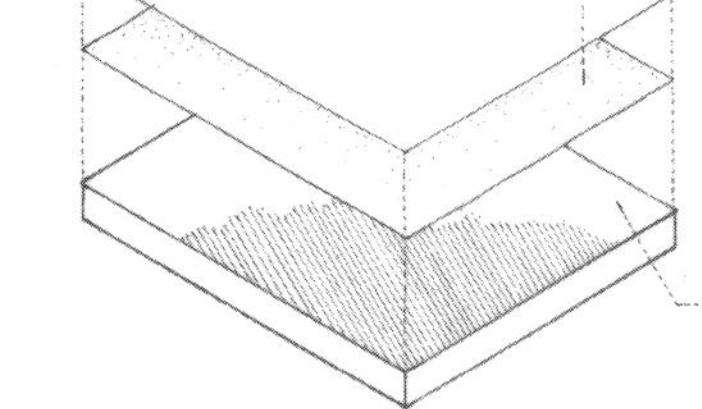

anticorrosive paint
A paint or primer specially formulated with rust-inhibiting pigments to prevent or reduce the corrosion of metal surfaces. Also called **rust-inhibiting paint**.

fire-retardant paint
A paint specially formulated with silicone, polyvinyl chloride, or other substance to reduce the flame-spread of a combustible material.

heat-resistant paint
A paint specially formulated with silicone resins to withstand high temperatures.

binder
The nonvolatile part of a paint vehicle that bonds particles of pigment into a cohesive film during the drying process.

solvent
The volatile part of a paint vehicle that evaporates during the drying process.

thinner
A volatile liquid used to dilute paint or varnish to the desired or proper consistency for ease in application.

mineral spirits
A volatile distillation of petroleum, used as a solvent and thinner for paints and varnishes.

turpentine
A colorless, volatile oil obtained by distilling oleoresin from various conifers and used as a thinner and solvent for paints and varnishes. Also called **oil of turpentine, spirits of turpentine**.

paint system
A combination of one or more coatings selected for compatibility with each other and the surface to which they are applied, as well as suitability for the expected exposure and desired decorative effect.

glaze coat
A thin coat of transparent color applied to enhance the color of a painted surface.

mistcoat
A thin, sometimes pigmented coat applied to a finish coat to improve its luster.

topcoat
The final coat of paint applied to a surface. Also called **finish coat**.

undercoat
A primer or intermediate coat applied to hide the color of the substrate and improve adhesion of the topcoat.

ground coat
A primer or basecoat of paint intended to show through a topcoat. Also called **ground color**.

basecoat
A first coat of paint or other liquid finish applied to a surface.

primer
A basecoat applied to a surface to improve the adhesion of subsequent coats of paint or varnish. Also called **prime coat**.

sealer
A basecoat applied to a surface to reduce the absorption of subsequent coats of paint or varnish, or to prevent bleeding through the finish coat.

pigment
A finely ground, insoluble substance suspended in a liquid vehicle to impart color and opacity to a paint.

+

vehicle
A liquid in which pigment is dispersed before being applied to a surface. to control consistency, adhesion, gloss, and durability.

drying oil
Any of various oily, organic liquids, as linseed oil, that oxidizes and hardens to form a tough elastic film when exposed in a thin layer to air.

oil paint
A paint in which the vehicle is a drying oil.

alkyd resin
Any of a group of synthetic resins derived from a polyvalent alcohol in reaction with an organic acid, used chiefly in adhesives and paints.

alkyd paint
A paint in which the vehicle is an alkyd resin.

epoxy paint
A paint having an epoxy resin as a binder for increased resistance to abrasion, corrosion, and chemicals.

latex
A water emulsion of synthetic rubber or plastic globules obtained by polymerization and used in paints and adhesives.

latex paint
A paint having a latex binder that coalesces as water evaporates from the emulsion. Also called **rubber-base paint, water-base paint**.

dye
A soluble coloring material that imparts color by absorption.

stain
A solution of dye or suspension of pigment in a vehicle, applied to penetrate and color a wood surface without obscuring the grain.

water stain
A penetrating stain made by dissolving dye in a water vehicle.

spirit stain
A penetrating stain made by dissolving dye in an alcohol or spirit vehicle.

penetrating stain
A stain that penetrates a wood surface, leaving a very thin film on the surface.

oil stain
A stain made by dissolving dye or suspending pigment in a drying oil or oil varnish vehicle.

pigmented stain
An oil stain containing pigments capable of obscuring the grain and texture of a wood surface. Also called **opaque stain**.

copal
A hard, lustrous resin obtained from various tropical trees, used chiefly in making varnishes.

varnish
A liquid preparation consisting of a resin dissolved in an oil (**oil varnish**) or in alcohol (**spirit varnish**), that when spread and allowed to dry forms a hard, lustrous, usually transparent coating.

spar varnish
A durable, weather-resistant varnish made from durable resins and linseed or tung oil. Also called **marine varnish**.

polyurethane varnish
An exceptionally hard, abrasion-resistant, and chemical-resistant varnish made from a plastic resin of the same name.

lac
A resinous secretion of the female of the lac insect, used in making shellac.

shellac
A spirit varnish made by dissolving purified lac flakes in denatured alcohol. Also called **shellac varnish**.

Chinese lacquer
A natural varnish obtained from an Asian sumac, used to produce a highly polished, lustrous surface on wood. Also called **Japanese lacquer**.

lacquer
Any of various clear or colored synthetic coatings consisting of nitrocellulose or other cellulose derivative dissolved in a solvent that dries by evaporation to form a high-gloss film.

PLASTER

A composition of gypsum or lime, water, sand, and sometimes hair or other fiber, applied in a pasty form to the surfaces of walls or ceilings in a plastic state and allowed to harden and dry.

gypsum plaster
A basecoat plaster made of calcined gypsum mixed with sand, water, and various additives to control its setting and working qualities.

calcined gypsum
Gypsum heated to drive off most of its chemically combined water.

plaster of Paris
Calcined gypsum in white, powdery form, containing no additives to control the set, used as a base for gypsum plaster, as an additive in lime plaster, and as a material for making ornamental casts.

gypsum
A soft mineral, hydrated calcium sulfate, used as a retarder in portland cement and in the making of gypsum plaster.

alabaster
A finely granular form of pure gypsum, often white and translucent, used for ornamental objects and work.

lime plaster
A mixture of lime, sand, and sometimes a fiber, used as a basecoat plaster.

cement temper
The addition of portland cement to lime plaster to improve its strength and durability.

three-coat plaster
Plasterwork applied in three successive coats, a scratch coat followed by a brown coat and a finish coat.

two-coat plaster
Plasterwork applied in two coats, a basecoat followed by a finish coat.

finish coat
The final coat of plaster, serving either as a finished surface or as a base for decoration.

skim coat
A thin leveling or finish coat of plaster.

brown coat
A roughly finished, leveling coat of plaster, either the second coat in three-coat plaster or the base coat in two-coat plaster applied over gypsum lath or masonry. Also called **floating coat.**

basecoat
Any plaster coat applied before the finish coat.

scratch coat
The first coat in three-coat plaster, which is scratched to provide a better bond for the second or brown coat.

gauged plaster
A finish coat in plastering, consisting of lime putty to which gauging plaster is added to control the setting time and counteract shrinkage.

gauging plaster
A specially ground gypsum plaster for mixing with lime putty, formulated to provide either a quick-set or a slow-set for a finish coat of plaster.

hard finish
A finish coat of lime putty and Keene's cement or gauging plaster, troweled to a smooth, dense finish.

lime putty
Quicklime slaked with sufficient water to form a thick paste. Also called **plasterer's putty.**

Keene's cement
Trademark for a brand of white anhydrous gypsum plaster that produces an exceptionally strong, dense, crack-resistant finish.

anhydrous
Having all water of crystallization removed.

white coat
A finish coat of lime putty and white gauging plaster, troweled to a smooth, dense finish.

veneer plaster
A ready-mixed gypsum plaster applied as a very thin, one- or two-coat finish over a veneer base. Also called **thin-coat plaster.**

acoustical plaster
A low-density plaster containing vermiculite or other porous material to enhance its ability to absorb sound.

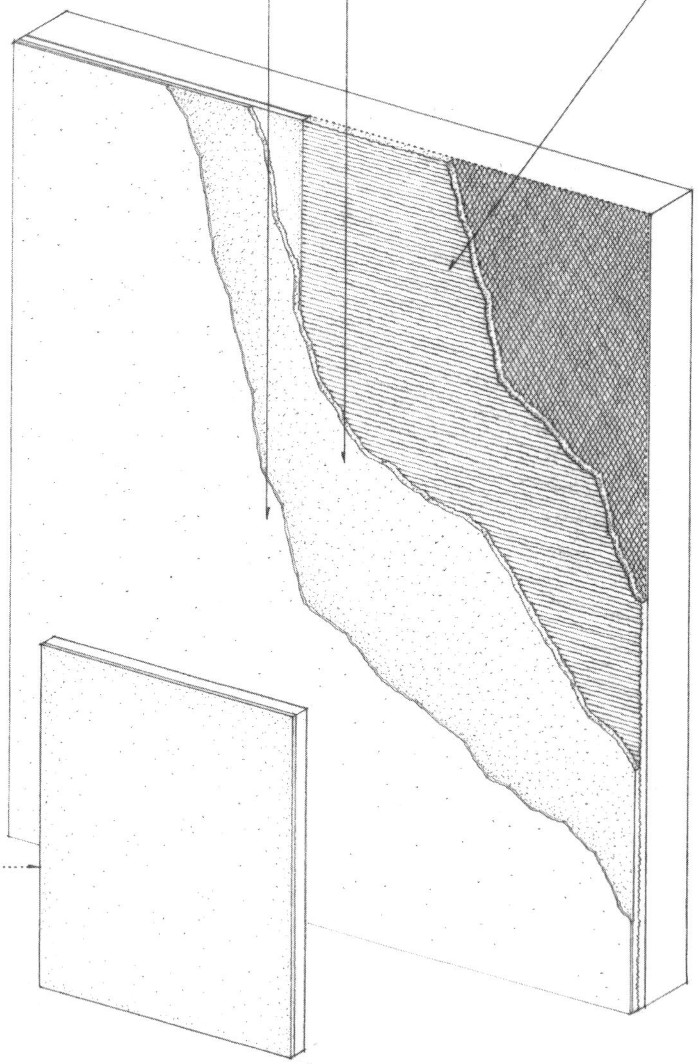

hardwall
A basecoat of neat gypsum plaster.

neat plaster
A gypsum basecoat plaster having no admixture except hair or other fiber, used for on-the-job mixing with aggregates.

wood-fibered plaster
A mill-mixed gypsum basecoat plaster containing coarse cellulose fibers for greater bulk, strength, and fire resistance, used neat or mixed with sand to obtain a basecoat of superior hardness.

bond plaster
A gypsum basecoat plaster containing a small amount of lime and chemical additives to improve the bond of succeeding coats to dense, nonporous surfaces.

gypsum-perlite plaster
A gypsum basecoat plaster containing perlite as an aggregate to reduce its weight and increase its thermal and fire resistance.

gypsum-vermiculite plaster
A gypsum basecoat plaster containing vermiculite as an aggregate to reduce its weight and increase its thermal and fire resistance.

ready-mixed plaster
Plaster that is formulated and dry-mixed by the manufacturer, requiring only the addition of water at the job site.

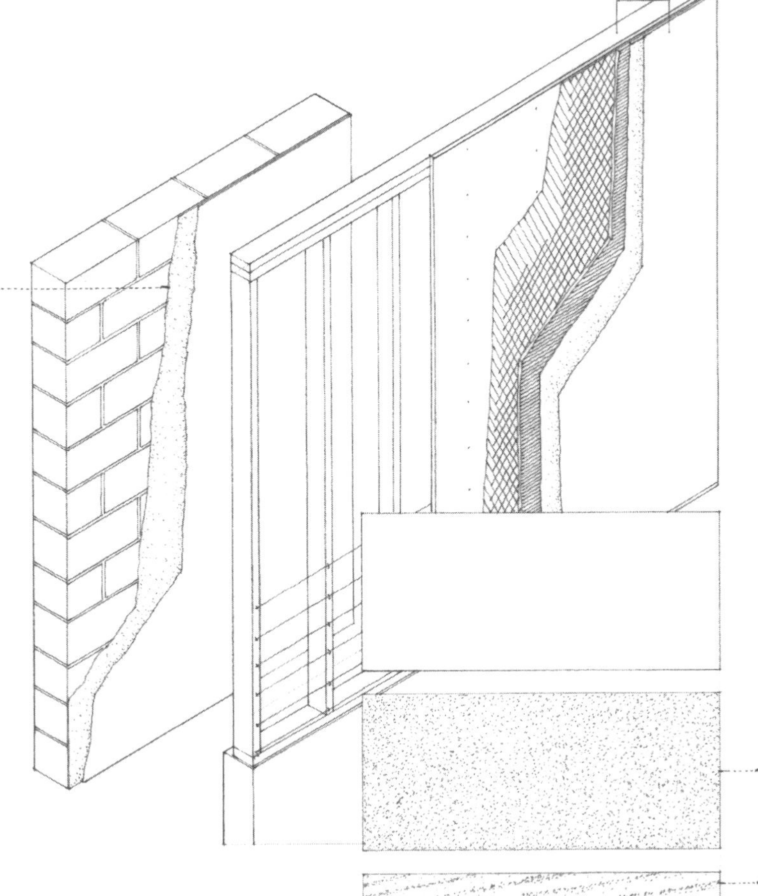

rendering coat
The first coat of plaster on a masonry wall. Also called **rough coat**.

spatter dash
A wet, rich mix of portland cement and sand thrown onto a smooth brick or concrete surface and allowed to harden to provide a key for a first coat of plaster.

key
A grooving or roughness applied to a surface to improve its bond with another surface.

stucco
A coarse plaster composed of portland or masonry cement, sand, and hydrated lime, mixed with water and applied in a plastic state to form a hard covering for exterior walls.

portland cement stucco
Stucco made with masonry cement or with portland cement mixed with less than 50% by volume of lime.

portland cement-lime stucco
Portland cement stucco to which lime is added in an amount greater than 50% by volume to improve the plasticity of the mix.

albarium
A stucco used in ancient times, made from powdered marble and lime mortar and often polished.

intonaco
A finish coat of plaster made with white marble dust to receive a fresco.

scagliola
Plasterwork imitating granite or marble.

sand-float finish
A textured finish coat of plaster containing sand, leveled and smoothed with a float.

float finish
A fine-textured stucco finish produced by smoothing with a carpet or rubber-faced float.

combed finish
A stucco finish produced by dragging a serrated tool across the stucco surface before it sets. Also called **dragged finish**.

dash-troweled finish
A stucco finish produced by troweling the high spots of a dashed stucco surface before it sets.

stipple-troweled finish
A stucco finish produced by troweling the high spots of a stippled stucco surface before it sets.

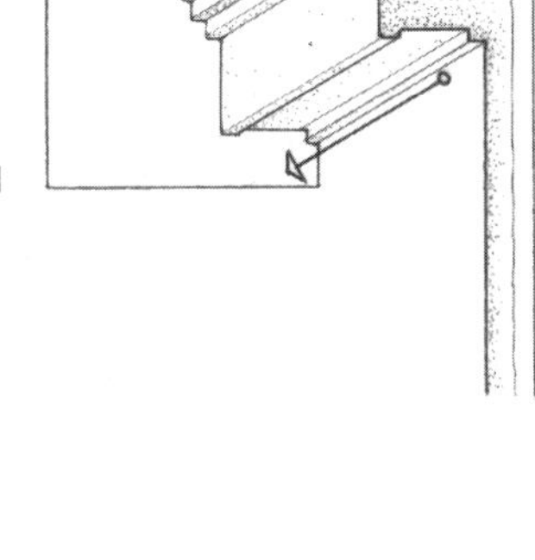

molding plaster
A plaster used in ornamental work, consisting of finely ground gypsum and hydrated lime.

running mold
A sheet-metal template cut to the desired profile, backed with wood, and pushed along between temporary grounds or rules to form a plaster molding along the angle between a wall and ceiling. Also called **horsed mold**.

horse
The wooden support for the sheet-metal template of a running mold.

daubing
The process of giving a wall a rough finish by throwing plaster against it.

pebble dash
An exterior wall finish produced by throwing and pressing small pebbles into unset stucco.

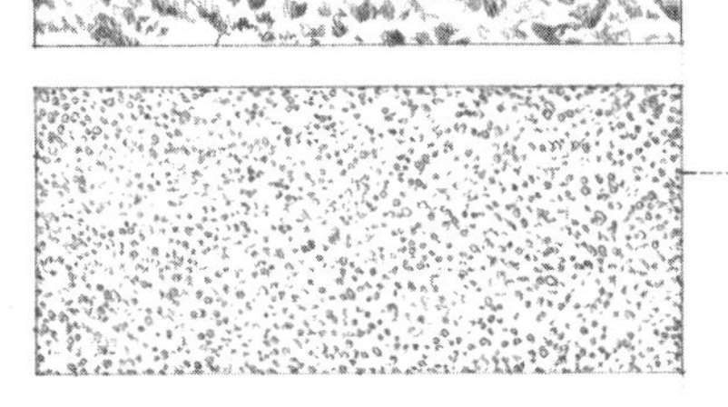

roughcast
An exterior wall finish composed of a stucco mixed with fine pebbles and dashed against a wall. Also called **spatter dash**.

pargeting
Fine ornamental plasterwork, esp. exterior plasterwork bearing designs in low relief. Also, **parget**.

lath
Any of a number of suitable surfaces for receiving plasterwork, as gypsum lath, metal lath, wood lath, masonry, or brickwork.

metal lath
A plaster base fabricated of expanded metal or of wire fabric, painted or galvanized for corrosion resistance.

expanded-metal lath
Metal lath fabricated by slitting and expanding a sheet of steel alloy to form a stiff network with diamond-shaped openings.

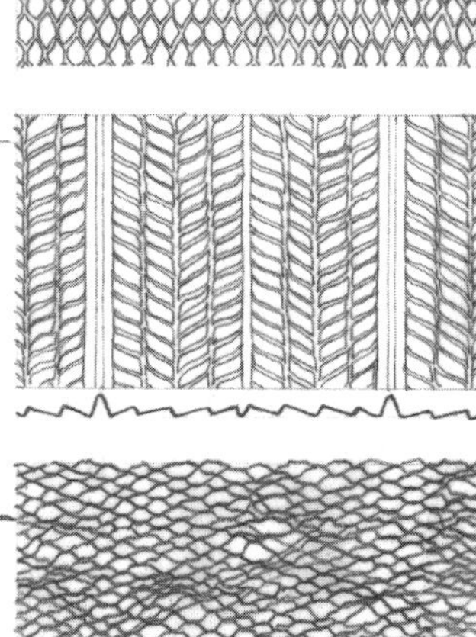

rib lath
An expanded-metal lath having V-shaped ribs to provide greater stiffness and permit wider spacing of the supporting framing members.

self-centering lath
A rib lath used over steel joists as formwork for concrete slabs, or as lathing in solid plaster partitions.

self-furring lath
Expanded-metal, welded-wire, or woven-wire lath that is dimpled to space itself from the supporting surface, creating a space for the keying of plaster or stucco.

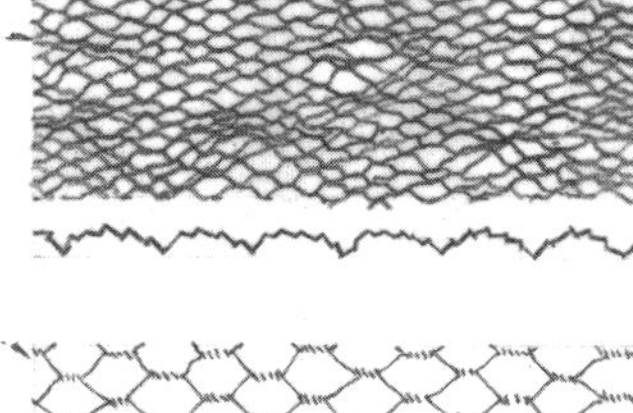

wire lath
Welded- or woven-wire fabric, usually with a paper backing, used as a base for plaster or stucco.

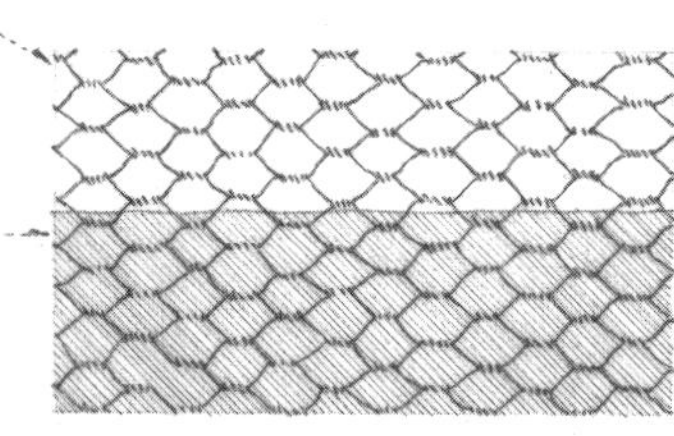

paper-backed lath
Expanded-metal or wire lath having a backing of perforated or building paper, used as a base for plaster or stucco.

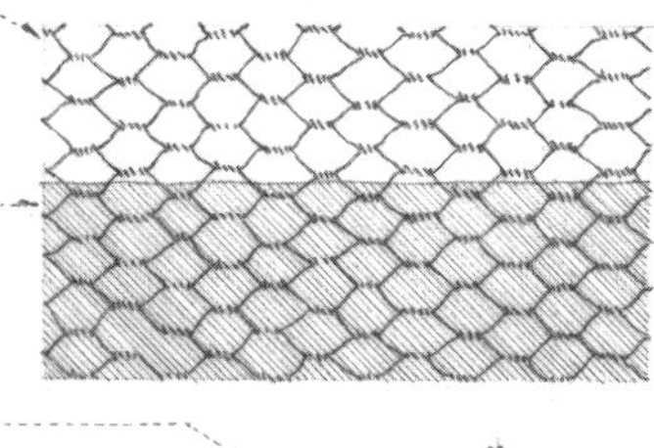

corner lath
A strip of expanded-metal lath bent to form a 90° angle, used at an internal corner to prevent cracks in plastering. Also called **corner reinforcement**.

strip lath
A narrow strip of expanded-metal lath for reinforcing joints in gypsum lath or junctures between different types of plaster bases.

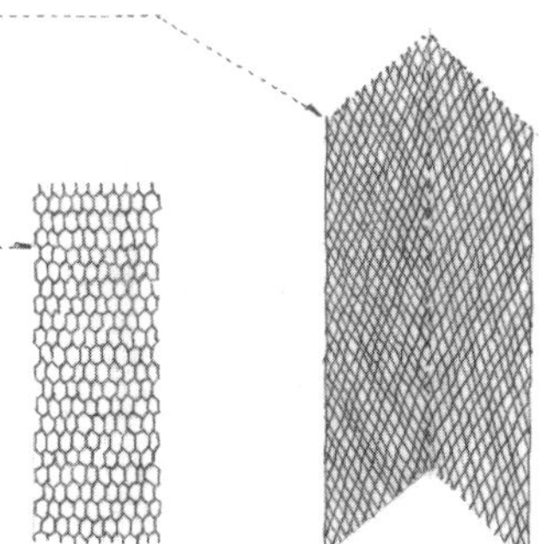

scrim
Coarse cotton, fiberglass, or metal mesh, used for bridging and reinforcing a joint or as a base for plastering or painting.

gypsum lath
Gypsum board having an air-entrained core faced with absorbent paper, used as a base for plaster. Also called **rock lath**.

perforated gypsum lath
Gypsum lath punched with small holes to provide a mechanical key for plaster.

insulating gypsum lath
Gypsum lath having an aluminum foil backing that serves as a vapor retarder and reflective thermal insulator.

veneer base
Gypsum lath having a special paper facing for receiving veneer plaster.

wood lath
A thin, narrow strip of wood used with other strips to form latticework, a backing for plaster or stucco, or a support for slates or other roofing material.

furring
The attaching of wood strips or metal channels to a wall or other surface, as to provide an even base for lath or a finish material, or to provide an air space between a wall and a finish material.

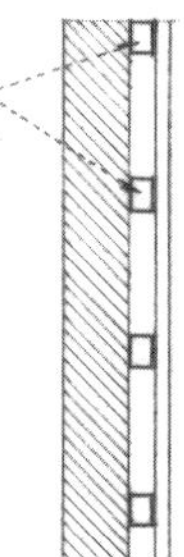

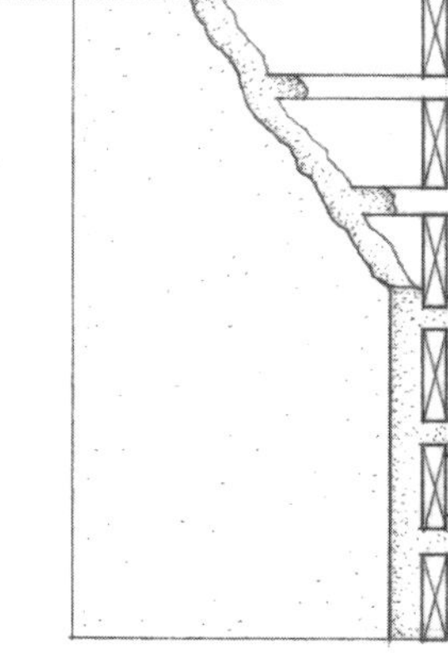

plaster bond
The adhesion of plaster to its base produced by mechanical or chemical means.

mechanical bond
The physical keying of a plaster coat to a plaster base or with another plaster coat roughened by scoring.

bonding agent
A chemical substance applied to a suitable substrate to improves its bond with a succeeding layer.

suction
The absorption of water from a finish coat of plaster by the basecoat or gypsum lath, resulting in a better bond.

ground
A strip of wood or a metal bead used at an opening as a guide for plastering to a given thickness and as a stop for the plasterwork.

screed
A strip of wood, plaster, or metal applied to a surface to be plastered to serve as a guide for making a true surface and plastering to a given thickness.

base screed
A preformed metal screed for separating a plastered surface from another material along the base of a wall.

vented screed
A perforated metal screed for venting a concealed space behind a plastered surface.

expansion screed
A preformed metal screed applied over joints in gypsum lath to control cracking.

control joint
A preformed metal strip installed to relieve shrinkage, temperature, or structural stresses within a large plastered or stuccoed area.

corner bead
A preformed metal strip having two expanded or perforated flanges and variously shaped projecting noses, used as a ground and to strengthen and protect an external angle in plasterwork or a gypsum board surface. Also called **angle bead**.

bullnose corner bead
A corner bead having a rounded edge.

arch corner bead
A flexible corner bead for forming and reinforcing the curved portion of an arched opening.

casing bead
A preformed metal strip having an expanded or perforated flange and variously shaped ends, used as a ground and to strengthen and reinforce the edges of plasterwork or a gypsum board surface.

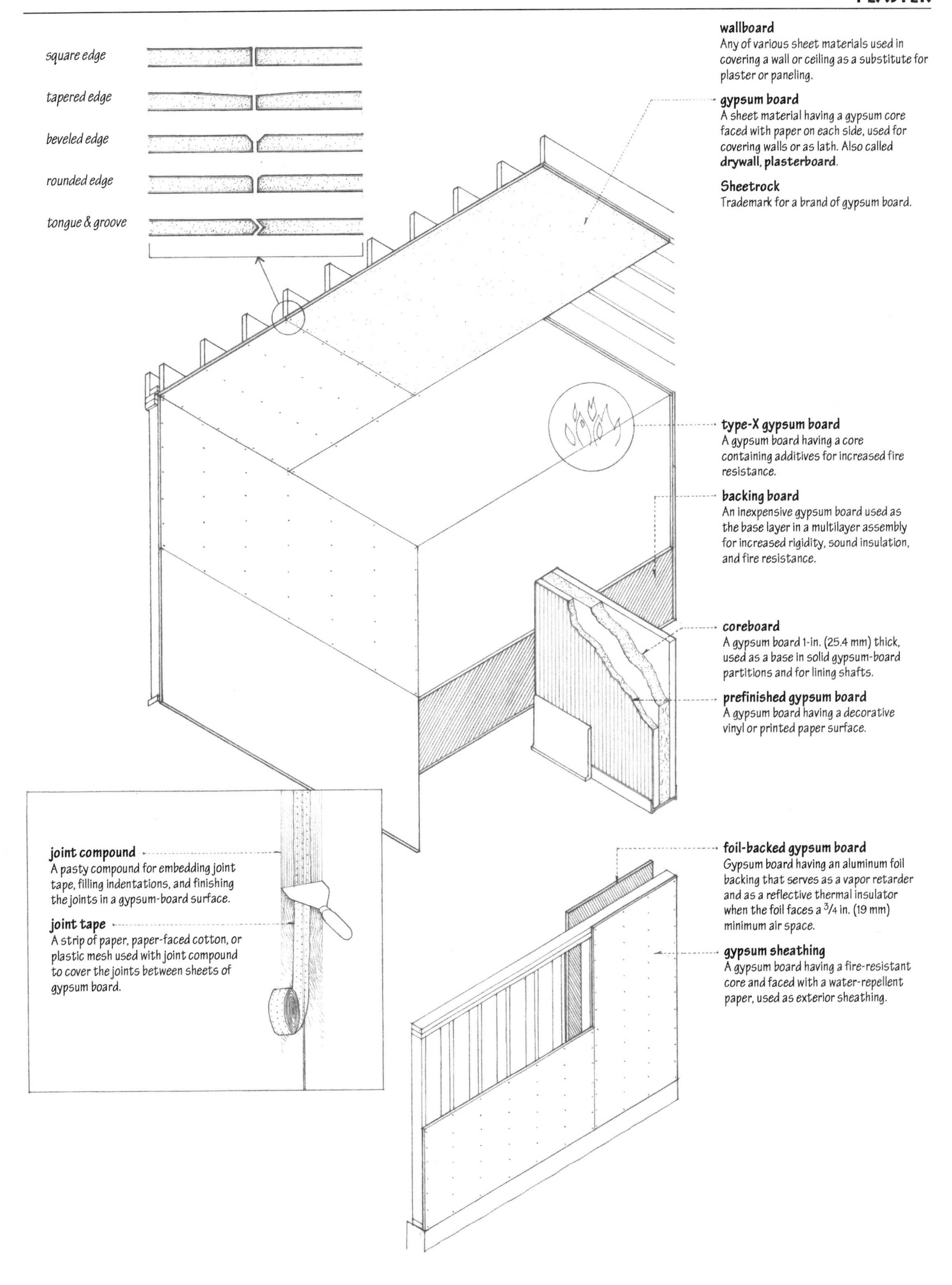

wallboard
Any of various sheet materials used in covering a wall or ceiling as a substitute for plaster or paneling.

gypsum board
A sheet material having a gypsum core faced with paper on each side, used for covering walls or as lath. Also called **drywall, plasterboard**.

Sheetrock
Trademark for a brand of gypsum board.

type-X gypsum board
A gypsum board having a core containing additives for increased fire resistance.

backing board
An inexpensive gypsum board used as the base layer in a multilayer assembly for increased rigidity, sound insulation, and fire resistance.

coreboard
A gypsum board 1-in. (25.4 mm) thick, used as a base in solid gypsum-board partitions and for lining shafts.

prefinished gypsum board
A gypsum board having a decorative vinyl or printed paper surface.

joint compound
A pasty compound for embedding joint tape, filling indentations, and finishing the joints in a gypsum-board surface.

joint tape
A strip of paper, paper-faced cotton, or plastic mesh used with joint compound to cover the joints between sheets of gypsum board.

foil-backed gypsum board
Gypsum board having an aluminum foil backing that serves as a vapor retarder and as a reflective thermal insulator when the foil faces a 3/4 in. (19 mm) minimum air space.

gypsum sheathing
A gypsum board having a fire-resistant core and faced with a water-repellent paper, used as exterior sheathing.

Any of numerous synthetic or natural organic materials that are mostly thermoplastic or thermosetting polymers of high molecular weight and that can be molded, extruded, or drawn into objects, films, or filaments.

polymerization
A chemical reaction in which the molecules of a monomer combine to form larger molecules that contain repeating structural units of the original molecules.

monomer
A molecule of low molecular weight that can be chemically bound as a unit of a polymer.

polymer
A compound of high molecular weight formed by polymerization and consisting essentially of repeating structural units.

high polymer
A polymer consisting of molecules that are large multiples of monomers.

copolymer
A compound of high molecular weight formed by polymerizing two or more different monomers together.

casting
A method of shaping a plastic object by pouring the material into a mold and allowing it to harden without the use of pressure.

blow molding
A method of forming hollow ware by injecting air under pressure into a molten mass, as of a thermoplastic or glass, and shaping the material within a mold.

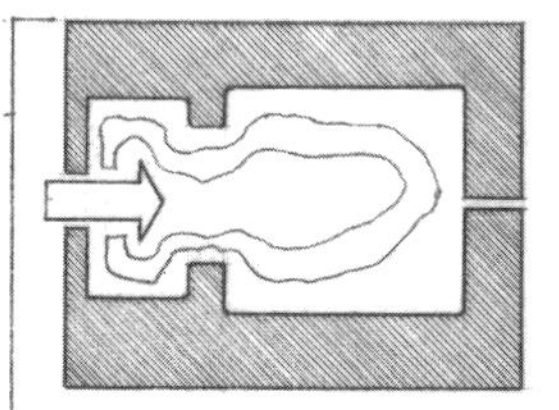

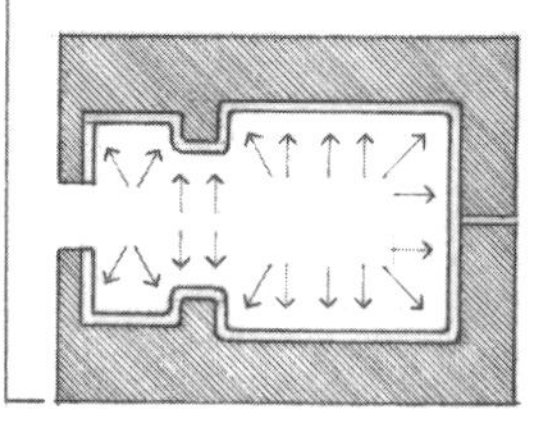

injection molding
A method of forming a thermoplastic, thermoset, metal, or ceramic material by rendering it fluid in a heating chamber and then forcing it under high pressure into a closed mold.

compression molding
A method of forming thermosetting plastic by closing a mold on it, forming the material by heat and pressure.

transfer molding
A method of forming thermosetting plastic by softening it in one chamber before it is forced into an adjacent mold where it is cured under heat and pressure.

thermoforming
A method of shaping a thermoplastic sheet by heating and forcing it against the contours of a mold by heat and pressure.

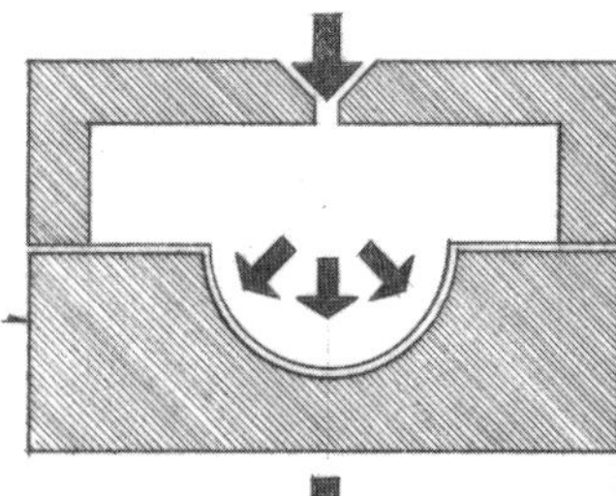

pressure forming
A method of thermoforming a plastic sheet by forcing it against the contours of a mold with compressed air.

vacuum forming
A method of thermoforming a plastic sheet by evacuating the space between the sheet and the contours of a mold.

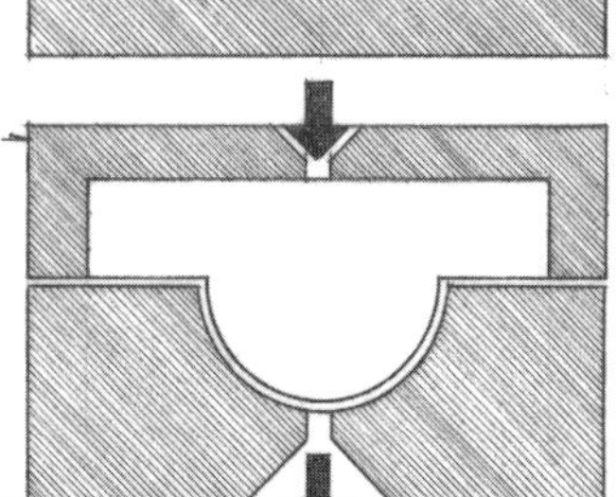

resin
Any of numerous solid or semisolid organic substances prepared by polymerization and used with fillers, stabilizers, and other components to form plastics.

filler
A relatively inert substance added to modify the bulk, strength, heat resistance, electrical resistance, or working properties of a resin.

stabilizer
A substance added to prevent or retard the degradation of a plastic when exposed to the ultraviolet radiation or other environmental conditions.

plasticizer
Any of various substances added to a resin to increase its workability and flexibility.

catalyst
A substance that causes or accelerates a chemical reaction without itself undergoing a permanent change in composition.

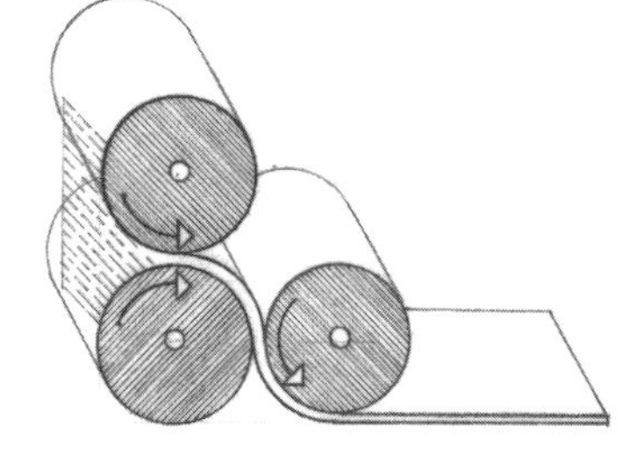

calendering
A method of producing plastic film or sheeting by passing the material between a series of revolving, heated rollers.

sheeting
A thin form of plastic, having a thickness very small in proportion to its length and width.

film
Sheeting having a nominal thickness not greater than 10 mils.

thermoplastic
A plastic capable of softening or fusing when heated without a change in any inherent properties, and of hardening again when cooled.

acrylic resin
Any of a class of thermoplastic resins used for casting or molding plastic parts that are exceptionally transparent, tough, and resistant to weather and chemicals, or as the main ingredient in coatings, adhesives, and caulking compounds.

Lucite
Trademark for a brand of transparent acrylic resin.

Plexiglas
Trademark for a brand of light, transparent, weather-resistant acrylic resin.

polycarbonate
A tough, transparent thermoplastic characterized by its high-impact strength and used for lighting fixtures, safety glazing, and hardware.

Lexan
Trademark for a brand of tough polycarbonate used for shatterproof windows.

polyethylene
A tough, light, and flexible thermoplastic used esp. in the form of sheeting and film for packaging, dampproofing, and as a vapor retarder. Also called **polythene**.

polypropylene
A tough, thermoplastic that is resistant to heat and chemicals and used for pipe fittings, electrical insulation, and carpeting fibers.

polystyrene
A hard, tough, stable thermoplastic that is easily colored and molded, expanded, or rolled into sheeting.

acrylonitrile-butadiene-styrene
A thermoplastic used for making plastic pipes and hardware products that are tough, rigid, and resistant to heat and chemicals. Abbr.: **ABS**

vinyl
Any of various tough, flexible plastics made from polyvinyl resin.

polyvinyl resin
Any of a class of thermoplastic resins formed by polymerizing or copolymerizing a vinyl compound. Also called **vinyl resin**.

polyvinyl chloride
A white, water-insoluble thermoplastic widely used in the manufacture of floor coverings, insulation, and piping. Abbr.: **PVC**

polyvinyl butyral
A thermoplastic resin used chiefly as the interlayer of safety glass.

nylon
Any of a class of thermoplastics characterized by extreme toughness, strength, and elasticity and capable of being extruded into filaments, fibers, and sheets.

thermosetting plastic
A plastic that becomes permanently rigid when heated and cannot be softened again. Also called **thermoset**.

polyurethane
Any of various thermoplastic or thermosetting resins used in flexible and rigid foams, elastomers, and resins for sealants, adhesives, and coatings.

polyester
Any of a group of thermosetting resins used in the manufacture of plastics and textile fibers.

fiberglass-reinforced plastic
A polyester reinforced with glass fibers and used in translucent roofs and skylights, facings for sandwich panels, and molded plumbing fixtures.

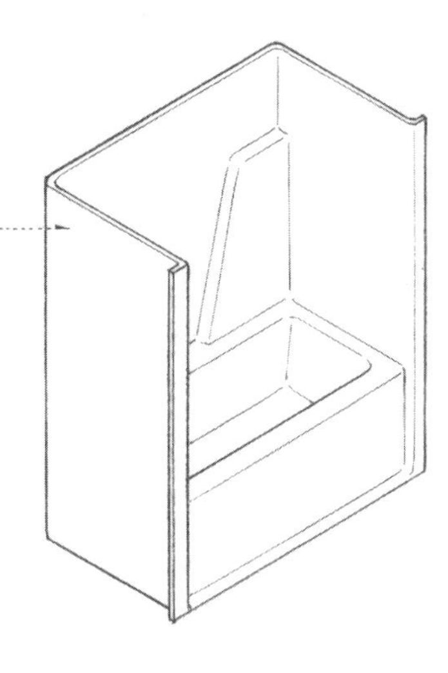

Dacron
Trademark for a brand of strong, wrinkle-resistant polyester fiber.

Mylar
Trademark for a brand of strong, thin polyester film used in photography, recording tapes, and electrical insulation.

epoxy resin
Any of various thermosetting resins capable of forming tight cross-linked polymer structures characterized by toughness, strong adhesion, and high corrosion and chemical resistance, used esp. in surface coatings and adhesives.

melamine resin
Any of a class of thermosetting resins formed by the interaction of melamine and formaldehyde and used for molded products, adhesives, and surface coatings.

phenolic resin
Any of a class of hard, heat-resistant thermosetting resins formed by the condensation of phenol with formaldehyde and used for molded products, adhesives, and surface coatings. Also called **phenoplast**.

Bakelite
Trademark for a brand of dark phenolic resin, invented by Dr. Leo Baekeland in 1916, and used for telephone receivers, radio cabinets, electric insulators, and molded plastic hardware.

urea-formaldehyde resin
Any of various thermosetting synthetic resin made by condensing urea with formaldehyde and used in appliance housings, electrical devices, adhesives, and surface coatings.

postforming
A method of shaping a fully or partially cured thermosetting laminate over a mold by heat and pressure.

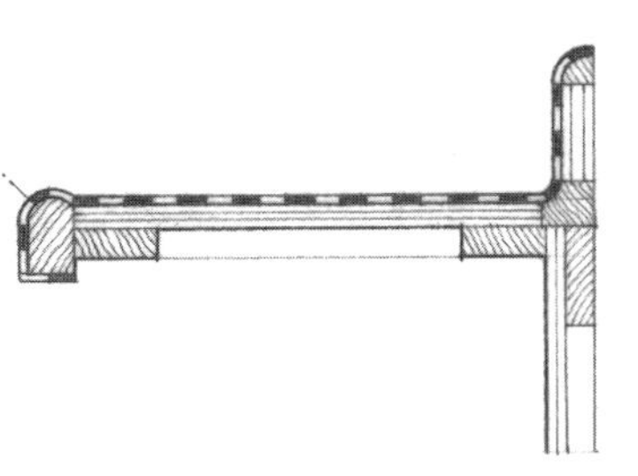

service temperature
The maximum temperature at which a plastic can be continuously employed without a noticeable reduction in any of its inherent properties.

softening point
The temperature at which a plastic changes from a rigid to a soft state.

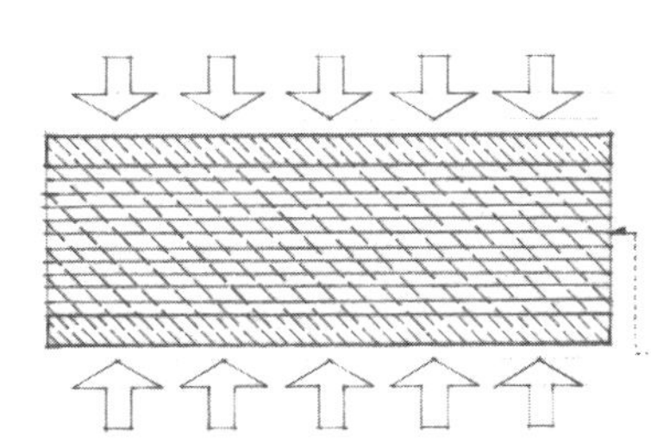

laminate
A product made by uniting two or more layers of material by an adhesive or other means, as plywood and plastic laminate.

plastic laminate
A hard surfacing material consisting of superposed layers of paper impregnated with melamine and phenolic resins, fused together under heat and pressure.

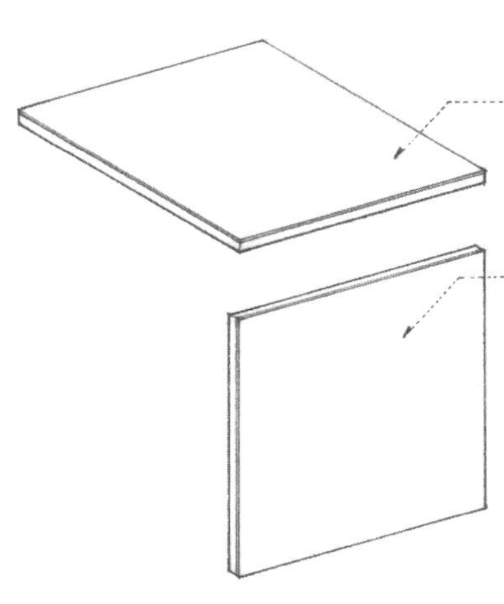

high-pressure laminate
A plastic laminate molded and cured in the range of pressures from 1,200 to 2,000 psi (84 to 140 kg per sq. cm), used for surfacing countertops and cabinetry.

low-pressure laminate
A plastic laminate molded and cured with a maximum pressure of 400 psi (28 kg per sq. m), used in vertical and low-wear applications.

Formica
Trademark for a brand of plastic laminate.

rubber
A material made by chemically treating and toughening natural rubber, valued for its elasticity, nonconduction of electricity, and resistance to shock and moisture.

natural rubber
A highly elastic solid substance, essentially a polymer of isoprene, obtained by coagulating the milky juice of rubber trees and plants. Also called **india rubber**.

foam rubber
A light, spongy, cellular rubber made by foaming latex before vulcanization.

vulcanization
The treatment of rubber with sulfur and heat to impart greater elasticity, strength, and durability.

synthetic rubber
An elastomer similar to natural rubber in properties and uses, produced by the polymerization of an unsaturated hydrocarbon, as butylene or isoprene, or by the copolymerization of hydrocarbons with styrene or butadiene.

elastomer
Any of various polymers having the elastic properties of natural rubber, as butyl rubber or neoprene.

butyl rubber
A synthetic rubber having exceptional resistance to sunlight and unusually low gaseous permeability, produced by polymerizing butylene and used in roofing membranes and waterproofing barriers.

Butyl
Trademark for a brand of butyl rubber.

neoprene
A synthetic rubber characterized by superior resistance to oils and sunlight, and used in paints, roofing membranes, flashing, gaskets, and bearings.

silicone rubber
A rubber made from silicone elastomers and noted for its retention of flexibility, resilience, and tensile strength over a wide temperature range.

silicone
Any of a group of polymers containing alternating silicon and oxygen atoms, characterized by thermal stability, chemical inertness, and extreme water repellence, and used in adhesives, lubricants, protective coatings, and synthetic rubber.

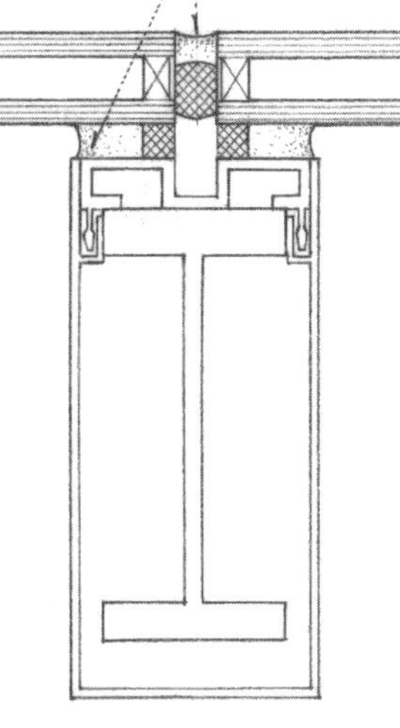

PLATE

A rigid, planar, usually monolithic structure that disperses applied loads in a multidirectional pattern, with the loads generally following the shortest and stiffest routes to the supports.

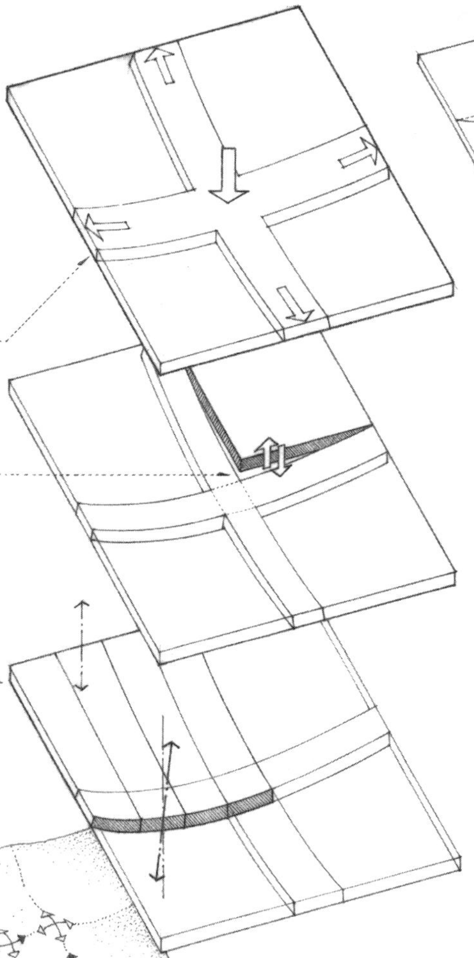

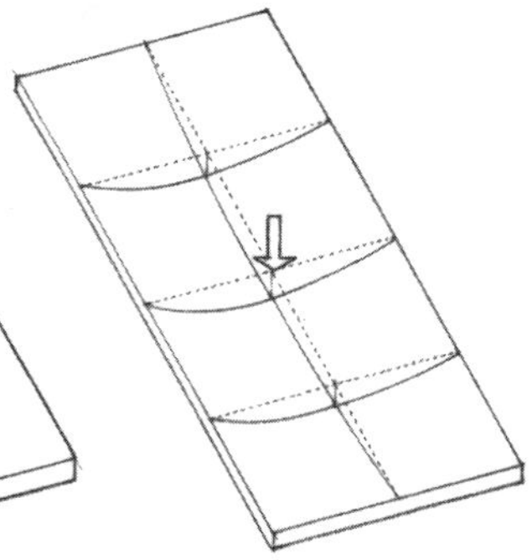

plate action
The manner in which an applied load is transmitted to the supports of a plate in a multidirectional pattern.

A plate can be envisioned as a series of adjacent beam strips interconnected continuously along their lengths.

As an applied load is transmitted to the supports through bending of one beam strip, the load is distributed over the entire plate by vertical shear transmitted from the deflected strip to adjacent strips.

The bending of one beam strip also causes twisting of transverse strips, whose torsional resistance increases the overall stiffness of the plate. Therefore, while bending and shear transfer an applied load in the direction of the loaded beam strip, shear and twisting transfer the load at right angles to the loaded strip.

A plate should be square or nearly square to ensure that it behaves as a two-way structure. As a plate becomes more rectangular than square, the two-way action decreases and a one-way system spanning the shorter direction develops since the shorter plate strips are stiffer and carry a greater portion of the load.

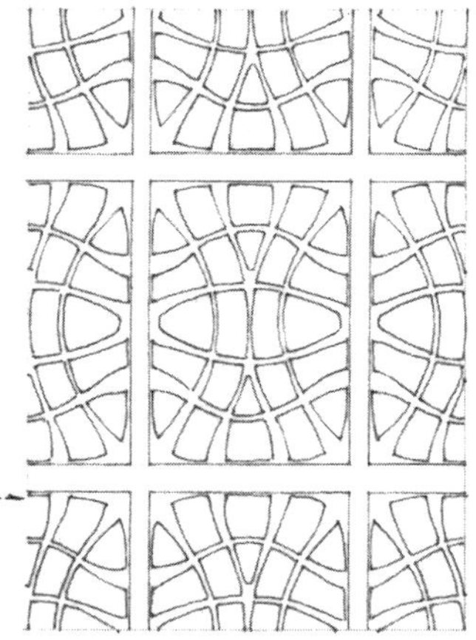

continuous plate
A plate extending as a structural unit over three or more supports in a given direction. A continuous plate is subject to lower bending moments than a series of discrete, simply supported plates.

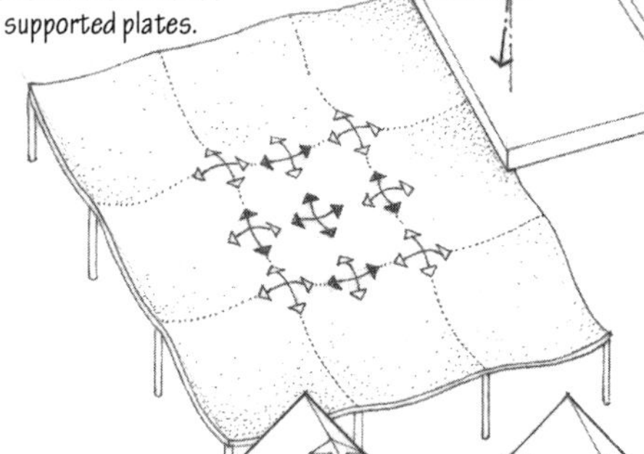

isostatic plate
A plate reinforced by a grid of curved ribs which follow the isostatics of the structure.

isostatics
Lines of principal stress indicating the flow of bending stresses and along which torsional shear stresses are zero.

folded plate
A plate structure composed of thin, deep elements joined rigidly along their boundaries and forming sharp angles to brace each other against lateral buckling. The resulting stiffness of the cross section enables a folded plate to span relatively long distances.

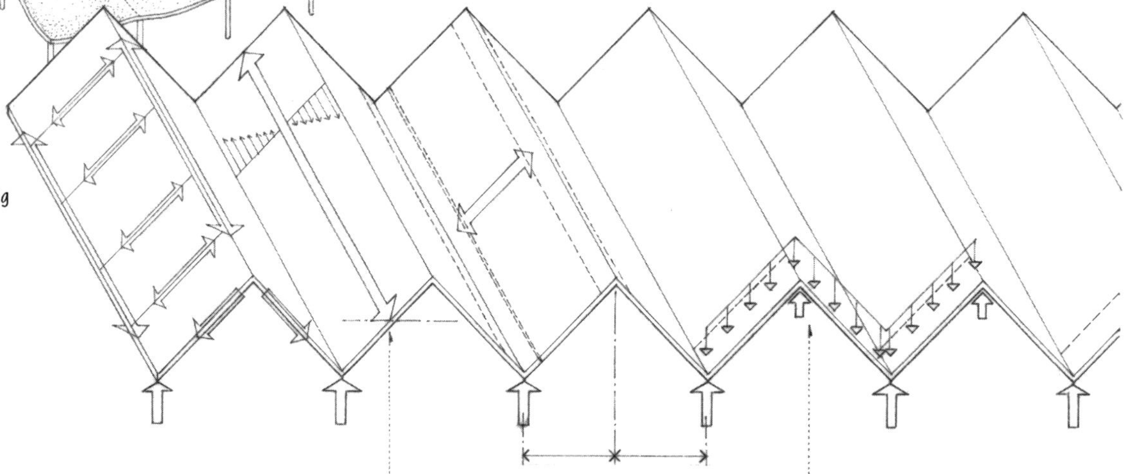

Each plane behaves as a beam in the longitudinal direction.

In the short direction, the span is reduced by each fold acting as a rigid support.

Transverse strips behave as a continuous beam supported at fold points.

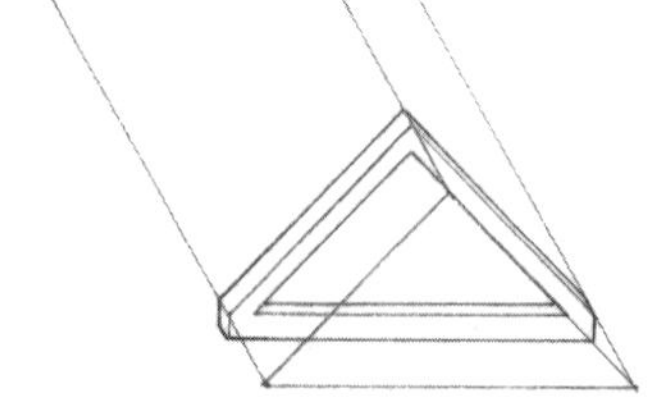

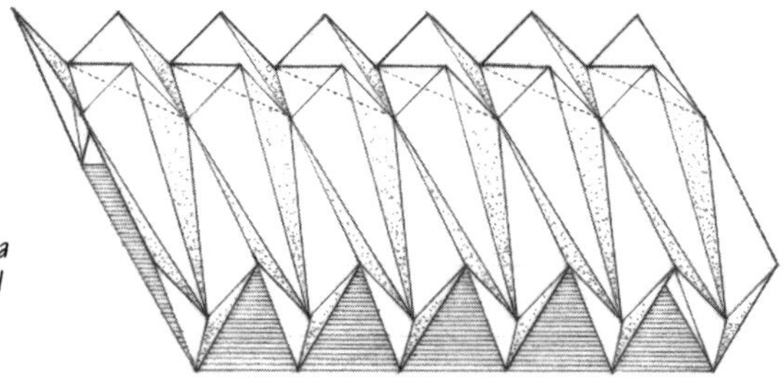

Vertical diaphragms or rigid frames stiffen a folded plate against deformation of the fold profile.

skew grid
A grid structure of beams or flat trusses running obliquely to the sides of the base rectangle in order to equalize their spans and stiffnesses. The shorter spans at the corners result in additional stiffness.

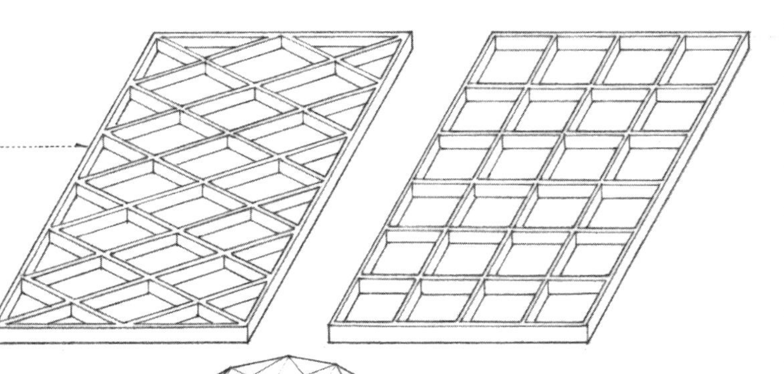

grid structure
A framework of crisscrossing beams connected at their intersections by rigid joints and dispersing an applied load in two directions according to the physical properties and dimensions of the beam elements.

All beam elements participate in carrying a load through a combination of bending and twisting. If two beams at right angles to each other are identical, they share an applied load equally in bending. If the beams have different lengths, however, the shorter beam carries more of the load since the stiffness of a beam is inversely proportional to the cube of its length and a load generally follows the path of least resistance to supports. For example, if two beams have a span ratio of 1:2, their stiffnesses will have a ratio of 1:8. Consequently, the shorter beam will carry $^8/_9$ of the load. The torsional resistance of beams against the twisting induced by the bending of a transverse beam increases the stiffness of the grid.

lamella roof
A vaulted roof composed of lamellae forming a crisscross pattern of parallel arches skewed with respect to the sides of the covered space.

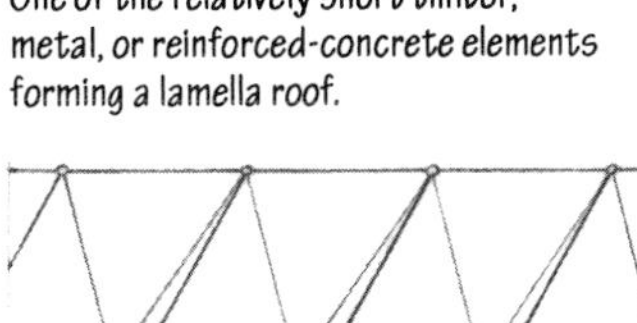

lamella
One of the relatively short timber, metal, or reinforced-concrete elements forming a lamella roof.

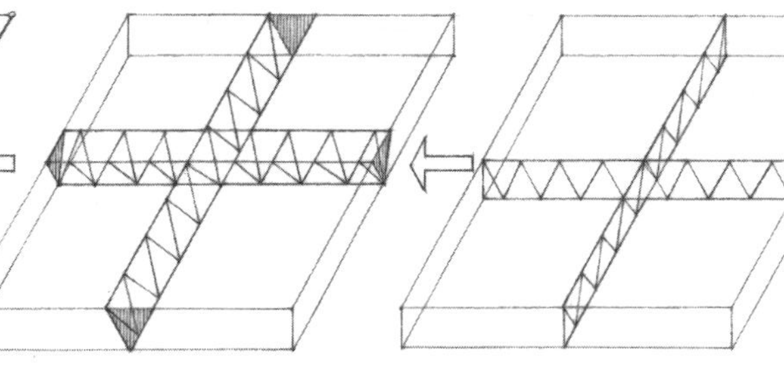

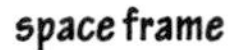

space frame
A three-dimensional structural frame based on the rigidity of the triangle and composed of linear elements subject only to axial tension or compression. The simplest spatial unit of a space frame is a tetrahedron having 4 joints and 6 structural members. As with plate structures, the supporting bay for a space frame should be square or nearly square to ensure that it acts as a two-way structure. Also called **space truss**.

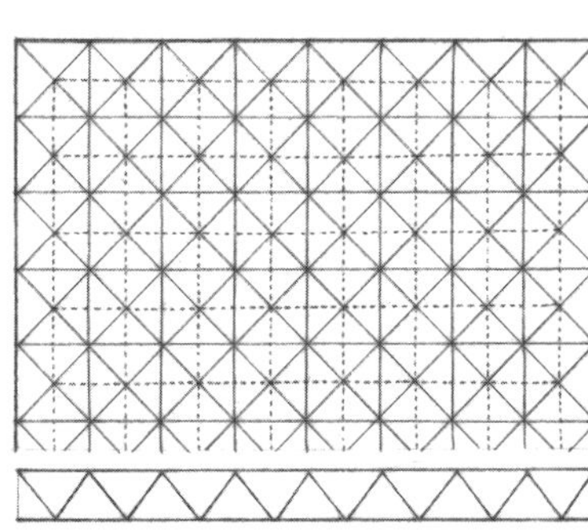

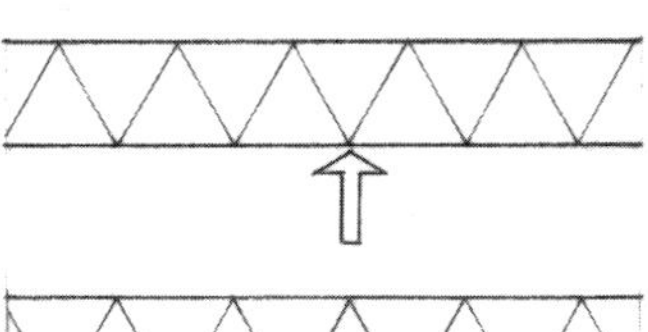

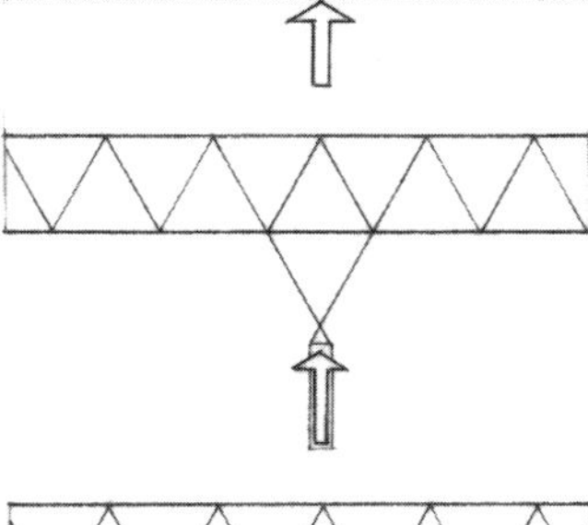

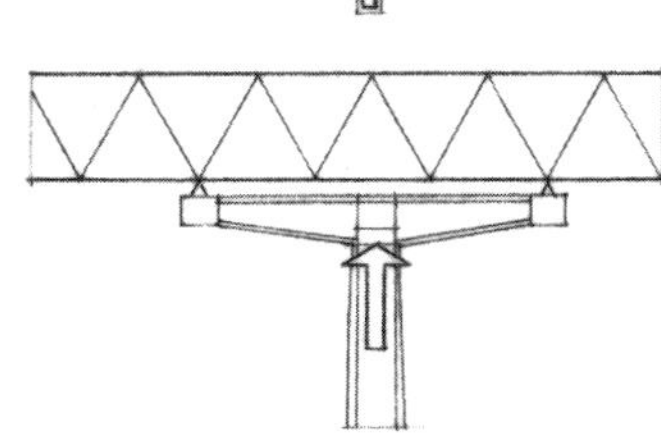

Increasing the bearing area of the supports increases the number of members into which shear is transferred and reduces the forces in the members.

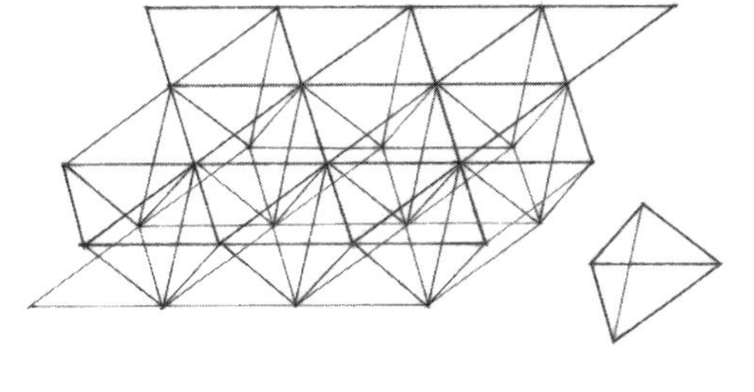

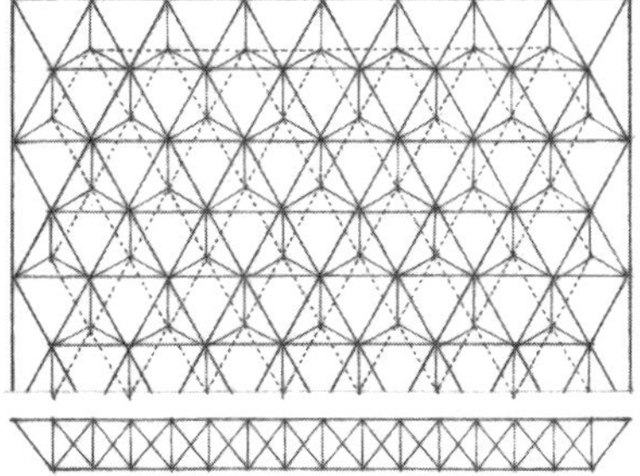

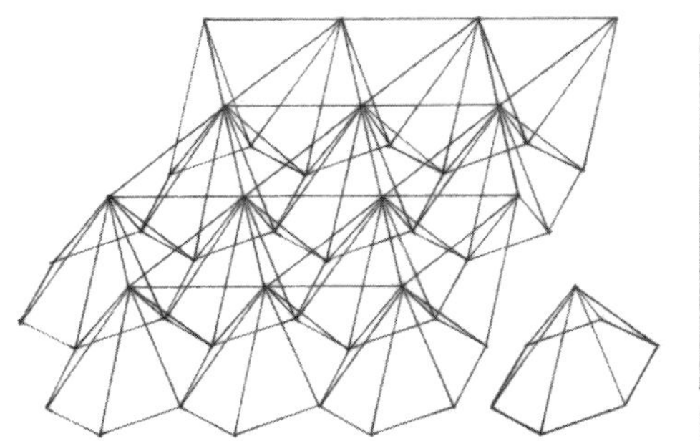

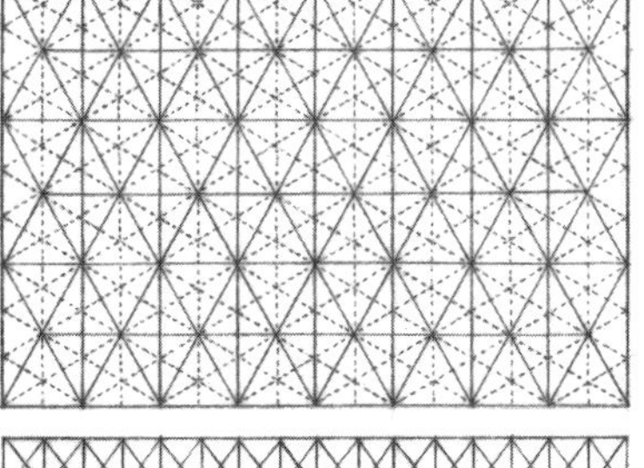

PLUMBING

The system of pipes, valves, fixtures, and other apparatus of a water supply or sewage system.

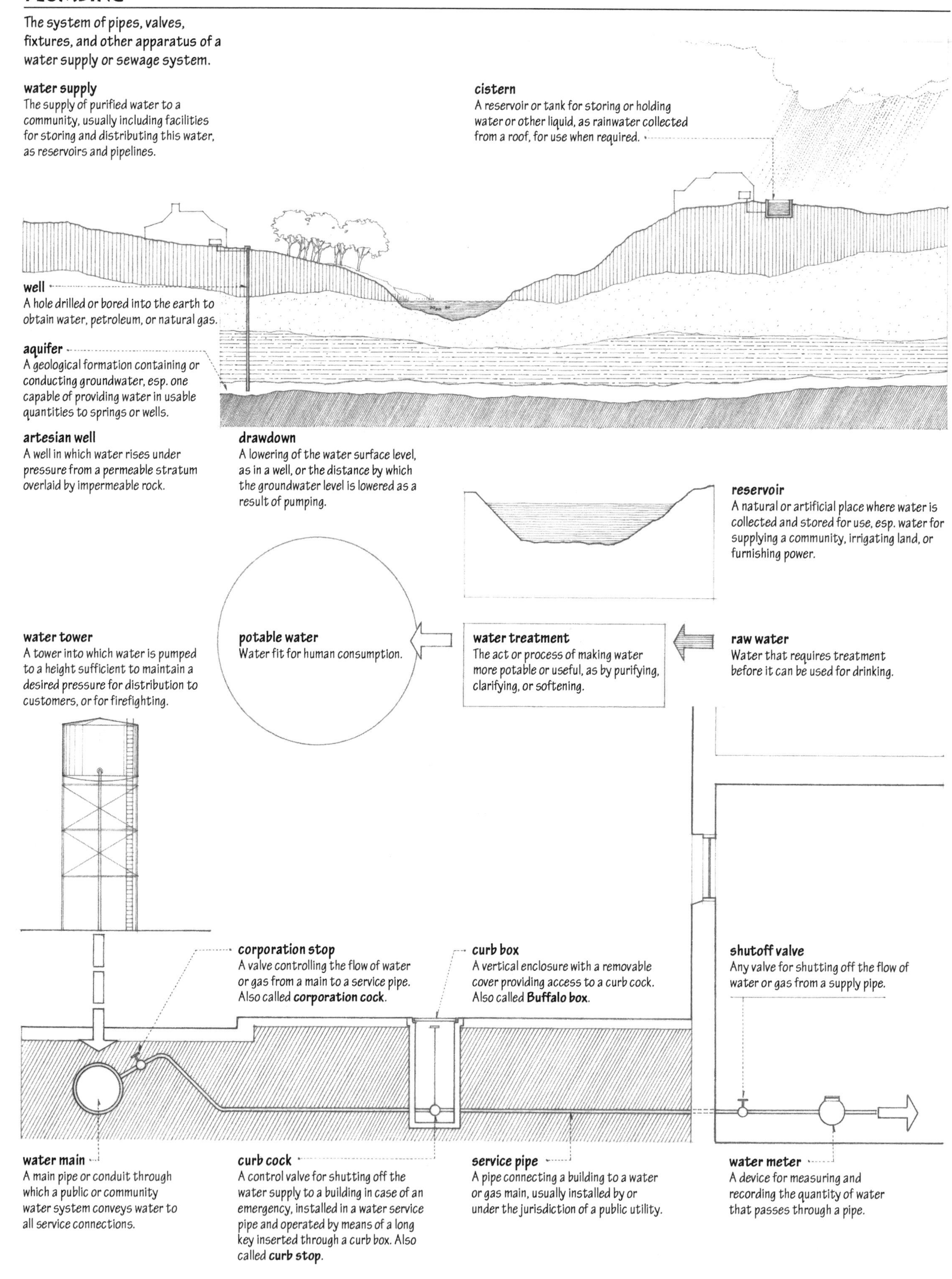

water supply
The supply of purified water to a community, usually including facilities for storing and distributing this water, as reservoirs and pipelines.

cistern
A reservoir or tank for storing or holding water or other liquid, as rainwater collected from a roof, for use when required.

well
A hole drilled or bored into the earth to obtain water, petroleum, or natural gas.

aquifer
A geological formation containing or conducting groundwater, esp. one capable of providing water in usable quantities to springs or wells.

artesian well
A well in which water rises under pressure from a permeable stratum overlaid by impermeable rock.

drawdown
A lowering of the water surface level, as in a well, or the distance by which the groundwater level is lowered as a result of pumping.

reservoir
A natural or artificial place where water is collected and stored for use, esp. water for supplying a community, irrigating land, or furnishing power.

water tower
A tower into which water is pumped to a height sufficient to maintain a desired pressure for distribution to customers, or for firefighting.

potable water
Water fit for human consumption.

water treatment
The act or process of making water more potable or useful, as by purifying, clarifying, or softening.

raw water
Water that requires treatment before it can be used for drinking.

corporation stop
A valve controlling the flow of water or gas from a main to a service pipe. Also called **corporation cock**.

curb box
A vertical enclosure with a removable cover providing access to a curb cock. Also called **Buffalo box**.

shutoff valve
Any valve for shutting off the flow of water or gas from a supply pipe.

water main
A main pipe or conduit through which a public or community water system conveys water to all service connections.

curb cock
A control valve for shutting off the water supply to a building in case of an emergency, installed in a water service pipe and operated by means of a long key inserted through a curb box. Also called **curb stop**.

service pipe
A pipe connecting a building to a water or gas main, usually installed by or under the jurisdiction of a public utility.

water meter
A device for measuring and recording the quantity of water that passes through a pipe.

water system
A system of pipes, valves, and fixtures for distributing and using water in a building.

gravity water system
A water supply and distribution system in which the water source is set at a height sufficient to maintain adequate supply pressure throughout the water distribution system. Also called **downfeed distribution system**.

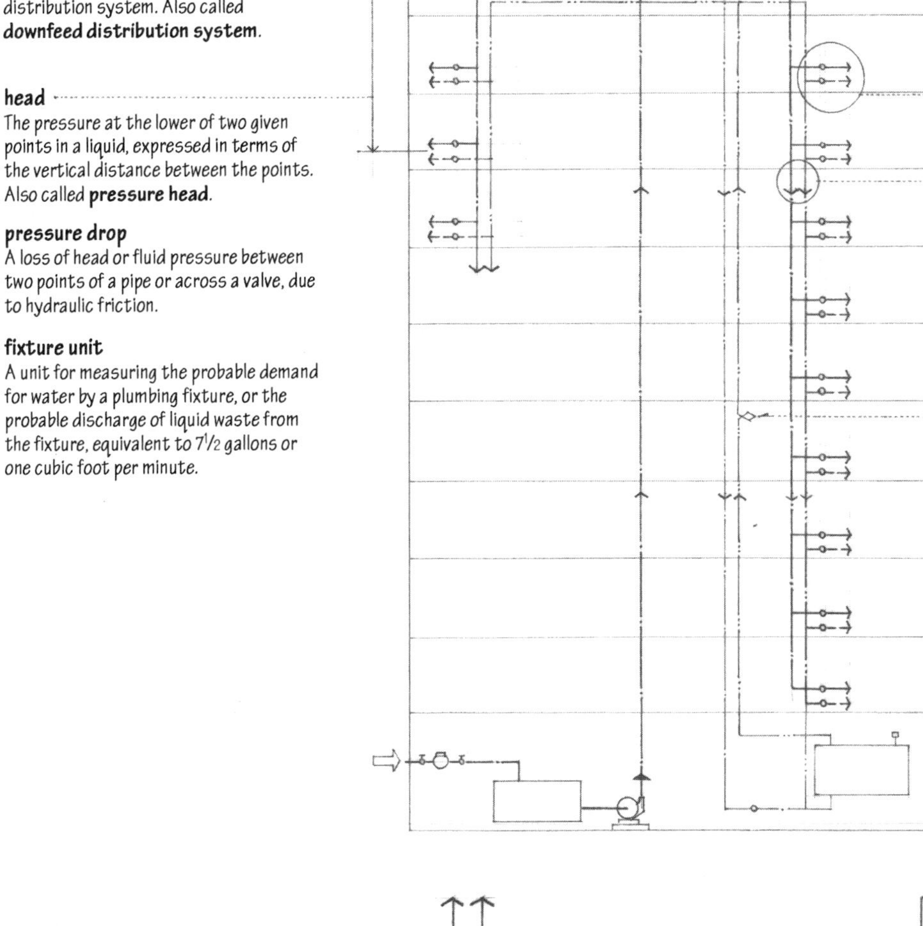

head
The pressure at the lower of two given points in a liquid, expressed in terms of the vertical distance between the points. Also called **pressure head**.

pressure drop
A loss of head or fluid pressure between two points of a pipe or across a valve, due to hydraulic friction.

fixture unit
A unit for measuring the probable demand for water by a plumbing fixture, or the probable discharge of liquid waste from the fixture, equivalent to 7½ gallons or one cubic foot per minute.

branch
Any member of a piping system other than a main, riser, or stack.

riser
A vertical pipe, conduit, or duct in a utility system.

main
A principal pipe, conduit, or duct in a utility system.

expansion bend
An expansion joint of pipe and pipe fittings permitting thermal expansion to occur in a long run of hot-water piping. Also called **expansion loop**.

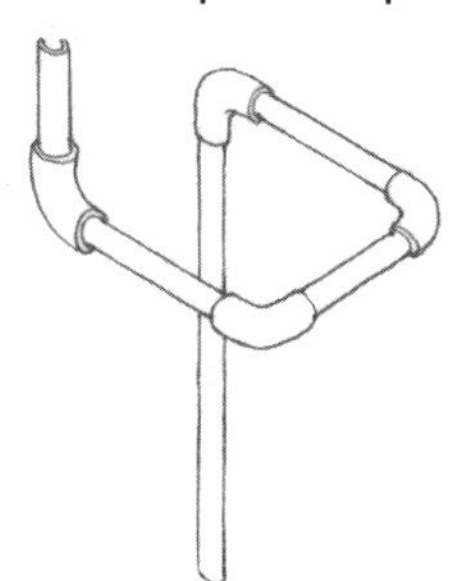

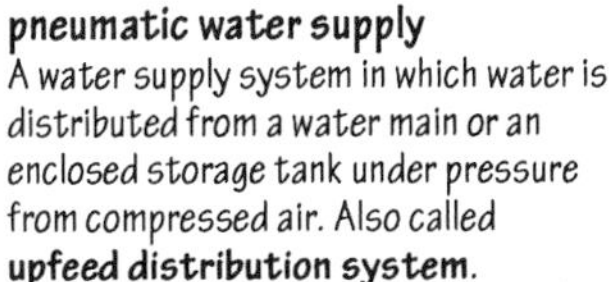

pneumatic water supply
A water supply system in which water is distributed from a water main or an enclosed storage tank under pressure from compressed air. Also called **upfeed distribution system**.

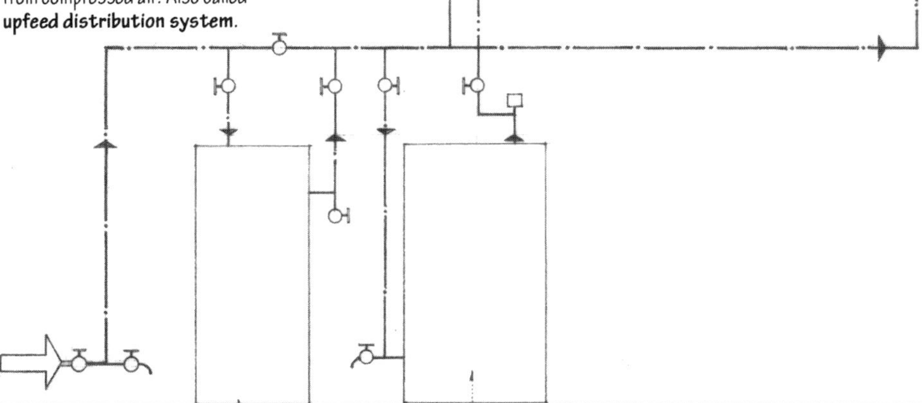

water softener
An apparatus that removes calcium and magnesium salts from hard water by ion exchange in order to give the water more efficient sudsing ability with soap.

hard water
Water containing dissolved salts of calcium or magnesium and forming soap lather with difficulty.

water heater
An electric or gas appliance for heating water to a temperature between 120°F and 140°F (50°C and 60°C) and storing it for use.

hose bibb
A threaded exterior faucet, as for attaching a garden hose, often attached to the side of a house at about the height of a sill. Also called **hosecock**, **sillcock**.

faucet
A device for controlling the flow of a liquid from a pipe by opening or closing an orifice. Also called **spigot**, **tap**.

flow pressure
The fluid pressure in a supply pipe at a faucet or other outlet while the faucet or outlet is wide open and water is flowing, expressed in psi (N/m^2).

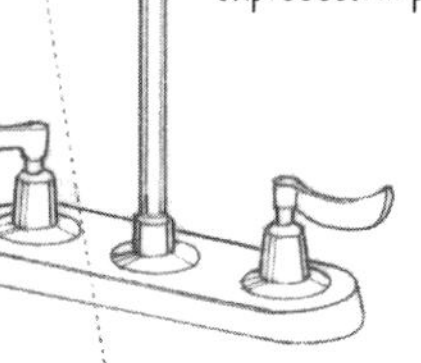

mixing faucet
A faucet having a single outlet for water from separately controlled hot-water and cold-water taps. Also called **mixer**.

aerator
A sievelike device for mixing air with the water flowing from the end of a spigot.

anti-scald faucet
A faucet having a thermostatically controlled valve for maintaining the desired water temperature regardless of pressure or flow.

plumbing fixture
Any of various receptacles for receiving water from a water system and discharging the liquid waste into a drainage system.

sanitary ware
Plumbing fixtures, as sinks and toilet bowls, made of vitreous china, porcelain enamel, or enameled metal.

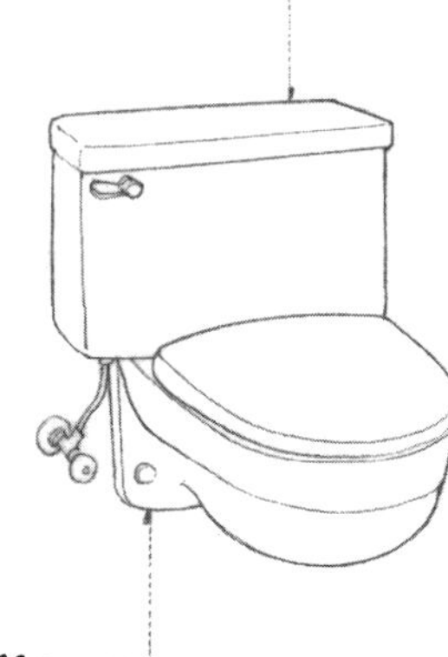

wall-hung
Designed to be attached to or hung from a wall.

ball cock
A device for regulating the supply of water in a flush tank by means of a hollow floating ball which by its rise or fall shuts or opens a supply valve. Also called **float valve**.

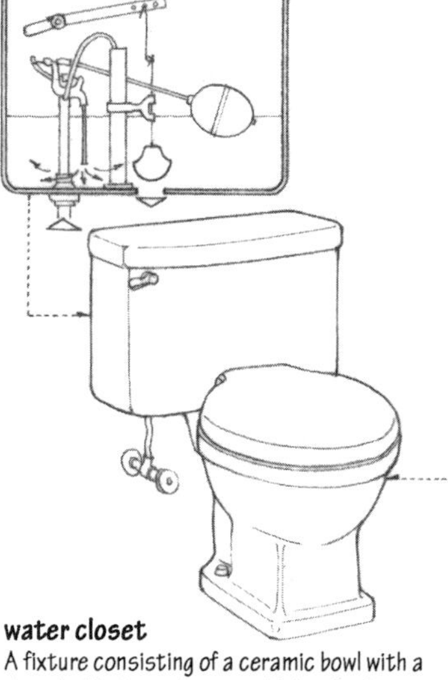

water closet
A fixture consisting of a ceramic bowl with a detachable, hinged seat and lid and a device for flushing with water, used for defecation and urination. Also called **toilet**.

flushometer valve
A valve that supplies a fixed quantity of water to fixtures for flushing purposes when actuated by direct water pressure.

siphon-jet
A toilet bowl in which the flushing water enters through the rim and siphonic action initiated by a water jet draws the contents of the bowl through the trapway.

reverse-trap
A toilet bowl similar to the siphon-jet, but having a smaller water surface and trapway.

siphon-vortex
A toilet bowl similar to the siphon-jet, but having the flushing water directed through the rim to create a vortex that scours the bowl.

wash-down
A toilet bowl having a simple washout action and emptying through a small, irregular passage: prohibited by some health codes.

bidet
A basinlike fixture designed to be straddled for bathing the genitals and posterior parts of the body.

urinal
A flushable fixture used by men for urinating.

toilet partition
A panel forming an enclosure around a water closet for privacy in a public lavatory.

bathtub
An oblong tub to bathe in, esp. one that is a permanent fixture in a bathroom.

shower
A bath in which water is sprayed on the body from an overhead nozzle or showerhead.

grab bar
A bar attached to a wall near a bathtub or shower to provide a hand grip for a person who is bathing.

receptor
The shallow base pan of a stall shower.

lavatory
A bowl or basin with running water for washing the face and hands.

sink
A basin, as in a kitchen or laundry, connected with a water supply and drainage system for washing.

disposal
An electrical device in the drain of a sink, for grinding food wastes to be washed down the drain. Also called **disposer**.

laundry tray
A deep sink for washing clothes.

service sink
A deep sink used in janitorial work. Also called **slop sink**.

water hammer
The concussion and banging noise that results when a volume of water moving in a pipe suddenly stops or loses momentum.

air chamber
A compartment in a water system containing air that elastically compresses and expands to equalize the pressure and flow of water in the system. Also called **air cushion**.

overflow
An outlet, pipe, or receptacle for excess liquid.

backflow
A flow of a liquid opposite to the usual or desired direction.

back-siphonage
A backflow of used or contaminated water from a plumbing fixture into a pipe supplying potable water due to negative pressure in the pipe.

backwater valve
A valve for preventing flowing liquid, as sewage, from reversing its direction. Also called **backflow valve**.

flow rate
The rate of discharge from a plumbing fixture, equal to the total number of gallons discharged per minute divided by 7.5 and expressed in fixture units.

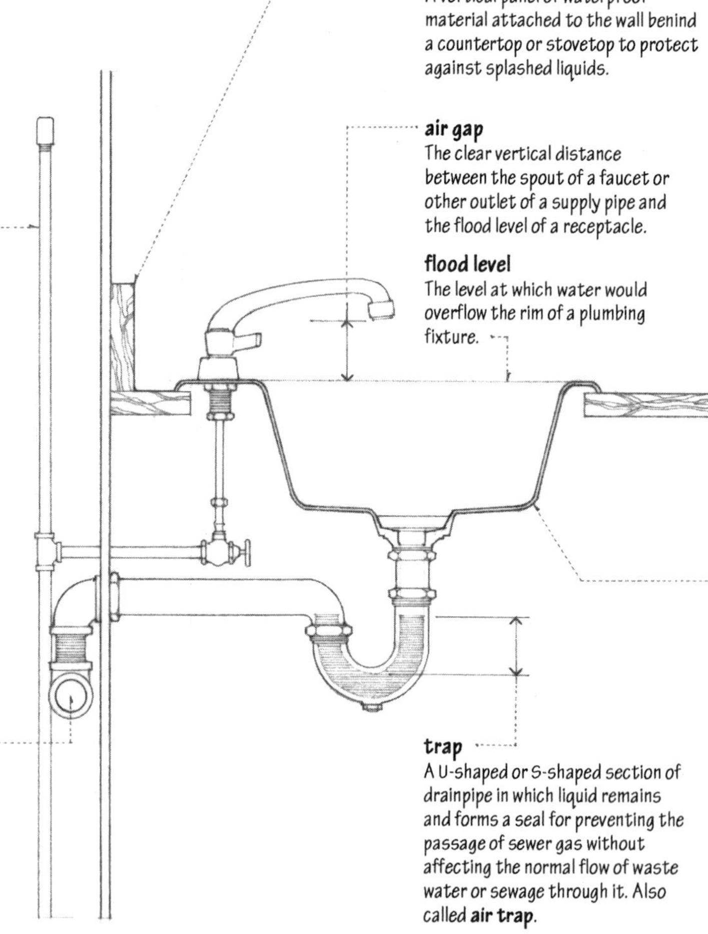

backsplash
A vertical panel of waterproof material attached to the wall behind a countertop or stovetop to protect against splashed liquids.

air gap
The clear vertical distance between the spout of a faucet or other outlet of a supply pipe and the flood level of a receptacle.

flood level
The level at which water would overflow the rim of a plumbing fixture.

trap
A U-shaped or S-shaped section of drainpipe in which liquid remains and forms a seal for preventing the passage of sewer gas without affecting the normal flow of waste water or sewage through it. Also called **air trap**.

drum trap
A cylindrical trap closed on the bottom and having a cover plate for access, usually installed on the drain line from a bathtub.

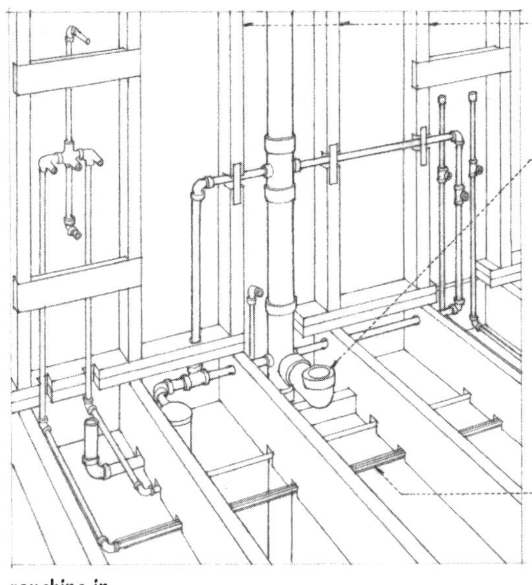

plumbing wall
A wall or partition containing vertical space for a plumbing stack. Also called **stack partition**.

closet bend
A 90° soil fitting installed directly beneath a water closet.

developed length
The length of a pipeline measured along the centerline of the pipe and pipe fittings.

molded insulation
Thermal insulation premolded to fit around pipes and pipe fittings.

roughing-in
The act or process of installing all parts of a plumbing system that will later be concealed, usually to the fixture connections.

valve
Any device for controlling or stopping the flow of a liquid or gas by a movable part that opens, partially obstructs, or shuts a passage, pipe, inlet, or outlet.

bonnet
The part of a valve casing through which the stem passes and that forms a guide and seal for the stem.

seat
The part or surface of a valve on which the stem is closed to stop flow completely.

globe valve
A valve with a globular body, closed by a disk seating on an opening in an internal wall.

gate valve
A shutoff valve closed by lowering a wedge-shaped gate across the passage.

angle valve
A globe valve having an outlet at a right angle to the inlet.

alignment valve
A washerless valve opened by aligning holes in a disk, cylinder, or ball.

mixing valve
A valve for controlling the relative amount of hot and cold water admitted from separate hot-water and cold-water lines.

check valve
A valve permitting a liquid or gas to flow in one direction only.

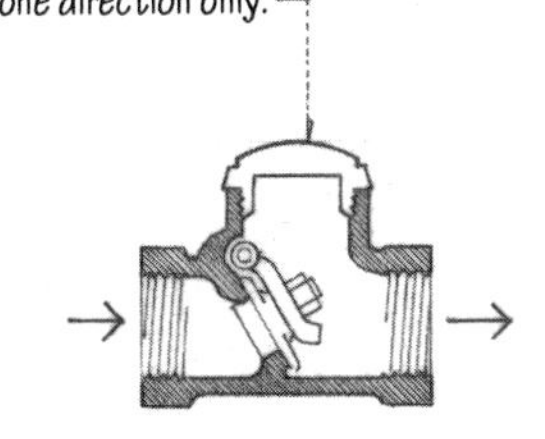

male
Made to fit into a corresponding open or recessed part.

female
Having a recessed part into which a corresponding part fits.

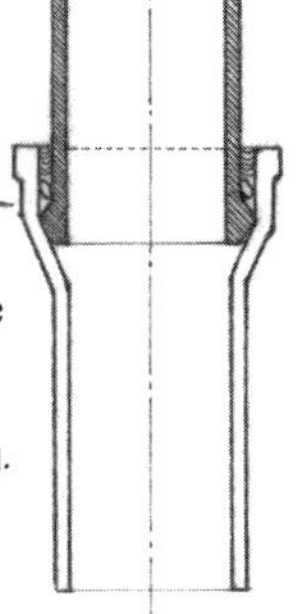

bell-and-spigot
A pipe joint made by fitting the end (**spigot**) of one pipe into the enlarged end (**bell**) of another pipe and sealing with a caulking compound or a compressible ring.

gasket
A rubber or metal ring inserted between two mating surfaces to make the joint watertight.

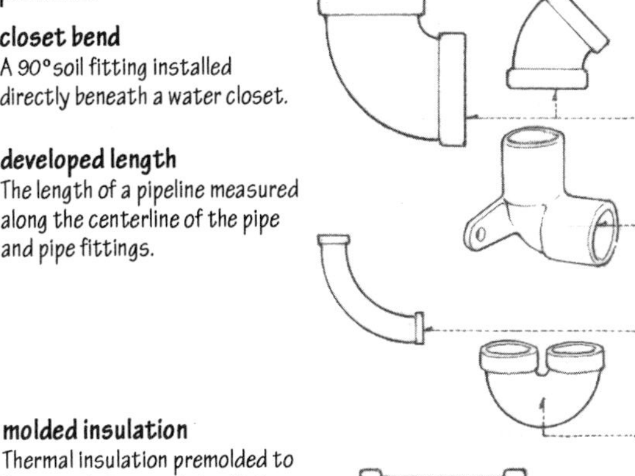

pipe
A hollow cylinder of metal or plastic used for the conveyance of water, steam, gas, or other fluid material.

pipe fitting
A standard part, as an elbow, union, or tee, for connecting two or more pipes.

elbow
A pipe fitting having an angled, usually 90° bend. Also called **ell, el**.

drop elbow
An elbow having lugs for attachment to a wall or joist. Also called **drop ell**.

sweep fitting
A pipe fitting having a large radius of curvature.

return bend
A 180° bend in a pipe.

tee
A T-shaped pipe fitting for making a three-way joint.

drop tee
A tee having lugs for attachment to a wall or joist.

sanitary tee
A tee having a slight curve in the 90° transition to channel the flow from a branch pipe in the direction of the main.

wye
A Y-shaped pipe fitting for joining a branch pipe with a main, usually at a 45° angle.

cross
A pipe fitting for making a four-way connection.

sanitary cross
A cross having a slight curve in each of the 90° transitions to channel the flow from branch pipes in the direction of the main.

crossover
A U-shaped pipe for bypassing another pipe.

nipple
A short length of pipe with threads on each end, used for joining couplings or other pipe fittings.

coupling
A short length of pipe having each end threaded on the inside, used for joining two pipes of the same diameter.

increaser
A coupling increasing in diameter at one end.

reducer
A coupling decreasing in diameter at one end.

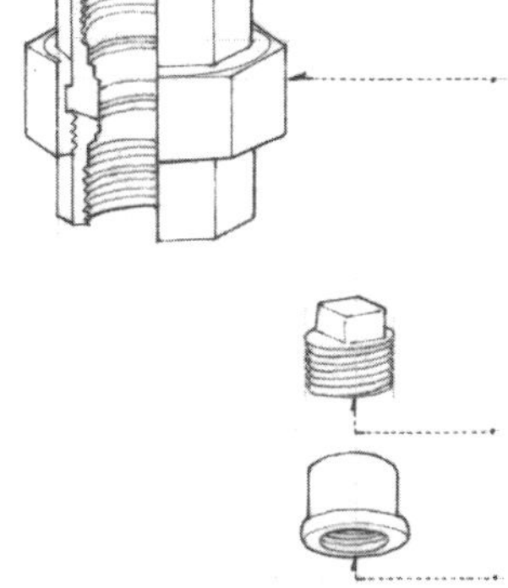

union
A coupling device for connecting two pipes neither of which can be turned, consisting of two internally threaded end pieces which are tightened around the pipe ends to be joined, and an externally threaded center piece, which draws the two end pieces together as it is rotated.

plug
An externally threaded fitting for closing the end of a pipe.

cap
An internally threaded fitting for enclosing the end of a pipe.

drainage system
A system of pipes, traps, and other apparatus for conveying sewage, waste water, or rainwater to a public sewer or a private treatment facility.

drain
Any pipe or channel by which a liquid is drawn off.

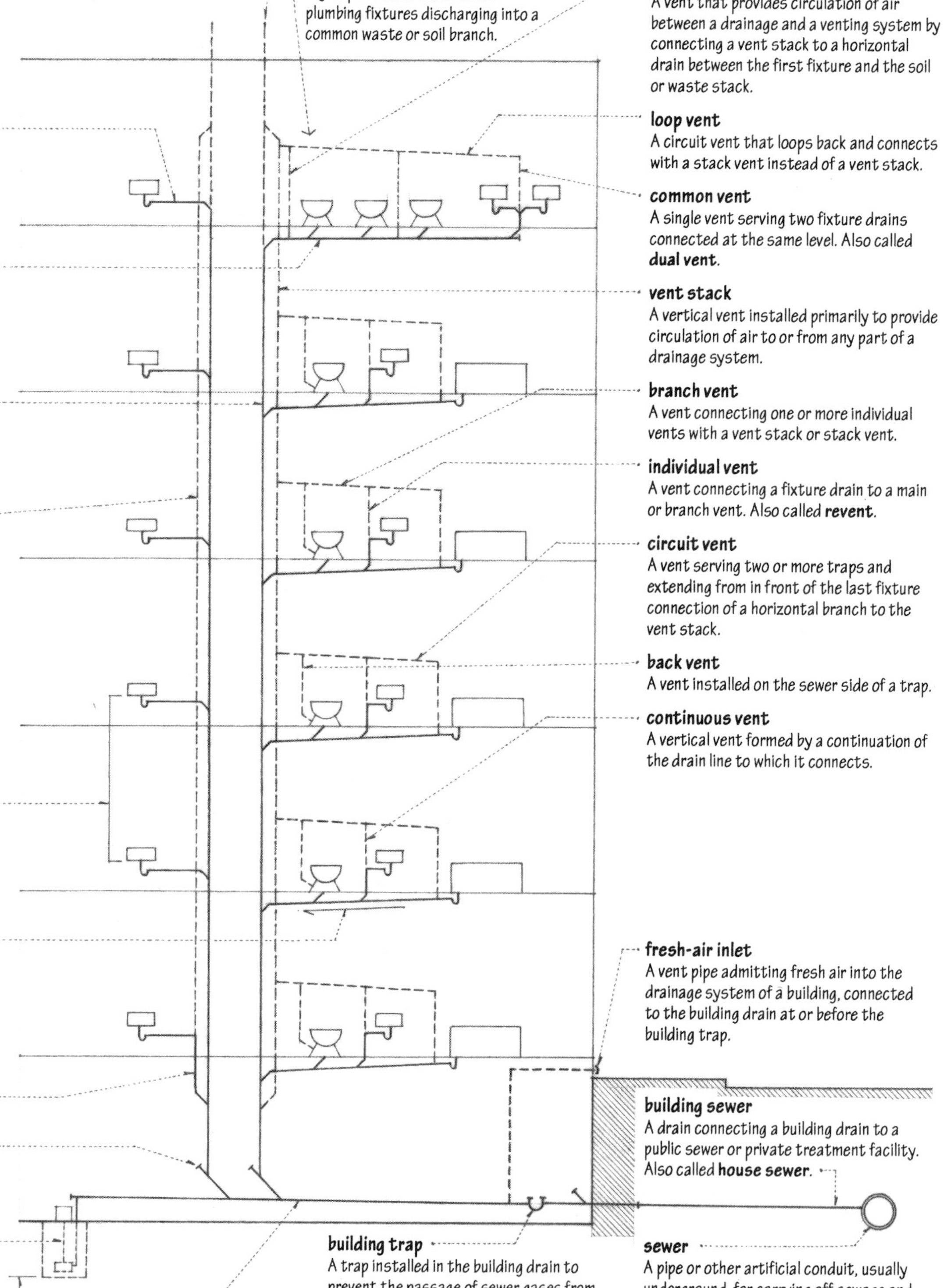

fixture drain
A drain extending from the trap of a plumbing fixture to a junction with a waste or soil stack.

branch drain
A drain connecting one or more fixtures to a soil or waste stack.

stack
A vertical waste pipe or vent pipe serving a number of floors.

soil stack
A vertical soil pipe.

soil pipe
Any pipe carrying the discharge from water closets or urinals to the building drain or building sewer.

waste stack
A vertical waste pipe.

waste pipe
Any pipe carrying the discharge from plumbing fixtures other than water closets or urinals.

indirect waste pipe
A waste pipe that is not connected directly with a drainage system, but discharges into it through a properly trapped plumbing fixture.

branch interval
A length of soil or waste stack corresponding to a story height but never less than 8 ft. (2.4 m), within which the horizontal branch drains from one floor are connected.

fall
The downward slope of a pipe, conduit, or channel, expressed either as a percentage or in inches per foot.

wet vent
An oversized pipe functioning both as a soil or waste pipe and a vent.

cleanout
A pipe fitting with a removable plug giving access to a soil or waste pipe for inspection or cleaning.

sump pump
A pump for removing the accumulations of liquid from a sump.

sump
A pit or reservoir serving as a drain or receptacle for water or other liquids.

invert
The lowest point on the interior of a drainpipe or sewer where the liquid is deepest.

vent system
A system of pipes supplying a flow of air to or from a drainage system or providing a circulation of air within the system to protect trap seals from siphonage and back pressure.

building drain
The lowest part of a drainage system that receives the discharge from soil and waste stacks inside the walls of a building and conveys it by gravity to the building sewer. Also called **house drain**.

stack vent
The extension of a soil or waste stack above the highest horizontal drain connected to the stack. Also called **soil vent, waste vent**.

battery
A group of two or more similar plumbing fixtures discharging into a common waste or soil branch.

building trap
A trap installed in the building drain to prevent the passage of sewer gases from the building sewer to the drainage system of a building. Not all plumbing codes require a building trap. Also called **house trap**.

vent
A pipe connecting a drain near one or more traps to a vent stack or stack vent.

relief vent
A vent that provides circulation of air between a drainage and a venting system by connecting a vent stack to a horizontal drain between the first fixture and the soil or waste stack.

loop vent
A circuit vent that loops back and connects with a stack vent instead of a vent stack.

common vent
A single vent serving two fixture drains connected at the same level. Also called **dual vent**.

vent stack
A vertical vent installed primarily to provide circulation of air to or from any part of a drainage system.

branch vent
A vent connecting one or more individual vents with a vent stack or stack vent.

individual vent
A vent connecting a fixture drain to a main or branch vent. Also called **revent**.

circuit vent
A vent serving two or more traps and extending from in front of the last fixture connection of a horizontal branch to the vent stack.

back vent
A vent installed on the sewer side of a trap.

continuous vent
A vertical vent formed by a continuation of the drain line to which it connects.

fresh-air inlet
A vent pipe admitting fresh air into the drainage system of a building, connected to the building drain at or before the building trap.

building sewer
A drain connecting a building drain to a public sewer or private treatment facility. Also called **house sewer**.

sewer
A pipe or other artificial conduit, usually underground, for carrying off sewage and other liquid waste to a treatment plant or other point of disposal.

sanitary sewer
A sewer conveying only the sewage from plumbing fixtures and excluding storm water.

sewage
The liquid waste containing animal or vegetable matter in suspension or solution that passes through a sewer.

scum
A layer of sewage matter that rises to the surface of the sewage in a septic tank.

scum clear space
The distance between the bottom of the layer of scum and the bottom of the outlet in a septic tank.

sludge clear space
The distance between the top of the sludge and the bottom of the outlet in a septic tank.

sludge
Sediment that settles out of sewage, forming a semi-solid mass on the bottom of a septic tank.

sewage treatment plant
Structures and appurtenances for receiving the discharge of a sanitary drainage system and reducing the organic and bacterial content of the waste so as to render it less offensive or dangerous.

cesspool
A covered pit for receiving the sewage from a house, having a perforated lining to allow the liquid portion of the sewage to leach into the ground while the sludge is retained in the pit to undergo decomposition. Cesspools are no longer acceptable as a means of sewage disposal.

septic tank
A covered watertight tank for receiving the discharge from a building sewer, separating out the solid organic matter which is decomposed and purified by anaerobic bacteria, and allowing the clarified liquid to discharge for final disposal.

dosing chamber
A chamber of a large septic tank employing siphonic action to automatically discharge a large volume of effluent when a predetermined quantity has accumulated.

effluent
Liquid sewage that has been treated in a septic tank or a sewage treatment plant.

seepage pit
A pit that is lined with a perforated masonry or concrete wall to allow effluent collected from a septic tank to seep or leach into the surrounding soil, sometimes used as a substitute for a drainfield.

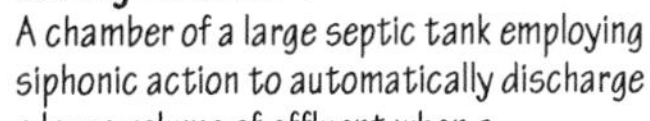

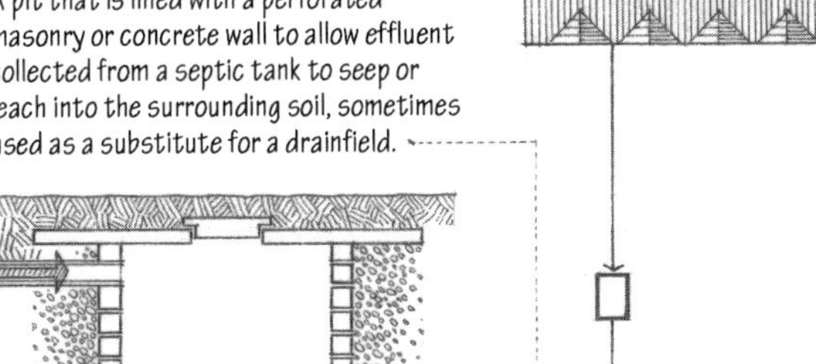

grease trap
A tank installed between a kitchen sink and a house sewer for retaining and removing grease from waste water. Also called **grease interceptor**.

distribution box
A box through which the flow of effluent from a septic tank is distributed to the drainage tiles of a drainfield. Also called **diversion box**.

drainfield
An open area containing an arrangement of absorption trenches through which septic-tank effluent from a septic tank may seep or leach into the surrounding soil. Also called **absorption field, disposal field**.

absorption trench
A narrow trench 12 to 36 in. (305 to 914 mm) wide containing coarse aggregate and a distribution pipe through which the effluent from a septic tank is allowed to seep into the soil.

sand filter
A filter for cleansing water or purifying effluent, consisting of layers of coarse stone, coarse gravel, and sand becoming finer toward the top.

subsurface sand filter
A sewage filtering system consisting of a number of distribution pipes surrounded by graded gravel, an intermediate layer of clean, coarse sand, and a system of underdrains to carry off the filtered effluent.

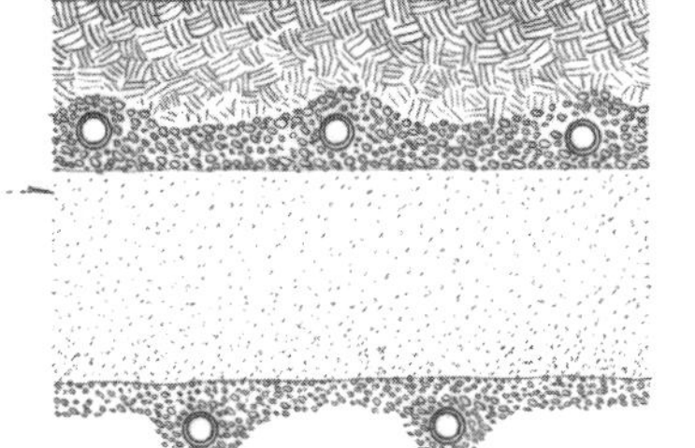

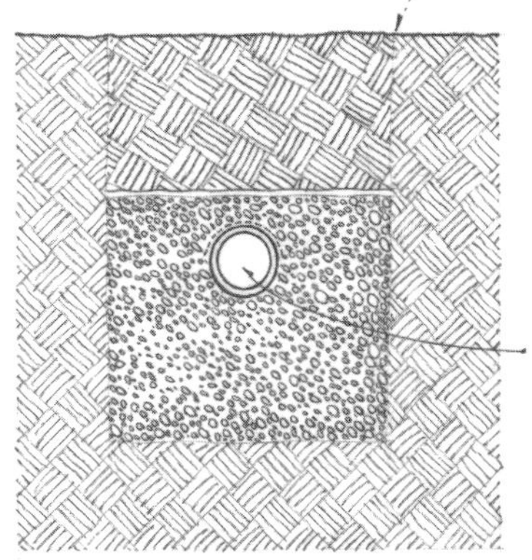

absorption bed
A trench wider than 36 in. (914 mm), containing coarse aggregate and two or more distribution pipes through which the effluent from a septic tank may seep into the surrounding soil. Also called **seepage bed**.

distribution pipe
Drain tiles laid with open joints or perforated pipe having sufficient openings for the distribution of the effluent from a septic tank. Also called **distribution line**.

serial distribution
A sequence of absorption trenches, absorption beds, or seepage pits so arranged that the total effective absorption area of one is utilized before effluent flows into the next.

percolation test
A test for determining the rate at which a soil will absorb effluent, made by measuring the rate at which the water level drops after a hole is dug in the soil and filled with water.

leach
To cause water or other liquid to percolate through something, so as to dissolve out soluble constituents.

drain tile
A hollow tile laid end to end with open joints to disperse effluent in a drainfield, or to drain water-saturated soil. Also, **drainage tile**.

Concrete in which steel reinforcement is embedded in such a manner that the two materials act together in resisting forces. Also called **béton armé, ferroconcrete**.

reinforcement
A system of steel bars, strands, or wires for absorbing tensile, shearing, and sometimes the compressive stresses in a concrete member or structure.

reinforcing bar
A steel bar for reinforcing concrete, usually specified by a number equivalent to its diameter in eighths of an inch. Also called **rebar**.

deformed bar
A reinforcing bar hot-rolled with surface deformations to develop a greater bond with concrete.

plain concrete
Concrete having no reinforcement, or reinforced only for drying shrinkage or thermal stresses.

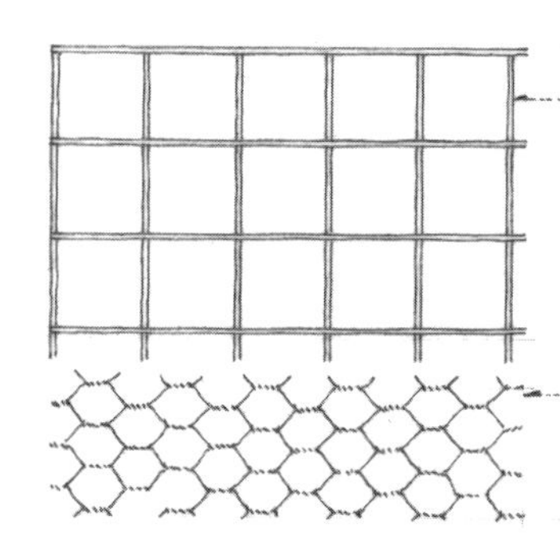

ferrocement
Constructed of cement-sand mortar over a wire mesh that has been preshaped over a mold.

fiber-reinforced concrete
Concrete reinforced with dispersed, randomly oriented fibers of glass or plastic.

gfrc
Abbreviation for glass-fiber-reinforced concrete.

welded-wire fabric
A grid of longitudinal and transverse steel wires or bars welded together at all points of intersection, usually specified by the size of the grid in inches and the wire gauge. Also called **welded-wire mesh**.

woven-wire fabric
A mesh of cold-drawn steel wires mechanically twisted together to form hexagonally shaped openings.

tension reinforcement
Reinforcement designed to absorb tensile stresses.

compression reinforcement
Reinforcement designed to absorb compressive stresses.

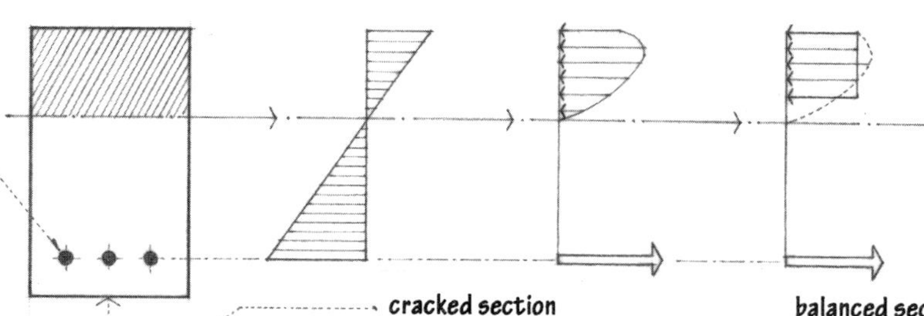

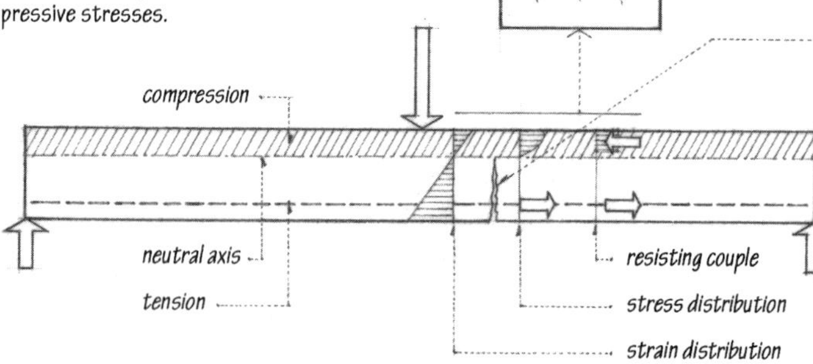

cracked section
A concrete section designed or analyzed on the assumption that concrete has no resistance to tensile stresses.

cracking load
A load that causes the tensile stress in a concrete member to exceed the tensile strength of the concrete.

balanced section
A concrete section in which the tension reinforcement theoretically reaches its specified yield strength as the concrete in compression reaches its assumed ultimate strain.

overreinforced section
A concrete section in which the concrete in compression reaches its assumed ultimate strain before the tension reinforcement reaches its specified yield strength. This is a dangerous condition since failure of the section could occur instantaneously without warning.

underreinforced section
A concrete section in which the tension reinforcement reaches its specified yield strength before the concrete in compression reaches its assumed ultimate strain. This is a desirable condition since failure of the section would be preceded by large deformations, giving prior warning of impending collapse.

effective depth
The depth of a concrete section measured from the compression face to the centroid of the tension reinforcement.

bar spacing
The center-to-center spacing of parallel reinforcing bars, the resulting clear distance between the bars being regulated by bar diameter, maximum size of coarse aggregate, and thickness of the concrete section.

cover
The amount of concrete required to protect steel reinforcement from fire and corrosion, measured from the surface of the reinforcement to the outer surface of the concrete section.

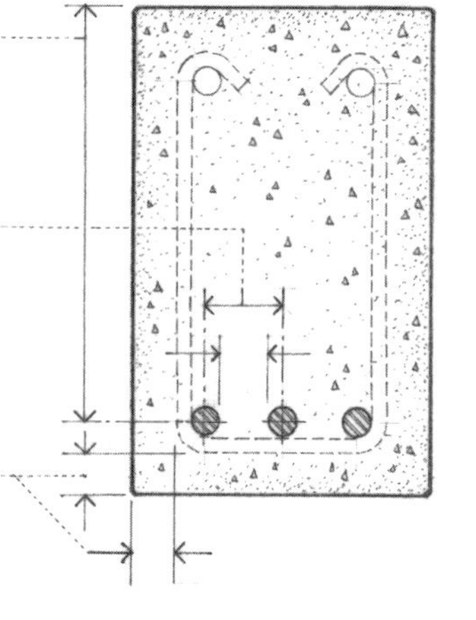

effective area of concrete
The area of a concrete section between the compression face and the centroid of the tension reinforcement.

effective area of reinforcement
The product of the right cross-sectional area of reinforcement and the cosine of the angle between its direction and the direction for which its effectiveness is considered.

percentage reinforcement
The ratio of effective area of reinforcement to effective area of concrete at any section of a reinforced concrete member, expressed as a percentage.

bond
The adhesion between two substances, as concrete and reinforcing bars.

bond stress
The adhesive force per unit area of contact between a reinforcing bar and the surrounding concrete developed at any section of a flexural member.

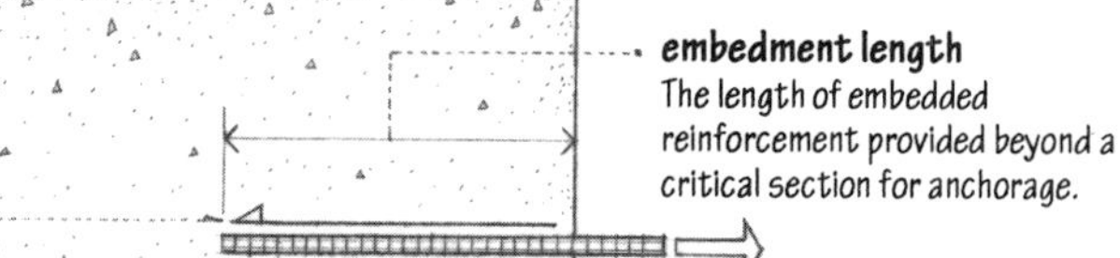

embedment length
The length of embedded reinforcement provided beyond a critical section for anchorage.

hook
A bend or curve given to the end of a tension bar to develop an equivalent embedment length, used where there is insufficient room to develop an adequate embedment length.

standard hook
A 90°, 135°, or 180° bend made at the end of a reinforcing bar according to industry standards with a radius based on the bar diameter.

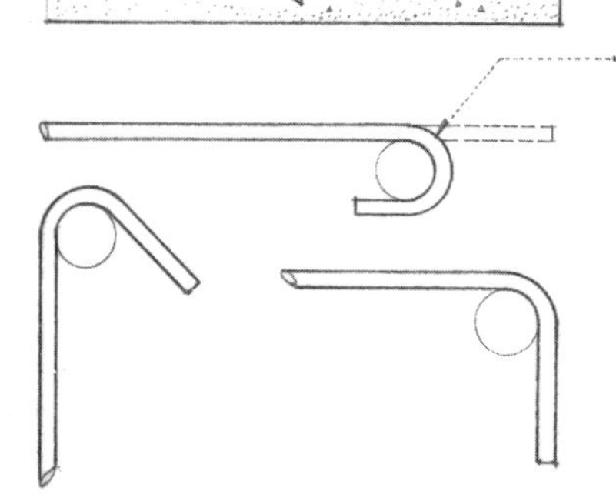

anchorage
Any of various means, as embedment length or hooked bars, for developing tension or compression in a reinforcing bar on each side of a critical section in order to prevent bond failure or splitting.

critical section
The section of a flexural concrete member at a point of maximum stress, a point of inflection, or a point within the span where tension bars are no longer needed to resist stress.

truss bar
A longitudinal bar bent up or down at points of moment reversal in a reinforced concrete beam.

top bar
Any of the longitudinal bars serving as tension reinforcement in the section of a concrete beam or slab subject to a negative moment.

reinforced concrete beam
A concrete beam designed to act together with longitudinal and web reinforcement in resisting applied forces.

longitudinal reinforcement
Reinforcement essentially parallel to the horizontal surface of a slab or to the long axis of a concrete beam or column.

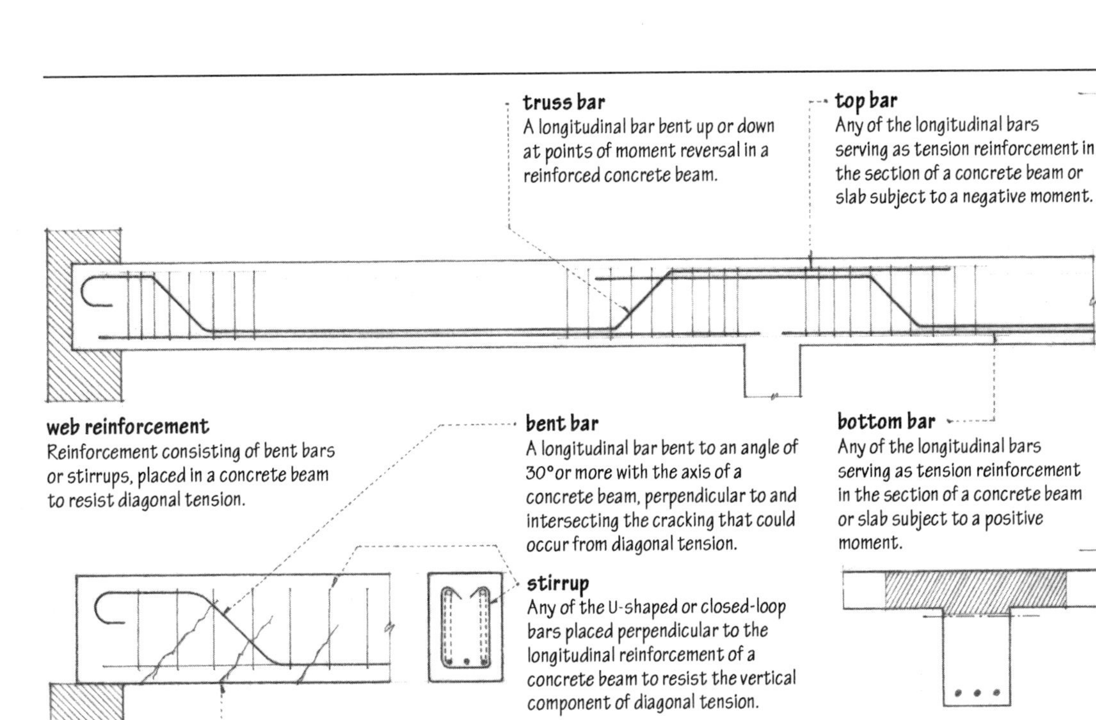

web reinforcement
Reinforcement consisting of bent bars or stirrups, placed in a concrete beam to resist diagonal tension.

bent bar
A longitudinal bar bent to an angle of 30° or more with the axis of a concrete beam, perpendicular to and intersecting the cracking that could occur from diagonal tension.

bottom bar
Any of the longitudinal bars serving as tension reinforcement in the section of a concrete beam or slab subject to a positive moment.

deep beam
A reinforced concrete beam having a depth-to-span ratio greater than 2:5 for continuous spans, or 4:5 for simple spans, subject to nonlinear distribution of stress and lateral buckling.

stirrup
Any of the U-shaped or closed-loop bars placed perpendicular to the longitudinal reinforcement of a concrete beam to resist the vertical component of diagonal tension.

T-beam
A monolithic reinforced concrete construction in which a portion of the slab on each side of a beam acts as a flange in resisting compressive stresses, and the portion of the beam projecting below the slab serves as a web or stem in resisting bending and shear stresses.

diagonal tension
The principle tensile stresses acting at an angle to the longitudinal axis of a beam.

vertical reinforcement
Longitudinal reinforcement placed in a concrete column to absorb compressive stresses, resist bending stresses, and reduce the effects of creep and shrinkage in the column. The effective cross-sectional area of vertical reinforcement should not be less than 0.01 nor more than 0.08 times the gross cross-sectional area of the column, with a minimum of four #5 bars for tied columns and a minimum of six #5 bars for spiral columns.

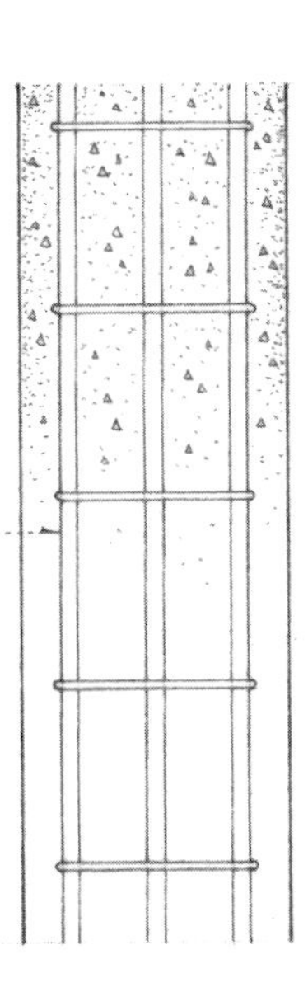

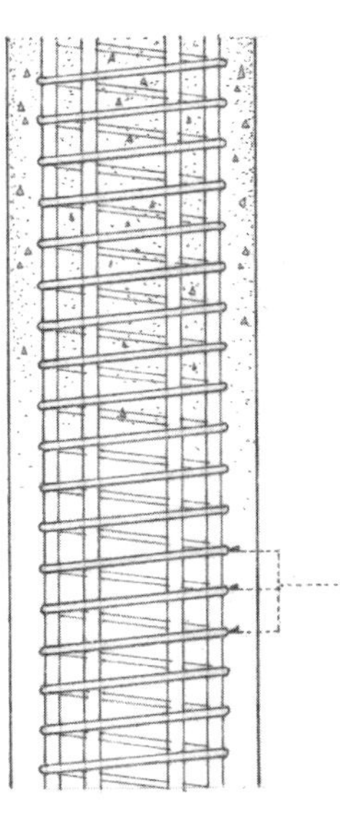

reinforced concrete column
A concrete column designed to act together with vertical and lateral reinforcement in resisting applied forces. Reinforced concrete columns constituting the principal supports for a floor or roof should have a minimum diameter of 10 in. (254 mm), or if rectangular in section, a minimum thickness of 8 in. (203 mm), and a minimum gross area of 96 sq. in. (61935 sq. mm).

lateral reinforcement
Spiral reinforcement or lateral ties placed in a concrete column to laterally restrain the vertical reinforcement and prevent buckling.

spiral reinforcement
Lateral reinforcement consisting of an evenly spaced continuous spiral held firmly in place by vertical spacers. Spiral reinforcement should have a diameter of at least 3/8 in. (9.5 mm), with a maximum center-to-center spacing between spirals of 1/6 of the core diameter, and a clear spacing between spirals not to exceed 3 in. (76 mm) nor be less than 1 3/8 in. (35 mm) or 1 1/2 times the size of the coarse aggregate.

lap splice
A splice for transferring tensile or compressive stresses from one longitudinal bar to another, made by lapping their ends for a length specified in bar diameters.

butt splice
A splice for transferring tensile or compressive stresses from one longitudinal bar to another, made by butting their ends together and connecting them in a positive fashion.

welded splice
A butt splice made by arc-welding the butted ends of two reinforcing bars.

compression splice
A butt splice made by connecting the butted ends of two reinforcing bars with a mechanical fastener, as a sleeve clamp.

offset bend
A bend displacing a section of longitudinal bar to a position parallel to the original bar, used esp. in the vertical reinforcement of concrete columns.

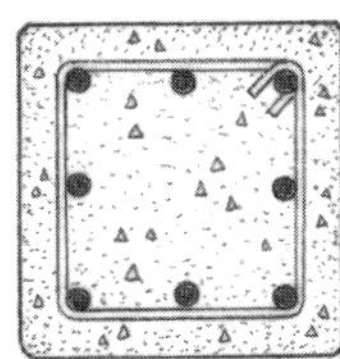

tied column
A concrete column reinforced with vertical bars and individual lateral ties. Lateral ties should have a diameter of at least 3/8 in. (9.5 mm), spaced apart not over 48 tie diameters, 16 bar diameters, or the least dimension of the column section. Each corner and alternate longitudinal bar should be laterally supported by the bend of a tie having an included angle of not more than 135°, with no bar being more than 6 in. (152 mm) clear from such a supported bar.

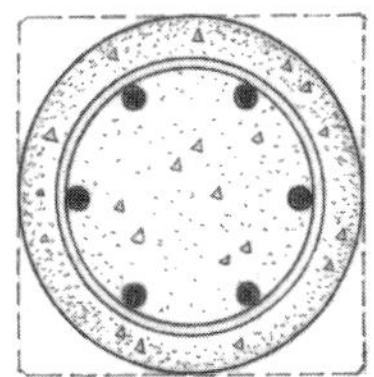

spiral column
A concrete column with spiral reinforcement enclosing a circular core reinforced with vertical bars.

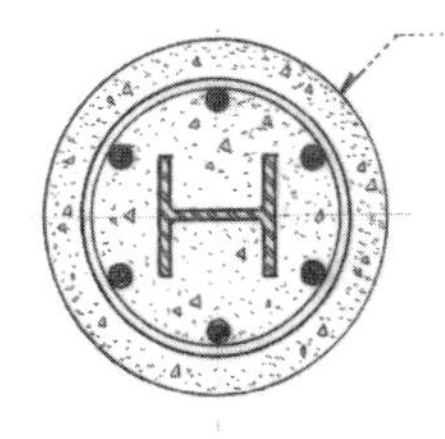

compound column
A structural steel column encased in concrete at least 2 1/2 in. (64 mm) thick, reinforced with wire mesh.

composite column
A structural steel column thoroughly encased in concrete reinforced with both vertical and spiral reinforcement.

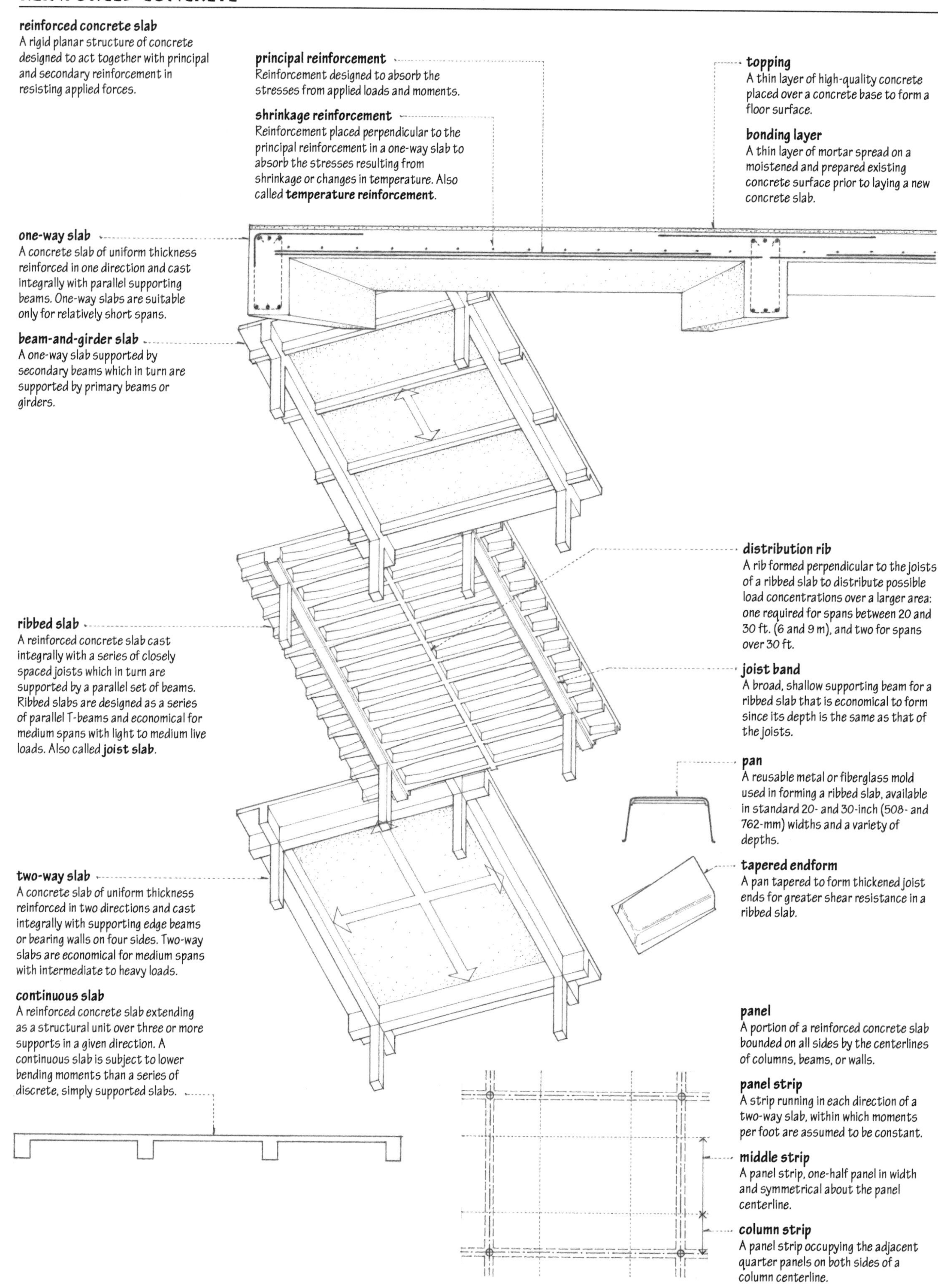

reinforced concrete slab
A rigid planar structure of concrete designed to act together with principal and secondary reinforcement in resisting applied forces.

principal reinforcement
Reinforcement designed to absorb the stresses from applied loads and moments.

shrinkage reinforcement
Reinforcement placed perpendicular to the principal reinforcement in a one-way slab to absorb the stresses resulting from shrinkage or changes in temperature. Also called **temperature reinforcement**.

topping
A thin layer of high-quality concrete placed over a concrete base to form a floor surface.

bonding layer
A thin layer of mortar spread on a moistened and prepared existing concrete surface prior to laying a new concrete slab.

one-way slab
A concrete slab of uniform thickness reinforced in one direction and cast integrally with parallel supporting beams. One-way slabs are suitable only for relatively short spans.

beam-and-girder slab
A one-way slab supported by secondary beams which in turn are supported by primary beams or girders.

ribbed slab
A reinforced concrete slab cast integrally with a series of closely spaced joists which in turn are supported by a parallel set of beams. Ribbed slabs are designed as a series of parallel T-beams and economical for medium spans with light to medium live loads. Also called **joist slab**.

distribution rib
A rib formed perpendicular to the joists of a ribbed slab to distribute possible load concentrations over a larger area: one required for spans between 20 and 30 ft. (6 and 9 m), and two for spans over 30 ft.

joist band
A broad, shallow supporting beam for a ribbed slab that is economical to form since its depth is the same as that of the joists.

pan
A reusable metal or fiberglass mold used in forming a ribbed slab, available in standard 20- and 30-inch (508- and 762-mm) widths and a variety of depths.

tapered endform
A pan tapered to form thickened joist ends for greater shear resistance in a ribbed slab.

two-way slab
A concrete slab of uniform thickness reinforced in two directions and cast integrally with supporting edge beams or bearing walls on four sides. Two-way slabs are economical for medium spans with intermediate to heavy loads.

continuous slab
A reinforced concrete slab extending as a structural unit over three or more supports in a given direction. A continuous slab is subject to lower bending moments than a series of discrete, simply supported slabs.

panel
A portion of a reinforced concrete slab bounded on all sides by the centerlines of columns, beams, or walls.

panel strip
A strip running in each direction of a two-way slab, within which moments per foot are assumed to be constant.

middle strip
A panel strip, one-half panel in width and symmetrical about the panel centerline.

column strip
A panel strip occupying the adjacent quarter panels on both sides of a column centerline.

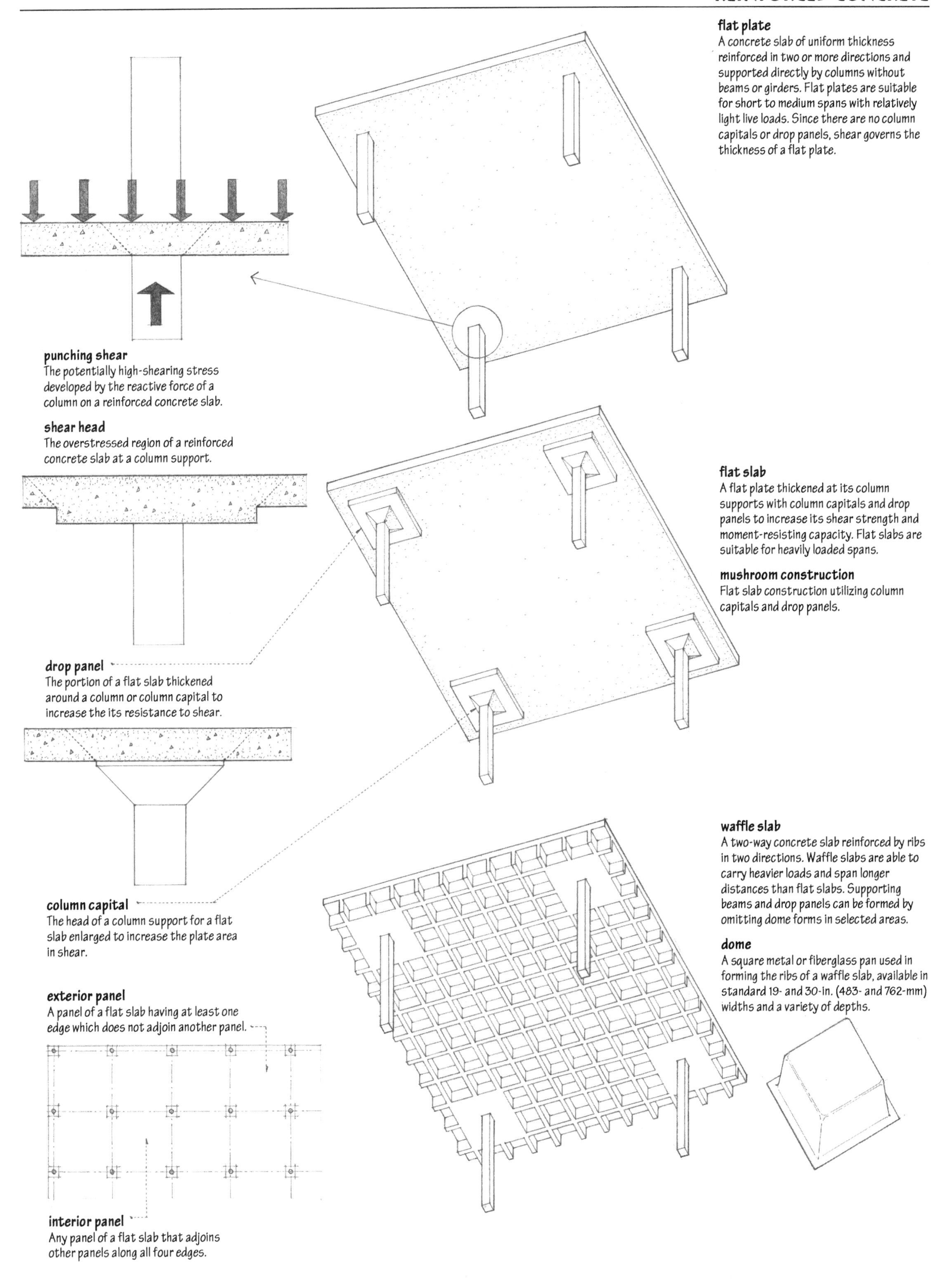

flat plate
A concrete slab of uniform thickness reinforced in two or more directions and supported directly by columns without beams or girders. Flat plates are suitable for short to medium spans with relatively light live loads. Since there are no column capitals or drop panels, shear governs the thickness of a flat plate.

punching shear
The potentially high-shearing stress developed by the reactive force of a column on a reinforced concrete slab.

shear head
The overstressed region of a reinforced concrete slab at a column support.

flat slab
A flat plate thickened at its column supports with column capitals and drop panels to increase its shear strength and moment-resisting capacity. Flat slabs are suitable for heavily loaded spans.

mushroom construction
Flat slab construction utilizing column capitals and drop panels.

drop panel
The portion of a flat slab thickened around a column or column capital to increase the its resistance to shear.

column capital
The head of a column support for a flat slab enlarged to increase the plate area in shear.

waffle slab
A two-way concrete slab reinforced by ribs in two directions. Waffle slabs are able to carry heavier loads and span longer distances than flat slabs. Supporting beams and drop panels can be formed by omitting dome forms in selected areas.

dome
A square metal or fiberglass pan used in forming the ribs of a waffle slab, available in standard 19- and 30-in. (483- and 762-mm) widths and a variety of depths.

exterior panel
A panel of a flat slab having at least one edge which does not adjoin another panel.

interior panel
Any panel of a flat slab that adjoins other panels along all four edges.

precast concrete
A concrete member or product that is cast and cured in a place other than where it is to be installed in a structure.

solid flat slab
A precast, prestressed concrete plank suitable for short spans and uniformly distributed floor and roof loads.

hollow-core slab
A precast, prestressed concrete plank internally cored to reduce dead weight. Hollow-core slabs are suitable for medium to long spans and uniformly distributed floor and roof loads.

topping
A layer of reinforced concrete cast to form a composite structural unit with a precast concrete floor or roof deck.

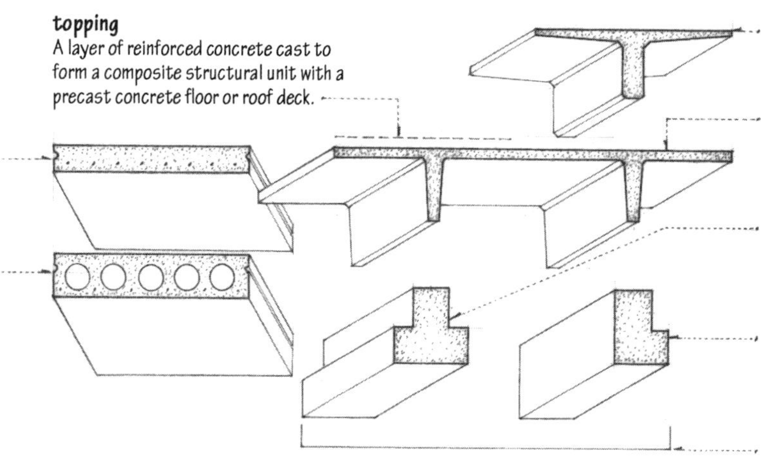

single tee
A precast, prestressed concrete slab having a broad, T-shaped cross section.

double tee
A precast, prestressed concrete slab having two stems and a broad cross section resembling the capital letters TT.

inverted tee
A precast, prestressed ledger beam having a cross section resembling an inverted capital T.

L-beam
A precast, prestressed ledger beam having a cross section resembling the capital letter L.

ledger beam
A reinforced concrete beam having projecting ledges for receiving the ends of joists or slabs.

prestressed concrete
Concrete reinforced by pretensioning or posttensioning high-strength steel tendons within their elastic limit to actively resist a service load. The tensile stresses in the tendons are transferred to the concrete, placing the entire cross section of a flexural member in compression. The resulting compressive stresses counteract the tensile-bending stresses from the applied load, enabling the prestressed member to deflect less, carry a greater load, or span a greater distance than a conventionally reinforced member of the same size, proportion, and weight.

prestress
To introduce internal stresses to a concrete member in order to counteract the stresses that will result from an applied load.

pretension
To prestress a concrete member by tensioning the reinforcing tendons before the concrete is cast. The tendons are first stretched between two abutments until a predetermined tensile force is developed. Concrete is then cast in formwork around the tendons and fully cured. Finally, the tendons are cut, and the tensile stress in the tendons are transferred to the concrete through bond stresses.

tendon
A high-strength steel strand or bar for prestressing concrete.

strand
A cable composed of high-strength steel wires twisted about a core.

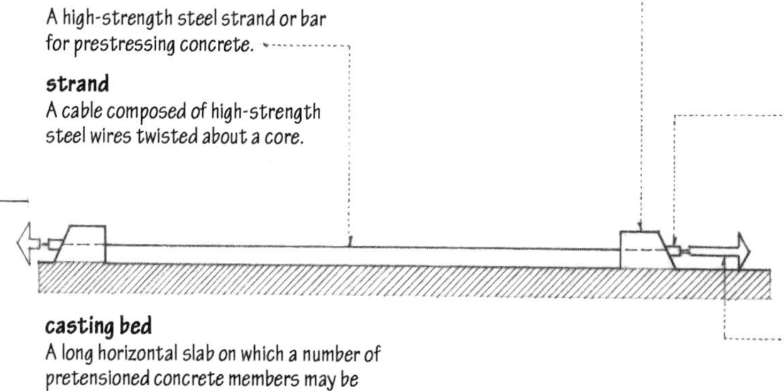

casting bed
A long horizontal slab on which a number of pretensioned concrete members may be prestressed, formed, and cast simultaneously.

abutment
A structure for anchoring the reinforcing tendons in the pretensioning of a concrete member.

anchor
A mechanical device for locking a stressed tendon in position and delivering the prestressing force to the concrete, either permanently in a posttensioned member or temporarily during hardening of a pretensioned concrete member. Also called **anchorage**.

jacking force
The tensile force exerted temporarily by a jack in the prestressing of a concrete member.

jack
A hydraulic device for stretching and stressing tendons in the prestressing of a concrete member.

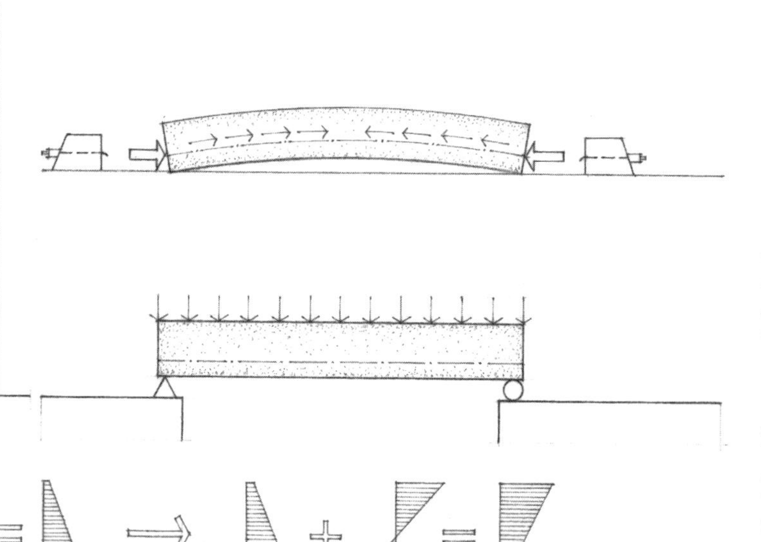

final prestress

dead load stresses

combined stresses

live load stresses

initial prestress
The tensile force in the reinforcing tendons transferred to a concrete member at the time of stressing.

loss of prestress
A reduction in initial prestress resulting from the combined effects of creep, shrinkage, or elastic shortening of the concrete, relaxation of the reinforcing steel, friction losses resulting from the curvature of draped tendons, and slippage at the anchorages.

final prestress
The internal stress that exists in a prestressed concrete member after all losses in prestress have occurred.

effective prestress
The final prestress in a prestressed concrete member, including the effect of the weight of the member but excluding the effect of any superimposed load.

partial prestressing
The prestressing of a concrete member to a level of stress such that nominal tensile stresses exist at design or service loads.

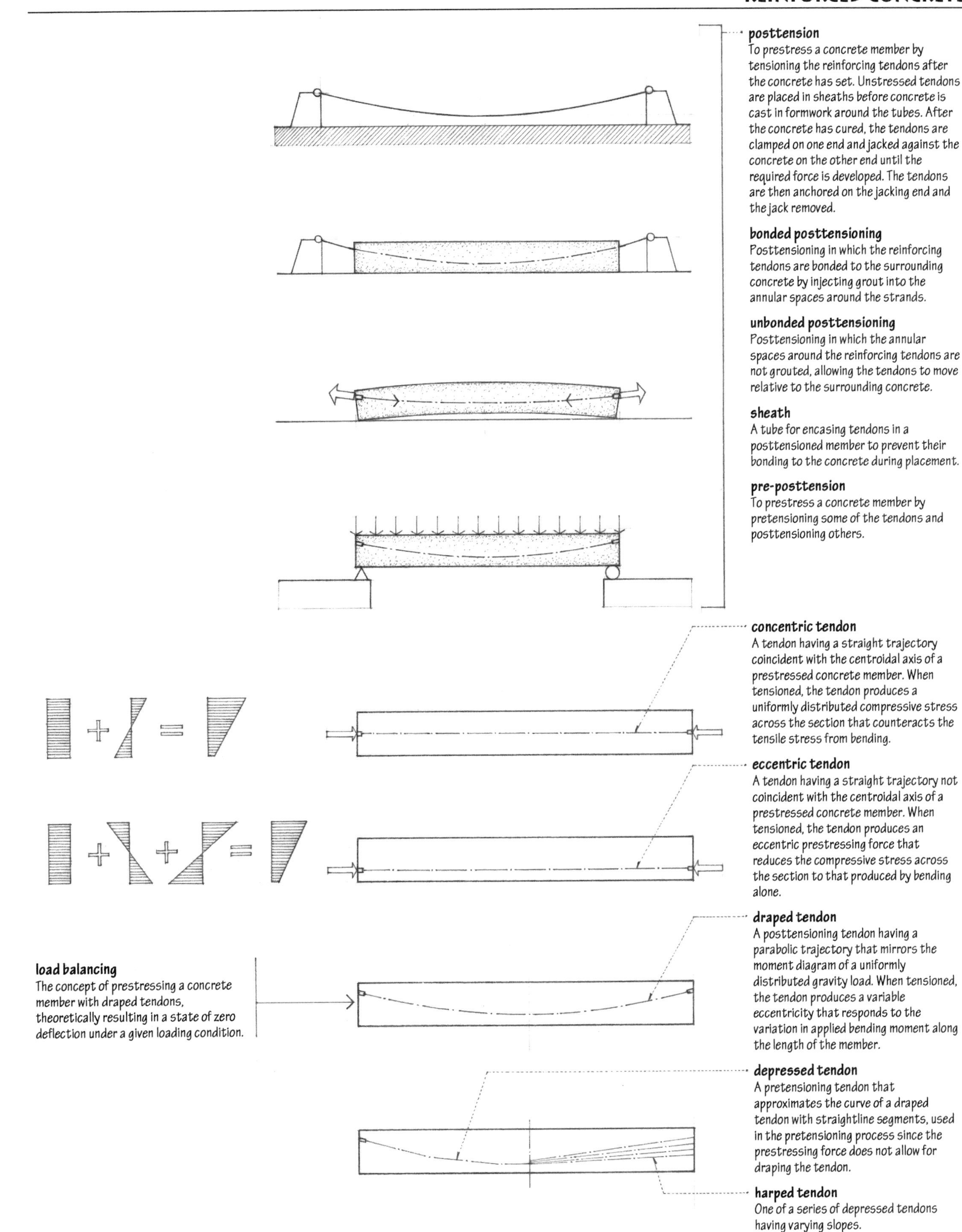

posttension
To prestress a concrete member by tensioning the reinforcing tendons after the concrete has set. Unstressed tendons are placed in sheaths before concrete is cast in formwork around the tubes. After the concrete has cured, the tendons are clamped on one end and jacked against the concrete on the other end until the required force is developed. The tendons are then anchored on the jacking end and the jack removed.

bonded posttensioning
Posttensioning in which the reinforcing tendons are bonded to the surrounding concrete by injecting grout into the annular spaces around the strands.

unbonded posttensioning
Posttensioning in which the annular spaces around the reinforcing tendons are not grouted, allowing the tendons to move relative to the surrounding concrete.

sheath
A tube for encasing tendons in a posttensioned member to prevent their bonding to the concrete during placement.

pre-posttension
To prestress a concrete member by pretensioning some of the tendons and posttensioning others.

concentric tendon
A tendon having a straight trajectory coincident with the centroidal axis of a prestressed concrete member. When tensioned, the tendon produces a uniformly distributed compressive stress across the section that counteracts the tensile stress from bending.

eccentric tendon
A tendon having a straight trajectory not coincident with the centroidal axis of a prestressed concrete member. When tensioned, the tendon produces an eccentric prestressing force that reduces the compressive stress across the section to that produced by bending alone.

load balancing
The concept of prestressing a concrete member with draped tendons, theoretically resulting in a state of zero deflection under a given loading condition.

draped tendon
A posttensioning tendon having a parabolic trajectory that mirrors the moment diagram of a uniformly distributed gravity load. When tensioned, the tendon produces a variable eccentricity that responds to the variation in applied bending moment along the length of the member.

depressed tendon
A pretensioning tendon that approximates the curve of a draped tendon with straightline segments, used in the pretensioning process since the prestressing force does not allow for draping the tendon.

harped tendon
One of a series of depressed tendons having varying slopes.

ROOF

The external upper covering of a building, including the frame for supporting the roofing.

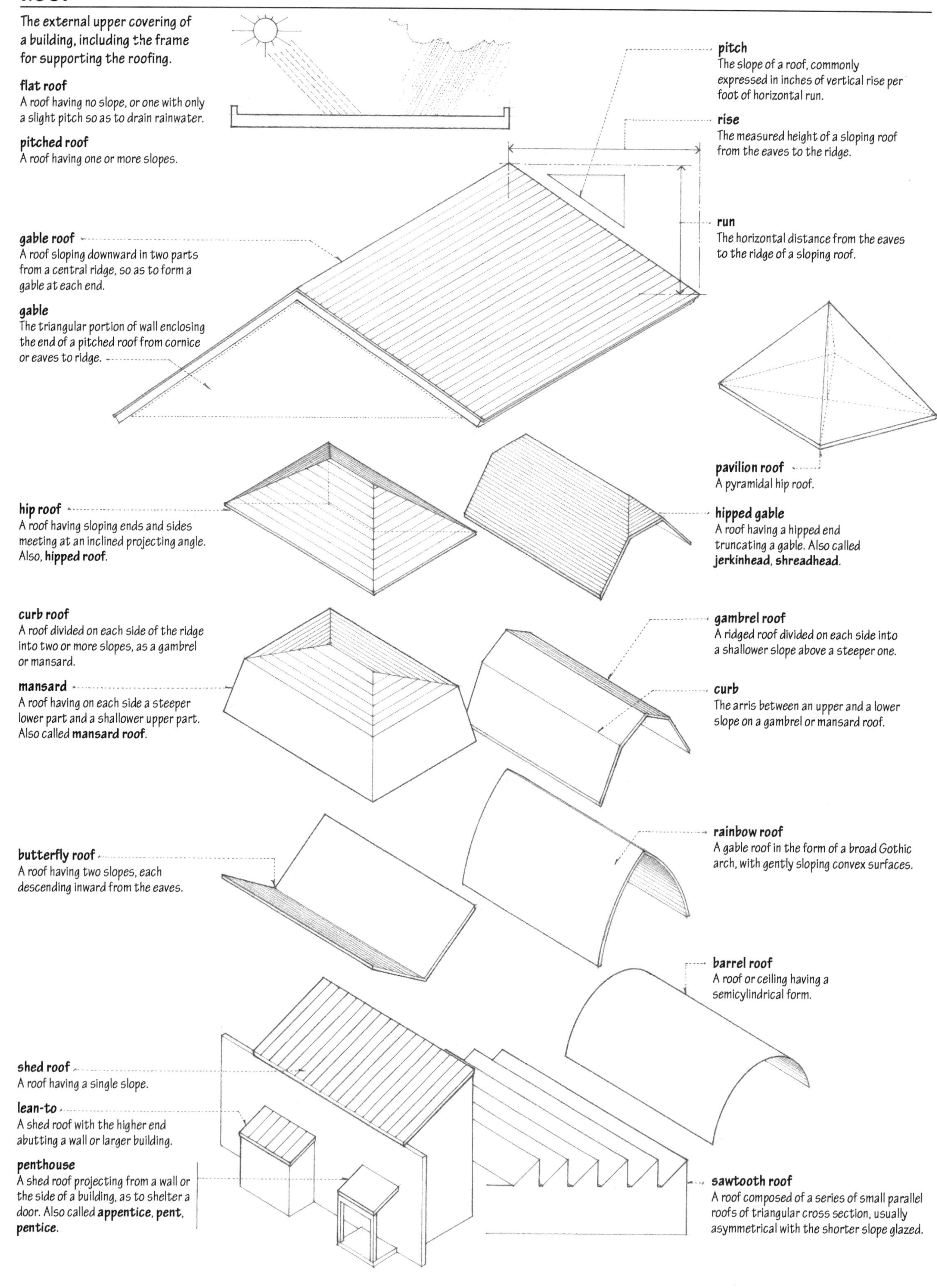

flat roof
A roof having no slope, or one with only a slight pitch so as to drain rainwater.

pitched roof
A roof having one or more slopes.

pitch
The slope of a roof, commonly expressed in inches of vertical rise per foot of horizontal run.

rise
The measured height of a sloping roof from the eaves to the ridge.

run
The horizontal distance from the eaves to the ridge of a sloping roof.

gable roof
A roof sloping downward in two parts from a central ridge, so as to form a gable at each end.

gable
The triangular portion of wall enclosing the end of a pitched roof from cornice or eaves to ridge.

pavilion roof
A pyramidal hip roof.

hip roof
A roof having sloping ends and sides meeting at an inclined projecting angle. Also, **hipped roof**.

hipped gable
A roof having a hipped end truncating a gable. Also called **jerkinhead, shreadhead**.

curb roof
A roof divided on each side of the ridge into two or more slopes, as a gambrel or mansard.

mansard
A roof having on each side a steeper lower part and a shallower upper part. Also called **mansard roof**.

gambrel roof
A ridged roof divided on each side into a shallower slope above a steeper one.

curb
The arris between an upper and a lower slope on a gambrel or mansard roof.

butterfly roof
A roof having two slopes, each descending inward from the eaves.

rainbow roof
A gable roof in the form of a broad Gothic arch, with gently sloping convex surfaces.

barrel roof
A roof or ceiling having a semicylindrical form.

shed roof
A roof having a single slope.

lean-to
A shed roof with the higher end abutting a wall or larger building.

penthouse
A shed roof projecting from a wall or the side of a building, as to shelter a door. Also called **appentice, pent, pentice**.

sawtooth roof
A roof composed of a series of small parallel roofs of triangular cross section, usually asymmetrical with the shorter slope glazed.

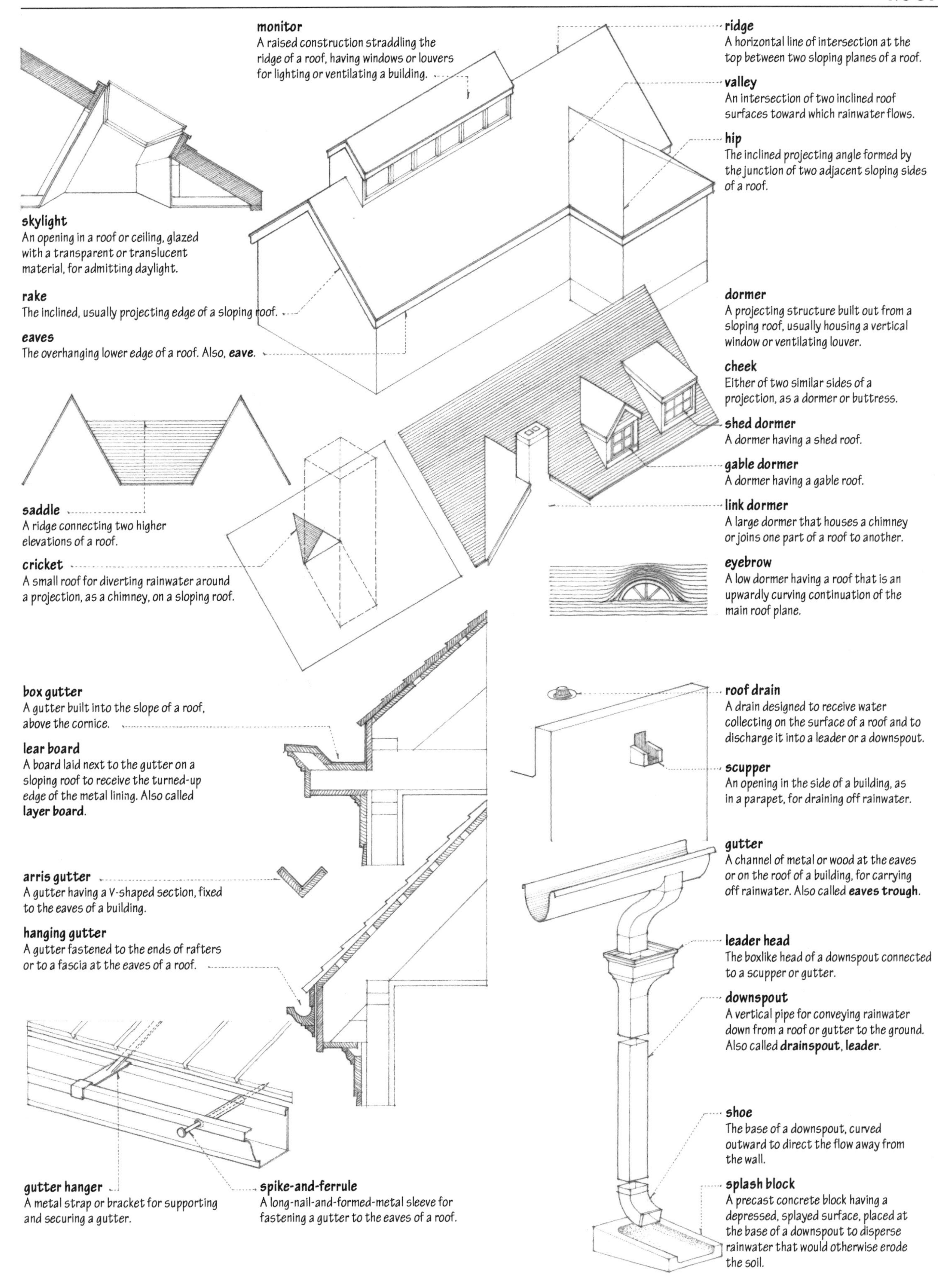

monitor
A raised construction straddling the ridge of a roof, having windows or louvers for lighting or ventilating a building.

ridge
A horizontal line of intersection at the top between two sloping planes of a roof.

valley
An intersection of two inclined roof surfaces toward which rainwater flows.

hip
The inclined projecting angle formed by the junction of two adjacent sloping sides of a roof.

skylight
An opening in a roof or ceiling, glazed with a transparent or translucent material, for admitting daylight.

rake
The inclined, usually projecting edge of a sloping roof.

eaves
The overhanging lower edge of a roof. Also, **eave**.

dormer
A projecting structure built out from a sloping roof, usually housing a vertical window or ventilating louver.

cheek
Either of two similar sides of a projection, as a dormer or buttress.

shed dormer
A dormer having a shed roof.

gable dormer
A dormer having a gable roof.

link dormer
A large dormer that houses a chimney or joins one part of a roof to another.

eyebrow
A low dormer having a roof that is an upwardly curving continuation of the main roof plane.

saddle
A ridge connecting two higher elevations of a roof.

cricket
A small roof for diverting rainwater around a projection, as a chimney, on a sloping roof.

box gutter
A gutter built into the slope of a roof, above the cornice.

lear board
A board laid next to the gutter on a sloping roof to receive the turned-up edge of the metal lining. Also called **layer board**.

arris gutter
A gutter having a V-shaped section, fixed to the eaves of a building.

hanging gutter
A gutter fastened to the ends of rafters or to a fascia at the eaves of a roof.

gutter hanger
A metal strap or bracket for supporting and securing a gutter.

spike-and-ferrule
A long-nail-and-formed-metal sleeve for fastening a gutter to the eaves of a roof.

roof drain
A drain designed to receive water collecting on the surface of a roof and to discharge it into a leader or a downspout.

scupper
An opening in the side of a building, as in a parapet, for draining off rainwater.

gutter
A channel of metal or wood at the eaves or on the roof of a building, for carrying off rainwater. Also called **eaves trough**.

leader head
The boxlike head of a downspout connected to a scupper or gutter.

downspout
A vertical pipe for conveying rainwater down from a roof or gutter to the ground. Also called **drainspout**, **leader**.

shoe
The base of a downspout, curved outward to direct the flow away from the wall.

splash block
A precast concrete block having a depressed, splayed surface, placed at the base of a downspout to disperse rainwater that would otherwise erode the soil.

double roof
A roof in which longitudinal members, as a ridge beam and purlins, are used as intermediate supports for common rafters. Also called **double-framed roof**.

purlin
A longitudinal member of a roof frame for supporting common rafters between the ridge and the eaves. Also, **purline**. Also called **binding rafter**.

subpurlin
A light structural member for carrying roofing materials, supported by and running at right angles to purlins.

king post
A vertical member from the apex to the bottom chord of a pitched truss.

joggle post
A king post having notches or raised areas for receiving and supporting the feet of inclined struts. Also called **joggle piece**.

joggle
An enlarged area of a post for supporting the foot of a strut or brace.

common rafter
A rafter extending from a wallplate to a ridgeboard or ridgebeam and having no function other than to support sheathing and covering of a roof.

pole plate
A beam perpendicular to the ends of tie beams in a trussed roof and supporting common rafters near their lower ends.

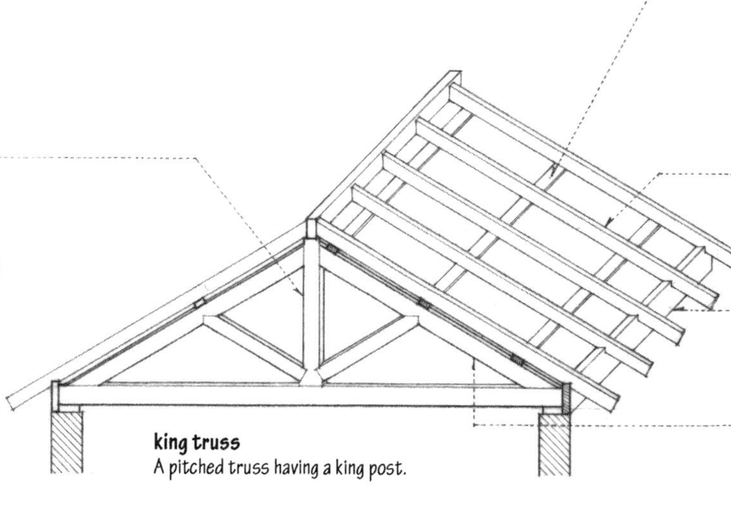

king truss
A pitched truss having a king post.

principal rafter
A diagonal member of a roof principal, usually forming part of a truss and supporting the purlins on which common rafters rest.

principal
A member in a frame structure upon which adjacent or similar members depend for support or reinforcement.

auxiliary rafter
A rafter reinforcing a principal rafter or a diagonal member of a queen truss. Also called **cushion rafter**.

straining piece
A horizontal tie beam uniting the tops of two queen posts. Also called **straining beam**.

queen post
Either of the two vertical web members set at equal distances from the apex of a pitched truss.

tie beam
A horizontal timber for connecting two structural members to keep them from spreading apart, as a beam connecting the feet of two principal rafters in a roof truss.

straining sill
A compression member lying along and dogged to the tie beam of a queen truss and separating the feet of the queen posts.

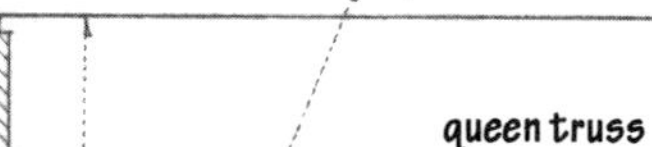

queen truss
A pitched truss having two queen posts connected by a straining piece.

arch brace
A curved brace, usually used in pairs to support a roof frame and give the effect of an arch.

hammer post
A vertical timber set on the inner end of a hammer beam and braced to a collar beam above to support a purlin.

hammer beam
One of pair of short horizontal members attached to the foot of a principal rafter at the level of the wall plate, used in place of a tie beam.

hammer brace
A bracket for supporting a hammer beam.

bracket
A support projecting horizontally from a wall to bear the weight of a cantilever or to strengthen an angle.

pendant post
A vertical timber supported at its lower end by a corbel and carrying at its upper end a hammer beam or tie beam.

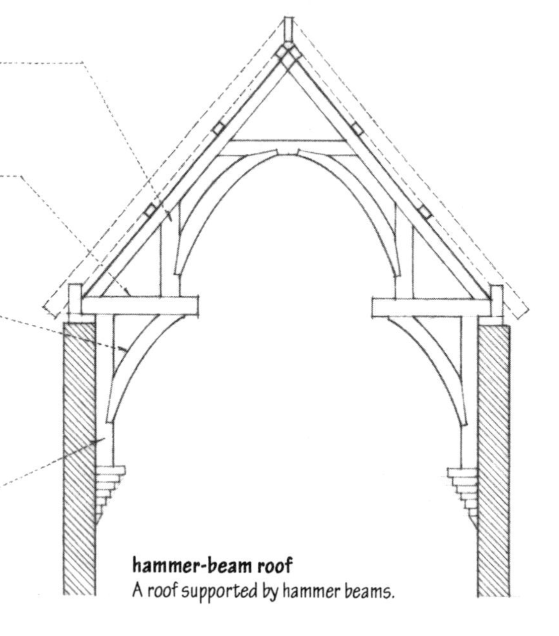

hammer-beam roof
A roof supported by hammer beams.

cruck
One of a pair of naturally curved timbers, forming one of several arched frames supporting the roof of an old English cottage or farm building.

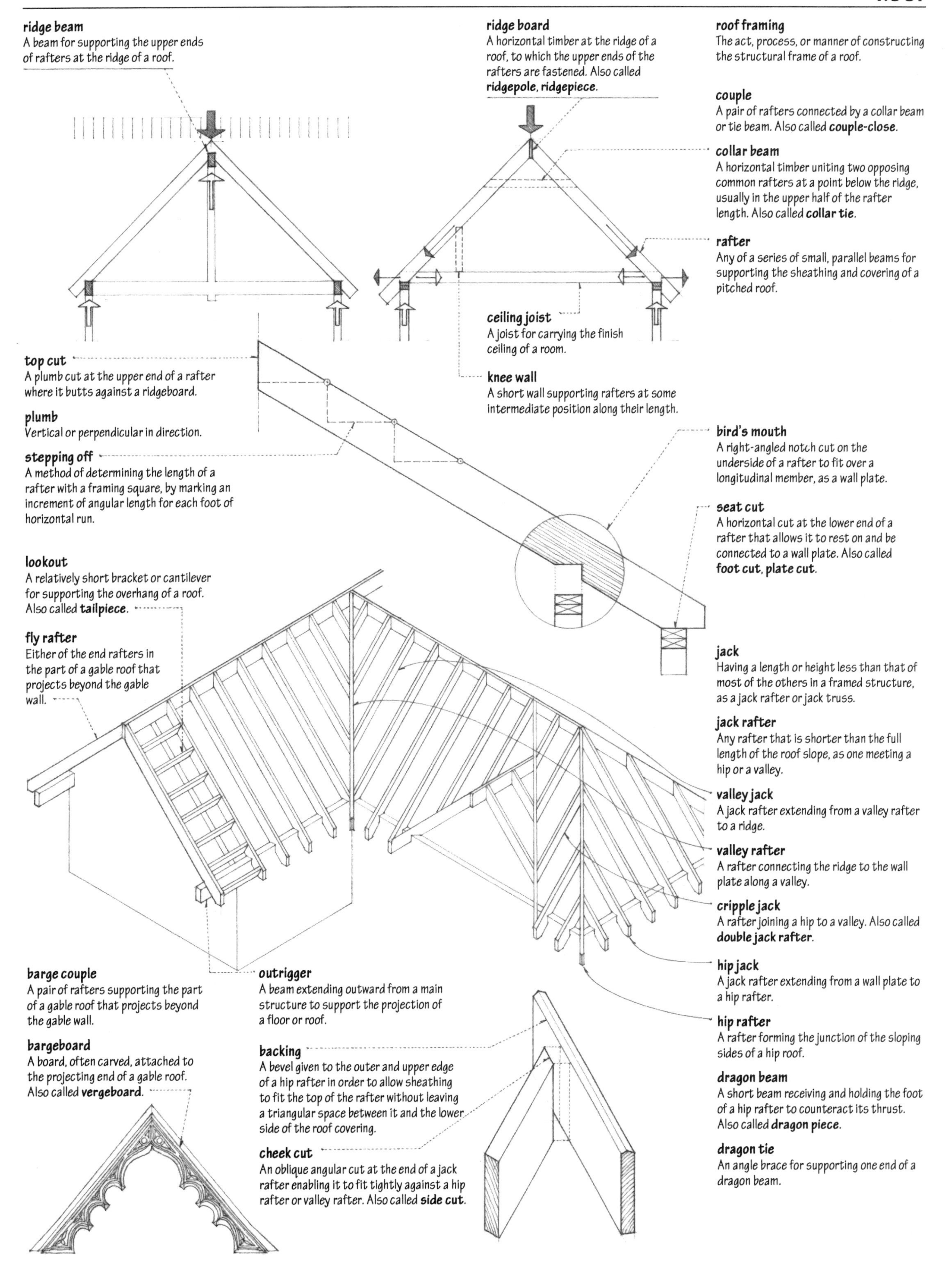

ridge beam
A beam for supporting the upper ends of rafters at the ridge of a roof.

top cut
A plumb cut at the upper end of a rafter where it butts against a ridgeboard.

plumb
Vertical or perpendicular in direction.

stepping off
A method of determining the length of a rafter with a framing square, by marking an increment of angular length for each foot of horizontal run.

lookout
A relatively short bracket or cantilever for supporting the overhang of a roof. Also called **tailpiece**.

fly rafter
Either of the end rafters in the part of a gable roof that projects beyond the gable wall.

barge couple
A pair of rafters supporting the part of a gable roof that projects beyond the gable wall.

bargeboard
A board, often carved, attached to the projecting end of a gable roof. Also called **vergeboard**.

ridge board
A horizontal timber at the ridge of a roof, to which the upper ends of the rafters are fastened. Also called **ridgepole, ridgepiece**.

ceiling joist
A joist for carrying the finish ceiling of a room.

knee wall
A short wall supporting rafters at some intermediate position along their length.

outrigger
A beam extending outward from a main structure to support the projection of a floor or roof.

backing
A bevel given to the outer and upper edge of a hip rafter in order to allow sheathing to fit the top of the rafter without leaving a triangular space between it and the lower side of the roof covering.

cheek cut
An oblique angular cut at the end of a jack rafter enabling it to fit tightly against a hip rafter or valley rafter. Also called **side cut**.

roof framing
The act, process, or manner of constructing the structural frame of a roof.

couple
A pair of rafters connected by a collar beam or tie beam. Also called **couple-close**.

collar beam
A horizontal timber uniting two opposing common rafters at a point below the ridge, usually in the upper half of the rafter length. Also called **collar tie**.

rafter
Any of a series of small, parallel beams for supporting the sheathing and covering of a pitched roof.

bird's mouth
A right-angled notch cut on the underside of a rafter to fit over a longitudinal member, as a wall plate.

seat cut
A horizontal cut at the lower end of a rafter that allows it to rest on and be connected to a wall plate. Also called **foot cut, plate cut**.

jack
Having a length or height less than that of most of the others in a framed structure, as a jack rafter or jack truss.

jack rafter
Any rafter that is shorter than the full length of the roof slope, as one meeting a hip or a valley.

valley jack
A jack rafter extending from a valley rafter to a ridge.

valley rafter
A rafter connecting the ridge to the wall plate along a valley.

cripple jack
A rafter joining a hip to a valley. Also called **double jack rafter**.

hip jack
A jack rafter extending from a wall plate to a hip rafter.

hip rafter
A rafter forming the junction of the sloping sides of a hip roof.

dragon beam
A short beam receiving and holding the foot of a hip rafter to counteract its thrust. Also called **dragon piece**.

dragon tie
An angle brace for supporting one end of a dragon beam.

roofing
Any of various water-resistant materials, as shingles, slates, or tiles, laid on a roof to shed or drain rainwater.

shingle
A thin, usually oblong piece of wood, asphaltic material, slate, metal, or concrete, laid in overlapping rows to cover the roof and walls of buildings.

imbrication
The overlapping of shingles or roofing tiles with break joints to form a weathertight covering.

break joints
The arranging of building units, as masonry, shingles, or siding, to ensure that vertical joints are not continuous in adjacent courses. Also called **staggered joints**.

common lap
A method of laying shingles by offsetting alternate courses one-half the width of a shingle.

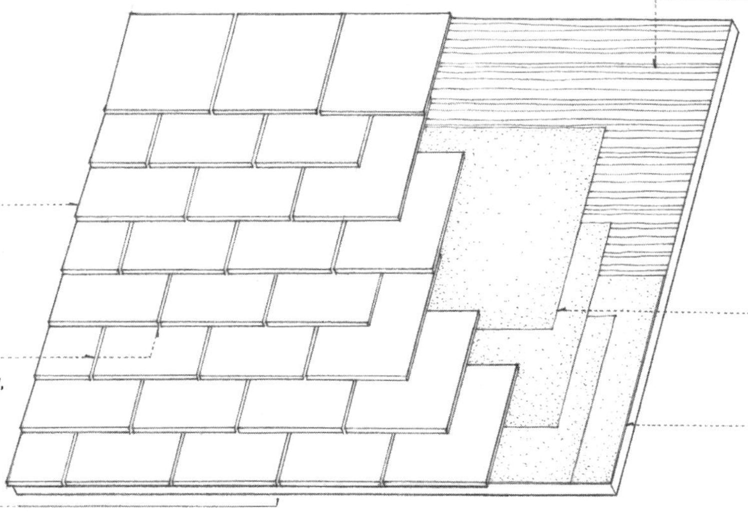

toplap
The distance by which a shingle, slate, or roofing tile overlaps another in the course immediately below it.

exposure
The portion of the length of a shingle, slate, or roofing tile left exposed to the weather when laid in place. Also called **gauge**, **margin**.

headlap
The distance by which a shingle, slate, or roofing tile overlaps another in the second course below it.

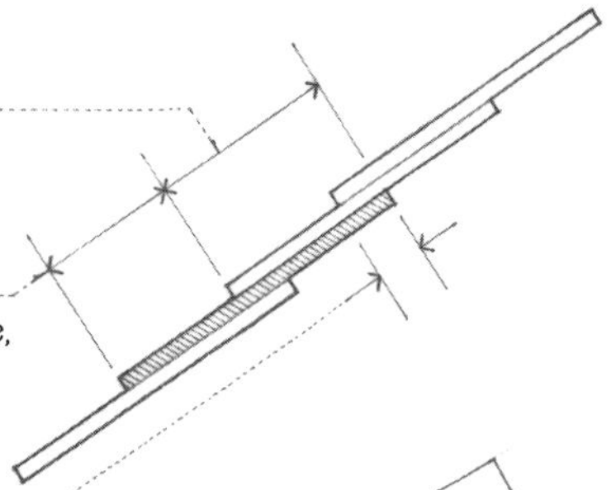

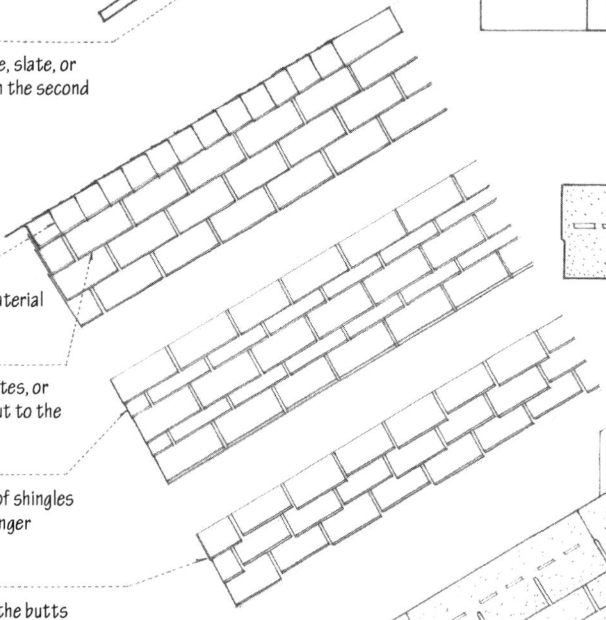

ridgecap
A course or layer of roofing material covering the ridge of a roof.

ridge course
The top course of shingles, slates, or roofing tiles next to a ridge, cut to the required length.

ribbon course
One of the alternate courses of shingles or slate laid with shorter or longer exposure.

staggered course
A course of shingles laid with the butts slightly above or below the one adjacent.

doubling course
A double layer of shingles or tiles laid at the foot of a roof slope or a vertical section of shingling.

starting course
The first course of shingles, slates, or tiles along the eaves of a roof before the first regular course is laid.

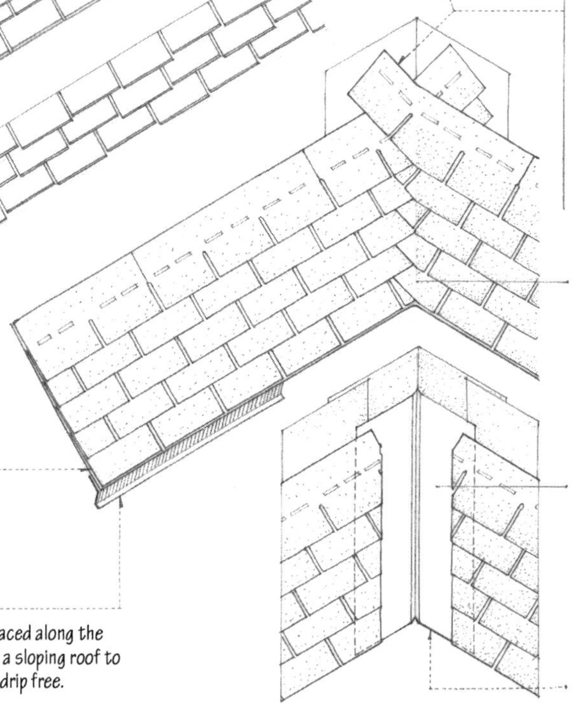

drip edge
A metal molding placed along the eaves and rakes of a sloping roof to allow rainwater to drip free.

sheathing
Boards or structural panels, as plywood, fastened to the frame of a wall or roof as a base for cladding or roofing.

panel clip
An H-shaped metal device for joining sheets of plywood roof sheathing at unsupported joints.

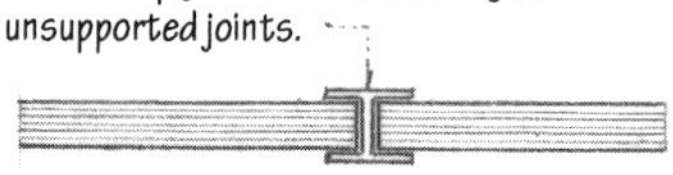

underlayment
A weather-resistant material, as roofing felt, for covering and protecting a roof deck before shingles are applied.

eaves flashing
An additional layer of underlayment cemented to a roof deck to prevent melting ice and snow from backing up under the roofing along the eaves.

ice dam
A buildup of snow and ice along the eave of a sloping roof.

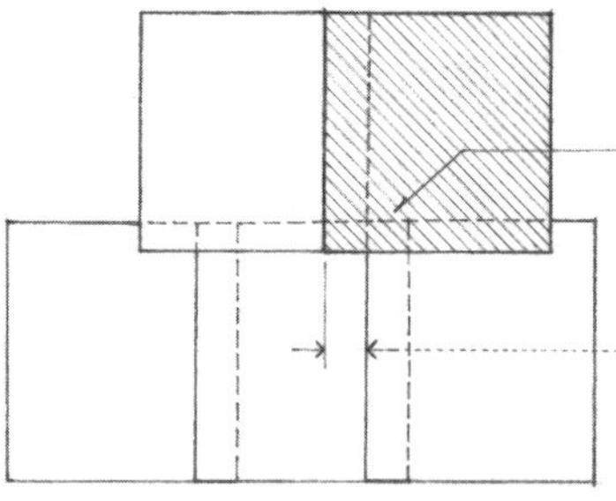

Dutch lap
A method of laying shingles or slates by lapping each shingle over one to the side and one below.

sidelap
The distance by which a shingle, slate, or roofing tile overlaps an adjacent one along its side edge. Also called **endlap**.

coverage
The amount of weather protection provided by the overlapping of shingles or slates.

square
A unit for measuring roofing materials, equal to 100 sq. ft. (9.3 sq. m) of coverage.

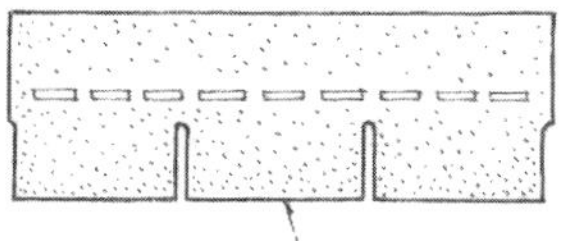

asphalt shingle
A composition shingle having an asphalt-impregnated felt base, surfaced on the weather side with colored mineral granules embedded in a hot asphaltic coating.

fiberglass shingle
A composition shingle having an inorganic fiberglass base, saturated with asphalt and surfaced on the weather side with colored ceramic granules.

closed valley
A valley formed by overlapping successive courses of shingles in alternate directions. Also called **laced valley**, **woven valley**.

open valley
A valley at which shingles or slates are not laid to the intersection, exposing a lining of sheet metal or roll roofing.

valley flashing
A wide strip of sheet metal or roofing felt for lining the valley of a roof.

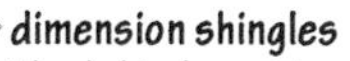

blue label
A premium grade of red cedar shingle of clear, edge-grained heartwood.

red label
An intermediate grade of red cedar shingle having a limited amount of flat grain and sapwood.

black label
A utility grade of red cedar shingle.

dimension shingles
Wood shingles cut to a uniform size.

random shingles
Wood shingles of uniform length, but of random width.

shake
A thick shingle formed by splitting a short log into a number of tapered radial sections.

tapersplit shake
A handsplit shake tapered by reversing the block with each split.

handsplit-and-resawn shake
A tapersplit shake having a split face and a sawn back.

straightsplit shake
A handsplit shake of uniform thickness.

butt
The thick, usually lower exposed end of a wood shingle or shake.

undercourse
A row of wood shingles laid along the rake of a sloping roof with the butts projecting outward to give an inward slope to the surface shingles. Also called **undercloak**.

spaced sheathing
Roofing boards laid some distance apart to provide ventilation for wood shingles and shakes. Also called **open boarding, skip sheathing**.

Boston hip
The weaving of shingles at the hip or ridge of a roof. Also called **Boston ridge**.

weaving
A method of laying shingles on adjoining surfaces of a roof or wall so that shingles on each face lap each other alternately.

sprocket
A strip of wood fixed to each rafter at the eaves in order to extend a sloping roof with a flatter pitch. Also called **cocking piece**.

rafter tail
The lower, sometimes exposed, end of a rafter that overhangs a wall.

tail cut
A sometimes ornamental cut at the lower end of a rafter tail.

open cornice
An eaves overhang exposing the ends of rafters and the underside of the roof sheathing. Also called **open eaves**.

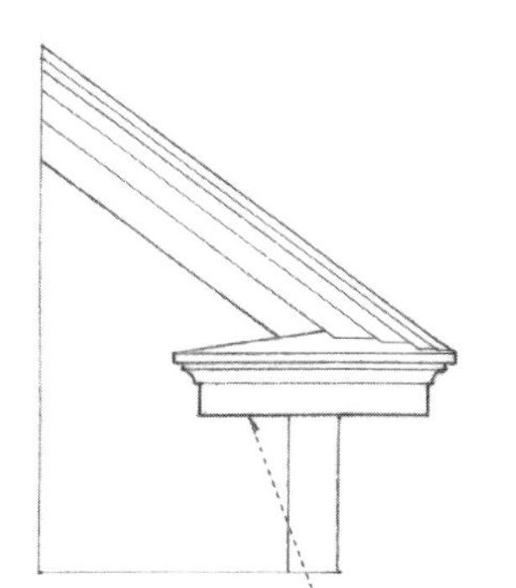

cornice return
The continuation of a cornice around the gable end of a house.

box cornice
A slightly projecting, hollow cornice of boards and moldings, nailed to rafters and lookouts. Also called **closed cornice**.

fascia
Any broad, flat, horizontal surface, as the outer edge of a cornice or roof.

fascia board
A wide board set vertically to cover the lower ends of rafters or the joint between the top of a wall and the projecting eaves.

diagonal slating
A method of laying roofing slates with the diagonal of each tile running horizontally. Also called **drop-point slating**.

honeycomb slating
Diagonal slating in which the tails are cut from the roofing slates.

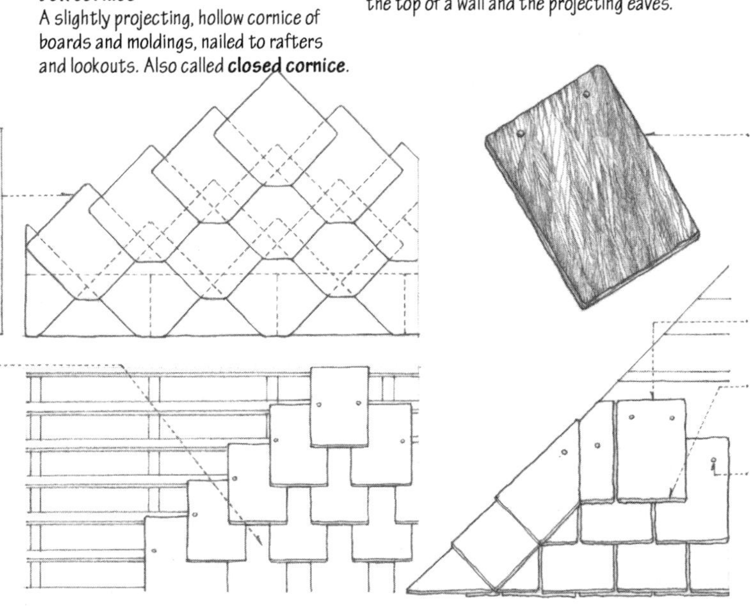

open slating
A method of laying roofing slates with spaces between adjacent tiles in a course. Also called **spaced slating**.

diminishing course
One of a number of courses of roofing slates that diminish in exposure, and sometimes width, from the eaves to the ridge.

sized slates
Roofing slates of uniform width.

random slates
Roofing slates of varying width, often laid in diminishing courses. Also called **rustic slates**.

head
The upper end of a roofing slate.

tail
The lower, exposed portion of a roofing slate.

slating nail
A copper nail having a large, flat head and a medium-diamond-shaped point, used esp. for fixing slates.

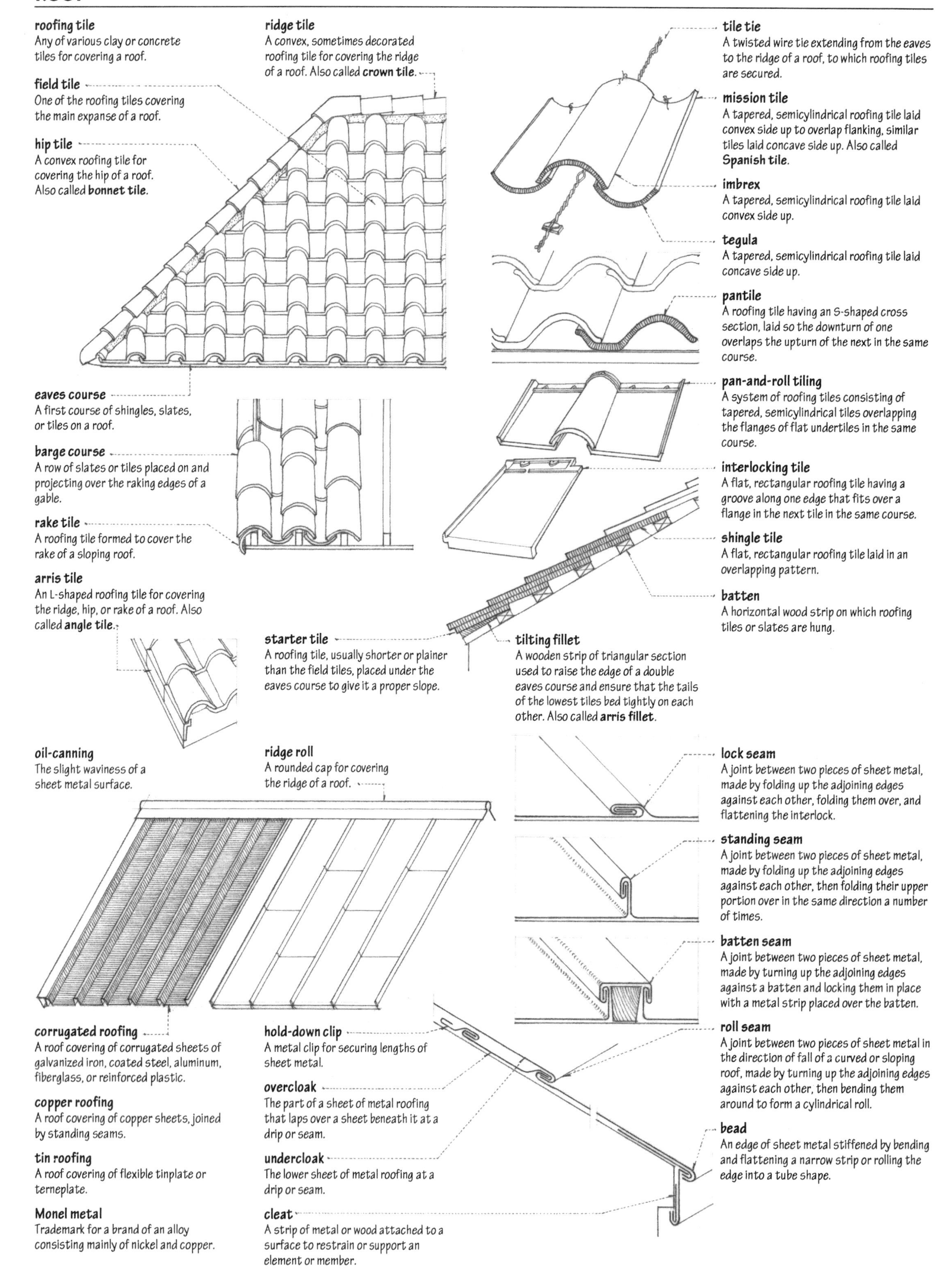

roofing tile
Any of various clay or concrete tiles for covering a roof.

field tile
One of the roofing tiles covering the main expanse of a roof.

hip tile
A convex roofing tile for covering the hip of a roof. Also called **bonnet tile.**

ridge tile
A convex, sometimes decorated roofing tile for covering the ridge of a roof. Also called **crown tile.**

eaves course
A first course of shingles, slates, or tiles on a roof.

barge course
A row of slates or tiles placed on and projecting over the raking edges of a gable.

rake tile
A roofing tile formed to cover the rake of a sloping roof.

arris tile
An L-shaped roofing tile for covering the ridge, hip, or rake of a roof. Also called **angle tile.**

tile tie
A twisted wire tie extending from the eaves to the ridge of a roof, to which roofing tiles are secured.

mission tile
A tapered, semicylindrical roofing tile laid convex side up to overlap flanking, similar tiles laid concave side up. Also called **Spanish tile.**

imbrex
A tapered, semicylindrical roofing tile laid convex side up.

tegula
A tapered, semicylindrical roofing tile laid concave side up.

pantile
A roofing tile having an S-shaped cross section, laid so the downturn of one overlaps the upturn of the next in the same course.

pan-and-roll tiling
A system of roofing tiles consisting of tapered, semicylindrical tiles overlapping the flanges of flat undertiles in the same course.

interlocking tile
A flat, rectangular roofing tile having a groove along one edge that fits over a flange in the next tile in the same course.

shingle tile
A flat, rectangular roofing tile laid in an overlapping pattern.

batten
A horizontal wood strip on which roofing tiles or slates are hung.

starter tile
A roofing tile, usually shorter or plainer than the field tiles, placed under the eaves course to give it a proper slope.

tilting fillet
A wooden strip of triangular section used to raise the edge of a double eaves course and ensure that the tails of the lowest tiles bed tightly on each other. Also called **arris fillet.**

oil-canning
The slight waviness of a sheet metal surface.

ridge roll
A rounded cap for covering the ridge of a roof.

corrugated roofing
A roof covering of corrugated sheets of galvanized iron, coated steel, aluminum, fiberglass, or reinforced plastic.

copper roofing
A roof covering of copper sheets, joined by standing seams.

tin roofing
A roof covering of flexible tinplate or terneplate.

Monel metal
Trademark for a brand of an alloy consisting mainly of nickel and copper.

hold-down clip
A metal clip for securing lengths of sheet metal.

overcloak
The part of a sheet of metal roofing that laps over a sheet beneath it at a drip or seam.

undercloak
The lower sheet of metal roofing at a drip or seam.

cleat
A strip of metal or wood attached to a surface to restrain or support an element or member.

lock seam
A joint between two pieces of sheet metal, made by folding up the adjoining edges against each other, folding them over, and flattening the interlock.

standing seam
A joint between two pieces of sheet metal, made by folding up the adjoining edges against each other, then folding their upper portion over in the same direction a number of times.

batten seam
A joint between two pieces of sheet metal, made by turning up the adjoining edges against a batten and locking them in place with a metal strip placed over the batten.

roll seam
A joint between two pieces of sheet metal in the direction of fall of a curved or sloping roof, made by turning up the adjoining edges against each other, then bending them around to form a cylindrical roll.

bead
An edge of sheet metal stiffened by bending and flattening a narrow strip or rolling the edge into a tube shape.

Hypalon
Trademark for a brand of chlorinated polyethylene.

EPDM
Ethylene propylene diene monomer, a synthetic rubber manufactured in sheets and used as a roofing membrane.

single-ply roofing
A sheet of elastomeric material, as neoprene, EPDM, or PVC, having seams fused by heat or a solvent, fixed to a roof deck with adhesive, mechanical fasteners, or by the weight of a gravel ballast. Also called **elastomeric roofing**.

elastomeric
Having the elastic qualities of natural rubber.

gravel stop
A metal strip with a vertical flange for retaining surfacing aggregate and preventing leaks around the edge of a built-up roof.

protected membrane roof
A single-ply roofing membrane protected from sunlight and extremes of temperature by a layer of rigid board insulation and an additional layer of gravel ballast.

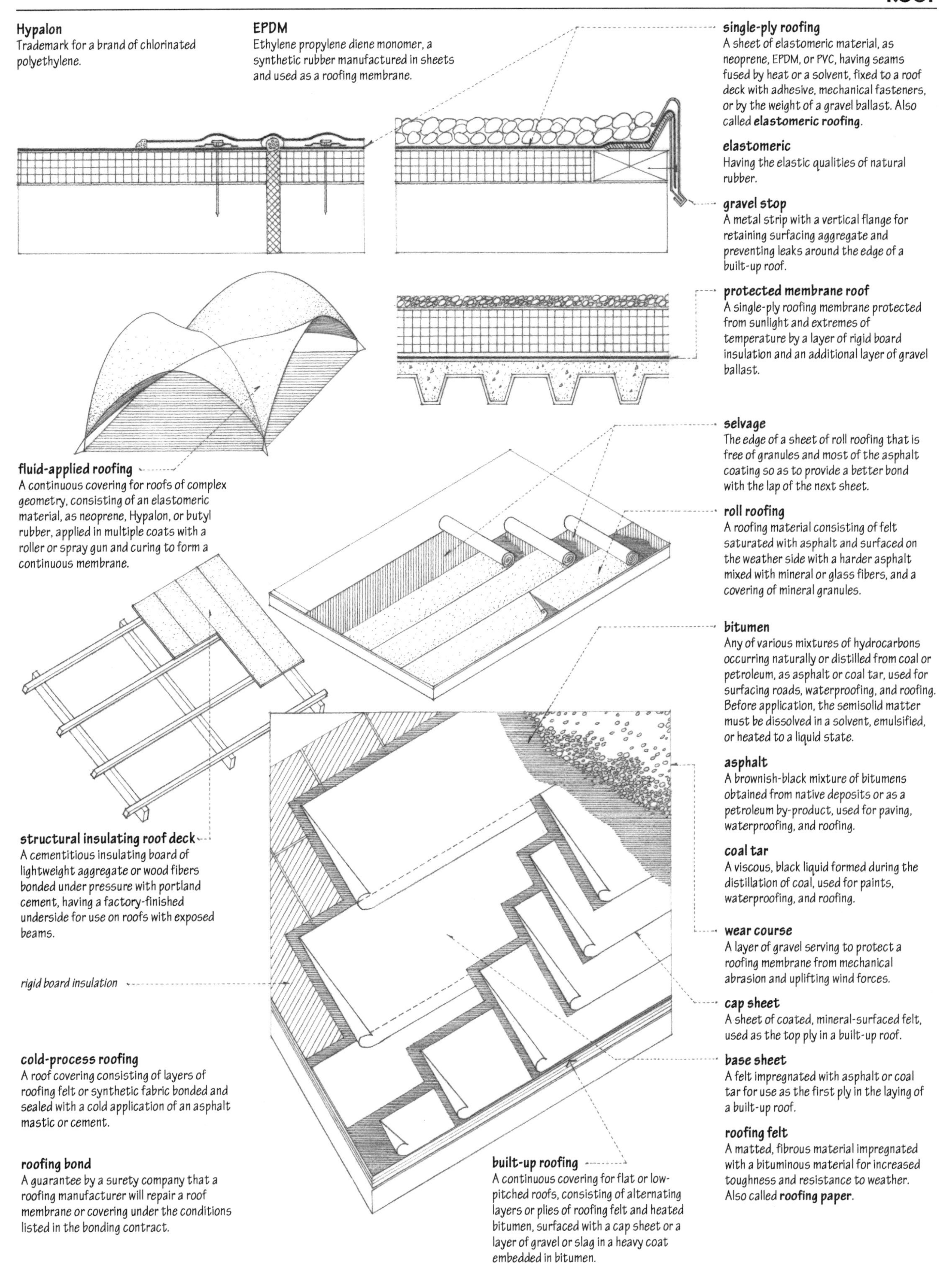

fluid-applied roofing
A continuous covering for roofs of complex geometry, consisting of an elastomeric material, as neoprene, Hypalon, or butyl rubber, applied in multiple coats with a roller or spray gun and curing to form a continuous membrane.

structural insulating roof deck
A cementitious insulating board of lightweight aggregate or wood fibers bonded under pressure with portland cement, having a factory-finished underside for use on roofs with exposed beams.

cold-process roofing
A roof covering consisting of layers of roofing felt or synthetic fabric bonded and sealed with a cold application of an asphalt mastic or cement.

roofing bond
A guarantee by a surety company that a roofing manufacturer will repair a roof membrane or covering under the conditions listed in the bonding contract.

built-up roofing
A continuous covering for flat or low-pitched roofs, consisting of alternating layers or plies of roofing felt and heated bitumen, surfaced with a cap sheet or a layer of gravel or slag in a heavy coat embedded in bitumen.

selvage
The edge of a sheet of roll roofing that is free of granules and most of the asphalt coating so as to provide a better bond with the lap of the next sheet.

roll roofing
A roofing material consisting of felt saturated with asphalt and surfaced on the weather side with a harder asphalt mixed with mineral or glass fibers, and a covering of mineral granules.

bitumen
Any of various mixtures of hydrocarbons occurring naturally or distilled from coal or petroleum, as asphalt or coal tar, used for surfacing roads, waterproofing, and roofing. Before application, the semisolid matter must be dissolved in a solvent, emulsified, or heated to a liquid state.

asphalt
A brownish-black mixture of bitumens obtained from native deposits or as a petroleum by-product, used for paving, waterproofing, and roofing.

coal tar
A viscous, black liquid formed during the distillation of coal, used for paints, waterproofing, and roofing.

wear course
A layer of gravel serving to protect a roofing membrane from mechanical abrasion and uplifting wind forces.

cap sheet
A sheet of coated, mineral-surfaced felt, used as the top ply in a built-up roof.

base sheet
A felt impregnated with asphalt or coal tar for use as the first ply in the laying of a built-up roof.

roofing felt
A matted, fibrous material impregnated with a bituminous material for increased toughness and resistance to weather. Also called **roofing paper**.

ROOM

A portion of space within a building, separated by walls or partitions from other similar spaces.

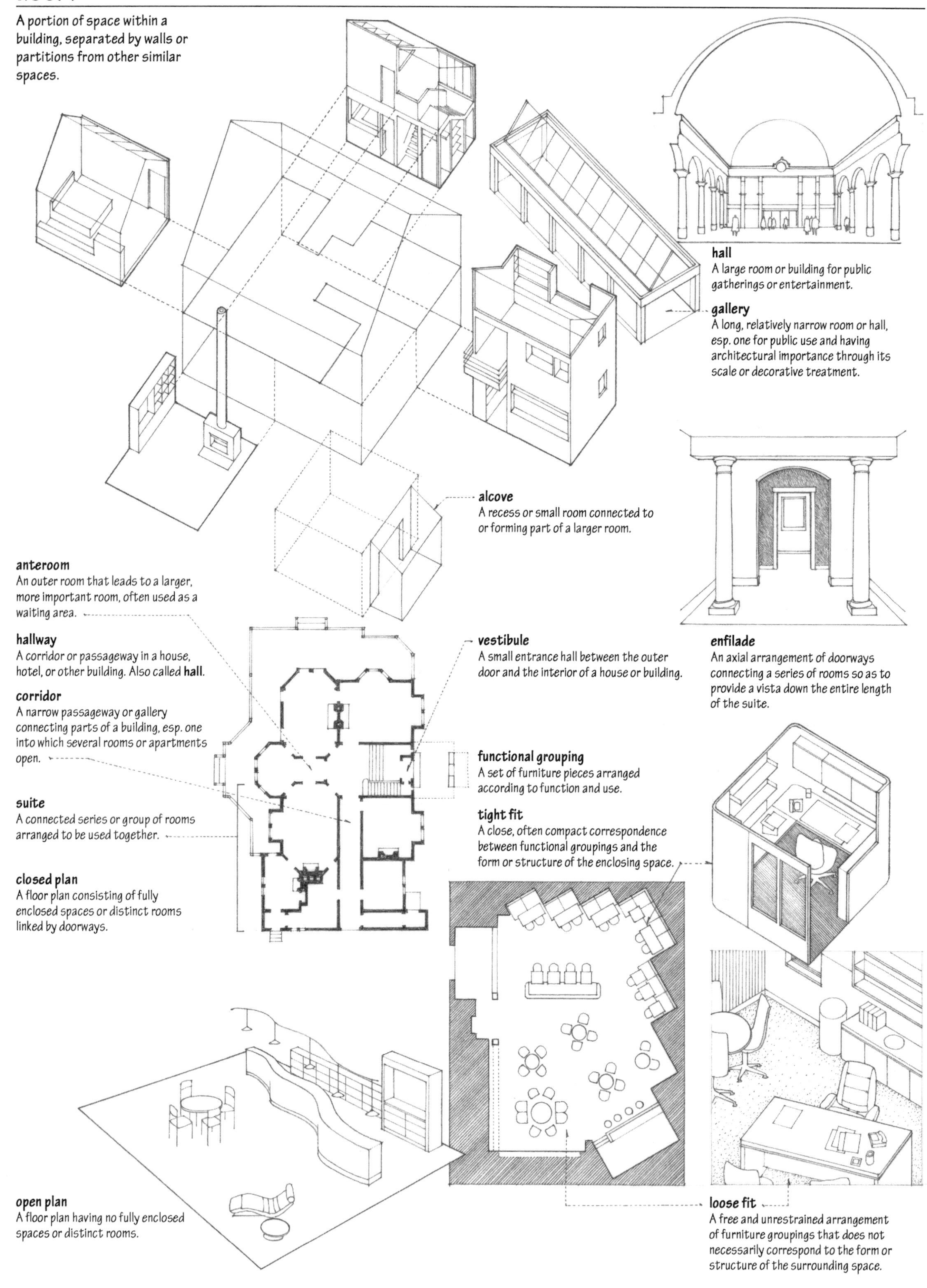

hall
A large room or building for public gatherings or entertainment.

gallery
A long, relatively narrow room or hall, esp. one for public use and having architectural importance through its scale or decorative treatment.

alcove
A recess or small room connected to or forming part of a larger room.

enfilade
An axial arrangement of doorways connecting a series of rooms so as to provide a vista down the entire length of the suite.

anteroom
An outer room that leads to a larger, more important room, often used as a waiting area.

hallway
A corridor or passageway in a house, hotel, or other building. Also called **hall**.

corridor
A narrow passageway or gallery connecting parts of a building, esp. one into which several rooms or apartments open.

suite
A connected series or group of rooms arranged to be used together.

closed plan
A floor plan consisting of fully enclosed spaces or distinct rooms linked by doorways.

vestibule
A small entrance hall between the outer door and the interior of a house or building.

functional grouping
A set of furniture pieces arranged according to function and use.

tight fit
A close, often compact correspondence between functional groupings and the form or structure of the enclosing space.

open plan
A floor plan having no fully enclosed spaces or distinct rooms.

loose fit
A free and unrestrained arrangement of furniture groupings that does not necessarily correspond to the form or structure of the surrounding space.

mass
The physical volume or bulk of a solid body.

space
The three-dimensional field in which objects and events occur and have relative position and direction, esp. a portion of that field set apart in a given instance or for a particular purpose.

Euclidean space
Ordinary two- or three-dimensional space in which Euclid's definitions and axioms apply. Also called **Cartesian space**.

void
An empty space contained within or bounded by mass.

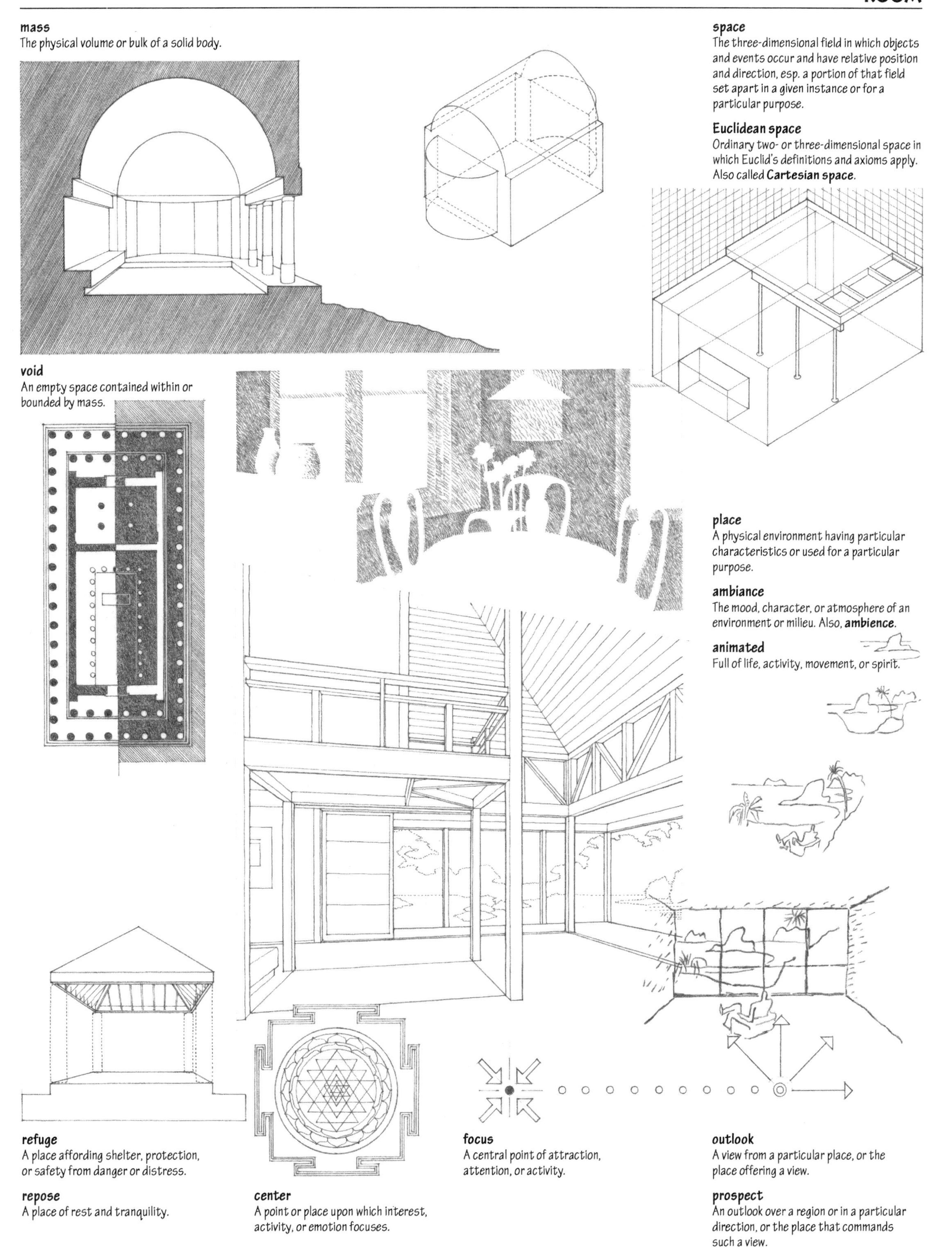

place
A physical environment having particular characteristics or used for a particular purpose.

ambiance
The mood, character, or atmosphere of an environment or milieu. Also, **ambience**.

animated
Full of life, activity, movement, or spirit.

refuge
A place affording shelter, protection, or safety from danger or distress.

repose
A place of rest and tranquility.

center
A point or place upon which interest, activity, or emotion focuses.

focus
A central point of attraction, attention, or activity.

outlook
A view from a particular place, or the place offering a view.

prospect
An outlook over a region or in a particular direction, or the place that commands such a view.

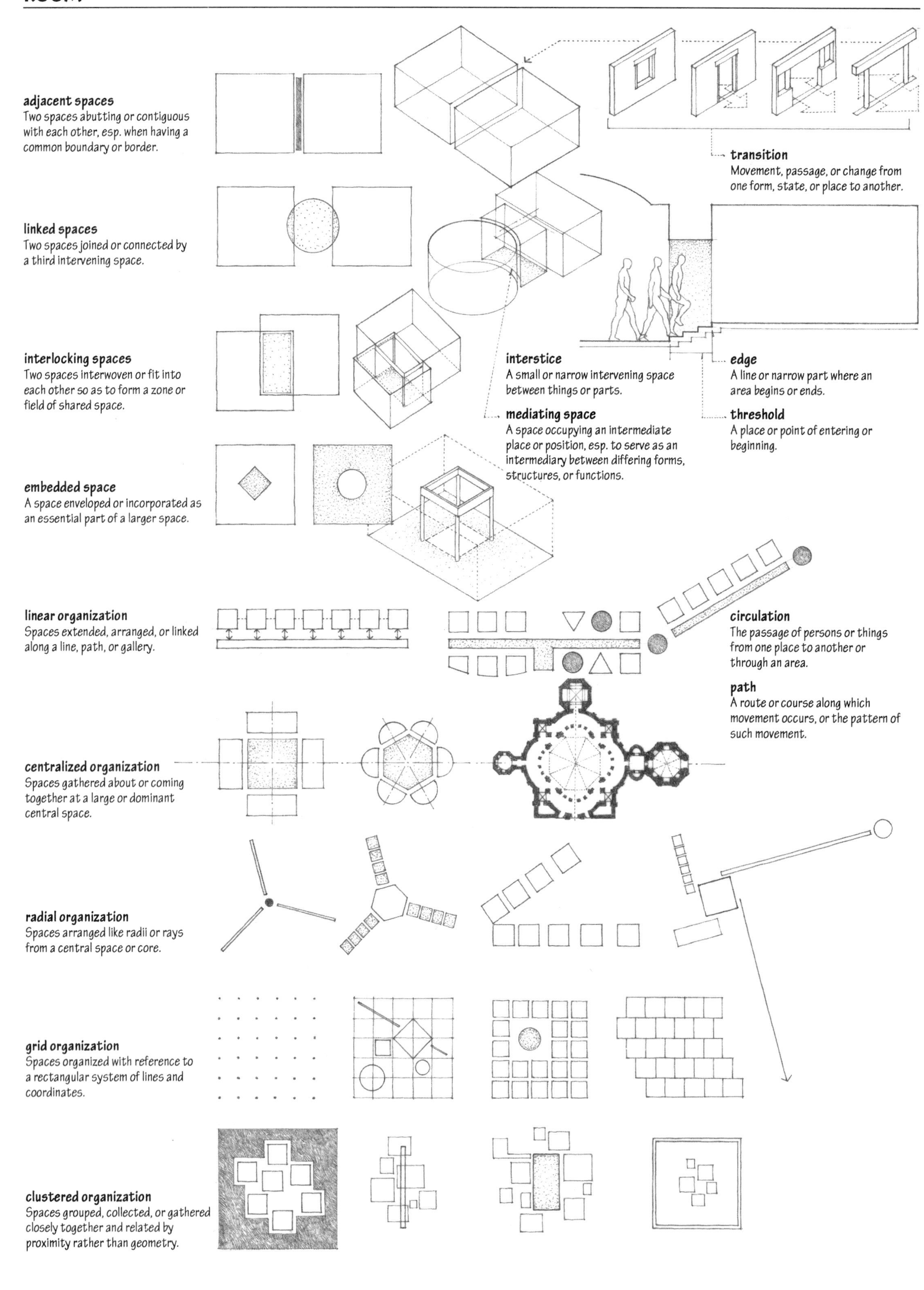

adjacent spaces
Two spaces abutting or contiguous with each other, esp. when having a common boundary or border.

transition
Movement, passage, or change from one form, state, or place to another.

linked spaces
Two spaces joined or connected by a third intervening space.

interlocking spaces
Two spaces interwoven or fit into each other so as to form a zone or field of shared space.

interstice
A small or narrow intervening space between things or parts.

mediating space
A space occupying an intermediate place or position, esp. to serve as an intermediary between differing forms, structures, or functions.

edge
A line or narrow part where an area begins or ends.

threshold
A place or point of entering or beginning.

embedded space
A space enveloped or incorporated as an essential part of a larger space.

linear organization
Spaces extended, arranged, or linked along a line, path, or gallery.

circulation
The passage of persons or things from one place to another or through an area.

path
A route or course along which movement occurs, or the pattern of such movement.

centralized organization
Spaces gathered about or coming together at a large or dominant central space.

radial organization
Spaces arranged like radii or rays from a central space or core.

grid organization
Spaces organized with reference to a rectangular system of lines and coordinates.

clustered organization
Spaces grouped, collected, or gathered closely together and related by proximity rather than geometry.

A thin, curved plate structure, shaped to transmit applied forces by compressive, tensile, and shear stresses acting in the plane of the surface.

membrane stresses
The compressive, tensile, and shear stresses acting in the plane of the surface of a shell structure. A shell can sustain relatively large forces if uniformly applied. Because of its thinness, however, a shell has little bending resistance and is unsuitable for concentrated loads.

thin shell
A shell structure constructed of reinforced concrete.

translational surface
A surface generated by sliding a plane curve along a straight line or over another plane curve.

barrel shell
A rigid cylindrical shell structure.

If the length of a barrel shell is three or more times its transverse span, it behaves as a deep beam with a curved section spanning in the longitudinal direction. Edges are stiffened with beams or adjoining shells.

If it is relatively short, it exhibits archlike action. Tie rods, transverse rigid frames, or the like are required to counteract the outward thrusts of the arching action.

cylindrical surface
A surface generated by sliding a straight line along a plane curve, or vice versa. Depending on the curve, a cylindrical surface may be circular, elliptic, or parabolic. Because of its straight line geometry, a cylindrical surface can be regarded as being either a translational or a ruled surface.

elliptic paraboloid
A surface generated by sliding a vertical parabola with downward curvature along a perpendicular parabola with downward curvature. Its horizontal sections are ellipses while its vertical sections are parabolas.

hyperbolic paraboloid
A surface generated by sliding a parabola with downward curvature along a parabola with upward curvature, or by sliding a straight line segment with its ends on two skew lines. It can be considered to be both a translational and a ruled surface. Also called **hypar**.

paraboloid
A surface all of whose intersections by planes are either parabolas and ellipses or parabolas and hyperbolas.

saddle surface
A surface having an upward curvature in one direction and a downward curvature in the perpendicular direction.
In a saddle-surfaced shell structure, regions of downward curvature exhibit archlike action,
while regions of upward curvature behave as a cable structure. If the edges of the surface are not supported, beam behavior may also be present.

anticlastic
Having opposite curvatures at a given point.

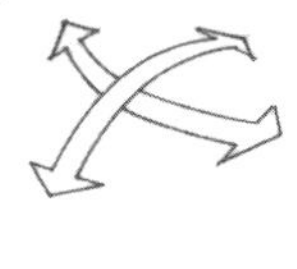

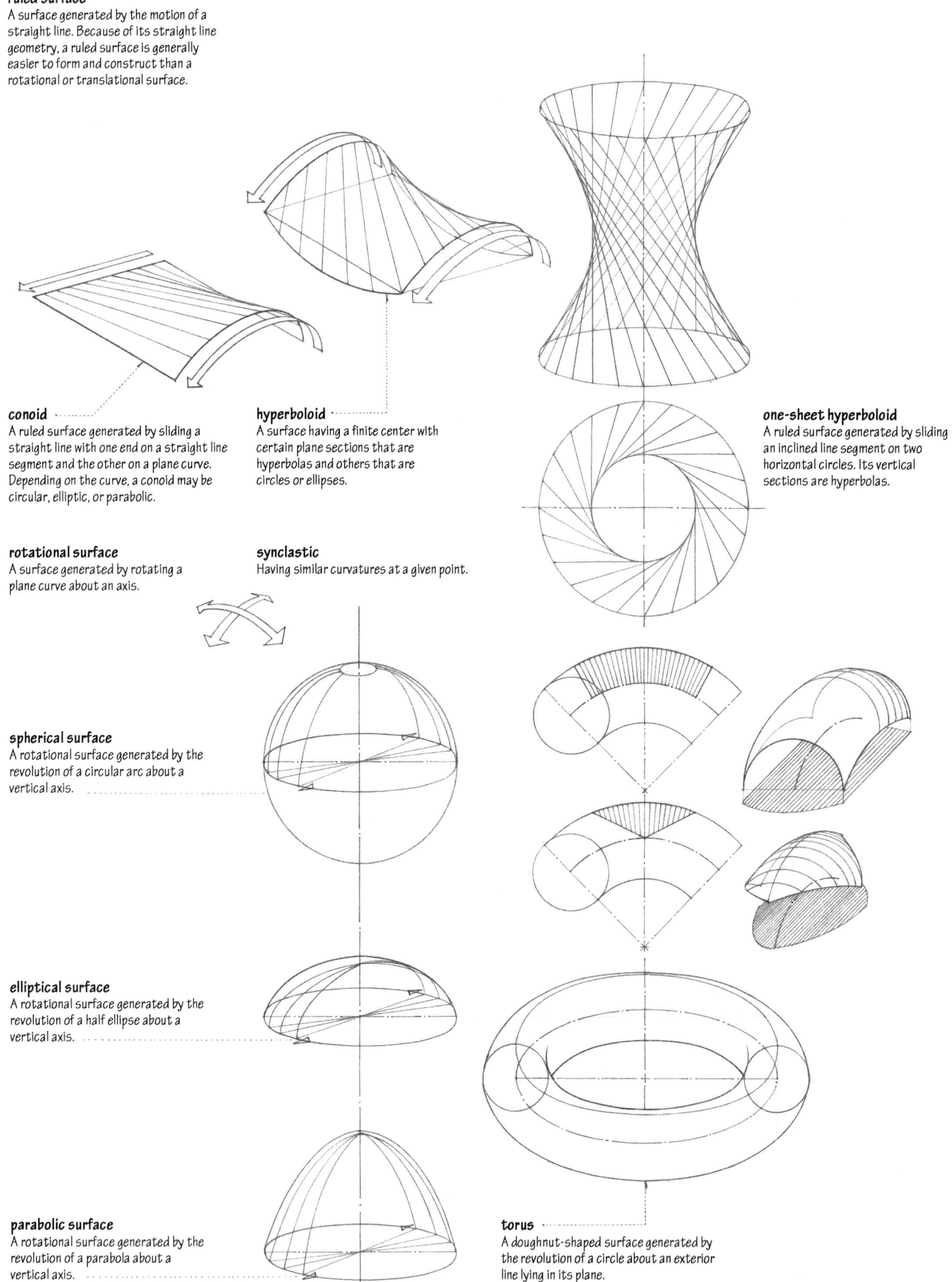

ruled surface
A surface generated by the motion of a straight line. Because of its straight line geometry, a ruled surface is generally easier to form and construct than a rotational or translational surface.

conoid
A ruled surface generated by sliding a straight line with one end on a straight line segment and the other on a plane curve. Depending on the curve, a conoid may be circular, elliptic, or parabolic.

hyperboloid
A surface having a finite center with certain plane sections that are hyperbolas and others that are circles or ellipses.

one-sheet hyperboloid
A ruled surface generated by sliding an inclined line segment on two horizontal circles. Its vertical sections are hyperbolas.

rotational surface
A surface generated by rotating a plane curve about an axis.

synclastic
Having similar curvatures at a given point.

spherical surface
A rotational surface generated by the revolution of a circular arc about a vertical axis.

elliptical surface
A rotational surface generated by the revolution of a half ellipse about a vertical axis.

parabolic surface
A rotational surface generated by the revolution of a parabola about a vertical axis.

torus
A doughnut-shaped surface generated by the revolution of a circle about an exterior line lying in its plane.

Work done at a site in preparation for a construction project, as excavation, sheeting, shoring, and grading.

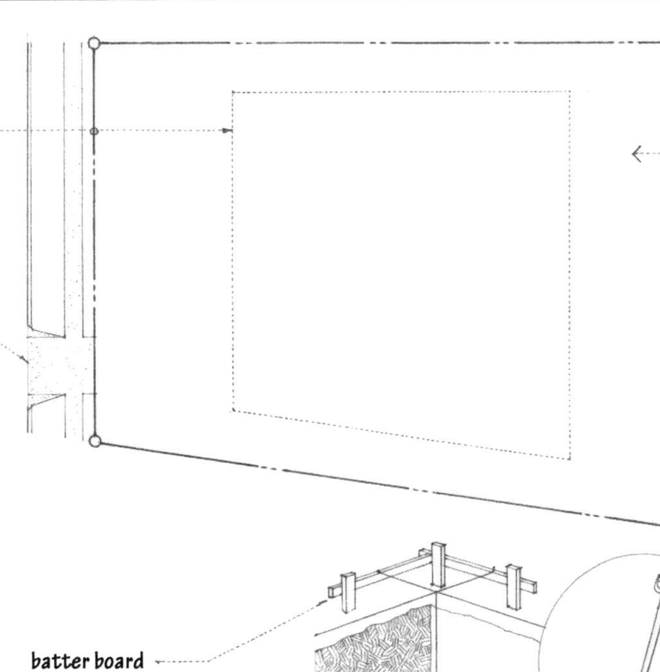

encroachment
The unauthorized extension of a building, or part thereof, on the property or domain of another.

setback
The minimum required distance from every structure to the property lines of a lot, established by a zoning ordinance to provide for air, light, solar access, and privacy.

curb cut
A depression in a curb providing vehicular access from a street to a driveway on private property.

contract limit
A perimeter line established on the drawings or elsewhere in the contract documents defining the boundaries of the site available to the contractor for construction purposes.

site
The geographic location of a construction project, usually defined by legal boundaries.

property line
One of the legally defined and recorded boundaries of a parcel of land. Also called **lot line**.

easement
A legal right held by specified persons or the public to make limited use of the land of another, as a right-of-way.

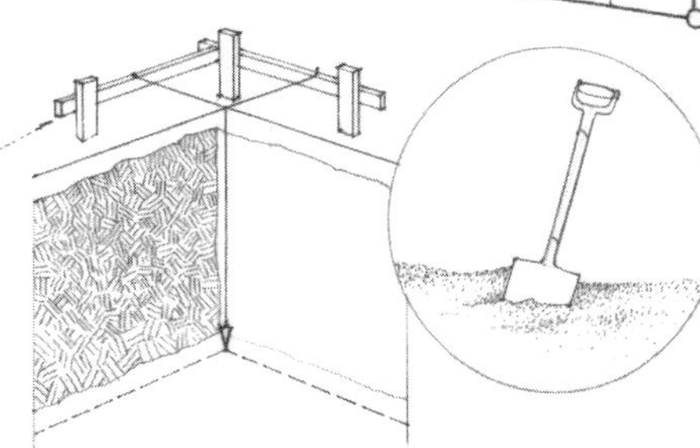

overburden
Waste earth and rock overlying a useful mineral deposit, bedrock, or a deposit of sand, gravel, or rock needed for construction. Also called **burden**.

test pit
A small pit dug to examine the existing soil conditions and determine the depth of the water table at a proposed building site.

shoring
A system of shores for bracing or supporting a wall or other structure.

shore
A temporary supporting strut, esp. one placed obliquely against the side of an excavation, formwork, or structure.

raker
An inclined shore for supporting a wall. Also called **raking shore**.

flying shore
A horizontal strut fixed between and supporting two walls above ground level.

cofferdam
A watertight enclosure constructed underwater or in water-bearing soil and pumped dry to allow access for construction or repairs.

batter board
One of a number of boards set horizontally with vertical stakes to support the strings outlining the foundation plan of a proposed building.

groundbreaking
The act or ceremony of breaking ground for a new construction project.

earthwork
The excavation and embankment of earth in connection with an engineering operation.

excavation
The digging and removal of earth from its natural position, or the cavity resulting from such removal.

tieback
A steel rod or tendon attached to a deadman or a rock or soil anchor to prevent lateral movement of a retaining wall or formwork.

sheet pile
Any of a number of timber, steel, or precast concrete planks driven vertically side by side to retain earth or prevent water from seeping into an excavation. Also called **sheath pile**.

lagging
A number of boards joined together side by side to retain the face of an excavation.

soldier pile
A steel H-section driven vertically into the ground to support horizontal sheeting or lagging. Also called **soldier beam**.

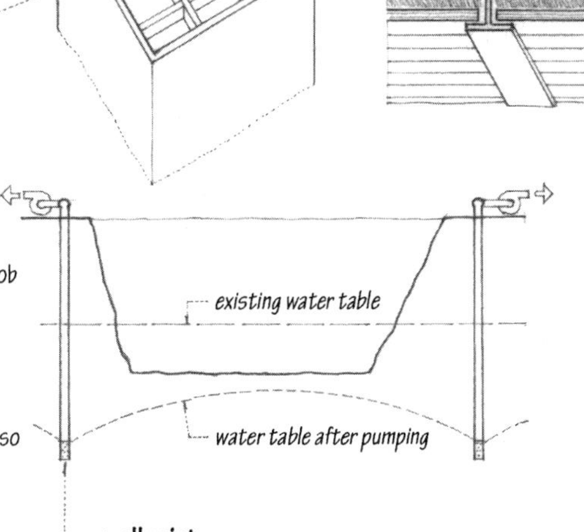

dewater
To remove water from an excavated job site, usually by draining or pumping.

boil
An unwanted flow of water and solid matter into an excavation, due to excessive outside water pressure. Also called **blow**.

Abyssinian well
A perforated pipe driven into the ground for pumping out collected ground water.

wellpoint
A perforated tube driven into the ground to collect water from the surrounding area so it can be pumped away, as to lower a water table or to prevent an excavation from filling with groundwater.

tremie
A funnellike device with a pipe or tube for depositing concrete underwater.

slurry wall
A concrete wall cast in a trench to serve as sheeting and often as a permanent foundation wall, constructed by excavating a trench in short lengths, filling it with a slurry of bentonite and water to prevent the sidewalls from collapsing, setting reinforcement, and placing concrete in the trench with a tremie to displace the slurry.

fill
To raise an existing grade with earth, stone, or other material, or the quantity of material used in building up the level of an area.

made ground
Ground that has been raised to a higher level by filling with hard rubble, as stone or broken brick. Also called **made-up ground**.

borrow pit
A pit from which sand, gravel, or other construction material is taken for use as fill in another location.

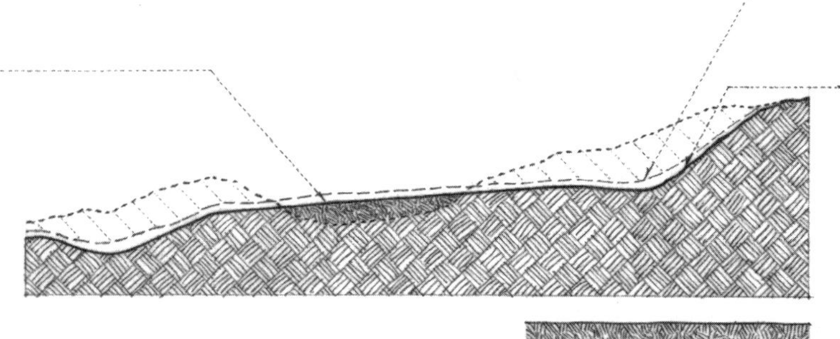

rough grading
The cutting, filling, and shaping of earth in preparation for finish grading.

fine grading
The precise grading of an area after rough grading to prepare for paving, seeding, or planting.

grade stake
A stake marking the amount of cut or fill required to bring the ground to a specified level.

controlled fill
Fill material that is placed in layers, compacted, and tested after each compaction for moisture content, depth of lift, and bearing capacity before additional layers are placed.

cut and fill
An excavating operation in which the excavated material is moved to another location and used as fill.

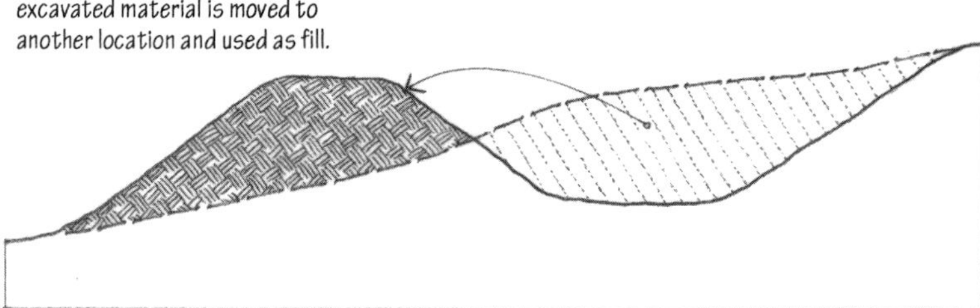

vertical curve
A smooth parabolic curve in the vertical plane for connecting two grades of different slope in order to avoid an abrupt transition.

bench terrace
An embankment constructed across sloping ground with a steep drop on the downside.

grade
The ground elevation at any specific point on a construction site, esp. where the ground meets the foundation of a building. Also called **grade line**.

existing grade
The elevation of the original ground surface before excavation or grading begins. Also called **natural grade**.

finish grade
The elevation of drives, walks, lawns, or other improved surfaces after completion of construction or grading operations. Also, **finished grade**.

below grade
Occurring or situated below the surface of the ground.

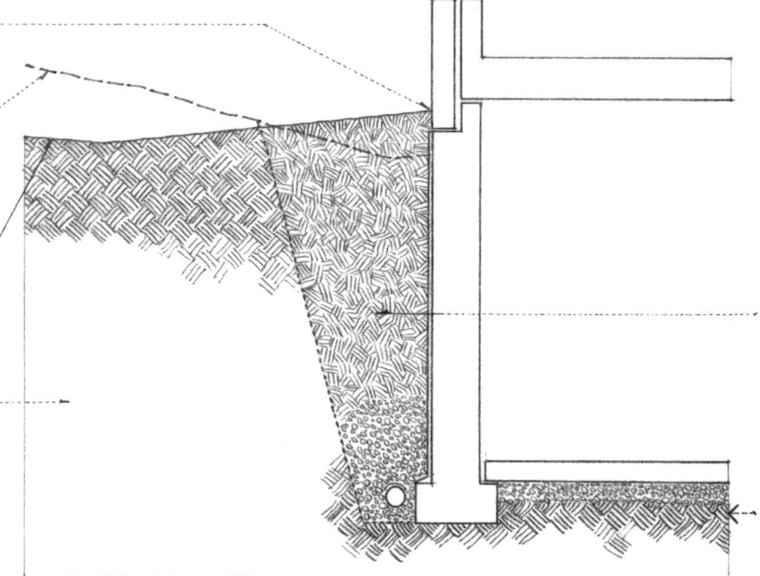

backfill
To refill an excavation with earth, stone, or other material, esp. the space around exterior foundation walls.

subgrade
The prepared earth surface upon which a pavement, concrete slab, or foundation is built. A subgrade should be stable, drain well, and be relatively free of frost action.

underpinning
A system of supports that enables an existing foundation to be rebuilt, strengthened, or deepened, esp. the additional support required when a new excavation in adjoining property is deeper than the existing foundation.

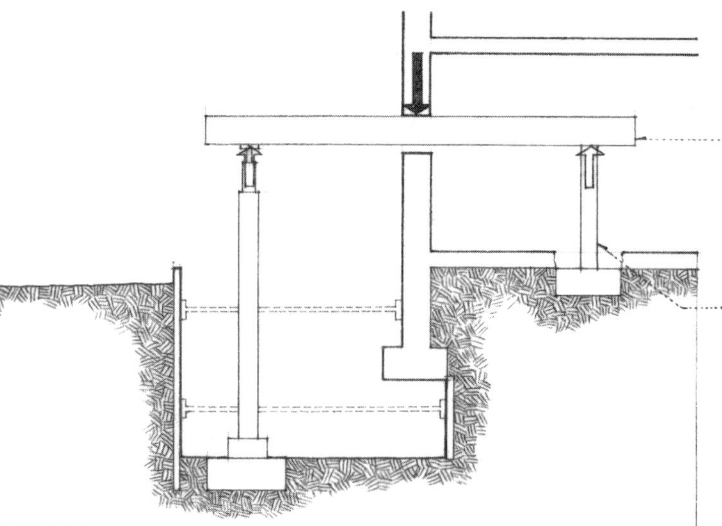

needle
A short beam passed through a wall as a temporary support while the foundation or part beneath is repaired, altered, or strengthened. Also called **needle beam**.

dead shore
An upright timber for supporting a dead load during the structural alteration of a building, esp. one of two supports for a needle.

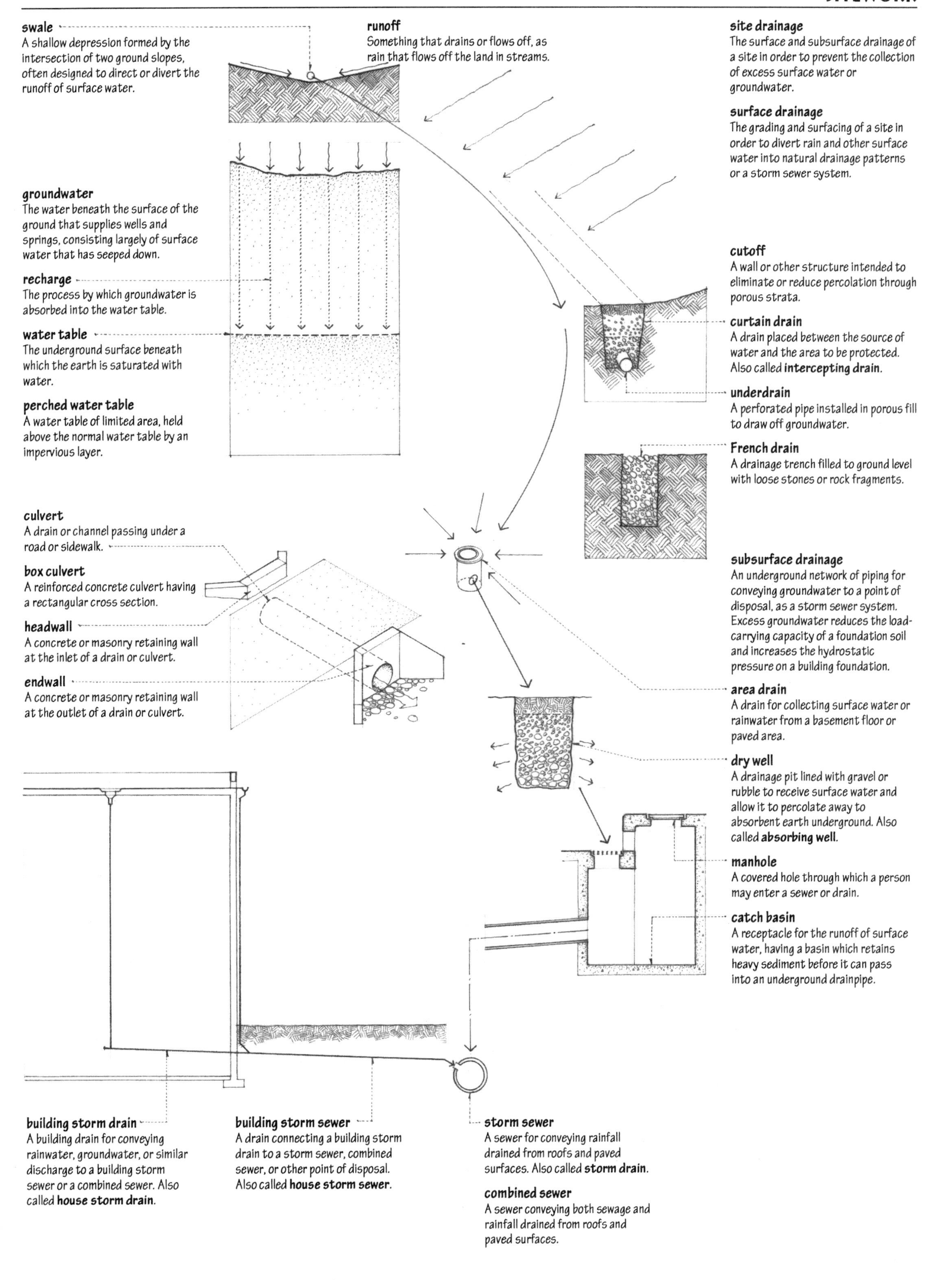

swale
A shallow depression formed by the intersection of two ground slopes, often designed to direct or divert the runoff of surface water.

runoff
Something that drains or flows off, as rain that flows off the land in streams.

site drainage
The surface and subsurface drainage of a site in order to prevent the collection of excess surface water or groundwater.

surface drainage
The grading and surfacing of a site in order to divert rain and other surface water into natural drainage patterns or a storm sewer system.

groundwater
The water beneath the surface of the ground that supplies wells and springs, consisting largely of surface water that has seeped down.

recharge
The process by which groundwater is absorbed into the water table.

water table
The underground surface beneath which the earth is saturated with water.

perched water table
A water table of limited area, held above the normal water table by an impervious layer.

cutoff
A wall or other structure intended to eliminate or reduce percolation through porous strata.

curtain drain
A drain placed between the source of water and the area to be protected. Also called **intercepting drain**.

underdrain
A perforated pipe installed in porous fill to draw off groundwater.

French drain
A drainage trench filled to ground level with loose stones or rock fragments.

culvert
A drain or channel passing under a road or sidewalk.

box culvert
A reinforced concrete culvert having a rectangular cross section.

headwall
A concrete or masonry retaining wall at the inlet of a drain or culvert.

endwall
A concrete or masonry retaining wall at the outlet of a drain or culvert.

subsurface drainage
An underground network of piping for conveying groundwater to a point of disposal, as a storm sewer system. Excess groundwater reduces the load-carrying capacity of a foundation soil and increases the hydrostatic pressure on a building foundation.

area drain
A drain for collecting surface water or rainwater from a basement floor or paved area.

dry well
A drainage pit lined with gravel or rubble to receive surface water and allow it to percolate away to absorbent earth underground. Also called **absorbing well**.

manhole
A covered hole through which a person may enter a sewer or drain.

catch basin
A receptacle for the runoff of surface water, having a basin which retains heavy sediment before it can pass into an underground drainpipe.

building storm drain
A building drain for conveying rainwater, groundwater, or similar discharge to a building storm sewer or a combined sewer. Also called **house storm drain**.

building storm sewer
A drain connecting a building storm drain to a storm sewer, combined sewer, or other point of disposal. Also called **house storm sewer**.

storm sewer
A sewer for conveying rainfall drained from roofs and paved surfaces. Also called **storm drain**.

combined sewer
A sewer conveying both sewage and rainfall drained from roofs and paved surfaces.

SOIL

The top layer of the earth's surface, consisting of disintegrated rock and decayed organic matter suitable for the growth of plant life.

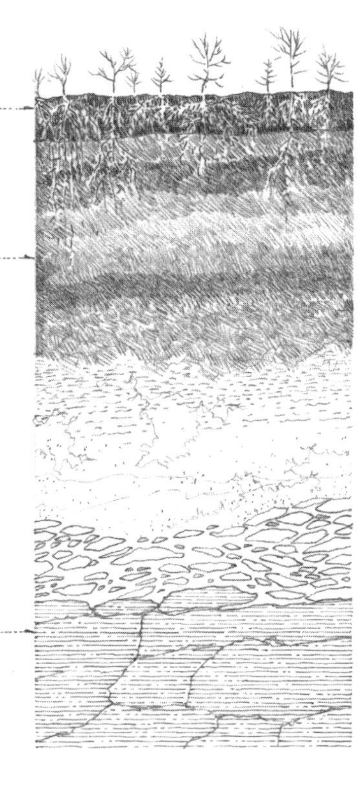

topsoil
The fertile surface layer of soil, as distinct from the subsoil.

subsoil
The bed or layer of earth immediately beneath the surface soil.

permafrost
Perennially frozen subsoil in arctic or subarctic regions. Also called **pergelisol**.

bedrock
The unbroken, solid rock that underlies all unconsolidated material on the earth's surface, as soil, clay, sand, or rock fragments.

organic soil
Soil containing a large amount of organic matter, usually very compressible and having poor load-sustaining properties.

soil profile
A diagram of a vertical section of soil from the ground surface to the underlying material, showing a succession of horizons developed by weathering, deposition, or both.

horizon
Any of a series of relatively distinct layers of soil or its underlying material found in a vertical section of land.

stratum
A single bed or layer of sedimentary earth or rock having the same composition throughout, lying between beds of another kind.

soil analysis
A process for determining the particle-size distribution in an aggregate, soil, or sediment.

soil class
A numerical classification of soil by texture, used by the U.S. Department of Agriculture: (1) gravel, (2) sand, (3) clay, (4) loam, (5) loam with some sand, (6) silt-loam, and (7) clay-loam.

boulder
A large, naturally rounded rock, lying on the surface of the ground or partially embedded in it.

cobble
A naturally rounded stone, smaller than a boulder and larger than a pebble, used for rough paving, walls, and foundations. Also called **cobblestone**.

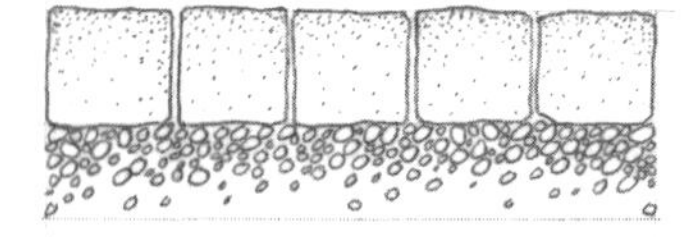

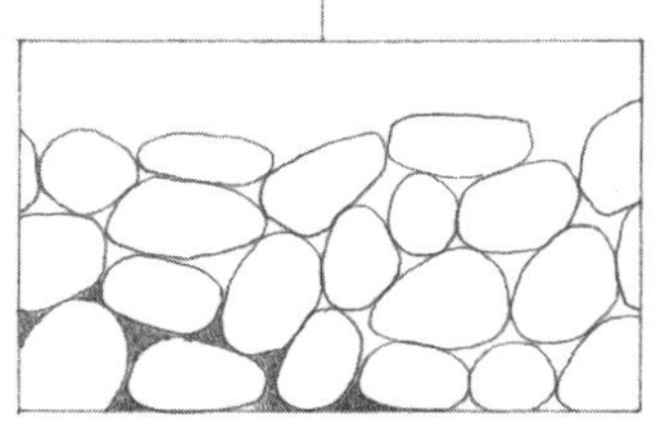

gravel
Small pebbles and stones, or a mixture of these with sand, formed either naturally or by crushing rock, esp. such material that will pass a 3-in. (76 mm) sieve and be retained on a No. 4 (4.8 mm) sieve.

crushed gravel
Gravel having one or more fractured faces produced by mechanical crushing.

crushed stone
Stone having well-defined edges produced by the mechanical crushing of rocks or boulders. Also called **crushed rock**.

pea gravel
A small-diameter, natural gravel, usually 1/4 to 3/8 in. (6.4 to 9.5 mm) in size, screened to specification.

pebble
A small, rounded stone, especially one worn smooth by the action of water.

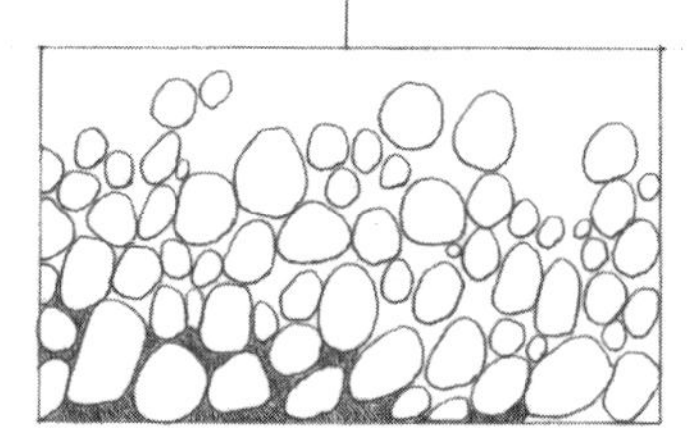

sand
A loose, granular material resulting from the disintegration of rocks, consisting of grains smaller than gravel but coarser than silt.

sand clay
A well-graded, naturally occurring sand often used as a base or subbase material, having about 10% clay or just enough to make the mixture bind tightly when compacted.

silt
Loose sedimentary material consisting of fine mineral particles between 0.002 mm and 0.05 mm in diameter.

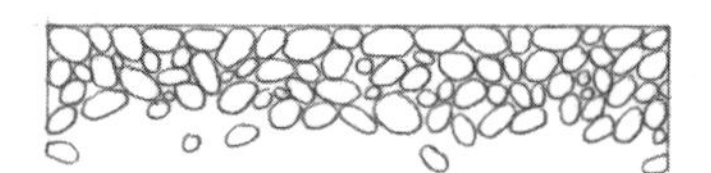

clay
A natural, earthy material that is plastic when moist but hard when fired and is used for making brick, tile, and pottery, composed mainly of fine particles of hydrous aluminum silicates less than 0.002 mm in diameter.

clay loam
Soil containing 27% to 40% clay and 20% to 45% sand.

bentonite
A clay formed by the decomposition of volcanic ash, having the ability to absorb large amounts of water and to expand to several times its natural volume.

loam
A rich soil containing a relatively equal mixture of sand and silt and a smaller proportion of clay and organic matter.

loess
An unstratified, cohesive, loamy deposit deposited by wind.

geotechnical
Of or pertaining to the practical applications of geological science in civil engineering.

foundation investigation
The investigation and classification of a foundation soil based on observation and tests of material disclosed by borings or excavations to obtain the information necessary for the design of a foundation system, including the shearing strength, compressibility, cohesion, expansiveness, permeability, and moisture content of the soil, the elevation of the water table, and the anticipated total and differential settlement. Also called **subsurface investigation**.

soil mechanics
The branch of civil engineering that deals with the mechanical behavior of soil when compressed or sheared, or when water flows through it.

soil structure
The arrangement and aggregation of soil particles in a soil mass.

core
An undisturbed, cylindrical sample of earth or rock obtained by means of a core drill and used for analysis and testing of bearing capacity. Also called **boring**.

Atterberg limits
The levels of water content defining the boundaries between the different states of consistency of a plastic or cohesive soil, as determined by standard tests.

liquid limit
The water content, expressed as a percentage of dry weight, at which a soil passes from a plastic to a liquid state.

plasticity index
The numerical difference between the liquid limit and the plastic limit of a soil.

plastic limit
The water content, expressed as a percentage of dry weight, at which a soil loses its plasticity and begins to behave as a solid.

plastic soil
A soil that can be rolled into 1/8 in.- (3.2-mm) diameter threads without crumbling.

shrinkage limit
The water content, expressed as a percentage of dry weight, at which a reduction in water content will not cause a further decrease in the volume of a soil mass.

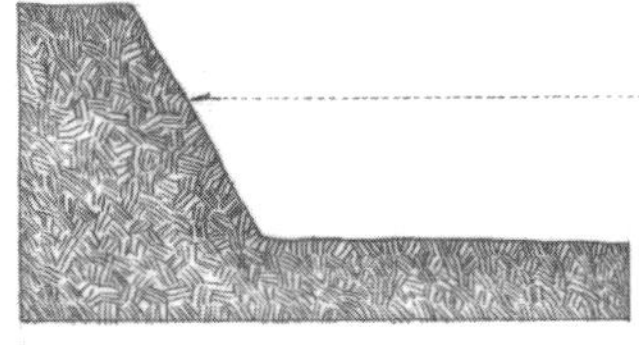

cohesive soil
Soil that has considerable strength when unconfined and air-dried, and significant cohesion when submerged.

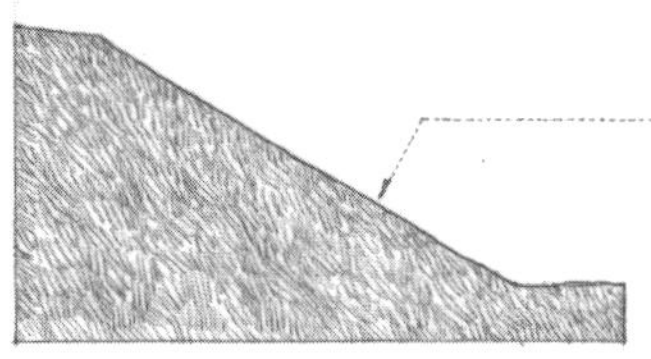

cohesionless soil
Soil that has little or no strength when unconfined and air-dried, and little or no cohesion when submerged.

granular material
Any gravel, sand, or silt that exhibits no cohesiveness or plasticity.

permeability
The property of a porous material that allows a gas or liquid to pass through its pore spaces.

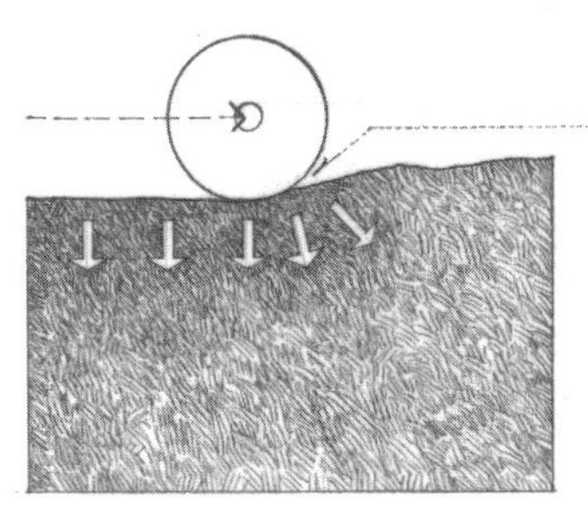

compaction
The consolidation of sediment by the weight of overlying deposits, or a similar compression of soil, aggregate, or cementitious material by rolling, tamping, or soaking.

optimum moisture content
The water content of a soil at which maximum density can be attained through compaction.

void ratio
The ratio of the volume of void spaces to the volume of solid particles in a soil mass.

critical void ratio
The void ratio corresponding to the critical density of a soil mass.

critical density
The unit weight of a saturated granular material above which it will gain strength and below which it will lose strength when subjected to rapid deformation.

penetration test
A test for measuring the density of granular soils and the consistency of some clays at the bottom of a borehole, recording the number of blows required by a hammer to advance a standard soil sampler.

penetration resistance
The unit load required to produce a specified penetration into a soil at a specified rate of penetration.

pervious soil
Any permeable soil that allows the relatively free movement of water.

impervious soil
Any fine-grained soil, as clay, having pores too small to permit water to pass except by slow capillary action.

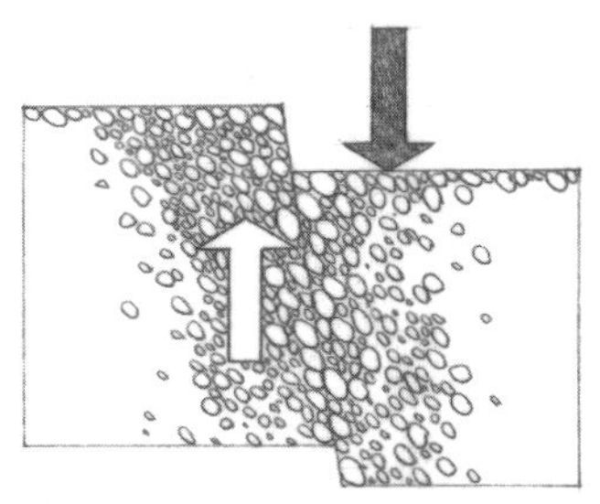

shearing strength
The property of a soil that enables its particles to resist displacement with respect to one another when an external force is applied, due largely to the combined effects of cohesion and internal friction. Also called **shearing resistance**.

SOLAR ENERGY

Energy derived from the sun in the form of solar radiation.

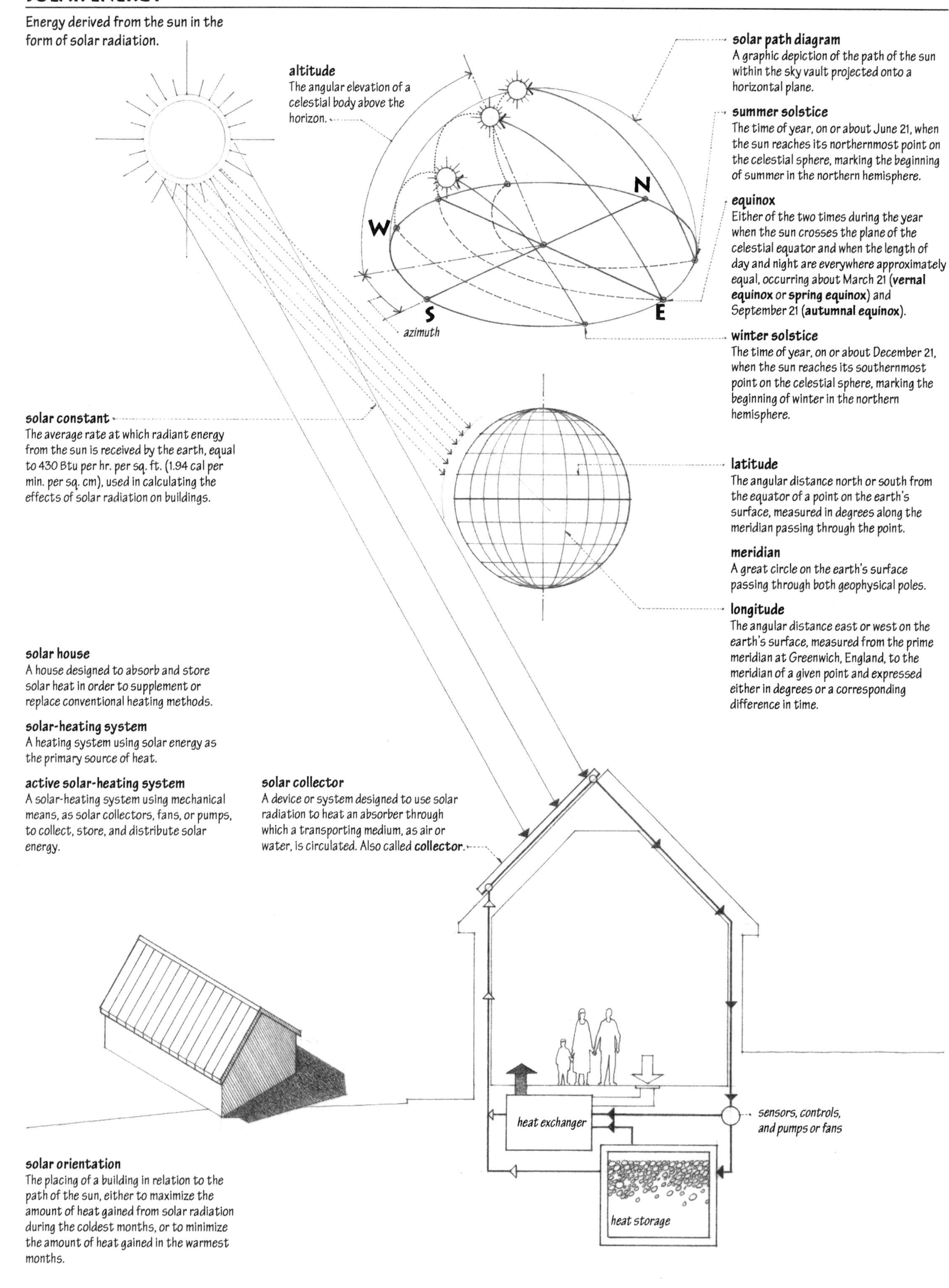

altitude
The angular elevation of a celestial body above the horizon.

solar path diagram
A graphic depiction of the path of the sun within the sky vault projected onto a horizontal plane.

summer solstice
The time of year, on or about June 21, when the sun reaches its northernmost point on the celestial sphere, marking the beginning of summer in the northern hemisphere.

equinox
Either of the two times during the year when the sun crosses the plane of the celestial equator and when the length of day and night are everywhere approximately equal, occurring about March 21 (**vernal equinox** or **spring equinox**) and September 21 (**autumnal equinox**).

winter solstice
The time of year, on or about December 21, when the sun reaches its southernmost point on the celestial sphere, marking the beginning of winter in the northern hemisphere.

solar constant
The average rate at which radiant energy from the sun is received by the earth, equal to 430 Btu per hr. per sq. ft. (1.94 cal per min. per sq. cm), used in calculating the effects of solar radiation on buildings.

latitude
The angular distance north or south from the equator of a point on the earth's surface, measured in degrees along the meridian passing through the point.

meridian
A great circle on the earth's surface passing through both geophysical poles.

longitude
The angular distance east or west on the earth's surface, measured from the prime meridian at Greenwich, England, to the meridian of a given point and expressed either in degrees or a corresponding difference in time.

solar house
A house designed to absorb and store solar heat in order to supplement or replace conventional heating methods.

solar-heating system
A heating system using solar energy as the primary source of heat.

active solar-heating system
A solar-heating system using mechanical means, as solar collectors, fans, or pumps, to collect, store, and distribute solar energy.

solar collector
A device or system designed to use solar radiation to heat an absorber through which a transporting medium, as air or water, is circulated. Also called **collector**.

solar orientation
The placing of a building in relation to the path of the sun, either to maximize the amount of heat gained from solar radiation during the coldest months, or to minimize the amount of heat gained in the warmest months.

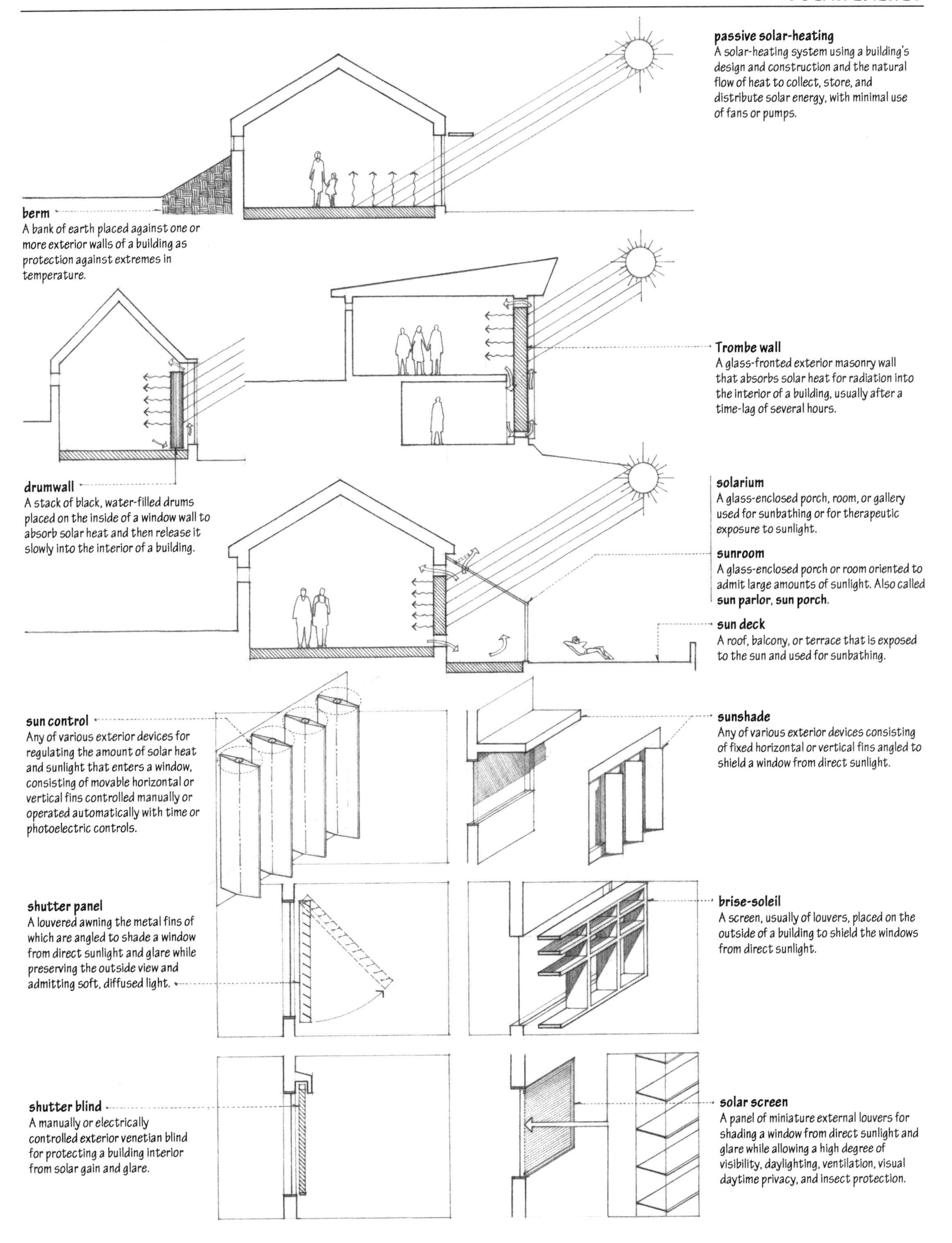

passive solar-heating
A solar-heating system using a building's design and construction and the natural flow of heat to collect, store, and distribute solar energy, with minimal use of fans or pumps.

berm
A bank of earth placed against one or more exterior walls of a building as protection against extremes in temperature.

Trombe wall
A glass-fronted exterior masonry wall that absorbs solar heat for radiation into the interior of a building, usually after a time-lag of several hours.

drumwall
A stack of black, water-filled drums placed on the inside of a window wall to absorb solar heat and then release it slowly into the interior of a building.

solarium
A glass-enclosed porch, room, or gallery used for sunbathing or for therapeutic exposure to sunlight.

sunroom
A glass-enclosed porch or room oriented to admit large amounts of sunlight. Also called **sun parlor**, **sun porch**.

sun deck
A roof, balcony, or terrace that is exposed to the sun and used for sunbathing.

sun control
Any of various exterior devices for regulating the amount of solar heat and sunlight that enters a window, consisting of movable horizontal or vertical fins controlled manually or operated automatically with time or photoelectric controls.

sunshade
Any of various exterior devices consisting of fixed horizontal or vertical fins angled to shield a window from direct sunlight.

shutter panel
A louvered awning the metal fins of which are angled to shade a window from direct sunlight and glare while preserving the outside view and admitting soft, diffused light.

brise-soleil
A screen, usually of louvers, placed on the outside of a building to shield the windows from direct sunlight.

shutter blind
A manually or electrically controlled exterior venetian blind for protecting a building interior from solar gain and glare.

solar screen
A panel of miniature external louvers for shading a window from direct sunlight and glare while allowing a high degree of visibility, daylighting, ventilation, visual daytime privacy, and insect protection.

The sensation stimulated in the organs of hearing by mechanical radiant energy transmitted as longitudinal pressure waves through the air or other medium.

sound wave
A longitudinal pressure wave in air or an elastic medium, esp. one producing an audible sensation.

wave
A disturbance or oscillation that transfers energy progressively from point to point in a medium or space without advance by the points themselves, as in the transmission of sound or light.

waveform
A graphic representation of the shape of a wave, obtained by plotting deviation at a fixed point versus time.

wavelength
The distance, measured in the direction of propagation of a wave, from any one point to the next point of corresponding phase.

phase
A particular point or stage in a periodic cycle or process.

amplitude
The maximum deviation of a wave or alternating current from its average value.

frequency
The number of cycles per unit time of a wave or oscillation.

hertz
The SI unit of frequency, equal to one cycle per second. Abbr.: **Hz**

wave front
A surface of a propagating wave composed at any instant of all points having identical phase, usually perpendicular to the direction of propagation.

fundamental
The lowest frequency at which a vibrating element or system will freely oscillate. Also called **fundamental frequency**.

harmonic
A vibration having a frequency that is an integral multiple of that of the fundamental.

band
A range of wavelengths or frequencies between two defined limits.

pitch
The predominant frequency of a sound as perceived by the human ear.

octave
The interval between two frequencies having a ratio of 2:1.

Doppler effect
An apparent shift in frequency occurring when an acoustic source and listener are in motion relative to each other, the frequency increasing when the source and listener approach each other and decreasing when they move apart.

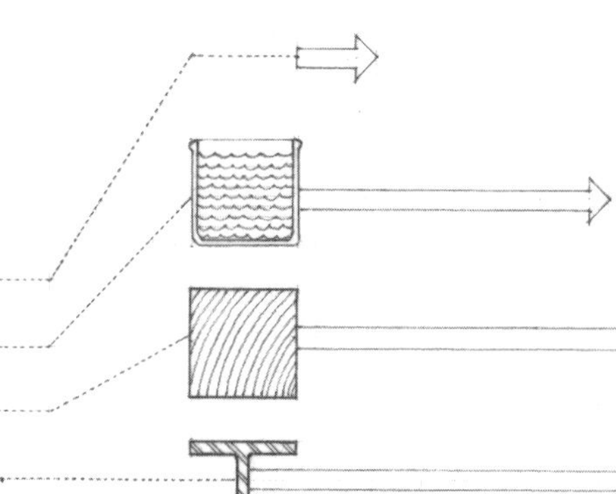

speed of sound
The velocity of sound traveling through air at approximately 1087 ft. (0.3 km) per second at sea level, through water at approximately 4500 ft. (1.4 km) per second, through wood at approximately 11,700 ft. (3.6 km) per second, and through steel at approximately 18,000 ft. (5.5 km) per second.

loudness
A subjective response to sound indicating the magnitude of the auditory sensation produced by the amplitude of a sound wave.

phon
A unit for measuring the apparent loudness of a sound, equal in number to the decibels of a 1000-Hz reference sound judged by a group of listeners to be equal in loudness to the given sound.

sone
A unit for measuring the apparent loudness of a sound, judged by a group of listeners to be equal to the loudness of a 1000-Hz reference sound having an intensity of 40 decibels.

decibel
A unit for expressing the relative pressure or intensity of sounds on a uniform scale from 0 for the least perceptible sound to about 130 for the average threshold of pain. Abbr.: **dB**

Decibel measurement is based on a logarithmic scale since increments of sound pressure or intensity are perceived as equal when the ratio between successive changes in intensity remain constant. The decibel levels of two sound sources, therefore, cannot be added mathematically:
e.g., 60 dB + 60 dB = 63 dB, not 120 dB.

hearing
The sense by which sound is perceived, involving the entire mechanism of the internal, middle, and external ear and including the nervous and cerebral operations that translate the physical operations into meaningful signals.

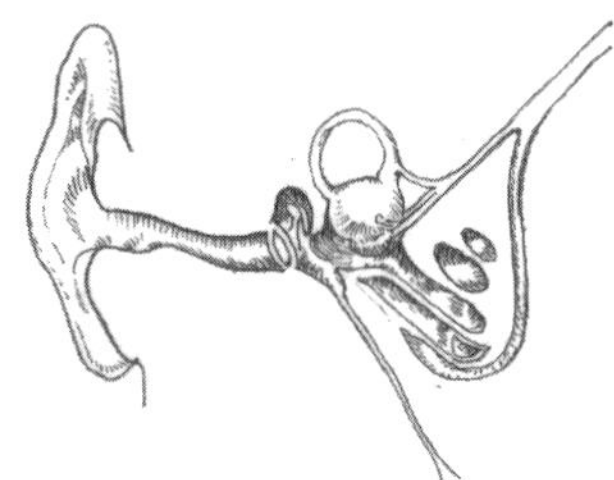

equal loudness contour
A curve representing the sound pressure level at which sounds of different frequencies are judged by a group of listeners to be equally loud.

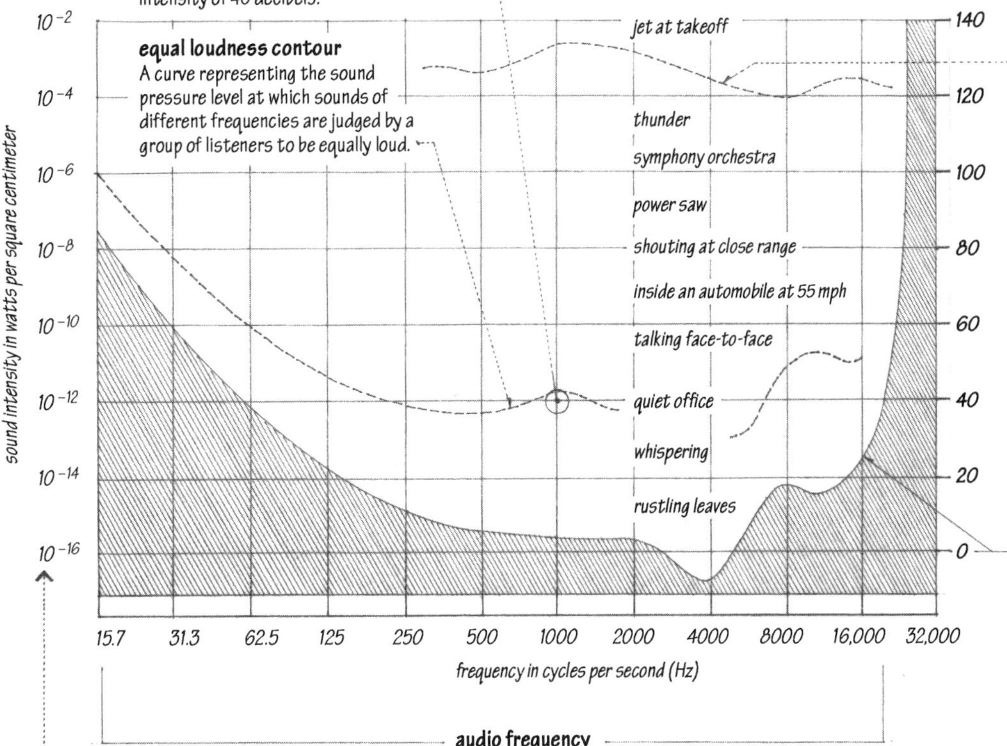

threshold of pain
The level of sound intensity high enough to produce the sensation of pain in the human ear, usually around 130 dB.

auditory fatigue
Physical or mental weariness caused by prolonged exposure to loud noises.

hearing loss
An increase in the threshold of audibility, at specific frequencies, caused by normal aging, disease, or injury to the hearing organs.

threshold of hearing
The minimum sound pressure capable of stimulating an auditory sensation, usually 20 micropascals or zero dB.

audio frequency
A range of frequencies from 15 Hz to 20,000 Hz audible to the normal human ear.

sound intensity
The rate at which acoustic energy flows through a medium, expressed in watts per square meter.

sound intensity level
Sound intensity measured on the decibel scale, equal to 10 times the common logarithm of the ratio of the sound intensity to a reference intensity, usually 10^{-12} watts per square meter (10^{-16} watts per square centimeter.)

logarithm
The exponent indicating the power to which a base number must be raised to arrive at a given number.

common logarithm
A logarithm having a base of 10.

sound pressure
The difference between the actual pressure at any point in the field of a sound wave and the static pressure at that point, expressed in pascals.

sound pressure level
Sound pressure measured on the decibel scale, equal to 10 times the common logarithm of the ratio of the sound pressure to a reference pressure, usually 20 micropascals.

micropascal
One-millionth (10^{-6}) part of a pascal. Symbol: **μPa**

sound power
The amount of acoustic energy radiated by a source per unit time, expressed in watts.

sound power level
The acoustic power of a source measured on the decibel scale, equal to 10 times the common logarithm of the ratio of the acoustic power to a reference power, usually 10^{-12} watts.

sound level meter
An electrical instrument for measuring sound pressure levels. To compensate for the way we perceive the relative loudness of different frequencies of sound, there are three networks: A, B, and C. These networks weight the recordings for different frequencies and combine the results in a single reading. The A-network scale, in dBA units, is most commonly used since it discriminates against the lower frequencies, as does the human ear at moderate sound levels.

acoustics
The branch of physics that deals with the production, control, transmission, reception, and effects of sound.

room acoustics
The qualities or characteristics of a room, auditorium, or concert hall that determine the audibility of speech or fidelity of musical sounds in it.

sounding board
A structure over or behind and above a speaker or orchestra to reflect the sound toward the audience.

reflecting surface
A nonabsorptive surface from which incident sound is reflected, used esp. to redirect sound in a space. To be effective, a reflecting surface should have a least dimension equal to or greater than the wavelength of the lowest frequency of the sound being reflected.

acoustical cloud
One of a number of acoustic panels installed near the ceiling of a concert hall to reflect sound for improving the acoustic quality of music.

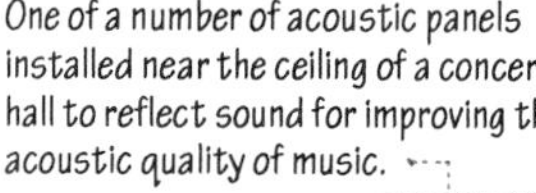

acoustical analysis
A detailed study of the use of a building, the location and orientation of its spaces, possible sources of noise, and the desirable acoustical environment in each usable area.

acoustical design
The planning, shaping, finishing, and furnishing of an enclosed space to establish the acoustical environment necessary for distinct hearing.

acoustical treatment
The application of absorbent or reflecting materials to the walls, ceiling, and floor of an enclosed space to alter or improve its acoustic properties.

diffracted sound
Airborne sound waves bent by diffraction around an obstacle in their path.

reflected sound
The return of unabsorbed airborne sound after striking a surface, at an angle equal to the angle of incidence.

airborne sound
Sound radiated directly into and transmitted through the air.

live
Highly reverberant or resonant, as an auditorium or concert hall.

dead
Without resonance, as a room free from echoes and reverberation.

soundproof
Impervious to audible sound.

direct sound
Airborne sound traveling directly from a source to the listener. In a room, the human ear always hears direct sound before it hears reflected sound. As direct sound loses intensity, the importance of reflected sound increases.

attenuation
A decrease in energy or pressure per unit area of a sound wave, occurring as the distance from the source increases as a result of absorption, scattering, or spreading in three dimensions.

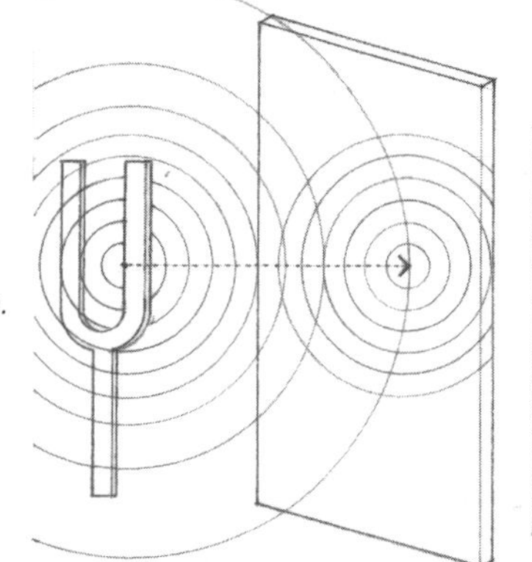

resonance
The intensification and prolongation of sound produced by sympathetic vibration.

sympathetic vibration
A vibration induced in one body by the vibrations of exactly the same period in a neighboring body.

echo
The repetition of a sound produced by the reflection of sound waves from an obstructing surface, loud enough and received late enough to be perceived as distinct from the source.

flutter
A rapid succession of echoes caused by the reflection of sound waves back and forth between two parallel surfaces, with sufficient time between each reflection to cause the listener to be aware of separate, discrete signals.

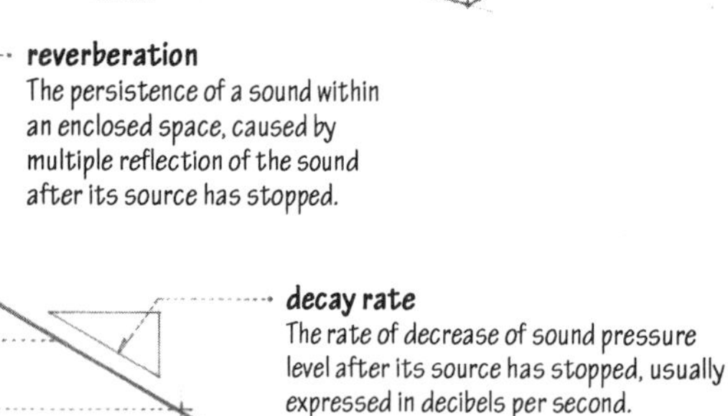

reverberation
The persistence of a sound within an enclosed space, caused by multiple reflection of the sound after its source has stopped.

decay rate
The rate of decrease of sound pressure level after its source has stopped, usually expressed in decibels per second.

reverberation time
The time in seconds required for a sound made in an enclosed space to diminish by 60 decibels.

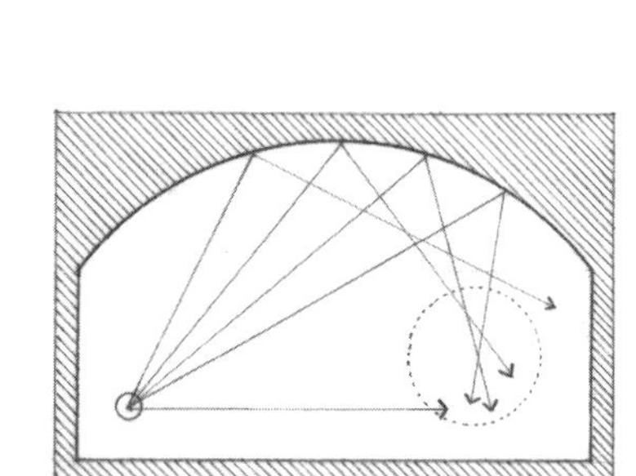

focusing
The convergence of sound waves reflected from a concave surface.

90
80
70
60
50
40
30
20
10
sound intensity level in dB
63 125 250 500 1000 2000 4000 8000
octave band center frequencies in Hz
very noisy
noisy
moderately noisy
quiet
very quiet
approximate threshold of hearing for continuous noise

noise criteria curve
One of a series of curves representing the sound pressure level across the frequency spectrum for background noise that should not be exceeded in various environments. Higher noise levels are permitted at the lower frequencies since the human ear is less sensitive to sounds in this frequency region. Also called **NC curves**.

noise
Any sound that is unwanted, annoying, or discordant, or that interferes with one's hearing of something.

noise reduction
The perceived difference in sound pressure levels between two enclosed spaces, due to the sound-isolating qualities of the separating barrier as well as the absorption present in the receiving room: expressed in decibels.

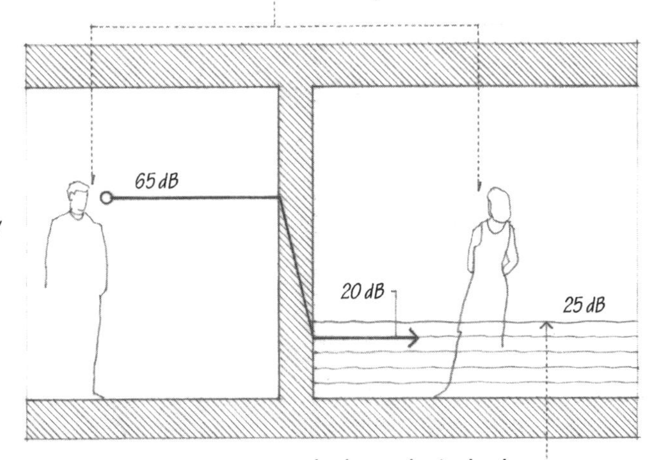

background noise level
The level of ambient sound normally present in a space, above which speech, music, or other sounds must be presented to be heard.

standing wave
A wave in which the amplitude of the resultant of a transmitted and a reflected wave is fixed in time and ranges from zero at the nodes to a maximum at the antinodes.

interference
The phenomenon in which two or more light or sound waves of the same frequency combine to reinforce or cancel each other, the amplitude of the resulting wave being equal to the algebraic or vector sum of the amplitudes of the combining waves.

white noise
An unvarying, unobtrusive sound having the same intensity for all frequencies of a given band, used to mask or obliterate unwanted sound. Also called **white sound**.

background noise
The sound normally present in an environment, usually a composite of sounds from both exterior and interior sources, none of which are distinctly identifiable by the listener. Also called **ambient sound**.

absorption
The interception and conversion of sound energy into heat or other form of energy by the structure of a material, measured in sabins or absorption units.

sabin
A unit of sound absorption, equal to one sq. ft. (0.09 sq. m) of a perfectly absorptive surface.

metric sabin
A unit of sound absorption, equal to 1 square meter of perfectly absorptive surface. Also called **absorption unit**.

absorption coefficient
A measure of the efficiency of a material in absorbing sound at a specified frequency, equal to the fractional part of the incident sound energy at that frequency absorbed by the material.

noise reduction coefficient
A measure of the sound-absorbing efficiency of a material, equal to the average of the absorption coefficients of the material, computed to the nearest 0.05 at four frequencies: 250, 500, 1000, and 2000 Hz.

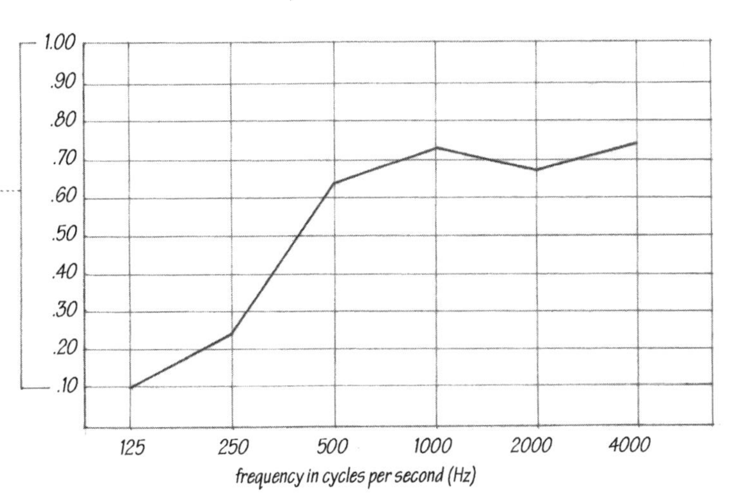

sound isolation
The use of building materials and construction assemblies designed to reduce the transmission of airborne and structure-borne sound from one room to another or from the exterior to the interior of a building. Also called **sound insulation**.

flanking path
A path for the transmission of sound other than through a floor, wall, or ceiling assembly, as along such interconnecting structures as ductwork or piping.

plenum barrier
An acoustic barrier erected in a plenum over a partition to reduce sound transmission between adjoining rooms.

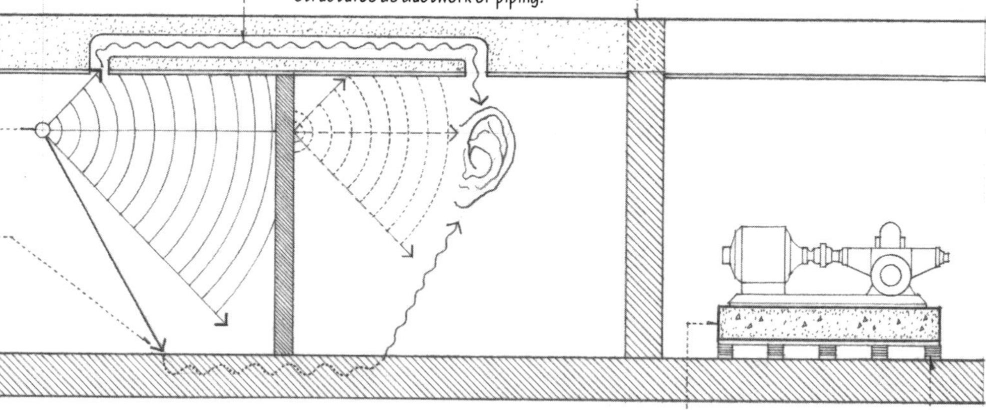

airborne sound transmission
Sound transmitted when a surface is set into vibration by the alternating air pressures of incident sound waves.

structure-borne sound transmission
Sound transmitted through the solid media of a building's structure as a result of direct physical contact or impact, as by vibrating equipment or footsteps.

acoustic mass
Resistance to the transmission of sound caused by the inertia and elasticity of the transmitting medium. In general, the heavier and more dense a body, the greater its resistance to sound transmission.

vibration isolator
A resilient base for mechanical equipment, installed to reduce the transmission of vibration and noise to the supporting structure. Also called **isolation mount**.

inertia block
A heavy concrete base for vibrating mechanical equipment, used in conjunction with vibration isolators to increase the mass of the equipment and decrease the potential for vibratory movement.

transmission loss
A measure of the performance of a building material or construction assembly in preventing the transmission of airborne sound, equal to the reduction in sound intensity as it passes through the material or assembly when tested at all one-third octave band center frequencies from 125 to 4000 Hz: expressed in decibels. Abbr.: **TL**

Three factors enhance the TL rating of a construction assembly: mass, separation into layers, and absorptive capacity.

average transmission loss
A single-number rating of the performance of a building material or construction assembly in preventing the transmission of airborne sound, equal to the average of its TL values at nine test frequencies.

sound transmission class
A single-number rating of the performance of a building material or construction assembly in preventing the transmission of airborne sound, derived by comparing the laboratory TL test curve for the material or assembly to a standard frequency curve. Abbr.: **STC**

The higher the STC rating, the greater the sound-isolating value of the material or construction. An open doorway has an STC rating of 10; normal construction has STC ratings from 30 to 60; special construction is required for STC ratings above 60.

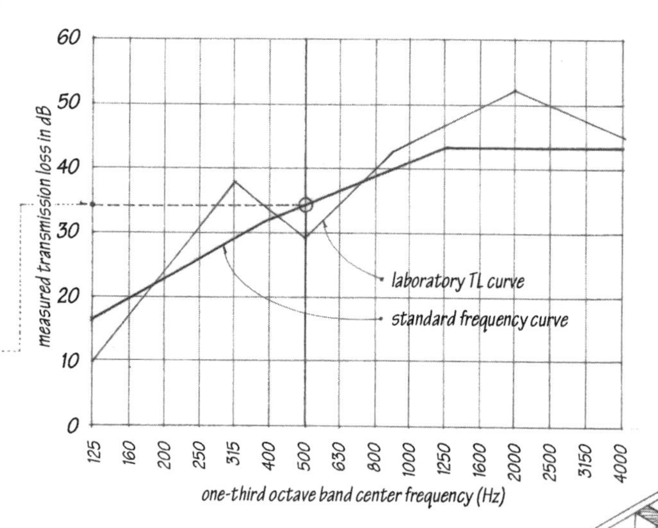

discontinuous construction
Any of several construction methods, as the use of staggered studs or resilient mountings, for breaking the continuity of a path through which structure-borne sound may be transmitted from one space to another.

staggered-stud partition
A partition for reducing sound transmission between rooms, framed with two separate rows of studs arranged in zigzag fashion and supporting opposite faces of the partition, sometimes with a fiberglass blanket between.

impact noise
Structure-borne sound generated by physical impact, as by footsteps or the moving of furniture.

impact insulation class
A single-number rating of the performance of a floor-ceiling construction in preventing the transmission of impact noise. Abbr.: **IIC**

The higher the IIC rating, the more effective is the construction in isolating impact noise. The IIC rating replaces the previously used Impact Noise Rating (INR) and is approximately equal to the INR rating +51 dB for a given construction.

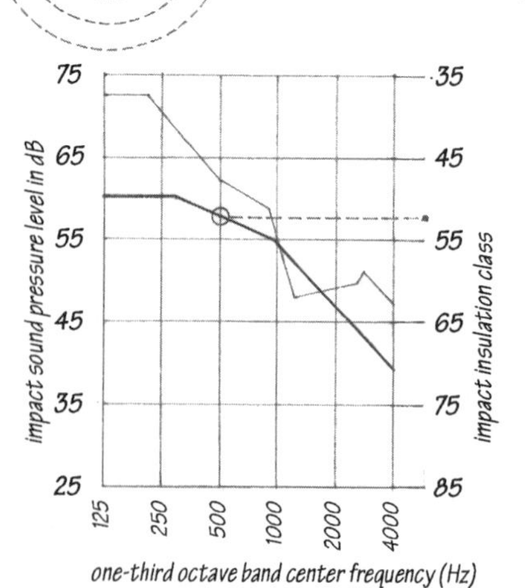

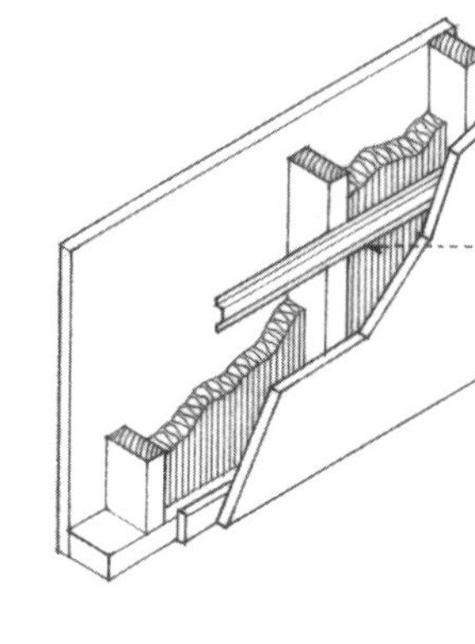

resilient mounting
A system of flexible attachments or supports that permits room surfaces to vibrate normally without transmitting the vibratory motions and associated noise to the supporting structure.

resilient channel
A metal channel for the resilient mounting of wallboard to studs or joists, used in sound-isolating construction to reduce the transmission of vibrations and noise.

resilient clip
A flexible metal device for the resilient mounting of wallboard or metal lath to studs or joists, used in sound-isolating construction to reduce the transmission of vibrations and noise.

One of a flight or series of steps for going from one level to another, as in a building.

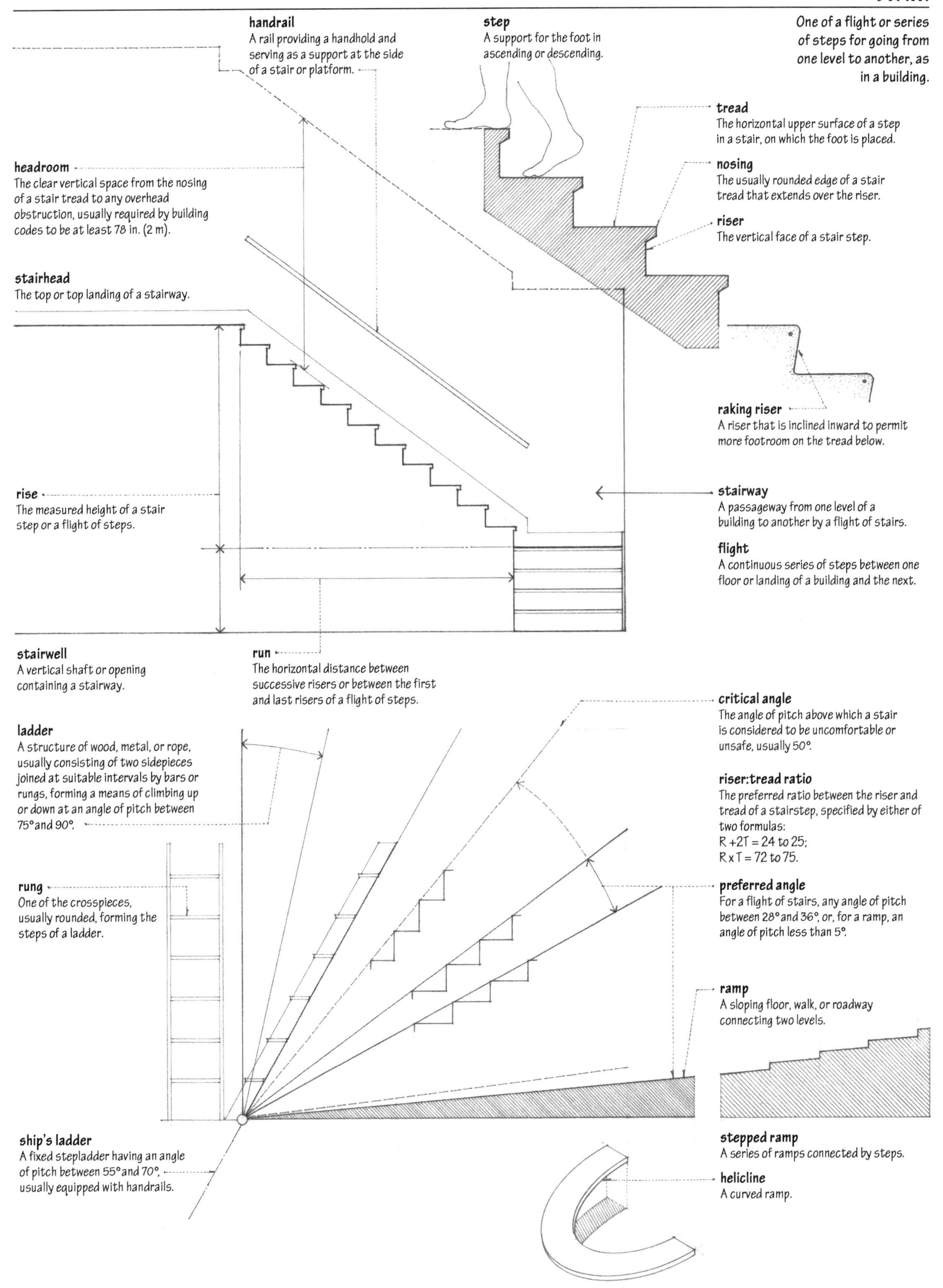

handrail
A rail providing a handhold and serving as a support at the side of a stair or platform.

step
A support for the foot in ascending or descending.

tread
The horizontal upper surface of a step in a stair, on which the foot is placed.

nosing
The usually rounded edge of a stair tread that extends over the riser.

riser
The vertical face of a stair step.

headroom
The clear vertical space from the nosing of a stair tread to any overhead obstruction, usually required by building codes to be at least 78 in. (2 m).

stairhead
The top or top landing of a stairway.

raking riser
A riser that is inclined inward to permit more footroom on the tread below.

rise
The measured height of a stair step or a flight of steps.

stairway
A passageway from one level of a building to another by a flight of stairs.

flight
A continuous series of steps between one floor or landing of a building and the next.

stairwell
A vertical shaft or opening containing a stairway.

run
The horizontal distance between successive risers or between the first and last risers of a flight of steps.

critical angle
The angle of pitch above which a stair is considered to be uncomfortable or unsafe, usually 50°.

ladder
A structure of wood, metal, or rope, usually consisting of two sidepieces joined at suitable intervals by bars or rungs, forming a means of climbing up or down at an angle of pitch between 75° and 90°.

riser:tread ratio
The preferred ratio between the riser and tread of a stairstep, specified by either of two formulas:
$R + 2T = 24$ to 25;
$R \times T = 72$ to 75.

rung
One of the crosspieces, usually rounded, forming the steps of a ladder.

preferred angle
For a flight of stairs, any angle of pitch between 28° and 36°, or, for a ramp, an angle of pitch less than 5°.

ramp
A sloping floor, walk, or roadway connecting two levels.

ship's ladder
A fixed stepladder having an angle of pitch between 55° and 70°, usually equipped with handrails.

stepped ramp
A series of ramps connected by steps.

helicline
A curved ramp.

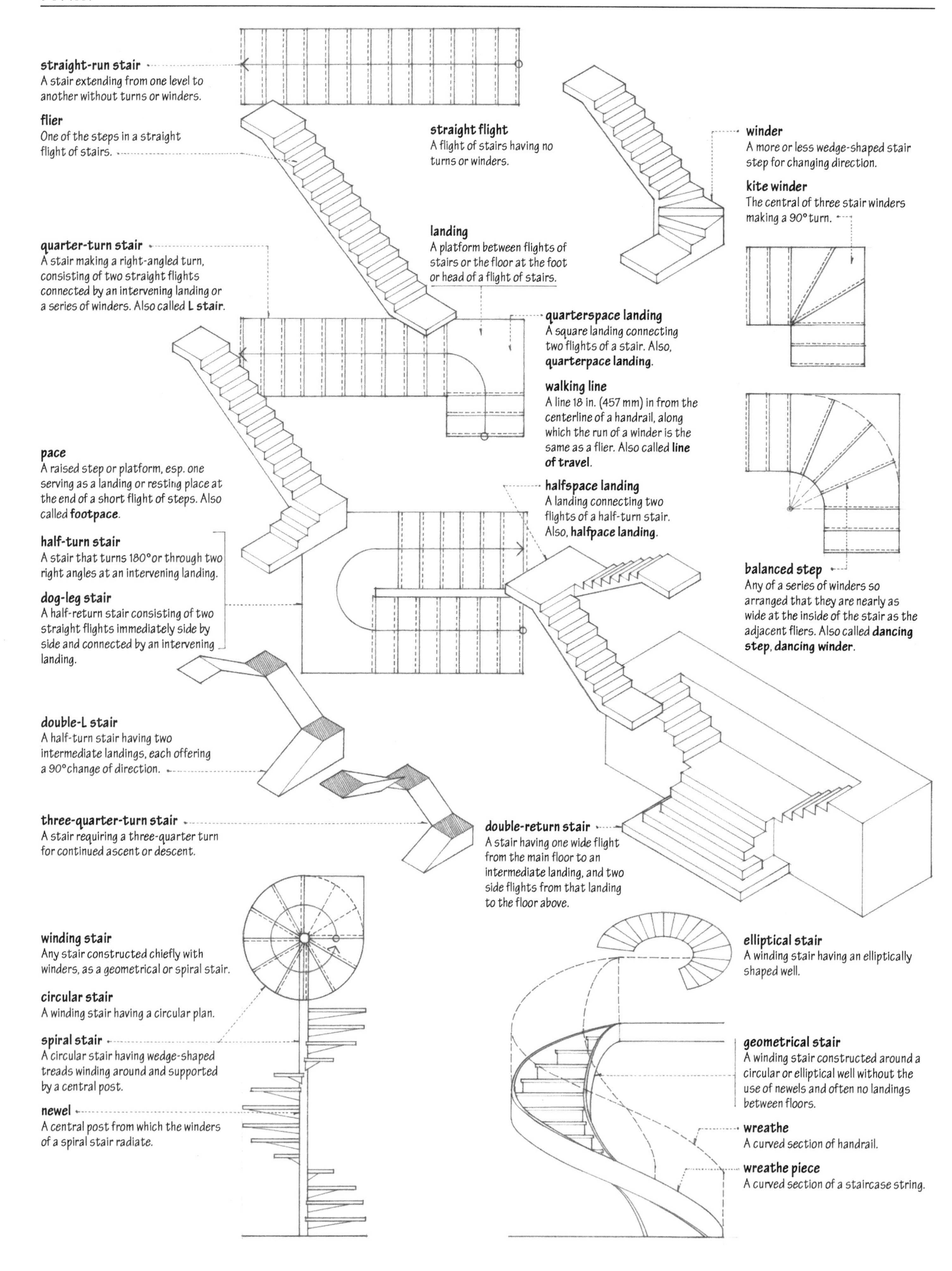

straight-run stair
A stair extending from one level to another without turns or winders.

flier
One of the steps in a straight flight of stairs.

straight flight
A flight of stairs having no turns or winders.

winder
A more or less wedge-shaped stair step for changing direction.

kite winder
The central of three stair winders making a 90° turn.

landing
A platform between flights of stairs or the floor at the foot or head of a flight of stairs.

quarter-turn stair
A stair making a right-angled turn, consisting of two straight flights connected by an intervening landing or a series of winders. Also called **L stair**.

quarterspace landing
A square landing connecting two flights of a stair. Also, **quarterpace landing**.

walking line
A line 18 in. (457 mm) in from the centerline of a handrail, along which the run of a winder is the same as a flier. Also called **line of travel**.

pace
A raised step or platform, esp. one serving as a landing or resting place at the end of a short flight of steps. Also called **footpace**.

halfspace landing
A landing connecting two flights of a half-turn stair. Also, **halfpace landing**.

half-turn stair
A stair that turns 180° or through two right angles at an intervening landing.

dog-leg stair
A half-return stair consisting of two straight flights immediately side by side and connected by an intervening landing.

balanced step
Any of a series of winders so arranged that they are nearly as wide at the inside of the stair as the adjacent fliers. Also called **dancing step**, **dancing winder**.

double-L stair
A half-turn stair having two intermediate landings, each offering a 90° change of direction.

three-quarter-turn stair
A stair requiring a three-quarter turn for continued ascent or descent.

double-return stair
A stair having one wide flight from the main floor to an intermediate landing, and two side flights from that landing to the floor above.

winding stair
Any stair constructed chiefly with winders, as a geometrical or spiral stair.

circular stair
A winding stair having a circular plan.

spiral stair
A circular stair having wedge-shaped treads winding around and supported by a central post.

newel
A central post from which the winders of a spiral stair radiate.

elliptical stair
A winding stair having an elliptically shaped well.

geometrical stair
A winding stair constructed around a circular or elliptical well without the use of newels and often no landings between floors.

wreathe
A curved section of handrail.

wreathe piece
A curved section of a staircase string.

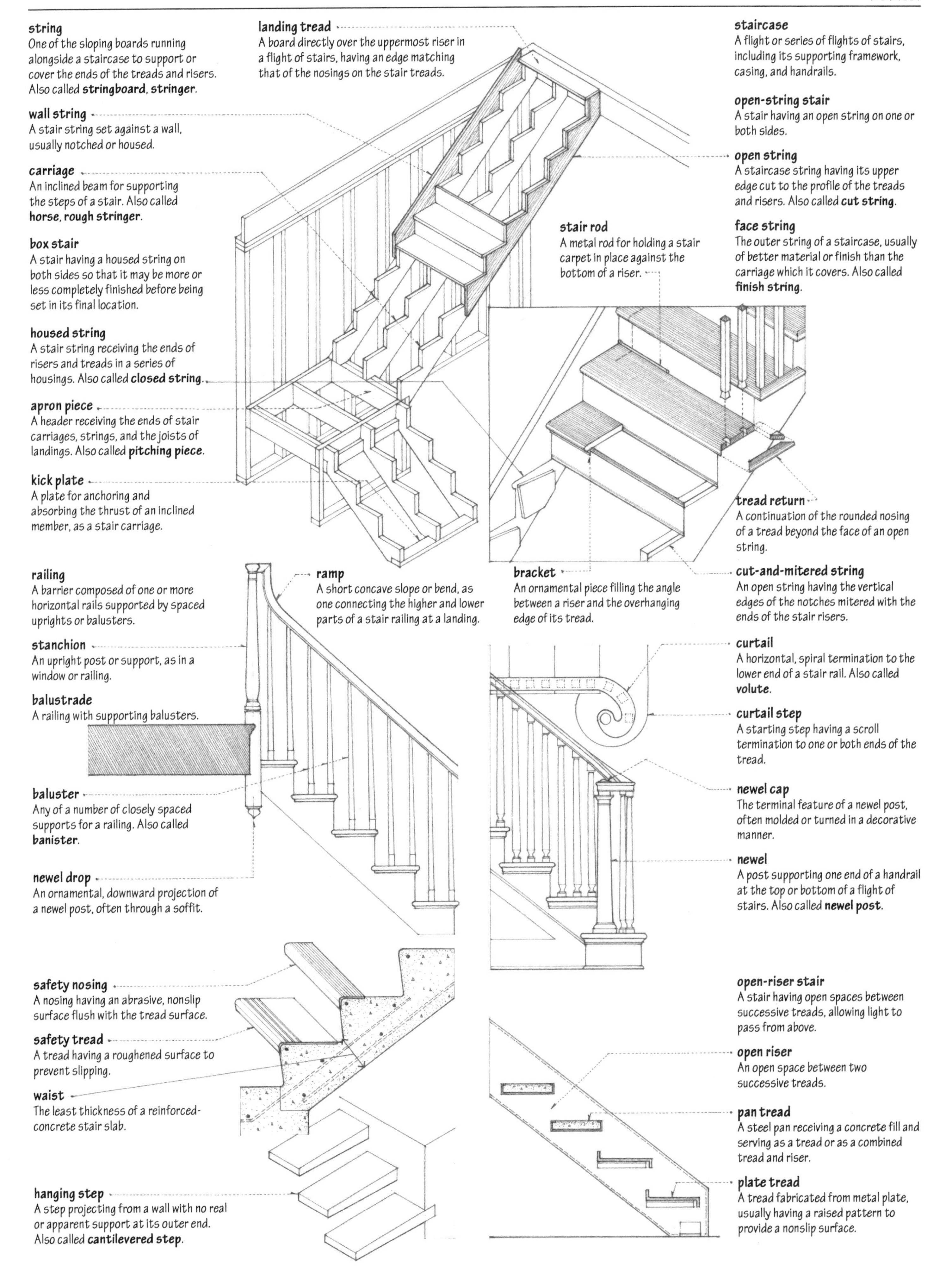

string
One of the sloping boards running alongside a staircase to support or cover the ends of the treads and risers. Also called **stringboard, stringer**.

wall string
A stair string set against a wall, usually notched or housed.

carriage
An inclined beam for supporting the steps of a stair. Also called **horse, rough stringer**.

box stair
A stair having a housed string on both sides so that it may be more or less completely finished before being set in its final location.

housed string
A stair string receiving the ends of risers and treads in a series of housings. Also called **closed string**.

apron piece
A header receiving the ends of stair carriages, strings, and the joists of landings. Also called **pitching piece**.

kick plate
A plate for anchoring and absorbing the thrust of an inclined member, as a stair carriage.

landing tread
A board directly over the uppermost riser in a flight of stairs, having an edge matching that of the nosings on the stair treads.

staircase
A flight or series of flights of stairs, including its supporting framework, casing, and handrails.

open-string stair
A stair having an open string on one or both sides.

open string
A staircase string having its upper edge cut to the profile of the treads and risers. Also called **cut string**.

stair rod
A metal rod for holding a stair carpet in place against the bottom of a riser.

face string
The outer string of a staircase, usually of better material or finish than the carriage which it covers. Also called **finish string**.

tread return
A continuation of the rounded nosing of a tread beyond the face of an open string.

bracket
An ornamental piece filling the angle between a riser and the overhanging edge of its tread.

cut-and-mitered string
An open string having the vertical edges of the notches mitered with the ends of the stair risers.

railing
A barrier composed of one or more horizontal rails supported by spaced uprights or balusters.

stanchion
An upright post or support, as in a window or railing.

balustrade
A railing with supporting balusters.

baluster
Any of a number of closely spaced supports for a railing. Also called **banister**.

newel drop
An ornamental, downward projection of a newel post, often through a soffit.

ramp
A short concave slope or bend, as one connecting the higher and lower parts of a stair railing at a landing.

curtail
A horizontal, spiral termination to the lower end of a stair rail. Also called **volute**.

curtail step
A starting step having a scroll termination to one or both ends of the tread.

newel cap
The terminal feature of a newel post, often molded or turned in a decorative manner.

newel
A post supporting one end of a handrail at the top or bottom of a flight of stairs. Also called **newel post**.

safety nosing
A nosing having an abrasive, nonslip surface flush with the tread surface.

safety tread
A tread having a roughened surface to prevent slipping.

waist
The least thickness of a reinforced-concrete stair slab.

hanging step
A step projecting from a wall with no real or apparent support at its outer end. Also called **cantilevered step**.

open-riser stair
A stair having open spaces between successive treads, allowing light to pass from above.

open riser
An open space between two successive treads.

pan tread
A steel pan receiving a concrete fill and serving as a tread or as a combined tread and riser.

plate tread
A tread fabricated from metal plate, usually having a raised pattern to provide a nonslip surface.

STONE

Rock or a piece of rock quarried and worked into a specific size and shape for a particular purpose.

rock
Solid mineral matter, naturally formed by the action of heat or water and occurring in fragments or large masses.

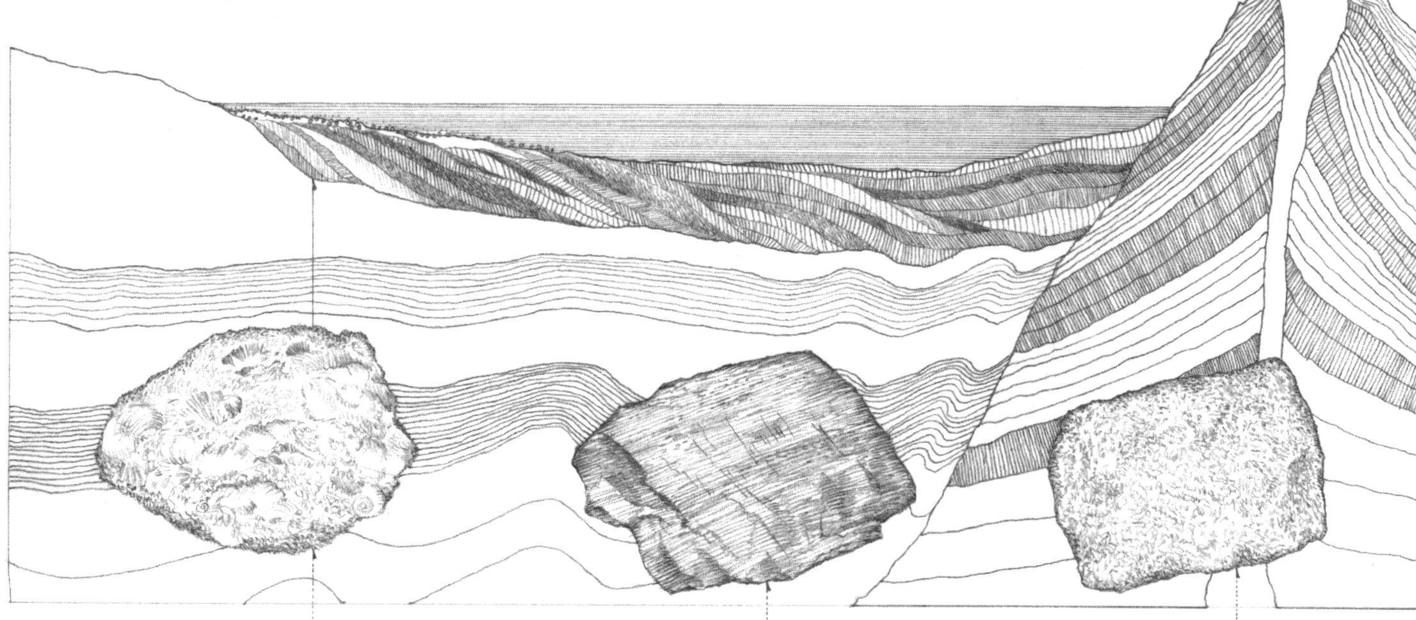

sedimentary rock
A class of rock formed by the deposition of sediment, as limestone, sandstone or shale.

metamorphic rock
A class of rock that has undergone a change in structure, texture, or composition due to natural agencies, as heat and pressure, esp. when the rock becomes harder and more crystalline.

igneous rock
A class of rock formed by the crystallization of molten magma, as granite.

limestone
A sedimentary rock formed chiefly by the accumulation of organic remains, as shells and coral, consisting mainly of calcium carbonate, and used as a building stone and in the manufacture of lime.

travertine
A variety of limestone deposited by spring waters, esp. hot springs, sold as marble in the building trade.

dolomite
A limestone rich in magnesium carbonate.

oolite
A limestone composed of small, round, calcerous grains resembling fish roe. Also called **egg stone**.

sandstone
A sedimentary rock consisting of sand, usually quartz, cemented together by various substances, as silica, clay, or calcium carbonate.

bluestone
A dense, fine-grained, argillaceous sandstone that splits easily along bedding planes to form thin slabs.

brownstone
A reddish-brown sandstone quarried and used extensively as a building material.

soapstone
A massive, soft rock containing a high proportion of talc, used as dimension stone for hearths, table tops, and carved ornaments. Also called **steatite**.

marble
A metamorphic rock of crystallized limestone, consisting mainly of calcite or dolomite, capable of taking a high polish, and used esp. in architecture and sculpture. The presence and distribution of numerous minerals account for the distinctive variegated appearance that many marbles have. The commercial term includes many dense limestones and some coarse-grained dolomites.

verd antique
A dark-green, mottled serpentine that takes a high polish and is sold as a marble. Also, **verde antique**.

slate
A dense, fine-grained metamorphic rock formed by the compression of various sediments, as clay or shale, having good cleavage along parallel planes.

quartzite
A compact, granular metamorphic rock consisting essentially of quartz, derived from sandstone.

gneiss
A banded or foliated metamorphic rock corresponding in composition to granite, in which the minerals are arranged in layers.

granite
A very hard, coarse-grained igneous rock composed mainly of quartz, feldspar, and mica or other colored minerals.

obsidian
A volcanic glass similar in composition to granite, usually black with a bright luster, and transparent in thin pieces.

malachite
A green to nearly black mineral, copper carbonate, used as a highly polished veneer and for making ornamental articles.

serpentine
A mineral or rock consisting of hydrous magnesium silicate, usually green in color and having a mottled appearance.

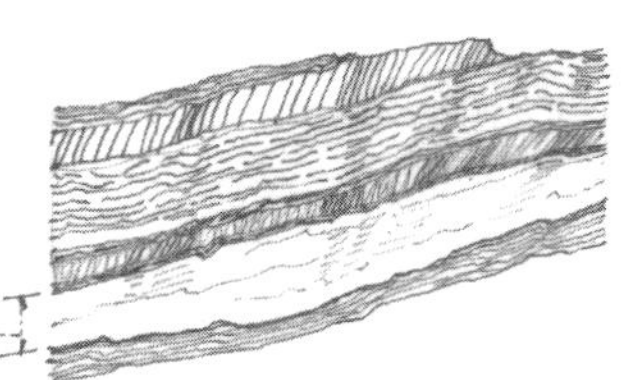

grain
The granular texture or appearance of a stone.

bedding plane
The surface that separates one stratum or layer of stratified rock from another.

cleavage plane
A relatively smooth surface along which certain rocks will tend to split.

split-faced
Noting a rough stone finish produced by splitting to expose the bedding planes.

freestone
Any fine-grained stone, as limestone or sandstone, that can be quarried or worked easily, esp. one that cuts well in all directions.

carved work
Hand-cut ornamental features in brick or stone masonry.

cast stone
A hardened mix of concrete with a fine stone aggregate, having a surface ground, polished, or molded to simulate natural stone.

cut stone
Building stone cut or machined to a relatively fine finish.

chat-sawn
Noting a coarse, pebbled stone finish produced by using a slurry of a loose abrasive and water in the sawing process.

shot-sawn
Noting a pebbled or rippled stone finish produced by using a slurry of water and hardened steel pellets in the sawing process.

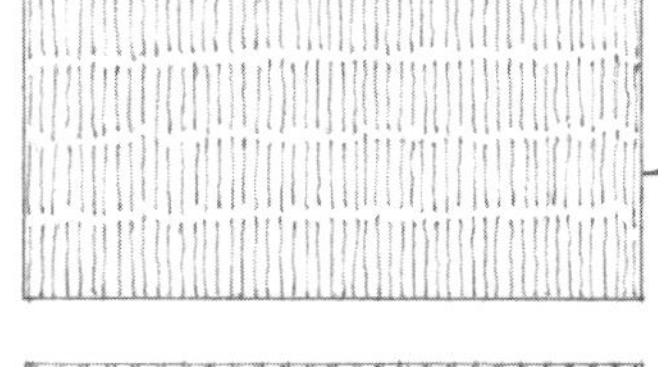

flame finish
A textured stone finish produced by superheating the surface so as to cause small chips to split off. Also called **thermal finish**.

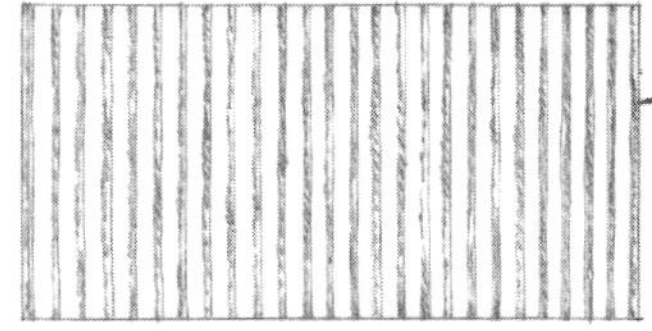

honed finish
A smooth stone finish having little or no gloss, obtained by rubbing with an abrasive.

polished work
A stone face of crystalline texture, as of marble or granite, ground and buffed to form a glasslike surface. Also called **glassed surface**.

building stone
Any stone suitable for use in building construction, as limestone, marble, or granite.

fieldstone
Loose, unfinished stone found on the surface or in the soil, esp. when used for building, as in dry masonry.

dimension stone
Quarried and squared stone 2 ft. (610 mm) or more in length and width and of specified thickness.

dressed stone
Stone worked to desired shape and smoothed on the face.

pitch-faced
Noting a stone having all arrises cut in the same plane and the faces roughly dressed with a pick.

draft
A line or border chiseled at the edge of a stone to guide the stonecutter in leveling the surfaces.

drafted margin
A smooth, uniform margin worked around a stone face.

sunk draft
A margin of a stone set below the rest of the face.

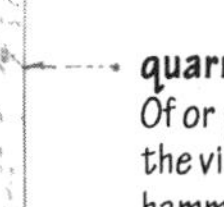

quarry-faced
Of or pertaining to a stone or stonework the visible face of which is dressed with a hammer. Also, **rock-faced**.

boasted surface
A stone finish obtained by chiseling roughly parallel grooves across the face.

batted surface
A scored stone surface made with a mason's chisel after the surface has been rubbed smooth. Also called **tooled surface**.

STRUCTURE

A stable assembly of structural elements designed and constructed to function as a whole in supporting and transmitting applied loads safely to the ground without exceeding the allowable stresses in the members.

linear structure
A structural member having a length that dominates its other two dimensions.

surface structure
A structural member having a length and width that dominates its thickness.

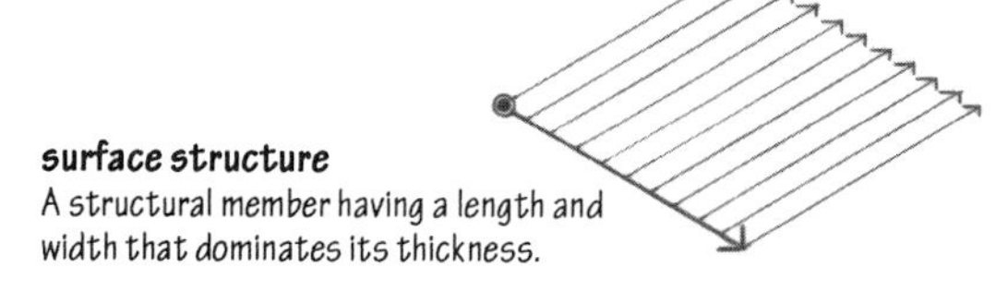

rigid
Of or pertaining to a structure or structural member having a shape that does not change appreciably under the action of an applied load or changing loads.

bulk-active structure
A structure or structural member that redirects external forces primarily through the bulk and continuity of its material, as a beam or column.

vector-active structure
A structure that redirects external forces primarily through the composition of tension and compression members, as a truss.

surface-active structure
A structure that redirects external forces primarily along the continuity of a surface, as a plate or shell.

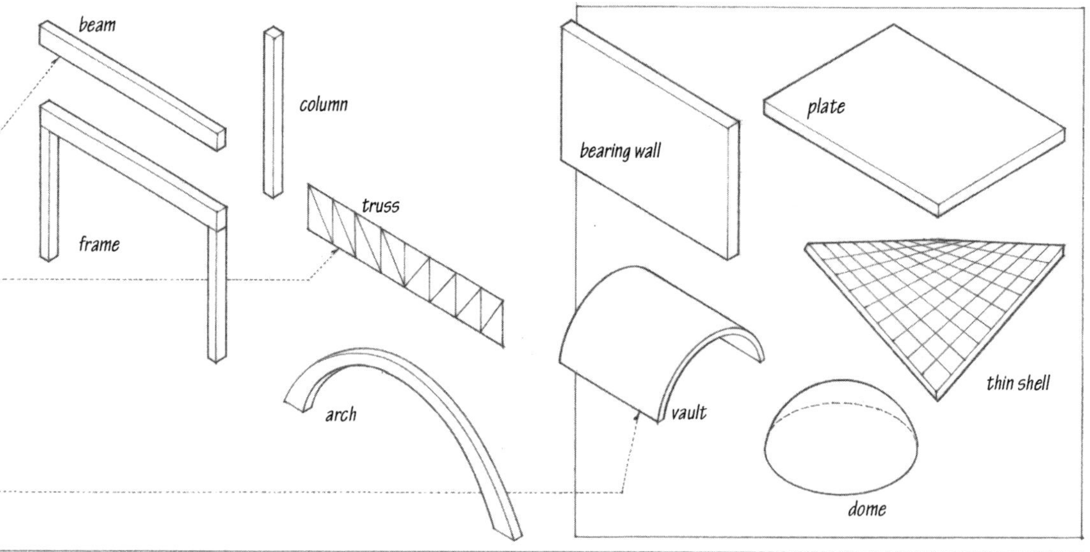

flexible
Of or pertaining to a structure or structural member characterized by a lack of stiffness and having a shape that responds to changes in loading.

form-active structure
A structure or structural member that redirects external forces primarily through the form of its material, as an arch or cable.

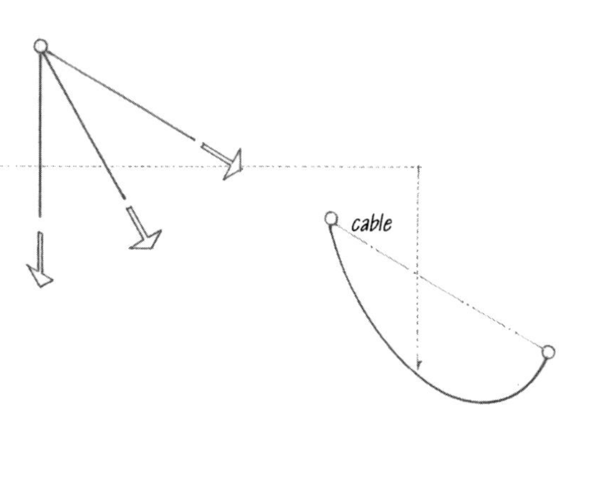

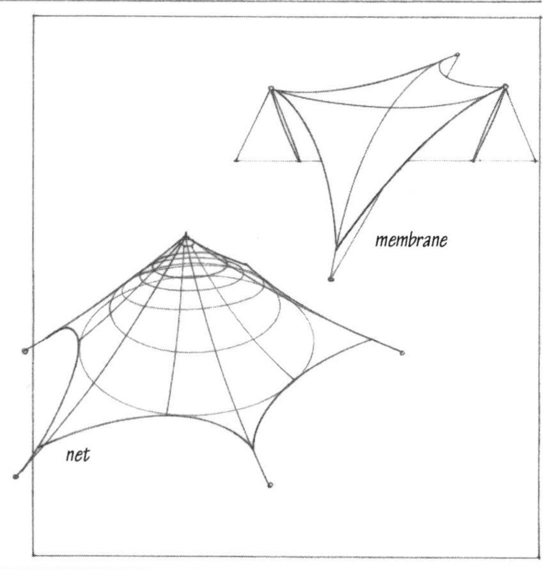

structural member
One of the constituent parts into which a structure may be resolved by analysis, having a unitary character and exhibiting a unique behavior under an applied load.

compression member
A structural member subject primarily to compressive forces.

strut
A structural member designed primarily to resist longitudinal compression.

tension member
A structural member subject primarily to tensile forces.

tie
A tension member designed to keep two structural members from spreading or separating.

bending member
A structural member subject primarily to transverse forces.

one-way
Of or pertaining to a structure or structural member having a load-carrying mechanism that acts in one direction only.

two-way
Of or pertaining to a structure or structural member having a load-carrying mechanism that acts in two or more directions.

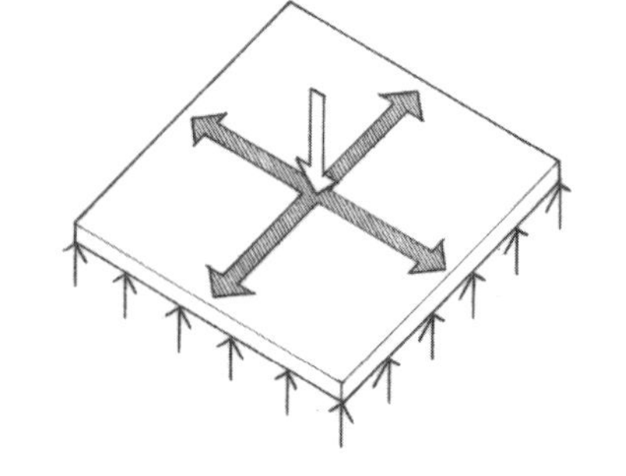

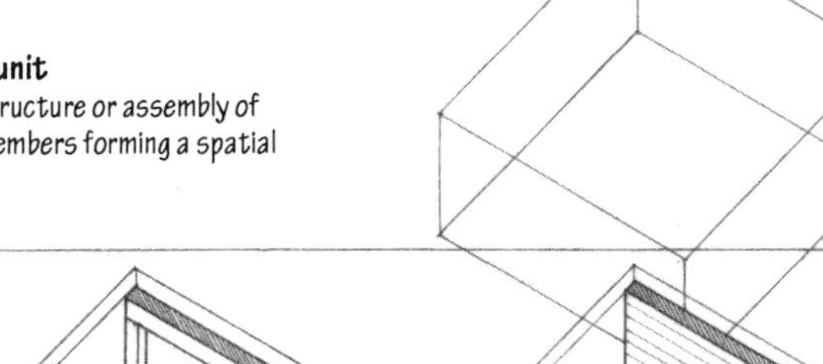

structural unit
A discrete structure or assembly of structural members forming a spatial volume.

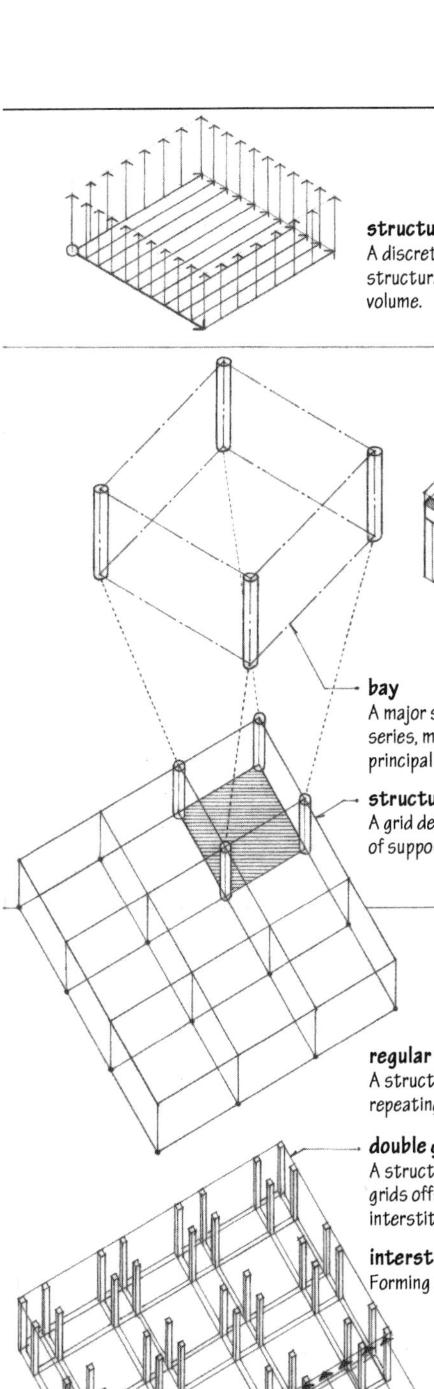

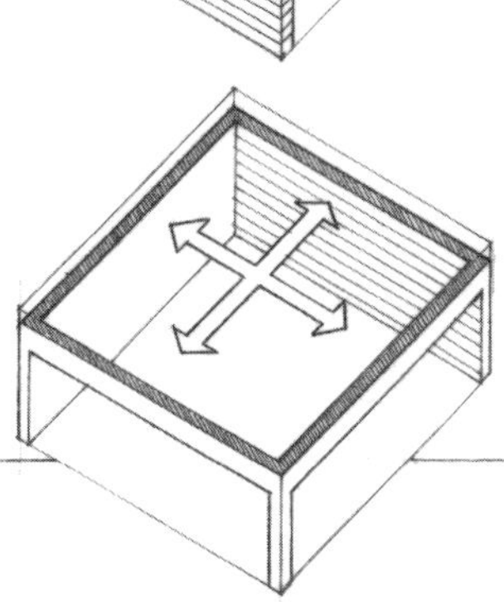

bay
A major spatial division, usually one of a series, marked or partitioned off by the principal vertical supports of a structure.

structural grid
A grid defining the principal points or lines of support for a structural system.

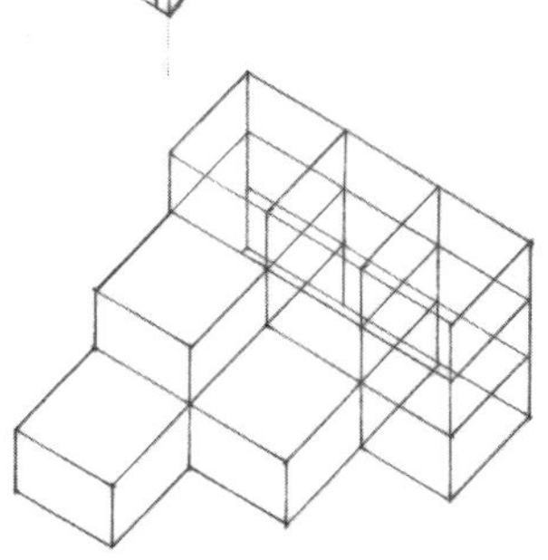

regular grid
A structural grid having regularly repeating bays in two directions.

double grid
A structural pattern consisting of two grids offset from each other and creating interstitial spaces between the bays.

interstitial
Forming an intervening space.

slipped grid
A structural grid having points or lines of supports spaced uniformly in one direction but varying in the other.

structural pattern
The arrangement of principal vertical supports for a structure, which influences the selection of an appropriate spanning system and establishes the possibilities for the ordering of spaces and functions.

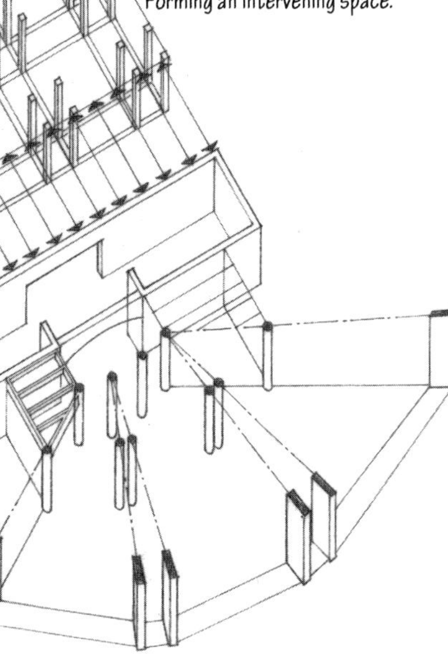

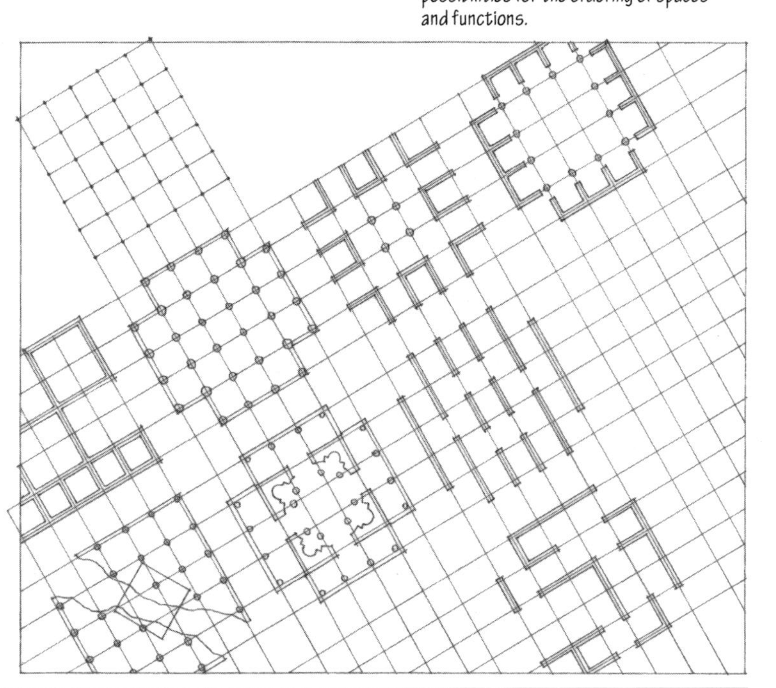

transition structure
A structure mediating between two or more different structural patterns.

irregular grid
A structural grid having irregularly shaped bays in one or more directions.

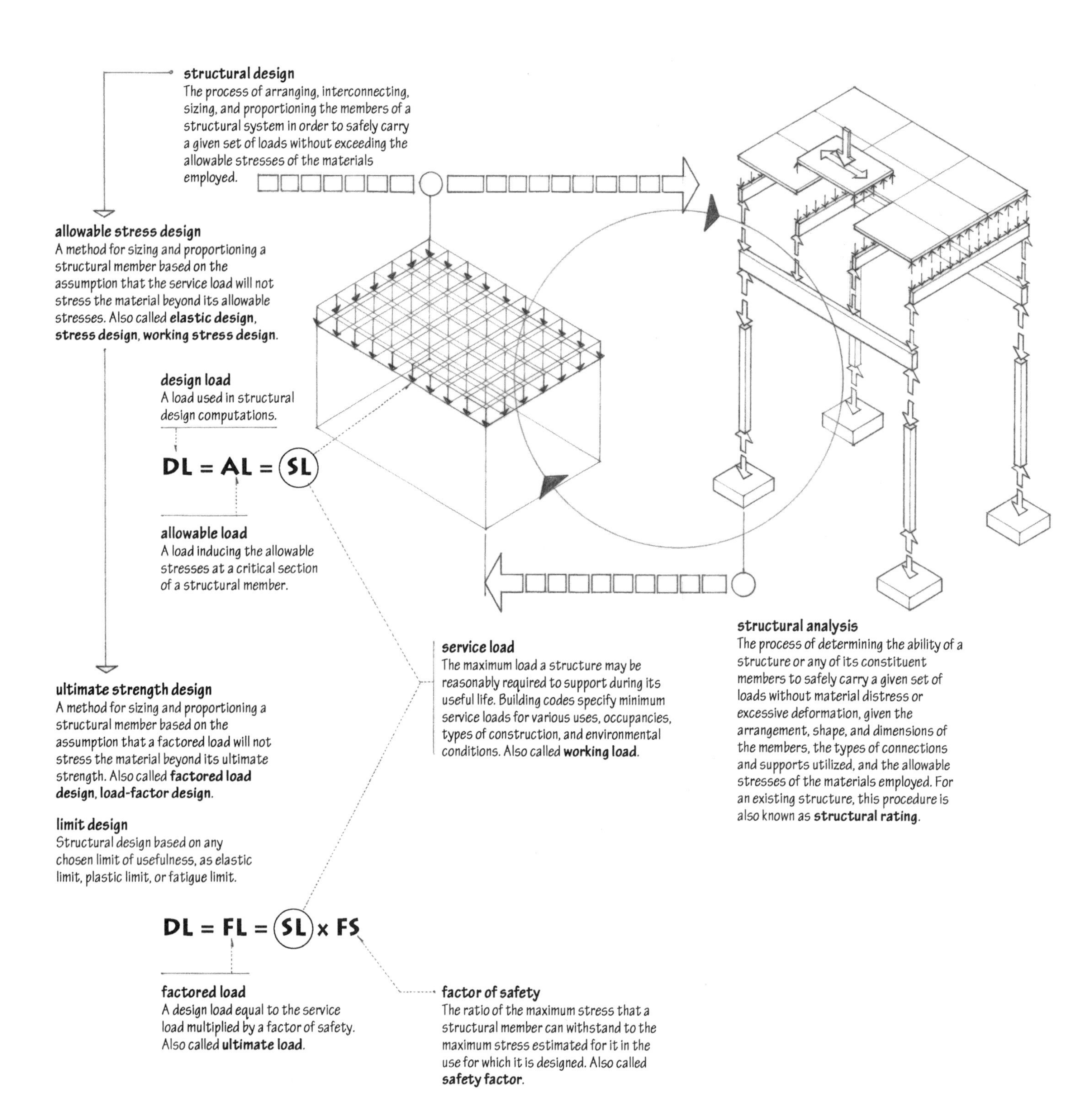

structural design
The process of arranging, interconnecting, sizing, and proportioning the members of a structural system in order to safely carry a given set of loads without exceeding the allowable stresses of the materials employed.

allowable stress design
A method for sizing and proportioning a structural member based on the assumption that the service load will not stress the material beyond its allowable stresses. Also called **elastic design, stress design, working stress design**.

design load
A load used in structural design computations.

$$DL = AL = SL$$

allowable load
A load inducing the allowable stresses at a critical section of a structural member.

service load
The maximum load a structure may be reasonably required to support during its useful life. Building codes specify minimum service loads for various uses, occupancies, types of construction, and environmental conditions. Also called **working load**.

structural analysis
The process of determining the ability of a structure or any of its constituent members to safely carry a given set of loads without material distress or excessive deformation, given the arrangement, shape, and dimensions of the members, the types of connections and supports utilized, and the allowable stresses of the materials employed. For an existing structure, this procedure is also known as **structural rating**.

ultimate strength design
A method for sizing and proportioning a structural member based on the assumption that a factored load will not stress the material beyond its ultimate strength. Also called **factored load design, load-factor design**.

limit design
Structural design based on any chosen limit of usefulness, as elastic limit, plastic limit, or fatigue limit.

$$DL = FL = SL \times FS$$

factored load
A design load equal to the service load multiplied by a factor of safety. Also called **ultimate load**.

factor of safety
The ratio of the maximum stress that a structural member can withstand to the maximum stress estimated for it in the use for which it is designed. Also called **safety factor**.

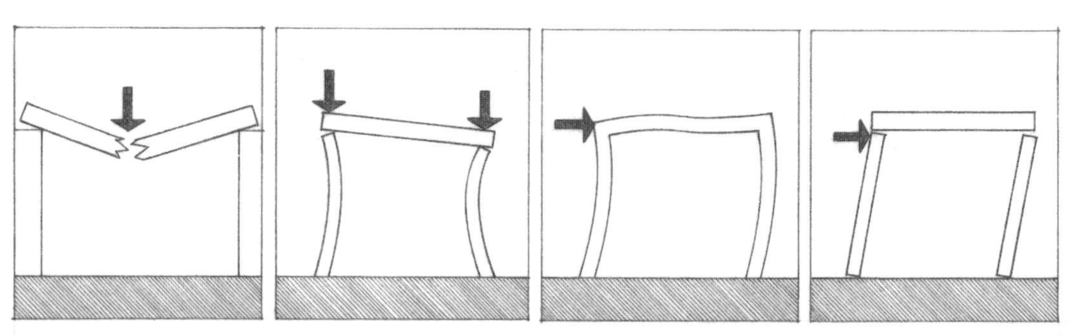

structural failure
Any condition, as fracturing, buckling, or plastic deformation, that renders a structural assembly, element, or joint incapable of sustaining the load-carrying function for which it was designed.

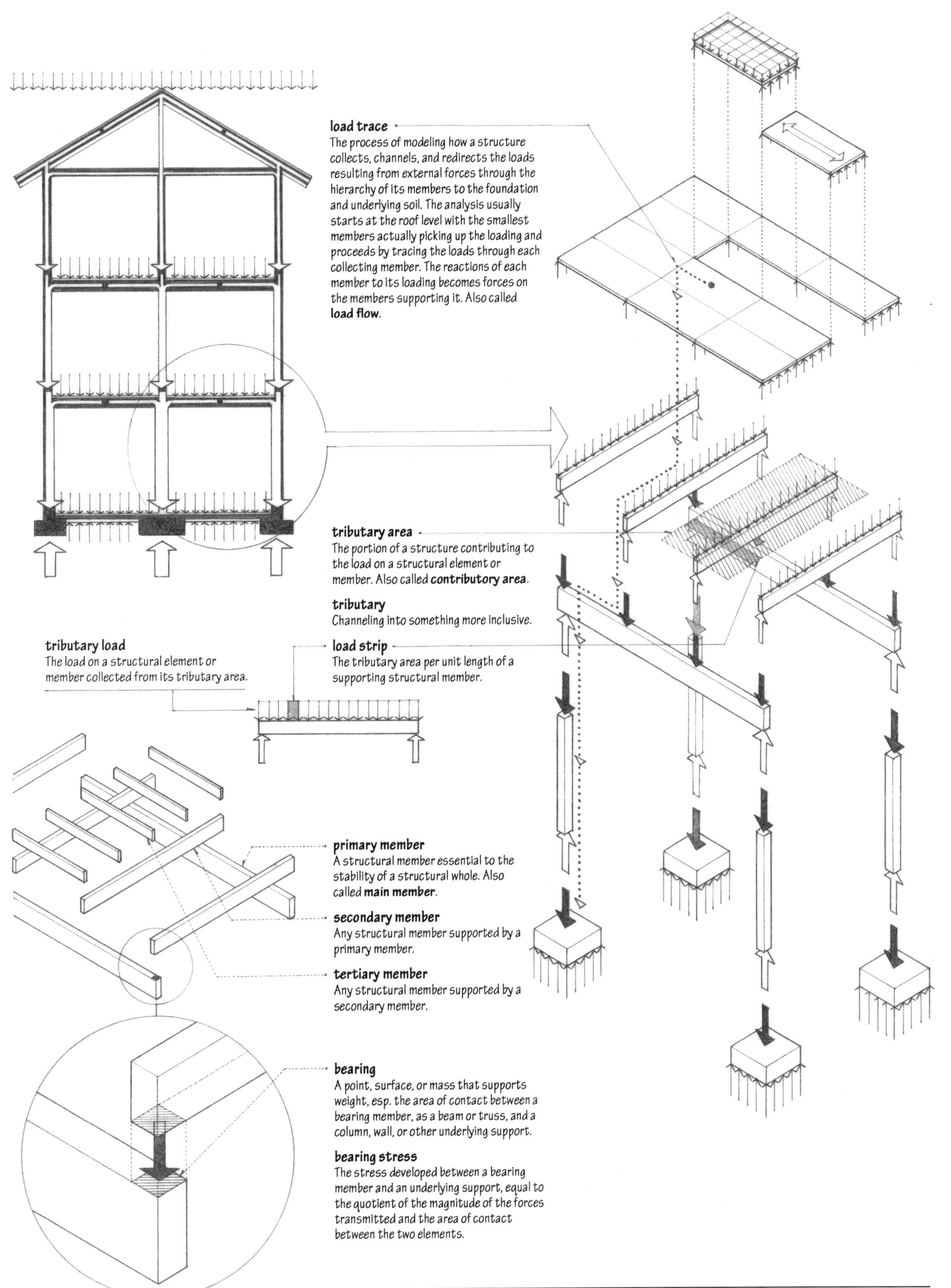

load trace
The process of modeling how a structure collects, channels, and redirects the loads resulting from external forces through the hierarchy of its members to the foundation and underlying soil. The analysis usually starts at the roof level with the smallest members actually picking up the loading and proceeds by tracing the loads through each collecting member. The reactions of each member to its loading becomes forces on the members supporting it. Also called **load flow**.

tributary area
The portion of a structure contributing to the load on a structural element or member. Also called **contributory area**.

tributary
Channeling into something more inclusive.

tributary load
The load on a structural element or member collected from its tributary area.

load strip
The tributary area per unit length of a supporting structural member.

primary member
A structural member essential to the stability of a structural whole. Also called **main member**.

secondary member
Any structural member supported by a primary member.

tertiary member
Any structural member supported by a secondary member.

bearing
A point, surface, or mass that supports weight, esp. the area of contact between a bearing member, as a beam or truss, and a column, wall, or other underlying support.

bearing stress
The stress developed between a bearing member and an underlying support, equal to the quotient of the magnitude of the forces transmitted and the area of contact between the two elements.

support condition
The manner in which a structural member is supported and connected to other members, affecting the nature of the reactive forces developed on the loaded member.

point of support
A point on a structural member at which its reaction to a load is transmitted as a force to a supporting member.

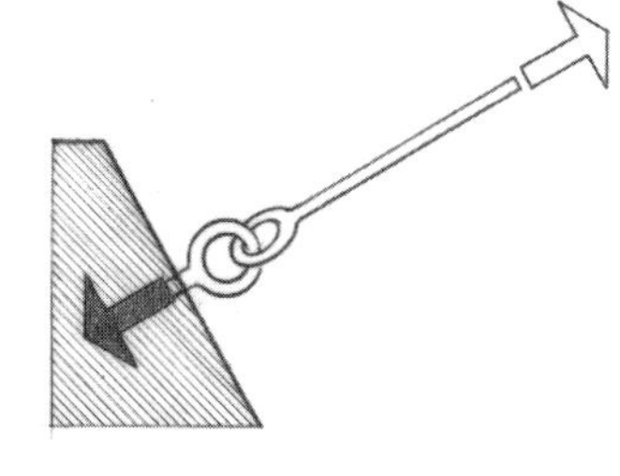

unrestrained member
A structural member permitted to rotate freely about a point of support.

roller support
A structural support that allows rotation but resists translation in a direction perpendicular into or away from its face. Also called **roller joint**.

cable support
A cable anchorage that allows rotation but resists translation only in the direction of the cable.

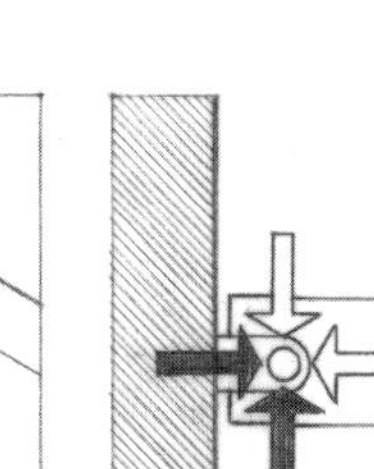

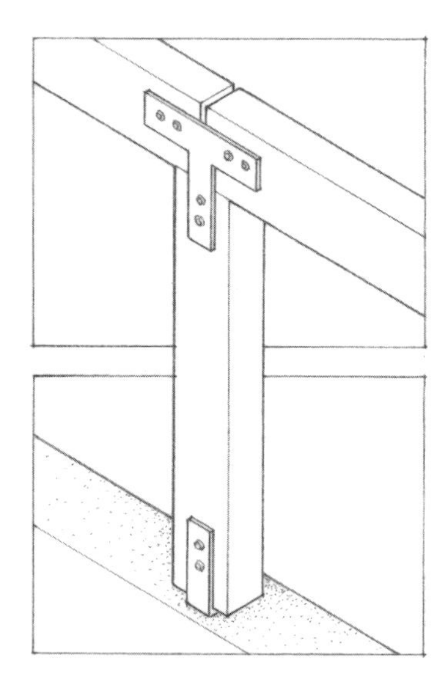

pin joint
A structural connection that allows rotation but resists translation in any direction. Also called **hinge joint**, **pinned connection**.

pin
A slender rod driven through holes in adjacent parts to keep the parts together or to permit them to move in one plane relative to each other.

rigid joint
A structural connection that maintains the angular relationship between the joined elements, restrains rotation and translation in any direction, and provides both force and moment resistance. Also called **fixed connection**, **fixed joint**, **rigid connection**.

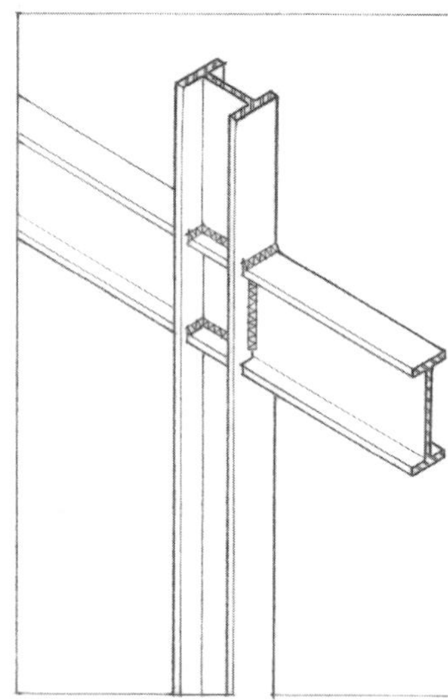

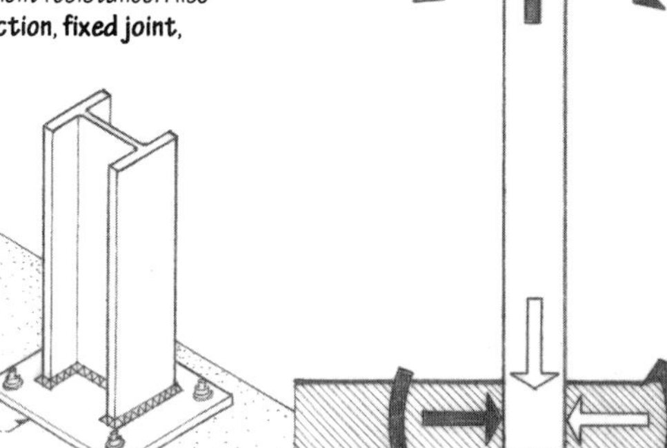

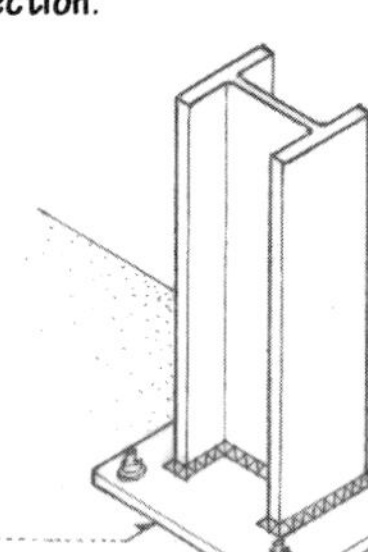

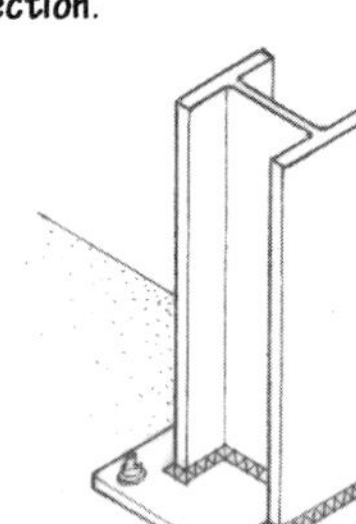

fixed-end connection
A rigid joint connecting the end of a structural member to a support.

anchorage
A means for binding a structural member to another or to its foundation, often to resist uplifting and horizontal forces.

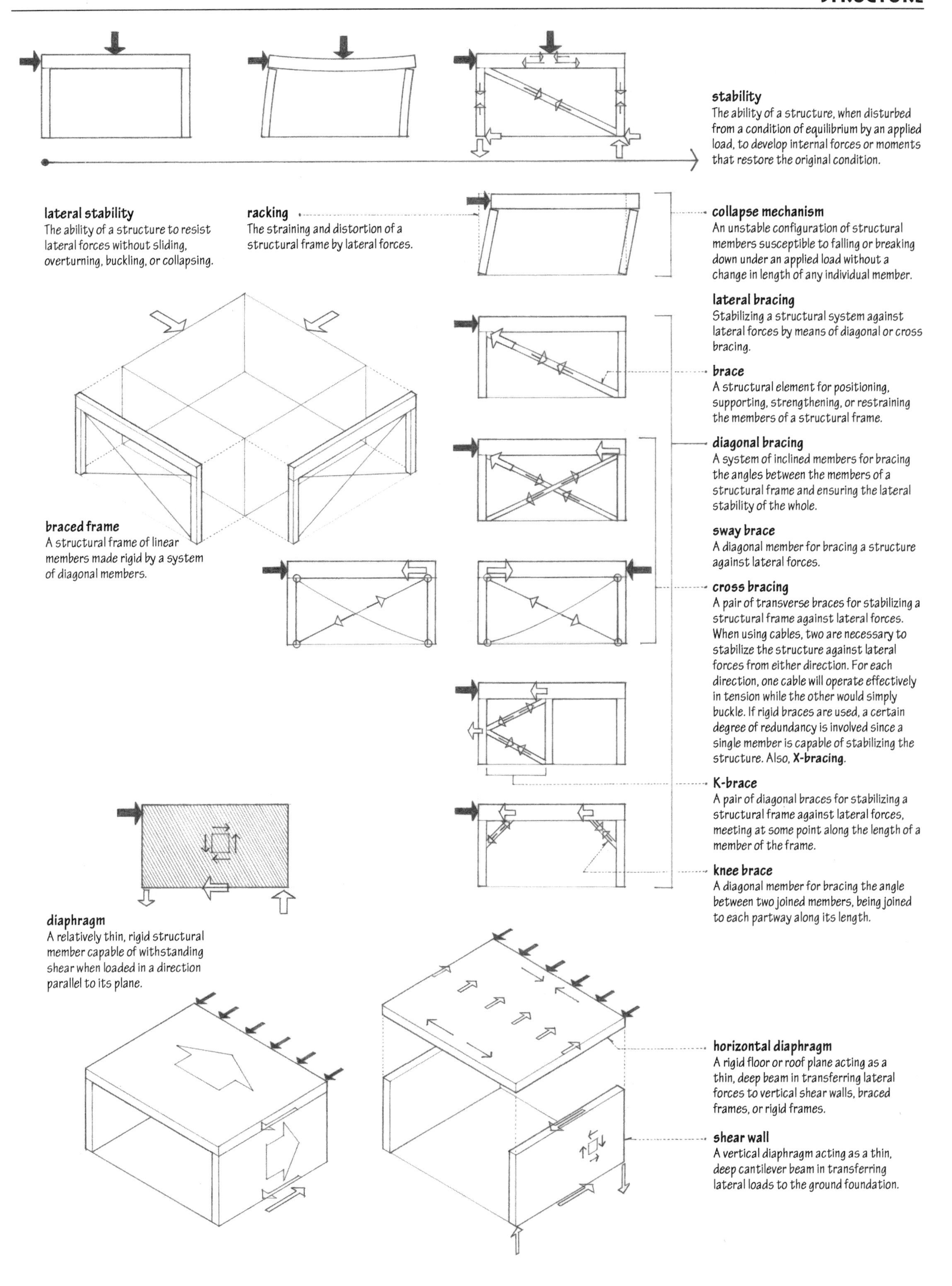

stability
The ability of a structure, when disturbed from a condition of equilibrium by an applied load, to develop internal forces or moments that restore the original condition.

lateral stability
The ability of a structure to resist lateral forces without sliding, overturning, buckling, or collapsing.

racking
The straining and distortion of a structural frame by lateral forces.

collapse mechanism
An unstable configuration of structural members susceptible to falling or breaking down under an applied load without a change in length of any individual member.

lateral bracing
Stabilizing a structural system against lateral forces by means of diagonal or cross bracing.

brace
A structural element for positioning, supporting, strengthening, or restraining the members of a structural frame.

diagonal bracing
A system of inclined members for bracing the angles between the members of a structural frame and ensuring the lateral stability of the whole.

braced frame
A structural frame of linear members made rigid by a system of diagonal members.

sway brace
A diagonal member for bracing a structure against lateral forces.

cross bracing
A pair of transverse braces for stabilizing a structural frame against lateral forces. When using cables, two are necessary to stabilize the structure against lateral forces from either direction. For each direction, one cable will operate effectively in tension while the other would simply buckle. If rigid braces are used, a certain degree of redundancy is involved since a single member is capable of stabilizing the structure. Also, **X-bracing**.

K-brace
A pair of diagonal braces for stabilizing a structural frame against lateral forces, meeting at some point along the length of a member of the frame.

knee brace
A diagonal member for bracing the angle between two joined members, being joined to each partway along its length.

diaphragm
A relatively thin, rigid structural member capable of withstanding shear when loaded in a direction parallel to its plane.

horizontal diaphragm
A rigid floor or roof plane acting as a thin, deep beam in transferring lateral forces to vertical shear walls, braced frames, or rigid frames.

shear wall
A vertical diaphragm acting as a thin, deep cantilever beam in transferring lateral loads to the ground foundation.

regular structure
A structural system characterized by the symmetrical configuration of mass and lateral force-resisting elements and having no significant discontinuities of stiffness or strength. The effects of lateral forces on regular structures may be determined by static methods.

dual system
A structural system for resisting lateral forces, combining the ductility of a moment-resisting frame with the rigidity of a shear wall.

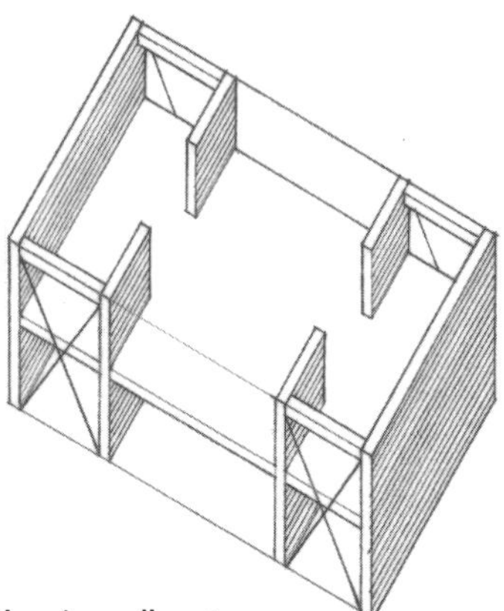

bearing wall system
A structural system consisting of vertical planar elements for supporting gravity loads and shear walls or braced frames for resisting lateral forces.

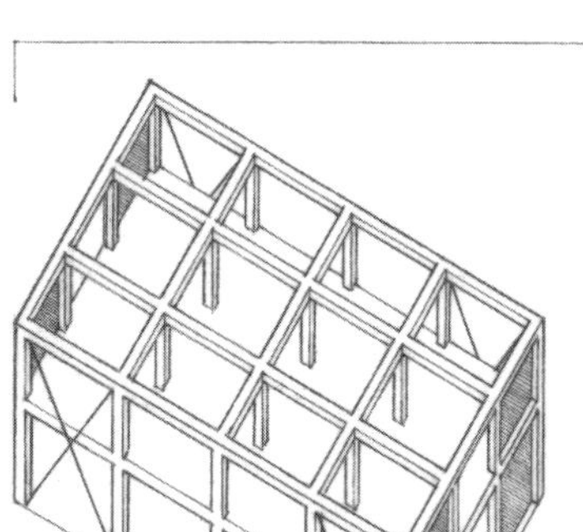

frame system
A structural system consisting of a three-dimensional array of interconnected linear members that functions as a complete, self-contained unit in supporting gravity loads and shear walls or braced frames for resisting lateral forces.

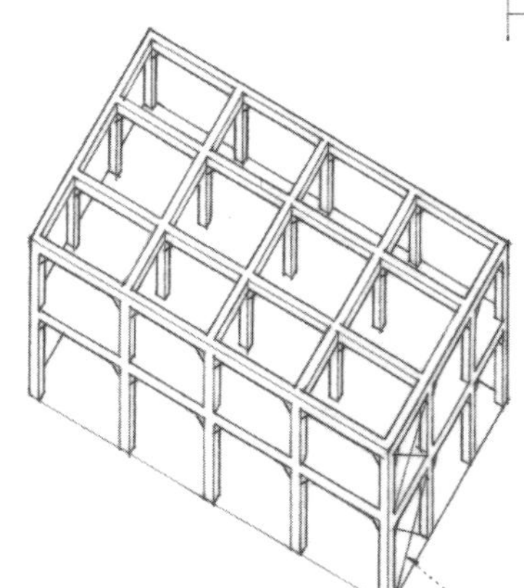

moment-resisting frame
A frame system designed to resist lateral forces primarily by flexure in the members and joints.

eccentric bracing
A structural system for resisting lateral forces, combining the ductility of a moment-resisting frame with the rigidity of a braced frame.

irregular structure
A structural system characterized by any of various plan or vertical irregularities, as a soft or weak story, a discontinuous shear wall or diaphragm, or the asymmetrical layout of mass or lateral-force resisting elements. Irregular structures generally require dynamic analysis in order to determine the torsional effects of lateral forces.

center of resistance
The centroid of the vertical elements of a lateral force-resisting system, through which the shear reaction to lateral forces acts. Also called **center of rigidity**.

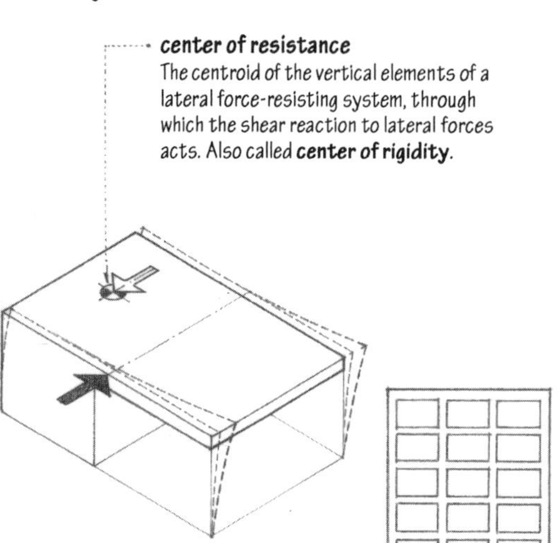

torsional irregularity
The asymmetrical layout of mass or lateral force-resisting elements, resulting in noncoincident centers of mass and resistance and causing the story drift at one end of the structure to be more than the average of the story drifts at both ends.

reentrant corner
The plan configuration of a structure and its lateral force-resisting system having projections beyond a corner significantly greater than the plan dimension in the given direction. A reentrant corner tends to produce differential motions between different portions of the structure, resulting in local stress concentrations at the corner. Solutions include providing a seismic joint to separate the building into simpler shapes, tying the building together more strongly at the corner, or splaying the corner.

seismic joint
A joint that physically separates two adjacent building masses so that free vibratory movement in each can occur independently of the other.

discontinuous diaphragm
A horizontal diaphragm having a large cutout or open area, or a stiffness significantly less than that of the story above or below.

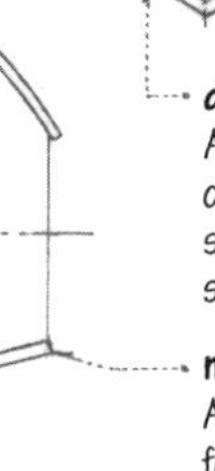

nonparallel system
A structural system having lateral force-resisting elements neither parallel nor symmetrical about the major orthogonal axes of the system.

soft story
A story having a lateral stiffness significantly less than that of the stories above.

weak story
A story having lateral strength significantly less than that of the stories above.

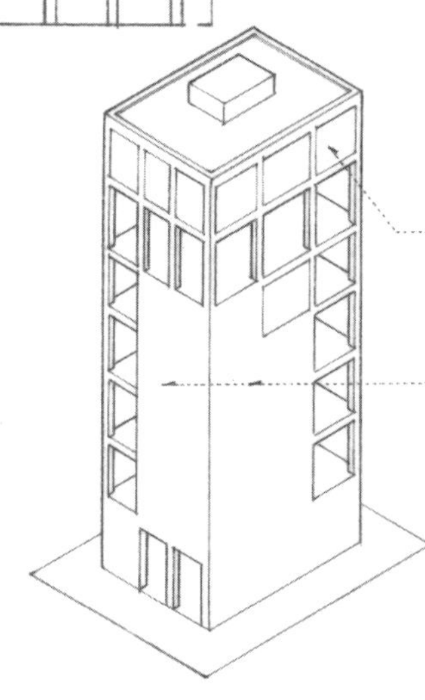

irregular mass
A story having an effective mass significantly greater than that of an adjacent story.

discontinuous shear wall
A shear wall having a large offset or a significant change in horizontal dimension.

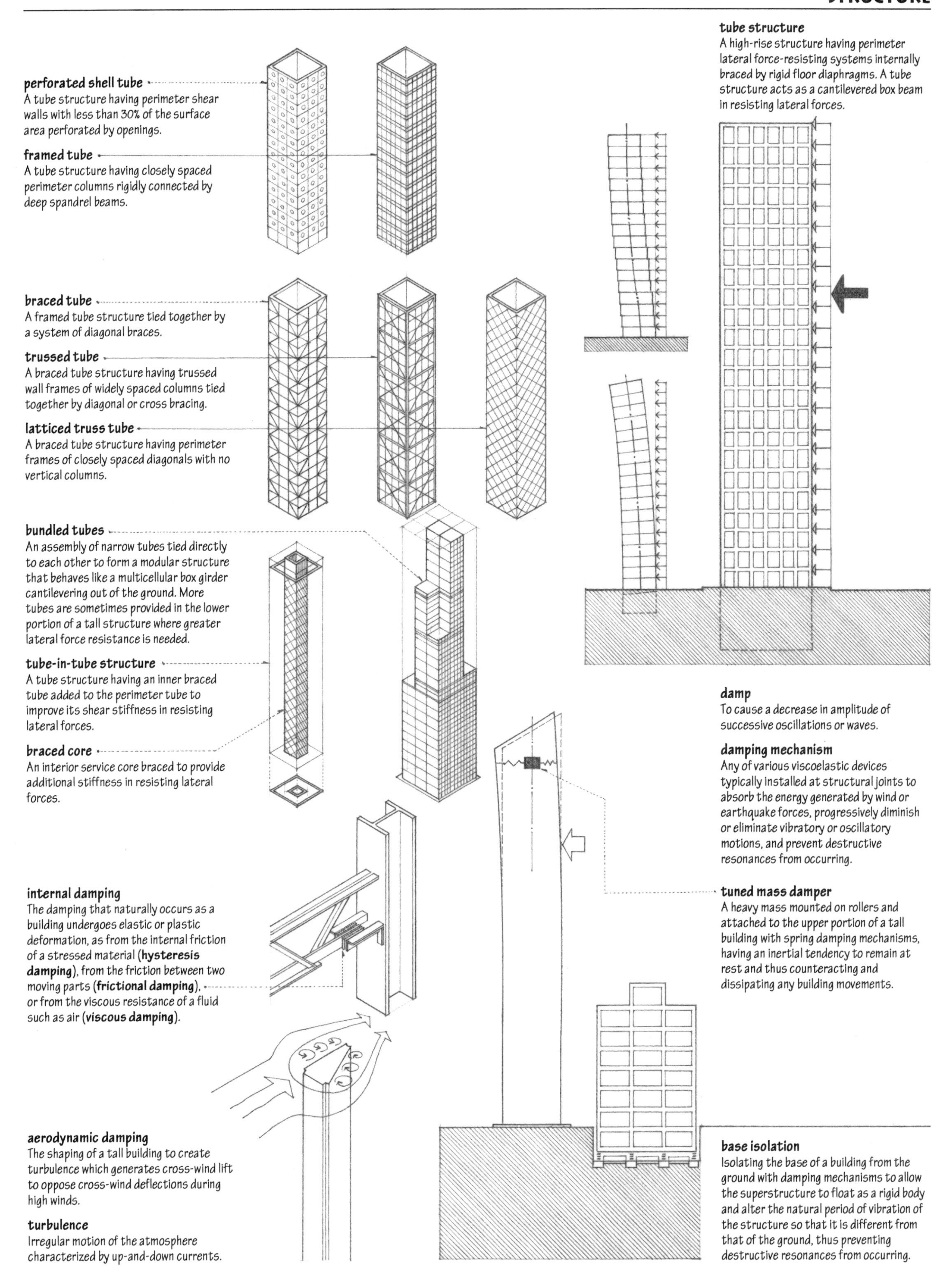

tube structure
A high-rise structure having perimeter lateral force-resisting systems internally braced by rigid floor diaphragms. A tube structure acts as a cantilevered box beam in resisting lateral forces.

perforated shell tube
A tube structure having perimeter shear walls with less than 30% of the surface area perforated by openings.

framed tube
A tube structure having closely spaced perimeter columns rigidly connected by deep spandrel beams.

braced tube
A framed tube structure tied together by a system of diagonal braces.

trussed tube
A braced tube structure having trussed wall frames of widely spaced columns tied together by diagonal or cross bracing.

latticed truss tube
A braced tube structure having perimeter frames of closely spaced diagonals with no vertical columns.

bundled tubes
An assembly of narrow tubes tied directly to each other to form a modular structure that behaves like a multicellular box girder cantilevering out of the ground. More tubes are sometimes provided in the lower portion of a tall structure where greater lateral force resistance is needed.

tube-in-tube structure
A tube structure having an inner braced tube added to the perimeter tube to improve its shear stiffness in resisting lateral forces.

braced core
An interior service core braced to provide additional stiffness in resisting lateral forces.

damp
To cause a decrease in amplitude of successive oscillations or waves.

damping mechanism
Any of various viscoelastic devices typically installed at structural joints to absorb the energy generated by wind or earthquake forces, progressively diminish or eliminate vibratory or oscillatory motions, and prevent destructive resonances from occurring.

internal damping
The damping that naturally occurs as a building undergoes elastic or plastic deformation, as from the internal friction of a stressed material (**hysteresis damping**), from the friction between two moving parts (**frictional damping**), or from the viscous resistance of a fluid such as air (**viscous damping**).

tuned mass damper
A heavy mass mounted on rollers and attached to the upper portion of a tall building with spring damping mechanisms, having an inertial tendency to remain at rest and thus counteracting and dissipating any building movements.

aerodynamic damping
The shaping of a tall building to create turbulence which generates cross-wind lift to oppose cross-wind deflections during high winds.

turbulence
Irregular motion of the atmosphere characterized by up-and-down currents.

base isolation
Isolating the base of a building from the ground with damping mechanisms to allow the superstructure to float as a rigid body and alter the natural period of vibration of the structure so that it is different from that of the ground, thus preventing destructive resonances from occurring.

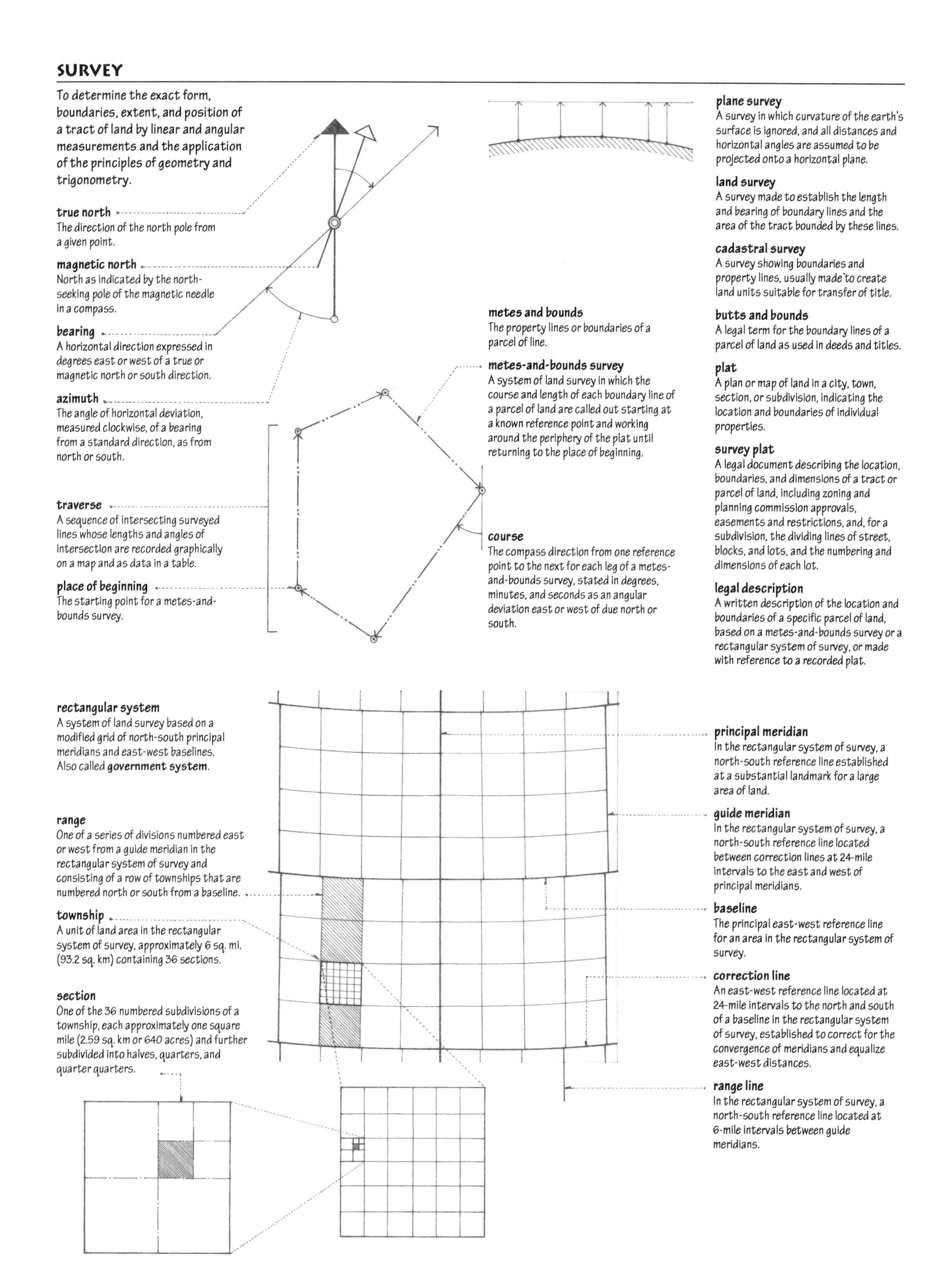

To determine the exact form, boundaries, extent, and position of a tract of land by linear and angular measurements and the application of the principles of geometry and trigonometry.

true north
The direction of the north pole from a given point.

magnetic north
North as indicated by the north-seeking pole of the magnetic needle in a compass.

bearing
A horizontal direction expressed in degrees east or west of a true or magnetic north or south direction.

azimuth
The angle of horizontal deviation, measured clockwise, of a bearing from a standard direction, as from north or south.

traverse
A sequence of intersecting surveyed lines whose lengths and angles of intersection are recorded graphically on a map and as data in a table.

place of beginning
The starting point for a metes-and-bounds survey.

metes and bounds
The property lines or boundaries of a parcel of line.

metes-and-bounds survey
A system of land survey in which the course and length of each boundary line of a parcel of land are called out starting at a known reference point and working around the periphery of the plat until returning to the place of beginning.

course
The compass direction from one reference point to the next for each leg of a metes-and-bounds survey, stated in degrees, minutes, and seconds as an angular deviation east or west of due north or south.

plane survey
A survey in which curvature of the earth's surface is ignored, and all distances and horizontal angles are assumed to be projected onto a horizontal plane.

land survey
A survey made to establish the length and bearing of boundary lines and the area of the tract bounded by these lines.

cadastral survey
A survey showing boundaries and property lines, usually made to create land units suitable for transfer of title.

butts and bounds
A legal term for the boundary lines of a parcel of land as used in deeds and titles.

plat
A plan or map of land in a city, town, section, or subdivision, indicating the location and boundaries of individual properties.

survey plat
A legal document describing the location, boundaries, and dimensions of a tract or parcel of land, including zoning and planning commission approvals, easements and restrictions, and, for a subdivision, the dividing lines of street, blocks, and lots, and the numbering and dimensions of each lot.

legal description
A written description of the location and boundaries of a specific parcel of land, based on a metes-and-bounds survey or a rectangular system of survey, or made with reference to a recorded plat.

rectangular system
A system of land survey based on a modified grid of north-south principal meridians and east-west baselines. Also called **government system**.

range
One of a series of divisions numbered east or west from a guide meridian in the rectangular system of survey and consisting of a row of townships that are numbered north or south from a baseline.

township
A unit of land area in the rectangular system of survey, approximately 6 sq. mi. (93.2 sq. km) containing 36 sections.

section
One of the 36 numbered subdivisions of a township, each approximately one square mile (2.59 sq. km or 640 acres) and further subdivided into halves, quarters, and quarter quarters.

principal meridian
In the rectangular system of survey, a north-south reference line established at a substantial landmark for a large area of land.

guide meridian
In the rectangular system of survey, a north-south reference line located between correction lines at 24-mile intervals to the east and west of principal meridians.

baseline
The principal east-west reference line for an area in the rectangular system of survey.

correction line
An east-west reference line located at 24-mile intervals to the north and south of a baseline in the rectangular system of survey, established to correct for the convergence of meridians and equalize east-west distances.

range line
In the rectangular system of survey, a north-south reference line located at 6-mile intervals between guide meridians.

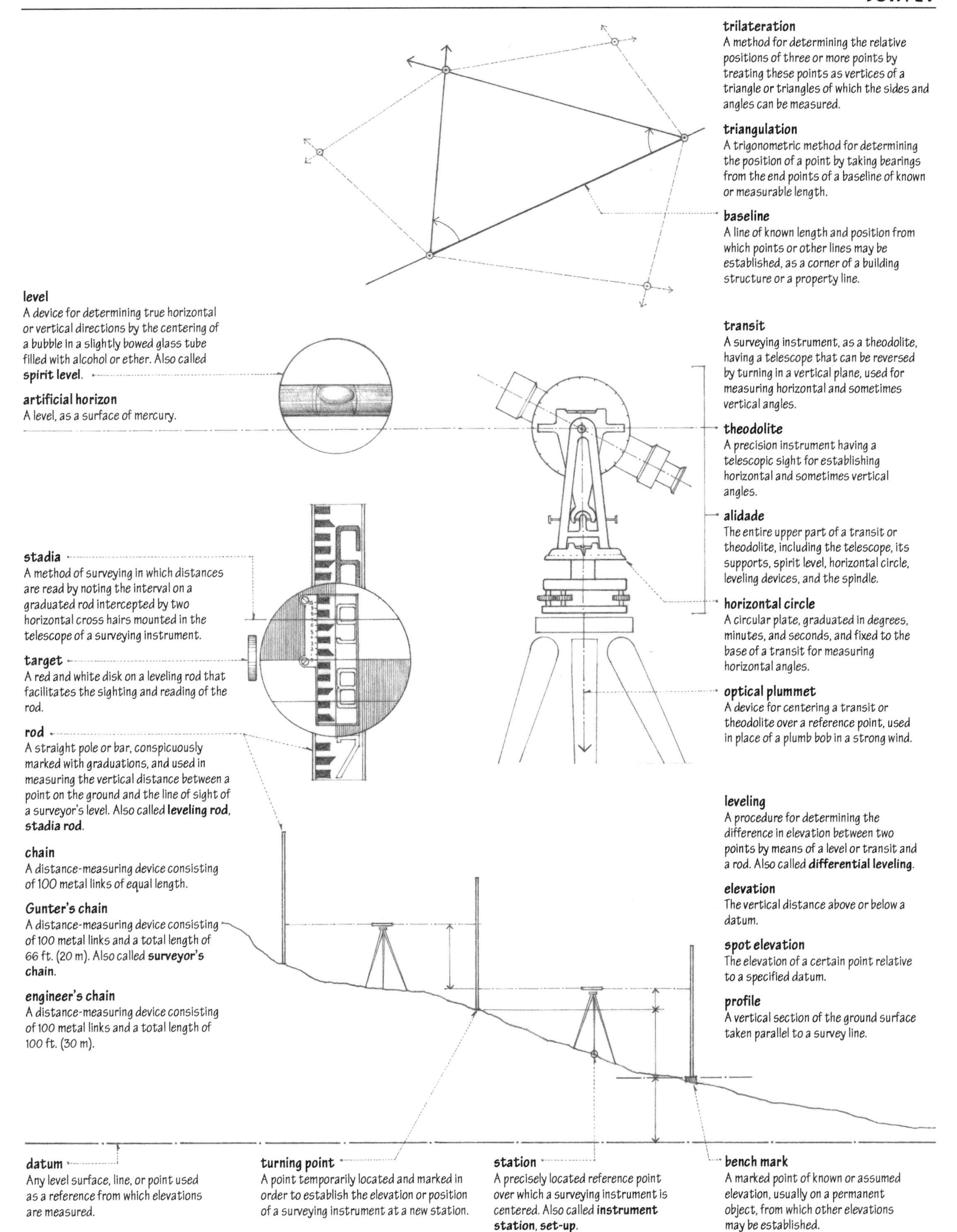

trilateration
A method for determining the relative positions of three or more points by treating these points as vertices of a triangle or triangles of which the sides and angles can be measured.

triangulation
A trigonometric method for determining the position of a point by taking bearings from the end points of a baseline of known or measurable length.

baseline
A line of known length and position from which points or other lines may be established, as a corner of a building structure or a property line.

level
A device for determining true horizontal or vertical directions by the centering of a bubble in a slightly bowed glass tube filled with alcohol or ether. Also called **spirit level**.

artificial horizon
A level, as a surface of mercury.

transit
A surveying instrument, as a theodolite, having a telescope that can be reversed by turning in a vertical plane, used for measuring horizontal and sometimes vertical angles.

theodolite
A precision instrument having a telescopic sight for establishing horizontal and sometimes vertical angles.

alidade
The entire upper part of a transit or theodolite, including the telescope, its supports, spirit level, horizontal circle, leveling devices, and the spindle.

horizontal circle
A circular plate, graduated in degrees, minutes, and seconds, and fixed to the base of a transit for measuring horizontal angles.

optical plummet
A device for centering a transit or theodolite over a reference point, used in place of a plumb bob in a strong wind.

stadia
A method of surveying in which distances are read by noting the interval on a graduated rod intercepted by two horizontal cross hairs mounted in the telescope of a surveying instrument.

target
A red and white disk on a leveling rod that facilitates the sighting and reading of the rod.

rod
A straight pole or bar, conspicuously marked with graduations, and used in measuring the vertical distance between a point on the ground and the line of sight of a surveyor's level. Also called **leveling rod**, **stadia rod**.

chain
A distance-measuring device consisting of 100 metal links of equal length.

Gunter's chain
A distance-measuring device consisting of 100 metal links and a total length of 66 ft. (20 m). Also called **surveyor's chain**.

engineer's chain
A distance-measuring device consisting of 100 metal links and a total length of 100 ft. (30 m).

leveling
A procedure for determining the difference in elevation between two points by means of a level or transit and a rod. Also called **differential leveling**.

elevation
The vertical distance above or below a datum.

spot elevation
The elevation of a certain point relative to a specified datum.

profile
A vertical section of the ground surface taken parallel to a survey line.

datum
Any level surface, line, or point used as a reference from which elevations are measured.

turning point
A point temporarily located and marked in order to establish the elevation or position of a surveying instrument at a new station.

station
A precisely located reference point over which a surveying instrument is centered. Also called **instrument station**, **set-up**.

bench mark
A marked point of known or assumed elevation, usually on a permanent object, from which other elevations may be established.

TEMPLE

An edifice or place dedicated to the worship or presence of a deity.

sacred
Of or pertaining to religious objects, rites, or practices, as opposed to the secular or profane.

secular
Of or pertaining to the temporal or worldly rather than the sacred or spiritual. Also, **profane**.

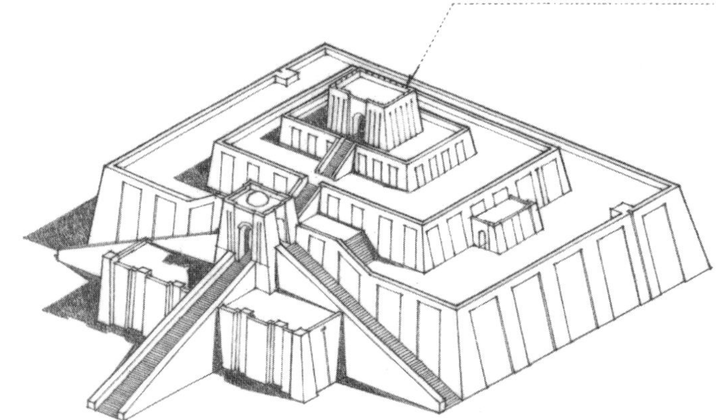

ziggurat
A temple-tower in Sumerian and Assyrian architecture, built in diminishing stages of mud brick with buttressed walls faced with burnt brick, culminating in a summit shrine or temple reached by a series of ramps; thought to be of Sumerian origin, dating from the end of the 3rd millennium B.C. Also, **zikkurat**.

Tower of Babel
A temple-tower presumed to be the great ziggurat at Babylon, which no longer survives, though it was seen and described by the Greek historian, Herodotus, in the 5th century B.C.:

"And they said to one another, Let us make brick, and burn it thoroughly. And they had brick for stone, and slime for mortar. And they said, Let us build a city and a tower, whose top may reach unto heaven; and let us make a name, lest we be scattered abroad upon the face of the whole earth."
—Genesis 11:4

Lamassu
The monumental stone sculptures of human-headed, winged bulls or lions that guarded the entrances to Mesopotamian palaces and temples.

menhir
A prehistoric monument consisting of an upright megalith, usually standing alone but sometimes aligned with others.

megalith
A very large stone used as found or roughly dressed, esp. in ancient construction work.

monolith
A single block of stone of considerable size, often in the form of an obelisk or column.

cairn
A heap of stones piled up as a monument, tombstone, or landmark. Also, **carn**.

dolmen
A prehistoric monument consisting of two or more large upright stones supporting a horizontal stone slab, found esp. in Britain and France and usually regarded as a tomb.

passage grave
A megalithic tomb of the Neolithic and early Bronze Ages found in the British Isles and Europe, consisting of a roofed burial chamber and narrow entrance passage, covered by a tumulus: believed to have been used for successive family or clan burials spanning a number of generations. Also called **chamber grave**.

tumulus
An artificial mound of earth or stone, esp. over an ancient grave. Also called **barrow**.

trilithon
Two upright megaliths supporting a horizontal stone. Also called **trilith**.

cromlech
A circular arrangement of megaliths enclosing a dolmen or burial mound.

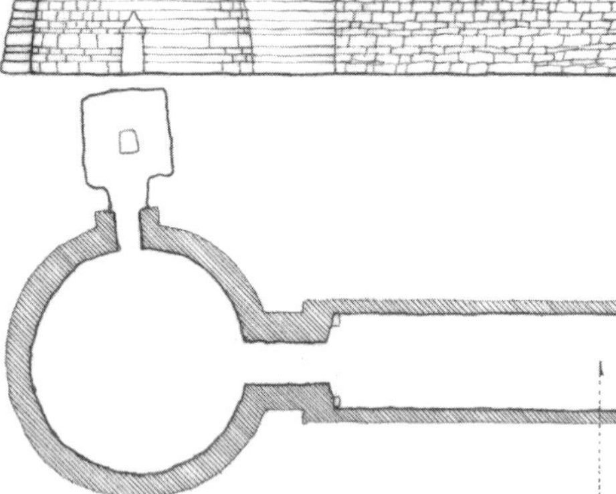

shaft grave
A tomb of the Aegean civilizations consisting of a deep rectangular cut into sloping rock and a roof of timber or stone.

beehive tomb
A stone-built subterranean tomb of the Mycenaean civilization consisting of a circular chamber covered by a corbeled dome and entered by a walled passage through a hillside. Also called **tholos**.

dromos
A long, deep passageway into an ancient subterranean tomb.

Stonehenge
A megalithic monument erected in the early Bronze Age c2700 B.C. on Salisbury Plain, Wiltshire, England, consisting of four concentric rings of trilithons and menhirs centered around an altar stone: believed to have been used by a sun cult or for astronomical observations.

mastaba
An ancient Egyptian tomb made of mud brick, rectangular in plan with a flat roof and sloping sides, from which a shaft leads to underground burial and offering chambers.

serdab
A small chamber inside a mastaba containing a statue of the deceased.

uraeus
The figure of the sacred asp, depicted on the headdress of ancient Egyptian rulers and deities as an emblem of supreme power.

pyramid
A massive masonry structure having a rectangular base and four smooth, steeply sloping sides facing the cardinal points and meeting at an apex, used in ancient Egypt as a tomb to contain the burial chamber and the mummy of the pharaoh. The pyramid was usually part of a complex of buildings within a walled enclosure, including mastabas for members of the royal family, an offering chapel and a mortuary temple. A raised causeway led from the enclosure down to a valley temple on the Nile, where purification rites and mummification were performed.

syrinx
A narrow rock-cut corridor in an ancient Egyptian tomb.

necropolis
A historic burial ground, esp. a large, elaborate one of an ancient city.

causeway
A raised passageway ceremonially connecting the valley temple with an ancient Egyptian pyramid.

pharaoh
Any of the rulers of ancient Egypt who were believed to be divine and had absolute power.

cavetto
A concave molding having an outline that approximates a quarter circle.

sphinx
A figure of an imaginary creature having the body of a lion and the head of a man, ram, or hawk, commonly placed along avenues leading to ancient Egyptian temples or tombs.

cavetto cornice
A characteristic cornice of Egyptian buildings, consisting of a large cavetto decorated with vertical leaves and a roll molding below. Also called **Egyptian gorge**.

cult temple
An ancient Egyptian temple for the worship of a deity, as distinguished from a mortuary temple.

mortuary temple
An ancient Egyptian temple for offerings and worship of a deceased person, usually a deified king. In the New Kingdom, cult and funerary temples had many features in common: an avenue of sphinxes leading to a tall portal guarded by a towering pylon, an axial plan with a colonnaded forecourt and a hypostyle hall set before a dark, narrow sanctuary in which stood a statue of the deity, and walls lavishly decorated with pictographic carvings in low or sunken relief. Many of the major temples grew by accretion due to the pious ambitions of successive pharaohs, who believed in the afterlife and were determined to create an enduring reputation through their buildings.

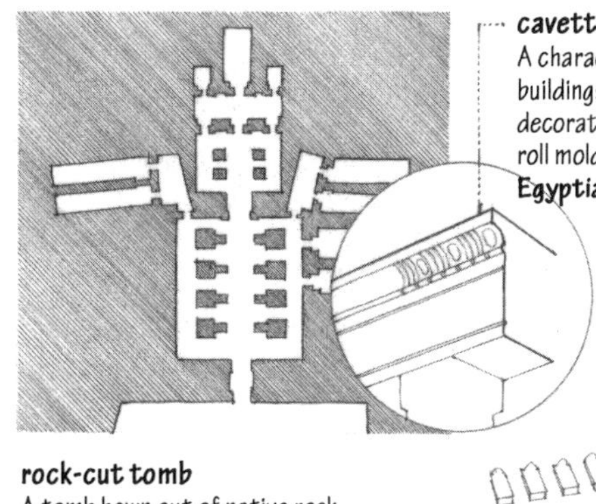

rock-cut tomb
A tomb hewn out of native rock, presenting only an architectural front with dark interior chambers, of which the sections are supported by masses of stone left in the form of solid pillars.

obelisk
A tall, four-sided shaft of stone that tapers as it rises to a pyramidal point, originating in ancient Egypt as a sacred symbol of the sun-god Ra and usually standing in pairs astride temple entrances.

pylon
A monumental gateway to an ancient Egyptian temple, consisting either of a pair of tall truncated pyramids and a doorway between them or of one such masonry mass pierced with a doorway, often decorated with painted reliefs.

propylon
A freestanding gateway having the form of a pylon and preceding the main gateway to an ancient Egyptian temple or sacred enclosure.

hypostyle hall
A large hall having many columns in rows supporting a flat roof, and sometimes a clerestory: prevalent in ancient Egyptian and Achaemenid architecture.

New Kingdom
The period in the history of ancient Egypt, c1550–1200 B.C., comprising the 18th to 20th dynasties: characterized by the dominance of its capital at Thebes.

Osirian column
An ancient Egyptian column incorporating the sculptured figure of Osiris, the Egyptian god of death and resurrection.

Hathor-headed
Noting an ancient Egyptian column having as its capital the head of Hathor, the Egyptian goddess of love and happiness, often represented with the head or horns of a cow. Also, **Hathoric**.

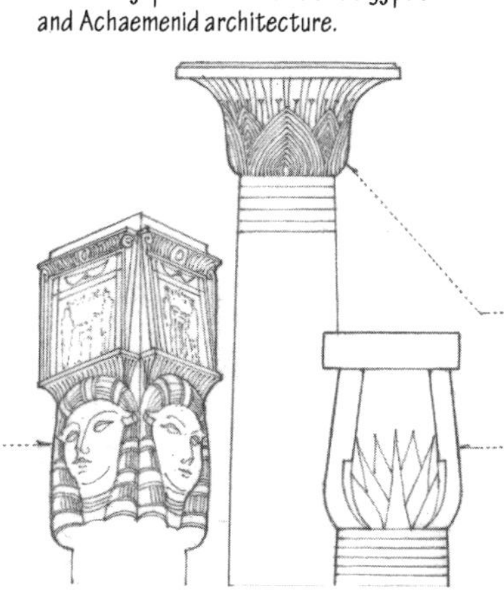

palm capital
An ancient Egyptian capital shaped like of the crown of a palm tree.

lotus capital
An ancient Egyptian capital having the shape of a lotus bud.

megaron
A building or semi-independent unit of a building, typically having a rectangular principal chamber with a center hearth and a porch, often of columns in antis: traditional in Greece since Mycenaean times and believed to be the ancestor of the Doric temple.

agora
A marketplace or public square in an ancient Greek city, usually surrounded with public buildings and porticoes and commonly used as a place for popular or political assembly.

stoa
An ancient Greek portico, usually detached and of considerable length, used as a promenade or meeting place around public places.

temenos
In ancient Greece, a piece of ground specially reserved and enclosed as a sacred place.

Greek temple
A temple built as a shrine to the ancient Greek god or goddess to whom it was dedicated. Since the temple was not intended for internal worship, it was built with special regard for external effect. It stood on a stylobate of three or more steps, with a cella containing the statue of the deity and front and rear porticoes, the whole being surmounted by a low gable roof of timber, covered in terra-cotta or marble tiles.

epinaos
The rear vestibule of a classical temple. Also called **opisthodomos**, **posticum**.

altar
An elevated place or structure upon which sacrifices are offered or incense burned in worship, or before which religious rites are performed.

cella
The principal chamber or enclosed part of a classical temple, where the cult image was kept. Also called **naos**.

pronaos
An open vestibule before the cella of a classical temple. Also called **anticum**.

stele
An upright stone slab or pillar with a carved or inscribed surface, used as a monument or marker, or as a commemorative tablet in the face of a building. Also, **stela**.

acroterium
A pedestal for a sculpture or ornament at the apex or at each of the lower corners of a pediment. Also called **acroterion**.

acropolis
The fortified high area or citadel of an ancient Greek city.

pediment
A wide, low-pitched gable surmounting a colonnade or a major division of a facade.

tympanum
The triangular space enclosed by the horizontal and raking cornices of a pediment, often recessed and decorated with sculpture.

antefix
An upright ornament at the eaves of a tile roof concealing the foot of a row of convex tiles that cover the joints of the flat tiles.

stylobate
A course of masonry forming the foundation for a row of columns, esp. the outermost colonnade of a classical temple.

stereobate
A solid mass of masonry visible above ground level and serving as the foundation of a building, esp. the platform forming the floor and substructure of a classical temple. Also called **crepidoma**, **podium**.

atlas
A sculptured figure of a man used as a column. Also called **telamon**.

caryatid
A sculptured female figure used as a column. Also called **canephora**.

tabernacle
The portable sanctuary in which the Hebrews carried the ark of the covenant through the desert until the building of the Temple of Jerusalem by Solomon.

holy of holies
The innermost chamber in the biblical Tabernacle and the Temple in Jerusalem where the ark of the covenant was kept. Also called **sanctum sanctorum**.

Ark of the Covenant
The chest containing two stone tablets inscribed with the Ten Commandments, carried by the Hebrews during their desert wanderings after the Exodus.

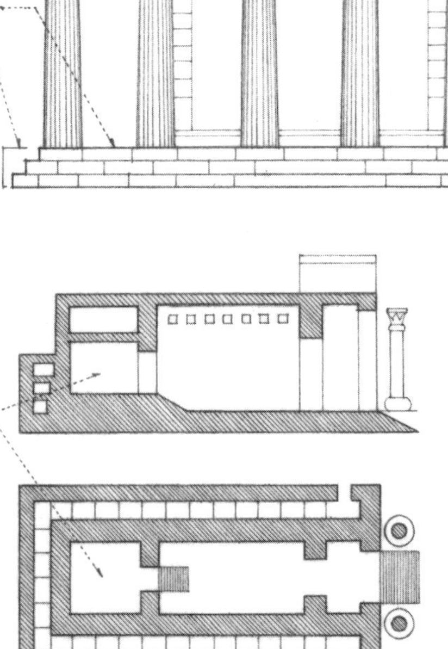

Temple of Solomon
The first Temple of Jerusalem, completed c950 B.C. by Phoenician artisans under the direction of King Solomon and destroyed by Nebuchadnezzar II in 586 B.C. Based on Canaanite and Phoenician prototypes, it was oblong in shape, and consisted of three main parts: an outer hall (ulam), the main sanctuary (hekhal), and the holy of holies (debir), all decorated with massive carvings in ivory, gold, and cedar.

synagogue
A building or place of assembly for Jewish worship and religious instruction.

bimah
The platform in a synagogue from which services are conducted. Also called **almemar**, **bema**.

Holy Ark
The cabinet in a synagogue in which the scrolls of the Torah are kept, set into or against the wall that faces toward Jerusalem.

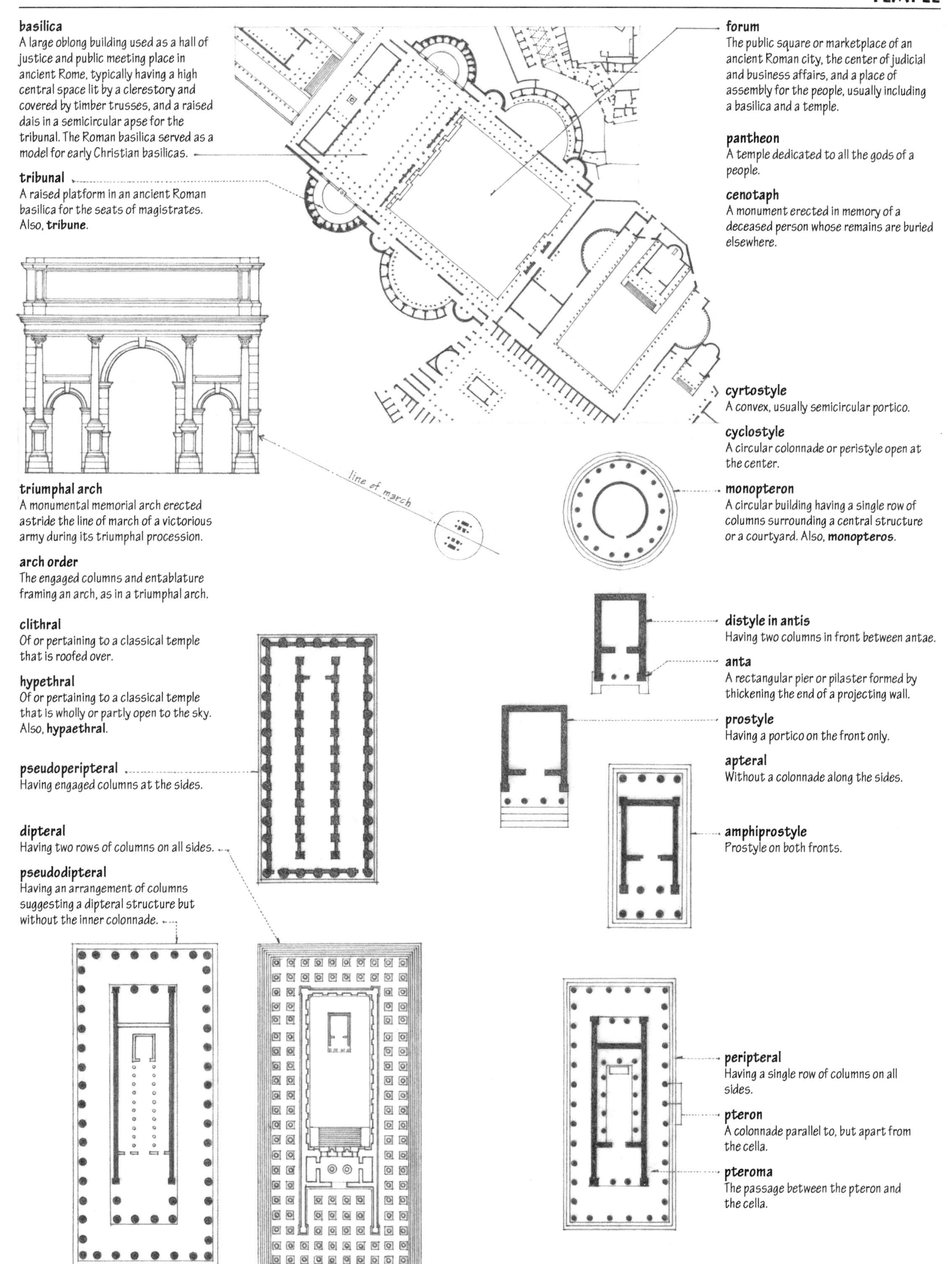

basilica
A large oblong building used as a hall of justice and public meeting place in ancient Rome, typically having a high central space lit by a clerestory and covered by timber trusses, and a raised dais in a semicircular apse for the tribunal. The Roman basilica served as a model for early Christian basilicas.

tribunal
A raised platform in an ancient Roman basilica for the seats of magistrates. Also, **tribune**.

triumphal arch
A monumental memorial arch erected astride the line of march of a victorious army during its triumphal procession.

arch order
The engaged columns and entablature framing an arch, as in a triumphal arch.

clithral
Of or pertaining to a classical temple that is roofed over.

hypethral
Of or pertaining to a classical temple that is wholly or partly open to the sky. Also, **hypaethral**.

pseudoperipteral
Having engaged columns at the sides.

dipteral
Having two rows of columns on all sides.

pseudodipteral
Having an arrangement of columns suggesting a dipteral structure but without the inner colonnade.

forum
The public square or marketplace of an ancient Roman city, the center of judicial and business affairs, and a place of assembly for the people, usually including a basilica and a temple.

pantheon
A temple dedicated to all the gods of a people.

cenotaph
A monument erected in memory of a deceased person whose remains are buried elsewhere.

cyrtostyle
A convex, usually semicircular portico.

cyclostyle
A circular colonnade or peristyle open at the center.

monopteron
A circular building having a single row of columns surrounding a central structure or a courtyard. Also, **monopteros**.

distyle in antis
Having two columns in front between antae.

anta
A rectangular pier or pilaster formed by thickening the end of a projecting wall.

prostyle
Having a portico on the front only.

apteral
Without a colonnade along the sides.

amphiprostyle
Prostyle on both fronts.

peripteral
Having a single row of columns on all sides.

pteron
A colonnade parallel to, but apart from the cella.

pteroma
The passage between the pteron and the cella.

mosque
A Muslim building or place of public worship. Also called **masjid**, **musjid**.

madrasah
A Muslim theological school arranged around a courtyard and attached to a mosque, found from the 11th century on in Egypt, Anatolia, and Persia. Also, **madrasa**.

maidan
The large open square of a city, used as a marketplace or parade ground, esp. in India. Also, **meidan**, **meydan**.

ziyada
A court or series of courts serving to shelter a mosque from immediate contact with secular buildings.

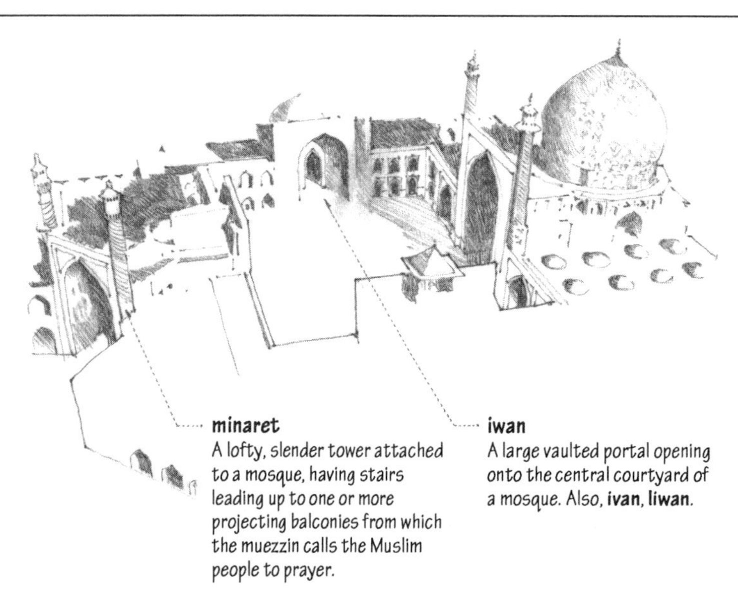

minaret
A lofty, slender tower attached to a mosque, having stairs leading up to one or more projecting balconies from which the muezzin calls the Muslim people to prayer.

iwan
A large vaulted portal opening onto the central courtyard of a mosque. Also, **ivan**, **liwan**.

Islam
The religious faith of Muslims, based on the teachings of the prophet Muhammad, the central themes of which are belief in the one God, Allah, the existence of Paradise and Hell, and the universal Judgment Day to come. Also called **Muhammadanism**.

Muslim
Of or pertaining to the law, religion, or civilization of Islam; a believer in Islam. Also, **Moslem**, **Muslem**.

Muhammad
Arab prophet and founder of Islam, A.D. 570–632. Also, **Mohammed**.

Koran
The sacred text of Islam, revered as the revelations made by Allah to Muhammad through the angel Gabriel and accepted as the foundation of Islamic law, religion, culture, and politics.

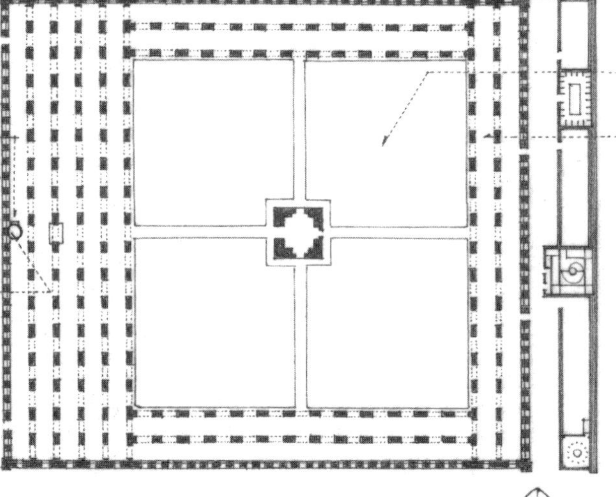

mimbar
A pulpit in a mosque, recalling the three steps from which Muhammad addressed his followers.

qibla
The wall in a mosque in which the mihrab is set, oriented to Mecca. Also, **qiblah**, **kibla**, **kiblah**.

mihrab
A niche or decorative panel in a mosque designating the qibla.

sahn
The central courtyard of a mosque.

riwaq
An arcaded hall of a mosque.

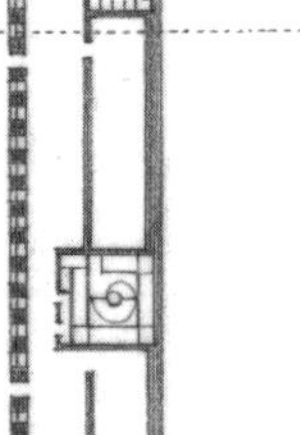

Mecca
A city in Saudi Arabia, birthplace of Muhammad and spiritual center of Islam.

Ka'ba
A small, cubical stone building in the courtyard of the Great Mosque at Mecca containing a sacred black stone and regarded by Muslims as the House of God, the objective of their pilgrimages, and the point toward which they turn in praying. Also, **Ka'aba**, **Ka'abah**.

melon dome
A bulbous ribbed dome, found esp. in Islamic architecture.

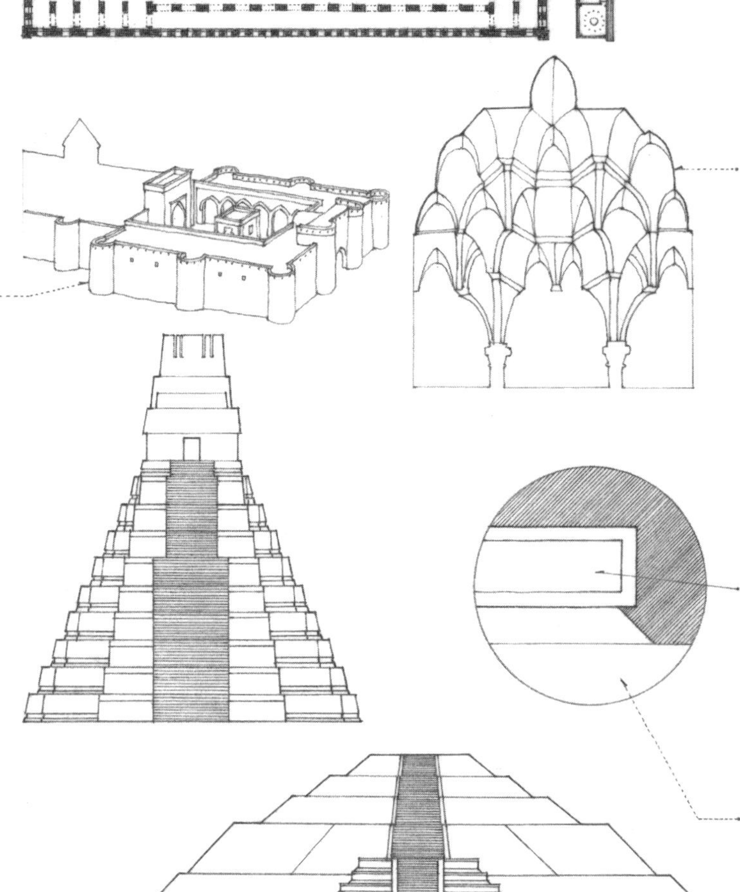

caravansary
An inn in the Near East for the overnight accommodation of caravans, usually having a large courtyard enclosed by a solid wall and entered through an imposing gateway. Also, **caravanserai**.

stalactite work
A system of decoration in Islamic architecture, formed by the intricate corbeling of brackets, squinches, and inverted pyramids; sometimes wrought in stone but more often in plaster. Also called **honeycomb work**, **muqarna**.

pendentive bracketing
Corbeling having the general form of a pendentive, commonly found in Moorish architecture.

maksoorah
An openwork screen or partition enclosing an area for prayer or a tomb in a mosque.

pyramid
A masonry mass having a rectangular base and four stepped and sloping faces culminating in a single apex, used in ancient Egypt and pre-Columbian Central America as a tomb or a platform for a temple.

tablero
A rectangular, strongly framed panel that overhangs a talud. An original contribution of Teotihuacán architecture, this tablero-talud combination was introduced cA.D. 150 to differentiate the stages of stepped pyramids and altar platforms. It is widely copied throughout Mesoamerica, with regional variations.

talud
In Mesoamerican architecture, an outer wall that slopes inward as it rises. The talud first appeared c800 B.C. at the Olmec site of La Venta, in Tabasco state, Mexico.

Hinduism
The dominant religion of India, based upon the religion of the original Aryan settlers as expounded and evolved in the Vedas, having a diverse body of philosophy and cultural practices, many popular cults, and a large pantheon symbolizing a supreme being of many forms and natures. Buddhism is outside the Hindu tradition but is regarded as a related religion.

pantheon
The officially recognized gods of a people.

Vedas
The oldest sacred writings of Hinduism, composed between 1500 and 800 B.C., incorporating four collections hymns, prayers, and liturgical formulas: Rig-Veda, Yajur-Veda, Sama-Veda, and Atharva-Veda.

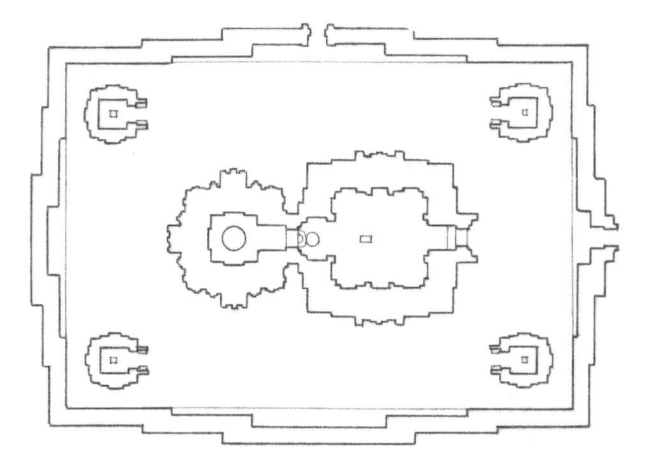

stamba
A freestanding memorial pillar in Indian architecture, bearing carved inscriptions, religious emblems, or a statue. Also, **stambha**.

lât
A monolithic stamba, as distinguished from one built up of stone courses.

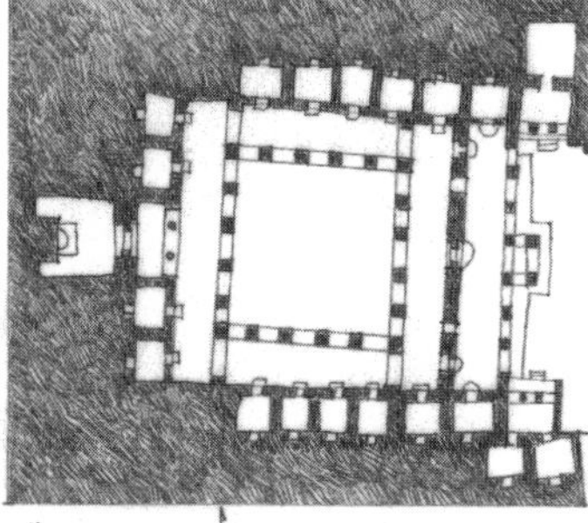

vihara
A Buddhist monastery in Indian architecture often excavated from solid rock, consisting of a central pillared chamber surrounded by a verandah onto which open small sleeping cells. Adjacent to this cloister was a courtyard containing the main stupa.

chaitya
A Buddhist shrine in India, usually carved out of solid rock on a hillside, having the form of an aisled basilica with a stupa at one end.

wat
A Buddhist monastery or temple in Thailand or Cambodia.

Khmer
A people of Cambodia who established an empire in the 5th century A.D. and dominated most of Indochina from the 9th to the 12th centuries.

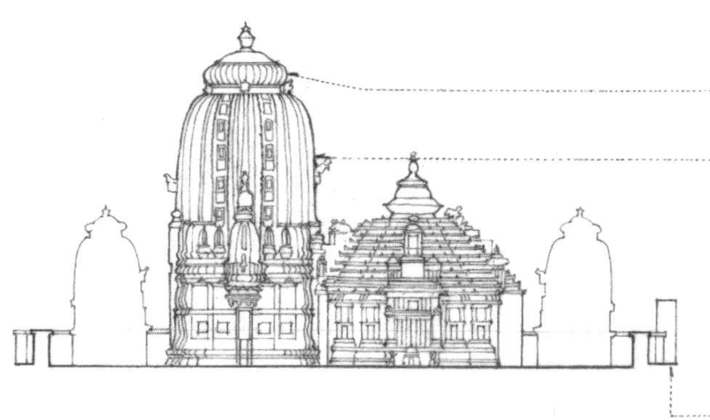

tee
A finial in the form of a conventionalized umbrella, used on stupas, topes, and pagodas.

chattri
An umbrella-shaped finial symbolizing dignity, composed of a stone disk on a vertical pole.

torana
An elaborately carved, ceremonial gateway in Indian Buddhist and Hindu architecture, having two or three lintels between two posts.

vedika
A railing enclosing a sacred area, as a stupa.

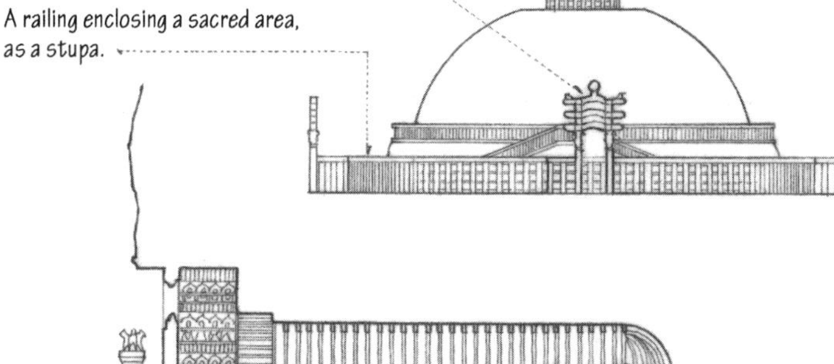

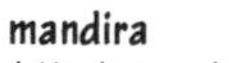

mandira
A Hindu temple.

rath
A Hindu temple cut out of solid rock to resemble a chariot. Also, **ratha**.

vimana
The sanctuary of a Hindu temple in which a deity is enshrined.

amalaka
The bulbous stone finial of a sikhara.

sikhara
A tower of a Hindu temple, usually tapered convexly and capped by an amalaka. Also, **sikra**.

mandapa
A large, porchlike hall leading to a Hindu temple and used for religious dancing and music.

gopuram
A monumental, usually ornate gateway tower to a Hindu temple enclosure, esp. in southern India. Also, **gopura**.

stupa
A Buddhist memorial mound erected to enshrine a relic of Buddha and to commemorate some event or mark a sacred spot. Modeled on a funerary tumulus, it consists of an artificial dome-shaped mound raised on a platform, surrounded by an outer ambulatory with a stone vedika and four toranas, and crowned by a chattri. The name for the stupa in Ceylon is **dagoba**, and in Tibet and Nepal, **chorten**. Also called **tope**.

Buddhism
A religion based on the Four Noble Truths, originated in India by Gautama Buddha and later spreading to China, Burma, Japan, Tibet, and parts of Southeast Asia.

Four Noble Truths
The doctrines of Buddha: all life is suffering; the cause of suffering is desire; cessation of suffering is possible through Nirvana – the extinction of craving; Nirvana can be reached through mental and moral self-purification.

Buddha
Title of Gautama Siddhartha *c*563–*c*483 B.C., Indian philosopher, religious leader, and founder of Buddhism. Also called **Gautama Buddha**.

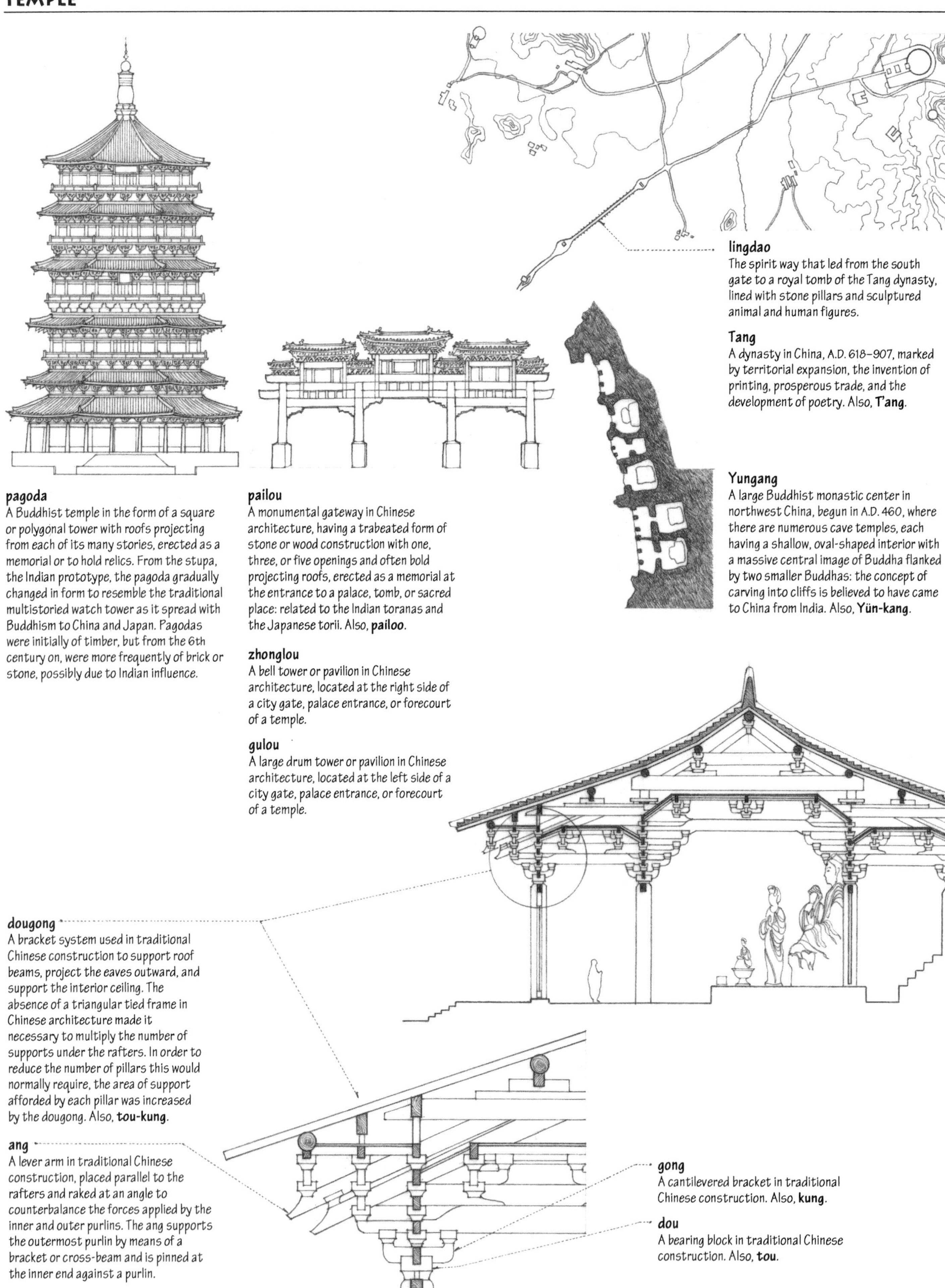

pagoda
A Buddhist temple in the form of a square or polygonal tower with roofs projecting from each of its many stories, erected as a memorial or to hold relics. From the stupa, the Indian prototype, the pagoda gradually changed in form to resemble the traditional multistoried watch tower as it spread with Buddhism to China and Japan. Pagodas were initially of timber, but from the 6th century on, were more frequently of brick or stone, possibly due to Indian influence.

pailou
A monumental gateway in Chinese architecture, having a trabeated form of stone or wood construction with one, three, or five openings and often bold projecting roofs, erected as a memorial at the entrance to a palace, tomb, or sacred place: related to the Indian toranas and the Japanese torii. Also, **pailoo.**

zhonglou
A bell tower or pavilion in Chinese architecture, located at the right side of a city gate, palace entrance, or forecourt of a temple.

gulou
A large drum tower or pavilion in Chinese architecture, located at the left side of a city gate, palace entrance, or forecourt of a temple.

lingdao
The spirit way that led from the south gate to a royal tomb of the Tang dynasty, lined with stone pillars and sculptured animal and human figures.

Tang
A dynasty in China, A.D. 618–907, marked by territorial expansion, the invention of printing, prosperous trade, and the development of poetry. Also, **T'ang.**

Yungang
A large Buddhist monastic center in northwest China, begun in A.D. 460, where there are numerous cave temples, each having a shallow, oval-shaped interior with a massive central image of Buddha flanked by two smaller Buddhas: the concept of carving into cliffs is believed to have came to China from India. Also, **Yün-kang.**

dougong
A bracket system used in traditional Chinese construction to support roof beams, project the eaves outward, and support the interior ceiling. The absence of a triangular tied frame in Chinese architecture made it necessary to multiply the number of supports under the rafters. In order to reduce the number of pillars this would normally require, the area of support afforded by each pillar was increased by the dougong. Also, **tou-kung.**

ang
A lever arm in traditional Chinese construction, placed parallel to the rafters and raked at an angle to counterbalance the forces applied by the inner and outer purlins. The ang supports the outermost purlin by means of a bracket or cross-beam and is pinned at the inner end against a purlin.

gong
A cantilevered bracket in traditional Chinese construction. Also, **kung.**

dou
A bearing block in traditional Chinese construction. Also, **tou.**

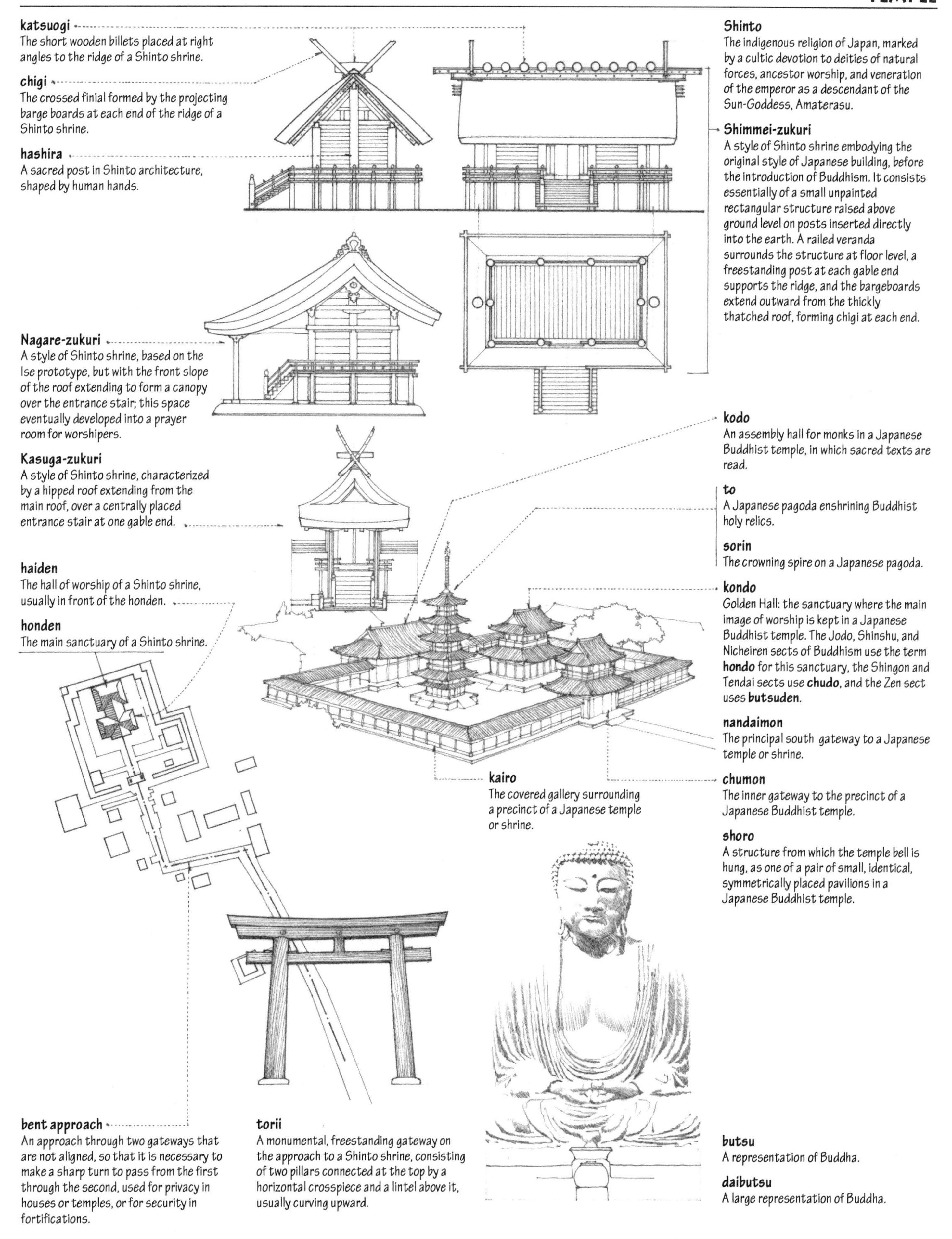

katsuogi
The short wooden billets placed at right angles to the ridge of a Shinto shrine.

chigi
The crossed finial formed by the projecting barge boards at each end of the ridge of a Shinto shrine.

hashira
A sacred post in Shinto architecture, shaped by human hands.

Shinto
The indigenous religion of Japan, marked by a cultic devotion to deities of natural forces, ancestor worship, and veneration of the emperor as a descendant of the Sun-Goddess, Amaterasu.

Shimmei-zukuri
A style of Shinto shrine embodying the original style of Japanese building, before the introduction of Buddhism. It consists essentially of a small unpainted rectangular structure raised above ground level on posts inserted directly into the earth. A railed veranda surrounds the structure at floor level, a freestanding post at each gable end supports the ridge, and the bargeboards extend outward from the thickly thatched roof, forming chigi at each end.

Nagare-zukuri
A style of Shinto shrine, based on the Ise prototype, but with the front slope of the roof extending to form a canopy over the entrance stair; this space eventually developed into a prayer room for worshipers.

Kasuga-zukuri
A style of Shinto shrine, characterized by a hipped roof extending from the main roof, over a centrally placed entrance stair at one gable end.

kodo
An assembly hall for monks in a Japanese Buddhist temple, in which sacred texts are read.

to
A Japanese pagoda enshrining Buddhist holy relics.

sorin
The crowning spire on a Japanese pagoda.

haiden
The hall of worship of a Shinto shrine, usually in front of the honden.

honden
The main sanctuary of a Shinto shrine.

kondo
Golden Hall: the sanctuary where the main image of worship is kept in a Japanese Buddhist temple. The Jodo, Shinshu, and Nicheiren sects of Buddhism use the term **hondo** for this sanctuary, the Shingon and Tendai sects use **chudo**, and the Zen sect uses **butsuden**.

nandaimon
The principal south gateway to a Japanese temple or shrine.

kairo
The covered gallery surrounding a precinct of a Japanese temple or shrine.

chumon
The inner gateway to the precinct of a Japanese Buddhist temple.

shoro
A structure from which the temple bell is hung, as one of a pair of small, identical, symmetrically placed pavilions in a Japanese Buddhist temple.

bent approach
An approach through two gateways that are not aligned, so that it is necessary to make a sharp turn to pass from the first through the second, used for privacy in houses or temples, or for security in fortifications.

torii
A monumental, freestanding gateway on the approach to a Shinto shrine, consisting of two pillars connected at the top by a horizontal crosspiece and a lintel above it, usually curving upward.

butsu
A representation of Buddha.

daibutsu
A large representation of Buddha.

THEATER

A building, part of a building, or an outdoor area for housing dramatic presentations, stage entertainment, or motion-picture shows.

Greek theater
An open-air theater, usually hollowed out of the slope of a hillside with a tiered seating area around and facing a circular orchestra backed by the skene, a building for the actors' use.

orchestra
The circular space in front of the stage in the ancient Greek theater, reserved for the chorus.

chorus
The group of actors in ancient Greece that served as major participants in or commentators on the main action of the drama.

skene
A structure facing the audience in an ancient Greek theater, forming the background before which performances were given.

proscenium
The front part of the stage of an ancient Greek or Roman theater upon which the actors performed.

parodos
One of the two side passageways to an ancient Greek theater, between the stage and the seating area, through which the chorus entered the orchestra.

parascenium
Either of two wings flanking and projecting forward from the skene of an ancient Greek theater, containing apartments for the actors.

diazoma
An aisle between the lower and upper tiers of seats in an ancient Greek theater, concentric with the orchestra and the outer wall and communicating with the radial aisles.

cercis
A wedge-shaped section of seats between two stepped passageways in an ancient Greek theater.

Roman theater
An open-air theater modeled upon that of the ancient Greeks, but often built on level ground with colonnaded galleries, a semicircular orchestra, and a raised stage backed by an elaborate architectural structure.

orchestra
A semicircular space in the front of the stage of an ancient Roman theater, reserved for senators and other distinguished spectators.

gradin
One of a series of steps or tiered seats, as in an amphitheater. Also, **gradine**.

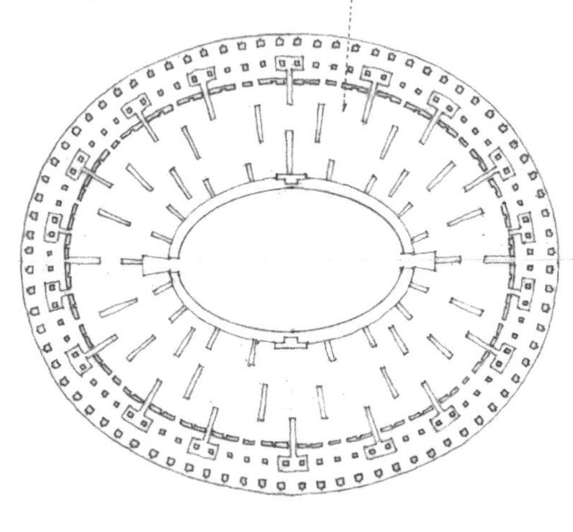

amphitheater
An oval or round building with tiers of seats around a central arena, as those used in ancient Rome for gladiatorial contests and spectacles.

velarium
A canvas awning drawn over an ancient Roman amphitheater to protect the audience from rain or sun.

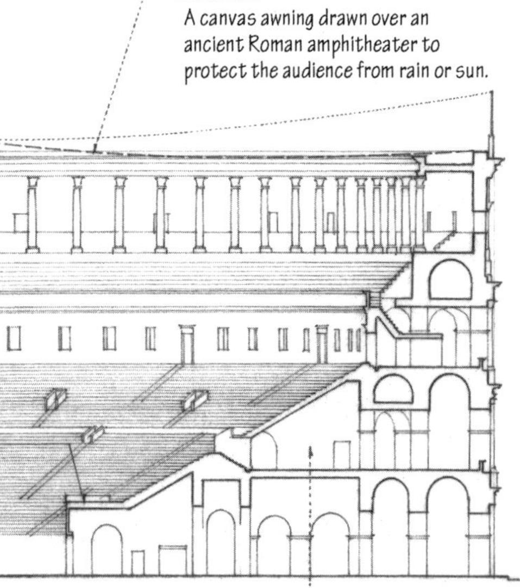

podium
A raised platform encircling the arena of an ancient Roman amphitheater, having on it the seats of privileged spectators.

vomitory
A large opening, as in an ancient Roman amphitheater or stadium, permitting large numbers of people to enter or leave. Also, **vomitorium**.

supercolumniation
The placing of one order of columns above another, usually with the more elaborate orders at the top.

proscenium stage
A stage that is framed by a proscenium arch.

proscenium arch
The arch that separates the stage from the auditorium. Also called **proscenium**.

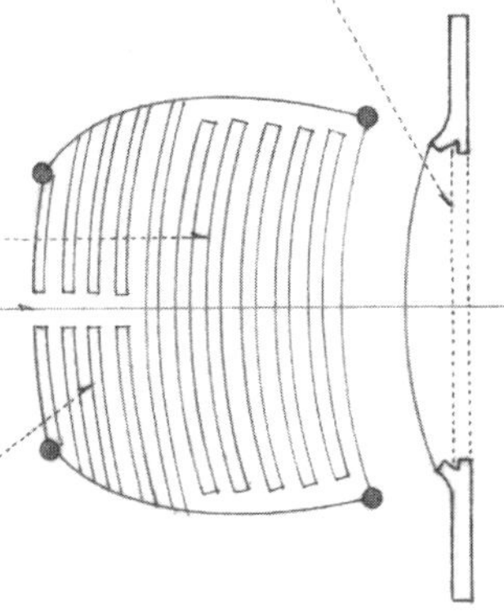

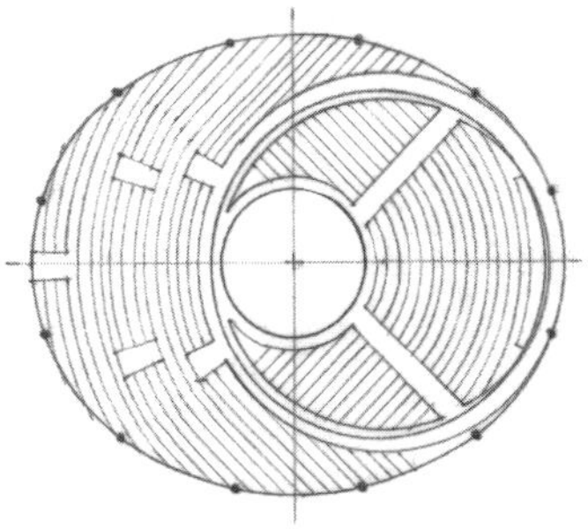

surround theater
A theater or concert hall in which the seating is arranged around or on all four sides of a central stage.

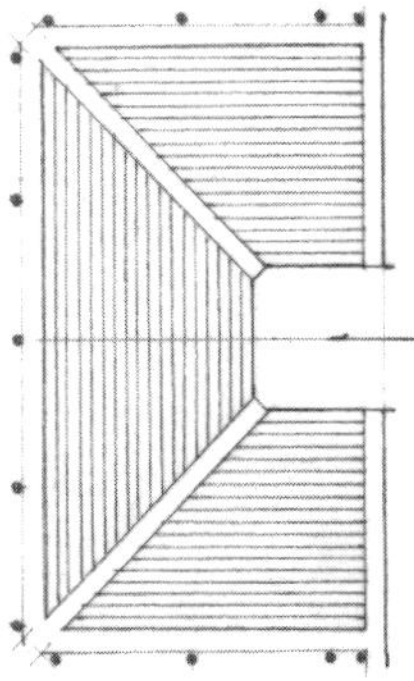

seating
The arrangement of seats in a theater, stadium, or other place of assembly.

continental seating
A theater seating plan in which there is no center aisle, but with wide spacing between each row of seats to permit ease of passage.

aisle
A walkway between or along sections of seats in a theater, auditorium, church, or other place of assembly.

blind row
A row of seats having its first seat at a side aisle and its last seat at a side wall.

arena theater
A theater with seats arranged on at least three sides around a central stage. Also called **theater-in-the-round**.

thrust stage
A stage that extends beyond the proscenium arch and is usually surrounded on three sides by seats.

stagehouse
The part of a theater on the stage side of the proscenium, including the stage, wings, and storage area.

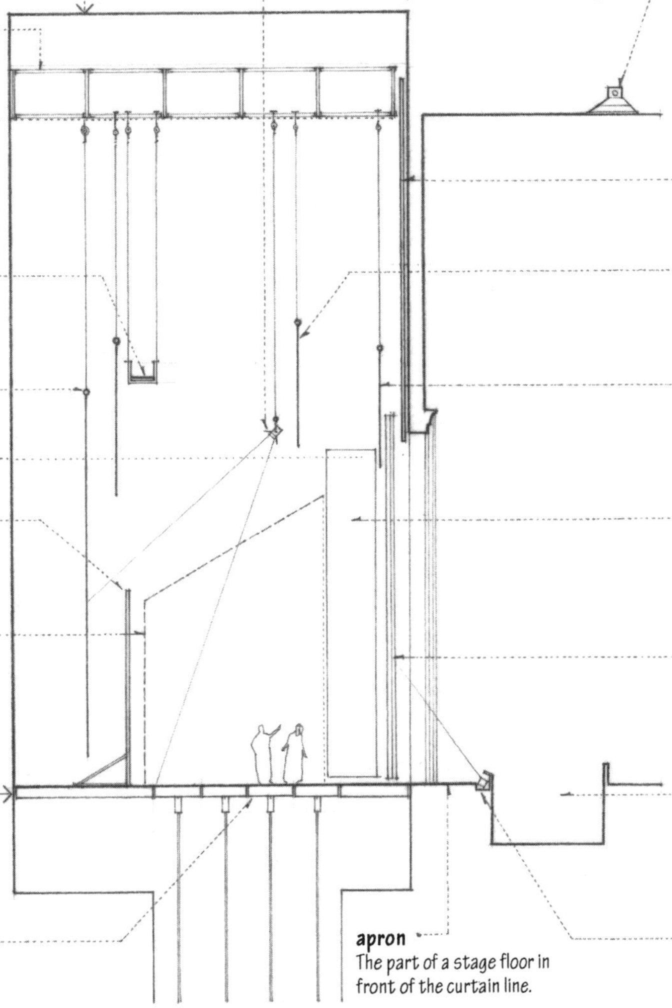

spotlight
A strong, focused beam of light for calling attention to an object, person, or group on a stage. Also called **spot**.

houselights
The lamps providing illumination of an auditorium or the seating area of a theater.

gridiron
A stell structure above the stage of a theater, from which hung scenery and equipment are manipulated. Also called **grid**.

flies
The space above the stage used chiefly for storing and hanging scenery and equipment. Also called **fly loft**.

bridge
A gallery or platform that can be raised or lowered over a stage and is used by technicians and stagehands.

batten
A length of metal pipe hung from the gridiron, for suspending scenery or equipment, as drop scenes, flats, or lighting units. Also called **pipe batten**.

flat
A piece of scenery consisting of a wooden frame, usually rectangular, covered with lightweight board or fabric.

orchestra shell
A sound-reflecting structure that closes off the flies and wings of a stage to form a performing area for music.

stage
The platform, usually raised, on which the actors perform in a theater. Also, the platform and all the parts of a theater back of the proscenium.

drop stage
A stage floor that moves vertically on an elevator, usually so that one set can quickly replace another. Also called **lift stage**.

apron
The part of a stage floor in front of the curtain line.

fire curtain
A curtain of asbestos or other fireproof material that can be lowered just inside the proscenium arch in case of fire, sealing off the backstage area from the auditorium. Also called **safety curtain**.

border
A narrow curtain or strip of painted canvas hung above the stage to mask the flies and form the top of the stage set.

teaser
A drapery or flat piece hung across the top of the proscenium arch to mask the flies and, together with the tormentors, frame the stage opening.

tormentor
A curtain or framed structure used directly behind the proscenium at each side of the stage to screen the wings and sidelights from the audience.

act curtain
A curtain for closing the proscenium opening between acts or scenes. Also called **act drop**, **house curtain**.

orchestra pit
The space reserved for musicians, usually the front part of the main floor, sometimes wholly or partly under the forward part of the stage.

footlights
The row of lights on the front of a stage, usually set in a trough, nearly on a level with the feet of the performers.

opera house
A theater devoted chiefly to the public performance of operas.

front of the house
The parts of a theater that are on the audience side of the fire wall.

balcony
A gallery that projects over the main floor of a theater to accommodate additional people.

gallery
An upper floor projecting over the main floor of a theater or hall.

wing balcony
The part of a balcony that extends along the sidewalls of an auditorium.

loge
A private seating area for a small group of spectators in a theater or opera house.

peanut gallery
The rearmost and cheapest section of seats in the uppermost balcony of a theater.

sight line
Any of the lines of sight between the spectators and the stage or playing area of a theater or stadium.

dress circle
A curved or circular division of seats in a theater, opera house, or the like, usually the first gallery, originally set apart for spectators in evening dress.

mezzanine
The lowest balcony or forward part of such a balcony in a theater.

grand tier
The first tier of boxes immediately above the parterre in a large opera house or theater.

tier
One of a number of galleries, as in a theater.

orchestra
The entire main-floor space for spectators in a theater or auditorium.

parterre
The rear section of seats, and sometimes also the side sections, of the main floor of a theater, opera house, or concert hall. Also called **parquet circle**.

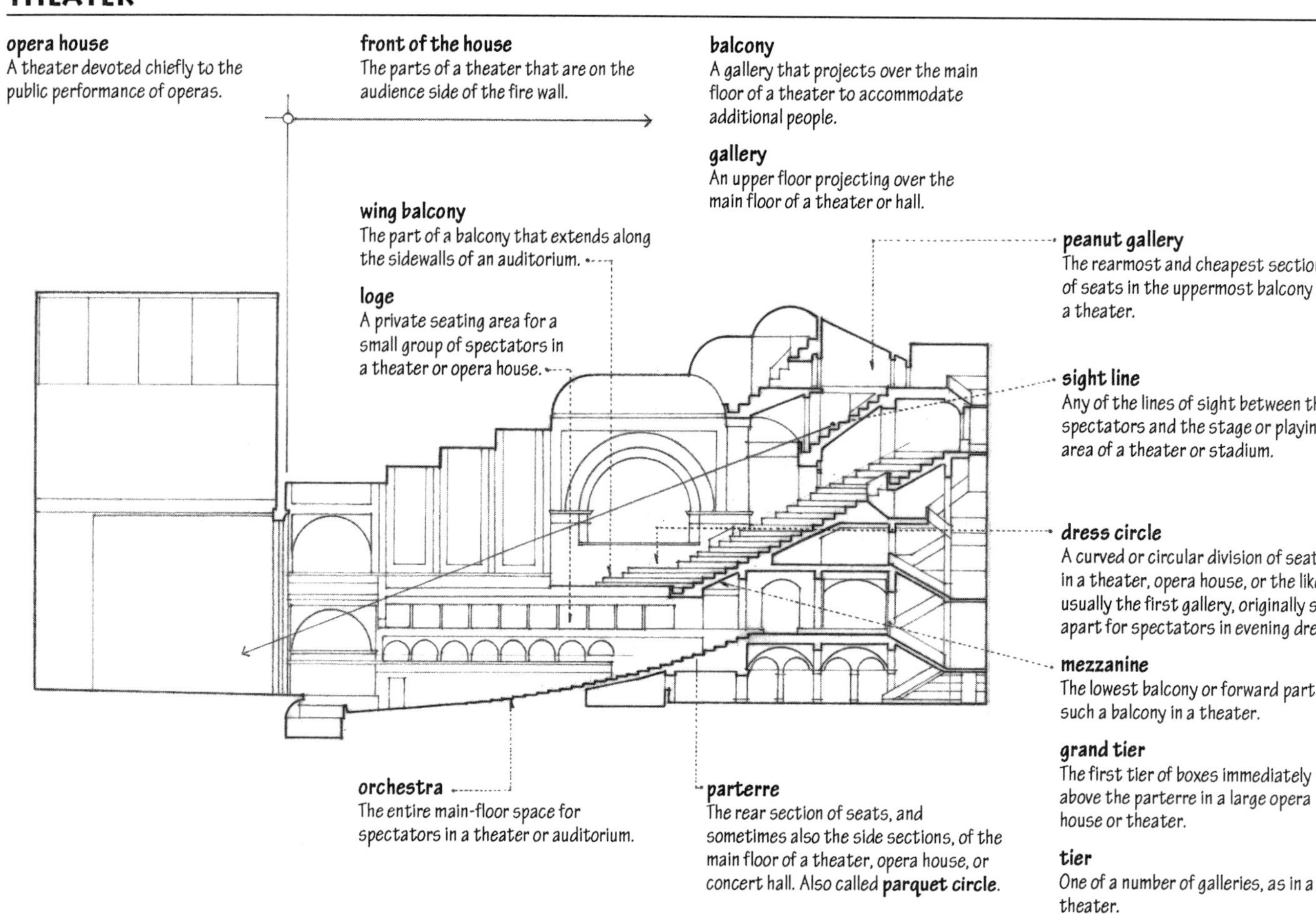

backstage
The area behind the proscenium in a theater, esp. in the wings and dressing rooms.

auditorium
The space set apart for the audience in a theater or meeting hall.

lobby
A hall serving as a passageway or waiting room at or near the entrance to a theater, hotel, or apartment house. Also called **foyer**.

lounge
A large public waiting room, as in a theater, hotel, or air terminal, often having adjoining washrooms.

box office
The office of a theater or stadium at which tickets are sold.

marquee
A tall rooflike projection above a theater entrance, usually containing the name of a currently featured play or film and its stars.

dressing room
A room for use in getting dressed, esp. one for performers backstage in a theater or television studio.

green room
A lounge in a theater, concert hall, or broadcasting studio, for use by performers when they are not on stage.

wing
The platform or space to the right or left of the stage proper.

runway
A narrow platform or ramp extending from a stage into the orchestra pit or into an aisle of an auditorium.

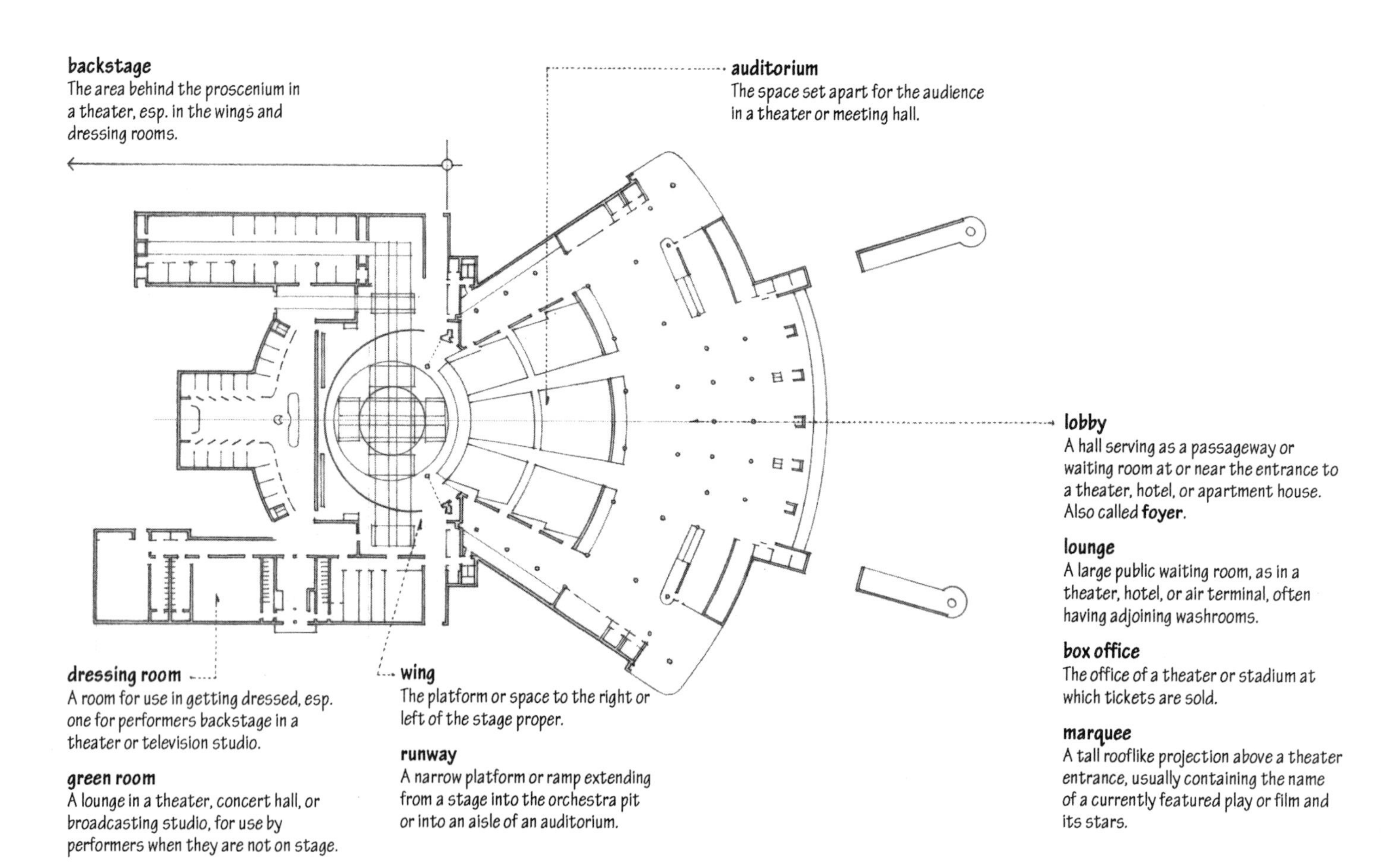

A structural frame based on the geometric rigidity of the triangle and composed of linear members subject only to axial tension or compression.

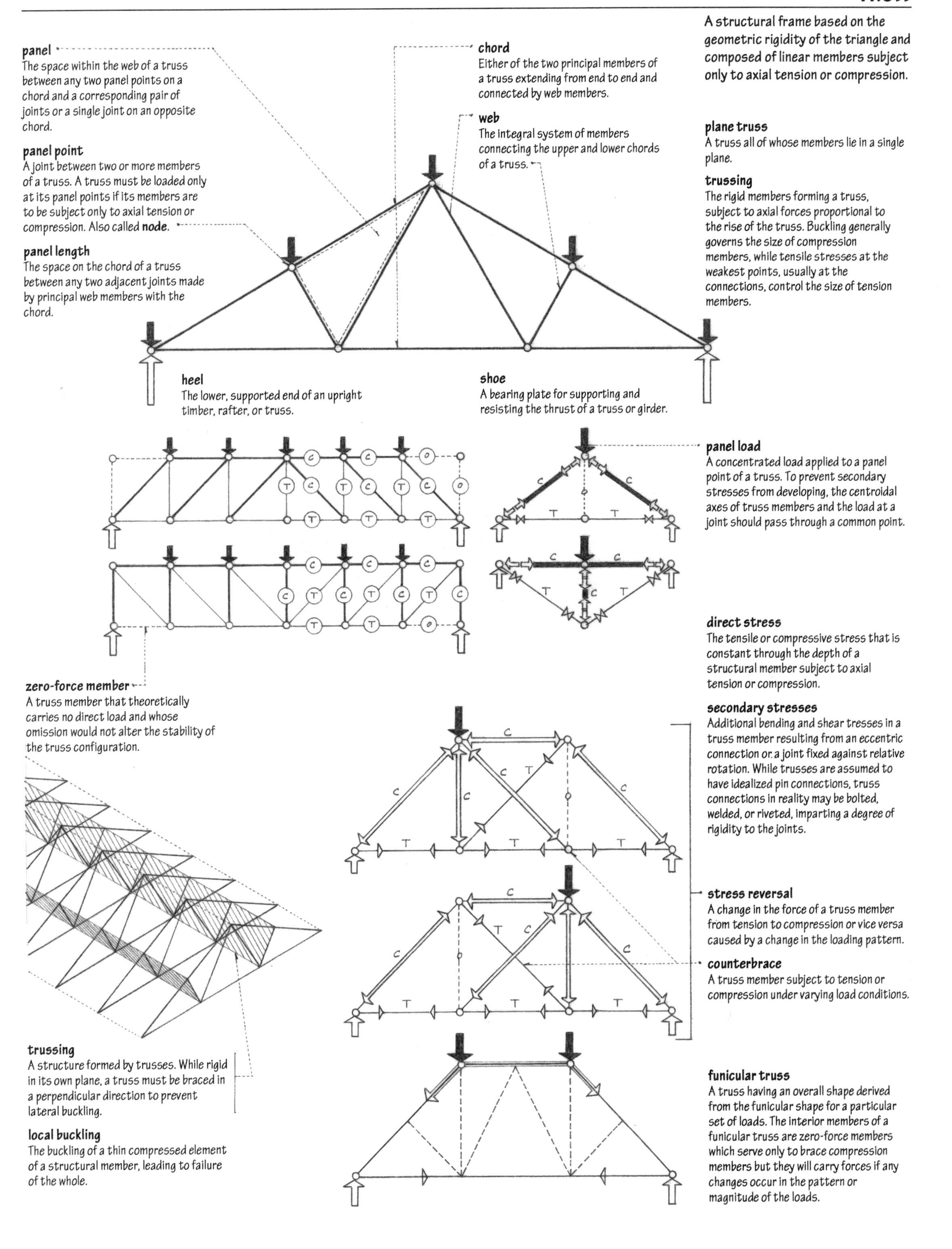

panel
The space within the web of a truss between any two panel points on a chord and a corresponding pair of joints or a single joint on an opposite chord.

panel point
A joint between two or more members of a truss. A truss must be loaded only at its panel points if its members are to be subject only to axial tension or compression. Also called **node**.

panel length
The space on the chord of a truss between any two adjacent joints made by principal web members with the chord.

chord
Either of the two principal members of a truss extending from end to end and connected by web members.

web
The integral system of members connecting the upper and lower chords of a truss.

heel
The lower, supported end of an upright timber, rafter, or truss.

shoe
A bearing plate for supporting and resisting the thrust of a truss or girder.

plane truss
A truss all of whose members lie in a single plane.

trussing
The rigid members forming a truss, subject to axial forces proportional to the rise of the truss. Buckling generally governs the size of compression members, while tensile stresses at the weakest points, usually at the connections, control the size of tension members.

panel load
A concentrated load applied to a panel point of a truss. To prevent secondary stresses from developing, the centroidal axes of truss members and the load at a joint should pass through a common point.

zero-force member
A truss member that theoretically carries no direct load and whose omission would not alter the stability of the truss configuration.

direct stress
The tensile or compressive stress that is constant through the depth of a structural member subject to axial tension or compression.

secondary stresses
Additional bending and shear tresses in a truss member resulting from an eccentric connection or a joint fixed against relative rotation. While trusses are assumed to have idealized pin connections, truss connections in reality may be bolted, welded, or riveted, imparting a degree of rigidity to the joints.

stress reversal
A change in the force of a truss member from tension to compression or vice versa caused by a change in the loading pattern.

counterbrace
A truss member subject to tension or compression under varying load conditions.

trussing
A structure formed by trusses. While rigid in its own plane, a truss must be braced in a perpendicular direction to prevent lateral buckling.

local buckling
The buckling of a thin compressed element of a structural member, leading to failure of the whole.

funicular truss
A truss having an overall shape derived from the funicular shape for a particular set of loads. The interior members of a funicular truss are zero-force members which serve only to brace compression members but they will carry forces if any changes occur in the pattern or magnitude of the loads.

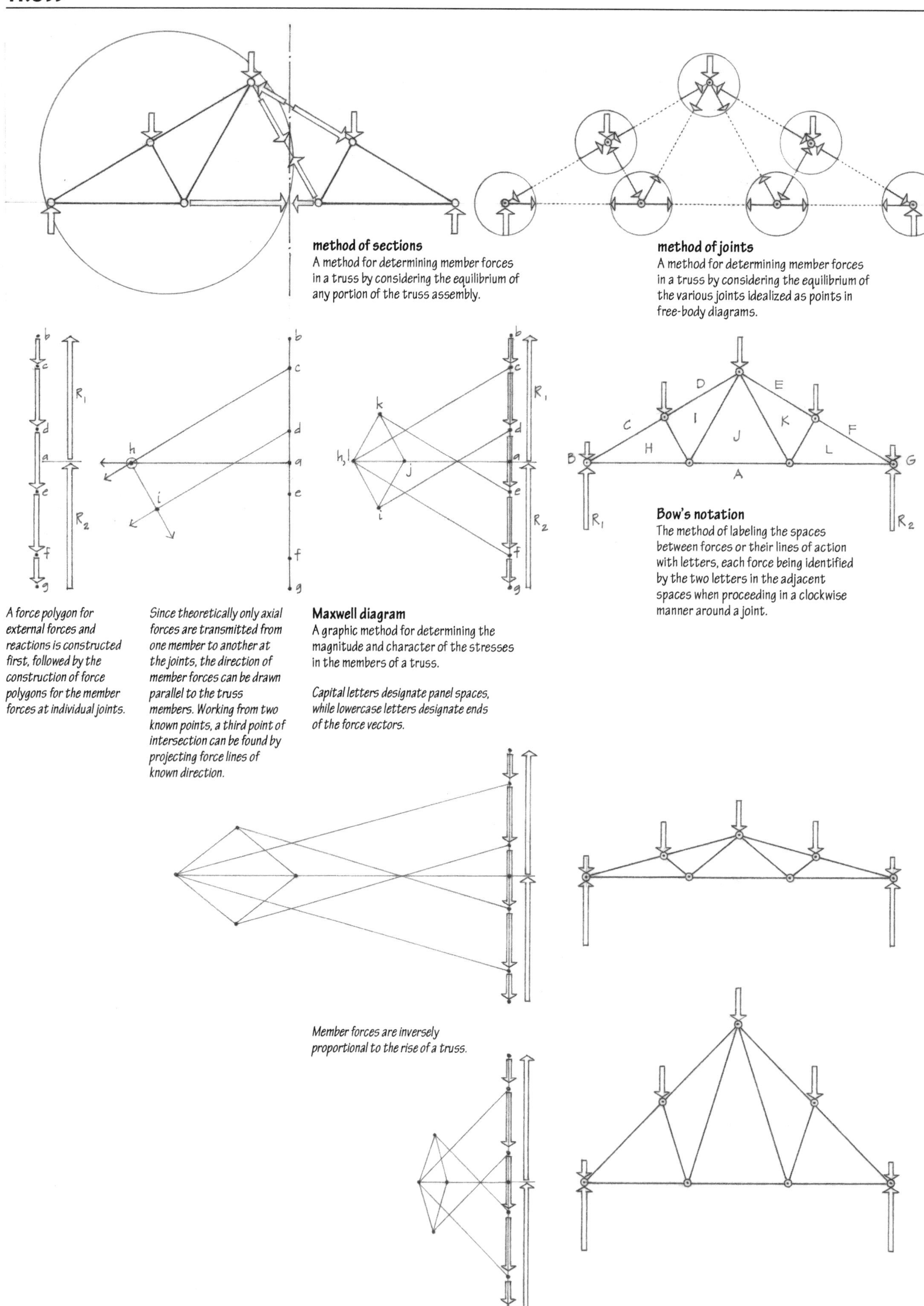

method of sections
A method for determining member forces in a truss by considering the equilibrium of any portion of the truss assembly.

method of joints
A method for determining member forces in a truss by considering the equilibrium of the various joints idealized as points in free-body diagrams.

A force polygon for external forces and reactions is constructed first, followed by the construction of force polygons for the member forces at individual joints.

Since theoretically only axial forces are transmitted from one member to another at the joints, the direction of member forces can be drawn parallel to the truss members. Working from two known points, a third point of intersection can be found by projecting force lines of known direction.

Maxwell diagram
A graphic method for determining the magnitude and character of the stresses in the members of a truss.

Capital letters designate panel spaces, while lowercase letters designate ends of the force vectors.

Bow's notation
The method of labeling the spaces between forces or their lines of action with letters, each force being identified by the two letters in the adjacent spaces when proceeding in a clockwise manner around a joint.

Member forces are inversely proportional to the rise of a truss.

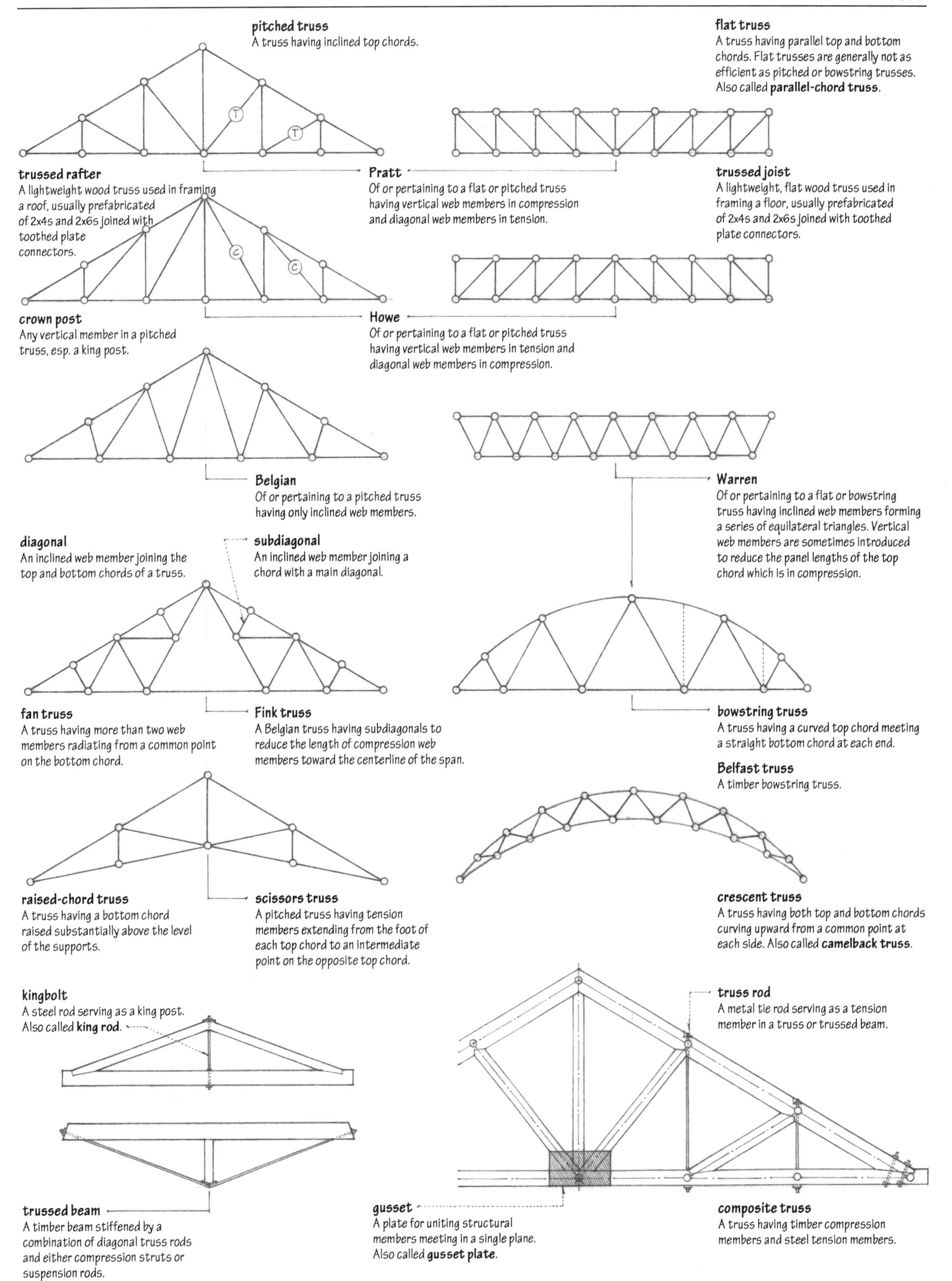
pitched truss
A truss having inclined top chords.
flat truss
A truss having parallel top and bottom chords. Flat trusses are generally not as efficient as pitched or bowstring trusses. Also called **parallel-chord truss.**
trussed rafter
A lightweight wood truss used in framing a roof, usually prefabricated of 2x4s and 2x6s joined with toothed plate connectors.
Pratt
Of or pertaining to a flat or pitched truss having vertical web members in compression and diagonal web members in tension.
trussed joist
A lightweight, flat wood truss used in framing a floor, usually prefabricated of 2x4s and 2x6s joined with toothed plate connectors.
crown post
Any vertical member in a pitched truss, esp. a king post.
Howe
Of or pertaining to a flat or pitched truss having vertical web members in tension and diagonal web members in compression.
Belgian
Of or pertaining to a pitched truss having only inclined web members.
Warren
Of or pertaining to a flat or bowstring truss having inclined web members forming a series of equilateral triangles. Vertical web members are sometimes introduced to reduce the panel lengths of the top chord which is in compression.
diagonal
An inclined web member joining the top and bottom chords of a truss.
subdiagonal
An inclined web member joining a chord with a main diagonal.
fan truss
A truss having more than two web members radiating from a common point on the bottom chord.
Fink truss
A Belgian truss having subdiagonals to reduce the length of compression web members toward the centerline of the span.
bowstring truss
A truss having a curved top chord meeting a straight bottom chord at each end.
Belfast truss
A timber bowstring truss.
raised-chord truss
A truss having a bottom chord raised substantially above the level of the supports.
scissors truss
A pitched truss having tension members extending from the foot of each top chord to an intermediate point on the opposite top chord.
crescent truss
A truss having both top and bottom chords curving upward from a common point at each side. Also called **camelback truss.**
kingbolt
A steel rod serving as a king post. Also called **king rod.**
truss rod
A metal tie rod serving as a tension member in a truss or trussed beam.
trussed beam
A timber beam stiffened by a combination of diagonal truss rods and either compression struts or suspension rods.
gusset
A plate for uniting structural members meeting in a single plane. Also called **gusset plate.**
composite truss
A truss having timber compression members and steel tension members.

VAULT

An arched structure of stone, brick, or reinforced concrete, forming a ceiling or roof over a hall, room, or other wholly or partially enclosed space.

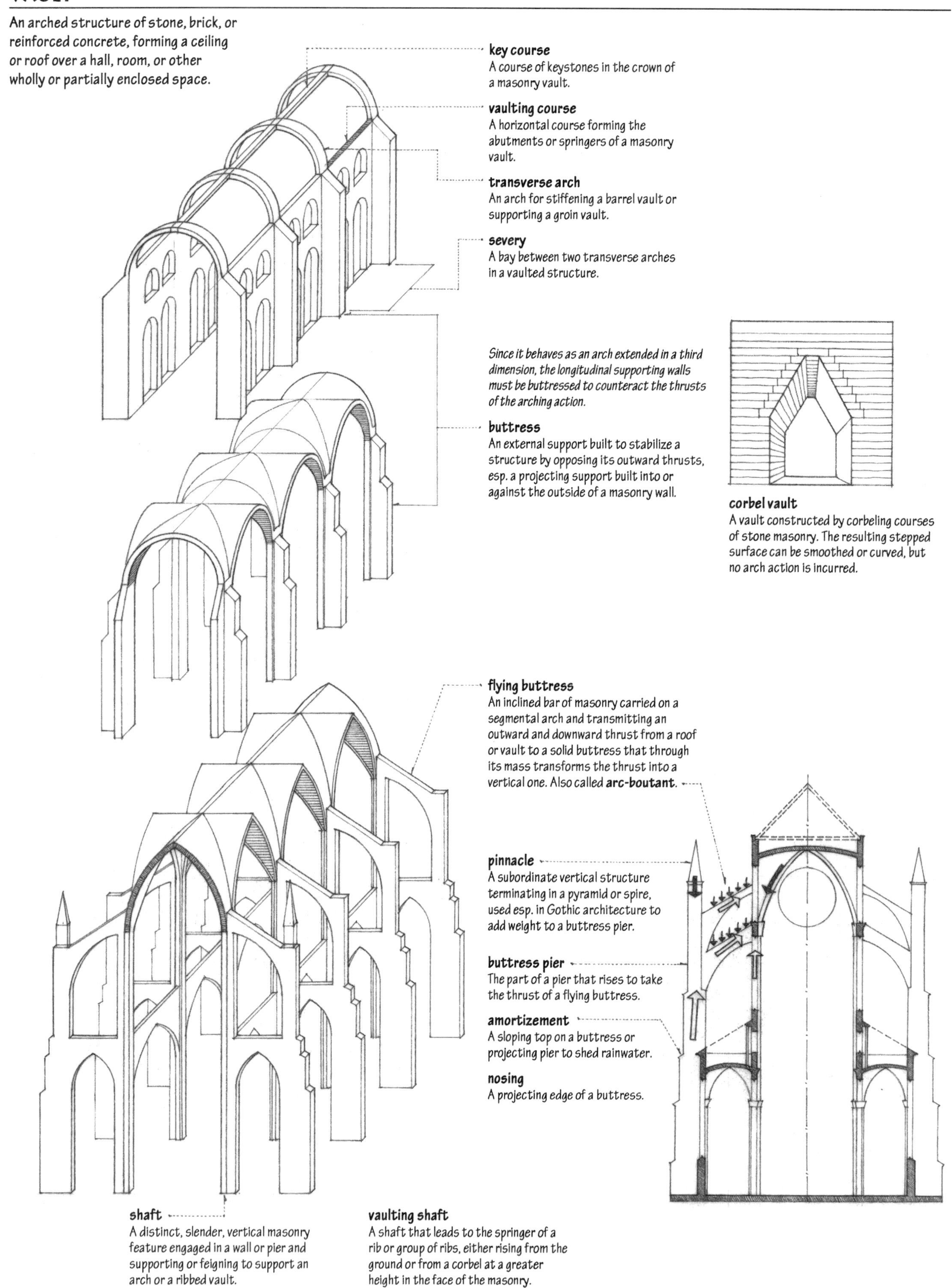

key course
A course of keystones in the crown of a masonry vault.

vaulting course
A horizontal course forming the abutments or springers of a masonry vault.

transverse arch
An arch for stiffening a barrel vault or supporting a groin vault.

severy
A bay between two transverse arches in a vaulted structure.

Since it behaves as an arch extended in a third dimension, the longitudinal supporting walls must be buttressed to counteract the thrusts of the arching action.

buttress
An external support built to stabilize a structure by opposing its outward thrusts, esp. a projecting support built into or against the outside of a masonry wall.

corbel vault
A vault constructed by corbeling courses of stone masonry. The resulting stepped surface can be smoothed or curved, but no arch action is incurred.

flying buttress
An inclined bar of masonry carried on a segmental arch and transmitting an outward and downward thrust from a roof or vault to a solid buttress that through its mass transforms the thrust into a vertical one. Also called **arc-boutant**.

pinnacle
A subordinate vertical structure terminating in a pyramid or spire, used esp. in Gothic architecture to add weight to a buttress pier.

buttress pier
The part of a pier that rises to take the thrust of a flying buttress.

amortizement
A sloping top on a buttress or projecting pier to shed rainwater.

nosing
A projecting edge of a buttress.

shaft
A distinct, slender, vertical masonry feature engaged in a wall or pier and supporting or feigning to support an arch or a ribbed vault.

vaulting shaft
A shaft that leads to the springer of a rib or group of ribs, either rising from the ground or from a corbel at a greater height in the face of the masonry.

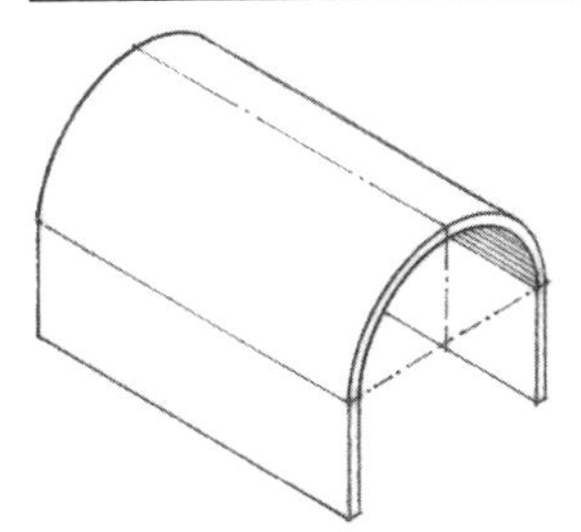

barrel vault
A vault having a semicircular cross section. Also called **cradle vault, tunnel vault, wagon vault**.

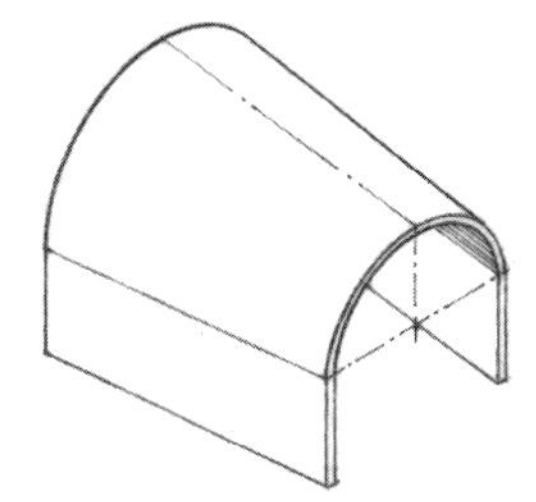

conical vault
A vault having a circular cross section that is larger at one end than the other.

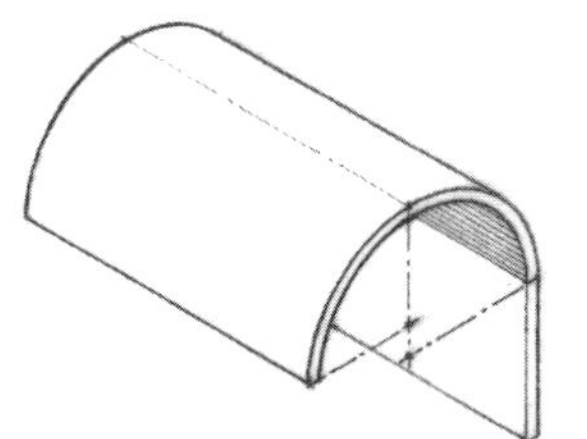

rampant vault
A vault springing from an abutment higher at one side than at the other.

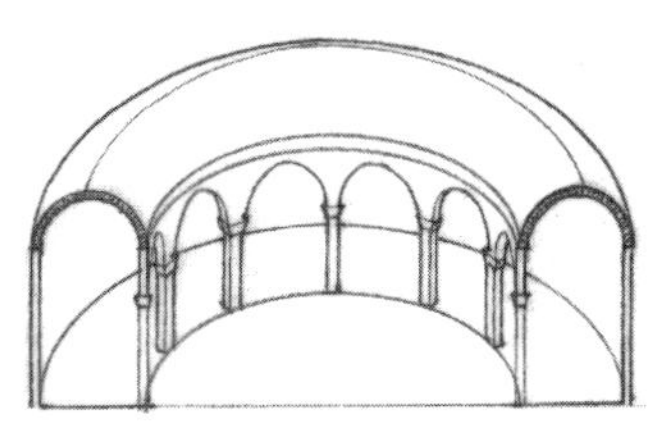

annular vault
A barrel vault having a circular plan in the shape of a ring.

groin
One of the curved lines or edges along which two intersecting vaults meet.

tripartite vault
A compound vault for covering a triangular space, formed by the intersection of three barrel vaults.

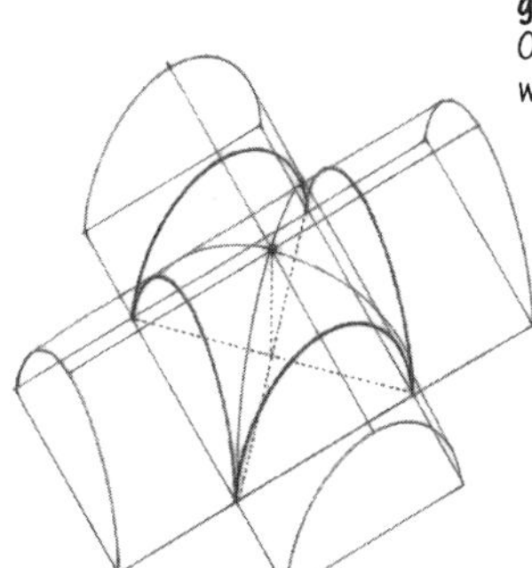

groin vault
A compound vault formed by the perpendicular intersection of two vaults, forming arched diagonal arrises called groins. Also called **cross vault**.

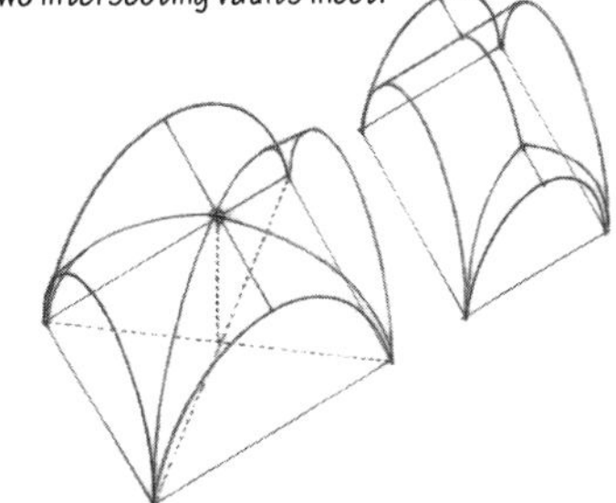

underpitch vault
A compound vault having a central vault intersected by vaults of lower pitch. Also called **Welsh vault**.

stilted vault
A compound vault having a narrower transverse vault springing from a higher level so that the ridges are at the same height.

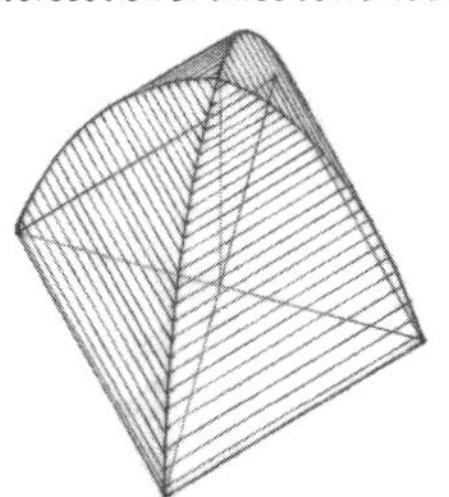

cloister vault
A compound vault formed by four coves meeting along diagonal vertical planes. Also called **coved vault**.

web
A surface framed by the ribs of a ribbed vault.

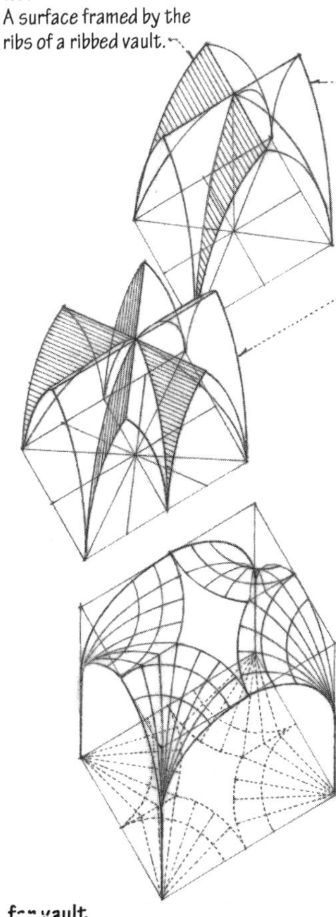

rib vault
A vault supported by or decorated with arched diagonal ribs. Also, **ribbed vault**.

quadripartite vault
A rib vault divided into four parts by intersecting diagonal ribs.

sexpartite vault
A rib vault divided into six compartments by two diagonal ribs and three transverse ribs.

rib
Any of several archlike members supporting a vault at the groins, defining its distinct surfaces or dividing these surfaces into panels.

arc doubleau
A rib spanning the longitudinal axis of a rib vault and dividing it into bays or compartments. Also called **transverse rib**.

tierceron
A rib springing from a point of support on either side of the ogives or transverse ribs of a rib vault. Also called **intermediate rib**.

formeret
A rib against a wall, parallel to the longitudinal axis of a rib vault. Also called **wall rib**.

boss
An ornamental, knoblike projection, as a carved keystone at the intersection of ogives.

pendant
A sculptured ornament suspended from a roof truss, vault, or ceiling. Also called **drop**.

f-- vault
A vault composed of a number of concave conoidal sections, usually four, springing from the corners of the vaulting compartment, often decorated with ribs that radiate from the springing like the framework of a fan.

key
The keystone at the crown of an arch or at the intersection of two or more vaulting ribs.

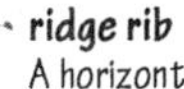

ridge rib
A horizontal rib marking the crown of a vaulting compartment.

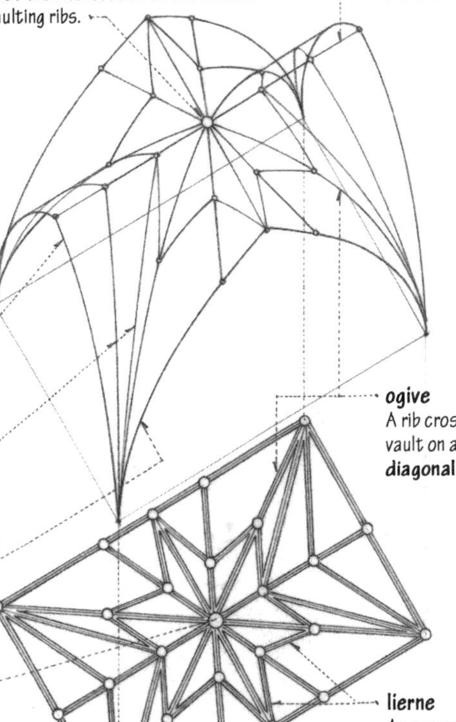

ogive
A rib crossing a compartment of a rib vault on a diagonal. Also called **diagonal rib, groin rib**.

lierne
An ornamental vaulting rib other than one springing from a pier or a ridge rib.

star vault
A vault having ribs, liernes, or tiercerons arranged in a star-shaped pattern. Also called **stellar vault**.

Sight: the act or power of sensing with the eyes.

see
To perceive with the eyes. The act of seeing is a dynamic and creative process. It is capable of delivering a stable, three-dimensional perception of the moving, changing images which make up our visual world. There are three steps in the swift and sophisticated processing which results in the images we see.

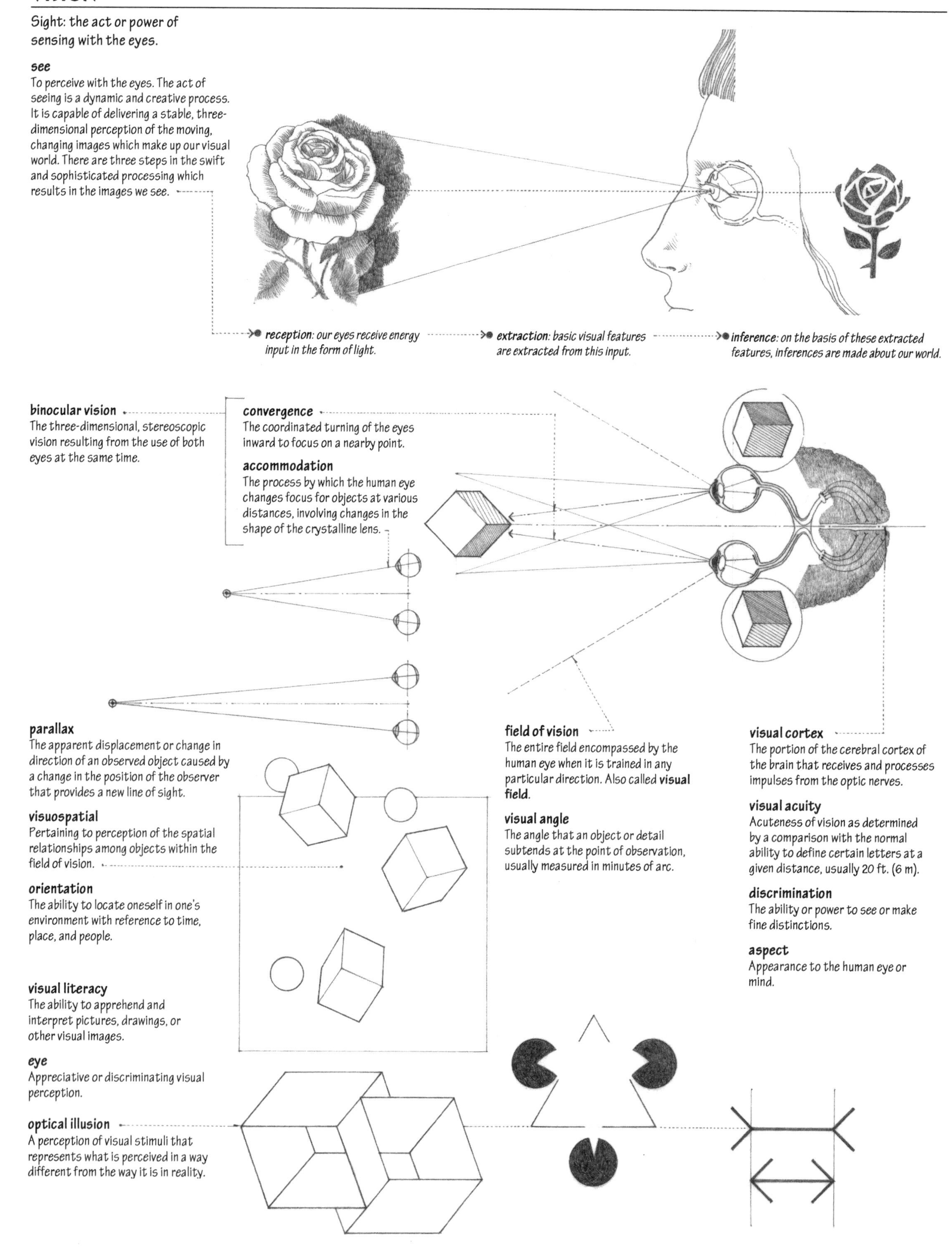

reception: *our eyes receive energy input in the form of light.*

extraction: *basic visual features are extracted from this input.*

inference: *on the basis of these extracted features, inferences are made about our world.*

binocular vision
The three-dimensional, stereoscopic vision resulting from the use of both eyes at the same time.

convergence
The coordinated turning of the eyes inward to focus on a nearby point.

accommodation
The process by which the human eye changes focus for objects at various distances, involving changes in the shape of the crystalline lens.

parallax
The apparent displacement or change in direction of an observed object caused by a change in the position of the observer that provides a new line of sight.

visuospatial
Pertaining to perception of the spatial relationships among objects within the field of vision.

orientation
The ability to locate oneself in one's environment with reference to time, place, and people.

visual literacy
The ability to apprehend and interpret pictures, drawings, or other visual images.

eye
Appreciative or discriminating visual perception.

optical illusion
A perception of visual stimuli that represents what is perceived in a way different from the way it is in reality.

field of vision
The entire field encompassed by the human eye when it is trained in any particular direction. Also called **visual field**.

visual angle
The angle that an object or detail subtends at the point of observation, usually measured in minutes of arc.

visual cortex
The portion of the cerebral cortex of the brain that receives and processes impulses from the optic nerves.

visual acuity
Acuteness of vision as determined by a comparison with the normal ability to define certain letters at a given distance, usually 20 ft. (6 m).

discrimination
The ability or power to see or make fine distinctions.

aspect
Appearance to the human eye or mind.

camouflage
The obscuring of a form or figure that occurs when its shape, pattern, texture, or coloration is similar to that of its surrounding field or background.

projection
A property of perception in which the mind's eye searches for meaning by imagining and projecting known or familiar images onto the seemingly amorphous shapes of a pattern until it finds a match which makes sense. This attempt to complete an incomplete pattern, or find a meaningful pattern embedded in a larger one, is in accordance with what we already know or expect to see. Once seen and understood, it is difficult to not see the image.

similarity
A property of perception in which there is a tendency to group things which have some visual characteristic in common, as a similarity of shape, size, color, orientation or detail.

proximity
A property of perception in which there is a tendency to group elements which are close together, to the exclusion of those which are further away.

continuity
A property of perception in which there is a tendency to group elements which continue along the same line or in the same direction. This search for continuity of line and direction can also lead to our perception of the simpler, more regular figures or patterns in a composition.

constancy
A perceptual phenomenon in which apparent differences in size are ignored in order to identify and categorize things, regardless of how distant they are, leading to the perception of a class of objects as having uniform size and constant color and texture.

closure
A property of perception in which there is a tendency for an open or incomplete figure to be seen as if it were a closed or complete and stable form.

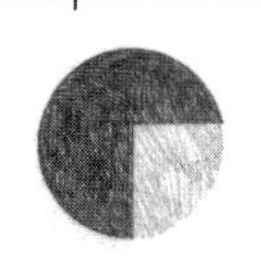
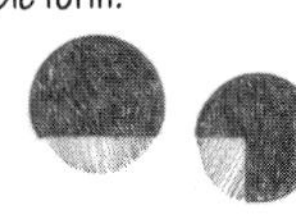

perception
The act or faculty of apprehending by means of the senses or of the mind.

visual perception
An awareness derived by the visual system in response to an external stimulus.

figure-ground
A property of perception in which there is a tendency to see parts of a visual field as solid, well-defined objects standing out against a less distinct background.

figure
A shape or form, as determined by outlines or exterior surfaces.

ground
The receding part of a visual field against which a figure is perceived. Also called **background**.

background
The parts or portion of a scene, situated in the rear, as opposed to foreground.

foreground
The parts or portion of a scene situated in the front, nearest to the viewer.

Gestalt psychology
The theory or doctrine that physiological or psychological phenomena do not occur through the summation of individual elements, as reflexes or sensations, but through gestalts functioning separately or interrelatedly. Also called **configurationism**.

gestalt
A unified configuration, pattern, or field of specific properties that cannot be derived from the summation of the component parts.

pattern
A consistent, characteristic, or coherent arrangement based on the interrelation of component parts.

successive contrast
A phenomenon of visual perception in which intense exposure to one color or value leads to the sensation of its complement, which is projected as an afterimage on another color or surface viewed immediately thereafter.

afterimage
A visual sensation that persists after the stimulus that caused it is no longer operative or present.

simultaneous contrast
A phenomenon of visual perception in which the stimulation of one color or value leads to the sensation of its complement, which is projected instantaneously on a juxtaposed color or value. Simultaneous contrast intensifies complementary colors and shifts analogous colors toward each other's complementary hue, esp. when the juxtaposed colors are similar in value. When two colors of contrasting value are juxtaposed, the lighter color will deepen the darker color while the darker color will lighten the lighter one.

WALL

Any of various upright constructions presenting a continuous surface and serving to enclose, divide, or protect an area.

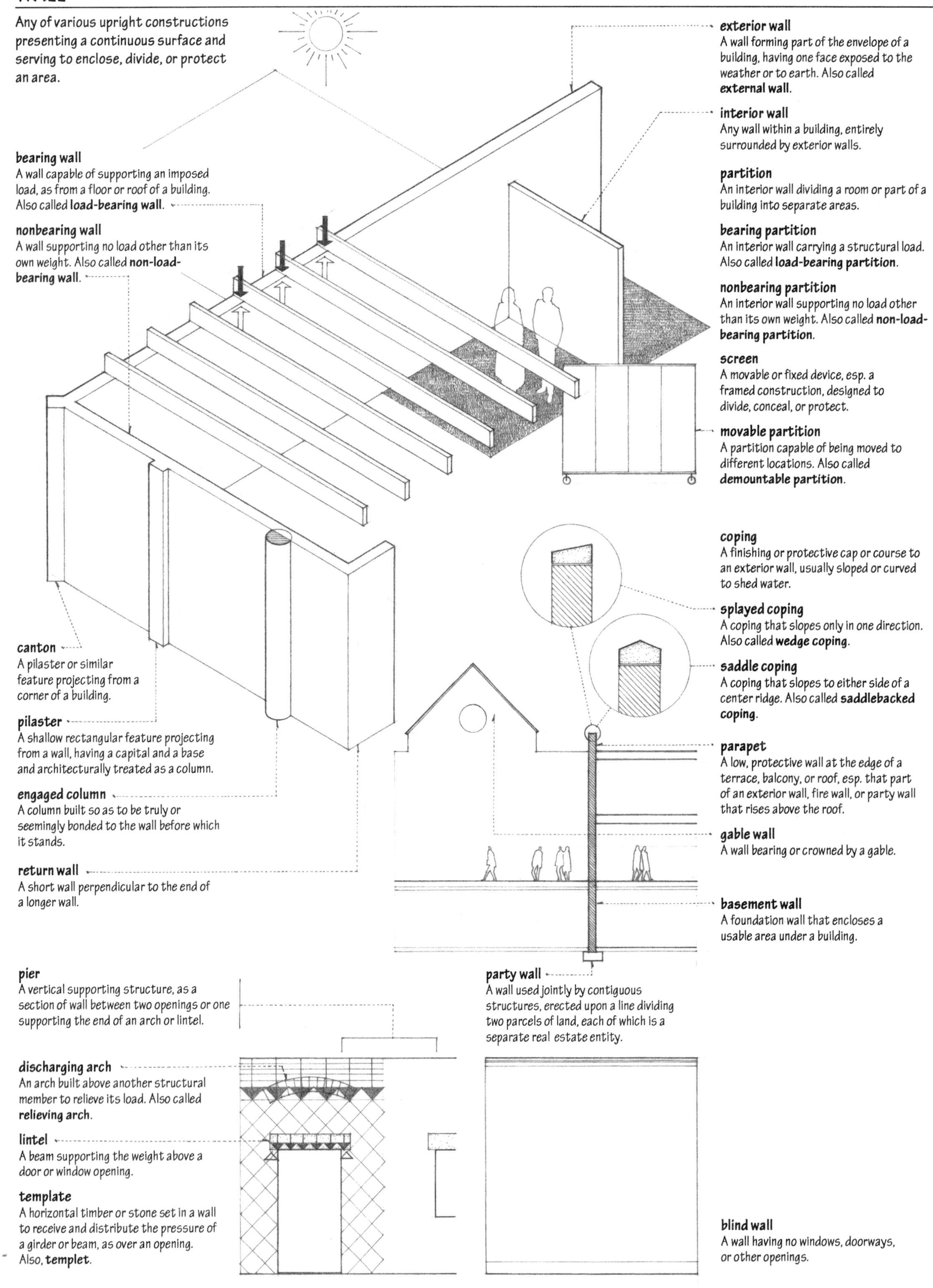

bearing wall
A wall capable of supporting an imposed load, as from a floor or roof of a building. Also called **load-bearing wall**.

nonbearing wall
A wall supporting no load other than its own weight. Also called **non-load-bearing wall**.

canton
A pilaster or similar feature projecting from a corner of a building.

pilaster
A shallow rectangular feature projecting from a wall, having a capital and a base and architecturally treated as a column.

engaged column
A column built so as to be truly or seemingly bonded to the wall before which it stands.

return wall
A short wall perpendicular to the end of a longer wall.

exterior wall
A wall forming part of the envelope of a building, having one face exposed to the weather or to earth. Also called **external wall**.

interior wall
Any wall within a building, entirely surrounded by exterior walls.

partition
An interior wall dividing a room or part of a building into separate areas.

bearing partition
An interior wall carrying a structural load. Also called **load-bearing partition**.

nonbearing partition
An interior wall supporting no load other than its own weight. Also called **non-load-bearing partition**.

screen
A movable or fixed device, esp. a framed construction, designed to divide, conceal, or protect.

movable partition
A partition capable of being moved to different locations. Also called **demountable partition**.

coping
A finishing or protective cap or course to an exterior wall, usually sloped or curved to shed water.

splayed coping
A coping that slopes only in one direction. Also called **wedge coping**.

saddle coping
A coping that slopes to either side of a center ridge. Also called **saddlebacked coping**.

parapet
A low, protective wall at the edge of a terrace, balcony, or roof, esp. that part of an exterior wall, fire wall, or party wall that rises above the roof.

gable wall
A wall bearing or crowned by a gable.

basement wall
A foundation wall that encloses a usable area under a building.

party wall
A wall used jointly by contiguous structures, erected upon a line dividing two parcels of land, each of which is a separate real estate entity.

pier
A vertical supporting structure, as a section of wall between two openings or one supporting the end of an arch or lintel.

discharging arch
An arch built above another structural member to relieve its load. Also called **relieving arch**.

lintel
A beam supporting the weight above a door or window opening.

template
A horizontal timber or stone set in a wall to receive and distribute the pressure of a girder or beam, as over an opening. Also, **templet**.

blind wall
A wall having no windows, doorways, or other openings.

frame house
A house constructed with a skeletal framework of timber, usually sheathed with siding or shingles.

plate
Any of various horizontal timbers laid flat across the heads of studding or upon floors to support joists, rafters, or studs at or near their ends.

wall plate
A horizontal member built into or laid along the top of a wall to support and distribute the load from joists or rafters. Also called **raising plate**.

top plate
The uppermost horizontal member of a framed wall on which joists or rafters rest.

blocking
A number of small wood pieces inserted to space, join, or reinforce members of a building frame, fill the spaces between them, or provide a nailing surface for finish materials.

stud wall
A wall or partition framed with studs and faced with sheathing, siding, wallboard, or plasterwork. Also called **stud partition**.

stud
Any of a series of slender, upright members of wood or metal forming the structural frame of a wall or partition.

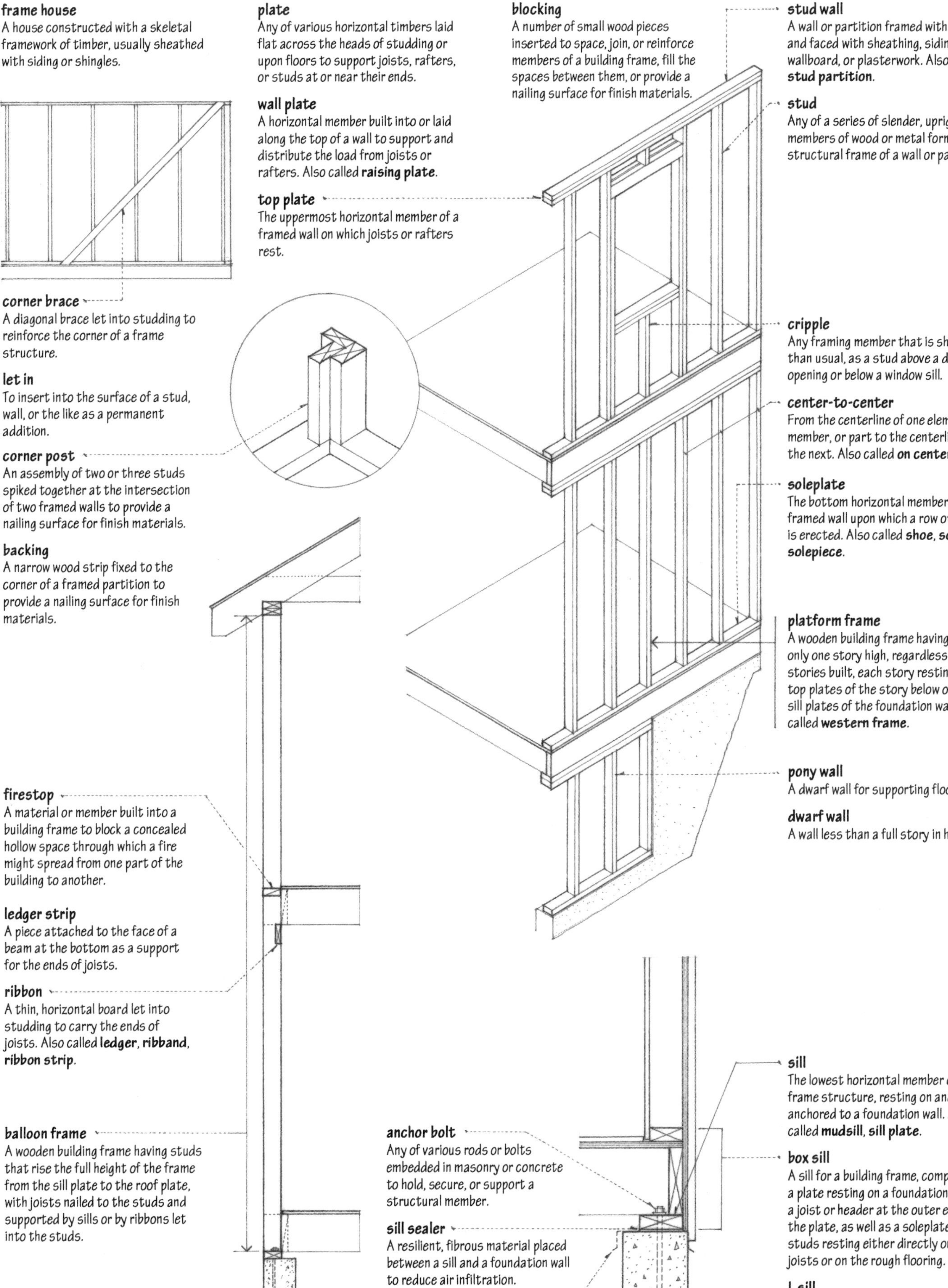

corner brace
A diagonal brace let into studding to reinforce the corner of a frame structure.

let in
To insert into the surface of a stud, wall, or the like as a permanent addition.

corner post
An assembly of two or three studs spiked together at the intersection of two framed walls to provide a nailing surface for finish materials.

backing
A narrow wood strip fixed to the corner of a framed partition to provide a nailing surface for finish materials.

cripple
Any framing member that is shorter than usual, as a stud above a door opening or below a window sill.

center-to-center
From the centerline of one element, member, or part to the centerline of the next. Also called **on center**.

soleplate
The bottom horizontal member of a framed wall upon which a row of studs is erected. Also called **shoe**, **sole**, **solepiece**.

platform frame
A wooden building frame having studs only one story high, regardless of the stories built, each story resting on the top plates of the story below or on the sill plates of the foundation wall. Also called **western frame**.

pony wall
A dwarf wall for supporting floor joists.

dwarf wall
A wall less than a full story in height.

firestop
A material or member built into a building frame to block a concealed hollow space through which a fire might spread from one part of the building to another.

ledger strip
A piece attached to the face of a beam at the bottom as a support for the ends of joists.

ribbon
A thin, horizontal board let into studding to carry the ends of joists. Also called **ledger**, **ribband**, **ribbon strip**.

balloon frame
A wooden building frame having studs that rise the full height of the frame from the sill plate to the roof plate, with joists nailed to the studs and supported by sills or by ribbons let into the studs.

anchor bolt
Any of various rods or bolts embedded in masonry or concrete to hold, secure, or support a structural member.

sill sealer
A resilient, fibrous material placed between a sill and a foundation wall to reduce air infiltration.

termite shield
Sheet metal installed atop a foundation wall or around pipes to prevent the passage of termites.

sill
The lowest horizontal member of a frame structure, resting on and anchored to a foundation wall. Also called **mudsill**, **sill plate**.

box sill
A sill for a building frame, composed of a plate resting on a foundation wall and a joist or header at the outer edge of the plate, as well as a soleplate for studs resting either directly on the joists or on the rough flooring.

L sill
A sill for a building frame, composed of a plate resting on a foundation wall and a joist or header at the outer edge of the plate.

siding
A weatherproof material, as shingles, boards, or units of sheet metal, used for surfacing the exterior walls of a frame building.

corner board
A board against which siding is fitted at the corner of a frame structure.

batten
A small board or strip of wood used for various building purposes, as to cover joints between boards, support shingles or roofing tiles, or provide a base for lathing.

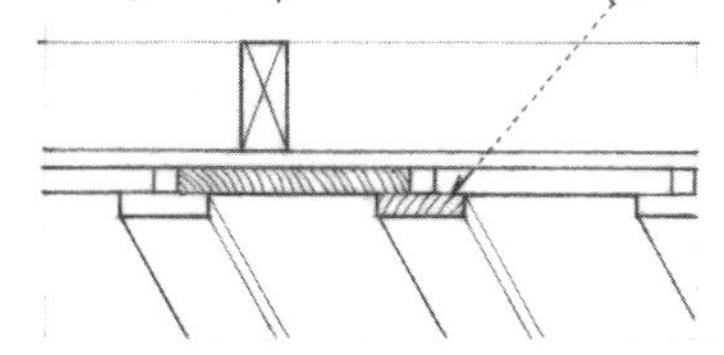

board and batten
Siding consisting of wide boards or plywood sheets set vertically with butt joints covered by battens.

rake
A board or molding placed along the sloping sides of a gable to cover the ends of the siding.

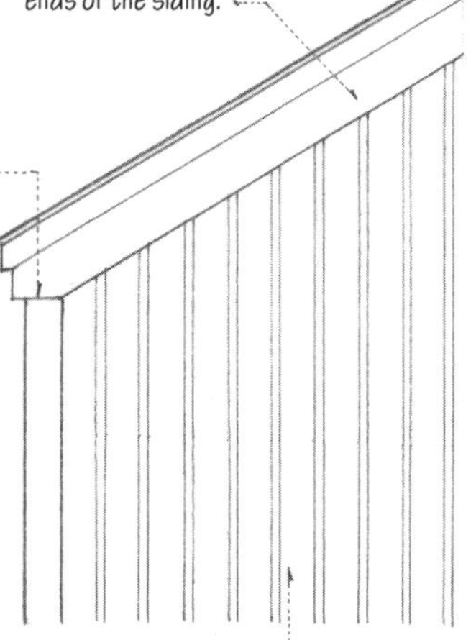

vertical siding
Siding consisting of matched boards applied vertically.

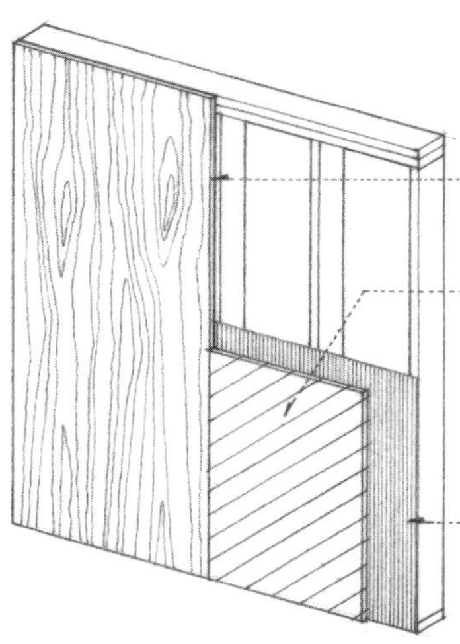

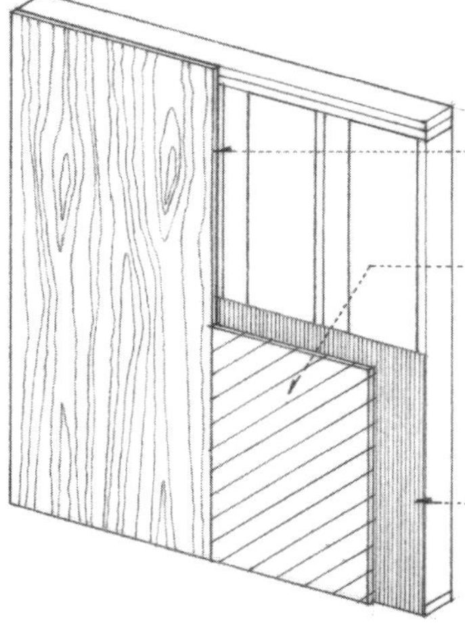

sheathing
A rough covering of boards, plywood, or other panel materials applied to a frame structure to serve as a base for siding, flooring, or roofing.

structural sheathing
Sheathing capable of bracing the plane of a framed wall or roof.

diagonal sheathing
A sheathing of boards applied diagonally for lateral strength.

boarding
A structure of boards, as for sheathing or subflooring.

building paper
Any of various papers, felts, or similar sheet material used in construction to prevent the passage of air or moisture.

clapboard
A long, thin board with one edge thicker than the other, laid horizontally as bevel siding.

shiplap
A flush, overlapping joint, as a rabbet, between two boards joined edge to edge. Also, the boarding joined with such overlapping joints.

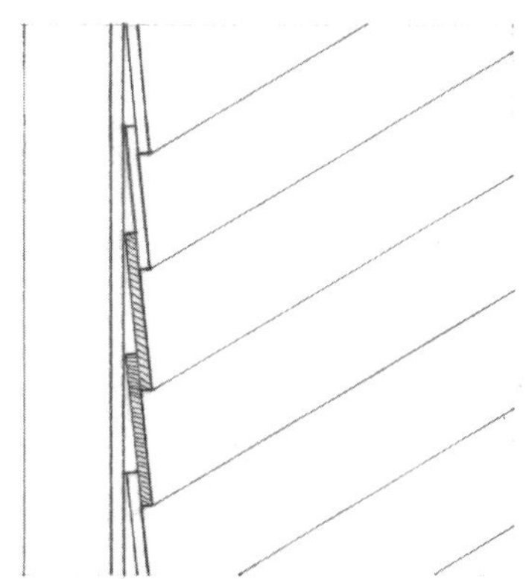

colonial siding
Siding composed of plain, square-edged boards laid horizontally so that the upper overlaps the one below.

bevel siding
Siding composed of tapered boards, as clapboards, laid horizontally with the thicker lower edge of each board overlapping the thinner upper edge of the board below it. Also called **lap siding**.

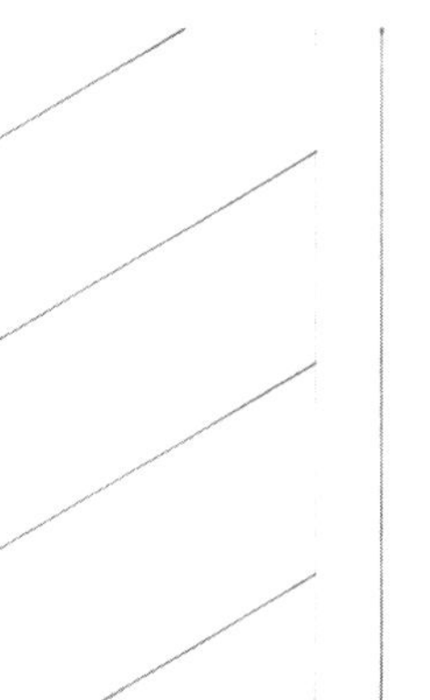

Dolly Varden siding
Bevel siding rabbeted along the lower edge to receive the upper edge of the board below it.

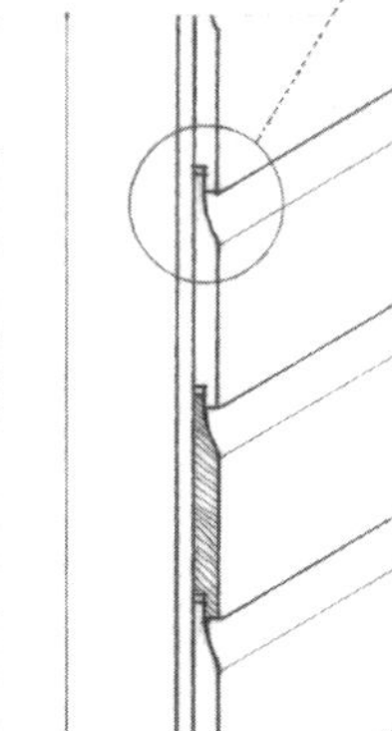

drop siding
Siding composed of boards narrowed along the upper edges to fit into rabbets or grooves in the lower edges, laid horizontally with their backs flat against the sheathing or studs of the wall. Also called **novelty siding, rustic siding**.

paneling
A series of panels, esp. decorative wood panels, joined in a continuous surface.

surround
An encircling area or border.

panel
A distinct portion, section, or division of a wall, wainscot, ceiling or door, esp. of any surface sunk below or raised above the surrounding area, or enclosed by a frame or border.

wainscot
A facing of wood paneling, esp. when covering the lower portion of an interior wall.

mullion
A vertical member dividing the panels in wainscoting.

dado
The lower portion of an interior wall when faced or treated differently from the upper section, as with paneling or wallpaper.

flush panel
A panel having a surface in the same plane as the surrounding frame.

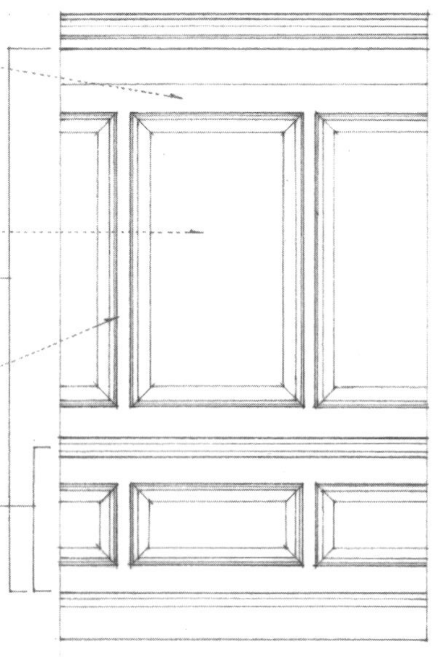

raised panel
A panel having a center portion thicker than the edges or projecting above the surrounding frame. Also called **fielded panel**.

sunk panel
A panel having a surface recessed below the surrounding frame or surface.

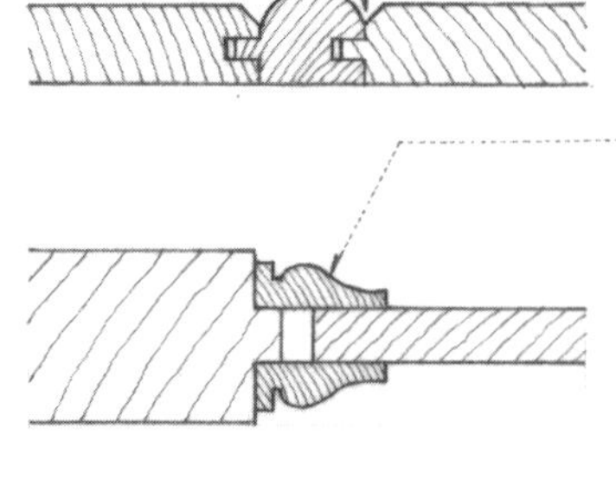

flush bead
A bead having its outer surface at the same level as the adjoining surfaces.

cock bead
A bead that projects above or beyond the adjoining surfaces.

quirk
A groove or acute angle dividing a bead or other molding from adjoining members or surfaces.

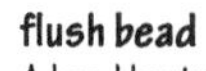

bolection
A raised molding for framing a panel, doorway, or fireplace, esp. when the meeting surfaces are at different levels. Also, **bilection**.

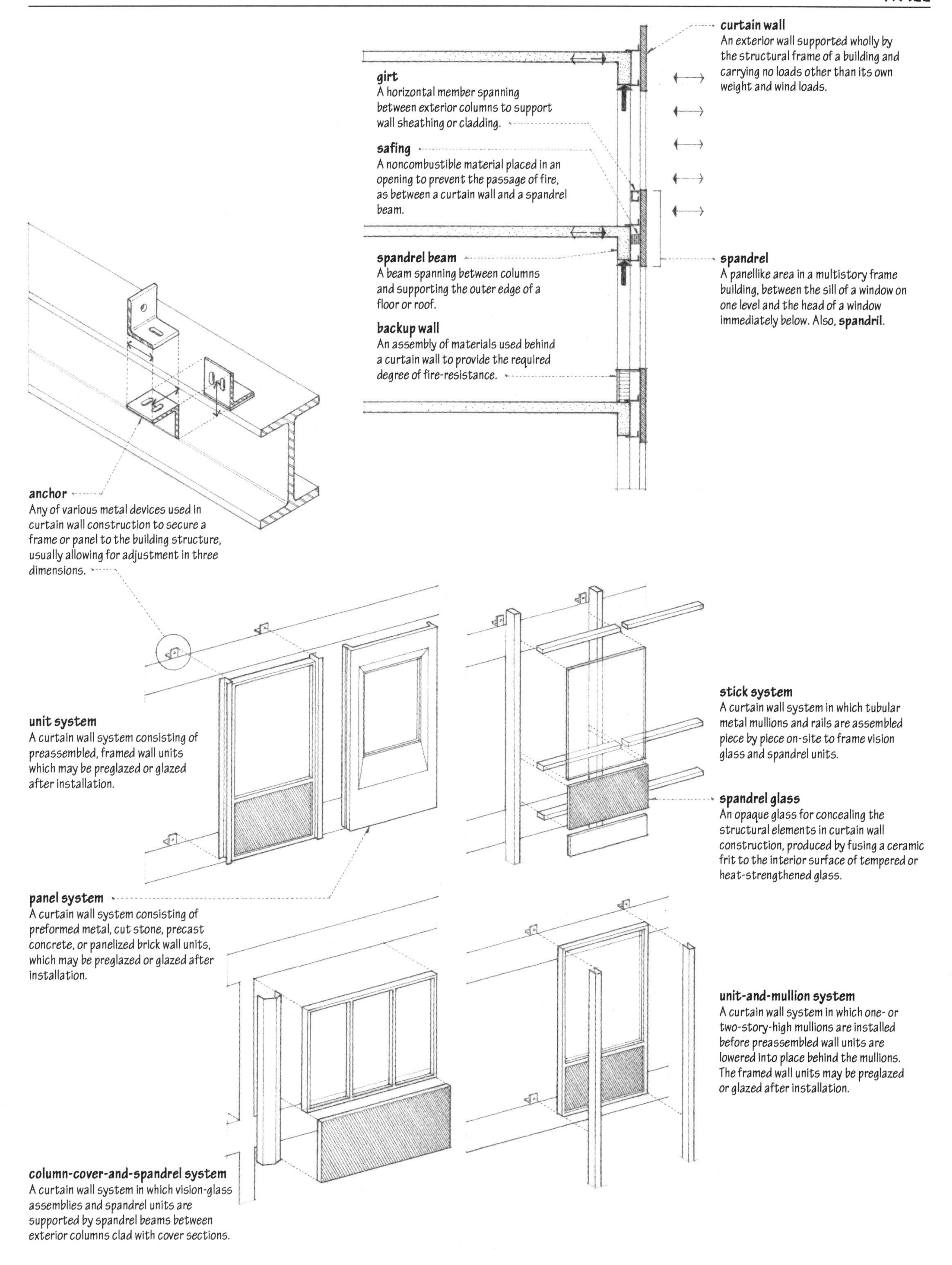

curtain wall
An exterior wall supported wholly by the structural frame of a building and carrying no loads other than its own weight and wind loads.

girt
A horizontal member spanning between exterior columns to support wall sheathing or cladding.

safing
A noncombustible material placed in an opening to prevent the passage of fire, as between a curtain wall and a spandrel beam.

spandrel beam
A beam spanning between columns and supporting the outer edge of a floor or roof.

backup wall
An assembly of materials used behind a curtain wall to provide the required degree of fire-resistance.

spandrel
A panellike area in a multistory frame building, between the sill of a window on one level and the head of a window immediately below. Also, **spandril**.

anchor
Any of various metal devices used in curtain wall construction to secure a frame or panel to the building structure, usually allowing for adjustment in three dimensions.

unit system
A curtain wall system consisting of preassembled, framed wall units which may be preglazed or glazed after installation.

stick system
A curtain wall system in which tubular metal mullions and rails are assembled piece by piece on-site to frame vision glass and spandrel units.

spandrel glass
An opaque glass for concealing the structural elements in curtain wall construction, produced by fusing a ceramic frit to the interior surface of tempered or heat-strengthened glass.

panel system
A curtain wall system consisting of preformed metal, cut stone, precast concrete, or panelized brick wall units, which may be preglazed or glazed after installation.

unit-and-mullion system
A curtain wall system in which one- or two-story-high mullions are installed before preassembled wall units are lowered into place behind the mullions. The framed wall units may be preglazed or glazed after installation.

column-cover-and-spandrel system
A curtain wall system in which vision-glass assemblies and spandrel units are supported by spandrel beams between exterior columns clad with cover sections.

retaining wall
A wall of treated timber, masonry, or concrete for holding in place a mass of earth. A retaining wall can fail by overturning, sliding, or settling. Also called **breast wall**.

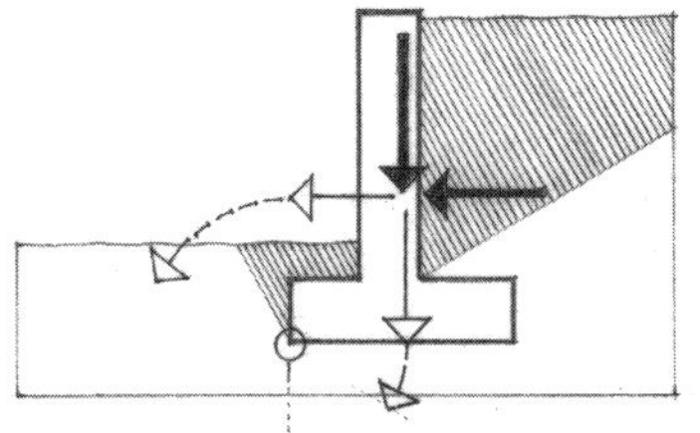

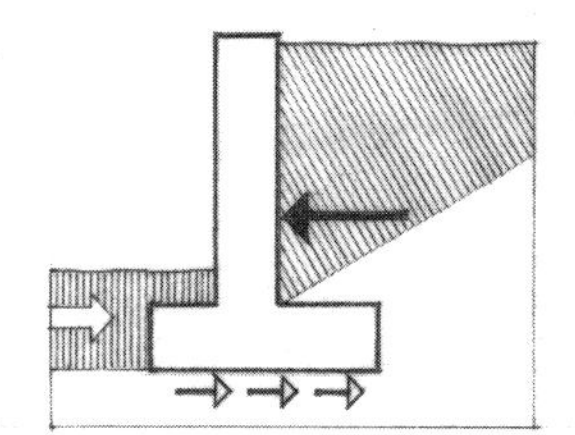

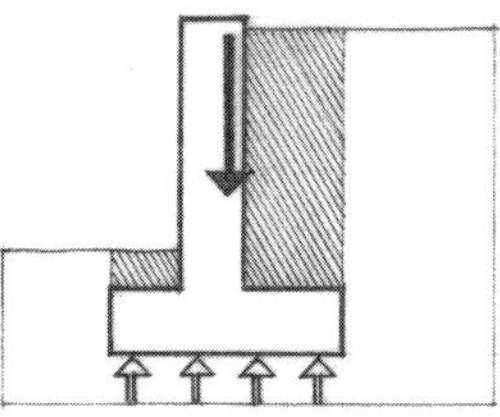

surcharge
An additional or excessive load or burden, as that of the earth above the level of the top of a retaining wall.

toe
The forward, lower tip of the base of a footing or retaining wall, extended to give broader bearing and greater stability.

counterfort
A triangular-shaped cross wall tying a concrete retaining wall to its base at regular intervals, built on the side of the material to be retained in order to stiffen the vertical slab and add weight to the base.

batter
A backward slope of the face of a wall as it rises.

cantilever wall
A retaining wall of reinforced concrete or reinforced concrete masonry, cantilevered from and securely tied to a spread footing that is shaped to resist overturning and sliding.

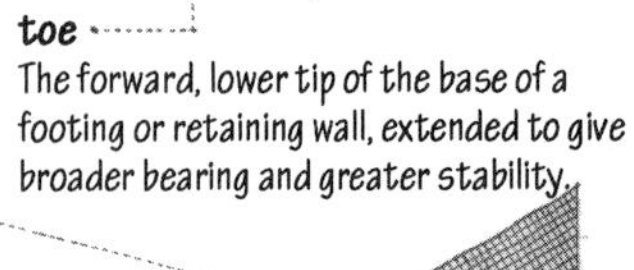

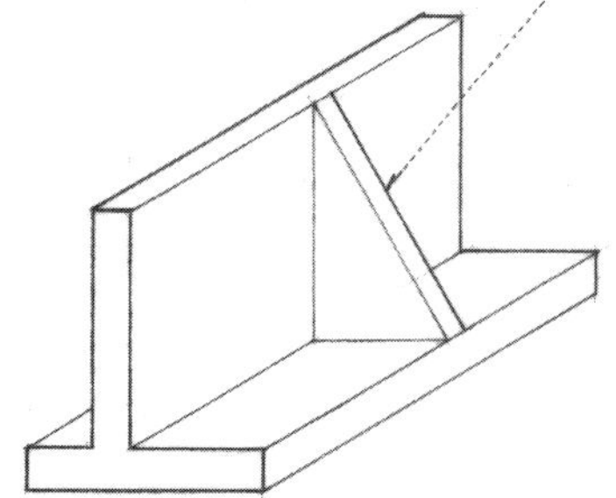

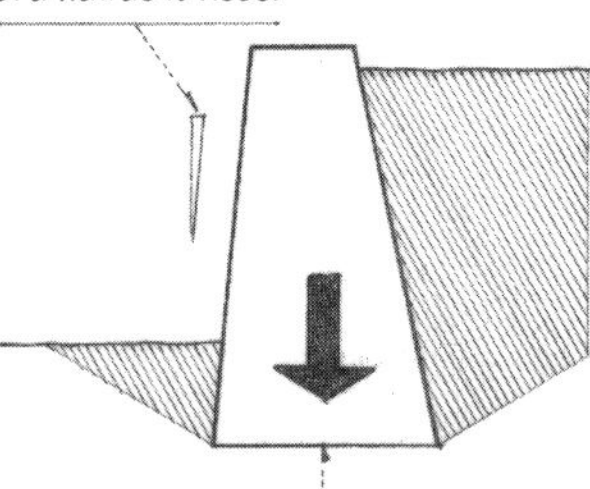

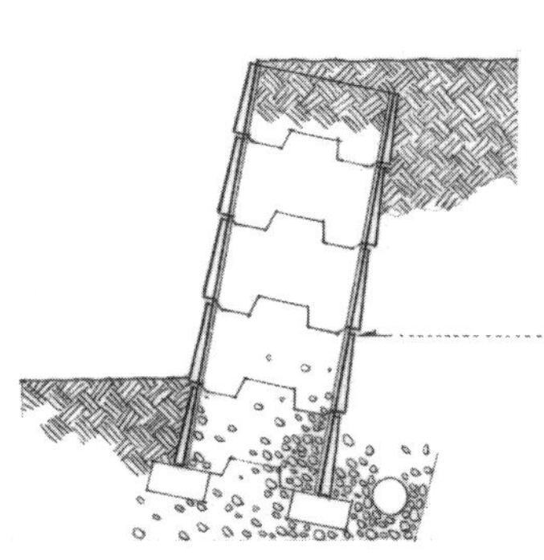

deadman
A log, concrete block, or similar mass buried in the ground as an anchor.

gravity wall
A masonry or concrete retaining wall that resists overturning and sliding by the sheer weight and volume of its mass.

bin wall
A type of gravity retaining wall formed by stacking modular, interlocking precast concrete units and filling the voids with crushed stone or gravel. Also called **cellular wall**.

cribbing
A system of cribs for retaining earth or for a building being moved or having its foundation rebuilt. Also called **cribwork**.

crib
A cellular framework of squared timbers, or steel or concrete members of similar form, assembled in layers at right angles, often filled with earth or stones and used in the construction of foundations and retaining walls.

earth tieback wall
A retaining wall consisting of precast concrete panels fastened to long galvanized steel straps extending into a compacted soil backfill.

critical height
The maximum height at which a vertical cut in a cohesive soil will stand without shoring.

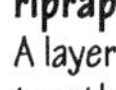

riprap
A layer of broken stones thrown together irregularly on an embankment slope to prevent erosion.

angle of repose
The maximum slope, measured in degrees from the horizontal, at which loose solid material will remain in place without sliding.

angle of slide
The minimum slope, measured in degrees from the horizontal, at which loose solid material will begin to slide or flow.

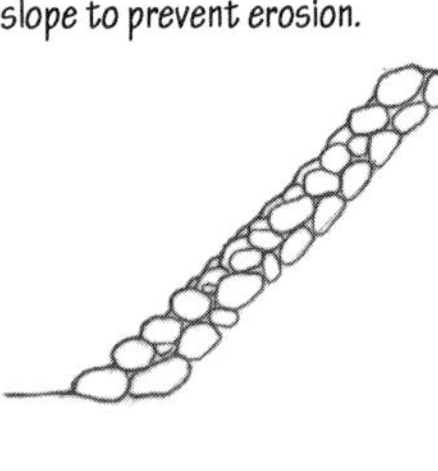

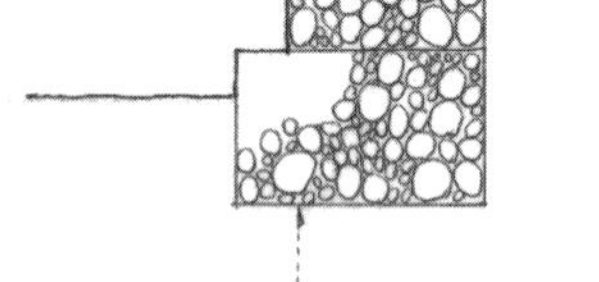

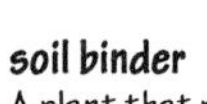

gabion
A galvanized wire basket filled with stones and used in constructing an abutment or retaining structure.

revet
To face a sloping surface or embankment with stone or other material.

revetment
A facing of masonry or other suitable material for protecting an embankment against erosion.

soil binder
A plant that prevents or inhibits erosion by providing a ground cover and forming a dense network of roots that hold the soil.

soil stabilizer
A chemical admixture for maintaining or increasing the stability of a soil mass.

An opening in the wall of a building for admitting light and air, usually fitted with a frame in which are set operable sashes containing panes of glass.

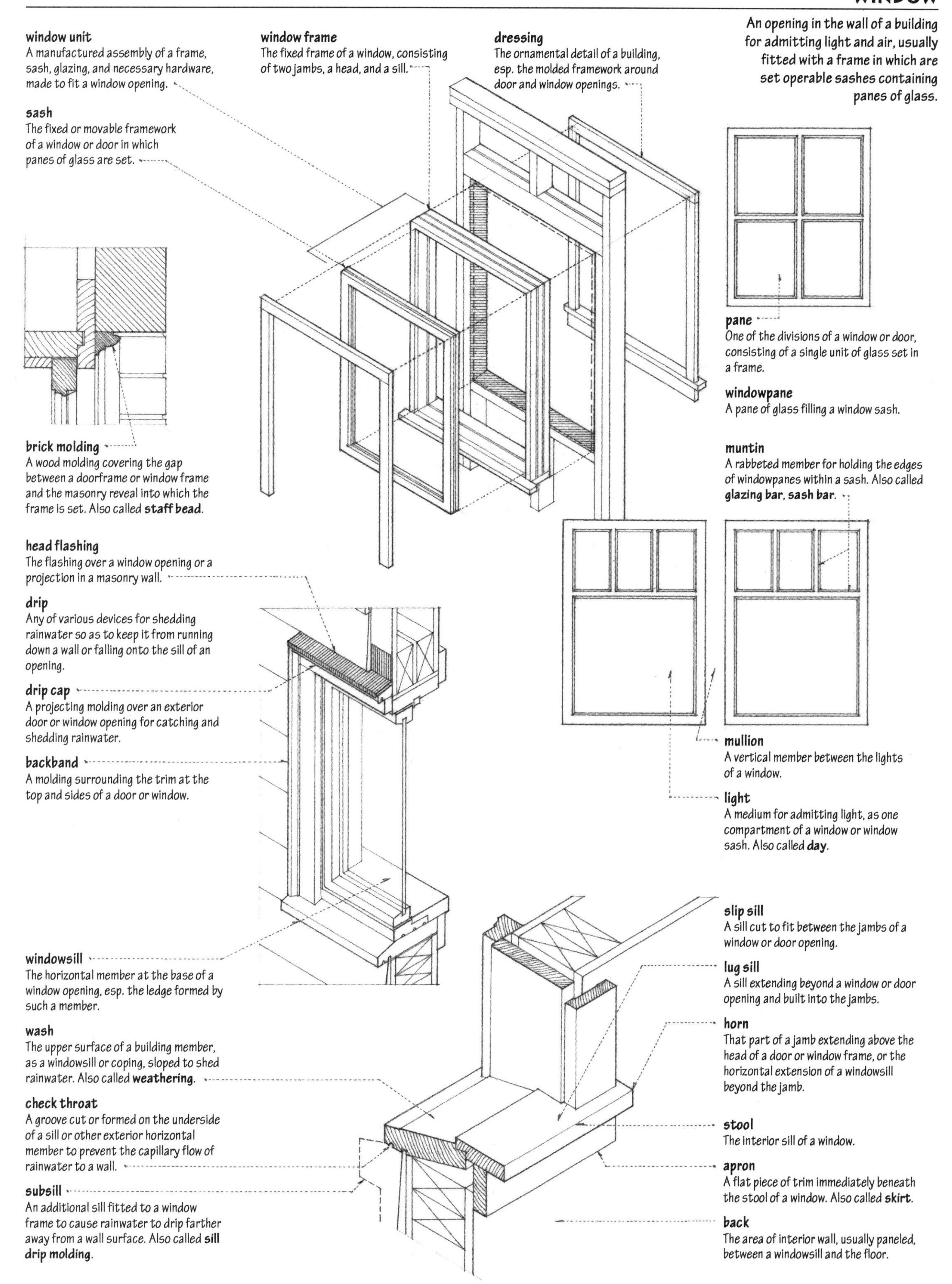

window unit
A manufactured assembly of a frame, sash, glazing, and necessary hardware, made to fit a window opening.

window frame
The fixed frame of a window, consisting of two jambs, a head, and a sill.

dressing
The ornamental detail of a building, esp. the molded framework around door and window openings.

sash
The fixed or movable framework of a window or door in which panes of glass are set.

pane
One of the divisions of a window or door, consisting of a single unit of glass set in a frame.

windowpane
A pane of glass filling a window sash.

brick molding
A wood molding covering the gap between a doorframe or window frame and the masonry reveal into which the frame is set. Also called **staff bead**.

muntin
A rabbeted member for holding the edges of windowpanes within a sash. Also called **glazing bar**, **sash bar**.

head flashing
The flashing over a window opening or a projection in a masonry wall.

drip
Any of various devices for shedding rainwater so as to keep it from running down a wall or falling onto the sill of an opening.

drip cap
A projecting molding over an exterior door or window opening for catching and shedding rainwater.

backband
A molding surrounding the trim at the top and sides of a door or window.

mullion
A vertical member between the lights of a window.

light
A medium for admitting light, as one compartment of a window or window sash. Also called **day**.

windowsill
The horizontal member at the base of a window opening, esp. the ledge formed by such a member.

wash
The upper surface of a building member, as a windowsill or coping, sloped to shed rainwater. Also called **weathering**.

check throat
A groove cut or formed on the underside of a sill or other exterior horizontal member to prevent the capillary flow of rainwater to a wall.

subsill
An additional sill fitted to a window frame to cause rainwater to drip farther away from a wall surface. Also called **sill drip molding**.

slip sill
A sill cut to fit between the jambs of a window or door opening.

lug sill
A sill extending beyond a window or door opening and built into the jambs.

horn
That part of a jamb extending above the head of a door or window frame, or the horizontal extension of a windowsill beyond the jamb.

stool
The interior sill of a window.

apron
A flat piece of trim immediately beneath the stool of a window. Also called **skirt**.

back
The area of interior wall, usually paneled, between a windowsill and the floor.

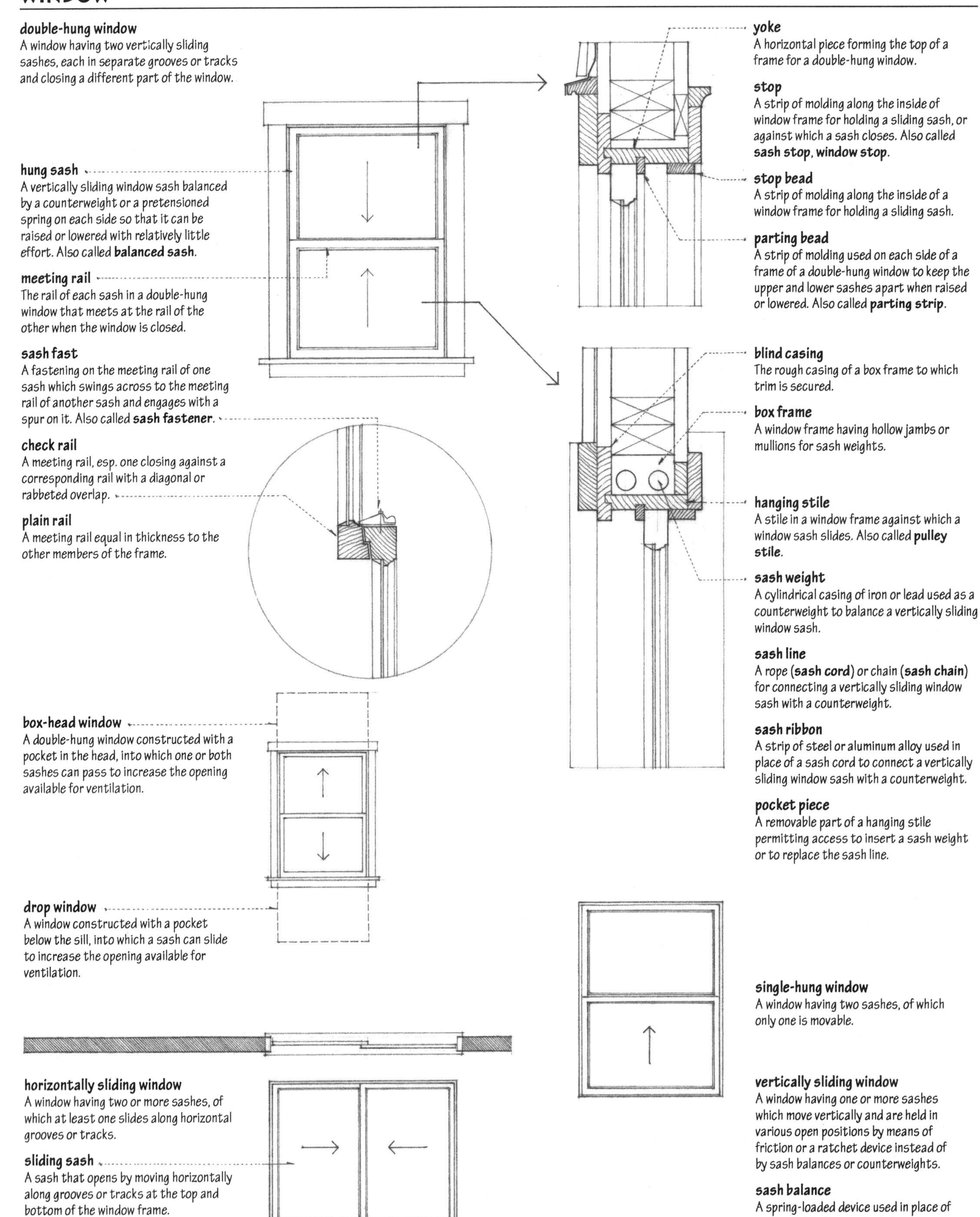

double-hung window
A window having two vertically sliding sashes, each in separate grooves or tracks and closing a different part of the window.

hung sash
A vertically sliding window sash balanced by a counterweight or a pretensioned spring on each side so that it can be raised or lowered with relatively little effort. Also called **balanced sash**.

meeting rail
The rail of each sash in a double-hung window that meets at the rail of the other when the window is closed.

sash fast
A fastening on the meeting rail of one sash which swings across to the meeting rail of another sash and engages with a spur on it. Also called **sash fastener**.

check rail
A meeting rail, esp. one closing against a corresponding rail with a diagonal or rabbeted overlap.

plain rail
A meeting rail equal in thickness to the other members of the frame.

box-head window
A double-hung window constructed with a pocket in the head, into which one or both sashes can pass to increase the opening available for ventilation.

drop window
A window constructed with a pocket below the sill, into which a sash can slide to increase the opening available for ventilation.

horizontally sliding window
A window having two or more sashes, of which at least one slides along horizontal grooves or tracks.

sliding sash
A sash that opens by moving horizontally along grooves or tracks at the top and bottom of the window frame.

yoke
A horizontal piece forming the top of a frame for a double-hung window.

stop
A strip of molding along the inside of window frame for holding a sliding sash, or against which a sash closes. Also called **sash stop, window stop**.

stop bead
A strip of molding along the inside of a window frame for holding a sliding sash.

parting bead
A strip of molding used on each side of a frame of a double-hung window to keep the upper and lower sashes apart when raised or lowered. Also called **parting strip**.

blind casing
The rough casing of a box frame to which trim is secured.

box frame
A window frame having hollow jambs or mullions for sash weights.

hanging stile
A stile in a window frame against which a window sash slides. Also called **pulley stile**.

sash weight
A cylindrical casing of iron or lead used as a counterweight to balance a vertically sliding window sash.

sash line
A rope (**sash cord**) or chain (**sash chain**) for connecting a vertically sliding window sash with a counterweight.

sash ribbon
A strip of steel or aluminum alloy used in place of a sash cord to connect a vertically sliding window sash with a counterweight.

pocket piece
A removable part of a hanging stile permitting access to insert a sash weight or to replace the sash line.

single-hung window
A window having two sashes, of which only one is movable.

vertically sliding window
A window having one or more sashes which move vertically and are held in various open positions by means of friction or a ratchet device instead of by sash balances or counterweights.

sash balance
A spring-loaded device used in place of sash weights to counterbalance a vertically sliding window sash. Also called **spring balance**.

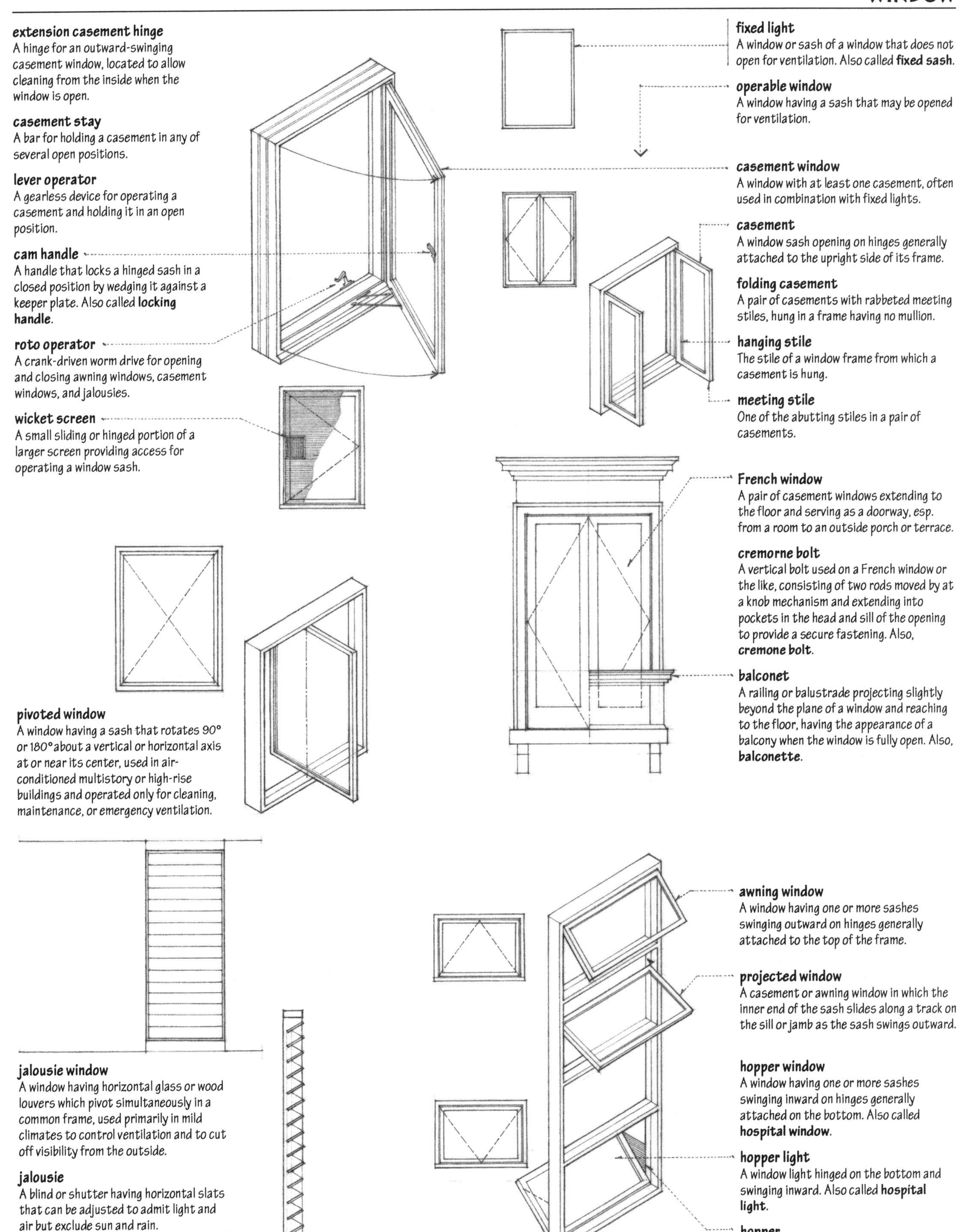

extension casement hinge
A hinge for an outward-swinging casement window, located to allow cleaning from the inside when the window is open.

casement stay
A bar for holding a casement in any of several open positions.

lever operator
A gearless device for operating a casement and holding it in an open position.

cam handle
A handle that locks a hinged sash in a closed position by wedging it against a keeper plate. Also called **locking handle**.

roto operator
A crank-driven worm drive for opening and closing awning windows, casement windows, and jalousies.

wicket screen
A small sliding or hinged portion of a larger screen providing access for operating a window sash.

pivoted window
A window having a sash that rotates 90° or 180° about a vertical or horizontal axis at or near its center, used in air-conditioned multistory or high-rise buildings and operated only for cleaning, maintenance, or emergency ventilation.

jalousie window
A window having horizontal glass or wood louvers which pivot simultaneously in a common frame, used primarily in mild climates to control ventilation and to cut off visibility from the outside.

jalousie
A blind or shutter having horizontal slats that can be adjusted to admit light and air but exclude sun and rain.

shielding angle
The angle below which something can be seen when viewed through a louver.

fixed light
A window or sash of a window that does not open for ventilation. Also called **fixed sash**.

operable window
A window having a sash that may be opened for ventilation.

casement window
A window with at least one casement, often used in combination with fixed lights.

casement
A window sash opening on hinges generally attached to the upright side of its frame.

folding casement
A pair of casements with rabbeted meeting stiles, hung in a frame having no mullion.

hanging stile
The stile of a window frame from which a casement is hung.

meeting stile
One of the abutting stiles in a pair of casements.

French window
A pair of casement windows extending to the floor and serving as a doorway, esp. from a room to an outside porch or terrace.

cremorne bolt
A vertical bolt used on a French window or the like, consisting of two rods moved by at a knob mechanism and extending into pockets in the head and sill of the opening to provide a secure fastening. Also, **cremone bolt**.

balconet
A railing or balustrade projecting slightly beyond the plane of a window and reaching to the floor, having the appearance of a balcony when the window is fully open. Also, **balconette**.

awning window
A window having one or more sashes swinging outward on hinges generally attached to the top of the frame.

projected window
A casement or awning window in which the inner end of the sash slides along a track on the sill or jamb as the sash swings outward.

hopper window
A window having one or more sashes swinging inward on hinges generally attached on the bottom. Also called **hospital window**.

hopper light
A window light hinged on the bottom and swinging inward. Also called **hospital light**.

hopper
One of the triangular draft barriers on each side of a hopper light.

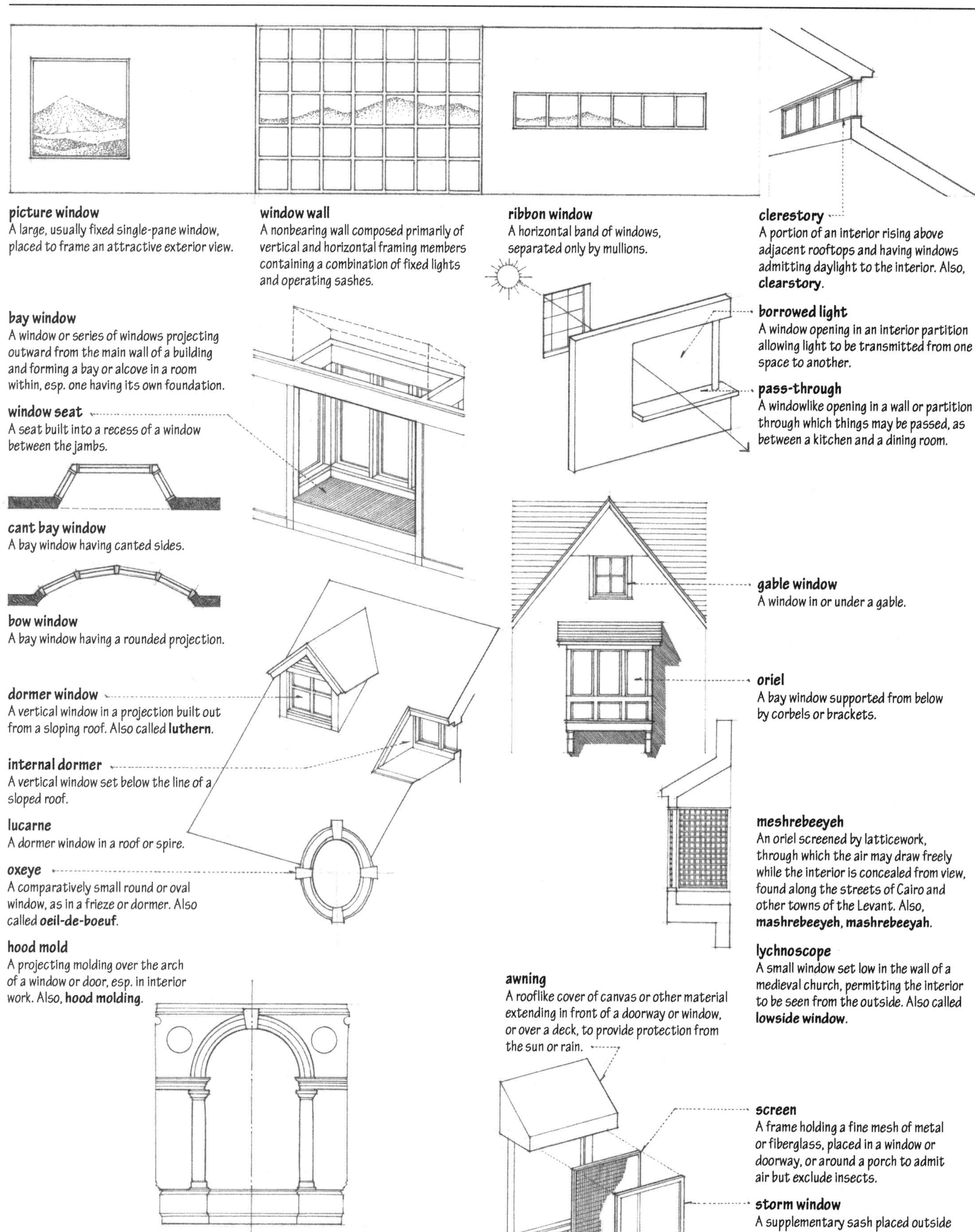

picture window
A large, usually fixed single-pane window, placed to frame an attractive exterior view.

window wall
A nonbearing wall composed primarily of vertical and horizontal framing members containing a combination of fixed lights and operating sashes.

ribbon window
A horizontal band of windows, separated only by mullions.

clerestory
A portion of an interior rising above adjacent rooftops and having windows admitting daylight to the interior. Also, **clearstory**.

bay window
A window or series of windows projecting outward from the main wall of a building and forming a bay or alcove in a room within, esp. one having its own foundation.

window seat
A seat built into a recess of a window between the jambs.

borrowed light
A window opening in an interior partition allowing light to be transmitted from one space to another.

pass-through
A windowlike opening in a wall or partition through which things may be passed, as between a kitchen and a dining room.

cant bay window
A bay window having canted sides.

bow window
A bay window having a rounded projection.

gable window
A window in or under a gable.

dormer window
A vertical window in a projection built out from a sloping roof. Also called **luthern**.

oriel
A bay window supported from below by corbels or brackets.

internal dormer
A vertical window set below the line of a sloped roof.

lucarne
A dormer window in a roof or spire.

oxeye
A comparatively small round or oval window, as in a frieze or dormer. Also called **oeil-de-boeuf**.

meshrebeeyeh
An oriel screened by latticework, through which the air may draw freely while the interior is concealed from view, found along the streets of Cairo and other towns of the Levant. Also, **mashrebeeyeh, mashrebeeyah**.

hood mold
A projecting molding over the arch of a window or door, esp. in interior work. Also, **hood molding**.

lychnoscope
A small window set low in the wall of a medieval church, permitting the interior to be seen from the outside. Also called **lowside window**.

awning
A rooflike cover of canvas or other material extending in front of a doorway or window, or over a deck, to provide protection from the sun or rain.

screen
A frame holding a fine mesh of metal or fiberglass, placed in a window or doorway, or around a porch to admit air but exclude insects.

storm window
A supplementary sash placed outside an existing window as additional protection against severe weather. Also called **storm sash**.

Palladian motif
A window or doorway in the form of a round-headed archway flanked on either side by narrower compartments, the side compartments being capped with entablatures on which the arch of the central compartment rests. Also called **Serlian motif**, **Venetian motif**.

window box
A box designed to hold soil for growing plants at or on a windowsill.

combination window
A window equipped with interchangeable screen and glass sections for summer and winter use.

tracery
Ornamental work of branchlike lines, esp. the lacy openwork in the upper part of a Gothic window.

plate tracery
Early Gothic tracery formed of pierced slabs of stone set on edge, the design being in the shape and disposition of the openings. Also called **perforated tracery**.

geometric tracery
Gothic tracery characterized by a pattern of geometric shapes, as circles and foils.

mouchette
A daggerlike motif found esp. in Gothic tracery, formed by elliptical and ogee curves.

curvilinear tracery
Gothic tracery characterized by a pattern of irregular, boldly curved forms. Also called **flowing tracery**.

bar tracery
Gothic tracery that succeeded plate tracery, consisting of molded stone mullions that divide into various branching elements which fill the window head.

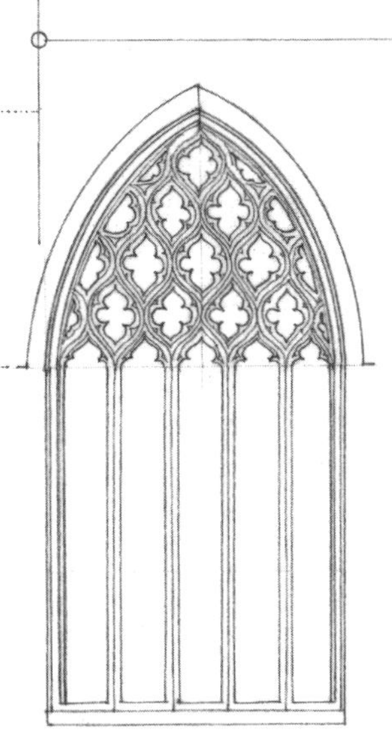

reticulated tracery
Gothic tracery consisting mainly of a netlike arrangement of repeated geometrical figures. Also called **net tracery**.

angel light
A triangular light in a Gothic window, formed by the arch of the window, an arch of a lower tier of tracery, and a mullion of an upper tier of tracery.

perpendicular tracery
Predominantly vertical Gothic tracery having mullions rising to the curve of the arch, crossed at intervals by horizontal transoms. Also called **rectilinear tracery**.

foil
Any of several arcs or rounded spaces divided by cusps and tangent to the interior of a larger arc, as of an arch or circle.

foliation
Ornamentation of an archway, window, or other opening with foils or representations of foliage.

cusp
A pointed projection formed by two intersecting arcs, used esp. to vary the outlines of intradoses or to form foils.

cuspidation
Decoration with cusps.

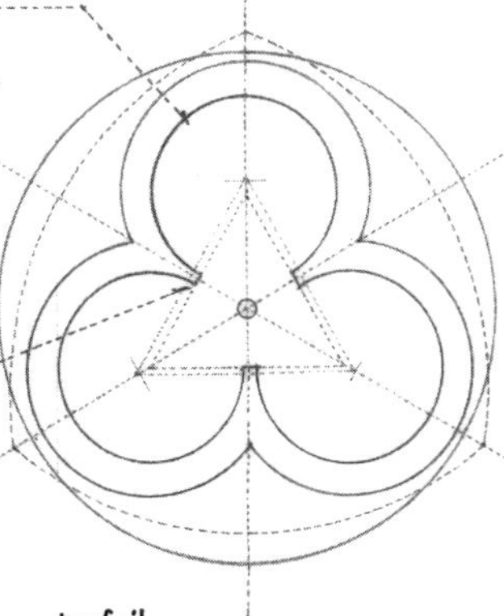

trefoil
An arrangement of three foils divided by cusps and radiating from a common center.

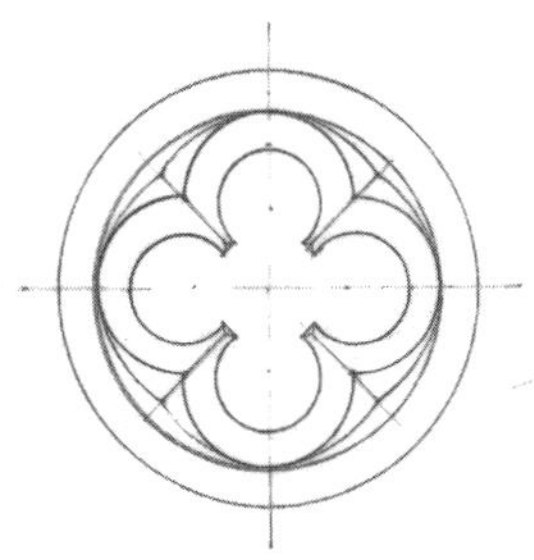

quatrefoil
An ornament composed of four foils, divided by cusps and radiating from a common center.

cinquefoil
A design composed of five foils, divided by cusps and radiating from a common center.

multifoil
Having more than five foils.

WOOD

The tough, fibrous cellular substance that makes up most of the stems and branches of trees beneath the bark.

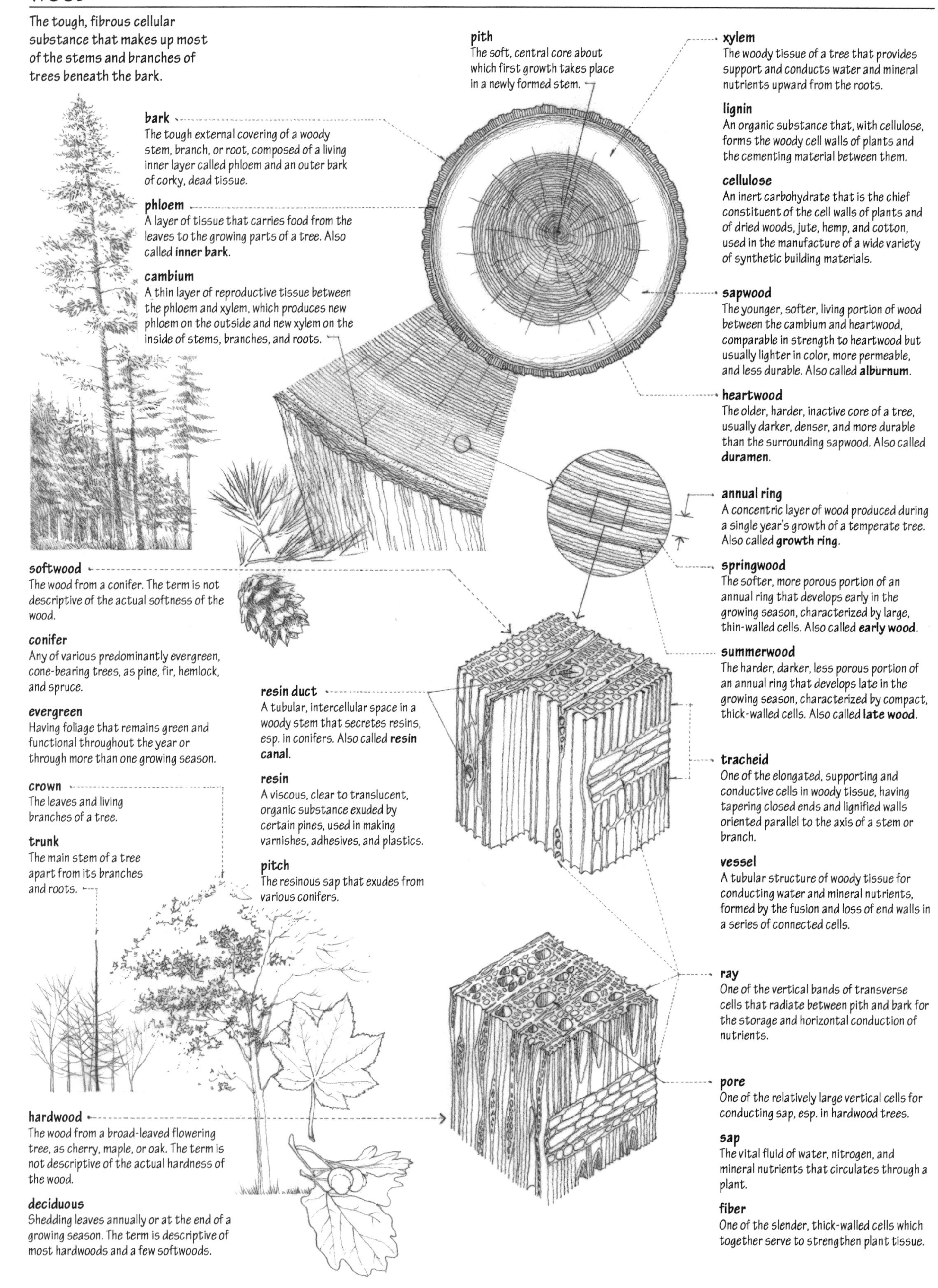

bark
The tough external covering of a woody stem, branch, or root, composed of a living inner layer called phloem and an outer bark of corky, dead tissue.

phloem
A layer of tissue that carries food from the leaves to the growing parts of a tree. Also called **inner bark**.

cambium
A thin layer of reproductive tissue between the phloem and xylem, which produces new phloem on the outside and new xylem on the inside of stems, branches, and roots.

pith
The soft, central core about which first growth takes place in a newly formed stem.

xylem
The woody tissue of a tree that provides support and conducts water and mineral nutrients upward from the roots.

lignin
An organic substance that, with cellulose, forms the woody cell walls of plants and the cementing material between them.

cellulose
An inert carbohydrate that is the chief constituent of the cell walls of plants and of dried woods, jute, hemp, and cotton, used in the manufacture of a wide variety of synthetic building materials.

sapwood
The younger, softer, living portion of wood between the cambium and heartwood, comparable in strength to heartwood but usually lighter in color, more permeable, and less durable. Also called **alburnum**.

heartwood
The older, harder, inactive core of a tree, usually darker, denser, and more durable than the surrounding sapwood. Also called **duramen**.

annual ring
A concentric layer of wood produced during a single year's growth of a temperate tree. Also called **growth ring**.

springwood
The softer, more porous portion of an annual ring that develops early in the growing season, characterized by large, thin-walled cells. Also called **early wood**.

summerwood
The harder, darker, less porous portion of an annual ring that develops late in the growing season, characterized by compact, thick-walled cells. Also called **late wood**.

softwood
The wood from a conifer. The term is not descriptive of the actual softness of the wood.

conifer
Any of various predominantly evergreen, cone-bearing trees, as pine, fir, hemlock, and spruce.

evergreen
Having foliage that remains green and functional throughout the year or through more than one growing season.

crown
The leaves and living branches of a tree.

trunk
The main stem of a tree apart from its branches and roots.

resin duct
A tubular, intercellular space in a woody stem that secretes resins, esp. in conifers. Also called **resin canal**.

resin
A viscous, clear to translucent, organic substance exuded by certain pines, used in making varnishes, adhesives, and plastics.

pitch
The resinous sap that exudes from various conifers.

tracheid
One of the elongated, supporting and conductive cells in woody tissue, having tapering closed ends and lignified walls oriented parallel to the axis of a stem or branch.

vessel
A tubular structure of woody tissue for conducting water and mineral nutrients, formed by the fusion and loss of end walls in a series of connected cells.

ray
One of the vertical bands of transverse cells that radiate between pith and bark for the storage and horizontal conduction of nutrients.

hardwood
The wood from a broad-leaved flowering tree, as cherry, maple, or oak. The term is not descriptive of the actual hardness of the wood.

deciduous
Shedding leaves annually or at the end of a growing season. The term is descriptive of most hardwoods and a few softwoods.

pore
One of the relatively large vertical cells for conducting sap, esp. in hardwood trees.

sap
The vital fluid of water, nitrogen, and mineral nutrients that circulates through a plant.

fiber
One of the slender, thick-walled cells which together serve to strengthen plant tissue.

timber
Wood suitable for use as a building material.

log
A length of trunk or large limb of a felled tree, ready for sawing.

rough lumber
Lumber that is sawn, edged and trimmed, but not surfaced.

dressed lumber
Lumber that is surfaced with a planing machine to attain a smooth surface and uniform size.

surfaced green
Of or pertaining to dressed lumber having a moisture content exceeding 19% at the time of manufacture.

surfaced dry
Of or pertaining to dressed lumber having at a moisture content of 19% or less at the time of manufacture.

lumber
The timber product manufactured by sawing, resawing, passing lengthwise through a planing machine, cross-cutting to length, and grading.

seasoned
Of or pertaining to lumber that has been dried to reduce its moisture content and improve its serviceability.

kiln-dried
Of or pertaining to lumber seasoned in a kiln under controlled conditions of heat, air circulation, and humidity.

air-dried
Of or pertaining to lumber seasoned by exposure to the atmosphere.

equilibrium moisture content
The moisture content at which wood neither gains nor loses moisture when surrounded by air at a given temperature and relative humidity.

fiber-saturation point
The stage in the drying or wetting of wood at which the cell walls are fully saturated but the cell cavities are void of water, ranging from a moisture content of 25% to 32% for commonly used species. Further drying results in shrinkage and generally greater strength, stiffness, and density of the wood.

oven-dry
Of or pertaining to lumber dried to a point at which no moisture can be extracted when exposed in a kiln to a temperature of 214° to 221°F (101° to 105°C).

moisture content
The amount of water contained in a wood piece, expressed as a percentage of the weight of the wood when oven-dry.

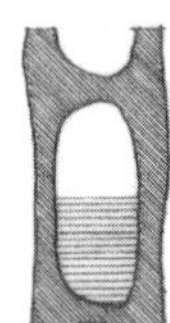

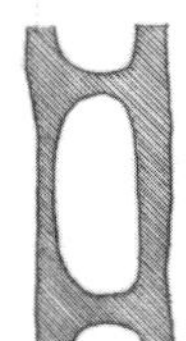

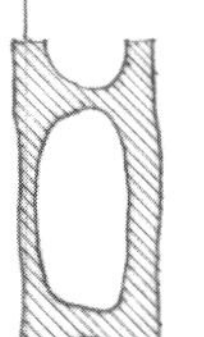

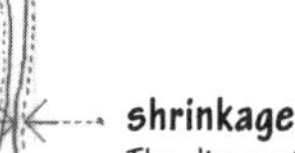

shrinkage
The dimensional contraction of a wood piece occurring when its moisture content falls below the fiber-saturation point. Shrinkage is very slight along the grain, but significant across the grain.

working
The alternate swelling and shrinkage of seasoned wood occurring with changes in moisture content caused by changes in relative humidity of the surrounding air.

acclimatize
To store wood products, as millwork and flooring, in an interior space until the materials adapt to the moisture content and temperature of the new environment.

tangential shrinkage
Wood shrinkage in a direction tangent to the growth rings, about double that of radial shrinkage.

radial shrinkage
Wood shrinkage perpendicular to the grain, across the growth rings.

longitudinal shrinkage
Wood shrinkage parallel to the grain, about 2% of radial shrinkage.

board foot
A unit of quantity for lumber equal to the volume of a piece whose nominal dimensions are 12 in. (304.8 mm) square and 1 in. (25.4 mm) thick.

board measure
Lumber measurement in board feet.

nominal dimension
The dimension of lumber before drying and surfacing, used for convenience in defining size and computing quantity. Nominal dimensions are always written without inch marks. Also called **nominal size**.

dressed size
The dimension of lumber after seasoning and surfacing, from 3/8 to 3/4 in. (9.5 to 19.1 mm) less than the nominal dimension. A dressed size is always written with inch marks ("). Also called **dressed dimension**.

grain
The direction, size, arrangement, and appearance of the fibers in a piece of dressed wood.

edge grain
Wood grain resulting from quartersawing, having the annual rings forming an angle of 45° or more with the broad faces of a piece. Also called **vertical grain**.

flat grain
Wood grain resulting from plain-sawing, having the annual rings forming an angle of less than 45° with the broad faces of a piece.

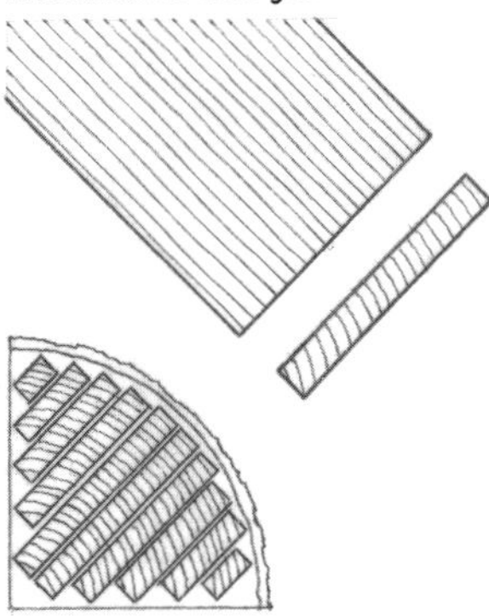

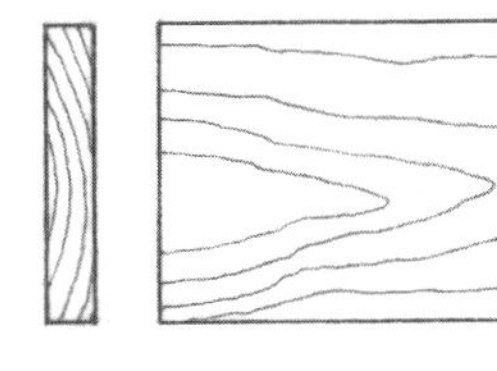

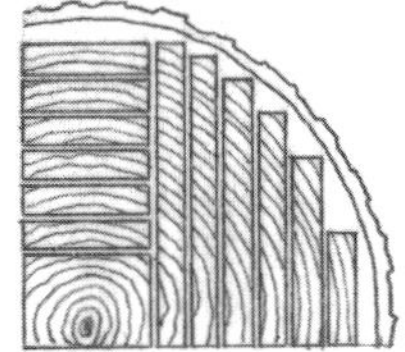

quartersaw
To saw quartered logs approximately at right angles to the annual rings.

plain-saw
To saw a squared log into boards with evenly spaced parallel cuts. Also called **bastard-saw**.

mixed grain
Any combination of edge-grained and flat-grained lumber.

end grain
Wood grain resulting from a cut across the grain.

crosscut
A cut made across the grain of wood.

rip
To saw wood in the direction of the grain. Also called **ripsaw**.

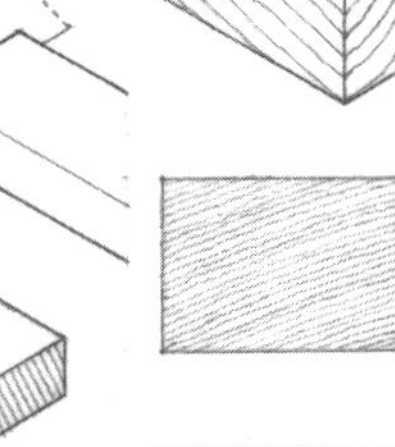

diagonal grain
Wood grain having the annual rings at an angle to the length of a piece, resulting from sawing at an angle to the axis of a log.

cross grain
Wood grain having the cells and fibers running transversely or diagonally to the length of a piece as a result of sawing, or irregularly as a result of a growth characteristic.

close grain
Wood grain characterized by narrow, inconspicuous annual rings with little difference in pore size between springwood and summer wood.

coarse grain
Wood grain characterized by wide, conspicuous annual rings with considerable contrast in pore size between springwood and summerwood.

coarse texture
Wood grain having large pores. Also called **open grain**.

fine texture
Wood grain having small, closely spaced pores.

raised grain
A dressed wood surface having the denser summerwood rising above the softer springwood.

warp
Any deviation from a plane or true surface of a board or panel, usually caused by uneven drying during the seasoning process or by a change in moisture content.

cup
A curvature across the width or face of a wood piece, measured at the point of greatest deviation from a straight line drawn from edge to edge of the piece.

bow
A curvature along the length of a wood piece, measured at the point of greatest deviation from a straight line drawn from end to end of the piece.

crook
A curvature along the edge of a wood piece, measured at the point of greatest deviation from a straight line drawn from end to end of the piece.

twist
A warp resulting from the turning of the edges of a wood piece in opposite directions.

shake
A separation along the grain of a wood piece, usually between the annual rings, caused by stresses on a tree while standing or during felling.

pitch pocket
A well-defined opening between the annual rings of a softwood, containing or having once contained solid or liquid pitch.

check
A lengthwise separation of wood across the annual rings, caused by uneven or rapid shrinkage during the seasoning process.

split
A check that extends completely through a board or wood veneer. Also called **through check**.

wane
The presence of bark or absence of wood at a corner or along an edge of a piece.

knot
The base of a woody branch enclosed by a subsequent growth of wood in the stem from which it rises. In the structural grading of a wood piece, knots are restricted by size and location.

live knot
A knot having annual rings intergrown with those of the surrounding wood. Live knots are allowable in structural timber within certain size limits. Also called **intergrown knot**.

sound knot
A knot that is solid across its face, at least as hard as the surrounding wood, and undecayed.

tight knot
A knot held firmly in place by growth or position.

dead knot
A knot having annual rings not intergrown with those of the surrounding wood. Encasement may be partial or complete, but a dead knot is considered to be a defect since it can easily loosen or be knocked out. Also called **encased knot, loose knot**.

decay
The decomposition of wood by fungi and other microorganisms, resulting in softening, loss of strength and weight, and often a change of texture and color.

dry rot
A decay of seasoned timber caused by fungi that consume the cellulose leaving a soft, brittle skeleton readily reduced to powder.

pecky
Having isolated spots of incipient decay from fungi, as pecky cypress or pecky cedar.

skip
An area on the surface of a board or panel missed by a planing machine.

machine burn
A surface charring caused by overheating of the cutting blades or abrasive belts during shaping or finishing of a material.

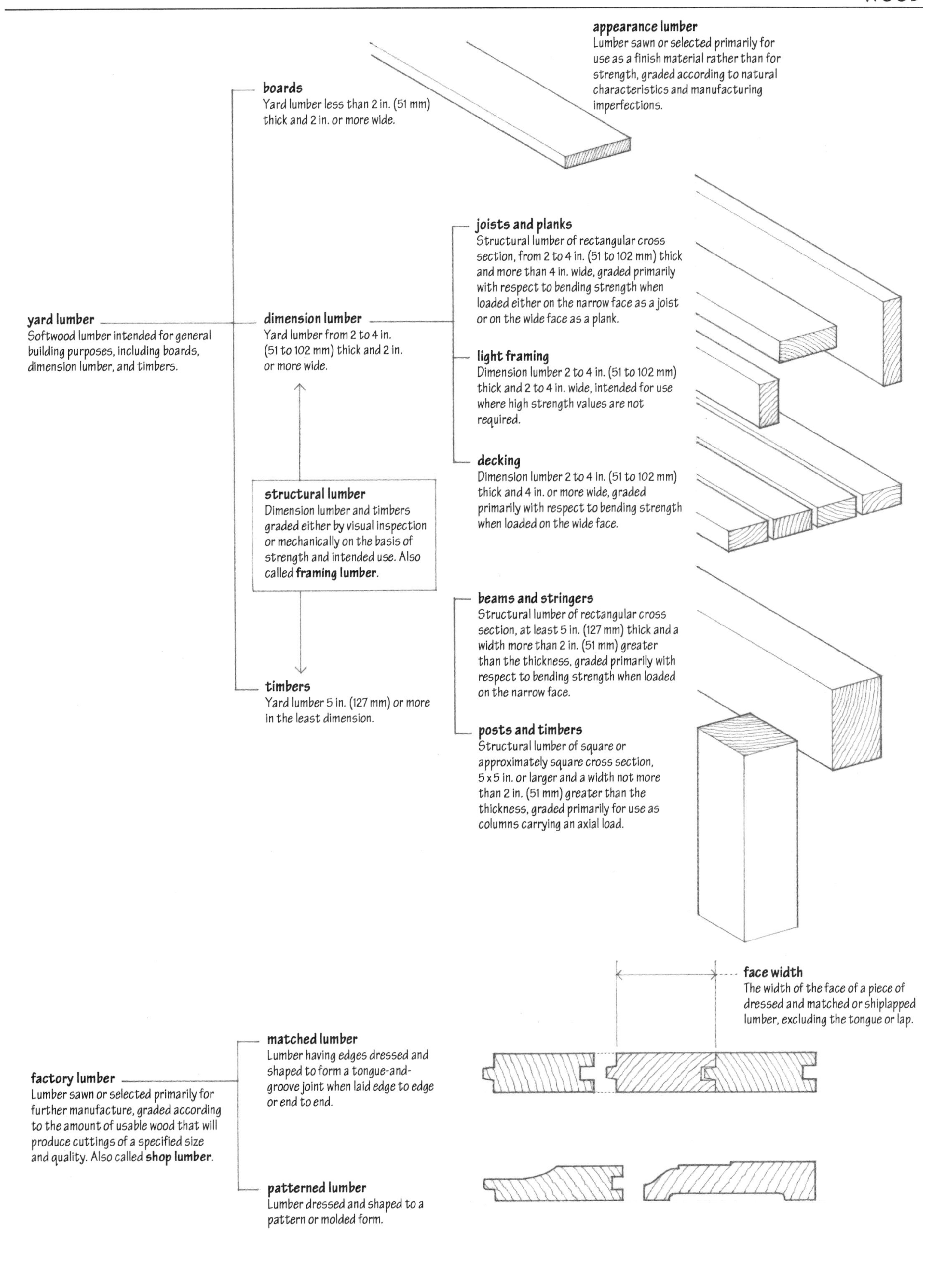
appearance lumber
Lumber sawn or selected primarily for use as a finish material rather than for strength, graded according to natural characteristics and manufacturing imperfections.
boards
Yard lumber less than 2 in. (51 mm) thick and 2 in. or more wide.
joists and planks
Structural lumber of rectangular cross section, from 2 to 4 in. (51 to 102 mm) thick and more than 4 in. wide, graded primarily with respect to bending strength when loaded either on the narrow face as a joist or on the wide face as a plank.
yard lumber
Softwood lumber intended for general building purposes, including boards, dimension lumber, and timbers.
dimension lumber
Yard lumber from 2 to 4 in. (51 to 102 mm) thick and 2 in. or more wide.
light framing
Dimension lumber 2 to 4 in. (51 to 102 mm) thick and 2 to 4 in. wide, intended for use where high strength values are not required.
decking
Dimension lumber 2 to 4 in. (51 to 102 mm) thick and 4 in. or more wide, graded primarily with respect to bending strength when loaded on the wide face.
structural lumber
Dimension lumber and timbers graded either by visual inspection or mechanically on the basis of strength and intended use. Also called framing lumber.
beams and stringers
Structural lumber of rectangular cross section, at least 5 in. (127 mm) thick and a width more than 2 in. (51 mm) greater than the thickness, graded primarily with respect to bending strength when loaded on the narrow face.
timbers
Yard lumber 5 in. (127 mm) or more in the least dimension.
posts and timbers
Structural lumber of square or approximately square cross section, 5 x 5 in. or larger and a width not more than 2 in. (51 mm) greater than the thickness, graded primarily for use as columns carrying an axial load.
face width
The width of the face of a piece of dressed and matched or shiplapped lumber, excluding the tongue or lap.
matched lumber
Lumber having edges dressed and shaped to form a tongue-and-groove joint when laid edge to edge or end to end.
factory lumber
Lumber sawn or selected primarily for further manufacture, graded according to the amount of usable wood that will produce cuttings of a specified size and quality. Also called shop lumber.
patterned lumber
Lumber dressed and shaped to a pattern or molded form.

visual grading
The visual examination and grading of structural lumber by trained inspectors according to quality-reducing characteristics that affect strength, appearance, durability, or utility.

machine rating
The grading of structural lumber by a machine that flexes a test specimen, measures its resistance to bending, calculates its modulus of elasticity, and electronically computes the appropriate stress grade, taking into account such factors as the effects of knots, slope of grain, growth rate, density, and moisture content. Also called **machine stress-rating**.

grademark
A stamp applied to each piece of lumber indicating the assigned stress grade, mill of origin, moisture content at time of manufacture, species or species group, and the grading authority.

slope of grain
The angle of grain relative to a line parallel to the length of a wood piece.

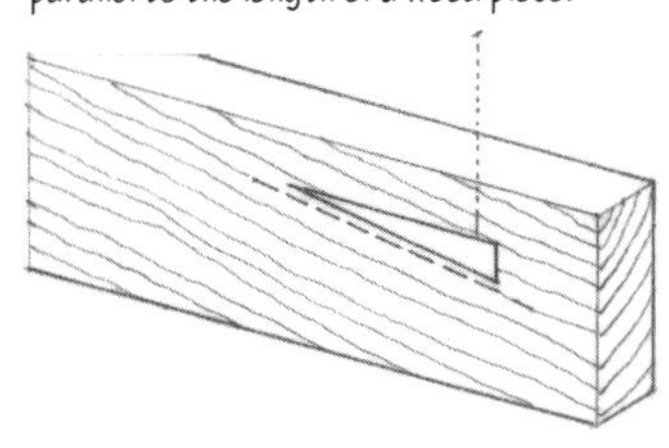

stress grade
Any of the grades of structural lumber for which a set of base values and corresponding modulus of elasticity is established for a species or group of species by a grading agency.

design value
Any of the allowable unit stresses for a species and grade of structural lumber obtained by modifying the base value by factors related to size and conditions of use.

=

size-adjusted value
A base value for a species or group of species of structural lumber, adjusted for cross-sectional size.

base value
Any of the allowable unit stresses for bending, compression perpendicular and parallel to grain, tension parallel to grain, horizontal shear, and corresponding modulus of elasticity, established by a grading agency for various species and grades of structural lumber. Base values must be adjusted first for size and then for conditions of use.

X

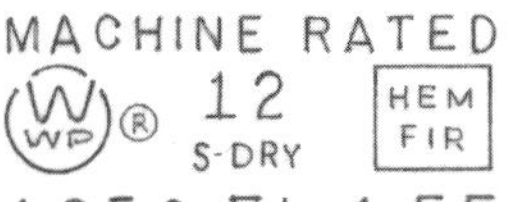

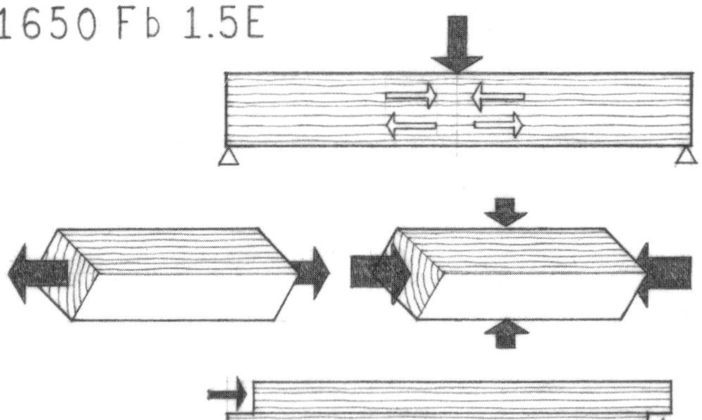

size factor
A coefficient for modifying the base values of a species and grade of lumber according to the cross-sectional size of the piece.

repetitive member factor
A coefficient for increasing the size-adjusted values of repetitive members, since the sharing of the load by the pieces enhances the strength of the entire assembly.

repetitive member
Any of a series of three or more light framing members, as joists or rafters, spaced not more than 24 in. (610 mm) on center and joined by sheathing, decking, or other load-distributing members.

duration of load factor
A coefficient for increasing the size-adjusted values of a wood member subject to a short-term load, since wood has the property of carrying substantially greater maximum loads for short durations than for long durations of loading.

horizontal shear factor
A coefficient for increasing the size-adjusted horizontal shear value of a wood member having shakes, checks, or splits when their length is known and any increase in length is not anticipated.

flat use factor
A coefficient for increasing the size-adjusted bending value for planking having a face width of 4 in. (102 mm) or more.

wet use factor
A coefficient for decreasing the size-adjusted values for wood members when their moisture content will likely exceed 19% in use.

treated wood
Wood that has been coated or impregnated with chemicals to improve its resistance to decay, insect infestation, or fire.

pressure-treated wood
Wood impregnated with chemicals applied under pressure to reduce its resistance to decay and insect infestation.

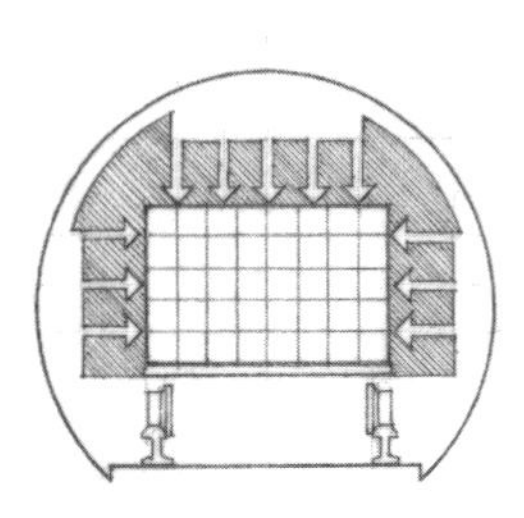

full-cell process
A process for pressure-treating wood in which a vacuum is first drawn to remove air from the wood fibers and allow the preservative to be absorbed by the cell walls, after which pressure is applied to force additional preservative into the cell cavities. The full-cell process leaves the maximum amount of preservative in the wood.

empty-cell process
A process for pressure-treating wood in which the pressure of the entering preservative entraps air in the wood fibers, which expands when the pressure is released to expel excess preservative from the cell cavities. The empty-cell process yields a drier product while ensuring deep, uniform penetration of the preservative.

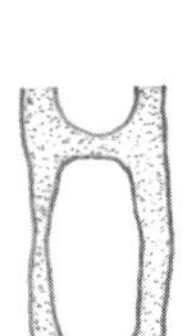

preservative
Any of various substances for coating or impregnating wood in order to protect it against wood-destroying fungi and insects.

water-borne preservative
An inorganic, water-soluble compound, as ammoniacal copper arsenite (ACA) or chromated copper arsenite (CCA), used as a wood preservative. ACA and CCA affix chemically to the wood cell walls and is resistant to leaching. The copper acts as a fungicide while the arsenate is toxic to wood-destroying insects. Wood treated with ACA and CCA is odorless and paintable.

oil-borne preservative
An organic chemical dissolved in a petroleum oil carrier, as pentachlorophenol or copper naphthenate, used as a wood preservative. Pentachlorophenol, the most commonly used oil-borne preservative, has a persistent odor, is insoluble in water, and is highly toxic not only to fungi and insects but also to humans and plants.

creosote
An oily liquid of aromatic hydrocarbons obtained by the distillation of coal tar, used as a wood preservative for marine installations or for severe exposures to wood-destroying fungi and insects. Creosote and creosote solutions have a penetrating odor and render wood unpaintable.

non-pressure-treated wood
Wood coated, dipped, or impregnated with a preservative under atmospheric pressure.

vacuum process
A non-pressure treatment in which a vacuum or partial vacuum exhausts air from the cells and pores of the wood while atmospheric pressure forces preservative into the wood.

fire-retardant wood
Wood treated with mineral salts impregnated under pressure to reduce flammability or combustibility. The salts react chemically at temperatures below the ignition point of wood, causing the combustible vapors normally generated in the wood to break down into water and carbon dioxide.

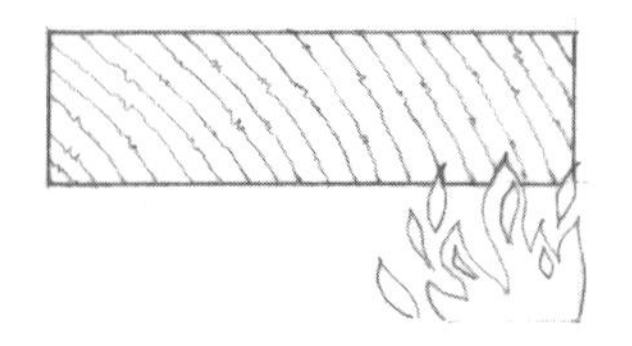

ferrule
A metal ring or cap placed around the end of a wooden post or handle to prevent splitting.

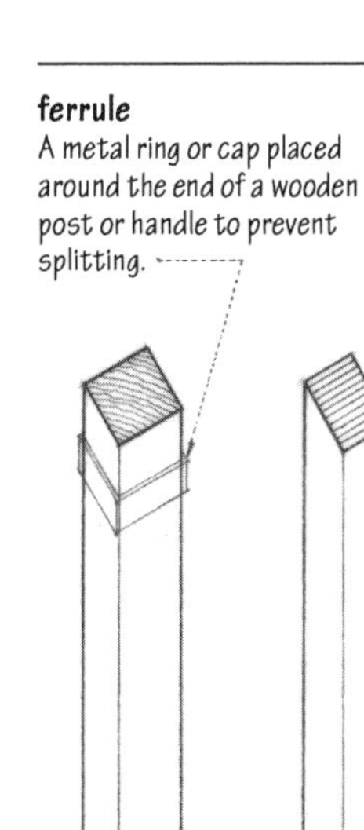

solid column
A wood column consisting of a single piece of solid-sawn or glued-laminated timber, usually square or rectangular in cross section.

bracket load
An eccentric load applied at some point below the upper end of a timber column, the static effect of which is assumed to be equivalent to the same load applied axially plus an additional side load applied at midheight.

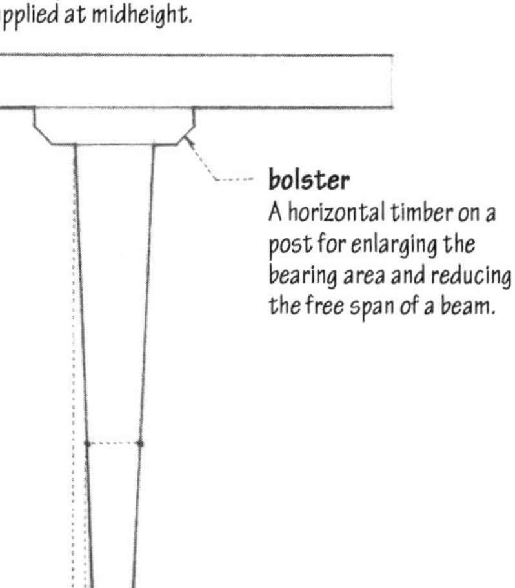

bolster
A horizontal timber on a post for enlarging the bearing area and reducing the free span of a beam.

tapered column
A wood column having a cross section that diminishes along its length. In determining the slenderness ratio for a tapered column, the least dimension is taken as the sum of the minimum diameter or least dimension and one-third the difference between the minimum and maximum diameters or lesser and greater dimensions.

box column
A built-up column having a hollow, square or rectangular cross section.

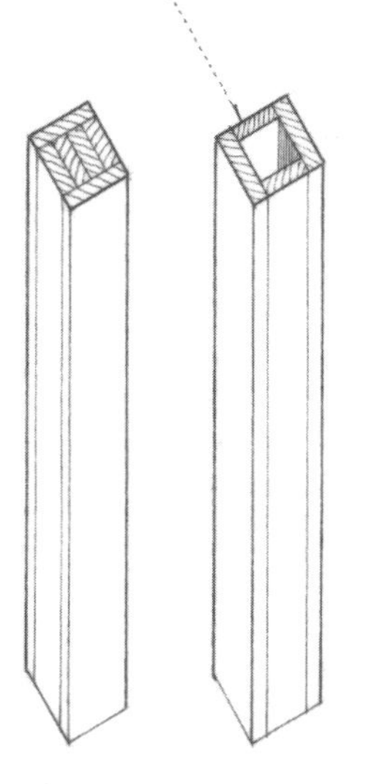

built-up column
A wood column formed by fastening or gluing cover plates to two or more parallel planks, or boxing planks around a solid core. A built-up column is never equal in strength to a solid column of comparable material and overall dimensions.

spaced column
A wood column consisting of two or more parallel members separated at their ends and midpoints by blocking, and joined at the ends by timber connectors capable of developing the required shear resistance.

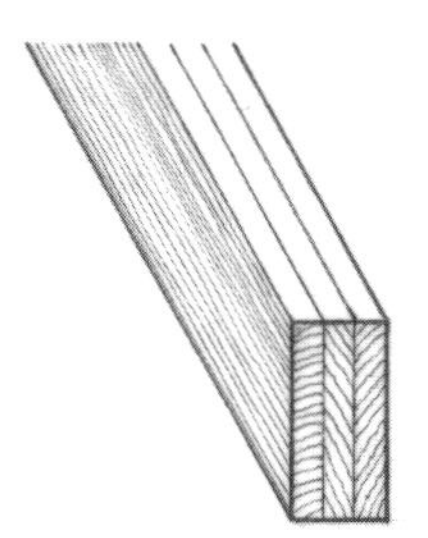

built-up beam
A vertically laminated wood beam made by fastening together two or more smaller members with bolts, lag screws, or spikes, equal in strength to the sum of the strengths of the individual pieces if none of the laminations are spliced.

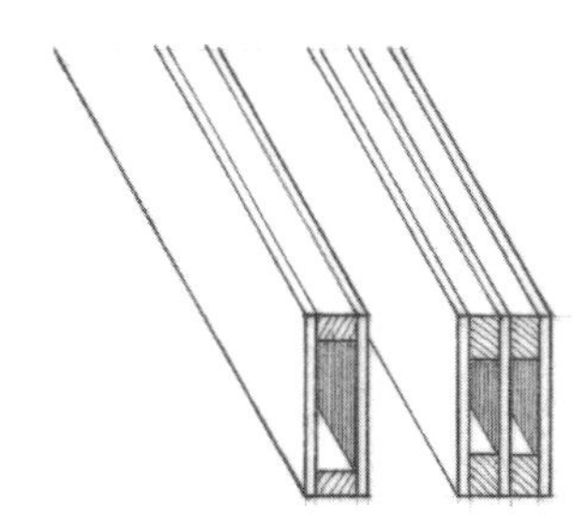

box beam
A beam having a hollow, rectangular cross section, made by gluing two or more plywood or oriented strandboard webs to sawn or laminated veneer lumber flanges.

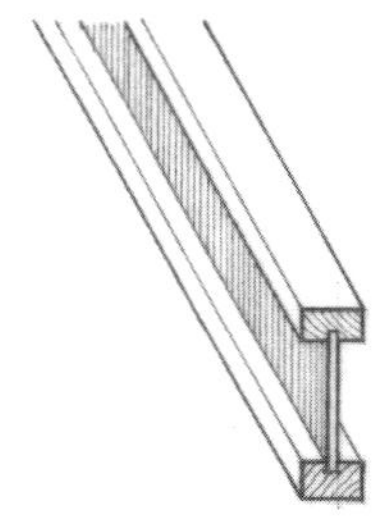

I-beam
A beam made by gluing sawn or laminated veneer lumber flanges along the top and bottom edges of a single plywood or oriented strandboard web. Also called **I-joist**.

flitchplate
A steel plate for reinforcing a flitch beam.

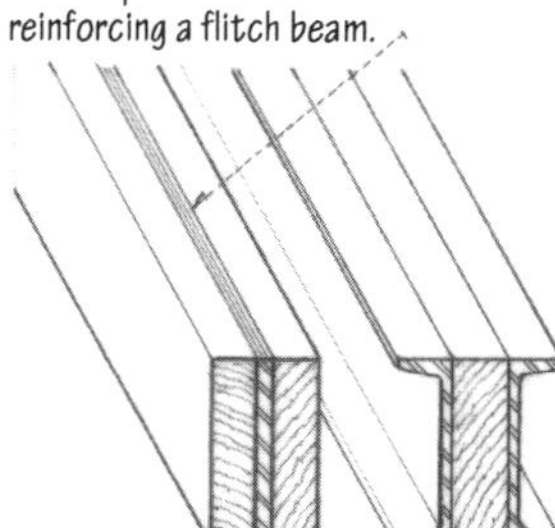

flitch beam
A vertically laminated beam consisting of timbers set on edge and bolted side by side to steel plates or sections. Also called **flitch girder**, **sandwich beam**.

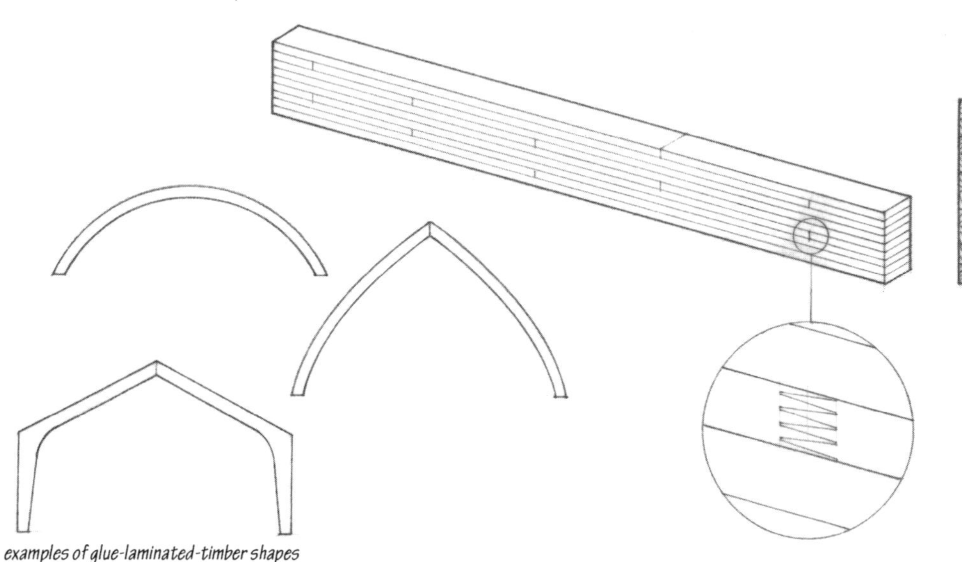

examples of glue-laminated-timber shapes

glued-laminated timber
A structural lumber product made by laminating stress-grade lumber with adhesive under controlled conditions, usually with the grain of all plies being parallel. The advantages of glued-laminated timber over dimension lumber are generally higher allowable unit stresses, improved appearance, and availability of various sectional shapes. Glue-laminated timbers may be end-joined with scarf or finger joints to any desired length, or edge-glued for greater width or depth. Also called **glulam**.

appearance grade
One of three grades of glue-laminated timber – premium, architectural, and industrial – based on surface appearance as affected by growth characteristics, wood fillers, and dressing operations.

plywood
A wood panel product made by bonding veneers together under heat and pressure, usually with the grain at right angles to each other and symmetrical about the center ply.

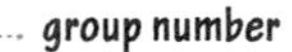

group number
A number identifying one of five groups of species used for the face and back veneers of a plywood panel, the species being classified on the basis of bending strength and stiffness, with Group 1 containing the stiffest species and Group 5 the least stiff.

APA
RATED SHEATHING
32/16 15/32 INCH
SIZED FOR SPACING
EXPOSURE 1
000
NRB-108

span rating
A number specifying the maximum recommended center-to-center spacing in inches of the supports for a structural wood panel spanning with its long dimension across three or more supports.

exposure durability
A classification of a wood panel product according to its ability to withstand exposure to weather or moisture without weakening or warping.

panel grade
The grade of a wood panel product identified by the face and back veneer grades or by its intended use.

engineered grade
The grade of a structural wood panel based on its intended use as sheathing, subflooring, or in the fabrication of box beams and stressed-skin panels.

exterior plywood
A plywood panel consisting of C-grade veneers or better, bonded with a fully waterproof glueline for permanent exposure to weather or moisture.

interior plywood
A plywood panel made with D-grade veneers or better, bonded with an exterior, intermediate, or interior glueline.

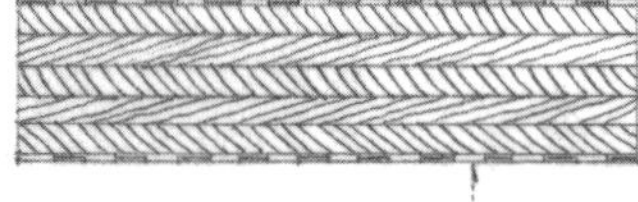

high-density overlay
An exterior wood panel having a resin-fiber overlay on both sides providing a smooth, hard, abrasion-resistant surface, used for concrete forms, cabinets, and countertops. Abbr.: **HDO**

medium-density overlay
An exterior wood panel having a phenolic or melamine resin overlay on one or both sides providing a smooth base for painting. Abbr.: **MDO**

specialty panel
Any of various wood panel products, as grooved or rough-sawn plywood, intended for use as siding or paneling.

texture 1-11
An exterior plywood panel having grooves 1/4 in. (6.4 mm) deep and 3/8 in. (9.5 mm) wide, spaced 4 or 8 in. (102 or 203 mm) on center.

exterior
An exposure durability classification for structural wood panels manufactured with a waterproof glueline for use as siding or other continuously exposed applications.

exposure 1
An exposure durability classification for structural wood panels manufactured with an exterior glueline for use in protected construction subject to repeated wetting.

exposure 2
An exposure durability classification for structural wood panels manufactured with an intermediate glueline for use in fully protected construction subject to a minimum of wetting.

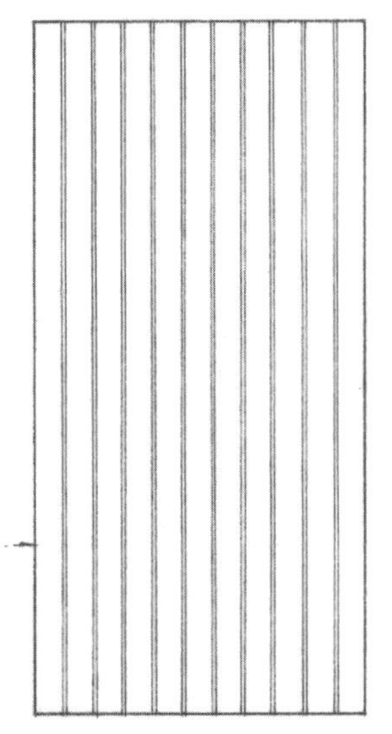

gradestamp
A trademark of the American Plywood Association (APA), stamped on the back of a structural wood panel product to identify the panel grade, thickness, span rating, exposure durability classification, mill number, and National Research Board (NRB) report number.

veneer grade
A grade defining the appearance of a veneer in terms of growth characteristics and the number and size of repairs that may be made during manufacture.

N-grade
A smooth softwood veneer of all heartwood or all sapwood, free from open defects with only a few well-matched repairs.

A-grade
A smooth, paintable softwood veneer with a limited number of neatly made repairs parallel to the grain.

B-grade
A softwood veneer having a solid surface with circular repair plugs, tight knots, and minor splits permitted.

C-grade
A softwood veneer having tight knots and knotholes of limited size, synthetic or wood repairs, and discoloration and sanding defects that do not impair the strength of the panel.

C-plugged grade
An improved C-grade softwood veneer having smaller knots and knotholes, some broken grain, and synthetic repairs.

D-grade
A softwood veneer having large knots and knotholes, pitch pockets, and tapering splits.

premium grade
The highest grade of hardwood veneer, permitting only a few small burls, pin knots, and inconspicuous patches.

good grade
A grade of hardwood veneer similar to premium grade except that matching of veneer faces is not required.

sound grade
A sound, smooth hardwood veneer free of open defects but containing streaks, discoloration, patches, and small sound tight knots.

utility grade
A hardwood veneer permitting discoloration, streaks, patches, tight knots, small knotholes and splits.

backing grade
A grade of hardwood veneer similar to utility grade but permitting larger defects not affecting the strength or durability of the panel.

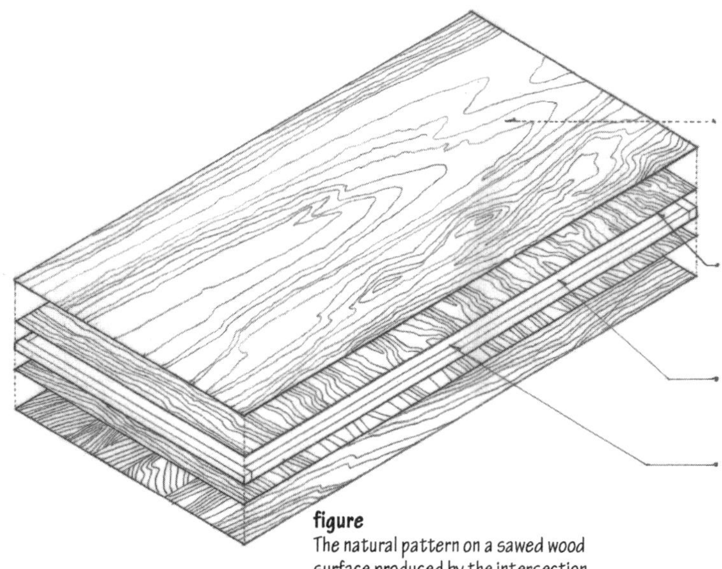

figure
The natural pattern on a sawed wood surface produced by the intersection of annual rings, knots, burls, rays, and other growth characteristics.

decorative plywood
Hardwood-faced plywood manufactured for use as paneling or in cabinetry and furniture.

veneer
A thin sheet of wood rotary cut, sliced, or sawn from a log or flitch and used as a superior facing to inferior wood or bonded together to form plywood.

crossband
A layer of veneer immediately adjacent to and at right angles to the face plies in a plywood panel.

core
The center of a plywood panel, consisting of veneers, sawn lumber, or composition board.

banding
The solid wood stock extending around the sides of a veneered panel, concealing the core and facilitating the shaping of the panel edges.

matching
Arranging sheets of veneers so as to emphasize the color and figure of the wood.

book matching
Arranging veneers from the same flitch alternately face up and face down to produce symmetrical mirror images about the joints between adjacent sheets.

herringbone matching
Book matching in which the figures in adjacent sheets slope in opposite directions.

slip matching
Arranging adjacent sheets of veneer from the same flitch side by side without turning so as to repeat the figure.

diamond matching
Arranging four diagonally cut sheets of a veneer to form a diamond pattern about a center.

random matching
Arranging veneers to intentionally create a casual, unmatched appearance.

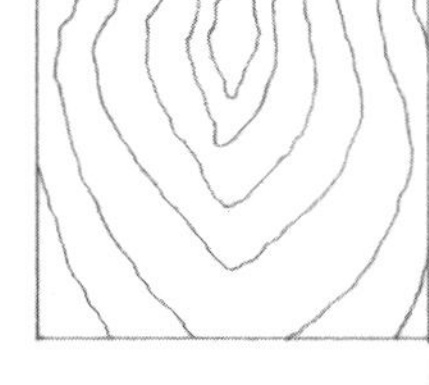

rotary cutting
The rotating of a log against the cutting edge of a knife in a lathe, producing a continuous veneer with a bold, variegated ripple figure.

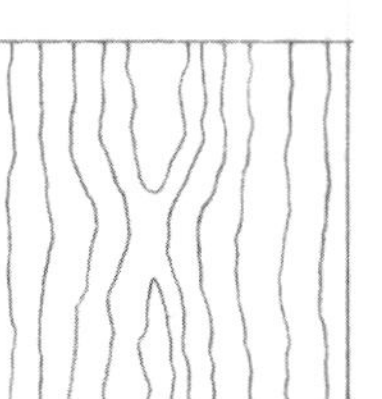

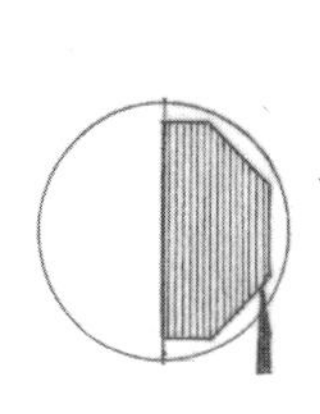

flat slicing
The longitudinal slicing of a half-log parallel to a line through its center, producing a veneer having a variegated wavy figure. Also called **plain slicing**.

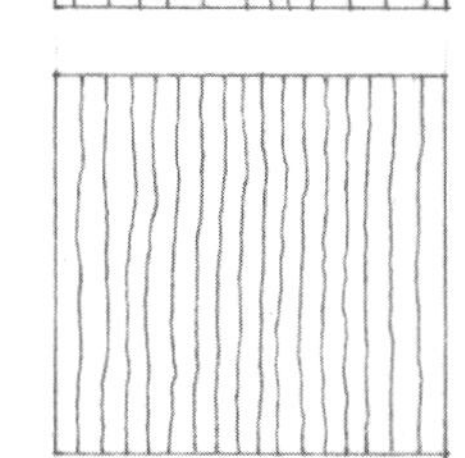

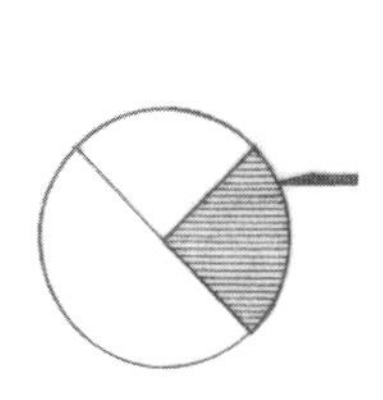

quarter slicing
The longitudinal slicing of a quarter log perpendicular to the annual rings, producing a series of straight or varied stripes in the veneer.

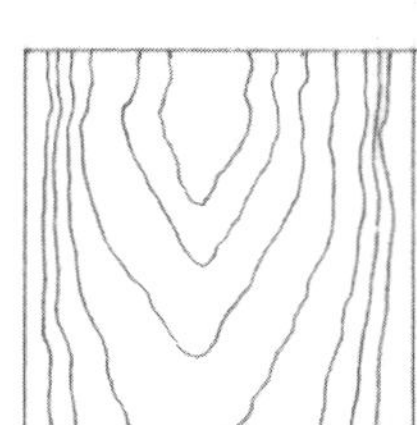

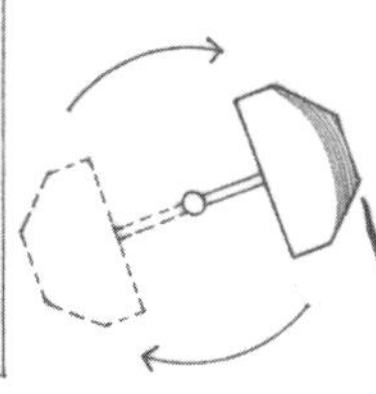

half-round slicing
The slicing of a flitch mounted off-center in the lathe, slightly across the annual rings, producing characteristics of both rotary cutting and flat slicing.

flitch
A longitudinal section of a log to be cut into veneers.

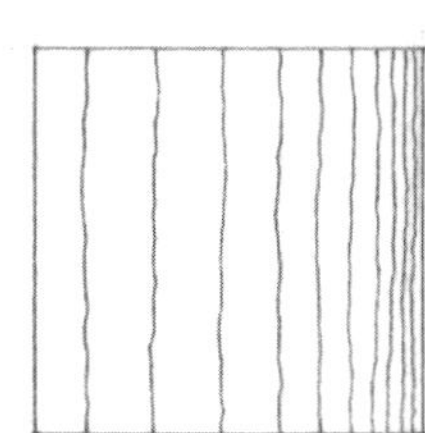

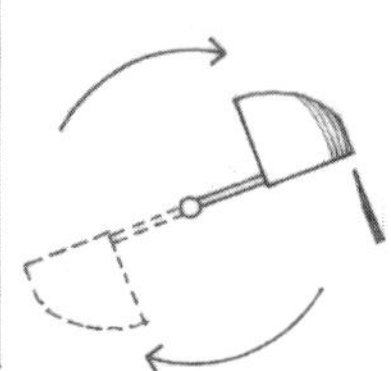

rift cutting
The slicing of oak and similar species perpendicular to the conspicuous, radiating rays so as to minimize their appearance.

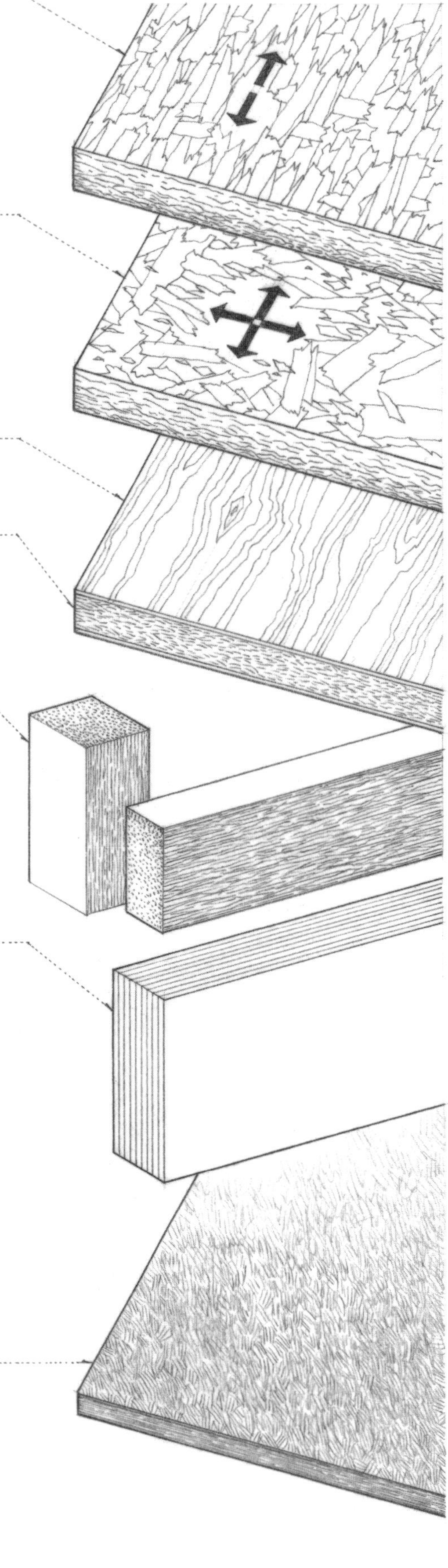

oriented strandboard
A nonveneered wood panel product commonly used for sheathing and as subflooring, made by bonding three or five layers of long, thin wood strands under heat and pressure using a waterproof adhesive. The surface strands are aligned parallel to the long axis of the panel, making the panel stronger along its length.
Abbr.: **OSB**

waferboard
A nonveneered panel product composed of large, thin wood flakes bonded under heat and pressure with a waterproof adhesive. The planes of the wafers are generally oriented parallel to the plane of the panel but their grain directions are random, making the panel approximately equal in strength and stiffness in all directions in the plane of the panel.

composite panel
A wood panel product consisting of two face veneers bonded to a reconstituted wood core.

particleboard
A nonveneered wood panel product made by bonding small wood particles under heat and pressure, commonly used as a core material for decorative panels and cabinetwork, and as underlayment for floors. Also called **chipboard**.

parallel strand lumber
A structural lumber product made by bonding long, narrow wood strands together under heat and pressure using a waterproof adhesive. Parallel strand lumber is a proprietary product marketed under the trademark, **Parallam**, used as beams and columns in post-and-beam construction and for beams, headers, and lintels in light frame construction.
Abbr.: **PSL**

laminated veneer lumber
A structural lumber product made by bonding layers of wood veneers together under heat and pressure using a waterproof adhesive. Having the grain of all veneers run in the same longitudinal direction results in a product that is strong when edge loaded as a beam or face loaded as a plank. Laminated veneer lumber is marketed under various brand names, as **Microlam**, and used as headers and beams or as flanges for prefabricated wood I-joists. Abbr.: **LVL**

fiberboard
A building material made of wood or other plant fibers compressed with a binder into rigid sheets.

hardboard
A very dense, compressed wood fiberboard.

tempered hardboard
A hardboard impregnated with a drying oil or other oxidizing resin and baked to improve its hardness and moisture resistance.

Masonite
Trademark for a brand of tempered hardboard.

Peg-Board
Trademark for a brand of tempered hardboard having regularly spaced perforations into which hooks may be inserted for the storage or display of articles.

Aa

Dd

Ee

Ff

Gg

Mm

Nn

Uu

Vv

Ww

Xx

Yy

Zz